| Case Name | Facts | LA stat (min'n cont) | FPSJ |
|---|---|---|---|
| Carp v. Dee. | • neyligace (preds liab) <br> • advertisemnt <br> • proximity <br> • prez rez | • tortias actw/in the state of MA. | dis 4 factors (719) |
| Pennoyer v. Neff. | | | |
| Asahi | | | |
| Nicastro. | | | |
| ALS. | | | |

# CIVIL PROCEDURE

**ASPEN CASEBOOK SERIES**

# CIVIL PROCEDURE

## Doctrine, Practice, and Context

## Fourth Edition

**STEPHEN N. SUBRIN**
Professor of Law
Northeastern University School of Law

**MARTHA L. MINOW**
Dean and Jeremiah Smith, Jr. Professor of Law
Harvard University Law School

**MARK S. BRODIN**
Professor of Law and Michael and Helen Lee Distinguished Scholar
Boston College Law School

**THOMAS O. MAIN**
William S. Boyd Professor of Law
William S. Boyd School of Law
University of Nevada, Las Vegas

**ALEXANDRA D. LAHAV**
Professor of Law
University of Connecticut School of Law

Published by Wolters Kluwer Law & Business in New York.

Wolters Kluwer Law & Business serves customers worldwide with CCH, Aspen Publishers, and Kluwer Law International products. (www.wolterskluwerlb.com)

To contact Customer Service, e-mail customer.service@wolterskluwer.com, call 1-800-234-1660, fax 1-800-901-9075, or mail correspondence to:

    Wolters Kluwer Law & Business
    Attn: Order Department
    PO Box 990
    Frederick, MD 21705

Printed in the United States of America.

1 2 3 4 5 6 7 8 9 0

ISBN 978-1-4548-0708-7

**Library of Congress Cataloging-in-Publication Data**

Civil procedure : doctrine, practice, and context / Stephen N. Subrin . . . [et al.].—4th ed.
  p. cm.—(Aspen casebook series)
Includes index.
ISBN 978-1-4548-0708-7
1. Civil procedure—United States. I. Subrin, Stephen, 1936-
KF8839.C452 2012
347.73′5—dc23

                                    2012005822

# About Wolters Kluwer Law & Business

Wolters Kluwer Law & Business is a leading global provider of intelligent information and digital solutions for legal and business professionals in key specialty areas, and respected educational resources for professors and law students. Wolters Kluwer Law & Business connects legal and business professionals as well as those in the education market with timely, specialized authoritative content and information-enabled solutions to support success through productivity, accuracy and mobility.

Serving customers worldwide, Wolters Kluwer Law & Business products include those under the Aspen Publishers, CCH, Kluwer Law International, Loislaw, Best Case, ftwilliam.com and MediRegs family of products.

**CCH** products have been a trusted resource since 1913, and are highly regarded resources for legal, securities, antitrust and trade regulation, government contracting, banking, pension, payroll, employment and labor, and healthcare reimbursement and compliance professionals.

**Aspen Publishers** products provide essential information to attorneys, business professionals and law students. Written by preeminent authorities, the product line offers analytical and practical information in a range of specialty practice areas from securities law and intellectual property to mergers and acquisitions and pension/benefits. Aspen's trusted legal education resources provide professors and students with high-quality, up-to-date and effective resources for successful instruction and study in all areas of the law.

**Kluwer Law International** products provide the global business community with reliable international legal information in English. Legal practitioners, corporate counsel and business executives around the world rely on Kluwer Law journals, looseleafs, books, and electronic products for comprehensive information in many areas of international legal practice.

**Loislaw** is a comprehensive online legal research product providing legal content to law firm practitioners of various specializations. Loislaw provides attorneys with the ability to quickly and efficiently find the necessary legal information they need, when and where they need it, by facilitating access to primary law as well as state-specific law, records, forms and treatises.

**Best Case Solutions** is the leading bankruptcy software product to the bankruptcy industry. It provides software and workflow tools to flawlessly streamline petition preparation and the electronic filing process, while timely incorporating ever-changing court requirements.

**ftwilliam.com** offers employee benefits professionals the highest quality plan documents (retirement, welfare and non-qualified) and government forms (5500/PBGC, 1099 and IRS) software at highly competitive prices.

**MediRegs** products provide integrated health care compliance content and software solutions for professionals in healthcare, higher education and life sciences, including professionals in accounting, law and consulting.

Wolters Kluwer Law & Business, a division of Wolters Kluwer, is headquartered in New York. Wolters Kluwer is a market-leading global information services company focused on professionals.

# *Dedication*

I dedicate this book to over three decades of
Northeastern Law students who have insisted that intelligence,
compassion, and justice must go hand in hand, and to Joan,
who has done the same—and then some.
**—Stephen N. Subrin**

I dedicate this book to law students past and future in hopes
that you will work to make procedure more civil, and to Joe Singer,
who inspires accessible casebooks and other improvements of daily life.
**—Martha L. Minow**

I dedicate this edition to all those who devote their talents and energies
to the pursuit of justice in the courts across the land.
**—Mark S. Brodin**

I dedicate this book to my parents, who always seem to know the way,
and to Paula, with whom I read maps.
**—Thomas O. Main**

I dedicate this book to Martha Minow for her thoughtful guidance;
Nick, Oona, and Moshe for every minute; Pnina Lahav, my inspiration
and imma; and to all the students who thought they wouldn't like
civil procedure, but found out that they do.
**—Alexandra D. Lahav**

# Summary of Contents

# Contents

# *Exercises*

## Chapter 4

## Chapter 5

## Chapter 6

## Chapter 7

## Chapter 8

## Chapter 9

# *Preface to the Fourth Edition*

Twelve years have passed since our first edition. We remain grateful to the dozens of professors who have adopted our book, many of whom have given us suggestions through the years that we continue to incorporate. Please keep advising us. And please tell us your questions about the book that arise in the course of your teaching.

Working on the book this time around has prompted us to reminisce about its origins and to consider whether we have remained true to our initial insights and goals. It's been two decades since Steve Subrin talked at Brooklyn Law School about *Teaching Civil Procedure While You Watch It Disintegrate*, 59 Brooklyn L. Rev. 1155 (1993). Thom Main, his student and research assistant at the time, attended the conference. We recall the backlash from those who claimed that our assertion of disintegration was overblown, and that we were overly pessimistic.

Fast forward to the last several months as we have been revising the book, and found that we had to revise our historical and contextual materials to take account of the multiple constrictions on civil litigation and the right to trial by jury that have continued to evolve. Maybe we weren't pessimistic enough two decades ago. In any event, with regard to the changes in pleading requirements, we decided to summarize *Twombly* and print the majority and dissenting opinions in *Iqbal*. We assure students in the materials that it is not their fault that the language of rules can remain the same, while their "interpretation" can dramatically change.

We have remained true throughout the book to our belief that historical context is necessary to truly understand doctrine; context allows students to see that procedure is neither dry nor devoid of important political and social consequences. We also continue to believe that practice – engaging in how lawyers actually use procedure – is essential to understanding the doctrine and becoming initiated in the challenges and joys of becoming a professional. We have added a couple of practice exercises and several new review problems. We continue to think that law students, like most people, learn best by doing. In short, we still embrace our title: Civil Procedure: Doctrine, Practice, and Context.

Those who have used the book before will notice a few other improvements. In addition to the normal exchange of a few cases for better ones and updating the commentary, we shifted the focus of Chapter Six, Questioning and Taming the Current System, to the strengths and limitations of courts, explored through the lens of structural injunctions and alternative dispute resolution. We have moved material on the adversary system to our chapter on discovery. Chapter Eleven, Class Actions, has been completely overhauled and streamlined. The chapter focuses on the due process requirements for class actions and the policies motivating approval for and opposition to the class action device. We give due attention to the requirements of Rule 23, and other issues in complex litigation, such as aggregate settlement and federal jurisdiction over class actions and mass court cases.

As we were finalizing this edition, The Federal Courts Jurisdiction and Venue Clarification Act of 2011 became law. Fortunately, we were able to include the changes and clarifications of this act. There is an improved Teacher's Manual which takes account of the changes in the book and what we have learned from our students and other professors about teaching the material.

The most important change has been the addition of Alexandra Lahav as a co-author. Alexandra joined Martha in revising the materials in Chapters One, Two, and Six, and she also revised Chapter Eleven. Having been relieved of that chapter, Thom and Steve revised Chapter Eight on Subject Matter Jurisdiction and Removal, and continued their work on Chapters Three, Four, and Five. Mark revised Chapters Seven, Nine, and Ten. Being obsessive law professors, we talked together (and even occasionally argued) about the final product. You now know whom best to call or write with your questions and suggestions with respect to particular chapters. Thom handles digital issues and technical problems. Despite our and the editors' proofreading, there are inevitably errors. Please tell Thom about them.

Once again we thank our families for putting up with us as we grappled with the decisions and minutia that come with revising casebooks. We thank Sonia McNeil and Kate Epstein of Harvard Law School for their research assistance. And we thank Gretchen Otto and all of our friends at Aspen Publishers for their editorial guidance and support. Finally, a word of appreciation to ourselves. Steve, Martha, Mark, and Thom have truly enjoyed collaborating with each other through these many years. The truth is that we have never exchanged a harsh word throughout this experiment in trying to improve the teaching of civil procedure. We are overjoyed to have Alexandra join us. She not only brings us her rare blend of intelligence, knowledge, and creativity, but also a wry sense of humor and a much appreciated infusion of energy and relative youth.

Stephen N. Subrin
Martha L. Minow
Mark S. Brodin
Thomas O. Main
Alexandra D. Lahav

March 2012

# *Preface to the First Edition*

The impetus for this book grew out of our own experience as law students and professors. We find that students learn most effectively when legal doctrine, its context, and how doctrine actually works in practice are integrated. Empirical and theoretical research support the notion that we learn and remember at our best as a result of intense, sustained experiences in which we must perform concrete tasks that call upon a number of our faculties. Many of our deepest learning experiences have come from teaching a new course, helping a client solve a problem, or writing an article or a book—experiences that call upon a combination of knowledge, insight, values, clarity, advocacy, judgment, and endurance. These are the lessons that stick.

We wanted a civil procedure course that created a more unified learning experience. Civil procedure doctrine can seem remote from the reality of torts, crimes, contracts, and land. And yet perhaps no other legal subject so calls into question the major issues of law and practicing law in the United States: separation of powers, federalism, the adversarial relationship, efficiency, fairness, power and powerlessness, justice, and fees. In a civil procedure course one finds, for example, the conceptual challenges of *Erie,* the ethical dimensions of discovery, and the practical necessities of hard and fast rules. Moreover, this is a field in flux, and studying the underlying values and historical context of procedure helps one make some sense of the inherent uncertainty and change.

Often students say that they know the doctrine, yet (frustratingly) they cannot meaningfully apply it. We wanted to develop a course in which students applied the doctrine they were learning. Seven years ago, Steve Subrin and several of his students at Northeastern University School of Law confronted the challenge of creating a more unified civil procedure course. They put two real cases, with practice-oriented exercises, at the center of a contextual, philosophic, and multidisciplinary study of civil procedure. They reprinted fewer opinions, but retained more of the procedure and factual context by not severely editing them. They also reprinted longer excerpts of pertinent articles to demonstrate the flow of an extended argument. The students were given challenging questions to contemplate or answer, but they were not given questions that required additional reading or expert knowledge. Finally, they employed *orientation essays* to illuminate certain doctrines and to elucidate the contextual and practical environments that influenced, and were influenced by, those doctrines.

We have remained true to the vision of Steve Subrin and his students—the vision of creating a civil procedure course that not only taught the doctrine but also applied it and illuminated the integral role of civil procedure in every substantive area of the law. Many features of this book promote that vision:

- Orientation essays that focus on doctrine, practice, or context, or a combination of these.
- Pleadings and files of two real cases are threaded throughout the book.
- To maintain a manageable size yet cover all of the essentials, the authors have carefully edited the book's cases.
- There is complete integration of contextual materials and practice exercises.
- Thomas Main helped design the founding materials as a law student, and became a co-author of this text as he entered practice and added a law-practice perspective to this course.
- Martha Minow and Mark Brodin brought original materials and different perspectives that contributed to this effort to reinvent a course in civil procedure.

We are grateful to those who aided and abetted this project. In particular, Jeff Stern, a distinguished trial lawyer at Sugarman, Rogers, Barshak & Cohen in Boston, Massachusetts, helped us develop the materials for the wrongful death action involving the roll-over of a Jeep. Jane Picker, Ken Kowalski, and the Fair Employment Law Clinic at Cleveland-Marshall College of Law, Cleveland State University, helped us develop the materials for the Title VII class action against the Cleveland Ohio Fire Department. In both cases, we have changed the names and, in a few instances for pedagogical purposes, certain facts.

Many Northeastern University School of Law students and graduates inspired Steve's vision for this book, and participated in its initial preparation and later iterations. He gives special thanks to Mary Azzarito, John Becker, David Brenner, Kent Brintnall, Kevin Brown, Shawn Bush, Genna Carver, Stephanie Cucurullo, Rachel Dimitruk, Liz Goldstein, Amy Hubert, Vik Kanwar, Dovie King, Amber Klinge, Aileen Lachs, Laura Matlow,

Mark McGrath, David Plotkin, Judy Prosper, Sasha Rosebush, Joel Rosen, Nicole Voigt, Jason Walta, Angela Wessels, and Debra Williams.

Martha thanks Laurie Corzett, Katie Cook, Naomi Ronen, and many generations of civil procedure students.

Mark thanks the hundreds of civil procedure students over the years who, he insists, have taught him far more than he has taught them.

Thomas thanks Grace Petrola, Sandy Heffley, and countless others who contributed time and expertise to this project. He also thanks Hill & Barlow, Boston, Massachusetts, and Platinum Equity Holdings, Los Angeles, California, who wittingly shared (and in important respects shouldered) his commitment to this text.

All of the authors sincerely thank Greg Pingree for helping to clarify the collective voice of this book. The authors also thank Bernard Johnston, Melody Davies, and Jay Boggis of Aspen Publishers for their assistance and patience. And finally, the authors thank Carol McGeehan, our Acquisitions Editor, for her support, guidance, and belief in this project. The final product is truly a collaborative effort.

Stephen N. Subrin
Martha L. Minow
Mark S. Brodin
Thomas O. Main

February 2000

# CIVIL PROCEDURE

# 1

# *An Introduction to Civil Procedure*

The rules and laws governing civil litigation are the domain of lawyers and not the typical subject for popular culture or public debate. Nonetheless, as this introduction explores, civil procedure rules and practices centrally structure private dispute resolution and many public controversies. This introduction also provides a brief explanation of sources for key rules and doctrines, suggestions for studying, and comments on the unique features of this casebook. Especially for students interested in theoretical understandings of law, the introduction offers analysis of law itself as a kind of theater with rules and practices for translating social harms into a drama recognized by the legal world.

The opening section introduces a central theme of the course through discussion of one notable case, *United States v. Hall*, 472 F.2d 261 (5th Cir. 1972). The theme is that the law imposes limitations on the power of courts. The doctrinal issue is the reach of the courts' contempt power— whether a court has power to hold a nonparty in contempt. Arising in the larger context of a school desegregation suit, *Hall* presents judicial analysis of both common law precedents and a rule about judicial power to punish non-parties for violating a court order.

The second section of this chapter addresses the constitutional foundations for due process, or the right to be heard, a right that guides the structure of procedure in the United States. Because landmark Supreme Court opinions have addressed the scope of due process in reviewing decisions by administrative agencies, these opinions provide the centerpiece, but the frameworks and values that emerge pervade procedural rules and practices in the courts as well. Indeed, the values behind due process are critical to the doctrines governing access to court, jurisdiction, and preclusion, which are developed in later parts of the book.

The final section of this chapter considers access to the courts and to lawyers. Access to the courts is prior to every other topic in the field of procedure. This chapter considers initial access to the court system and to representation, while other parts of the book continue the thread in considering how various procedural rules affect litigants' access to justice.

## A. WHAT STUDENTS SHOULD KNOW FROM THE START

### 1. Why Procedure Matters

Most starting law students have some sense of the subjects to be addressed in criminal law, property, contracts, and torts. The media and personal encounters make these fields familiar to nonlawyers. Many students have signed leases for apartments and entered into oral or written employment contracts. Some have been involved in automobile accidents or injured by defective products. Others have had close encounters with the criminal law through following highly visible murder trials, serving on juries, or watching the experiences of friends and family members. However, few students, if any, have thought about why some cases are in federal court and some in state court, or whether an accident victim may file successive suits for each separate injury suffered in an incident, or what steps initiate and terminate a lawsuit.

Yet from the moment a lawyer meets a prospective client and begins to learn the details of the problem for which assistance is sought, the lawyer must think about such procedural dimensions. How could the client's story be translated into a "complaint," which is the document that commences litigation? What elements would comprise a viable "claim for relief" and thus survive the defendant's available procedural challenges, which may charge lack of jurisdiction, improper venue, failure to join a necessary party, or failure to plead with sufficient specificity? How can the "discovery" (pretrial fact investigation) process be used to develop evidence sufficient to support the "allegations" in the complaint? Is the amount of money likely to be recovered on a prevailing claim adequate to make the litigation worth the costs, including attorneys' fees? Or should the lawyer encourage the client to drop the claim, settle the claim, or pursue mediation or another alternative to litigation?

Even lawyers who never plan to go to court (the majority of the profession) must concern themselves with procedural matters. The business lawyer who drafts a contract must consider what could happen if either party fails to perform and litigation arises. Will my client have to chase the breaching party to its distant home state to file a suit to enforce the contract, or will we have to defend a suit charging breach in that distant forum? Should we negotiate for a "forum selection clause" and a "choice of law clause" to specify where any litigation over the contract would take place, and under what normative rules? Should we include an arbitration provision?

The skills used in mastering the world of procedure are highly useful in other legal endeavors. Drafting complaints and answers helps lawyers refine the skill of sorting out points of agreement and disagreement. Studying the Federal Rules of Civil Procedure and procedural statutes highlights the delicate art of statutory construction and interpretation. Mastering the line of Supreme Court opinions governing personal jurisdiction involves close reading of evolving case law and learning to see how legal concepts and factual distinctions matter over time in judge-made law. Fact gathering and managing information to prepare for litigation are skills crucial even to lawyers who never pursue court actions.

Although at times procedure may seem to involve petty details (do weekends count in assessing when a ten-day deadline kicks in?), it also engages the largest questions law can engage: What should a society value? How should it resolve disputes? What role should citizens have in governance? What are the roles and limits of democratic institutions such as legislatures? What power should be held and used by the nonmajoritarian institution of the court? Can words restrict the actions of people entrusted with power? What can remedy a wrong? What is a lie? How should economic disparities affect access to justice? These large questions underlie and shape the subject. Now let's consider what that subject is.

## 2. *What Is "Civil Procedure"?*

The "civil" in "civil procedure" means noncriminal. Although a criminal case may result in imprisonment or a fine and the moving party is always the government, in a civil case the remedies include monetary compensation or an order directing the defendant to do or stop doing something. Often, both plaintiff and defendant are private parties, although in some instances the government may be either plaintiff or defendant. As we will see in *Turner v. Rogers*, reproduced at the end of this chapter, in some cases the line between criminal and civil adjudication is blurred.

"Procedure" is meant to contrast with "substance." The rights and duties governing daily activities of people and institutions constitute substantive law. For instance, a torts course covers the various forms of conduct about which a plaintiff can complain and obtain redress under such doctrines as negligence, assault, and defamation; the doctrines themselves are composed of elements that a litigant must prove before a court can order a remedy.

In contrast, a procedure course concentrates on the *methods* by which the substantive law can be enforced, typically, although not exclusively, by courts. Thus, procedure determines how disputes are channeled into a legal form; civil procedure addresses the channeling of disputes into courts and the methods for resolving them there. The topics range from the mundane, such as what documents must be filed and when, to those basic to defining governmental power in the United States. The procedural laws define the balance of power between the federal government and the states, including what power to resolve disputes is retained by the states and what by the federal government (subject matter jurisdiction) and which source of law—state or federal—applies to a dispute when it is litigated (the federalism issue epitomized by the case of *Erie Railroad v. Tomkins*, 304 U.S. 64 (1938)). Procedural law also defines the scope of the government's power, including when a person's liberty may be affected by the courts (due process, personal jurisdiction). Every issue, even the most mundane or technical, also involves important social policies and values. The doctrine of pleadings, for example, controls the ability of plaintiffs to access the court system. Summary judgment raises the fundamental question of whether disputes should be resolved by the professional judge or by lay citizens summoned to serve on juries. In sum, the civil procedure course concerns the premises and operations of the adversarial system of justice, the scope of due process, the ethical issues posed for a lawyer entrusted with representing the interests of another, and the proper balance between efficiency and fairness.

The basic line between procedure and substance, so central to the definition of civil procedure, will not always be clear or obvious. Indeed, in this respect, the debates over the line between procedure and substance mirror debates over most other lines drawn by the law. Procedure and substance are often closely connected as well as mutually defining; because some rules depend on the distinction between procedure and substance, that distinction itself at times becomes the site of disputes.

## 3. Meeting the Players and the Institutions

If substantive law announces norms and the consequences for their breach, procedural law converts a conflict over norms and breach into a case amenable to trial. Procedures translate conflicts into cases capable of being brought to trial, even when the dispute never gets that far and instead ends in settlement or moves through alternative processes such as mediation or arbitration. Procedural law translates disputants into parties. As parties, people appear in court; party or potential party status affects even out-of-court conversations. This section will briefly introduce procedural terms used in the federal courts, terms that you need to know in order to work with the materials in this chapter. A more comprehensive survey of terms appears in Chapter 3 and describes both the elements and stages of a lawsuit, and the issues that procedural rules address. You will soon see why civil procedure is often described as "lawyers' law," because the basic vocabulary is foreign to nonlawyers and the vocabulary actually reflects institutions and professional practices that compose the world of lawyers.

### a. Parties

The complaining party, who may be an individual, a corporation, or a collection of individuals, becomes the *plaintiff* or plaintiffs; those named in terms of fault or responsibility for the plaintiffs' claims become the *defendant* or defendants. Thus identified, the plaintiffs and defendants are adversaries on opposite sides of the lawsuit. Historically in the American system, progress in pursuing a civil case depends on the parties' initiatives rather than on the decision of a judge or prosecutor. Even with court changes enlarging the roles of judges and administrators as managers of the docket, the tradition of party control in practice puts the burden on the parties' lawyers. Lawyers, in turn, will be influenced by their own assessment of the merits of their client's position, by their predictions of the outcome, and by the method they will use for assessing attorneys' fees. The general rule is that each party pays its own attorneys' fees, so estimates of the party's ability to pay influence the attorney. Many lawyers in the tort field offer clients contingency fee arrangements, meaning a promise by the client to give the lawyer a percentage (typically one-third) of any recovered damages, with no obligation to pay if there is no recovery. Some statutes require that a losing defendant pay the attorneys' fees incurred by a prevailing plaintiff. Variations in these payment methods affect the attorney's calculus of the costs and risks of filing the suit, undertaking extensive investigation, hiring expert witnesses, and settling before trial or before judgment.

Sometimes, disputes involve more than two sides, such that simple opposition cannot capture the varied interests and obligations at issue. The Federal Rules of Civil Procedure permit plaintiffs and defendants to construct lawsuits that vary the bipolar two-party lawsuit structure through devices such as joinder, intervention, class action, and interpleader, each of which will be explored later in the course.

### b. Jurisdiction

This general term refers to the power of a tribunal over a case. It actually has two dimensions: *jurisdiction over the subject matter* and *jurisdiction over the person*. To have subject matter jurisdiction, a court must be authorized by the Constitution and statutes to decide cases dealing with this kind of subject. The federal district (trial) courts have power to hear only the kinds of lawsuits specified by Congress under two categories: (i) the suit raises a federal question, under federal statutes or the U.S. Constitution, or (ii) the suit involves parties satisfying diversity of citizenship (the plaintiff and defendant are citizens of different states or one of them is a citizen of a foreign country) *and* more than a statutory minimum amount is in controversy (currently set by Congress at $75,000). Specialized courts (dealing, for example, with patents or tax matters) have even more restricted spheres of subject matter jurisdiction. State trial courts include some with *general jurisdiction*—able to decide most cases—and those with specialized jurisdiction, such as the housing court (for landlord/tenant matters) or juvenile court (for offenses by minors).

Trial courts hear the initial dispute and presentation of evidence; appellate courts review the record developed in the course of the trial in light of claims of error in legal interpretation or application. The federal system has thirteen U.S. Courts of Appeals, each of which hears cases from a geographic area called a circuit. An appeal from a district court in Texas, for example, will be heard in the U.S. Court of Appeals for the Fifth Circuit. The Supreme Court of the United States is the court of last resort in the federal system. It has discretionary appellate jurisdiction over cases coming from the federal courts of appeals as well as from state supreme courts if, and only if, those cases depend on an issue of federal law. State systems have varying names for their trial, appellate, and highest courts.

Jurisdiction over the person, or personal jurisdiction, must also be satisfied before a court can proceed with a case. This means that the court selected by the plaintiff must have authority to direct the defendant to appear and to bind the defendant with a judgment. Thus, the defendant must be subject to suit in the state in which the court is located, which in turn means that the defendant resides there or has engaged in conduct with sufficient connection to the state to make it fair to impose personal jurisdiction there.

### c. Remedies

There are various kinds of relief a court may order after being persuaded that the plaintiff's claims are meritorious. Remedies may include money damages to compensate the plaintiff; money damages to punish the defendant; a declaration of the rights and duties of the parties; and orders, called injunctions, that direct the defendant to stop the harmful conduct or to start new conduct as required by law.

## 4. Sources for the Rules and Doctrines

The rules governing civil procedure come from several sources. Most law school civil procedure courses focus heavily on the federal courts and thus rely substantially on the Federal Rules of Civil Procedure. Congress has authorized the Supreme Court to prescribe rules to govern the conduct of federal district courts and courts of appeals (as well as rules of evidence), so long as those rules do not "abridge, enlarge or modify any substantive right." 28 U.S.C. § 2072(b).* Congress specified the mechanism for developing these rules: the Judicial Conference, composed of the Chief Justice of the

---

*Congressional enactments are codified and organized by numbered titles. Title 28 collects the laws governing the federal judiciary and judicial procedure.

Supreme Court, the chief judge of each court of appeals, one district judge from each regional circuit, and the chief judge of the Court of International Trade, authorizes the appointment of a standing committee that screens proposed rules. *See* 28 U.S.C. § 2073. The Judicial Conference also authorizes the appointment of advisory committees to focus on particular topics, such as civil rules or evidence rules. The advisory committees, comprising judges, practitioners, and scholars, consider proposed amendments and new rules, gather comments from judges and lawyers, and send revised proposals to the standing Committee on Practice and Procedure. That committee reports to the Judicial Conference, which recommends rule changes to the Supreme Court. The Supreme Court then decides whether to transmit such proposed rules to Congress, which in turn has the chance to reject the proposal or else, through inaction, let the proposal become part of the rules. 28 U.S.C. § 2074. In addition, Congress has on its own initiative adopted legislation to alter one or more rules or promote alternative processes for reforming rules. *See, e.g.*, Civil Justice Reform Act of 1990, Pub. L. No. 101-650, 104 Stat. 5089 (codified as amended at 28 U.S.C. §§ 471-482). Federal district courts also have large numbers of local rules. Approximately half of the states have adopted the Federal Rules of Civil Procedure for their own state procedural rules.

No less important, however, are court-made doctrines. Some predate the codified rules of procedure; some interpret those rules; and some interpret constitutional or legislative norms to provide for procedural rules. Thus, for example, the doctrines governing a right to a hearing and what a hearing must include interpret the Due Process Clauses of the Fifth and Fourteenth Amendments to the U.S. Constitution. The doctrines governing the remedial powers of the courts grow from common law practices and statutory interpretation. The doctrine of personal jurisdiction stems from the Due Process Clauses of the Fifth and Fourteenth Amendments as well as interpretations of state statutes. (In this and other areas, experts' judgments about the trends in case law and about admirable decisions are collected in a Restatement of Law, under the auspices of the American Law Institute.) Subject matter jurisdiction involves judicial interpretations of Article III of the U.S. Constitution and of statutes governing the courts. Allocation of power between the trial judge and jury depends on interpretations of the Seventh Amendment, common law and constitutional doctrines about burden of proof, as well as judicial interpretation of rules governing juries and the conduct of trials. Doctrines addressing the effects of a prior judgment on a subsequent lawsuit—the preclusion, or *res judicata* rules—grow from common law decisions as well as from interpretations of the Full Faith and Credit Clause of the Constitution (Art. IV, § 1), the Due Process Clauses, and judicial interpretations of statutes; a restatement of the law of judgments reflects the views of experts. Finally, special rules governing complex litigation have grown not only from the Federal Rules of Civil Procedure but also from congressional action, precedents, and the work of a multidistrict panel of judges addressing the subject.

Procedural design and rules, as well as judicial interpretations of these rules, can generate political debate and controversy. In this sense procedure is no different than the substantive law you will learn in courses such as torts or criminal law. In later chapters, we will see how the courts have reinterpreted the Federal Rules over time and the criticisms of those reinterpretations.

## 5. How to Approach Studying

Learning procedure, like learning most of the law, requires that you actively engage the materials. Develop a habit of pursuing questions and imagining the events surrounding the materials you read. Rather than memorizing the materials, you will get more out of the course if you focus your time in some or all of these ways:

First, carefully read all assignments before class, and read them critically. You should argue with the material. Ask: Why was the case decided this way? Does the doctrine announced by the court make sense? Does its application to this circumstance make sense? What alternatives are there, and would they be better? Generate hypothetical situations, or "what ifs." What if the facts were slightly different? Would that produce a different result in the eyes of the court that produced the opinion? Should it produce a different result? What if the motion were a different motion? What if the case were in state rather than federal court? What if the judge sat without a jury? Learning in law requires playing with the facts and doctrine, not memorizing and repeating rules.

Second, always ask where a given case is in the life cycle of procedure. Has there already been a trial, and is the case now on appeal—and if so, in what court? Or is the case at an earlier stage, such as a challenge to the complaint through a motion to dismiss? Is a trial court's grant or rejection of such a motion now on appeal? These questions will arise in all your courses; become aware of the procedural posture of every case you study. Also ask what will happen next, procedurally?

Third, look up what you do not know. If a rule or statute is mentioned and seems relevant, look it up. It will often be in your rule and statute supplement.

Fourth, when analyzing a rule or statute, always start with a close reading of the language of the relevant rule or statute, just as courts do. Consider if there are any ambiguous words; in what ways can the ambiguity be resolved?

Fifth, think hard about facts. What "facts" are described in the judicial opinion? What is the source for those facts—an adversarial trial, the statements in the plaintiff's complaint, an empirical study, one witness's sworn statement? What is contested or contestable about the facts? What could resolve the contest? Which facts seem crucial to the judgment by a court or by you? Legal doctrine, abstracted from facts, is slippery if not worthless.

It is the facts of any case that shape its ultimate result, putting the matter on one side or another of a legal rule or convincing a decision maker to change the rule. A wise lawyer once said, "I could find the law easier than the facts. When I was stumped or made a mistake, it was usually because of elusive facts."

Sixth, try to make sense of what you read by learning about its historical and political context. This book offers sources toward that end. Statutes and cases are made by people who reflect the times in which they live and respond to the world they have known. Many procedural issues are explicable only in relationship to prior debates and reforms. Being mindful of such context will help you remember and understand the law, and will also help you explain it and persuade others about your views.

Seventh, remember that law is about real people and groups. Ask what effect the law has on them and what happened after the cases were over. What do these outcomes make you think about the policies and rules you have studied?

Eighth, develop your own study materials as the course proceeds. An outline that you construct from your notes on the readings and class discussion will help you to get your hands around the material and to manage the large amount of information and analysis you will need to know by the end of the course. It is best to do this as you go along. Include not only cases and their results but also statements of rules and exceptions and the values and policies underlying the rules and judicial interpretations of them.

Ninth, form a study group to discuss and debate the materials with your classmates. Propose hypotheticals and try to work them out together. By the middle of the course, take a look at old exams and tackle them together or use the practice questions provided in this book. This will help you *practice* law rather than simply study it; you want to get in the habit of applying doctrine, forming arguments, predicting court action, and evaluating unsatisfactory decisions. All of this is easier and more fun to do when learning with and from other students.

Tenth, do not worry if many aspects of this and other courses do not make immediate sense or hang entirely together. Much understanding of law depends on understanding each part's relationship to the others; many aspects of each course will make more sense as you learn other aspects. Be patient and determined.

### 6. *About This Book*

This book includes leading and illustrative judicial opinions, relevant statutes and rules, and exercises that place you in the role of lawyer and judge to help develop the critical skills of analysis, research, fact investigation, strategy formulation, document drafting, written and oral advocacy, and ability to make informed judgments in the face of necessarily limited information. The book further includes historical, empirical, and jurisprudential materials to help you see the litigation system in its broader contexts and to expose the value choices behind both the existing system and proposals for reform. Understanding the context in which rules are made and interpreted and the policies that they embody is critical to becoming a great advocate because advocates draw on context, values, and policies in framing their arguments and convincing the courts to rule in favor of their clients. In this way, doctrine, context, and practice are linked to one another—to become an accomplished practitioner you will need to master both doctrine and context.

The aspiring lawyer who uses this book should become a problem solver, considering each case and issue from the perspective of a legal practitioner, who faces key decisions along the path of litigation. Based on an initial meeting with a potential client, the lawyer asks: Is there a claim for relief? What remedies are available, and do they make litigation worthwhile? Who will pay attorneys' fees? What is an appropriate court? Who should be designated as a party? What should the complaint include? What facts should be investigated through discovery? When should settlement be pursued? What motions should be filed and when?

For focus and coherence, this book continually uses the files of two actual cases. The first, brought by a surviving spouse, is a wrongful death action arising out of a motor vehicle accident. The second is an employment discrimination class action. By offering materials that reveal how these two cases move through the litigation process, the book provides chronological set pieces around which you can organize and remember what you have learned. The two cases also permit a realistic and sophisticated exploration of procedural doctrine and procedural decision making. They allow you to see the relationship between decisions made early on and those made in the later stages of the litigation. They also vividly demonstrate the importance of facts and how one arranges them into different stories for different audiences or purposes. Because practicing lawyers follow through with individual cases, rather than jump each day to new problems, these materials simulate real features of practice, in which procedural topics remain interconnected in the life history of particular cases. Finally, the two cases provide a good deal of substantive law, to create a realistic sense of the interplay between substance and process.

## 7. *Law as Theater*

Fundamentally, legal procedures enable the process of translating harms in the world into terms that are recognized by lawyers and judges. Crucial to that process of translation are the facts and the substantive law (rules of contract, tort, and so forth). Yet also vital are elements of presentation: style, tone, rhetoric, and drama. For the process to succeed, such elements must combine to form the appearance of fairness and impartiality, both to the specific players in a given legal dispute and to the society at large. Professor Milner Ball has proposed a way of understanding these elements by exploring the significance of metaphor and the function of courts as theater.

■ **MILNER S. BALL, THE PROMISE OF AMERICAN LAW: A THEOLOGICAL, HUMANISTIC VIEW OF LEGAL PROCESS**
*48-62, 136-138 (1981) Reprinted with permission of University of Georgia Press.*

### THE ELEMENT OF METAPHOR

The elements of presentation—rules of evidence, the case of the opposing side, the dynamics of the proceeding (including surprise and improvisation), the quality of evidence and witnesses, and the compellingness of the law—are considered just as carefully by an attorney as are the facts and the law. The dominant element in the presentation with which he will be concerned is the need to persuade the appropriate decisionmakers, first to a judgment that the claim is judicially cognizable, and then to a judgment favorable to the party represented. The consequential logic, which to a degree governs the selection of facts and law, coupled with the attorney's need for a persuasive presentation, distinguishes the legal case from a scientific investigation. . . . The methods are better understood as those of playwrights, actors, and directors, and may be described as the making of metaphor.

The passage from fact to metaphor is what the advocate seeks. It is the passage from the materials of fact and law (the text) by means of courtroom presentation (the performance) to a persuasive statement of what is to be done in a given situation (the metaphor).

### THE FUNCTIONS OF JUDICIAL THEATER

#### REDIRECTING AGGRESSION

. . . [T]he theatrical character of lawsuits . . . allows them to redirect aggression. Aggression, the need to fight and have revenge, is acted out and is thereby ritually expressed and controlled. It is in this sense that "[t]he right to sue and defend in the courts is the alternative of force."

Acceptance of judicial proceedings must be voluntary and is consequently dependent upon the perceived fairness of the courts. . . .

Participants . . . bring with them a willing suspension of disbelief. It is manifested in their willingness to observe the rules and forms of the proceedings, their willingness to abide by the outcome of the proceedings, and their willingness not to dismiss the legitimacy of the legal system, characterized though it may be by curious formulae, arcane rites, and untoward results. Like the license granted theater, this willingness will answer for any sustained length of time only to the system's reasonable degree of success in doing what it promises, in this case, justice.

#### ENCOURAGING IMPARTIALITY

Courts may not always or even frequently do justice, but their theatrical quality does contribute to their potential for doing justice by encouraging disinterestedness in the decision-makers. As actors, the judge and jury are asked to play parts in a government of laws and not of people. Fulfillment of the roles enables judgments that rise above prejudice and that, therefore, will more likely be just. . . .

### THE PERFORMANCE AS A WHOLE

If the advocate's presentation of his client's case is a form of theater which is played to the judge or jury and which contributes to judgment, there is also the theater of the courtroom itself—embracing all that goes on within—played to the public at large. It is the function of this drama to provide an image of legitimate society. In this sense, it is importantly an end in itself. As is true of theater generally, so of judicial theater: the performance is the "good" consumed. The courts are not so much in the business of producing decisions—finding facts, fixing liability, convicting the guilty, protecting the innocent, etc.—as they are of giving a performance. . . .

## B. AN OPENING CASE: THE POWER AND LIMITS OF COURTS

In *United States v. Hall*, 472 F.2d 261 (5th Cir. 1972), the Court of Appeals for the Fifth Circuit asks whether the district court judge may punish—or indeed do anything to—someone who was not a party to the relevant lawsuit. What are the limits of judicial power as announced in this opinion? Have those limits changed because of this decision, or does this decision simply confirm pre-existing limits? When the court looks to a rule to answer the question before it, where does that rule come from? When there is more than one relevant rule, what should a court do? When applying established rules to new facts, does the court change the rules, and if so, how?

## 1. *Reading the Case*

As you read the opinions in this and other cases that follow, please consider the following different ways you can analyze opinions in procedural cases and be prepared to discuss them in class. These methods will serve you well for the entire course and beyond.

*The underlying story*. First, it is often helpful to try to figure out what led to the dispute prior to the lawsuit. Who were the parties, what did they do prior to the litigation that led to the dispute, and what do they want to achieve in the lawsuit?

*The procedural posture*. Second, you can read a case in order to follow and understand the procedure. This approach has three aspects: (1) You must consider the precise procedural question before each court. (2) You should analyze what procedural steps took place previously. This will help you preview procedural concepts before you get to them in greater detail, and it will help you review what you already know. (3) Finally, you should also consider the outcome at each level of court, from trial through the appellate process. In this case, you might ask what the circuit court did with the district court decision. Also ask what will happen next in the case now that the circuit court has spoken.

*Lawyer and judge strategies.* Third, you can consider the strategies of each of the participants. Why did the lawyers act as they did? This includes analyzing why they made their procedural choices and why plaintiffs seek particular types of relief. What is the judge's strategy in writing the opinion? When looking at cases with multiple opinions, such as concurrences or dissents, especially at the Supreme Court level, you might ask what are the Justices' strategies in writing their opinions? The judges may be trying to gain votes from other judges, and to influence future behavior and subsequent decisions.

*Holdings and procedural doctrine.* Fourth (some students and teachers like to start with this), you will want to consider what the case holds. What doctrine will lawyers and legislators take from the case? Is there reasoning that will be valuable to later cases? How closely does the judge try to link his decision to the facts of the particular case?

*Other viewpoints of your choice.* Fifth, you might consider judicial opinions from the points of view of other disciplines that interest you. For example, take history: What does this case tell you about the procedural, intellectual, and factual history of the times? If you like novels, consider the plot and characters involved. If you like film, imagine the courtroom scenes and others that precede and follow them.

## 2. Reading a Federal Rule of Civil Procedure

Civil procedure may differ from your other classes in that statutes and rules in addition to judicial decisions are central to this subject. Many of the cases you read will be interpretations of procedural rules. *United States v. Hall,* the introductory case in this book, required the judge to interpret Rule 65 of the Federal Rules of Civil Procedure. Lawyers and judges interpret the Federal Rules using the same tools that they use to interpret statutes. But the Federal Rules differ from other laws in two ways that are useful to know. First, the process for passing Federal Rules differs from that for statutes because the Federal Rules are written by the advisory committee to the Committee on the Rules of Practice and Procedure, approved by the Supreme Court and ratified by Congress. By contrast, federal statutes are passed by both houses and presented to the President. When judges interpret the Federal Rules, they are interpreting rules written by the judicial branch rather than the legislative. Nevertheless, the Federal Rules have the force of statutes; after a Federal Rule comes into effect, any law that conflicts with that rule is supplanted. *See* 28 U.S.C. § 2072.

Second, the Federal Rules are accompanied by a set of comments written by the advisory committee, known as "Advisory Committee Notes," which appear at the end of each rule. There is a dispute as to how these comments are to be used to help courts and litigants understand the meaning of the Federal Rules. Most judges see these comments as analogous to legislative history, to be referred to or ignored depending on one's philosophy of statutory interpretation. Some scholars argue that the Notes ought to be seen as definitive because of the process by which rules are adopted. *See* Catherine Struve, *The Paradox of Delegation: Interpreting the Rules of Civil Procedure*, 150 U. Pa. L. Rev. 1099 (2002). Disputes over the weight of the comments suggest the potentially significant disagreements over the scope and meaning of the rules as well as the elements of their interpretation.

Here is a recommended approach to reading a Federal Rule:

*Look at the structure of the rule.* Before you read the entire rule, first look at its structure. Most rules have different parts addressing particular questions that might arise in the course of their application. Often these are in bold. At this point it is useful to step back and ask yourself: What is this rule about? At what point in the litigation does this rule become relevant? Think about the rule in the larger context of the lawsuit (the forest) before delving into its more specific language (the trees).

*Read the text of the rule carefully. Then read it again.* Careful reading is the key to interpreting rules and statutes. This is difficult because rules have no narrative. Instead, the case or hypothetical assigned with the rule provides the story. You might see yourself as trying to figure out how the rule will affect the way the story turns out. As you read the rule the second time, ask yourself which of the provisions of the rule are relevant to the problem that arises in the case or hypothetical you have been assigned. Of those provisions, what are alterative interpretations that will benefit one side or the other? How would you choose between them if you were the judge? Which interpretation is best for this litigant, which is best for society, and which fits most neatly with your ideas about how judges should interpret legal texts?

*Interpreting the rule.* Sometimes the plain text of the rule will be clear. Other times, the words used will be subject to different interpretations; in other words, parts of the rule will be ambiguous. Often a term that seems clear on an initial reading can seem more ambiguous in context and application. As you read the *Hall* case and Rule 65, consider what parts of the rule are ambiguous and what parts are clear. Then consider what tools the defendant uses to interpret the rule and what interpretive tools the judge uses to reach a different conclusion. Which approach do you find more convincing?

The same interpretative strategies are generally used for interpreting rules and statutes. You will encounter various methods of statutory interpretation as you move through the course and may choose to take a course devoted to statutory interpretation. As an introduction, three tools are useful to know:

*Plain meaning.* The first place that a court is to look for meaning is the text of the statute. Courts begin with the statute itself. But, of course, words do not exist in a vacuum. Sometimes the statute will specifically define a word. Other times the context in which the word is being used provides a basis for how it should be interpreted. If a term is not specifically defined in the statute, courts may interpret its "ordinary" meaning, sometimes relying on a dictionary. Justice Scalia, an ardent proponent of the plain text tool of statutory interpretation, explained that statutory construction "is a holistic endeavor. A provision that may seem ambiguous in isolation is often clarified by the remainder of the statutory scheme—because the same terminology is used elsewhere in a context that makes its meaning clear, or because only one of the permissible meanings produces a substantive effect that is compatible with the rest of the law." *United Savings Ass'n v. Timbers of Inwood Forest Associates*, 484 U.S. 365, 371 (1988) (internal citations omitted).

*Purpose*. Judges will also look to the purpose of the statute to interpret it, sometimes expressed in a statement of findings and purposes. Justice Jackson summarized this approach: "courts will construe the details of an act in conformity with its dominating general purpose, will read text in the light of context and will interpret the text so far as the meaning of the words fairly permits so as to carry out in particular cases the generally expressed legislative policy." *SEC v. Joiner*, 320 U.S. 344, 350-351 (1943). The general purpose of the Federal Rules of Civil Procedure is set forth in Rule 1. After reading the *Hall* case, consider to what extent Rule 1 provides justification for the parties' desired results and the court's ultimate decision.

*Legislative history*. Courts will sometimes use legislative history—contemporaneous statements by lawmakers and other materials—to illuminate the meaning of the text and the purpose of the statute as a whole. The use of legislative history is controversial. One of the difficulties of using legislative history is that legislators who voted for a law may not all agree as to its purpose or likely effects. With respect to the Federal Rules, we have a more definitive expression of the intent of the rules drafters in the form of the "Advisory Committee Notes." Courts and litigators rely on these Notes to shed light on how language in the rule ought to be interpreted. Not all judges agree, however, on the force that ought to be given to the Notes when interpreting rules. Justice Scalia summarizes this position: "The Advisory Committee's insights into the proper interpretation of a Rule's text are useful to the same extent as any scholarly commentary. But the Committee's *intentions* have no effect on the Rule's meaning. Even assuming that we and the Congress that allowed the Rule to take effect read and agreed with those intentions, it is the text of the Rule that controls." *Krupski v. Costa Corciere S. p. A.*, 130 S. Ct. 2485, 2499 (2010) (Scalia, J. concurring).

## 3. *Background of* United States v. Hall*

Eric Hall was arrested on March 9, 1972, for violating an emergency ex parte injunction issued pursuant to one of a series of decisions involving the Duval County, Florida, public schools, then the thirteenth largest school

*Thanks to Vik Kanwar and Dovie Yoana King, graduates of Northeastern University School of Law, for their research.

district in the country. Duval County maintained a dual school system divided along racial lines despite the U.S. Supreme Court's decision in *Brown v. Board of Education*, 347 U.S. 482 (1954), forbidding such deliberate segregation. In 1960, a group of black parents sued the school board on behalf of their school-aged children. The court found that the school board had maintained a racially divided school system "as a matter of policy, custom and usage" and had "not adopted any plan whatever for eliminating racial discrimination in the public system." *Braxton v. Board of Public Instruction for Duval County*, 326 F.2d 616, 620 (5th Cir. 1964).

By 1971, the Duval County School Board remained either incapable of or unwilling to comply with the court's order. Only 60 of the 30,000 black students in the school system participated in desegregated schooling; most black students attended all-black schools, even if that required commuting to distant schools. *Mims v. Duval County School Board*, 329 F. Supp. 123, 125 (D. Fla. 1971). The district court therefore ordered remedial action, including a plan to pair Ribault and Raines High Schools, which would yield two integrated schools. This decision was in line with the Supreme Court's 1971 opinion in *Swann v. Charlotte-Mecklenburg Board of Education*, 402 U.S. 1 (1971), which detailed the duties of school districts and the powers of district courts to ensure plans to work realistically and effectively to end racial segregation in public schools.

Soon after the court's desegregation order was put into effect, racial violence erupted at Ribault High School—the formerly predominantly white school. In response to the violence, administrators shut down the school on at least two occasions. These and subsequent events were reported in Otis Perkins, *End to Disruptions at Schools Ordered Here*, Florida Times-Union, March 6, 1972. On February 18, 1972, black students at Ribault organized a walkout; white students and black students then engaged in fights that damaged school property. Despite the participation of both groups of students, school officials blamed the black students and charged and suspended 12 of them. The administrators then recruited 30 extra teachers to be present on campus. The administration also alerted sheriffs in the vicinity, rearranged lunch schedules, and eliminated one class period to avoid confrontations between the racial groups. Then, a white faculty member removed from the cafeteria bulletin board several posters relating to Black History week, including one with a picture of philosopher and prisoner advocate Angela Davis and the caption, "THIS IS WAR."* Black students replaced the posters, and then white students took them down. This incident produced a 20-minute delay in classes, and 50 white students and 125 black students then gathered on the school patio in a "free for all" fight. Black students then tried to organize another boycott.

---

*Angela Davis became a fugitive after August 7, 1970, when she was accused of involvement in Jonathan Jackson's attempted hostage trade for the Soledad Brothers—an effort that ended in a deadly shootout. She later became a philosopher and university professor.

School authorities held black students largely responsible for the unrest that day. The authorities also believed that black adults from outside the school were encouraging students to defy police and school authorities. The school administrators petitioned the district court for injunctive relief to bar such outsiders from school premises. In response, the court issued an ex parte injunction on Sunday, March 5, 1972. Among those intended to be covered by the injunction were members of the Florida Black Front, an organization that modeled itself on the Black Panthers. The injunction was served directly on some members of that group, but not to Eric Hall, who was associated with the group. Eric Hall's lawyer, William Sheppard, recalled that Eric intended to go to the school to support the black students following the incident over the posters. Whether Hall supported or opposed integration was not entirely clear; he did seek to inspire active strategies for asserting rights.*

Hall learned of the injunction from another member of the Black Front. He asked his lawyer what would happen if he went to the high school. Sheppard recalled his response: "I told him honestly that I thought he'd get picked up in three minutes." Sheppard also recalls that Hall next telephoned the famous leftist lawyer, William Kunstler, for a second opinion.** Kunstler reportedly told Hall that as a nonparty to the suit, he could do what he wanted to do. Hall entered the campus, was immediately arrested, and was then charged with contempt. The case that bears his name has been cited with approval by the U.S. Supreme Court. *See Washington v. Washington State Commercial Passenger Fishing Vessel Assn.*, 443 U.S. 658, 692 n.32 (1979); *Golden State Bottling Co. v. NLRB*, 414 U.S. 168, 180 (1973).

Duval County never fully integrated its school system, and controversy still surrounds its schools. Despite a court-approved agreement with the National Association for the Advancement of Colored People (NAACP) in 1996, Duval County administrators prefer voluntary integration through specialized magnet programs. The NAACP, by contrast, favors a school choice plan limiting students' options in order to ensure racial balance in the schools and is concerned that the school system plans to build new schools solely in predominantly white suburbs. The school board filed a motion to end the federal court involvement in the system. The litigation ultimately ended in 2001 when the 11th Circuit, over the NAACP's objection, lifted the injunction and ended the suit because, in the court's estimation, its purpose had been achieved. *N.A.A.C.P., Jacksonville Branch v. Duval County School*, 273 F.3d 960 (2001).

A final word or two on the principals involved in the case: The senior judge on the appellate panel assigned to the case, Judge John Minor Wisdom, was one of the champions of the civil rights movement who enforced Supreme Court school desegregation rulings despite personal attacks and threats of physical violence.

---

*Interviews by Vik Kanwar with William Sheppard, Jan. 10, 1998, and Mar. 17, 1998.
**Kunstler, a cofounder of the Center for Constitutional Rights, represented the Chicago 7 defendants and many Black Panthers.

Less than a week after completing his jail term for contempt, Eric Hall was shot by a security guard in a Jacksonville, Florida, nightclub. After his photograph appeared in a newspaper story about the incident, a former parole officer from southern Florida recognized him as someone known as Kenneth Hall, wanted for robbery in southern Florida. Hall was removed from his hospital bed and tried and convicted in southern Florida. Reportedly, by the early 1980s, he had become a prisoners' rights activist.

## 4. *The Opinion*

### ■ UNITED STATES v. HALL*
472 F.2d 261 (5th Cir. 1972)

Wisdom, Circuit Judge:

This case presents the question whether a district court has power to punish for criminal contempt a person who, though neither a party nor bearing any legal relationship to a party, violates a court order designed to protect the court's judgment in a school desegregation case. We uphold the district court's conclusion that in the circumstances of this case it had this power, and affirm the defendant's conviction for contempt.

On June 23, 1971, the district court entered a "Memorandum Opinion and Final Judgment" in the case of *Mims v. Duval County School Board*. The court required the Duval County Florida school board to complete its desegregation of Duval County schools, in accordance with the Supreme Court's decision in *Swann v. Charlotte-Mecklenburg Board of Education*, 402 U.S. 1 (1971), by pairing and clustering a number of schools which had theretofore been predominantly one-race schools. This order culminated litigation begun eleven years before, *Braxton v. Board of Public Instruction*. This Court affirmed the district court's order in *Mims v. Duval County School Board*, 447 F.2d 1330 (5th Cir. 1971). The district court retained jurisdiction to enter such orders as might be necessary in the future to effectuate its judgment.

Among the schools marked for desegregation under the plan approved by the district court was Ribault Senior High School, a predominantly white school. The plan directed pairing of Ribault with William E. Raines Senior High School, a predominantly black school, so that the black enrollment would be 59 percent at Raines and 57 percent at Ribault. After the desegregation order was put into effect racial unrest and violence developed at Ribault, necessitating on one occasion the temporary closing of the school. On March 5, 1972, the superintendent of schools and the sheriff of Jacksonville filed a petition for injunctive relief in the case with the district court. This petition alleged that certain black adult "outsiders" had caused or

*Eds.' Note:* In this case and throughout this book we have omitted textual citations; textual omissions are indicated with ellipses. We have retained the original footnote numbering.

abetted the unrest and violence by their activities both on and off the Ribault campus. The petition identified the appellant Eric Hall, allegedly a member of a militant organization known as the "Black Front," as one of several such outsiders who, in combination with black students and parents, were attempting to prevent the normal operation of Ribault through student boycotts and other activities. As relief the petitioners requested an order "restraining all Ribault Senior High School students and any person acting independently or in concert with them from interfering with the orderly operation of the school and the Duval County School system, and for such other relief as the court may deem just and proper."

At an *ex parte* session on March 5, 1972, the district court entered an order providing in part:

> 1. All students of Ribault Senior High School, whether in good standing or under suspension, and other persons acting independently or in concert with them and having notice of this order are hereby enjoined and restrained from
>
> (a) Obstructing or preventing the attendance in classes of students and faculty members;
>
> (b) Harassing, threatening or intimidating any faculty, staff member or employee of Ribault Senior High School or the Duval County School Board;
>
> (c) Harassing, threatening or intimidating any student en route to and from school;
>
> (d) Destroying or attempting to destroy, defacing or attempting to deface any structure, buildings, materials or equipment of Ribault Senior High School or the Duval County School Board;
>
> (e) Committing any other act to disrupt the orderly operation of Ribault Senior High School or any other school of the Duval County School System;
>
> 2. Until further order of this Court, no person shall enter any building of the Ribault Senior High School or go upon the school's grounds except the following:
>
> (a) Students of Ribault Senior High School while attending classes or official school functions;
>
> (b) The faculty, staff, and administration of Ribault Senior High School and other employees of the Duval County School Board having assigned duties at the school;
>
> (c) Persons having business obligations which require their presence on the school's premises;
>
> (d) Parents of Ribault Senior High School students or any other person who has the prior permission of the principal or his designee to be present on the school's premises;
>
> (e) Law enforcement officials of the City of Jacksonville, the State of Florida or the United States Government.

The order went on to provide that "anyone having notice of this order who violates any of the terms thereof shall be subject to arrest, prosecution and punishment by imprisonment or fine, or both, for criminal contempt under the laws of the United States of America. . . ." The court ordered the sheriff to serve copies of the order on seven named persons, *including Eric Hall*. Hall was neither a party plaintiff nor a party defendant in the *Mims* litigation, and in issuing this order the court did not join Hall or any of the other persons named in the order as parties.

On March 9, 1972, four days after the court issued its order, Hall violated that portion of the order restricting access to Ribault High School by appearing on the Ribault campus. When questioned by a deputy United States marshal as to the reasons for his presence, Hall replied that he was on the grounds of Ribault for the purpose of violating the March 5 order. The marshal then arrested Hall and took him into custody. After a nonjury trial, the district court found Hall guilty of the charge of criminal contempt and sentenced him to sixty days' imprisonment.

On this appeal Hall raises two related contentions. Both contentions depend on the fact that Hall was not a party to the *Mims* litigation and the fact that, in violating the court's order, he was apparently acting independently of the *Mims* parties. He first points to the common law rule that a nonparty who violates an injunction solely in pursuit of his own interests cannot be held in contempt. Not having been before the court as a party or as the surrogate of a party, he argues that in accordance with this common law rule he was not bound by the court's order. Second, he contends that Rule 65(d) of the Federal Rules of Civil Procedure prevents the court's order from binding him, since Rule 65(d) limits the binding effect of injunctive orders to "parties to the action, their officers, agents, servants, employees, and attorneys, and . . . those persons in active concert or participation with them who receive actual notice of the order by personal service or otherwise." We reject both contentions.

For his first contention, that a court of equity has no power to punish for contempt a nonparty acting solely in pursuit of his own interests, the appellant relies heavily on the two leading cases of *Alemite Manufacturing Corp. v. Staff*, 42 F.2d 832 (2d Cir. 1930), and *Chase National Bank v. City of Norwalk*, 291 U.S. 431 (1934). In *Alemite* the district court had issued an injunction restraining the defendant and his agents, employees, associates, and confederates from infringing the plaintiff's patent. Subsequently a third person, not a party to the original suit and acting entirely on his own initiative, began infringing the plaintiff's patent and was held in contempt by the district court. The Second Circuit reversed in an opinion by Judge Learned Hand, stating that "it is not the act described which the decree may forbid, but only that act when the defendant does it." 42 F.2d at 833. In *Chase National Bank* the plaintiff brought suit against the City of Norwalk to obtain an injunction forbidding the removal of poles, wires, and other electrical equipment belonging to the plaintiff. The district court issued a decree enjoining the City, its officers, agents, and employees, "and all persons whomsoever to whom notice of this order shall come" from removing the equipment or otherwise interfering with the operation of the plaintiff's power plant. The Supreme Court held that the district court had violated "established principles of equity jurisdiction and procedure" insofar as its order applied to persons who were not parties, associates, or confederates of parties, but who merely had notice of the order. *See also Regal Knitwear Co. v. NLRB*, 324 U.S. 9, 13 (1945); *Scott v. Donald*, 165 U.S. 107 (1896).

This case is different. In *Alemite* and *Chase National Bank* the activities of third parties, however harmful they might have been to the plaintiffs' interests, would not have disturbed in any way the adjudication of rights and obligations as between the original plaintiffs and defendants. Infringement of the *Alemite* plaintiff's patent by a third party would not have upset the defendant's duty to refrain from infringing or rendered it more difficult for the defendant to perform that duty. Similarly, the defendant's duty in *Chase National Bank* to refrain from removing the plaintiff's equipment would remain undisturbed regardless of the activities of third parties, as would the plaintiff's right not to have its equipment removed by the defendant. The activities of Hall, however, threatened both the plaintiffs' right and the defendant's duty as adjudicated in the *Mims* litigation. In *Mims* the plaintiffs were found to have a constitutional right to attend an integrated school. . . . In short, the activities of persons contributing to racial disorder at Ribault imperiled the court's fundamental power to make a binding adjudication between the parties properly before it.

Courts of equity have inherent jurisdiction to preserve their ability to render judgment in a case such as this. This was the import of the holding in *United States v. United Mine Workers of America*, 330 U.S. 258 (1947). There the district court had issued a temporary restraining order forbidding a union from striking, though there was a substantial question of whether the Norris-LaGuardia Act had deprived the district court of jurisdiction to issue such an order. The Supreme Court upheld the defendants' contempt conviction for violation of this order. As an alternative holding the Court stated that the contempt conviction would have been upheld even if the district court had ultimately been found to be without jurisdiction. This holding affirmed the power of a court of equity to issue an order to preserve the status quo in order to protect its ability to render judgment in a case over which it might have jurisdiction. . . .

The integrity of a court's power to render a binding judgment in a case over which it has jurisdiction is at stake in the present case. . . .

The principle that courts have jurisdiction to punish for contempt in order to protect their ability to render judgment is also found in the use of *in rem* injunctions. Federal courts have issued injunctions binding on all persons, regardless of notice, who come into contact with property which is the subject of a judicial decree. . . . A court entering a decree binding on a particular piece of property is necessarily faced with the danger that its judgment may be disrupted in the future by members of an undefinable class—those who may come into contact with the property. The *in rem* injunction protects the court's judgment. The district court here faced an analogous problem. The judgment in a school case, as in other civil rights actions, inures to the benefit of a large class of persons, regardless of whether the original action is cast in the form of a class action. . . . At the same time court orders in school cases, affecting as they do large numbers of people, necessarily depend on the cooperation of the entire community for their implementation.

As this Court is well aware, school desegregation orders often strongly excite community passions. School orders are, like *in rem* orders, particularly vulnerable to disruption by an undefinable class of persons who are neither parties nor acting at the instigation of parties. In such cases, as in voting rights cases, courts must have the power to issue orders similar to that issued in this case, tailored to the exigencies of the situation and directed to protecting the court's judgment. . . .

The appellant also asserts that Rule 65(d) of the Federal Rules of Civil Procedure prevents the court's order from binding him.[3] He points out that he was not a party to the original action, nor an officer, agent, servant, employee, or attorney of a party, and denies that he was acting in "active concert or participation" with any party to the original action.

In examining this contention we start with the proposition that Rule 65 was intended to embody "the common-law doctrine that a decree of injunction not only binds the parties defendant but also those identified with them in interest, in 'privity' with them, represented by them or subject to their control." . . . Literally read, Rule 65(d) would forbid the issuance of *in rem* injunctions. Note, *Binding Nonparties to Injunction Decrees*, 49 Minn. L. Rev. 719, 736 (1965). But courts have continued to issue *in rem* injunctions notwithstanding Rule 65(d), since they possessed the power to do so at common law and since Rule 65(d) was intended to embody rather than to limit their common law powers.

Similarly, we conclude that Rule 65(d), as a codification rather than a limitation of courts' common-law powers, cannot be read to restrict the inherent power of a court to protect its ability to render a binding judgment. We hold that Hall's relationship to the *Mims* case fell within that contemplated by Rule 65(d). By deciding *Mims* and retaining jurisdiction the district court had, in effect, adjudicated the rights of the entire community with respect to the racial controversy surrounding the school system. Moreover, as we have noted, in the circumstances of this case third parties such as Hall were in a position to upset the court's adjudication. This was not a situation which could have been anticipated by the draftsmen of procedural rules. In meeting the situation as it did, the district court did not overstep its powers.

3. Rule 65(d) provides:

*Form and Scope of Injunction or Restraining Order.* Every order granting an injunction and every restraining order shall set forth the reasons for its issuance; shall be specific in terms; shall describe in reasonable detail, and not by reference to the complaint or other document, the act or acts sought to be restrained; and is binding only upon the parties to the action, their officers, agents, servants, employees, and attorneys, and upon those persons in active concert or participation with them who receive actual notice of the order by personal service or otherwise.

*Eds.' Note*: When you compare the version of Rule 65 reproduced in the opinion to that in your Federal Rules supplement, you will note that the version of Rule 65(d) in effect in 1972 is similar in substance to the modern rule, but the format is quite different. This is because all of the Federal Rules were restyled in 2007.

We do not hold that courts are free to issue permanent injunctions against all the world in school cases. Hall had notice of the court's order. Rather than challenge it by the orderly processes of law, he resorted to conscious, willful defiance. *See Walker v. Birmingham*, 388 U.S. 307 (1967).

It is true that this order was issued without a hearing, and that ordinarily injunctive relief cannot be granted without a hearing. *See* 7 J. Moore, *Moore's Federal Practice* ¶ 65.04[3] & n.8a (1972). But we need not hold that this order has the effect of a preliminary or permanent injunction. Rather, the portion of the court's order here complained of may be characterized as a temporary restraining order, which under Rule 65(b) may be issued *ex parte*. . . .

We hold, then, that the district court had the inherent power to protect its ability to render a binding judgment between the original parties to the *Mims* litigation by issuing an interim *ex parte* order against an undefinable class of persons. We further hold that willful violation of that order by one having notice of it constitutes criminal contempt. The judgment of the district court is affirmed.

## Comments and Questions

1. The use of injunctions arising from public nuisance suits against gangs has gained popularity in many cities as a tool against criminal activity. Typically a city will identify a neighborhood as the focus of an anti-gang effort, bringing suit against named defendants as alleged gang members. Often, defendants fail to appear at the preliminary injunction hearing, and those who do appear are rarely represented by counsel. Being a civil proceeding, the "reasonable doubt" standard is not used. Thus, an injunction is often issued, prohibiting defendants from engaging in illegal as well as otherwise legal activity, such as congregating with other gang members. Once the injunction is issued, a violation of its terms constitutes criminal contempt, punishable by imprisonment. In this way judges become de facto legislatures, criminalizing various types of behavior by specific individuals on the grounds of preventing a public nuisance. The use of such injunctions and subsequent prosecutions for criminal contempt were upheld in a landmark decision by the Supreme Court of California in *People ex rel. Gallo v. Acuna*, 929 P.2d 596 (Cal. 1997). An attempt by the Chicago City Council to criminalize similar activity (loitering in a public place by gang members) through legislation was held to be unconstitutionally vague by the Supreme Court in *City of Chicago v. Morales*, 527 U.S. 41 (1999). Nonetheless, the Court hinted at more restricted alternatives, and the use of gang injunctions has become more and more popular.

Two recent developments have raised further questions concerning the constitutionality of such injunctions. First, the areas covered by such injunctions have become larger in scope. Second, gangs have been sued as unincorporated associations, leading to injunctions issued against the gangs as associations rather than individually named defendants. This leaves determination of gang membership to police officers enforcing the injunctions and eventually to judges overseeing contempt hearings. Doubts have been raised concerning the vagueness and excessive discretion involved in such procedures. Can the decision in *Hall* be used to support the use of such injunctions and the subsequent enforcement of injunctions against unnamed parties? Is the use of the court's contempt power in such cases necessary to ensuring the court's ability to remedy the initial nuisance? Do other considerations outweigh the potential benefits? *See* Scott E. Atkinson, *The Outer Limits of Gang Injunctions*, 59 Vand. L. Rev. 1693 (2006); Matthew Mickle Werdegar, *Enjoining the Constitution: The Use of Public Nuisance Abatement Injunctions Against Urban Street Gangs*, 51 Stan. L. Rev. 409 (1999).

2. In a suit filed by an abortion clinic against a group of regular protesters, a state court granted the clinic an injunction prohibiting various types of activities in the vicinity, such as blocking or obstructing passage to the clinic or producing loud noises that could be heard inside. According to the terms of the injunction, it applied to "all persons with actual notice" of the judgment. In a subsequent suit, the clinic attempted to apply the injunction to a new set of picketers, unrelated to the first group. The court held that the "actual notice" provision of the injunction was invalid, as it could not be made to apply to the world at large. *Planned Parenthood Golden Gate v. Garibaldi*, 132 Cal. Rptr. 2d 46 (Ct. App. 2003). The court emphasized that its role is limited to remedying deprivations as between two parties, as opposed to drafting rules applicable to the general public. Is this consistent with the decision in *Hall*?

## C. THE RIGHT TO BE HEARD: ELEMENTS AND HISTORY OF DUE PROCESS

> ". . . nor shall any State deprive any person of life, liberty, or property, without due process of law . . ."
> U.S. Constitution, amend. XIV, § 1*

The phrase "due process of law" is the Constitution's most basic notion of procedure. But what does it mean? The phrase most simply refers to a right to be heard, but as interpreted by theorists and courts, the meaning of that right has evolved and changed shape over time. A heated debate over these issues in the context of a highly charged political period produced six separate opinions in the Supreme Court case of *Joint Anti-Fascist Refugee Committee v. McGrath*, 341 U.S. 123 (1951). In that case, three organizations challenged the decision of the Attorney General of the United States both to list them as "totalitarian, fascist, communist, or subversive" and to furnish that

---

*\*Eds.' Note:* The Fourteenth Amendment specifically sets limits on what state governments may do. For limitations on the federal government, see Amendment Five: "nor [shall any person] be deprived of life, liberty, or property, without due process of law."

information to the Loyalty Review Board of the United States Civil Service Commission. The three organizations claimed that this governmental action was taken without notice to them or an opportunity for them to present a defense, and injured them in a national climate that was decidedly anti-Communist. The majority view of the Supreme Court Justices interpreted "due process" to require that the organizations be given the opportunity to be heard and to present their own evidence before being labeled pejoratively by the Attorney General.

In his concurring opinion in the case, Justice Felix Frankfurter suggested two reasons for notice and hearing: "No better instrument has been devised for *arriving at truth* than to give a person in jeopardy of a serious loss notice of the case against him and opportunity to meet it. Nor has a better way been found for *generating the feeling*, so important to a popular government, *that justice has been done*." 341 U.S. 149, 171-172 (emphasis added). He explained: "The heart of the matter is that democracy implies respect for the elementary rights of men, however suspect or unworthy; a democratic government must therefore practice fairness; and fairness can rarely be obtained by secret, one-sided determination of facts decisive of rights."

At the same time, Justice Frankfurter acknowledged that "'due process,' unlike some legal rules, is not a technical conception with a fixed content unrelated to time, place and circumstances. Expressing as it does in its ultimate analysis respect enforced by law for that feeling of just treatment which has evolved through centuries of Anglo-American constitutional history and civilization, 'due process' cannot be imprisoned within the treacherous limits of any formula. . . . It is a delicate process of adjustment inescapably involving the exercise of judgment by those whom the Constitution entrusted with the unfolding of the process." 341 U.S. at 162-163.

Nearly twenty years later, a group of attorneys for poor people gave the Justices a further opportunity to interpret due process. *Goldberg v. Kelly* posed the question: Does due process require notice and a hearing before the government terminates public assistance (or welfare) benefits? As you read the background to the case and the Supreme Court opinions, consider the values behind the idea of due process and the specific contours that idea took in this setting.

## 1. Background of Goldberg v. Kelly

Presidents John F. Kennedy and Lyndon B. Johnson promoted programs to address poverty; these became the "War on Poverty" declared by President Johnson in 1964. These federal programs included public assistance, health care, housing assistance, job training, public education, and legal services for poor people. Activists and lawyers working on behalf of poor people found a model in the civil rights movement. "Activists, perhaps naively and certainly optimistically, viewed the federal courts as the ultimate protectors of individual rights and, under the appropriate circumstances, arbiters of social change." Martha F. Davis, *Brutal Need: Lawyers and the Welfare Rights Movement, 1960-1973* at 1 (1993).

Activists and lawyers hoped to use law to make public assistance more certain and reliable, even though the state had long treated welfare as a gift rather than a right. Even progressive lawyers in the 1960s stopped short of arguing that the Constitution mandated welfare as a right. Instead, the lawyers argued that once an individual established eligibility, under a statute, for public assistance, the state had to comply with constitutional principles, such as equal protection and the right to travel in the implementation of the benefit. Before *Goldberg v. Kelly*, federal and state welfare laws had allowed benefits to be terminated as soon as a caseworker determined that the recipient was ineligible. Sometimes, caseworkers used the threat of termination to shake up recipients and make them pliant.

For due process to apply, however, public assistance had to somehow fit the predicates of "life, liberty, or property." Here, a landmark article written by Charles Reich helped. The Yale Law School professor argued that government benefits including licenses and jobs, as well as welfare payments, effectively operate like property and deserve legal protections like property, if the state is not to require extraordinary abilities to coerce those who depend on these resources.* Recent legislative changes have altered the underlying benefits program established in the 1970s, as described in a Comment that follows the Court's opinion in *Goldberg v. Kelly*.

## 2. The Complaint

Civil litigation starts with a complaint, filed by the plaintiff. As you read the complaint that launched the decision now known as *Goldberg v. Kelly*, note that the initial filing is captioned *Kelly v. Wyman*. Why? The plaintiff class was led by Kelly; the plaintiffs won at the district court level, and the caption for the appeal listed the appellant (defendant) first. But by that time, the head of the state agency had changed, so the name had changed. Consider how the plaintiffs' lawyers framed the lawsuit. Why did they frame the suit to include more than one plaintiff? The Federal Rule governing complaints requires only a "short and plain statement of the claim showing that the pleader is entitled to relief" along with a demand for that relief. Fed. R. Civ. P. 8. Yet this complaint includes considerable detail. What might have been the benefit to the plaintiffs of providing more detail than was required?

---

*For a thorough discussion of the influences on Reich's thought, see Martha Davis, *Brutal Need: Lawyers and the Welfare Rights Movement 1960-1973*, at 82-86 (1993). Lawyers for poor people, notably those working at the federally funded Mobilization for Youth Legal Unit in New York City, and others at the Center on Social Welfare Policy in New York City, took up these ideas in a test case challenging terminations of public benefits. That case became *Goldberg v. Kelly*.

| | |
|---|---|
| JOHN KELLY, et al.,<br>Plaintiffs<br>v.<br><br>GEORGE K. WYMAN,<br>et al., Defendants. | Civil Action No. 394-1968<br><br><br>COMPLAINT<br>FOR DECLARATORY JUDGMENT,<br>INJUNCTIVE RELIEF |

## I

This is an action for injunctive and declaratory relief authorized by Title 42 U.S.C. 1983 to secure rights, privileges and immunities established by the Fourteenth Amendment to the Constitution of the United States and the Social Security Act, Title 42 U.S.C. 301 et seq., and the regulations promulgated thereunder. Jurisdiction is conferred on this Court by Title 28 U.S.C. 1343(3) and (4) providing for original jurisdiction of this Court in suits authorized by Title 42 U.S.C. 1983; and jurisdiction is further conferred on this Court by 28 U.S.C. 2201 and 2202 relating to declaratory judgments.

## II

This is a proper case for determination by a three-judge court pursuant to Title 28 U.S.C. 2281 and 2284,* in that it seeks an injunction to restrain the defendants from applying, enforcing, executing and implementing Sections 213(2), 214, 304, 325, 350(2) (6), and 353(2) of the New York Social Services Law, Section 351.22 and 356.4 of Volume 18, Official Compilation of Code Rules and Regulations of the State of New York (hereafter referred to as 18 N.Y.C.R.R.), Sections 84.2-84.23 of 18 N.Y.C.R.R., promulgated by the New York State Board of Social Welfare to supersede Section 351.22 and 356.4 on March 1, 1968, and related statutes, rules and regulations, insofar as these statutes and regulations require termination or suspension of financial aid in the form of public assistance [Aid to Families with Dependent Children (AFDC), Aid to the Aged, Blind and Disabled (AABD), and Home Relief (HR)] prior to the granting of adequate notice and opportunity to be heard on the grounds of the invalidity of said statutes and regulations under the Constitution and laws of the United States.

## III

This action seeks an injunction and declaratory judgment restraining the enforcement of, and declaring unconstitutional the aforesaid state

---

*Eds.' Note:* Section 2281 was repealed in 1976. Section 2284 sets forth the current law concerning three-judge courts.

statutes and state-wide rules and regulations, on their face and as applied and interpreted by defendants, on the grounds that said statutes, rules and regulations, and actions taken pursuant thereto deprive plaintiffs of the due process of law guaranteed by the Fourteenth Amendment to the United States Constitution and, so far as the AFDC and AABD programs are concerned, deprive plaintiffs of the "fair hearing" guaranteed by the Social Security Act, in that said statutes, rules and regulations deny to plaintiffs an opportunity for a hearing prior to termination or suspension of financial aid under the public assistance program.

## IV

Plaintiffs John Kelly, Randolph Young, and Juan DeJesus are adult citizens of the United States and residents of the City and State of New York who received public assistance until aid was terminated without notice and without a hearing.

Plaintiffs Pearl McKinney and Pearl Frye are adult citizens of the United States and residents of the City and State of New York who received public assistance until aid was terminated without a hearing.

Plaintiff Altagracia Guzman is an adult citizen of the United States who faces imminent termination of her public assistance benefits if she does not accede to a demand of the New York City Department of Social Service, for which demand the Department has no basis in law.

## V

Plaintiffs bring this action pursuant to Rule 23 of the Federal Rules of Civil Procedure on behalf of themselves and all other recipients of public assistance who are similarly situated. All public assistance recipients are similarly affected by the statutes, rules and regulations challenged herein in that all are by statute, rule and regulation made subject to peremptory *ex parte* termination of their aid. The persons in the class are so numerous as to make joinder impractical; there are common questions of law and fact; plaintiffs' claims are typical of the claims of the class; and the representative plaintiffs will fairly and adequately protect the interests of the class. The parties opposing the class have acted or refused to act on grounds generally applicable to the class.

## VI

Defendant George K. Wyman is the Commissioner of the Department of Social Services of the State of New York and is charged with statewide administration of the public assistance program and with establishing regulations to carry out the statutory provisions of said program.

Defendant Maurice C. Hunt is Acting Commissioner of the Department of Social Services of the City of New York and is responsible for administering the public assistance program in the City of New York.

Defendants Hugh R. Jones, as Chairman of the State Board of Social Welfare, and Mrs. Omar Adams, Dorothy I. Height, Richard G. Kimmerer, John M. Galbraith, Edward J. Johannes, Jr., Arthur G. Hopkins, Mrs. Monica M. McConville, John P. Hale, Mrs. Alexander E. Holstein, Jr., Frederick A. Klingenstein, George F. Berlinger, Theodore C. Jackson, Jose Lopez, and David Bernstein, as members of the State Board of Social Welfare, are responsible for the promulgation of rules governing the policies and conduct of the Department of Social Services of the State of New York.

## VII

The aforesaid public assistance programs created by the New York Social Services law provide financial aid to certain needy persons. Persons who meet the statutory criteria receive financial aid as a matter of statutory entitlement.

## VIII

At all times relevant hereto the State of New York and defendants, in order to receive federal funds for the Aid to Families with Dependent Children and Aid to the Aged, Blind, and Disabled programs have been required by the Social Security Act, Title 42 U.S.C. § 301 et seq., to have formulated a "state plan" for said programs in conformity with the provisions of the Act and the United States Constitution. The Social Security Act, as interpreted by regulations of the United States Department of Health, Education and Welfare requires that a "state plan" provide for granting an opportunity for a fair hearing before the State agency to any individual aggrieved by an action of a local Department of Social Services.

## IX

1. Plaintiff John Kelly is twenty-nine years old and was a recipient of Home Relief in the amount of $80.05 semi-monthly from August 1967, until January 1, 1968.

2. Plaintiff Kelly was the victim of a hit and run accident in June, 1966, which resulted in serious injury, repeated hospitalization and inability to work.

3. On December 16, 1967, plaintiff Kelly was ordered by his caseworker to move out of the Broadway Central Hotel in which he was then residing and in which he desired to reside and into the Barbara Hotel which charged equal rates but which Mr. Kelly knew to be inhabited by drug addicts and drunkards.

4. Plaintiff Kelly moved into the Barbara Hotel as a result of his caseworker's order, but moved out of this hotel within a short time since he considered it a serious threat to his health and safety. Mr. Kelly moved into the apartment of a friend.

5. On January 8, 1968, plaintiff Kelly was informed by the hotel desk clerk at the Barbara Hotel where he received his mail that Mr. Kelly's caseworker

had terminated his case and had instructed the clerk to return a check which was mailed to Mr. Kelly for a winter coat which the Department had previously decided Mr. Kelly required.

6. Plaintiff Kelly did not receive his assistance check due January 16, 1968.

7. Plaintiff Kelly attempted to visit his caseworker at the Gramercy Welfare Center, 110 East 28th Street, New York, N.Y. on January 8 and January 16, 1968, and on both occasions was refused an interview.

8. Plaintiff Kelly was informed on both occasions that his case had been terminated because he had violated his caseworker's instructions to move into the Barbara Hotel and remain there or suffer immediate termination of his case.

9. On January 23, 1968, a social worker at Mobilization for Youth, Inc. telephoned the Gramercy Welfare Center and was informed that Mr. Kelly's case had been terminated. Her efforts to re-open Mr. Kelly's case were ineffective.

10. Plaintiff Kelly has no assets, no means of support and remains unable to work pending further surgery which was occasioned by his 1966 automobile accident. Since his termination Mr. Kelly has been living on the charity of his friends.

[The complaint provides details of the background and situation of additional plaintiffs including financial status and the manner in which public assistance was terminated.] . . .

## XV

Sections 213(2), 304, 325 and 353(2) of the New York Social Services Law, and 18 N.Y.C.R.R. Section 356.4 as in effect and as amended by 18 N.Y.C.R.R. Section 84.2-84.23. effective March 1, 1968, prescribing the hearing procedure in the public assistance program, and Sections 214, 304(6), 325 and 350(2) (b) and 18 N.Y.C.R.R. 351.22 prescribing the manner of termination or suspension of aid in the public assistance program, on their face, and as interpreted and applied to plaintiffs and members of their class, deprive the plaintiffs of the right of due process of law guaranteed by the Fourteenth Amendment to the United States Constitution and, to the extent applicable, of the "Fair Hearing" guaranteed by the Social Security Act in that said statutes and the regulations adopted in enforcement thereof authorize and require effective action terminating and suspending financial aid prior to the granting of reasonable notice and opportunity for a hearing which meets due process standards. The termination and withdrawal of financial aid may, under the present regulations, extend for a period of several months before a hearing is held and a decision is rendered, even though plaintiffs had been receiving such aid and are in vital need of such aid for food, shelter and medical care and even though plaintiffs are prepared to prove that they are and have been eligible. Such deprivation is contrary to the purpose of the Social Security Act.

## XVI

Plaintiffs have no adequate remedy at law and defendants will continue to cause and threaten to cause irreparable injury to plaintiffs unless enjoined by this Court. Plaintiffs Kelly, Young and Dejesus will not be afforded any administrative hearing since they received aid through the Home Relief program. Plaintiff Frye is awaiting the hearing she has requested. Plaintiff McKinney only received her notice of termination on Friday, January 26.

## XVII

Plaintiffs have no adequate resources with which to support themselves and their families in the absence of their public assistance grants.

WHEREFORE, plaintiffs respectfully pray on behalf of themselves and all others similarly situated that this Court:

1. Assume jurisdiction of this cause and convene a three-judge Court pursuant to Title 28 U.S.C. § 2281.

2. Enter a temporary restraining order and a preliminary injunction ordering the defendants to refrain from

1. refusing to pay the named plaintiffs herein their regular public assistance grants and

2. terminating aid to any recipient of public assistance without giving advance written notice stating the reasons for such action and without affording such recipients an opportunity for a hearing prior to withdrawal of aid.

3. Enter a declaratory judgment pursuant to Title 28 U.S.C. Sections 2201 and 2202 and Rule 57 of the Federal Rules of Civil Procedure declaring that Sections 213(2), 214, 304, 325, 350(2) (b) and 353(2) of the New York Social Service Law and related provisions, and the regulations and rules issued pursuant thereto, violate the Fourteenth Amendment to the United States Constitution and the Social Security Act on their face and as applied, insofar as they authorize and require termination or suspension of public assistance prior to granting reasonable notice and opportunity for a hearing meeting due process standards.

4. Enter a preliminary and permanent injunction restraining the defendants, their successors in office, agents and employees from terminating or suspending the aid of any public assistance recipient prior to the granting of reasonable and adequate notice and opportunity for a hearing which satisfies the standards of due process of law.

5. Allow plaintiffs their costs herein, grant them and all others similarly situated such additional or alternative relief including payment of all monies wrongfully withheld, as the Court may deem to be just and appropriate.

Respectfully submitted,
[Attorneys' names]

(Sworn to January 26, 1968.)

## 3. *The Supreme Court's Response*

### ■ GOLDBERG v. KELLY
#### 397 U.S. 254 (1970)

Justice BRENNAN delivered the opinion of the Court:

The question for decision is whether a State that terminates public assistance payments to a particular recipient without affording him the opportunity for an evidentiary hearing prior to termination denies the recipient procedural due process in violation of the Due Process Clause of the Fourteenth Amendment.

This action was brought in the District Court for the Southern District of New York by residents of New York City receiving financial aid under the federally assisted program of Aid to Families with Dependent Children (AFDC) or under New York State's general Home Relief program.[1] Their complaint alleged that the New York State and New York City officials administering these programs terminated, or were about to terminate, such aid without prior notice and hearing, thereby denying them due process of law. At the time the suits were filed there was no requirement of prior notice or hearing of any kind before termination of financial aid. However, the State and city adopted procedures for notice and hearing after the suits were brought, and the plaintiffs, appellees here, then challenged the constitutional adequacy of those procedures.

The State Commissioner of Social Services amended the State Department of Social Services' Official Regulations to require that local social services officials proposing to discontinue or suspend a recipient's financial aid do so . . . [by] giving notice to the recipient of the reasons for a proposed discontinuance or suspension at least seven days prior to its effective date, with notice also that upon request the recipient may have the proposal reviewed by a local welfare official holding a position superior to that of the supervisor who approved the proposed discontinuance or suspension, and, further, the recipient may submit, for purposes of the review, a written statement to demonstrate why his grant should not be discontinued or suspended. The decision by the reviewing official whether to discontinue or suspend aid must be made expeditiously, with written notice of the decision to the recipient. . . .

[Under an additional city procedure, a] caseworker who has doubts about the recipient's continued eligibility must first discuss them with the recipient. If the caseworker concludes that the recipient is no longer eligible, he recommends termination of aid to a unit supervisor. If the latter concurs, he sends the recipient a letter stating the reasons for proposing to terminate aid and notifying him that within seven days he may request that a higher

---

1. AFDC was established by the Social Security Act of 1935, 49 Stat. 627, as amended, 42 U.S.C. § 601-610 (1964 ed. and Supp. IV). It is a categorical assistance program supported by federal grants-in-aid but administered by the state according to regulations of the Secretary of Health, Education and Welfare. . . . Home Relief is a general assistance program financed and administered solely by New York state and local governments. . . .

official review the record, and may support the request with a written statement prepared personally or with the aid of an attorney or other person. If the
reviewing official affirms the determination of ineligibility, aid is stopped
immediately and the recipient is informed by letter of the reasons for the
action. Appellees' challenge to this procedure emphasizes the absence of
any provisions for the personal appearance of the recipient before the reviewing official, for oral presentation of evidence, and for confrontation and cross-
examination of adverse witnesses. However, the letter does inform the
recipient that he may request a post-termination "fair hearing," This is a
proceeding before an independent state hearing officer at which the recipient
may appear personally, offer oral evidence, confront and cross-examine the
witnesses against him, and have a record made of the hearing. If the recipient
prevails at the "fair hearing" he is paid all funds erroneously withheld. . . . A
recipient whose aid is not restored by a "fair hearing" decision may have
judicial review. . . .

The constitutional issue to be decided, therefore, is the narrow one
whether the Due Process Clause requires that the recipient be afforded an
evidentiary hearing *before* the termination of benefits. The District Court
held that only a pre-termination evidentiary hearing would satisfy the
constitutional command, and rejected the argument of the state and city
officials that the combination of the post-termination "fair hearing" with
the informal pre-termination review disposed of all due process claims. . . .
Although state officials were party defendants in the action, only the Commissioner of Social Services of the City of New York appealed. We noted
probable jurisdiction. . . . We affirm. . . .

Appellant does not contend that procedural due process is not applicable
to the termination of welfare benefits. Such benefits are a matter of statutory
entitlement for persons qualified to receive them. Their termination involves
state action that adjudicates important rights. The constitutional challenge
cannot be answered by an argument that public assistance benefits are "a
'privilege' and not a 'right.'" *Shapiro v. Thompson*, 394 U.S. 618, 627 n.6
(1969). Relevant constitutional restraints apply as much to the withdrawal
of public assistance benefits as to disqualification for unemployment compensation, *Sherbert v. Verner*, 374 U.S. 398 (1963); or to denial of a tax exemption,
*Speiser v. Randall*, 357 U.S. 513 (1958); or to discharge from public employment, *Slochower v. Board of Higher Education*, 350 U.S. 551 (1956). The
extent to which procedural due process must be afforded the recipient is
influenced by the extent to which he may be "condemned to suffer grievous
loss," *Joint Anti-Fascist Refugee Committee v. McGrath*, 341 U.S. 123, 168
(1951) (Frankfurter, J., concurring), and depends upon whether the recipient's interest in avoiding that loss outweighs the governmental interest in
summary adjudication. Accordingly, as we said in *Cafeteria & Restaurant
Workers Union v. McElroy*, 367 U.S. 886, 895 (1961), "consideration of
what procedures due process may require under any given set of circumstances must begin with a determination of the precise nature of the government function involved as well as of the private interest that has been

affected by governmental action." *See also Hannah v. Larche*, 363 U.S. 420, 440, 442 (1960).

It is true, of course, that some governmental benefits may be administratively terminated without affording the recipient a pre-termination evidentiary hearing. But we agree with the District Court that when welfare is discontinued, only a pre-termination evidentiary hearing provides the recipient with procedural due process. For qualified recipients, welfare provides the means to obtain essential food, clothing, housing, and medical care. Thus the crucial factor in this context—a factor not present in the case of the blacklisted government contractor, the discharged government employee, the taxpayer denied a tax exemption, or virtually anyone else whose governmental entitlements are ended—is that termination of aid pending resolution of a controversy over eligibility may deprive an eligible recipient of the very means by which to live while he waits. Since he lacks independent resources, his situation becomes immediately desperate. His need to concentrate upon finding the means for daily subsistence, in turn, adversely affects his ability to seek redress from the welfare bureaucracy.

Moreover, important governmental interests are promoted by affording recipients a pre-termination evidentiary hearing. From its founding the Nation's basic commitment has been to foster the dignity and well-being of all persons within its borders. We have come to recognize that forces not within the control of the poor contribute to their poverty. This perception, against the background of our traditions, has significantly influenced the development of the contemporary public assistance system. Welfare, by meeting the basic demands of subsistence, can help bring within the reach of the poor the same opportunities that are available to others to participate meaningfully in the life of the community. At the same time, welfare guards against the societal malaise that may flow from a widespread sense of unjustified frustration and insecurity. Public assistance, then, is not mere charity, but a means to "promote the general Welfare, and secure the Blessings of Liberty to ourselves and our Posterity." The same governmental interests that counsel the provision of welfare, counsel as well its uninterrupted provision to those eligible to receive it; pre-termination evidentiary hearings are indispensable to that end.

Appellant does not challenge the force of these considerations but argues that they are outweighed by countervailing governmental interests in conserving fiscal and administrative resources. These interests, the argument goes, justify the delay of any evidentiary hearing until after discontinuance of the grants. Summary adjudication protects the public fisc by stopping payments promptly upon discovery of reason to believe that a recipient is no longer eligible. Since most terminations are accepted without challenge, summary adjudication also conserves both the fisc and administrative time and energy by reducing the number of evidentiary hearings actually held.

We agree with the District Court, however, that these governmental interests are not overriding in the welfare context. The requirement of a prior hearing doubtless involves some greater expense, and the benefits paid to ineligible recipients pending decision at the hearing probably cannot be recouped, since these recipients are likely to be judgment-proof. But the State is not without weapons to minimize these increased costs. Much of the drain on fiscal and administrative resources can be reduced by developing procedures for prompt pre-termination hearings and by skillful use of personnel and facilities. Indeed, the very provision for a post-termination evidentiary hearing in New York's Home Relief program is itself cogent evidence that the State recognizes the primacy of the public interest in correct eligibility determinations and therefore in the provision of procedural safeguards. Thus, the interest of the eligible recipient in uninterrupted receipt of public assistance, coupled with the State's interest that his payments not be erroneously terminated, clearly outweighs the State's competing concern to prevent any increase in its fiscal and administrative burdens. . . .

## II

We also agree with the District Court, however, that the pre-termination hearing need not take the form of a judicial or quasi-judicial trial. We bear in mind that the statutory "fair hearing" will provide the recipient with a full administrative review.[14] Accordingly, the pre-termination hearing has one function only: to produce an initial determination of the validity of the welfare department's grounds for discontinuance of payments in order to protect a recipient against an erroneous termination of his benefits. . . . Thus, a complete record and a comprehensive opinion, which would serve primarily to facilitate judicial review and to guide future decisions, need not be provided at the pre-termination stage. We recognize, too, that both welfare authorities and recipients have an interest in relatively speedy resolution of questions of eligibility, that they are used to dealing with one another informally, and that some welfare departments have very burdensome caseloads. These considerations justify the limitation of the pre-termination hearing to minimum procedural safeguards, adapted to the particular characteristics of welfare recipients, and to the limited nature of the controversies to be resolved. We wish to add that we, no less than the dissenters, recognize the importance of not imposing upon the States or the Federal Government in this developing field of law any procedural requirements beyond those demanded by rudimentary due process. . . .

In the present context these principles require that a recipient have timely and adequate notice detailing the reasons for a proposed termination, and an effective opportunity to defend by confronting any adverse witnesses and by presenting his own arguments and evidence orally. These rights are important in cases such as those before us, where recipients have challenged proposed terminations as resting on incorrect or misleading factual premises or on misapplication of rules or policies to the facts of particular cases.

---

14. Due process does not, of course, require two hearings. If, for example, a State simply wishes to continue benefits until after a "fair" hearing there will be no need for a preliminary hearing.

We are not prepared to say that the seven-day notice currently provided by New York City is constitutionally insufficient per se, although there may be cases where fairness would require that a longer time be given. Nor do we see any constitutional deficiency in the content or form of the notice. New York employs both a letter and a personal conference with a caseworker to inform a recipient of the precise questions raised about his continued eligibility. Evidently the recipient is told the legal and factual bases for the Department's doubts. This combination is probably the most effective method of communicating with recipients.

The city's procedures presently do not permit recipients to appear personally with or without counsel before the official who finally determines continued eligibility. Thus a recipient is not permitted to present evidence to that official orally, or to confront or cross-examine adverse witnesses. These omissions are fatal to the constitutional adequacy of the procedures.

The opportunity to be heard must be tailored to the capacities and circumstances of those who are to be heard. It is not enough that a welfare recipient may present his position to the decision maker in writing or secondhand through his caseworker. Written submissions are an unrealistic option for most recipients, who lack the educational attainment necessary to write effectively and who cannot obtain professional assistance. Moreover, written submissions do not afford the flexibility of oral presentations; they do not permit the recipient to mold his argument to the issues the decision maker appears to regard as important. Particularly where credibility and veracity are at issue, as they must be in many termination proceedings, written submissions are a wholly unsatisfactory basis for decision. The secondhand presentation to the decision maker by the caseworker has its own deficiencies; since the caseworker usually gathers the facts upon which the charge of ineligibility rests, the presentation of the recipient's side of the controversy cannot safely be left to him. Therefore a recipient must be allowed to state his position orally. Informal procedures will suffice; in this context due process does not require a particular order of proof or mode of offering evidence. . . .

In almost every setting where important decisions turn on questions of fact, due process requires an opportunity to confront and cross-examine adverse witnesses. . . . Welfare recipients must therefore be given an opportunity to confront and cross-examine the witnesses relied on by the department.

"The right to be heard would be, in many cases, of little avail if it did not comprehend the right to be heard by counsel." *Powell v. Alabama*, 287 U.S. 45, 68-69 (1932). We do not say that counsel must be provided at the pretermination hearing, but only that the recipient must be allowed to retain an attorney if he so desires. . . .

Finally, the decision maker's conclusion as to a recipient's eligibility must rest solely on the legal rules and evidence adduced at the hearing. To demonstrate compliance with this elementary requirement, the decision maker should state the reasons for his determination and indicate the evidence he relied on, though his statement need not amount to a full opinion or even formal findings of fact and conclusions of law. And, of course, an impartial decision maker is essential. We agree with the District Court that prior involvement in some aspects of a case will not necessarily bar a welfare official from acting as a decision maker. He should not, however, have participated in making the determination under review. Affirmed.

Justice BLACK, dissenting:

In the last half century the United States, along with many, perhaps most, other nations of the world, has moved far toward becoming a welfare state, that is, a nation that for one reason or another taxes its most affluent people to help support, feed, clothe, and shelter its less fortunate citizens. The result is that today more than nine million men, women, and children in the United States receive some kind of state or federally financed public assistance in the form of allowances or gratuities, generally paid them periodically, usually by the week, month, or quarter. Since these gratuities are paid on the basis of need, the list of recipients is not static, and some people go off the lists and others are added from time to time. These ever-changing lists put a constant administrative burden on government and it certainly could not have reasonably anticipated that this burden would include the additional procedural expense imposed by the Court today.

. . . [W]hen federal judges use this judicial power for legislative purposes, I think they wander out of their field of vested powers and transgress into the area constitutionally assigned to the Congress and the people. That is precisely what I believe the Court is doing in this case. Hence my dissent.

The more than a million names on the relief rolls in New York, and the more than nine million names on the rolls of all the 50 States were not put there at random. The names are there because state welfare officials believed that those people were eligible for assistance. Probably in the officials' haste to make out the lists many names were put there erroneously in order to alleviate immediate suffering, and undoubtedly some people are drawing relief who are not entitled under the law to do so. Doubtless some draw relief checks from time to time who know they are not eligible, either because they are not actually in need or for some other reason. Many of those who thus draw undeserved gratuities are without sufficient property to enable the government to collect back from them any money they wrongfully receive. But the Court today holds that it would violate the Due Process Clause of the Fourteenth Amendment to stop paying those people weekly or monthly allowances unless the government first affords them a full "evidentiary hearing" even though welfare officials are persuaded that the recipients are not rightfully entitled to receive a penny under the law. In other words, although some recipients might be on the lists for payment wholly because of deliberate fraud on their part, the Court holds that the government is helpless and must continue, until after an evidentiary hearing, to pay money that it does not owe, never has owed, and never could owe. I do not believe there is any provision in our Constitution that should thus paralyze the government's efforts to protect itself against making payments to people who are not entitled to them.

Particularly do I not think that the Fourteenth Amendment should be given such an unnecessarily broad construction. That Amendment came into being primarily to protect Negroes from discrimination, and while some of its language can and does protect others, all know that the chief purpose behind it was to protect ex-slaves. . . .

I would have little, if any, objection to the majority's decision in this case if it were written as the report of the House Committee on Education and Labor, but as an opinion ostensibly resting on the language of the Constitution I find it woefully deficient. . . .

The procedure required today as a matter of constitutional law finds no precedent in our legal system. Reduced to its simplest terms, the problem in this case is similar to that frequently encountered when two parties have an ongoing legal relationship that requires one party to make periodic payments to the other. Often the situation arises where the party "owing" the money stops paying it and justifies his conduct by arguing that the recipient is not legally entitled to payment. The recipient can, of course, disagree and go to court to compel payment. But I know of no situation in our legal system in which the person alleged to owe money to another is required by law to continue making payments to a judgment-proof claimant without the benefit of any security or bond to insure that these payments can be recovered if he wins his legal argument. . . .

The Court apparently feels that this decision will benefit the poor and needy. In my judgment the eventual result will be just the opposite. . . . Thus the end result of today's decision may well be that the government, once it decides to give welfare benefits, cannot reverse that decision until the recipient has had the benefits of full administrative and judicial review, including, of course, the opportunity to present his case to this Court. Since this process will usually entail a delay of several years, the inevitable result of such a constitutionally imposed burden will be that the government will not put a claimant on the rolls initially until it has made an exhaustive investigation to determine his eligibility. . . .

For the foregoing reasons I dissent from the Court's holding. The operation of a welfare state is a new experiment for our Nation. For this reason, among others, I feel that new experiments in carrying out a welfare program should not be frozen into our constitutional structure. They should be left, as are other legislative determinations, to the Congress and the legislatures that the people elect to make our laws.

[Chief Justice BURGER and Justice STEWART also dissented.]

## Comments and Questions

1. In what court did this case start—and where did it end?
2. Which Due Process Clause is invoked in this case—from the Fifth or Fourteenth Amendment—and why?

3. Describe the underlying story: Who are the plaintiffs and defendants, and how do they disagree? What happened that led to the disagreement, and what do the parties want to achieve through the lawsuit?

4. Does the Supreme Court rule that welfare is property for purposes of triggering the due process protections? How does the majority on the Court deal with this question? Does the Court respond to Justice Black's argument in dissent? What are the strongest elements of Justice Black's view?

5. What would be the "full service," maximum elements of procedure that could ever be "due"? Use the formal court trial as a model for comparing expansive elements of process with the narrower elements at issue in *Goldberg v. Kelly*. How important are the following: advance notice, access to counsel, the opportunity to testify in person, language translation services, the opportunity to cross-examine witnesses, the requirement of a written record of testimony, and the requirement of a statement of reasons accompanying the decision? Which elements of process does the *Goldberg* Court find necessary in the termination of welfare benefits, and which ones not necessary? What principles or factors affect this set of distinctions?

6. Who will pay for the additional process required by the Court? Will the moneys available for benefits need to be reduced by the administrative costs in conducting pre-termination hearings? How will the Court's opinion influence termination decisions by the state agency? How will the Court's opinion influence the agency's initial decisions about who is eligible for benefits?

7. What values are served by the particular elements of process discussed by the majority? Remember Justice Frankfurter's emphasis on arriving at the truth and on generating the feeling that justice has been done (*Joint Anti-Fascist Refugee Committee v. McGrath, supra*)? Some researchers have found that people report greater perceptions of satisfaction with dispute resolution based on their perceptions of the process than on the actual results. *See, e.g.*, E. Allan Lind and Tom R. Tyler, *The Social Psychology of Procedural Justice* (1988); John Thibaut and Laurens Walker, *Procedural Justice: A Psychological Analysis* (1975). *But see* Dan Simon and Nicholas Scurich, *Lay Judgment of Judicial Decision-Making*, 8 J. of Empirical Legal Stud. 709 (2011) (presenting findings that evaluation of the merits of a judicial decision by lay persons correlates with their evaluation of the process of decision making in that case).

8. In 1996, Congress enacted the Personal Responsibility and Work Opportunity Reconciliation Act of 1996 (PRWORA), Pub. L. No. 104-193, 110 Stat. 2105, which explicitly declared that welfare benefits under the law are not entitlements and also granted flexibility to the states to limit the benefits, based on fiscal constraints. Given that the decision in *Goldberg* was based on the finding that welfare benefits were an entitlement, some observers predicted that this change would lead courts to find that no due process protections attach when an individual is denied or terminated from the temporary assistance program. *See, e.g.*, Christine N. Cimini, *Welfare Entitlements in the Era of Devolution*, 9 Geo. J. on Poverty L. & Pol'y 89

(2002); Richard J. Pierce, Jr., *The Due Process Counterrevolution of the 1990s?*, 96 Colum. L. Rev. 1973 (1996). In *Cleveland Board of Education v. Loudermill*, 470 U.S. 532 (1985), the Supreme Court made clear that the legislature may determine the scope of a government entitlement but *cannot* determine what minimum level of process must attach to satisfy constitutional requirements once that entitlement is granted. Does PRWORA attempt to legislate constitutional requirements, or merely provide a more limited form of entitlement? *See* Risa E. Kaufman, *Bridging the Federalism Gap: Procedural Due Process and Race Discrimination in a Devolved Welfare System*, 3 Hastings Race & Poverty L.J. 1 (2005). Courts have found that at least some due process protections still apply under PRWORA. The Colorado Court of Appeals ruled that welfare benefit recipients had a limited property right in the continued receipt of benefits under PRWORA and were entitled to due process, which was violated by the state's use of sanction notices that lacked full or accurate information about the sanctions and the appeal process. *Weston v. Cassata*, 37 P.3d 469 (Colo. App. 2001), *cert. denied*, 536 U.S. 923 (2002). The Supreme Court of Appeals of West Virginia held that, under PRWORA, former recipients of welfare benefits had no due process right to a pre-termination hearing when benefits were terminated due to a five-year time limit placed on assistance. *State ex rel. K.M. v. West Virginia Dept. of Health and Human Resources*, 575 S.E.2d 393 (W. Va. 2002). Even so, the court held that the state appeals system violated due process because it prevented review of the decision to refuse a six-month extension.

9. Since PRWORA, most states have retained their previous welfare systems, including hearing requirements. Wisconsin, however, has privatized its administration of welfare benefits; local nongovernmental agencies administer the program, including initial hearings and terminations. *See* Vicki Lens, *Bureaucratic Disentitlement After Welfare Reform: Are Fair Hearings the Cure?*, 12 Geo. J. Poverty L. & Pol'y 13 (2005). Will due process apply to a private corporation under contract with the state that terminates an individual's benefits? *See* David J. Kennedy, *Due Process in a Privatized Welfare System*, 64 Brook. L. Rev. 231 (1998).

In the following excerpt, Frank Michelman identifies values behind process in his discussion of access fees, such as filing fees, that make it difficult if not impossible for impoverished individuals to file lawsuits. Which of the values he identifies persist, even for potential parties who have little or no chance of prevailing on the merits?

In the second excerpt, Tom Tyler and Allan Lind consider procedural values in light of social psychology and political stability. Again, consider what aspects of their argument stand independent from any claims by parties that should prevail on the merits. Can and should the legitimacy of the legal system be secured by procedural rights, even if outcomes are systematically biased against certain groups?

# ■ FRANK L. MICHELMAN, THE SUPREME COURT AND LITIGATION ACCESS FEES: THE RIGHT TO PROTECT ONE'S RIGHTS

*1973 Duke L.J. 1153, 1172-1177*

[T]here are generally accepted reasons for making litigation possible. I think we take little risk of serious distortion if we try to frame those reasons in terms of the values (ends, interests, purposes) that are supposed to be furthered by allowing persons to litigate.

I have been able to identify four discrete, though interrelated, types of such values, which may be called dignity values, participation values, deterrence values, and (to choose a clumsily neutral term) effectuation values. *Dignity values* reflect concern for the humiliation or loss of self-respect which a person might suffer if denied an opportunity to litigate. *Participation values* reflect an appreciation of litigation as one of the modes in which persons exert influence, or have their wills "counted" in societal decisions they care about. *Deterrence values* recognize the instrumentality of litigation as a mechanism for influencing or constraining individual behavior in ways thought socially desirable.[73] *Effectuation values* see litigation as an important means through which persons are enabled to get, or are given assurance of having, whatever we are pleased to regard as rightfully theirs. . . .

*Dignity values.* These seem most clearly offended when a person confronts a formal, state-sponsored, public proceeding charging wrongdoing, failure, or defect, and the person is either prevented from responding or forced to respond without the assistance and resources that a self-respecting response necessitates.

The damage to self-respect from the inability to defend oneself properly seems likely to be most severe in the case of criminal prosecution, where representatives of civil society attempt in a public forum to brand one a violator of important societal norms. . . .

Of course, one immediately sees that there are some nominally "civil" contexts where the would-be litigant is trying to fend off accusatory action by the government threatening rather dire and stigmatizing results (for example, a proceeding to divest a parent of custody of a child on grounds of unfitness), which are exceedingly difficult to distinguish from standard criminal contexts in dignity value terms. Still these cases do not by themselves show that the dignity notion is uncontainable. Challenging though it may be in a few cases to draw the line between the quasi-criminal and the noncriminal context, the determination usually will not be insuperably difficult.

---

73. A possibly more accurate (but less distinct) label would have been "social welfare values." The category is intended to stand for all interpretations of litigation as a means for maximizing value across society, as distinguished from securing to the victorious party his due. In a given case, value maximization might be effectuated through an act of redistribution of wealth (the immediate impact of the judgment or decree itself), rather than through an act of (negative or affirmative) deterrence strictly speaking (the impact on future behavior of knowledge of the decision and its grounds). . . .

But this is hardly to say that dignity considerations are entirely absent from civil contexts. Perhaps there is something generally demeaning, humiliating, and infuriating about finding oneself in a dispute over legal rights and wrongs and being unable to uphold one's own side of the case. How serious these effects are seems to depend on various factors including, possibly, the identity of the adversary (is it the government?), the origin of the argument (did the person willingly start it himself?), the possible outcomes (will the person, or others, feel that he has been determined to be a wrongdoer?), and how public the struggle has become (has it reached the courts yet?). . . .

*Participation values.* The illumination that may sometimes flow from viewing litigation as a mode of politics has escaped neither courts nor legal theorists. But I can see no way of trenchantly deploying that insight so as to rank litigation contexts for purposes of a selective access-fee relief rule. (Certainly the Supreme Court's emergent rule cannot be construed to reflect any such ranking.)

But if participation values cannot help us differentiate among litigation contexts, they can contribute significantly to the argument for a broad constitutional right of court access. Participation values are at the root of the claim that such a right can be derived from the first amendment, a claim that I shall not pursue. And they also help inspire the analogy between general litigation rights and general voting rights. . . .

*Deterrence values.* Litigation is often, and enlighteningly, viewed as a process, or part of a process, for constraining all agents in society to the performance of duties and obligations imposed with a view to social welfare. A possible link between deterrence values and access fees is, of course, supplied by the obvious frustration of those values which results if the person in the best position, or most naturally motivated, to pursue judicial enforcement of such constraints is prevented by access fees from doing so. . . .

*Effectuation values.* In the effectuation perspective we view the world from the standpoint of the prospective litigant as distinguished from that of society as a whole or as a collectivity. Value is ascribed to the actual protection and realization of those interests of the litigant which the law purports to protect and effectuate (in this perspective one would shamelessly refer to those interests as the litigant's "rights") and more generally to a prevailing assurance that those interests will be protected; and litigation is regarded as a process, or as a part of a process, for providing such protection and assurance. . . .

# ■ TOM R. TYLER AND E. ALLAN LIND, A RELATIONAL MODEL OF AUTHORITY IN GROUPS

*25 Advances in Experimental Social Psychology 115, 133-140 (1992)*

The research . . . shows that a key factor affecting legitimacy across a variety of settings is the person's evaluation of the fairness of the procedures used by the authority in question. The studies that have included behavioral measures show much the same pattern of results with respect to measures of obedience and other behaviors linked to authority. Evaluations of both the favorability of the authority's decision and its fairness, in distributive justice terms, have occasionally been found to exert an effect on legitimacy independent of that exerted by procedural fairness. Nevertheless, it is clear that in terms of both the strength of effects and the ubiquity of effects, neither outcome factor is nearly as important as procedural justice in determining whether an authority is viewed as legitimate.[12]

Why is procedural justice so central to legitimacy? One explanation can be found in some of the original theorizing on procedural justice issues. In their discussion of the problems of dispute resolution in groups, Thibaut and Walker (1975) noted the potential harm that the process of resolving disputes could do to social relationships within a group or society: poorly resolved disputes can threaten enduring relationships. They suggested that the use of procedures regarded by all parties as fair facilitates the maintenance of positive relations among group members—preserving the "fabric of society"—even in the face of the conflict of interest that exists in any group whose members have different preference structures and different beliefs with respect to what the group should strive for and how it should manage its affairs (Thibaut & Walker, 1975, p. 67).

A second reason for the pre-eminence of procedural justice concerns in judgments of the legitimacy of authority is found in another analysis by Thibaut and Walker (1978). In many social situations it is not at all clear what decision or action is correct in an objective sense. Indeed, it could be argued that most group decisions concern questions for which, at least at the time the decision is made, there is no way of knowing what course of action will work out best. In these circumstances, Thibaut and Walker argue, what is critical to good decision making is the appearance of fairness, and fairness is most obviously achieved when procedures that are accepted as just are used to generate the decision. In other words, absent objective indicators of the correctness of a decision, the best guarantee of decision quality is the use of good—which is to say fair—procedures. . . .

A third and final reason for the importance accorded procedural justice concerns in judgments of legitimacy has to do with links between perceptions of procedures and other cognitions about groups. In an earlier analysis (Lind & Taylor, 1988) we have argued that procedures are widely viewed as essential elements of groups, that perceptions of procedures are key features of cognitions about groups. It is no accident, for example, that the

---

12. As noted above, it is important to distinguish personal satisfaction from attitudes such as legitimacy. We are not saying that people are happy if they receive unfavorable outcomes through a fair procedure. We are saying, however, that they 1) are more likely to accept the decision and 2) are less likely to blame the authorities and/or institutions they have dealt with. As a consequence, they are more likely to follow the authority's directives in the future.

drafting of a constitution is generally one of the first enterprises of any group that intends to function on a continuing basis. Through the design of procedures a group gives itself form and makes specific its values and goals. Because procedures are widely viewed as manifestations of group values, we argue, they take on enormous symbolic significance in cognitions about groups. According to this line of thought, perceptions of procedures have greater impact on evaluations of groups than do perceptions of outcomes, because outcomes are generally viewed as one-time responses to particular situations while procedures have an enduring quality that makes an unfair procedure much more threatening than a single unfair outcome. In much the same way, the procedures used by an authority to reach a decision might be seen as an expression of the authority's values, and the judgment that an authority uses unfair procedures might be viewed with greater concern than the judgment that a particular decision is unfair.

Whatever the explanation, the results reviewed above suggest that the use of fair procedures is an important element, perhaps the key element, for the effective exercise of legitimate authority. . . .

Effectively exercising authority is a core issue within any organized group. Hence, the questions which we have been examining are always important. But they become especially important in situations of resource scarcity, where social conflict is more likely and where allocation is especially problematic. As we noted above, the empowerment of authorities seems to be a response of groups to problems such as social conflict and the allocation of scarce or diminishing resources, and yet it is precisely in such situations that the actions of authorities are most likely to be controversial. . . .

The possibility of heightened social conflict was viewed as especially problematic for American government authorities during the 1970s because the United States was in an historic period during which it seemed particularly vulnerable to social unrest. Alienation from and distrust of legal, political, and industrial authorities was quite high. Since the legitimacy of authorities is often viewed as a "cushion of support" that helps societies to survive difficult periods in history, the weakness of the support underlying the American legal, political, and economic systems seemed to point to a potentially dangerous vulnerability to destructive social unrest. . . .

### 4. Costs of Process

Process has costs. What role should costs play in determining how much process is due in a given circumstance? The Supreme Court addressed this issue in *Mathews v. Eldridge*, which followed shortly after *Goldberg v. Kelly*. As you read *Eldridge*, consider whether the Court simply applies *Goldberg*'s standard for interpreting how much process is due, or instead changes the standard. In either instance, why did this decision come out differently?

# ■ MATHEWS, SECRETARY OF HEALTH, EDUCATION, AND WELFARE v. ELDRIDGE
## *424 U.S. 319 (1976)*

Justice POWELL delivered the opinion of the Court:

The issue in this case is whether the Due Process Clause of the Fifth Amendment requires that prior to the termination of Social Security disability benefit payments the recipient be afforded an opportunity for an evidentiary hearing.

Cash benefits are provided to workers during periods in which they are completely disabled under the disability insurance benefits program created by the 1956 amendments to Title II of the Social Security Act. 70 Stat. 815, 42 U.S.C. § 423. Respondent Eldridge was first awarded benefits in June 1968. In March 1972, he received a questionnaire from the state agency charged with monitoring his medical condition. Eldridge completed the questionnaire, indicating that his condition had not improved and identifying the medical sources, including physicians, from whom he had received treatment recently. The state agency then obtained reports from his physician and a psychiatric consultant. After considering these reports and other information in his file the agency informed Eldridge by letter that it had made a tentative determination that his disability had ceased in May 1972. The letter included a statement of reasons for the proposed termination of benefits, and advised Eldridge that he might request reasonable time in which to obtain and submit additional information pertaining to his condition.

In his written response, Eldridge disputed one characterization of his medical condition and indicated that the agency already had enough evidence to establish his disability. The state agency then made its final determination that he had ceased to be disabled in May 1972. This determination was accepted by the Social Security Administration (SSA), which notified Eldridge in July that his benefits would terminate after that month. The notification also advised him of his right to seek reconsideration by the state agency of this initial determination within six months.

Instead of requesting reconsideration Eldridge commenced this action challenging the constitutional validity of the administrative procedures established by the Secretary of Health, Education and Welfare for assessing whether there exists a continuing disability. He sought an immediate reinstatement of benefits pending a hearing on the issue of his disability. 361 F. Supp. 520 (W.D. Va. 1973). The Secretary moved to dismiss on the grounds that Eldridge's benefits had been terminated in accordance with valid administrative regulations and procedures and that he had failed to exhaust available remedies. In support of his contention that due process requires a pre-termination hearing, Eldridge relied exclusively upon this Court's decision in *Goldberg v. Kelly*, 397 U.S. 254 (1970), which established a right to an "evidentiary hearing" prior to termination of welfare benefits. The Secretary contended that *Goldberg* was not controlling since eligibility for disability benefits, unlike eligibility for welfare benefits, is not based on financial need and since issues of credibility and veracity do not play a significant role in the disability entitlement decision, which turns primarily on medical evidence. . . .

Procedural due process imposes constraints on governmental decisions which deprive individuals of "liberty" or "property" interests within the meaning of the Due Process Clause of the Fifth or Fourteenth Amendment. The Secretary does not contend that procedural due process is inapplicable to terminations of Social Security disability benefits. . . . Rather, the Secretary contends that the existing administrative procedures, detailed below, provide all the process that is constitutionally due before a recipient can be deprived of that interest.

This Court consistently has held that some form of hearing is required before an individual is finally deprived of a property interest. *Wolff v. McDonnell*, 418 U.S. 539, 557-558 (1974). The "right to be heard before being condemned to suffer grievous loss of any kind, even though it may not involve the stigma and hardships of a criminal conviction, is a principle basic to our society." *Joint Anti-Fascist Comm. v. McGrath*, 341 U.S. 123, 168 (1951) (Frankfurter, J., concurring). The fundamental requirement of due process is the opportunity to be heard "at a meaningful time and in a meaningful manner." Eldridge agrees that the review procedures available to a claimant before the initial determination of ineligibility becomes final would be adequate if disability benefits were not terminated until after the evidentiary hearing stage of the administrative process. The dispute centers upon what process is due prior to the initial termination of benefits, pending review.

In recent years this Court increasingly has had occasion to consider the extent to which due process requires an evidentiary hearing prior to the deprivation of some type of property interest even if such a hearing is provided thereafter. In only one case, *Goldberg v. Kelly*, 397 U.S. at 266-271, has the Court held that a hearing closely approximating a judicial trial is necessary. In other cases requiring some type of pre-termination hearing as a matter of constitutional right the Court has spoken sparingly about the requisite procedures. *Sniadach v. Family Finance Corp.*, 395 U.S. 337 (1969), involving garnishment of wages, was entirely silent on the matter. In *Fuentes v. Shevin*, 407 U.S. 67, 96-97 (1972), the Court said only that in a replevin suit between two private parties the initial determination required something more than an *ex parte* proceeding before a court clerk. Similarly, *Bell v. Burson*, 402 U.S. 535, 540 (1971), held, in the context of the revocation of a state-granted driver's license, that due process required only that the pre-revocation hearing involve a probable-cause determination as to the fault of the licensee, noting that the hearing "need not take the form of a full adjudication of the question of liability." In *Arnett v. Kennedy*, 416 U.S. 134 (1974), we sustained the validity of procedures by which a federal employee could be dismissed for cause. They included notice of the action sought, a copy of the charge, reasonable time for filing a written response, and an opportunity for an oral appearance. Following dismissal, an evidentiary hearing was provided.

These decisions underscore the truism that "'[d]ue process,' unlike some legal rules, is not a technical conception with a fixed content unrelated to time, place and circumstances." *Cafeteria Workers v. McElroy*, 367 U.S. 886, 895 (1961). "[D]ue process is flexible and calls for such procedural protections as the particular situation demands." *Morrissey v. Brewer*, 408 U.S. 471, 481 (1972). Accordingly, resolution of the issue whether the administrative procedures provided here are constitutionally sufficient requires analysis of the governmental and private interests that are affected. More precisely, our prior decisions indicate that identification of the specific dictates of due process generally requires consideration of three distinct factors: First, the private interest that will be affected by the official action; second, the risk of an erroneous deprivation of such interest through the procedures used, and the probable value, if any, of additional or substitute procedural safeguards; and finally, the Government's interest, including the function involved and the fiscal and administrative burdens that the additional or substitute procedural requirement would entail. *See, e.g., Goldberg v. Kelly.*

The principal reasons for benefits terminations are that the worker is no longer disabled or has returned to work. As Eldridge's benefits were terminated because he was determined to be no longer disabled, we consider only the sufficiency of the procedures involved in such cases.

The continuing-eligibility investigation is made by a state agency acting through a "team" consisting of a physician and a nonmedical person trained in disability evaluation. The agency periodically communicates with the disabled worker, usually by mail—in which case he is sent a detailed questionnaire—or by telephone, and requests information concerning his present condition, including current medical restrictions and sources of treatment, and any additional information that he considers relevant to his continued entitlement to benefits.

Information regarding the recipient's current condition is also obtained from his sources of medical treatment. If there is a conflict between the information provided by the beneficiary and that obtained from medical sources such as his physician, or between two sources of treatment, the agency may arrange for an examination by an independent consulting physician. Whenever the agency's tentative assessment of the beneficiary's condition differs from his own assessment, the beneficiary is informed that benefits may be terminated, provided a summary of the evidence upon which the proposed determination to terminate is based, and afforded an opportunity to review the medical reports and other evidence in his case file. He also may respond in writing and submit additional evidence.

The state agency then makes its final determination, which is reviewed by an examiner in the SSA Bureau of Disability Insurance. If, as is usually the case, the SSA accepts the agency determination it notifies the recipient in writing, informing him of the reasons for the decision, and of his right to seek de novo reconsideration by the state agency. Upon acceptance by the SSA, benefits are terminated effective two months after the month in which medical recovery is found to have occurred.

If the recipient seeks reconsideration by the state agency and the determination is adverse, the SSA reviews the reconsideration determination and notifies the recipient of the decision. He then has a right to an evidentiary hearing before an SSA administrative law judge. The hearing is nonadversary, and the SSA is not represented by counsel. As at all prior and subsequent stages of the administrative process, however, the claimant may be represented by counsel or other spokesmen. . . .

Despite the elaborate character of the administrative procedures provided by the Secretary, the courts below held them to be constitutionally inadequate, concluding that due process requires an evidentiary hearing prior to termination. In light of the private and governmental interests at stake here and the nature of the existing procedures, we think this was error.

Since a recipient whose benefits are terminated is awarded full retroactive relief if he ultimately prevails, his sole interest is in the uninterrupted receipt of this source of income pending final administrative decision on his claim. His potential injury is thus similar in nature to that of the welfare recipient in *Goldberg*, the nonprobationary federal employee in *Arnett*, and the wage earner in *Sniadach*.

Only in *Goldberg* has the Court held that due process requires an evidentiary hearing prior to a temporary deprivation. It was emphasized there that welfare assistance is given to persons on the very margin of subsistence. . . . Eligibility for disability benefits, in contrast, is not based upon financial need. Indeed, it is wholly unrelated to the worker's income or support from many other sources, such as earnings of other family members, workmen's compensation awards, tort claims awards, savings, private insurance, public or private pensions, veterans' benefits, food stamps, public assistance, or the "many other important programs, both public and private, which contain provisions for disability payments affecting a substantial portion of the work force. . . ." *Richardson v. Belcher*, 404 U.S. 84, 85-87 (Douglas, J., dissenting).

As *Goldberg* illustrates, the degree of potential deprivation that may be created by a particular decision is a factor to be considered in assessing the validity of any administrative decisionmaking process. The potential deprivation here is generally likely to be less than in *Goldberg*, although the degree of difference can be overstated. . . . Thus, in contrast to the discharged federal employee in *Arnett*, there is little possibility that the terminated recipient will be able to find even temporary employment to ameliorate the interim loss.

As we recognized last Term in *Fusari v. Steinberg*, 419 U.S. 379, 389 (1975), "the possible length of wrongful deprivation of . . . benefits [also] is an important factor in assessing the impact of official action on the private interests." The Secretary concedes that the delay between a request for a hearing before an administrative law judge and a decision on the claim is currently between 10 and 11 months. Since a terminated recipient must first obtain a reconsideration decision as a prerequisite to invoking his right to an evidentiary hearing, the delay between the actual cutoff of benefits and final decision after a hearing exceeds one year.

In view of the torpidity of this administrative review process, and the typically modest resources of the family unit of the physically disabled worker, the hardship imposed upon the erroneously terminated disability recipient may be significant. Still, the disabled worker's need is likely to be less than that of a welfare recipient. In addition to the possibility of access to private resources, other forms of government assistance will become available where the termination of disability benefits places a worker or his family below the subsistence level. In view of these potential sources of temporary income, there is less reason here than in *Goldberg* to depart from the ordinary principle, established by our decisions, that something less than an evidentiary hearing is sufficient prior to adverse administrative action.

An additional factor to be considered here is the fairness and reliability of the existing pre-termination procedures, and the probable value, if any, of additional procedural safeguards. Central to the evaluation of any administrative process is the nature of the relevant inquiry. *See Mitchell v. W. T. Grant Co.*, 416 U.S. 600, 617 (1974); Friendly, *Some Kind of Hearing*, 123 U. Pa. L. Rev. 1267, 1281 (1975). In order to remain eligible for benefits the disabled worker must demonstrate by means of "medically acceptable clinical and laboratory diagnostic techniques," 42 U.S.C. § 423(d)(3), that he is unable "to engage in any substantial gainful activity by reason of any medically determinable physical or mental impairment. . . ." In short, a medical assessment of the worker's physical or mental condition is required. This is a more sharply focused and easily documented decision than the typical determination of welfare entitlement. In the latter case, a wide variety of information may be deemed relevant, and issues of witness credibility and veracity often are critical to the decisionmaking process. *Goldberg* noted that in such circumstances "written submissions are a wholly unsatisfactory basis for decision."

By contrast, the decision whether to discontinue disability benefits will turn, in most cases, upon "routine, standard, and unbiased medical reports by physician specialists," *Richardson v. Perales*, 402 U.S. 389, 404 (1971), concerning a subject whom they have personally examined. . . . To be sure, credibility and veracity may be a factor in the ultimate disability assessment in some cases. But procedural due process rules are shaped by the risk of error inherent in the truthfinding process as applied to the generality of cases, not the rare exceptions. The potential value of an evidentiary hearing, or even oral presentation to the decisionmaker, is substantially less in this context than in *Goldberg*.

The decision in *Goldberg* also was based on the Court's conclusion that written submissions were an inadequate substitute for oral presentation because they did not provide an effective means for the recipient to communicate his case to the decisionmaker. Written submissions were viewed as an unrealistic option, for most recipients lacked the "educational attainment necessary to write effectively" and could not afford professional assistance. In addition, such submissions would not provide the "flexibility of oral presentations" or "permit the recipient to mold his argument to the issues the decision maker appears to regard as important." 397 U.S., at 269. In the context of the disability-benefits-entitlement assessment the administrative procedures under review here fully answer these objections. . . .

A further safeguard against mistake is the policy of allowing the disability recipient's representative full access to all information relied upon by the state agency. In addition, prior to the cutoff of benefits the agency informs the recipient of its tentative assessment, the reasons therefor, and provides a summary of the evidence that it considers most relevant. Opportunity is then afforded the recipient to submit additional evidence or arguments, enabling him to challenge directly the accuracy of information in his file as well as the correctness of the agency's tentative conclusions. These procedures, again as contrasted with those before the Court in *Goldberg*, enable the recipient to "mold" his argument to respond to the precise issues which the decision-maker regards as crucial. . . .

In striking the appropriate due process balance the final factor to be assessed is the public interest. This includes the administrative burden and other societal costs that would be associated with requiring, as a matter of constitutional right, an evidentiary hearing upon demand in all cases prior to the termination of disability benefits. The most visible burden would be the incremental cost resulting from the increased number of hearings and the expense of providing benefits to ineligible recipients pending decision. No one can predict the extent of the increase, but the fact that full benefits would continue until after such hearings would assure the exhaustion in most cases of this attractive option. Nor would the theoretical right of the Secretary to recover undeserved benefits result, as a practical matter, in any substantial offset to the added outlay of public funds. The parties submit widely varying estimates of the probable additional financial cost. We only need say that experience with the constitutionalizing of government procedures suggests that the ultimate additional cost in terms of money and administrative burden would not be insubstantial.

Financial cost alone is not a controlling weight in determining whether due process requires a particular procedural safeguard prior to some administrative decision. But the Government's interest, and hence that of the public, in conserving scarce fiscal and administrative resources is a factor that must be weighed. At some point the benefit of an additional safeguard to the individual affected by the administrative action and to society in terms of increased assurance that the action is just, may be outweighed by the cost. Significantly, the cost of protecting those whom the preliminary administrative process has identified as likely to be found undeserving may in the end come out of the pockets of the deserving since resources available for any particular program of social welfare are not unlimited.

But more is implicated in cases of this type than ad hoc weighing of fiscal and administrative burdens against the interests of a particular category of claimants. The ultimate balance involves a determination as to when, under our constitutional system, judicial-type procedures must be imposed upon administrative action to assure fairness. We reiterate the wise admonishment of Mr. Justice Frankfurter that differences in the origin and function of administrative agencies "preclude wholesale transplantation of the rules of procedure, trial, and review which have evolved from the history and experience of courts." *FCC v. Pottsville Broadcasting Co.*, 309 U.S. 134, 143 (1940). The judicial model of an evidentiary hearing is neither a required, nor even the most effective, method of decisionmaking in all circumstances. The essence of due process is the requirement that "a person in jeopardy of serious loss [be given] notice of the case against him and opportunity to meet it." *Joint Anti-Fascist Comm. v. McGrath*, 341 U.S., at 171-172 (Frankfurter, J., concurring). All that is necessary is that the procedures be tailored, in light of the decision to be made, to "the capacities and circumstances of those who are to be heard," *Goldberg v. Kelly*, 397 U.S., at 268-269 (footnote omitted), to insure that they are given a meaningful opportunity to present their case. In assessing what process is due in this case, substantial weight must be given to the good-faith judgments of the individuals charged by Congress with the administration of social welfare programs that the procedures they have provided assure fair consideration of the entitlement claims of individuals. *See Arnett v. Kennedy*, 416 U.S. 17, 202 (White, J., concurring in part and dissenting in part). This is especially so where, as here, the prescribed procedures not only provide the claimant with an effective process for asserting his claim prior to any administrative action, but also assure a right to an evidentiary hearing, as well as to subsequent judicial review, before the denial of his claim becomes final.

We conclude that an evidentiary hearing is not required prior to the termination of disability benefits and that the present administrative procedures fully comport with due process. The judgment of the Court of Appeals is

*Reversed.*

Justice STEVENS took no part in the consideration or decision of this case.

Justice BRENNAN, with whom Justice MARSHALL concurs, dissented:
. . . [T]he Court's consideration that a discontinuance of disability benefits may cause the recipient to suffer only a limited deprivation is no argument. It is speculative. Moreover, the very legislative determination to provide disability benefits, without any prerequisite determination of need in fact, presumes a need by the recipient which is not this Court's function to denigrate. Indeed, in the present case, it is indicated that because disability benefits were terminated there was a foreclosure upon the Eldridge home and the family's furniture was repossessed, forcing Eldridge, his wife, and their children to sleep in one bed. Finally, it is also no argument that a worker, who has been placed in the untenable position of having been denied disability benefits, may still seek other forms of public assistance.

## Comments and Questions

1. Note that the membership of the Court changed between the times of the decisions in *Goldberg* and *Mathews*. Sitting in 1970 were Justices

Hugo Black, Harry A. Blackmun, William J. Brennan, Warren E. Burger, William O. Douglas, John M. Harlan, Thurgood Marshall, Potter Stewart, and Byron R. White. By 1976, President Nixon's nominees, Lewis F. Powell and William H. Rehnquist, had replaced Hugo Black and John Harlan, and President Ford's nominee, John Paul Stevens, replaced William O. Douglas (although Justice Stevens did not participate in the *Mathews* decision). How relevant is this to explaining the results?

2. Congress responded to *Mathews* in 1983 by requiring pre-termination hearings for disability benefits upon request. 42 U.S.C. § 423(g), amended by Pub. L. No. 97-455 (1983). Continuation of aid is provided while termination is under appeal. That aid is not required to be paid back unless there is a showing that the recipient did not appeal in good faith.

3. The Court in *Mathews v. Eldridge* articulates a three-factor test. Does this balancing test better guide judicial interpretations of due process than the pre-existing calls for flexible, evolving judgments? Does the balancing test make any difference to the actual results in cases like *Goldberg* and *Mathews*?

How does the balancing test build upon or move away from the basic values of due process? Materials from two leading commentators help address this question.

## ■ JERRY L. MASHAW, THE SUPREME COURT'S DUE PROCESS CALCULUS FOR ADMINISTRATIVE ADJUDICATION: THREE FACTORS IN SEARCH OF A THEORY OF VALUE
### *44 U. Chi. L. Rev. 28, 28-30, 46-59 (1976)*

During the 1970s the Supreme Court has undertaken an intensive review of administrative hearing procedures for conformity with constitutional requirements of due process of law. The landmark case of *Goldberg v. Kelly* in 1970 confirmed the Court's unwillingness to limit its review by traditional notions of property interests and also suggested, in its specification of the constitutionally requisite elements of adjudicatory procedure, that the Court was prepared to assume a highly interventionist posture. What followed was a "due process revolution"—a flood of cases seeking to extend, or simply to apply, *Goldberg*'s precepts.

The basic task that this burgeoning due process case load has presented to the courts has been to give content to the requirements of due process while maintaining an appropriate judicial role in the design of administrative procedures. Although *Goldberg* may have indicated the Court's willingness to impose a detailed model of requisite adjudicatory procedure upon a particular administrative function, no recent Supreme Court has believed that a single model is readily and consistently applicable to all administrative functions. What is required, therefore, are general criteria for review that will lend consistency and principle to the Court's decisions while permitting different administrative functions to be reviewed on their own terms. At the same time, those general criteria should be sufficiently concrete to structure administrative behavior without resort to a judicial test of every procedure that lacks some element of the paradigm process advanced by *Goldberg*.

In the Court's latest attempt to formulate this due process calculus, *Mathews v. Eldridge*, Justice Powell's majority opinion articulates a set of criteria with a comprehensiveness that suggests a preliminary integration of the Court's recent efforts. In the majority's words, from which there is no dissent, the Court must consider:

> first, the private interest that will be affected by the official action; second, the risk of an erroneous deprivation of such interest through the procedures used, and the probable value, if any, of additional or substitute procedural safeguards; and finally, the Government's interest, including the function involved and the fiscal and administrative burdens that the additional or substitute procedural requisites would entail.

Although this functional formulation impliedly invites an intrusive, particularistic review and specification of procedures, it is tempered by judicial restraint. "In assessing what process is due in this case, substantial weight must be given to the good-faith judgment of the individuals charged by Congress with the administration of the social welfare system that the procedures they have provided assure fair consideration of the entitlement claims of individuals."

The thesis of this article is that the *Eldridge* approach is unsatisfactory both as employed in that case and as a general formulation of due process review of administrative procedures. The failing of *Eldridge* is its focus on questions of technique rather than on questions of value. That focus, it is argued, generates an inquiry that is incomplete because unresponsive to the full range of concerns embodied in the due process clause. . . .

The Supreme Court's analysis in *Eldridge* is not informed by systematic attention to any theory of the values underlying due process review. The approach is implicitly utilitarian but incomplete, and the Court overlooks alternative theories that might have yielded fruitful inquiry. My purpose is, first, to articulate the limits of the Court's utilitarian approach, both in *Eldridge* and as a general schema for evaluating administrative procedures, and second, to indicate the strengths and weaknesses of three alternative theories—individual dignity, equality, and tradition. These theories, at the level of abstraction here presented, require little critical justification: they are widely held, respond to strong currents in the philosophic literature concerning law, politics, and ethics, and are supported either implicitly or explicitly by the Supreme Court's due process jurisprudence.[61]

---

61. In early due process cases the Supreme Court concentrated on tradition. The oft-cited statement in *Davidson v. New Orleans*, 96 U.S. 97, 104 (1877), that the Court's approach to due process problems should be "by the gradual process of judicial inclusion and exclusion," epitomizes the conservative, precedent-oriented, historical approach. As governmental functions increased, however, the Court was faced

## A. UTILITARIANISM

Utility theory suggests that the purpose of decisional procedures—like that of social action generally—is to maximize social welfare. Indeed, the three-factor analysis enunciated in *Eldridge* appears to be a type of utilitarian, social welfare function. That function first takes into account the social value at stake in a legitimate private claim; it discounts that value by the probability that it will be preserved through the available administrative procedures, and it then subtracts from that discounted value the social cost of introducing additional procedures. When combined with the institutional posture of judicial self-restraint, utility theory can be said to yield the following plausible decision-rule: "Void procedures for lack of due process only when alternative procedures would so substantially increase social welfare that their rejection seems irrational."

The utilitarian calculus is not, however, without difficulties. The *Eldridge* Court conceives of the values of procedure too narrowly: it views the sole purpose of procedural protections as enhancing accuracy, and thus limits its calculus to the benefits or costs that flow from correct or incorrect decisions. No attention is paid to "process values" that might inhere in oral proceedings or to the demoralization costs that may result from the grant-withdrawal-grant-withdrawal sequence to which claimants like *Eldridge* are subjected. Perhaps more important, as the Court seeks to make sense of a calculus in which accuracy is the sole goal of procedure, it tends erroneously to characterize disability hearings as concerned almost exclusively with medical impairment and thus concludes that such hearings involve only medical evidence, whose reliability would be little enhanced by oral procedure.

---

with due process problems that had no compelling historical analogies. If the Court was not to be a continual stumbling block to "progress," a more flexible approach was needed. Indeed, the history of due process in the Supreme Court might be characterized as a continuous search for a theory of due process review that combines the legitimacy of the evolutionary theory with a flexibility that permits adaptation to contemporary circumstances. Dignitary or natural right, utilitarian, and egalitarian theories have all been incorporated to this end.

Dignitary ideas, although used occasionally in a supportive role both before 1900 and in some contemporary cases, were employed most frequently as the primary mode of analysis from about 1933 through the early 1950s. The proliferation of new government functions associated with the New Deal legislation and, later, with emergency war measures, stimulated a judicial reaction that was captured in the Court's emphasis on individual rights and dignitary values. The reactive natural rights style, predicated upon the Justices' perception of the "fair" solution in each case, had an ad hoc quality that soon became disturbing. The apparent inconsistency of the Supreme Court's due process jurisprudence led Sanford Kadish in a seminal article to describe the Supreme Court's decisions as in "chaotic array." Kadish, *Methodology and Criteria in Due Process Adjudication—A Survey and Criticism*, 66 Yale L.J. 319 (1957).

In the late 1950s and early 1960s various utilitarian formulations began to supply a structure for analysis. In *Cafeteria & Restaurant Workers Local 473 v. McElroy*, 367 U.S. 886, 895 (1961), for example, the Court, per Mr. Justice Stewart, stated that two factors must be considered in due process cases: "the precise nature of the government function involved . . . [and] of the private interest that has been affected by government action." The statement of the utilitarian approach culminates in the *Eldridge* opinion's three-factor calculus.

Equality as a due process value has received considerable attention in criminal (or quasi-criminal) cases, but little outside that area. Perhaps the best example of the explicit use of equality concerns with respect to an administrative function is found in *Ashbacker Radio Corp. v. FCC*, 326 U.S. 327, 330 (1945). There the Court, per Mr. Justice Douglas, stated that the right to a hearing "becomes an empty thing" unless all parties affected by the process have an equal opportunity to be heard.

As applied by the *Eldridge* Court the utilitarian calculus tends, as cost-benefit analyses typically do, to "dwarf soft variables" and to ignore complexities and ambiguities.

The problem with a utilitarian calculus is not merely that the Court may define the relevant costs and benefits too narrowly. However broadly conceived, the calculus asks unanswerable questions. For example, what is the social value, and the social cost, of continuing disability payments until after an oral hearing for persons initially determined to be ineligible? Answers to those questions require a technique for measuring the social value and social cost of government income transfers, but no such technique exists. Even if such formidable tasks of social accounting could be accomplished, the effectiveness of oral hearings in forestalling the losses that result from erroneous terminations would remain uncertain. In the face of these pervasive indeterminacies the *Eldridge* Court was forced to retreat to a presumption of constitutionality.

Finally, it is not clear that the utilitarian balancing analysis asks the constitutionally relevant questions. The due process clause is one of those Bill of Rights protections meant to insure individual liberty in the face of contrary collective action. Therefore, a collective legislative or administrative decision about procedure, one arguably reflecting the intensity of the contending social values and representing an optimum position from the contemporary social perspective, cannot answer the constitutional question of whether due process has been accorded. A balancing analysis that would have the Court merely redetermine the question of social utility is similarly inadequate. There is no reason to believe that the Court has superior competence or legitimacy as a utilitarian balancer except as it performs its peculiar institutional role of insuring that libertarian values are considered in the calculus of decision. . . .

## B. INDIVIDUAL DIGNITY

The increasingly secular, scientific, and collectivist character of the modern American state reinforces our propensity to define fairness in the formal, and apparently neutral language of social utility. Assertions of natural or "inalienable" rights seem, by contrast, somewhat embarrassing. Their ancestry, and therefore their moral force, are increasingly uncertain. Moreover, their role in the history of the due process clause makes us apprehensive about their eventual reach. It takes no peculiar acuity to see that the tension in procedural due process cases is the same as that in the now discredited substantive due process jurisprudence—a tension between the efficacy of the state and the individual's right to freedom from coercion or socially imposed disadvantage.

Yet the popular moral presupposition of individual dignity, and its political counterpart, self-determination, persist. State coercion must be legitimized, not only by acceptable substantive policies, but also by political processes that respond to a democratic morality's demand for participation in decisions affecting individual and group interests. At the level of individual administrative decisions this demand appears in both the layman's and the lawyer's language as the right to a "hearing" or "to be heard," normally meaning orally and in person. To accord an individual less when his property or status is at stake requires justification, not only because he might contribute to accurate determinations, but also because a lack of personal participation causes alienation and a loss of that dignity and self-respect that society properly deems independently valuable. . . .

Notwithstanding its difficulties, the dignitary theory of due process might have contributed significantly to the *Eldridge* analysis. The questions of procedural "acceptability" which the theory poses may initially seem vacuous or at best intuitive, but they suggest a broader sensitivity than the utilitarian factor analysis to the nature of governmental decisions. Whereas the utilitarian approach seems to require an estimate of the quantitative value of the claim, the dignitary approach suggests that the Court develop a qualitative appraisal of the type of administrative decision involved. While the disability decision in *Eldridge* may be narrowly characterized as a decision about the receipt of money payments, it may also be considered from various qualitative perspectives which seem pertinent in view of the general structure of the American income-support system.

That system suggests that a disability decision is a judgment of considerable social significance, and one that the claimant should rightly perceive as having a substantial moral content. The major cash income-support programs determine eligibility, not only on the basis of simple insufficiency of income, but also, or exclusively, on the basis of a series of excuses for partial or total nonparticipation in the work force: agedness, childhood, family responsibility, injury, disability. A grant under any of these programs is an official, if sometimes grudging, stamp of approval of the claimant's status as a partially disabled worker or nonworker. It proclaims, in effect, that those who obtain it have encountered one of the politically legitimate hazards to self-sufficiency in a market economy. The recipients, therefore, are entitled to society's support. Conversely, the denial of an income maintenance claim implies that the claim is socially illegitimate, and the claimant, however impecunious, is not excused from normal work force status.

These moral and status dimensions of the disability decision indicate that there is more at stake in disability claims than temporary loss of income. They also tend to put the disability decision in a framework that leads away from the superficial conclusion that disability decisions are a routine matter of evaluating medical evidence. Decisions with substantial "moral worth" connotations are generally expected to be highly individualized and attentive to subjective evidence. The adjudication of such issues on the basis of documents submitted largely by third parties and by adjudicators who have never confronted the claimant seems inappropriate. Instead, a court approaching an analysis of the disability claims process from the dignitary perspective might emphasize those aspects of disability decisions that focus on a particular claimant's vocational characteristics, his unique response to his medical condition, and the ultimate predictive judgment of whether the claimant should be able to work.

## C. EQUALITY

Notions of equality can . . . significantly inform the evaluation of any administrative process. One question we might ask is whether an investigative procedure is designed in a fashion that systematically excludes or undervalues evidence that would tend to support the position of a particular class of parties. If so, those parties might have a plausible claim that the procedure treated them unequally. Similarly, in a large-scale inquisitorial process involving many adjudicators, the question that should be posed is whether like cases receive like attention and like evidentiary development so that the influence of such arbitrary factors as location are minimized. In order to take such equality issues into account, we need only to broaden our due process horizons to include elements of procedural fairness beyond those traditionally associated with adversary proceedings. These two inquiries might have been pursued fruitfully in *Eldridge*. First, is the state agency system of decision making, which is based on documents, particularly disadvantageous for certain classes of claimants? There is some tentative evidence that it is. Cases such as *Eldridge* involving muscular or skeletal disorders, neurological problems, and multiple impairments, including psychological overlays, are widely believed to be both particularly difficult, due to the subjectivity of the evidence, and particularly prone to be reversed after oral hearing.

Second, does the inquisitorial process at the state agency level tend to treat like cases alike? If the GAO's* study is indicative, the answer is decidedly no. According to that study, many, perhaps half, of the decisions are made on the basis of records that other adjudicators consider so inadequate that a decision could not be rendered. The relevance of such state agency variance to *Eldridge*'s claim is twofold: first, it suggests that state agency determinations are unreliable and that further development at the hearing stage might substantially enhance their reliability; alternatively, it may suggest that the hierarchical or bureaucratic mode of decision making, with overhead control for consistency, does not accurately describe the Social Security disability system. And if consistency is not feasible under this system, perhaps the more compelling standard for evaluating the system is the dignitary value of individualized judgment, which . . . implies claimant participation.

## D. TRADITION OR EVOLUTION

Judicial reasoning, including reasoning about procedural due process, is frequently and self-consciously based on custom or precedent. In part,

---

*The Federal General Accounting Office surveyed state disability determinations to assess consistency. The study found definite inconsistencies both among state agencies and between state agencies and the federal adjudicators.

reliance on tradition or "authority" is a court's institutional defense against illegitimacy in a political democracy. But tradition serves other values, not the least of which are predictability and economy of effort. More importantly, the inherently conservative technique of analogy to custom and precedent seems essential to the evolutionary development and the preservation of the legal system. Traditional procedures are legitimate not only because they represent a set of continuous expectations, but because the body politic has survived their use.

The use of tradition as a guide to fundamental fairness is vulnerable, of course, to objection. Since social and economic forces are dynamic, the processes and structures that proved functional in one period will not necessarily serve effectively in the next. Indeed, evolutionary development may as often end in the extinction of a species as in adaptation and survival. For this reason alone tradition can serve only as a partial guide to judgment.

Furthermore, it may be argued that reasoning by analogy from traditional procedures does not actually provide a perspective on the values served by due process. Rather, it is a decisional technique that requires a specification of the purposes of procedural rules merely in order that the decision maker may choose from among a range of authorities or customs the particular authority or custom most analogous to the procedures being evaluated.

This objection to tradition as a theory of justification is weighty, but not devastating. What is asserted by an organic or evolutionary theory is that *the purposes of legal rules cannot be fully known*. Put more cogently, while procedural rules, like other legal rules, should presumably contribute to the maintenance of an effective social order, we cannot expect to know precisely how they do so and what the long-term effects of changes or revisions might be. Our constitutional stance should therefore be preservative and incremental, building carefully, by analogy, upon traditional modes of operation. So viewed, the justification "we have always done it that way" is not so much a retreat from reasoned and purposive decision making as a profound acknowledgment of the limits of instrumental rationality.

Viewed from a traditionalist's perspective, the Supreme Court's opinion in *Eldridge* may be said to rely on the traditional proposition that property interests may be divested temporarily without hearing, provided a subsequent opportunity for contest is afforded. *Goldberg v. Kelly* is deemed an exceptional case, from which *Eldridge* is distinguished.

## CONCLUSION

The preceding discussion has emphasized the way that explicit attention to a range of values underlying due process of law might have led the *Eldridge* Court down analytic paths different from those that appear in Justice Powell's opinion. The discussion has largely ignored, however, arguments that would justify the result that the Court reached in terms of the alternative value theories here advanced. Those arguments are now set forth.

First, focus on the dignitary aspects of the disability decision can hardly compel the conclusion that an oral hearing is a constitutional necessity prior to the termination of benefits when a full hearing is available later. Knowledge that an oral hearing will be available at some point should certainly lessen disaffection and alienation. Indeed, Eldridge seemed secure in the knowledge that a just procedure was available. His desire to avoid taking a corrective appeal should not blind us to the support of dignitary values that the de novo appeal provides.

Second, arguments premised on equality do not necessarily carry the day for the proponent of prior hearings. The Social Security Administration's attempt to routinize and make consistent hundreds of thousands of decisions in a nationwide income-maintenance program can be criticized both for its failures in its own terms and for its tendency to ignore the way that disability decisions impinge upon perceptions of individual moral worth. On balance, however, the program that Congress enacted contains criteria that suggest a desire for both consistency and individualization. No adjudicatory process can avoid tradeoffs between the pursuit of one or the other of these goals. Thus a procedural structure incorporating (1) decisions by a single state agency based on a documentary record and subject to hierarchical quality review, followed by (2) appeal to de novo oral proceedings before independent administrative law judges, is hardly an irrational approach to the necessary compromise between consistency and individualization.

Explicit and systematic attention to the values served by a demand for due process nevertheless remains highly informative in *Eldridge* and in general. The use of analogy to traditional procedures might have helped rationalize and systematize a concern for the "desperation" of claimants that seems as impoverished in *Eldridge* as it seems profligate in *Goldberg*; and the absence in *Eldridge* of traditionalist, dignitary, or egalitarian considerations regarding the disability adjudication process permitted the Court to overlook questions of both fact and value—questions that, on reflection, seem important. The structure provided by the Court's three factors is an inadequate guide for analysis because its neutrality leaves it empty of suggestive value perspectives.

Furthermore, an attempt by the Court to articulate a set of values that informs due process decision making might provide it with an acceptable judicial posture from which to review administrative procedures. The *Goldberg* decision's approach to prescribing due process—specification of the attributes of adjudicatory hearings by analogy to judicial trial—makes the Court resemble an administrative engineer with an outdated professional education. It is at once intrusive and ineffectual. Retreating from this stance, the *Eldridge* Court relies on the administrator's good faith—an equally troublesome posture in a political system that depends heavily on judicial review for the protection of countermajoritarian values. . . .

## ■ LOUIS KAPLOW, THE VALUE OF ACCURACY IN ADJUDICATION: AN ECONOMIC ANALYSIS

*23 J. Legal Stud. 307, 307-311, 356-357, 370-376, 389-399*
*(1994)*

### I. INTRODUCTION

. . . Accuracy is a central concern with regard to a wide range of legal rules. One might go so far as to say that a large portion of the rules of civil, criminal, and administrative procedure and rules of evidence involve an effort to strike a balance between accuracy and legal costs. . . .

Accurate damage determination may improve individuals' incentives to behave properly. If I contemplate committing an act that is unusually harmful, I will be more careful or more likely to refrain from the act if I will be held responsible for the true, higher level of harm, rather than for the lower, average level of harm for the class of acts. (Similarly, if my act is less harmful than is usual, holding me liable for an accordingly low amount will prevent excessive deterrence of my activity or avoid creating excessive incentives to be cautious.) In contrast, if at the time I act I am unaware whether my act will cause an atypically high or low level of harm, knowledge that an adjudicator will determine harm precisely ex post will not cause me to adjust my behavior accordingly. . . .

Determining the value of accuracy with regard to future events consists largely of identifying the social benefits associated with different outcomes. For example, with entitlements to social security disability payments, one would be concerned with the benefit of supporting the truly disabled, the implicit cost of public expenditures, and the extent to which giving payments to those not truly disabled produces benefits that fall short of the cost of public funds. While this formulation does not appear to deviate substantially from conventional understandings . . . arguments about accuracy in this context often confuse changes in accuracy with implicit changes in the burden of proof. . . .

Initially, it is useful to define a shift in the burden of proof in isolation—that is, taking as given all other aspects of the system, including its accuracy. When a decision-maker hears all the evidence, there inevitably remains some uncertainty about what actually happened. A higher proof burden is taken here to mean that the decision-maker must have a higher level of confidence that the party is responsible for committing the illegal act in order to impose a sanction. Thus, raising the burden of proof increases the rate of mistaken acquittals and decreases the rate of mistaken convictions.

In contrast, increasing accuracy [reduces] the rate of mistaken acquittals and convictions. This arises when better information is available to the decision-maker or a more capable decision-maker is used. For a given burden of proof, better information or better analysis of given information reduces mistakes of both types. . . .

Consider some alternative policies. Suppose there is a subsidy of defendants' legal counsel and a simultaneous downward shift in the express burden of proof to an extent that the portion of detected individuals who are ultimately convicted remains the same. Then, the only effect would be on accuracy.

The question thus becomes whether the additional accuracy is worth the cost, the burden-of-proof question being disposed of separately. For example, what if increasing resources available to the prosecution by the same amount increased accuracy more? Then, one could accompany this change by an increase in the express burden of proof, producing more accuracy at the same cost. Similarly, if what one really desired in advocating a subsidy to defendants' legal counsel was making the de facto burden of proof higher, one might accomplish this directly or through other indirect means (such as by reducing resources available to the prosecution). Thus, it is possible in principle to view accuracy and the burden of proof separately. Any policies affecting both can be analyzed with regard to each component because if one aspect is desirable and the other not, it would be possible to benefit from the former and do without the latter. . . .

### 1. THE VALUE OF ACCURACY

Consider a scenario in which individuals apply for disability benefits. Eligibility for benefits depends on whether one is disabled. The system of adjudication involves two types of mistakes. . . . Some disabled individuals will be mistakenly denied benefits, and some individuals who are not disabled will be mistakenly granted benefits. Expenditures to increase accuracy are assumed to reduce both types of errors, so that with more accurate procedures a higher portion of the truly disabled receive benefits, and fewer individuals who are not disabled receive benefits. . . .

In order to assess the value of accuracy, consider first the effect on the disabled. Providing more of them benefits has an element of social gain and a cost. The gain corresponds to the social value of a disabled person receiving benefits, rather than being left to other means of support. The cost is that of the funds, which may be supplied by increasing taxes, diverting revenue from other programs, or reducing benefit levels. The net effect should be positive, for otherwise it would be best to eliminate the program.

Second, consider those not disabled. Denying them benefits involves a cost (for, after all, providing payments to those not disabled is not a complete waste of resources) and a gain. The gain here corresponds to the cost with the truly disabled: reducing expenditures allows one to reduce taxes, increase funding of other programs, or raise benefit levels. The net effect here should be positive as well, for otherwise it would be best to expand the program to include those not disabled.

Finally, there is the cost of providing more accurate procedures themselves. Because this cost must be financed, it also has the character described previously. To determine whether a posited increase in accuracy is desirable, one would determine how much it reduced each type of error and sum the gains and losses just described.

An alternative way to view this cost-benefit calculus is to group all the financial costs and benefits together. More disabled receiving benefits increases the revenue requirement; fewer individuals who are not disabled receiving benefits reduces required revenues; and enhanced accuracy affects administrative costs. Taken together, the net effect on direct costs could be positive or negative. To determine whether increasing accuracy is desirable, one would add to this the benefit of more disabled individuals receiving payments and the cost that fewer individuals not disabled receive payments.

### 2. CLAIMANTS' INCENTIVES TO PRESENT INFORMATION

Subsection 1 indicates that the appropriate level of accuracy is determined by a number of factors. But the claimant will only be concerned with the value of benefits to himself and the costs he incurs in attempting to demonstrate eligibility. Thus, claimants' incentives to provide information to enhance their chance of receiving benefits will be excessive because claimants do not take into account the cost of providing benefits.

To illustrate, suppose that a claimant seeks to receive $10,000 in public benefits. To receive these benefits, the claimant would be willing to spend up to $9,999. But the social benefit of the claimant being found eligible is always less—and often much less—than this amount. The reason is that paying the $10,000 in benefits involves an expenditure of public funds, which may require increasing taxes, reducing others' benefits, or cutting other programs. Hence, the social value of the transfer is less than the private value, regardless of whether the claimant is truly eligible or ineligible.

In practice, of course, claimants usually would choose to spend far less than $9,999. For example, if a claimant can spend $500 to achieve a 95 percent chance of receiving benefits, he surely would not spend an additional $9,499 to increase the probability to 100 percent, even if this were possible. The argument in the previous paragraph, however, applies equally to incentives at the margin. When a claimant contemplates an additional expenditure to increase the likelihood of receiving benefits, he considers only the cost of the expenditure and the gain from receiving the benefits, and not the social cost of funding the program. Therefore, whatever the amount individuals choose to spend, the amount will be socially excessive unless they are restrained or discouraged from undertaking as much effort in establishing eligibility as they would like. A system designed to determine benefit eligibility should generally constrain to some extent the ability of individuals to expend resources establishing their claims.

### 3. COURTS AND COMMENTATORS' VIEWS

Much of the attention to accuracy in the context of benefit eligibility has been with regard to the Supreme Court's approach to procedural due process that was first articulated precisely in *Mathews v. Eldridge*:

"Identification of the specific dictates of due process generally requires consideration of three distinct factors: First, the private interest that will be affected by the official action; second, the risk of an erroneous deprivation of such interest through the procedures used, and the probable value, if any, of additional or substitute procedural safeguards; and finally, the Government's interest, including the function involved and the fiscal and administrative burdens that the additional or substitute procedural requirement would entail." Much subsequent criticism has focused either on whether the Court in this case or others applied this analysis correctly or on the appropriateness of a cost-benefit framework. The present discussion will instead concern whether the cost-benefit framework is properly conceived. . . .

A generous interpretation of the Court's discussion suggests that the first factor refers to the interest of the disabled in receiving benefits, the second to the reduction of false negatives, and the third to costs of the added procedure plus something else, presumably involving the cost of paying benefits to the ineligible. . . . Even so, this interpretation is not really a formulation. Rather, it is a heterogeneous listing of relevant factors. There is little care either in specifying each relevant component or in ruling out irrelevant ones. And it does not attempt to indicate how the components fit together. These limitations of the Court's test need not create significant problems as long as those who apply the test take it to represent a more coherent formulation. It does not appear, however, that clear thinking always results. In particular, there seems to be systematic confusion about the relationship between accuracy and the burden of proof. . . .

This confusion is reflected in the Court's third factor, which is generally seen as suggesting that government functions will be adversely affected, even aside from the added costs incurred in funding additional procedural safeguards. This seems to assume that the added procedure will involve an increase in the rate at which benefits are paid to individuals who are not disabled. Procedures that increase accuracy in isolation do not produce this sort of effect: more accuracy would reduce the rate of mistaken grants of benefits. Instead, this pattern of results—a higher rate of granting benefits to both the disabled and those who are not disabled—is what follows from a reduction in the implicit burden of proof. In other words, the Court and subsequent interpreters and commentators implicitly have in mind procedures that involve a de facto shift in the burden of proof, without regard to their effect on accuracy.

This makes the Court's test and discussion of it easier to understand. The origin is apparent: those who challenge existing procedures are individuals who lose under them, and they will seek an additional procedure that will improve their circumstances. But there remains the problem of justification. Is there a constitutional requirement that burdens of proof not be too high in determining benefit eligibility? If not, what is the basis for demanding a reduction in the burden of proof? . . .

## C. ACCURACY IN ESTABLISHING FUTURE RIGHTS AND OBLIGATIONS

### 1. THE RIGHT TO APPEAR

In the context of determining future entitlements, a commonly expressed objection to employing an economic analysis to determine appropriate procedures is that the process value of allowing individuals to be heard is ignored. There remains some question, however, about the justification for such a process value—in particular, one not already subsumed in the value of accuracy or in setting the burden of proof.

One suspects that claimants who object to not being heard are those who are, for example, denied benefits. If only losers complain, however, one should be suspicious that the complaint is motivated by a concern for the result, and thus an objection to a lack of process may implicitly be an instrumental argument. An entirely plausible reason to object to not being heard is that one may believe (perhaps feel certain) that the decision was adverse precisely because the decision-maker was deprived of information one had to offer. Thus, the decision may have been inaccurate. . . .

To test this, one must consider a hypothetical situation—one probably too far removed from the typical disappointed applicant's mind for him to take seriously—in which the applicant is heard but it is certain that the decision would be unaffected by the hearing. Would individuals value appearing if they knew in advance that they would be ignored or that they would be "heard" but that hearing them could have no effect whatever on the decision?

From one perspective, this is simply an empirical question that could be tested directly. There is indirect evidence relevant to how much people value such appearances for their own sake. One type of evidence noted previously is the high rate of settlement in most civil litigation. Another is the form of dispute resolution typically specified by contract, and these often are of a simple sort. Of particular relevance for *Mathews v. Eldridge*, individuals' private disability contracts presumably do not provide for personal appearances in formal hearings. Moreover, in such instances, individuals who agree to summary procedures forgo not only the benefits of greater personal involvement per se but also any positive effect such involvement may have on the accuracy of outcomes. Finally, it is important to recall . . . that individuals' incentives to promote their interests in claims proceedings, by personal appearance or otherwise, tend to be socially excessive. Thus, even if individuals, at the time disputes arose, did value further participation and were willing to pay for it, satisfying such preferences may be socially undesirable. . . .

### 2. APPEARANCES AND LEGITIMACY

Perhaps a system that allows additional procedures appears to be more "legitimate." Consider first the possibility that the system would be seen as more legitimate because it would appear to be more accurate. If the procedures indeed make the system more accurate, this suggests that accuracy is more valuable than economic analysis typically assumes. The idea may be that compliance with legal commands is enhanced not only by more precisely tailored incentives but also by a belief that the system functions well.

A second possibility is that additional procedures would make the system appear more legitimate even though it is not assumed that the procedures make it more accurate. Again, there is the problem from Subsection 1 that few if any individuals actually focus carefully on a hypothetical situation in which a new procedure is added and it has no effect on the outcome. If such a procedure were, nonetheless, seen as contributing to legitimacy, one would wish to know why. One possibility is that a procedure enhances legitimacy because it furthers the sorts of values addressed in Subsection 1. . . . In recent decades, one has heard more complaints about the litigation explosion, the excessive monetary cost and other burdens associated with particular types of lawsuits, and excessive procedures delaying or denying justice than about a serious shortage of procedures or an inadequacy of opportunities to be involved with lawyers or the legal system. Although such views in substantial part involve an unsophisticated understanding of the legal system, an approach that privileged them may warrant less accuracy and concern for procedure than indicated by the economic analysis presented here. . . .

Some commentators have remarked that a cost-benefit calculus such as that employed in *Mathews v. Eldridge* is not obviously suited to implementation by appellate courts rather than by legislative bodies or specialized agencies. Moreover, the Due Process Clause is a component of the Bill of Rights, much of which is designed to protect individuals against potential government abuse. Thus, it is not necessarily appropriate for the courts' tests of the constitutionality of procedures to mirror an economic analysis designed to determine which procedures are socially best.

## Comments and Questions

1. The substantial literature bringing economic analysis into procedure and administration of justice includes Judge Richard A. Posner's general work, *Economic Analysis of Law* (5th ed. 1998); an argument for replacing fairness concerns with analysis from welfare economics advanced by Louis Kaplow and Steven Shavell, *Fairness Versus Welfare*, 114 Harv. L. Rev. 971 (2001); and empirical work such as Geoffrey P. Miller, *The Legal-Economic Analysis of Comparative Civil Procedure*, 45 Am. J. Comp. L. 905 (1997), and the articles reviewed in William M. Landes, *The Empirical Side of Law & Economics*, 70 U. Chi. L. Rev. 167 (2003). A good general overview is Robert Bone, *The Economics of Civil Procedure* (2003). For criticism of these approaches, see Michael B. Dorff, *Why Welfare Depends on Fairness: A Reply to Kaplow and Shavell*, 75 S. Cal. L. Rev. 847 (2002); Herbert Hovenkamp, *Positivism in Law & Economics*, 78 Cal. L. Rev. 815 (1990); and Arthur A. Leff, *Economic Analysis of Law: Some Realism About Nominalism*, 60 Va. L. Rev. 45 (1974).

2. As the Kaplow excerpt indicates, litigation has a private and a public function. The private function is to provide a resolution to a controversy between two people. But that process has implications for the society as a whole, in terms of the cost to the broader society of providing a forum for adjudication as well as the cost to society of inaccurate results and, perhaps, suboptimal incentives such as over- or under-deterrence of misconduct. For a discussion see Steven Shavell, *The Fundamental Divergence Between the Private and Social Motive to Use the Legal System*, 26 J. Legal Stud. 575 (1997). These issues will arise again in the discussion of settlement and of the jury right later in the course.

## 5. *Enemy Combatants and Due Process*

New frontiers of due process doctrine have become front-page news as the United States responds to terrorist attacks and combat with detention centers.

## ■ HAMDI v. RUMSFELD
### *542 U.S. 507 (2004)*

Justice O'CONNOR announced the judgment of the Court, and delivered an opinion, in which THE CHIEF JUSTICE, Justice KENNEDY, and Justice BREYER join:

At this difficult time in our Nation's history, we are called upon to consider the legality of the Government's detention of a United States citizen on United States soil as an "enemy combatant" and to address the process that is constitutionally owed to one who seeks to challenge his classification as such. The United States Court of Appeals for the Fourth Circuit held that petitioner Yaser Hamdi's detention was legally authorized and that he was entitled to no further opportunity to challenge his enemy-combatant label. We now vacate and remand. We hold that although Congress authorized the detention of combatants in the narrow circumstances alleged here, due process demands that a citizen held in the United States as an enemy combatant be given a meaningful opportunity to contest the factual basis for that detention before a neutral decisionmaker.

### I

On September 11, 2001, the al Qaeda terrorist network used hijacked commercial airliners to attack prominent targets in the United States. Approximately 3,000 people were killed in those attacks. One week later, in response to these "acts of treacherous violence," Congress passed a resolution authorizing the President to "use all necessary and appropriate force against those nations, organizations, or persons he determines planned, authorized, committed, or aided the terrorist attacks" or "harbored such organizations or persons, in order to prevent any future acts of international terrorism against the United States by such nations, organizations or persons." Authorization for Use of Military Force (AUMF), 115 Stat. 224. Soon thereafter, the President ordered United States Armed Forces to Afghanistan, with a mission to subdue al Qaeda and quell the Taliban regime that was known to support it.

This case arises out of the detention of a man whom the Government alleges took up arms with the Taliban during this conflict. His name is Yaser Esam Hamdi. Born in Louisiana in 1980, Hamdi moved with his family to Saudi Arabia as a child. By 2001, the parties agree, he resided in Afghanistan. At some point that year, he was seized by members of the Northern Alliance, a coalition of military groups opposed to the Taliban government, and eventually was turned over to the United States military. The Government asserts that it initially detained and interrogated Hamdi in Afghanistan before transferring him to the United States Naval Base in Guantanamo Bay in January 2002. In April 2002, upon learning that Hamdi is an American citizen, authorities transferred him to a naval brig in Norfolk, Virginia, where he remained until a recent transfer to a brig in Charleston, South Carolina. The Government contends that Hamdi is an "enemy combatant," and that this status justifies holding him in the United States indefinitely—without formal charges or proceedings—unless and until it makes the determination that access to counsel or further process is warranted.

In June 2002, Hamdi's father, Esam Fouad Hamdi, filed the present petition for a writ of habeas corpus under 28 U.S.C. § 2241 in the Eastern District of Virginia, naming as petitioners his son and himself as next friend. The elder Hamdi alleges in the petition that he has had no contact with his son since the Government took custody of him in 2001, and that the Government has held his son "without access to legal counsel or notice of any charges pending against him." . . . [T]he Government filed a response and a motion to dismiss the petition. It attached to its response a declaration from one Michael Mobbs (hereinafter Mobbs Declaration), who identified himself as Special Advisor to the Under Secretary of Defense for Policy. . . .

Mobbs then set forth what remains the sole evidentiary support that the Government has provided to the courts for Hamdi's detention. The declaration states that Hamdi "traveled to Afghanistan" in July or August 2001, and that he thereafter "affiliated with a Taliban military unit and received weapons training." It asserts that Hamdi "remained with his Taliban unit following the attacks of September 11" and that, during the time when Northern Alliance forces were "engaged in battle with the Taliban," "Hamdi's Taliban unit surrendered" to those forces, after which he "surrender[ed] his Kalishnikov assault rifle" to them. The Mobbs Declaration also states that, because al Qaeda and the Taliban "were and are hostile forces engaged in armed conflict with the armed forces of the United States," "individuals associated with" those groups "were and continue to be enemy combatants." Mobbs states that Hamdi was labeled an enemy combatant "[b]ased upon his interviews and in light of his association with the Taliban." According to the declaration, a series of "U.S. military screening team[s]" determined that Hamdi met "the criteria for enemy combatants," and "[a] subsequent interview of Hamdi has confirmed the fact that he surrendered and gave his firearm to Northern Alliance forces, which supports his classification as an enemy combatant. . . ."

The District Court found that the Mobbs Declaration fell "far short" of supporting Hamdi's detention. It criticized the generic and hearsay nature of the affidavit, calling it "little more than the government's 'say-so.'" It ordered the Government to turn over numerous materials for in camera review . . . indicat[ing] that all of these materials were necessary for "meaningful judicial review" of whether Hamdi's detention was legally authorized and whether Hamdi had received sufficient process to satisfy the Due Process Clause of the Constitution and relevant treaties or military regulations. . . .

The Fourth Circuit reversed, . . . stress[ing] that, because it was "undisputed that Hamdi was captured in a zone of active combat in a foreign theater of conflict," no factual inquiry or evidentiary hearing allowing Hamdi to be heard or to rebut the Government's assertions was necessary or proper. Concluding that the factual averments in the Mobbs Declaration, "if accurate," provided a sufficient basis upon which to conclude that the President had constitutionally detained Hamdi pursuant to the President's war powers, it ordered the habeas petition dismissed.

## II

[Justice O'CONNOR then explained that the AUMF authorized capture and detention of individuals who were part of hostile forces taking up arms against the United States in Afghanistan. This satisfied 18 U.S.C. § 4001(a), which states that "[n]o citizen shall be imprisoned or otherwise detained by the United States except pursuant to an Act of Congress."]

## III

Even in cases in which the detention of enemy combatants is legally authorized, there remains the question of what process is constitutionally due to a citizen who disputes his enemy-combatant status. Hamdi argues that he is owed a meaningful and timely hearing and that "extra-judicial detention [that] begins and ends with the submission of an affidavit based on third-hand hearsay" does not comport with the Fifth and Fourteenth Amendments. The Government counters that any more process than was provided below would be both unworkable and "constitutionally intolerable." . . .

### C

. . . The ordinary mechanism that we use for balancing such serious competing interests, and for determining the procedures that are necessary to ensure that a citizen is not "deprived of life, liberty, or property, without due process of law," U.S. Const., Amdt. 5, is the test that we articulated in

*Mathews v. Eldridge*, 424 U.S. 319 (1976). *Mathews* dictates that the process due in any given instance is determined by weighing "the private interest that will be affected by the official action" against the Government's asserted interest, "including the function involved" and the burdens the Government would face in providing greater process. 424 U.S., at 335. The *Mathews* calculus then contemplates a judicious balancing of these concerns, through an analysis of "the risk of an erroneous deprivation" of the private interest if the process were reduced and the "probable value, if any, of additional or substitute procedural safeguards." *Ibid*. We take each of these steps in turn.

**1**

It is beyond question that substantial interests lie on both sides of the scale in this case. Hamdi's "private interest . . . affected by the official action," is the most elemental of liberty interests—the interest in being free from physical detention by one's own government. . . . Moreover, as critical as the Government's interest may be in detaining those who actually pose an immediate threat to the national security of the United States during ongoing international conflict, history and common sense teach us that an unchecked system of detention carries the potential to become a means for oppression and abuse of others who do not present that sort of threat. . . . We reaffirm today the fundamental nature of a citizen's right to be free from involuntary confinement by his own government without due process of law, and we weigh the opposing governmental interests against the curtailment of liberty that such confinement entails.

**2**

On the other side of the scale are the weighty and sensitive governmental interests in ensuring that those who have in fact fought with the enemy during a war do not return to battle against the United States. As discussed above, the law of war and the realities of combat may render such detentions both necessary and appropriate, and our due process analysis need not blink at those realities. Without doubt, our Constitution recognizes that core strategic matters of warmaking belong in the hands of those who are best positioned and most politically accountable for making them.

The Government also argues at some length that its interests in reducing the process available to alleged enemy combatants are heightened by the practical difficulties that would accompany a system of trial-like process. In its view, military officers who are engaged in the serious work of waging battle would be unnecessarily and dangerously distracted by litigation half a world away, and discovery into military operations would both intrude on the sensitive secrets of national defense and result in a futile search for evidence buried under the rubble of war. To the extent that these burdens are triggered by heightened procedures, they are properly taken into account in our due process analysis.

**3**

Striking the proper constitutional balance here is of great importance to the Nation during this period of ongoing combat. But it is equally vital that our calculus not give short shrift to the values that this country holds dear or to the privilege that is American citizenship. It is during our most challenging and uncertain moments that our Nation's commitment to due process is most severely tested; and it is in those times that we must preserve our commitment at home to the principles for which we fight abroad. . . .

We therefore hold that a citizen-detainee seeking to challenge his classification as an enemy combatant must receive notice of the factual basis for his classification, and a fair opportunity to rebut the Government's factual assertions before a neutral decisionmaker. "For more than a century the central meaning of procedural due process has been clear: 'Parties whose rights are to be affected are entitled to be heard; and in order that they may enjoy that right they must first be notified.' It is equally fundamental that the right to notice and an opportunity to be heard 'must be granted at a meaningful time and in a meaningful manner.'" *Fuentes v. Shevin*, 407 U.S. 67, 80 (1972) (quoting *Baldwin v. Hale*, 1 Wall. 223, 233, 17 L.Ed. 531 (1864)). These essential constitutional promises may not be eroded.

At the same time, the exigencies of the circumstances may demand that, aside from these core elements, enemy-combatant proceedings may be tailored to alleviate their uncommon potential to burden the Executive at a time of ongoing military conflict. Hearsay, for example, may need to be accepted as the most reliable available evidence from the Government in such a proceeding. Likewise, the Constitution would not be offended by a presumption in favor of the Government's evidence, so long as that presumption remained a rebuttable one and fair opportunity for rebuttal were provided. Thus, once the Government puts forth credible evidence that the habeas petitioner meets the enemy-combatant criteria, the onus could shift to the petitioner to rebut that evidence with more persuasive evidence that he falls outside the criteria. A burden-shifting scheme of this sort would meet the goal of ensuring that the errant tourist, embedded journalist, or local aid worker has a chance to prove military error while giving due regard to the Executive once it has put forth meaningful support for its conclusion that the detainee is in fact an enemy combatant. In the words of *Mathews*, process of this sort would sufficiently address the "risk of an erroneous deprivation" of a detainee's liberty interest while eliminating certain procedures that have questionable additional value in light of the burden on the Government. 424 U.S., at 335.

We think it unlikely that this basic process will have the dire impact on the central functions of warmaking that the Government forecasts. The parties agree that initial captures on the battlefield need not receive the process we have discussed here; that process is due only when the determination is made to continue to hold those who have been seized. The Government has made clear in its briefing that documentation regarding battlefield detainees already is kept in the ordinary course of military affairs. Any factfinding imposition created by requiring a knowledgeable affiant to summarize these records to an independent tribunal is a minimal one. Likewise, arguments that military officers ought not have to wage war under the threat of litigation lose much of their steam when factual disputes at enemy-combatant hearings are limited to the alleged combatant's acts. This focus meddles little, if at all, in the strategy or conduct of war, inquiring only into the appropriateness of continuing to detain an individual claimed to have taken up arms against the United States. While we accord the greatest respect and consideration to the judgments of military authorities in matters relating to the actual prosecution of a war, and recognize that the scope of that discretion necessarily is wide, it does not infringe on the core role of the military for the courts to exercise their own time-honored and constitutionally mandated roles of reviewing and resolving claims like those presented here. The judgment of the United States Court of Appeals for the Fourth Circuit is vacated, and the case is remanded for further proceedings.

It is so ordered.

Justice SOUTER, with whom Justice GINSBURG joins, concurring in part, dissenting in part, and concurring in the judgment.

. . . The plurality rejects [the limits asserted by the Government] on the exercise of jurisdiction and so far I agree with its opinion. The plurality does, however, accept the Government's position that if Hamdi's designation as an enemy combatant is correct, his detention (at least as to some period) is authorized by [the AUMF]. Here I disagree and respectfully dissent. The Government has failed to demonstrate that the Force Resolution authorizes the detention complained of here even on the facts the Government claims . . .

. . . It should go without saying that in joining with the plurality to produce a judgment, I do not adopt the plurality's resolution of constitutional issues that I would not reach. It is not that I could disagree with the plurality's determinations (given the plurality's view of the Force Resolution) that someone in Hamdi's position is entitled at a minimum to notice of the Government's claimed factual basis for holding him, and to a fair chance to rebut it before a neutral decisionmaker; nor, of course, could I disagree with the plurality's affirmation of Hamdi's right to counsel. On the other hand, I do not mean to imply agreement that the Government could claim an evidentiary presumption casting the burden of rebuttal on Hamdi, or that an opportunity to litigate before a military tribunal might obviate or truncate enquiry by a court on habeas. . . .

Justice SCALIA, with whom Justice STEVENS joins, dissenting:

## I

. . . The gist of the Due Process Clause, as understood at the founding and since, was to force the Government to follow those common-law procedures traditionally deemed necessary before depriving a person of life, liberty, or property. When a citizen was deprived of liberty because of alleged criminal conduct, those procedures typically required committal by a magistrate followed by indictment and trial. The Due Process Clause "in effect affirms the right of trial according to the process and proceedings of the common law."

To be sure, certain types of permissible *non* criminal detention—that is, those not dependent upon the contention that the citizen had committed a criminal act—did not require the protections of criminal procedure. However, these fell into a limited number of well-recognized exceptions—civil commitment of the mentally ill, for example, and temporary detention in quarantine of the infectious. *See Opinion on the Writ of Habeas Corpus*, Wilm. 77, 88-92, 97 Eng. Rep. 29, 36-37 (H.L.1758) (Wilmot, J.). It is unthinkable that the Executive could render otherwise criminal grounds for detention noncriminal merely by disclaiming an intent to prosecute, or by asserting that it was incapacitating dangerous offenders rather than punishing wrongdoing. *Cf. Kansas v. Hendricks*, 521 U.S. 346, 358 (1997) ("A finding of dangerousness, standing alone, is ordinarily not a sufficient ground upon which to justify indefinite involuntary commitment").

These due process rights have historically been vindicated by the writ of habeas corpus. In England before the founding, the writ developed into a tool for challenging executive confinement.

The writ of habeas corpus was preserved in the Constitution—the only common-law writ to be explicitly mentioned. *See* Art. I, § 9, cl. 2. Hamilton lauded "the establishment of the writ of habeas corpus" in his Federalist defense as a means to protect against "the practice of arbitrary imprisonments . . . in all ages, [one of] the favourite and most formidable instruments of tyranny." The Federalist No. 84, at 444. . . .

## II

The allegations here, of course, are no ordinary accusations of criminal activity. Yaser Esam Hamdi has been imprisoned because the Government believes he participated in the waging of war against the United States. The relevant question, then, is whether there is a different, special procedure for imprisonment of a citizen accused of wrongdoing *by aiding the enemy in wartime.*

### A

Justice O'Connor, writing for a plurality of this Court, asserts that captured enemy combatants (other than those suspected of war crimes) have traditionally been detained until the cessation of hostilities and then released. That is probably an accurate description of wartime practice with respect to enemy *aliens*. The tradition with respect to American citizens, however, has been quite different. Citizens aiding the enemy have been treated as traitors subject to the criminal process.

. . . The Constitution provides: "Treason against the United States, shall consist only in levying War against them, or in adhering to their Enemies, giving them Aid and Comfort"; and establishes a heightened proof requirement (two witnesses) in order to "convic[t]" of that offense. Art. III, § 3, cl. 1.

**B**

There are times when military exigency renders resort to the traditional criminal process impracticable. English law accommodated such exigencies by allowing legislative suspension of the writ of habeas corpus for brief periods.

Our Federal Constitution contains a provision explicitly permitting suspension, but limiting the situations in which it may be invoked: "The Privilege of the Writ of Habeas Corpus shall not be suspended, unless when in Cases of Rebellion or Invasion the public Safety may require it." Art. I, § 9, cl. 2. Although this provision does not state that suspension must be effected by, or authorized by, a legislative act, it has been so understood, consistent with English practice and the Clause's placement in Article I. *See Ex parte Bollman*, 4 Cranch 75, 101, 2 L.Ed. 554 (1807); *Ex parte Merryman*, 17 F. Cas. 144, 151-152 (C.D.Md. 1861) (Taney, C. J., rejecting Lincoln's unauthorized suspension); 3 Story § 1336, at 208-209.

The Suspension Clause was by design a safety valve, the Constitution's only "express provision for exercise of extraordinary authority because of a crisis," *Youngstown Sheet & Tube Co. v. Sawyer*, 343 U.S. 579, 650 (1952) (Jackson, J., concurring).

**III**

Even if suspension of the writ on the one hand, and committal for criminal charges on the other hand, have been the only traditional means of dealing with citizens who levied war against their own country, it is theoretically possible that the Constitution does not *require* a choice between these alternatives.

I believe, however, that substantial evidence does refute that possibility. First, the text of the 1679 Habeas Corpus Act makes clear that indefinite imprisonment on reasonable suspicion is not an available option of treatment for those accused of aiding the enemy, absent a suspension of the writ. . . .

**V**

It follows from what I have said that Hamdi is entitled to a habeas decree requiring his release unless (1) criminal proceedings are promptly brought, or (2) Congress has suspended the writ of habeas corpus. A suspension of the writ could, of course, lay down conditions for continued detention, similar to those that today's opinion prescribes under the Due Process Clause. *Cf.* Act of Mar. 3, 1863, 12 Stat. 755. But there is a world of difference between the people's representatives' determining the need for that suspension (and prescribing the conditions for it), and this Court's doing so. . . .

Having found a congressional authorization for detention of citizens where none clearly exists; and having discarded the categorical procedural protection of the Suspension Clause; the plurality then proceeds, under the guise of the Due Process Clause, to prescribe what procedural protections it thinks appropriate. It "weigh[s] the private interest . . . against the Government's asserted interest," (internal quotation marks omitted), and—just as though writing a new Constitution—comes up with an unheard-of system in which the citizen rather than the Government bears the burden of proof, testimony is by hearsay rather than live witnesses, and the presiding officer may well be a "neutral" military officer rather than judge and jury. It claims authority to engage in this sort of "judicious balancing" from *Mathews v. Eldridge*, 424 U.S. 319 (1976), a case involving . . . *the withdrawal of disability benefits*! Whatever the merits of this technique when newly recognized property rights are at issue (and even there they are questionable), it has no place where the Constitution and the common law already supply an answer.

There is a certain harmony of approach in the plurality's making up for Congress's failure to invoke the Suspension Clause and its making up for the Executive's failure to apply what it says are needed procedures—an approach that reflects what might be called a Mr. Fix-it Mentality. The plurality seems to view it as its mission to Make Everything Come Out Right, rather than merely to decree the consequences, as far as individual rights are concerned, of the other two branches' actions and omissions. . . . The problem with this approach is not only that it steps out of the courts' modest and limited role in a democratic society; but that by repeatedly doing what it thinks the political branches ought to do it encourages their lassitude and saps the vitality of government by the people. . . .

Because the Court has proceeded to meet the current emergency in a manner the Constitution does not envision, I respectfully dissent.

Justice THOMAS, dissenting:
The Executive Branch, acting pursuant to the powers vested in the President by the Constitution and with explicit congressional approval, has determined that Yaser Hamdi is an enemy combatant and should be detained. That detention falls squarely within the Federal Government's war powers, and we lack the expertise and capacity to second-guess that decision. As such, petitioners' habeas challenge should fail, and there is no reason to remand the case. . . .

Although I do not agree with the plurality that the balancing approach of *Mathews v. Eldridge*, 424 U.S. 319 (1976) is the appropriate analytic tool with which to analyze this case, I cannot help but explain that the plurality misapplies its chosen framework, one that if applied correctly would probably lead to the result I have reached. The plurality devotes two paragraphs to its discussion of the Government's interest, though much of those two paragraphs explain why the Government's concerns are misplaced. . . . At issue here is the . . . significant interest of the security of the Nation. The Government seeks to further that interest by detaining an enemy soldier not only to prevent him from rejoining the ongoing plains, detention can serve to gather critical intelligence regarding the intentions and capabilities of our adversaries, a function that the Government avers has become all the more important in the war on terrorism.

Additional process, the Government explains, will destroy the intelligence gathering function. It also does seem quite likely that, under the process envisioned by the plurality, various military officials will have to take time to litigate this matter. And though the plurality does not say so, a meaningful ability to challenge the Government's factual allegations will probably require the Government to divulge highly classified information to the purported enemy combatant, who might then upon release return to the fight armed with our most closely held secrets.

The plurality manages to avoid these problems by discounting or entirely ignoring them. . . .

The plurality next opines that "[w]e think it unlikely that this basic process will have the dire impact on the central functions of warmaking that the Government forecasts." . . . [T]his highlights serious difficulties in applying the plurality's balancing approach here. First, in the war context, we know neither the strength of the Government's interests nor the costs of imposing additional process.

Second, it is at least difficult to explain why the result should be different for other military operations that the plurality would ostensibly recognize as "central functions of warmaking." . . . Because a decision to bomb a particular target might extinguish *life* interests, the plurality's analysis seems to require notice to potential targets. . . . I offer these examples not because I think the plurality would demand additional process in these situations but because it clearly would not. The result here should be the same. . . .

Undeniably, Hamdi has been deprived of a serious interest, one actually protected by the Due Process Clause. Against this, however, is the Government's overriding interest in protecting the Nation. . . .

## Comments and Questions

1. The *Hamdi* decision is a plurality decision, meaning that a majority of the Justices agreed on the outcome but not on the reasoning. Here six Justices concurred on the judgment, that is, on the ultimate decision to vacate the Fourth Circuit decision and remand to the district court. Four Justices (O'Connor, Roberts, Kennedy, Breyer) signed on to the plurality opinion reprinted here. What type of hearing do they propose for the accused? How do they determine this? Contrast the position of Justice O'Connor's plurality opinion with the dissent of Justices Scalia and Stevens. How would Justice Thomas balance the interests at stake differently than the majority?

2. You may wonder about the precedential value of a plurality decision. The Supreme Court has held that "[w]hen a fragmented Court decides a case and no single rationale explaining the result enjoys the assent of five Justices, 'the holding of the Court may be viewed as that position taken by those

Members who concurred in the judgments on the narrowest grounds. . . . '"
Marks v. U.S., 430 U.S. 188, 193 (1977). What is the "holding" in *Hamdi*?

   3. After the decision in *Hamdi*, the Supreme Court ruled 5-4 in *Hamdan v. Rumsfeld*, 548 U.S. 557 (2006), that the President's convening of military commissions to try detainees held in Guantanamo Bay, Cuba, exceeded constitutional limitations on executive power and contravened the Uniform Code of Military Justice and Common Article 3 of the Geneva Conventions that the United States signed in 1949. Consistent with the Court's decision, Congress subsequently responded by authorizing the President to proceed with military commissions and to foreclose access to the federal court through the traditional writ of habeas corpus. The Military Commissions Act of 2006, 10 U.S.C. §§ 948a-950t. In *Boumediene v. Bush*, 553 U.S. 723, 798 (2008), the Supreme Court upheld federal court habeas jurisdiction over detainees held in Guantanamo Bay, despite the lack of statutory authorization, but expressly left open what standards would apply. The D.C. Circuit has de facto exclusive jurisdiction over habeas petitions brought by Guantanamo detainees. For a critical discussion of the D.C. Circuit's evolving case law in this area, see Stephen I. Vladeck, *The D.C. Circuit After* Boumediene, 41 Seton Hall L. Rev. 1451 (2011).

## Practice Exercise No. 1: Designing a Sound Dispute Resolution Process

   At the beginning of this section you learned of a due process case brought in the 1950s by organizations that had been designated "totalitarian, fascist, communist, or subversive" by the Attorney General. Today, under the Antiterrorism and Effective Death Penalty Act of 1996 (AEDPA), the Secretary of State may designate an entity as a Foreign Terrorist Organization if she determines that (A) the entity is foreign, (B) it engages in "terrorist activity" or "terrorism," and (C) the terrorist activity threatens the security of the United States or its nationals. 8 U.S.C. § 1189(a)(1). "Terrorist activity," as defined by the statute, includes hijacking, sabotage, kidnapping, assassination, and the use of explosives, firearms, or biological, chemical, or nuclear weapons with intent to endanger people or property, or a threat or conspiracy to do any of the foregoing. To "engage in terrorist activity" may involve soliciting funds or affording material support for terrorist activities. When an organization is designated as a Foreign Terrorist Organization, its assets may be frozen and its members forbidden from entering the United States. The statute permits organizations to appeal their designation to the federal courts. Using the cases you have read so far and the case below, *Connecticut v. Doehr*, prepare answers to the following hypotheticals for discussion in class.

   1. Imagine that you are a lawyer working in the State Department and
      have been asked to draft an administrative procedure for designating

Foreign Terrorist Organizations under the AEDPA. What procedure would you propose? As you draft the procedure, remember that the Secretary of State is concerned about two things: (i) sharing classified information with potential terrorist organizations and (ii) the ability of terrorist organizations to abscond with unlawful funds before the determination is made.

2. Now imagine that the Secretary of State has decided on the following procedure for designating an organization a Foreign Terrorist Organization: State Department personnel will review classified and non-classified material and make a designation. To prevent organizations from liquidating their assets, the State Department will issue the designation and freeze the organization's assets. The organization will be notified within 5 days of the designation and, at that point, will be given access to non-classified information and the opportunity to dispute the designation through written submissions. One organization, the Sovereignty Coalition, was designated a Foreign Terrorist Organization and had their assets frozen. They have appealed to the federal courts. What is their best argument? How should the government respond? How should the federal district court rule?

# ■ CONNECTICUT v. DOEHR
### *501 U.S. 1 (1991)*

Justice WHITE delivered an opinion, Parts I, II, and III of which are the opinion of the Court:

This case requires us to determine whether a state statute that authorizes prejudgment attachment of real estate without prior notice or hearing, without a showing of extraordinary circumstances, and without a requirement that the person seeking the attachment post a bond, satisfies the Due Process Clause of the Fourteenth Amendment. We hold that, as applied to this case, it does not.

## I.

On March 15, 1988, petitioner John F. DiGiovanni submitted an application to the Connecticut Superior Court for an attachment in the amount of $75,000 on respondent Brian K. Doehr's home in Meriden, Connecticut. DiGiovanni took this step in conjunction with a civil action for assault and battery that he was seeking to institute against Doehr in the same court. The suit did not involve Doehr's real estate, nor did DiGiovanni have any pre-existing interest either in Doehr's home or any of his other property.

Connecticut law authorizes prejudgment attachment of real estate without affording prior notice or the opportunity for a prior hearing to the individual whose property is subject to the attachment. The State's prejudgment remedy statute provides, in relevant part:

> "The court or a judge of the court may allow the prejudgment remedy to be issued by an attorney without hearing as provided in sections 52-278c and 52-278d upon verification by oath of the plaintiff or of some competent affiant, that there is probable cause to sustain the validity of the plaintiff's claims and (1) that the prejudgment remedy requested is for an attachment of real property. . . ." Conn. Gen. Stat. § 52-278e (1991).

The statute does not require the plaintiff to post a bond to insure the payment of damages that the defendant may suffer should the attachment prove wrongfully issued or the claim prove unsuccessful.

As required, DiGiovanni submitted an affidavit in support of his application. In five one-sentence paragraphs, DiGiovanni stated that the facts set forth in his previously submitted complaint were true; that "I was willfully, wantonly and maliciously assaulted by the defendant, Brian K. Doehr"; that "[s]aid assault and battery broke my left wrist and further caused an ecchymosis to my right eye, as well as other injuries"; and that "I have further expended sums of money for medical care and treatment." The affidavit concluded with the statement, "In my opinion, the foregoing facts are sufficient to show that there is probable cause that judgment will be rendered for the plaintiff."

On the strength of these submissions the Superior Court Judge, by an order dated March 17, found "probable cause to sustain the validity of the plaintiff's claim" and ordered the attachment on Doehr's home "to the value of $75,000." The sheriff attached the property four days later, on March 21. Only after this did Doehr receive notice of the attachment. He also had yet to be served with the complaint, which is ordinarily necessary for an action to commence in Connecticut. As the statute further required, the attachment notice informed Doehr that he had the right to a hearing: (1) to claim that no probable cause existed to sustain the claim; (2) to request that the attachment be vacated, modified, or dismissed or that a bond be substituted; or (3) to claim that some portion of the property was exempt from execution. Conn. Gen. Stat. § 52-278e(b) (1991).

Rather than pursue these options, Doehr filed suit against DiGiovanni in Federal District Court, claiming that § 52-278e(a)(1) was unconstitutional under the Due Process Clause of the Fourteenth Amendment. . . .

## II

With this case we return to the question of what process must be afforded by a state statute enabling an individual to enlist the aid of the State to deprive another of his or her property by means of the prejudgment attachment or similar procedure. Our cases reflect the numerous variations this type of remedy can entail. In *Sniadach v. Family Finance Corp. of Bay View*,

395 U.S. 337 (1969), the Court struck down a Wisconsin statute that permitted a creditor to effect prejudgment garnishment of wages without notice and prior hearing to the wage earner. In *Fuentes v. Shevin*, 407 U.S. 67 (1972), the Court likewise found a due process violation in state replevin provisions that permitted vendors to have goods seized through an ex parte application to a court clerk and the posting of a bond. Conversely, the Court upheld a Louisiana ex parte procedure allowing a lienholder to have disputed goods sequestered in *Mitchell v. W.T. Grant Co.*, [416 U.S. 600 (1974)]. *Mitchell*, however, carefully noted that *Fuentes* was decided against "a factual and legal background sufficiently different . . . that it does not require the invalidation of the Louisiana sequestration statute." *Id.*, 416 U.S. at 615. Those differences included Louisiana's provision of an immediate postdeprivation hearing along with the option of damages; the requirement that a judge rather than a clerk determine that there is a clear showing of entitlement to the writ; the necessity for a detailed affidavit; and an emphasis on the lienholder's interest in preventing waste or alienation of the encumbered property. In *North Georgia Finishing, Inc. v. Di-Chem, Inc.*, 419 U.S. 601 (1975), the Court again invalidated an ex parte garnishment statute that not only failed to provide for notice and prior hearing but also failed to require a bond, a detailed affidavit setting out the claim, the determination of a neutral magistrate, or a prompt postdeprivation hearing.

These cases "underscore the truism that '"[d]ue process," unlike some legal rules, is not a technical conception with a fixed content unrelated to time, place and circumstances.'" *Mathews v. Eldridge, supra*, 424 U.S., at 334. In *Mathews*, we drew upon our prejudgment remedy decisions to determine what process is due when the government itself seeks to effect a deprivation on its own initiative. That analysis resulted in the now familiar threefold inquiry requiring consideration of "the private interest that will be affected by the official action"; "the risk of an erroneous deprivation of such interest through the procedures used, and the probable value, if any, of additional or substitute safeguards"; and lastly "the Government's interest, including the function involved and the fiscal and administrative burdens that the additional or substitute procedural requirement would entail." *Id.*, at 335.

Here the inquiry is similar, but the focus is different. Prejudgment remedy statutes ordinarily apply to disputes between private parties rather than between an individual and the government. Such enactments are designed to enable one of the parties to "make use of state procedures with the overt, significant assistance of state officials," and they undoubtedly involve state action "substantial enough to implicate the Due Process Clause." *Tulsa Professional Collection Services, Inc. v. Pope*, 485 U.S. 478, 486 (1988). Nonetheless, any burden that increasing procedural safeguards entails primarily affects not the government, but the party seeking control of the other's property. For this type of case, therefore, the relevant inquiry requires, as in *Mathews*, first, consideration of the private interest that will be affected by the prejudgment measure; second, an examination of the risk of erroneous deprivation through the procedures under attack and the probable value of additional or alternative safeguards; and third, in contrast to *Mathews*, principal attention to the interest of the party seeking the prejudgment remedy, with, nonetheless, due regard for any ancillary interest the government may have in providing the procedure or forgoing the added burden of providing greater protections.

We now consider the *Mathews* factors in determining the adequacy of the procedures before us, first with regard to the safeguards of notice and a prior hearing, and then in relation to the protection of a bond.

## III

We agree with the Court of Appeals that the property interests that attachment affects are significant. For a property owner like Doehr, attachment ordinarily clouds title; impairs the ability to sell or otherwise alienate the property; taints any credit rating; reduces the chance of obtaining a home equity loan or additional mortgage; and can even place an existing mortgage in technical default where there is an insecurity clause. Nor does Connecticut deny that any of these consequences occurs.

Instead, the State correctly points out that these effects do not amount to a complete, physical, or permanent deprivation of real property; their impact is less than the perhaps temporary total deprivation of household goods or wages. But the Court has never held that only such extreme deprivations trigger due process concern. To the contrary, our cases show that even the temporary or partial impairments to property rights that attachments, liens, and similar encumbrances entail are sufficient to merit due process protection. . . .

We also agree with the Court of Appeals that the risk of erroneous deprivation that the State permits here is substantial. By definition, attachment statutes premise a deprivation of property on one ultimate factual contingency—the award of damages to the plaintiff which the defendant may not be able to satisfy. For attachments before judgment, Connecticut mandates that this determination be made by means of a procedural inquiry that asks whether "there is probable cause to sustain the validity of the plaintiff's claim." Conn. Gen. Stat. § 52-278e(a) (1991).

. . . Permitting a court to authorize attachment merely because the plaintiff believes the defendant is liable, or because the plaintiff can make out a facially valid complaint, would permit the deprivation of the defendant's property when the claim would fail to convince a jury, when it rested on factual allegations that were sufficient to state a cause of action but which the defendant would dispute, or in the case of a mere good-faith standard, even when the complaint failed to state a claim upon which relief could be granted. The potential for unwarranted attachment in these situations is self-evident and too great to satisfy the requirements of due process absent any countervailing consideration.

Even if the provision requires the plaintiff to demonstrate, and the judge to find, probable cause to believe that judgment will be rendered in favor of the plaintiff, the risk of error was substantial in this case. As the record shows, and as the State concedes, only a skeletal affidavit need be, and was, filed. The State urges that the reviewing judge normally reviews the complaint as well, but concedes that the complaint may also be conclusory. It is self-evident that the judge could make no realistic assessment concerning the likelihood of an action's success based upon these one-sided, self-serving, and conclusory submissions. . . . The likelihood of error that results illustrates that "fairness can rarely be obtained by secret, one-sided determination of facts decisive of rights. . . . [And n]o better instrument has been devised for arriving at truth than to give a person in jeopardy of serious loss notice of the case against him and opportunity to meet it." *Joint Anti-Fascist Refugee Comm. v. McGrath*, 341 U.S. 123, 170-172 (1951) (Frankfurter, J., concurring).

What safeguards the State does afford do not adequately reduce this risk. Connecticut points out that the statute also provides an "expeditiou[s]" post-attachment adversary hearing; notice for such a hearing; judicial review of an adverse decision; and a double damages action if the original suit is commenced without probable cause. . . . It is true that a later hearing might negate the presence of probable cause, but this would not cure the temporary deprivation that an earlier hearing might have prevented. "The Fourteenth Amendment draws no bright lines around three-day, 10-day or 50-day deprivations of property. Any significant taking of property by the State is within the purview of the Due Process Clause." *Fuentes*, 407 U.S., at 86.

. . . Finally, we conclude that the interests in favor of an ex parte attachment, particularly the interests of the plaintiff, are too minimal to supply such a consideration here. The plaintiff had no existing interest in Doehr's real estate when he sought the attachment. His only interest in attaching the property was to ensure the availability of assets to satisfy his judgment if he prevailed on the merits of his action. Yet there was no allegation that Doehr was about to transfer or encumber his real estate or take any other action during the pendency of the action that would render his real estate unavailable to satisfy a judgment. Our cases have recognized such a properly supported claim would be an exigent circumstance permitting postponing any notice or hearing until after the attachment is effected. . . .

No interest the government may have affects the analysis. The State's substantive interest in protecting any rights of the plaintiff cannot be any more weighty than those rights themselves. Here the plaintiff's interest is *de minimis*. Moreover, the State cannot seriously plead additional financial or administrative burdens involving predeprivation hearings when it already claims to provide an immediate post-deprivation hearing. . . .

Connecticut's statute appears even more suspect in light of current practice. A survey of state attachment provisions reveals that nearly every State requires either a preattachment hearing, a showing of some exigent circumstance, or both, before permitting an attachment to take place. . . . We do not mean to imply that any given exigency requirement protects an attachment from constitutional attack. Nor do we suggest that the statutory measures we have surveyed are necessarily free of due process problems or other constitutional infirmities in general. We do believe, however, that the procedures of almost all the States confirm our view that the Connecticut provision before us, by failing to provide a preattachment hearing without at least requiring a showing of some exigent circumstance, clearly falls short of the demands of due process. . . .

### V

Because Connecticut's prejudgment remedy provision, Conn. Gen. Stat. § 52-278e(a)(1), violates the requirements of due process by authorizing prejudgment attachment without prior notice or a hearing, the judgment of the Court of Appeals is affirmed, and the case is remanded to that court for further proceedings consistent with this opinion.

It is so ordered.

## D. ACCESS TO LAWYERS AND TO THE LEGAL SYSTEM

When should the due process right to be heard ensure a right to a lawyer? When should that right encompass rights of access to the formal setting of the courtroom? The following due process cases address these questions. Complicating the question of access to a lawyer is the issue of communication between clients and lawyers who may come from different social, economic, and cultural worlds. Questions of access could be resolved outside the constitutional framework through legislation, voluntary contributions by the bar, or the creation of cheaper, quicker processes inside and outside the formal judicial setting. When would such alternatives be desirable?

### 1. Access to Court

### ■ BODDIE v. CONNECTICUT
*401 U.S. 371 (1971)*

Justice HARLAN delivered the opinion of the Court:

Appellants, welfare recipients residing in the State of Connecticut, brought this action in the Federal District Court for the District of Connecticut on behalf of themselves and others similarly situated, challenging, as applied to them, certain state procedures for the commencement of litigation, including requirements for payment of court fees and costs for service of process, that restrict their access to the courts in their effort to bring an action for divorce.

It appears from the briefs and oral argument that the average cost to a litigant for bringing an action for divorce is $60. Section 52-259 of the Connecticut General Statutes provides: "There shall be paid to the clerks of the supreme court or the superior court, for entering each civil cause, forty-five dollars. . . ." An additional $15 is usually required for the service of process by the sheriff, although as much as $40 or $50 may be necessary where notice must be accomplished by publication.

There is no dispute as to the inability of the named appellants in the present case to pay either the court fees required by statute or the cost incurred for the service of process. The affidavits in the record establish that appellants' welfare income in each instance barely suffices to meet the costs of the daily essentials of life and includes no allotment that could be budgeted for the expense to gain access to the courts in order to obtain a divorce. Also undisputed is appellants' "good faith" in seeking a divorce.

Assuming, as we must on this motion to dismiss the complaint, the truth of the undisputed allegations made by the appellants, it appears that they were unsuccessful in their attempt to bring their divorce actions in the Connecticut courts, simply by reason of their indigency. The clerk of the Superior Court returned their papers "on the ground that he could not accept them until an entry fee had been paid." Subsequent efforts to obtain a judicial waiver of the fee requirement and to have the court effect service of process were to no avail.

Appellants thereafter commenced this action in the Federal District Court seeking a judgment declaring that Connecticut's statute and service of process provisions, "requiring payment of court fees and expenses as a condition precedent to obtaining court relief [are] unconstitutional [as] applied to these indigent [appellants] and all other members of the class which they represent." As further relief, appellants requested the entry of an injunction ordering the appropriate officials to permit them "to proceed with their divorce actions without payment of fees and costs." Our conclusion is that, given the basic position of the marriage relationship in this society's hierarchy of values and the concomitant state monopolization of the means for legally dissolving this relationship, due process does prohibit a State from denying, solely because of inability to pay, access to its courts to individuals who seek judicial dissolution of their marriages.

At its core, the right to due process reflects a fundamental value in our American constitutional system. Our understanding of that value is the basis upon which we have resolved this case.

Perhaps no characteristic of an organized and cohesive society is more fundamental than its erection and enforcement of a system of rules defining the various rights and duties of its members, enabling them to govern their affairs and definitively settle their differences in an orderly, predictable manner. Without such a "legal system," social organization and cohesion are virtually impossible; with the ability to seek regularized resolution of conflicts individuals are capable of interdependent action that enables them to strive for achievements without the anxieties that would beset them in a disorganized society. Put more succinctly, it is this injection of the rule of law that allows society to reap the benefits of rejecting what political theorists call the "state of nature."

American society, of course, bottoms its systematic definition of individual rights and duties, as well as its machinery for dispute settlement, not on custom or the will of strategically placed individuals, but on the common-law model. It is to courts, or other quasi-judicial official bodies, that we ultimately look for the implementation of a regularized, orderly process of dispute settlement. Within this framework, those who wrote our original Constitution, in the Fifth Amendment, and later those who drafted the Fourteenth Amendment, recognized the centrality of the concept of due process in the operation of this system. Without this guarantee that one may not be deprived of his rights, neither liberty nor property, without due process of law, the State's monopoly over techniques for binding conflict resolution could hardly be said to be acceptable under our scheme of things. Only by providing that the social enforcement mechanism must function strictly within these bounds can we hope to maintain an ordered society that is also just. It is upon this premise that this Court has through years of adjudication put flesh upon the due process principle. . . .

Such litigation has, however, typically involved rights of defendants— not, as here, persons seeking access to the judicial process in the first instance. This is because our society has been so structured that resort to the courts is not usually the only available, legitimate means of resolving private disputes. Indeed, private structuring of individual relationships and repair of their breach is largely encouraged in American life, subject only to the caveat that the formal judicial process, if resorted to, is paramount. Thus, this Court has seldom been asked to view access to the courts as an element of due process. The legitimacy of the State's monopoly over techniques of final dispute settlement, even where some are denied access to its use, stands unimpaired where recognized, effective alternatives for the adjustment of differences remain. But the successful invocation of this governmental power by plaintiffs has often created serious problems for defendants' rights. For at that point, the judicial proceeding becomes the only effective means of resolving the dispute at hand and denial of a defendant's full access to that process raises grave problems for its legitimacy.

Recognition of this theoretical framework illuminates the precise issue presented in this case. As this Court on more than one occasion has recognized, marriage involves interests of basic importance in our society. *See, e.g.,* *Loving v. Virginia*, 388 U.S. 1 (1967); *Skinner v. Oklahoma*, 316 U.S. 535 (1942); *Meyer v. Nebraska*, 262 U.S. 390 (1923). It is not surprising, then, that the States have seen fit to oversee many aspects of that institution. . . .

[A]lthough they assert here due process rights as would-be plaintiffs, we think appellants' plight, because resort to the state courts is the only avenue to dissolution of their marriages, is akin to that of defendants faced with exclusion from the only forum effectively empowered to settle their disputes. Resort to the judicial process by these plaintiffs is no more voluntary in a realistic sense than that of the defendant called upon to defend his interests in court. For both groups this process is not only the paramount dispute-settlement technique, but, in fact, the only available one. In this posture we think that this appeal is properly to be resolved in light of the principles enunciated in our due process decisions that delimit rights of defendants compelled to litigate their differences in the judicial forum.

These due process decisions, representing over a hundred years of effort by this Court to give concrete embodiment to this concept, provide, we think, complete vindication for appellants' contentions. In particular, precedent has firmly embedded in our due process jurisprudence two important principles upon whose application we rest our decision in the case before us.

Prior cases establish, first, that due process requires, at a minimum, that absent a countervailing state interest of overriding significance, persons forced to settle their claims of right and duty through the judicial process must be given a meaningful opportunity to be heard. . . .

Due process does not, of course, require that the defendant in every civil case actually have a hearing on the merits. . . . What the Constitution does require is "an opportunity . . . granted at a meaningful time and in a meaningful manner," *Armstrong v. Manzo*, 380 U.S. 545, 552 (1965) (emphasis added), "for [a] hearing appropriate to the nature of the case," *Mullane v. Central Hanover Bank & Trust Co.*, 339 U.S. 306, 313 (1950).

Our cases further establish that a statute or a rule may be held constitutionally invalid as applied when it operates to deprive an individual of a protected right although its general validity as a measure enacted in the legitimate exercise of state power is beyond question. Thus, in cases involving religious freedom, free speech or assembly, this Court has often held that a valid statute was unconstitutionally applied in particular circumstances because it interfered with an individual's exercise of those rights.

No less than these rights, the right to a meaningful opportunity to be heard within the limits of practicality, must be protected against denial by particular laws that operate to jeopardize it for particular individuals. . . .

The State's obligations under the Fourteenth Amendment are not simply generalized ones; rather, the State owes to each individual that process which, in light of the values of a free society, can be characterized as due.

Drawing upon the principles established by the cases just canvassed, we conclude that the State's refusal to admit these appellants to its courts, the sole means in Connecticut for obtaining a divorce, must be regarded as the equivalent of denying them an opportunity to be heard upon their claimed right to a dissolution of their marriages, and, in the absence of a sufficient countervailing justification for the State's action, a denial of due process.

The arguments for this kind of fee and cost requirement are that the State's interest in the prevention of frivolous litigation is substantial, its use of court fees and process costs to allocate scarce resources is rational, and its balance between the defendant's right to notice and the plaintiff's right to access is reasonable.

In our opinion, none of these considerations is sufficient to override the interest of these plaintiff-appellants in having access to the only avenue open for dissolving their allegedly untenable marriages. . . .

We are thus left to evaluate the State's asserted interest in its fee and cost requirements as a mechanism of resource allocation or cost recoupment. Such a justification was offered and rejected in *Griffin v. Illinois*, 351 U.S. 12 (1956). In *Griffin* it was the requirement of a transcript beyond the means of the indigent that blocked access to the judicial process. While in *Griffin* the transcript could be waived as a convenient but not necessary predicate to court access, here the State invariably imposes the costs as a measure of allocating its judicial resources. Surely, then, the rationale of *Griffin* covers this case.

In concluding that the Due Process Clause of the Fourteenth Amendment requires that these appellants be afforded an opportunity to go into court to obtain a divorce, we wish to re-emphasize that we go no further than necessary to dispose of the case before us, a case where the bona fides of both appellants' indigency and desire for divorce are here beyond dispute. We do not decide that access for all individuals to the courts is a right that is, in all circumstances, guaranteed by the Due Process Clause of the Fourteenth Amendment so that its exercise may not be placed beyond the reach of any individual, for, as we have already noted, in the case before us this right is the exclusive precondition to the adjustment of a fundamental human relationship. . . .

Reversed.

[Justice DOUGLAS's and Justice BRENNAN's concurring opinions are omitted.]

Justice BLACK, dissenting:

This is a strange case and a strange holding. Absent some specific federal constitutional or statutory provision, marriage in this country is completely under state control, and so is divorce. When the first settlers arrived here the power to grant divorces in Great Britain was not vested in that country's courts but in its Parliament. And as recently as 1888 this Court in *Maynard v. Hill*, 125 U.S. 190, upheld a divorce granted by the Legislature of the Territory of Oregon. Since that time the power of state legislatures to grant divorces or vest that power in their courts seems not to have been questioned. It is not by accident that marriage and divorce have always been considered to be under state control. The institution of marriage is of peculiar importance to the people of the States. . . .

The Court here holds, however, that the State of Connecticut has so little control over marriages and divorces of its own citizens that it is without power to charge them practically nominal initial court costs when they are without ready money to put up those costs. The Court holds that the state law requiring payment of costs is barred by the Due Process Clause of the Fourteenth Amendment of the Federal Constitution. Two members of the majority believe that the Equal Protection Clause also applies. I think the Connecticut court costs law is barred by neither of those clauses.

It is true, as the majority points out, that the Court did hold in *Griffin v. Illinois*, 351 U.S. 12 (1956), that indigent defendants in criminal cases must be afforded the same right to appeal their convictions as is afforded to a defendant who has ample funds to pay his own costs. . . . [T]here are strong reasons for distinguishing between the two types of cases.

Criminal defendants are brought into court by the State or Federal Government to defend themselves against charges of crime. They go into court knowing that they may be convicted, and condemned to lose their lives, their liberty, or their property, as a penalty for their crimes. Because of this great governmental power the United States Constitution has provided special protections for people charged with crime. . . .

Civil lawsuits, however, are not like government prosecutions for crime. Civil courts are set up by government to give people who have quarrels with their neighbors the chance to use a neutral governmental agency to adjust their differences. In such cases the government is not usually involved as a party, and there is no deprivation of life, liberty, or property as punishment for crime. Our Federal Constitution, therefore, does not place such private disputes on the same high level as it places criminal trials and punishment. There is consequently no necessity, no reason, why government should in civil trials be hampered or handicapped by the strict and rigid due process rules the Constitution has provided to protect people charged with crime.

. . . The rules set out in the Constitution itself provide what is governmentally fair and what is not. Neither due process nor equal protection permits state laws to be invalidated on any such nonconstitutional standard as a judge's personal view of fairness. The people and their elected representatives, not judges, are constitutionally vested with the power to amend the Constitution. . . .

## Comments and Questions

1. Which of these values are crucial to the majority opinion, and why? What is their role in the Court's analysis?

a. The interests of individuals involved in marriage and divorce are so fundamental that the state must act very carefully in governing them.

b. The state monopoly over the techniques of binding conflict resolution in the area of divorce cannot be conducted in a mode that deprives an individual of liberty or property.

c. The state monopoly over the techniques of binding conflict resolution cannot be conducted in a mode that deprives an individual of liberty or property.

d. The individual plaintiffs have untenable marriages.

e. The state here offers no mechanisms for waiving access fees for divorce upon demonstration of the parties' indigency.

2. Which of the rationales offered by Justice Black in dissent do you find most persuasive?

    a. Accommodation of indigents in criminal litigation is not a compelling analogy for the treatment of indigents in civil litigation, where the state itself does not threaten to deprive a person of life, liberty, or property.

    b. Nothing in the language of the Constitution empowers a judge to invalidate state laws on the basis of personal views of fairness.

    c. Dissatisfaction with the system should lead to action by the people and their elected representatives, not by judges.

3. What rejoinders does the majority offer to the arguments in the dissent? Which do you find most persuasive?

4. How can the *Boddie* decision support an indigent mother's claim to waive the costs of a transcript necessary to appeal a civil court judgment terminating her parental rights for abuse or neglect? How can the decision in *Boddie* be distinguished to avoid supporting that mother's claim? For the Supreme Court's decision on the subject, see *M.L.B. v. S.L.J.*, 519 U.S. 102 (1996).

5. Should a person be able to file for bankruptcy protection without having to pay the filing fee? *See United States v. Kras*, 409 U.S. 434 (1973) (rejecting an indigent person's request to waive the filing fee on due process grounds).

## 2. *Access to a Lawyer*

## ■ LASSITER v. DEPARTMENT OF SOCIAL SERVICES OF DURHAM COUNTY, NORTH CAROLINA
### *452 U.S. 18 (1981)*

Justice STEWART delivered the opinion of the Court:

In the late spring of 1975, after hearing evidence that the petitioner, Abby Gail Lassiter, had not provided her infant son William with proper medical care, the District Court of Durham County, N.C., adjudicated him a neglected child and transferred him to the custody of the Durham County Department of Social Services, the respondent here. A year later, Ms. Lassiter was charged with first-degree murder, was convicted of second-degree murder, and began a sentence of 25 to 40 years of imprisonment.[1] In 1978 the

---

1. The North Carolina Court of Appeals, in reviewing the petitioner's conviction, indicated that the murder occurred during an altercation between Ms. Lassiter, her mother, and the deceased:

"Defendant's mother told [the deceased] to 'come on.' They began to struggle and deceased fell or was knocked to the floor. Defendant's mother was beating deceased with a broom. While deceased was still on the floor and being beaten with the broom, defendant entered the apartment. She went into the kitchen

Department petitioned the court to terminate Ms. Lassiter's parental rights because, the Department alleged, she "has not had any contact with the child since December of 1975" and "has willfully left the child in foster care for more than two consecutive years without showing that substantial progress has been made in correcting the conditions which led to the removal of the child, or without showing a positive response to the diligent efforts of the Department of Social Services to strengthen her relationship to the child, or to make and follow through with constructive planning for the future of the child."

Ms. Lassiter was served with the petition and with notice that a hearing on it would be held. Although her mother had retained counsel for her in connection with an effort to invalidate the murder conviction, Ms. Lassiter never mentioned the forthcoming hearing to him (or, for that matter, to any other person except, she said, to "someone" in the prison). At the behest of the Department of Social Services' attorney, she was brought from prison to the hearing, which was held August 31, 1978. The hearing opened, apparently at the judge's insistence, with a discussion of whether Ms. Lassiter should have more time in which to find legal assistance. Since the court concluded that she "has had ample opportunity to seek and obtain counsel prior to the hearing of this matter, and [that] her failure to do so is without just cause," the court did not postpone the proceedings. Ms. Lassiter did not aver that she was indigent, and the court did not appoint counsel for her.

A social worker from the respondent Department was the first witness. She testified that in 1975 the Department "received a complaint from Duke Pediatrics that William had not been followed in the pediatric clinic for medical problems and that they were having difficulty in locating Ms. Lassiter. . . ." She said that in May 1975 a social worker had taken William to the hospital, where doctors asked that he stay "because of breathing difficulties [and] malnutrition and [because] there was a great deal of scarring that indicated that he had a severe infection that had gone untreated." The witness further testified that, except for one "prearranged" visit and a chance meeting on the street, Ms. Lassiter had not seen William after he had come into the State's custody, and that neither Ms. Lassiter nor her mother had "made any contact with the Department of Social Services regarding that child." When asked whether William should be placed in his grandmother's custody, the social worker said he should not, since the grandmother "has indicated to me on a number of occasions that she was not able to take responsibility for the child" and since "I have checked with people in the community and from Ms. Lassiter's church who also feel that this additional

---

and got a butcher knife. She took the knife and began stabbing the deceased who was still prostrate. The body of deceased had seven stab wounds. . . ." *State v. Lassiter*, No. 7614SC1054 (June 1, 1977).

After her conviction was affirmed on appeal, Ms. Lassiter sought to attack it collaterally. Among her arguments was that the assistance of her trial counsel had been ineffective because he had failed to "seek to elicit or introduce before the jury the statement made by [Ms. Lassiter's mother,] 'And I did it, I hope she dies.'" Ms. Lassiter's mother had, like Ms. Lassiter, been indicted on a first-degree murder charge; however, the trial court granted the elder Ms. Lassiter's motion for a nonsuit. The North Carolina General Court of Justice, Superior Court Division, denied Ms. Lassiter's motion for collateral relief. File No. 76-CR-3102 (Mar. 20, 1979).

responsibility would be more than she can handle." The social worker added that William "has not seen his grandmother since the chance meeting in July of '76 and that was the only time."

After the direct examination of the social worker, the judge said:

> I notice we made extensive findings in June of '75 that you were served with papers and called the social services and told them you weren't coming; and the serious lack of medical treatment. And, as I have said in my findings of the 16th day of June '75, the Court finds that the grandmother, Ms. Lucille Lassiter, mother of Abby Gail Lassiter, filed a complaint on the 8th day of May, 1975, alleging that the daughter often left the children, Candina, Felicia and William L. with her for days without providing money or food while she was gone.

Ms. Lassiter conducted a cross-examination of the social worker, who firmly reiterated her earlier testimony. The judge explained several times, with varying degrees of clarity, that Ms. Lassiter should only ask questions at this stage; many of her questions were disallowed because they were not really questions, but arguments.

Ms. Lassiter herself then testified, under the judge's questioning, that she had properly cared for William. Under cross-examination, she said that she had seen William more than five or six times after he had been taken from her custody and that, if William could not be with her, she wanted him to be with her mother since, "He knows us. Children know they family. . . . They know they people, they know they family and that child knows us anywhere. . . . I got four more other children. Three girls and a boy and they know they little brother when they see him." Ms. Lassiter's mother was then called as a witness. She denied, under the questioning of the judge, that she had filed the complaint against Ms. Lassiter, and on cross-examination she denied both having failed to visit William when he was in the State's custody and having said that she could not care for him.

The court found that Ms. Lassiter "has not contacted the Department of Social Services about her child since December, 1975, has not expressed any concern for his care and welfare, and has made no efforts to plan for his future." Because Ms. Lassiter thus had "wilfully failed to maintain concern or responsibility for the welfare of the minor," and because it was "in the best interests of the minor," the court terminated Ms. Lassiter's status as William's parent.

On appeal, Ms. Lassiter argued only that, because she was indigent, the Due Process Clause of the Fourteenth Amendment entitled her to the assistance of counsel, and that the trial court had therefore erred in not requiring the State to provide counsel for her. The North Carolina Court of Appeals decided that "[while] this State action does invade a protected area of individual privacy, the invasion is not so serious or unreasonable as to compel us to hold that appointment of counsel for indigent parents is constitutionally mandated." *In re Lassiter*, 43 N.C. App. 525. The Supreme Court of North Carolina summarily denied Ms. Lassiter's application for discretionary review, and we granted certiorari to consider the petitioner's claim under the Due Process Clause of the Fourteenth Amendment.

For all its consequence, "due process" has never been, and perhaps can never be, precisely defined. "[Unlike] some legal rules," this Court has said, due process "is not a technical conception with a fixed content unrelated to time, place and circumstances." *Cafeteria Workers v. McElroy*, 367 U.S. 886, 895. Rather, the phrase expresses the requirement of "fundamental fairness," a requirement whose meaning can be as opaque as its importance is lofty. Applying the Due Process Clause is therefore an uncertain enterprise which must discover what "fundamental fairness" consists of in a particular situation by first considering any relevant precedents and then by assessing the several interests that are at stake.

The pre-eminent generalization that emerges from this Court's precedents on an indigent's right to appointed counsel is that such a right has been recognized to exist only where the litigant may lose his physical liberty if he loses the litigation. Thus, when the Court overruled the principle of *Betts v. Brady*, 316 U.S. 455, that counsel in criminal trials need be appointed only where the circumstances in a given case demand it, the Court did so in the case of a man sentenced to prison for five years. *Gideon v. Wainwright*, 372 U.S. 335. And thus *Argersinger v. Hamlin*, 407 U.S. 25, established that counsel must be provided before any indigent may be sentenced to prison, even where the crime is petty and the prison term brief.

That it is the defendant's interest in personal freedom, and not simply the special Sixth and Fourteenth Amendments right to counsel in criminal cases, which triggers the right to appointed counsel is demonstrated by the Court's announcement in *In re Gault*, 387 U.S. 1, that "the Due Process Clause of the Fourteenth Amendment requires that in respect of proceedings to determine delinquency *which may result in commitment to an institution in which the juvenile's freedom is curtailed*," the juvenile has a right to appointed counsel even though those proceedings may be styled "civil" and not "criminal." *Id.* at 41 (emphasis added). Similarly, four of the five Justices who reached the merits in *Vitek v. Jones*, 445 U.S. 480, concluded that an indigent prisoner is entitled to appointed counsel before being involuntarily transferred for treatment to a state mental hospital. The fifth Justice differed from the other four only in declining to exclude the "possibility that the required assistance may be rendered by competent laymen in some cases." *Id.* at 500 (separate opinion of Powell, J.).

Significantly, as a litigant's interest in personal liberty diminishes, so does his right to appointed counsel. In *Gagnon v. Scarpelli*, 411 U.S. 778, the Court gauged the due process rights of a previously sentenced probationer at a probation-revocation hearing. In *Morrissey v. Brewer*, 408 U.S. 471, 480, which involved an analogous hearing to revoke parole, the Court had said: "Revocation deprives an individual, not of the absolute liberty to which every citizen is entitled, but only of the conditional liberty properly dependent on observance of special parole restrictions." Relying on that discussion, the Court in *Scarpelli* declined to hold that indigent probationers have, per se, a right to counsel at revocation hearings, and instead left the decision whether counsel should be appointed to be made on a case-by-case basis.

Finally, the Court has refused to extend the right to appointed counsel to include prosecutions which, though criminal, do not result in the defendant's loss of personal liberty. The Court in *Scott v. Illinois*, 440 U.S. 367, for instance, interpreted the "central premise of *Argersinger*" to be "that actual imprisonment is a penalty different in kind from fines or the mere threat of imprisonment," and the Court endorsed that premise as "eminently sound and [warranting] adoption of actual imprisonment as the line defining the constitutional right to appointment of counsel." *Id.*, at 373. The Court thus held "that the Sixth and Fourteenth Amendments to the United States Constitution require only that no indigent criminal defendant be sentenced to a term of imprisonment unless the State has afforded him the right to assistance of appointed counsel in his defense." *Id.*, at 373-374.

In sum, the Court's precedents speak with one voice about what "fundamental fairness" has meant when the Court has considered the right to appointed counsel, and we thus draw from them the presumption that an indigent litigant has a right to appointed counsel only when, if he loses, he may be deprived of his physical liberty. It is against this presumption that all the other elements in the due process decision must be measured.

The case of *Mathews v. Eldridge*, 424 U.S. 319, 335, propounds three elements to be evaluated in deciding what due process requires, viz., the private interests at stake, the government's interest, and the risk that the procedures used will lead to erroneous decisions. We must balance these elements against each other, and then set their net weight in the scales against the presumption that there is a right to appointed counsel only where the indigent, if he is unsuccessful, may lose his personal freedom.

This Court's decisions have by now made plain beyond the need for multiple citation that a parent's desire for and right to "the companionship, care, custody, and management of his or her children" is an important interest that "undeniably warrants deference and, absent a powerful countervailing interest, protection." *Stanley v. Illinois*, 405 U.S. 645, 651. Here the State has sought not simply to infringe upon that interest, but to end it. If the State prevails, it will have worked a unique kind of deprivation. A parent's interest in the accuracy and justice of the decision to terminate his or her parental status is, therefore, a commanding one.

Since the State has an urgent interest in the welfare of the child, it shares the parent's interest in an accurate and just decision. For this reason, the State may share the indigent parent's interest in the availability of appointed counsel. If, as our adversary system presupposes, accurate and just results are most likely to be obtained through the equal contest of opposed interests, the State's interest in the child's welfare may perhaps best be served by a hearing in which both the parent and the State acting for the child are represented by counsel, without whom the contest of interests may become unwholesomely unequal. North Carolina itself acknowledges as much by providing that where a parent files a written answer to a termination petition, the State must supply a lawyer to represent the child. N.C. Gen. Stat. § 7A-289.29 (Supp. 1979).

The State's interests, however, clearly diverge from the parent's insofar as the State wishes the termination decision to be made as economically as possible and thus wants to avoid both the expense of appointed counsel and the cost of the lengthened proceedings his presence may cause. But though the State's pecuniary interest is legitimate, it is hardly significant enough to overcome private interests as important as those here, particularly in light of the concession in the respondent's brief that the "potential costs of appointed counsel in termination proceedings . . . is [sic] admittedly *de minimis* compared to the costs in all criminal actions."

Finally, consideration must be given to the risk that a parent will be erroneously deprived of his or her child because the parent is not represented by counsel. North Carolina law now seeks to assure accurate decisions by establishing the following procedures: A petition to terminate parental rights may be filed only by a parent seeking the termination of the other parent's rights, by a county department of social services or licensed child-placing agency with custody of the child, or by a person with whom the child has lived continuously for the two years preceding the petition. § 7A289.24. A petition must describe facts sufficient to warrant a finding that one of the grounds for termination exists, § 7A289.25 (6), and the parent must be notified of the petition and given 30 days in which to file a written answer to it, § 7A289.27. If that answer denies a material allegation, the court must, as has been noted, appoint a lawyer as the child's guardian ad litem and must conduct a special hearing to resolve the issues raised by the petition and the answer. § 7A-289.29. If the parent files no answer, "the court shall issue an order terminating all parental and custodial rights . . . ; provided the court shall order a hearing on the petition and may examine the petitioner or others on the facts alleged in the petition." § 7A289.28. Findings of fact are made by a court sitting without a jury and must "be based on clear, cogent, and convincing evidence." § 7A289.30. Any party may appeal who gives notice of appeal within 10 days after the hearing. § 7A289.34.

The respondent argues that the subject of a termination hearing—the parent's relationship with her child—far from being abstruse, technical, or unfamiliar, is one as to which the parent must be uniquely well informed and to which the parent must have given prolonged thought. The respondent also contends that a termination hearing is not likely to produce difficult points of evidentiary law, or even of substantive law, since the evidentiary problems peculiar to criminal trials are not present and since the standards for termination are not complicated. In fact, the respondent reports, the North Carolina Departments of Social Services are themselves sometimes represented at termination hearings by social workers instead of by lawyers.

Yet the ultimate issues with which a termination hearing deals are not always simple, however commonplace they may be. Expert medical and psychiatric testimony, which few parents are equipped to understand and fewer still to confute, is sometimes presented. The parents are likely to be people with little education, who have had uncommon difficulty in dealing with life, and who are, at the hearing, thrust into a distressing and disorienting situation. That these factors may combine to overwhelm an uncounseled parent is evident from the findings some courts have made. . . . The respondent is able to point to no presently authoritative case, except for the North Carolina judgment now before us, holding that an indigent parent has no due process right to appointed counsel in termination proceedings.

The dispositive question, which must now be addressed, is whether the three *Eldridge* factors, when weighed against the presumption that there is no right to appointed counsel in the absence of at least a potential deprivation of physical liberty, suffice to rebut that presumption and thus to lead to the conclusion that the Due Process Clause requires the appointment of counsel when a State seeks to terminate an indigent's parental status. . . .

If, in a given case, the parent's interests were at their strongest, the State's interests were at their weakest, and the risks of error were at their peak, it could not be said that the *Eldridge* factors did not overcome the presumption against the right to appointed counsel, and that due process did not therefore require the appointment of counsel. But since the *Eldridge* factors will not always be so distributed, and since "due process is not so rigid as to require that the significant interests in informality, flexibility and economy must always be sacrificed," *Gagnon v. Scarpelli*, 411 U.S. at 788, neither can we say that the Constitution requires that appointment of counsel in every parental termination proceeding. We therefore adopt the standard found appropriate in *Gagnon v. Scarpelli*, and leave the decision whether due process calls for the appointment of counsel for indigent parents in termination proceedings to be answered in the first instance by the trial court, subject, of course, to appellate review. . . .

The Department of Social Services was represented at the hearing by counsel, but no expert witnesses testified, and the case presented no specially troublesome points of law, either procedural or substantive. While hearsay evidence was no doubt admitted, and while Ms. Lassiter no doubt left incomplete her defense that the Department had not adequately assisted her in rekindling her interest in her son, the weight of the evidence that she had few sparks of such an interest was sufficiently great that the presence of counsel for Ms. Lassiter could not have made a determinative difference. True, a lawyer might have done more with the argument that William should live with Ms. Lassiter's mother—but that argument was quite explicitly made by both Lassiters, and the evidence that the elder Ms. Lassiter had said she could not handle another child, that the social worker's investigation had led to a similar conclusion, and that the grandmother had displayed scant interest in the child once he had been removed from her daughter's custody was, though controverted, sufficiently substantial that the absence of counsel's guidance on this point did not render the proceedings fundamentally unfair.

Finally, a court deciding whether due process requires the appointment of counsel need not ignore a parent's plain demonstration that she is not interested in attending a hearing. Here, the trial court had previously found that Ms. Lassiter had expressly declined to appear at the 1975 child custody hearing, Ms. Lassiter had not even bothered to speak to her retained lawyer after being notified of the termination hearing, and the court specifically found that Ms. Lassiter's failure to make an effort to contest the termination proceeding was without cause. In view of all these circumstances, we hold that the trial court did not err in failing to appoint counsel for Ms. Lassiter. . . .

For the reasons stated in this opinion, the judgment is affirmed.

[Chief Justice BURGER's concurring opinion is omitted.]

Justice BLACKMUN, with whom Justice BRENNAN and Justice MARSHALL join, dissenting:

The Court today denies an indigent mother the representation of counsel in a judicial proceeding initiated by the State of North Carolina to terminate her parental rights with respect to her youngest child. The Court most appropriately recognizes that the mother's interest is a "commanding one," and it finds no countervailing state interest of even remotely comparable significance. Nonetheless, the Court avoids what seems to me the obvious conclusion that due process requires the presence of counsel for a parent threatened with judicial termination of parental rights, and, instead, revives an ad hoc approach thoroughly discredited nearly 20 years ago in *Gideon v. Wainwright*, 372 U.S. 335 (1963). Because I believe that the unique importance of a parent's interest in the care and custody of his or her child cannot constitutionally be extinguished through formal judicial proceedings without the benefit of counsel, I dissent.

This Court is not unfamiliar with the problem of determining under what circumstances legal representation is mandated by the Constitution. In *Betts v. Brady*, 316 U.S. 455 (1942), it reviewed at length both the tradition behind the Sixth Amendment right to counsel in criminal trials and the historical practices of the States in that area. The decision in *Betts*—that the Sixth Amendment right to counsel did not apply to the States and that the due process guarantee of the Fourteenth Amendment permitted a flexible, case-by-case determination of the defendant's need for counsel in state criminal trials—was overruled in *Gideon v. Wainwright*, 372 U.S., at 345. . . .

Outside the criminal context, however, the Court has relied on the flexible nature of the due process guarantee whenever it has decided that counsel is not constitutionally required. The special purposes of probation revocation determinations, and the informal nature of those administrative proceedings, including the absence of counsel for the State, led the Court to conclude that due process does not require counsel for probationers. *Gagnon v. Scarpelli*, 411 U.S. 778, 785-789 (1973). In the case of school disciplinary proceedings, which are brief, informal, and intended in part to be educative, the Court also found no requirement for legal counsel. *Goss v. Lopez*, 419 U.S. 565, 583 (1975). Most recently, the Court declined to intrude the presence of counsel for a minor facing voluntary civil commitment by his parent, because of the parent's substantial role in that decision and because of the decision's essentially medical and informal nature. *Parham v. J.R.*, 442 U.S. 584, 604-609 (1979).

In each of these instances, the Court has recognized that what process is due varies in relation to the interests at stake and the nature of the governmental proceedings. Where the individual's liberty interest is of diminished or less than fundamental stature, or where the prescribed procedure involves informal decisionmaking without the trappings of an adversarial trial-type proceeding, counsel has not been a requisite of due process. Implicit in this analysis is the fact that the contrary conclusion sometimes may be warranted. Where an individual's liberty interest assumes sufficiently weighty constitutional significance, and the State by a formal and adversarial proceeding seeks to curtail that interest, the right to counsel may be necessary to ensure fundamental fairness. To say this is simply to acknowledge that due process allows for the adoption of different rules to address different situations or contexts.

It is not disputed that state intervention to terminate the relationship between petitioner and her child must be accomplished by procedures meeting the requisites of the Due Process Clause. Nor is there any doubt here about the kind of procedure North Carolina has prescribed. North Carolina law requires notice and a trial-type hearing before the State on its own initiative may sever the bonds of parenthood. The decisionmaker is a judge, the rules of evidence are in force, and the State is represented by counsel. The question, then, is whether proceedings in this mold, that relate to a subject so vital, can comport with fundamental fairness when the defendant parent remains unrepresented by counsel. As the Court today properly acknowledges, our consideration of the process due in this context, as in others, must rely on a balancing of the competing private and public interests, an approach succinctly described in *Mathews v. Eldridge*. As does the majority, I evaluate the "three distinct factors" specified in *Eldridge*. . . .

At stake here is "the interest of a parent in the companionship, care, custody, and management of his or her children." *Stanley v. Illinois*, 405 U.S. 645, 651 (1972). This interest occupies a unique place in our legal culture, given the centrality of family life as the focus for personal meaning and responsibility. "[Far] more precious . . . than property rights," *May v. Anderson*, 345 U.S. 528, 533 (1953), parental rights have been deemed to be among those "essential to the orderly pursuit of happiness by free men," *Meyer v. Nebraska*, 262 U.S. 390, 399 (1923), and to be more significant and priceless than "'liberties which derive merely from shifting economic arrangements.'" *Stanley v. Illinois*, 405 U.S., at 651, quoting *Kovacs v. Cooper*, 336 U.S. 77, 95 (1949) (Frankfurter, J., concurring). Accordingly, although the Constitution is verbally silent on the specific subject of families, freedom of personal choice in matters of family life long has been viewed as a fundamental liberty interest worthy of protection under the Fourteenth Amendment. Within the general ambit of family integrity, the Court has accorded a high degree of constitutional respect to a natural parent's interest both in controlling the details of the child's upbringing, and in retaining the custody and companionship of the child.

In this case, the State's aim is not simply to influence the parent-child relationship but to extinguish it. A termination of parental rights is both total and irrevocable. Unlike other custody proceedings, it leaves the parent with no right to visit or communicate with the child, to participate in, or even to know about, any important decision affecting the child's religious, educational, emotional, or physical development. . . .

The magnitude of this deprivation is of critical significance in the due process calculus, for the process to which an individual is entitled is in part determined "by the extent to which he may be 'condemned to suffer grievous loss.'" *Goldberg v. Kelly*, 397 U.S. 254, 263 (1970), quoting *Joint Anti-Fascist Refugee Committee v. McGrath*, 341 U.S. 123, 168 (1951) (Frankfurter, J., concurring). Surely there can be few losses more grievous than the abrogation of parental rights. Yet the Court today asserts that this deprivation somehow is less serious than threatened losses deemed to require appointed counsel, because in this instance the parent's own "personal liberty" is not at stake.

I do not believe that our cases support the "presumption" asserted, that physical confinement is the only loss of liberty grievous enough to trigger a right to appointed counsel under the Due Process Clause. Indeed, incarceration has been found to be neither a necessary nor a sufficient condition for requiring counsel on behalf of an indigent defendant. The prospect of canceled parole or probation, with its consequent deprivation of personal liberty, has not led the Court to require counsel for a prisoner facing a revocation proceeding. On the other hand, the fact that no new incarceration was threatened by a transfer from prison to a mental hospital did not preclude the Court's recognition of adverse changes in the conditions of confinement and of the stigma that presumably is associated with being labeled mentally ill. *Vitek v. Jones*, 445 U.S. 480, 492, 494 (1980). For four Members of the Court, these "other deprivations of liberty," coupled with the possibly diminished mental capacity of the prisoner, compelled the provision of counsel for any indigent prisoner facing a transfer hearing.

Moreover, the Court's recourse to a "pre-eminent generalization," misrepresents the importance of our flexible approach to due process. . . .

Rather than opting for the insensitive presumption that incarceration is the only loss of liberty sufficiently onerous to justify a right to appointed counsel, I would abide by the Court's enduring commitment to examine the relationships among the interests on both sides, and the appropriateness of counsel in the specific type of proceeding. The fundamental significance of the liberty interests at stake in a parental termination proceeding is undeniable, and I would find this first portion of the due process balance weighing heavily in favor of refined procedural protections. The second *Eldridge* factor, namely, the risk of error in the procedure provided by the State, must then be reviewed with some care.

The method chosen by North Carolina to extinguish parental rights resembles in many respects a criminal prosecution. Unlike the probation revocation procedure reviewed in *Gagnon v. Scarpelli*, on which the Court so heavily relies, the termination procedure is distinctly formal and adversarial. The State initiates the proceeding by filing a petition in district court.

In addition, the proceeding has an obvious accusatory and punitive focus. In moving to terminate a parent's rights, the State has concluded that it no longer will try to preserve the family unit, but instead will marshal an array of public resources to establish that the parent-child separation must be made permanent. . . .

[T]he State here has prescribed virtually all the attributes of a formal trial as befits the severity of the loss at stake in the termination decision—every attribute, that is, except counsel for the defendant parent. The provision of counsel for the parent would not alter the character of the proceeding, which is already adversarial, formal, and quintessentially legal. It, however, would diminish the prospect of an erroneous termination, a prospect that is inherently substantial, given the gross disparity in power and resources between the State and the uncounseled indigent parent.

The prospect of error is enhanced in light of the legal standard against which the defendant parent is judged. As demonstrated here, that standard commonly adds another dimension to the complexity of the termination proceeding. Rather than focusing on the facts of isolated acts or omissions, the State's charges typically address the nature and quality of complicated ongoing relationships among parent, child, other relatives, and even unrelated parties. . . .

The legal issues posed by the State's petition are neither simple nor easily defined. The standard is imprecise and open to the subjective values of the judge. A parent seeking to prevail against the State must be prepared to adduce evidence about his or her personal abilities and lack of fault, as well as proof of progress and foresight as a parent that the State would deem adequate and improved over the situation underlying a previous adverse judgment of child neglect. The parent cannot possibly succeed without being able to identify material issues, develop defenses, gather and present sufficient supporting nonhearsay evidence, and conduct cross-examination of adverse witnesses.

The Court, of course, acknowledges, that these tasks "may combine to overwhelm an uncounseled parent." I submit that that is a profound understatement. . . .

The risk of error . . . is several-fold. The parent who actually has achieved the improvement or quality of parenting the State would require may be unable to establish this fact. The parent who has failed in these regards may be unable to demonstrate cause, absence of willfulness, or lack of agency diligence as justification. And errors of fact or law in the State's case may go unchallenged and uncorrected. Given the weight of the interests at stake, this risk of error assumes extraordinary proportions. By intimidation, inarticulateness, or confusion, a parent can lose forever all contact and involvement with his or her offspring.

The final factor to be considered, the interests claimed for the State, do not tip the scale against providing appointed counsel in this context. The State hardly is in a position to assert here that it seeks the informality of a rehabilitative or educative proceeding into which counsel for the parent would inject an unwelcome adversarial edge. As the Assistant Attorney General of North Carolina declared before this Court, once the State moves for termination, it "has made a decision that the child cannot go home and should not go home. It no longer has an obligation to try and restore that family."

The State may, and does, properly assert a legitimate interest in promoting the physical and emotional well-being of its minor children. But this interest is not served by terminating the rights of any concerned, responsible parent. . . .

The State also has an interest in avoiding the cost and administrative inconvenience that might accompany a right to appointed counsel. But, as the Court acknowledges, the State's fiscal interest "is hardly significant enough to overcome private interests as important as those here." . . .

The Court's analysis is markedly similar to mine; it, too, analyzes the three factors listed in *Mathews v. Eldridge*, and it, too, finds the private interest weighty, the procedure devised by the State fraught with risks of error, and the countervailing governmental interest insubstantial. Yet, rather than follow this balancing process to its logical conclusion, the Court abruptly pulls back and announces that a defendant parent must await a case-by-case determination of his or her need for counsel. . . .

The Court's own precedents make this clear. In *Goldberg v. Kelly*, the Court found that the desperate economic conditions experienced by welfare recipients as a class distinguished them from other recipients of governmental benefits. In *Mathews v. Eldridge*, the Court concluded that the needs of Social Security disability recipients were not of comparable urgency, and, moreover, that existing pre-termination procedures, based largely on written medical assessments, were likely to be more objective and evenhanded than typical welfare entitlement decisions. . . .

Moreover, the case-by-case approach advanced by the Court itself entails serious dangers for the interests at stake and the general administration of justice. . . .

The problem of inadequate representation is painfully apparent in the present case. . . .

It is perhaps understandable that the District Court judge experienced difficulty and exasperation in conducting this hearing. But both the difficulty and the exasperation are attributable in large measure, if not entirely, to the lack of counsel. An experienced attorney might have translated petitioner's reaction and emotion into several substantive legal arguments. The State charged petitioner with failing to arrange a "constructive plan" for her child's future or to demonstrate a "positive response" to the Department's intervention. A defense would have been that petitioner had arranged for the child to be cared for properly by his grandmother, and evidence might have been adduced to demonstrate the adequacy of the grandmother's care of the other children.

The Department's own "diligence" in promoting the family's integrity was never put in issue during the hearing, yet it is surely significant in light of petitioner's incarceration and lack of access to her child. Finally, the asserted willfulness of petitioner's lack of concern could obviously have been attacked since she was physically unable to regain custody or perhaps even to receive meaningful visits during 21 of the 24 months preceding the action.

Petitioner plainly has not led the life of the exemplary citizen or model parent. It may well be that if she were accorded competent legal representation, the ultimate result in this particular case would be the same. But the issue before the Court is not petitioner's character; it is whether she was given a meaningful opportunity to be heard when the State moved to terminate absolutely her parental rights. In light of the unpursued avenues of defense, and of the experience petitioner underwent at the hearing, I find virtually incredible the Court's conclusion today that her termination proceeding was fundamentally fair. . . .

Finally, I deem it not a little ironic that the Court on this very day grants, on due process grounds, an indigent putative father's claim for state-paid blood grouping tests in the interest of according him a meaningful opportunity to disprove his paternity, *Little v. Streater*, but in the present case rejects, on due process grounds, an indigent mother's claim for state-paid legal assistance when the State seeks to take her own child away from her in a termination proceeding. In *Little v. Streater*, the Court stresses and relies upon the need for "procedural fairness," the "compelling interest in the accuracy of [the] determination," the "not inconsiderable" risk of error, the indigent's "fac[ing] the State as an adversary," and "fundamental fairness. . . ."

If the Court in *Boddie v. Connecticut*, 401 U.S. 371 (1971), was able to perceive as constitutionally necessary the access to judicial resources required to dissolve a marriage at the behest of private parties, surely it should perceive as similarly necessary the requested access to legal resources when the State itself seeks to dissolve the intimate and personal family bonds between parent and child. It will not open the "floodgates" that, I suspect, the Court fears. On the contrary, we cannot constitutionally afford the closure that the result in this sad case imposes upon us all. I respectfully dissent.

[Justice STEVENS's dissenting opinion is omitted.]

## Comments and Questions

1. What are the benefits and problems of the *Lassiter* Court's case-by-case decision making about the right to publicly funded counsel?

2. Note that in the termination of parental rights at issue in *Lassiter*, the state assumes the role of moving party, or plaintiff, and the parent is the defendant. The child is not a party to the lawsuit. Even if the parent has no attorney, the state agency will have counsel, and in many circumstances, the child will also have an attorney, a guardian *ad litem* (pending the litigation), appointed by the court to protect his or her interests.

3. Picking up on the Court's view that although not always required by due process, legal representation would be wise policy, North Carolina amended its statutes to make legal representation available for indigent parents facing termination of parental rights. *See* N.C. Gen. Stat. 7(b)-1109(b) (1999). Some state courts interpreted their own due process clauses as requiring provision of counsel in parental termination hearings. *See, e.g., In re Ella R.B.*, 30 N.Y.2d 352 (1972); *In re K.L.J.*, 813 P.2d 276 (Alaska 1991). Now many other states have created a statutory right. A 2010 study found that in all but six states, parents have an absolute right to counsel in termination proceedings. However, that study notes that "[e]ven in states in which a strong statutory right exists, many problems exist as it relates to attorney compensation, training requirements, and the timing of appointments, among other issues." Vivek Sankaran, *A National Survey on a Parent's Right to Counsel in Termination of Parental Rights and Dependency Cases*, available at *http://www.law.umich.edu/centersandprograms/ccl/specialprojects/Documents/National%20Survey%20on%20a%20Parent's%20Right%20to%20Counsel.pdf.* Children also may be entitled to representation by counsel or a guardian *ad litem*. Howard Davidson, *The Child's Right to Be Heard and Represented in Judicial Proceedings*, 18 Pepp. L. Rev. 258, 268 (1991). For a thoughtful treatment of due process and legal representation of mothers facing the removal of children for safety reasons in the face of spousal abuse, see *Sharwline Nicholson v. Nicholas Scopetta*, 203 F. Supp. 2d 153 (E.D.N.Y. 2002).

4. In contrast to *Lassiter*, most other Western democracies uphold a general right to counsel in civil litigation and do not leave the matter to legislation, which can be repealed. Two years before the Supreme Court's decision, the European Court of Human Rights held that the right to a fair hearing in civil cases included the right to counsel. *Airey v. Ireland*, judgment of 9 October 1979, Series A no. 32. See also *Steel and Morris v. The United Kingdom*, no. 68416/01, ECHR 2005-II. While these cases did not declare a right to counsel in *all* civil litigation, both provided for a right to counsel in any circumstances in which individuals cannot adequately represent themselves, including divorce proceedings and defamation suits. The rulings apply to the forty-five European nations that are signatories to the European Convention on Human Rights. A right to counsel in civil litigation has also been included in almost all European Constitutions, as well as those of Canada and South Africa. *See* Andrew Scherer, *Securing a Civil Right to Counsel: The Importance of Collaborating*, 30 N.Y.U. Rev. of Law & Soc. Change 675, 680 (2006).

In August 2006, the American Bar Association passed a resolution calling for state governments and the federal government to provide a right to counsel "in those categories of adversarial proceedings where basic human needs are at stake, such as those involving shelter, sustenance, safety, health, or child custody. . . ." ABA, Resolution 112A (Aug. 7, 2006), reprinted in Raven Lidman, *Civil Gideon as a Human Right: Is the U.S. Going to Join Step with the Rest of the Developed World?*, 15 Temp. Pol. & Civ. Rts. L. Rev.

769 (2006). *See also* Michael S. Greco, *Court Access Should Not Be Rationed*, A.B.A. Journal, Dec. 2005, at 91.

### 3. Civil Legal Assistance

Legal representation is not the only type of assistance that a court system can provide litigants forced to appear before them. As you read the case below, consider how the Court draws the line between criminal proceedings, where in some cases the state must provide a lawyer, and civil proceedings where the state is under no such obligation. Consider also the Court's arguments about the type of legal assistance to which litigants ought to be entitled when liberty is at stake. What are the differences and similarities between Mr. Turner's situation and Ms. Lassiter's?

### ■ TURNER v. ROGERS
#### 131 S. Ct. 2507 (2011)

Justice BREYER delivered the opinion of the Court.

South Carolina's Family Court enforces its child support orders by threatening with incarceration for civil contempt those who are (1) subject to a child support order, (2) able to comply with that order, but (3) fail to do so. We must decide whether the Fourteenth Amendment's Due Process Clause requires the State to provide counsel (at a civil contempt hearing) to an indigent person potentially faced with such incarceration. We conclude that whereas here the custodial parent (entitled to receive the support) is unrepresented by counsel, the State need not provide counsel to the noncustodial parent (required to provide the support). But we attach an important caveat, namely, that the State must nonetheless have in place alternative procedures that assure a fundamentally fair determination of the critical incarceration-related question, whether the supporting parent is able to comply with the support order.

### I

#### A

South Carolina family courts enforce their child support orders in part through civil contempt proceedings. Each month the family court clerk reviews outstanding child support orders, identifies those in which the supporting parent has fallen more than five days behind, and sends that parent an order to "show cause" why he should not be held in contempt. S.C. Rule Family Ct. 24 (2011). The "show cause" order and attached affidavit refer to the relevant child support order, identify the amount of the arrearage, and set a date for a court hearing. At the hearing that parent may demonstrate that he is not in contempt, say, by showing that he is not able to make the required payments. If he fails to make the required showing, the court may hold him in civil contempt. And it may require that he be imprisoned unless and until he purges himself of contempt by making the required child support payments (but not for more than one year regardless).

**B**

In June 2003 a South Carolina family court entered an order, which (as amended) required petitioner, Michael Turner, to pay $51.73 per week to respondent, Rebecca Rogers, to help support their child. (Rogers' father, Larry Price, currently has custody of the child and is also a respondent before this Court.) Over the next three years, Turner repeatedly failed to pay the amount due and was held in contempt on five occasions. The first four times he was sentenced to 90 days' imprisonment, but he ultimately paid the amount due (twice without being jailed, twice after spending two or three days in custody). The fifth time he did not pay but completed a 6-month sentence.

After his release in 2006 Turner remained in arrears. On March 27, 2006, the clerk issued a new "show cause" order. And after an initial postponement due to Turner's failure to appear, Turner's civil contempt hearing took place on January 3, 2008. Turner and Rogers were present, each without representation by counsel.

The hearing was brief. The court clerk said that Turner was $5,728.76 behind in his payments. The judge asked Turner if there was "anything you want to say." Turner replied,

> Well, when I first got out, I got back on dope. I done meth, smoked pot and everything else, and I paid a little bit here and there. And, when I finally did get to working, I broke my back, back in September. I filed for disability and SSI. And, I didn't get straightened out off the dope until I broke my back and laid up for two months. And, now I'm off the dope and everything. I just hope that you give me a chance. I don't know what else to say. I mean, I know I done wrong, and I should have been paying and helping her, and I'm sorry. I mean, dope had a hold to me.

The judge then said, "[o]kay," and asked Rogers if she had anything to say. After a brief discussion of federal benefits, the judge stated,

> If there's nothing else, this will be the Order of the Court. I find the Defendant in willful contempt. I'm [going to] sentence him to twelve months in the Oconee County Detention Center. He may purge himself of the contempt and avoid the sentence by having a zero balance on or before his release. I've also placed a lien on any SSI or other benefits.

The judge added that Turner would not receive good-time or work credits, but "[i]f you've got a job, I'll make you eligible for work release." When Turner asked why he could not receive good-time or work credits, the judge said, "[b]ecause that's my ruling."

The court made no express finding concerning Turner's ability to pay his arrearage (though Turner's wife had voluntarily submitted a copy of Turner's application for disability benefits). . . . Nor did the judge ask any followup questions or otherwise address the ability-to-pay issue. After the hearing, the judge filled out a prewritten form titled "Order for Contempt of Court," which included the statement:

"Defendant (was) (was not) gainfully employed and/or (had) (did not have) the ability to make these support payments when due."

But the judge left this statement as is without indicating whether Turner was able to make support payments.

### C

While serving his 12-month sentence, Turner, with the help of pro bono counsel, appealed. He claimed that the Federal Constitution entitled him to counsel at his contempt hearing. The South Carolina Supreme Court decided Turner's appeal after he had completed his sentence. And it rejected his "right to counsel" claim. The court pointed out that civil contempt differs significantly from criminal contempt. The former does not require all the "constitutional safeguards" applicable in criminal proceedings. And the right to government-paid counsel, the Supreme Court held, was one of the "safeguards" not required.

Turner sought certiorari. In light of differences among state courts (and some federal courts) on the applicability of a "right to counsel" in civil contempt proceedings enforcing child support orders, we granted the writ.

\* \* \*

### III

We must decide whether the Due Process Clause grants an indigent defendant, such as Turner, a right to state-appointed counsel at a civil contempt proceeding, which may lead to his incarceration. This Court's precedents provide no definitive answer to that question. This Court has long held that the Sixth Amendment grants an indigent defendant the right to state-appointed counsel in a criminal case. *Gideon v. Wainwright*, 372 U.S. 335 (1963). And we have held that this same rule applies to *criminal contempt* proceedings (other than summary proceedings). *United States v. Dixon*, 509 U.S. 688, 696 (1993).

But the Sixth Amendment does not govern civil cases. Civil contempt differs from criminal contempt in that it seeks only to "coerc[e] the defendant to do" what a court had previously ordered him to do. *Gompers v. Bucks Stove & Range Co.*, 221 U.S. 418, 442 (1911). A court may not impose punishment "in a civil contempt proceeding when it is clearly established that the alleged contemnor is unable to comply with the terms of the order." *Hicks v. Feiock*, 485 U.S. 624, 638, n. 9 (1988). And once a civil contemnor complies with the underlying order, he is purged of the contempt and is free. *Id.*, at 633 (he "carr[ies] the keys of [his] prison in [his] own pockets" (internal quotation marks omitted)).

Consequently, the Court has made clear (in a case not involving the right to counsel) that, where civil contempt is at issue, the Fourteenth Amendment's Due Process Clause allows a State to provide fewer procedural protections than in a criminal case.

This Court has decided only a handful of cases that more directly concern a right to counsel in civil matters. And the application of those decisions to the present case is not clear. On the one hand, the Court has held that the Fourteenth Amendment requires the State to pay for representation by counsel in a civil "juvenile delinquency" proceeding (which could lead to incarceration). *In re Gault*, 387 U.S. 1, 35-42 (1967). Moreover, in *Vitek v. Jones*, 445 U.S. 480, 496-497 (1980), a plurality of four Members of this Court would have held that the Fourteenth Amendment requires representation by counsel in a proceeding to transfer a prison inmate to a state hospital for the mentally ill. Further, in *Lassiter v. Department of Social Services of Durham County*, 452 U.S. 18 (1981), a case that focused upon civil proceedings leading to loss of parental rights, the Court wrote that

> the preeminent generalization that emerges from this Court's precedents on an indigent's right to appointed counsel is that such a right has been recognized to exist only where the litigant may lose his physical liberty if he loses the litigation. *Id.*, at 25.

And the Court then drew from these precedents "the presumption that an indigent litigant has a right to appointed counsel only when, if he loses, he may be deprived of his physical liberty." *Id.*, at 26-27.

On the other hand, the Court has held that a criminal offender facing revocation of probation and imprisonment does not ordinarily have a right to counsel at a probation revocation hearing. *Gagnon v. Scarpelli*, 411 U.S. 778 (1973). And, at the same time, *Gault*, *Vitek*, and *Lassiter* are readily distinguishable. The civil juvenile delinquency proceeding at issue in *Gault* was "little different" from, and "comparable in seriousness" to, a criminal prosecution. 387 U.S., at 28, 36. In *Vitek*, the controlling opinion found no right to counsel. 445 U.S., at 499-500 (Powell, J., concurring in part) (assistance of mental health professionals sufficient). And the Court's statements in Lassiter constitute part of its rationale for denying a right to counsel in that case. We believe those statements are best read as pointing out that the Court previously had found a right to counsel *"only"* in cases involving incarceration, not that a right to counsel exists in *all* such cases (a position that would have been difficult to reconcile with *Gagnon*).

**B**

Civil contempt proceedings in child support cases constitute one part of a highly complex system designed to assure a noncustodial parent's regular payment of funds typically necessary for the support of his children.

Often the family receives welfare support from a state-administered federal program, and the State then seeks reimbursement from the noncustodial parent. Other times the custodial parent (often the mother, but sometimes the father, a grandparent, or another person with custody) does not receive government benefits and is entitled to receive the support payments herself.

The Federal Government has created an elaborate procedural mechanism designed to help both the government and custodial parents to secure the payments to which they are entitled. These systems often rely upon wage withholding, expedited procedures for modifying and enforcing child support orders, and automated data processing. 42 U.S.C. §§ 666(a), (b), 654(24). But sometimes States will use contempt orders to ensure that the custodial parent receives support payments or the government receives reimbursement. Although some experts have criticized this last-mentioned procedure, and the Federal Government believes that "the routine use of contempt for non-payment of child support is likely to be an ineffective strategy," the Government also tells us that "coercive enforcement remedies, such as contempt, have a role to play." Brief for United States as *Amicus Curiae* 21-22, and n. 8 (citing Dept. of Health and Human Services, *National Child Support Enforcement, Strategic Plan: FY 2005-2009*, pp. 2, 10). South Carolina, which relies heavily on contempt proceedings, agrees that they are an important tool.

We here consider an indigent's right to paid counsel at such a contempt proceeding. It is a civil proceeding. And we consequently determine the "specific dictates of due process" by examining the "distinct factors" that this Court has previously found useful in deciding what specific safeguards the Constitution's Due Process Clause requires in order to make a civil proceeding fundamentally fair. *Mathews v. Eldridge*, 424 U.S. 319, 335 (1976) (considering fairness of an administrative proceeding). As relevant here those factors include (1) the nature of "the private interest that will be affected," (2) the comparative "risk" of an "erroneous deprivation" of that interest with and without "additional or substitute procedural safeguards," and (3) the nature and magnitude of any countervailing interest in not providing "additional or substitute procedural requirement [s]." *Ibid.*

The "private interest that will be affected" argues strongly for the right to counsel that Turner advocates. That interest consists of an indigent defendant's loss of personal liberty through imprisonment. The interest in securing that freedom, the freedom "from bodily restraint," lies "at the core of the liberty protected by the Due Process Clause." And we have made clear that its threatened loss through legal proceedings demands "due process protection."

Given the importance of the interest at stake, it is obviously important to assure accurate decisionmaking in respect to the key "ability to pay" question. Moreover, the fact that ability to comply marks a dividing line between civil and criminal contempt reinforces the need for accuracy. That is because an incorrect decision (wrongly classifying the contempt proceeding as civil) can increase the risk of wrongful incarceration by depriving the defendant of the procedural protections (including counsel) that the

Constitution would demand in a criminal proceeding. And since 70% of child support arrears nationwide are owed by parents with either no reported income or income of $10,000 per year or less, the issue of ability to pay may arise fairly often.

On the other hand, the Due Process Clause does not always require the provision of counsel in civil proceedings where incarceration is threatened. And in determining whether the Clause requires a right to counsel here, we must take account of opposing interests, as well as consider the probable value of "additional or substitute procedural safeguards." *Mathews*, supra, at 335.

Doing so, we find three related considerations that, when taken together, argue strongly against the Due Process Clause requiring the State to provide indigents with counsel in every proceeding of the kind before us.

First, the critical question likely at issue in these cases concerns, as we have said, the defendant's ability to pay. That question is often closely related to the question of the defendant's indigence. But when the right procedures are in place, indigence can be a question that in many—but not all—cases is sufficiently straightforward to warrant determination *prior* to providing a defendant with counsel, even in a criminal case. Federal law, for example, requires a criminal defendant to provide information showing that he is indigent, and therefore entitled to state-funded counsel, before he can receive that assistance. *See* 18 U.S.C. § 3006A(b).

Second, sometimes, as here, the person opposing the defendant at the hearing is not the government represented by counsel but the custodial parent *un*represented by counsel. *See* Dept. of Health and Human Services, Office of Child Support Enforcement, *Understanding Child Support Debt: A Guide to Exploring Child Support Debt in Your State* 5, 6 (2004) (51% of nationwide arrears, and 58% in South Carolina, are not owed to the government). The custodial parent, perhaps a woman with custody of one or more children, may be relatively poor, unemployed, and unable to afford counsel. Yet she may have encouraged the court to enforce its order through contempt. *Cf.* Tr. Contempt Proceedings (Sept. 14, 2005), App. 44a-45a (Rogers asks court, in light of pattern of nonpayment, to confine Turner). She may be able to provide the court with significant information. *Cf.* id., at 41a-43a (Rogers describes where Turner lived and worked). And the proceeding is ultimately for her benefit.

A requirement that the State provide counsel to the noncustodial parent in these cases could create an asymmetry of representation that would "alter significantly the nature of the proceeding." *Gagnon*, at 787. Doing so could mean a degree of formality or delay that would unduly slow payment to those immediately in need. And, perhaps more important for present purposes, doing so could make the proceedings *less* fair overall, increasing the risk of a decision that would erroneously deprive a family of the support it is entitled to receive. The needs of such families play an important role in our analysis.

Third, as the Solicitor General points out, there is available a set of "substitute procedural safeguards," *Mathews*, 424 U.S., at 335, which, if employed together, can significantly reduce the risk of an erroneous deprivation of liberty. They can do so, moreover, without incurring some of the drawbacks inherent in recognizing an automatic right to counsel. Those safeguards include (1) notice to the defendant that his "ability to pay" is a critical issue in the contempt proceeding; (2) the use of a form (or the equivalent) to elicit relevant financial information; (3) an opportunity at the hearing for the defendant to respond to statements and questions about his financial status (*e.g.*, those triggered by his responses on the form); and (4) an express finding by the court that the defendant has the ability to pay. In presenting these alternatives, the Government draws upon considerable experience in helping to manage statutorily mandated federal-state efforts to enforce child support orders. It does not claim that they are the only possible alternatives, and this Court's cases suggest, for example, that sometimes assistance other than purely legal assistance (here, say, that of a neutral social worker) can prove constitutionally sufficient. But the Government does claim that these alternatives can assure the "fundamental fairness" of the proceeding even where the State does not pay for counsel for an indigent defendant.

While recognizing the strength of Turner's arguments, we ultimately believe that the three considerations we have just discussed must carry the day. In our view, a categorical right to counsel in proceedings of the kind before us would carry with it disadvantages (in the form of unfairness and delay) that, in terms of ultimate fairness, would deprive it of significant superiority over the alternatives that we have mentioned. We consequently hold that the Due Process Clause does not *automatically* require the provision of counsel at civil contempt proceedings to an indigent individual who is subject to a child support order, even if that individual faces incarceration (for up to a year). In particular, that Clause does not require the provision of counsel where the opposing parent or other custodian (to whom support funds are owed) is not represented by counsel and the State provides alternative procedural safeguards equivalent to those we have mentioned (adequate notice of the importance of ability to pay, fair opportunity to present, and to dispute, relevant information, and court findings).

We do not address civil contempt proceedings where the underlying child support payment is owed to the State, for example, for reimbursement of welfare funds paid to the parent with custody. Those proceedings more closely resemble debt-collection proceedings. The government is likely to have counsel or some other competent representative. And this kind of proceeding is not before us. Neither do we address what due process requires in an unusually complex case where a defendant "can fairly be represented only by a trained advocate."

## IV

The record indicates that Turner received neither counsel nor the benefit of alternative procedures like those we have described. He did not receive clear notice that his ability to pay would constitute the critical question in his civil contempt proceeding. No one provided him with a form (or the equivalent) designed to elicit information about his financial circumstances. The court did not find that Turner was able to pay his arrearage, but instead left the relevant "finding" section of the contempt order blank. The court nonetheless found Turner in contempt and ordered him incarcerated. Under these circumstances Turner's incarceration violated the Due Process Clause.

We vacate the judgment of the South Carolina Supreme Court and remand the case for further proceedings not inconsistent with this opinion.

It is so ordered.

Justice THOMAS, with whom Justice SCALIA joins, and with whom THE CHIEF JUSTICE and Justice ALITO join as to Parts I-B and II, dissenting.

The Due Process Clause of the Fourteenth Amendment does not provide a right to appointed counsel for indigent defendants facing incarceration in civil contempt proceedings. Therefore, I would affirm. Although the Court agrees that appointed counsel was not required in this case, it nevertheless vacates the judgment of the South Carolina Supreme Court on a different ground, which the parties have never raised. Solely at the invitation of the United States as *amicus curiae*, the majority decides that Turner's contempt proceeding violated due process because it did not include "alternative procedural safeguards." Consistent with this Court's longstanding practice, I would not reach that question.

## I

The only question raised in this case is whether the Due Process Clause of the Fourteenth Amendment creates a right to appointed counsel for all indigent defendants facing incarceration in civil contempt proceedings. It does not.

### A

Under an original understanding of the Constitution, there is no basis for concluding that the guarantee of due process secures a right to appointed counsel in civil contempt proceedings. It certainly does not do so to the extent that the Due Process Clause requires "'that our Government must proceed according to the "law of the land"—that is, according to written constitutional and statutory provisions.'" *Hamdi v. Rumsfeld*, 542 U.S. 507, 589 (2004) (Thomas, J., dissenting) (quoting *In re Winship*, 397 U.S. 358, 382 (1970) (Black, J., dissenting)). . . . Although the Sixth Amendment secures a right to "the Assistance of Counsel," it does not apply here because civil contempt proceedings are not "criminal prosecutions." U.S. Const., Amdt. 6 . . . .

### B

Even under the Court's modern interpretation of the Constitution, the Due Process Clause does not provide a right to appointed counsel for all indigent defendants facing incarceration in civil contempt proceedings.

Such a reading would render the Sixth Amendment right to counsel—as it is currently understood—superfluous. Moreover, it appears that even cases applying the Court's modern interpretation of due process have not understood it to categorically require appointed counsel in circumstances outside those otherwise covered by the Sixth Amendment. . . .

## II

The majority agrees that the Constitution does not entitle Turner to appointed counsel. But at the invitation of the Federal Government as *amicus curiae*, the majority holds that his contempt hearing violated the Due Process Clause for an entirely different reason, which the parties have never raised: The family court's procedures "were inadequate to ensure an accurate determination of [Turner's] present ability to pay." Brief for United States as *Amicus Curiae* 19 (capitalization and boldface type deleted). I would not reach this issue. . . .

## III

For the reasons explained in the previous two sections, I would not engage in the majority's balancing analysis. But there is yet another reason not to undertake the *Mathews v. Eldridge* balancing test here. 424 U.S. 319 (1976). That test weighs an individual's interest against that of the Government. It does not account for the interests of the child and custodial parent, who is usually the child's mother. But their interests are the very reason for the child support obligation and the civil contempt proceedings that enforce it. . . .

Because of the difficulties in collecting payment through traditional enforcement mechanisms, many States also use civil contempt proceedings to coerce "deadbeats" into paying what they owe. The States that use civil contempt with the threat of detention find it a "highly effective" tool for collecting child support when nothing else works. . . .

Although I think that the majority's analytical framework does not account for the interests that children and mothers have in effective and flexible methods to secure payment, I do not pass on the wisdom of the majority's preferred procedures. Nor do I address the wisdom of the State's decision to use certain methods of enforcement. Whether "deadbeat dads" should be threatened with incarceration is a policy judgment for state and federal lawmakers, as is the entire question of government involvement in the area of child support. This and other repercussions of the shift away from the nuclear family are ultimately the business of the policymaking branches.

## Comments and Questions

1. For the poor, the decision to seek child support and to amend support agreements is sometimes regulated by law. The Personal Responsibility and

Work Opportunity Reconciliation Act of 1996 provides that states must reduce welfare payments by not less than 25 percent for parents who do not seek or amend their request for child support and may eliminate welfare payments altogether for parents found in noncompliance. 42 U.S.C.A. § 608(2). Some states impose criminal sanctions for noncompliance. *See* Kaaryn S. Gustafson, *The Criminalization of Poverty*, 99 J. Crim. L. & Criminology 643, 665, n. 105 (2009). Ought these laws change the evaluation of the state's involvement in bringing the action in the first place and thereby the Court's calculus?

2. In the United States, civil legal assistance comes in various forms. Some lawyers take on indigent clients with the hope of receiving court-awarded attorneys' fees—which are available if specifically provided for by a fee-shifting statute—or contingency fees—in case there is a good chance of monetary recovery—both of which are discussed in Chapter 2. Additionally, many governmentally and privately financed legal clinics provide legal services to indigent parties. For example, the federal Legal Services Corporation (LSC) funds legal assistance lawyers, but LSC-funded organizations turn away as many potential clients as they accept due to a lack of resources. Such publicly funded legal services programs either hire salaried attorneys or provide contracts with private attorneys to represent low-income individuals in certain cases. Given the limited resources currently available for this purpose, how should such attorneys' services be allocated? Does due process require a certain minimum level of funding for civil legal representation, or does the level of available governmental funding for civil legal representation determine what due process requires? If due process does require an attorney to be provided in a given case but the government does not have the funds to do so, how should such a case be resolved? *See, e.g.*, Trisha M. Anklam, *The Price of Justice: In Light of* Lavallee, *What Should Massachusetts Courts Do When Attorneys Are Not Available to Represent Indigent Parents Involved in Care and Protection Matters?*, 32 New Eng. J. on Crim. & Civ. Confinement 111 (2006). Do the due process considerations regarding the private interest at stake help determine the relative importance of claims about divorce, termination of parental rights, housing, income support, and health care access?

3. People who cannot afford to pay lawyers may find access to legal representation through the donated legal services of individual lawyers or law firms. A long tradition of such *pro bono publico*\* service among lawyers today takes many forms, and some estimate that pro bono services provide one-quarter to almost one-third of the civil legal needs of the poor. *See, e.g.*, Rebecca L. Sandefur, *Lawyers' Pro Bono Service and American-Style Civil Legal Assistance*, 41 Law & Soc'y Rev. 79 (2007). Some large law firms and law departments of corporations include pro bono work as an important part of their own practice, and expect individual lawyers to participate. Other firms offer individual lawyers opportunities to spend time working in legal aid clinics or public defender services. Many law schools house clinics that

---

\**Pro bono publico* means for the public good or general welfare; pro bono legal work is usually understood as offering services to indigents without charge. *Black's Legal Dictionary* 1203 (6th ed. 1990).

serve low-income clients and support student work at legal aid clinics and governmental agencies. Some bar associations promote and organize pro bono efforts. The American Bar Association, in its Model Rules of Professional Responsibility, exhorts its members to undertake pro bono service. For decades, lawyers have debated whether pro bono service should be required for all lawyers. To date, no state bar has made pro bono service mandatory. However, the ABA reports that five states now require attorneys to report their pro bono hours, while twelve states provide for voluntary reporting, and eight states have rejected proposals to require reporting. At least thirty law schools require participation in a pro bono or public service program as a condition of graduation. Directory of Law School Public Interest and Pro Bono Programs, American Bar Association, *www.abanet.org/legalservices/ pro-bono/lawschools*. The American Bar Association has consistently rejected proposals for a mandatory pro bono service duty. Should all law schools institute mandatory pro bono programs?

4. A recent study investigated the effects of an offer of representation to claimants seeking unemployment benefits from the Harvard Legal Aid Bureau (HLAB), "a student-run, faculty-overseen legal services office that is part of the clinical educational program at Harvard Law School." The authors carefully summarized their findings as follows:

> Within the limits of statistical uncertainty, and with respect to HLAB's unemployment practice, and with respect to the claimants HLAB's outreach and intake system allowed it to reach, and with respect to outcomes measurable from official records (which concern a claimant's pecuniary interests), the randomized evaluation determined that an offer of HLAB representation had no statistically significant effect on the probability that a claimant would prevail, but that the offer did delay the adjudicatory process. This finding does not mean that we know that the HLAB offer had no positive effect on a claimant's probability of success. We can say, however, that the any such effect is unlikely to be large (or the data probably would have shown it), and that we do have a high degree of confidence in the delay finding.

See D. James Greiner and Cassandra Wolos Pattanayak, *Randomized Evaluation in Legal Assistance: What Difference Does Representation (Offer and Actual Use) Make?*, 121 Yale L.J. (forthcoming 2012). Approximately 39 percent of the group not receiving an HLAB offer found representation elsewhere and approximately 8 percent of the group receiving an HLAB offer elected to proceed *pro se*. The finding that offers of representation delayed proceedings and did not cause a robust increase in the probability of success was troubling. The authors also found that actual use of legal representation delayed proceedings. HLAB responded to an early version of the study:

> In light of recent reports on the unpublished paper ["Randomized Evaluation in Legal Assistance"] . . . and subsequent concern about the breadth and impact of the study's conclusions, we thought we should respond with some thoughts

about why we entered into the study in the first place, and what we think the study does and does not tell us about the provision of free legal services. . . .

HLAB . . . has a history of experimentation, change, and self-evaluation. . . . We had some reason to believe that claimants in the system did relatively well. A retrospective study conducted by one of our clinical students three years ago found that pro se claimants won approximately 50 percent of their cases. In entering into Professor Greiner's study, we had hoped to determine what subset of clients we could help most, and then to redirect our resources to those populations—or, if it turned out the unemployment hearings system was effectively serving pro se claimants, to shift resources to our other practice areas, which include housing law, family law, wage and hour, and other government benefits.

. . . Although we had hoped that the study could tell us about the effect on case outcomes of legal representation—this too had been Professor Greiner's goal—as the study developed, it became clear that the study could not meet this goal. First, a number of the study participants who were offered representation . . . never accepted or followed up on that offer. Second, nearly half of those who did not receive an offer of representation from HLAB ended up receiving representation from other local legal services providers. . . . Because the two groups are so heterogeneous, and because we have not been able to parse out the outcomes of the two subgroups within the control group, the offer/no offer distinction does not appear to be a sufficient proxy for representation/no representation. . . .

Although the study cannot tell us whether representation makes a difference in unemployment insurance hearings in Boston, it does tell us whether an offer of representation—at least from HLAB—does, but that is as compared to the study's heterogeneous control group. At present, it is unclear how helpful that information is for decision-making, either internally at HLAB or more broadly in the legal services community.

Best,
Rachel Lauter
President, Harvard Legal Aid Bureau

David Grossman
Faculty Director, Harvard Legal Aid Bureau Clinical Professor
of Law, Harvard Law School

In a reply, Greiner and Pattanayak contended that a study of the effect of offers of representation was useful because legal aid organizations attempt to improve their potential clients' lives by making offers of representation. These organizations cannot control whether the offers are accepted, or whether those to whom no offers are made find representation elsewhere.

Greiner and Pattanayak explored three possible explanations for their findings. First, HLAB depends on clients reaching out to the organization. Perhaps these clients possess characteristics that make them less likely to need representation, such as the kind of savvy and resourcefulness necessary to reach out to a legal services provider in the first place. A second explanation was that the adjudicatory system for unemployment hearings is a simplified system that is not purely adversarial; the judge may play a role in eliciting facts during the proceedings. Perhaps administrative judges made a special effort with pro se litigants in that system. Third, it is possible that the legal issues HLAB clients faced were simple ones that did not require expert testimony or other presentation of evidence so that lawyers did not add special value. The data itself did not prove the authors' hypothesized explanations. The underlying assumption for all these explanations is that both an HLAB offer and HLAB representation delayed proceedings without causing a robust increase in success. In light of this debate, consider the following questions:

- Why did the researchers elect not to proceed in a controlled experiment where participant clients were randomly assigned to either receive HLAB representation or no representation? What ethical issues might this research method raise?
- What light do the stories in *Lassiter* and *Turner*, combined with the study, shed on the value of legal services as compared with alternative procedures? What would you want to know as a policymaker to decide these questions?
- What role should empirical study of legal representation and other types of legal assistance (from lawyers and nonlawyers) have in the determination of due process entitlements to representation?

# 2

<br>

# *Remedies and Stakes*

## A. INTRODUCTION

Voltaire wrote: "I was never ruined but twice: once when I lost a lawsuit, and once when I won one." *An Editor's Treasury: A Continuing Anthology of Prose, Verse, and Literary Curiosities* 1032 (Herbert Meyer ed. 1968). The costs—economic and emotional—of litigation should never be underestimated; what, then, are the benefits? The ability of courts to order remedies stands as the most concrete benefit, and these remedies can include money damages, orders to direct a defendant to cease the offending behavior or to undertake new behavior, and declarations of rights and duties. Although most remedies must await the plaintiffs' success in demonstrating entitlement to relief, courts are also authorized under special circumstances to order provisional, temporary relief even before the litigation is completed.

This chapter explores the range of remedial options as well as the practices limiting their availability. In other words, this chapter covers the results that litigation can be used to achieve for clients. The end of litigation should always be on the lawyer's mind in considering whether to bring a case and what to ask for in the complaint (addressed in the next chapter). What a party seeks to achieve in litigation also determines when parties will settle and for how much. The chapter also introduces attorneys' fees and the ways individuals and corporations can finance litigation. For example, under limited circumstances, one party may be ordered to pay another party's attorneys' fees. These issues are included because the ways litigation is financed—through fee shifting or other methods—affects the plaintiffs' decision to bring a case at all and to see their case through. As a result, attorneys' fees have an impact on deterrence and settlement just as money damages and other remedies do. Broadly speaking, judicial power over remedies can be understood as part of the larger topic of what is at stake in litigation.

The chapter closes with a section on judicial power to enforce court-ordered remedies through use of the contempt power, revisiting some themes introduced in Chapter 1. The final section also raises the question of the availability of methods other than litigation to achieve goals. For example, peaceful protest is an alternative to the courts often pursued by social movements.

As you learn about the remedies early in the litigation, such as attachments, temporary restraining orders and preliminary injunctions, and remedies that come at the end of litigation, such as damages, injunctions, and declaratory judgments, consider the context in which plaintiffs seek these remedies. When are they appropriate and how does the doctrine police their use? Consider also the historical context that gave rise to various attorneys' fee regimes and litigation financing—how do changing economic and policy climates influence the doctrine?

## B. PROVISIONAL RELIEF

Should a plaintiff ever be able to use the law to obtain relief before proving the elements of the claim? Exceptional, but still frequently used, are devices for *securing the judgment* and for *maintaining the status quo*. Both stem from the equity powers of courts. The remedies in equity primarily were injunctive relief, while at law the remedies ordinarily were limited to money damages.

The Federal Rules of Civil Procedure joined law and equity in the federal court system in 1938. Originally, on this continent these two judicial systems were largely separate and reflected the English judicial system, which had separate courts of law and equity until the passage of the Judicature Acts of the 1870s. The law and equity courts in England evolved as complementary systems, with the King's equity courts affording relief where the common law courts, the only courts with juries, did not. Equitable relief was a last resort, available when the formalities and limitations of the common law system precluded a just result. Nevertheless, equitable relief is now common in the merged system and is explicitly provided for by some statutes.

Before the merger, law and equity involved different sets of procedures. For example, no jury existed at equity; the jury served only the law courts. This fact still limits when a jury is available in federal court, as we will see in the materials on the jury right in Chapter 5. As interpreted by American courts, the Seventh Amendment directs courts to use tests informed by the historical line between equity and common law jurisdictions in determining which cases will have a jury, if the parties so request. Pleadings at law faced strict categories; joinder was a rarity. Fact-finding mechanisms now known as discovery originated with equity. Yet common law courts in the United States permitted some discovery by the mid-nineteenth century. Similarly, equity courts would find procedural ways to refer particular factual issues to common law courts to be decided by a jury. Over time, a kind of interdependency grew between the two systems, which made merger all the more welcome. Currently, the Federal Rules cover the entire system of merged law and equity and tend to reflect the flexibility of equity rather than the rigidity of law. Vestiges of the old division remain, however, in the tensions between justice and efficiency, and in many standards and rules.

## 1. Securing the Judgment: Attachments, Garnishments, and Sequestration

Plaintiffs often bring a civil lawsuit in order to obtain or recover real or personal property or to receive money. Their lawyers would very much like to "tie up" defendants' property, pending the outcome of litigation. Sometimes, this is called "securing the judgment." For instance, plaintiffs' lawyers would like to put an attachment or a lien on real estate belonging to the defendant. The real estate could be the subject of the lawsuit or could be unrelated, but would represent the defendants' assets and thus their ability to pay the judgment. Alternatively, plaintiffs' attorneys could seek a preliminary injunction to enjoin the defendant from transferring the real estate. In many jurisdictions, lawyers, after obtaining a lien, a restraining order, or a preliminary injunction, will then file a notice of *lis pendens* in the registry of deeds, warning anyone who may want to acquire an interest in the realty of the pending litigation that the attachment could prevent them from obtaining unburdened title to the property. This is the procedure that was at issue in *Connecticut v. Doehr*, 501 U.S. 1 (1991), reproduced in Chapter 1, which considered the due process requirements prior to attachment of property.

More frequently, plaintiffs' lawyers prefer to trigger a process that would direct a public official, such as a sheriff, to take defendants' personal property to a neutral location or order the defendants' banks or employers to cut off the defendants' access to funds or wages. This process, often called sequestration, attaches property or funds pending the outcome of litigation; often this procedure removes property from the person in possession, pending some further action or proceedings affecting the property. This helps plaintiffs in two major ways. First, plaintiffs are assured that the defendants' resources will be available to collect if the plaintiffs win their lawsuits. If the property that has been secured is the very item at issue in the lawsuit (for instance, an installment vendor as plaintiff has sought to *replevy* the merchandise sold to the defendant), then the winning plaintiff will have less trouble turning a paper victory in court into actual recovery of the asset in question. Second, tying up a defendant's asset—such as a bank account or wages—puts intense pressure on the defendant to settle, regardless of the merits of the case. Plaintiffs generally like to secure such attachments prior to notifying defendants. Otherwise, defendants could harm or transfer the asset or dissipate the money before the end of the lawsuit.

The plaintiff (or other party seeking the injunction) may post a bond to cover any losses the enjoined party would face from damages, court costs, and attorneys' fees should the injunction turn out to have been erroneously granted. With the moving party's bond in place, the court will issue an attachment order, which can involve literally seizing the property (through sequestration) or placing it under a *receiver*. A receiver is an official designated by the court to "hold and manage property . . . [m]ost frequently [] corporate property" usually because the property may be "endangered by fraud, by mismanagement or by dissension." Alternatively, the court may require the enjoined party to post a monetary bond to ensure compliance and pay for any judgment that will be rendered against him or her. *See Developments in the Law—Injunctions*, 78 Harv. L. Rev. 1086, 1091-1093 (1964).

## 2. Preserving the Status Quo

Sometimes a plaintiff wants to ensure that the defendant will stop engaging in a harmful activity or refrain from undertaking one. Yet during the pendency of the litigation, the defendant may act in harmful ways that would make a final remedy inadequate or unable to protect the plaintiff. In that situation, the Federal Rules make available forms of provisional relief known as temporary restraining orders (TROs) and preliminary injunctions. Typically such orders are issued after a short hearing. In the case of TROs, the Federal Rules limit the order to ten days (with a possible ten-day extension). *See* Fed. R. Civ. P. 65(b). In an emergency, a TRO may even be issued without prior notice or participation of the party to be bound.

"A plaintiff seeking a preliminary injunction must establish that he is likely to succeed on the merits, that he is likely to suffer irreparable harm in the absence of preliminary relief, that the balance of equities tips in his favor, and that an injunction is in the public interest." *Winter v. Natural Res. Def. Council, Inc.*, 129 U.S. 365, 374 (2008). The standard for a preliminary injunction requires courts to choose between incommensurable values and make judgments in the face of gross uncertainty. Courts in this context are charged with defining the "public interest," although in political life there is no widespread agreement about what that is. In the face of uncertainty about the magnitude and probability of harm, courts are nevertheless called upon to issue decisions. Consider these challenges, as well as what it means to "preserve the status quo" pending the outcome of the litigation, as you read the following case.

## ■ U.S. v. NEW YORK TIMES CO., et al.
### *328 F. Supp. 324 (S.D.N.Y. 1971)*

GURFEIN, District Judge.

On Motion for Preliminary Injunction

On June 12, June 13 and June 14, 1971 The New York Times published summaries and portions of the text of two documents—certain volumes from a 1968 Pentagon study relating to Vietnam and a summary of a 1965 Defense Department study relating to the Tonkin Gulf incident. The United States sues to enjoin the Times from "further dissemination, disclosure or divulgence" of materials contained in the 1968 study of the decision making process with respect to Vietnam and the summary of the 1965 Tonkin Gulf study. In its application for a temporary restraining order the United States also asked the Court to order the Times the furnish to the Court all the documents involved so that they could be impounded pending a determination. On June 15 upon the argument of the order to show cause the Court entered a temporary restraining order against The New York Times in substance preventing the further publication until a determination by the Court upon the merits of the Government's application for a preliminary injunction. The Court at that time, in the absence of any evidence, refused to require the documents to be impounded.

The Government contends that the documents still unpublished and the information in the possession of the Times involve a serious breach of the security of the United States and that the further publication will cause "irreparable injury to the national defense."

The articles involved material that has been classified as Top Secret and Secret, although the Government concedes that these classifications are related to volumes rather than individual documents and that included within the volumes may be documents which should not be classified in such high categories. The documents involved are a 47 volume study entitled "HISTORY OF UNITED STATES DECISION MAKING PROCESS ON VIETNAM POLICY" and a document entitled "THE COMMAND AND CONTROL STUDY OF THE TONKIN GULF INCIDENT DONE BY THE DEFENSE DEPARTMENT'S WEAPONS SYSTEM EVALUATION GROUP IN 1965." There is no question that the documents are in the possession of the Times.

The issue of fact with respect to national security was resolved in the following manner. In view of the claim of the Government that testimony in support of its claim that publication of the documents would involve a serious security danger would in itself be dangerous the Court determined that under the 'Secrets of State' doctrine an in camera proceeding should be held at which only the attorneys for each side, witnesses for the Government and two designated representatives of The New York Times would be present. It was believed that this would enable the Government to present its case forcefully and without restraint so that the accommodation of the national security interest with the rights of a free press could be determined with no holds barred. It was with reluctance that the Court granted a hearing from which the public was excluded, but it seemed that there was no other way to serve the needs of justice. My finding with respect to the testimony on security will be adverted to below.

1. This case is one of first impression. In the researches of both counsel and of the Court nobody has been able to find a case remotely resembling this one—where a claim is made that national security permits a prior restraint

on the publication of a newspaper. The Times in affidavits has indicated a number of situations in which classified information has been 'leaked' to the press without adverse governmental or judicial action. It cites news stories and the memoirs of public officials who have used (shortly after the events) classified material in explaining their versions of the decision making process. They point out that no action has ever been taken against any such publication of "leaks." The Government on the other hand points out that there has never been an attempt to publish such a massive compilation of documents which is probably unique in the history of "leaks." The Vietnam study had been authorized by Secretary of Defense McNamara, continued under Secretary Clifford and finally delivered to Secretary of Defense Laird. The White House was not given a copy. The work was done by a group of historians, including certain persons on contract with the Government. It is actually called a "history." The documents in the Vietnam study relate to the period from 1945 to early 1968. There is no reference to any material subsequent to that date. The Tonkin Gulf incident analysis was prepared in 1965, six years ago. The Times contends that the material is historical and that the circumstance that it involves the decision making procedures of the Government is no different from the descriptions that have emerged in the writings of diarists and memoirists. The Government on the other hand contends that by reference to the totality of the studies an enemy might learn something about United States methods which he does not know, that references to past relationships with foreign governments might affect the conduct of our relations in the future and that the duty of public officials to advise their superiors frankly and freely in the decision making process would be impeded if it was believed that newspapers could with impunity publish such private information. These are indeed troublesome questions.

This case, in the judgment of the Court, was brought by the Government in absolute good faith to protect its security and not as a means of suppressing dissident or contrary political opinion. The issue is narrower—as to whether and to what degree the alleged security of the United States may "chill" the right of newspapers to publish. That the attempt by the Government to restrain the Times is not an act of attempted precensorship as such is also made clear by the historic nature of the documents themselves. It has been publicly stated that the present Administration had adopted a new policy with respect to Vietnam. Prior policy must, therefore, be considered as history rather than as an assertion of present policy the implementation of which could be seriously damaged by the publication of these documents.

2. The Times contends that the Government has no inherent power to seek injunction against publication and that the power of the Court to grant such an injunction can be derived only from a statute. The Government has asserted a statutory authority for the injunction, namely, the Act of June 25, 1948, c. 645, 62 Stat. 736; Sept. 23, 1950, c. 1024, Tit. I, Sec. 18, 64 Stat. 1003 (18 U.S.C. 793). The Government contends moreover, that it has an inherent right to protect itself in its vital functions and that hence an injunction will lie even in the absence of a specific statute.

There seems little doubt that the Government may ask a Federal District Court for injunctive relief even in the absence of a specific statute authorizing such relief. [The court then evaluated the relevant statutes and determined that the publication of the documents would not disclose classified information prohibited by statute.] . . .

The injunction sought by the Government must, therefore, rest upon the premise that in the absence of statutory authority there is inherent power in the Executive to protect the national security. It was conceded at the argument that there is Constitutional power to restrain serious security breaches vitally affecting the interests of the Nation. This Court does not doubt the right of the Government to injunctive relief against a newspaper that is about to publish information or documents absolutely vital to current national security. But it does not find that to be the case here. Nor does this Court have to pass on the delicate question of the power of the President in the absence of legislation to protect the functioning of his prerogatives—the conduct of foreign relations, the right to impartial advice and military security, for the responsibility of which the Executive is charged against private citizens who are not Government officials. For I am constrained to find as a fact that the *in camera* proceedings at which representatives of the Department of State, Department of Defense and the Joint Chiefs of Staff testified, did not convince this Court that the publication of these historical documents would seriously breach the national security. It is true, of course, that any breach of security will cause the jitters in the security agencies themselves and indeed in foreign governments who deal with us. But to sustain a preliminary injunction the Government would have to establish not only irreparable injury, but also the probability of success in the litigation itself. It is true that the Court has not been able to read through the many volumes of documents in the history of Vietnam, but it did give the Government an opportunity to pinpoint what it believed to be vital breaches to our national security of sufficient impact to controvert the right of a free press. Without revealing the content of the testimony, suffice it to say that no cogent reasons were advanced as to why these documents except in the general framework of embarrassment previously mentioned, would vitally affect the security of the Nation. In the light of such a finding the inquiry must end. If the statute (18 U.S.C. 793) were applicable (which I must assume as an alternative so that this decision may be reviewed by an appellate court), it is doubtful that it could be applied to the activities of the New York Times. For it would be necessary to find as an element of the violation a willful belief that the information to be published "could be used to the injury of the United States or to the advantage of any foreign nation." That this is an essential element of the offense is clear.

I find that there is no reasonable likelihood of the Government successfully proving that the actions of the Times were not in good faith, nor is there irreparable injury to the Government. This has been an effort on the part of the Times to vindicate the right of the public to know. It is not a case involving an intent to communicate vital secrets for the benefit of a foreign government or to the detriment of the United States.

3. As a general matter we start with the proposition that prior restraint on publication is unconstitutional. *Near v. Minnesota ex rel. Olson*, 283 U.S. 697 (1931). . . . Yet the free press provision of the First Amendment is not absolute. In the *Near* case the Court said that "no one would question but that a government might prevent actual obstruction to its recruiting service or the publication of the sailing dates of transports or the number and location of troops." The illustrations accent how limited is the field of security protection in the context of the compelling force of First Amendment right. The First Amendment concept of a 'free press' must be read in the light of the struggle of free men against prior restraint of publication. From the time of Blackstone it was a tenet of the founding fathers that precensorship was the primary evil to be dealt with in the First Amendment. Fortunately upon the facts adduced in this case there is no sharp clash such as might have appeared between the vital security interest of the Nation and the compelling Constitutional doctrine against prior restraint. If there be some embarrassment to the Government in security aspects as remote as the general embarrassment that flows from any security breach, we must learn to live with it. The security of the Nation is not at the ramparts alone. Security also lies in the value of our free institutions. A cantankerous press, an obstinate press, an ubiquitous press must be suffered by those in authority in order to preserve the even greater values of freedom of expression and the right of the people to know. In this case there has been no attempt by the Government at political suppression. There has been no attempt to stifle criticism. Yet in the last analysis it is not merely the opinion of the editorial writer or of the columnist which is protected by the First Amendment. It is the free flow of information so that the public will be informed about the Government and its actions.

These are troubled times. There is no greater safety valve for discontent and cynicism about the affairs of Government than freedom of expression in any form. This has been the genius of our institutions throughout our history. It is one of the marked traits of our national life that distinguish us from other nations under different forms of government.

For the reasons given the Court will not continue the restraining order which expires today and will deny the application of the Government for a preliminary injunction. The temporary restraining order will continue, however, until such time during the day as the Government may seek a stay from a Judge of the Court of Appeals for the Second Circuit.

The foregoing shall constitute the Court's findings of fact and conclusions of law under Rule 52(a) of the Federal Rules of Civil Procedure.

It is so ordered.

## Comments and Questions

1. After the "Pentagon Papers" case was decided at the district court level, the United States government appealed to the Second Circuit, which issued

an injunction staying the case and limiting publication of the Pentagon Papers by the *New York Times* until the government could appeal to the Supreme Court. 444 F.2d 544 (2d Cir. 1971). The Supreme Court ultimately agreed with the district court and lifted the stay. 403 U.S. 713 (1971). The Court issued an unsigned *per curiam* opinion only lifting the stay and affirming the district court's ruling on the preliminary injunction. The Court was deeply divided on the principles at stake in the case. In addition to the *per curiam*, the Justices also issued five concurring and three dissenting opinions. Justice Black was of the opinion that the First Amendment's bar on laws regulating publication by the press was absolute. He wrote that "every moment's continuance of the injunctions against these newspapers amounts to a flagrant, indefensible, and continuing violation of the First Amendment." 403 U.S. at 715. He explained, "The word 'security' is a broad, vague generality whose contours should not be invoked to abrogate the fundamental law embodied in the First Amendment." 403 U.S. at 719. Justice Douglas's concurrence approved of the district court's analysis that the statutes in question did not authorize the government to enjoin the *Times* from publishing the Pentagon Papers and explained the rationale for prohibiting the government from seeking an injunction absent Congressional authorization: "Secrecy in government is fundamentally anti-democratic, perpetuating bureaucratic errors. Open debate and discussion of public issues are vital to our national health. On public questions there should be 'uninhibited, robust, and wide-open' debate." 403 U.S. at 724 (quoting *New York Times v. Sullivan*, 376 U.S. 254 (1964)). Justice Brennan concurred to underscore that the Court did not decide whether an injunction against a newspaper could ever issue, only that no injunction was appropriate in this case and "[u]nless and until the Government has clearly made out its case, the First Amendment commands that no injunction may issue." 403 U.S. at 727. Justice Stewart, in a concurrence joined by Justice White, underscored the importance of a free press, but also the values served by government secrecy, writing, "[I]t is elementary that the successful conduct of international diplomacy and the maintenance of an effective national defense require both confidentiality and secrecy. Other nations can hardly deal with this Nation in an atmosphere of mutual trust unless they can be assured that their confidences will be kept. And within our own executive departments, the development of considered and intelligent international policies would be impossible if those charged with their formulation could not communicate with each other freely, frankly, and in confidence." 403 U.S. at 728. The executive, he explained, may act to keep such things secret, but the courts, applying the First Amendment, cannot issue an injunction. Justice White, in a concurrence joined by Justice Stewart, wrote that he saw how publication of the Pentagon Papers would be damaging, but that the government had not met the heavy burden of demonstrating a "grave and irreparable" injury to the national interest. 403 U.S. at 732. Chief Justice Burger dissented, finding that the case had proceeded too quickly, with insufficient deliberation to say what dangers to national security were posed by publication and would permit the district courts to complete a trial while preserving the status quo (that is, continuing to enjoin the publication of the materials). 403 U.S. at 750. Justice Harlan, with whom the Chief Justice and Justice Blackmun joined, agreed that the case had moved too quickly for proper deliberation and described the timeline as follows:

> Both the Court of Appeals for the Second Circuit and the Court of Appeals for the District of Columbia Circuit rendered judgment on June 23. The New York Times' petition for certiorari, its motion for accelerated consideration thereof, and its application for interim relief were filed in this Court on June 24 at about 11 a.m. The application of the United States for interim relief in the Post case was also filed here on June 24 at about 7:15 p.m. This Court's order setting a hearing before us on June 26 at 11 a.m., a course which I joined only to avoid the possibility of even more peremptory action by the Court, was issued less than 24 hours before. The record in the Post case was filed with the Clerk shortly before 1 p.m. on June 25; the record in the Times case did not arrive until 7 or 8 o'clock that same night. The briefs of the parties were received less than two hours before argument on June 26.

Justice Harlan also believed that the Executive's determination of national security needs was not given sufficient deference by the courts below. Finally, Justice Blackmun filed a separate dissent, arguing that the rush to decision was unnecessary and explaining: "The country would be none the worse off were the cases tried quickly, to be sure, but in the customary and properly deliberative manner. The most recent of the material, it is said, dates no later than 1968, already about three years ago, and the Times itself took three months to formulate its plan of procedure and, thus, deprived its public for that period." 403 U.S. at 761.

What role might the existence of other media outlets prepared to publish the same material have played in the Court's decision and the timing of the case?

2. What is the relationship between a preliminary injunction and the merits? What does it mean to preserve the "status quo"? That is, does the status quo change once an injunction is issued? Consider how the disagreements among the Supreme Court justices described above illuminate this relationship.

3. Most recently, the Supreme Court revisited the doctrine of preliminary injunctions in *Winter v. Natural Res. Def. Council, Inc.*, 129 U.S. 365 (2008). In that case the Court held that it is not enough that the plaintiff demonstrate that she *may* possibly succeed on the merits, but rather she must show that she is *likely* to succeed. The Supreme Court left open the question of how the other parts of the test relate to one another. Can a stronger showing on one part of the test make up for a weaker showing on another? For example, if plaintiff is able to make a strong showing of irreparable harm but her showing that the balance of equities tips in her favor is weak, can the Court grant a preliminary injunction? Courts continue to struggle with this question.

4. *Winter* also demonstrated how difficult it is to weigh the balance of equities and to consider the public interest. That case involved a motion

for a preliminary injunction brought by the Natural Resource Defense Council, an environmental nonprofit organization, seeking to stop the United States Navy from conducting training exercises off the coast of California until an environmental impact statement could be prepared. The plaintiff's argument was that the sonar used in those exercises was likely to harm marine mammals. Since preparing the environmental impact statement is a lengthy process, requiring it would effectively stop the training exercises. According to the Navy such an injunction would have endangered national security. The Court was put in the position of balancing the potential harms to the environment by proceeding with training and the harms to the national security of stopping the training. The Court ruled in favor of the Navy, concluding that there was insufficient evidence that marine mammals had actually been harmed in the past by similar exercises.

5. Compare the process for a preliminary injunction with the process for a temporary restraining order under the Federal Rules of Civil Procedure. Does it make sense that the due process cases you read in the last chapter insisted on the requirement of notice and the right to be heard prior to deprivation, but that temporary restraining orders can be granted *ex parte*? Why or why not? How are the situations different?

6. How do the procedures for obtaining temporary restraining orders square with the due process doctrines you studied in the previous chapter? In *Walker v. City of Birmingham*, which is reproduced later in this chapter, the lawyers for the City of Birmingham were able to obtain an injunction against civil rights marchers *ex parte* without even attempting to notify the other side. This was because the Alabama state rules of procedure permitted the courts to issue temporary restraining orders without notice to the opposing party. 7 Ala. Code Ann. § 1054 (Michie 1960). The Alabama state court judge who issued the initial injunction—which was later held unconstitutional by the Supreme Court—was the same one who heard the contempt case arising out of the refusal of members of the Southern Christian Leadership Conference to obey his injunction against marching. Do you think the procedure in *Walker* for issuing the preliminary injunction was constitutional?

## Practice Exercise No. 2: Motion for a Preliminary Injunction

Generic Comics is a comic book publisher in the United States. Its properties include thousands of comic book characters. It uses or licenses the use of its characters on products, for special events, and in connection with animated and live-action television series, television motion pictures, and feature films. Among these properties are a series of comic books called Justice, Inc. and the characters appearing in those books. Justice, Inc. is a group of superheroes who save the world from a group of recognizable villains.

In 2000, Generic Comics entered into an agreement with a movie studio, Motion Pictures, pursuant to which Generic Comics licensed the exclusive right to create, produce, distribute, and market theatrical motion pictures based on the "Justice Inc. Property" (or "Property"), defined in the agreement as "the Justice Inc. comic book series" and including "all related characters." The scope of the grant of rights was broad, although the media within which they could be exploited (i.e., theatrical motion pictures) was narrow. Generic Comics received $3 million for the license as well as a percentage of the gross proceeds. It also retained some rights, which are at the center of this dispute. These are summed up in ¶ 8 of the Agreement:

> 8. Generic Comics reserves all television rights [based on the Property] (other than television rights with respect to the Pictures produced hereunder). Generic Comics shall not, without Motion Picture's prior written consent, which consent may be withheld in Motion Picture's sole discretion, produce, distribute, or exploit or authorize the production, distribution, or exploitation of any live-action motion picture for free television exhibition, pay television exhibition, non-theatrical exhibition, or home video exhibition (on cassettes or discs) or any feature-length animated motion picture for non-theatrical exhibition or home video exhibition (on cassettes or discs).

In early 2011, after ten years in development, Motion Pictures released a feature film called "Justice, Inc." and launched an extensive media and promotional campaign costing approximately $70 million. The movie generated $250 million in gross receipts from foreign and domestic sales, as well as millions more from sales of videotapes, DVDs, and associated merchandising. Motion Pictures estimates that it will net a profit of approximately $130 million and that Generic Comics will receive approximately $5 million over the life of the film. Motion Pictures is preparing a sequel to the film.

At the same time that the "Justice, Inc." movie was released, Generic Comics developed a weekly television series called "Justice Task Force." In this series, siblings of the original Justice, Inc. characters travel to an alternate universe where the villains in the "Justice, Inc." comic books are reimagined as heroes. Notwithstanding Generic Comics' claim that they took care to eliminate any elements reminiscent of Justice, Inc. in the "Justice Task Force" television show, the promotional material for the show, including television previews, referenced Justice, Inc. and associated characters. Generic Comics entered into broadcast licenses with television stations across the country and is currently in the process of selling advertising for the first season of the show. Generic Comics expects the show to run for five seasons, netting a total of approximately $60 million.

Motion Pictures filed a lawsuit in United States Federal Court for the Southern District of California in July 2011 seeking to enjoin Generic Comics from advertising or airing the "Justice Task Force" television show and requiring Generic Comics to remove all characters related to "Justice, Inc." from that show before airing. Motion Pictures argues that the term "live-action motion picture for free television" in ¶ 8 of the Agreement includes the television program "Justice Task Force." Generic Comics disputes this assertion, stating that although the term is ambiguous it can only refer to a long-form film, not short television episodes lasting under one hour. Motion Pictures asserts that it will suffer irreparable harm because the series will dilute the value of the Justice, Inc. franchise, especially if the television series is of low quality.

Be prepared to argue in favor of either side in the preliminary injunction motion in this case.

## C. FINAL RELIEF

### 1. Equitable Relief

At the conclusion of trial, if the plaintiff prevails, the court may issue an award for money damages, historically considered a remedy at law, or instead equitable relief such as a permanent injunction—like a preliminary injunction but with enduring effect—to direct the defendant to halt the offending conduct or perform acts under a legal duty. The law courts generally used procedures and techniques thought to be more predictable than their equitable counterparts. The usual remedy available in the law courts was money damages; the equity courts, in contrast, offered injunctions; an accounting (reviewing of financial books, with reallocation of any monies wrongly placed in one account rather than another); rescission and reformation of contracts; and other tailor-made remedies. In the contemporary American federal system, which has merged law and equity, courts can consider requests for both kinds of relief. However, equitable relief is supposed to be available only when money damages would not be adequate.

Historically, courts announced that a permanent injunction, like a preliminary injunction, would issue only to avoid irreparable injury. (Unlike the test for a preliminary injunction, the inquiry leading to a permanent injunction does not involve predicting the likelihood of plaintiff success on the merits because the merits have already been decided.) Yet some courts have minimized the importance of this traditional requirement and instead called for evaluating the choice between money damages and an injunction in light of the relative ease of specifying each. Consider and assess the argument for this kind of analysis offered in the following case.

## ■ WALGREEN CO. v. SARA CREEK PROPERTY CO.
### 966 F.2d 273 (7th Cir. 1992)

Posner, Circuit Judge:

This appeal from the grant of a permanent injunction raises fundamental issues concerning the propriety of injunctive relief. The essential facts are simple. Walgreen has operated a pharmacy in the Southgate Mall in

Milwaukee since its opening in 1951. Its current lease, signed in 1971 and carrying a 30-year, 6-month term, contains, as had the only previous lease, a clause in which the landlord, Sara Creek, promises not to lease space in the mall to anyone else who wants to operate a pharmacy or a store containing a pharmacy. Such an exclusivity clause, common in shopping-center leases, is occasionally challenged on antitrust grounds—implausibly enough, given the competition among malls; but that is an issue for another day, since in this appeal Sara Creek does not press the objection it made below to the clause on antitrust grounds.

In 1990, fearful that its largest tenant—what in real estate parlance is called the "anchor tenant"—having gone broke was about to close its store, Sara Creek informed Walgreen that it intended to buy out the anchor tenant and install in its place a discount store operated by Phar-Mor Corporation, a "deep discount" chain, rather than, like Walgreen, just a "discount" chain. Phar-Mor's store would occupy 100,000 square feet, of which 12,000 would be occupied by a pharmacy the same size as Walgreen's. The entrances to the two stores would be within a couple of hundred feet of each other.

Walgreen filed this diversity suit for breach of contract against Sara Creek and Phar-Mor and asked for an injunction against Sara Creek's letting the anchor premises to Phar-Mor. After an evidentiary hearing, the judge found a breach of Walgreen's lease and entered a permanent injunction against Sara Creek's letting the anchor tenant premises to Phar-Mor until the expiration of Walgreen's lease. He did this over the defendants' objection that Walgreen had failed to show that its remedy at law—damages—for the breach of the exclusivity clause was inadequate. Sara Creek had put on an expert witness who testified that Walgreen's damages could be readily estimated, and Walgreen had countered with evidence from its employees that its damages would be very difficult to compute, among other reasons because they included intangibles such as loss of goodwill.

Sara Creek reminds us that damages are the norm in breach of contract as in other cases. Many breaches, it points out, are "efficient" in the sense that they allow resources to be moved into a more valuable use. Perhaps this is one—the value of Phar-Mor's occupancy of the anchor premises may exceed the cost to Walgreen of facing increased competition. If so, society will be better off if Walgreen is paid its damages, equal to that cost, and Phar-Mor is allowed to move in rather than being kept out by an injunction. That is why injunctions are not granted as a matter of course, but only when the plaintiff's damages remedy is inadequate. Walgreen's is not, Sara Creek argues; the projection of business losses due to increased competition is a routine exercise in calculation. Damages representing either the present value of lost future profits or (what should be the equivalent, *Carusos v. Briarcliff, Inc.*, 76 Ga. App. 346, 351-52 (1947)) the diminution in the value of the leasehold have either been awarded or deemed the proper remedy in a number of reported cases for breach of an exclusivity clause in a shopping-center lease. . . . Why, Sara Creek asks, should they not be adequate here?

Sara Creek makes a beguiling argument that contains much truth, but we do not think it should carry the day. For if, as just noted, damages have been awarded in some cases of breach of an exclusivity clause in a shopping-center lease, injunctions have been issued in others. . . . The choice between remedies requires a balancing of the costs and benefits of the alternatives. *Hecht Co. v. Bowles*, 321 U.S. 321, 329 (1944); *Yakus v. United States*, 321 U.S. 414, 440 (1944). The task of striking the balance is for the trial judge, subject to deferential appellate review in recognition of its particularistic, judgmental, fact-bound character. . . . As we said in an appeal from a grant of a preliminary injunction—but the point is applicable to review of a permanent injunction as well—"The question for us [appellate judges] is whether the [district] judge exceeded the bounds of permissible choice in the circumstances, not what we would have done if we had been in his shoes. . . ."

The plaintiff who seeks an injunction has the burden of persuasion—damages are the norm, so the plaintiff must show why his case is abnormal. But when, as in this case, the issue is whether to grant a permanent injunction, not whether to grant a temporary one, the burden is to show that damages are inadequate, not that the denial of the injunction will work irreparable harm. "Irreparable" in the injunction context means not rectifiable by the entry of a final judgment. . . . It has nothing to do with whether to grant a permanent injunction, which, in the usual case anyway, is the final judgment. The use of "irreparable harm" or "irreparable injury" as synonyms for inadequate remedy at law is a confusing usage. It should be avoided.

The benefits of substituting an injunction for damages are twofold. First, it shifts the burden of determining the cost of the defendant's conduct from the court to the parties. If it is true that Walgreen's damages are smaller than the gain to Sara Creek from allowing a second pharmacy into the shopping mall, then there must be a price for dissolving the injunction that will make both parties better off. Thus, the effect of upholding the injunction would be to substitute for the costly processes of forensic fact determination the less costly processes of private negotiation. Second, a premise of our free-market system, and the lesson of experience here and abroad as well, is that prices and costs are more accurately determined by the market than by government. . . .

The costs and benefits of the damages remedy are the mirror of those of the injunctive remedy. The damages remedy avoids the cost of continuing supervision and third-party effects, and the cost of bilateral monopoly as well. It imposes costs of its own, however, in the form of diminished accuracy in the determination of value, on the one hand, and of the parties' expenditures on preparing and presenting evidence of damages, and the time of the court in evaluating the evidence, on the other.

The weighing up of all these costs and benefits is the analytical procedure that is or at least should be employed by a judge asked to enter a permanent injunction, with the understanding that if the balance is even the injunction should be withheld. The judge is not required to explicate every detail of the analysis and he did not do so here, but as long we are satisfied that his approach is broadly consistent with a proper analysis we shall affirm; and we are satisfied here. The determination of Walgreen's damages would have been costly in forensic resources and inescapably inaccurate. . . . The lease had ten years to run. So Walgreen would have had to project its sales revenues and costs over the next ten years, and then project the impact on those figures of Phar-Mor's competition, and then discount that impact to present value. All but the last step would have been fraught with uncertainty. . . .

Damages are not always costly to compute, or difficult to compute accurately. . . . But this is not such a case and here damages would be a costly and inaccurate remedy; and on the other side of the balance some of the costs of an injunction are absent and the cost that is present seems low. The injunction here, like one enforcing a covenant not to compete (standardly enforced by injunction), is a simple negative injunction—Sara Creek is not to lease space in the Southgate Mall to Phar-Mor during the term of Walgreen's lease—and the costs of judicial supervision and enforcement should be negligible. There is no contention that the injunction will harm an unrepresented third party. It may harm Phar-Mor but that harm will be reflected in Sara Creek's offer to Walgreen to dissolve the injunction. (Anyway, Phar-Mor is a party.) . . .

The only substantial cost of the injunction in this case is that it may set off a round of negotiations between the parties. In some cases, illustrated by *Boomer v. Atlantic Cement Co.*, 26 N.Y.2d 219 (1970), this consideration alone would be enough to warrant the denial of injunctive relief. The defendant's factory was emitting cement dust that caused the plaintiffs harm monetized at less than $200,000, and the only way to abate the harm would have been to close down the factory, which had cost $45 million to build. An injunction against the nuisance could therefore have created a huge bargaining range (could, not would, because it is unclear what the current value of the factory was), and the costs of negotiating to a point within it might have been immense. If the market value of the factory was actually $45 million, the plaintiffs would be tempted to hold out for a price to dissolve the injunction in the tens of millions and the factory would be tempted to refuse to pay anything more than a few hundred thousand dollars. Negotiations would be unlikely to break down completely, given such a bargaining range, but they might well be protracted and costly. There is nothing so dramatic here. Sara Creek does not argue that it will have to close the mall if enjoined from leasing to Phar-Mor. Phar-Mor is not the only potential anchor tenant. *Liza Danielle, Inc. v. Jamko, Inc.*, 408 So. 2d 735, 740 (Fla. App. 1982), on which Sara Creek relies, presented the converse case where the grant of the injunction would have forced an existing tenant to close its store. The size of the bargaining range was also a factor in the denial of injunctive relief in *Gitlitz v. Plankinton Building Properties, Inc.*, 228 Wis. 334, 339-40 (1938).

To summarize, the judge did not exceed the bounds of reasonable judgment in concluding that the costs (including forgone benefits) of the damages remedy would exceed the costs (including forgone benefits) of an injunction. . . .

## Comments and Questions

1. Note that the precise question before the Court of Appeals for the Seventh Circuit was whether the district court had exceeded the bounds of reasonable discretion in issuing the injunction. Did the appellate court simply apply or instead modify the standard for issuing permanent injunctions?

2. One way to understand the facts in *Walgreen Co. v. Sara Creek Property* draws on the concept of bilateral monopoly in economics. A bilateral monopoly involves a single buyer and a single seller who must negotiate a price even though, in the general market, the seller is a dominant seller and thus can charge a higher-than-market price, and in the general market the buyer dominates and thus can pay a lower-than-market price. The result of their negotiation could end up anywhere between the higher price that the seller can command and the lower price that the buyer can demand, and will reflect their relative bargaining power. In this case, the landlord, as seller of space, has bargaining power in part because Walgreen Co. is established in the mall and would not want to leave. Yet Walgreen Co., as the buyer of space, has bargaining power because its general position in the market enabled it to negotiate the exclusivity clause in the first place. The economic analysis suggests that actual bargaining power will be necessary to work out a deal rather than a general market assessment of the value of the breached clause at issue.

3. How can nonmonetary costs and benefits be included in the comparison of equitable relief and damages? Consider a case in which the plaintiffs demonstrated that unconstitutional race discrimination by public officials explains the pattern of student enrollment in the public schools. Would it be possible or desirable to imagine money damages as an alternative to an injunctive order directing the officials to change the method of student assignment to the schools?

4. A court may issue a negative injunction, directing the defendant to cease the offending conduct. Such relief may be available even without a showing of irreparable harm. (Remember that irreparable harm is the standard for obtaining preliminary but not permanent injunctive relief.) *See Continental Airlines Inc. v. Intra Brokers, Inc.*, 24 F.3d 1099 (9th Cir. 1994) (affirming injunction against the selling of airline discount coupons).

5. Equitable relief has been granted in the form of long-term injunctions directing the desegregation of racially segregated schools, the improvement of prison conditions found to violate the Eighth Amendment ban on cruel and unusual punishment, the alteration of institutions for persons with mental disabilities in light of demonstrated statutory violations, and the redirection of public housing management found to violate statutory and constitutional guarantees. *See, e.g., Finney v. Hutto*, 410 F. Supp. 251 (E.D. Ark. 1976) (prison conditions); *Halderman v. Pennhurst State School and Hosp.*, 673 F.2d 647 (3d Cir. 1982) (en banc) (mental hospital); *Perez v. Bos. Hous. Auth.*, 379 U.S. 703 (1980) (public housing); *Swann v. Charlotte-Mecklenburg Bd. of Educ.*, 402 U.S. 1 (1971) (school desegregation). These injunctive orders often are very

specific, indicating, for example, how the defendants should assign and transport students and teachers to schools; how patients should be evaluated and treated; how health and safety standards in housing should be devised and administered; and what resources should be available to individual prisoners. To assist a court in monitoring the implementation of such orders, judges have exercised their authority to appoint judicial officers, such as masters or monitors. *See* Fed. R. Civ. P. 53. Some conceptual and legal issues raised by these types of injunctions are addressed in Chapter 6.

6. Settlement of lawsuits that seek injunctive relief can produce *consent decrees*, which are settlements negotiated by parties but approved and enforced by the court which retains jurisdiction over the dispute. *See* Larry Kramer, *Consent Decrees and the Rights of Third Parties*, 87 Mich. L. Rev. 321 (1988). This form of dispute resolution resembles both a private contract and a court judgment. It is often used to terminate public law and institutional reform litigation where the goal is to ensure enforcement of a statute or government regulation, such as antitrust and employment discrimination regulations. Although the terms of the consent decree must be approved by the court, the parties contribute language, ideas, and voluntary compliance to the process. Violations of either kind of consent decree can trigger judicial enforcement through contempt hearings and sanctions. A court may approve a consent decree after finding liability or violation by the defendant; alternatively, the parties may propose and the judge may approve a consent decree prior to such a finding. This flexibility promotes settlement, but also may prompt questions about the use of judicial resources to enforce a privately constructed settlement. *See* Jeremy A. Ralkin and Neal E. Devins, *Averting Government by Consent Decree: Constitutional Limits on the Enforcement of Settlements with the Federal Government*, 40 Stan. L. Rev. 203 (1987).

What difference would it make—to the parties and to the public—for a court to enforce a consent decree right after the suit is filed, compared with one produced after the introduction of massive evidence at trial? *See United States v. Am. Telephone and Telegraph Co.*, 522 F. Supp. 131 (D.D.C. 1982). The Supreme Court has addressed further questions about consent decrees, such as the binding of third parties and the circumstances permitting modification. *See Martin v. Wilks*, 490 U.S. 755 (1989) (effect on third parties); *Rufo v. Inmates of the Suffolk Cty. Jail*, 502 U.S. 367 (1992) (modification permitted in light of significant change in facts or law warranting suitably tailored revision).

7. Courts often issue injunctions or use consent decrees without a termination date; for example, injunctions and consent decrees addressing school desegregation, prison conditions, and improvement of foster care systems can last for years or even decades. How do they end? Termination of the relief and associated judicial monitoring typically ends with a motion by one or both parties, triggered either by compliance or a demonstration of changed circumstances. At times, the court will shift the burden of proof on the motion to terminate the relief from plaintiff to defendant, depending on the kind of case and the particular factual circumstances.

A party seeking the dissolution of a desegregation plan bears the burden of proving that the school complied with the decree in good faith, *see Hampton v. Jefferson Cnty. Bd. of Educ.*, 102 F. Supp. 2d 358 (W.D. Ky. 2000), and has desegregated to the extent practicable. *See id.; Arthur v. Nyquist*, 566 F. Supp. 511, 692 (W.D.N.Y. 1983). Similarly, a school district will bear the burden of justifying its desegregation plan, *see United States v. Crucial*, 722 F.2d 1182 (5th Cir. 1983), if it moves to modify it. The criteria courts use to evaluate whether a previously "dual" or segregated school district has achieved "unitary" or desegregated status include the extent and degree of segregation among students, faculty, staff, extracurricular activities, transportation, and facilities. *See Bd. of Educ. of Oklahoma City Pub. Schools, Indep. School Dist. No. 89, Oklahoma Cnty., Okla. v. Dowell*, 498 U.S. 237 (1991). If a school board whose district has been subject to a desegregation decree can prove that forces unrelated to *de jure* segregation, such as demographic shifts, cause the current segregation, then it establishes that desegregation has been achieved to the extent practicable and will be able to have the order dissolved. *See Holton v. City of Thomasville School Dist.*, 425 F.3d 1325 (11th Cir. 2005); *N.A.A.C.P., Jacksonville Branch v. Duval Cnty. School*, 273 F.3d 960, 539 (11th Cir. 2001). Once a school district has established that the district has achieved unitary status, the burden shifts back to the plaintiffs to prove that any future racial disparities or de facto segregation stem from intentional segregation. *Hoots v. Pennsylvania*, 272 F. Supp. 2d 539 (W.D. Pa. 2003). Courts prefer to return schools to the full control of local school districts rather than uphold injunctions. *N.A.A.C.P., Jacksonville Branch v. Duval Cnty. School*, 273 F.3d 960 (11th Cir. 2001). Occasionally, parents will bring an action against the school system either to reopen an earlier case or on the grounds that it had not fulfilled its obligation to eliminate de jure segregation, and the court may find that the school system has already desegregated to the extent practicable and terminate the desegregation decree. *See, e.g, Holton v. City of Thomasville School Dist.*, 425 F.3d 1325 (11th Cir. 2005).

In suits charging prisons with violating inmates' constitutional rights, courts have issued injunctions and consent decrees that require structural prison reform. The most recent example is the Supreme Court's decision in *Brown v. Plata*, 131 S. Ct. 1910 (2011), in which the Court upheld a District Court order requiring California to reduce its prison population to remedy long-standing constitutional violations arising from prison overpopulation. Until the mid-1990s, decrees usually ended when one party, usually the prison itself, moved to terminate or modify these decrees based on changed circumstances, specifically that structural elements identified by the court as constitutionally problematic now conformed to constitutional standards. The measures courts instituted varied widely. *See* Malcolm M. Feeley and Edward L. Rubin, *Judicial Policy Making and the Modern State: How the Courts Reformed America's Prisons* 40-41 (1998) (listing matters on which courts imposed institutional standards and monitored for constitutional compliance, including facilities, food, sanitation, education, the frequency of showers, and the wattage of cell light bulbs). In 1996, Congress passed the Prison Litigation Reform Act of 1996 (PLRA), Pub. L. No. 104-34, 110 Stat. 1321 (codified as amended at 11 U.S.C. § 523(a)(2000), at 18 U.S.C. §§ 3624(a) and 3626 (2000), and in scattered sections of 28 and 42 U.S.C.). In addition to limiting the remedies courts can provide, 18 U.S.C. § 3626 (2000), the PLRA imposes a two-year expiration date on injunctions; currently, an injunction will terminate unless the court makes a new finding that affirmative relief is still required to end an ongoing constitutional violation. 18 U.S.C. §§ 3626(b)(1)(A)(i), (b)(3) (2000). After the expiration date, the PLRA shifts the burden from the defendant to the plaintiff. While this shift does impose new burdens on plaintiffs, it has not prevented some long-term prison litigation aimed at structural reform. *See, e.g., Sheppard v. Phoenix*, 210 F. Supp. 2d 450 (S.D.N.Y. 2002); *see also* Chantale Fiebig, Note, *Legislating from the Bench: Judicial Activism in California and Its Increasing Impact on Adult Prison Reform*, 3 Stan. J. C. R. & C. L. 131, 134-142 (2007) (documenting long-running consent decrees, several involving the appointment of Special Masters to run the prisons, in California's prison system).

8. What role does a judge play in crafting the elements of equitable relief—and does this task draw the judge beyond the conventional role assigned in the adversary system? Debates over judicial action in cases yielding complex injunctions appear in both scholarly and the popular media. *See, e.g.*, Derrick Bell, *The Dialectics of School Desegregation*, 32 Ala. L. Rev. 281 (1981); Colin Diver, *The Judge as Political Powerbroker: Superintending Structural Change in Public Institutions*, 65 Va. L. Rev. 43 (1979); Owen Fiss, *The Forms of Justice*, 93 Harv. L. Rev. 1 (1979).

## Practice Exercise No. 3: Equitable Relief in *Carpenter* and *City of Cleveland*

Equitable remedies, including injunctions and declaratory relief, combine with money damages to create the range of possible remedies available in a lawsuit. How does a plaintiff come to know what relief to seek? It helps to consult a lawyer to learn about what relief might be available and in what scope. The lawyer, in turn, will investigate relevant case law, assess probabilities of success in the litigation, and estimate the costs of litigation. But even before this kind of investigation, the lawyer's counsel about the contrasts between equitable and damage remedies can help a client clarify goals and choices. It is this kind of advice that you should try to develop in this exercise in the context of two situations, both of which became real cases. These two cases will recur throughout this book to show unfolding stages of litigation and decision points for lawyers and clients. As you read the following descriptions, keep in mind the difference between the types of final relief that may be sought in each case. Imagine that the plaintiff(s) in each case have asked you what kind of relief they could obtain if they prevail in their lawsuits. What would you tell them?

1. The *Carpenter* Case: Nancy Carpenter wants to file a suit in Massachusetts following the death of her husband, Charles Carpenter, who was a passenger in a Jeep CJ-7. Randall Dee was driving the jeep at the time of the fatal accident. Dee allegedly lost control of the jeep, and it rolled over, pinning Charles Carpenter under the vehicle and killing him. Dee could have been acting recklessly in at least the following acts and omissions: speeding, failing to stop at an intersection, and modifying the jeep with the use of a suspension lift kit and hugely oversized tires. At the time of the incident, the jeep was owned by Twyla Burrell, the ex-girlfriend of Randall Dee. Burrell maintained a minimum liability insurance policy on the jeep, worth a total of $10,000. You have not yet had the jeep inspected.

Apparently, Randall Dee is not a wealthy man. He is unmarried and lives with his brother in a house they bought from the estate of their deceased father. Randall Dee's interest in the home may be his only substantial asset.

2. The *City of Cleveland* Case: A group of women believe they have faced sex discrimination in recruitment, training, testing, hiring, and other employment practices affecting firefighters at the Cleveland, Ohio, Fire Department. They may have claims under federal civil rights statutes such as Title VII (deprivation of employment opportunities on the basis of sex) and under the U.S. Constitution (equal protection). The defendants are likely to be the City of Cleveland, the officers and members of the Civil Service Commission of Cleveland, and the Fire Chief.

Given their claims, what would you tell each client about potential equitable relief? Assume that the Federal Rules of Civil Procedure or identical state rules apply; you may want to re-read Fed. R. Civ. P. 65. What kinds of injunctions could be available—and how would they redress the plaintiffs' injuries? Is there any way to indicate that monetary damages would be inadequate, and that therefore equitable relief would be in order?

## 2. Enforcement of Equitable Relief

Sometimes described as "the least dangerous branch," courts lack police or other direct resources to ensure enforcement of their rulings. Thus, even when a plaintiff wins and a court renders a final judgment, the dispute may not be over. First, the claimant needs a document, which is entitled a judgment, Fed. R. Civ. P. 58. *See also* Fed. R. Civ. P. 54(a) ("judgment" in federal court applies to decrees including equitable decrees). Executing or enforcing that judgment, when the defendant does not comply voluntarily, can lead to further proceedings. Under Fed. R. Civ. P. 70, the court can enforce some equitable decrees by appointing a person to engage in the required behavior (such as conveying title to property) at the cost of the disobedient party.

If the recalcitrant defendant fails to comply with an equitable order (Fed. R. Civ. P. 70), the court—at its own motion or at the request of the plaintiff—may hold contempt proceedings. Civil contempt proceedings are brought by the dissatisfied party trying to enforce the court order and are conducted according to the Rules of Civil Procedure, but in a more summary fashion. They can entail either an order to pay the plaintiff for damage done by failure to comply with the original order or a penalty for failure to comply, including fines and imprisonment. (Of course, imposing fines is somewhat strange as a response for failure to comply with an equitable order, since equitable relief itself is available only if money damages would be inadequate.)

In criminal contempt proceedings, based on government prosecutions of the original defendant under a reasonable doubt standard, the court may punish disobedience through fines or imprisonment; the focus is less enforcement of the original order or redressing the plaintiff's wrong than ensuring respect for the court. The distinction between criminal and civil contempt remains unclear; the Supreme Court has called this area of law a "hodge-podge," and for good reason. *United States v. United Mine Workers*, 330 U.S. 258, 364 (1947). More about the law of contempt follows later in this chapter.

### 3. Note on Declaratory Relief

Sometimes, the relief a party wants most is a clarification of the law as applied to particular facts. For example, an investor may be reluctant to finance an entrepreneur without a clear announcement that the proposed enterprise will breach no patents owned by someone else; or the administrator of a new governmental task force may want a declaratory judgment that the meetings will be held in private before proceeding with the risk of litigation over this issue. Congress has empowered courts to issue clarifications, or declaratory judgments, under the Declaratory Judgment Act, 28 U.S.C. §§ 2201 and 2202, and most states have similar legislation authorizing suits that permit parties to obtain a declaration of rights. Also, a request for a declaratory judgment may be coupled with a request for other relief, including damages or an injunction. The difficulty posed by declaratory relief on its own arises from the constitutional requirement that courts refrain from acting in the absence of a concrete, live controversy; Article III of the Constitution limits federal courts to considering only actual cases or controversies, rather than hypothetical issues.

### 4. Damages

Stemming from law rather than equity, the remedy of money damages poses often difficult questions of valuation. How much money does a specific legal violation warrant? The substantive law governing contracts, torts, antitrust, and other matters will give considerable direction to a court about the measurement of damages in terms of compensation, replacement value, expectation interests, and the like. More ambiguity arises in the context of efforts to enforce constitutional rights since the U.S. Constitution itself gives no indication about how to measure monetary damages. Indeed, the very procedural predicate for a suit for monetary damages under the U.S. Constitution stems from a federal statute, 42 U.S.C. § 1983, authorizing suits by individuals against every person acting under the color of law who deprives an individual of "rights, privileges or immunities secured by the Constitution and laws," leaving courts to determine the measurement of damages to be awarded for such deprivations unless injunctive relief is granted instead. The following case considers the measurement of monetary damages in light of a prior precedent holding that public school officials cannot suspend enrolled students without first holding a due process hearing. *Goss v. Lopez*, 419 U.S. 565 (1975). What, if any, monetary damages should a public school student receive if suspended without a prior hearing?

## ■ CAREY v. PIPHUS
*435 U.S. 247 (1978)*

Justice POWELL delivered the opinion of the Court:

In this case, brought under 42 U.S.C. § 1983, we consider the elements and prerequisites for recovery of damages by students who were suspended from public elementary and secondary schools without procedural due process. The Court of Appeals for the Seventh Circuit held that the students are entitled to recover substantial nonpunitive damages even if their suspensions were justified, and even if they do not prove that any other actual injury was caused by the denial of procedural due process. We disagree, and hold that in the absence of proof of actual injury, the students are entitled to recover only nominal damages.

### I

Respondent Jarius Piphus was a freshman at Chicago Vocational High School during the 1973-1974 school year. On January 23, 1974, during school hours, the school principal saw Piphus and another student standing outdoors on school property passing back and forth what the principal described as an irregularly shaped cigarette. The principal approached the students unnoticed and smelled what he believed was the strong odor of burning marihuana. He also saw Piphus try to pass a packet of cigarette papers to the other student. When the students became aware of the principal's presence, they threw the cigarette into a nearby hedge.

The principal took the students to the school's disciplinary office and directed the assistant principal to impose the "usual" 20-day suspension for violation of the school rule against the use of drugs. The students protested that they had not been smoking marihuana, but to no avail. Piphus was allowed to remain at school, although not in class, for the remainder of the school day while the assistant principal tried, without success, to reach his mother. . . .

A suspension notice was sent to Piphus' mother, and a few days later two meetings were arranged among Piphus, his mother, his sister, school officials, and representatives from a legal aid clinic. The purpose of the meetings was not to determine whether Piphus had been smoking marihuana, but rather to explain the reasons for the suspension. Following an unfruitful exchange of views, Piphus and his mother, as guardian ad litem, filed suit against petitioners in Federal District Court under 42 U.S.C. § 1983 and its jurisdictional counterpart, 28 U.S.C. § 1343, charging that Piphus had been suspended without due process of law in violation of the Fourteenth Amendment. The complaint sought declaratory and injunctive relief, together with actual and punitive damages in the amount of $3,000. Piphus was readmitted to school under a temporary restraining order after eight days of his suspension.

Respondent Silas Brisco was in the sixth grade at Clara Barton Elementary School in Chicago during the 1973-1974 school year. On September 11, 1973, Brisco came to school wearing one small earring. The previous school year the school principal had issued a rule against the wearing of earrings by male students because he believed that this practice denoted membership in certain street gangs and increased the likelihood that gang members would terrorize other students. Brisco was reminded of this rule, but he refused to remove the earring, asserting that it was a symbol of black pride, not of gang membership.

The assistant principal talked to Brisco's mother, advising her that her son would be suspended for 20 days if he did not remove the earring. Brisco's mother supported her son's position, and a 20-day suspension was imposed. Brisco and his mother, as guardian ad litem, filed suit in Federal District Court under 42 U.S.C. § 1983 and 28 U.S.C. § 1343, charging that Brisco had been suspended without due process of law in violation of the Fourteenth Amendment. The complaint sought declaratory and injunctive relief, together with actual and punitive damages in the amount of $5,000. Brisco was readmitted to school during the pendency of proceedings for a preliminary injunction after 17 days of his suspension.

Piphus' and Brisco's cases were consolidated for trial and submitted on stipulated records. The District Court held that both students had been suspended without procedural due process. It also held that petitioners were not entitled to qualified immunity from damages under the second branch of *Wood v. Strickland*, 420 U.S. 308 (1975), because they "should have known that a lengthy suspension without any adjudicative hearing of any type" would violate procedural due process. . . . Despite these holdings, the District Court declined to award damages because: "Plaintiffs put no evidence in the record to qualify their damages, and the record is completely devoid of any evidence which could even form the basis of a speculative inference measuring the extent of their injuries. Plaintiffs' claims for damages therefore fail for complete lack of proof."

The court also stated that the students were entitled to declaratory relief and to deletion of the suspensions from their school records, but for reasons that are not apparent the court failed to enter an order to that effect. Instead, it simply dismissed the complaints. No finding was made as to whether respondents would have been suspended if they had received procedural due process.

On respondents' appeal, the Court of Appeals reversed and remanded. It first held that the District Court erred in not granting declaratory and injunctive relief. It also held that the District Court should have considered evidence submitted by respondents after judgment that tended to prove the pecuniary value of each day of school that they missed while suspended. The court said, however, that respondents would not be entitled to recover damages representing the value of missed school time if petitioners showed on remand "that there was just cause for the suspension[s] and that therefore [respondents] would have been suspended even if a proper hearing had been held."

Finally, the Court of Appeals held that even if the District Court found on remand that respondents' suspensions were justified, they would be entitled to recover substantial "nonpunitive" damages simply because they had been denied procedural due process. *Id.*, at 31. Relying on its earlier decision in *Hostrop v. Board of Junior College Dist. No. 515*, 523 F.2d 569 (7th Cir. 1975), *cert. denied*, 425 U.S. 963 (1976), the court stated that such damages should be awarded "even if, as in the case at bar, there is no proof of individualized injury to the plaintiff, such as mental distress. . . ." 545 F.2d, at 31. We granted certiorari to consider whether, in an action under § 1983 for the deprivation of procedural due process, a plaintiff must prove that he actually was injured by the deprivation before he may recover substantial "nonpunitive" damages. 430 U.S. 964 (1977).

## II

Title 42 U.S.C. § 1983, Rev. Stat. § 1979, derived from § 1 of the Civil Rights Act of 1871, 17 Stat. 13, provides:

> Every person who, under color of any statute, ordinance, regulation, custom, or usage, of any State or Territory, subjects, or causes to be subjected, any citizen of the United States or other person within the jurisdiction thereof to the deprivation of any rights, privileges, or immunities secured by the Constitution and laws, shall be liable to the party injured in an action at law, suit in equity, or other proper proceeding for redress.

The legislative history of § 1983, elsewhere detailed, *e.g., Monroe v. Pape*, 365 U.S. 167, 172-183 (1961); *id.*, at 225-234 (Frankfurter, J., dissenting in part), demonstrates that it was intended to "[create] a species of tort liability" in favor of persons who are deprived of "rights, privileges, or immunities secured" to them by the Constitution.

Petitioners contend that the elements and prerequisites for recovery of damages under this "species of tort liability" should parallel those for recovery of damages under the common law of torts. In particular, they urge that the purpose of an award of damages under § 1983 should be to compensate persons for injuries that are caused by the deprivation of constitutional rights; and, further, that plaintiffs should be required to prove not only that their rights were violated, but also that injury was caused by the violation, in order to recover substantial damages. Unless respondents prove that they actually were injured by the deprivation of procedural due process, petitioners argue, they are entitled at most to nominal damages.

Respondents seem to make two different arguments in support of the holding below. First, they contend that substantial damages should be awarded under § 1983 for the deprivation of a constitutional right whether or not any injury was caused by the deprivation. This, they say, is appropriate both because constitutional rights are valuable in and of themselves, and because of the need to deter violations of constitutional rights. Respondents believe that this view reflects accurately that of the Congress that enacted § 1983. Second, respondents argue that even if the purpose of a § 1983 damages award is, as petitioners contend, primarily to compensate persons for injuries that are caused by the deprivation of constitutional rights, every deprivation of procedural due process may be presumed to cause some injury. This presumption, they say, should relieve them from the necessity of proving that injury actually was caused.

### A

Insofar as petitioners contend that the basic purpose of a § 1983 damages award should be to compensate persons for injuries caused by the deprivation of constitutional rights, they have the better of the argument. Rights, constitutional and otherwise, do not exist in a vacuum. Their purpose is to protect persons from injuries to particular interests, and their contours are shaped by the interests they protect. . . .

The Members of the Congress that enacted § 1983 did not address directly the question of damages, but the principle that damages are designed to compensate persons for injuries caused by the deprivation of rights hardly could have been foreign to the many lawyers in Congress in 1871. Two other sections of the Civil Rights Act of 1871 appear to incorporate this principle, and no reason suggests itself for reading § 1983 differently. To the extent that Congress intended that awards under § 1983 should deter the deprivation of constitutional rights, there is no evidence that it meant to establish a deterrent more formidable than that inherent in the award of compensatory damages.[10]

---

10. This is not to say that exemplary or punitive damages might not be awarded in a proper case under § 1983 with the specific purpose of deterring or punishing violations of constitutional rights. [The Court cited several lower court decisions upholding punitive awards in § 1983 cases.] Although we imply no approval or disapproval of any of these cases, we note that there is no basis for such an award in this case. The District Court specifically found that petitioners did not act with malicious intention to deprive respondents of their rights or to do them other injury, and the Court of Appeals approved only the award of "non-punitive" damages.

We also note that the potential for liability of § 1983 defendants for attorney's fees, *see* Civil Rights Attorney's Fees Awards Act of 1976, 42 U.S.C. § 1988, provides additional—and by no means inconsequential—assurance that agents of the State will not deliberately ignore due process rights.

B

It is less difficult to conclude that damages awards under § 1983 should be governed by the principle of compensation than it is to apply this principle to concrete cases. But over the centuries the common law of torts has developed a set of rules to implement the principle that a person should be compensated fairly for injuries caused by the violation of his legal rights. These rules, defining the elements of damages and the prerequisites for their recovery, provide the appropriate starting point for the inquiry under § 1983 as well.

It is not clear, however, that common-law tort rules of damages will provide a complete solution to the damages issue in every § 1983 case. In some cases, the interests protected by a particular branch of the common law of torts may parallel closely the interests protected by a particular constitutional right. In such cases, it may be appropriate to apply the tort rules of damages directly to the § 1983 action. In other cases, the interests protected by a particular constitutional right may not also be protected by an analogous branch of the common law torts. In those cases, the task will be the more difficult one of adapting common-law rules of damages to provide fair compensation for injuries caused by the deprivation of a constitutional right.

Although this task of adaptation will be one of some delicacy—as this case demonstrates—it must be undertaken. The purpose of § 1983 would be defeated if injuries caused by the deprivation of constitutional rights went uncompensated simply because the common law does not recognize an analogous cause of action. . . .

C

The Due Process Clause of the Fourteenth Amendment provides: "[N]or shall any State deprive any person of life, liberty, or property, without due process of law." This Clause "raises no impenetrable barrier to the taking of a person's possessions," or liberty, or life. *Fuentes v. Shevin*, 407 U.S. 67, 81 (1972). Procedural due process rules are meant to protect persons not from the deprivation, but from the mistaken or unjustified deprivation of life, liberty, or property. Thus, in deciding what process constitutionally is due in various contexts, the Court repeatedly has emphasized that "procedural due process rules are shaped by the risk of error inherent in the truth-finding process."

In this case, the Court of Appeals held that if petitioners can prove on remand that "[respondents] would have been suspended even if a proper hearing had been held," 545 F.2d, at 32, then respondents will not be entitled to recover damages to compensate them for injuries caused by the suspensions. The court thought that in such a case, the failure to accord procedural due process could not properly be viewed as the cause of the suspensions. The court suggested that in such circumstances, an award of damages for injuries caused by the suspensions would constitute a windfall, rather than compensation, to respondents. 545 F.2d at 32. We do not understand the parties to disagree with this conclusion. Nor do we.

The parties do disagree as to the further holding of the Court of Appeals that respondents are entitled to recover substantial—although unspecified—damages to compensate them for "the injury which is 'inherent in the nature of the wrong,'" 545 F.2d, at 31, even if their suspensions were justified and even if they fail to prove that the denial of procedural due process actually caused them some real, if intangible, injury. Respondents, elaborating on this theme, submit that the holding is correct because injury fairly may be "presumed" to flow from every denial of procedural due process. Their argument is that in addition to protecting against unjustified deprivations, the Due Process Clause also guarantees the "feeling of just treatment" by the government. *Anti-Fascist Committee v. McGrath*, 341 U.S.123, 162 (1951) (Frankfurter, J., concurring). They contend that the deprivation of protected interests without procedural due process, even where the premise for the deprivation is not erroneous, inevitably arouses strong feelings of mental and emotional distress in the individual who is denied this "feeling of just treatment." They analogize their case to that of defamation per se, in which "the plaintiff is relieved from the necessity of producing any proof whatsoever that he has been injured" in order to recover substantial compensatory damages. C. McCormick, *Law of Damages* § 116 at 423 (1935).

... Petitioners' argument is ... that such injury cannot be presumed to occur, and that plaintiffs at least should be put to their proof on the issue, as plaintiffs are in most tort actions.

We agree with petitioners in this respect. As we have observed in another context, the doctrine of presumed damages in the common law of defamation per se "is an oddity of tort law, for it allows recovery of purportedly compensatory damages without evidence of actual loss." The doctrine has been defended on the grounds that those forms of defamation that are actionable per se are virtually certain to cause serious injury to reputation, and that this kind of injury is extremely difficult to prove. Moreover, statements that are defamatory per se by their very nature are likely to cause mental and emotional distress, as well as injury to reputation, so there arguably is little reason to require proof of this kind of injury either. But these considerations do not support respondents' contention that damages should be presumed to flow from every deprivation of procedural due process. ...

First, it is not reasonable to assume that every departure from procedural due process, no matter what the circumstances or how minor, inherently is as likely to cause distress as the publication of defamation per se is to cause injury to reputation and distress. ...

Moreover, where a deprivation is justified but procedures are deficient, whatever distress a person feels may be attributable to the justified deprivation rather than to deficiencies in procedure. But as the Court of Appeals held, the injury caused by a justified deprivation, including distress, is not properly compensable under § 1983. This ambiguity in causation, which is absent in the case of defamation per se, provides additional need for requiring the plaintiff to convince the trier of fact that he actually suffered distress because of the denial of procedural due process itself.

Finally, we foresee no particular difficulty in producing evidence that mental and emotional distress actually was caused by the denial of procedural due process itself. . . . In sum, then, although mental and emotional distress caused by the denial of procedural due process itself is compensable under § 1983, we hold that neither the likelihood of such injury nor the difficulty of proving it is so great as to justify awarding compensatory damages without proof that such injury actually was caused. . . .

Because the right to procedural due process is "absolute" in the sense that it does not depend upon the merits of a claimant's substantive assertions, and because of the importance to organized society that procedural due process be observed, *see Boddie v. Connecticut*, 401 U.S. 371, 375 (1971); *Anti-Fascist Committee v. McGrath*, 341 U.S. at 171-172 (Frankfurter, J., concurring), we believe that the denial of procedural due process should be actionable for nominal damages without proof of actual injury. We therefore hold that if, upon remand, the District Court determines that respondents' suspensions were justified, respondents nevertheless will be entitled to recover nominal damages not to exceed one dollar from petitioners.

The judgment of the Court of Appeals is reversed, and the case is remanded for further proceedings consistent with this opinion.

## Comments and Questions

1. The traditional common law concept of compensatory damages seeks to return to the plaintiff the position he or she enjoyed prior to the harm. Nominal damages, in contrast, represent a token amount simply to signify the recognition that harm was done. What is the significance of the Court's decision to approve only nominal damages? Does this suggest that due process is not worth very much in financial terms, or that deterrence of due process violations should be secured through means other than the threat of money damages? How does footnote 10 bear on this issue? Under what circumstances could the plaintiffs have obtained more than nominal damages for a due process violation?

2. If you served as counsel to a school board after this decision, what guidelines would you advise for designing procedures for school suspensions?

3. Valuations problems arise even where damages are sought for harm to a building or piece of land. Thus, in *Trinity Church in the City of Bos. v. John Hancock Mutual Life Ins. Co.*, 399 Mass. 43 (1987), the Church claimed that the life insurance company and other defendants caused structural damage to the church building while constructing the John Hancock Tower Building; the construction caused physical settlement, which in turn undermined the structural integrity of the church building. For relief, the plaintiff sought to recover the cost of repairing the interior and exterior of the church, as well as compensation for the structural damage. Fair market value, the usual measure of damages, proved unavailing. The court therefore considered using the cost of reproduction less depreciation, and ruled in favor of

replacement or restoration costs. *Id.* at 51. *See also Peevyhouse v. Garland Coal & Mining Co.*, 382 P.2d 109 (Okla. 1963), *cert. denied*, 375 U.S. 906 (1963) (measure of damages to land from strip-mining normally would be cost of restoration unless economic waste would result; here, recovery is to be measured by diminution of market value).

## 5. *Punitive Damages*

If nominal damages simply direct a token amount to signify the recognition of harm, and compensatory damages seek to return the plaintiff to the position he or she enjoyed prior to the harm, what should be the role of punitive damages? Sometimes, further monetary relief seems appropriate to deter future wrongful conduct and to express public disapproval of the injuring behavior. The common law thus developed *punitive damages*, typically left to the jury to assess, based on "'the gravity of the wrong and the need to deter similar wrongful conduct.'" *Pacific Mutual Life Ins. Co. v. Haslip*, 499 U.S. 1 (1991). That jury determination would in turn be reviewed by the trial and appellate courts under a standard of reasonableness. In recent years, reformers have argued that punitive damage awards are increasing in frequency, amounts, and unpredictability. *See, e.g.*, Cass R. Sunstein, Daniel Kahneman, and David Schkade, *Assessing Punitive Damages*, 107 Yale L.J. 2071 (1998). Others respond that the problems have been much overstated and reflect faulty generalizations from a few outlying cases. *See, e.g.*, Geoffrey T. Miller, *Behind the Battle Lines: A Comparative Analysis of the Necessity to Enact Comprehensive Federal Products Liability Reforms*, 45 Buff. L. Rev. 241 (1997); Product Liability Fairness Act, 1995: Hearings on S. 565 Before the S. Subcomm. on Consumer Affairs, Foreign Commerce, and Tourism, 104th Cong. 505 (1995) (testimony of Dr. Stephen Daniels, Senior Research Fellow, American Bar Foundation). Besides generating legislative proposals, the debate over punitive damages has inspired a search by litigants for federal constitutional authority to limit the scope of punitive damages. The Court has rejected claims that the Excessive Fines Clause of the Eighth Amendment sets a limit on punitive damages, *Browning-Ferris Indus. of V. v. Kelco Disposal, Inc.*, 492 U.S. 257 (1989), but has concluded that the Due Process Clause of the Fourteenth Amendment does, in certain cases, limit jury and judicial discretion in this area. *Pacific Mutual Life Ins. Co. v. Haslip, supra.*

In *Honda Motor Co. v. Oberg*, 512 U.S. 415 (1994), the Supreme Court found a procedural defect in an Oregon rule prohibiting judicial review of the jury's award of punitive damages unless the court could affirmatively say there was no evidence for the verdict. After reviewing eighteenth- and nineteenth-century English and American cases addressing excessive damages, the Court reasoned that judicial review had long been an important part of the process of awarding punitive damages. Oregon's constitutional provision to the contrary departed from tradition and thus presumptively violated due process without adequate substitutes to guard against arbitrary awards. Justice Ginsburg, joined by Chief Justice Rehnquist, dissented, not from the idea that due process should restrict punitive damage procedures, but from the application of due process to the Oregon context.

In *BMW v. Gore*, 517 U.S. 559 (1996), the Court rejected a punitive damages award in Alabama despite the state court's adherence to the procedural safeguard of judicial review. The Court found the award of punitive damages "grossly excessive," and, therefore, a violation of Fourteenth Amendment due process. Dr. Ira Gore sued the auto distributor, BMW of North America, for fraud after discovering that the $40,000 new auto he had purchased from an authorized dealer had been repainted. BMW admitted a nationwide nondisclosure policy on its routine practice of repairing and repainting damaged new cars where the damage amounted to less than 3 percent of the car's total value. An Alabama jury found BMW liable for $4,000 diminution in value to Gore's car, then imposed $4 million in punitive damages, calculated by multiplying Gore's $4,000 in damages by the approximate number of undisclosed repaintings nationwide. The Alabama Supreme Court reduced the award to $2 million after concluding that the jury had erred in including in its calculations BMW's acts outside the jurisdiction.

Writing for the majority, Justice Stevens, who also had written the majority opinion in *Honda*, found the $2 million punitive damages grossly excessive in light of the state's legitimate interests in punishing and deterring illegal conduct within the state. The Court identified three "guideposts" to clarify what constitutes unconstitutional excessiveness in punitive damage awards. Most important is (1) how reprehensible is the defendant's conduct? Less important, but also relevant are (2) the ratio of the award to the actual or potential harm inflicted and (3) a comparison of the award to civil or criminal penalties that could be imposed for comparable misconduct. The Court found BMW's conduct not reprehensible because it only involved monetary loss, it reflected a reasonable effort to comport with uninterpreted state statutes, and it ceased upon a finding of unlawfulness. Noting that no "mathematical bright line" could demarcate constitutionality, the Court found the 500:1 ratio of award to damages excessive in light of precedents and reason and when compared with comparable legislatively created sanctions. A concurring opinion by Justice Breyer cited procedural defects in the Alabama judicial review of punitive awards. Dissenting opinions by Justices Scalia and Ginsburg expressed concern about this federal intrusion into state law.

In 2003, the Supreme Court held that an award of $145 million in punitive damages violated due process in a case where the compensatory judgment amounted to $1 million. In *State Farm Mut. Aut. Ins. Co. v. Campbell*, 538 U.S. 408 (2003), Mr. and Mrs. Curtis Campbell claimed that their insurance company's refusal to settle a claim falling within the limits of their insurance policy constituted bad faith, fraud, and intentional infliction of emotional distress. As later established at trial on the underlying claim, the Campbells were 100 percent responsible for an automobile accident that killed one individual and rendered another permanently disabled, yet their insurance company resisted settlement and pursued trial and appeals in the state courts. In their suit against State Farm Mutual Automobile Insurance Co., the Campbells introduced evidence that the insurance company declined to settle the underlying claim as part of a national scheme to meet corporate fiscal goals by capping the payouts on claims and engaging in fraudulent practices nationwide. Applying the guideposts for interpreting due process from *BMW v. Gore*, the Court reasoned first that "the reprehensibility guidepost does not permit courts to expand the scope of the case so that a defendant may be punished for any malfeasance," and therefore, damages should arise only in relation to the specific type of conduct that harmed the plaintiffs, not to the company's nationwide policies. Applying the second guidepost, the Court reasoned that there should be a presumption against an award with a 145:1 ratio between harm or potential harm suffered by the plaintiff and the punitive damages award, and consideration of the defendant's wealth could not justify an otherwise unconstitutional award. Using the third guidepost—the disparity between the punitive damages award and the civil penalties authorized in comparable cases—the Court found that $145 million in punitive damage "dwarfed" the $10,000 authorized under state law for an act of fraud. Further, the Court reasoned that the substantial compensatory damage award itself included a punitive element, and its $1 million level indicated the approximate level for a proper measure of punitive damages in the case. Justices Scalia, Thomas, and Ginsburg dissented. In her dissent, Justice Ginsburg questioned the Court's substitution of its judgment for that of the state courts and emphasized that the trial court specifically found that State Farm's national scheme was directly relevant to the Campbells' case. Justice Ginsburg also observed that the Court had swiftly converted guideposts into "instructions that begin to resemble marching orders." 538 U.S. at 439.

Most recently, in *Philip Morris USA v. Williams*, 549 U.S. 346 (2007), the Court addressed whether a jury can increase punitive damages in order to punish a defendant for harming nonparties. The suit was brought on behalf of deceased smoker Jesse D. Williams, alleging negligence and deceit by tobacco company Philip Morris. At trial, after plaintiff's attorney made reference to all the past Oregon smokers that were likely harmed by Philip Morris, defense counsel requested an instruction to the jury clarifying that they could not increase punitive damages to punish Philip Morris for harm to such nonparties; the request was denied. The jury went on to award $821,000 in compensatory damages and $79.5 million in punitive damages. Writing for the Court, Justice Breyer explained that allowing punitive damages for harm to nonparties would indeed constitute a taking of defendants' property without due process of law. Because nonparties would not be present, defendants would be deprived of the right to present every available defense. At the same time, the Court held that harm to nonparties would still be relevant to the level of reprehensibility of defendant's conduct, and remanded the case to the Oregon Supreme Court for reconsideration under the clarified standard. "This nuance eludes me," Justice Stevens wrote in his dissent, arguing that punishing for reprehensibility due to third-party harm is the same as punishing for the third-party harm itself. Justice Ginsburg also dissented, joined by Justices Thomas and Scalia, arguing that the punitive damages awarded in the case were in fact the result of a judgment of reprehensibility, and thus legitimate. The subsequent history of the case illustrates the limits of the reach of the federal courts. On remand, the Oregon Supreme Court held on independent state law grounds that the trial court had not erred in refusing to adopt the defendant's proffered jury instructions, reinstating the original verdict. *Williams v. Phillip Morris, Inc.*, 176 P.3d 1255 (2008). The defendant again appealed, and although the Supreme Court initially granted certiorari, 553 U.S. 1093 (2008), it subsequently denied the writ of certiorari as improvidently granted, 556 U.S. 178 (2009).

Finally, in *Exxon Shipping Co. v. Baker*, 554 U.S. 471 (2008), the Supreme Court gave a clue as to how far it was willing to go to limit punitive damages. That case concerned the propriety of a punitive damages award of $2.5 billion arising out of the grounding of the supertanker the *Exxon Valdez* and the resulting oil spill on the coast of Alaska in 1989. The issue before the Court was whether this punitive damages award was reasonable under maritime law, a species of federal common law (which you will learn more about when you learn *Erie* doctrine in Chapter 7). Unlike the previous cases, *Baker* was not a due process case. Expressing concern over variability in punitive damages awards and relying on studies demonstrating relatively low ratios between compensatory and punitive damages, the Court held that the appropriate award would represent a 1:1 ratio between punitive and compensatory damages. This limited the award amount to $507.5 million. For a critique of the Court's reliance on statistical studies of punitive damages awards, see Theodore Eisenberg, M. Heise, and M. Wells, *Variability in Punitive Damages: Empirically Assessing* Exxon Shipping Co. v. Baker, 166 J. Inst. & Theoretical Econ. 5 (2010).

## Comments and Questions

1. States' rights arguments are invoked both by justices who support due process review of punitive damages and by those who oppose it. Try to map out the way both sides of the controversy use states' rights arguments. How can this be?

2. In *BMW v. Gore*, Justice Scalia expressed the view that the Fourteenth Amendment affords "an opportunity to contest the reasonableness of a damages judgment in state court; but [not a] federal guarantee [that] a damages award actually be reasonable." *BMW*, 517 U.S. at 599. How do you assess this position?

3. Assess the Court's guideposts for constitutional review of punitive damages awards. How do you think lower courts will interpret it? Would a bright-line rule be better, and can you articulate such a rule? What ought to be the relationship between compensatory and punitive damages?

4. What kind of proof and what legal standard are needed for punitive damages? In typical common law cases, the moving party must show that the defendant acted egregiously, and usually this involves acting with malice or with reckless or callous indifference. The interaction between this standard and an underlying claim that itself requires demonstration of defendant's intention or state of mind can be very complex. In *Kolstad v. Am. Dental Assn.*, 527 U.S. 526 (1999), the Supreme Court held that although a plaintiff may seek punitive damages in a Title VII employment discrimination case, success in proving intentional discrimination does not itself guarantee evidence to support punitive damages. The Court rejected a standard of egregiousness and approved the standard of malice or reckless or callous indifference for demonstrating a basis for punitive damages. The Court also ruled that common law agency principles would limit liability on supervisors or the entire entity for conduct by individuals that might itself justify punitive damages.

## Practice Exercise No. 4: Damages in *Carpenter* and *City of Cleveland*

Imagine that the *Carpenter* and *City of Cleveland* plaintiffs have asked you to predict the scope of damages they could receive if they prevailed in their claims.

1. What types and categories of damages would be available for Nancy Carpenter, the plaintiff in the *Carpenter* case? Of what significance is the fact that she was pregnant at the time her husband Charles was killed? (How *specifically* would this affect her recoverable damages?) If it is ultimately determined that Charles did not die instantly, but rather remained conscious for minutes or hours after the accident, does this affect the amount of recoverable damages? Substantive law usually guides answers to these questions, and we expect you to use the statutes in the Case Files to answer these questions about what types and categories of damages may be recoverable. We only want you to begin thinking about specific dollar amounts; what specific information will you need to value these claims? What witnesses, including experts, would you need to establish such value(s) at trial? (You may wish to take an early look at the letter from the valuation expert that is intended primarily for use in Practice Exercise No. 30. The letter, prepared by Economics Specialists of Boston, Inc., appears in the Case Files.)

2. What types and categories of damages would be available to women plaintiffs in the *City of Cleveland* case who claim they were denied recruitment, training, testing, hiring, and employment opportunities at the Cleveland Fire Department?

## 6. *Enforcement of Damages*

If the defendant refuses to pay money damages, the plaintiff must first be sure to obtain a judgment, which in federal court is described in Fed. R. Civ.

P. 58. That judgment must be entered in the docket. Fed. R. Civ. P. 79(a); *see also* Forms 70 and 71 (at the end of the Federal Rules). The original judgment merely identifies the defendant's obligation to the plaintiff; it does not order payment (compared with an injunction, which directly orders conduct). Fed. R. Civ. P. 69 provides the process for enforcing a judgment for the payment of money. This involves a writ of execution, absent an alternative specified by the court or a relevant federal statute. Federal law does not provide many details of the enforcement process; therefore, the law of the state in which enforcement is sought will govern. State laws permit the use of proceedings to supplement or aid the enforcement of a judgment; these may include actions for garnishment of wages, contempt, and appointment of a receiver.

To collect from a defendant who does not pay on his own initiative, the plaintiff (now called the judgment creditor because she is owed a sum by the defendant/judgment debtor) must initiate another legal proceeding. Some state statutes permit judgment creditors to obtain a lien on property by recording the judgment in a registry of deeds or in the location for filings under the Uniform Commercial Code. The judgment creditor also can obtain a writ of execution for a piece of defendant's property, which authorizes the sheriff to seize the property, sell it—generally at public auction—and turn over the proceeds to the plaintiff. Through a discovery process, the plaintiff may even compel the defendant to disclose the location of assets to satisfy the judgment. Another option for the plaintiff is to execute the judgment against the income of the defendant, resulting in garnishment of wages if the defendant does not pay the installment as ordered. Even if assets exist or income exists, however, the plaintiff may have difficulty taking control of them. Many state statutes exempt certain property from liens so that the defendant can remain able to house, clothe, and feed his or her family; many statutes also limit wage garnishment. (It is worth asking, to what extent should due process "notice and right to be heard" principles apply to procedures to execute a final judgment?)

Other hurdles for the plaintiff include the sheltering effects of bankruptcy, under which the defendant's total assets may be outweighed by total debts, and the prioritization of creditors, which assures secured creditors first dibs on the defendant's assets.

It may also be difficult or impossible to collect on a judgment because of a lack of assets owned by the judgment debtor, because assets are exempt, or because prior liens exist. Consequently, plaintiffs and their lawyers often try to locate defendants who have insurance or sufficient assets to pay a judgment without causing the plaintiff to spend additional money and time to collect.

## D. SETTLEMENT

The vast majority of cases settle before trial. Settlement occurs when a plaintiff agrees to abandon his legal claim(s) in exchange for payment or other relief by the defendant. A settlement is a contract and is subject to the laws governing contracts. Behind the scenes of litigation, parties are often negotiating a settlement price. Why do parties choose to settle? Steven Shavell provides an economic analysis of settlement in the following excerpt.

# ■ STEVEN SHAVELL, FOUNDATIONS OF ECONOMIC ANALYSIS OF LAW
### 401-407, 410 (2004)

I now take up the question of whether parties will reach a settlement or instead go to trial. A settlement is a legally enforceable agreement, usually involving a payment from the defendant to the plaintiff, in which the plaintiff agrees not to pursue his claim further. If the parties do not reach a settlement, we will assume that they go to trial, that is, that the court will determine the outcome of their case. . . .

**Simple model.** Let us suppose for simplicity that the plaintiff and the defendant each has somehow formed beliefs—which may differ—about the trial outcome. Then we can discuss settlement possibilities in terms of two quantities. Consider first the minimum amount that the plaintiff would accept in settlement. Assuming that the plaintiff is risk neutral, this minimum acceptable amount equals his expected gain from trial less the cost of going to trial. For instance, if the plaintiff believes he will prevail with probability 70 percent, would obtain $100,000 upon prevailing, and the trial would involve expenses to him of $20,000, the minimum amount he would accept in settlement is 70% × $100,000 − $20,000 = $70,000 − $20,000 = $50,000; if he were offered anything less than this amount, he would be better off going to trial. If the defendant believes the odds of the plaintiff's winning are, say, only 50 percent, and the defendant's trial costs would be $25,000, then he would pay at most 50% × $100,000 + $25,000 = $50,000 + $25,000 = $75,000 in settlement.

It is evident that *if the plaintiff's minimum acceptable amount is less than the defendant's maximum acceptable amount, a mutually beneficial settlement is possible*—a settlement equal to any amount in between these two figures would be preferable to a trial for each party. Thus, if the plaintiff's minimum is $50,000 and defendant's maximum is $75,000, any amount in between, such as $60,000, would be preferred by each to going to trial. But if the plaintiff's chances of winning were only 20 percent, the defendant's maximum amount would be $20,000 + $25,000 = $45,000, so the most he would pay is less than the minimum $50,000 that the plaintiff would be willing to accept, and settlement could not occur.

Can more be said about when a mutually beneficial settlement will exist? That is, under what conditions will the plaintiff's minimum acceptable demand be less than the defendant's maximum acceptable payment? It is clear that if the plaintiff and the defendant have the same beliefs about the trial outcome, then there should always exist mutually beneficial settlements, because they can each escape trial costs by settling. Suppose that they both believe that $50,000 is the expected judgment the defendant will have to pay if there is a trial. Then the trial costs that the plaintiff would bear would lead to his willingness to accept a lower figure than $50,000; if his trial costs would be $10,000, he would accept $40,000, and so forth. Conversely, any trial costs that the defendant would have to bear would increase above $50,000 what he would be willing to pay; if his trial costs would be $10,000, he would be willing to pay $60,000. Thus, the settlement range would be from $40,000 to $60,000. For settlement possibilities to be eliminated, the plaintiff's minimum amount must rise far enough from $40,000 and/or the defendant's fall far enough from $60,000 such that the plaintiff's minimum turns out to exceed the defendant's maximum. That can occur only if they have different beliefs about the trial outcome. This line of thought suggests the following conclusion: A mutually beneficial settlement amount exists as long as the plaintiff's and defendant's estimates of the expected judgment do not diverge too much. Indeed, it can be shown that *a mutually beneficial settlement exists as long as the plaintiff's estimate of the expected judgment does not exceed the defendant's estimate by more than the sum of their costs of trial.* . . .

**Interpretation of the model.** A number of comments may help us to interpret and understand the foregoing model.

(a) *Does the existence of a mutually beneficial settlement amount imply that settlement will occur?* Although we know that there cannot be a settlement when a mutually beneficial settlement amount does *not* exist, what can be said about the outcome when a mutually beneficial settlement amount does exist? The answer is that there may or may not be a settlement, depending on the nature of bargaining between the parties and the information they have about each other. . . .

(b) *Parties' beliefs.* The effect of parties' beliefs on the existence of mutually beneficial settlement amounts, and thus on the tendency toward settlement, can be easily understood from the italicized conditions stated in the preceding section. Specifically, the greater the amount by which the plaintiff's estimate the likelihood of winning exceeds the defendant's, the smaller the tendency toward settlement, because it is the excess of the plaintiff's expected judgment over the defendant's expected payment that leads to trial. It is important to emphasize that what leads to trial is not that a plaintiff is confident of winning, but rather that he is *more* confident than the defendant thinks he has a right to be. . . .

Of course, if the plaintiff assesses his chances of winning as lower than the defendant assesses the plaintiff's chances, there will be a range of mutually beneficial settlements. If, for example, the plaintiff thinks his chances of winning are 30 percent and the defendant thinks the plaintiff's chances are 50 percent, then, given the figures mentioned above, the plaintiff would accept any amount over $50,000, and the defendant would pay any amount up to $80,000. (Note also that in such cases, this italicized condition automatically holds, because the difference in the plaintiff's expected gain and defendant's expected loss is negative and therefore definitely is less than the sum of trial costs.)

What would we expect the parties' beliefs about the likelihood of trial outcomes to be? The parties may, and often will, be in possession of different information about a case when it begins. For instance, the defendant may know more about whether he would be found liable than the plaintiff knows. Also, the two sides may initially have in mind different legal arguments that they can make. But the parties may elect to share information or may be forced to do so . . . and parties often can independently acquire information that the other side possesses (for instance, plaintiff could interview witnesses to an accident and learn more about the defendant's behavior). To the degree that the parties do come to similar beliefs, settlement becomes more likely.

We would not predict, though, that beliefs will always converge. For example, the parties might not want to share certain legal arguments with each other, believing that if a trial comes about, they would lose the advantage of surprise; yet in light of these arguments, each party might believe it is more likely to win than the other. Another factor standing in the way of convergence of beliefs is the element of natural optimism about one's chances. . . .

But, by and large, especially because parties have legal counsel who are likely to be familiar with the same body of law and because of opportunities for acquisition of information about facts material to disputes, we would expect beliefs about trial outcomes to be relatively close by the time of a trial, leading toward settlement.

(c) *Judgment amount.* If the size of the judgment rises, then the likelihood of trial rises, other things being constant. This is because the effect of a divergence in the assessments of the likelihood of winning is magnified if the judgment that would be awarded becomes larger. If there is, for instance, a 20 percent difference in beliefs and the judgments award would be $10,000, the difference in expected judgments would be only $2,000, perhaps not enough to exceed the sum of legal costs of trial and thus not enough to cause trial. But if the judgment would be $1,000,000, the 20 percent difference in trial outcomes would signify a $200,000 difference in expected awards, and thus be more likely to exceed the sum of trial costs, leading to trial.

Another point about the judgment amount is that, although we have assumed for simplicity that the parties agree on what the judgment amount would be, that might not be so. Differences in the parties' beliefs about the amount that would be won affect their expected judgments and thus the existence of mutually beneficial settlements, according to the italicized condition. If the plaintiff thinks he would win a larger amount than the defendant thinks, then again this would lead toward trial. . . .

(d) *Legal expenses.* The larger are the legal expenses of either party, the greater are the chances of settlement, clearly, since the sum of legal costs will rise, and thus the greater will be the likelihood that the sum of legal costs will exceed any excess of the plaintiff's expectation over the defendant's expectation. One would expect legal expenses to rise with the size of the potential judgment. This factor tends to increase the chances of settlement for large stakes cases, and thus works opposite to the tendency just discussed in (c) toward litigation.

(e) *Risk aversion.* When we introduce risk aversion into the basic model, we see that it leads to a greater likelihood of settlement. The reason is simply that a trial is a risky venture because its outcome is unknown. To a risk-averse party, settlement is more attractive than it is to a risk-neutral party. Further, as the degree of risk aversion of either party increases, or as the amount at stake increases—the size of the judgment or the size of legal fees—settlement becomes more likely, other things being equal. . . .

**Actual amount of trial versus settlement.** In fact, the vast majority of cases settle. Data on state courts show that over 96 percent of civil cases do not go to trial. Similarly, recent data on federal courts demonstrate that, for fiscal year 2001, almost 98 percent of federal civil cases were resolved without trial. These figures, however, may either overstate or understate the true rate: Because cases that are not tried may have been dismissed by a court, 96 percent or 98 percent is the settlement rate plus the dismissal rate, not the settlement rate; but because many disputes are settled before any complaint is filed, 96 percent or 98 percent may understate the settlement rate. In any event, it is evident that the vast majority of cases settle.

## Comments and Questions

1. Under the economic model, settlement is an efficient way to avoid the costs of litigation. Yet in practice, there can be shortfalls from efficiency—or values not captured by efficiency. The classic article condemning settlement is Owen Fiss, *Against Settlement*, 93 Yale L.J. 1073 (1984). Professor Fiss argues that settlement often involves a stark imbalance of bargaining power, that consent is often coerced, and that the bargain may be struck by someone without authority. In such situations, the interests of the party are not properly represented, and the party is often misinformed. Recently, at least one federal court attempted to remedy such problems by providing settlement assistance to pro se litigants who face a settlement conference. Laurie Wardell, *Sidebar: Settlement Assistance Program for Pro Se Cases*, 54 JAN. Fed. Lawyer 33 (2007).

2. Why does Professor Shavell call his model the "simple model"? What assumptions must be made, and what other factors might change the analysis or provide for an unexpected result? Settlement can often be motivated by more than the brute economics of legal costs and payment of damages. For example, a defendant may be extremely concerned with the public nature of a trial and might seek a confidential settlement to protect itself from negative publicity, copycat litigation, or other related costs. Can a defendant's desire for a confidential settlement be accurately represented by the simple model?

Some argue that confidential settlements are too costly because they often conceal public harm, and there has been a recent rise of legislation prohibiting or reducing confidential settlements in certain areas. *See* Alison Lothes, *Quality, Not Quantity: An Analysis of Confidential Settlements and Litigants' Economic Incentives*, 154 U. Pa. L. Rev. 433 (2005). For an economic analysis of confidential settlements reaching counterintuitive results, *see* Scott A. Moss, *Illuminating Secrecy: A New Economic Analysis of Confidential Settlements*, 105 Mich. L. Rev. 867 (2007). Confidentiality clauses in settlements can have ethical dimensions for lawyers as well. *See* Jon Bauer, *Buying Witness Silence: Evidence Suppressing Settlements and Lawyer's Ethics*, 87 Or. L. Rev. 481 (2008).

3. While everyone knows that most cases settle, there is little empirical evidence of exactly what proportion of cases settle as opposed to being disposed of in other ways by courts during pretrial process (such as on a motion to dismiss or by summary judgment) or through arbitration. It is wrong to assume that a case will either settle or go to trial, because there are many intermediate means of resolving a case, which you will begin learning about in the next chapter. For a discussion of the difficulty of determining what proportion of cases settle in the federal courts, see Gillian Hadfield, *Where Have All the Trials Gone? Settlements, Non-trial Adjudications and Statistical Artifacts in the Changing Disposition of Federal Civil Cases*, 1 J. of Emp. Legal Stud. 705 (2004). One example of a settlement/trial hybrid is the high-low agreement, where the parties agree on a floor and a ceiling of damages prior to going to trial.

# E. FINANCING LITIGATION

The way litigation is financed has an inextricable effect on plaintiffs' remedies and on settlement, creating incentives or disincentives to bring lawsuits, to settle them early, or to pursue them to trial. In most cases in the United States each party is responsible for paying her own attorneys' fees. This is known as the "American Rule." That rule and alterations to it (by statute, regulation, or judicial decision) have significant effect on lawyers' decisions to take a case and on the timing of settlement. In some areas of the law, such as civil rights litigation and some consumer protection laws, fee-shifting statutes require the defendant to pay the plaintiff's reasonable attorneys' fees if plaintiff prevails. *See, e.g.,* 42 U.S.C. § 1988. In other areas of the law, especially but not exclusively personal injury cases, the practice of contingency fees allows the plaintiff to finance the litigation by agreeing to pay the lawyer a percentage of her recovery, often 30 percent, in lieu of an hourly fee. Finally, an emerging and controversial business model involves third-party financing of litigation. Judicial rules, ethical rules, and statutes governing fee arrangements and awards are crucial to an understanding of what litigation can bring to parties, and more broadly, of how the American legal system operates.

## 1. The "American Rule"

Under the "American Rule," the losing party does not pay the prevailing party's attorneys' fees. As the name might imply, this is not the rule everywhere else. In England and much of Europe, for example, losing parties typically are required to pay the opposing lawyer's fees as well as their own lawyer's fees; costs follow victory. What differences emerge in practice under these rules?

Defenders of the American Rule maintain that it permits the poor, as well as the rich, to litigate. Poor folks would not otherwise be able to sue, the argument goes, because of the fear that if they lose they will have to pay the opponent's legal fees. Moreover, the American Rule encourages innovative claims, while the English Rule directs plaintiffs, and their lawyers, to be more risk averse.

Advocates of the English Rule emphasize that it deters frivolous or marginal litigation and that it more fully compensates the prevailing party for the troubles of litigation. It is worth noting that in practice, the English Rule exempts cases where the losing party's lawyer is financed through legal aid, which, in turn, is available to low-income people. Also, in the English practice a taxing officer determines fees (for both solicitors and barristers) with reference to a fee schedule, which tends to run 60-70 percent of actual fees. Insurance may also cover some of the costs. Further, applications for taxation of costs may be made at points before the end of the litigation, such as the award of preliminary relief, and therefore fees may be awarded to a party that does not prevail in the end. In Germany, the losing party pays fees to the degree that the winning party was successful, or what may be known as "less-than-full" fee compensation. Thus, "if the remedy sought was payment of 300,000 euros, and if the plaintiff is successful only in relation to the amount of 100,000 euros, the plaintiff has to bear two-thirds of the costs." *See* Peter F. Schlosser, *Lectures on Civil-Law Litigation Systems and American Cooperation with Those Systems*, 45 U. Kan. L. Rev. 9, 18 (1996). This rule deters plaintiffs from seeking enormous damages.

Fee rules also reflect other differences between the English and U.S. legal systems and cultures. England virtually abolished juries in civil cases (except for libel and malicious prosecution) over fifty years ago. Cases are tried before judges, whose decisions on damages as well as liability are narrowly bound by precedent. England does not have distinct sovereign states that apply their own common law rules. For all these reasons, outcomes tend to be more predictable in England than in the United States.

In contrast, the jury remains a vital part of the U.S. civil justice system, and a case that might seem marginal when filed may nonetheless persuade a jury. Moreover, substantive and procedural rules evolve rapidly and in varied directions across the fifty states, producing a more volatile and less precedent-bound legal world than in England. Propositions that might at one time have been thought highly speculative have become accepted law.

For a comparison of the two attorneys' fees models and an assessment of their probable impact on attorney conduct and results in particular cases, using economics to model the risk preferences of lawyers and their clients, see Steven Shavell, *Suit, Settlement and Trial: A Theoretical Analysis Under Alternative Methods for the Allocation of Legal Costs*, 11 J. Legal Stud. 55 (1982), and John J. Donohue III, *Opting for the British Rule, or If Posner and Shavell Can't Remember the Coase Theorem, Who Will?* 104 Harv. L. Rev. 1093 (1991).

## 2. Fee-Shifting Statutes

Even at common law, the American Rule governing attorneys' fees had exceptions. The Supreme Court has concluded that when a party acts in "bad faith," courts have inherent authority to assess fees to reimburse the opposing party. Some courts have ruled that when a lawyer or litigant acts in a way that creates a "common fund" for the benefit of others, the resulting fund can be "taxed" for the fair value of the lawyer's work, to prevent a windfall to the beneficiaries. In the 1960s and 1970s, some lower federal courts adopted the theory that losing defendants could be ordered to pay plaintiffs' attorneys' fees where those plaintiffs acted as "private attorneys general." The Supreme Court rejected this theory in *Alyeska Pipeline Serv. Co. v. Wilderness Soc'y*, 421 U.S. 240 (1975), and concluded that Congress, rather than the courts, should determine the kinds of cases warranting a fee shift. The Court recognized that a fee shift fundamentally provides an incentive to plaintiffs to file suit, an incentive to lawyers to represent those plaintiffs, and a deterrent to defendants at risk of such suits.

Congress responded to *Alyeska* by adopting the Civil Rights Attorney's Fees Act of 1976, 42 U.S.C. § 1988. By 1995, Congress had included fee-shifting provisions in over 180 pieces of legislation that addressed topics ranging from environmental protection and civil rights to intellectual property and banking. *See, e.g.*, Clean Air Act Amendments of 1977, 42 U.S.C. § 7622(e)(2); Equal Access to Justice Act, 28 U.S.C. § 2412(b); Handicapped Children's Protection Act of 1988, 20 U.S.C. § 1415(e)(4)(B); Patent Infringement Act, 35 U.S.C. § 285; Electronic Fund Transfer Act, 15 U.S.C. §§ 1693m(a) and (f). By creating monetary incentives for attorneys to pursue these and other claims, Congress intended to promote enforcement of selected federal statutory rights.

Yet unlike the English Rule, which directs that the loser pay the attorneys' fees of the opponent, many of these American statutes, as interpreted by the courts, provide only for shifting *prevailing* plaintiffs' fees to the defendants; a losing plaintiff is not obliged to pay the defendants' attorneys' fees. This pro-plaintiff, one-way shift structure encourages enforcement efforts without penalizing the unsuccessful plaintiff. Yet even under a statute with this structure, a court may order the plaintiff who brings a totally frivolous or groundless suit to pay the defendant's attorneys' fees. *See, e.g., Fox v. Vice*, 131 S. Ct. 2205 (2011). Such sanctions are also available under Fed. R. Civ. P. 11, which provides that a court may order "payment of some or all of the reasonable attorneys' fees and other expenses" as a sanction for filing a pleading or motion without adequate inquiry, unwarranted by existing law or fact, or based on a frivolous argument for new law.

Finally, at least one state has recently passed "loser pays" legislation, requiring losing parties in some civil cases to pay their opponents' legal fees. *See* H.B. 274, 82 (R) Leg. (Tex. 2011).

### 3. The Effect of Rule 68 Settlement Offers on Attorneys' Fees

As a monetary incentive and deterrent, attorneys' fees become part of the package of possibilities that influence settlement of lawsuits. If Congress authorizes attorneys' fees for a prevailing plaintiff, then the defendant must include the possible liability for plaintiff's attorneys' fees in the calculus of the costs and benefits of proceeding to trial, compared with the costs and benefits of settlement. Similarly, the plaintiff must consider the risk of losing not only on the merits, but also of forgoing attorneys' fees, in deciding whether to file initially, as well as whether to proceed or to settle. How should a statutory policy promoting certain kinds of lawsuits be reconciled with a judicial policy promoting settlement? When should the value of attorneys' fees themselves be on the bargaining table for settlement of a lawsuit? The following cases address these complex issues.

### ■ MAREK v. CHESNY
#### *473 U.S. 1 (1985)*

Chief Justice BURGER delivered the opinion of the Court:

We granted certiorari to decide whether attorney's fees incurred by a plaintiff subsequent to an offer of settlement under Federal Rule of Civil Procedure 68 must be paid by the defendant under 42 U.S.C. § 1988, when the plaintiff recovers a judgment less than the offer.

#### I

Petitioners, three police officers, in answering a call on a domestic disturbance, shot and killed respondent's adult son. Respondent, in his own behalf and as administrator of his son's estate, filed suit against the officers in the United States District Court under 42 U.S.C. § 1983 and state tort law.

Prior to trial, petitioners made a timely offer of settlement "for a sum, including costs now accrued and attorney's fees, of ONE HUNDRED THOUSAND ($100,000) DOLLARS." Respondent did not accept the offer. The case went to trial and respondent was awarded $5,000 on the state-law "wrongful death" claim, $52,000 for the § 1983 violation, and $3,000 in punitive damages.

Respondent filed a request for $171,692.47 in costs, including attorney's fees. This amount included costs incurred after the settlement offer. Petitioners opposed the claim for postoffer costs, relying on Federal Rule of Civil Procedure 68, which shifts to the plaintiff all "costs" incurred subsequent to an offer of judgment not exceeded by the ultimate recovery at trial. Petitioners argued that attorney's fees are part of the "costs" covered by Rule 68, The District Court agreed with petitioners and declined to award respondent "costs, including attorney's fees, incurred after the offer of judgment." 547 F. Supp. 542, 547 (N.D. Ill. 1982). The parties subsequently agreed that $32,000 fairly represented the allowable costs, including attorney's fees, accrued prior to petitioners' offer of settlement. Respondent appealed the denial of postoffer costs.

The Court of Appeals reversed. The court rejected what it termed the "rather mechanical linking up of Rule 68 and section 1988." It stated that the District Court's reading of Rule 68 and § 1988, while "in a sense logical," would put civil rights plaintiffs and counsel in a "predicament" that "cuts against the grain of section 1988." Plaintiffs' attorneys, the court reasoned, would be forced to "think very hard" before rejecting even an inadequate offer, and would be deterred from bringing good-faith actions because of the prospect of losing the right to attorney's fees if a settlement offer more favorable than the ultimate recovery were rejected. The court concluded that "[t]he legislators who enacted section 1988 would not have wanted its effectiveness blunted because of a little known rule of court." We granted certiorari. We reverse.

## II

Rule 68 provides that if a timely pretrial offer of settlement is not accepted and "the judgment finally obtained by the offeree is not more favorable than the offer, the offeree must pay the costs incurred after the making of the offer." The plain purpose of Rule 68 is to encourage settlement and avoid litigation. The Rule prompts both parties to a suit to evaluate the risks and costs of litigation, and to balance them against the likelihood of success upon trial on the merits. This case requires us to decide whether the offer in this case was a proper one under Rule 68, and whether the term "costs" as used in Rule 68 includes attorney's fees awardable under 42 U.S.C. § 1988.

. . . [Does] the term "costs" in Rule 68 include[] attorney's fees awardable under 42 U.S.C. § 1988[?] By the time the Federal Rules of Civil Procedure were adopted in 1938, federal statutes had authorized and defined awards of costs to prevailing parties for more than 85 years. *See* Act of Feb. 26, 1853, 10 Stat. 161; *see generally Alyeska Pipeline Service Co. v. Wilderness Society*, 421 U.S. 240 (1975). Unlike in England, such "costs" generally had not included attorney's fees; under the "American Rule," each party had been required to bear its own attorney's fees. The "American Rule" as applied in federal courts, however, had become subject to certain exceptions by the late 1930's. Some of these exceptions had evolved as a product of the "inherent power in the courts to allow attorney's fees in particular situations." *Alyeska, supra*, at 259. . . .

The authors of Federal Rule of Civil Procedure 68 were fully aware of these exceptions to the American Rule. The Advisory Committee's Note to Rule 54(d), 28 U.S.C. App., p. 621, contains an extensive list of the federal statutes which allowed for costs in particular cases; of the 35 "statutes as to costs" set forth in the final paragraph of the Note, no fewer than 11 allowed for attorney's fees as part of costs. Against this background of varying definitions of "costs," the drafters of Rule 68 did not define the term; nor is there any explanation whatever as to its intended meaning in the history of the Rule.

In this setting, given the importance of "costs" to the Rule, it is very unlikely that this omission was mere oversight; on the contrary, the most reasonable inference is that the term "costs" in Rule 68 was intended to refer to all costs properly awardable under the relevant substantive statute or other authority. In other words, all costs properly awardable in an action are to be considered within the scope of Rule 68 "costs." Thus, absent congressional expressions to the contrary, where the underlying statute defines "costs" to include attorney's fees, we are satisfied such fees are to be included as costs for purposes of Rule 68. . . .

Here, respondent sued under 42 U.S.C. § 1983. Pursuant to the Civil Rights Attorney's Fees Awards Act of 1976, 90 Stat. 2641, as amended, 42 U.S.C. § 1988, a prevailing party in a § 1983 action may be awarded attorney's fees "as part of the costs." Since Congress expressly included attorney's fees as "costs" available to a plaintiff in a § 1983 suit, such fees are subject to the cost-shifting provision of Rule 68. This "plain meaning" interpretation of the interplay between Rule 68 and § 1988 is the only construction that gives meaning to each word in both Rule 68 and § 1988.

Unlike the Court of Appeals, we do not believe that this "plain meaning" construction of the statute and the Rule will frustrate Congress' objective in § 1988 of ensuring that civil rights plaintiffs obtain "'effective access to the judicial process.'" *Hensley v. Eckerhart*, 461 U.S. 424, 429 (1983), *quoting* H.R. Rep. No. 94-1558, p. 1 (1976). Merely subjecting civil rights plaintiffs to the settlement provision of Rule 68 does not curtail their access to the courts, or significantly deter them from bringing suit. Application of Rule 68 will serve as a disincentive for the plaintiffs' attorney to continue litigation after the defendant makes a settlement offer. There is no evidence, however, that Congress, in considering § 1988, had any thought that civil rights claims were to be on any different footing from other civil claims insofar as settlement is concerned. Indeed, Congress made clear its concern that civil rights plaintiffs not be penalized for "helping to lessen docket congestion" by settling their cases out of court. . . .

Moreover, Rule 68's policy of encouraging settlements is neutral, favoring neither plaintiffs nor defendants; it expresses a clear policy of favoring settlement of all lawsuits. Civil rights plaintiffs—along with other plaintiffs—who reject an offer more favorable than what is thereafter recovered at trial will not recover attorney's fees for services performed after the offer is rejected. But, since the Rule is neutral, many civil rights plaintiffs will benefit from the offers of settlement encouraged by Rule 68. . . .

To be sure, application of Rule 68 will require plaintiffs to "think very hard" about whether continued litigation is worthwhile; that is precisely what Rule 68 contemplates. This effect of Rule 68, however, is in no sense inconsistent with the congressional policies underlying § 1983 and § 1988. Section 1988 authorizes courts to award only "reasonable" attorney's fees to prevailing parties. In *Hensley v. Eckerhart, supra*, we held that "the most critical factor" in determining a reasonable fee "is the degree of success obtained." *Id.*, at 436. We specifically noted that prevailing at trial "may say little about whether the expenditure of counsel's time was reasonable in relation to the success achieved." *Ibid.* In a case where a rejected settlement offer exceeds the ultimate recovery, the plaintiff—although technically the prevailing party—has not received any monetary benefits from the postoffer services of his attorney. This case presents a good example: the $139,692 in postoffer legal services resulted in a recovery $8,000 less than petitioners' settlement offer. Given Congress' focus on the success achieved, we are not persuaded that shifting the postoffer costs to respondent in these circumstances would in any sense thwart its intent under § 1988.

Rather than "cutting against the grain" of § 1988, as the Court of Appeals held, we are convinced that applying Rule 68 in the context of a § 1983 action is consistent with the policies and objectives of § 1988. Section 1988 encourages plaintiffs to bring meritorious civil rights suits; Rule 68 simply encourages settlements. There is nothing incompatible in these two objectives.

## III

Congress, of course, was well aware of Rule 68 when it enacted § 1988, and included attorney's fees as part of recoverable costs. The plain language of Rule 68 and § 1988 subjects such fees to the cost-shifting provision of Rule 68. Nothing revealed in our review of the policies underlying § 1988 constitutes "the necessary clear expression of congressional intent" required "to exempt . . . [the] statute from the operation of" Rule 68. *Califano v. Yamasaki*, 442 U.S. 682, 700 (1979). We hold that petitioners are not liable for costs of $139,692 incurred by respondent after petitioners' offer of settlement. The judgment of the Court of Appeals is Reversed.

[Concurring opinions of Justices POWELL and REHNQUIST are omitted.]

Justice BRENNAN, with whom Justice MARSHALL and Justice BLACKMUN join, dissenting:

The question presented by this case is whether the term "costs" as it is used in Rule 68 of the Federal Rules of Civil Procedure and elsewhere throughout the Rules refers simply to those taxable costs defined in 28 U.S.C. § 1920 and traditionally understood as "costs"—court fees, printing expenses, and the like—or instead includes attorney's fees when an underlying fees-award statute happens to refer to fees "as part of" the awardable costs. Relying on what it recurrently emphasizes is the "plain language" of one such statute, 42 U.S.C. § 1988, the Court today holds that a prevailing civil rights litigant entitled to fees under that statute is per se barred by Rule 68 from recovering any fees for work performed after rejecting a settlement offer where he ultimately recovers less than the proffered amount in settlement.

I dissent. The Court's reasoning is wholly inconsistent with the history and structure of the Federal Rules, and its application to the over 100 attorney's fees statutes enacted by Congress will produce absurd variations in Rule 68's operation based on nothing more than picayune differences in statutory phraseology. Neither Congress nor the drafters of the Rules could possibly have intended such inexplicable variations in settlement incentives. Moreover, the Court's interpretation will "seriously undermine the purposes behind the attorney's fees provisions" of the civil rights laws, *Delta Air Lines, Inc. v. August*, 450 U.S. 346, 378 (1981) (Rehnquist, J., dissenting)—provisions imposed by Congress pursuant to § 5 of the Fourteenth Amendment. Today's decision therefore violates the most basic limitations on our rulemaking authority as set forth in the Rules Enabling Act, 28 U.S.C. § 2072, and as summarized in *Alyeska Pipeline Co. v. Wilderness Society*, 421 U.S. 240 (1975). Finally, both Congress and the Judicial Conference of the United States have been engaged for years in considering possible amendments to Rule 68 that would bring attorney's fees within the operation of the Rule. That process strongly suggests that Rule 68 has not previously been viewed as governing fee awards, and it illustrates the wisdom of deferring to other avenues of amending Rule 68 rather than ourselves engaging in "standardless judicial lawmaking." *Delta Air Lines, Inc. v. August, supra* 450 U.S. at 378 (Rehnquist, J., dissenting).

# I

The Court's "plain language" analysis, goes as follows: Section 1988 provides that a "prevailing party" may recover "a reasonable attorney's fee as part of the costs." Rule 68 in turn provides that, where an offeree obtains a judgment for less than the amount of a previous settlement offer, "the offeree must pay the costs incurred after the making of the offer." Because "attorney's fees" are "costs," the Court concludes, the "plain meaning" of Rule 68 per se prohibits a prevailing civil rights plaintiff from recovering fees incurred after he rejected the proposed out-of-court settlement.

The Court's "plain language" approach is, as Judge Posner's opinion for the court below noted, "in a sense logical." 720 F.2d 474, 478 (7th Cir. 1983). However, while the starting point in interpreting statutes and rules is always the plain words themselves, "[t]he particular inquiry is not what is the abstract force of the words or what they may comprehend, but in what sense were they intended to be understood or what understanding they convey when used in the particular act," We previously have been confronted with "superficially appealing argument[s]" strikingly similar to those adopted by the Court today, and we have found that they "cannot survive careful consideration." *Roadway Express, Inc. v. Piper*, 447 U.S. 752, 758 (1980). So it is here. . . .

For a number of reasons, "costs" as that term is used in the Federal Rules should be interpreted uniformly in accordance with the definition of costs set forth in § 1920:

*First.* The limited history of the costs provisions in the Federal Rules suggests that the drafters intended "costs" to mean only taxable costs traditionally allowed under the common law or pursuant to the statutory predecessor of § 1920. Nowhere was it suggested that the meaning of taxable "costs" might vary from case to case depending on the language of the substantive statute involved—a practice that would have cut against the drafters' intent to create uniform procedures applicable to "every action" in federal court. Fed. Rule Civ. Proc. 1.

*Second.* The Rules provide that "costs" may automatically be taxed by the clerk of the court on one day's notice, Fed. Rule Civ. Proc. 54(d)—strongly suggesting that "costs" were intended to refer only to those routine, readily determinable charges that could appropriately be left to a clerk, and as to which a single day's notice of settlement would be appropriate. Attorney's fees, which are awardable only by the court and which frequently entail lengthy disputes and hearings, obviously do not fall within that category.

*Third.* When particular provisions of the Federal Rules are intended to encompass attorney's fees, they do so explicitly. Eleven different provisions of the Rules authorize a court to award attorney's fees as "expenses" in particular circumstances, demonstrating that the drafters knew the difference, and intended a difference, between "costs," "expenses," and "attorney's fees."

*Fourth.* With the exception of one recent Court of Appeals opinion and two recent District Court opinions, the Court can point to no authority suggesting that courts or attorneys have ever viewed the cost-shifting provisions of Rule 68 as including attorney's fees. . . .

*Fifth.* We previously have held that words and phrases in the Federal Rules must be given a consistent usage and be read *in pari materia*, reasoning that to do otherwise would "attribute a schizophrenic intent to the drafters." *Id.*, at 353. Applying the Court's "plain language" approach consistently throughout the Rules, however, would produce absurd results that would turn statutes like § 1988 on their heads and plainly violate the restraints imposed on judicial rulemaking by the Rules Enabling Act. For example, Rule 54(d) provides that "costs shall be allowed as of course to the prevailing party unless the court otherwise directs." Similarly, the plain language of Rule 68 provides that a plaintiff covered by the Rule "must pay the costs incurred after the making of the offer"—language requiring the plaintiff to bear both his postoffer costs and the defendant's postoffer costs. If "costs" as used in these provisions were interpreted to include attorney's fees by virtue of the wording of § 1988, losing civil rights plaintiffs would be required by the "plain language" of Rule 54(d) to pay the defendant's attorney's fees, and prevailing plaintiffs falling within Rule 68 would be required to bear the defendant's postoffer attorney's fees.

Had it addressed this troubling consequence of its "plain language" approach, perhaps the Court would have acknowledged that such a reading would conflict directly with § 1988, which allows an award of attorney's fees to a prevailing defendant only where "the suit was vexatious, frivolous, or brought to harass or embarrass the defendant," and that the substantive standard set forth in § 1988 therefore overrides the otherwise "plain meaning" of Rules 54(d) and 68. But that is precisely the point, and the Court cannot have it both ways. . . .

*Sixth.* As with all of the Federal Rules, the drafters intended Rule 68 to have a uniform, consistent application in all proceedings in federal court. In accordance with this intent, Rule 68 should be interpreted to provide uniform, consistent incentives "to encourage the settlement of litigation." *Delta Air Lines, Inc. v. August, supra,* 450 U.S. at 352. Yet today's decision will lead to dramatically different settlement incentives depending on minor variations in the phraseology of the underlying fees-award statutes—distinctions that would appear to be nothing short of irrational and for which the Court has no plausible explanation.

Congress has enacted well over 100 attorney's fees statutes, many of which would appear to be affected by today's decision. . . . Under the "plain language" approach of today's decision, Rule 68 will operate to include the potential loss of otherwise recoverable attorney's fees as an incentive to settlement in litigation under these statutes. . . .

The result is to sanction a senseless patchwork of fee shifting that flies in the face of the fundamental purpose of the Federal Rules—the provision of uniform and consistent procedure in federal courts. Such a construction will "introduce into [Rule 68] distinctions unrelated to its goal . . . and [will] result in virtually random application of the Rule." . . .

In sum, there is nothing in the history and structure of the Rules or in the history of any of the underlying attorney's fee statutes to justify such incomprehensible distinctions based simply on fine linguistic variations among the underlying fees-award statutes—particularly where, as in *Roadway Express,* the cost provision can be read as embodying a uniform definition derived from § 1920. As partners with Congress, we have a responsibility not to carry "plain language" constructions to the point of producing "untenable distinctions and unreasonable results." *American Tobacco Co. v. Patterson,* 456 U.S. 63, 71 (1982). . . .

## II

### A

Although the Court's opinion fails to discuss any of the problems reviewed above, it does devote some space to arguing that its interpretation of Rule 68 "is in no sense inconsistent with the congressional policies underlying § 1983 and § 1988." The Court goes so far as to assert that its interpretation fits in smoothly with § 1988 as interpreted by *Hensley v. Eckerhart,* 461 U.S. 424 (1983).

The Court is wrong. Congress has instructed that attorney's fee entitlement under § 1988 be governed by a reasonableness standard. Until today the Court always has recognized that this standard precludes reliance on any mechanical "bright-line" rules automatically denying a portion of fees, acknowledging that such "mathematical approach[es]" provide "little aid in determining what is a reasonable fee in light of all the relevant factors." 461 U.S. at 435-436, n.11. Although the starting point is always "the number of hours reasonably expended on the litigation," this "does not end the inquiry": a number of considerations set forth in the legislative history of § 1988 "may lead the district court to adjust the fee upward or downward." *Id.*, at 433-434. We also have emphasized that the district court "necessarily has discretion in making this equitable judgment" because of its "superior understanding of the litigation." *Id.*, at 437. Section 1988's reasonableness standard is, in sum, "acutely sensitive to the merits of an action and to antidiscrimination policy." *Roadway Express, Inc. v. Piper*, 447 U.S. at 762.

Rule 68, on the other hand, is not "sensitive" at all to the merits of an action and to antidiscrimination policy. It is a mechanical per se provision automatically shifting "costs" incurred after an offer is rejected, and it deprives a district court of all discretion with respect to the matter by using "the strongest verb of its type known to the English language—'must.'" *Delta Air Lines, Inc. v. August, supra*, 450 U.S. at 369. The potential for conflict between § 1988 and Rule 68 could not be more apparent.

Of course, a civil rights plaintiff who unreasonably fails to accept a settlement offer, and who thereafter recovers less than the proffered amount in settlement, is barred under § 1988 itself from recovering fees for unproductive work performed in the wake of the rejection. This is because "the extent of a plaintiff's success is a crucial factor in determining the proper amount of an award of attorney's fees," 461 U.S. at 440 (emphasis added); hours that are "excessive, redundant, or otherwise unnecessary" must be excluded from that calculus, *id.*, at 434. To this extent, the results might sometimes be the same under either § 1988's reasonableness inquiry or the Court's wooden application of Rule 68. Had the Court allowed the Seventh Circuit's remand in the instant case to stand, for example, the District Court after conducting the appropriate inquiry might well have determined that much or even all of the respondent's postoffer fees were unreasonably incurred and therefore not properly awardable.

But the results under § 1988 and Rule 68 will not always be congruent, because § 1988 mandates the careful consideration of a broad range of other factors and accords appropriate leeway to the district court's informed discretion. Contrary to the Court's protestations, it is not at all clear that "[t]his case presents a good example" of the smooth interplay of § 1988 and Rule 68, *ante*, at 9, because there has never been an evidentiary consideration of the reasonableness or unreasonableness of the respondent's fee request. It is clear, however, that under the Court's interpretation of Rule 68 a plaintiff who ultimately recovers only slightly less than the proffered amount in settlement will per se be barred from recovering trial fees even if he otherwise "has obtained excellent results" in litigation that will have far-reaching benefit to the public interest. . . .

To discuss but one example, Rule 68 allows an offer to be made any time after the complaint is filed and gives the plaintiff only 10 days to accept or reject. The Court's decision inevitably will encourage defendants who know they have violated the law to make "low-ball" offers immediately after suit is filed and before plaintiffs have been able to obtain the information they are entitled to by way of discovery to assess the strength of their claims and the reasonableness of the offers. The result will put severe pressure on plaintiffs to settle on the basis of inadequate information in order to avoid the risk of bearing all of their fees even if reasonable discovery might reveal that the defendants were subject to far greater liability. Indeed, because Rule 68 offers may be made recurrently without limitation, defendants will be well advised to make ever-slightly-larger offers throughout the discovery process and before plaintiffs have conducted all reasonably necessary discovery.

This sort of so-called "incentive" is fundamentally incompatible with Congress' goals. Congress intended for "private citizens . . . to be able to assert their civil rights" and for "those who violate the Nation's fundamental laws" not to be able "to proceed with impunity." . . .

Other difficulties will follow from the Court's decision. For example, if a plaintiff recovers less money than was offered before trial but obtains potentially far-reaching injunctive or declaratory relief, it is altogether unclear how the Court intends judges to go about quantifying the "value" of the plaintiff's success. . . .

**B**

Indeed, the judgment of the Court of Appeals below turned on its determination that an interpretation of Rule 68 to include attorney's fees is beyond the pale of the judiciary's rulemaking authority. *Ibid.* Congress has delegated its authority to this Court "to prescribe by general rules . . . the practice and procedure of the district courts and courts of appeals of the United States in civil actions." 28 U.S.C. § 2072. This grant is limited, however, by the condition that "[s]uch rules shall not abridge, enlarge or modify any substantive right." *Ibid.* The right to attorney's fees is "substantive" under any reasonable definition of that term.

## Comments and Questions

1. The ruling in *Marek v. Chesney* encourages parties to make realistic offers to their opponent by penalizing the party who refuses an offer of judgment and later receives a less favorable judgment at trial. But before *Marek* the penalty was minor: it provided for a shift only of "costs" as a penalty, and costs (such as filing fees) are generally quite small. *Marek* adds teeth to the penalty in civil rights cases by construing "costs" to include attorneys' fees. This means that where a fee-shifting statute allows a prevailing party to

recover attorneys' fees as part of costs, Rule 68 can curtail any fees otherwise due if the prevailing party rejected a settlement offer more favorable than the ultimate judgment. Fee-shifting statutes that do not include attorneys' fees as part of costs apparently avoid this operation of Rule 68.

2. What is the method that the Court uses to interpret Rule 68? What is the dissent's response?

3. Importantly, *Marek* was decided at a time when § 1988 (the Civil Rights Attorney's Fees Act) was the most commonly used of the federal fee-shifting statutes and the most common exception to the American Rule. Previous to *Marek* (*see Christiansburg Garment Co. v. EEOC*, 434 U.S. 412 (1978)), the Supreme Court had interpreted § 1988 as authorizing courts to order defendants to pay the attorneys' fees of prevailing plaintiffs, but generally *not* to authorize courts to order plaintiffs to pay the attorneys' fees of prevailing defendants (the exception is where the plaintiffs suit is "frivolous, unreasonable, or without foundation"—much like a Rule 11 violation). *Marek* is therefore a "one-way" fee-shift rule, permitting shifts of attorneys' fees only from plaintiff to defendant; it is a "pro-plaintiff" rule, given the Court's view of the importance of encouraging enforcement of the civil rights laws.

Consider the plaintiff who wins a lawsuit brought under § 1983. Normally that plaintiff would then be entitled also to obtain attorneys' fees under § 1988. *Marek* ruled that Fed. R. Civ. P. 68 includes attorneys' fees within the scope of "costs" that can be shifted to the plaintiff who rejects a settlement offer that turns out to be greater than ultimate recovery. In the following simple hypothetical, how much must defendant pay in attorneys' fees?

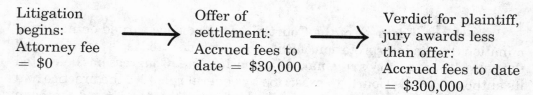

Litigation begins: Attorney fee = $0 → Offer of settlement: Accrued fees to date = $30,000 → Verdict for plaintiff, jury awards less than offer: Accrued fees to date = $300,000

By rejecting a settlement offer that exceeded ultimate judgment, under Fed. R. Civ. P. 68, the plaintiff now cannot shift to the defendant his attorneys' fees incurred after rejecting the settlement offer and will have to pay those fees unless the plaintiff's prior arrangement with the attorney imposed no such obligation on the plaintiff. Under what circumstances might an attorney sign such a contract?

The basic idea in *Marek*'s majority view is that the value of the attorneys' work up until the settlement offer deserves acknowledgment, but that the attorneys' work subsequent to a rejected settlement offer is not worthwhile when the ultimate recovery is less than the offer. But can the plaintiff who rejected the settlement offer now be liable for the defendant's attorneys' fees? The language of Fed. R. Civ. P. 68 suggests as much, once "costs" is construed to include "fees": "If the judgment finally obtained by the offeree is not more favorable than the offer, the offeree must pay the costs incurred after the making of the offer." Yet the Court in *Marek* does not direct the plaintiff to pay the attorneys' fees of the defendant that were incurred subsequent to the rejection of the settlement offer. The opinion's only comment on this issue appears in its footnote 1, where the Court notes that the District Court refused to shift the petitioner-defendant's attorneys' fees to the respondent-plaintiff, and the petitioner-defendant did not contest this issue before the Supreme Court.

This decision makes sense in light of the interpretation of § 1988. Because § 1988 has been construed as a one-way shift (absent extreme circumstances), the courts will not direct plaintiffs in § 1983 cases to pay the attorneys' fees of defendants even if Fed. R. Civ. P. 68 is triggered. Moreover, a defendant who makes a successful Rule 68 offer still is not a "prevailing party" if the plaintiff did have some recovery. Several courts thus have concluded that a defendant cannot recover its fees after making a successful Rule 68 offer. *See, e.g., EEOC v. Bailey Ford, Inc.*, 26 F.3d 570, 571 (5th Cir. 1994); *Payne v. Milwaukee Cnty.*, 288 F.3d 1021, 1027 (7th Cir. 2002).

4. Is an accepted settlement offer adequate to be substantially "prevailing" for purposes of triggering attorneys' fees under § 1988 (or other fee-shifting statutes that permit a shift of fees to benefit the prevailing party)? It is if the accepted Rule 68 offer is filed with the court and signed as a judgment by the clerk. You may review the language of Rule 68(a) on this point. If there is no judgment, such as when litigation serves as a catalyst for the defendant's decision to change its policies, the plaintiff is not entitled to fees. *See Buckhannon Bd. and Care Home, Inc. v. W. Va. Dep't of Health & Human Res.*, 532 U.S. 598 (2001) (holding that federal laws providing for fee shifting to prevailing parties are inapplicable in the absence of an actual judgment or court-approved settlement). When cases to which no fee-shifting statute applies settle, there is no need to file the settlement with the court. Instead, the plaintiff simply dismisses the suit with prejudice.

5. Fed. R. Civ. P. 54(d) provides that costs other than attorneys' fees are to be awarded to prevailing parties unless the court otherwise directs or particular statutory provisions apply. Although "costs" covered by federal awards of costs to prevailing parties are usually quite limited, they can include the costs of a plaintiff's experts following a judgment for the plaintiff. *See* Peter L. Murray, *A Comparative Law Experiment*, 8 Ind. Intl. & Comp. L. Rev. 2115, 2138 (1998). Expert fees may be paid for by the other side under Fed. R. Civ. P. 26(a)(4)(C), which authorizes the judge to require a party seeking discovery to pay the reasonable fee of an expert responding to the discovery, or a fair portion of the fees and expenses incurred by the opposing party in obtaining facts and opinions from the expert.

6. By its own terms, Rule 68 requires that offers allow judgment to be taken for both damages and costs. After *Marek*, if an underlying statute defines attorneys' fees as costs, then attorneys' fees must also be included in Rule 68 offers. The Court in *Marek* noted that this requirement can be met either by an offer that includes or specifies an amount for costs, or by an offer that does not include costs but that nevertheless allows judgment to be taken, costs to be determined and awarded by the court. If a rejected offer does not

include costs, final judgment will be compared to the amount of the offer. In contrast, if a rejected offer includes costs, the final judgment will presumably be compared to the amount of the offer minus the costs accrued at the time of the offer. Thus, courts must often determine whether an offer included costs in order to determine whether Rule 68 applies. Unfortunately, Rule 68 does not provide guidance on how to draft a Rule 68 offer, nor how courts are to interpret such offers. If a defendant has offered "$100,000 with costs," has the defendant offered $100,000 including costs, or $100,000 in addition to costs? Courts have struggled with such ambiguities and have often reached contrary results. *See, e.g., Kyreakakis v. Paternoster*, 732 F. Supp. 1287 (D.N.J. 1990); *Christian v. R. Wood Motors, Inc.*, 1995 WL 238981 (N.D.N.Y. 1995). Other complications, such as claims involving requests for injunctive relief, have proved equally difficult.

## Practice Exercise No. 5: Revising Fed. R. Civ. P. 68

States have been experimenting with methods for encouraging settlement that are more robust than Rule 68. For example, as part of tort reform measures the State of Georgia adopted the following provision:

> If a defendant makes an offer of settlement which is rejected by the plaintiff, the defendant shall be entitled to recover reasonable attorney's fees and expenses of litigation incurred by the defendant . . . from the date of the rejection of the offer of settlement through the entry of judgment if the final judgment is one of no liability or the final judgment obtained by the plaintiff is less than 75 percent of such offer of settlement.

OCGA § 9-11-68(b)(1) (West 2011), *limited on constitutional grounds by Fowler Prop., Inc. v. Dowland*, 646 S.E.2d 197, 197 (Ga. 2007) (holding that statute could not be applied retroactively). Texas has enacted an offer of settlement statute that is trigged when "a settlement offer is made and rejected and the judgment to be rendered will be significantly less favorable to the rejecting party than was the settlement offer." V.T.C.A., Civil Practice & Remedies Code § 42.004 (West 2011). In that event, the party rejecting settlement must pay all the offering party's costs, including reasonable attorneys' fees, with the caveat that "[t]he litigation costs that may be awarded under this chapter to any party may not be greater than the total amount that the claimant recovers or would recover before adding an award of litigation costs under this chapter in favor of the claimant or subtracting as an offset an award of litigation costs under this chapter in favor of the defendant." Some states have offer of settlement rules geared to specific type of cases. For example, Maryland enacted an offer of judgment statute applicable to medical malpractice claims. Md. Code, Courts and Judicial Proceedings, § 3-2A-08A(f) (West 2011).

Imagine that you have been appointed to an Advisory Committee considering proposed changes to Fed. R. Civ. P. 68; what would you recommend? As you draft your revisions, keep in mind the *Marek* dissent's concern that the Rules Enabling Act boundaries may be breached by a procedural rule with substantive effects. Try to work out the specific language for a new rule, and explain what you are pursuing and how the rule would handle different cases.

For detailed analysis of the problems under the current regime and for alternative approaches, *see* Danielle M. Shelton, *Rewriting Rule 68: Realizing the Benefits of the Federal Settlement Rule by Injecting Certainty into Offers of Judgment*, 91 Minn. L. Rev. 865 (2007); Robert G. Bone, *"To Encourage Settlement": Rule 68, Offers of Judgment, and the History of the Federal Rules of Civil Procedure*, 102 Nw. U. L. Rev. 1561 (2008).

## 4. Conditional Offer of Settlement

What if the defendant offers a settlement whose terms include waiver of the attorneys' fees, notwithstanding a statutory provision calling for the defendant to pay the fee of a prevailing plaintiff? In *Evans v. Jeff D.*, 475 U.S. 717 (1986), the lawyers for a class-action plaintiff group of children with disabilities faced precisely this question when the defendant offered to settle and provide "virtually all of the injunctive relief" to improve the children's health care treatment as sought in the complaint—provided that the plaintiffs would waive statutory attorneys' fees. The plaintiff's attorney claimed that this offer violated the statute and would undermine its purpose of promoting precisely this kind of successful lawsuit. The lawyer claimed that he faced an ethical conflict between the interests of his current client and the interests of potential future clients with similar claims whose cases he would not be able to take because of the risk of forgoing attorneys' fees even in a successful case. The Supreme Court rejected this argument:

> Although respondents contend that Johnson, as counsel for the class, was faced with an "ethical dilemma" when petitioners offered him relief greater than that which he could reasonably have expected to obtain for his clients at trial (if only he would stipulate to a waiver of the statutory fee award), . . . we do not believe that the "dilemma" was an "ethical" one in the sense that Johnson had to choose between conflicting duties under the prevailing norms of professional conduct. Plainly Johnson had no *ethical* obligation to seek a statutory fee award. His ethical duty was to serve his clients loyally and competently. Since the proposal to settle the merits was more favorable than the probable outcome of the trial, Johnson's decision to recommend acceptance was consistent with the highest standards of our profession.

475 U.S. at 727-728.

# Comments and Questions

1. Special problems in *Evans v. Jeff D.* arose because the case was a class action composed of children with disabilities. Therefore, the option of a full discussion between attorney and client about whether to accept a settlement that waives attorneys' fees was unavailable. Could an individual, competent adult client make a sensible choice about whether or not to waive attorneys' fees as part of a settlement offer?

2. Perhaps the most widespread response to the issue presented in *Evans v. Jeff D.* is the use of contractual provisions between lawyers and their clients that forbid the client from waiving court-awarded fees. Are there any problems with this kind of agreement? Should the rules of professional ethics forbid it?

3. Taking *Evans v. Jeff D.* and *Marek v. Chesny* together, what policies provide the basis for the federal tendency toward settlement and toward litigation encouraged by pro-plaintiff fee shifts? Would you strike the balance differently? What factors are most relevant to this judgment? Note how the balance affects (a) when lawsuits should be filed; (b) when already filed lawsuits should be settled; and (c) when lawsuits should be followed through to judgments and precedential effects.

4. A series of additional Supreme Court decisions have addressed fee shifting, largely acting to limit access to fees. Plaintiffs cannot obtain attorneys' fees when their lawsuit was merely a "catalyst" that led the defendant to change an illegal practice. *Buckhannon Bd. & Care Home, Inc. v. W. Va. Dep't of Health & Human Res.*, 532 U.S. 598, 600-601 (2001). Nor can plaintiffs be awarded attorneys' fees when they obtain a preliminary injunction if that injunction is subsequently dissolved or reversed. *Sole v. Wyner*, 551 U.S. 74, 86 (2007). How do these limitations on fees alter the calculus for plaintiff's lawyers? Do they raise any ethical issues for defense lawyers?

## 5. *Frivolous Claims*

As noted in the introduction to this section, a defendant may receive an award of fees under § 1988 in lawsuits bringing frivolous claims, but only for fees and costs that the defendant would not have incurred but for the frivolous claims. *Fox v. Vice*, 131 S. Ct. 2205 (2011). Defining a frivolous claim is notoriously difficult. In *Fox*, Justice Kagan explained:

> . . . In enacting § 1988, we stated, Congress sought "to protect defendants from burdensome litigation having no legal or factual basis." Accordingly, § 1988 authorizes a district court to award attorney's fees to a defendant "upon a finding that the plaintiff's action was frivolous, unreasonable, or without foundation." . . . These standards would be easy to apply if life were like the movies, but that is usually not the case. In Hollywood, litigation most often concludes

with a dramatic verdict that leaves one party fully triumphant and the other utterly prostrate. The court in such a case would know exactly how to award fees (even if that anti-climactic scene is generally left on the cutting-room floor). But in the real world, litigation is more complex, involving multiple claims for relief that implicate a mix of legal theories and have different merits. Some claims succeed; others fail. Some charges are frivolous; others (even if not ultimately successful) have a reasonable basis. In short, litigation is messy, and courts must deal with this untidiness in awarding fees.

131 S. Ct. at 2214.

The issue of frivolous claims is raised here because fee shifting enables litigation, raising concerns in some circles that it enables too much litigation. These issues will be revisited in Chapter 3's discussion of pleadings doctrine and sanctions under Fed. R. Civ. P. 11.

## 6. Assessing the Value of Legal Services

When a court awards attorneys' fees, how should those fees be calculated? Billing practices by attorneys vary widely. Traditionally, lawyers in this country have billed for each hour of service, but lawyers charge different hourly rates based on their years of experience, demonstrated expertise, access to colleagues with other expertise, or other reputational features. Percentage contingent fees are a long-standing alternative, especially in the field of personal injuries; the attorney and client agree by contract that the attorney will share a specified percentage of any award or settlement. Increasingly, lawyers explore other billing practices, including set fees for certain services, yearly salary (for in-house counsel, prepaid legal services plans, or legal aid lawyers), or a mixture of methods. Should the attorneys' fees awarded under a fee-shifting statute be subjected to a judicial inquiry as to their reasonableness—and if so, how should they be measured? Should the court inquire about the relationship between the fees and the amount recovered? The following case illuminates these questions.

## ■ CITY OF RIVERSIDE v. RIVERA
### 477 U.S. 561 (1986)

Justice BRENNAN announced the judgment of the Court and delivered an opinion in which Justice MARSHALL, Justice BLACKMUN and Justice STEVENS join:

The issue presented in this case is whether an award of attorney's fees under 42 U.S.C. § 1988 is per se "unreasonable" within the meaning of the statute if it exceeds the amount of damages recovered by the plaintiff in the underlying civil rights action.

**I**

Respondents, eight Chicano individuals, attended a party on the evening of August 1, 1975, at the Riverside, California, home of respondents Santos and Jennie Rivera. A large number of unidentified police officers, acting without a warrant, broke up the party using tear gas and, as found by the District Court, "unnecessary physical force." Many of the guests, including four of the respondents, were arrested. The District Court later found that "[t]he party was not creating a disturbance in the community at the time of the break-in." . . . Criminal charges against the arrestees were ultimately dismissed for lack of probable cause.

On June 4, 1976, respondents sued the city of Riverside, its Chief of Police, and 30 individual police officers under 42 U.S.C. §§ 1981, 1983, 1985(3), and 1986 for allegedly violating their First, Fourth, and Fourteenth Amendment rights. The complaint, which also alleged numerous state-law claims, sought damages and declaratory and injunctive relief. On August 5, 1977, 23 of the individual police officers moved for summary judgment; the District Court granted summary judgment in favor of 17 of these officers. The case against the remaining defendants proceeded to trial in September 1980. The jury returned a total of 37 individual verdicts in favor of the respondents and against the city and five individual officers, finding 11 violations of § 1983, 4 instances of false arrest and imprisonment, and 22 instances of negligence. Respondents were awarded $33,350 in compensatory and punitive damages: $13,300 for their federal claims, and $20,050 for their state-law claims.

Respondents also sought attorney's fees and costs under § 1988. They requested compensation for 1,946.75 hours expended by their two attorneys at a rate of $125 per hour, and for 84.5 hours expended by law clerks at a rate of $25 per hour, a total of $245,456.25. The District Court found both the hours and rates reasonable, and awarded respondents $245,456.25 in attorney's fees. The court rejected respondents' request for certain additional expenses, and for a multiplier sought by respondents to reflect the contingent nature of their success and the high quality of their attorneys' efforts.

Petitioners appealed only the attorney's fees award, which the Court of Appeals for the Ninth Circuit affirmed. *Rivera v. City of Riverside*, 679 F.2d 795 (1982). Petitioners sought a writ of certiorari from this Court. We granted the writ, vacated the Court of Appeals' judgment, and remanded the case for reconsideration in light of *Hensley v. Eckerhart*, 461 U.S. 424 (1983). On remand, the District Court held two additional hearings, reviewed additional briefing, and reexamined the record as a whole. The court made extensive findings of fact and conclusions of law, and again concluded that respondents were entitled to an award of $245,456.25 in attorney's fees, based on the same total number of hours expended on the case and the same hourly rates. The court again denied respondents' request for certain expenses and for a multiplier.

Petitioners again appealed the fee award. And again, the Court of Appeals affirmed, finding that "the district court correctly reconsidered the case in light of *Hensley*. . . ." 763 F.2d 1580, 1582 (1985). The Court of Appeals rejected three arguments raised by petitioners. First, the court rejected petitioners' contention that respondents' counsel should not have been compensated for time spent litigating claims other than those upon which respondents ultimately prevailed. Emphasizing that the District Court had determined that respondents' attorneys had "spent no time on claims unrelated to the successful claims," *ibid.*, the Court of Appeals concluded that "[t]he record supports the district court's findings that all of the plaintiffs' claims involve a 'common core of facts' and that the claims involve related legal theories." *Ibid.* The court also observed that, consistent with *Hensley*, the District Court had "considered the degree of success [achieved by respondents' attorneys] and found a reasonable relationship between the extent of that success and the amount of the fee award." 763 F.2d, at 1582. Second, the Court of Appeals rejected the argument that the fee award was excessive because it exceeded the amount of damages awarded by the jury. Examining the legislative history of § 1988, the court found no support for the proposition that an award of attorney's fees may not exceed the amount of damages recovered by a prevailing plaintiff. Finally, the court found that the District Court's "extensive findings of fact and conclusions of law" belied petitioners' claim that the District Court had not reviewed the record to determine whether the fee award was justified. . . .

## II

### A

. . . Congress enacted the Civil Rights Attorney's Fees Awards Act of 1976, 42 U.S.C. § 1988, which authorized the district courts to award reasonable attorney's fees to prevailing parties in specified civil rights litigation. [T]he statute itself does not explain what constitutes a reasonable fee. . . .

*Hensley v. Eckerhart*, 461 U.S. 424 (1983), announced certain guidelines for calculating a reasonable attorney's fee under § 1988. *Hensley* stated that "[t]he most useful starting point for determining the amount of a reasonable fee is the number of hours reasonably expended on the litigation multiplied by a reasonable hourly rate." *Id.*, at 433. This figure, commonly referred to as the "lodestar," is presumed to be the reasonable fee contemplated by § 1988. The opinion cautioned that "[t]he district court . . . should exclude from this initial fee calculation hours that were not 'reasonably expended'" on the litigation. *Id.*, at 434 (quoting Senate Report, at 6). . . .

### B

Petitioners argue that the District Court failed properly to follow *Hensley* in calculating respondents' fee award. We disagree. The District Court carefully considered the results obtained by respondents pursuant to the instructions set forth in *Hensley*, and concluded that respondents were entitled to recover attorney's fees for all hours expended on the litigation. First, the court found that "[t]he amount of time expended by counsel in conducting this litigation was reasonable and reflected sound legal judgment under the circumstances." The court also determined that counsel's excellent performances in this case entitled them to be compensated at prevailing market rates, even though they were relatively young when this litigation began. *See Johnson*, 488 F.2d, at 718-719 ("If a young attorney demonstrates the skill and ability, he should not be penalized for only recently being admitted to the bar").

The District Court then concluded that it was inappropriate to adjust respondents' fee award downward to account for the fact that respondents had prevailed only on some of their claims, and against only some of the defendants. The court first determined that "it was never actually clear what officer did what until we had gotten through with the whole trial," so that "[u]nder the circumstances of this case, it was reasonable for plaintiffs initially to name thirty-one individual defendants . . . as well as the City of Riverside as defendants in this action." . . .

The District Court also considered the amount of damages recovered, and determined that the size of the damages award did not imply that respondents' success was limited:

> [T]he size of the jury award resulted from (a) the general reluctance of jurors to make large awards against police officers, and (b) the dignified restraint which the plaintiffs exercised in describing their injuries to the jury. For example, although some of the actions of the police would clearly have been insulting and humiliating to even the most insensitive person and were, in the opinion of the Court, intentionally so, plaintiffs did not attempt to play up this aspect of the case.

*Id.*, at 188-189. The court paid particular attention to the fact that the case "presented complex and interrelated issues of fact and law," *id.*, at 187, and that "[a] fee award in this civil rights action will . . . advance the public interest." . . .

Based on our review of the record, we agree with the Court of Appeals that the District Court's findings were not clearly erroneous. We conclude that the District Court correctly applied the factors announced in *Hensley* in calculating respondents' fee award, and that the court did not abuse its discretion in awarding attorney's fees for all time reasonably spent litigating the case.

## III

Petitioners, joined by the United States as amicus curiae, maintain that *Hensley*'s lodestar approach is inappropriate in civil rights cases where a plaintiff recovers only monetary damages. In these cases, so the argument goes, use of the lodestar may result in fees that exceed the amount of damages recovered and that are therefore unreasonable. Likening such cases to private tort actions, petitioners and the United States submit that attorney's fees in such cases should be proportionate to the amount of damages a plaintiff recovers. Specifically, they suggest that fee awards in damages cases should be modeled upon the contingent-fee arrangements commonly used in personal injury litigation. In this case, assuming a 33% contingency rate, this would entitle respondents to recover approximately $11,000 in attorneys fees.

The amount of damages a plaintiff recovers is certainly relevant to the amount of attorney's fees to be awarded under § 1988. *See Johnson*, 488 F.2d, at 718. It is, however, only one of many factors that a court should consider in calculating an award of attorney's fees. We reject the proposition that fee awards under § 1988 should necessarily be proportionate to the amount of damages a civil rights plaintiff actually recovers.

### A

As an initial matter, we reject the notion that a civil rights action for damages constitutes nothing more than a private tort suit benefiting only the individual plaintiffs whose rights were violated. Unlike most private tort litigants, a civil rights plaintiff seeks to vindicate important civil and constitutional rights that cannot be valued solely in monetary terms. . . .

### B

A rule that limits attorney's fees in civil rights cases to a proportion of the damages awarded would seriously undermine Congress' purpose in enacting § 1988. Congress enacted § 1988 specifically because it found that the private market for legal services failed to provide many victims of civil rights violations with effective access to the judicial process. These victims ordinarily cannot afford to purchase legal services at the rates set by the private market. . . . Moreover, the contingent fee arrangements that make legal services available to many victims of personal injuries would often not encourage lawyers to accept civil rights cases, which frequently involve substantial expenditures of time and effort but produce only small monetary recoveries. . . .

Justice POWELL, concurring in the judgment:

I join only the Court's judgment. The plurality opinion reads our decision in *Hensley v. Eckerhart*, 461 U.S. 424 (1983), more expansively than I would, and more expansively than is necessary to decide this case. For me affirmance—quite simply—is required by the District Court's detailed findings of fact, which were approved by the Court of Appeals. On its face, the fee award seems unreasonable. But I find no basis for this Court to reject the findings made and approved by the courts below. . . .

Federal Rule of Civil Procedure 52(a) provides that "[f]indings of fact [by a district court] shall not be set aside unless clearly erroneous. . . ." The Court of Appeals did not disagree with any of the foregoing findings by the District Court. I see no basis on which this Court now could hold that these findings are clearly erroneous. To be sure, some of the findings fairly can be viewed as conclusions or matters of opinion, but the findings that are critical to the judgments of the courts below are objective facts. . . .

Petitioners argue for a rule of proportionality between the fee awarded and the damages recovered in a civil rights case. Neither the decisions of this Court nor the legislative history of § 1988 support such a "rule." The facts and circumstances of litigation are infinitely variable. . . .

Chief Justice BURGER, dissenting:

I join Justice Rehnquist's dissenting opinion. I write only to add that it would be difficult to find a better example of legal nonsense than the fixing of attorney's fees by a judge at $245,456.25 for the recovery of $33,350 damages.

The two attorneys receiving this nearly quarter-million-dollar fee graduated from law school in 1973 and 1974; they brought this action in 1975, which resulted in the $33,350 jury award in 1980. Their total professional experience when this litigation began consisted of Gerald Lopez' 1-year service as a law clerk to a judge and Roy Cazares' two years' experience as a trial attorney in the Defenders' Program of San Diego County. For their services the District Court found that an hourly rate of $125 per hour was reasonable.

Can anyone doubt that no private party would ever have dreamed of paying these two novice attorneys $125 per hour in 1975, which, considering inflation, would represent perhaps something more nearly a $250 per hour rate today? . . .

This fee award plainly constitutes a grave abuse of discretion which should be rejected by this Court—particularly when we have already vacated and remanded this identical fee award previously—rather than simply affirming the District Court's findings as not being either "clearly erroneous" or an "abuse of discretion." The Court's result will unfortunately only add fuel to the fires of public indignation over the costs of litigation.

Justice REHNQUIST, with whom the CHIEF JUSTICE, Justice WHITE, and Justice O'CONNOR join, dissenting:

I see no escape from the conclusion that the District Court's finding that respondents' attorneys "reasonably" spent 1,946.75 hours to recover a money judgment of $33,350 is clearly erroneous, and that therefore the District Court's award of $245,456.25 in attorney's fees to respondents should be reversed. The Court's affirmance of the fee award emasculates the principles laid down in *Hensley*, and turns § 1988 into a relief Act for lawyers.

A brief look at the history of this case reveals just how "unreasonable" it was for respondents' lawyers to spend so much time on it. Respondents filed their initial complaint in 1976, seeking injunctive and declaratory relief and compensatory and punitive damages from the city of Riverside, its Chief of Police, and 30 police officers, based on 256 separate claims allegedly arising out of the police breakup of a single party. Prior to trial, 17 of the police officers were dismissed from the case on motions for summary judgment, and respondents dropped their requests for injunctive and declaratory relief. More significantly, respondents also dropped their original allegation that the police had acted with discriminatory intent. The action proceeded to trial, and the jury completely exonerated nine additional police officers. Respondents ultimately prevailed against only the city and five police officers on various § 1983, false arrest and imprisonment, and common negligence claims. No restraining orders or injunctions were ever issued against petitioners, nor was the city ever compelled to change a single practice or policy as a result of respondents' suit. The jury awarded respondents a total of $33,350 in compensatory and punitive damages. Only about one-third of this total, or $13,300, was awarded to respondents based on violations of their federal constitutional rights. . . .

The analysis of whether the extraordinary number of hours put in by respondents' attorneys in this case was "reasonable" must be made in light of both the traditional billing practices in the profession, and the fundamental principle that the award of a "reasonable" attorney's fee under § 1988 means a fee that would have been deemed reasonable if billed to affluent plaintiffs by their own attorneys. . . .

## Comments and Questions

1. What response did the plurality give to the dissent's claim that it was wasteful to spend $245,456.25 in attorneys' fees to win $33,350 in compensation? What response would you have given?

2. Should attorneys' fees be calculated any differently when the relief is injunctive, versus when the relief is money damages?

3. Consider as alternatives to the method for determining attorneys' fees used in *City of Riverside* a simple percentage of recovery, William J. Lynk, *The Court and Plaintiff's Bar: Awarding the Attorney's Fees in Class Action Litigation*, 23 J. Legal Stud. 185, 187 (1994), or modeling what an auction for the right to serve as lawyer would generate in an actual market, *see The Paths of Civil Litigation: Class Actions: Market Models for Attorneys' Fees in Class Action Litigation*, 113 Harv. L. Rev. 1827 (2000).

4. Does the central difficulty in *City of Riverside* stem from hourly billing? What other ways of assessing the value of lawyers' work could provide compensation and incentive to lawyers to undertake appropriate cases? Most attorneys in private practice base their fees on the number of hours they work on a matter, often billing in six-minute increments. Annual billings in excess of 2,000 hours per year is common in larger firms and firms link billed hours to substantial bonuses awarded to their associates. The hourly billing model raises three concerns. First, hourly billing may encourage inefficiency. Second, it may encourage excessive litigation. Third, it may encourage fraud. It is difficult to determine how much unethical billing goes on. In the increasingly tight legal market, clients are extremely cost sensitive and firms are increasingly required to justify their bills with detailed explanations of the work performed. A 1991 study found that most lawyers denied engaging in unethical billing practices such as "padding" hours. *See* William G. Ross, *The Ethics of Hourly Billing by Attorneys*, 44 Rutgers L. Rev. 1 (1991). As you learn

more about the process of civil litigation, consider how the Rules of Civil Procedure might provide opportunities for increasing billed hours in ways that do not necessarily benefit the client. The discovery process, which you will read about in Chapter 4, has been a particular subject of criticism for encouraging unnecessary attorney labor and a concomitant increase in fees. Some law firms have sought to encourage business by switching to a flat rate approach, such as billing a flat rate per task. Another alternative is the contingency fee, discussed next.

## 7. *The Contingency Fee*

An American innovation, the contingency fee is the leading alternative to hourly billing by attorneys. Typically, the client signs an agreement drafted by the attorney that promises to pay the attorney a specified percentage, usually one-third, of any recovery achieved through the litigation, and simultaneously makes it clear that the client will owe no fee if there is no recovery. Under state judicial and ethics rules, such arrangements do not violate traditional norms against champerty, in which a person not a party to a suit agrees to invest in it in return for a share in the profits, while also providing for judicial review to ensure reasonable terms in contingency agreements.

What effect does this billing practice have on attorneys? The contingency fee in a real sense makes the lawyer an investor or joint venturer with the client. To proceed with the lawsuit, the lawyer has to invest time and potentially further resources for experts, court costs, and investigative work. The lawyer therefore must make judgments about which cases are worth taking "on speculation"; some must pay off if the lawyer is to stay in business over time.

The contingency fee also affects how much time a lawyer puts into a case, what the lawyer does with that time, and how the lawyer views settlements (and clients). One economic analysis suggests that the lawyer "should continue to devote hours to [a given contingency fee case] only as long as each additional hour increased his fee by at least as much as his opportunity cost," meaning the cost of forgoing work on another matter. Kevin M. Clermont and John D. Currivan, *Improving on the Contingent Fee*, 63 Cornell L. Rev. 529 (1978). Perhaps lawyers paid on a contingent fee basis will spend fewer hours on a case than would be optimal for the client (if the case appears to be a losing one), and lawyers paid on an hourly basis will put in more than the optimal number of hours. One study, based on court records and interviews with 371 hourly fee lawyers and 267 contingent fee lawyers from twelve state and federal courts concluded that:

> . . . the contingent fee lawyer appears sensitive to the potential return to be achieved from a case, which is closely related to the stakes. The hourly fee lawyer's return from a case is not as tied to stakes, and other types of considerations (*e.g.*, the client's goals, the nature of the forum, etc.) have a greater influence.

Herbert M. Kritzer, William L.F. Felstiner, Austin Sarat, and David M. Tru-bek, *The Impact of Fee Arrangement on Lawyer Effort*, 19 L. & Soc'y Rev. 251, 271 (1985).

In *Venegas v. Mitchell*, 495 U.S. 82 (1990), the Supreme Court considered whether a federal fee-shifting statute invalidates contingent-fee contracts that would require a prevailing plaintiff to pay his attorney more than the statutory award against the defendant. Mitchell was hired three months before the trial of Venegas' civil rights suit against city police officers (alleging false arrest and perjured trial), after the bulk of preparation had been completed. Mitchell obtained a $10,000 non-refundable retainer and a right to share in 40 percent of the gross amount of any recovery. After trial, the defendants unsuccessfully moved to set aside the judgment and then appealed. Mitchell pursued and obtained statutory attorneys' fees under 42 U.S.C. § 1988, which the court calculated by multiplying the hours of attorney time by a market-based hourly rate. Mitchell then sought 40 percent of the judgment proceeds. The court agreed to enforce the contingency fee arrangement. On review, the Supreme Court concluded that private fee arrangements may exist alongside statutory fee shifts, and therefore permitted enforcement of the contingency fee arrangement at issue. Perhaps the problem in the case arose from the method for assessing the value of the lawyer's time.

An advocacy group called Common Good has launched a proposal to coordinate incentives to settle and attorneys' fees by limiting the scope of contingency fees (essentially limited to tort cases). *See* Adam Liptak, *In 13 States, a Push to Limit Lawyers' Fees*, N.Y. Times, May 26, 2003. The proposal would limit the fees in many cases to 10 percent of the first $100,000 of a settlement, with 5 percent of any further settlement amount. Under the proposal, at the start of the case a plaintiff's attorney must write the defendant's attorney with a description of the injury and explanation of the defendant's liability. If the defense responds with a settlement offer and the plaintiff accepts it, the cap on the contingency fee for the plaintiff's attorney would apply. If that attorney neglected to send such a letter at all, the fee would be similarly capped regardless of how many hours or what degree of success for the plaintiff emerge. Consider how the proposal would affect the adversary system, the settlement rate, and the balance of power between plaintiff and defendant; would you support the proposal?

## 8. *Third-Party Litigation Financing*

Traditionally, contingency fee lawyers self-funded litigation. The newest development in litigation financing is financing by third-party investors. Consider the limits and possibilities of third-party litigation financing laid out in the following excerpt.

# ■ JONATHAN T. MOLOT, LITIGATION FINANCE: A MARKET SOLUTION TO A PROCEDURAL PROBLEM
*99 Geo. L.J. 65, 92-100 (2010)*

There are several different ways that U.S. investors have sought to profit from investments in litigation claims, each of which is briefly discussed below.

*a. The Cash Advance Industry for Personal Injury Victims.* Over the last decade or so, a relatively new "cash advance" industry has developed. Cash advance firms offer personal injury victims cash advances while their personal injury lawsuits are pending. Most of these firms structure their advances as nonrecourse loans. The transactions are loans insofar as the cash advance firm charges a fixed interest rate on the funds advanced, rather than receiving a specified percentage of the plaintiffs' recovery the way attorneys do under a contingent fee arrangement. Yet, they are nonrecourse loans because the plaintiff need only pay back the advance if the lawsuit succeeds. The cash advance firm accepts the risk that the lawsuit will result in a defense verdict or a recovery that is less than the amount owed by the plaintiff.

There are serious problems with this cash advance system. The problems stem from the very high interest rates charged by cash advance firms— typically 3% to 5% monthly interest, and often much higher. The high interest rate is a problem for two reasons. First, it strips the risk-transfer mechanism of much of its value for the plaintiff. If our goal is to ensure that plaintiffs receive what they are entitled to under substantive law, it does no good if the plaintiff must pay away much of that value in interest. Second, the rapid accumulation of interest undermines our goal of bolstering plaintiffs' bargaining position vis-à-vis repeat player defendants. A plaintiff whose net recovery declines the longer he or she goes without settling will have strong incentives to settle quickly, and have a much harder time rejecting low settlement offers and holding out for more. . . .

The high interest rates charged by cash advance firms are partly a product of the risk involved, but they are also partly a byproduct of government regulation. Cash advance firms structure their products to avoid two areas of government regulation. First, by charging a fixed interest rate, rather than taking a share of the plaintiffs' recovery, cash advance firms avoid prohibitions against champerty and maintenance that historically have prevented third parties from funding litigation in exchange for a share of the recovery. . . . To avoid usury restrictions imposed on traditional loans, the cash advance firms make repayment of the advances entirely conditional on success in the lawsuit. . . .

Rather than paying a high, compounding interest rate a plaintiff might be far better-off simply selling a percentage of his recovery to a cash advance firm, just as he does to his attorney. . . . Just as plaintiffs today can use contingent fee arrangements to protect themselves from the downside risk of losing and being on the hook for legal fees, so too could plaintiffs sell an interest in a third of their cases to cash advance firms, thereby protecting themselves from the risk of collecting nothing. . . .

There are two obstacles to this shift from charging high interest rates to taking a share of the recovery. The first is economic. The diligence required of a cash advance firm to ensure that a lawsuit is worth more than a fixed amount is not as great as the diligence required to put a precise value on the suit. . . .

State regulation is a second obstacle that prevents cash advance firms from charging a percentage of the recovery. . . . [A]lthough many states have done away with champerty and maintenance restrictions, others have not. Before cash advance firms could routinely take shares of recoveries from personal injury victims, they would need to seek clarification or reform of the law and would have to structure their transactions very carefully.

*b. Investment in Commercial Litigation by Investment Funds.* . . . Some investment funds and investment banks have begun to buy interests in commercial lawsuits. . . . Hedge funds, and some traders at investment banks, have long viewed litigation risk as attractive because it is uncorrelated with markets—the outcome of a lawsuit will not depend upon fluctuations in the stock or bond markets. . . . Even if a fund can accurately predict the outcome of a pending lawsuit, [however,] the stock price of the company that is a party to that lawsuit will depend upon many factors outside of the pending litigation. . . .

For a fund that wants to make a clean bet on a lawsuit—a bet that will expose it to pure litigation risk while neutralizing other factors that can affect a company's share price—the most attractive course is to make a direct investment in the lawsuit. The hedge fund can offer the plaintiff cash for a portion of the recovery where the plaintiff needs cash or simply wants to reduce his exposure to litigation risk. . . . By selling part of its claim, the plaintiff can both eliminate the cost of pursuing the claim and monetize a portion of the claim to fuel the company's growth. . . . By enlisting the help and cash of a third party, the plaintiff may be able to bolster its negotiating position vis-à-vis the defendant, thereby increasing its recovery. . . .

Where commercial claims are involved, rather than personal injury claims, it is easy to structure transactions so that the capital provider takes a percentage of the recovery without running afoul of any potentially applicable maintenance or champerty restrictions. Lawsuits that are held by corporate entities can be sold simply by selling ownership interests in the relevant corporate entities—ownership interests with returns that may be tied to the recovery in the relevant lawsuit. Indeed, complicated structuring may be entirely unnecessary because most champerty and maintenance laws are confined to "personal" actions, like personal injury suits, and do not restrict the sale of commercial claims. Moreover, the pricing problems that may get in the way of cash advance firms buying a percentage of a personal injury claim are less daunting in the commercial claim context. It is much less costly and time consuming to value one $50 million commercial suit than to value one-thousand different $50,000 lawsuits, provided that each suit has its own individual set of facts and legal issues. Expected returns can cover the diligence expenses associated with such a large investment. . . .

   *c. Law-Firm Finance.* Investment-fund capital has been of some use not only to small companies with large commercial claims, but also, in some instances, to law firms that want to take in capital and off-load risk associated with contingent fee cases. Recall that one limitation of the contingent fee system is that it does not permit lawyers to share fees with nonlawyers. However, some of the same entities that buy interests in lawsuits from plaintiffs have recently found ways to make investments in litigation via law firms. These investments in law firms, like investments in personal injury claims, are structured as loans rather than as the sale of a portion of claims. Unlike maintenance and champerty restrictions that have been relaxed in many states to permit litigation plaintiffs to sell portions of their claims, the ethical prohibition against attorney fee sharing is uniform. Only the District of Columbia permits lawyers to share fees with nonlawyers, though this permission is limited to other professionals, like accountants or lobbyists, who work side-by-side with lawyers in partnerships and take a share of profits for their work. No state permits lawyers to give away a portion of their legal fees—whether contingent fees or hourly fees—in exchange for a capital infusion from an investment fund.

   Lawyers are, however, permitted to borrow money. And, just as cash advance firms make nonrecourse loans to personal injury victims, so too might investors make loans to law firms that are recoverable only out of the law firms' revenues for legal services rendered. The interest rates for these law-firm loans might not be quite as high as for personal injury victims, but they would still be quite high—25% per year or greater, depending upon the risk involved. . . .

   Why, one might wonder, would a law firm ever agree to pay such a high rate of interest? Do law firms really need outside financing? Outside the U.S., the answer has been yes, and at least regulators in Australia have moved toward allowing lawyers to raise capital from outside investors and even toward offering shares to the public. . . . In the United States, where equity-based financing is prohibited, would lawyers similarly be inclined to resort to outside financing, even if it must be in the form of debt, rather than equity? Different law firms may have different reasons for raising capital from outside investors or lenders. A law firm that generally works for a contingent fee may find that it has taken on a large, potentially quite profitable case, but lacks the resources to litigate a large, drawnout battle with the defendant. . . . Conventional bank loans may not suffice given the extent of the risk involved. For lawyers unwilling or unable to guarantee their law firms' loans personally, borrowing money from an investment fund at a high rate of interest may make sense. If the cases are sufficiently large and promising, the lawyers may still hope to make a great deal of money after paying off loans at a 25% interest rate . . . Outside financing might also be of value to a risk-averse law firm that generally bills by the hour and is presented with attractive contingent fee opportunities. . . .

Law-firm finance represents a way for attorneys to take on risk through contingent fee arrangements, and then spread that risk over a broader pool of investors who are better able to bear it. As with the cash advance industry, however, the high-interest loan structure is not ideal if the ultimate goal is to bolster the bargaining power of risk-averse plaintiffs pitted against repeat-player defendants. A law firm paying interest on an outstanding loan, like a plaintiff who has received a cash advance, will have a strong incentive to settle early and repay its debt from the proceeds.

## Comments and Questions

1. Consider the three forms of litigation financing in light of the discussion in Chapter 1 about access to justice. Would these different types of litigation financing allow more access to the courts for the underserved, would they increase litigation needlessly, or would they have no effect? How would one go about finding out?

2. The Federal Rules do not explicitly take into account the cost of financing litigation, although they have been revised with those costs in mind, nor do the rules apply differently to different types of litigation. Instead, the Rules are trans-substantive. Should the Rules explicitly take into account the different types of financing available for different litigants?

## Practice Exercise No. 6: Fee Arrangements in *Carpenter* and *City of Cleveland*

Return to the *Carpenter* and *City of Cleveland* cases. Assume that you have been approached by the plaintiff(s) in each case to represent them. Estimate the relief available and the statutory attorneys' fees (if any). Should you take these cases, and, if so, under what contractual terms for attorneys' fees? How would you handle costs and disbursements?

## F. CONTEMPT

A party or lawyer who disobeys a court order or court rule risks being found in contempt of court. A court's contempt power extends to both civil and criminal contempt, but the distinction between the two types of contempt has caused much confusion among courts and law students alike. In the leading case distinguishing the two types of contempt, the Supreme Court stated that "[c]ontempts are neither wholly civil nor altogether criminal. And it may not always be easy to classify a particular act as belonging to either one of these two classes. It may partake of the characteristics of both." *Gompers v. Buck's Stove & Range Co.*, 221 U.S. 418 (1911) (internal quotations omitted).

Generally speaking, civil contempt is tied up with ongoing litigation, and is meant to induce some sort of outcome or remedy. The punishment is remedial and thus can be indefinite; the contempt is alleviated when the individual in contempt acquiesces to the court's will. For example, a party may be found to be in civil contempt for refusing to provide requested documents. The party may be conditionally punished until such time that the party agrees to produce the required documents. In *Turner v. Rogers*, reproduced in Chapter 1, a South Carolina court held a father who did not pay child support in civil contempt. By contrast, criminal contempt involves punishment for violating a court order or interfering with court power. While civil contempt is intended to compel, criminal contempt is expressly punitive. Thus, punishment of criminal contempt must be definite and in accordance with the rules and procedures of criminal law, including a higher burden of proof. Unlike civil contempt, criminal contempt is adjudicated independently from other litigation. Examples of acts giving rise to criminal contempt proceedings include threatening a judge and obstructing court proceedings. For a useful comparison of civil and criminal contempt, see Jennifer Fleischer, *In Defense of Civil Contempt Sanctions*, 36 Colum. J .L. & Soc. Probs. 35 (2002).

On occasion, individuals deliberately disobey court orders just as they may disobey a statute in order to protest or challenge a rule or norm they consider unjust. In recent years, protestors have violated rules governing access to abortion clinics and military settings. *See, e.g., Jayne Bray v. Alexandria Women's Health Clinic*, 506 U.S. 263 (1993) (pro-life protest); *United States and Connecticut v. Carmen E.F. Vasquez*, 145 F.3d 74 (2d Cir. 1998) (same); *United States v. Albertini*, 472 U.S. 676 (1985) (anti-nuclear protest); *United States v. Springer*, 51 F.3d 861 (9th Cir. 1995) (same). When someone disobeys a *statute* and faces criminal or civil consequences, there usually is a chance to offer a defense and a challenge to the law at issue in the course of a judicial hearing. After a court finds a party in contempt for violating its order, should that party be able to defend the noncompliance by arguing the order was itself unlawful? Would failing to give such an opportunity undermine due process or substantive justice? Or would giving such an opportunity invite further violations of court orders and disrespect for judicial power? The leading case on the subject grew out of the civil rights effort, led by the Reverend Martin Luther King, Jr., to challenge racial segregation in Birmingham, Alabama. David Luban described the historical context for the case in the following excerpt.

## ■ DAVID LUBAN, LEGAL MODERNISM
### *218-220 (1994)*

In January 1963, the Southern Christian Leadership Conference (SCLC) held a retreat in Georgia to discuss strategy for a concerted attack on segregation in Birmingham, Alabama. Project C for "confrontation"—would consist of demonstrations and boycotts of Birmingham's downtown businesses during the normally busy Easter shopping season.

Birmingham itself had recently begun to display some sentiment for change in its segregationist ways. A group of whites headed by the Chamber of Commerce president campaigned to alter Birmingham's municipal government by abolishing the offices of the three segregationist commissioners (including the notoriously racist commissioner of public safety, Theophilus Eugene "Bull" Connor) who then ran the city. The voters agreed to move to a mayoral system, and in a special election, Connor was defeated by a more moderate segregationist named Albert Boutwell. Connor went to court to demand that he be allowed to finish his term of office as commissioner of public safety and while this matter was pending, Birmingham was governed by what were in effect two city governments, each passing its own laws and conducting city business after its own fashion; municipal checks were signed by both Connor and Boutwell. Some Birmingham whites hoped that the SCLC would cancel the Easter demonstrations to give the new government a chance to show what it could do, but the SCLC leadership—which had previously canceled demonstrations to allow the run-off election between Connor and Boutwell to proceed without the pressure of demonstrations—went ahead with Project C.

A Birmingham city ordinance required the demonstrators to obtain a parade permit from the city commission. On April 3, Mrs. Lola Hendricks, representing the demonstrators, approached Connor to request a permit; Connor replied, "No, you will not get a permit in Birmingham, Alabama to picket. I will picket you over to the City Jail." On April 5—one week before Good Friday—Connor replied to a second, telegraphic, request for a parade permit with another refusal. The demonstrators proceeded with their protests.

Project C included plans for the Reverend Martin Luther King, Jr., to place himself in a position to be arrested on Good Friday, April 12.

Late Wednesday evening, April 10, Connor obtained an ex parte injunction from Alabama Circuit Court Judge W. A. Jenkins, Jr., forbidding civil rights leaders, including all the leaders of Project C, from taking part in or encouraging demonstrations. The injunction was served at 1:00 A.M. on Thursday, and the SCLC leadership debated how to respond to it. King feared that complying with the injunction would deflate the protest, as had happened the previous summer in Albany, Georgia. He went ahead with the planned demonstration the following day and was arrested; a second demonstration took place on Easter Sunday, April 14. Subsequently, Judge Jenkins found several of the demonstrators guilty of criminal contempt and sentenced each of them (including King) to five days in jail and a $50 fine. It is this conviction that the *Walker v. City of Birmingham* Court upheld.

This ends the sequence of events recounted in *Walker* and King's Letter. But the largest chronicle of the Birmingham campaign did not end with King's arrest. The demonstrators subsequently embarked on a strategy of marches by schoolchildren, leading to literally thousands of arrests. As the demonstrations continued, Bull Connor upped the level of official response, ordering that fire hoses and police dogs be turned on the demonstrators. Television news horrified its audiences with the spectacle of children bowled over by hoses that hit with enough force to rip the bark off trees. White moderates and the SCLC leadership undertook negotiations that led to a settlement announced on May 10. On May 11, the Ku Klux Klan staged a rally; after the meeting, the motel where King had been staying and the home of his brother were bombed. Crowds of angry blacks rioted, and President Kennedy eventually sent in federal troops. A month later, Alabama Governor George Wallace personally blocked the entrance of a University of Alabama building to prevent the entrance of two black students whose admission had been ordered by a federal court. Evidently this action was the last straw. The same day, President Kennedy spoke on national television to announce that he was seeking comprehensive civil rights legislation that eventually became the Civil Rights Act. This announcement and the march were the culminating events of Project C.

But let us return to King's original April arrest. While King was in jail, eight white clergymen—significantly, they were liberals who had publicly opposed Governor George Wallace's "Segregation Forever!" speech—took out a full-page advertisement in the Birmingham News denouncing the demonstrations. King responded from his cell, writing in the newspaper's margins until he was able to obtain paper; after he was permitted visitors, King's manuscript was typed by his friends and returned to him in jail for revisions. His Letter from Birmingham Jail attracted little attention at first. It was eventually printed by the American Friends Service Committee and reprinted in numerous periodicals; its fame and influence grew, and by now it is perhaps the most famous document to emerge from the civil rights movement. . . .

Point and counterpoint: King's Letter has become one of the great classics in the literature of civil disobedience, both for its philosophy and for the soul-stirring magnificence of its language. No one has called Potter Stewart's *Walker* opinion a classic (in what might be called the literature of civil obedience), but its status as a Supreme Court precedent makes it the functional equivalent of a classic. Both *Walker* and the *Letter* address an ancient question, a question that more than any other defines the very subject of legal philosophy: that, of course, is the question whether we lie under an obligation to obey unjust legal directives, including directives ordering our punishment for disobeying other unjust directives. All political philosophy, from Plato's *Apology* and *Crito* on, is driven by this question; all our political hopes and aspirations are contained in the descriptive and argumentative materials we use to answer it.

# ■ WALKER v. CITY OF BIRMINGHAM
### 388 U.S. 307 (1967)

Justice STEWART delivered the opinion of the Court:
On Wednesday, April 10, 1963, officials of Birmingham, Alabama, filed a bill of complaint in a state circuit court asking for injunctive relief against 139

individuals and two organizations. The bill and accompanying affidavits stated that during the preceding seven days:

> [R]espondents (had) sponsored and/or participated in and/or conspired to commit and/or to encourage and/or to participate in certain movements, plans or projects commonly called "sit-in" demonstrations, "kneel-in" demonstrations, mass street parades, trespasses on private property after being warned to leave the premises by the owners of said property, congregating in mobs upon the public streets and other public places, unlawfully picketing private places of business in the City of Birmingham, Alabama; violation of numerous ordinances and statutes of the City of Birmingham and State of Alabama. . . .

It was alleged that this conduct was "calculated to provoke breaches of the peace," threaten[ed] the safety, peace and tranquility of the City, and placed an undue burden and strain upon the manpower of the Police Department.

The bill stated that these infractions of the law were expected to continue and would "lead to further imminent danger to the lives, safety, peace, tranquility and general welfare of the people of the City of Birmingham," and that the "remedy by law [was] inadequate." The circuit judge granted a temporary [*state circuit judge*] injunction as prayed in the bill, enjoining the petitioners from, among other things, participating in or encouraging mass street parades or mass processions without a permit as required by a Birmingham ordinance.

Five of the eight petitioners were served with copies of the writ early the next morning. Several hours later four of them held a press conference. There a statement was distributed, declaring their intention to disobey the injunction because it was "raw tyranny under the guise of maintaining law and order." At this press conference one of the petitioners stated: "That they had respect for the Federal Courts, or Federal Injunctions, but in the past the State Courts had favored local law enforcement, and if the police couldn't handle it, the mob would."

That night a meeting took place at which one of the petitioners announced that "[i]njunction or no injunction we are going to march tomorrow." The next afternoon, Good Friday, a large crowd gathered in the vicinity of Sixteenth Street and Sixth Avenue North in Birmingham. A group of about 50 or 60 proceeded to parade along the sidewalk while a crowd of 1,000 to 1,500 onlookers stood by, "clapping, and hollering, and [w]hooping." Some of the crowd followed the marchers and spilled out into the street. At least three of the petitioners participated in this march.

Meetings sponsored by some of the petitioners were held that night and the following night, where calls for volunteers to "walk" and go to jail were made. On Easter Sunday, April 14, a crowd of between 1,500 and 2,000 people congregated in the midafternoon in the vicinity of Seventh Avenue and Eleventh Street North in Birmingham. One of the petitioners was seen organizing members of the crowd in formation. A group of about 50, headed by three other petitioners, started down the sidewalk two abreast. At least one other petitioner was among the marchers. Some 300 or 400 people from among the onlookers followed in a crowd that occupied the entire width of the street and overflowed onto the sidewalks. Violence occurred. Members of the crowd threw rocks that injured a newspaperman and damaged a police motorcycle.

The next day the city officials who had requested the injunction applied to the state circuit court for an order to show cause why the petitioners should not be held in contempt for violating it. At the ensuing hearing the petitioners sought to attack the constitutionality of the injunction on the ground that it was vague and overbroad, and restrained free speech. They also sought to attack the Birmingham parade ordinance upon similar grounds, and upon the further ground that the ordinance had previously been administered in an arbitrary and discriminatory manner.

The circuit judge refused to consider any of these contentions, pointing out that there had been neither a motion to dissolve the injunction, nor an effort to comply with it by applying for a permit from the city commission before engaging in the Good Friday and Easter Sunday parades. Consequently, the court held that the only issues before it were whether it had jurisdiction to issue the temporary injunction, and whether thereafter the petitioners had knowingly violated it. Upon these issues the court found against the petitioners, and imposed upon each of them a sentence of five days in jail and a $50 fine, in accord with an Alabama statute.

The Supreme Court of Alabama affirmed. That court, too, declined to consider the petitioners' constitutional attacks upon the injunction and the underlying Birmingham parade ordinance. . . .

Without question the state court that issued the injunction had, as a court of equity, jurisdiction over the petitioners and over the subject matter of the controversy. And this is not a case where the injunction was transparently invalid or had only a frivolous pretense to validity. We have consistently recognized the strong interest of state and local governments in regulating the use of their streets and other public places. . . . When protest takes the form of mass demonstrations, parades, or picketing on public streets and sidewalks, the free passage of traffic and the prevention of public disorder and violence become important objects of legitimate state concern. As the Court stated, in *Cox v. State of Louisiana,* "We emphatically reject the notion . . . that the First and Fourteenth Amendments afford the same kind of freedom to those who would communicate ideas by conduct such as patrolling, marching, and picketing on streets and highways, as these amendments afford to those who communicate ideas by pure speech." 379 U.S. 536, 555. . . .

The generality of the language contained in the Birmingham parade ordinance upon which the injunction was based would unquestionably raise substantial constitutional issues concerning some of its provisions. *Schneider v. State of New Jersey,* 308 U.S. 147; *Saia v. People of State of New York,* 334 U.S. 558; *Kunz v. People of State of New York,* 340 U.S. 290. The petitioners, however, did not even attempt to apply to the Alabama courts for an authoritative construction of the ordinance. Had they done so, those courts might have given the licensing authority granted in the

ordinance a narrow and precise scope. . . . [Here] it could not be assumed that
this ordinance was void on its face.

The breadth and vagueness of the injunction itself would also unquestionably be subject to substantial constitutional question. But the way to raise
that question was to apply to the Alabama courts to have the injunction
modified or dissolved. The injunction in all events clearly prohibited mass
parading without a permit, and the evidence shows that the petitioners fully
understood that prohibition when they violated it.

The petitioners also claim that they were free to disobey the injunction
because the parade ordinance on which it was based had been administered
in the past in an arbitrary and discriminatory fashion. In support of this
claim they sought to introduce evidence that, a few days before the injunction
issued, requests for permits to picket had been made to a member of the city
commission. One request had been rudely rebuffed, and this same official had
later made clear that he was without power to grant the permit alone, since
the issuance of such permits was the responsibility of the entire city
commission. Assuming the truth of this proffered evidence, it does not follow
that the parade ordinance was void on its face. The petitioners, moreover, did
not apply for a permit either to the commission itself or to any commissioner
after the injunction issued. Had they done so, and had the permit been
refused, it is clear that their claim of arbitrary or discriminatory administration of the ordinance would have been considered by the state circuit court
upon a motion to dissolve the injunction.

This case would arise in quite a different constitutional posture if the petitioners, before disobeying the injunction, had challenged it in the Alabama
courts, and had been met with delay or frustration of their constitutional
claims. . . .

The rule of law that Alabama followed in this case reflects a belief that in
the fair administration of justice no man can be judge in his own case,
however exalted his station, however righteous his motives, and irrespective
of his race, color, politics, or religion. This Court cannot hold that the petitioners were constitutionally free to ignore all the procedures of the law and
carry their battle to the streets. . . .

Affirmed.

## APPENDIX TO OPINION OF COURT

### [THE FULL TEXT OF DR. KING'S SPEECH]

In our struggle for freedom we have anchored our faith and hope in the
rightness of the Constitution and the moral laws of the universe.

Again and again the Federal judiciary has made it clear that the privileges guaranteed under the First and the Fourteenth Amendments are too
sacred to be trampled upon by the machinery of state government and police
power. In the past we have abided by Federal injunctions out of respect for the
forthright and consistent leadership that the Federal judiciary has given in
establishing the principle of integration as the law of the land.

However we are now confronted with recalcitrant forces in the Deep South that will use the courts to perpetuate the unjust and illegal system of racial separation.

Alabama has made clear its determination to defy the law of the land. Most of its public officials, its legislative body and many of its law enforcement agents have openly defied the desegregation decision of the Supreme Court. We would feel morally and legally responsible to obey the injunction if the courts of Alabama applied equal justice to all of its citizens. This would be sameness made legal. However the issuance of this injunction is a blatant [example] of difference made legal.

Southern law enforcement agencies have demonstrated now and again that they will utilize the force of law to misuse the judicial process.

This is raw tyranny under the guise of maintaining law and order. We cannot in all good conscience obey such an injunction, which is an unjust, undemocratic and unconstitutional misuse of the legal process.

We do this not out of any disrespect for the law but out of the highest respect for the law. This is not an attempt to evade or defy the law or engage in chaotic anarchy. Just as in all good conscience we cannot obey unjust laws, neither can we respect the unjust use of the courts.

We believe in a system of law based on justice and morality. Out of our great love for the Constitution of the U.S. and our desire to purify the judicial system of the state of Alabama, we risk this critical move with an awareness of the possible consequences involved.

Chief Justice WARREN, with whom Justice BRENNAN and Justice FORTAS join, dissenting:

Petitioners in this case contend that they were convicted under an ordinance that is unconstitutional on its face because it submits their First and Fourteenth Amendment rights to free speech and peaceful assembly to the unfettered discretion of local officials. They further contend that the ordinance was unconstitutionally applied to them because the local officials used their discretion to prohibit peaceful demonstrations by a group whose political viewpoint the officials opposed. The Court does not dispute these contentions, but holds that petitioners may nonetheless be convicted and sent to jail because the patently unconstitutional ordinance was copied into an injunction—issued ex parte without prior notice or hearing on the request of the Commissioner of Public Safety—forbidding all persons having notice of the injunction to violate the ordinance without any limitation of time. I dissent because I do not believe that the fundamental protections of the Constitution were meant to be so easily evaded, or that "the civilizing hand of law" would be hampered in the slightest by enforcing the First Amendment in this case.

The salient facts can be stated very briefly. Petitioners are Negro ministers who sought to express their concern about racial discrimination in Birmingham, Alabama, by holding peaceful protest demonstrations in that city on Good Friday and Easter Sunday 1963. For obvious reasons, it was important for the significance of the demonstrations that they be held on those particular dates. A representative of petitioners' organization went to the City Hall and asked to see the person or persons in charge to issue permits, permits for parading, picketing, and demonstrating. She was directed to Public Safety Commissioner Connor, who denied her request for a permit in terms that left no doubt that petitioners were not going to be issued a permit under any circumstances. He said, "No you will not get a permit in Birmingham, Alabama to picket. I will picket you over to the City Jail," and he repeated that twice. A second, telegraphic request was also summarily denied, in a telegram signed by Eugene "Bull" Connor, with the added information that permits could be issued only by the full City Commission, a three-man body consisting of Commissioner Connor and two others. According to petitioners' offer of proof, the truth of which is assumed for purposes of this case, parade permits had uniformly been issued for all other groups by the city clerk on the request of the traffic bureau of the police department, which was under Commissioner Connor's direction. The requirement that the approval of the full Commission be obtained was applied only to this one group.

Understandably convinced that the City of Birmingham was not going to authorize their demonstrations under any circumstances, petitioners proceeded with their plans despite Commissioner Connor's orders. On Wednesday, April 10, at 9 in the evening, the city filed in a state circuit court a bill of complaint seeking an ex parte injunction. The complaint recited that petitioners were engaging in a series of demonstrations as "part of a massive effort . . . to forcibly integrate all business establishments, churches, and other institutions" in the city, with the result that the police department was strained in its resources and the safety, peace, and tranquility were threatened. It was alleged as particularly menacing that petitioners were planning to conduct "kneel-in" demonstrations at churches where their presence was not wanted. The city's police dogs were said to be in danger of their lives. Faced with these recitals, the Circuit Court issued the injunction in the form requested, and in effect ordered petitioners and all other persons having notice of the order to refrain for an unlimited time from carrying on any demonstrations without a permit. A permit, of course, was clearly unobtainable; the city would not have sought this injunction if it had any intention of issuing one.

Petitioners were served with copies of the injunction at various times on Thursday and on Good Friday. Unable to believe that such a blatant and broadly drawn prior restraint on their First Amendment rights could be valid, they announced their intention to defy it and went ahead with the planned peaceful demonstrations on Easter weekend. On the following Monday, when they promptly filed a motion to dissolve the injunction, the court found them in contempt, holding that they had waived all their First Amendment rights by disobeying the court order.

These facts lend no support to the court's charges that petitioners were presuming to act as judges in their own case, or that they had a disregard for the judicial process. They did not flee the jurisdiction or refuse to appear in the Alabama courts. Having violated the injunction, they promptly submitted themselves to the courts to test the constitutionality of the injunction and the ordinance it parroted. They were in essentially the same position as persons who challenge the constitutionality of a statute by violating it, and then defend the ensuing criminal prosecution on constitutional grounds. It has never been thought that violation of a statute indicated such a disrespect for the legislature that the violator always must be punished even if the statute was unconstitutional. On the contrary, some cases have required that persons seeking to challenge the constitutionality of a statute first violate it to establish their standing to sue. Indeed, it shows no disrespect for law to violate a statute on the ground that it is unconstitutional and then to submit one's case to the courts with the willingness to accept the penalty if the statute is held to be valid.

The Court concedes that "[t]he generality of the language contained in the Birmingham parade ordinance upon which the injunction was based would unquestionably raise substantial constitutional issues concerning some of its provisions." That concession is well-founded but minimal. I believe it is patently unconstitutional on its face. . . . When local officials are given totally unfettered discretion to decide whether a proposed demonstration is consistent with "public welfare, peace, safety, health, decency, good order, morals or convenience," as they were in this case, they are invited to act as censors over the views that may be presented to the public. The unconstitutionality of the ordinance is compounded, of course, when there is convincing evidence that the officials have in fact used their power to deny permits to organizations whose views they dislike. . . .

I do not believe that giving this Court's seal of approval to such a gross misuse of the judicial process is likely to lead to greater respect for the law any more than it is likely to lead to greater protection for First Amendment freedoms. The ex parte temporary injunction has a long and odious history in this country, and its susceptibility to misuse is all too apparent from the facts of the case. . . . Respect for the courts and for judicial process was not increased by the history of the labor injunction.

Justice DOUGLAS, with whom the CHIEF JUSTICE, Justice BRENNAN, and Justice FORTAS concur, dissenting:

The record shows that petitioners did not deliberately attempt to circumvent the permit requirement. Rather they diligently attempted to obtain a permit and were rudely rebuffed and then reasonably concluded that any further attempts would be fruitless.

The right to defy an unconstitutional statute is basic in our scheme. Even when an ordinance requires a permit to make a speech, to deliver a sermon, to picket, to parade, or to assemble, it need not be honored when it is invalid on its face. . . .

Yet by some inscrutable legerdemain these constitutionally secured rights to challenge prior restraints invalid on their face are lost if the

State takes the precaution to have some judge append his signature to an ex parte order which recites the words of the invalid statute. The State neatly insulates its legislation from challenge by mere incorporation of the identical stifling, overbroad, and vague restraints on exercise of the First Amendment freedoms into an even more vague and pervasive injunction obtained invisibly and upon a stage darkened lest it be open to scrutiny by those affected. . . .

The Court today lets loose a devastatingly destructive weapon for infringement of freedoms jealously safeguarded not so much for the benefit of any given group of any given persuasion as for the benefit of all of us. We cannot permit fears of "riots" and "civil disobedience" generated by slogans like "Black Power" to divert our attention from what is here at stake—not violence or the right of the State to control its streets and sidewalks, but the insulation from attack of ex parte orders and legislation upon which they are based even when patently impermissible prior restraints on the exercise of First Amendment rights, thus arming the state courts with the power to punish as a "contempt" what they otherwise could not punish at all. Constitutional restrictions against abridgments of First Amendment freedoms limit judicial equally with legislative and executive power. Convictions for contempt of court orders which invalidly abridge First Amendment freedoms must be condemned equally with convictions for violation of statutes which do the same thing. I respectfully dissent.

## Comments and Questions

1. After its decision in *Walker*, the Supreme Court held that the Birmingham parade-permit ordinance violated the First Amendment because it gave unfettered discretion to city officials to restrict speech. *Shuttlesworth v. City of Birmingham*, 394 U.S. 147 (1967). The Court also ruled there that Reverend Shuttlesworth could overturn his conviction for parading without a permit. Why do you think the Supreme Court treated Reverend Shuttlesworth's action in violation of the law differently from Reverend King's violation of a court order predicated on the same law? Do you think there is a distinction here worth maintaining? For one effort to address these issues, see Alexander Bickel, *Civil Disobedience and the Duty to Obey*, 8 Gonz. L. Rev. 199 (1973).

2. The rule requiring obedience to a court order even if it is later found to be unconstitutional has been called the *collateral bar rule* because it forbids challenge by anyone who first disobeys the rule and then seeks to challenge it in court. In *Walker*, the U.S. Supreme Court defers to Alabama's collateral bar rule but also announces exceptions to that rule. What are those exceptions? How would you apply them to the facts of the *Shuttlesworth* case? To the facts of *Walker* itself?

3. What kind of rule is the collateral bar rule, and how can it be changed? Note that in *Walker*, the state's collateral bar rule was found to apply even in

the face of federal constitutional claims. Indeed, the majority opinion attached the following footnote, discussing *Kasper v. Brittain*, 245 F.2d 92 (6th Cir. 1957), to its statement that "in the fair administration of justice no man can be judge in his own case, however exalted his station, however righteous his motives, and irrespective of his race, color, politics, or religion":

> There, a federal court had ordered the public high school in Clinton, Tennessee, to desegregate. Kasper . . . organized a campaign "to run the Negroes out of the school." The federal court issued an ex parte restraining order enjoining Kasper from interfering with desegregation. Relying upon the First Amendment, Kasper harangued a crowd "to the effect that although he had been served with the restraining order, it did not mean anything . . ." His conviction for criminal contempt was affirmed by the Court of Appeals for the Sixth Circuit. That court concluded that "'an injunctional order issued by a court must be obeyed,'" whatever its seeming invalidity, citing *Howat v. Kansas*, 258 U.S. 181 (1922). This Court denied certiorari.

Does this footnote affect your assessment of the collateral bar rule? Some state courts have rejected the collateral bar rule. *See In re Berry*, 68 Cal. 2d 137 (1968). What are the arguments for retaining and rejecting it?

4. What light does *Walker v. Birmingham* shed on the appellate court's decision in *United States v. Hall, supra*?

5. In the contempt proceeding that gave rise to the *Walker* litigation, the defendants were represented by some of the best lawyers in the United States. Contrast this with the situation in *Turner v. Rogers*, the contempt case reproduced in Chapter 1. How do these two cases influence your thinking about the line between criminal and civil actions? How is the context of the *Walker* case—in terms of subject matter of the underlying lawsuit and the moment in history in which the suit was brought—differ from that in *Turner*? Do these differences explain the different approaches of the court?

6. Given the remedial powers to order contempt, preliminary injunctions and temporary restraining orders, money damages, permanent injunctions, and attorneys' fees, do you agree with the characterization of the courts as "the least dangerous branch"? What powers, in contrast, do legislatures and executives have—and what procedural restrictions and oversight exist to restrain their powers?

7. Further historical context can be found in Alan Westin and Barry Mahoney, *The Trial of Martin Luther King* (1974), Taylor Branch, *Parting the Waters* (1988), and the award-winning Public Broadcasting Service series, *Eyes on the Prize* (1987).

8. Long before the Supreme Court's decision in *Walker*, back at the time of his arrest for violating the Alabama court order, Reverend Martin Luther King, Jr., wrote a response to a statement by eight Alabama clergymen urging him and others in the black community to stop their program of "direct action," including sit-ins, boycotts, and marches against racial segregation. King's direct-action approach pursued tenets of civil disobedience in response to the Southern resistance to integration, which had been mandated by the

Supreme Court since its decision in *Brown v. Bd. of Educ.of Topeka, Shawnee County, Kan.*, 347 U.S. 483 (1954). King was awarded the Nobel Peace Prize for his struggle for civil rights. He was murdered in Memphis in April 1968. Following his assassination, major urban areas in the United States erupted in violence. As you read portions of Reverend King's letter, consider what you find persuasive, and why, and whether any of his arguments join issue with the majority opinion in *Walker*. You can also find the full text of King's letter in *Civil Disobedience: Theory and Practice* 72-89 (Hugo Bedav ed. 1969).

## ■ MARTIN LUTHER KING, JR., LETTER FROM BIRMINGHAM CITY JAIL*

*A Testament of Hope: The Essential Writings and Speeches of Martin Luther King, Jr., 289 (James M. Washington, ed. 1986)*

*The following is the public statement directed to Martin Luther King, Jr., by eight Alabama clergymen:*

We the undersigned clergymen are among those who, in January, issued "An Appeal for Law and Order and Common Sense," in dealing with racial problems in Alabama. We expressed understanding that honest convictions in racial matters could properly be pursued in the courts, but urged that decisions of those courts should in the meantime be peacefully obeyed.

Since that time there had been some evidence of increased forbearance and a willingness to face facts. Responsible citizens have undertaken to work on various problems which cause racial friction and unrest. In Birmingham, recent public events have given indication that we all have opportunity for a new constructive and realistic approach to racial problems.

However, we are now confronted by a series of demonstrations by some of our Negro citizens, directed and led in part by outsiders. We recognize the natural impatience of people who feel that their hopes are slow in being realized. But we are convinced that these demonstrations are unwise and untimely.

We agree rather with certain local Negro leadership which has called for honest and open negotiation of racial issues in our area. And we believe this kind of facing of issues can best be accomplished by citizens of our own metropolitan area, white and Negro, meeting with their knowledge and experience of the local situation. All of us need to face that responsibility and find proper channels for its accomplishment.

Just as we formerly pointed out that "hatred and violence have no sanction in our religious and political traditions," we also point out that such actions as incite to hatred and violence, however technically peaceful those actions may be, have not contributed to the resolution of our local problems. We do not believe that these days of new hope are days when extreme measures are justified in Birmingham.

We commend the community as a whole, and the local news media and law enforcement officials in particular, on the calm manner in which these demonstrations have been handled. We urge the public to continue to show restraint should the demonstrations continue, and the law enforcement officials to remain calm and continue to protect our city from violence.

We further strongly urge our own Negro community to withdraw support from these demonstrations, and to unite locally in working peacefully for a better Birmingham. When rights are consistently denied, a cause should be pressed in the courts and in negotiations among local leaders, and not in the streets. We appeal to both our white and Negro citizenry to observe the principles of law and order and common sense.

*Bishop C. C. J. Carpenter, Bishop Joseph A. Durick, Rabbi Milton L. Grafman, Bishop Paul Hardin, Bishop Nolan B. Harmon, Rev. George M. Murray, Rev. Edward V. Ramage, Rev. Earl Stallings*

April 12, 1963

My dear Fellow Clergymen.

While confined here in the Birmingham City Jail, I came across your recent statement calling our present activities "unwise and untimely." Seldom, if ever, do I pause to answer criticism of my work and ideas. If I sought to answer all of the criticisms that cross my desk, my secretaries would be engaged in little else in the course of the day, and I would have no time for constructive work. But since I feel that you are men of genuine goodwill and your criticisms are sincerely set forth, I would like to answer your statement in what I hope will be patient and reasonable terms. . . .

Several months ago our local affiliate here in Birmingham invited us to be on call to engage in a nonviolent direct action program if such were deemed necessary. We readily consented and when the hour came we lived up to our promises. So I am here, along with several members of my staff, because we were invited here. I am here because I have basic organizational ties here.

Beyond this, I am in Birmingham because injustice is here. Just as the eighth century prophets left their little villages and carried their "thus saith the Lord" far beyond the boundaries of their home towns; and just as the Apostle Paul left his little village of Tarsus and carried the gospel of Jesus Christ to practically every hamlet and city of the Graeco-Roman world, I too am compelled to carry the gospel of freedom beyond my particular home town. Like Paul, I must constantly respond to the Macedonian call for aid.

Moreover, I am cognizant of the interrelatedness of all communities and states. I cannot sit idly by in Atlanta and not be concerned about what happens in Birmingham. Injustice anywhere is a threat to justice everywhere. We are caught in an inescapable network of mutuality, tied in a single garment of destiny. Whatever affects one directly affects all indirectly. Never again can we afford to live with the narrow, provincial "outside agitator" idea. Anyone who lives inside the United States can never be considered an outsider anywhere in this country.

You deplore the demonstrations that are presently taking place in Birmingham. But I am sorry that your statement did not express a similar concern for the conditions that brought the demonstrations into being. I am sure that each of you would want to go beyond the superficial social analyst who looks merely at effects, and does not grapple with underlying causes. I would not hesitate to say that it is unfortunate that so-called demonstrations are taking place in Birmingham at this time, but I would say in even more emphatic terms that it is even more unfortunate that the white power structure of this city left the Negro community with no other alternative.

In any nonviolent campaign there are four basic steps: 1) Collection of the facts to determine whether injustices are alive. 2) Negotiation. 3) Self-purification and 4) Direct Action. We have gone through all of these steps in Birmingham. There can be no gainsaying of the fact that racial injustice engulfs this community.

Birmingham is probably the most thoroughly segregated city in the United States. Its ugly record of police brutality is known in every section of this country. Its unjust treatment of Negroes in the courts is a notorious reality. There have been more unsolved bombings of Negro homes and churches in Birmingham than any city in this nation. These are the hard, brutal and unbelievable facts. On the basis of these conditions Negro leaders sought to negotiate with the city fathers. But the political leaders consistently refused to engage in good faith negotiation. . . .

When we discovered that Mr. Connor was in [a run-off election], we decided again to postpone action so that the demonstrations could not be used to cloud the issues. At this time we agreed to begin our nonviolent witness the day after the run-off.

This reveals that we did not move irresponsibly into direct action. We too wanted to see Mr. Connor defeated; so we went through postponement after postponement to aid in this community need. After this we felt that direct action could be delayed no longer.

### CREATIVE TENSION

You may well ask, "Why direct action? Why sit-ins, marches, etc.? Isn't negotiation a better path?" You are exactly right in your call for negotiation. Indeed, this is the purpose of direct action. Nonviolent direct action seeks to create such a crisis and establish such creative tension that a community that has constantly refused to negotiate is forced to confront the issue. It seeks so to dramatize the issue that it can no longer be ignored. I just referred to the creation of tension as a part of the work of the nonviolent resister. This may sound rather shocking. But I must confess that I am not afraid of the word tension. I have earnestly worked and preached against violent tension, but there is a type of constructive nonviolent tension that is necessary for growth. Just as Socrates felt that it was necessary to create a tension in the mind so that individuals could rise from the bondage of myths and half-truths to the unfettered realm of creative analysis and objective appraisal, we must see the need of having nonviolent gadflies to create the kind of tension in society that will help men to rise from the dark depths of prejudice and racism to the majestic heights of understanding and brotherhood. So the purpose of the direct action is to create a situation so crisis-packed that it will inevitably open the door to negotiation. We, therefore, concur with you in your call for negotiation. Too long has our beloved Southland been bogged down in the tragic attempt to live in monologue rather than dialogue.

One of the basic points in your statement is that our acts are untimely. Some have asked. "Why didn't you give the new administration time to act?" The only answer that I can give to this inquiry is that the new administration must be prodded about as much as the outgoing one before it acts. We will be sadly mistaken if we feel that the election of Mr. Boutwell will bring the millennium to Birmingham. While Mr. Boutwell is much more articulate and gentle than Mr. Connor, they are both segregationists, dedicated to the task of maintaining the status quo. The hope I see in Mr. Boutwell is that he will be reasonable enough to see the futility of massive resistance to desegregation. But he will not see this without pressure from the devotees of civil rights. My friends, I must say to you that we have not made a single gain in civil rights without determined legal and nonviolent pressure. History is the long and tragic story of the fact that privileged groups seldom give up their privileges voluntarily. Individuals may see the moral light and voluntarily give up their unjust posture; but as Reinhold Niebuhr has reminded us, groups are more immoral than individuals.

We know through painful experience that freedom is never voluntarily given by the oppressor; it must be demanded by the oppressed. Frankly, I have never yet engaged in a direct action movement that was "well timed," according to the timetable of those who have not suffered unduly from the disease of segregation. For years now I have heard the words "Wait!" It rings in the ear of every Negro with a piercing familiarity. This "Wait" has almost always meant "Never." It has been a tranquilizing thalidomide, relieving the emotional stress for a moment, only to give birth to an ill-formed infant of frustration. We must come to see with the distinguished jurist of yesterday that "justice too long delayed is justice denied." We have waited for more than three hundred and forty years for our constitutional and God-given rights. The nations of Asia and Africa are moving with jet-like speed toward the goal of political independence, and we still creep at horse and buggy pace toward the gaining of a cup of coffee at a lunch counter. I guess it is easy for those who have never felt the stinging darts of segregation to say, "Wait." But when you have seen vicious mobs lynch your mothers and fathers at will and drown your sisters and brothers at whim; when you have seen hate-filled policemen curse, kick, brutalize and even kill your black brothers and sisters with impunity; when you see the vast majority of your twenty million Negro brothers smothering in an airtight cage of poverty in the midst of an affluent society; when you suddenly find your tongue twisted and your speech stammering as you seek to explain to your six-year-old daughter why she can't go to the public amusement park that has just been advertised on television, and see tears welling up in her little eyes when she is told that Funtown is closed to colored children, and see the depressing clouds of inferiority begin to form in her little mental sky, and see her begin to distort her little personality to unconsciously developing a bitterness toward white people; when you have to concoct an answer for a five-year-old son asking in agonizing pathos: "Daddy, why do white people treat colored people so mean?"; when you take a cross country drive and find it necessary to sleep night after night in the uncomfortable corners of your automobile because no motel will accept you; when you are humiliated day in and day out by nagging signs reading "white" and "colored"; when your first name becomes "nigger" and your middle name becomes "boy" (however old you are) and your last name becomes "John," and when your wife and mother are never given the respected title "Mrs."; when you are harried by day and haunted at night by the fact that you are a Negro, living constantly at tip-toe stance never quite knowing what to expect next, and plagued with inner fears and outer resentments; when you are forever fighting a degenerating sense of "nobodiness"; then you will understand why we find it difficult to wait. There comes a time when the cup of endurance runs over, and men are no longer willing to be plunged into an abyss of injustice where they experience the blackness of corroding despair. I hope, sirs, you can understand our legitimate and unavoidable impatience.

### BREAKING THE LAW

You express a great deal of anxiety over our willingness to break laws. This is certainly a legitimate concern. Since we so diligently urge people to obey the Supreme Court's decision of 1954 outlawing segregation in the public schools, it is rather strange and paradoxical to find us consciously breaking laws. One may well ask, "how can you advocate breaking some laws and obeying others?" The answer is found in the fact that there are two types of laws: There are *just* and there are *unjust* laws. I would agree with Saint Augustine that "An unjust law is no law at all."

Now what is the difference between the two? How does one determine when a law is just or unjust? A just law is a man-made code that squares with the moral law or the law of God. An unjust law is a code that is out of harmony with the moral law. To put it in the terms of Saint Thomas Aquinas, an unjust law is a human law that is not rooted in eternal and natural law. Any law that uplifts human personality is just. Any law that degrades human personality is unjust. All segregation statutes are unjust because segregation distorts the soul and damages the personality. It gives the segregator a false sense of superiority, and the segregated a false sense of inferiority. To use the words of Martin Buber, the great Jewish philosopher, segregation substitutes an "I-it" relationship for the "I-thou" relationship, and ends up relegating persons to the status of things. So segregation is not only politically, economically and sociologically unsound, but it is morally wrong and sinful. Paul Tillich has said that sin is separation. Isn't segregation an existential expression of man's tragic separation, an expression of his awful estrangement, his terrible sinfulness? So I can urge men to disobey segregation ordinances because they are morally wrong.

Let us turn to a more concrete example of just and unjust laws. An unjust law is a code that a majority inflicts on a minority that is not binding on itself. This is difference made legal. On the other hand a just law is a code that a majority compels a minority to follow that it is willing to follow itself. This is sameness made legal.

Let me give another explanation. An unjust law is a code inflicted upon a minority which that minority had no part in enacting or creating because they did not have the unhampered right to vote. Who can say that the legislature of Alabama which set up the segregation laws was democratically elected? Throughout the state of Alabama all types of conniving methods are used to prevent Negroes from becoming registered voters and there are some counties without a single Negro registered to vote despite the fact that the Negro constitutes a majority of the population. Can any law set up in such a state be considered democratically structured?

These are just a few examples of unjust and just laws. There are some instances when a law is just on its face and unjust in its application. For instance, I was arrested Friday on a charge of parading without a permit. Now there is nothing wrong with an ordinance which requires a permit for a parade, but when the ordinance is used to preserve segregation and to deny citizens the First Amendment privilege of peaceful assembly and peaceful protest, then it becomes unjust.

I hope you can see the distinction I am trying to point out. In no sense do I advocate evading or defying the law as the rabid segregationist would do. This would lead to anarchy. One who breaks an unjust law must do it *openly, lovingly* (not hatefully as the white mothers did in New Orleans when they were seen on television screaming "nigger, nigger, nigger"), and with a willingness to accept the penalty. I submit that an individual who breaks a law that conscience tells him is unjust, and willingly accepts the penalty by staying in jail to arouse the conscience of the community over its injustice, is in reality expressing the very highest respect for law.

Of course, there is nothing new about this kind of civil disobedience. It was seen sublimely in the refusal of Shadrach, Meshach and Abednego to obey the laws of Nebuchadnezzar because a higher moral law was involved. It was practiced superbly by the early Christians who were willing to face hungry lions and the excruciating pain of chopping blocks, before submitting to certain unjust laws of the Roman empire. To a degree academic freedom is a reality today because Socrates practiced civil disobedience.

## THE WHITE MODERATE

We can never forget that everything Hitler did in Germany was "legal" and everything the Hungarian freedom fighters did in Hungary was "illegal." It was "illegal" to aid and comfort a Jew in Hitler's Germany. But I am sure that if I had lived in Germany during that time I would have aided and comforted my Jewish brothers even though it was illegal. If I lived in a Communist country today where certain principles dear to the Christian faith are suppressed, I believe I would openly advocate disobeying these anti-religious laws. I must make two honest confessions to you, my Christian and Jewish brothers. First, I must confess that over the last few years I have been gravely disappointed with the white moderate. I have almost reached the regrettable conclusion that the Negro's great stumbling block in the stride toward freedom is not the White Citizen's Councilor or the Ku Klux Klanner, but the white moderate who is more devoted to "order" than to justice; who prefers a negative peace which is the absence of tension to a positive peace which is the presence of justice; who constantly says "I agree with you in the goal you seek, but I can't agree with your methods of direct action"; who paternalistically feels that he can set the timetable for another man's freedom; who lives by the myth of time and who constantly advises the Negro to wait until a "more convenient season." Shallow understanding from people of good will is more frustrating than absolute misunderstanding from people of ill will. Lukewarm acceptance is much more bewildering than outright rejection.

I had hoped that the white moderate would understand that law and order exist for the purpose of establishing justice, and that when they fail to do this they become dangerously structured dams that block the flow of social progress. . . .

You spoke of our activity in Birmingham as extreme. At first, I was rather disappointed that fellow clergymen would see my nonviolent efforts as those of the extremist. I started thinking about the fact that I stand in the middle of two opposing forces in the Negro community. One is a force of complacency made up of Negroes who, as a result of long years of oppression, have been so completely drained of self-respect and a sense of "somebodiness" that they have adjusted to segregation, and of a few Negroes in the middle class who, because of a degree of academic and economic security, and because at points they profit by segregation, have unconsciously become insensitive to the problems of the masses. The other force is one of bitterness and hatred and comes perilously close to advocating violence. It is expressed in the various black nationalist groups that are springing up over the nation, the largest and best known being Elijah Muhammad's Muslim movement. This movement is nourished by the contemporary frustration over the continued existence of racial discrimination. It is made up of people who have lost faith in America, who have absolutely repudiated Christianity, and who have concluded that the white man is an incurable "devil." I have tried to stand between these two forces saying that we need not follow the "do-nothingism" of the complacent or the hatred and despair of the black nationalist. There is the more excellent way of love and nonviolent protest. I'm grateful to God that, through the Negro church, the dimension of nonviolence entered our struggle. If this philosophy had not emerged, I am convinced that by now many streets of the South would be flowing with floods of blood. And I am further convinced that if our white brothers dismiss as "rabble rousers" and "outside agitators" those of us who are working through the channels of nonviolent direct action and refuse to support our nonviolent efforts, millions of Negroes, out of frustration and despair, will seek solace and security in black nationalist ideologies, a development that will lead inevitably to a frightening racial nightmare. . . .

### EXTREMISTS FOR LOVE

. . . [A]s I continued to think about the matter, I gradually gain[ed] a bit of satisfaction from being considered an extremist. Was not Jesus an extremist in love—"Love your enemies, bless them that curse you, pray for them that despitefully use you." Was not Amos an extremist for justice—"Let justice roll down like waters and righteousness like a mighty stream." Was not Paul an extremist for the gospel of Jesus Christ—"I bear in my body the marks of the Lord Jesus." Was not Martin Luther an extremist—"Here I stand; I can do none other so help me God." Was not John Bunyan an extremist—"I will stay in jail to the end of my days before I make a butchery of my conscience." Was not Abraham Lincoln an extremist—"This nation cannot survive half slave and half free." Was not Thomas Jefferson an extremist—"We hold these truths to be self-evident, that all men are created equal." So the question is not whether we will be extremist but what kind of extremist will we be. Will we be extremists for hate or will we be extremists for love? Will we be extremists for the preservation of injustice—or will we be extremists for the cause of justice? In that dramatic scene on Calvary's hill, three men were crucified. We must not forget that all three were crucified for the same crime—the crime of extremism. Two were extremists for immorality, and thusly fell below their environment. The other, Jesus Christ, was an extremist for love, truth, and goodness, and thereby rose above his environment. So, after all, maybe the South, the nation and the world are in dire need of creative extremists. . . .

[In this portion of his letter, Doctor King criticizes white churches that "stand on the sideline and merely mouth pious irrelevancies and sanctimonious trivialities, and speak about obeying law, but neither about 'right' nor 'injustice.'" He also criticizes most moderate whites: "I guess I should have realized that few members of a race that has oppressed race can understand or appreciate the deep groans and passionate yearnings of those that have been oppressed and still fewer have the vision to see that injustice must be rooted out by strong, persistent and determined action."]

### BULL CONNOR'S POLICE

I must close now. But before closing, I am impelled to mention one other point in your statement that troubled me profoundly. You warmly commended the Birmingham police force for keeping "order" and "preventing violence." I don't believe you would have so warmly commended the police force if you had seen its angry violent dogs literally biting six unarmed, nonviolent Negroes. I don't believe you would so quickly commend the policemen if you would observe their ugly and inhuman treatment of Negroes here in the city jail; if you would watch them push and curse old Negro women and young Negro girls; if you would see them slap and kick old Negro men and young boys; if you will observe them, as they did on two occasions, refuse to give us food because we wanted to sing our grace together. I'm sorry that I can't join you in your praise for the police department.

It is true that they have been rather disciplined in their public handling of the demonstrators. In this sense they have been rather publicly "nonviolent." But for what purpose? To preserve the evil system of segregation. Over the last few years I have consistently preached that nonviolence demands that the means we use must be as pure as the ends we seek. So, I have tried to make it clear that it is wrong to use immoral means to attain moral ends. But now I must affirm that it is just as wrong, or even more so, to use moral means to preserve immoral ends. Maybe Mr. Connor and his policemen have been rather publicly nonviolent, as Chief Pritchett was in Albany, Georgia, but they have used the moral means of nonviolence to maintain the immoral end of flagrant racial injustice. T. S. Eliot has said that there is no greater treason than to do the right deed for the wrong reason.

I wish you had commended the Negro sit-inners and demonstrators of Birmingham for their sublime courage, their willingness to suffer and their amazing discipline in the midst of the most inhuman provocation. One day the South will recognize its real heroes. They will be the James Merediths, courageously and with a majestic sense of purpose facing jeering and hostile mobs and the agonizing loneliness that characterizes the life of the pioneer. They will be old oppressed, battered Negro women, symbolized in a seventy-two year old woman of Montgomery, Alabama, who rose up with a sense of dignity and with her people decided not to ride the segregated buses, and responded to one who inquired about her tiredness with ungrammatical profundity: "My feet is tired, but my soul is rested." They will be the young high school and college students, young ministers of the gospel and a host of their elders courageously and nonviolently sitting-in at lunch counters and willingly going to jail for conscience's sake. One day the South will know that when these disinherited children of God sat down at lunch counters they were in reality standing up for the best in the American dream and the most sacred values in our Judeo-Christian heritage, and thusly, carrying our whole nation back to those great wells of democracy which were dug deep by the founding fathers in the formulation of the Constitution and the Declaration of Independence.

Never before have I written a letter this long (or should I say a book?). I'm afraid that it is much too long to take your precious time. I can assure you that it would have been much shorter if I had been writing from a comfortable desk, but what else is there to do when you are alone for days in the dull monotony of a narrow jail cell other than write long letters, think strange thoughts, and pray long prayers?

If I have said anything in this letter that is an overstatement of the truth and is indicative of an unreasonable impatience, I beg you to forgive me. If I have said anything in this letter that is an understatement of the truth and is indicative of my having a patience that makes me patient with anything less than brotherhood, I beg God to forgive me.

I hope this letter finds you strong in the faith. I also hope that circumstances will soon make it possible for me to meet each of you, not as an integrationist or a civil rights leader, but as a fellow clergyman and a Christian brother. Let us all hope that the dark clouds of racial prejudice will soon pass away and the deep fog of misunderstanding will be lifted from our fear-drenched communities and in some not too distant tomorrow the radiant stars of love and brotherhood will shine over our great nation with all of their scintillating beauty.

Yours for the cause of Peace and Brotherhood
Martin Luther King, Jr.

9. One possible rejoinder to King's Letter from Birmingham City Jail follows the logic of civil disobedience: If a person or group wants to dramatize the injustice of a law by disobeying it, they should be willing to take the consequences of that disobedience. This would strengthen their impact, either by producing martyrs or by dramatizing the perceived injustice. It would also express ultimate respect for the rule of law and the law's rules for bringing about change. According to this view, we see the outer limit of judicial remedies for potential injustices when protestors take their claims to the streets rather than to the courts. How should defenders of Reverend King respond? How does this debate affect your view of the collateral bar rule? These issues are discussed in Abe Fortas, *Concerning Dissent and Civil Disobedience* (1968). Justice Fortas joined the dissenting opinion in *Walker*.

# 3

# Thinking Like a Trial Lawyer, Pleadings, and Joinder

## A. INTRODUCTION

In Chapters 3, 4, and 5, we turn to the major steps in civil litigation. Chapter 3 covers the requirements for a complaint and also considers how many plaintiffs and defendants must, can, and should be joined, and what responses the defendant can and should make. Chapter 4 addresses the discovery process, which is central to the civil litigation process. Chapter 5 discusses the right of trial by jury and the many methods that have evolved to instruct and constrain juries.

It is important that you begin to internalize your own sense of the chronological flow of a civil lawsuit from the filing of the initial pleadings; through discovery and motions; through trial, verdict, and judgment; and then to the concept of finality. To this end, we have provided various ways in which you can gain perspective on the entire process. After this introduction, we provide a brief description of the major aspects of a case in the chronological order in which they typically take place. You may find it helpful to refer back to this section whenever you are learning a new topic, so that you can appreciate where the concept that you are studying fits into the larger picture.

## B. THE STAGES AND ESSENTIAL CONCEPTS OF A CIVIL LITIGATION

Most civil cases are introduced to plaintiffs' lawyers when a client comes to the office and expresses dissatisfaction with the behavior of others. As the client describes what is wrong, the lawyer considers whether this is a situation for which the law gives any relief. Assume, for instance, the potential client, Joe, says, "I was in an elevator yesterday, and a passenger, Sally, didn't say hello to me." If this is the whole story, the lawyer would probably think that the law does not recognize snubbing as a wrong. In other words, the action of Sally the passenger was not legally "cognizable." Thus, whether the law will give relief is sometimes called a question of *cognizability*.

The underlying concept (or "unit of measurement" if you like scientific analogies) the lawyer would use in reaching this result is called the *cause of action* or *claim showing that the pleader is entitled to relief*. Causes of action are a shorthand for what events or circumstances must have taken place (or, in some instances, will take place) before a court will grant relief under some applicable substantive law.

Each cause of action or claim has components, called *elements*. Through your substantive law courses (torts, contracts, property, environmental law, employment discrimination, etc.) you will learn the elements of many different causes of action. So let us suppose Joe said instead: "I was walking down the street and I think Sally tripped me, or perhaps she was just careless in sticking out her leg." The attorney might now think about two potential causes of action: negligence and battery. The lawyer might say to herself: "Sally, as another pedestrian, had a 'duty' to Joe to refrain from unreasonable conduct, and perhaps she breached that duty by acting 'unreasonably' in tripping Joe, and that caused him harm ('cause in fact') which was foreseeable or within the risk Sally took ('proximate cause'), and since he broke his leg as a result of her action, he has suffered 'harm' or sustained 'damages.' So if the facts are true, there may be a cause of action for negligence because all five elements (of the negligence cause of action) are present: duty, unreasonable conduct (breach of duty), cause in fact, proximate cause, and harm or damages."

Perhaps Sally acted intentionally. If so, there may be a cause of action for battery with these elements: (1) an intentional act by defendant; (2) resulting in harmful or offensive contact; (3) without consent; and (4) causing injury. Of course, even within this single cause of action there may be multiple factual *theories* of the case. For instance, a battery could result from a punch in the face, pulling a chair out from underneath someone, creating an electric shock, tainting someone's food, and so forth. Multiple factual theories could arise even within a single case.

Throughout this course, we will deal with many causes of action from many different substantive areas of the law. This will require us to consider what are the elements of those causes of action. Please remember that different jurisdictions, lawyers, and law professors choose to treat or express the elements somewhat differently. So, do not be alarmed if in your torts class "negligence" and "battery" are explained a bit differently than in this rendition.

If, after talking to the potential client and possibly performing further investigation, a lawyer is satisfied that there is at least one provable cause of action, she will discuss fees and perhaps take the case. Joe's lawyer, at some point, will want to discuss with Joe whether commencing a lawsuit is the best way to begin. Perhaps a call to Sally, or to her insurance company or her lawyer, if they exist, makes more sense. A demand letter, and perhaps the suggestion of mediation or some other method of alternative dispute resolution (ADR), should be considered. We will discuss some specific ADR techniques later in the course, but understand that the parties will usually be negotiating a resolution of their dispute before, during, and even after the formal phases of litigation. The formal processes of litigation, however, will alter the parties' expectations and settlement positions.

If a lawsuit is to be filed, then the lawyer will have to decide in which states the defendant can be sued; this is a question of *personal jurisdiction.* Let's say you are an Oregon lawyer, and Sally, who lives in California, allegedly caused Joe to trip on a street in Oregon. He has come to discuss the case with you in Oregon. You would probably conclude quickly, since Oregon has typical personal jurisdiction statutes, that Sally could be sued on the facts of this case either in Oregon or in California. If you decide California is a better *forum* state—a state in which a court sits, and where a suit has been or will be brought—you would help Joe find a lawyer in California, since you have probably not been admitted to practice law there.

It probably makes sense to sue in Oregon, where your client lives and where the accident occurred; this would also mean that you could handle the case and earn a fee. Next, you would have to decide in which Oregon court to commence suit. Oregon, like all other states, has a state court system and at least one federal district court (remember, federal district courts are trial courts). The issue of "what court is empowered to hear this type of case" is called a question of *subject matter jurisdiction.* A combination of constitutional provisions and statutes grant different courts the right to hear different types of cases. For instance, in any given state, either the state constitution or statutes will give at least one trial court the authority to hear most types of cases. This broad grant of power to a trial court is called a grant of *general subject matter jurisdiction.*

Article III of the U.S. Constitution describes what cases Congress is permitted to authorize the federal district courts to hear. This grant of power is considerably narrower than the authorization provided in state constitutions and statutes. Thus, subject matter jurisdiction in the federal courts is commonly called *limited subject matter jurisdiction.* The limited subject matter jurisdiction for federal district courts can be found primarily in Title 28, in the "1330" sections of the U.S. Code. (After Congress passes a bill, it becomes an Act. Acts are assigned to a Title, by subject matter. Peruse these sections either in your rules supplement or in the U.S. Code volumes in the library or online.) The two major grants of limited subject matter jurisdiction to the federal district courts are called *federal question* and *diversity of citizenship.* See if you can find where these grants appear in your rules supplement. Sometimes, grants of limited subject matter jurisdiction to the federal district courts appear in various substantive statutes granting specific rights (scattered throughout the Code), so Title 28 is not the only title in which one can find such grants of federal subject matter jurisdiction.

Even after the lawyer decides in what court system and in what state to commence a suit (and please keep in mind that litigation is not the only rational alternative to resolve disputes), she must determine where—within the state or within the federal system—the case can be brought. This question is geographic, but it is different from personal jurisdiction or subject matter jurisdiction. This additional issue is called *venue*. For instance, if the suit of Joe against Sally is brought in an Oregon Circuit Court, a trial court of the Oregon state judicial system, one still must decide in which geographic section of the state to bring the case. Typical state venue statutes look to the county in which the cause of action arose (in this instance, it would be where Sally allegedly tripped Joe) or where the defendant resides. *See, e.g.*, Or. Rev. Stat. § 14.080. Congress has placed venue restrictions on where plaintiffs can commence cases in federal court. Try to find the relevant section(s) in your rules supplement.

The plaintiff must have not only personal jurisdiction over the defendant or defendants, subject matter jurisdiction in the appropriate court, and proper venue, but the defendants must also be appropriately notified of the commencement of suit. The "due process" requirements of notice and the right to be heard are explored at length in Chapter 1 and again in several cases concerning provisional relief in Chapter 2. These issues of personal jurisdiction, subject matter jurisdiction, venue, and notice raise fascinating and complex issues of federalism, separation of powers, and elemental fairness, and they occupy much of the second half of the materials in this book.

In the case of *Joe v. Sally*, as Joe's lawyer, you may have the opportunity to choose either a state court in Oregon or California, or a federal court in either state, if the potential damages were in excess of $75,000. Assuming Joe is a citizen of Oregon and Sally is a citizen of California, and the potential damages were sufficient, there would be diversity of citizenship within the meaning of Title 28, § 1332. Note that this would then be a case where there is *concurrent subject matter jurisdiction* among state courts and federal courts. Unless Congress makes a grant of *exclusive subject matter jurisdiction*, then a case that would have federal subject matter jurisdiction will also have state subject matter jurisdiction. On the other hand, if, for instance, Congress says that only federal courts can hear a certain type of case, such as actions alleging certain types of anti-competitive behavior specifically prescribed in the Sherman Anti-Trust Act (15 U.S.C. § 4), then the plaintiff's lawyer would be unable to bring that exact violation into a state trial court. Many first-year law students assume that if there is a federal question, such as a violation of a federal civil rights act, then the case can only be brought in federal court. This is *not* true. Again, unless Congress grants exclusivity to the federal court system, there is concurrent subject matter jurisdiction and the plaintiff has the choice of state or federal courts.

Returning to the case of *Joe v. Sally*, let us assume as Joe's lawyer that you have decided to bring the case in the Circuit Court of Oregon (a state court with general subject matter jurisdiction) sitting in the County of Yamhill. You will have checked what is called the *long-arm statute* of Oregon to make sure that Sally, a California citizen, can be sued in Oregon for a tort she allegedly committed there (Rule 4(c) of the Oregon Rules of Civil Procedure would indeed permit this exercise of personal jurisdiction). Also, you will have checked the applicable Oregon venue statute and complied with it in choosing the location of the court in Oregon in which to sue. You will then draft a *complaint* in accordance with Oregon's procedural rules. If the case were in a federal court, such pleading rules would appear in the Federal Rules of Civil Procedure. The pleading rules and cases interpreting them (as well as local culture, and in some instances, local rules) will tell you how precise you must be in your complaint about the facts and the specific relevant causes of action and their elements. You will have to check the applicable *statute of limitations* to make certain that the complaint has been filed within a statutorily prescribed time or, depending on the state law, that each defendant (in this case, "Sally") is "served" the complaint (*service of process*) or (again depending on statutes and their constitutionality) otherwise notified about the case. You will also have to decide whether you can and desire to demand a *jury* trial. This is usually a question of both constitutional right and trial strategy.

A plaintiff's lawyer also must consider *joinder* issues at the beginning of a case. If you choose to raise both negligence and battery causes of action against Sally, that would be called joinder of causes of action or, in the language of the Federal Rules, *joinder of claims*. If Joe tells you that the doctor who treated him for his broken leg after Sally tripped him did a bad job in setting the splint, then you will consider whether Joe has a negligence action against the doctor (often called a *medical malpractice* cause of action). Whether one can and should join Sally and the doctor as defendants in the same lawsuit is called a *joinder of parties* issue.

One reason that plaintiffs' lawyers begin their analysis of potential cases by considering causes of action is that the defendant, in answering the plaintiff, can promptly bring a *motion to dismiss* the case because of the plaintiff's failure to state a cause of action, or, in the words of Fed. R. Civ. P. 12(b)(6), "failure to state a claim upon which relief can be granted." This includes the concept of cognizability: a complaint may be dismissed for failure to state a claim when the circumstances alleged are not considered a wrong by the substantive law, even if everything that is alleged in the complaint actually happened exactly as plaintiff described it. Such a motion may also be brought on the basis that the plaintiff has alleged insufficient facts.

As you will find out, the defendant, either by motion or in its answer, has many options and many responsibilities. The defendant can challenge personal jurisdiction, subject matter jurisdiction, venue, and notice (service of process). The defendant, if filing an *answer*, must admit or deny the allegations. The defendant must state, or risk waiving by not stating, *affirmative defenses*. Affirmative defenses are defenses that the defendant has to the plaintiff's causes of action, even if the case is in an appropriate court and the plaintiff otherwise has a good cause of action. In the case of Joe against Sally, Sally might claim, for example, that Joe's own negligence contributed to the fall, or that he consented to contact, or that the applicable statute of limitations has already run. The defendant can also *counterclaim* against the plaintiff for damages or relief that the defendant seeks from the plaintiff. In some instances, such counterclaims are compulsory, in the sense that if the defendant does not bring the claim within the restricted period of time, it will be treated as waived and not permitted in the future. In federal court, for example, Fed. R. Civ. P. 13(a) mandates *compulsory counterclaims* if the defendant has a claim that "arises out of the transaction or occurrence that is the subject matter of the opposing party's claim" (although the rule is more complicated than this abbreviated statement of it). Perhaps Joe slandered Sally immediately after the incident. Lawyers might then debate whether this is a compulsory or *permissive counterclaim*.

Sally may have good reason to believe that if she is responsible to Joe, someone else is responsible to her for what she owes Joe. Let's say that Sally was acting as a messenger for a delivery company when the accident happened, and that the company had agreed to indemnify her for any harm caused while she made deliveries. Sally could bring a complaint for indemnification against the company, called an *impleader* or *third-party practice*. In federal court, impleader is covered by Fed. R. Civ. P. 14. If there are co-defendants, they may have claims against each other, which are called *cross-claims* in some states and in Fed. R. Civ. P. 13(g).

In some instances a plaintiff must join certain parties, or the case cannot go forward. These are called issues of *necessary and indispensable parties*, and are covered by Fed. R. Civ. P. 19. There are also more complex joinder issues, such as *intervention* (Fed. R. Civ. P. 24), *interpleader* (Fed. R. Civ. P. 22), and *class actions* (Fed. R. Civ. P. 23). These devices are introduced in this casebook but are explored more fully in a Complex Litigation course.

Assuming that the case survives preliminary motions that challenge the pleadings, the parties may then engage in *discovery*. Most states, as well as the federal courts, have a group of procedures whereby one party may gain information from the other parties, and, in some instances, even from non-party witnesses. Fed. R. Civ. P. 26 through 37 cover the discovery provisions, and are drafted to permit quite liberal discovery. In federal courts and some state courts, selected information is subject to *mandatory disclosure* in the earliest stages of the litigation. Additional discovery is obtained by other methods, including written questions to opposing parties called *interrogatories*, written and oral *depositions*, requests to inspect documents, and motions to inspect real or personal property. In oral depositions, one party normally forces another and/or other witnesses to appear in person before a stenographer (or another method of recording) to answer a series of oral questions under oath. Court orders may limit the amount and scope of discovery; there are sanctions for interfering with legitimate discovery and for abuse of the discovery rules; and many district courts also have local rules that limit discovery. All ninety-four federal district courts, and many state trial courts, have *local rules* and *standing orders* of judges that supplement the rules found throughout the country or in a given state. Consequently, a lawyer in federal court, for example, must know not only the Federal Rules of Civil Procedure, but also the applicable local rules and standing orders of the individual judges.

To understand the procedure that logically likely comes next, you must understand the concepts of the *burden of production* and the *burden of persuasion.* At the trial of a case, the party with the burden of proof, usually the plaintiff, must have a sufficiency of evidence as to each element of at least one cause of action to permit a reasonable fact finder to find that each element is true. This is called the *burden of production.* Let's say that Joe in fact sued Sally for negligence, the case reached a jury trial, and Joe's lawyer examined the witnesses in court and offered whatever evidence she had in favor of Joe. Assume that she was done with her part of the case, which is called *resting.* If the defendant's lawyer does not think there was a sufficiency of evidence to permit reasonable juries to find that all of the elements are true, that lawyer can move for a *judgment as a matter of law* under Fed. R. Civ. P. 50(a). (This motion was once labeled and is still often referred to as a motion for a *directed verdict.*) For instance, in the case of Joe against Sally, if Joe's lawyer offered no evidence from which reasonable people could infer that Sally acted intentionally or unreasonably, then the trial judge, upon the defendant's motion, would grant a directed verdict, meaning that the jury would have to find for the defendant. This is because Joe would not have met his "production" burden.

But it is logical that even if Joe survives a motion for directed verdict, he may not ultimately win. Let's say that Joe describes in open court how Sally carelessly tripped him, and also presents other potentially believable evidence of each element of his negligence case. This would mean that he would survive a directed verdict motion because he has met his production burden, that is, produced a sufficiency of evidence to permit reasonable jurors to find that each element is true. But the jury may not actually believe all or part of Joe's testimony, or it may find that what he said to Sally did not in their minds add up to negligence or unreasonable conduct. Thus the jury might find for the defendant, because Joe did not persuade them that each element is true. In that instance, Joe did not meet the persuasion burden. In civil cases, the plaintiff must ordinarily persuade the fact finder by a *preponderance of the evidence* that each element is more likely than not to be true (or, as it is sometimes said, that the scale of justice tips at least a little bit in favor of the plaintiff as to each and every element of the plaintiff's cause of action). You can now see that in the normal case, the plaintiff has three burdens with respect to the merits of his or her case: He or she must plead correctly in the complaint, then meet the production burden, and then, in order to ultimately win, meet the persuasion burden.

If, after discovery, it appears that there is no way a plaintiff can win his or her case because it is predictable that at the trial the plaintiff will not have a sufficiency of evidence to meet the production burden, the defendant can then bring a motion for *summary judgment*. This will dispose of the case after (or during) discovery but before trial. This motion is described in Fed. R. Civ. P. 56.

A plaintiff can win a case at summary judgment or directed verdict, though this is far less common than a defendant prevailing on such motions. But let's say that the cause of action is nonpayment of a promissory note, and that it is undisputed after discovery that the plaintiff lent the defendant money, got a valid promissory note in return, and that the defendant, without any affirmative defense, has not paid. If the elements of a plaintiff's cause of action are self-evident, why have a trial? Put another way, if it is clear that every element of the plaintiff's claim *must be* true, then the plaintiff should win without the necessity of a trial. This plaintiff should win on a summary judgment motion. And if the plaintiff has not filed a summary judgment motion, she could still win this case, after defendant has rested, at the directed verdict stage.

There are other important motions, such as the motion for *renewed judgment as a matter of law* under Fed. R. Civ. P. 50(b). (This motion was once labeled and is still often referred to as a motion for a *judgment notwithstanding the verdict* or *JNOV*.) Other motions include new trial motions and motions to vacate judgment; we will tackle all of these in Chapter 5. The JNOV motion raises precisely the same question as a directed verdict motion, and requires the judge to apply exactly the same test, but the motion is brought *after* the jury has rendered its verdict. (The Federal Rules refer to both directed verdict and JNOV as motions for judgment as a matter of law, with the latter being a *renewed* form of the former.) You will discuss later in the course why a judge might deny a motion for directed verdict, and then, after the jury has found for one party (usually the plaintiff), grant a JNOV on behalf of the opposing party (usually the defendant).

Before you read what happens at trial, we want to caution that civil trials have become very rare. Probably fewer than 2 percent of terminated cases in state and federal courts are terminated by a trial. Many cases are disposed of through a dispositive motion, such as a motion to dismiss for failure to state a claim for which relief can be granted or a motion for summary judgment; some cases are dismissed because the plaintiff has failed to prosecute the claim for a prolonged period of time. A large percentage—maybe even 60-70 percent in some courts—of commenced cases are terminated by settlement. Most settlements are achieved solely by the lawyers or the parties, but increasingly mediators (often judges or magistrates) assist the lawyers and the parties in their negotiations.

You should also be aware that in federal courts, and increasingly in state courts as well, the cases do not just go, unsupervised by the courts, from pleadings, discovery, and motions to settlement or trial. There are often several stages of *case management* in which the judges or other court personnel exercise control over the time sequence of the case and the amount and order of pretrial discovery. Especially in federal courts, much litigation time and expense is frequently spent on pretrial conferences and documents that are designed to focus the case, whittle it down to essentials, and provide the opposing lawyers and the judge with a description of the witnesses, evidence, and potential evidentiary problems that would be present in the unlikely event a trial actually occurs. You might wish to look at this time at Fed. R. Civ. P. 16 in order to get a preliminary sense of the ways in which case management has become an essential characteristic of much civil litigation.

That many, if not most, cases settle does not mean that litigators are not concerned about the facts that would likely come out, the law that would be applied, or the verdicts or orders that might be rendered after a full-scale trial. It is frequently said that settlement discussion is "in the shadow of the law,"* in an attempt to indicate how lawyers, and mediators or judges who assist them in helping to achieve settlement, tend to think and talk in terms of what the results might be if the case is ultimately decided by a judge or jury. Trials are important to the disposition of civil cases in several ways. A firm trial date is one of the strongest inducements to serious settlement talks. The costs of trial, and the uncertainty of trial results, also encourage settlement. What has happened in the trial of similar cases, and the potential verdicts in the case at hand, inform settlement discussion. That one is willing to try a case and is fully prepared for trial can influence settlement demands and offers. And sometimes, trials actually happen.

Trials usually begin with each side giving *opening statements*. The plaintiff's lawyer then introduces her case first, with *direct examination* of each witness. Then the defendant's lawyer will ordinarily *cross-examine* those witnesses. At the trial, as the parties introduce evidence, the attorneys may raise *objections* to some of the questions asked or exhibits offered. The judge will apply *rules of evidence* in assessing the validity of the counsel's objections. If the question is a proper one, the judge will *overrule* the objection, and the witness must answer the question. If the judge finds that the question is improperly framed by counsel or that counsel seeks *inadmissible* testimony, she will *sustain* the objection, which means that the lawyer will have to reframe the question or move on to another matter.

Assume this is a jury case. Once both sides rest, assuming neither side wins on a motion for directed verdict, each side will give *closing arguments*. These will be preceded or followed by the judge's *instructing* the jury. The jury will render its *verdict*. The verdict will later become a *judgment*. If the plaintiff wins, he, she, or it can use formal methods to *execute* on the judgment—that is, force the defendant to pay it. Bear in mind, though, that in some cases the plaintiff will be seeking injunctive relief. She may seek a *temporary restraining order* at the beginning of the case to stop the defendant from doing irreparable harm, and then seek to have that judgment become a

---

*This expression comes from the oft-cited article *Bargaining in the Shadow of the Law: The Case of Divorce*, 88 Yale L.J. 950 (1979). The authors, Robert Mnookin and Lewis Kornhauser, discuss how divorce negotiations occur "in the shadow of the law" in the sense that they are shaped by what the parties suspect a court will do if no agreement is reached and they are forced instead to go to trial.

*preliminary* injunction, stopping the defendant from doing something prior to trial. If the plaintiff wins, the injunction may become a *permanent injunction.*

In most instances, in both state and federal courts, the losing party can appeal only from a *final judgment.* In the federal court system, the party that loses at the district court level has a right to appeal to the U.S. Court of Appeals. If the appeal is lost at this level, the losing party can apply to the U.S. Supreme Court for review. This is called a petition for a *writ of certiorari.* (Supreme Court review is governed by 28 U.S.C. §§ 1253-1258.)

If a party loses in the state trial court of general jurisdiction, then the party usually has the right to appeal to an intermediate appellate court. If the appeal is lost at this level, the losing party can appeal to the state's highest court, but that court usually has discretion over which cases it will hear. Some of the appellate decisions at the highest state court level can be reviewed by the U.S. Supreme Court, but only if that decision involved federal law. *See* 28 U.S.C. § 1257.

Generally, appellate courts insist that the party seeking review has objected to the decision or ruling it is appealing at the time the decision was originally made. Additionally, appellate courts usually require that the trial court's decision be based on the same point. Consequently, a good trial lawyer is always keeping a close eye on the proceedings, looking to object to questionable decisions so that she has a viable, appealable point in the event of a later unfavorable final judgment.

Can you imagine why appellate courts are reluctant to let a party who only loses on a preliminary matter appeal that point at that time to an appellate court? What if, for instance, Sally files a motion to dismiss for improper venue and loses. Why shouldn't she be permitted to appeal immediately on this matter? This would be called an *interlocutory appeal.* Appeals of interlocutory orders sometimes are allowed under 28 U.S.C. § 1292(b) if (i) the question involved is one of law; (ii) the question is controlling; (iii) there are substantial grounds for a difference of opinion; and (iv) immediate appeal materially advances the ultimate termination of litigation. For example, appeals from interlocutory orders of the district courts regarding injunctions are sometimes allowed because of the final and irreparable effect on the rights of the parties, and because the evaluation is completely separate from the merits of the case and is unreviewable on appeal. 28 U.S.C. § 1292(a).

Once a case reaches final judgment, the concept of *res judicata* (literally "a matter adjudged") applies. Let's say that a jury renders a defendant's verdict in the case of *Joe v. Sally*, which then becomes a judgment. A year later, Joe decides to go to another lawyer to try again. Intuitively, this would be both unfair to Sally and expensive for the court system. The defense to the second case would be *res judicata*, because plaintiffs are not permitted to bring the same case twice. Even if Joe decided to sue in case one alleging only battery, and now tries to bring a case for negligence arising from the same incident, *res judicata* would apply. In modern parlance, one would say that Joe is not permitted to split his claim, a concept also called *claim preclusion.*

Sometimes, an issue is decided in one case, and is relevant to a new claim between the same parties in a subsequent case. Assume that *A* sues *B* on a promissory note and wins a case for installments not paid up until the time of the verdict. (Assume further that the note does not have an "acceleration clause" making all of the installments due upon any single failure to pay.) Subsequently, *B* continues not to pay, and *A* sues for the subsequent installments owed. *A* will probably not have to reprove the validity of the promissory note, because that issue has already been litigated between the same parties. The second court would say that *A* can *collaterally estop B* from denying that the note was valid. In other words, the second fact finder, whether judge or jury, would summarily have to find that the note was a valid one. This concept is usually called *issue preclusion*.

Unfortunately some courts use the term *res judicata* to cover both claim preclusion and issue preclusion. In any event, the issues of *res judicata* and collateral estoppel are covered near the end of this book—appropriate, given their finality.

It is now time to explore more deeply the concepts of claims, causes of action, and elements as a prelude to lessons on pleading and the history of pleading.

## C. CLAIMS, CAUSES OF ACTION, AND ELEMENTS

At the heart of a trial lawyer's thinking and strategy about civil litigation are the fundamental concepts of claims or causes of action (these terms frequently mean the same thing*) and elements. A lawsuit usually begins when there has been a dispute and a party or parties to that dispute, and their lawyers, believe that they are entitled to relief because the law recognizes the injury they have suffered, and permits the court to intervene and provide injunctive, monetary, or declaratory relief. A *cause of action* is one shorthand term for what the plaintiff must prove in order to win a litigation. The corresponding term used by the Federal Rules of Civil Procedure, however, is a *claim showing that the pleader is entitled to relief*. Why the Federal Rules use the phrase "claim showing that the pleader is entitled to relief" rather than the previously used term, "cause of action," is something you should consider throughout this chapter. (One relevant factor is the period during which the Federal Rules were drafted, 1935-1937. The New Deal, which enlarged the power of the federal government through a myriad of new agencies and programs, was in full swing.) Each cause of action or claim connotes a group of circumstances for which a court will grant relief. These circumstances, in turn, are divided into parts called elements. In this section, we

---

*The term "claim" is also often used to denote one transaction or occurrence that may permit multiple causes of action.

will provide several examples of causes of action and their elements. In civil litigation, a judge often asks the plaintiff's lawyer what her *prima facie case* is. This can mean that the judge is asking either for an enumeration of the elements of the plaintiff's claim (or cause of action) or for a short description of the evidence as to each of those elements.

Putting aside for now jurisdictional and notice issues, we have seen that plaintiffs have three obligations in order to win in civil litigation. First, whether in state or federal court, plaintiffs must state in their initial pleading that they are entitled to relief. Depending on the court system, the procedural rules may also require a statement of the facts underlying the cause of action. Second, after satisfying their initial pleading obligation, plaintiffs must meet a production burden. This is shorthand for the idea that a plaintiff must present sufficient evidence to permit a reasonable person to find that each element of the claim (or cause of action) is true. Finally, in order to prevail, a plaintiff must meet a burden of persuasion by persuading the fact finder that each element is true. Although a lawyer must, when deciding whether to take a case, assess the likelihood of satisfying the pleading obligation, meeting the production burden, and persuading the fact finder, this chapter focuses on the pleading obligation. We will focus on burdens of production and burdens of persuasion in Chapter 5.

A lawyer cannot responsibly draft a complaint without analyzing her client's situation in order to see if there is a cognizable claim, a claim for which the law will give her client relief. In order to do this analysis, she will have to analyze the elements of her claim or claims. Indeed, much of your law school curriculum will deal with the exploration of causes of action and elements from a wide variety of fields. Causes of action and their elements constitute the substantive law that it is the responsibility of procedure to "process." Lawyers thus can spend much creative energy trying to convince courts to expand older causes of action and to create new ones. Lawyers, lobbyists, and legislators also may create new causes of action through statutes.

The library offers hundreds of places in which to research available causes of action and their elements (as well as the type of evidence one might find to meet both production and persuasion burdens). Each state, for instance, is likely to have at least one or more volumes in a "practice" series that explains causes of action in that state. Volumes in the library containing "pattern jury instructions" will also give you insight into how the substantive law is expressed through causes of action that, in turn, are composed of elements.

What follows is a summary of some popular causes of action. Please realize that this is a limited list with only a summary group of elements. Once you begin to prepare an actual case, you will gain sophistication in articulating the elements. It is also important to remember that different jurisdictions (and law school instructors) may teach the elements of a claim or cause of action in a different manner than you see them here.

*Assault:* (1) intent to cause harmful or offensive contact; and (2) imminent apprehension of such contact.

*Battery:* (1) intentional act; (2) resulting in harmful or offensive contact; (3) lack of consent; and (4) causing injury.

*Breach of Contract:* (1) valid contract; (2) breach; (3) performance by plaintiff; and (4) damage.

*Conversion:* (1) right to property; (2) right to possession; (3) demand for possession; and (4) wrongful possession or control by defendant.

*Copyright Infringement:* (1) ownership of valid copyright; and (2) copying of constituent elements of the work that are original.

*Defamation (or Libel):* (1) false and defamatory statement; (2) publication not privileged; (3) fault (ranging from negligence to malice, depending on the publisher); (4) harm (may be presumed); and (5) recipient understood communication refers to plaintiff.

*Failure to Warn of a Product Defect:* (1) danger existing with foreseeable use of product; (2) inadequate warning of the danger; (3) product was defective and unreasonably dangerous; (4) defect existed at the time it left the control of the manufacturer; (5) product reached user without substantial change; (6) causation; and (7) injury.

*False Imprisonment:* (1) deprivation of liberty; (2) lack of consent; and (3) no legal justification.

*Fraud:* (1) false representation; (2) knowledge of falsity; (3) intent to induce reliance; (4) reasonable reliance; and (5) damage.

*Fraudulent Conveyance:* (1) conveyance without fair consideration; (2) knowledge of an impending obligation; and (3) obligation not satisfied.

*Intentional Infliction of Emotional Distress:* (1) intent; (2) extreme and outrageous conduct; (3) causation; and (4) severe emotional distress.

*Medical Malpractice:* (1) professional standard of care in the community; (2) departure from the standard; (3) causation; and (4) injury.

*Negligence:* (1) duty; (2) breach; (3) cause-in-fact; (4) proximate cause; and (5) harm.

*Negligent Entrustment of a Vehicle:* (1) entrustment by the owner; (2) to a known unlicensed, incompetent, or reckless driver; (3) negligence by driver; and (4) driver's negligence proximately caused the accident.

*Nuisance (Private):* (1) substantial interference; (2) intentional act; (3) unreasonable interference with right to use and enjoy land; and (4) causation.

*Patent Infringement:* (1) unauthorized use or sale; (2) of a patented invention; (3) within or imported into the United States.

*Spoliation of Evidence:* (1) pending or probable litigation involving the plaintiff; (2) defendant's knowledge that litigation exists or is probable; (3) destruction of evidence; (4) disruption of plaintiff's case; (5) proximate cause; and (6) damages.

*Strict Products Liability (Design Defect):* (1) sale of a product by one engaged in the business of selling such products; (2) product reached consumer without substantial change in condition; (3) product was in a defective condition unreasonably dangerous to the user; (4) causation; and (5) injury.

*Tortious Interference with Contractual Relations:* (1) existing contract; (2) defendant aware of that contract; (3) defendant intentionally procured breach of that contract; (4) lack of justification; and (5) resulting damage.

*Trademark Infringement:* (1) plaintiff possessed a mark; (2) defendant used the mark; (3) use of mark occurred in commerce; and (4) use was likely to confuse customers.

*Trespass:* (1) unauthorized entry by defendant; (2) property possessed by plaintiff; and (3) damage.

*Trespass to Chattel:* (1) dispossession by defendant of plaintiff's chattel; and (2) impairment of chattel's condition, quality, or value, or deprivation of use for a substantial period of time.

*Unjust Enrichment:* (1) benefit conferred on defendant; (2) defendant appreciated or knew of benefit; and (3) circumstances would make it inequitable for the receiving party to benefit without paying for its value.

*Wrongful Death:* (1) tort; (2) resulting death; and (3) damages suffered by heirs. (This cause of action is usually statutory, as you will see later in the course.)

This list of causes of action and their elements primarily includes common law private causes of action. Claims of a more public nature often incorporate burden shift problems and more sophisticated issues of definition. For instance, much civil rights litigation is brought under 42 U.S.C. § 1983, the post-Civil War statute now utilized to enforce constitutional and other federal law violations committed by state actors. Much employment discrimination litigation is brought under Title VII. Each of these statutes can raise sophisticated issues with respect to definitions and burdens. We address many of these problems in materials relating to the *City of Cleveland* case, with those Case Files reprinted in the back of this book. You might want to look at the initial Memorandum and the Memorandum Re: Directed Verdict in the Case Files to see how elements are treated in a more complex public litigation matter.

## Practice Exercise No. 7:
## Initial Strategy Session in *Carpenter*

Assume that you are an associate in a law firm and have received a memorandum in preparation for a strategy session. The memorandum on the potential client, which you should read for the exercise, is the first document in the Case Files for *Carpenter v. Dee.* (The documents relating to this case are printed at the end of your book in the section labeled Case Files.) Prepare to discuss with the senior partner the causes of action that may be available to Nancy Carpenter (and against whom) if the firm chooses to represent her. Consider each element of a potential claim and, using the facts of the case, note where you will need additional information. Of course, at this early stage in the litigation the memorandum is not a complete statement of the case; indeed, some important facts are missing. Although you do not know much about specific claims or causes of action yet, consider the sampling of causes of action and elements that you just read; also read the three brief Massachusetts statutes in the Case Files that follow the initial memorandum. Do you think the firm should take this case? Why?

## D. PLEADINGS AND AMENDMENTS

Having considered how plaintiffs' lawyers think about a potential litigation, we now address the documents and motions that parties draft in the beginning stages of a lawsuit. Although most cases are brought in state courts, we concentrate our inquiry on the Federal Rules of Civil Procedure that control litigation in the federal trial courts. These rules have been highly influential on state rules and practices, and provide a common reservoir of procedural learning for most law students in the United States. Fed. R. Civ. P. 7, 8, 9, and 10 lay out the requirements for a federal complaint, and 12(b)(6) describes the motion that a defendant may bring to challenge whether the plaintiff's complaint correctly describes a claim for which relief can be granted.

At this point in the course both you, the student, and your professor encounter a severe conceptual and practical problem. The Federal Rules of Civil Procedure were drafted from 1935 to 1937, and became law in 1938. The underlying assumptions that animated the Rules included the importance of simplicity and liberality in pleading. Later in this chapter we provide history about the evolution of different procedural regimes; you should already recognize, however, that although the pleading rules have remained essentially the same since 1938, their interpretation has materially changed. Changes first occurred as a result of some federal district and circuit court judges acting on their own, and more recently by Supreme Court decisions. The trend has been in the direction of more rigorous pleading requirements, with plaintiffs obligated to provide more facts in the complaint, rather than waiting for the discovery stage for each side to explore in detail the underlying facts. As you will later study, other aspects of civil procedure, such as summary judgment, have moved in the same direction of requiring more of plaintiffs than was previously required. Again, this has been accomplished with only modest changes in the Rules themselves.

It is not your fault that the Rules and attached Forms in the Federal Rules say one thing, but the interpretation is now often different than in the past and different from what one might expect from the words themselves. We try to help you adjust to this predicament by providing three types of information: the Rules themselves and opinions interpreting them (doctrine), information about how and why the transformations have occurred (context), and practice exercises in which you make arguments in the course of applying the Rules to concrete situations. We think that you, as well as the accomplished lawyer, can act more successfully as advocates for clients and in policy arenas by studying how and why judges and others make their decisions. Your advocacy should be informed by knowledge of the political, social, and economic forces that influence those you are trying to persuade.

In any event, as you will see, the goal of simplicity and liberality in pleading has been the subject of recent, dramatic, and controversial reform. Of course, though, even with modest pleading requirements, there may be strategic reasons to plead with greater specificity than the rules require. For instance, a more extensive story in a pleading may help educate the judge to see the case in a more favorable light, or it may lead to an earlier and more advantageous settlement.

In this section, you will also study the responses that a defendant must make, and may make, to a complaint. This will require close attention to Rules 8 and 12. You will discover, for example, that the defendant will have the choice, if appropriate, of challenging, either through a motion or in an answer, whether the complaint sufficiently states a claim for which relief can be granted. This section will also expose you to the rules for amending pleadings. Indeed, a fundamental tenet of the simplicity theme of the drafters of the Federal Rules was ease of amendment. Amending complaints may have become a more frequent and necessary occurrence with the trend that requires more factual information in complaints.

By the end of this section, you should know the fundamental rules of pleading complaints and answers, as well as the rules governing amendments. You should also be thinking about pleadings from the points of view of a variety of essential actors and audiences in litigation: parties, lawyers, judges, the court system, and society.

## 1. The Purpose and Doctrine of Complaints

We now introduce the civil complaint and modern-day pleading standards. How much detail to require in pleadings raises a perplexing dilemma. If rules require too much specificity, some meritorious cases will either not be brought or will be terminated early in the process for failure to meet the standard. If rules require little precision, suits without merit will be more likely to be instituted. In a later section in this chapter, as mentioned previously, we provide some of the history behind attempts to improve this and other aspects of American procedure; we think, though, that the history and its importance will make more sense if you have some of the relevant rules and case law in mind before reading the history.

The Federal Rules of Civil Procedure became law in 1938. Their principal draftsman, Professor Charles E. Clark, subsequently became a judge on the U.S. Court of Appeals for the Second Circuit. In *Dioguardi v. Durning*, 139 F.2d 774 (2d Cir. 1944), Judge Clark had the opportunity to interpret the pleading rule that he had drafted. Read (or re-read) Federal Rule 1, 8(a)(2), 12(b)(6), and Form 11 in your rules supplement, and then consider the complaint that Harry Durning filed in that case. (In fact, Mr. Durning's initial complaint had been dismissed, and the following is his *amended* complaint. It is reprinted here verbatim.)

Plaintiff, as and for his bill of amended complaint the defendant, respectfully alleges:

FIRST: I want justice done on the basis of my medicinal extracts which have disappeared saying that they had leaked, which could never be true in the manner they were bottled.

SECOND: Mr. E.G. Collord Clerk in Charge, promised to give me my merchandise as soon as I paid for it. Then all of a sudden payments were stopped.

THIRD: Then, he didn't want to sell me my merchandise at catalogue price with the 5% off, which was very important to me, after I had already paid $5,000 for them, beside a few other expenses.

FOURTH: Why was the medicinaly given to the Springdale Distilling Co. with my betting price of $110; and not their price of $120.

FIFTH: It isn't so easy to do away with two cases with 37 bottles of one quart. Being protected, they can take this chance.

SIXTH: No one can stop my rights upon my merchandise, because of both the duly and the entry.

WHEREFORE: Plaintiff demands judgment against the defendant, individually and as Collector of Customs at the Port of New York, in the sum of Five Thousand Dollars ($5,000) together with interest from the respective dates of payment as set forth herein, together with the costs and disbursements of this action.

The district judge had dismissed this amended complaint for failure to state a claim. Why do you think Judge Clark reversed the lower courts and found the claims, "however inartistically they may be stated," satisfactory under Federal Rule 8(a)? (Hint: In the opinion Judge Clark wrote: "[H]ere is another instance of judicial haste which in the long run makes waste.")

Thirteen years later, the U.S. Supreme Court confronted a similar situation and had the opportunity either to reinforce Judge Clark's vision or to outline a different course. Justice Black authored the opinion for a unanimous Court.

## ■ CONLEY v. GIBSON
### *355 U.S. 41 (1957)*

Justice BLACK delivered the opinion of the Court:

Once again Negro employees are here under the Railway Labor Act asking that their collective bargaining agent be compelled to represent them fairly. In a series of cases beginning with *Steele v. Louisville & Nashville R. Co.*, 323 U.S. 192, this Court has emphatically and repeatedly ruled that an exclusive bargaining agent under the Railway Labor Act is obligated to represent all employees in the bargaining unit fairly and without discrimination because of race and has held that the courts have power to protect employees against such invidious discrimination.

This class suit was brought in a Federal District Court in Texas by certain Negro members of the Brotherhood of Railway and Steamship Clerks, petitioners here, on behalf of themselves and other Negro employees similarly situated against the Brotherhood, its Local Union No. 28 and certain officers of both. In summary, the complaint made the following allegations relevant to our decision: Petitioners were employees of the Texas and New Orleans Railroad at its Houston Freight House. Local 28 of the Brotherhood was the designated bargaining agent under the Railway Labor Act for the bargaining unit to which petitioners belonged. A contract existed between the Union and the Railroad which gave the employees in the bargaining unit certain protection from discharge and loss of seniority. In May 1954, the Railroad purported to abolish 45 jobs held by petitioners or other Negroes all of whom were either discharged or demoted. In truth the 45 jobs were not abolished at all but instead filled by whites as the Negroes were ousted, except for a few instances where Negroes were rehired to fill their old jobs but with loss of seniority. Despite repeated pleas by petitioners, the Union, acting according to plan, did nothing to protect them against these discriminatory discharges and refused to give them protection comparable to that given to white employees. The complaint then went on to allege that the Union had failed in general to represent Negro employees equally and in good faith. It charged that such discrimination constituted a violation of petitioners' right under the Railway Labor Act to fair representation from their bargaining agent. And it concluded by asking for relief in the nature of declaratory judgment, injunction and damages.

The respondents appeared and moved to dismiss the complaint on several grounds: (1) the National Railroad Adjustment Board had exclusive jurisdiction over the controversy; (2) the Texas and New Orleans Railroad, which had not been joined, was an indispensable party defendant; and (3) the complaint failed to state a claim upon which relief could be given. The District Court granted the motion to dismiss holding that Congress had given the Adjustment Board exclusive jurisdiction over the controversy. The Court of Appeals for the Fifth Circuit, apparently relying on the same ground, affirmed. 229 F.2d 436. Since the case raised an important question concerning the protection of employee rights under the Railway Labor Act we granted certiorari.

[Justice Black then provided his rationale for overturning the district and circuit court determinations of the jurisdictional issue. Although "the District Court did not pass on the other reasons advanced for dismissal of the complaint," he thought it "timely and proper for" the Supreme Court to consider the other two arguments for dismissal. The "indispensable party" contention was swiftly rejected, and Black proceeded to address the 12(b)(6) motion.]

[W]e hold that . . . the complaint adequately set forth a claim upon which relief could be granted. In appraising the sufficiency of the complaint we follow, of course, the accepted rule that a complaint should not be dismissed for failure to state a claim unless it appears beyond doubt that the plaintiff can prove no set of facts in support of his claim which would entitle him to relief. Here, the complaint alleged, in part, that petitioners were discharged wrongfully by the Railroad and that the Union, acting according to plan, refused to protect their jobs as it did those of white employees or to help them with their grievances all because they were Negroes. If these allegations are proven there has been a manifest breach of the Union's statutory duty to represent fairly and without hostile discrimination all of the employees in the bargaining unit. This Court squarely held in *Steele* and subsequent cases that discrimination in representation because of race is prohibited by the Railway Labor Act. The bargaining representative's duty not to draw "irrelevant and invidious" distinctions among those it represents does not come to an abrupt end, as the respondents seem to contend, with the making of an agreement between union and employer. Collective bargaining is a continuing process. Among other things, it involves day-to-day adjustments in the contract and other working rules, resolution of new problems not covered by existing agreements, and the protection of employee rights already secured by contract. The bargaining representative can no more unfairly discriminate in carrying out these functions than it can in negotiating a collective agreement. A contract may be fair and impartial on its face yet administered in such a way, with the active or tacit consent of the union, as to be flagrantly discriminatory against some members of the bargaining unit.

The respondents point to the fact that under the Railway Labor Act aggrieved employees can file their own grievances with the Adjustment Board or sue the employer for breach of contract. Granting this, it still furnishes no sanction for the Union's alleged discrimination in refusing to represent petitioners. The Railway Labor Act, in an attempt to aid collective action by employees, conferred great power and protection on the bargaining agent chosen by a majority of them. As individuals or small groups the employees cannot begin to possess the bargaining power of their representative in negotiating with the employer or in presenting their grievances to him. Nor may a minority choose another agent to bargain in their behalf. We need not pass on the Union's claim that it was not obliged to handle any grievances at all because we are clear that once it undertook to bargain or present grievances for some of the employees it represented it could not refuse to take similar action in good faith for other employees just because they were Negroes.

The respondents also argue that the complaint failed to set forth specific facts to support its general allegations of discrimination and that its dismissal is therefore proper. The decisive answer to this is that the Federal Rules of Civil Procedure do not require a claimant to set out in detail the facts upon which he bases his claim. To the contrary, all the Rules require is "a short and plain statement of the claim" that will give the defendant fair notice of what the plaintiff's claim is and the grounds upon which it rests. The illustrative forms appended to the Rules plainly demonstrate this. Such simplified "notice pleading" is made possible by the liberal opportunity for discovery and the other pretrial procedures established by the Rules to disclose more precisely the basis of both claim and defense and to define more narrowly the disputed facts and issues. Following the simple guide of Rule 8(f) that "all pleadings shall be so construed as to do substantial justice,"* we have no doubt that petitioners' complaint adequately set forth a claim and gave the respondents fair notice of its basis. The Federal Rules reject the approach that pleading is a game of skill in which one misstep by counsel may be decisive to the outcome and accept the principle that the purpose of pleading is to facilitate a proper decision on the merits.

The judgment is reversed and the cause is remanded to the District Court for further proceedings not inconsistent with this opinion. . . .

## Comments and Questions

1. In order to defend or criticize a pleading standard one must consider the goals of a system of pleading. Is the goal to screen out claims that lack merit? If so, wouldn't a more rigorous pleading standard require plaintiffs to do their legal and factual homework prior to filing? Is that such a bad idea? What are the competing goals?

2. Some lower federal courts reacted to the regime of "notice pleading" by requiring stricter pleading in some types of cases—most notably civil rights cases. Indeed, during the 1970s and 1980s all federal courts of appeals applied a standard demanding factual specificity of civil rights plaintiffs filing cases in federal courts. For example, in a 1992 case before the U.S. Court of Appeals for the Fifth Circuit, the court summarized some of the allegations in the complaint:

> This civil rights case arose out of [an incident] involving the execution of search warrants by law enforcement officers with the Tarrant County Narcotics Intelligence and Coordination Unit. . . . Charlene Leatherman, her son Travis, and her two dogs, Shakespeare and Ninja. Ms. Leatherman and Travis were driving in Fort Worth when they were suddenly stopped by police cars. Police officers surrounded the two of them, shouting instructions and threatening to shoot them. The officers informed Ms. Leatherman that other law enforcement officers were in the process of searching her residence. The officers also informed her that the search team had shot and killed their two dogs. Ms. Leatherman and Travis returned to their home to find Shakespeare lying dead some twenty-five feet from the front door. He had been shot three times, once in the stomach, once in the leg, and once in the head. Ninja was lying in a pool of blood on the bed in the master bedroom. He had been shot in the head at close range, evidently with a shotgun, and brain matter was splattered across the bed, against the wall, and on the floor around the bed. The officers found nothing in the home relevant to their investigation. Rather than departing with dispatch, they proceeded to lounge on the front lawn of the Leatherman home for over an hour, drinking, smoking, talking, and laughing, apparently celebrating their seemingly unbridled power.

*Eds.' Note:* This mandate now appears at Fed. R. Civ. P. 8(e).

*Leatherman v. Tarrant County Narcotics Intelligence and Coordination Unit*, 954 F.2d 1054 (5th Cir. 1992). In opinions that featured such topical headings as "Dog Day Afternoon," "These Dogs Want Their Day," and "Let Sleeping Dogs Lie," the Fifth Circuit concluded that the plaintiff's complaint was "All Bark, No Bite":

> In *Elliott v. Perez*, 751 F.2d 1472 (5th Cir. 1985), this circuit adopted the heightened pleading requirement for cases against state actors in their individual capacities. Reasoning that the doctrine of immunity should accord the defendant-official not only immunity from liability, but also immunity from defending against the lawsuit, *id.* at 1477-78, the *Elliott* court held that: In cases against government officials involving the likely defense of qualified immunity we require of trial judges that they demand that the plaintiff's complaint state with factual detail and particularity the basis for the claim which necessarily includes why the defendant-official cannot successfully maintain the defense of immunity. *Id.* at 1473. . . .
>
> With the heightened pleading requirement as our guide, we turn to the particulars of this case. Quite plainly, plaintiffs' complaint falls short of alleging the requisite facts to establish a policy of inadequate training. Where, as here, a lawsuit brought against a municipality is predicated on inadequate training of its police officers, this circuit has cautioned that "to make such a showing in such a case, there would have to be demonstrated 'at least a pattern of similar incidents in which the citizens were injured' . . . [in order] to establish the official policy requisite to municipal liability under section 1983." *Rodriguez*, 871 F.2d at 554-55. . . .

*Id.* at 1057. The Fifth Circuit also affirmed the district court's *sua sponte* dismissal of the claims against certain of the defendants who had not even moved to dismiss for failure to state a claim.

3. The Supreme Court reversed the Fifth Circuit. Then-Chief Justice Rehnquist wrote a unanimous opinion for the Court: "We think that it is impossible to square the 'heightened pleading standard' applied by the Fifth Circuit in this case with the liberal system of 'notice pleading' set up by the Federal Rules. . . . Perhaps if Rules 8 and 9 were rewritten today, claims against municipalities under § 1983 might be subjected to the added specificity requirement of Rule 9(b). But that is a result which must be obtained by the process of amending the Federal Rules, and not by judicial interpretation." 507 U.S. 163, 168 (1992). Should Federal Rule 8(a) and/or 9(b) be amended to require a heightened degree of particularity when pleading claims against municipalities? Is it unrealistic to expect a single pleading standard to apply to all types of actions (other than fraud and mistake)?

4. Notwithstanding the Court's decision in *Leatherman*, lower courts persisted in imposing higher pleading standards for civil rights cases. This phenomenon led, in turn, to another Supreme Court decision. Reversing a decision of the U.S. Court of Appeals for the Second Circuit in an employment discrimination case, the Court, in another unanimous opinion, made clear that a plaintiff need not allege facts to support each element of its prima facie

case: The prima facie case is "an evidentiary standard, not a pleading requirement." *Swierkiewicz v. Sorema*, 534 U.S. 500 (2002).

5. More recently, however, the tide has turned, revealing a deep divide within the Supreme Court. To the surprise of many, in 2007, a majority of the Court rejected *Conley*'s "no set of facts" language and imposed a plausibility requirement at the pleading stage of a federal antitrust action. *See Bell Atlantic v. Twombly*, 550 U.S. 544 (2007). The facts and legal issues in the *Twombly* antitrust class action are described in the *Iqbal* opinions, which follow. Although suggesting that the complaint need not contain detailed factual allegations, the court in *Twombly* noted that "a plaintiff's obligation to provide the 'grounds' of his 'entitle[ment] to relief' requires more than labels and conclusions, and a formulaic recitation of the elements of a cause of action will not do. Factual allegations must be enough to raise a right to relief above the speculative level." In a footnote, the court added that "Rule 8(a)(2) still requires a 'showing,' rather than a blanket assertion, of entitlement to relief." Over a vigorous dissent, the Court denied that it was requiring "heightened fact pleading of specifics, but only enough facts to state a claim to relief that is plausible on its face. Because the plaintiffs here have not nudged their claims across the line from conceivable to plausible, their complaint must be dismissed." After *Twombly*, two questions lingered: (i) did the new plausibility requirement at the pleading stage significantly alter the notice pleading regime? and (ii) did it apply outside the antitrust context? Some commentators also speculated that *Twombly* might only apply to cases like it, in which one could anticipate extraordinarily extensive, cumbersome, and costly discovery. In any event, the Court took another pleading case two years later.

# ■ ASHCROFT v. IQBAL
### *556 U.S. 662 (2009)*

Justice KENNEDY delivered the opinion of the Court, in which CHIEF JUSTICE ROBERTS, Justice SCALIA, Justice THOMAS, and Justice ALITO joined:

Respondent Javaid Iqbal is a citizen of Pakistan and a Muslim. In the wake of the September 11, 2001, terrorist attacks he was arrested in the United States on criminal charges and detained by federal officials. Respondent claims he was deprived of various constitutional protections while in federal custody. To redress the alleged deprivations, respondent filed a complaint against numerous federal officials, including John Ashcroft, the former Attorney General of the United States, and Robert Mueller, the Director of the Federal Bureau of Investigation (FBI). Ashcroft and Mueller are the petitioners in the case now before us. As to these two petitioners, the complaint alleges that they adopted an unconstitutional policy that subjected respondent to harsh conditions of confinement on account of his race, religion, or national origin.

In the District Court petitioners raised the defense of qualified immunity and moved to dismiss the suit, contending the complaint was not sufficient to state a claim against them. The District Court denied the motion to dismiss, concluding the complaint was sufficient to state a claim despite petitioners' official status at the times in question. Petitioners brought an interlocutory appeal in the Court of Appeals for the Second Circuit. The court, without discussion, assumed it had jurisdiction over the order denying the motion to dismiss; and it affirmed the District Court's decision.

Respondent's account of his prison ordeal could, if proved, demonstrate unconstitutional misconduct by some governmental actors. But the allegations and pleadings with respect to these actors are not before us here. This case instead turns on a narrower question: Did respondent, as the plaintiff in the District Court, plead factual matter that, if taken as true, states a claim that petitioners deprived him of his clearly established constitutional rights. We hold respondent's pleadings are insufficient.

## I

Following the 2001 attacks, the FBI and other entities within the Department of Justice began an investigation of vast reach to identify the assailants and prevent them from attacking anew. . . .

In the ensuing months the FBI questioned more than 1,000 people with suspected links to the attacks in particular or to terrorism in general. Of those individuals, some 762 were held on immigration charges; and a 184-member subset of that group was deemed to be "of 'high interest'" to the investigation. The high-interest detainees were held under restrictive conditions designed to prevent them from communicating with the general prison population or the outside world.

Respondent was one of the detainees. According to his complaint, in November 2001 agents of the FBI and Immigration and Naturalization Service arrested him on charges of fraud in relation to identification documents and conspiracy to defraud the United States. *Iqbal v. Hasty*, 490 F.3d 143, 147-148 (2d Cir. 2007). Pending trial for those crimes, respondent was housed at the Metropolitan Detention Center (MDC) in Brooklyn, New York. Respondent was designated a person "of high interest" to the September 11 investigation and in January 2002 was placed in a section of the MDC known as the Administrative Maximum Special Housing Unit (ADMAX SHU). . . . ADMAX SHU detainees were kept in lockdown 23 hours a day, spending the remaining hour outside their cells in handcuffs and leg irons accompanied by a four-officer escort.

Respondent pleaded guilty to the criminal charges, served a term of imprisonment, and was removed to his native Pakistan. *Id.*, at 149. He then filed a *Bivens* action in the United States District Court for the Eastern District of New York against 34 current and former federal officials and 19 "John Doe" federal corrections officers. *See Bivens v. Six Unknown Fed. Narcotics Agents*, 403 U.S. 388 (1971). The defendants range from the correctional officers who had day-to-day contact with respondent during the term of his confinement, to the wardens of the MDC facility, all the way to petitioners—officials who were at the highest level of the federal law enforcement hierarchy. First Amended Complaint in No. 04-CV1809 (JG)(JA), ¶¶ 10-11 (hereinafter Complaint).

The 21-cause-of-action complaint does not challenge respondent's arrest or his confinement in the MDC's general prison population. Rather, it concentrates on his treatment while confined to the ADMAX SHU. The complaint sets forth various claims against defendants who are not before us. For instance, the complaint alleges that respondent's jailors "kicked him in the stomach, punched him in the face, and dragged him across" his cell without justification, *id.*, ¶ 113; subjected him to serial strip and body-cavity searches when he posed no safety risk to himself or others, *id.*, ¶¶ 143-145; and refused to let him and other Muslims pray because there would be "[n]o prayers for terrorists," *id.*, ¶ 154.

The allegations against petitioners are the only ones relevant here. The complaint contends that petitioners designated respondent a person of high interest on account of his race, religion, or national origin, in contravention of the First and Fifth Amendments to the Constitution. The complaint alleges that "the [FBI], under the direction of Defendant Mueller, arrested and detained thousands of Arab Muslim men . . . as part of its investigation of the events of September 11." *Id.*, ¶ 47. It further alleges that "[t]he policy of holding post-September-11th detainees in highly restrictive conditions of confinement until they were 'cleared' by the FBI was approved by Defendants Ashcroft and Mueller in discussions in the weeks after September 11, 2001." *Id.*, ¶ 69. Lastly, the complaint posits that petitioners "each knew of, condoned, and willfully and maliciously agreed to subject" respondent to harsh conditions of confinement "as a matter of policy, solely on account of [his] religion, race, and/or national origin and for no legitimate penological interest." *Id.*, ¶ 96. The pleading names Ashcroft as the "principal architect" of the policy, *id.*, ¶ 10, and identifies Mueller as "instrumental in [its] adoption, promulgation, and implementation." *Id.*, ¶ 11.

Petitioners moved to dismiss the complaint for failure to state sufficient allegations to show their own involvement in clearly established unconstitutional conduct. The District Court denied their motion. Accepting all of the allegations in respondent's complaint as true, the court held that "it cannot be said that there [is] no set of facts on which [respondent] would be entitled to relief as against" petitioners. Invoking the collateral-order doctrine petitioners filed an interlocutory appeal in the United States Court of Appeals for the Second Circuit. While that appeal was pending, this Court decided *Bell Atlantic Corp. v. Twombly*, 550 U.S. 544 (2007), which discussed the standard for evaluating whether a complaint is sufficient to survive a motion to dismiss.

The Court of Appeals considered *Twombly*'s applicability to this case. Acknowledging that *Twombly* retired the *Conley* [*v. Gibson*, 355 U.S. 41 (1957)] no set-of-facts test relied upon by the District Court, the Court of Appeals' opinion discussed at length how to apply this Court's "standard for assessing the adequacy of pleadings." 490 F.3d, at 155. It concluded that *Twombly* called for a "flexible 'plausibility standard,' which obliges a pleader to amplify a claim with some factual allegations in those contexts where such amplification is needed to render the claim plausible." *Id.*, at 157-158. The court found that petitioners' appeal did not present one of "those contexts" requiring amplification. As a consequence, it held respondent's pleading adequate to allege petitioners' personal involvement in discriminatory decisions which, if true, violated clearly established constitutional law. *Id.*, at 174.

Judge Cabranes concurred . . . [but] nonetheless expressed concern at the prospect of subjecting high-ranking Government officials—entitled to assert the defense of qualified immunity and charged with responding to "a national and international security emergency unprecedented in the history of the American Republic"—to the burdens of discovery on the basis of a complaint as nonspecific as respondent's. . . .

We granted certiorari, and now reverse.

## II

[In this Part the Court concluded that the Court of Appeals had subject matter jurisdiction to affirm the District Court's denial of the motion to dismiss, and that an interlocutory appeal to the Supreme Court was permitted, even though there was not yet a final judgment.]

## III

. . . [W]e begin by taking note of the elements a plaintiff must plead to state a claim of unconstitutional discrimination against officials entitled to assert the defense of qualified immunity.

In *Bivens*—proceeding on the theory that a right suggests a remedy—this Court "recognized for the first time an implied private action for damages against federal officers alleged to have violated a citizen's constitutional rights." *Correctional Services Corp. v. Malesko*, 534 U.S. 61, 66 (2001). . . . [W]e assume, without deciding, that respondent's First Amendment claim is actionable under *Bivens*.

In the limited settings where *Bivens* does apply, the implied cause of action is the "federal analog to suits brought against state officials under Rev. Stat. § 1979, 42 U.S.C. § 1983." *Hartman v. Moore*, 547 U.S. 250, 254 n.2 (2006). Based on the rules our precedents establish, respondent correctly concedes that Government officials may not be held liable for the unconstitutional conduct of their subordinates under a theory of respondeat superior. . . . Because vicarious liability is inapplicable to *Bivens* and § 1983 suits, a plaintiff must plead that each Government-official defendant, through the official's own individual actions, has violated the Constitution.

The factors necessary to establish a *Bivens* violation will vary with the constitutional provision at issue. Where the claim is invidious discrimination in contravention of the First and Fifth Amendments, our decisions make clear that the plaintiff must plead and prove that the defendant acted with discriminatory purpose. Under extant precedent purposeful discrimination requires more than "intent as volition or intent as awareness of consequences." *Personnel Administrator of Mass. v. Feeney*, 442 U.S. 256, 279 (1979). It instead involves a decision maker's undertaking a course of action "'because of,' not merely 'in spite of,' [the action's] adverse effects upon an identifiable group." *Ibid.* It follows that, to state a claim based on a violation of a clearly established right, respondent must plead sufficient factual matter to show that petitioners adopted and implemented the detention policies at issue not for a neutral, investigative reason but for the purpose of discriminating on account of race, religion, or national origin. . . .

## IV

### A

We turn to respondent's complaint. Under Federal Rule of Civil Procedure 8(a)(2), a pleading must contain a "short and plain statement of the claim showing that the pleader is entitled to relief." As the Court held in *Twombly*, 550 U.S. 544, the pleading standard Rule 8 announces does not require "detailed factual allegations," but it demands more than an unadorned, the-defendant-unlawfully-harmed-me accusation. *Id.*, at 555.

A pleading that offers "labels and conclusions" or "a formulaic recitation of the elements of a cause of action will not do." 550 U.S., at 555. Nor does a complaint suffice if it tenders "naked assertion[s]" devoid of "further factual enhancement." *Id.*, at 557.

To survive a motion to dismiss, a complaint must contain sufficient factual matter, accepted as true, to "state a claim to relief that is plausible on its face." *Id.*, at 570. A claim has facial plausibility when the plaintiff pleads factual content that allows the court to draw the reasonable inference that the defendant is liable for the misconduct alleged. *Id.*, at 556. The plausibility standard is not akin to a "probability requirement," but it asks for more than a sheer possibility that a defendant has acted unlawfully. *Ibid.* Where a complaint pleads facts that are "merely consistent with" a defendant's liability, it "stops short of the line between possibility and plausibility of 'entitlement to relief.'" *Id.*, at 557 (brackets omitted).

Two working principles underlie our decision in *Twombly*. First, the tenet that a court must accept as true all of the allegations contained in a complaint is inapplicable to legal conclusions. Threadbare recitals of the elements of a cause of action, supported by mere conclusory statements, do not suffice. *Id.*, at 555 (although for the purposes of a motion to dismiss we must take all of the factual allegations in the complaint as true, we "are not bound to accept as true a legal conclusion couched as a factual allegation" (internal quotation marks omitted)). Rule 8 marks a notable and generous departure from the hyper-technical, code-pleading regime of a prior era, but it does not unlock the doors of discovery for a plaintiff armed with nothing more than conclusions. Second, only a complaint that states a plausible claim for relief survives a motion to dismiss. *Id.*, at 556. Determining whether a complaint states a plausible claim for relief will, as the Court of Appeals observed, be a context-specific task that requires the reviewing court to draw on its judicial experience and common sense. 490 F.3d, at 157-158. But where the well-pleaded facts do not permit the court to infer more than the mere possibility of misconduct, the complaint has alleged—but it has not "show[n]"—"that the pleader is entitled to relief." Fed. Rule Civ. Proc. 8(a)(2).

In keeping with these principles a court considering a motion to dismiss can choose to begin by identifying pleadings that, because they are no more than conclusions, are not entitled to the assumption of truth. While legal conclusions can provide the framework of a complaint, they must be supported by factual allegations. When there are well-pleaded factual allegations, a court should assume their veracity and then determine whether they plausibly give rise to an entitlement to relief.

Our decision in *Twombly* illustrates the two-pronged approach. There, we considered the sufficiency of a complaint alleging that incumbent telecommunications providers had entered an agreement not to compete and to forestall competitive entry, in violation of the Sherman Act, 15 U.S.C. § 1. Recognizing that § 1 enjoins only anticompetitive conduct "effected by a contract, combination, or conspiracy," the plaintiffs in *Twombly* flatly pleaded that the defendants "ha[d] entered into a contract, combination or conspiracy to prevent competitive entry . . . and ha[d] agreed not to compete with one another." 550 U.S., at 551 (internal quotation marks omitted). The complaint also alleged that the defendants' "parallel course of conduct . . . to prevent competition" and inflate prices was indicative of the unlawful agreement alleged. *Ibid.* (internal quotation marks omitted). . . . Because the well-pleaded fact of parallel conduct, accepted as true, did not plausibly suggest an unlawful agreement, the Court held the plaintiffs' complaint must be dismissed. *Id.*, at 570.

**B**

Under *Twombly*'s construction of Rule 8, we conclude that respondent's complaint has not "nudged [his] claims" of invidious discrimination "across the line from conceivable to plausible." *Ibid.*

We begin our analysis by identifying the allegations in the complaint that are not entitled to the assumption of truth. Respondent pleads that petitioners "knew of, condoned, and willfully and maliciously agreed to subject [him]" to harsh conditions of confinement "as a matter of policy, solely on account of [his] religion, race, and/or national origin and for no legitimate penological interest." Complaint ¶ 96. The complaint alleges that Ashcroft was the "principal architect" of this invidious policy, *id.*, ¶ 10, and that Mueller was "instrumental" in adopting and executing it, *id.*, ¶ 11. These bare assertions, much like the pleading of conspiracy in *Twombly*, amount to nothing more than a "formulaic recitation of the elements" of a constitutional discrimination claim, 550 U.S., at 555, namely, that petitioners adopted a policy "'because of,' not merely 'in spite of,' its adverse effects upon an identifiable group." *Feeney*, 442 U.S., at 279. As such, the allegations are conclusory and not entitled to be assumed true. *Twombly*, *supra*, 550 U.S., at 554-555. To be clear, we do not reject these bald allegations on the ground that they are unrealistic or nonsensical. We do not so characterize them any more than the Court in *Twombly* rejected the plaintiffs' express allegation of a "'contract, combination or conspiracy to prevent competitive entry,'" *id.*, at 551, because it thought that claim too chimerical to be maintained. It is the conclusory nature of respondent's allegations, rather than their extravagantly fanciful nature, that disentitles them to the presumption of truth.

We next consider the factual allegations in respondent's complaint to determine if they plausibly suggest an entitlement to relief. The complaint alleges that "the [FBI], under the direction of Defendant Mueller, arrested and detained thousands of Arab Muslim men . . . as part of its investigation of the events of September 11." Complaint ¶ 47. It further claims that "[t]he policy of holding post-September-11th detainees in highly restrictive conditions of confinement until they were 'cleared' by the FBI was approved by Defendants Ashcroft and Mueller in discussions in the weeks after September 11, 2001." *Id.*, ¶ 69. Taken as true, these allegations are consistent with petitioners' purposefully designating detainees "of high interest" because of their race, religion, or national origin. But given more likely explanations, they do not plausibly establish this purpose. . . .

On the facts respondent alleges the arrests Mueller oversaw were likely lawful and justified by his nondiscriminatory intent to detain aliens who were illegally present in the United States and who had potential connections to those who committed terrorist acts. As between that "obvious alternative explanation" for the arrests, *Twombly*, *supra*, at 567, and the purposeful, invidious discrimination respondent asks us to infer, discrimination is not a plausible conclusion.

But even if the complaint's well-pleaded facts give rise to a plausible inference that respondent's arrest was the result of unconstitutional discrimination, that inference alone would not entitle respondent to relief. It is important to recall that respondent's complaint challenges neither the constitutionality of his arrest nor his initial detention in the MDC. Respondent's constitutional claims against petitioners rest solely on their ostensible "policy of holding post-September-11th detainees" in the ADMAX SHU once they were categorized as "of high interest." Complaint ¶ 69. To prevail on that theory, the complaint must contain facts plausibly showing that petitioners purposefully adopted a policy of classifying post-September-11 detainees as "of high interest" because of their race, religion, or national origin.

This the complaint fails to do. [T]he complaint does not show, or even intimate, that petitioners purposefully housed detainees in the ADMAX SHU due to their race, religion, or national origin. All it plausibly suggests is that the Nation's top law enforcement officers, in the aftermath of a devastating terrorist attack, sought to keep suspected terrorists in the most secure conditions available until the suspects could be cleared of terrorist activity. . . . [R]espondent's complaint does not contain any factual allegation sufficient to plausibly suggest petitioners' discriminatory state of mind. His pleadings thus do not meet the standard necessary to comply with Rule 8.

It is important to note, however, that we express no opinion concerning the sufficiency of respondent's complaint against the defendants who are not before us. . . .

### C

Respondent offers three arguments that bear on our disposition of his case, but none is persuasive.

### 1

Respondent first says that our decision in *Twombly* should be limited to pleadings made in the context of an antitrust dispute. This argument is not supported by *Twombly* and is incompatible with the Federal Rules of Civil Procedure. . . . Our decision in *Twombly* expounded the pleading standard for "all civil actions," and it applies to antitrust and discrimination suits alike. *See* 550 U.S., at 555-556.

### 2

Respondent next implies that our construction of Rule 8 should be tempered where, as here, the Court of Appeals has "instructed the district court to cabin discovery in such a way as to preserve" petitioners' defense of qualified immunity "as much as possible in anticipation of a summary judgment motion." We have held, however, that the question presented by a motion to dismiss a complaint for insufficient pleadings does not turn on the controls placed upon the discovery process. *Twombly, supra,* at 559. . . .

We decline respondent's invitation to relax the pleading requirements on the ground that the Court of Appeals promises petitioners minimally intrusive discovery. That promise provides especially cold comfort in this pleading context, where we are impelled to give real content to the concept of qualified immunity for high-level officials who must be neither deterred nor detracted from the vigorous performance of their duties. Because respondent's complaint is deficient under Rule 8, he is not entitled to discovery, cabined or otherwise.

### 3

Respondent finally maintains that the Federal Rules expressly allow him to allege petitioners' discriminatory intent "generally," which he equates with a conclusory allegation. Iqbal Brief 32 (citing Fed. Rule Civ. Proc. 9). It follows, respondent says, that his complaint is sufficiently well pleaded because it claims that petitioners discriminated against him "on account of [his] religion, race, and/or national origin and for no legitimate penological interest." Complaint ¶ 96. Were we required to accept this allegation as true, respondent's complaint would survive petitioners' motion to dismiss. But the Federal Rules do not require courts to credit a complaint's conclusory statements without reference to its factual context.

It is true that Rule 9(b) requires particularity when pleading "fraud or mistake," while allowing "[m]alice, intent, knowledge, and other conditions of a person's mind [to] be alleged generally." But "generally" is a relative term. In the context of Rule 9, it is to be compared to the particularity requirement applicable to fraud or mistake. Rule 9 merely excuses a party from pleading discriminatory intent under an elevated pleading standard. . . .

## V

We hold that respondent's complaint fails to plead sufficient facts to state a claim for purposeful and unlawful discrimination against petitioners. The Court of Appeals should decide in the first instance whether to remand to the District Court so that respondent can seek leave to amend his deficient complaint.

The judgment of the Court of Appeals is reversed, and the case is remanded for further proceedings consistent with this opinion. It is so ordered.

Justice SOUTER, with whom Justice STEVENS, Justice GINSBURG, and Justice BREYER join, dissenting.

This case is here on the uncontested assumption that *Bivens v. Six Unknown Fed. Narcotics Agents*, 403 U.S. 388 (1971), allows personal liability based on a federal officer's violation of an individual's rights under the First and Fifth Amendments, and it comes to us with the explicit concession of petitioners Ashcroft and Mueller that an officer may be subject to *Bivens* liability as a supervisor on grounds other than respondeat superior. The Court apparently rejects this concession and, although it has no bearing on the majority's resolution of this case, does away with supervisory liability under *Bivens*. The majority then misapplies the pleading standard under *Bell Atlantic Corp. v. Twombly*, 550 U.S. 544 (2007), to conclude that the complaint fails to state a claim. I respectfully dissent from both the rejection of supervisory liability as a cognizable claim in the face of petitioners' concession, and from the holding that the complaint fails to satisfy Rule 8(a)(2) of the Federal Rules of Civil Procedure.

## I

### A

. . . Iqbal claims that on the day he was transferred to the special unit, prison guards, without provocation, "picked him up and threw him against the wall, kicked him in the stomach, punched him in the face, and dragged him across the room." First Amended Complaint in No. 04-CV-1809 (JG)(JA), ¶ 113 (hereinafter Complaint). He says that after being attacked a second time he sought medical attention but was denied care for two weeks. *Id.*, ¶¶ 187-188. According to Iqbal's complaint, prison staff in the special unit subjected him to unjustified strip and body cavity searches, *id.*, ¶¶ 136-140, verbally berated him as a "'terrorist'" and "'Muslim killer,'" *id.*, ¶ 87, refused to give him adequate food, *id.*, ¶ 91, and intentionally turned on air conditioning during the winter and heating during the summer, *id.*, ¶ 84. He claims that prison staff interfered with his attempts to pray and engage in religious study, *id.*, ¶¶ 153-154, and with his access to counsel, *id.*, ¶¶ 168, 171.

The District Court denied Ashcroft and Mueller's motion to dismiss Iqbal's discrimination claim, and the Court of Appeals affirmed. Ashcroft and Mueller then asked this Court to grant certiorari on two questions:

> 1. Whether a conclusory allegation that a cabinet-level officer or other high-ranking official knew of, condoned, or agreed to subject a plaintiff to allegedly unconstitutional acts purportedly committed by subordinate officials is sufficient to state individual-capacity claims against those officials under *Bivens*.
>
> 2. Whether a cabinet-level officer or other high-ranking official may be held personally liable for the allegedly unconstitutional acts of subordinate officials on the ground that, as high-level supervisors, they had constructive notice of the discrimination allegedly carried out by such subordinate officials.

Pet. for Cert. I.

The Court granted certiorari on both questions. The first is about pleading; the second goes to the liability standard.

In the first question, Ashcroft and Mueller did not ask whether "a cabinet-level officer or other high-ranking official" who "knew of, condoned, or agreed to subject a plaintiff to allegedly unconstitutional acts committed by subordinate officials" was subject to liability under *Bivens*. In fact, they conceded in their petition for certiorari that they would be liable if they had "actual knowledge" of discrimination by their subordinates and exhibited "'deliberate indifference'" to that discrimination. Pet. for Cert. 29. Instead, they asked the Court to address whether Iqbal's allegations against them (which they call conclusory) were sufficient to satisfy Rule 8(a)(2), and in particular whether the Court of Appeals misapplied our decision in *Twombly* construing that rule. Pet. for Cert. 11-24.

In the second question, Ashcroft and Mueller asked this Court to say whether they could be held personally liable for the actions of their subordinates based on the theory that they had constructive notice of their subordinates' unconstitutional conduct. *Id.*, at 25-33. This was an odd question to pose, since Iqbal has never claimed that Ashcroft and Mueller are liable on a constructive notice theory. Be that as it may, the second question challenged only one possible ground for imposing supervisory liability under *Bivens*. In sum, both questions assumed that a defendant could raise a *Bivens* claim on theories of supervisory liability other than constructive notice, and neither question asked the parties or the Court to address the elements of such liability.

The briefing at the merits stage was no different. Ashcroft and Mueller argued that the factual allegations in Iqbal's complaint were insufficient to overcome their claim of qualified immunity; they also contended that they could not be held liable on a theory of constructive notice. Again they conceded, however, that they would be subject to supervisory liability if they "had actual knowledge of the assertedly discriminatory nature of the classification of suspects as being 'of high interest' and they were deliberately indifferent to that discrimination." Brief for Petitioners 50. Iqbal argued that the allegations in his complaint were sufficient under Rule 8(a)(2) and *Twombly*, and conceded that as a matter of law he could not recover under a theory of respondeat superior. Thus, the parties agreed as to a proper standard of supervisory liability, and the disputed question was whether Iqbal's complaint satisfied Rule 8(a)(2).

Without acknowledging the parties' agreement as to the standard of supervisory liability, the Court asserts that it must sua sponte decide the scope of supervisory liability here. I agree that, absent Ashcroft and Mueller's concession, that determination would have to be made; without knowing the elements of a supervisory liability claim, there would be no way to determine whether a plaintiff had made factual allegations amounting to grounds for relief on that claim. *See Twombly*, 550 U.S., at 557-558. But deciding the scope of supervisory *Bivens* liability in this case is uncalled for. There are several reasons, starting with the position Ashcroft and Mueller have taken and following from it.

First, Ashcroft and Mueller have, as noted, made the critical concession that a supervisor's knowledge of a subordinate's unconstitutional conduct and deliberate indifference to that conduct are grounds for *Bivens* liability. . . .

Second, because of the concession, we have received no briefing or argument on the proper scope of supervisory liability, much less the full-dress argument we normally require. We consequently are in no position to decide the precise contours of supervisory liability here, this issue being a complicated one that has divided the Courts of Appeals. . . .

**B**

The majority, however, does ignore the concession. According to the majority, because Iqbal concededly cannot recover on a theory of respondeat superior, it follows that he cannot recover under any theory of supervisory liability. The majority says that in a *Bivens* action, "where masters do not answer for the torts of their servants," "the term 'supervisory liability' is a misnomer," and that "[a]bsent vicarious liability, each Government official, his or her title notwithstanding, is only liable for his or her own misconduct." Lest there be any mistake, in these words the majority is not narrowing the scope of supervisory liability; it is eliminating *Bivens* supervisory liability entirely. The nature of a supervisory liability theory is that the supervisor may be liable, under certain conditions, for the wrongdoing of his subordinates, and it is this very principle that the majority rejects. . . .

The dangers of the majority's readiness to proceed without briefing and argument are apparent in its cursory analysis, which rests on the assumption that only two outcomes are possible here: respondeat superior liability, in which "an employer is subject to liability for torts committed by employees while acting within the scope of their employment," Restatement (Third) of Agency § 2.04 (2005), or no supervisory liability at all. The dichotomy is false. . . .

In fact, there is quite a spectrum of possible tests for supervisory liability: it could be imposed where a supervisor has actual knowledge of a subordinate's constitutional violation and acquiesces [citations omitted]; or where supervisors " 'know about the conduct and facilitate it, approve it, condone it, or turn a blind eye for fear of what they might see' " [citations omitted]; or where the supervisor has no actual knowledge of the violation but was reckless in his supervision of the subordinate [citations omitted]; or where the supervisor was grossly negligent [citations omitted]. I am unsure what the general test for supervisory liability should be, and in the absence of briefing and argument I am in no position to choose or devise one.

Neither is the majority, but what is most remarkable about its foray into supervisory liability is that its conclusion has no bearing on its resolution of the case. The majority says that all of the allegations in the complaint that Ashcroft and Mueller authorized, condoned, or even were aware of their subordinates' discriminatory conduct are "conclusory" and therefore are "not entitled to be assumed true." As I explain below, this conclusion is unsound, but on the majority's understanding of Rule 8(a)(2) pleading standards, even if the majority accepted Ashcroft and Mueller's concession and asked whether the complaint sufficiently alleges knowledge and deliberate indifference, it presumably would still conclude that the complaint fails to plead sufficient facts and must be dismissed.

## II

Given petitioners' concession, the complaint satisfies Rule 8(a)(2). Ashcroft and Mueller admit they are liable for their subordinates' conduct if they "had actual knowledge of the assertedly discriminatory nature of the classification of suspects as being 'of high interest' and they were deliberately indifferent to that discrimination." Brief for Petitioners 50. Iqbal alleges that after the September 11 attacks the Federal Bureau of Investigation (FBI) "arrested and detained thousands of Arab Muslim men," Complaint ¶ 47, that many of these men were designated by high-ranking FBI officials as being " 'of high interest,' " *id.*, ¶¶ 48, 50, and that in many cases, including Iqbal's, this designation was made "because of the race, religion, and national origin of the detainees, and not because of any evidence of the detainees' involvement in supporting terrorist activity," *id.*, ¶ 49. The complaint further alleges that Ashcroft was the "principal architect of the policies and practices challenged," *id.*, ¶ 10, and that Mueller "was instrumental in the adoption, promulgation, and implementation of the policies and practices challenged," *id.*, ¶ 11. According to the complaint, Ashcroft and Mueller "knew of, condoned, and willfully and maliciously agreed to subject [Iqbal] to these conditions of confinement as a matter of policy, solely on account of [his] religion, race, and/or national origin and for no legitimate penological interest." *Id.*,

¶ 96. The complaint thus alleges, at a bare minimum, that Ashcroft and Mueller knew of and condoned the discriminatory policy their subordinates carried out. Actually, the complaint goes further in alleging that Ashcroft and Muller affirmatively acted to create the discriminatory detention policy. If these factual allegations are true, Ashcroft and Mueller were, at the very least, aware of the discriminatory policy being implemented and deliberately indifferent to it.

Ashcroft and Mueller argue that these allegations fail to satisfy the "plausibility standard" of *Twombly*. They contend that Iqbal's claims are implausible because such high-ranking officials "tend not to be personally involved in the specific actions of lower-level officers down the bureaucratic chain of command." Brief for Petitioners 28. But this response bespeaks a fundamental misunderstanding of the enquiry that *Twombly* demands. *Twombly* does not require a court at the motion-to-dismiss stage to consider whether the factual allegations are probably true. We made it clear, on the contrary, that a court must take the allegations as true, no matter how skeptical the court may be. . . .

Under *Twombly*, the relevant question is whether, assuming the factual allegations are true, the plaintiff has stated a ground for relief that is plausible. That is, in *Twombly*'s words, a plaintiff must "allege facts" that, taken as true, are "suggestive of illegal conduct." 550 U.S., at 564, n. 8. In *Twombly*, we were faced with allegations of a conspiracy to violate § 1 of the Sherman Act through parallel conduct. . . . Here, by contrast, the allegations in the complaint are neither confined to naked legal conclusions nor consistent with legal conduct. The complaint alleges that FBI officials discriminated against Iqbal solely on account of his race, religion, and national origin, and it alleges the knowledge and deliberate indifference that, by Ashcroft and Mueller's own admission, are sufficient to make them liable for the illegal action. Iqbal's complaint therefore contains "enough facts to state a claim to relief that is plausible on its face." *Id.*, at 570.

I do not understand the majority to disagree with this understanding of "plausibility" under *Twombly*. Rather, the majority discards the allegations discussed above with regard to Ashcroft and Mueller as conclusory, and is left considering only two statements in the complaint: that "the [FBI], under the direction of Defendant Mueller, arrested and detained thousands of Arab Muslim men . . . as part of its investigation of the events of September 11," Complaint ¶ 47, and that "[t]he policy of holding post-September-11th detainees in highly restrictive conditions of confinement until they were 'cleared' by the FBI was approved by Defendants Ashcroft and Mueller in discussions in the weeks after September 11, 2001," *id.*, ¶ 69. . . .

But these allegations do not stand alone as the only significant, nonconclusory statements in the complaint, for the complaint contains many allegations linking Ashcroft and Mueller to the discriminatory practices of their subordinates. *See* Complaint ¶ 10 (Ashcroft was the "principal architect" of the discriminatory policy); *id.*, ¶ 11 (Mueller was "instrumental" in adopting and executing the discriminatory policy); *id.*, ¶ 96 (Ashcroft and Mueller "knew of, condoned, and willfully and maliciously agreed to subject" Iqbal to harsh conditions "as a matter of policy, solely on account of [his] religion, race, and/or national origin and for no legitimate penological interest").

The majority says that these are "bare assertions" that, "much like the pleading of conspiracy in *Twombly*, amount to nothing more than a 'formulaic recitation of the elements' of a constitutional discrimination claim" and therefore are "not entitled to be assumed true." The fallacy of the majority's position, however, lies in looking at the relevant assertions in isolation. The complaint contains specific allegations that, in the aftermath of the September 11 attacks, the Chief of the FBI's International Terrorism Operations Section and the Assistant Special Agent in Charge for the FBI's New York Field Office implemented a policy that discriminated against Arab Muslim men, including Iqbal, solely on account of their race, religion, or national origin. *See* Complaint ¶¶ 47-53. Viewed in light of these subsidiary allegations, the allegations singled out by the majority as "conclusory" are no such thing. Iqbal's claim is not that Ashcroft and Mueller "knew of, condoned, and willfully and maliciously agreed to subject" him to a discriminatory practice that is left undefined; his allegation is that "they knew of, condoned, and willfully and maliciously agreed to subject" him to a particular, discrete, discriminatory policy detailed in the complaint. Iqbal does not say merely that Ashcroft was the architect of some amorphous discrimination, or that Mueller was instrumental in an ill-defined constitutional violation; he alleges that they helped to create the discriminatory policy he has described. Taking the complaint as a whole, it gives Ashcroft and Mueller "'fair notice of what the . . . claim is and the grounds upon which it rests.'" *Twombly*, 550 U.S., at 555 (quoting *Conley v. Gibson*, 355 U.S. 41, 47 (1957) (omission in original)).

That aside, the majority's holding that the statements it selects are conclusory cannot be squared with its treatment of certain other allegations in the complaint as nonconclusory. For example, the majority takes as true the statement that "[t]he policy of holding post-September-11th detainees in highly restrictive conditions of confinement until they were 'cleared' by the FBI was approved by Defendants Ashcroft and Mueller in discussions in the weeks after September 11, 2001." Complaint ¶ 69. This statement makes two points: (1) after September 11, the FBI held certain detainees in highly restrictive conditions, and (2) Ashcroft and Mueller discussed and approved these conditions. If, as the majority says, these allegations are not conclusory, then I cannot see why the majority deems it merely conclusory when Iqbal alleges that (1) after September 11, the FBI designated Arab Muslim detainees as being of "'high interest'" "because of the race, religion, and national origin of the detainees, and not because of any evidence of the detainees' involvement in supporting terrorist activity," Complaint ¶¶ 48-50, and (2) Ashcroft and Mueller "knew of, condoned, and willfully and maliciously agreed" to that discrimination, *id.*, ¶ 96. By my lights, there is no principled basis for the majority's disregard of the allegations linking Ashcroft and Mueller to their subordinates' discrimination.

Justice BREYER, dissenting.

I agree with Justice Souter and join his dissent. I write separately to point out that, like the Court, I believe it important to prevent unwarranted litigation from interfering with "the proper execution of the work of the Government." But I cannot find in that need adequate justification for the Court's interpretation of *Bell Atlantic Corp. v. Twombly*, 550 U.S. 544 (2007), and Federal Rule of Civil Procedure 8. The law, after all, provides trial courts with other legal weapons designed to prevent unwarranted interference. As the Second Circuit explained, where a Government defendant asserts a qualified immunity defense, a trial court, responsible for managing a case and "mindful of the need to vindicate the purpose of the qualified immunity defense," can structure discovery in ways that diminish the risk of imposing unwarranted burdens upon public officials. A district court, for example, can begin discovery with lower level government defendants before determining whether a case can be made to allow discovery related to higher level government officials. Neither the briefs nor the Court's opinion provides convincing grounds for finding these alternative case-management tools inadequate, either in general or in the case before us. For this reason, as well as for the independently sufficient reasons set forth in Justice Souter's opinion, I would affirm the Second Circuit.

## Comments and Questions

1. The language of Fed. R. Civ. P. 8(a)(2), requiring "a short and plain statement of the claim showing that the pleader is entitled to relief," carefully avoids using either the words "facts" or "causes of action," which are a part of some state pleading rules. The Federal Rule does not state that the pleader must identify facts for each element of the claim or cause of action. Does *Iqbal* change this, and if so, how? Is the Court identifying the quantum of notice that plaintiff must plead or is it abandoning "notice pleading" altogether?

2. The Court's *Twombly* and *Iqbal* decisions—sometimes collectively referred to as "TwIqbal"—have generated a considerable amount of scholarly attention. *See, e.g.*, David L. Noll, *The Indeterminacy of Iqbal*, 99 Geo. L.J. 117 (2010); Arthur R. Miller, *From Conley to Twombly to Iqbal*, 60 Duke L.J. 1 (2010); Adam N. Steinman, *The Pleading Problem*, 62 Stan. L. Rev. 1293 (2010). Further, Volume 74 of the Lewis & Clark Law Review contains a rich collection of articles in a symposium edition.

As the book goes to press, collections of empirical data on the practical consequences of *Twombly* and *Iqbal* are only starting to emerge, and the effect is not yet clear. *See* Patricia W. Hatamyar, *The Tao of Pleading: Do Twombly and Iqbal Matter Empirically?*, 59 Am. U. L. Rev. 553 (2010); Patricia W. Hatamyar, *An Updated Quantitative Study of Iqbal's Impact on 12(b)(6) Motions*, U. Rich. L. Rev. (2012) (forthcoming), available at *http://ssrn.com/abstract=1883650*; Joe S. Cecil et al., *Motions to Dismiss for Failure to State a Claim After* Iqbal: *Report to the Judicial Conference Advisory Committee on Civil Rules*, available at *http://ssrn.com/abstract=1878646*.

3. Re-read the second sentence of Federal Rule 9(b). How does the majority interpret this mandate? Does that interpretation make sense?

4. Look at Form 11 of the Federal Rules in your Rule Book and Federal Rule 84. Can you reconcile Form 11 with *TwIqbal*? What about Rule 11(b)(3), which you will get to later in this chapter?

5. How would the dissenters rule on a motion to dismiss a complaint that provided only: "Defendant, my former employer, discriminated against me on the basis of my race"?

6. It is not easy to define what constitutes frivolous litigation, but whatever it is, there is the risk that a liberal pleading requirement will let such cases continue to the discovery stage of litigation, or will result in some defendants paying off the plaintiff through settlement in order to avoid litigation costs. On the other hand, a pleading rule that requires specificity before the plaintiff is entitled to discovery may deter the bringing of some meritorious suits or lead to the dismissal of meritorious suits. In order to make rational judgments about what type of rule makes sense for what types of cases, one has to factor in variables such as who is likely to have the required information prior to discovery and what are the costs to the parties, the lawyers, and the court system under different pleading regimes. To complicate even further the problem of designing desirable pleading rules, one should also consider the role that pleading rules play in deterring untoward pre-litigation conduct of defendants. *See* Robert Bone, *Modeling Frivolous Suits*, 145 U. Pa. L. Rev. 519 (1997); Richard L. Marcus, *The Puzzling Persistence of Pleading Practice*, 76 Tex. L. Rev. 1749, 1757 (1998); Christopher Fairman, *The Myth of Notice Pleading*, 45 Ariz. L. Rev. 987 (2003).

7. Congress, and some state legislatures, on occasion integrate specific pleading requirements into the substantive law. For instance, some states imposed stringent pleading requirements for medical malpractice cases as part of tort reform. Congress, in order to deter allegedly frivolous or weak securities fraud class action cases, passed the Private Securities Litigation Reform Act (PSLRA), Pub. L. No. 104-67, 109 Stat. 737 (1995). These rules require that the complaint "specify each statement alleged to have been misleading [and] the reason or reasons why the statement is misleading." When liability depends on defendant's state of mind (such as intent or reckless disregard), the plaintiffs must "state with *particularity* the facts giving rise to a *strong inference* that the defendant acted with the required state of mind." 15 U.S.C. § 78u-4(b)(2) (emphasis added).

In the same term that it decided *Twombly*, the Court heard a case involving the pleading standard required under the PSLRA. In *Tellabs, Inc. v. Makor Issues & Rights, Ltd.*, 551 U.S. 308 (2007), the Court noted that "[e]xacting pleading requirements are among the control measures Congress included in the [Reform Act]" as a "check against abusive litigation." Because Congress left the term "strong inference" undefined, the Court articulated the standard: "To qualify as 'strong' within the intendment of [the PSLRA] an inference of scienter must be more than merely plausible or reasonable—it must be cogent and at least as compelling as any opposing inference of nonfraudulent intent." Justice Ginsburg explained that a "court must take into account plausible opposing inferences" because "[t]he strength of an inference cannot be decided in a vacuum." The Court further held that in assessing whether a plaintiff's allegations satisfy these standards, "omissions and ambiguities count against inferring scienter."

Some scholars suggest that, after *Twombly* and *Iqbal*, the pleading standard under Rule 8(a) may be more exacting and onerous than the *heightened* pleading standard under the PSLRA. *See, e.g.*, Marc I. Steinberg and Diego E. Gomez-Cornejo, *Blurring the Lines Between Pleading Doctrines: The Enhanced Rule 8(a)(2) Plausibility Pleading Standard Converges with the Heightened Fraud Pleading Standards Under Rule 9(b) and the PSLRA*, 30 Rev. Litig. 1 (2010).

8. The Court mentions that the amount of specificity required is somewhat context-specific. What does this suggest about the nature of trans-substantive rules of procedure?

9. We have now seen two different grounds for prevailing on a 12(b)(6) motion: (1) Plaintiff fails to state a cognizable claim—i.e., the substantive law offers no relief for this type of injury; and (2) plaintiff has failed to plead sufficient facts—i.e., such a cause of action exists, but the plaintiff does not provide sufficient allegations within the meaning of *Twombly* and *Iqbal*. *Bower v. Weisman* shows still a third way that a portion of a claim may be deficient. How is it different from the other two?

## ■ BOWER v. WEISMAN
### 639 F. Supp. 532 (S.D.N.Y. 1986)

SWEET, District Judge:

. . . [I]n July, 1985, Bower and Weisman terminated a fifteen-year close personal and business relationship. According to Bower, in exchange for valuable business and social assistance which Bower rendered to Weisman during their relationship, Weisman promised to provide Bower with an economic interest in his affairs and to provide Bower and her daughter with financial security. Bower contends that Weisman agreed to provide these benefits even after their relationship terminated, as long as Bower, a Japanese citizen, did not remarry or leave the United States and that Weisman breached a series of written and oral agreements, codifying Weisman's promise of financial security.

Bower asserts that in the final version of this agreement dated July 6, 1985, Weisman agreed (1) to purchase a house in California for Bower at a cost of $6.5 million; (2) to provide Bower with an irrevocable trust in the amount of $3.9 million and $100,000 in trust for Bower's daughter; (3) to pay Bower an annual sum of $120,000 for ten years over and above a promissory note held by Frederick Weisman Company (FWC) dated November 1, 1983; (4) to pay Bower's living expenses until her remarriage or departure from the United States; (5) to provide rent-free possession of Weisman's

New York townhouse until her remarriage or departure from the United States. Provision number (3) concerns a promissory note and consultant agreement executed on November 1, 1983 by FWC and Preferred Capital International Inc. (Preferred Capital), a corporation wholly owned by Bower.

In mid-July, 1985, the Bower-Weisman relationship terminated, and according to Bower, Weisman reneged on this agreement and attempted to coerce her to leave the townhouse, which she asserts was purchased with her own money but which she sold to Weisman in 1980 at his request to accommodate his tax needs in reliance on his promises of a rent-free tenancy. In September and November, 1985, Weisman instructed his agents to enter the apartment, to strip it of artwork and furniture which was purportedly the property of Weisman, to change the locks on Bower's door when she was at work and her daughter was home ill, and to station three armed guards in the townhouse lobby, with instructions to prevent the entry of "unauthorized" individuals. Furthermore, Bower claims that Weisman's real estate agents and attorneys made unauthorized visits to the apartment and disturbed her personal belongings.

The complaint alleges seven claims arising from the July 6, 1985 agreement outlined above, each of which is challenged in [defendant's] motion. Claim One asserts tort and contract claims for money damages arising from the "breach of express agreements"; Claim Two alleges fraud, misrepresentation and deceit in connection with the agreement; Claim Three is for "breach of contract and conversion" and concerns Weisman's attempt to remove Bower from the townhouse and his alleged conversion of art and furniture. Claims Four and Five charge the defendants with trespass and false imprisonment in connection with the townhouse, and Claims Six and Seven concern intentional infliction of emotional distress, and private nuisance, also in connection with Weisman's actions to recover the townhouse. . . .

## MOTION FOR A MORE DEFINITE STATEMENT

Weisman [next] argues that pursuant to Fed. R. Civ. P. 12(e), he is entitled to a more definite statement with respect to two aspects of the complaint. First, Weisman asserts that the complaint fails to disclose the specific provisions of the alleged agreements upon which plaintiff relies. Moreover, he argues that the complaint fails to reveal which parts of the agreements have been modified and which provisions remain in effect after these modifications. Second, Weisman urges that the complaint fails to identify which of the three defendants is charged with each act and merely discusses all as "defendant." . . . For the following reasons, this motion for a more definite statement is granted.

A motion for a more definite statement may be granted if "a pleading . . . is so vague and ambiguous that a party cannot reasonably be required to frame a responsive pleading . . ." Fed. R. Civ. P. 12(e). A motion pursuant to Rule 12(e) should not be granted "unless the complaint is so excessively vague and ambiguous as to be unintelligible and as to prejudice the defendant seriously in attempting to answer it." *Boothe v. TRW Credit Data*, 523 F. Supp. 631, 635 (S.D.N.Y. 1981). With respect to Weisman's first assertion, Bower's complaint is not so unintelligible as to preclude Weisman from drafting a responsive pleading. The essence of a complaint is to inform the defendant as to the general nature of the action and as to the incident out of which a cause of action arose. *Id.* Bower's complaint satisfies this requirement as it clearly identifies the offending acts. The complaint traced in detail the interactions of Bower and Weisman which led to the first written agreement of July, 1983, and the series of subsequent modifications that occurred in September through November of 1983, September, 1984, October, 1984, culminating in the final agreement of July 6, 1985, embodied in paragraph 25. Moreover, paragraph 26 describes the provisions of the agreement that were allegedly violated by Weisman. Weisman has been given fair notice of the claims against him, and nothing prevents him from formulating a responsive pleading.

Weisman seeks to remove the ambiguity that is present in paragraphs 36, 40, 43-47, 50 and 52-55. These paragraphs employ the term "defendant" without specifying which particular defendant is referred to. Obviously, Weisman cannot effectively respond to Bower's complaint until he knows which claims Bower is asserting against him in his individual capacity. Although Rare Properties is a wholly owned subsidiary of FWC, of which Weisman is the sole owner, Bower has not produced any evidence that the proper corporate forms have not been observed with respect to these corporations. The motion for a more particular statement will be granted on this ground. . . .

## MOTION TO DISMISS FOR FAILURE TO STATE FRAUD WITH PARTICULARITY

Fed. R. Civ. P. 9(b) requires that: "In all averments of fraud or mistake, the circumstances constituting fraud or mistake shall be stated with particularity." There is tension between the specificity required under Rule 9(b) and the liberal pleading allowances of Fed. R. Civ. P. 8(a)(2) which requires only a "short and plain statement of the claim showing that the pleader is entitled to relief." However, Rule 9(b) does not render Rule 8 meaningless in fraud cases. The two rules must be read in conjunction with each other. Courts have not struck a balance between these rules by devising an easily applied test. Thus, the degree of specificity required will be dependent upon the facts of each case.

Bower's allegations do no more than state generally that all three defendants intentionally misrepresented and defrauded the plaintiff by making promises and representations. In paragraph 32, Bower alleges that "[t]hose representations of the defendants were false and deceitful at the time they were made to the plaintiff. . . ." Such sweeping statements fail to clarify which alleged agreements form the basis of Bower's claim for fraud.

"[A well-pleaded claim of fraud] normally includes the time, place, and content of the false representations, the facts misrepresented, and the nature of the detrimental reliance. . . ." *Elster v. Alexander*, 75 F.R.D. 458, 461 (N.D. Ga. 1977). Bower's claim fails with respect to all of these particulars. Moreover, Bower's failure to separate Weisman from the two corporate defendants involved in this case makes it impossible for Weisman to frame an effective response.

Rule 9(b) seeks, in part, to assure that defendants ". . . are given notice of the exact nature of the fraud claimed, sufficient to permit responsive measures." *Todd v. Oppenheimmer & Co., Inc.*, 78 F.R.D. 415, 419 (S.D.N.Y. 1978). Here, Bower's pleadings are vague and fail to provide the specificity required by Rule 9(b). Therefore, Bower's second claim for misrepresentation, fraud and deceit is dismissed with leave to replead.

When determining whether to grant a Rule 12(b)(6) motion, the court must primarily consider allegations in the complaint. However, at this early stage of the proceedings, a court's review of the sufficiency of the complaint is a very limited one. The allegations are accepted as true, and the complaint is construed in a light most favorable to the pleader. . . .

### MOTION TO DISMISS FOR FAILURE TO STATE A CLAIM UPON WHICH RELIEF CAN BE GRANTED

The motion to dismiss for failure to state a claim is disfavored and is seldom granted. The reason for such a policy is two-fold. First, "[t]he salvaged minutes that may accrue from circumventing these procedures can turn to wasted hours if the appellate court feels constrained to reverse the dismissal of the action." *Rennie & Laughlin, Inc. v. Chrysler Corporation*, 242 F.2d 208, 213 (9th Cir. 1957). Second, courts are wary of dismissal in view of the policy of the federal rules which seeks to have determinations reached on the merits. *Id.* The test that is in accord with these goals is that ". . . a complaint should not be dismissed for failure to state a claim unless it appears beyond doubt that the plaintiff can prove no set of facts in support of his claim which would entitle him to relief." *Conley v. Gibson*, 355 U.S. 41, 45-46 (1957). Thus, this court must determine in the light most favorable to the plaintiff whether the following claims state any basis for relief.

#### A. TRESPASS

Plaintiff has alleged the necessary elements to sustain a cause of action in trespass. From July, 1983 to July, 1985, the agreements between Bower and Weisman contained a provision that in the event of the breakup of the parties' relationship, Bower would be permitted to reside rent-free at the 73rd Street townhouse so long as she paid all maintenance expenses and did not remarry or move out of the country. Upon termination of the relationship in August, 1985, plaintiff alleges that she was in actual possession of the townhouse and that she shared this residence only with her daughter, Teru. "Trespass is an action for injury to possession for which an action may be maintained even against an owner by the one entitled to possession." *Meadow Point Properties v. Nick Mazzoferro & Sons*, 219 N.Y.S.2d 908, 909 (Sup. Ct. Suffolk Co. 1961). Because Bower alleges to have been in actual (and exclusive) possession of the townhouse, she may maintain an action for trespass. . . .

Considering the allegations in the light most favorable to the plaintiff, Bower's complaint asserts a possessory interest in the townhouse beyond a licensing arrangement. . . .

Bower has also successfully pleaded the other requisite elements of trespass. . . . Bower asserts that Weisman, through his agents, intentionally entered the townhouse property without her consent. She alleges that artwork was removed from the premises by defendant and/or his agents. Bower also states that defendant changed her apartment locks and placed three armed guards at the entrance of the property. . . .

Defendant's motion to dismiss the trespass claim is denied.

### B. FALSE IMPRISONMENT

The action for the tort of false imprisonment seeks to protect an individual's freedom from restraint of movement. The Court of Appeals of New York has set forth the following elements as constituting a cause of action for false imprisonment: (1) defendant intended to confine the plaintiff; (2) plaintiff was conscious of the confinement; (3) plaintiff did not consent to the confinement, and (4) confinement was not otherwise privileged.

Plaintiff's fifth claim for false imprisonment fails to set forth any facts which would support the allegation that plaintiff was confined at the 73rd Street townhouse. Bower alleges that due to the posting of three armed guards at the townhouse entrance, she "has been unable to freely enter and exit her home in the unfettered manner to which she is accustomed and . . . has become a prisoner by virtue of the defendant's acts." However, other paragraphs of Bower's Second Amended Complaint are entirely at odds with the proposition set forth above. Paragraph 42 states that on November 5, 1985, plaintiff left her house to go to work. Paragraph 44 states that the three armed guards were instructed "not to permit access to anyone other than the plaintiff, her daughter, or a person seeking access for emergency and/or medical purposes." This indicates that plaintiff was permitted ingress and egress from the townhouse. Moreover, paragraph 47 alleges that unauthorized persons entered the townhouse while Bower was not home. Plaintiff's own allegations support the conclusion that her movement was unrestrained. . . . Plaintiff's fifth claim for false imprisonment is dismissed with leave to replead within twenty (20) days.

### C. INTENTIONAL INFLICTION OF EMOTIONAL DISTRESS

The following components form a claim for intentional infliction of emotion distress: (1) an extreme and outrageous act by the defendant; (2) an intent to cause severe emotional distress; (3) resulting severe emotional distress; (4) caused by the defendant's conduct. Plaintiff's complaint pleads each of the necessary elements of this cause of action to survive a 12(b)(6) challenge.

Paragraph 63 sets forth the "outrageous" acts by defendant that were directed at the plaintiff. First, three armed guards were placed in the lobby of the townhouse to prevent all persons except Bower, her child and medical personnel from entering or exiting from the townhouse. Second, the locks to Bower's apartment were changed without her consent which caused her to become "frightened and distraught." Third, Weisman, through his agents, entered plaintiff's apartment without her permission and removed artwork without her consent. Bower contends that defendant intended that such acts would cause her severe emotional distress, and that she has, in fact, "suffered severe mental anguish, anxiety, and unwarranted pain and suffering."

These allegations demonstrate that defendant embarked upon a course of conduct that was designed to intimidate, threaten and humiliate the plaintiff and which resulted in emotional upset. It will be for the trier of fact to determine whether defendant's conduct went beyond all reasonable bounds of decency, and would arouse resentment against the defendant as to cause the trier of fact to exclaim that such conduct was "outrageous." *Restatement (Second) of Torts* § 46 comment (d) (1965).

### D. PRIVATE NUISANCE

The elements of a private nuisance in New York are: (1) an interference substantial in nature, (2) intentional in origin, (3) unreasonable in character, (4) with a person's property right to use and enjoy land, (5) caused by another's conduct in acting or failure to act. Plaintiff's seventh claim for private nuisance must be dismissed since Bower has failed to allege an interference which is substantial in nature and unreasonable in character.

The "substantial" and "unreasonable" interference requirements distinguish an action for private nuisance from that of trespass. . . . The substantial interference requirement is to satisfy the need for a showing that the land is reduced in value because of the defendant's conduct. "The law does not concern itself with trifles and there must be a real and appreciable invasion of the plaintiff's interests before he can have an action for either a public or private nuisance." Restatement (Second) of Torts § 821F comment c.

In paragraph 68, Bower asserts that defendant trespassed upon the townhouse, removed articles from the premises, changed locks and positioned guards in the lobby. However, plaintiff failed to allege that these acts caused a reduction in the value of the property. . . . Plaintiff's failure to plead a substantial and unreasonable interference with the land is fatal to her claim for private nuisance. . . .

In summary, Weisman's motion for a more definite statement pursuant to Fed. R. Civ. P. 12(e) and motion to dismiss the second claim in the Complaint for failure to state fraud with particularity pursuant to Rule 9(b) is granted, and Bower has leave to replead within thirty (30) days of this opinion. In addition, Bower's Fifth Claim for false imprisonment, and Seventh Claim for private nuisance are dismissed, as they fail to state a claim upon which relief can be granted, Fed. R. Civ. P. 12(b)(6). All other motions are denied. . . .

## Comments and Questions

1. The last comment before the *Bower* opinion identified two different grounds for prevailing on a 12(b)(6) motion, and Judge Sweet's discussion of the false imprisonment count gives us a third. In which of these three categories does the dismissal of the private nuisance count fall?

2. A dismissal without prejudice gives plaintiff the opportunity to refile the claim. Why would a court bother writing an opinion dismissing a count (or an entire complaint) and yet leave the door open for plaintiff to file again? Put another way: Has defendant accomplished anything by getting an action dismissed when the court orders that that dismissal is without prejudice?

3. Judges ordinarily do not look beyond the "four corners" of the complaint when ruling on a 12(b)(6) motion. Fed. R. Civ. P. 10(c) states, however, that "[a] copy of a written instrument that is an exhibit to a pleading is a part of the pleading for all purposes." Professor Marcus observes that "[c]ourts have energetically seized this opportunity and permitted defendants to bring a range of materials to bear on the complaint in support of motions to dismiss, even where not attached as exhibits." (His footnote 57 gives examples of courts' taking consideration of unattached informational brochures, an unattached partnership agreement, and an EEOC charge that was not attached to the complaint.) Richard L. Marcus, *The Puzzling Persistence of Pleading Practice*, 76 Tex. L. Rev. 1749, 1757 (1998).

4. Rule 8(d)(3) provides that a party may state "as many separate claims or defenses as it has, *regardless of consistency*" (emphasis added). Is this approach consistent with a liberal standard of notice pleading?

5. If inconsistency is tolerated, why, then, did Judge Sweet grant the defendant's 12(b)(6) motion as to the false imprisonment count in *Bower v. Weisman*?

6. You already have a good deal of information to help you consider the goals that pleading requirements should achieve. It is important that you understand these various goals, because they will help you make arguments for and against motions to dismiss, and they will also help you decide on your own strategy for drafting complaints in different types of cases. One way to consider goals is to think about the underlying values of a procedural system that we explored in Chapter 1. Another way to approach goals for a pleading system is to consider the relationship of the complaint to other stages of the litigation. What is the relationship of pleading requirements to discovery? To *res judicata*, in the claim preclusion sense? Finally, consider your various audiences. Are there times when you would plead more than is required by the pleading rules themselves? See the discussion of strategy considerations that follows.

7. In the field of civil procedure we are fortunate to have the benefit of several exceptionally well written single-volume treatises, including Jack H. Friedenthal, Mary Kay Kane, and Arthur R. Miller, *Civil Procedure* (4th ed. 2005); Geoffrey C. Hazard, Jr., John Leubsdorf, and Debra Lyn Basset, *Civil Procedure* (6th ed. 2011); and Charles A. Wright and Mary Kay Kane, *Law of Federal Courts* (7th ed. 2011). The Wright and Kane single volume, as its title

connotes, concentrates almost exclusively on the federal court system. The late Professor Wright also authored a multi-volume treatise entitled *Federal Practice and Procedure*. Many of the volumes of this treatise were co-authored with Arthur Miller, and the treatise thus is often referred to as *Wright & Miller*. The other most frequently cited multi-volume treatise in the federal procedure field is called *Moore's Federal Practice*, named after William Moore, who was its initial author. Find out where these books are in your law library. When you are stumped on a procedure question during this course, or want to know more about a given topic, take a look at these books. You can usually find an answer quickly—and it is great practice.

8. Rule 9(b), which the court applied in *Bower v. Weisman*, required "particularity" in the pleading of the "circumstances constituting fraud or mistake." Why? Note that Rule 9(g) requires that "if an item of special damage is claimed, it must be specifically stated." The purpose of the rule is to notify the defendant when the type of loss is unusual for the type of claim being sued upon, so that the defendant is not unfairly surprised. For instance, the defendant might not know, absent specific pleading, that a plaintiff incurred expenses to minimize a loss. We have only provided one example here, because the question of what is a "special damage" for pleading purposes is just the type of question that gives you an opportunity to begin using the treatises we have described (or to find other sources in your school's library that might answer the question). If you were unsure whether a type of damage was "special," would you plead it?

## Practice Exercise No. 8: Analyzing 12(b)(6) and 12(e) Motions in *Carpenter*

After an initial client interview and strategy session, Attorney Carol Coblentz decided to represent Nancy Carpenter. Some legal research and factual investigation were done, and a complaint was filed. The defendants filed a 12(b)(6) motion to dismiss and a 12(e) motion for a more definite statement. You are a law clerk to a trial judge who soon will have to rule on the two motions. What rulings do you suggest and why? Assume that the pleading rules applicable in the state courts of the Commonwealth of Massachusetts are identical to the Federal Rules of Civil Procedure. The complaint, relevant statutes, and motions can be found (with the initial memorandum) in the *Carpenter v. Dee* Case Files. These motions were actually filed in this case. How would you assess their quality? Their likelihood of success?

### 2. Strategy Considerations

Many litigation decisions require the lawyer to consider three different questions: What must I do? What may I do? What should I do? As you have seen, the Federal Rules of Civil Procedure instruct the lawyer about the minimum requirements for a complaint. But lawyers can compose a much more comprehensive complaint if they choose, including even more facts than mandated by *Twombly* and *Iqbal*. In addition to drafting a complaint so that it will survive a 12(b)(6) motion, a plaintiff's lawyer will have a number of audiences she may wish to persuade or influence. The obvious ones are the judge and the opposing party and her lawyer. But who are other target audiences? Does the complaint in *Carpenter* adequately tell Nancy's *story*? Is it a sterile legal document? Could it be more literary—or a better advocacy document—without compromising (or perhaps even while advancing) its other important functions?

Importantly, pleadings within the formal system are not the only outlet for the skilled lawyer to advocate. Indeed, there is something of a parallel system that has no procedural rulebook, is largely ignored in law schools, and is seldom mentioned by judges. Yet it is a methodical and logical system that civil litigators are aware of and, increasingly, rely on as a necessary complement to the formal system:

> [M]any civil litigators, particularly those representing plaintiffs, seem to find it both desirable and necessary (in order to achieve optimum results for their clients) to prepare various written documents, notebooks, and even videos containing narratives that integrate the law and facts of their cases in ways that may persuade their relevant audiences—the opposing lawyer, the opposing lawyer's client, their own client, insurance companies, and mediators. These advocacy materials appear in myriad forms, including demand letters, other settlement correspondence, notebooks, mediation statements, edifying brochures, and documentary videos.

Stephen N. Subrin and Thomas O. Main, *The Integration of Law and Fact in an Uncharted Parallel Procedural Universe*, 79 Notre Dame L. Rev. 1981, 1983 (2004). Does the emergence of this parallel system suggest that the formal system does not adequately allow the expression of narrative and advocacy? Notice that, in the formal system, Fed. R. Civ. P. 12(f) authorizes a motion to strike material from a pleading that is "redundant, immaterial, impertinent, or scandalous." Is this mandate unduly restrictive?

### Practice Exercise No. 9: Considering the *City of Cleveland* Complaint

As an associate in a law firm, you have received an initial memorandum introducing a case involving women firefighters in the City of Cleveland. The memorandum is printed in the Case Files, under *City of Cleveland Firefighters*. The senior partner in the firm wants you to read the memorandum in order to acquaint yourself with the facts and law in the case. The partner wants you to be prepared to talk with her and other partners and associates about the type of complaint to be drafted in this case. At the strategy session, the partner wants you to be prepared to explain the causes of action and their elements, and to discuss what audiences the complaint should be written for, what major problems you anticipate in drafting, what tone you would advise for the complaint, how specific the complaint should be, and what additional factual and legal information you think is needed. The partner asks that you focus primarily on the Section 1983 and disparate treatment claims.

Your professor may instead ask you to prepare a demand letter, on behalf of plaintiffs, addressed to the City of Cleveland. Although we will talk more about the nonformal elements of dispute resolution in a later chapter, it is useful at this stage to consider why (and when) an attorney would send a demand letter. One reason to send a demand letter is to encourage the defendant to make a reasonable offer of settlement that might resolve the case in a manner that satisfies your client without the expense, delay, and risks of litigation. The tone of a demand letter thus is often determined by what the lawyer thinks will persuade the other parties to settle. An article in the *Student Lawyer* suggested that the letter "should be reasonable and realistic," and further advised the nascent lawyer to

> . . . achieve the right tone and level of specificity. One legitimate purpose of a demand letter is to intimidate, so adopt a formal tone. Be sure the recipient understands (1) your client's point of view, (2) what your client wants, (3) the specific deadline for complying, and (4) that you have taken account of the recipient's essential position and found it either wholly or partly unmeritorious.

Bryan A. Garner, *Legal Writing—Demand Letters Are Designed to Produce Results for Your Clients*, April, 2002 Student Lawyer 9. As you draft the demand letter for the plaintiffs in the *City of Cleveland*, compare the rhetoric and tone of the demand letter with the rhetoric and tone of the formal complaint. Why might they differ even though both documents are drawing from common facts and law?

## 3. Technical Pleading Requirements

In this part we emphasize some important, but more technical, pleading requirements. Technical requirements are traps for the unwary that can be costly and embarrassing if not followed. We will focus on the Federal Rules, but remember that the rules of practice and procedure in state court may differ.

First, re-read Rule 10. This rule addresses such matters as the contents of the "caption" (the introductory content that provides a heading for each pleading and motion) and the form of the allegations. These are important requirements, but should be self-explanatory. If the *Carpenter v. Dee* complaint were filed in federal court, would it comply with these mandates?

Second, re-read Rule 17(a). This rule requires that an action be prosecuted in the name of the *real party in interest*. The real party in interest is the person who has the right to come to court and seek the relief, as recognized by the law. Usually this is a matter of consulting the applicable substantive law to ascertain to whom the substantive law allows recovery for a particular cause of action. If your friend was damaged by the negligent conduct of x and you (rather than your friend) filed the lawsuit against x, the lawsuit would fail because the substantive law of negligence gives the cause of action to the injured party. Now consider a trickier problem: If Charlie Carpenter is deceased, to whom do his causes of action belong—his wife, his child, his parents? What if Charlie had a lover, or an ex-wife, or a child by another woman? The answer, again, would turn on the applicable substantive laws and to whom each of those laws gives the cause of action. We answer the *procedural* question as to the real party in interest by consulting the applicable *substantive* law.

Third, re-read Rule 17(b) and (c). Capacity to sue (or be sued) raises similar but different concerns than those implicated by Rule 17(a). With this part of the rule we are concerned with the ability of certain entities to sue. For example, if a contractor performs faulty work on a church, can the church sue in its own name? What if this "church" is just a handful of folks who meet in someone's basement each Sunday morning? And now, what about the contractor? If the church's check was issued to "Dan's Construction Services," is that necessarily the right defendant? What if that business is not a corporation or otherwise registered? The Rule explains where you will look to answer these questions. Importantly, though, you must be on the lookout and recognize that these questions lurk. Also, remember that a party may be the real party in interest yet lack the capacity to sue. For example, a minor or mentally incompetent person who is injured in a car wreck may be the real party in interest in the outcome of the litigation yet lack the capacity to sue. Such a party would need a surrogate to stand in for her/him and make the important decisions relating to the lawsuit.

## Comments and Questions

1. Why doesn't the "real party in interest" Rule 17(a) cover defendants? Can you come up with a credible argument that such a rule is not needed for plaintiffs (either)?

2. Assume that an action is not brought by the real party in interest. What should you file? Similarly, by what motion (or otherwise) would you challenge the lack of capacity to sue or be sued?

3. If you wanted to sue your law school for a personal injury that occurred on campus, what—exactly—would you name as the defendant? The University? The Regents of the University? The law school? Or something else?

## 4. Anonymous Plaintiffs

Occasionally parties want to initiate a lawsuit without disclosing their identity in court filings, which ordinarily are accessible to the press and to the public. It may be obvious to understand why someone would prefer not to disclose certain details about themselves, their past, prior jobs, business dealings, relationships, and so forth. These plaintiffs are willing to have their identities known to the defendant, but wish to remain anonymous in court filings. Should this be allowed under (some) circumstances? Or is disclosure part of the price a litigant must pay in litigation? What do the Federal Rules require?

# ■ DOE v. UNITED SERVICES LIFE INSURANCE COMPANY
### 123 F.R.D. 437 (S.D.N.Y. 1988)

SWEET, District Judge:

Plaintiff "John Doe" ("Doe") has moved for an order granting him leave to prosecute this action under a pseudonym, sealing all court records in which his actual name, address, or employer appear and withholding this information from defendant United Services Life Insurance Company ("United Services") and any of United Services's witnesses unless they agree to a confidentiality order. United Services seeks to dismiss the complaint for failure to identify the plaintiff as Rule 10(a) of the Federal Rules of Civil Procedure requires. For the reasons set forth below, Doe's motion is granted to the extent set forth below and United Services's motion is denied.

Doe currently works as a law clerk to a federal judge. During Doe's last year of law school, Doe and his father agreed to obtain a life insurance policy on Doe's life to secure his father's obligations as guarantor of Doe's student loans. In November of 1987, Doe and his father allegedly applied to United Services to purchase a $100,000 life insurance policy on Doe's life, naming Doe's father as beneficiary.

As part of the application process, a United Services representative interviewed Doe and the company required that Doe undergo a physical examination. Doe alleges that United Services takes extra precautions in processing homosexuals' life insurance applications and that the company required the interview and blood test because as a single male living in Greenwich Village with another male at the time of his application, Doe fit a homosexual profile.

Because Doe allegedly admitted at the interview that he previously had been arrested for public intoxication and because his blood test revealed abnormally high levels of liver enzymes often associated with alcohol abuse, United Services added a $105 surcharge to Doe's premium, raising it from $155 to $260.

Upon learning of his abnormal blood test results, Doe offered to retake the blood test, but United Services declined. After undergoing an independent blood test that yielded no abnormal results, Doe brought this lawsuit. Doe alleges he is heterosexual.

Doe originally filed the complaint in this action in the Supreme Court of the State of New York, alleging violations of New York insurance law and discrimination based on sex, marital status, and sexual orientation. United Services removed the action and made the instant motion prior to answer.

Pursuant to a state court ex parte order authorizing service of the pleading under the name "John Doe," Doe served United Services with the complaint and an order to show cause returnable August 12, 1988, seeking leave to prosecute the action under a pseudonym and other protection of his identity. That motion was pending at the time United Services removed the case to federal court. Because motions pending in state court at the time of removal survive removal, this court made Doe's motion returnable September 16, 1988, upon the moving papers originally filed in state court.

After Doe initiated the lawsuit, United Services invited Doe to submit to another blood test and offered to issue him a standard rate policy if his liver enzyme tests were within normal range. Doe declined, presumably to defeat a mootness claim and to assert his rights as alleged in the complaint.

According to Doe, the public's interest in eliminating unfair practices in the sale of insurance, Doe's privacy interest in not being publicly identified as a homosexual, and Doe's concern for his status as a law clerk for a federal judge favor permitting him to proceed pseudonymously. United Services denies that this case will require Doe to reveal confidential information about his sexual preference or practices and characterizes the action as involving a challenge to the company's decision to charge Doe a higher premium "due to a health risk unrelated to sexual activities," not one regarding homosexuality or susceptibility to AIDS. United Services also argues that permitting Doe to proceed pseudonymously will injure it by involving it in a highly publicized case while denying it the ability to defend itself from publicity or to set the record straight by a full response.

"Generally, lawsuits are public events and the public has a legitimate interest in knowing the pertinent facts." *Free Market Compensation v. Commodity Exch.*, 98 F.R.D. 311, 312 (S.D.N.Y. 1983). Accordingly, parties to a lawsuit usually should proceed under their real names. *See* Fed. R. Civ. P. 10(a) ("In the complaint the title of the action shall include the names of all the parties. . . ."); Fed. R. Civ. P. 17 ("Every action shall be prosecuted in the name of the real party in interest."); *see also Coe v. United States Dist. Court for the Dist. of Colo.*, 676 F.2d 411, 415 (10th Cir. 1982); *Southern Methodist Univ. Assn. v. Wynne & Jaffe*, 599 F.2d 707, 712 (5th Cir. 1979).

Under special circumstances, however, courts have allowed parties to use fictitious names, particularly where necessary to "protect privacy in a very private matter." *Doe v. Deschamps*, 64 F.R.D. 652, 653 (D. Mont. 1974); *see, e.g., Roe v. Wade*, 410 U.S. 113 (1973) (abortion); *Poe v. Ullman*, 367 U.S. 497 (1961) (birth control); *Doe v. Mundy*, 514 F.2d 1179 (7th Cir. 1975) (abortion); *Doe v. Alexander*, 510 F. Supp. 900 (D. Minn. 1981) (transsexuality); *Doe v. Harris*, 495 F. Supp. 1161 (S.D.N.Y. 1980) (mental illness); *Doe v. McConn*, 489 F. Supp. 76 (S. D. Tex. 1980) (transsexuality); *Doe v. Shapiro*, 302 F.

Supp. 761 (D. Conn. 1969) (welfare rights of illegitimate children), *appeal dismissed*, 396 U.S. 488 (1970).

Cases where a party risks public identification as a homosexual also raise privacy concerns that have supported an exception to the general rule of disclosure. *See, e.g., Doe v. Weinberger*, 820 F.2d 1275 (D.C. Cir. 1987), *cert. granted*, —U.S.—, 108 S. Ct. 1073 (1988); *Doe v. United States Air Force*, 812 F.2d 738 (D.C. Cir. 1987); *Doe v. Commonwealth's Attorney for City of Richmond*, 403 F. Supp. 1199 (E.D. Va. 1975), *aff'd*, 425 U.S. 901 (1976); *Doe v. Chaffee*, 355 F. Supp. 112 (N.D. Cal. 1973). Concern to avoid public identification as a homosexual is heightened in light of widespread public fear engendered by the Acquired Immunodeficiency Syndrome ("AIDS") crisis. *Cf. Doe v. Rostker*, 89 F.R.D. 158, 161 (proceeding anonymously is appropriate where issues in case present a risk of "some social stigma").

Doe may well be publicly identified as homosexual, despite the fact that Doe contends—and United Services concedes—that he is heterosexual. Doe's complaint alleges that United Services discriminated against him because it suspected that he was homosexual, and by bringing this action Doe seeks to vindicate the rights of homosexuals. Moreover, Doe is represented in this case by attorneys cooperating with Lambda Legal Defense and Education Fund, Inc., an organization widely recognized for its efforts in defending the rights of lesbians and gay men. [In a footnote, the court stated, "One of the reasons Doe offers for prosecuting this case under a pseudonym involves the effect this case might have on his status as a law clerk to a federal judge. This court's decision to permit Doe to proceed pseudonymously reflects a concern for his public identification as a homosexual, not a concern for his employment status. Courts should not permit parties to proceed pseudonymously just to protect the parties' professional or economic life. *See Coe v. United States District Court for the District of Colo.*, 676 F.2d 411 (10th Cir. 1982); *Southern Methodist University Assn. v. Wynne & Jaffe*, 599 F.2d 707 (5th Cir. 1979)."]

Significantly, this is not a case in which permitting Doe to proceed pseudonymously will disadvantage United Services. United Services already knows Doe's true identity, it will have full discovery rights as the case progresses, and it will only be barred from using or disclosing the fruits of its discovery for purposes other than the defense of this action.

For the reasons set forth above, Doe's motion is granted upon the conditions set forth in connection with the denial of United Services's motion. It is so ordered.

## Comments and Questions

1. What specific Federal Rules are relevant to the decision to be made by the court in this case?

2. Where does the court get the authority to alter the clear language of the Rules, for instance, Rule 10(a)? What about the Rules Enabling Act, 28 U.S.C. § 2072?

3. Why is the plaintiff allowed to plead anonymously, when in most discrimination cases plaintiffs must reveal their true identities? Does the court succeed in distinguishing the facts of this case from those in which courts have not permitted the plaintiffs to proceed anonymously?

4. Is tremendous embarrassment sufficient grounds to proceed anonymously? In *Doe v. Smith*, 429 F.3d 706 (7th Cir. 2005), a plaintiff suing her former boyfriend wanted to proceed anonymously in an action alleging that his distribution of a videotape of them having sexual relations violated the Wiretap Act. The Seventh Circuit remanded the case and instructed the trial judge to revisit this question (among others):

> The judge granted her application to do so without discussing this circuit's decisions, which disfavor anonymous litigation. The public has an interest in knowing what the judicial system is doing, an interest frustrated when any part of litigation is conducted in secret. Plaintiff was a minor when the recording occurred but is an adult today. She has denied Smith the shelter of anonymity—yet it is Smith, and not the plaintiff, who faces disgrace if the complaint's allegations can be substantiated. And if the complaint's allegations are false, then anonymity provides a shield behind which defamatory charges may be launched without shame or liability.
>
> Everyone at the high school who saw the recording already knows who "Doe" is, and most people acquainted with Smith could find out whether or not they had seen the recording. (Their dating relationship was no secret.) Now perhaps anonymity still could be justified if the tape has been circulated more widely (as counsel asserted at oral argument), and disclosure would allow strangers to identify the person in the recording and thus add to her humiliation. That question should be explored in the district court—and, if the judge decides that anonymous litigation is inappropriate, the plaintiff should be allowed to dismiss the suit in lieu of revealing her name.

*Id.* at 710. On remand, the district court delayed ruling on this issue and ordered the parties to commence discovery. 412 F. Supp. 2d 944, 947 (2006). The parties eventually settled.

5. Based on the values inherent in our procedural system, under what circumstances does it make sense to permit plaintiffs to proceed anonymously? When should plaintiffs not be obliged to "pay to play"? In one case, a group of named and unnamed union leaders and laborers in Colombia filed a complaint against certain U.S. corporations alleging that the company's executives had, in combination with their Colombian subsidiaries, hired Colombian paramilitaries to kill and torture plaintiffs and others. The district court allowed many of the plaintiffs to proceed anonymously based on their alleged concern for their safety in Colombia. *See Romero v. Drummond Co., Inc.*, 480 F.3d 1234 (11th Cir. 2007). What showing should be required of these plaintiffs?

6. You will find that "John Doe" parties appear in another context—where a plaintiff must name an unidentified defendant in a complaint in order to avoid a statute of limitations bar. But appreciate that *unknown* is different than *anonymous*. Circumstances involving unknown defendants are often governed by statutes that provide a means of tolling (putting on hold) the statute of limitations while the plaintiff, often through discovery, attempts to uncover the identity of John Doe defendants named in the complaint. Once a plaintiff discovers the identity of defendants named fictitiously in the complaint, she must amend the complaint by naming the actual defendants in lieu of the John Doe defendants. Under the Federal Rules, as long as the amendments conform to requirements of Fed. R. Civ. P. 15(c), they will relate back to the time of the filing of the original complaint, thus avoiding the statute of limitations time bar. In *Jacobson v. Osborne*, 133 F.2d 315 (5th Cir. 1998), however, the court would not permit the plaintiff to use Rule 15(c) in a situation where "John Doe" defendants were so named, because of the inability to identify them, rather than as a result of a mistake. For a critique of the federal approach to fictitious party pleading, see Carol M. Rice, *Meet John Doe: It Is Time for Federal Civil Procedure to Recognize John Doe Parties*, 57 U. Pitt. L. Rev. 883 (1996). Some states' statutes and decisions have allowed plaintiffs greater leeway in using fictitiously named defendants. California law is particularly liberal in allowing plaintiffs to plead John Doe defendants. We will address the subject of amendments later in this chapter.

## 5. Answers, Motions, and Affirmative Defenses

### a. Preliminary Motions

Assume that you are an attorney with a client who has been served with a civil complaint. You will first note how much time is remaining in which you have to act, because you will not want your client to lose by *default* for failing to respond. If you were in federal district court, you would examine Rule 12(a) to determine the applicable time period. If you needed an extension, you would turn to Rule 6(b). You would also want to check the local rules of the court in question to determine if there were special rules for seeking an enlargement of time. Do not assume that you can deal with extensions by merely obtaining the consent of the plaintiff's lawyer, although such consent (in writing, when possible) is desirable. The safest course is to have the court grant a motion to extend time within the initial period allowed. Check with a knowledgeable person in your office or with a clerk at the court in question to determine how gaining an extension of time is correctly accomplished in the court in question. It makes sense to satisfy yourself that not only are you in tune with the court's customs, but that you can back up your behavior with the specific language in a rule.

What are your options when faced with a complaint, assuming that you have now solved the timing question? In federal court, a good place to begin is Fed. R. Civ. P. 12 and 8, probably in that order.

*A motion for a more definite statement* (Fed. R. Civ. P. 12(e)) is available if the complaint is so vague or ambiguous that your client cannot reasonably be required to formulate a response. The rule mandates that the motion include a description of the "defects complained of and the details required." This motion must be made, as Rule 12(e) states, "before interposing a responsive pleading." You cannot answer and *then* successfully bring the motion. (There was a 12(e) Motion in Practice Exercise No. 8; you can find the motion in the *Carpenter v. Dee* Case Files.) Given that *Twombly* and *Iqbal* seem to require a good deal more from the plaintiff than *Conley v. Gibson* had suggested, won't defendants now usually file a 12(b)(6) motion rather than a 12(e) motion?

The courts have tried to prevent the motion for a more definite statement from being used as a substitute for discovery. Previous language in Federal Rule 12(e) permitted motions for a bill of particulars, but this method was deleted in 1946 because, according to the Advisory Committee, "[w]ith respect to the preparations for trial, the party is properly relegated to the various methods of examination and discovery provided in the rules for that purpose."

*A motion to strike* (Fed. R. Civ. P. 12(f)) asks the court to delete from a pleading "any insufficient defense or any redundant, immaterial, impertinent, or scandalous matter." Note that Rule 12(f) also imposes time limits, although the court can act on its "own initiative at any time" to strike the matters described in the rule. If a plaintiff lists several potential causes of action, and one of them "fails to state a claim upon which relief can be granted," the defendant can use Rule 12(f) on the ground that the particular count is "immaterial" or, more typically, can use a 12(b)(6) motion to seek the dismissal of that count. Assume you want examples of what courts have previously found to be insufficient defenses or "redundant, immaterial, impertinent, or scandalous" matters; name (or find) at least two different sources in the library where you could quickly find them.

## b. Motions to Dismiss

Re-read Federal Rule 12(b) to find the seven permitted motions to dismiss. Note that 12(b) gives you the choice of either raising these defenses as part of your answer, or by preliminary motions prior to filing an answer. You should consider as a matter of the defendant's strategy why you would choose to answer first, including your 12(b) defenses in the answer, rather than acting by motions and delaying your answer. One very practical consideration is whether defense counsel is prepared to file an answer. As you will see, an answer must contain the defendant's theories and contentions, and this research, investigation, and preparation may take time. The deadline for defendant's response is short: see Fed. R. Civ. P. 12(a)(1)(A). Can you come up with other strategic considerations for taking the answer or motion route?

You are already familiar with the *motion to dismiss for failure to state a claim* (12(b)(6)). Each of the other "12(b)'s" will be taken up when they are covered later in the course. For example, Chapters 7 and 8 deal with, among other things, jurisdictional issues and service of process. Consequently, the defenses (or motions to dismiss) based on *lack of jurisdiction over the subject matter* (12(b)(1)), *lack of jurisdiction over the person* (12(b)(2)), *improper venue* (12(b)(3)), *insufficiency of process* (12(b)(4)), and *insufficiency of service of process* (12(b)(5)) will be examined then. Perhaps you cannot wait to find out the difference between an "insufficiency of process" and an "insufficiency of service of process." In fact, lawyers often move under both subsections when they are challenging service of process. Technically, the former addresses a failure to conform the summons with the requirements of Rules 4(a) and 4(b), and the latter challenges a failure to properly serve the opponent. For instance, the form of a summons could be correct, but not served at all or not served correctly upon the defendant.

The final 12(b) defense, Fed. R. Civ. P. 12(b)(7), *failure to join a party under Rule 19,* refers to the failure to join an indispensable party in accordance with Rule 19. You will later learn that defendants can use Rule 19 strategically to insist that an indispensable party be joined in circumstances where such joinder is impossible, because it would destroy subject matter jurisdiction or because the plaintiff is unable to obtain personal jurisdiction over the omitted Rule 19 party in the court where the case has been commenced. The net result may be dismissal.

Remember that although we are discussing the 12(b) defenses or motions in the context of a defendant's answering a plaintiff's complaint, such defenses or motions will also have to be considered in other situations, such as by a plaintiff when she faces a counterclaim or a co-defendant who faces a cross-claim. Rule 8(a) gives the requirements for all claims, whether an original claim, counterclaim, cross-claim, or third-party claim, and Rule 8(b) requires defenses and admissions or denials to allegations when one is faced with an adverse claim (such as a plaintiff faced with a counterclaim).

Before moving on to the drafting of an answer (with admissions and denials and affirmative defenses), you should consider Rules 12(g) and 12(h), which deal with consolidating defenses in a motion and the waiver or preserving certain defenses. There are several ways that by omission you can lose the right to bring four of the 12(b) defenses or motions. (We will explain in a moment the "favored" three defenses, which receive greater protection against waiver.) One way to lose 12(b) defenses is to bring one 12(b) motion, but omit others. This is the purpose of 12(g). Let's say you, as defendant's counsel, bring a motion to dismiss for failure of personal jurisdiction (for instance, the defendant has never had any affiliation with the forum state and has not consented to be sued there), the motion is denied, and you then bring a motion to dismiss for lack of venue. Rule 12(h) forbids this, and you will have lost your challenge to venue by failure to consolidate the two motions.

Consider the same example, but this time you try to circumvent Rule 12(g) by filing an answer with your challenge to venue after losing the personal jurisdiction motion. Again, you will be stymied, but this time by Rule 12(h)(1); read it, and you will see why.

Or let's say that you do not raise any 12(b) defenses by motion, but instead put a 12(b)(2) defense—lack of jurisdiction over the person—in your answer. Later you try to add a challenge to venue. This is prohibited by Rule 12(h)(1). An amendment to add the defense will usually not save you from your waiver. Can you see why?

Another possibility is that you do not bring any 12(b) motions prior to answering, nor do you include any in your answer. You will have waived your personal jurisdiction (12(b)(2)), venue (12(b)(3)), and process (12(b)(4) and (12(b)(5)) defenses—the nonfavored defenses—by your inaction.

The long and short of it is this: (1) If you file a 12(b) motion prior to your answer, include any plausible less-favored defenses in your motion at the same time; and (2) if you answer, without having first brought 12(b) motions, include plausible less-favored defenses in your answer. Do these rules regarding consolidation and waiver of 12(b) defenses make sense to you? Why or why not?

We have yet to discuss why the defenses of failure to state a claim upon which relief can be granted, failure to join an indispensable party under Rule 19, and lack of subject matter jurisdiction are not waived by a failure to consolidate them with other 12(b) motions nor by failing to include them in your answer. Notice that Rule 12(h)(3) goes even further.

We will discuss the sanctity of subject matter jurisdiction and indispensable party when we confront those concepts later. Similarly, we will discuss the common sense of having waiver provisions for personal jurisdiction, venue, and process issues when we reach those topics. But you are already equipped to figure out why 12(b)(6) is protected against waiver. Consider, for instance, what would happen at trial in a case where there was one alleged cause of action, but it was clear from the pleading that it did not cover the transaction in question. In other words, a 12(b)(6) motion would have been granted had it been filed or included in the answer as a defense. What if the court could not now consider the motion because of waiver? Would this make sense? Why or why not?

Rule 12(h) goes on to say that "an objection of failure to state a legal defense to a claim" may also "be made in any pleading permitted or ordered under Rule 7(a), or by a motion for judgment on the pleadings, or at the trial on the merits." Why is the plaintiff's objection—of failure to state a legal defense to a claim—also protected against waiver?

Although the favored 12(b) defenses relating to subject matter jurisdiction, Rule 19, and failure to state a claim are not waived by omission in the answer or failure to consolidate with other 12(b) motions, it is common practice for a defendant's lawyers to include them in their answer if applicable. Sometimes, however, defendants refrain from including such a defense. For instance, defense counsel may think that the plaintiff's counsel is lazy and will not realize the weakness of a particular element in its case if it does not have to defend against a 12(b)(6) motion. The defendant may omit the 12(b)(6) defense in its answer, knowing that it can raise it later or perhaps deciding to wait for the directed verdict stage—after it is usually too late for the plaintiff to cure an omission—before pointing out the failure to have any evidence of an element. (It is true that 12(b)(6) relates to the allegations of the complaint and directed verdict to the evidence. However, since some courts have been reluctant to grant 12(b)(6) motions, or to grant them only with leave to amend, a defendant's lawyer might wish not to draw attention to a potential weakness in the plaintiff's case, as demonstrated by a weakness in its complaint, at an early stage of the litigation.)

There is one final matter on the 12(b) defenses. Whether they are raised by preliminary motion, or in the answer, or—in the case of the "favored" defenses—after the answer, Rule 12(i) states that such defenses "must be heard and decided before trial unless the court orders a deferral until trial." Why do the Rules encourage the early determination of the 12(b) defenses?

You should also be aware of the Rule 12(c) motion for judgment on the pleadings, although it is infrequently used. It is possible that upon considering all of the pleadings, which usually will be a complaint and an answer, it is clear that the plaintiff or defendant must win. An example of the latter would be a complaint in which the allegations, taken as true, show that the statute of limitations has run, coupled with an answer that raises the statute of limitations as an affirmative defense. An example of the former would be an answer that admits all of plaintiff's allegations and raises a nonapplicable defense, such as contributory negligence in a contract case. In this case, a plaintiff could win a motion for judgment on the pleadings.

### c. Answers

It is now time to consider what you, as defense counsel, will put in your answer. Let us assume that you have decided not to bring 12(b) defenses by separate motion. Your answer will potentially contain at least four types of material. The four most common types of materials in the answer are: (1) *admissions* and *denials* to the averments in the plaintiff's complaint (Fed. R. Civ. P. 8(b)); (2) *12(b) defenses*; (3) *affirmative defenses* (Fed. R. Civ. P. 8(c)); and (4) *counterclaims* and *cross-claims* (Fed. R. Civ. P. 13). Recognizing that the answer is an advocacy document, defendants may also use the answer to assert their theory(ies) of their case; defendants often include as additional "defenses," for example, that there was no negligence, that there is a lack of causation, etc.

In addition, when filing their answer, defense counsels simultaneously consider whether they wish to *implead* a third party (Fed. R. Civ. P. 14) or *otherwise seek to add parties.* For instance, the defendant might consider adding an additional defendant to a counterclaim in accordance with Rule 13(h). Defense counsel might further attempt to enlarge the case through a motion to consolidate (Fed. R. Civ. P. 42(a)), or by encouraging someone else to intervene (Fed. R. Civ. P. 24). And defense counsel might seek to *reduce the number of parties* through a motion for misjoinder pursuant to Rule 21. Finally, defense counsel should also consider at the time of answering whether to *claim a jury trial.* The jury claim is often stated in the answer. We will discuss the topic of jury trials in Chapter 5.

### d. Admissions and Denials

The doctrine on admissions and denials is fairly straightforward. Read Rule 8(b). The rule requires the admission or denial of each averment, except when a party "lacks knowledge or information sufficient to form a belief about the truth of an allegation," a topic we explore in greater detail in a moment. A pleader may deny specific allegations (or averments), whole paragraphs of the complaint, or even the entire complaint. But all pleadings are subject to Rule 11, a rule that we will study later. It is typical to deny entire paragraphs, as you will note by looking at the answers in the *Carpenter v. Dee* case. Rule 8(b)(6) prescribes that when a responsive pleading is required, allegations not denied will be deemed admitted. One exception is "the amount of damages." Try thinking of an example of a pleading to which no responsive pleading is required. *See* Rule 7(a). When no responsive pleading is required, "an allegation is considered denied or avoided."

A major purpose of an answer is to narrow the issues and to apprise the parties of what is still in dispute. Defense counsels are very careful not to admit anything that they in fact dispute, because once the defendant admits an averment, absent an amendment changing the admission to a denial, it will be taken as true for the remainder of the case. Consequently, admissions in pleadings are more binding than evidence given at a trial, which the fact finder can believe or disbelieve. Thus, it is very difficult to get a defendant to admit a legal conclusion, such as "duty" or "negligence," if there is *any* ground for denying the allegation. Sometimes, defense counsels state that the plaintiff has alleged a "legal conclusion" that does not require admission or denial, although the Rules do not specifically cover the situation. More frequently, the defendant will just deny the allegation. If a plaintiff desires to use the pleadings as a mechanism for reducing the legal battlefield, she is better off pleading very specific facts so that opposing counsel has more difficulty stating an unconditional denial.

Penalties exist for denying an entire group of averments when in fact the pleader denies only a portion (and could admit the remainder). A favorite example of casebooks is *Zielinski v. Philadelphia Piers, Inc.*, 139 F. Supp. 408 (D.C. Pa. 1956), where the plaintiff alleged in the complaint that a vehicle owned, operated, and controlled by the defendant, its agents, servants, and employees was managed so negligently and carelessly that it came into contact with the plaintiff and caused him injuries. The defendant denied the entire paragraph of averments in the complaint, but could have admitted that (1) the accident happened; (2) it owned the vehicle that came into contact with the plaintiff; and (3) there was some injury to plaintiff. The defendant denied the group of allegations, however, presumably because it had leased the vehicle to another entity, which, in turn, had hired the allegedly negligent driver. The plaintiff thus had sued the wrong defendant, and the statute of limitations on its claim (against the proper defendant) had expired sometime after the defendant answered but before the plaintiff ascertained the identity of the correct defendant. Although the named defendant arguably was responsible under certain theories of agency, the court ruled that the defendant should be treated as if it had admitted operation and control of the vehicle, in part because it had not more carefully admitted and denied specific averments in the complaint. This is an unusual case, and in fact the court thought the plaintiff had been misled in additional ways. Nonetheless, the case is a reminder to defendants not to be casual in their admissions and denials.

Frequently, a defense lawyer has insufficient knowledge or information to form a belief about an allegation, and therefore wants to deny it. Although some courts have not required that the language in Rule 8(b) in this regard be precisely followed, others have required strict adherence and do not permit the language "neither admits nor denies." *See, e.g., Aster Telesolutions, Inc. v. Premier Technical Solutions, Inc.*, 2006 WL 1547980 (N.D. Ill. 2006) (citing *State Farm Mut. Auto. Ins. Co. v. Riley*, 199 F.R.D. 276 (N.D. Ill. 2001)).

Some courts have insisted that parties not use the "lacks knowledge or information sufficient to form a belief" phrase of Rule 8(b) as an excuse to avoid making reasonable inquiry prior to admitting or denying averments. Much like denying a factual allegation that should have been admitted, a court may later deem the defendant to have admitted that allegation. Consider the following excerpt from a district court opinion rebuking the defendant, the U.S. government, for its answer:

> The preparation of this case by the Government has been quite casual. There have been delays in service of third-party complaints and answers. . . . [F]ailure to make reasonable investigation of even Government files in the preparation of this case prevented defendant from actually responding to plaintiff's allegation that he was a business invitee. In answer to that averment in plaintiff's original and amended complaints defendant stated that it lacked sufficient knowledge or information to admit or deny, in accord with Fed. R. Civ. P. 8(b).
>
> An answer of lack of knowledge or information will usually be deemed a denial. A party, however, may be held to the duty to exert reasonable effort to obtain knowledge of a fact. . . . In the present case defendant failed to examine available, highly relevant Government documents which would have given a basis for the belief that plaintiff was not a business invitee and that the Court did not have jurisdiction under the FTCA. A fact which is denied for lack of knowledge or information may be deemed admitted if the matter is one to which

the party does have knowledge or information. . . . The Government will be held to an admission that plaintiff was a business invitee at the time of the accident. . . .

*Greenbaum v. United States*, 360 F. Supp. 784 (E.D. Pa. 1973).

There is another thorny situation that often confronts defense counsel. The lawyer has been given some information about the plaintiff's averment that leads her to the belief it is false and should therefore be denied, but she is uncertain. This is not the situation where there is an insufficiency of knowledge or information, but rather an honest and justifiable hesitancy to express certainty in one's denial because of inability to test the reliability of sources. Wright and Miller put it this way:

> A party who lacks first-hand or personal knowledge of the validity of one or more of the allegations in the preceding pleading, but who has sufficient information to form a belief concerning the truth or falsity of those allegation may interpose a denial upon "information and belief." This form of denial is not authorized expressly by Rule 8(b), as is the denial based upon a lack of knowledge or information sufficient to form belief. However . . . federal courts have permitted allegations on information and belief, presumably because it was accepted under the codes that preceded the federal rule . . . and because of the provision in Rule 11 stating that when an attorney signs the pleading that signature constitutes a certificate "that to the best of the person's knowledge, information, and belief formed after an inquiry reasonable under the circumstances. . . ."

Charles A. Wright and Arthur R. Miller, 5 *Federal Practice and Procedure* § 1263.

### e. Affirmative Defenses

Affirmative defenses are the counterpart to the "confession and avoidance" of the common law. In effect, the defendant is saying, "Even if you prove your cause of action" (i.e., the confession), "I still win because of another rule or an exception" (i.e., the avoidance). For instance, plaintiff might prove all of the elements of a negligence case, and yet lose because of the defense of statute of limitations or contributory negligence (if that is a complete defense under the applicable law). Usually, but not always, defendants have the burdens of pleading, production, and persuasion as to all elements of the affirmative defense, just as plaintiffs usually have the same burdens as to the elements of their causes of action.

Rule 8(c) lists eighteen matters as affirmative defenses, but makes clear that these are merely illustrative, and that the defendant has the obligation to plead "any avoidance or affirmative defense." Other affirmative defenses to be pled under certain circumstances and causes of action include comparative negligence, gift, truth, privilege, multiplicity of suits, rescission, election of remedies, and many others. In the same fashion that causes of action have elements, affirmative defenses likewise have constituent elements that must be pled and, ultimately, proved.

It used to be commonplace for those practicing law under the Federal Rules to assume that the failure to list an affirmative defense in the answer would mean that the defendant has waived it and could not present evidence with respect to it at trial, unless an amendment was permitted. It is still safer practice for defense counsel to include all of the potential affirmative defenses in the answer. Some circuit courts, however, have concluded that a defendant does not waive an affirmative defense by failing to raise it in the answer, absent a showing of prejudice to the plaintiff. For example, in the case that follows, the plaintiff, who had been injured in an industrial accident at an acrylic manufacturing plant, sued the contractor (Fluor Enterprises), which had been hired to provide construction, maintenance, and engineering technicians. After a jury returned a verdict for plaintiff in the amount of $2.5 million, defendant appealed. One of the issues on appeal was whether defendant should have been allowed to invoke the affirmative defense of borrowed servant. Under this doctrine, an entity who "borrows" another employee's worker may be shielded from tort liability by worker's compensation statutes. The district court had concluded that the defendant had waived this defense:

> In general, a party's failure to raise an affirmative defense in the pleadings results in a waiver of the defense. In deciding waiver issues under Rule 8(c), this Court in some cases has examined whether a plaintiff had notice of the unpled defense or was prejudiced by the lack of notice. *See Sweet v. Sec'y, Dep't. of Corr.*, 467 F.3d 1311, 1321 n.4 (11th Cir. 2006) (concluding that a plaintiff is not prejudiced by a defendant's failure to comply with Rule 8(c) if the plaintiff has notice of the affirmative defense by some other means), *cert. denied*, — U.S.—, 127 S. Ct. 2139, (2007). . . .
>
> On appeal, Fluor contends it implicitly pled the borrowed servant doctrine in its answer by claiming an affirmative defense under the Alabama Worker's Compensation Act's (AWCA) exclusivity provisions, because the only basis for asserting an affirmative defense under the AWCA's exclusivity provisions would have been under the theory that Lawrence [Fluor's technician, who allegedly caused the accident] was a borrowed servant. . . . Fluor also contends that Proctor had other notice of the defense and was not prejudiced. The district court concluded that Fluor had not actually pled the defense and thus waived the defense "regardless of whether the Plaintiff realized, recognized, or inquired as to facts that may give rise to such a defense. . . ." The district court said nothing about, much less made a finding about, whether Proctor, in fact, either had notice of Fluor's borrowed servant defense or would be surprised and prejudiced. Instead, the district court considered Proctor's notice of the defense to be unimportant.
>
> We conclude that, given the circumstances presented in this case, the district court abused its discretion by concluding that Fluor waived the borrowed servant defense by failing to plead it separately in its answer. The

general rule of waiver is more easily applied when a party fails to set forth one of the nineteen defenses specifically listed in Rule 8(c); waiver becomes less clear when a party fails to assert affirmatively some "other matter" that pre-existing federal case law has not clearly construed as "constituting an avoidance or affirmative defense" under Rule 8(c).

*Proctor v. Fluor Enterprises, Inc.*, 494 F.3d 1337, 1350-1351 (11th Cir. 2007).

Usually, lawyers know or are able to find out in advance and with certainty the elements of causes of action and the applicable affirmative defenses. The same sources that describe causes of action also usually describe affirmative defenses. On those rare occasions when a court must decide whether a circumstance should be part of the plaintiff's prima facie case or an affirmative defense of the defendant, the opinions discuss such matters as accessibility to the evidence, whether the potential defense is an exception to ordinary events, and whether the parties should be hampered or aided in proving their cases. If a statute is involved, the court will attempt to discern whether its language implies what is an affirmative defense (such as an "except" clause in the statute) or whether legislative intent helps resolve the question.

Sometimes, a court or legislature will wish to place some burden on a defendant, but not a total affirmative defense. For instance, consider the case where a plaintiff takes a suit to the dry cleaners for cleaning (a bailment) and it is not returned in as good condition as when the cleaner received it or it is not returned at all. Who has the burden of showing negligence or lack thereof? Some courts put the burden of proving negligence on the plaintiff, but then say that if the fact finder believes that the plaintiff took the suit to the dry cleaner in good condition and the dry cleaner accepted it and did not return it in at least as good condition (the triggering facts), then negligence is presumed, unless the defendant produces enough evidence to permit a finding that it was not negligent (production burden) and then the burden of persuasion is again on the plaintiff. Some courts use such a presumption to shift the entire burden of proof to the defendant, thus effectively creating an affirmative defense, but only after the plaintiff proves the triggering facts.

Another device courts occasionally use is to place the pleading burden on the plaintiff, but to require the defendant to plead the nonexistence of the element as an affirmative defense and to prove it. For instance, usually the plaintiff must allege nonpayment in a promissory note case, but the defendant must allege payment as an affirmative defense and has both the production and persuasion burdens with respect to payment.

## Practice Exercise No. 10: Analyzing the Answer in *Carpenter*

The purpose of this exercise is to help you learn the differences among 12(b)(6) defenses, denials, and affirmative defenses. The Answer of Randall

Dee to the initial Complaint is in the Case Files. Analyze the Answer in *Carpenter* in light of the Complaint. (Assume that the pleading rules in Massachusetts are the same as the Federal Rules of Civil Procedure.)

(a) What effect will the admissions in paragraphs four and five of Randall Dee's answer have on the trial?

(b) Assuming that the defendant has reasonable knowledge, is the answer to paragraph six in compliance with the applicable Massachusetts rules?

(c) What does the denial to the allegations in paragraph eleven put in issue? Assuming that further stages of this case (such as discovery, summary judgment, pretrial conference) do not bring closure to the issue and that it remains as defined by the pleadings, how will the judge instruct the jury on the question of conscious suffering, including instructions on burden of proof?

(d) Examine each of Randall Dee's defenses, and explain what type of defense it is. Is it a defense at all or a mislabeled "denial"?

(e) Should *Twombly* and *Iqbal* change the pleading standard for *defendants*? How would a more rigorous pleading standard for defendants change the content of Randall Dee's answer? Could Randall Dee plead with greater specificity? Who is in the better position to plead details about what happened and why: Nancy Carpenter or Randall Dee?

(f) Notice that Randall Dee's counsel lumps different types of defenses together, rather than separating affirmative defenses from other types. This is common practice, although some lawyers divide their answer by making distinct categories, such as "12(b) defenses" and "affirmative defenses." Some lawyers begin their answers with affirmative defenses and thus take advantage of this opportunity for rhetoric. What order and method of labeling do the forms attached to the Federal Rules suggest? Which specific forms are you relying on in giving your answer?

(g) If you were a legislator or judge faced with the question, would you make the second defense an affirmative defense? Why or why not?

# Review Exercise No. 1

The following question will help you review the material to ensure that you are integrating doctrine, practice, and context. Consider the facts given in this problem, including the details from the given complaint, and answer the four questions that follow. It should take you at least ninety minutes to answer these questions fully.

On May 18, 2012, Tristan Plord, a lifelong resident of Miami, Florida, filed a complaint in a United States federal district court asserting claims for false representation and for promissory estoppel against Denver Home Finance, Inc. ("Denver"). (Don't worry, we will state the elements of these causes of action.) Denver, a Colorado corporation with a principal place of business in Denver, Colorado, was served with that complaint the same day. The complaint included the following allegations:

(1)   On May 19, 2009, Plord purchased a home in Miami, Florida.

(2)   Plaintiff financed that home with Denver.

(3)   As a condition to close on the purchase agreement, Denver insisted that plaintiff present proof of fire, flood, and wind insurance for the property.

(4)   Plaintiff purchased fire, flood, and wind insurance through Imbler Insurance Co. ("Imbler"), and presented proof thereof to Denver. Denver agreed to make the quarterly insurance payments to Imbler out of an escrow account established by Plaintiff.

(5)   On November 1, 2010, Imbler notified Plord that the company was not renewing her insurance policy, and that the policy would terminate as of November 30, 2010.

(6)   Plaintiff notified Denver of the insurance termination by telephone on November 5, 2010, and they told her that they would promptly obtain insurance for the home, and that the insurance payments would be paid out of escrow (as was occurring with the payments to Imbler).

(7)   On September 23, 2011, Hurricane Ishtar hit the southern coast of Florida causing damage to plaintiff's home.

(8)   Damages to the roof, building structure, and contents are an amount in excess of $215,000.

(9)   When plaintiff attempted to make a claim for insurance benefits for the damage, she learned that there was no insurance coverage on the home.

### Count One: Promissory Estoppel

(10)   Denver is liable on a theory of promissory estoppel.

### Count Two: False Representation—Fraud

(11)   Denver made material false representations with knowledge of their falsity.

In answering this question you should assume that (1) you are answering this question on December 8, 2012; (2) the complaint was accurately captioned, contained a valid allegation of subject matter jurisdiction, and was properly signed by the plaintiff's attorney; (3) the statute of limitations on all claims is two years; (4) the statute of frauds does not present any obstacles to plaintiff's recovery; and (5) there are only two substantive causes of action that could serve as the basis for Plord's claim against Denver, and the details for these follow: *False Representation*, for which the elements are (i) a false statement; (ii) known by the speaker to be false or made recklessly without any knowledge of the truth; (iii) made with the intent that the other party would act upon it; (iv) reliance by the other party; and (v) damages; and *Promissory Estoppel*, for which the elements are (i) a promise clear and unambiguous on its terms; (ii) reliance by the party to whom the promise is made; (iii) that reliance is both reasonable and foreseeable; and (iv) damages.

Question No. 1: How should the court rule if Denver moves to dismiss Plord's complaint under Fed. R. Civ. P. 12(b)(6) for failure to state a claim?

Question No. 2: Imagine that you represent Denver, and that you are discussing the allegations of the complaint with your client's representative, the chief executive officer of the company. Assume that it is general knowledge that a terribly destructive hurricane named Ishtar hit Miami, Florida, on September 23, 2011. With regard (only) to paragraph 7 of the complaint, will you recommend that the answer admit it, deny it, or something else?

Question No. 3: Who should sign the Answer in this case? Be specific, and give your reason.

Question No. 4: Should the Answer include the affirmative defense that the plaintiff's claim is barred by the statute of limitations? If yes, state the Federal Rule by which you will seek to have the case adjudicated in your client's favor. If no, what risk do you take by not including this defense in your answer?

## 6. Amendments

When judges and lawyers want a quick introduction to a civil lawsuit, they often first look at the complaint and answer in order to educate themselves on the factual background of the case and the claims and defenses. Unless altered by a pretrial conference order, the pleadings also set the boundaries for the trial, confining the parties to the alleged claims and defenses and instructing the judge and the lawyers as to what facts have been admitted. But much of modern civil litigation revolves around discovery, and during that stage new facts, and consequently previously unpleaded causes of action and defenses, often emerge. It is true that the most plaintiff-friendly reading of Rule 8(a)(2) would permit the plaintiff simply to state a claim showing one cause of action, and that the plaintiff would then be able to prove at trial any cause of action within the story told in the complaint. But lawyers are cautious and want to be certain that at trial they can introduce evidence on their entire case. Since the trial judge may tell them that they cannot introduce evidence of causes of action and defenses absent from their pleadings (or outside the limits of a pretrial order under Rule 16 or a similar state rule), lawyers frequently want to amend their pleadings. In federal court civil litigation, Rule 15 controls whether one can amend a pleading, although sometimes local rules provide further requirements and limitations.

Rule 15 has four subparagraphs. The most critical portions are (1) the sentence in 15(a)(2) stating that the "court should freely give leave when justice so requires"; and (2) 15(c), which describes when an amendment "relates back to the date of the original pleading."

You should be aware, though, of the situations covered by Fed. R. Civ. P. 15(b) and 15(d). Rule 15(b) is there to help solve the problem of proffered or admitted evidence that seems to go beyond the confines of the pleadings. The first sentence to Rule 15(b)(2) places trial lawyers in somewhat of a dilemma. It states: "When an issue not raised by the pleadings is tried by the parties' express or implied consent, it must be treated in all respects as if raised in the pleadings." Consider opposing counsel's options when the plaintiff introduces a cause of action that is slightly different from what is explicit in the complaint (or when the defendant raises an affirmative defense that was not pleaded). If one objects, the opponent will move to amend and leave is "freely given when justice so requires." (Fed. R. Civ. P. 15(a).) Yet if one doesn't object, the risk is that one has given "implied" consent.

In general, it is probably better to object when you think your opponent is introducing evidence beyond the pleadings. First, it is important to know whether a new issue has in fact been raised, so that you know whether you have to meet it through cross-examination or by introducing your own evidence. Sometimes it is not clear what your opponent is driving at when she introduces evidence, and you do not want to invite her to invent a new theory that perhaps she didn't see. So there may be occasions when you do not object because you do not want to educate the opposition. But the ambiguity may be resolved against you later (as a result of your "implied" consent by your not objecting to the admissibility of the evidence), so you are often better off knowing exactly where you and opposing counsel stand.

Second, you might win by your objection, and in fact keep a new cause of action, theory, or defense out of the case. Your arguments for keeping out evidence on a new theory will be similar to the arguments that you normally raise against an amendment. In other words, here are arguments that parties make as to why "justice" does not require granting the right to amend within the meaning of Rule 15(a). The stock ones (in addition to the argument that the statute of limitations has run, which we will take up later) are (1) the opponent has unreasonably delayed raising the issue, although this argument usually fails without an additional argument about prejudice; (2) you have been prejudiced in your preparation of the case by the delay; (3) the new issue is raised in bad faith, such as for the purpose of clouding real issues or confusing the fact finder or making the other side look "bad" on a largely irrelevant question; or (4) the new issue is "futile" in the sense that the party pressing it cannot win on it. The last sentence of 15(b)(1) permits the court to grant a continuance to the objecting party so she can prepare to meet the new issue without prejudice, but this option is particularly unappealing to judges in the middle of a jury trial or when the party introducing the new issue has had ample opportunity to raise the question by seeking a formal amendment.

Sometimes, events have happened since the date of the original pleading that are relevant to the case, but could not have been pleaded specifically at the time because they had not yet occurred. This is the reason for Fed. R. Civ. P. 15(d) on "Supplemental Pleadings." For instance, there may be subsequent breaches of the contract sued upon, or additional installment payments due, or patent, copyright, or trademark infringements that occurred after the initial complaint. A 1963 amendment to 15(d) makes clear that the trial court is empowered to grant a supplemental pleading even if the new material cures a defect in the original complaint. If a new claim is involved and the statute of limitations has now run, the pleader who seeks the supplemental pleading will have to rely on the provisions of 15(c) dealing with "relation back" of amendments.

Probably the most litigated provisions of Rule 15, or of any rules regarding amendments, concern statute of limitations problems and whether such a statute can be met by having the additional claim or defense relate back to the date of the original pleading. For example, if a plaintiff brought the initial cause of action within the statute of limitations, and the new claim or new cause of action to be "amended in" is now beyond the statutory period, the plaintiff will want the "amended in" claim or cause of action to "relate back" to the commencement date of the initial case. Can you see why it is the intersection of statutes of limitations and motions to amend that raises the most controversial amendment issues?

It is important to know clearly what a statute of limitations is. Most states have statutes requiring that certain causes of action be brought within a certain number of years from when the cause of action accrued. Some federal statutes provide limitations periods for specific federal claims.* Usually, the cause of action accrues when every element of the cause of action has taken place, and usually the last element to occur is the damage or harm. A typical statute of limitations for tort claims is three years. Consequently, if an automobile accident happened on Day One, and the plaintiff was therefore injured on Day One, the plaintiff would have to bring her lawsuit within three years from Day One. (A typical statute of limitations for contract claims is six years.)

Sometimes, potential parties will agree to stop the running of a statute of limitations. A defendant may not want a complaint to be filed and may be willing to agree to forestall the running of the period of time under the statute of limitations pending settlement negotiations. These are often called "tolling agreements."

Reasons for the existence of statutes of limitations include (1) giving potential parties a sense of repose or peace after time has expired (one shouldn't have to worry a lifetime about potential wrongdoing); (2) permitting accused parties to amass evidence while it is still fresh; (3) helping courts to avoid depleting their scarce resources on stale cases in which it will be difficult, if not impossible, to find out what happened. These rationales should help you see why the amendment doctrine becomes more complicated when amendments are sought after the expiration of a statute of limitations.

Consider the facts of *Carpenter v. Dee.* Let's say that *prior* to the running of the applicable statute of limitations, Nancy Carpenter's lawyer, who initially pleaded only a wrongful death count, decided that it was necessary to add a count for conscious suffering. Or assume that her lawyer, through discovery, found plausible defendants in addition to the Dee brothers, such as the retailer that sold the tires and the suspension lift kit. Such

---

*28 U.S.C. § 1658, enacted in 1990, provides a general four-year statute of limitations (absent a specific limitations period in the applicable federal law) for all civil actions "arising under an Act of Congress enacted after the date of enactment of this section."

amendments normally will not cause parties or courts much trouble. Why? Then consider the same motions to amend *after* the applicable statute of limitations has expired. Why is it now more problematic?

Before reading an amendment/statute of limitations case, you should note two conceptual problems. One is whether the amendment concerns merely adding a claim or defense, as opposed to adding a party. Re-read Fed. R. Civ. P. 15(c). Assume a federal cause of action that does not have any special "relationship back" law attached to it. (If you were in federal court and there were a claim grounded in state law, the federal court, by virtue of 15(c)(1)(A), would apply the "relation back" doctrine of the state law if it were more lenient than the Federal Rules.) If you sought to add a second federal claim to your first, after the statute of limitations had run, "relation back" would be governed by 15(c)(1)(B). But if you sought to add a new party to your initial federal cause of action after the applicable statute of limitations had run, the more stringent provisions of 15(c)(1)(C) would apply. Why are the provisions different?

The second conceptual problem arises from the fact that Fed. R. Civ. P. 15(a) and 15(c) impose different tests. Justice may require adding a claim, defense, or a party within the meaning of 15(a), but if the applicable statute of limitations has already expired, there may be a sound affirmative defense, unless the 15(c) "relation back" provisions save the amending party. A court could first grant the amendment and then, after the affirmative defense of statute of limitations is raised in answer to the amended pleading, examine whether 15(c) permits the amending party to surmount the defense. Or a court could decide not to permit the amendment unless it first determines that the amending party will be able to bring the amendment within the contours of the applicable statute of limitations. Some judges prefer the first route (decide the issues of amendment and relation back separately) and some prefer the second (deny the amendment if there is no relation back).

A practical point: Careful lawyers often place the exact language to be amended (added or subtracted) within the motion to amend, and then attach the entire pleading in the form it would take if the amendment were granted. If you do this, the court can then merely ask the clerk to docket the amended pleading when the motion is granted. Often, local rules or special court rules will spell out the method you should use in seeking amendments.

In reading *Singletary*, make sure that you can articulate every portion of Rule 15(c) that must be met, and how the court handles each requirement. Unfortunately, the Third Circuit here was interpreting an earlier iteration of Federal Rule 15. We have changed the references within the text to correspond with the current numbering.

We print the *Singletary* and *Krupski* cases successively. Consider, and be able to explain, whether they are dealing with the same or different problems under Rule 15.

# ■ SINGLETARY v. PENNSYLVANIA DEPARTMENT OF CORRECTIONS
### *266 F.3d 186 (3d Cir. 2001)*

BECKER, Chief Judge:

This is an appeal from a grant of summary judgment for defendants Pennsylvania Department of Corrections (PADOC), State Correctional Institute at Rockview (SCI-Rockview), and former Superintendent of SCI-Rockview, Joseph Mazurkiewicz, in a 42 U.S.C. § 1983 civil rights lawsuit brought against them by Dorothy Singletary, the mother of Edward Singletary, a prisoner who committed suicide while incarcerated at Rockview. The plaintiff does not appeal from the grant of summary judgment for PADOC and SCI-Rockview. She does appeal the District Court's grant of summary judgment in favor of defendant Mazurkiewicz, but there is plainly no merit to this challenge for there is no evidence that Mazurkiewicz exhibited deliberate indifference to Edward Singletary's medical needs.

In her original complaint, the plaintiff also included as defendants "Unknown Corrections Officers." The only chance for the plaintiff to prevail depends on her ability to succeed in: (1) amending her original complaint to add as a defendant Robert Regan, a psychologist at SCI-Rockview, against whom the plaintiff has her only potentially viable case; and (2) having this amended complaint relate back to her original complaint under Federal Rule of Civil Procedure [15(c)(1)(C)] so that she overcomes the defense of the statute of limitations. Rule [15(c)(1)(C)] provides for the "relation back" of amended complaints that add or change parties if certain conditions are met, in which case the amended complaint is treated, for statute of limitations purposes, as if it had been filed at the time of the original complaint.

The District Court denied the plaintiff's motion for leave to amend because it concluded that the amended complaint would not meet the conditions required for relation back under [15(c)(1)(C)]. . . .

We conclude that the District Court was correct in ruling that the amended complaint did not meet the notice requirements of Rule [15(c)(1)(C)(i)]. . . .

## I

Edward Singletary was serving a 6-12 year sentence at SCI-Rockview for his conviction of rape. In November 1995, Singletary was transferred to the maximum security restricted housing unit (MSRHU) of SCI-Rockview as a result of "threatening an employee or family with bodily harm." Over the next ten months, Singletary became increasingly agitated, acting hostilely to the staff and accusing them of tampering with his food and mail. During this period, Singletary was given chances to leave the MSRHU and re-enter the general population unit of SCI-Rockview, but he refused each time.

During his stay in the MSRHU, Singletary was seen weekly by a counselor, monthly by a three-person Program Review Committee, and by medical psychological staff as needed. A staff psychiatrist, Dr. Abdollah Nabavi, prescribed an anti-depressant to help Singletary with his sleeplessness and anxiety. Nabavi also offered Singletary Trilafon, an anti-psychotic drug, because he "felt [Singletary] was agitated, he was over suspicious, he was just very uncomfortable in the environment. . . . I think he was [psychotic]. If he was not, he was very close to being psychotic." Dep. of Dr. Nabavi at 31-32. Singletary, however, refused the Trilafon.

On October 3, 1996, Singletary became agitated when he was told to remove some magazines that had accumulated in his cell, and he threatened a prison officer. Because of the threat, the next day Singletary was transferred to a cell in the "Deputy Warden" (DW) building with the approval of the prison Superintendent, defendant Joseph Mazurkiewicz. After placement in a DW cell, Singletary was seen on October 4, 1996 by Kevin Burke, a psychiatrist consultant for SCI-Rockview, and by Robert Regan, a psychological services staff member and the person whom Dorothy Singletary seeks to add as a defendant. Regan was working as a "psychological service specialist" at SCI-Rockview at this time; his duties included the psychological testing and assessment of inmates, parole evaluations, group therapy, mental health intervention, and suicide risk evaluation and prevention. Regan did not have any administrative or supervisory duties at the prison. Beginning in late 1994, Regan had met with and evaluated Singletary on a weekly basis.

In their meetings with Singletary on October 4, Regan and Burke talked separately with him to assess his mental state. Singletary vehemently denied to both of them at that time that he was suicidal. On the basis of these examinations, neither Regan nor Burke saw any reason to take further precaution for Singletary. Just after midnight on October 6, 1996, Singletary committed suicide by hanging himself with a bedsheet.

On October 6, 1998, Dorothy Singletary filed in the District Court for the Eastern District of Pennsylvania a § 1983 deliberate indifference lawsuit alleging cruel and unusual punishment in violation of the Eighth Amendment along with pendent state law claims for wrongful death. Named as defendants were PADOC, SCI-Rockview, Mazurkiewicz, and "Unknown Corrections Officers." The action was ordered transferred to the Middle District of Pennsylvania on January 12, 1999 to correct a venue deficiency, and that order and the original file were officially docketed by the Middle District on February 16, 1999. On April 16, 1999, PADOC and SCI-Rockview moved for judgment on the pleadings pursuant to Federal Rule of Civil Procedure 12(c), and on May 28, 1999, the District Court granted this motion in part by dismissing Singletary's § 1983 claims against these defendants on Eleventh Amendment grounds, but denied their motion to dismiss the pendent state claims on sovereign immunity grounds.

The parties then conducted discovery, and on June 23, 2000, the defendants moved for summary judgment. On July 28, 2000, about a week after filing her response to the summary judgment motion, the plaintiff moved to amend her complaint to add Regan as a defendant. In two orders dated September 20, 2000, the District Court: (1) denied the plaintiff leave to amend her complaint to add Regan as a defendant on the grounds that that claim would be barred by the statute of limitations because it did not meet the conditions for relation back in Federal Rule of Civil Procedure [15(c)(1)(C)]; (2) granted summary judgment for defendant Mazurkiewicz on the deliberate indifference claim on the basis that the plaintiff had not presented any evidence of what Mazurkiewicz knew or should have known about Edward Singletary; (3) granted summary judgment for defendants PADOC and SCI-Rockview on the plaintiff's pendent state law claims because they were barred by the Eleventh Amendment; and (4) dismissed the remaining state law claims without prejudice because there were no federal law claims remaining in the lawsuit. This appeal followed.

## II

We find the plaintiff's assertion that the District Court erred in granting summary judgment to defendant Mazurkiewicz to be clearly lacking in merit and dispose of it in the margin.[2] We thus turn to Singletary's contention that the court erred by not granting her leave to amend her complaint to add Regan as a defendant. We review a district court's decision granting or denying leave to amend a complaint for abuse of discretion. However, if we are reviewing the factual conclusions that a district court made while considering the Rule 15 motion, our standard of review is clear error. Furthermore, if the district court's decision regarding a Rule 15(c) motion was based on the court's interpretation of the Federal Rules of Civil Procedure, our review is plenary.

### A. RULE [15(C)(1)(C)]

The parties agree that the statute of limitations for this action is two years, which expired on October 6, 1998, the day that Singletary filed her original complaint. The plaintiff then moved to amend her complaint by adding Regan as a defendant on July 28, 2000, almost two years after the statute of limitations had run. The plaintiff argues that this proposed amendment did not violate the statute of limitations because the amendment would relate back to the original, timely filed complaint under Federal Rule of Civil Procedure [15(c)(1)(C)]. Rule 15(c) can ameliorate the running of the statute of limitations on a claim by making the amended claim relate back to the original, timely filed complaint. *See Nelson v. County of Allegheny*, 60 F.3d 1010, 1015 (3d Cir. 1995). . . .

---

2. The District Court granted summary judgment for Mazurkiewicz because it found that the plaintiff had not presented any evidence that tended to show that Mazurkiewicz had been deliberately indifferent to Edward Singletary's medical needs as that concept has been developed in Supreme Court and Third Circuit case law. . . .

The issue in the case is whether the plaintiff can use [15(c)(1)(C)] to have her amended complaint substituting Regan as a defendant in place of "Unknown Corrections Officers" relate back to her original complaint. The Rule is written in the conjunctive, and courts interpret [15(c)(1)(C)] as imposing three conditions, all of which must be met for a successful relation back of an amended complaint that seeks to substitute newly named defendants. *See Urrutia v. Harriburg County Police Dept.*, 91 F.3d 451, 457 (3d Cir. 1996). The parties do not dispute that the first condition—that the claim against the newly named defendants must have arisen "out of the conduct, transaction, or occurrence set forth or attempted to be set forth in the original pleading"—is met. The second and third conditions are set out in [15(c)(1)(C)(i) & (ii)], respectively, and must be met "within the period provided by Rule 4(m) for service of the summons and complaint," Fed. R. Civ. P. [15(c)(1)(C)], which is "120 days after the filing of the complaint," Fed. R. Civ. P. 4(m). The second condition is that the newly named party must have "received such notice of the institution of the action [within the 120-day period] that the party will not be prejudiced in maintaining a defense on the merits." Fed. R. Civ. P. [15(c)(1)(C)(i)]. *Urrutia* states that this condition "has two requirements, notice and the absence of prejudice, each of which must be satisfied." 91 F.3d at 458. The third condition is that the newly named party must have known, or should have known, (again, within the 120 day period) that "but for a mistake" made by the plaintiff concerning the newly named party's identity, "the action would have been brought against" the newly named party in the first place. Fed. R. Civ. P. [15(c)(1)(C)(ii)].

Under these facts, we are concerned with three issues: (1) did Regan receive notice of the institution of the action before February 3, 1999 (which is 120 days after the complaint was filed); (2) was the notice that Regan received sufficient that he was not prejudiced in maintaining his defense; and (3) did Regan know (or should he have known) by February 3, 1999 that but for a mistake Singletary would have named him as a party in the original complaint? As explained above, the answers to all of these questions must be "Yes" for Singletary to prevail on her Rule [15(c)(1)(C)] argument. The District Court concluded that Regan did not receive any notice of the litigation or of his role in that litigation during the 120 day period. The court also concluded that Regan would be unfairly prejudiced by having to mount his defense at this late date, and that he neither knew nor should have known that, but for a mistake, he would have been named in the original complaint.

Notice is the main issue, and we will address that first . . . [T]he unfair prejudice issue is closely dependent on the outcome of our notice inquiry; because we agree with the District Court that Regan did not receive notice within the 120 day period (and because the District Court based its decision on notice and mentioned prejudice only in passing), we will not address prejudice.[3]

---

3. Prejudice and notice are closely intertwined in the context of Rule [15(c)(1)(C)], as the amount of prejudice a defendant suffers under [15(c)(1)(C)] is a direct effect of the type of notice he receives. . . .

### B. NOTICE

This court has seldom spoken on the meaning of "notice" in the context of Rule [15(c)(1)(C)]. Still, we can glean some general instruction from the few cases that address the issue. First, Rule [15(c)(1)(C)] notice does not require actual service of process on the party sought to be added; notice may be deemed to have occurred when a party who has some reason to expect his potential involvement as a defendant hears of the commencement of litigation through some informal means. *See Varlack v. SWC Caribbean, Inc.*, 550 F.2d 171, 175 (3d Cir. 1977) (holding that a person who the plaintiff sought to add as a defendant had adequate notice under [15(c)(1)(C)] when, within the relevant period, the person by happenstance saw a copy of the complaint naming both the place where he worked and an "unknown employee" as a defendant, which he knew referred to him). . . . At the same time, the notice received must be more than notice of the event that gave rise to the cause of action; it must be notice that the plaintiff has instituted the action.

The plaintiff does not argue that Regan received formal or even actual notice within the 120 day period; instead, she contends that Regan received "constructive or implied notice" of the institution of the action. She cites to several district court cases within this Circuit for the proposition that "notice concerning the institution of an action may be actual, constructive, or imputed." The plaintiff then advances two methods of imputing notice to Regan that she argues are implicated here: (1) the shared attorney method (Regan received timely notice because he shared his attorney with SCI-Rockview, an originally named party); and (2) the identity of interest method (Regan received timely notice because he had an identity of interest with SCI-Rockview). The central question before us is whether the facts of this case support the application of one or the other of these forms of notice.

### 1. Notice via sharing an attorney with an original defendant

The "shared attorney" method of imputing Rule [15(c)(1)(C)] notice is based on the notion that, when an originally named party and the party who is sought to be added are represented by the same attorney, the attorney is likely to have communicated to the latter party that he may very well be joined in the action. This method has been accepted by other Courts of Appeals and by district courts within this Circuit. We endorse this method of imputing notice under Rule [15(c)(1)(C)].

The relevant inquiry under this method is whether notice of the institution of this action can be imputed to Regan within the relevant 120 day period, i.e., by February 3, 1999, by virtue of representation Regan shared with a defendant originally named in the lawsuit. The plaintiff contends that Regan shared an attorney with all of the originally named defendants; more precisely, she submits that appellee's attorney, Deputy (State) Attorney General Gregory R. Neuhauser, entered an appearance as "Counsel for Defendants" in the original lawsuit, and hence that Neuhauser represented the "several Unknown Corrections Officers" defendants, one of whom turned out to be Regan. The plaintiff submits that Neuhauser's investigation for this lawsuit, must have included interviewing Regan (as he was one of the last counselors to evaluate Edward Singletary's mental state), so that Regan would have gotten notice of the institution of the lawsuit at that time.

The plaintiff notes further that Neuhauser responded to all of the allegations in the complaint including those governing the unknown corrections officers; that Neuhauser defended at Regan's deposition; and that nothing in Neuhauser's Answer to the Complaint was inconsistent with jointly representing employees like Regan. The defendants counter that, even if Regan were made a defendant in this suit, Regan would not have to accept Neuhauser as his counsel: Pennsylvania law specifically allows state employees to engage their own counsel when sued for actions taken in the course of their employment.

The plaintiff's contentions raise an interesting issue: whether an attorney's original entry of appearance as "Counsel for Defendants" can be used to establish, at the time of that appearance, a sufficient relationship for Rule [15(c)(1)(C)] notice purposes with a party who is later substituted as a defendant for a "John Doe" (or its functional equivalent) named in the original complaint. Because we are concerned with the notice that the newly named defendant received, the fundamental issue here is whether the attorney's later relationship with the newly named defendant gives rise to the inference that the attorney, within the 120 day period, had some communication or relationship with, and thus gave notice of the action to, the newly named defendant.

In this case, however, the record is clear that Neuhauser did not become the attorney for the defendants until well after the relevant 120 day period had run. . . .

Furthermore, the plaintiff has not made a "shared attorney" argument regarding the original attorney Shellenberger (the defendants' attorney of record during the 120 day period), but even if she did, Shellenberger has not represented, and will never represent, Regan at any point in this action. . . .

### 2. Notice via an identity of interest with an originally named defendant

The "identity of interest" method of imputing Rule [15(c)(1)(C)] notice to a newly named party is closely related to the shared attorney method. Identity of interest is explained by one commentator as follows: "Identity of interest generally means that the parties are so closely related in their business operations or other activities that the institution of an action against one serves to provide notice of the litigation to the other." . . .

In *Schiavone v. Fortune*, 477 U.S. 21 (1986), the Supreme Court seemingly endorsed the identity of interest method of imputing notice for Rule [15(c)(1)(C)]: "Timely filing of a complaint, and notice within the limitations period to the party named in the complaint, permit imputation of notice to a subsequently named and sufficiently related party." *Id*. at 29. District courts within this Circuit have interpreted this passage to mean that the Supreme Court has accepted the identity of interest notice method, *see, e.g., Keitt v. Doe*, 1994 WL 385333 at [*]4 (E.D. Pa. Jul. 22, 1994), and we find this reading of

*Schiavone* plausible. At all events, we adopt it as a logical construction of the Rule. Thus, the relevant issue is whether Regan has a sufficient identity of interest with an originally named defendant to impute the notice that defendant received to Regan.

The plaintiff does not substantially develop her identity of interest argument (she concentrates mainly on the shared attorney method of imputing notice), but she does advance the argument that Regan shared an identity of interest with SCI-Rockview because he was employed by SCI-Rockview. The question before us is therefore whether an employee in Regan's position (staff psychologist) is so closely related to his employer for the purpose of this type of litigation that these two parties have a sufficient identity of interest so that the institution of litigation against the employer serves to provide notice of the litigation to the employee.

There is not a clear answer to this question in the case law. The parties do not cite, and we have not found, any Third Circuit case that addresses this issue. . . .

We believe, however, that Regan does not share sufficient identity of interest with SCI-Rockview so that notice given to SCI-Rockview can be imputed to Regan for Rule [15(c)(1)(C)] purposes. Regan was a staff level employee at SCI-Rockview with no administrative or supervisory duties at the prison. Thus, Regan's position at SCI-Rockview cannot alone serve as a basis for finding an identity of interest, because Regan was clearly not highly enough placed in the prison hierarchy for us to conclude that his interests as an employee are identical to the prison's interests. That is, Regan and SCI-Rockview are not "so closely related in their business operations or other activities that the institution of an action against one serves to provide notice of the litigation to the other." . . .

[A]bsent other circumstances that permit the inference that notice was actually received, a non-management employee like Regan does not share a sufficient nexus of interests with his or her employer so that notice given to the employer can be imputed to the employee for Rule [15(c)(1)(C)] purposes. For this reason, we reject the plaintiff's identity of interest argument, and conclude that the District Court did not err in denying the plaintiff leave to amend her complaint to add Regan as a defendant.

### C. But for a mistake concerning the identity of the proper party

Rule [15(c)(1)(C)(ii)] provides a further requirement for relating back an amended complaint that adds or changes a party; the newly added party knew or should have known that "but for a mistake concerning the identity of the proper party, the action would have been brought against the party." Fed. R. Civ. P. [15(c)(1)(C)(ii)]. The plaintiff argues that this condition is met in her proposed amended complaint, but the District Court found otherwise. The defendants also contend that (1) the plaintiff did not make a *mistake* as to Regan's identity, and (2) Regan did not know, nor should he have known, that the action would have been brought against him had his identity been known, because the original complaint named "Unknown Corrections Officers" and Regan is not a corrections officer but a staff psychologist.

The issue whether the requirements of Rule [15(c)(1)(C)(ii)] are met in this case is a close one. We begin by noting that the bulk of authority from other Courts of Appeals takes the position that the amendment of a "John Doe" complaint—i.e., the substituting of real names for "John Does" or "Unknown Persons" named in an original complaint—does not meet the "but for a mistake" requirement in [15(c)(1)(C)(ii)], because not knowing the identity of a defendant is not a mistake concerning the defendant's identity. This is, of course, a plausible theory, but in terms of both epistemology and semantics it is subject to challenge.

In *Varlack v. SWC Caribbean, Inc.*, 550 F.2d 171, 175 (3d Cir. 1977), this Court appeared to have reached the opposite conclusion insofar as we held that the amendment of a "John Doe" complaint met all of the conditions for Rule [15(c)(1)(C)] relation back, including the "but for a mistake" requirement. In *Varlack*, the plaintiff had filed a complaint against, *inter alia*, an "unknown employee" of a branch of the Orange Julius restaurant chain, alleging that this employee had hit him with a two-by-four in a fight, which caused him to fall through a plate glass window, injuring his arm so severely that it had to be amputated. After the statute of limitations had run, the plaintiff sought to amend his complaint to change "unknown employee" to the employee's real name, using Rule [15(c)(1)(C)] to have the amended complaint relate back to the original. The newly named defendant testified that he had coincidentally seen a copy of the complaint naming both Orange Julius and an "unknown employee" as defendants, and that he had known at that time that he was the "unknown employee" referred to. This Court affirmed the district court's grant of the [15(c)(1)(C)] motion, holding that the plaintiff met all the requirements of [15(c)(1)(C)], including the requirement that the newly named defendant "knew or should have known but for a mistake concerning the identity of the proper party." *See id.* at 175.

We are, of course, bound by *Varlack* insofar as it held that the plaintiff's lack of knowledge of a particular defendant's identity can be a mistake under Rule [15(c)(1)(C)(ii)]. *See* Internal Operating Procedures of the United States Court of Appeals for the Third Circuit 9.1 (2000). Moreover, as is also noted above, every other Court of Appeals that has considered this issue (specifically, the First, Second, Fourth, Fifth, Sixth, Seventh, and Eleventh Circuits) has come out contrary to *Varlack*, generally speaking, the analysis in these other cases centers on the linguistic argument that a lack of knowledge of a defendant's identity is not a "mistake" concerning that identity. However, even assuming that *Varlack* allows for amended "John Doe" complaints to meet Rule [15(c)(1)(C)(ii)]'s "mistake" requirement, it is questionable whether the other parts of [15(c)(1)(C)(ii)] are met in this case, namely, whether Regan knew or should have known that he would have been named in the complaint if his identity were known. Because the original complaint named "Unknown *Corrections Officers*," it is surely arguable that psychologist Regan would have no way of knowing that the plaintiff meant to name him.

These are sticky issues. Because, as we explained above, the plaintiff's argument on the applicability of Rule [15(c)(1)(C)] to her case fails on notice grounds, we do not need to decide these questions here. We do, however, take this opportunity to express in the margin our concern over the state of the law on Rule [15(c)(1)(C)] (in particular the other Circuits' interpretation of the "mistake" requirement) and to recommend to the Advisory Rules Committee a modification of Rule [15(c)(1)(C)] to bring the Rule into accord with the weight of the commentary about it.[5]

---

5. As we note in the text, some Courts of Appeals have held that proposed amended complaints that seek to replace a "John Doe" or other placeholder name in an original complaint with a defendant's real name do not meet Rule [15(c)(1)(C)(ii)]'s "but for a mistake" requirement. We find this conclusion to be highly problematic. It is certainly not uncommon for victims of civil rights violations (e.g. an assault by police officers or prison guards) to be unaware of the identity of the person or persons who violated those rights. This information is in the possession of the defendants, and many plaintiffs cannot obtain this information until they have had a chance to undergo extensive discovery following institution of a civil action. If such plaintiffs are not allowed to relate back their amended "John Doe" complaints, then the statute of limitations period for these plaintiffs is effectively substantially shorter than it is for other plaintiffs who bring the exact same claim but who know the names of their assailants; the former group of plaintiffs would have to bring their lawsuits well before the end of the limitations period, immediately begin discovery and hope that they can determine the assailants' names before the statute of limitations expires. There seems to be no good reason to disadvantage plaintiffs in this way simply because for example, they were not able to see the name tag of the offending state actor.

The rejoinder to this argument is that allowing the relation back of amended "John Doe" complaints risks unfairness to defendants, who, under the countervailing *Varlack* interpretation of Rule [15(c)(1)(C)(ii)], may have a lawsuit sprung upon them well after the statute of limitations period has run. But fairness to the defendants is accommodated in the other requirements of Rule [15(c)(1)(C)], namely the requirements that (1) the newly named defendants had received "such notice of the institution of the action" during the relevant time period "that the party will not be prejudiced in the maintaining a defense on the merits"; and (2) the newly named defendants knew or should have known that the original complaint was directed towards them ("the action would have been brought against the party"). These requirements generally take care of the "springing a claim on an unsuspecting defendant" problem. . . .

We also note that Rule [15(c)(1)(C)(ii)]'s mistake requirement has been held to be met (and thus relation back clearly permitted) for an amended complaint that adds or substitutes a party when a plaintiff makes a mistake by suing the state but not individual officers in a § 1983 action. See *Lundy v. Adamar of New Jersey, Inc.*, 34 F.3d 1173, 1192 n. 13 (3d Cir. 1994) (Becker, J., concurring in part and dissenting in part) (listing cases in which plaintiffs have been permitted to have their complaints relate back when they made mistakes in the naming of defendants in their complaints including naming states and state agencies instead of state officials in § 1983 cases). We think that it makes no sense to allow plaintiffs who commit such a clear pleading error to have their claims relate back, while disallowing such an option for plaintiffs who, usually through no fault of their own, do not know the names of the individuals who violated their rights. This disparity of treatment of § 1983 plaintiffs seems to have no principled basis and should not be codified in our Rules of Civil Procedure.

All of the commentators who address this issue (at least those that we found in our research) call for Rule [15(c)(1)(C)] to allow relation back in cases in which a "John Doe" complaint is amended to substitute real defendants' names. . . . In his manuscript "Rule [15(c)(1)(C)] Puzzles," Professor Edward H. Cooper of the University of Michigan Law School suggests the following alteration (in italics) in subsection [15(c)(1)(C)(ii)] of the Rule in order to make it clear that the relation back of "John Doe" amended complaints is allowed: "the party to be brought in by amendment . . . knew or should have known that, but for a mistake *or lack of information* concerning the identity of the proper party. . . ." Cooper *supra*, (manuscript at 8). We believe that a change in Rule [15(c)(1)(C)] along the lines advocated by the Professor Cooper would fix the lack of fairness to plaintiffs with "John Doe" complaints that currently inheres in the other Circuits' interpretation of the Rule, and would bring the Rule more clearly into alignment with the liberal pleading practice policy of the Federal Rules of Civil Procedure.

For these reasons, we encourage the Rules Advisory Committee to amend Rule [15(c)(1)(C)] so that it clearly embraces the Cooper approach to the relation back of "John Doe" complaints. As the Supreme Court has said, "the requirements of the rules of procedure should be liberally construed and . . . 'mere technicalities' should not stand in the way of consideration of a case on its merits." *Torres v. Oakland Scavenger Co.*, 487 U.S. 312, 316 (1988). Rule [15(c)(1)(C)] is clearly meant to further the policy of considering claims on their merits rather than dismissing them on technicalities, and this policy is substantially furthered by the Cooper approach to Rule [15(c)(1)(C)(ii)].

### III. CONCLUSION

For the above reasons, the District Court's grant of summary judgment for the defendants and the court's order denying the plaintiff's motion to amend her complaint will be affirmed. The Clerk is directed to send copies of this opinion to the Chairman and Reporter of the Judicial Conference Advisory Committee on Civil Rules and the Standing Committee on Practice and Procedure, calling attention to footnote 5.

## ■ KRUPSKI v. COSTA CROCIERE S.P.A.
### 130 S. Ct. 2485 (2010)

Justice SOTOMAYOR delivered the opinion of the Court.

Rule 15(c) of the Federal Rules of Civil Procedure governs when an amended pleading "relates back" to the date of a timely filed original pleading and is thus itself timely even though it was filed outside an applicable statute of limitations. Where an amended pleading changes a party or a party's name, the Rule requires, among other things, that "the party to be brought in by amendment . . . knew or should have known that the action would have been brought against it, but for a mistake concerning the proper party's identity." Rule 15(c)(1)(C). In this case, the Court of Appeals held that Rule 15(c) was not satisfied because the plaintiff knew or should have known of the proper defendant before filing her original complaint. The court also held that relation back was not appropriate because the plaintiff had unduly delayed in seeking to amend. We hold that relation back under Rule 15(c)(1)(C) depends on what the party to be added knew or should have known, not on the amending party's knowledge or its timeliness in seeking to amend the pleading. Accordingly, we reverse the judgment of the Court of Appeals.

### I

On February 21, 2007, petitioner, Wanda Krupski, tripped over a cable and fractured her femur while she was on board the cruise ship Costa Magica. Upon her return home, she acquired counsel and began the process of seeking compensation for her injuries. Krupski's passenger ticket—which explained that it was the sole contract between each passenger and the carrier—included a variety of requirements for obtaining damages for an injury suffered on board one of the carrier's ships. The ticket identified the carrier as

"Costa Crociere S. p. A., an Italian corporation, and all Vessels and other ships owned, chartered, operated, marketed or provided by Costa Crociere, S.p.A., and all officers, staff members, crew members, independent contractors, medical providers, concessionaires, pilots, suppliers, agents and assigns onboard said Vessels, and the manufacturers of said Vessels and all their component parts."

The ticket required an injured party to submit "written notice of the claim with full particulars . . . to the carrier or its duly authorized agent within 185 days after the date of injury." The ticket further required any lawsuit to be "filed within one year after the date of injury" and to be "served upon the carrier within 120 days after filing." For cases arising from voyages departing from or returning to a United States port in which the amount in controversy exceeded $75,000, the ticket designated the United States District Court for the Southern District of Florida in Broward County, Florida, as the exclusive forum for a lawsuit. The ticket extended the "defenses, limitations and exceptions . . . that may be invoked by the Carrier" to "all persons who may act on behalf of the Carrier or on whose behalf the Carrier may act," including "the Carrier's parents, subsidiaries, affiliates, successors, assigns, representatives, agents, employees, servants, concessionaires and contractors" as well as "Costa Cruise Lines N. V.," identified as the "sales and marketing agent for the Carrier and the issuer of this Passage Ticket Contract." The front of the ticket listed Costa Cruise Lines' address in Florida and stated that an entity called "Costa Cruises" was "the first cruise company in the world" to obtain a certain certification of quality.

On July 2, 2007, Krupski's counsel notified Costa Cruise Lines of Krupski's claims. On July 9, 2007, the claims administrator for Costa Cruise requested additional information from Krupski "[i]n order to facilitate our future attempts to achieve a pre-litigation settlement." The parties were unable to reach a settlement, however, and on February 1, 2008—three weeks before the 1-year limitations period expired—Krupski filed a negligence action against Costa Cruise, invoking the diversity jurisdiction of the Federal District Court for the Southern District of Florida. The complaint alleged that Costa Cruise "owned, operated, managed, supervised and controlled" the ship on which Krupski had injured herself; that Costa Cruise had extended to its passengers an invitation to enter onto the ship; and that Costa Cruise owed Krupski a duty of care, which it breached by failing to take steps that would have prevented her accident. The complaint further stated that venue was proper under the passenger ticket's forum selection clause and averred that, by the July 2007 notice of her claims, Krupski had complied with the ticket's pre-suit requirements. *Id.*, at 23. Krupski served Costa Cruise on February 4, 2008.

Over the next several months—after the limitations period had expired—Costa Cruise brought Costa Crociere's existence to Krupski's attention three times. First, on February 25, 2008, Costa Cruise filed its answer, asserting that it was not the proper defendant, as it was merely the North American sales and marketing agent for Costa Crociere, which was the actual carrier and vessel operator. Second, on March 20, 2008, Costa Cruise listed Costa Crociere as an interested party in its corporate disclosure statement. Finally, on May 6, 2008, Costa Cruise moved for summary judgment, again stating that Costa Crociere was the proper defendant.

On June 13, 2008, Krupski responded to Costa Cruise's motion for summary judgment, arguing for limited discovery to determine whether Costa

Cruise should be dismissed. According to Krupski, the following sources of information led her to believe Costa Cruise was the responsible party: The travel documents prominently identified Costa Cruise and gave its Florida address; Costa Cruise's Web site listed Costa Cruise in Florida as the United States office for the Italian company Costa Crociere; and the Web site of the Florida Department of State listed Costa Cruise as the only "Costa" company registered to do business in that State. Krupski also observed that Costa Cruise's claims administrator had responded to her claims notification without indicating that Costa Cruise was not a responsible party. With her response, Krupski simultaneously moved to amend her complaint to add Costa Crociere as a defendant.

On July 2, 2008, after oral argument, the District Court denied Costa Cruise's motion for summary judgment without prejudice and granted Krupski leave to amend, ordering that Krupski effect proper service on Costa Crociere by September 16, 2008. Complying with the court's deadline, Krupski filed an amended complaint on July 11, 2008, and served Costa Crociere on August 21, 2008. On that same date, the District Court issued an order dismissing Costa Cruise from the case pursuant to the parties' joint stipulation, Krupski apparently having concluded that Costa Cruise was correct that it bore no responsibility for her injuries.

Shortly thereafter, Costa Crociere—represented by the same counsel who had represented Costa Cruise—moved to dismiss, contending that the amended complaint did not relate back under Rule 15(c) and was therefore untimely. The District Court agreed. Rule 15(c), the court explained, imposes three requirements before an amended complaint against a newly named defendant can relate back to the original complaint. First, the claim against the newly named defendant must have arisen "out of the conduct, transaction, or occurrence set out—or attempted to be set out—in the original pleading." Fed. Rules Civ. Proc. 15(c)(1)(B), (C). Second, "within the period provided by Rule 4(m) for serving the summons and complaint" (which is ordinarily 120 days from when the complaint is filed, see Rule 4(m)), the newly named defendant must have "received such notice of the action that it will not be prejudiced in defending on the merits." Rule 15(c)(1)(C)(i). Finally, the plaintiff must show that, within the Rule 4(m) period, the newly named defendant "knew or should have known that the action would have been brought against it, but for a mistake concerning the proper party's identity." Rule 15(c)(1)(C)(ii).

The first two conditions posed no problem, the court explained: The claim against Costa Crociere clearly involved the same occurrence as the original claim against Costa Cruise, and Costa Crociere had constructive notice of the action and had not shown that any unfair prejudice would result from relation back. But the court found the third condition fatal to Krupski's attempt to relate back, concluding that Krupski had not made a mistake concerning the identity of the proper party. Relying on Eleventh Circuit precedent, the court explained that the word "mistake" should not be construed to encompass a deliberate decision not to sue a party whose identity the plaintiff knew before the statute of limitations had run. Because Costa Cruise informed Krupski that Costa Crociere was the proper defendant in its answer, corporate disclosure statement, and motion for summary judgment, and yet Krupski delayed for months in moving to amend and then in filing an amended complaint, the court concluded that Krupski knew of the proper defendant and made no mistake.

The Eleventh Circuit affirmed in an unpublished per curiam opinion. Rather than relying on the information contained in Costa Cruise's filings, all of which were made after the statute of limitations had expired, as evidence that Krupski did not make a mistake, the Court of Appeals noted that the relevant information was located within Krupski's passenger ticket, which she had furnished to her counsel well before the end of the limitations period. Because the ticket clearly identified Costa Crociere as the carrier, the court stated, Krupski either knew or should have known of Costa Crociere's identity as a potential party. It was therefore appropriate to treat Krupski as having chosen to sue one potential party over another. Alternatively, even assuming that she first learned of Costa Crociere's identity as the correct party from Costa Cruise's answer, the Court of Appeals observed that Krupski waited 133 days from the time she filed her original complaint to seek leave to amend and did not file an amended complaint for another month after that. In light of this delay, the Court of Appeals concluded that the District Court did not abuse its discretion in denying relation back.

We granted certiorari to resolve tension among the Circuits over the breadth of Rule 15(c)(1)(C)(ii), and we now reverse.

## II

Under the Federal Rules of Civil Procedure, an amendment to a pleading relates back to the date of the original pleading when:

"(A) the law that provides the applicable statute of limitations allows relation back;

"(B) the amendment asserts a claim or defense that arose out of the conduct, transaction, or occurrence set out-or attempted to be set out-in the original pleading; or

"(C) the amendment changes the party or the naming of the party against whom a claim is asserted, if Rule 15(c)(1)(B) is satisfied and if, within the period provided by Rule 4(m) for serving the summons and complaint, the party to be brought in by amendment:

"(i) received such notice of the action that it will not be prejudiced in defending on the merits; and

"(ii) knew or should have known that the action would have been brought against it, but for a mistake concerning the proper party's identity." Rule 15(c)(1).

In our view, neither of the Court of Appeals' reasons for denying relation back under Rule 15(c)(1)(C)(ii) finds support in the text of the Rule. We consider each reason in turn.

**A**

The Court of Appeals first decided that Krupski either knew or should have known of the proper party's identity and thus determined that she had made a deliberate choice instead of a mistake in not naming Costa Crociere as a party in her original pleading. By focusing on Krupski's knowledge, the Court of Appeals chose the wrong starting point. The question under Rule 15(c)(1)(C)(ii) is not whether Krupski knew or should have known the identity of Costa Crociere as the proper defendant, but whether Costa Crociere knew or should have known that it would have been named as a defendant but for an error. Rule 15(c)(1)(C)(ii) asks what the prospective defendant knew or should have known during the Rule 4(m) period, not what the plaintiff knew or should have known at the time of filing her original complaint.

Information in the plaintiff's possession is relevant only if it bears on the defendant's understanding of whether the plaintiff made a mistake regarding the proper party's identity. For purposes of that inquiry, it would be error to conflate knowledge of a party's existence with the absence of mistake. A mistake is "[a]n error, misconception, or misunderstanding; an erroneous belief." Black's Law Dictionary 1092 (9th ed.2009); see also Webster's Third New International Dictionary 1446 (2002) (defining "mistake" as "a misunderstanding of the meaning or implication of something"; "a wrong action or statement proceeding from faulty judgment, inadequate knowledge, or inattention"; "an erroneous belief"; or "a state of mind not in accordance with the facts"). That a plaintiff knows of a party's existence does not preclude her from making a mistake with respect to that party's identity. A plaintiff may know that a prospective defendant—call him party A—exists, while erroneously believing him to have the status of party B. Similarly, a plaintiff may know generally what party A does while misunderstanding the roles that party A and party B played in the "conduct, transaction, or occurrence" giving rise to her claim. If the plaintiff sues party B instead of party A under these circumstances, she has made a "mistake concerning the proper party's identity" notwithstanding her knowledge of the existence of both parties. The only question under Rule 15(c)(1)(C)(ii), then, is whether party A knew or should have known that, absent some mistake, the action would have been brought against him.

Respondent urges that the key issue under Rule 15(c)(1)(C)(ii) is whether the plaintiff made a deliberate choice to sue one party over another. We agree that making a deliberate choice to sue one party instead of another while fully understanding the factual and legal differences between the two parties is the antithesis of making a mistake concerning the proper party's identity. We disagree, however, with respondent's position that any time a plaintiff is aware of the existence of two parties and chooses to sue the wrong one, the proper defendant could reasonably believe that the plaintiff made no mistake. The reasonableness of the mistake is not itself at issue. As noted, a plaintiff might know that the prospective defendant exists but nonetheless harbor a misunderstanding about his status or role in the events giving rise to the claim at issue, and she may mistakenly choose to sue a different defendant based on that misimpression. That kind of deliberate but mistaken choice does not foreclose a finding that Rule 15(c)(1)(C)(ii) has been satisfied.

This reading is consistent with the purpose of relation back: to balance the interests of the defendant protected by the statute of limitations with the preference expressed in the Federal Rules of Civil Procedure in general, and Rule 15 in particular, for resolving disputes on their merits. *See, e.g.,* Advisory Committee's 1966 Notes 122; 3 Moore's Federal Practice §§ 15.02[1], 15.19[3][a] (3d ed. 2009). A prospective defendant who legitimately believed that the limitations period had passed without any attempt to sue him has a strong interest in repose. But repose would be a windfall for a prospective defendant who understood, or who should have understood, that he escaped suit during the limitations period only because the plaintiff misunderstood a crucial fact about his identity. Because a plaintiff's knowledge of the existence of a party does not foreclose the possibility that she has made a mistake of identity about which that party should have been aware, such knowledge does not support that party's interest in repose. . . .

**B**

The Court of Appeals offered a second reason why Krupski's amended complaint did not relate back: Krupski had unduly delayed in seeking to file, and in eventually filing, an amended complaint. The Court of Appeals offered no support for its view that a plaintiff's dilatory conduct can justify the denial of relation back under Rule 15(c)(1)(C), and we find none. The Rule plainly sets forth an exclusive list of requirements for relation back, and the amending party's diligence is not among them. Moreover, the Rule mandates relation back once the Rule's requirements are satisfied; it does not leave the decision whether to grant relation back to the district court's equitable discretion. *See* Rule 15(c)(1) ("An amendment . . . relates back . . . when" the three listed requirements are met (emphasis added)).

The mandatory nature of the inquiry for relation back under Rule 15(c) is particularly striking in contrast to the inquiry under Rule 15(a), which sets forth the circumstances in which a party may amend its pleading before trial. By its terms, Rule 15(a) gives discretion to the district court in deciding whether to grant a motion to amend a pleading to add a party or a claim. Following an initial period after filing a pleading during which a party may amend once "as a matter of course," "a party may amend its pleading only with the opposing party's written consent or the court's leave," which the court "should freely give . . . when justice so requires." Rules 15(a)(1)-(2). We have previously explained that a court may consider a movant's "undue delay" or "dilatory motive" in deciding whether to grant leave to amend under Rule 15(a). *Foman v. Davis,* 371 U.S. 178, 182 (1962). As the contrast between Rule 15(a) and Rule 15(c) makes clear, however, the speed with which a plaintiff moves to amend her complaint or files an amended complaint after obtaining leave to do so has no bearing on whether the amended complaint relates back. Cf. 6A C. Wright, A. Miller, & M. Kane,

Federal Practice and Procedure § 1498, pp. 142-143, and nn. 49-50 (2d ed. 1990 and Supp. 2010).

Rule 15(c)(1)(C) does permit a court to examine a plaintiff's conduct during the Rule 4(m) period, but not in the way or for the purpose respondent or the Court of Appeals suggests. As we have explained, the question under Rule 15(c)(1)(C)(ii) is what the prospective defendant reasonably should have understood about the plaintiff's intent in filing the original complaint against the first defendant. To the extent the plaintiff's postfiling conduct informs the prospective defendant's understanding of whether the plaintiff initially made a "mistake concerning the proper party's identity," a court may consider the conduct. Cf. *Leonard v. Parry*, 219 F.3d 25, 29 (C.A.1 2000) ("[P]ost-filing events occasionally can shed light on the plaintiff's state of mind at an earlier time" and "can inform a defendant's reasonable beliefs concerning whether her omission from the original complaint represented a mistake (as opposed to a conscious choice)"). The plaintiff's postfiling conduct is otherwise immaterial to the question whether an amended complaint relates back.

C

Applying these principles to the facts of this case, we think it clear that the courts below erred in denying relation back under Rule 15(c)(1)(C)(ii). The District Court held that Costa Crociere had "constructive notice" of Krupski's complaint within the Rule 4(m) period. Costa Crociere has not challenged this finding. Because the complaint made clear that Krupski meant to sue the company that "owned, operated, managed, supervised and controlled" the ship on which she was injured, and also indicated (mistakenly) that Costa Cruise performed those roles, Costa Crociere should have known, within the Rule 4(m) period, that it was not named as a defendant in that complaint only because of Krupski's misunderstanding about which "Costa" entity was in charge of the ship—clearly a "mistake concerning the proper party's identity."

Respondent contends that because the original complaint referred to the ticket's forum requirement and presuit claims notification procedure, Krupski was clearly aware of the contents of the ticket, and because the ticket identified Costa Crociere as the carrier and proper party for a lawsuit, respondent was entitled to think that she made a deliberate choice to sue Costa Cruise instead of Costa Crociere. As we have explained, however, that Krupski may have known the contents of the ticket does not foreclose the possibility that she nonetheless misunderstood crucial facts regarding the two companies' identities. Especially because the face of the complaint plainly indicated such a misunderstanding, respondent's contention is not persuasive. Moreover, respondent has articulated no strategy that it could reasonably have thought Krupski was pursuing in suing a defendant that was legally unable to provide relief.

Respondent also argues that Krupski's failure to move to amend her complaint during the Rule 4(m) period shows that she made no mistake in that period. But as discussed, any delay on Krupski's part is relevant only to the extent it may have informed Costa Crociere's understanding during the Rule

4(m) period of whether she made a mistake originally. Krupski's failure to add Costa Crociere during the Rule 4(m) period is not sufficient to make reasonable any belief that she had made a deliberate and informed decision not to sue Costa Crociere in the first instance. Nothing in Krupski's conduct during the Rule 4(m) period suggests that she failed to name Costa Crociere because of anything other than a mistake.

It is also worth noting that Costa Cruise and Costa Crociere are related corporate entities with very similar names; "crociera" even means "cruise" in Italian. Cassell's Italian Dictionary 137, 670 (1967). This interrelationship and similarity heighten the expectation that Costa Crociere should suspect a mistake has been made when Costa Cruise is named in a complaint that actually describes Costa Crociere's activities. . . . In addition, Costa Crociere's own actions contributed to passenger confusion over "the proper party" for a lawsuit. The front of the ticket advertises that "Costa Cruises" has achieved a certification of quality without clarifying whether "Costa Cruises" is Costa Cruise Lines, Costa Crociere, or some other related "Costa" company. . . .

In light of these facts, Costa Crociere should have known that Krupski's failure to name it as a defendant in her original complaint was due to a mistake concerning the proper party's identity. We therefore reverse the judgment of the Court of Appeals for the Eleventh Circuit and remand the case for further proceedings consistent with this opinion.

Justice SCALIA, concurring in part and concurring in the judgment.

I join the Court's opinion except for its reliance on the Notes of the Advisory Committee as establishing the meaning of Federal Rule of Civil Procedure 15(c)(1)(C). The Advisory Committee's insights into the proper interpretation of a Rule's text are useful to the same extent as any scholarly commentary. But the Committee's intentions have no effect on the Rule's meaning. Even assuming that we and the Congress that allowed the Rule to take effect read and agreed with those intentions, it is the text of the Rule that controls.

## Comments and Questions

1. Be prepared to explain with precision which provisions of Rule 15 the *Singletary* and *Krupski* decisions are interpreting, and how and why each court decides the issues the way that they do.

2. Judge Becker's opinion in *Singletary* notes the controversy over the interpretation of the "mistake" requirement for relation back in the context of adding new parties. *See* Fed. R. Civ. P. 15(c)(1)(C)(ii). What does Judge Becker recommend? Does *Krupski* resolve this controversy?

3. Remember that when a party seeks to amend a pleading she must meet the "justice so requires" language of 15(a), whether or not 15(c) is applicable. Review the types of arguments that should be relevant as to whether "justice

so requires" which are given in our preliminary discussion of amendments. Also be prepared to discuss the policies behind statutes of limitations which are frequently relevant to arguments on whether to grant or deny a motion to amend.

4. *Singletary* and *Krupski* are interpreting the Federal Rule on amendments. The practice and procedure for amendments is one of the rules where there can be significant variation between state and federal practice—even in those states that have largely replicated the Federal Rules. In some states, like Massachusetts, for example (remember this for Practice Exercise No. 11), the rule on relation back—whether adding parties or claims—provides "Whenever the claim or defense asserted in the amended pleading arose out of the conduct, transaction, or occurrence set forth or attempted to be set forth in the original pleading, the amendment (including an amendment changing a party) relates back to the original pleading." In fact, this is the old Federal Rule before it was amended.

5. Statutes of limitation, tolling, and the "discovery rule" (which states that a statute of limitations period should not commence until the cause of action is discovered) are creatures both of statute and of case law. For instance, a federal statute tolls the statute of limitations when a potential plaintiff is in the armed forces. *See* Soldiers and Sailors Relief Act, 50 App. U.S.C.A. § 525. Also, states often have statutes that toll the statute of limitations for minors, so that the limitations period begins when the minor reaches majority, such as eighteen or twenty-one, depending on the applicable law. You will discover in your tort course that the statutes of limitations may not begin to run in circumstances where a reasonable potential plaintiff would not know she has been harmed. For example, in the situation in which a surgeon leaves a sponge in the patient's stomach, the statute may not begin running until the plaintiff becomes aware that the sponge was left in her stomach. The following case excerpt should give you a sense of how these issues arise, and how each inquiry may be fact-specific:

> Equitable tolling applies only in the rare and exceptional circumstance. . . . The burden of demonstrating the appropriateness of equitable tolling lies with the party seeking to invoke it. . . . In order to avail himself of equitable tolling, [plaintiff] must demonstrate (1) the existence of the aforementioned rare and exceptional circumstances, and (2) that those circumstances prevented him from filing a timely petition despite the exercise of due diligence. . . . To merit application of equitable tolling, the petitioner must demonstrate that he acted with reasonable diligence during the period he wishes to have tolled, but that despite his efforts, extraordinary circumstances beyond his control prevented successful filing during that time. A petitioner must demonstrate a causal relationship between the extraordinary circumstances on which the claim for equitable tolling rests and the lateness of his filing, a demonstration that cannot be made if the petitioner, acting with reasonable diligence, could have filed on time notwithstanding the extraordinary circumstances.
>
> The district courts within this circuit have recognized that illness, including mental incapacity, can be an exceptional circumstance "for the purposes of

equitable tolling. . . . Depending on the recency and severity of . . . mental conditions, they might well amount to an extraordinary circumstance that, in an appropriate case, would warrant equitable tolling."). However, the existence of a mental illness alone is insufficient to toll the statute of limitations. Rather, illness or mental incapacity will only constitute an exceptional circumstance if it rendered the petitioner unable to pursue his legal rights during the relevant time period. . . . While mental illness can form the basis of an equitable tolling argument, without a particularized description of how his condition adversely affected his capacity to function generally or in relationship to the pursuit of his rights, defendant's claim is manifestly insufficient to justify equitable tolling. . . . To justify tolling, a petitioner must show that his mental health problems left him unable to pursue his legal rights during the relevant time period.

*Stephenson v. Ercole*, 2009 WL 3872358 (E.D.N.Y. 2009) (internal quotations and citations omitted).

## Practice Exercise No. 11: Argument on Plaintiff's Motion to Amend in *Carpenter*

Except as modified in this exercise, assume that the facts in the initial memo concerning *Carpenter v. Dee* are still the same (including that the plaintiff's lawyer did not know where Randall Dee bought the tires and suspension kit until she took Randall Dee's deposition). Assume that Nancy Carpenter's attorney did not file her suit until February 23, 2014, and that the Dees were served on April 30, 2014. Assume also that on February 19, 2012 (about six months after the accident), the plaintiff, through an attorney, gave written notice of her claim to the City of Lowell. After discovery, the plaintiff moved to file an amended complaint.

Assume the following timeline of relevant events: Randall Dee's deposition was first noticed by the plaintiff for June 30, 2014; that deposition was then delayed several times, usually to meet Randall's needs (to meet his work schedule, a death in his family, and, on one occasion, his illness). The deposition finally took place more than two months later, on September 6, 2014. At his deposition, Randall Dee stated that he purchased the oversized tires and suspension lift kit from Ultimate Auto. The following day, Carpenter's lawyer once again notified the city of Lowell of their responsibility. Of course, Lowell police knew of the accident at the time it occurred and, according to the plaintiff, knew or should have known of statutory violations even before the accident occurred.

Assume further that according to Dee's deposition, he told the owner of Ultimate Auto about the accident on or about September 3, 2011, a few days after the accident happened. Years later, and approximately one month after Dee had been served, Dee again mentioned the accident to him (Mr. Jenkins), and also told him that the Dees had been sued.

On October 4, 2014, Carpenter's counsel received the transcript from the deposition and, the following week, moved to amend the complaint by adding Ultimate Auto and the City of Lowell as defendants.

Assume that the applicable statute of limitations in this case is three years.

The motion to amend was first scheduled to be heard on December 14, 2014, but the judge then postponed the hearing for two weeks and asked Carpenter's lawyer to notify Ultimate Auto and the Legal Department of the City of Lowell, informing them of the pending motion and inviting them to participate in a hearing upon that motion. (Incidentally, note that notice to and the participation of putative parties is *not* required.) Assume that Carpenter's lawyers notified Ultimate Auto and the City, and lawyers for those parties are present at the hearing that is about to take place.

You should assume that the hearing on the motion to amend is taking place on December 28, 2014. You know that the judge hearing this motion usually calls first on the moving party. Think about what rule and, thus, what standards the court will apply in deciding this motion. (Except for the relation-back provision described in Comment and Question No. 4 above, the Massachusetts and Federal Rules on amendments are the same in all relevant respects.) Consider what each party would lose or gain if the motion is granted or denied. Attached to the motion to amend (in the Case Files) is the amended complaint that plaintiff seeks to file if the motion to amend is allowed. Reasonable inferences can be made about what records might be available to the City of Lowell and to Ultimate Auto.

The amended complaint, if allowed, mentions implied warranties and Mass. General Laws, chapter 90, § 7P. Massachusetts has adopted the Uniform Commercial Code provisions on implied warranties, and those provisions follow the amended complaint. You will also find other relevant Massachusetts law (statutory provisions relating to wrongful death, conscious suffering, and fraudulent conveyance) in the Case Files.

If your last name begins with a letter from A through H, you are plaintiff's counsel and thus should prepare arguments in favor of the motion to amend. Persons with last names beginning with the letters I and J will represent the defendants Randall and Peter Dee. Persons with last names beginning with the letters K through P will represent Ultimate Auto in opposition to the motion. Persons with last names beginning with a letter from Q through V will represent the City of Lowell in opposition to the motion. And persons with last names beginning with the letters W through Z will act as clerks to the judge. (Judicial clerks ordinarily help the judge prepare for a motion session by informing the judge about the legal standard, summarizing essential facts, and offering suggestions for questions to pose to the parties. Judges also will often ask their clerks how they would decide the motion, and why.)

For purposes of the discussion that may follow the motion session, please consider the following questions:

(1) Would the issues be different had this been a (diversity) case brought in the federal district court for the U.S. District Court for the District of Massachusetts? Focus on Fed. R. Civ. P. 15(c)(1)(A).

(2) Would the issues be different had Massachusetts adopted the federal version of Fed. R. Civ. P. 15?

## Note: Tips on Arguing Motions

It is not patronizing and, in fact, is prudent advocacy to assume that a judge in a motion session knows very little or even nothing about your case, the motion before the court, or even the controlling standard of law. Judges at motion sessions are often presiding over many cases and dozens of motions in any given day. Often the judges are looking at your motion papers for the first time the minute before argument begins.

First, state who you are and whom you represent. Then inform the judge of the precise thing that is before the court. (For example, "Your Honor, before this court is a motion brought pursuant to Fed. R. Civ. P. 12(b)(6) to dismiss the first count of the plaintiff's complaint for failure to state a claim for which relief may be granted.") If you are speaking first, tell the judge enough about the facts of the case and its procedural posture that she can easily follow your argument. As you introduce a rule or statute, tell the judge precisely which provisions and words are implicated, and why those provisions and words should lead the court to reach the conclusion you seek. Explain why what you seek is permitted, reasonable, and fair, or even compelled, given the facts of this case. If you rely on case law, you will probably need to tell the judge enough about the facts of the case upon which you rely so that she can understand its holding in context and can determine whether the case you rely upon is similar to the case then before her.

Listen to the judge's questions. Answer them directly, honestly, and forthrightly. Do not ignore your opponent's strong arguments or the judge's skepticism. Anticipate these statements and meet them head on. Throughout, be polite but not obsequious. Usually, common sense arguments in plain English work the best. Make sure the judge understands the impact (the unfairness, the inefficiency, etc.) if the judge were to rule against your client on this motion. (Of course, you will not want to be confrontational with the court, and thus, some subtlety may be necessary.) As you conclude your argument, make sure the judge knows exactly what you want her to do. (For example, "Therefore, we ask Your Honor to grant the motion for a more definite statement and require that plaintiffs include the specific dates of the publications that they claim were libelous.")

We wish to point out here that many, indeed most, pretrial motions are no longer heard at oral argument; rather they are decided on the basis of arguments made in written motions and memoranda. When oral arguments are allowed, judges may appear impatient or distracted, as they have much work to do. Nevertheless, assume that the judge is unfamiliar with your case, the motion before the court, and the controlling standard of law. Effective advocacy thus may require a *succinct* summary, overview, and introduction; take your cues from the judge to ascertain how much background she needs to decide the motion before her in favor of your client.

# E. THE HISTORICAL BACKGROUND OF CIVIL PROCEDURE

The next doctrine you will encounter in this course is Fed. R. Civ. P. 11, which has evolved through the years. We think it is important that you first get a sense of historical context to help you understand both the current procedural debates and the tensions that appear in most procedural systems. We hope that learning about the historical background of the Federal Rules, and the systems that preceded them, will help you make sense of the contradictions in, and problems confronting, current procedure. You will also be introduced to the Rules of Decision Act, Process and Conformity Acts, and the Enabling Act, all of which are critical to a thorough understanding of current procedural issues and debates. Early in the course you looked at procedural values, and now you can explore those same values in the historical context of actual people who, like you, had complex needs, ideologies, and agendas that influenced their proposals and arguments.

## 1. Where Are We Heading?

Current American civil procedure is in a period of flux. You may recall that we addressed this turmoil in the context of the *Twombly* and *Iqbal* decisions at the beginning of the section on pleadings. Although we do not yet have sufficient perspective to be certain, it looks as if we are heading to, or are already in, a period of change as significant as that which took place after New York adopted a new procedural code in 1848 and the Federal Rules of Civil Procedure were adopted in 1938. You will be learning much of your civil procedure by reading and applying the Federal Rules of Civil Procedure. Those rules were based on a procedural philosophy that emphasized helping lawsuits get to their "merits," either through voluntary settlement or at a trial in open court. The ingredients of a good procedural system were thought to be procedural simplicity, uniformity of procedure from court to court and for all types of cases (called *trans-substantive procedure*), and flexible rules that give lawyers latitude to make choices and judges discretion to resolve disputes.

Judicial discretion is still emphasized, and indeed has been expanded by *Twombly* and *Iqbal*, and by cases you will read when you later encounter summary judgment. The other goals and principles, however, have taken a severe beating, particularly since 1980. Consequently, you will be practicing under allegedly liberal procedural rules that in fact have become increasingly stringent and non-lawyer-friendly. Numerous indicia reflect this breakdown of the procedural order that dominated American law for fifty years. For example, review virtually any daily newspaper and observe the congressional hostility to lawyer-dominated civil litigation. When you get to the materials on discovery, in Chapter 4, you will find that the wide-open discovery of the original Federal Rules was constricted by amendments in 1980 (adding Rule 26(f) on discovery conferences) and in 1983 (amending Rule 26 and expanding the purposes of pretrial conference in Rule 16). In 1993 (adding initial mandatory disclosure and limiting the number of interrogatories and depositions) and 2000 (reducing the scope of permitted discovery and limiting the duration of depositions), further amendments were made to the discovery rules continuing the attempt to contain wide-open discovery. Consequently, lawyers have less latitude in discovery, while the courts use a stronger hand. You will soon learn how Rule 11 was amended in 1983 specifically to curtail attorney freedom, bringing the Federal Rules a bit closer to the more restricted spirit of pleading under the nineteenth-century Field Code. Rule 11 was amended yet again in 1993, heading in a slightly different direction.

The idea of procedural uniformity from court to court has been eroded by the proliferation of local rules. *See* Fed. R. Civ. P. 83. The Local Rules Project of the Committee on Rules of Practice and Procedure of the Judicial Conference of the United States collected the local rules of all district courts, and reported in 1988:

> The ninety-four district courts currently have an aggregate of approximately 5,000 local rules, not including many "sub-rules," standing orders and standard operating procedures. These rules are extraordinarily diverse and their numbers continue to grow rapidly. To give one stark example, the Central District of California, based in Los Angeles, has about thirty-one local rules with 434 "sub-rules," supplemented by approximately 275 standing orders. At the other extreme, the Middle District of Georgia has only one local rule and just one standing order. These local rules cover the entire spectrum of federal practice, from attorney admission and discipline, through the various stages of trial, including pleading and filing requirements, pre-trial discovery procedures, and taxation of costs.

The Civil Justice Reform Act of 1990, P.L. 101-650, Title I, 28 U.S.C. §§ 471-482, virtually mandated procedural diversity from district court to district court, by obligating each district court to implement its own civil justice expense and delay reduction plan within three years after enactment of the legislation. A major purpose of the Act was to encourage courts to experiment with different types of case management systems and also to experiment with a variety of alternative dispute resolution (ADR) methods. The expiration of this Act has also caused a considerable lack of clarity. *See* Carl Tobias, *The Expiration of the Civil Justice Reform Act of 1990*, 59 Wash. & Lee L. Rev. 541 (2002).

You have already learned something about the current unrest and instability in American civil procedure. Even before *Twombly* and *Iqbal*, some federal courts sanctioned more stringent pleading for civil rights cases than one might anticipate by reading the federal pleading rules and their historic interpretation. And as you have seen, *Twombly* and *Iqbal* signal a significantly more rigorous federal pleading standard. Congress also has attempted to curtail what are thought to be abuses inherent in the more open-textured federal procedural system, by passing the Private Securities Litigation Reform Act of 1995 (PSLRA), Publ. 104-67, 109 Stat. 737 (1995). Written to address class action lawsuits alleging fraud in the securities market, the PSLRA uses myriad procedural devices, including more stringent pleading requirements, to curtail what Congress has called "unmeritorious claims that were stifling free enterprise." *Class-Action Lawsuits by Investors Are Not Turning Out Exactly as Congress Planned*, New York Times, Feb. 27, 1997, at D:8:3. For instance, in making a complaint, a plaintiff must specifically enumerate and explain each alleged misleading statement by a defendant. Further, the complaint must state with particularity facts giving rise to a strong inference that the defendant acted with the required state of mind. *Tellabs, Inc. v. Makor Issues & Rights, Ltd.*, 551 U.S. 308 (2007).

The ongoing amendments to Rule 11 provide another example of the struggle over how much factual and legal information and certainty a lawyer and client should have prior to commencing suit. Once again, civil rights litigation provides an important battlefield, for the greater the investigation and detail (and thus the cost) required in advance, the less likely a typical civil rights plaintiff and her lawyers will be willing or able to commence suit.

These examples reveal two goals or values that seem to be in tension in each period of Anglo-American civil procedure. First, procedure is looked at as a formal means of containing civil disputes. Procedural law is seen as a means, along with substantive law, of reducing the number of variables that the decision maker will consider. It is also seen as a means of providing definition, focus, and constraints of time. Some would say that the very purpose of law is to provide such formalized definition and restraint. Justice Harlan put it this way in *Boddie v. Connecticut*, 401 U.S. 371, 374 (1971):

> Perhaps no characteristic of an organized and cohesive society is more fundamental than its erection and enforcement of a system of rules defining the various rights and duties of its members, enabling them to govern their affairs and definitively settle their differences in an orderly predictable manner. Without such a "legal system," social organization and cohesion are

virtually impossible. . . . Put more succinctly, it is this injection of the rule of law that allows society to reap the benefits of rejecting what political theorists call "the state of nature."

The second goal or value is to attempt to do justice based on the facts in each dispute. Human situations and particularly human disputes do not easily lend themselves to rigidity and formalism. The story, what many now call the "narrative," inevitably seeps beyond the narrowness of causes of actions and their elements. Indeed, it may be impossible to understand a claim without knowing the full story that gives rise to it; one meaning of "claim" under the federal rules is the entirety of a transaction or occurrence, and you will find out later in the course that principles of *res judicata* and preclusion law track this understanding. Professor James White, a professor of both law and English at the University of Michigan, has argued that the discipline of law is not unique in its inability to reduce life's circumstances to a selected set of variables captured in words that mean exactly what they say. *See* James B. White, *The Legal Imagination: Studies in the Nature of Legal Thought* (1973). Lawyers, like poets, novelists, and historians, are inevitably telling a story larger than the precise meaning of words. Trial lawyers know that the art of persuasion is in large measure the art of creating and telling stories. As you will soon see, this tension between on the one hand the narrowing focus of the story confined by substantive law and procedure and, on the other, the need to tell larger stories is played out in some measure in the history of the different procedures of law courts and equity courts dating back to the Middle Ages.

This tension between formalism and narrative does not take place in a human vacuum. Issues of power underlie many of the most perplexing questions of civil procedure. This is not a recent phenomenon. As you read about the use of jury in the common law courts, it is important to realize that by establishing the jury in common law courts, the King sought to gain the loyalty of the citizens of England. And by requiring that land disputes be resolved in his courts, rather than in those of barons or the county, the King sought to centralize his emerging nation and bring power to himself. The emerging power of the entrepreneurial class and the desire of lawyers to earn a better living (an issue of professional power) were important factors in the mid-nineteenth-century American procedural reform called the "Field Code."

As you read the following materials on equity and the common law, the Field Code, and the Federal Rules, bear in mind these themes of the formalism/narrative tension and how the quest for power influenced civil procedure in the past; surely, both themes will influence current and future reform movements as well. As you proceed through the various stages of litigation in this course and you consider the choices that former and current procedural reformers have made, and continue to make, the theme of formalism in tension with narrative, and the theme of power (with its own tensions: judge and jury; client and lawyer; lawyer and judge; judiciary and legislature) should provide lenses through which you can begin to understand what was and is at stake at both conceptual and political levels. And, of course, the formalism/narrative and power themes are themselves related. Formal procedural rules are often an attempt to confine power, just as narrative may be a means of broadening discretion (adding power to the judiciary) or democratizing the procedural system (if power is allocated to juries).

## 2. *The Common Law and Equity**

"Common law" has several meanings. It describes the English system of judge-made law, as opposed to the Continental system (such as in France and Germany) contained primarily in Codes. "Common law" is also used in the United States to distinguish law developed through judicial opinions from that enacted by legislative statutes. In addition, it is used to describe one of the two sets of courts in which formal litigation took place in England at least as early as the thirteenth century. On one hand, there were the three central law courts—King's Bench, Exchequer, and Common Pleas—which used "common law" procedures. On the other, there was the Chancery or equity court.

The law courts and equity court each had its own distinct procedural system, jurisprudence, and outlook; it is difficult to understand the development of American procedure without considering the differences.

### a. Common Law Procedure

The law courts had three major characteristics: the writs, single-issue pleading, and the jury. Ironically, the writ system developed in Chancery, which later housed the equity court. As early as the thirteenth century, subjects of the King would bring grievances to the Chancellor, who served as the King's secretary, advisor, and agent. The Chancellor's staff sold writs, royal orders that authorized a court to hear a case and instructed a sheriff to secure the defendant's attendance. Over time, the writs became organized into categories of often-used complaints. They became formalized, so that a plaintiff could not get into court without fitting into a specific category, such as trespass, replevin, or covenant. Each writ implied a range of procedural, remedial, and evidentiary incidents, such as subject matter and personal jurisdiction, burden of proof, and method of execution. Writs began to connote what events would permit what remedy; a body of substantive law ultimately evolved.

---

*Stephen N. Subrin has described the development of nineteenth- and twentieth-century civil procedure in the United States, and the antecedents to that procedure in England, in two articles: Stephen N. Subrin, *How Equity Conquered Common Law: The Federal Rules of Civil Procedure in Historical Perspective*, 135 U. Pa. L. Rev. 909 (1987), and Stephen N. Subrin, *David Dudley Field and the Field Code: An Historical Analysis of an Earlier Procedural Vision*, 6 L. & Hist. Rev. 311 (1988). Much of the history contained in the following pages borrows from those articles.

Accompanying the writ system was a process that we would call "single-issue pleading." At an earlier time, pleading designed to reduce cases to a single issue took place orally before a judge in London. Later, this developed into exchanges of documents. A defendant could plead jurisdictional defenses, demur to test a legal question, or traverse to raise a factual dispute. Alternatively, the defendant could plead a "confession and avoidance," today's affirmative defense. Unless a jurisdictional plea was granted, the parties pleaded back and forth until one side either demurred, resulting in a legal issue, or traversed, requiring the resolution of a factual dispute.

A factual dispute would be brought to a jury. The jury replaced earlier common law trial methods by which the parties were tested before God through ordeal, battle, or the swearing of neighbors ("compurgators") that they believed the parties. Like the writ system and single-issue pleading, the jury evolved as an attempt to make the resolution of human disputes more rational and predictable. Because human beings, instead of God, were to hear and decide cases, it became advantageous for parties to present facts that could change the minds of the now-human dispute resolvers.

The technicality and rigidity of the common law writ and single-issue system drew ridicule. To be called a "special pleader" was an insult. But given the complexity of many lawsuits today, with so many legal issues and so much discovery, one can perhaps sympathize with our procedural ancestors' attempts to reduce and focus cases, achieve a degree of predictability, and, through the writ system, use defined procedures to integrate the ends sought and means used. Moreover, today one can perhaps appreciate the historical development of the lay jury, for most current citizens have few opportunities other than jury service to partake in government.

### b. Equity Procedure

By the early sixteenth century it was apparent that the common law system was accompanied by a substantially different one called equity, probably based on the historical power of the Chancellor to fashion new writs. The formulary writ system's defined cubbyholes did not readily allow for individual assistance in unusual and unfair circumstances, such as a contract based on mistake or fraud, or a beneficiary's being deprived of the benefits of property where title was in the name of another. Bills in equity were written to persuade the Chancellor to relieve the petitioner from an alleged injustice that would result from the rigorous application of the common law. One could turn to equity only if there was no adequate remedy at law.

The equity court and its procedure were distinguishable from that of the common law courts in several ways. The bill in equity permitted, and often required, the joinder of multiple parties. While in the law courts the self-interest of the parties was thought too great to permit them to testify, the

Chancellor in equity compelled the defendant personally to come before him to answer under oath each sentence of the petitioner's bill. As a precursor to modern pretrial discovery, a petitioner in equity could attach interrogatories to the petition, requiring answers from the defendant. The Chancellor did not take testimony in open court, but relied on documents to decide a case. The Chancellor, not juries, decided equity cases. The Chancellor was able to fashion injunctive relief, such as compelling a defendant to give the use and profit of a property to a beneficiary, rather than being limited to awarding a specific amount of damages, as in common law courts. Finally, a Chancellor was less bound by the rigidity of the common law writ and pleading system, and could exercise more discretion in an attempt to do justice in the particular case.

### c. The Common Law Mentality in Pre-Twentieth-Century America

Just as the common law system provoked ridicule for injustice through technicality, the equity system brought complaints arising from the burdens of too many parties, issues, and papers. Many colonists in the New World brought with them a deep distrust of the royal Chancellor, who for them symbolized the unjust King. To them equity represented uncontrolled discretion, arbitrariness, and needless delay and expense.

Some of the earliest colonial courts had jurisdiction over disputes and lawmaking functions that in England would have fallen to several different courts and even to legislators. From 1680 to 1820, there was a gradual movement from the relatively unstructured, nontechnical procedural systems of the early colonists to a greater reliance on common law forms and procedures. Pleadings were usually limited to a few simple steps; joinder was restricted; and only a single form of action was allowed. Ironically, after the Revolution brought victory over the British, many states more formally followed the British system not only in pleading requirements, but in establishing separate equity courts or permitting common law judges to hear equity cases and grant equitable remedies.

Through the entire colonial period, great confidence was reposed in juries. Upon attaining statehood, each of the thirteen original colonies, as well as the federal government, provided citizens with the right to a jury trial in both criminal and civil cases. The jury was viewed as a means of permitting laymen to partake in governing themselves, educating the citizenry, and controlling the discretion and possible arbitrariness of judges. But by the beginning of the nineteenth century, American judges had begun to fashion ways for constricting and controlling the role of juries. Over time, many lawyers and judges began to view the jury as a cumbersome and unreliable mode of dispute resolution, rather than as an integral part of democratic government.

# Comments and Questions

1. This may be a good occasion for you to browse through the historical section of the law library. There exist several fine descriptions of the historical English bifurcated common law-equity system. The two courses of lectures of Frederick W. Maitland, *Equity and the Forms of Action at Common Law* (1913), and Stroud Francis Charles Milsom, *Historical Foundation of the Common Law* (1969), deserve special mention. The latter requires careful reading and re-reading. An easier and more comprehensive single volume is Theodore F.T. Plucknett, *A Concise History of the Common Law* 139-156 (5th ed. 1956). Two well-regarded multivolume histories of the law in England are William S. Holdsworth, *A History of the Common Law* (2d ed. 1937), and Frederick Pollock and Frederick W. Maitland, *History of English Law* (2d ed. 1905). For copies of common law documents (such as writs), see a set of volumes published through the years by the Selden Society. Perhaps the most engaging way to learn about the Chancery Court in England, however, is to read *Bleak House* (1853), a classic by Charles Dickens.

2. The most cited, if not the best, single-volume history of American law is the extremely readable *A History of American Law*, by Lawrence M. Friedman (3d ed. 2005). This is available in paperback. A useful single volume on early American law is the compilation of essays reprinted in *Essays in the History of Early American Law* (David H. Flaherty, ed. 1969). On the colonial experience, and the early faith in juries, William Nelson, *Americanization of the Common Law* (1975), is extremely useful. Morton J. Horwitz, *The Transformation of American Law 1780-1860* (1977), and Morton J. Horwitz, *The Transformation of American Law, 1870-1960: The Crisis of Legal Orthodoxy* (1993), invite one to think about the socioeconomic agendas of those who developed American law. Edward Purcell has authored two fascinating historical works that place important procedural issues into their social-economic-political context: Edward A. Purcell, Jr., *Litigation and Inequality: Federal Diversity Litigation in Industrial America, 1870-1958* (1992), and *Brandeis and the Progressive Constitution: Erie, the Judicial Power, and the Politics of the Federal Courts in Twentieth-Century America* (2000).

For a light and very entertaining account of the evolution of American civil procedure, see Charles Rembar, *The Law of the Land: The Evolution of Our Legal System* (1980). It is available in paperback and will also provide context for other first-year courses.

3. Consider this paragraph from Frederick W. Maitland, *Selected Essays* 19 (H.D. Hazeltine et al. eds. 1936):

We ought not to think of common law and equity as of two rival systems. Equity was not a self-sufficient system, at every point it presupposed the existence of common law. Common law was a self-sufficient system. I mean this: that if the legislature had passed a short act saying "Equity is hereby abolished," we might still have got on fairly well; in some respects our law would have been barbarous, unjust, absurd, but still the great elementary rights, the right to immunity from violence, the right to one's good name, the rights of ownership and of possession would have been decently protected and contract would have been enforced. On the other hand had the legislature said, "Common Law is hereby abolished," this decree if obeyed would have meant anarchy. At every point equity presupposed the existence of common law. Take the case of the trust. It's of no use for Equity to say that A is a trustee of Blackacre for B, unless thereby some court that can say that A is the owner of Blackacre. Equity without common law would have been a castle in the air, an impossibility.

What is Maitland talking about? Could you explain to another person why he found equity standing alone "anarchy" or "a castle in the air"? Maitland is apparently talking about equity as a repository of substantive law. Would his insight retain force with respect to procedural law?

Maitland sees common law and equity as complementary. In terms of procedure, how do common law and equity perspectives relate to each other? What are the advantages and disadvantages of each?

## 3. David Dudley Field and the Field Code: The Multiple Agendas of Procedural Reformers

During the first half of the nineteenth century, objections developed to the common law-equity system that the United States had inherited from the English. In 1846, a new constitution in New York eliminated the chancery court and created a court "having general jurisdiction in law and equity." It also provided for the legislature to appoint a commission of three members to "revise, reform, simplify, and abridge the rules of practice, pleading, forms, and proceeding of the courts of record of this state, and to report thereon to the legislature." This commission became known as the Practice Commission.

David Dudley Field (1805-1894) was an enormously talented and successful trial lawyer in New York City who participated in some of the most important litigation of his day. For instance, he represented Jim Fisk and Jay Gould in their struggle for control of the Erie Railroad and also represented Boss Tweed. Later in his career, in unpublished notes for an autobiography he contemplated writing, he concluded, probably accurately: "My practice was the largest and my income from it the most that any lawyer had at the New York Bar, and probably at any Bar in the country." His firm, Field and Shearman, later became the prestigious firm of Shearman and Sterling.

Although not among the original members of the Practice Commission, Field was appointed to replace an original member in 1847 and became the most dominant and well-known commissioner. The New York procedural code, adopted in that state in 1848, became known as the Field Code. It eventually was adopted in twenty-seven states, including such populous states as California and Ohio. As of 1890, 38 million Americans out of 63 million (60 percent of the population) lived in Field Code states. Field also wrote codes for almost all substantive law, but those codes were not adopted in New York nor in many other states.

The Field Code eliminated the forms of action and, for the most part, provided the same procedure for all types of cases. It reduced the number of pleadings to the complaint, answer, reply, and demurrer, and discarded the stylized search for a single issue. It required that complaints contain: "A statement of the facts constituting the cause of action in ordinary and concise language, without repetition, and in such a manner as to enable a person of common understanding to know what is intended." (N.Y. Laws 1848, c. 379, § 120 (2).) In 1851, this was amended to read: "A plain and concise statement of the facts constituting a cause of action without unnecessary repetition." (N.Y. Laws 1851, c. 479, § 1.)

The Code liberalized a party's ability to amend pleadings and to enter evidence at variance with a pleading. It expanded—but not to the same degree as the Federal Rules later would—the number of potential parties, causes of action, and defenses that could be joined in one suit. The Field Code eliminated equitable bills of discovery and interrogatories, but provided for limited discovery through requests to inspect and copy "a paper" in the other's possession or control "relating to the merits of the action, or the defense therein" (§ 342), and for limited requests to admit the genuineness of writings (§ 341). The Code permitted oral depositions of the opposing party. But unlike the Federal Rules, the Code deposition was in lieu of calling the adverse party at the trial; the deposition was before a judge, who would rule on evidentiary objections (§ 345). The Code permitted the court to grant the plaintiff "any relief consistent with the case made by the complaint, and embraced within the issue" (§ 231).

Procedural reform has recurrent themes. To understand this better, try to isolate the rationale of the Field Code reformers and compare it to the reform purposes behind the Federal Rules of Civil Procedure as well as those undercurrents of present-day reform efforts. The following are portions of an essay on procedural reform written by David Dudley Field on January 1, 1847.

## ■ DAVID DUDLEY FIELD, WHAT SHALL BE DONE WITH THE PRACTICE OF THE COURTS?

Speeches, arguments and miscellaneous papers of
David Dudley Field
*226-260 (A.P. Sprague, ed. 1884)*

The Constitution of this State, which goes into effect today, will render great changes necessary in our system of legal procedure. It remodels our Courts; unites the administration of law and equity in the same tribunal; directs testimony to be taken in like manner in both classes of cases; abolishes the offices of Master and Examiner in Chancery, hitherto important parts of our equity system; and, finally, directs that the next Legislature shall provide for the appointment of three commissioners, "whose duty it shall be to revise, reform, simplify, and abridge the rules and practice, pleadings, forms, and proceedings of the courts of record," and report thereon to the Legislature for its action. . . .

What I propose . . . in respect to cases of legal cognizance, is this: that the present forms of action be abolished, and in their stead a complaint and answer required, each setting forth the real claim and defense of the parties. Such pleadings would be precisely similar to those proposed for equity cases, *and we should thus have a uniform course of pleading for all cases, legal and equitable.* The distinction between the two classes of cases is now merely a distinction in the forms of proceeding. . . .

Let the plaintiff set forth his cause of action in his complaint briefly, in ordinary language, and without repetition; and let the defendant make his answer in the same way. Let each party verify his allegation by making oath that he believes it to be true. The complaint will then acquaint the defendant with the real charge, while the answer will inform the plaintiff of the real defense. The disputed facts will be sifted from the undisputed, and the parties will go to trial knowing what they have to answer. The plaintiff will state his case as he believes it, and as he expects to prove it. The defendant, on his part, will set forth what he believes and expects to establish, and he need set forth no more. He will not be likely to aver what he does not believe. His answer will disclose the whole of his defense, because he will not be allowed to prove anything which the answer does not contain. He will not be perplexed with questions of double pleading, nor shackled by ancient technical rules. . . .

The most ample power of amendment should likewise be given to the Courts. . . .

The legitimate end of every administration of law is to do justice, with the least possible delay and expense. Every system of pleading is useful only as it tends to this end. This it can do but in one of two ways: *either by enabling the parties the better to prepare for trial, or by assisting the jury and the court in judging the cause.* Let us consider it, then, in these two aspects:

*First, as it enables the parties to prepare for trial.* This it can only do by informing them of each other's case. To make them settle beforehand wherein they disagree, so as to enable them to dispense with unnecessary proofs, and to be prepared with those which are necessary, is the legitimate end of pleadings, so far as the parties are concerned. Now, no system could accomplish this more effectually than the one proposed. The plaintiff's whole case is stated in his complaint, the defendant's whole case in his answer; and nothing beyond what is contained in one of these is to be received in evidence, except, perhaps, such rebutting proof as may have been specified in written points, filed a certain number of days before the trial. . . .

*Second, as it assists the jury and the Court in performing their functions.* An opinion prevails that nothing but common-law issues are fit for a jury. Many lawyers are wedded to the system of pleading according to the ancient rules, though they admit and deplore the imperfections of our present practice. It is said that the production of the issue disentangles the case, lessens the number of questions of fact, and separates them from the questions of law.

Now, I deny, in the first place, that the production of an issue, according to the course of the common law, does really lessen the number of questions of fact. The declaration may contain any number of counts, each setting forth different causes of action, or the same cause of action in different forms. If the same plea is put into all the counts, there will be as many issues as there are counts. But the defendant may plead as many pleas to each count as he likes; and the plaintiff, with leave of the Court, may put in as many replications to each plea as he may happen to have answers to it. Suppose, now, a declaration containing five counts—no uncommon thing—three pleas to each count, and a single replication to each plea. Here are fifteen issues; and, if there be two replications to each plea, there will be thirty. . . .

The attempt to reduce questions to all their elements before trial, must commonly fail. What subordinate ones may arise can scarcely be known till the evidence is all disclosed. The greatest diligence and skill will lead only to an approximation, greater or less according to the nature of the original questions. The first one is always this: Has the plaintiff the right, or the defendant? This depends upon others. You may go on, if you please, to reduce them as far as possible, but you will scarcely ever reach the elementary ones till the cause is brought to trial, and the evidence produced. Then, by a strict analysis, they are rapidly sifted; and the cause turns at last upon two or three. . . .

## Comments and Questions

1. Common law procedure emphasized pleading. What stage of the litigation was most important to Field?

2. Most procedural reformers tend to ignore potential problems in their own proposals; consequently, most procedural reform gives way to later reform. What miscalculations, if any, do you think Field made?

3. The Field siblings may rank with the Adams and James families among the most productive and important in the early history of our country: Henry was the editor of a Presbyterian newspaper for forty-four years; Jonathan was a leader in the Massachusetts legislature; Matthew built the longest suspension bridge of his time; Cyrus laid the first transatlantic cable; and Stephen became a U.S. Supreme Court justice. Not many women were allowed to progress in the legal profession (or any other) at the time, but Field's only sister, Emelia, gave birth to David Brewer, who joined his uncle on the Supreme Court.

4. Usually, sound procedural reasons support procedural reform. But procedural reform has many faces. Field and his reforms had several progressive elements. He wanted litigation to be less costly and more efficient, and strove to make law understandable and accessible to ordinary people. He fervently believed in equality of opportunity. One law professor

summarized the progressive elements in Field and his work, concluding that Field had worked for "scientific law reform, international peace, feminism, and abolition of slavery."* But at the same time, there were several less liberal aspects undergirding Field's reforms.† At a time of mounting complaints about the technicality of law and a movement to eliminate the legal profession, Field stressed the need for well-trained legal experts both to represent clients and to "reform" the law. His reforms eliminated state regulation of lawyer's litigation fees and permitted Field and his extremely wealthy clients to make their own fee arrangements. At a time when a farmers' rebellion in the state of New York questioned the entire socioeconomic fabric of the country, Field emphasized a need to reform the judicial system and civil procedure. He wanted a well-defined substantive and procedural law that would both tie the hands of judges and permit clients to act freely, except where the law specifically prohibited such activity.

5. The American Law Institute and UNIDROIT, an international law-reform organization headquartered in Rome, have drafted Principles and Rules of Transnational Civil Procedure that a country could adopt for adjudication of disputes arising from international commercial transactions. And in these principles and rules, the influence of David Dudley Field is apparent—although it is perhaps more accurate to say that Field himself was largely influenced by European procedure and that most of the world requires more specificity in pleading than do the Federal Rules. The Transnational Rule Reporters have acknowledged that the pleading rule they have incorporated is essentially the Field Code standard. Transnational Rule 12, entitled "Statement of Claim (Complaint)," requires the plaintiff to "state the facts on which the claim is based, describe the evidence to support those statements, and refer to the legal grounds that support the claim, including foreign law, if applicable." Rule 12.1.

## 4. The Historical Background of the Federal Rules of Civil Procedure

### a. The Rules of Decision Act, Process and Conformity Acts, and the Enabling Act

A major decision to be made in a federal system is what law should apply in the state and federal courts. In 1789, the same year as the first presidential election, the Federal Judiciary Act provided for the establishment of the

---

*Peggy A. Rabkin, *The Origins of Law Reform: The Social Significance of the Nineteenth Century Codification Movement and Its Early Contribution to the Passage of the Early Married Women's Property Acts*, 24 Buffalo L. Rev. 683, 714 (1974).

†For a fuller exploration of the conservative aspects of Field's philosophy and reform efforts, see Stephen N. Subrin, *David Dudley Field and the Field Code: A Historical Analysis of an Earlier Procedural Vision*, 6 L. & Hist. Rev. 311, 319-327 (1988) (Subrin defends aspects of Field's procedural philosophy at 328-345).

Supreme Court, as well as thirteen district and three circuit courts. Section 34 of the Judiciary Act of 1789 provided "that the laws of the several states, except where the constitution, treaties, or statutes of the United States shall otherwise require or provide, shall be regarded as the rules of decision in trials at common law in the courts of the United States in cases where they apply." This section became known as the "Rules of Decision Act" and is now found, in slightly different form, in 28 U.S.C. § 1652. The exception clause in the Rules of Decision Act tracks the Supremacy Clause in Article VI of the Constitution.

It was unclear whether the Rules of Decision section of the Judiciary Act of 1789 covered procedural law, but the Process Act of the same year supplied the same basic formula: Apply state law in federal court, unless a federal law provides otherwise. Act of Sept. 29, 1789, ch. 21, § 2, 1 Stat. 93 (Process Act). Subsequent process and conformity acts repeated the pattern of requiring federal trial courts, for the most part, to apply the procedure of the state in which the federal court sat. Therefore, absent applicable federal law, state substantive and procedural law applied in both state and federal courts.

Until 1872, the Conformity Acts were what have been called "static conformity acts," for they required the federal courts to apply the state procedural law in existence at the time the federal act was passed. It was thought to be unwise, if not unconstitutional, to permit the states to effectively pass laws that would become federal laws of procedure. The problem was thought to be mitigated if Congress could look at the procedure of the states at the time of any one conformity act, and then vote to conform the federal procedure to the state procedure in a static way as of that date.

By 1872, it was clear that the static conformity acts presented some severe problems for practitioners. Most lawyers were applying procedural provisions similar to the Field Code in their state courts, but were required to apply previous common law procedures in federal court, because static conformity required the federal court to apply the state procedural law as of the time the federal conformity act was passed. In the Conformity Act of 1872, Congress moved to what is called "dynamic conformity," requiring federal courts, for the most part, to apply the same procedural law of the state that the state courts would then apply, thus keeping the federal courts up to date—in a dynamic way—with the then current state procedures.

Yet for several practical reasons, lawyers in federal court in their own state could not just apply the state procedural law with which they were familiar. The Conformity Act of 1872 provided that the federal trial judges should conform the federal procedure to state procedure "as near as may be." Federal judges used this language to apply some federal procedures that they favored, such as rules permitting them to supervise, if not control, juries through instructions and the granting of new trial motions. The Conformity Act (along with the Supremacy Clause and the exception clause of the Rules of Decision Act) also obligated federal trial judges to apply any specific procedural laws that Congress had passed for the federal courts.

The potential for state-federal court procedural uniformity was further eroded by equity practice in the federal courts. In 1789, when the first process act was passed, equity jurisdiction, jurisprudence, and procedure either did not exist or were under-developed in many state courts. Therefore, in some states, there would be little or no distinct equity law to conform to. The solution in the succession of process and conformity acts was to have federal courts apply historical equity law, and not state law, in equity cases. The Supreme Court adopted specific procedural rules for equity cases to be applied in the federal trial courts. The Supreme Court adopted the Federal Equity Rules of 1912, which became effective in 1913, to replace the outdated Equity Rules of 1842, which had been drafted to operate in the context of historical equity practice. Drawing heavily upon simplified practice under the English Judicature Acts of 1873 and 1875, technical pleadings and demurrers were eliminated, and the right to amend was liberalized. Although not unanimous, the opinion of most contemporaneous commentators was that the Equity Rules of 1912 were simple and efficient, and greatly improved equity practice by appropriately freeing judges from procedural technicalities.

Many of those who argued for uniform federal rules to be applied in all federal district courts premised their position on the failure of the conformity acts to provide true procedural uniformity between state and federal courts, and on the efficacy of the Equity Rules of 1912 as a model for uniform federal rules of procedure. Proponents of uniform federal procedural rules further argued that once the Supreme Court had provided simple, flexible, uniform rules for the federal courts, the states would follow suit, thus finally achieving the conformity of state and federal practice that had failed to be accomplished under the series of process and conformity acts.

Starting in 1911, the American Bar Association (ABA), at the urging of a Virginia lawyer, Thomas Wall Shelton, lobbied in Congress for a bill that would enable the Supreme Court to promulgate uniform procedural rules for all district courts—an "Enabling Act." Many of the arguments were based on the often cited, and little read, 1906 address of Roscoe Pound, then Dean of the Nebraska College of Law School, to the annual meeting of the ABA. In his historic address on *The Causes of Popular Dissatisfaction with the Administration of Justice*, 29 A.B.A. Rep. 395, 409-413 (1906), Pound—in addressing the topic suggested by the title of his speech—argued that the public was mistaken in its criticisms of the judiciary. The problem was not the power of judges under our constitutional system to hold legislative enactments unconstitutional, nor was it that judges were inevitably thrown into political controversy as a result of our tripartite government. According to Pound, much of the real fault was procedure, particularly "contentious procedure," and the "sporting theory of justice" whereby lawyers took advantage of procedural technicalities that stood in the way of justice. During the decade starting in 1905, he argued that it was the formalism of the common law writ system (which in his view survived the Field Code) and its rigid and inflexible procedural steps that hindered the just application of substantive law and the adjustment of law to modern circumstances. Pound complained that American judges were unduly constrained by procedural rules designed to control them and handicapped by their inability to "search independently for truth and justice."

Pound turned to equity as a model for expanded judicial discretion and for more liberal principles of pleading and joinder in order to meet the needs of modern jurisprudence. In this argument, he was later joined by Charles E. Clark, a professor and later dean at the Yale Law School. In 1935, Clark became the Reporter (the chief drafter) to the Advisory Committee appointed by the Supreme Court to draft the initial Federal Rules. He consistently turned to equity as the model for modern procedure.

Pound and Clark stressed the waste of time and the injustices that were perpetrated by having two types of jurisdiction—law and equity—in federal courts and in some state systems. Some litigants were thrown out of court because they mistakenly chose law or equity, and the statute of limitations had then run. Clark and other proponents complained at how complicated and lengthy the Field Code had become because of unsound legislative amendments. They complained that judges had made the Field Code too technical by insisting on precision in "fact" pleading, by narrowing the potential joinder of parties, and by allowing plaintiffs only a single theory of recovery in any one case.

Between 1912 and 1932, the ABA succeeded in creating a bill for an Enabling Act to authorize the Supreme Court to draft uniform federal rules that was proposed in almost every session of Congress. President and later Chief Justice William Howard Taft, presidential candidate and later Chief Justice Charles Evan Hughes, virtually every luminary in the American Bar Association, and legions of local bar leaders and law school scholars supported the ABA effort. But for twenty years the bill was usually held up in the Senate Judiciary Committee, and on one occasion killed on the floor, because of the determined opposition of Senator Thomas Walsh. Walsh was a Montana Progressive Democrat who was first elected to the Senate in 1912, at the same time Woodrow Wilson was elected President. Walsh was a brilliant constitutional and trial lawyer, who argued and wrote passionately for the confirmation of Louis D. Brandeis to the Supreme Court, for judicial recall, against judicial control of juries, and for enhancing jury power in labor disputes.

Walsh had many objections to proposals for an Enabling Act that would empower the Supreme Court to promulgate uniform federal procedural rules.* A trip to England and its courts had convinced him that legal culture was considerably more influential than procedural rules on the professional conduct of lawyers. He thought, based on his own experience as a trial lawyer in Montana, that the Conformity Act rarely caused procedural uncertainty

---

*For a more detailed description of Walsh's opposition to the Enabling Act, see Stephen N. Subrin, *How Equity Conquered Common Law: The Federal Rules of Civil Procedure in Historical Perspective*, 135 U. Pa. L. Rev. 909, 996-998 (1987).

and that the Field Code, which had been adopted in his state, worked well. He argued that uniform federal rules, as opposed to conforming to state practice, would prejudice the vast majority of lawyers because, although they knew their state procedure, they rarely appeared in federal court. Walsh thought that Supreme Court members, far removed from the trial of cases, were ill-adapted for what he saw as the legislative function of procedural rule making. Finally, he urged that equity rules, which he correctly assumed would form the basis for new uniform federal rules, were complex in practice and would not lead to uniformity and simplicity as the Enabling Act proponents contended. Walsh's death on the way to President Franklin Roosevelt's inauguration in 1933, after which Walsh was to have been sworn in as Attorney General, removed the major opponent to uniform federal procedural rules.

### b. The Enabling Act and the Drafting of the Federal Rules of Civil Procedure

In 1932, the ABA gave up trying to get Congress to pass an Enabling Act. Homer Cummings, Franklin Roosevelt's first Attorney General, was perfectly typecast to resubmit the Enabling Act to Congress in 1934, after conservatives had failed to accomplish its passage for twenty years. This Democratic liberal spokesperson was, like Taft and Hughes, familiar with big cases and with clients that were major banks, corporations, and utilities. When he sponsored the Act in 1934, he echoed the themes already developed by Pound and Clark: Now was the time for lawyers to give up their technical rules and to aid the government in drafting and implementing new legislation to solve national problems.

In 1934, the Enabling Act was passed with only modest resistance. It is now found in 28 U.S.C. § 2072. At first, the Supreme Court seemed reluctant to centralize the drafting of uniform federal rules or to take advantage of a provision in the Enabling Act that permitted the Court to merge law and equity procedure. During the first six months of 1935, Clark lobbied vigorously and effectively to have the Supreme Court exercise its authority under the Enabling Act to adopt the same procedural rules for both law and equity cases, to have those rules patterned on equity practice (particularly on the Federal Equity Rules of 1912), and to have a centralized drafting committee of experts to accomplish these aims. Later in 1935, the Supreme Court appointed a fourteen-person committee "to Draft Unified System of Equity and Law Rules," which became known as the Advisory Committee. 295 U.S. 774 (1935).

The composition of the Advisory Committee reflected both the political conservatives and the academic liberals who had joined in supporting uniform federal rules. Clark, Professor Edson Sunderland of the University of Michigan Law School (who was primarily responsible for drafting the liberal discovery provisions), Professor Edmund Morgan of Harvard Law School, the Dean of the University of Virginia Law School, and a Professor of Law at the University of Minnesota were joined by nine lawyers, most of whom were in large firm practice or were active participants in the ABA—in most cases, both. The chairman of the committee, William D. Mitchell, had been Solicitor General under President Coolidge and Attorney General under President Hoover before setting up his partnership in New York. The firms with partners on the committee, such as Cadwalader, Wickersham & Taft in New York City and Palmer, Dodge, Gardner & Bradford in Boston, represented leading banks, insurance companies, industries, railroads, and utilities in their communities throughout the country. Nevertheless, the original Federal Rules drafted by the Advisory Committee appear to have been conducive to the needs of plaintiffs, to the activism of liberal federal judges, and to the creation of new rights that have helped minorities, the poor, and the underrepresented, along with other citizens.

During the drafting process, the Pound-Clark equity-based vision prevailed, as you will see throughout the remainder of this course. Perhaps the predominant theme was that procedure should be subordinate to and should not interfere with substance. The rules became law in 1938 by congressional inaction. A later comment will explain how amendments to the rules are accomplished today.

## Comments and Questions

1. Before continuing, please have clear in your mind the major purpose and gist of the Rules of Decision Act, the Supremacy Clause, the Process and Conformity Acts, and the Enabling Act. These provisions recur throughout a civil procedure course. We will cover the precise provisions of the Enabling Act in more detail in the second half of the course, particularly when we cover *Erie* and *Hanna v. Plumer*.

2. The most comprehensive history of the Enabling Act is Stephen Burbank, *The Rules Enabling Act of 1934*, 130 U. Pa. L. Rev. 1015 (1982). This meticulously researched and reasoned article also provides in its footnotes exhaustive cites to historical material on the Process and Conformity Acts. For a thorough exploration of the early process acts and the Rules of Decision Act, see J. Goebel, *History of the Supreme Court of the United States: Antecedents and Beginnings to 1801* (1971).

3. Consider now the views of Clark on the Rules he drafted as Reporter.

## ■ CHARLES E. CLARK, COMMENTS

PROCEEDINGS OF THE INSTITUTE AT WASHINGTON, D.C. ON THE FEDERAL
RULES OF CIVIL PROCEDURE
*(American Bar Association, Oct. 6, 1938), at 34-44*

. . . I have the function here this afternoon of discussing particularly Rules 7 to 25, and I am glad to do that because in some ways these seem to me the quintessence of the whole system we are here planning. I think that if you follow the general plans and principles that we have in mind here you will agree with all the other rules. In fact, I might put it this way, that if you are likely to be shocked at all by the new rules I think that it probably is in this material that the shock will come. . . .

[T]here should be a considerable amount of flexibility permitted in the way in which lawyers present cases to the court. In fact, I think if there is one advance we have made it is that we realize there are more ways than one of telling a story, and so long as we get it out clearly and forcefully and simply to the court, the court ought not to try to tell the lawyers that they should have told the story in a different way. In other words, at the present time there are possibilities of various differences in statement, and that is going to be true under the new system just as before. Hence, if there are garrulous lawyers (and I am informed there are) they may still—probably with impunity—be garrulous in their pleadings. Therefore you have a good deal of opportunity of following your own previous plans and practices as before. After all, you are writing the story of your case for the court, and just as there should be a choice if you were writing any other type of essay—for, as I like to tell my class, the making of pleadings is one type of essay writing, a particular type, of course, where you should be above all else direct and forceful and see that you get your point over—so, since there is a choice here, you are entitled to make it.

But beyond that I would say this, that I think you will see at once these pleadings follow a general philosophy which is that detail, fine detail, in statement is not required and is in general not very helpful. . . .

I suggest that it is not the function of the pleadings to supply the place of evidence. It is not the function of the pleadings to give you admissions on the case except in a very broad way, except as to things that the parties or their counsel are perfectly ready to admit at any time, at the opening of the trial and so on. The function of the pleadings, as it now develops, is other than this. It is, in the first place, to distinguish the case from all others so that you can properly send it through the processes of the court, send it to the proper tribunals for trial, decide on such preliminary steps as may be necessary, the taking of depositions, reference to a Master, claim of jury trial, and so forth; in other words, to determine the proper routing of the case through the tribunal; and then secondly to serve as a basis for the binding force of the judgment, that is, for the application of the principle of *res judicata.*

For that purpose the more general pleadings are amply sufficient. Let me say that if any of you feel you need more information to develop your own case, if you need more information from your opponent, we have provided for that, and I think have provided for that much more directly and simply than ever you will obtain by attempting to force the correction of the pleadings. That is in the section on Deposition and Discovery. I think that is the device you should use to secure that information: Those rules will be explained to you tomorrow. . . .

In order to give you a concrete example of what I am talking about before I go to the separate rules, let us turn, if you will, to the appendix of forms. Let me say just a moment what those forms are intended to do. Those forms are not intended to be a desk manual so that whenever you have a case you won't have to do any thinking but simply say to your secretary, "Use official form No. So-and-so." That is not the purpose. The purpose is to illustrate the rules. These are the pictures that we hope will make the rules alive to you, and it seems to me if you look at the forms with that in mind you will get a great deal of the general philosophy which I am trying to state. . . . [Clark then used the form complaint for negligence as his example. *See* Fed. R. Civ. P. Form 11.]

Now I find that a great many lawyers feel, "Why, that is a very skinny statement. That is not the kind of thing to which we are accustomed." But I ask you, if you have in mind what I was suggesting before, that you are not looking for admissions or for something that will take the place of proof, if you are looking for a general statement which will send the case through the proper channels of the court and eventually provide for *res judicata*, how could you ask anything more? You have the case here differentiated from all the other situations giving rise to legal relations requiring court action. It is the case of the pedestrian-automobile accident. . . .

I think anyone who has had experience with the sort of case will know what to expect, and the addition of all those details will really add nothing to the real picture you have. . . .

## Comments and Questions

1. How would you summarize Clark's procedural philosophy? Now would be a good time to look again at some rules you have already studied, such as Fed. R. Civ. P. 7(a), 7(c), 8(a), 8(d), 8(e), and 12(b)(6). Consider the historical context in which the Advisory Committee was drafting.

2. Clark's procedural philosophy is manifest in *Dioguardi v. Durning*, 139 F.2d 774 (2d Cir. 1944), which was mentioned earlier in this chapter.

3. You were previously asked what misconceptions Field might have had in drafting his Code. What about the proponents of the Enabling Act and its drafters, such as Clark?

4. How is it that Clark, who was appointed by President Roosevelt to be a judge on the illustrious Second Circuit Court in 1939, could have ended up agreeing basically with Pound, Taft, Shelton, and the ABA leadership on procedural reform, and how did he end up in the opposite camp from Tom Walsh? After all, Clark and Walsh would have been considered political allies. Did the conservative and liberal supporters of the Enabling Act and the Federal Rules in fact have a great deal in common?

5. In the debate over the Enabling Act and in discussions surrounding the drafting of the Federal Rules, there was very little explicit talk about the fact that the rules (or procedural options within the rules) were the same for all cases (trans-substantive civil procedure). There was, of course, a good deal of discussion concerning the merger of law and equity. How, then, did this

procedural choice of trans-substantive rules come about? Was it inherent in the proponents' other assumptions about civil procedure?

6. Two related debates are now raging about the appropriate direction for civil procedure. One is whether current procedure is or should be non-trans-substantive. In other words, should some procedures be specifically developed for given types of cases? A related question is how much civil procedure knowingly favors some types of litigants or some types of cases, and to what extent this is purposeful. For a discussion of these issues on the occasion of the fiftieth anniversary of the Federal Rules of Civil Procedure, see Stephen N. Subrin, *Fireworks on the Fiftieth Anniversary of the Federal Rules of Civil Procedure*, 73 Judicature 4 (1989). *See also* 137 U. Pa. L. Rev. 1873-2257 (1989) (symposium issue). The regrettable politicization of the rulemaking process is explored in Jeffrey Stempel, *Ulysses Tied to the Generic Whipping Post: The Continuing Odyssey of Discovery "Reform,"* 64 Law & Contemp. Probs. 197 (2001). Professor Stempel uses discovery "reform" in 2000 as his prime example.

7. The current procedural rulemaking provisions are contained in 28 U.S.C. §§ 2071-2072. Proposals for amendments to the Federal Rules of Civil Procedure are first considered and drafted in the Advisory Committee on Civil Rules and are then reviewed, with the power to change them, in the Standing Committee on Rules of Practice and Procedure. There are also Advisory Committees on Criminal, Bankruptcy, Evidence, and Appellate Rules. The Chief Justice appoints members to the Advisory Committees and the Standing Committee.

The Standing Committee proposes rules to the Judicial Conference of the United States, which in turn proposes rules to the Supreme Court. The Judicial Conference of the United States is defined in 28 U.S.C. § 331. It begins:

> The Chief Justice of the United States shall summon annually the chief judge of each judicial circuit, the chief judge of the Court of International Trade and a district judge from each judicial circuit to a conference at such time and place in the United States as he may designate. He shall preside at such conference which shall be known as the Judicial Conference of the United States.

The Supreme Court decides what, if any, rules to present to Congress. In accordance with Title 28, § 2072, "[s]uch rules shall not take effect until they have been reported to Congress by the Chief Justice at or after the beginning of a regular session thereof but not later than the first day of May, and until the expiration of ninety days after they have been thus reported." Congress has specifically refused to allow some amendments to become law by this method of inaction, and, although infrequently, has even passed its own rule. Given these exceptions, Federal Rules of Civil Procedure are not actually statutes, for they have not gone through the normal congressional committee process, been voted on by both houses, or signed by the President. Section 2072, however, does state that "all laws in conflict with such rules shall be of no further force or effect after such rules have taken effect."

## 5. *Civil Procedure Today*

You have now read about the Common Law (accompanied by Equity), Field Code, and Federal Rule procedural regimes. One might say, although simplistically, that the Common Law jurisprudence concentrated on rigorous pleading, with the goals of confinement and predictability; the Field Code centered on verified pleading, with the goal of enlightened settlement or trial; and the Federal Rules were based on simple pleading, broad joinder, liberal discovery, and the avoidance of technicality, all toward the ends of termination by motion (although rarely), or settlement or trial based on the merits.

It is more difficult to encapsulate where we are today. Some have posited that the current goals of the civil litigation process are to terminate cases without trial and to discourage litigation. *See* Andrew M. Siegel, *The Court Against the Courts: Hostility to Litigation as an Organizing Theme in the Rehnquist Court's Jurisprudence*, 84 Tex. L. Rev. 1097 (2006); Jack M. Balkin and Sanford Levinson, *Understanding the Constitutional Revolution*, 87 Va. L. Rev. 1045 (2001); Judith Resnik, *Constricting Remedies: The Rehnquist Judiciary, Congress, and Federal Power*, 78 Ind. L.J. 223 (2003); Owen M. Fiss, *Against Settlement*, 93 Yale L.J. 1073 (1984); Stephen B. Burbank and Stephen N. Subrin, *Litigation and Democracy: Restoring a Realistic Prospect of Trial*, 46 Harv. C.R.-C.L. L. Rev. 399 (2011).

It is true that fewer than 2 percent of federal civil cases are terminated as a result of trial. It is also true that starting in the mid-1970s federal judges and others began applauding case management and alternative dispute resolution, and complaining about the high cost of litigation and the burdensome nature of discovery (which you will read about in the next chapter). And it cannot be reasonably denied that in most areas of civil procedure covered by the Federal Rules, whether pleading, summary judgment, discovery, or joinder—especially class actions—the changes since the 1980s have been in the direction of constraining and discouraging litigation, and generally have had an anti-plaintiff, pro-defendant slant.

It is very difficult to gain perspective on historical currents while change is taking place. We do not have a snappy way of reliably describing the present condition of American civil procedure, with such brief titles as "Common Law," "Field Code," and "Federal Rule." We are tempted by "Anti-Litigation," but we do not trust our ability to conquer our own biases to be comfortable in labeling, especially at a time when the procedure is still in flux.

We can, though, identify some of the factors that we think have led to the current state of civil procedure, and we can describe why we think some of the changes may be ill-advised. Starting in the late 1960s, and leveling off only in the past five years or so, there was a huge increase in the number of commenced civil cases, at both the federal and state levels, without a commensurate increase in judges. For example, federal filings grew nearly fourfold, from approximately 71,000 civil cases in 1966 to about 270,000 cases in 1996. (In 2010, the number of filings was approximately 283,000.) Some of the causes for the increase of cases were the Civil Rights Act of 1964, the civil rights and consumer-protection movements, and generally an increase in citizen awareness of rights. According to the Administrative Office of the United States Courts, between 1974 and 1998, more than 470 new federal causes of action were created.

There was also a huge increase in the number of law school graduates and lawyers. Almost simultaneously came the increase of criminal cases, in large measure caused by drug-related arrests and drug policy, including harsher drug laws and mandatory sentencing. These and other factors put pressure on judges to dispose of cases without trial.

Especially in federal courts, the costs of litigation kept rising. Discovery, especially in large cases, was an important factor. Defense lawyers, especially in larger firms, started charging by the hour; the temptations to increase discovery, and the number of lawyers working on discovery, proved irresistible. One could always defend the use of discovery as required by zealous advocacy. *See* Stephen C. Yeazell, *Re-Financing Civil Litigation*, 51 DePaul L. Rev. 183 (2001). Plaintiffs' lawyers could and did use discovery, as well as class actions, both to protect their clients and, undeniably in many cases, to pressure defendants into settlement because the transactional costs were so high and because the risks of loss at trial were too daunting. Particularly in the large cases, in which the stakes were highest, there were preposterous amounts of discovery, as you will learn about in the next chapter. Technological advances, such as photocopiers, fax machines, computers, and cell phones, added materially to the amount of discovery, particularly in large cases. These were cases that understandably most drew the attention of judges and the press. Some verdicts were enormous, and seemed disproportionate to injury. Some cases that brought the attention of the media—like suing because of an alleged mistake by a referee that caused one's favorite football team to lose—were by any definition frivolous. It is not hard to see reasons for trying to rein in a process that permitted such untoward manifestations of expense and greed.

But there are other sides of the story that make us skeptical of the wisdom of the multiple pro-defendant, anti-litigation trends in contemporary civil procedure. Empirical data does not support much of the current attack on the original Federal Rule process. Most cases, state and federal, have little or no discovery; the discovery that does occur is usually proportionate to the stakes involved. (We will discuss this in Chapter 4.) When the Rules or judicial opinions add new requirements, such as more rigorous pleading, mandatory discovery, discovery conferences, and pretrial conferences, they do it for all cases. But many cases did not seem to pose efficiency problems to begin with; yet the added procedural steps add substantial costs of time and money for all cases.

The data do not support the allegations that juries tend to give inflated awards or that the country is rampant with frivolous litigation. (We will discuss this in Chapter 5.) In fact, although there is not a lot of data, it is probable that Americans sue considerably less than those in other Western countries, and that most Americans with legal grievances and legal needs do not find their way to a lawyer; costs are obviously an important factor. *See* Gillian K. Hadfield, *Higher Demand, Lower Supply? A Comparative Assessment of the Legal Resource Landscape for Ordinary Americans*, 37 Fordham Urb. L.J. 129, 143 (2010); *see also* Gillian Hadfield, *The Price of Law: How the Market for Lawyers Distorts the Justice System*, 98 Mich. L. Rev. 953 (2000).

The attacks on civil litigation and civil procedure, and the subsequent altered interpretation of the Rules, often came from conservatives who were not friendly to the new civil rights statutes to begin with, or to consumer protection, or to plaintiffs generally. *See, e.g.*, Jeffrey W. Stempel, *Politics and Sociology in Federal Civil Rulemaking: Errors of Scope*, 52 Ala. L. Rev. 529, 530, 629 (2001). Many of the changes, such as *Iqbal* and the recent *Wal-Mart* decision (which you will study in the final chapter on class actions), have been accomplished by a 5-4 majority in the Supreme Court, generally thought to be conservative, pro-business, and unsympathetic to civil rights. The changes in procedure in the past thirty years have generally been prejudicial to the rights of the injured, consumers, and minorities.

When you get to Chapter 5 on the jury trial and attempts to curtail jury power, you will see why we believe that civil trials, especially jury trials, play an important part in our democracy. The drastic diminution of trials worries us. Among other reasons, Congress has relied on the private enforcement of rights in dozens of the most important statutes. That Congress has included plaintiff fee shifting and multiple damages as incentives for private enforcement is some indication of how important private enforcement had become in our legal-social-economic system. Congress, until recently, could have relied on liberal pleading, discovery, and joinder as part of the procedural regime. Contraction in these areas means less private enforcement of congressionally imposed social-economic norms. We cannot help but believe that some of this has been politically motivated. By this we mean that civil procedure is, in important respects, molded by those who seek power and that civil procedure grants power to some and detracts it from others. How else can one legitimately read what has happened and continues to happen in such as arenas as pleading, discovery, summary judgment, and class actions?

That systems of civil procedure are influenced by political currents should not surprise us. The Common Law process in England was influenced by the King's desire to centralize the legal system in London. The Field Code was part of American nineteenth-century political maneuvering for a laissez-faire social-economic system. The Federal Rules became law as a New Deal reform. Moreover, in both the instances of the Field Code and the Federal Rule reforms, there was some coalescence of both liberal and conservative thought. In 1976, Chief Justice Burger convened what was called the Pound Conference on Civil Justice Reform, in part commemorating Roscoe Pound's famous procedural reform speech of 1906. In the following excerpts of speeches given at the Pound Conference, you will observe many of the themes that frame the contemporary discourse of civil procedure reform—alternative dispute resolution, discovery, pleading standards, and power.

We will leave it to you to label this new era of American Civil Procedure that you are studying, and to decide on your own its advantages and disadvantages. But of one thing we are certain. Civil procedure, and changes to it, have never been and cannot be politically neutral. Some classes of litigants will benefit from changes; other will not.

## ■ CHIEF JUSTICE WARREN E. BURGER, *AGENDA FOR 2000 A.D.—A NEED FOR SYSTEMATIC ANTICIPATION*

*The Pound Conference: Perspectives on Justice in the Future 23, 29-32 (1979)*

The conference we open tonight is significant because it is the first time that the chief justices of the highest state courts, the leaders of the federal courts, leaders of the organized Bar, legal scholars and thoughtful members of other disciplines have joined forces to take a hard look at how our system of justice is working. We will ask whether it can cope with the demands of the future, and being a process of inquiry into needed change. But this meeting will be judged not on its unique composition but on what it stimulates for the years ahead. . . . If we are to justify taking two days' time of more than 200 leaders of the law, it will be useful to make clear what we are not here to do. That is a task easier, perhaps, than to say with precision what we hope to accomplish. We are not here to deal primarily with specifics and details but with fundamentals. . . .

Whatever risks may be involved in our probing and talking, we must be prepared to take them. There is nothing dangerous about studying and considering basic change, if the alterations will preserve old values and "deliver" justice at the lowest possible cost in the shortest feasible time. I do not, for example, think it subversive to ask why England, the source of all our legal institutions, found it prudent and helpful 40 years ago to abandon jury trials for most civil cases. . . .

[We should not] be surprised at the loss of public confidence caused by lawyers' using the courts for their own ends rather than with a consideration of the public interest. If Pound was correct in his analysis that excessive contentiousness was an impediment to fair administration of justice in 1906, I doubt that anyone could prove it less so today. Correct or not, there is also a widespread feeling that the legal profession and judges are overly tolerant of lawyers who exploit the inherently contentious aspects of the adversary system to their own private advantage at public expense. The willingness of some of the participants to elevate procedural maneuvering above the search for truth, as Pound said, sends out "to the whole community a false notion of the purpose and end of law." And he saw this as a large factor in the American cynicism about the law and the urge to want to "beat the law." . . . I believe that American lawyers, by and large, are the equal of any in the world, but a handful of members of any profession can inflict harm out of proportion to their number, on both the public and on the image of their profession.

Other conditions that caused dissatisfaction in 1906 are still with us. Jurors, witnesses and litigants continue to have their time squandered. They are often shuffled about courthouses in confusion caused by poor management within the courts. The delays and high costs in resolving civil disputes continue to frighten away potential litigants, and those who persist and ultimately gain a verdict often see up to half of the recovery absorbed by fees and expenses. . . .

There is nothing incompatible between efficiency and justice. Inefficient courts cause delay and expense, and diminish the value of the judgment. . . . Efficiency—like the trial itself—is not an end in itself. It has as its objective the very purpose of the whole system—to do justice. Inefficiency drains the value of even a just result either by delay or excessive cost, or both.

It is time, therefore, to ask ourselves whether the tools of procedure, the methods of judicial process that developed slowly through the evolution of the common law, and were fitted to a rural, agrarian society, are entirely suited, without change, to the complex modern society of the late 20th and the 21st centuries.

## ■ SIMON H. RIFKIND, *ARE WE ASKING TOO MUCH OF OUR COURTS?*
### *The Pound Conference: Perspectives on Justice in the Future 51-63 (1979)*

When Roscoe Pound spoke from the podium seventy years ago, he chose as his title, "The Causes of Popular Dissatisfaction with the Administration of Justice." When this conference was convened, it was taken for granted that the same title could appropriately be used. Everyone knows that dissatisfaction with the administration of justice continues today. That should not surprise as—Pound termed such dissatisfaction as "old as the law."

However, our ability to borrow Pound's title for our deliberations should not mislead us into the belief that we are looking at the same landscape. From my vantage point as a working trial lawyer, I venture the opinion that much of today's dissatisfaction springs not from failure but from conspicuous judicial success. The courts have been displaying a spectacular performance; it enjoys a constant "Standing Room Only" attendance. The cause of complaint is that the queues are getting too long. No problem seems to be beyond the desire of the American people to entrust to the courts; many litigants are clamoring for attention.

In consequence, there is a growing—and justified—apprehension that

(1) Quantitatively, the courts are carrying too heavy a burden—and probably a burden beyond the capability of mitigation by merely increasing the number of judges.
(2) Qualitatively, the courts are being asked to solve problems for which they are not institutionally equipped, or not as well equipped as other available agencies.

I do not perceive the role of the panelists—and certainly it is not my role—to invent or reveal the solutions to the problems facing the administration of justice. Rather, this is a place from which, as I perceive it, we are to be encouraged and stimulated to probe deeply—to question and to explore, and to create instruments for further probing and exploration. If we are successful, we shall have formulated an agenda for reform which will occupy our attention during the next decade. . . .

The cause of dissatisfaction which is most important today is [a function] of the peculiarities of the Anglo-American legal system, as they find expression in the environment of our judicial administration.

It is quite easy to document support for the proposition that our courts have become the handymen of our society. The American public today perceives courts as jacks-of-all-trades, available to furnish the answer to whatever may trouble us: Shall we build nuclear plants, and if so, where? Shall the Concorde fly to our shores? How do we tailor dismissal and lay-off programs during the depression, without undoing all of the progress achieved during prosperity by anti-discrimination statutes? All these are now the continuous grist of the judicial mills. . . . Thus, it is not surprising to learn that a lawsuit was recently filed in the Southern District of New York seeking to prevent the United States Postal Service from issuing a commemorative stamp honoring Alexander Graham Bell—on the grounds that someone else invented the telephone.

It is equally easy to compile reports—both state and federal—attesting to the backbreaking burden which the courts are carrying. Students of the subject report that caseloads in both the federal and state courts are increasing at a pace far beyond the growth in population. . . .

It is clear to me that one item on our agenda for the future must include efforts to lighten the workload of the courts if we are to eliminate public dissatisfaction with the administration of justice.

At this point, allow me to lay to rest some apprehension that I have heard expressed about the investigation launched by this conference. A large percentage of the increase in the business which has come into our courts in recent years has related to the protection of civil rights. That circumstance has generated a fear that this conference is conspiring to promote a counter-revolution; in the guise of an inquiry into whether the courts are being asked to do too much, and to do that for which they are ill-equipped, it is suggested we are seeking to erect an impassible barrier against the growing recognition of the rights of the accused, the voter, the consumer, the stockholder, the victims of racial and sexual discrimination; and indeed to reverse the generation-long movement for expansion of their rights.

Let me at once disengage myself from any such enterprise. The exploration of the Constitution, and discovery therein, progressively, of more commands for the humanization of our society have by no means run their course. . . . However, new rights—newly acknowledged and only recently enjoyed—will inevitably supply the pressure for judicial innovation to continue. If that momentum is to proceed without the artificial impediment of overladen courts, we must relieve the courts of burdens that do not require their special expertise.

Innovations of the future, whether the work-product of judges or legislators, will inevitably have to pass through courthouse strainers and filters. If these are clogged and stuffed, the passage is bound to be more sluggish, less reflective, and probably less sagacious.

What I suggest is that the direction of our search should be guided by our view of our courts as institutions of last resort. We should require them to do nothing which other, less irreplaceable institutions can do as well, and, as far as possible, preserve the courts for doing that which cannot be done elsewhere.

There are two main routes we can take toward the goal of lightening the workload of the courts—substantive and procedural.

The most important method of proceeding along the substantive route is to address the question: Shall the courts continue to be not only the dispute-resolvers, but also the problem-solvers of our society?

Heretofore, the accepted model of an American court was that of an institution devoted to the resolution of disputes. . . . The adversary process is a well honed tool for use in such a contest. . . .

Problem-solving is an enterprise of a different sort altogether. The problem-solver finds no refuge in the burden of proof. He does not confine his edict to the parties before him. The consequences of his pronouncement of a solution cannot be confined to tile-sized changes. He frequently administers avulsive changes. Problem-solving is, thus, a chancy business requiring, in a democracy, not only wisdom and inventiveness but a keen perception of the political implications. Moreover, it imposes a duty upon the problem-solver to hear all those who have a significant interest in the problem. Very frequently the problem-solver tends to become a champion of a cause and not a neutral decider. . . .

If we remove problem-solving from the courts, we will improve the administration of the *courts*. To improve the administration of *justice*, we must, in addition, change the manner in which the legislatures and executives respond to difficult social and political problems, so that very few will need to bring them to the courthouse door. The courts should not be the only place in which justice is administered. . . .

We must also explore the procedural route to lessening the burdens on the courts. This route is, of course, one which has often been used both to keep certain business out of the courts and to guide other business through the courts. . . . What more can we do to keep out the worthless, the trivial, and those litigations which, by a definition not yet formulated, ought not to be in the courts?. . . .

It would seem to me that the higher threshold in front of the courthouse door should be built on the probable merit of the claim. That suggests the question whether it would be prudent to borrow from our criminal practice and require a civil litigant to show "probable merit" before he cranks into action the prodigious machinery of the judicial process. . . . Further exploration might reveal whether the requirement for such a showing of merit would favorably affect the judicial burden.

One stage at which a requirement of showing probable merit might be especially useful is the point at which discovery is to begin. I believe it is fair to say that currently the power for the most massive invasion into private papers and private information is available to anyone willing to take the trouble to file a civil complaint. A foreigner watching the discovery proceedings in a civil suit would never suspect that this country has a highly-prized tradition of privacy enshrined in the fourth amendment.

Unless my experience is unique, I hazard the opinion that such discovery proceeds with no attempt at serious regulation. If the threshold for admission to discovery were lifted so as to require a showing of probable merit, the flow of several classes of litigation would tend to diminish. Many actions are instituted on the basis of a hope that discovery will reveal a claim. To some extent, this is the result of the liberalized requirements of pleading, heralded at the beginning of this century, which reduced the requirements of the petition and left for discovery the opportunity to define the facts and issues. The theory was that this would prevent pleading from being a "game of skill" and prevent trials from becoming "sporting matches." The practice—in many areas of the law—has been to make discovery the "sporting match" and an endurance contest. Is this a luxury which an overtaxed judicial system can afford?

The federal system has long recognized that a claim may be too small to warrant the attention of its courts. The states have not enjoyed this luxury. They have struggled with inferior courts and small claims courts. Is it possible to define a class of controversies, modest in amount, not very significant in principle, which need resolution for the peace and harmony of the community, but which do not need the courts? If so, can provision be made for the lay arbitration of such "neighborhood disputes"? Refusal to have recourse to such extrajudicial tribunals might be so burdened as to make the arbitration almost compulsory.

## ■ FRANK E. A. SANDER, *VARIETIES OF DISPUTE PROCESSING*
*The Pound Conference: Perspectives on Justice in the Future 65, 66, 83-84 (1979)*

[One] way of reducing the judicial caseload is to explore alternative ways of resolving disputes outside the courts. . . . By and large we lawyers and law teachers have been far too single-minded when it comes to dispute resolution. Of course . . . good lawyers have always tried to prevent disputes from coming about, but when that was not possible, we have tended to assume that the courts are the natural and obvious dispute resolvers. In point of fact there is a rich variety of different processes, which I would submit, singly or in combination may provide far more "effective" conflict resolution. . . .

What I am . . . advocating is a flexible and diverse panoply of dispute resolution processes, with particular types of cases being assigned to differing processes (or combinations of processes). . . . Conceivably such allocation might be accomplished for a particular class of cases at the outset by the legislature; that in effect is what was done by the Massachusetts legislature for malpractice cases. Alternatively one might envision by the year 2000 not simply a courthouse but a Dispute Resolution Center, where the grievant would be channeled through a screening clerk who would then direct him to the process (or sequence of processes) most appropriate to his type of case. The room directory in the lobby of such a Center might look as follows:

| | |
|---|---|
| Screening Clerk | Room 1 |
| Mediation | Room 2 |
| Arbitration | Room 3 |
| Fact Finding | Room 4 |
| Malpractice Screening Panel | Room 5 |
| Superior Court | Room 6 |
| Ombudsman | Room 7 |

. . . [One concern is] the need to retain the courts as the ultimate agency capable of effectively protecting the rights of the disadvantaged. This is a legitimate concern which I believe to be consistent with the goals I have advocated. I am not maintaining that cases asserting novel constitutional claims ought to be diverted to mediation or arbitration. On the contrary, the goal is to reserve the courts for those activities for which they are best suited and to avoid swamping and paralyzing them with cases that do not require their unique capabilities.

## ■ LAURA NADER, *COMMENTARY*
### *The Pound Conference: Perspectives on Justice in the Future 114 (1979)*

I come to this conference as a citizen, an anthropologist, an outsider to your profession. And I would like to make comments as an outsider. . . . I've been struck by a number of observations here. . . .

One is the absence of data undergirding statements by several people here. Associated with the absence of data is the absence of detachment—the ability to step back and see the problem. Associated with that is the absence of thinking in a broader context. Associated with that is the absence of reality-testing. I also notice in the discussions thus far . . . that there is an absence of a discussion of power. And related to this is an absence of a serious discussion of block solutions. I also find that there is a total lack of self-consciousness in discussing judges as workers—workers who have all the alienation problems that are common to employees and the problems that relate alienation to questions having to do with empathy.

Justice Burger asked us yesterday, to take a hard look at our own system of justice, and how it is working. In fact, we can only take a soft look because of the absence of data. I am puzzled . . . that we really know more about the workings of justice in non-western legal systems than we know about the workings of justice in the United States. We have law trained personnel for whom data means cases. You can't take a serious hard look at the system of justice solely on the basis of cases, although cases are important. . . . [W]e need to understand some things—and basic data is a requirement: we need to know who uses the American legal system; we need to know what it costs to run the system; we need to know whether in fact litigation is increasing at a pace beyond the needs of an industrial society and the growth of population. Some people agree, some people disagree. . . . The first thing that struck me when I began the study of how Americans complain—all we had were anecdotes. We did not have any idea, systematic or unsystematic, about what Americans do with legal problems when they feel they can't take them to court for whatever reason. . . .

I refer here to a *set of mind* which insists that problems of justice be phrased in terms of court case load, and the like—most certainly a problem in developing a just legal system. This is, at the least, a limited technical view. . . .

The most dramatic changes in social relationship in the past hundred years, has to do with the fact that most people's potential disputes are between individuals or between parties who do not know each other and never will. When a complainant has a complaint about General Motors, or about the federal government, or Social Security, or any number of things, these are not problems that can be settled in neighborhood courts. . . .

What is important is that we get some sense of reality, if we're going to make policy. Reality-testing is the way a psychiatrist judges whether somebody's insane or not—to measure the gap between what an individual thinks he is and what he in fact is. We're here to solve *problems*, and I would say that *the first step is to see them*. You can't solve them until you see them. I'm concerned that nothing was said yesterday, specifically about alleviating peoples' ills, and I think we need to look at specific examples. . . . It is the details that we should pay attention to. Now we need to understand in this reality-testing, that for example, people are not always equal before the law. People will not always have access to law. People will be afraid to take cases to law, which should go to law, because of extra-legal retaliation. I think these observations need to be considered here. . . .

## F. SANCTIONS

You have now learned about the liberalizing aspects of the pleading rules, which were an important part of the 1938 Federal Rules of Civil Procedure. You have seen that in procedure, revolutions seem to bring counterrevolutions. Scholars, judges, and lawyers now question whether the Federal Rules make it too easy to commence litigation. In the face of allegations that frivolous litigation is facilitated, if not invited, by the ease of pleading under Fed. R. Civ. P. 8(a), some advocate a return to more fact-specific pleading requirements. Others question whether Fed. R. Civ. P. 11's sanctions effectively discourage lawyers from making ungrounded allegations in their complaints.

Read Rule 11. That rule provides that a lawyer, by presenting to the court a pleading, motion, or other paper, certifies that to the best of that lawyer's knowledge, information, or belief, formed after an inquiry reasonable under the circumstances, that she or he has complied with all of the requirements of the rule. The rule is targeted at frivolous litigation and is intended to ensure that litigants "stop-and-think" before filing pleadings, motions, and other papers.

Since its inception in 1938, Federal Rule 11 has been substantively changed twice—first in 1983, and then again in 1993. But the Rule continues to be the target of reformers. (For a recent reform effort, *see, e.g.*, Lawsuit Abuse Reduction Act of 2011, H.R. 966, 112th Cong. (2011).) There are six parts of the current and prior versions of the Rule that have drawn (or draw) the most attention:

1. *The triggering conduct.* Reasonable minds disagree about whether a lawyer should be subject to sanctions if she violates the rule even when acting in good faith. Does the current rule provide that good faith is an acceptable excuse for failing to do reasonable prefiling factual and legal inquiry?

2. *Judicial discretion to sanction.* Some argue that sanctions should be *mandatory* once there has been a violation of the rule. Does the current rule give the district court discretion to withhold a sanction notwithstanding a violation of the rule?

3. *The nature of sanctions.* Sanctions can be monetary or nonmonetary, and the availability of or preference for monetary sanctions can alter litigation behavior by those with novel claims or by those who are risk-averse. When monetary sanctions are allowed, should they be based on the attorneys' fees incurred by the side seeking the sanctions? When monetary sactions are allowed, another question arises: to whom should the sanction be paid—the court or the other party? What does the current rule provide as to the nature of sanctions?

4. *The timing of the compliance obligation.* A lawyer's signature on a pleading or motion constitutes a series of representations to the court. But are those representations static—meaning that the certifications are accurate (only) at the time the pleading or motion is filed (the "snap-shot" approach)—or are those representations dynamic and continuing thereafter? Again, review the current rule to understand the lawyer's obligation.

5. *The ability to avoid sanctions.* Reasonable minds differ on whether the lawyer should have notice and an opportunity to correct a sanctionable document before a sanction may be imposed. The current rule has what is referred to as a "safe harbor" provision. When does that safe harbor apply and what—exactly—does it require?

6. *The target of sanctions.* The current rule permits the court to impose a sanction on more than simply the attorney who signed the pleading or motion. Who or what else may be sanctioned?

---

The following case illustrates an application of Federal Rule 11. Use the case to focus, in particular, on exactly what a lawyer certifies to the court when she or he puts her or his signature on a pleading (or motion).

## ■ CHAPLIN v. DUPONT ADVANCE FIBER SYSTEMS

*303 F. Supp. 2d 766 (E.D. Va. 2004), aff'd, 124 Fed. Appx. 771 (4th Cir. 2005)*

HUDSON, District Judge:

[In September 2000, DuPont Advance Fiber Systems, DuPont Spruance, and DuPont Textiles & Interiors, Incorporated (collectively, "DuPont") instituted a policy banning the display of offensive symbols on DuPont property. Included in the policy is a ban on the display of the Confederate battle flag on DuPont's Spruance Plant in Richmond, Virginia. Each of the seven plaintiffs is an employee at DuPont's Spruance plant, and each professes to be a Caucasian, a Christian, and a Confederate Southern American. As a result of DuPont's policy, plaintiffs brought a Title VII action, 42 U.S.C.A. § 2000e et seq., alleging employment discrimination based upon their national origin (Count 1), their religion (Count II), and their race (Count III).

[More specifically, the plaintiffs allege that DuPont committed a number of acts of direct and indirect discrimination against them. At the root of these, it appears, was DuPont's decision, in approximately September of 2000, to issue a ban on the wearing or displaying of Confederate symbols on clothing, newspapers, pictures, photographs, and bumper stickers. Am. Compl. ¶ 40. Thereafter, Jones was ordered to discontinue wearing clothing bearing Confederate symbols. *Id.* at ¶ 39. Lewis was told "it was not a good idea" to wear his Confederate belt buckle. *Id.* at ¶ 41. Oliver was ordered to remove a bumper sticker and window decal from his vehicle. *Id.* at ¶ 42. Ritenour was ordered to remove Confederate bumper stickers from his car "to avoid problems." *Id.* at ¶ 43. Rowlette was told to cease wearing a Confederate t-shirt or risk a reprimand, and he was ordered to sit in the back of the room during an off-site, DuPont-sponsored multi-cultural workshop because he wore such a shirt. *Id.* at ¶ 44. Of his own accord and as a result of the ban, Turley also ceased wearing his Confederate attire. *Id.* at ¶ 45.

[Since then, it appears that each of the plaintiffs has had some discussion with his supervisor about the ban. Defendants' Site Staff Manager, Mike Mayberry ("Mayberry"), is said to have responded, at one time, with a declaration to Chaplin that, "I'm discriminating against you and there ain't nothing you can do about it . . ." Am. Compl. ¶ 40. On another occasion, Mayberry explained to Turley that the ban was imposed because "the Confederate flag has been declared a hate symbol, is used by the Klan, represents slavery and is offensive to some black employees." *Id.* at ¶ 45. Thereafter, Plaintiffs told their supervisors, managers, and/or co-workers that the DuPont ban discriminates against them based on their national origin, their religion, and their race. *Id.* at ¶ 46.

[Additionally, Plaintiffs Oliver, Lewis, and Jones aver that in July of 2001, the defendants denied their request for approval of a "Heritage Preservation Network," which was to be a network for Confederate Southern Americans. *Id.* at ¶ 38. DuPont apparently supports other such networks, similar in nature, for groups of women, African American, Asian American, Italian American, Greek American, Irish American, Native American, Hispanic, and gay and lesbian employees. *Id.* at ¶¶ 38, 48, 49.

[As a result of DuPont's actions, Plaintiffs contend that racial tensions have increased in the plant and that they fear the "potential and dangerous result of this tension." Am. Compl. ¶ 50. Further, DuPont has caused them to "fear the loss of their job and career opportunities," and to suffer from humiliation, embarrassment, and emotional distress. *Id.*

[The District Court for the Eastern District of Virginia dismissed plaintiffs' action as to all counts pursuant to Fed. R. Civ. P. 12(b)(6). Prior to the ruling of the court, DuPont served upon plaintiffs its Rule 11 motion for sanctions, along with a letter requesting that they voluntarily dismiss the action within twenty-one days. Thereafter, when plaintiffs failed to dismiss their claims, DuPont filed its sanctions motion with the district court.]

## . . . I. DEFENDANTS' MOTION FOR RULE 11 SANCTIONS

Within their Rule 11 motion, Defendants argued that Plaintiffs' counsel, Kirk Lyons, Esquire ("Lyons"), should be sanctioned (1) for filing an Amended Complaint that contains claims not warranted by existing law, by a non-frivolous extension, modification, or reversal thereof, or by the establishment of new law; and (2) for filing claims that contain allegations and other factual contentions without current or potential future evidentiary support. At an earlier stage, this Court reviewed Defendants' motion and deferred its ruling pending supplemental briefing on critical sub-issues. Additionally, at that time, the Court raised a third Rule 11 issue, which was whether Lyons's actions, in filing pleadings without having the sponsorship of an attorney admitted to practice in the Eastern District of Virginia, comported with Local Rule 83.1. Subsequently, the parties analyzed all three issues in light of the Rule 11 jurisprudence of the Fourth Circuit.

First, as it relates to pleadings in general, Federal Rule of Civil Procedure 11(b) states that:

> By presenting to the court (whether by signing, filing, submitting, or later advocating) a pleading, written motion, or other paper, an attorney . . . is certifying that to the best of the person's knowledge, information, and belief, formed after an inquiry reasonable under the circumstances,—
>
> (1) it is not being presented for any improper purpose, such as to harass or to cause unnecessary delay or needless increase in the cost of litigation;
>
> (2) the claims, defenses, and other legal contentions therein are warranted by existing law or by a nonfrivolous argument for the extension, modification, or reversal of existing law or the establishment of new law; [and]
>
> (3) the allegations and other factual contentions have evidentiary support or, if specifically so identified, are likely to have evidentiary support after a reasonable opportunity for further investigation or discovery. . . .

Fed. R. Civ. P. 11(b). In other words, whether a civil complaint satisfies the requirements of Rule 11 depends upon how it measures up against three criteria. First, the complaint must be filed for a proper purpose. Second, each count of the complaint must have a sufficient basis in law. And third, each of the claims must have a sufficient basis in fact.

With respect to the first factor, Defendants argue that Plaintiffs' "crusading," repeat litigation of identical claims and subject matter, in the face of a number of adverse rulings from various courts and circuits, supports an inference that the immediate litigation was meant to harass DuPont. Under the circumstances of this case, which emphasizes Plaintiffs' claim of national origin discrimination, the Court does not agree.

Rule 11 "is not intended to chill an attorney's enthusiasm or creativity in pursuing factual or legal theories." *See* Fed. R. Civ. P. 11 (notes of advisory committee on 1983 amendment). Likewise, Rule 11 "does not seek to stifle the exuberant spirit of skilled advocacy or to require that a claim be proven before a complaint can be filed." *Cleveland Demolition Co. v. Azcon Scrap Corp.*, 827 F.2d 984, 988 (4th Cir. 1987). "Creative claims, coupled even with ambiguous or inconsequential facts, may merit dismissal, but not punishment." *Davis v. Carl*, 906 F.2d 533, 538 (11th Cir. 1990).

Here, it is the opinion of the Court that, regardless of the merits of the claims, Lyons's purpose in filing the immediate lawsuit was not to harass DuPont but, rather, to create or expand Title VII jurisprudence. As the Fourth Circuit has said, "if a complaint is filed to vindicate rights in court, and for some other purpose, a court should not sanction counsel for an intention that the court does not approve, so long as the added purpose is not undertaken in bad faith and is not so excessive as to eliminate a proper purpose. Thus, the purpose to vindicate rights in court must be central and sincere." *In re Kunstler*, 914 F.2d 505, 518 (4th Cir. 1990), *cert. denied*, 499 U.S. 969 (1991). Whatever Lyons's collateral intentions were, this Court is convinced that he filed the immediate action, on behalf of the plaintiffs, primarily to broaden the Fourth Circuit's interpretation of "national origin" protection. Consequently, the Court finds no proof that Lyons filed this action for an improper purpose.

Second, Defendants request sanctions because Lyons filed the immediate case in spite of the contrary Fourth Circuit ruling in *Terrill v. Chao*, 31 Fed. Appx. 99, 2002 WL 376681 (4th Cir. 2002) (per curiam), *cert. denied*, 537 U.S. 823 (2002). In so arguing, Defendants remind this Court that, in Terrill, the Fourth Circuit ruled against Lyons when he argued that Title VII included "Confederate Southern American" as a protected class. In light of Terrill, it is Defendants' position that the immediate case "ha[d] absolutely no chance of success under the existing precedent." *Lewin v. Cooke*, 95 F. Supp. 2d 513, 527 (E.D. Va. 2000).

For his part, Lyons concedes that an argument that "has absolutely no chance of success under the existing precedent" may be sanctionable. *Hunter v. Earthgrains Co. Bakery*, 281 F.3d 144, 153 (4th Cir. 2002) (citation omitted). He insists, however, that the precedent precluding the claim must be authoritative. *See Goldstein v. Malcolm G. Fries & Assocs.*, 72 F. Supp. 2d 620, 628 (E.D. Va. 1999). The Fourth Circuit agrees. In *Hogan v. Carter*, 85 F.3d 1113 (4th Cir. 1996), the Fourth Circuit noted that:

> [S]ince unpublished opinions are not even regarded as binding precedent in our circuit, such opinions cannot be considered in deciding whether particular conduct violated clearly established law. . . . We could not allow liability to be imposed . . . based upon unpublished opinions that we ourselves have determined will be binding only upon the parties immediately before the court.

*Id.* at 1118 (refusing to reject qualified immunity based upon an unpublished opinion that was not directly on point). In this case, although the Court has found no authoritative case law anywhere in the nation to support Plaintiffs' claim of national origin discrimination, neither has it found a single, binding case to the contrary. Thus, this Court cannot say that the plaintiffs' claim is "[un]warranted by existing law or by a nonfrivolous argument for the extension, modification, or reversal of existing law or the establishment of new law." Fed. R. Civ. P. 11(b)(2). Thus, Defendants' motion for sanctions will not be granted on that basis.

On the other hand, when compared with the requirements of Rule 11(b)(3), Lyons's Amended Complaint gives this Court great pause. According to Rule 11(b)(3), before filing Plaintiffs' claims, Lyons was required to assure that "the allegations and other factual contentions [therein had] evidentiary support or, if specifically so identified, [were] likely to have evidentiary support. . . ." Fed. R. Civ. P. 11(b)(3). This means that Lyons was required to conduct a reasonable investigation of the factual bases underlying each of his clients' claims before filing them. *See Cleveland Demolition Co.*, 827 F.2d at 987. When there is no factual basis for a particular claim, that claim violates Rule 11(b)(3). *See In re Kunstler*, 914 F.2d at 516.

In this case, Plaintiffs' amended complaint included three allegations. In sum, it averred that DuPont's ban on the display of the Confederate flag discriminated against them based upon their national origin, their religion, and their race. With respect to Count I, Plaintiffs provided the Court with voluminous facts, both supported and unsupported, purporting to back their claim of national origin discrimination. Irrespective of the merits of that claim, it marginally satisfies Rule 11(b)(3).

[With regard to Count II,] however, the Court is convinced that Lyons had absolutely no factual foundation upon which to base a claim of religious discrimination. [N]owhere in the Amended Complaint did Plaintiffs allege that they had both requested and been denied a religious accommodation. Even Plaintiffs' belated letter-writing effort failed to support such a claim. Accordingly, it is the opinion of this Court that Count II is so lacking in reasonable evidentiary support that the Court must impose Rule 11 sanctions for the filing of that claim.

[Likewise,] the Court finds that Plaintiffs' Count III racial discrimination claim is neither factually supported nor supportable. The plaintiffs are all Caucasian, but never once did they suggest that DuPont's policy discriminates, directly or indirectly, against Caucasians. On the contrary, Plaintiffs' averred class, Southern Confederate Americans, is multiracial. This fact alone practically eviscerates Plaintiffs' claim that DuPont discriminated against them on the basis of race. Thus, Plaintiffs' amended complaint contains no factual basis whatsoever to support an allegation that DuPont's ban discriminates by race. Lyons's prefiling inquiry could not have revealed otherwise.

Consequently, . . . it is clear that Count III is both frivolous and unwarranted such that it fails to satisfy the requirements of Rule 11(b)(3). . . . [T]he Court . . . grants the Defendants' motion for sanctions on that count.

The purposes of Rule 11 are to compensate the victims of the violation, to punish present litigation abuse, to streamline court dockets, to facilitate court management, and to deter future litigation abuse. *In re Kunstler*, 914 F.2d at 522-23. Whether Counts II and III are the product of bad faith or just poor judgment, it is the opinion of the Court that each is so devoid of merit as to warrant Rule 11 sanctions. Consequently, although the Court denies Defendants' Rule 11 motion for sanctions with respect to Count I of the Amended Complaint, the motion is granted with respect to Counts II and III. Fed. R. Civ. P. 11(b)(3). . . .

[The Court sanctioned counsel for the plaintiffs in the amount of $10,000.]

## Comments and Questions

1. Rule 11 is not a pleading rule. But (how) does it affect the pleading requirements under Rule 8(a)? Focus, in particular, on 11(b)(3). What role does (and should) *evidence* play in determining the sufficiency of a pleading under Rule 12(b)(6)?

2. If a complaint contains factual allegations that are "specifically . . . identified" as allegations that are likely to "have evidentiary support after a reasonable opportunity for further investigation or discovery," are those allegations included or excluded from the threshold analysis required by *Iqbal*?

3. The safe harbor provision of the new Rule, albeit a procedural technicality of sorts, has generated a substantial amount of litigation. Most of these disputes regard circumstances where a litigant has won the case and, thereafter, pursues sanctions, seeking some sort of compensation (or retribution) for the expense and delay caused by the other party's baseless assertions and/or arguments. However, unless the moving party also complied with the safe harbor provisions—thereby giving the other party the opportunity to withdraw or otherwise cure—the court will typically deny the motion. *See, e.g., Lawrence v. Richman Group of LT LLC*, 620 F.3d 153 (2d Cir. 2010); *Roth v. Green*, 466 F.3d 1179, 1193 (10th Cir. 2006).

4. Importantly, the "safe harbor" does not apply when a court awards a sanction on its own initiative. Most circuit courts have held that a *sua sponte* award of sanctions requires the issuance of a show cause order and a reasonable opportunity to respond. *See, e.g., Brunig v. Clark*, 560 F.3d 292 (5th Cir. 2009); *Laurino v. Tate*, 220 F.3d 1213 (10th Cir. 2000). Moreover, *sua sponte* sanctions are to be examined closely because of the unavailability of a "safe harbor." *Hunter v. Earthgrains Co. Bakery*, 281 F.3d 144 (4th Cir. 2002); *In re Pennie & Edmonds, LLP*, 323 F.3d 86 (2d Cir. 2003).

5. Several cases have suggested that it is not necessary to find that an attorney acted in bad faith in order to assess sanctions under Rule 11. *See, e.g., Hochen v. Bobst Group, Inc.*, 198 F.R.D. 11 (D. Mass. 2000) (violation of Rule 11 may be the result of inexperience, incompetence, willfulness, or deliberate choice), *aff'd sub nom. Nyer v. Winterthur Intl.*, 290 F.3d 456 (1st Cir. 2002). The fact that an attorney has done a good deal of prefiling investigation (150 hours, for example) does not relieve her of potential sanctions when her client's own deposition shows that her case is without factual merit. *Mercury Air Group, Inc. v. Mansour et al.*, 237 F.3d 542 (5th Cir. 2001).

In the *Earthgrains* case mentioned previously, the Fourth Circuit demonstrated how carefully it will review a district court's *sua sponte* Rule 11 sanction (in that case a lawyer's suspension of practice for five years in the Western District of North Carolina) when based on an allegedly frivolous contention of law. The plaintiff's lawyer had asserted that she could file a Title VII employment discrimination case in federal court, notwithstanding a mandatory arbitration clause in the applicable collective bargaining agreement. The lawyer had argued that the collective bargaining agreement was not sufficiently specific as to this particular cause of action, and that language in a previous U.S. Supreme Court opinion supported her view of the law. A decision in the Fourth Circuit, the circuit in question, was contrary to the lawyer's position. Other circuit courts disagreed with the Fourth Circuit (thus supporting the lawyer), and ultimately the Supreme Court probably agreed with the lawyer's position. In reversing the lower court's Rule 11 sanction, the Fourth Circuit provided several comforting quotes for lawyers attempting novel claims. "[T]he legal . . . argument must have 'absolutely no chance of success under the existing precedent.' . . . Although a legal claim may be so inartfully pled that it cannot survive a motion to dismiss, such a flaw will not in itself support Rule 11 sanctions—only the lack of any legal or factual basis is sanctionable." The circuit court cited a previous opinion of its chief judge suggesting that if it were forbidden to argue a position contrary to precedent, "the parties and counsel who in the early 1950's brought the case of *Brown v. Board of Ed.* . . . might have been thought by some district court to have engaged in sanctionable conduct for pursuing their claims in the face of the contrary precedent of *Plessy v. Ferguson*. . . ." 281 F.3d at 156.

6. Several studies might be read to indicate that the 1983-1993 version of Rule 11 was dramatically pro-defendant and particularly detrimental to plaintiffs in civil rights cases. Some are summarized in Georgene M. Vairo, *Rule 11: Where We Are and Where We Are Going*, 60 Fordham L. Rev. 475 (1991). Perhaps the most thorough study of the operation of the 1983 Rule 11 is the report of a task force of the U.S. Court of Appeals for the Third Circuit published by the American Judicature Society in *Rule 11 in Transition: The Report of the Third Circuit Task Force on Federal Rule of Civil Procedure 11* (Stephen B. Burbank, Reporter, 1989). Among other things, the Third Circuit study examined all Rule 11 motions in the Third Circuit for one year, and found that "motions for sanctions under the Rule were made in only approximately one half of one percent of the civil cases in the district courts of the Third Circuit. . . ." *Id.* at xiii. "In assessing the costs and benefits of Rule 11 in the Third Circuit, the Task Force found evidence in responses to its attorney questionnaire and in interviews with attorneys that the Rule has had widespread effects on conduct of the sort hoped for by the rulemakers and other evidence that it has yielded benefits (*e.g.*, contributing to case dismissal or settlement). . . . It also found that directly associated costs (such as, the costs of litigating Rule 11 issues to litigants and courts) do not appear to be clearly incommensurate with probable benefits. . . ." *Id.* at xiv.

But the Third Circuit Task Force also reported:

According to the data from our survey, sanctions are imposed pursuant to 13.6% (18/132) of Rule 11 motions. . . . Plaintiffs (and/or their counsel) are the "targets" of 66.7% (88/132) of such motions . . . ; defendants (and/or their counsel) of 33.3% (44/132). Plaintiffs are sanctioned pursuant to 15.9% (14/88) of the motions made against them . . . ; defendants pursuant to 9.1% (4/44) of the motions made against them. . . . Civil rights and employment discrimination cases account for 18.2% (24/132) of the Rule 11 motions in the survey. . . . Plaintiffs are the "targets" of 70.8% (17/24) of the motions in such cases . . . , and they are sanctioned pursuant to 47.1% (8/17) of such motions. . . .

*Id.* at 57. It is important to note that the Third Circuit Task Force found that "[r]equests for sanctions in civil rights cases constituted only a slightly larger slice of our pie (24/132 or 18.2%) than one would expect on the basis of civil filings in this circuit (16% of civil filings in the period [were civil rights cases]. . . ." *Id.* at 69.

What might be the reasons that Rule 11 sanctions were sought more frequently against plaintiffs than defendants, and that civil rights plaintiffs may be sanctioned substantially more frequently (47.1% compared to 8.45% in the Third Circuit for one year) than other plaintiffs? *Id.* at 69. Are there possible legitimate reasons? Even after the 1993 amendments, Rule 11 may be having an unjust chilling effect on civil rights plaintiffs. *See* Danielle Kie Hart, *Still Chilling After All These Years: Rule 11 of the Federal Rules of Civil Procedures and Its Impact on Civil Rights Plaintiffs After the 1993 Amendments*, 37 Val. U. L. Rev. 1 (2002). If a reformer were (1) concerned about an adverse chilling effect on civil rights plaintiffs, but (2) thought Rule 11 was generally salutary, what changes would she propose? To whom should such a proposal be made? This might be a good time for you to revisit yet again the exact language of the Rules Enabling Act.

7. Why is the Advisory Committee reluctant to see Rule 11 as a fee-shifting device? What is wrong with the goal of compensation in addition to that of deterrence? Is the Committee afraid that attorneys will bring questionable Rule 11 motions? Wouldn't the threat of a countermotion under Rule 11 take care of that?

8. In 1993 the Judicial Conference of the United States recommended that the amendments to Rule 11 (and other rules) be approved by the Supreme Court and transmitted to Congress. The Supreme Court submitted the amendments (without change) to the Congress, but noted that the transmittal did not "necessarily indicate that the Court itself would have proposed these amendments in the form submitted." Letter from William H. Rehnquist, Chief Justice of the U.S. Supreme Court, to Thomas S. Foley, Speaker of the House of Representatives (April 22, 1993), reprinted in 146 F.R.D. 403 (1993). The transmittal of the Promulgated Rules was accompanied by a statement from Justice White challenging the wisdom of the current rule-making process, and a dissent from Justice Scalia (joined by Justice Thomas with respect to amendments to Rule 11) challenging the wisdom of the proposed amendments. *Id.* at 507. With regard to the 1993 amendment to Rule 11, Justice Scalia wrote:

It is undeniably important to the Rules' goal of "the just, speedy, and inexpensive determination of every action," Fed. R. Civ. P. 1, that frivolous pleadings and motions be deterred. The current [1983-1993] Rule 11 achieves that objective by requiring sanctions when its standards are violated (though leaving the court broad discretion as to the manner of sanction), and by allowing compensation for the moving party's expenses and attorney's fees. The proposed revision would render the Rule toothless, by allowing judges to dispense with sanction, by disfavoring compensation for litigation expenses, and by providing a 21-day "safe harbor" within which, if the party accused of a frivolous filing withdraws the filing, he is entitled to escape with no sanction at all.

To take the last first: In my view, those who file frivolous suits and pleadings should have no "safe harbor." The Rules should be solicitous of the abused (the courts and the opposing party), and not of the abuser. Under the revised Rule, parties will be able to file thoughtless, reckless, and harassing pleadings, secure in the knowledge that they have nothing to lose: If objection is raised, they can retreat without penalty. The proposed revision contradicts what this Court said only three years ago: "Baseless filing puts the machinery of justice in motion, burdening courts and individuals alike with needless expense and delay. Even if the careless litigant quickly dismisses the action, the harm triggering Rule 11's concerns has already occurred. Therefore a litigant who violates Rule 11 merits sanctions even after a dismissal." *Cooter & Gell v. Hartmarx Corp.*, 496 U.S. 384, 398 (1990). The advisory committee itself was formerly of the same view. *Ibid.* (quoting Letter from Chairman, Advisory Committee on Civil Rules).

The proposed Rule also decreases both the likelihood and the severity of punishment for those foolish enough not to seek refuge in the safe harbor after an objection is raised. Proposed subsection (c) makes the issuance of any sanction discretionary, whereas currently it is *required*. Judges, like other human beings, do not like imposing punishment when their duty does not require it, especially upon their own acquaintances and members of their own profession. They do not immediately see, moreover, the system-wide benefits of serious Rule 11 sanctions, though they are intensely aware of the amount of their own time it would take to consider and apply sanctions in the case before them. For these reasons, I think it important to the effectiveness of the scheme that the sanctions remain mandatory.

Finally, the likelihood that frivolousness will even be *challenged* is diminished by the proposed Rule, which restricts the award of compensation to "unusual circumstances," with monetary sanctions "ordinarily" to be payable to the court. Advisory Committee Notes to Proposed Rule 11, pp 53-54. Under Proposed Rule 11(c)(2),* a court may order payment for "some or all of the reasonable attorneys' fees and other expenses incurred as a direct result of the violation" only when that is "warranted for effective deterrence." Since the deterrent effect of a fine is rarely increased by altering the identity of the payee, it takes imagination to conceive of instances in which this provision will ever apply. And the commentary makes it clear that even when compensation is granted it should be granted stingily—only for costs "directly and unavoidably caused by the violation." *Id.* at 54. As seen from the viewpoint of the victim of an abusive litigator, these revisions convert Rule 11 from a means of obtaining compensation to an invitation to throw good money after bad. The net effect is to decrease the incentive on the part of the person best situated to alert the court to perversion of our civil justice system.

---

*Eds.' Note:* This portion of the rule now appears at Fed. R. Civ. P. 11(c)(4).

I would not have registered this dissent if there were convincing indication that the current Rule 11 regime is ineffective, or encourages excessive satellite litigation. But there appears to be general agreement, reflected in a recent report of the advisory committee itself, that Rule 11, as written, basically works. According to that report, a Federal Judicial Center survey showed that 80% of district judges believe Rule 11 has had an overall positive effect and should be retained in its present form, 95% believed the Rule had not impeded development of the law, and about 75% said the benefits justify the expenditure of judicial time. *See* "Interim Report on Rule 11, Advisory Committee on Civil Rules," reprinted in Georgene M. Vairo, *Rule 11 Sanctions: Case Law Perspectives and Preventive Measures*, App. I-8-I-10 (2d ed. 1991). True, many lawyers do not like Rule 11. It may cause them financial liability, it may damage their professional reputation in front of important clients, and the cost-of-litigation savings it produces are savings not to lawyers but to litigants. But the overwhelming approval of the Rule by the federal district judges who daily grapple with the problem of litigation abuse is enough to persuade me that it should not be gutted as the proposed revision suggests. . . .

9. Would Randall Dee's motion to dismiss for failure to state a claim be sanctionable under Rule 11?

10. Is the complaint in *Iqbal* sanctionable?

11. In 1982, Professor John Oakley of the University of California used a nine-variable test to determine which states had procedural rules that "replicated" the Federal Rules. He found that in 1975, Massachusetts became the last of twenty-two states plus the District of Columbia to conform its procedure substantially to the Federal Rules through judicially promulgated rules; if one included statutorily adopted versions of the Federal Rules, there were four additional states, making a total of twenty-six. However, of the ten most populous states, only Ohio was a replica state. John B. Oakley and Arthur F. Coon, *The Federal Rules in State Courts: A Survey of State Court Systems of Civil Procedure*, 61 Wash. L. Rev. 1367 (1986). *See also* John B. Oakley, *A Fresh Look at the Federal Rules in State Courts*, 3 Nev. L.J. 354 (Winter 2002/2003).

The influence of the Federal Rules procedural system is even more widespread, however. The most important attributes of the Federal Rules—merger of law and equity, relative ease of pleading and amendment, liberal joinder of parties and theories, broad discovery, and summary judgment—are part of the rules governing civil litigation in courts of general jurisdiction in virtually every state. *See* Thomas O. Main, *Procedural Uniformity and the Exaggerated Role of Rules*, 46 Vill. L. Rev. 311 (2001).

Because many states have replicated the federal model for their own state rules of civil procedure, these states must decide with every amendment to the Federal Rules whether also to adopt the federal amendments. If you were a member of a state Advisory Committee on Civil Rules, would you urge adoption of the 1983 amendment to Rule 11? Is amending Rule 8(a) a better means to achieve the ends sought by the recent amendment to Rule 11? What are the advantages of uniform state and federal rules? Does intra-state procedural uniformity compromise other procedural values?

12. The materials in this chapter lend the impression that there is an abundance of frivolous litigation in the present court system. This may or may not be true. Because there has been little data collected regarding the behavior of the court system, no one really knows. Michael Saks, a law professor at Arizona State University, summarized much of the literature on this subject in the seminal law review article, *Do We Really Know Anything About the Behavior of the Tort Litigation System—And Why Not?*, 140 U. Pa. L. Rev. 1147 (1992). His introductory words epitomize the article: "Much of what we know about the tort litigation system is untrue, unknown, or unknowable." *Id.*

13. Rule 11 is not the only means to sanction improper conduct in the federal courts. Because Rule 11 is inapplicable to discovery disputes (*see* Rule 11(d)), courts use Rule 37 to enforce the discovery rules. Further, 28 U.S.C. § 1927 permits the court to make attorneys liable for excessive "costs, expenses and attorneys fees reasonably incurred because of such unreasonable and vexatious conduct." *Id.* A court can also "rely on its inherent power" to impose appropriate sanctions to control its proceedings. *Chambers v. NASCO, Inc.*, 501 U.S. 32, 50 (1991).

14. The 1993 Advisory Committee Notes elaborate on the variety of non-monetary sanctions available for a Rule 11 violation. These sanctions include (1) striking the offending paper; (2) issuing an admonition; (3) requiring participation in seminars or other educational programs; and (4) referring the matter to disciplinary authorities. Some judges have been more creative. *See, e.g., Patsy's Brand, Inc. v. I.O.B. Realty, Inc.*, Misc. Action No. 02-194, 2002 WL 59434 (S.D.N.Y. Jan. 16, 2002) (requiring dissemination of the district court's opinion to each lawyer in the represented firm, accompanied by a memorandum regarding ethics); *Balthazar v. Atlantic City Med. Center*, 279 F. Supp. 2d 574, 595 (D.N.J. 2003) (ordering plaintiff's counsel to attend and complete two continuing legal education courses, one in court practice and procedure and one in attorney professionalism); *Curran v. Price*, 150 F.R.D. 85 (D. Md. 1993) (ordering counsel to copy, in his own handwriting, a chapter of a procedure treatise).

Of course there are limits on a trial judge's discretion to sanction. *See In re Tutu Wells Contamination Litig.*, 120 F.3d 368, 381-385 (3d Cir. 1997) (district court did not have power to require sanctioned party to contribute to halfway house, since sanction was legislative in nature); *Whelan v. Heffler, Radetich & Saitta, LLP*, No. 3:99-CV-0337-P, 1999 WL 818749 at *5 (N.D. Tex. Oct. 13, 1999) (lifetime permanent injunction enjoining attorney from local bankruptcy practice was excessive).

## Practice Exercise No. 12: Reviewing the *City of Cleveland* Complaint Under Rule 11

Re-read the introductory memorandum in the *City of Cleveland* Case Files and prepare to discuss at a firm strategy session whether a partner can safely sign and file the complaint (in the Case Files) in light of the requirements of current Rule 11. Consider all four counts of the complaint, and be prepared to advise what, if any, additional factual or legal investigation is needed as to any count. The partner realizes that current Fed. R. Civ. P. 11 has a "safe harbor" provision, but she does not want to be forced to withdraw or amend portions of the complaint if the defendants make a Rule 11 motion for sanctions. Are there any allegations in the complaint for which the partner should use the hedging language permitted by Fed. R. Civ. P. 11(b)(3)? Do not concern yourself at this time with the class action aspects of the complaint. Assume that both the specific factual information in the introductory memorandum and the specific factual allegations in the complaint are true and have ample evidentiary support.

## G. SIMPLE JOINDER

When drafting a complaint, a lawyer must think not only about her causes of action or claims, but also about how many claims to join against the same defendant, and how many plaintiffs and defendants to include in one suit. As usual, there are three different types of questions: What must I do? What may I do? And what should I do?

In federal court, the breadth of permissible joinder of claims is fairly simple. Fed. R. Civ. P. 18 provides that a plaintiff can include as many claims against a defendant as she wants, even if they are totally unrelated. You can sue someone for breaching a contract with you, slandering you, defrauding you, and negligently running you over, even if these happened on different dates and are not connected in any way. Rule 42(b), however, allows a judge to separate claims for trial for reasons of convenience, avoiding prejudice, and economy. When you later study *res judicata* and claim preclusion, you will find that the joinder of claims is a bit less friendly than Rule 18 implies. If you do not bring all of your potential causes of action and remedies that arise from the same transaction at the same time (sometimes called "splitting your claim"), a final judgment will normally result in your not being able to bring those other causes of action or remedies later.

This concept of "transaction" pervades joinder issues, as well as other questions in federal procedure. At common law and under the Field Code, joinder of both claims and parties in law cases was severely limited. The joinder provisions, and the interpretation of those provisions by most courts, tended to prohibit joinder unless the writs or causes of action were the same and unless there were joint interests or joint ownership between the plaintiffs or defendants who were to be joined. In equity, the courts tended to permit, and often require, the joinder of all parties who played a part in the underlying factual situation giving rise to the litigation and of all equitable claims falling within that fact pattern. (In later equity practice, legal claims could be joined to equity claims in equity court.) Convenience was the key, rather than strict analytic cubbyholes such as provided by writs. Rule 26 of the Federal Equity Rules of 1912 had a catchall provision that permitted joinder of causes of action if "sufficient grounds . . . appear[ed] for uniting causes of action in order to promote the convenient administration of justice." The Rule ended with language familiar to the current federal court litigator: "If it appears that any such causes of action cannot be conveniently disposed of together, the court may order separate trials."

Rule 20, covering the permissive joinder of parties, is, like the pleading provisions and Rule 18, a further example of how Charles Clark and the others who drafted the Federal Rules attempted to liberalize litigation practice by making it more permissive, flexible, and inclusive. Once again, they turned to an idea prevalent in equity practice, the seeking of a convenient litigation package, rather than worrying whether the causes of action were identical. Rule 20 requires that the persons joining or joined in an action have rights "arising out of the same transaction, occurrence, or series of transactions or occurrences," and that there be a common "question of law or fact." Rule 20(b) permits the court to separate parties for purposes of trial or otherwise.

You have previously encountered the terms "transaction" and "occurrence" (along with "conduct") in Rule 15(c), with respect to whether an amendment subsequent to the expiration of the statute of limitations can "relate back" to the date of the original pleading. "Transaction" and "occurrence" appear again in Rule 13's definition of compulsory counterclaims, identifying claims that must be brought with an answer or otherwise be waived; in defining permissible "cross-claims" (claims between co-defendants) in Rule 13(g); and in portions of Rule 14, covering third-party practice. You have already read how this concept of the "same transaction" sets the contours for modern claim preclusion law. When you study subject matter jurisdiction, you will learn how the concept of pendent jurisdiction (now called supplemental jurisdiction) also looks to the underlying transaction in order to discern whether a state claim that lacks subject matter jurisdiction on its own can be constitutionally "appended" to a companion federal question claim; basically, if they arise from the same transaction (for this purpose called "the same nucleus of operative facts," which may be somewhat different from the same transaction), the state claim can ride the back of the federal, and stay in federal court.

Consequently, it is important that you begin to learn to make arguments about what constitutes the same transaction or occurrence. The courts tend to look to whether there is a sufficient overlap of facts or evidence, and to whether claims are logically related to each other. You will want to emphasize different points dependent on the purpose of the Rule's use of the term "transaction." For example, is the Rule or concept that utilizes a transactional test in your case concerned with efficiency, fairness, convenience, or constitutional restraint? It is conclusory (which is bad in legal discourse) just to say that claims obviously arise from the same underlying transaction or obviously are related. You must learn to support this conclusion with analysis of exactly which facts and which evidence are the same for distinct claims or distinct parties. In close cases, trial judges will want to know why it will be convenient, efficient, or fair for the court or the parties to keep the claims joined: exactly which evidence will not have to be entered twice, precisely which witnesses would otherwise have to be inconvenienced multiple times.

Another Rule associated with these Rules, Rule 21, permits the court to drop or add any dispensable party on its own initiative or as a result of a motion by any party. Because this Rule is very straightforward, this chapter does not provide a case for illustration. Simply put, Rule 21 permits the court to drop or add any non-necessary party at any stage in the action on any terms "as are just." Further, the court may sever any claim against any party and proceed with the severed claim separately.

# ■ LOPEZ v. CITY OF IRVINGTON
### *2008 WL 565776 (D.N.J. Feb. 28, 2008)*

GREENAWAY, JR., District Judge:

This matter comes before this Court on the motion of Defendants City of Irvington (the "City"), Irvington Police Department (the "PD"), Alfredo Aleman ("Aleman"), and Christopher Burrell ("Burrell") (collectively "Defendants"), to sever the trial of Plaintiffs Jaime Lopez ("Lopez"), Arnold Daniels ("Daniels"), Willie McKenzie ("McKenzie"), and Hilbert Gresham ("Gresham") (collectively "Plaintiffs"), pursuant to Fed. R. Civ. P. 21. For the reasons set forth below, Defendants' motion is denied.

## I. BACKGROUND

On November 4, 2005, Plaintiffs filed a Complaint alleging, inter alia, that the City of Irvington and the Irvington Police Department "fail[ed] to properly supervise and monitor [the] K-9 Unit [of the PD,] and in particular its officer Alfredo Aleman. . . ." (Compl.3.) Plaintiffs argue that as a result of such failure, the City and PD "allow[ed] for a pattern and practice of conduct to exist whereby various suspected felons, while in custody and control of law enforcement officers[,]" were mauled, maimed, and disfigured by Bullet, a canine under Defendant Aleman's control.

Specifically, Plaintiff Lopez claims that he was attacked by Defendant Aleman and Bullet. The parties agree that on or about May 2, 2004 Lopez was engaged in a burglary when Aleman apprehended and arrested him. At the time of the arrest, Aleman "was the [c]anine handler [ ] of the K-9 Bullet." Lopez alleges, and Defendants dispute, that during the arrest Aleman kicked Lopez in the ribs, and held him down on the floor while Bullet "bit [Lopez] and tore flesh from his left arm." Lopez also claims that Aleman ordered Bullet to "get" him. Finally, Lopez claims that after he was handcuffed and placed in the back seat of a squad car, "Aleman released Bullet into the back seat with the doors closed[,] and watched as the dog tore into [Lopez's] body and left shoulder."

Next, Plaintiff Daniels claims that he was attacked by Bullet on June 29, 2005. The parties agree that Daniels was arrested while "in the attic of an unoccupied house . . . for crimes associated with entry into the unoccupied house." Daniels alleges, and Defendants dispute, that he followed the directions of the police officers involved in the arrest. In addition, Daniels states that Defendant Aleman grabbed and threw him to the ground. At this time, Daniels claims, that Bullet bit him. Daniels also alleges that Aleman picked Daniels up, threw him against a wall, and held him down while instructing Bullet to "get" him. It was at Aleman's command that Bullet "repeatedly bit [Daniels'] legs." Daniels claims that even after he was handcuffed, he continued to be bitten by Bullet.

Plaintiff McKenzie alleges that he was also attacked by Bullet. The parties agree that "[o]n or about August 24, 2005, . . . [McKenzie] was observed exiting from a stolen vehicle and was pursued, apprehended and arrested by police with the assistance of K-9 Police Dog, Bullet." McKenzie claims, and Defendants dispute, that after he was handcuffed, "Defendant[ ] Aleman released Bullet to attack [McKenzie] by biting and tearing at him."

The next day, August 25, 2005, Plaintiff Gresham alleges that Bullet attacked him. The parties agree that "[o]n or about August 25, 2005, Plaintiff Gresham ran from police officers and was eventually caught, arrested by police with the assistance of K-9 Police Dog Bullet. . . ." Gresham also argues, and Defendants dispute, that "[a]fter being handcuffed by police, Defendant [ ] Aleman released Bullet to attack [Gresham]. [Gresham] was bitten and ripped at by the dog."

Defendants filed the instant motion to sever seeking to separate the trial of each Plaintiff. Defendants argue that Plaintiffs' claims should be severed because the claims "do not arise out of the same transaction or occurrence," and because "Defendants will be seriously prejudiced by the fact that each of the plaintiff's [sic] will not be subject to sequestration thus restricting and otherwise harnessing efforts to prevent them from parroting each other's testimony."

## II. STANDARD OF REVIEW

"A district court has broad discretion in deciding whether to sever a party pursuant to Federal Rule of Civil Procedure 21." *Boyer v. Johnson Matthey, Inc.*, No. 02-8382, 2004 U.S. Dist. LEXIS 9802, *3, 2004 WL 835082 (E.D.Pa. Apr. 16, 2004). . . . "Rule 21 is 'most commonly invoked to sever parties improperly joined under Rule 20.'" *Id.* at *4. However, the Rule may also be invoked to prevent prejudice or promote judicial efficiency. . . . Official Comm. of Unsecured Creditors v. Shapiro, 190 F.R.D. 352, 355 (E.D. Pa.2000) (stating that Rule 21 also "may be used to organize problematic issues other than joinder problems").

In order to determine whether plaintiffs have been misjoined, a court must decide whether "they assert any right to relief jointly, severally, or in the alternative with respect to or arising out of the same transaction, occurrence, or a series of transactions or occurrences[,] and [ ] any question of law or fact common to all plaintiffs will arise in the action." Fed. R. Civ. P. 20(a)(1). . . . "Both the same transaction(s) and the common question elements must be satisfied before joinder can be permitted." . . .

"[C]ourts generally apply a case-by-case approach" when considering whether the facts of several claims constitute a single transaction or occurrence, or a series of transactions or occurrences. "'Transaction' is a word of flexible meaning[, and] may comprehend a series of many occurrences, depending not so much upon the immediateness of their connection as upon their logical relationship." . . . The second element, however, "does not require precise congruence of all factual and legal issues; indeed, joinder may be permissible if there is but one question of law or fact common to the parties."

Once the court has resolved these threshold questions, it may then consider additional factors in determining whether to grant a motion to sever. These factors include (1) whether the issues sought to be tried separately are significantly different from one another, (2) whether the separable issues require the testimony of different witnesses and different documentary proof, (3) whether the party opposing the severance will be prejudiced if it is granted, and (4) whether the party requesting the severance will be prejudiced if it is not granted.

### III. DISCUSSION

First, Defendants argue that Plaintiffs are misjoined because the "factual predicate surrounding each apprehensi[on] and arrest do not arise out of the same transaction or occurrence[, and the plaintiffs] were arrested on different days at different locations by different officers." Plaintiffs counter and argue that "[t]he actions of these four plaintiffs arise from a similar series of transactions or occurrences, and common questions of law and fact will arise in the trial of the action." This Court finds Plaintiffs' position more persuasive.

Plaintiffs claim that the City and PD "failed to properly supervise and monitor its K-9 Unit," and as a result of such failure, permitted a pattern or practice of excessive force to exist among the police officers of the K-9 unit. Each Plaintiffs' [sic] example of excessive force is alleged to have resulted from this pattern or practice. (Compl. 4) (stating that "[s]uch actions were so significant and so similar in nature as to indicate such a pattern and practice of accepted conduct by defendant[ ] Aleman[,] including the handcuffing of such suspects prior to the K-9 dogs being let loose to maul, maim and disfigure the suspects."). . . . "Other courts [within this circuit] have found the common transaction element met when the plaintiffs alleged that a pattern or practice of discrimination existed." . . . This Court, therefore, finds that the allegations in the Complaint arise from the same transaction, occurrence, or series of transactions or occurrences.

Similarly, this Court finds that there exists a common question of law or fact. Although Plaintiffs allegedly suffered different incidents of force, by different police officers and at different times and locations, the allegation of a pattern or practice of excessive force is a common question of fact central to each claim. *See also Boyer*, 2004 U.S. Dist. LEXIS 9802, at *8, 2004 WL 835082 ("Though Plaintiffs allegedly suffered different incidents of discrimination, some occurring on different work shifts, at the hands of different supervisors, and at different times, the purported existence of a discriminatory pattern or practice is a common question of fact that Plaintiffs' claims share."). . . .

Second, Defendants argue that they will be seriously prejudiced if this Court does not sever Plaintiffs' claims. However, Defendants do not offer any persuasive indication of prejudice.

When considering a motion to sever, a court may consider the following factors: (1) whether the issues sought to be tried separately are significantly different from one another, (2) whether the separable issues require the testimony of different witnesses and different documentary proof, (3) whether the party opposing the severance will be prejudiced if it is granted, and (4) whether the party requesting the severance will be prejudiced if it is not granted. Applying these factors to the case sub judice, this Court finds that the factors weigh in favor of denying the motion.

The first factor, regarding the issues sought to be tried separately, has been discussed above. Plaintiffs each allege that Defendants engaged in a pattern or practice of excessive force. Similarly, each Plaintiff alleges that the attacks by Bullet indicate that the City and PD failed to supervise the officers of the K-9 unit.

Next, and by Defendants' own admission, several witnesses are common to each Plaintiffs' [sic] claim. For example, Defendants Aleman and Burrell, and Sergeant Burghardt are witnesses to the allegations underlying Plaintiffs Lopez's and Gresham's claims. Defendant Aleman and Sergeant Burghardt are also witnesses to Plaintiff Daniels' claims. Officer Love is a witness to Plaintiffs Lopez's and Daniels' claims; and Defendants Aleman and Burrell are witnesses to Plaintiff McKenzie's claims. Although there are other witnesses to each of the plaintiffs' claims, there is significant overlap.

Finally, this Court finds that Plaintiffs will be prejudiced if the motion is granted, while Defendants will not be prejudiced if the motion is denied. Because Plaintiffs have alleged a pattern or practice of excessive force, they will need to provide the jury with sufficient evidence to meet their burden that a pattern or practice actually existed. This will be difficult, if not impossible, if separate trials commence. In addition, Defendants have offered no support for their allegation of prejudice.

## IV. Conclusion

For the foregoing reasons, the motion of Defendants City of Irvington, Irvington Police Department, Alfredo Aleman, and Christopher Burrell, to sever Plaintiffs Jaime Lopez, Arnold Daniels, Willie McKenzie, and Hilbert Gresham, pursuant to Fed. R. Civ. P. 21, is denied.

## Comments and Questions

1. Use this case as an opportunity to truly "get your hands dirty" with facts and with the precise application of doctrine to those facts. Exactly why could these plaintiffs be joined? A major difference between good and sloppy legal analysis is whether the lawyer is excruciatingly precise with what particular facts make the doctrine apply. For example, don't just say that it's the "same transaction, occurrence, or series of transactions or occurrences," and that there is a "question of law or fact common to all" the persons who have been joined. Prove your points to a skeptic by including the particular facts in the case. Much of civil procedure is proving the commonality of events that happened to different people. One way to focus your analysis is to ask which particular facts and legal questions are relevant to each element of each cause of action that applies to each party. For instance, think about the case of *Joe v. Sally* from the beginning of this chapter. Assume that Sally allegedly tripped Mary the following day. It is difficult to come up with any overlapping questions of law or fact, or any commonality of transaction, without going to such a level of generality that a judge would dismiss the commonality out of hand. You could argue that a common question of law is whether tripping can ever be intentional (or an act of unreasonable care), but surely a more precise bit of commonality is required by either the same transaction test or the "common question of law or fact" test in Rule 20.

One reason we have given you *Carpenter v. Dee* is to provide you a set of facts that you can return to in order to prove to yourself that you can apply procedural rules. Can Nancy Carpenter join the various causes of action and theories you came up with in former assignments? What if Randall Dee owed Charlie Carpenter $1000 on a debt unrelated to the jeep or the accident? Could the plaintiff join that claim? What if Randall Dee had borrowed $1000 from Nancy Carpenter after the accident and now refuses to repay that debt. Can she join that claim in her complaint? Can she join Randall Dee, his brother, Ultimate Auto (where Dee bought the oversize tires and suspension lift kit), McGill's Garage, Inc. (where the jeep passed inspection), the City of Lowell (whose police evidently let the infractions relating to height pass without comment), and the manufacturer of the tires (assuming you can come up with a cause of action) as defendants in the same case? Prove your conclusion—using specific facts! What if Scott was injured in a similar incident a week later by Keefe, who also bought tires and a suspension lift kit from Ultimate Auto and lifted his jeep in the same manner? Can Carpenter and Scott draft one complaint against Ultimate Auto—a joinder of plaintiffs? What if Randall Dee and Keefe were racing their jeeps against each other when each tipped, injuring Charlie Carpenter and Scott? Could Nancy Carpenter and Scott join in a suit against Dee, Keefe, and Ultimate Auto? At the beginning of the course, we wrote that learning procedure permits you to exercise a great deal of imagination by considering "what ifs." Get in the habit of constructing your own hypotheticals to analyze alone or with your study group. The facts of the jeep case and the Cleveland firefighters case are rich with potential hypotheticals.

2. Rules 18 and 20 do not mention other procedural rules, concepts, and laws that might impose their own restraints, but those restraints are present. For instance, the Advisory Committee Notes to Rule 18 remind lawyers that jurisdictional and venue requirements must still be met. Issues of subject matter jurisdiction, personal jurisdiction, venue, and notice would of course apply to each party joined under Rule 20 as well. These topics are covered elsewhere in the course. Moreover, although Rule 18 (joinder of claims) is permissive, you must consider another field of civil procedure to decide what causes of action or theories to join. For example, in the case of *Joe v. Sally*, what would happen if Joe sued for battery and omitted negligence? Let's say Sally wins, and the case goes to final judgment. Could Joe then sue Sally again in negligence for the same tripping? Maybe you should put *res judicata* or *preclusion* in the margin of Rule 18 to remind yourself that the law does not allow as much permissiveness as Rule 18 would lead you to believe.

3. As previously mentioned, throughout the course you should keep a very close watch on the expression "transaction or occurrence"—the phrase is a malleable guideline, but it is also a favorite of the drafters of the Federal Rules. Pay special attention to *which* rules use the phrase and notice *how* (as explained in the appellate holdings). Why did Charles Clark use a concept such as "transaction" as his unit of measure for the limits of joinder? What role does this "transactional" approach play in the overall philosophy of the Federal Rules? Why did the common law procedure inherently have much more limited joinder of claims and parties? Why would Field have wanted less joinder, particularly if he knew the types of cases brought today? When making arguments to courts, lawyers often go to the rationale of a rule in order to convince the court of the rule/application they want on the facts of the case. In *Lopez*, do the plaintiffs have policy arguments that would help them convince the court of a broad meaning for "transaction, occurrence, or series of transactions or occurrences"?

4. Strategic considerations matter in deciding how many claims and parties to try to put in any one lawsuit. For example, the size of the lawsuit will have a tremendous impact on (1) discovery (e.g., interrogatories can only be sent to actual parties of the suit); (2) costs (e.g., the more parties and theories, the more discovery and the more costs to your client); (3) evidence (e.g., different hearsay restrictions and altering what is relevant evidence depend on what claims and parties you have joined); (4) the jury (e.g., you may or may not want several defendants all pointing at each other, or you

may or may not want to associate yourself with another party whose case or personality may rub off on your client); (5) *res judicata* (e.g., you may not want all of your eggs in one basket, but you don't want to be barred from plausible claims); and (6) control (e.g., with more parties it may or may not be harder to settle, depending on how you assess the situation; more defendants mean more pockets from which to pay your client, but may also mean that no one of them will want to give very much; more parties may also mean more lawyers who want to control the litigation in various ways). Use *Lopez* and *Carpenter v. Dee* to assess some of the strategic concerns relating to joinder. What did the Lopez plaintiffs gain by joining as plaintiffs? Was it worth more than the expense of litigating the motion to sever that led to the opinion that you just read? (How many hours of factual and legal research must it have taken for plaintiffs' attorneys to prepare their opposition to the defendants' motion? How many hours of court time were billed to the client? How long did their opposition to the motion delay the completion of the case?)

5. The defendants didn't make their motion to sever until shortly before trial was scheduled to begin. Would the motion have been stronger (or weaker) if it had been filed earlier, during the pleading stage?

6. Do the values "codified" in Rules 18 and 20 further the goal of making remedial justice more accessible? The goal of efficiency? Are these goals a zero-sum trade-off? For example, in *Lopez*, what do the plaintiffs and defendants gain or lose by broad joinder rules? What does society gain or lose? What about the values inherent in the tremendous discretion offered the trial judge by Rule 20(b) and Rule 42? If you were drafting the joinder provisions, would you grant this discretion to judges? In all cases?

7. Some federal judges have read Rule 20 very narrowly—more narrowly, some argue, than a reasonable construction of the rule would allow. *See, e.g.,* Robin J. Effron, *The Shadow Rules of Joinder*, 100 Georgetown L.J. _____ (2012) (forthcoming); Douglas D. McFarland, *Seeing the Forest for the Trees: The Transaction or Occurrence and the Claim Interlock Civil Procedure*, 12 Fla. Coastal L. Rev. 247 (2011). What are the risks and consequences of tolerating district judges who act without authority derived from amendments to the Federal Rules or from Supreme Court decisions? Or does Rule 42 indicate that district judges are supposed to have broad discretion in joinder matters?

8. Consider a hypothetical where the holder of a patent sues a number of unrelated defendants who are alleged to have infringed that patent independently of the others. Would all of those defendants be properly joined under Rule 20? In 2011, Congress passed the Leahy-Smith America Invents Act (H.R. 1249), which, *inter alia*, altered the rules of joinder for patent claims. Under that law multiple defendants in a single lawsuit may not be joined based solely upon the fact that they are all alleged to infringe the same patent. Can you reconcile this legislation that affects procedure only in patent cases with the goal of trans-substantive procedure? Should Rule 20 instead have been amended— and, if so, amended for *all* cases or with a special mandate for patent cases?

9. How and why is the rule for consolidation (Fed. R. Civ. P. 42(a)) different from the rule for joinder of parties (Fed. R. Civ. P. 20(a))?

## H. COUNTERCLAIMS AND CROSS-CLAIMS

A counterclaim is a claim asserted against an opposing party, usually by a defendant against a plaintiff. A counterclaim may seek any kind of relief that the court is competent to give. The relief may or may not be related to the plaintiff's claim. A counterclaim may ask for relief that merely neutralizes or cancels out the plaintiff's claim, or it may seek relief that exceeds the plaintiff's desired relief. Under the Federal Rules, counterclaims can be either compulsory or permissive. *See* Fed. R. Civ. P. 13.

A cross-claim is a claim between co-parties, usually defendants. In contrast to the blanket permissiveness of the counterclaim, a cross-claim may not assert every claim that possibly exists between co-parties. Instead, a cross-claim must be closely related to the transaction of the original claim asserted by plaintiff. (However, once a cross-claim has been legitimately asserted, consider the expansiveness permitted by Rule 18(a).) Cross-claims are always permissive. A party who does not bring a claim under 13(g) will not be barred by *res judicata*, waiver, or estoppel from asserting the claim at another time.

## ■ PODHORN v. PARAGON GROUP, INC.
### 606 F. Supp. 185 (D. Mo. 1985)

HUNGATE, District Judge:

This matter is before the Court on defendants' joint motion to dismiss plaintiffs' complaint.

Plaintiffs [Paul E. Podhorn, Jr., Liana E. Podhorn, and Renata A. Podhorn] bring this civil action alleging constructive eviction, breach of implied warranty of habitability, false swearing, false credit report, breach of implied covenant of quiet enjoyment, negligence, abuse of process, prima facie tort, conversion, and initiation of malicious prosecution by defendants. Defendant Paragon Group, Inc., is the owner of defendant San Miguel Apartments. All of these claims arose out of plaintiffs' tenancy at defendants' apartment building from April 1 to July 31, 1983.

On or about November 17, 1983, defendant Paragon Group, Inc., filed a petition in the Circuit Court of St. Louis County against the plaintiffs in this case, Paul and Liana Podhorn, for rent due. The state court action arose out of the same tenancy that gives rise to this federal cause. The Podhorns did not file a counterclaim in the state court action, and on March 28, 1984, a judgment in default was entered against the Podhorns in the sum of $1,113.33, plus costs.

Defendants move to dismiss plaintiffs' claim in this case asserting that it should have been filed as a compulsory counterclaim in the state court action.

Missouri Supreme Court Rule 55.32(a) requires the filing of compulsory counterclaims:

A pleading shall state as a counterclaim any claim which at the time of serving the pleading the pleader has against the opposing party, if it arises out of the transaction or occurrence that is the subject matter of the opposing party's claim and does not require for its adjudication the presence of third parties of whom the court cannot acquire jurisdiction. . . .

The Court finds plaintiffs' claims in this case arise out of the transaction or occurrence that gave rise to Paragon's rent action in the earlier state court case, namely plaintiffs' tenancy at defendants' apartment. Accordingly, plaintiffs were required to file the instant claims as compulsory counterclaims and their failure to do so bars them from having those claims heard.

Plaintiffs contend that associate circuit judges are granted limited authority and may not properly hear a civil case where the sum demanded, exclusive of interest and cost, exceeds $5,000. Mo. Rev. Stat. § 478.225.2(1). Plaintiffs argue that since their claims then and now exceed the statutory limit, the state court was without jurisdiction to hear their counterclaim if filed. Plaintiffs assert that the compulsory counterclaim rule does not apply in this action before an associate circuit judge.

Mo. Rev. Stat. § 517 governs the procedural dispute in this matter. The Supreme Court rule which requires the filing of compulsory counterclaims in the circuit court also applies to cases before an associate circuit judge. Mo. Rev. Stat. § 517.020.1(3). In the event the counterclaim is not triable before an associate circuit judge, as in this case where the counterclaim exceeds $5,000, the case is to be certified for assignment to a judge who may hear the claim. In short, although plaintiffs' counterclaim may not have been triable before the associate circuit judge, plaintiffs were not relieved of their obligation to file it.

Therefore, plaintiffs' claim is barred and this Court will grant defendants' motion to dismiss.

## Comments and Questions

1. Wright and Miller describe four tests for applying the words *"transaction or occurrence"* within the meaning of Rule 13(a):

   a. Are the issues of fact and law raised by the claim and counterclaim largely the same?
   b. Would *res judicata* bar a subsequent suit on defendant's claim absent the compulsory counterclaim rule?
   c. Will substantially the same evidence support or refute plaintiff's claim as well as defendant's counterclaim?
   d. Is there any logical relation between the claim and the counterclaim?

Charles A. Wright, Arthur R. Miller, and Mary Kay Kane, *Federal Practice and Procedure* § 1410.

2. A discussion of the important facts is conspicuously absent in the *Podhorn* opinion. Is this because there are *no* claims that could have arisen during the tenancy that would not also have been compulsory counterclaims in the first action? Revisit plaintiffs' causes of action and consider whether those

causes of action would necessarily be part of the "transaction or occurrence" that was the subject of the previous suit. For example, imagine that when the Podhorns were moving into the apartment on April 1, 1983, Renata Podhorn suffered serious injuries because the landlord negligently failed to warn the family about some dangerous defect in the apartment. Would Renata's claim be a compulsory counterclaim in the nonpayment of rent action later filed against Paul and Liana? How about a conversion claim if the landlord had entered the Podhorns' apartment without their permission or knowledge on June 15, and confiscated and sold many of the family's valuables?

3. Should it matter whether the Podhorns were represented by counsel in the first action?

4. Why is this case decided on a motion to dismiss? Is it obvious from the face of the complaint that defendant must win? Of what significance to these questions is the fact that *res judicata* is an affirmative defense?

5. You have now seen the terms "transaction" or "occurrence" as a portion of different rules: Fed. R. Civ. P. 20 (permissive joinder of parties); Fed. R. Civ. P. 15(c) (relation back of amendments); Fed. R. Civ. P. 13(a) (compulsory counterclaims); Fed. R. Civ. P. 13(g) (cross-claims against a co-party). Should the words be interpreted the same way, regardless of these different contexts, or might their interpretations take on slightly different shades of meaning? One way to approach such a question is to consider the purposes for using the terms in each context. Why are "transaction" and "occurrence" relevant to relationship back? Why are they relevant to joinder of parties or whether a counterclaim is compulsory? Would such a functional analysis lead one to different meanings? Professor Kane has explained how the term "transaction" has been used in the Federal Rules and elsewhere for differing purposes, and argues that those divergent purposes lead to different interpretations of the same word. Mary Kay Kane, *Original Sin and the Transaction in Federal Civil Procedure*, 76 Tex. L. Rev. 1723 (1998).

6. What does it mean to say that a counterclaim is "compulsory" or "permissive"? In what circumstances will the question of whether a potential counterclaim was compulsory normally be raised? For instance, assume that A and B are in a motor vehicle accident, each potentially having driven negligently into the other. A sues B. Will a court have to face the issue of whether B should have counterclaimed against A in the first suit, or in a later suit? As a defendant, how will you plead if you are in doubt as to whether a counterclaim is compulsory?

7. What place would Rule 13(a) counterclaims play in the overall procedural philosophy of Charles Clark? If you were on a committee drafting procedural rules, would you consider that a compulsory counterclaim provision would lead to "efficiency" or "inefficiency" or both? Consider the viewpoints of the court system, litigants, and their attorneys.

8. What are the reasons for the two exceptions in Rule 13(a)(2)?

9. The courts are in disagreement as to why there is a bar of the compulsory counterclaim that had not been brought in the first case. Some say it is a result of waiver, and others apply *res judicata* or estoppel doctrine. From the

point of view of the defendant in the first case, whose attorney neglected to bring the compulsory counterclaim (such that she cannot bring that claim in a subsequent case), it is difficult to see how it matters which theory causes the inability to now bring the claim.

10. Cross-claims must be closely related to at least one claim in the action. Consider the purpose of this requirement:

> When plaintiff brings suit against defendant, he is not free to object at some later time if defendant utilizes the forum to assert some unrelated claim against him in the forum of his own choice. But plaintiff's suit could become unduly complicated and prejudice might result to him if defendant is allowed to raise a claim against a co-defendant in which the original plaintiff has no interest.

Charles A. Wright, Arthur R. Miller, and Mary Kay Kane, *Federal Practice and Procedure* § 1431.

11. Make up a hypothetical involving a potential cross-claim. Why aren't cross-claims compulsory?

### Practice Exercise No. 13: Considering Counterclaims, Cross-Claims, and Rule 13(h) Additional Parties in *Carpenter*

*Counterclaims.* Consider the following possible counterclaim in the *Carpenter* case. Shortly after the accident in which her husband was killed, Nancy Carpenter calls a friend of the family who works at Raytheon (where Randall Dee was and is employed) and tells her that Randall Dee is an alcoholic. Randall Dee is then fired from his job. Does Randall Dee have a defamation claim against Nancy Carpenter for slander? Would this be a compulsory counterclaim? A permissive counterclaim? Would you need to do some legal research before you could answer this question?

*Cross-claims.* Assume that the judge in the motions session in the previous class has granted the motion of Nancy Carpenter to add Ultimate Auto, Inc. and the City of Lowell as named defendants, and the complaint is now filed as amended. Assume further that you represent the defendant driver of the jeep in question, Randall Dee. Do you have a plausible cross-claim? Prove it. Focus on the language of Mass. R. Civ. P. 13(g), which is the same as Fed. R. Civ. P. 13(g). If you do have a plausible cross-claim, how many counts would it have? What are the strategic reasons for filing it or not filing it? Regardless, try your hand at drafting such a cross-claim. Will you draft *de novo*, or can you get some help from a form somewhere near at hand?

You should also now look at the Massachusetts Contribution Statute in the Case Files. Consider other possible cross-claims, as well as Mass. R. Civ. P. 13(h) (which is also the same as the Federal Rule). Are there parties you might wish to bring in through the 13(h) route? Would you be able to?

# I. THIRD-PARTY PRACTICE

Rule 14 governs the procedure through which a defendant can bring a third party into the action. The rule permits the court to allow a defendant to *implead* a person not already a party to the action who is purportedly liable to the defendant for all or part of the defendant's liability to the plaintiff. In such an instance, the original defendant, now acting as a *third-party plaintiff*, impleads a *third-party defendant.* The case below illustrates.

## ■ GROSS v. HANOVER INS. CO.
### *138 F.R.D. 53 (S.D.N.Y. 1991)*

LEISURE, District Judge:

This is an action arising out of an insurance claim following the alleged loss of a substantial amount of jewelry. Defendant Hanover Insurance Company has now moved, pursuant to Federal Rule of Civil Procedure 14(a), to implead as third-party defendants Joseph Rizzo and Anthony Rizzo. For the reasons stated below, defendant's motion is granted.

### BACKGROUND

The facts necessary to decide the instant motion are not complex. Plaintiff alleges that he suffered a loss consisting of approximately $217,800 worth of diamonds consigned to one "3-R Jewelers" ("3-R"), a retail jewelry store, and approximately $48,000 worth of diamonds and emeralds left by plaintiff at 3-R for safekeeping. 3-R was at the relevant time owned by one Anthony Rizzo ("Anthony"), who employed his brother Joseph Rizzo ("Joseph") at the store. Plaintiff thereafter made a claim under a jewelers' block insurance policy issued to him by defendant, seeking $50,000 for loss of consignment goods and $25,000 for loss of goods left for safekeeping. The parties agree that the loss of the jewels was the result of a theft that occurred at the 3-R store.

Defendant alleges, however, that on December 16, 1989, the evening of the theft, a witness observed a man enter the 3-R store and begin talking to Joseph. Shortly thereafter, the man talking with Joseph walked out, then returned with a paper bag and proceeded to walk behind the counter and into a back room. When the witness left 3-R, the man was still in the store. Affidavit of Stephen H. Marcus, Esq., sworn to on June 28, 1991 ("Marcus Aff."), Exhibit H. In a statement he gave to the police, Joseph stated that he was in the store preparing to close for the night when two men entered and asked to purchase a watch. Joseph stated that he left the two men in the front of the store and went to the back to get a warranty card for the watch. He stated that he then heard the front door slam. When he returned to the front of the store the men were gone and a box and case of jewels were missing from the safe, which he had left open. Marcus Aff., Exhibit G. Defendant also claims that

Joseph was addicted to cocaine, and that Anthony was aware of this fact but nevertheless continued to employ Joseph at 3-R. The police report includes statements from Anthony that Joseph had a cocaine habit, that he thought the habit was under control, but "guess bigger problem than he [Anthony] thought," and that it "[l]ooked like Joey was setting place up." Marcus Aff., Exhibit F.

Defendant's proposed third-party complaint thus seeks to implead Joseph and Anthony on the ground that they will be liable to defendant, should defendant be found to be liable to plaintiff. Marcus Aff., Exhibit E. Specifically, the proposed third-party complaint asserts claims against Joseph for negligent handling of the jewels as plaintiff's consignee or bailee, or as the agent of 3-R; against Joseph for actual conversion of the jewels; and against Anthony for the negligent hiring, retention and supervision of Joseph.

## DISCUSSION

Rule 14(a) provides in relevant part that "[a]t any time after commencement of the action a defending party, as a third-party plaintiff, may cause a summons and complaint to be served upon a person not a party to the action who is or may be liable to the third-party plaintiff for all or part of the plaintiff's claim against the third-party plaintiff." Fed. R. Civ. P. 14(a). Where, as here, the defendant seeks to file the third-party complaint more than ten days after serving its original answer, the defendant "must obtain leave on motion upon notice to all parties to the action." Fed. R. Civ. P. 14(a). "The purpose of this rule is to promote judicial efficiency by eliminating the necessity for the defendant to bring a separate action against a third individual who may be secondarily or derivatively liable to the defendant for all or part of the plaintiff's original claim." *McLaughlin v. Biasucci*, 688 F. Supp. 965, 967 (S.D.N.Y. 1988). Accordingly, the district court has considerable discretion in deciding whether to permit a third-party complaint. *See Consolidated Rail Corp. v. Metz*, 115 F.R.D. 216, 218 (S.D.N.Y. 1987); *Old Republic Insurance Co. v. Concast.*, 99 F.R.D. 566, 568 (S.D.N.Y. 1983). "The court must balance the benefits derived from impleader—that is, the benefits of settling related matters in one suit—against the potential prejudice to the plaintiff and third-party defendants." *Oliner v. McBride's Industries, Inc.*, 106 F.R.D. 14, 20 (S.D.N.Y. 1985).

In the case at bar, defendant's proposed third-party claims arise from "'the same aggregate or core of facts which is determinative of the plaintiff's claim,'" and thus the interest in judicial economy would be served by permitting those claims to proceed in the instant action. *National Bank of Canada v. Artex Industries, Inc.*, 627 F. Supp. 610, 613 (S.D.N.Y. 1986) (quoting *Dery v. Wyer*, 265 F.2d 804, 807 (2d Cir. 1959)). Plaintiff argues, however, that the proposed third-party claims are "speculative," and thus the motion to implead should be denied. This argument fails for several reasons.

First, there is some question as to whether plaintiff may attack the merits of the proposed third-party claims at this stage of the proceedings. Second, it is well established that the words "is or may be liable" in Rule 14(a) make it clear that impleader is proper even though the third-party defendant's liability is not automatically established once the third-party plaintiff's liability to the original plaintiff has been determined. . . . Finally, the proposed third-party claims are sufficiently alleged, for Rule 14(a) purposes. "The federal and New York state court decisions hold that third-party impleader practice encompasses subrogation claims." . . .

Plaintiff's second argument in opposition to the instant motion consists of a claim that defendant has been dilatory in seeking to implead, and that plaintiff will suffer prejudice if discovery is expanded to include the third-party claims. There is, however, little evidence to suggest that defendant was so slow in bringing its Rule 14(a) motion that that motion should be denied. More importantly, the Court believes that the prejudice to be felt by plaintiff—if any—due to the need for additional discovery, is sufficiently outweighed by the benefits of more efficient litigation to be gained by permitting impleader. . . . If, in the future, plaintiff believes that defendant is using its third-party claims to delay the progress of the principal complaint in this action, he should so inform the Court. Needless to say, the Court would not countenance such tactics. . . .

## CONCLUSION

For the reasons stated above, defendant's motion to implead Joseph Rizzo and Anthony Rizzo, pursuant to Federal Rule of Civil Procedure 14(a), is granted. SO ORDERED.

## Comments and Questions

1. Perhaps the most difficult concept to grasp with impleaders is who can be brought in as a third-party defendant. Note the following words carefully: "[W]ho is or may be liable to it [the third-party plaintiff] for all or part of the claim against it." Fed. R. Civ. P. 14(a)(1). Consequently, in order for a defendant (third-party plaintiff) to implead a new party (the third-party defendant), three conditions must be met (leaving out for now jurisdiction and notice problems, which are addressed elsewhere in the course). First, and easiest, impleader can be used only in order to bring in one who is not already a party. Second, the defendant (third-party plaintiff) has to have a claim against the new party it is trying to implead (the third-party defendant). In other words, if A sues B, and B says, in effect, "It's not my fault, it is C's fault," that alone does *not* a good impleader make. Instead, B needs a theory of liability *against C*. By the way, nothing prevents B from pointing the finger at C throughout the trial, or even subpoenaing C to testify at the trial. C doesn't have to be a party in order for one side to blame C, assuming the evidence is relevant.

Third, for B to have a valid impleader against C, B not only needs a theory of liability against C, but it has to be "for all or part of" A's claim against B. Here is an example of a good impleader: A lent money to C, and B agreed to be C's guarantor. Under guaranty or surety law, if the guarantor or surety has to pay the lender, then the guarantor ordinarily has a claim against the borrower for what the guarantor was forced to pay the lender because of the borrower's debt. Therefore, if *A* (lender) sues *B* (guarantor), then *B* could implead *C* (borrower) because *B* will have a claim against *C* for all of what *B* will have to pay *A*. Notice that *B* has a claim against *C* if, but *only* if, *A* prevails on *A*'s claim against *B*. If *B* has a claim regardless of the outcome of *A v. B*, then this is not a valid impleader.

2. As you read the following excerpt from *United States v. Olavarrieta*, 812 F.2d 640 (11th Cir. 1987), see if you agree with the court that it is an improper impleader, and consider the tactical issues facing a litigator who has the option of impleader versus separate trials. Assuming Olavarrieta's impleader against the Board of Regents was proper, could Olavarrieta claim more from the Board of Regents than the United States was claiming from him? Precisely where would you look to find an answer to this?

The United States, as guarantor of Jose Olavarrieta's federally insured student loans totaling $4,000, filed suit against Olavarrieta in order to collect the unpaid balance and interest on the loans. Inter-National Bank of Miami made the loans to Olavarrieta under the Federal Insured Student Loan Program, Title IV-B of the Higher Education Act of 1965, 20 U.S.C.A. §§ 1071-88. After Olavarrieta defaulted on the loans, the bank sought payment from the government. The government paid off Olavarrieta's liability to the bank and then sought reimbursement from Olavarrieta by filing this suit.

Olavarrieta filed a third party complaint against the University of Florida, claiming that it had violated the Higher Education Act of 1965 and had breached its contract with him by failing to award him a J.D. degree. Olavarrieta amended this complaint to add the Board of Regents of the Division of Universities of the Florida Department of Education as a third party defendant and to add a claim for indemnification by the third party defendants for any sums he was found to owe the government. The district court granted the University of Florida's motion to dismiss. . . .

[W]e hold that the district court properly dismissed the third party complaint against the University of Florida. The capacity to be sued is determined by state law. Fed. R. Civ. P. 17(b). Under Florida law, the University of Florida is not endowed with an independent corporate existence or the capacity to be sued in its own name. Rather, those characteristics are bestowed on the Board of Regents as the head of Florida's university system. Therefore, the University of Florida is not a proper party in this action, and the district court was correct in dismissing the third party complaint asserted against it.

The district court was also correct in dismissing the third party complaint against the Board of Regents. Olavarrieta simply has failed to state any legal or factual grounds for indemnification. Furthermore, to the extent the third party complaint seeks relief on account of the University's failure to award Olavarrieta a J.D. degree as promised, it does not set forth proper grounds for a third party claim under Fed. R. Civ. P. 14(a). Rule 14(a) allows a defendant to assert a claim against any person not a party to the main action only if that third person's liability on that claim is in some way dependent upon the outcome of the main claim. Rule 14(a) does not allow the defendant to assert a separate and independent claim even though the claim arises out of the same general set of facts as the main claim. . . . Olavarrieta's third party claim alleging breach of contract or fraud on account of the University of Florida's failure to award him a J.D. degree as promised is a separate and independent action from the government's action against him. Whether Olavarrieta is entitled to any relief on this claim is wholly independent of his liability to the government for defaulting on his student loans. Therefore, Olavarrieta has failed to state any appropriate grounds for maintaining a third party complaint against the Board of Regents.

3. The Rule 8(a) pleading requirements explicitly apply to a Rule 14 third-party complaint. Rule 7 makes clear that a third-party complaint is ordinarily a "pleading" and that a third-party answer is required if a "third-party complaint is served." An answer by the third-party defendant should include Rule 8(b) admissions and denials and 8(c) affirmative defenses. Moreover, Rule 12(b) requires that all defenses to a "claim for relief in any pleading," explicitly including third-party claims, "shall be asserted in the responsive pleading thereto if one is required," and then excepts the 12(b) defenses that can be made by motion. Therefore, the third-party defendant should raise 12(b) defenses against the third-party plaintiff either by answer or motion. The third-party defendant may also, according to Rule 14(a)(2)(C), "assert against the plaintiff any defense that the third-party plaintiff has to the plaintiff's claim." Why should the third-party defendant be able to assert the initial defendant's defenses against the plaintiff?

4. Be sure to read all of Rule 14. It contains some details regarding transactions or occurrences that you should know. For instance, the third-party defendant may, but is not required to, assert any claims arising out of the same transaction or occurrence against the plaintiff. Also, the (original) plaintiff may assert a claim against the third-party defendant if the claim arises out of the same transaction or occurrence.

5. Note how third-party plaintiffs may implead someone whom plaintiff could not have sued directly; also, note how they might implead someone whom plaintiff could have sued directly (but chose not to).

6. Return to the *Carpenter* facts and assume that the only named parties in the suit are Nancy Carpenter (as administratrix), Ultimate Auto, and Randall Dee. List all the ways that another entity could be added to this suit—using only the Rules we have learned so far. For example, (1) plaintiff could move to amend pursuant to Rule 15 and add an additional defendant; (2) plaintiff could move to amend pursuant to Rule 15 and add an additional plaintiff. There are at least eight other possibilities to be added to this list.

## Practice Exercise No. 14: Considering Cross-Claims and Impleaders in *City of Cleveland*

You are in your first week as a summer associate in the firm that has been hired to represent the City of Cleveland. In scenario 1, you are to assume that the plaintiffs have included Dr. Marshall among the defendants named in the complaint. In scenario 2, you are to assume that Dr. Marshall is not named as a defendant.

For *both* scenarios, the partner to whom you have been assigned is contemplating the assertion of a claim by our client, the City, against Dr. Marshall. For each of the two scenarios, alert the partner of (1) the Rule, if any, that authorizes the claim; (2) any legal questions that need to be answered before we can assert the claim; and (3) any factual questions that need to be answered before we can assert the claim. Be precise—you will want to make a good impression.

## J. AN INTRODUCTION TO NECESSARY AND INDISPENSABLE PARTIES

Federal Rule 19 identifies persons who have not been named as parties but are necessary for a just adjudication of the underlying dispute. Such persons were not initially named as parties either because the plaintiff decided not to join the additional persons, or could not join them for jurisdictional reasons, or because the additional persons refused the plaintiff's invitation to join. Fed. R. Civ. P. 19(a) identifies three situations in which an absentee should be joined: where the plaintiff cannot get relief from the named party (read Rule 19(a)(1)(A)); where the absentee may be prejudiced by the failure to join (read Rule 19(a)(1)(B)(i)); and where the defendant may be prejudiced by the failure to join the absentee (read Rule 19(a)(1)(B)(ii)). Thus any party whose absence results in any of the problems identified in part (a) of the Rule is a party whose joinder is compulsory, if feasible.

For reasons that are explored elsewhere in the course, sometimes the absentee cannot be joined in this lawsuit. And when joinder is not feasible, the court must choose one of two difficult options: Either dismiss the plaintiff's case or proceed without a necessary party. The four factors enumerated in Rule 19(b) guide that inquiry. The labels "necessary" and "indispensable" are conclusory and inexact; they are simply vestiges of a prior version of Rule 19. Nevertheless, lawyers and judges use the terms frequently in the Rule 19 context, with "necessary" parties defined by Rule 19(a), and with those parties whose presence is deemed "indispensable" described by Rule 19(b).

We consider first the parameters of Rule 19(a).

## ■ TEMPLE v. SYNTHES CORPORATION, LTD.
### *498 U.S. 1042 (1991)*

PER CURIAM:
Petitioner Temple, a Mississippi resident, underwent surgery in October 1986 in which a "plate and screw device" was implanted in his lower spine. The device was manufactured by respondent Synthes Corp., Ltd. ("Synthes"),

a Pennsylvania corporation. Dr. S. Henry LaRocca performed the surgery at St. Charles General Hospital in New Orleans, Louisiana. Following surgery, the device's screws broke off inside Temple's back.

Temple filed suit against Synthes in the United States District Court for the Eastern District of Louisiana. The suit, which rested on diversity jurisdiction, alleged defective design and manufacture of the device. At the same time, Temple . . . filed suit against the doctor and the hospital in Louisiana state court.

Synthes did not attempt to bring the doctor and the hospital into the federal action by means of a third-party complaint, as provided in Federal Rule of Civil Procedure 14(a). Instead, Synthes filed a motion to dismiss Temple's federal suit for failure to join necessary parties pursuant to Federal Rule of Civil Procedure 19. Following a hearing, the District Court ordered Temple to join the doctor and the hospital as defendants within 20 days or risk dismissal of the lawsuit. According to the court, the most significant reason for requiring joinder was the interest of judicial economy. The court relied on this Court's decision in *Provident Tradesmens Bank & Trust Co. v. Patterson*, 390 U.S. 102 (1968), wherein we recognized that one focus of Rule 19 is "the interest of the courts and the public in complete, consistent, and efficient settlement of controversies." *Id.* at 111. When Temple failed to join the doctor and the hospital, the court dismissed the suit with prejudice.

Temple appealed, and the United States Court of Appeals for the Fifth Circuit affirmed. The court deemed it "obviously prejudicial to the defendants to have the separate litigations being carried on," because Synthes' defense might be that the plate was not defective but that the doctor and the hospital were negligent, while the doctor and the hospital, on the other hand, might claim that they were not negligent but that the plate was defective. The Court of Appeals found that the claims overlapped and that the District Court therefore had not abused its discretion in ordering joinder under Rule 19. A petition for rehearing was denied.

In his petition for certiorari to this Court, Temple contends that it was error to label joint tortfeasors as indispensable parties under Rule 19(b) and to dismiss the lawsuit with prejudice for failure to join those parties. We agree. Synthes does not deny that it, the doctor, and the hospital are potential joint tortfeasors. It has long been the rule that it is not necessary for all joint tortfeasors to be named as defendants in a single lawsuit. Nothing in the 1966 revision of Rule 19 changed that principle. The Advisory Committee Notes to Rule 19(a) explicitly state that "a tortfeasor with the usual 'joint-and-several' liability is merely a permissive party to an action against another with like liability." There is nothing in Louisiana tort law to the contrary. . . .

Here, no inquiry under Rule 19(b) is necessary, because the threshold requirements of Rule 19(a) have not been satisfied. As potential joint tortfeasors with Synthes, Dr. LaRocca and the hospital were merely permissive parties. The Court of Appeals erred by failing to hold that the District Court abused its discretion in ordering them joined as defendants and in dismissing the action when Temple failed to comply with the court's order. For these reasons, we grant the petition for certiorari, reverse the judgment of the Court of Appeals for the Fifth Circuit, and remand for further proceedings consistent with this opinion.

## Comments and Questions

1. Assuming that it would be more efficient to require the joinder of joint tortfeasors, what interests are instead given priority here?

2. Given the narrow scope of Rule 19(a), the *Temple* Court seems to have found it unnecessary to parse the language of the three categories of "necessary party" status. Work carefully through the language of Rule 19(a) and be able to explain why a joint tortfeasor is not a necessary party.

3. Subtle issues of interpretation are presented in each of the provisions of part (a). Consider, first, the language of Fed. R. Civ. P. 19(a)(1)(A). This provision confers necessary status upon the absentee only if "in that person's absence, the court cannot accord complete relief among existing parties."

The 19(a)(1)(A) inquiry focuses on the relief that is sought and the ability of the named parties to render that relief, if so ordered by the court. If a plaintiff seeks equitable relief that the named defendant(s) cannot alone effect, then the additional parties needed to effect that relief could be necessary parties. For example, if a lawsuit seeking specific performance of the conveyance of land is filed against only one of two joint owners of the property, the single defendant could not alone effect the transfer even if so ordered by the court.

*Temple* makes clear that in damages cases, joint tortfeasors are not necessary parties. But what if the named defendant is judgment-proof? Can a plaintiff obtain "complete relief" from the named defendant if he is unable to collect on the judgment? Although, as a practical matter, he may not be able to obtain complete relief, the inability to collect on a judgment typically will *not* satisfy the "complete relief" criterion of 19(a)(1)(A).

Some commentators consider this first category of Rule 19(a) a "null set." *See, e.g.*, Richard D. Freer, *Rethinking Compulsory Joinder: A Proposal to Restructure Federal Rule 19*, 60 N.Y.U. L. Rev. 1061, 1062 (1985). Indeed, the rule's narrow construction makes it applicable in very few cases, and Rule 19(a)(1)(A) may be misapplied more often than it is properly invoked. *Id.* at 1081-1082.

4. Next, Fed. R. Civ. P. 19(a)(1)(B)(i) confers necessary party status if the interests of the absentee would be prejudiced from the adverse effects of a judgment rendered in their absence. The challenge here is to determine which interests are protected and what quantum of impairment is required.

Courts typically recognize only "legally protected" interests. This interest must be more than a financial stake. One's family, for example, may be greatly affected by a judgment in one's favor or by a judgment against one, but this ordinarily would not make them necessary parties. These absentees would not have a direct stake or "interest relating to the subject matter of the action."

The joinder of an absent party is compulsory under Rule 19(a)(1)(B)(i) if the litigation would have a preclusive effect against the absent party in subsequent litigation. If collateral estoppel could be invoked against the absentee in other litigation, continuation of the federal action could "as a practical matter impair or impede" the absentee's interests and so Rule 19(a)(1)(B)(i) would require its joinder if joinder were feasible. One might expect the Due Process Clause to solve the problem, as no absentee can be bound unless it is named as a party in the litigation. The exception, of course, is for an absentee that is in privity with a named party; but, in that instance, the absent party will, in effect, have had its day in court by virtue of its privity with the named party. However, consider the facts of *Lopez v. Martin Luther King, Jr., Hospital*, 97 F.R.D. 24 (C.D. Cal. 1983). There the parents of a child sued the hospital and various doctors, alleging medical malpractice in the course of childbirth, for recovery of damages suffered by them (and not the child). (Under California law, the parents had a cause of action separate from the child's.) The child was not named as a plaintiff, because it would have destroyed the diversity jurisdiction of the federal court. (The Lopez parents were Mexican nationals; the child was a citizen of California.) The district court held that the child was a necessary party because the child might later have been precluded if a California court found privity. Importantly, however, courts disagree on the extent to which the likelihood of preclusion must be demonstrated. *See Janney Montgomery Scott, Inc. v. Shepard Niles, Inc.*, 11 F.3d 399 (3d Cir. 1993) (holding "[m]ere presentation of an argument that issue preclusion is possible is not enough to trigger Rule 19(a) . . .").

A second classic example is the group of cases involving a limited pie. A fixed fund that a court is asked to allocate may create a protectable interest in putative beneficiaries of the fund. (Consider, for example, the proceeds of a trust account.) Allocation to the plaintiff could "as a practical matter" impair the absentee's interest therein. Similarly, a judgment decreeing that the plaintiff is the owner of land will not bind absentees who claim title; but the absentee may be a necessary party if it casts a cloud on their title.

Further, courts are disinclined to find necessary parties in litigation involving the vindication of public rights. *See National Licorice Co. v. NLRB*, 309 U.S. 350 (1940).

In some cases, the courts have not insisted on Rule 19 joinder of those whose interests will "be impaired or impeded" by a litigation if their position is already advanced by another party . . . , if mandatory joinder would be unwieldy or impossible, and if there was a strong public interest that the case proceed. In an environmental suit brought by the Sierra Club, for example, the District Court for the Eastern District of California held that although miners' property rights would be affected, the miners were not necessary parties: "where what is at stake are essentially issues of public concern and the nature of the case would require joinder of a large number of persons, Rule 19's joinder requirements need not be satisfied." [*Sierra Club v. Watt*, 608 F. Supp. 305, 321-324 (E.D. Cal. 1985).] Also citing Federal Rule 1, the district court reasoned that "[s]urely justice cannot be done if public interest litigation is precluded by virtue of the requirements of joinder."

Phyllis Tropper Bauman et al., *Substance in the Shadow of Procedure: The Integration of Substantive and Procedural Law in Title VII Cases*, 33 B.C. L. Rev. 211, 281-282 (1992) (footnotes omitted).

5. Finally, consider Fed. R. Civ. P. 19(a)(1)(B)(ii) and the meaning of "inconsistent obligations." In *Carpenter*, assume that Nancy Carpenter sued (only) Randall Dee and, in that trial, a jury found for the plaintiff and awarded damages of $100,000. Assume, then, that Carpenter brought a second action against (only) Ultimate Auto and, in that second trial, a jury found for the plaintiff and awarded damages of $500,000. (And assume further that Ultimate Auto could not use nonmutual defensive collateral estoppel against Carpenter on the amount of her harm.) Would this constitute "inconsistent obligations" within the meaning of Fed. R. Civ. P. 19(a)(1)(B)(ii)? The answer is *no*, even though the verdicts certainly are inconsistent. Inconsistent verdicts are not uncommon. Frequently, when non-joined plaintiffs sue a defendant on the same theory (e.g., asbestos, tobacco, handguns, mass disaster), some plaintiffs win and others lose— even if the relevant facts are identical. An inconsistent *obligation* occurs if one court orders a party to do one thing (e.g., deed Blackacre to *A*) and another court orders the same party to perform an inconsistent act (e.g., deed Blackacre to *B*).

6. In *Carpenter*, if two passengers were killed, would both of them be necessary parties who should be joined as plaintiffs, if feasible? Why or why not? (What else would you need to know?) Would Randall Dee and Ultimate Auto have to be joined as defendants? Were Twyla Burrell and/or Peter Dee necessary parties given the construction of the original complaint?

7. What if Randall Dee had a liability insurance policy on the jeep requiring the insurer to indemnify the insured (Dee) for liability as a result of driving the jeep, with certain exclusions that are not relevant here? You will find out when you study preclusion law in Chapter 10 that insurers are in privity with the insured when the insurer can control the litigation. A provision granting such control is typical in liability policies and so the insurer is normally bound by a judicial liability determination against the insured. Do you think that the insurer in the jeep case cannot only be *impleaded* by Randall Dee but is also a Rule 19(a) *necessary party*?

The next case reviews all of the Rule 19(a) categories of necessary party status and also introduces the indispensability analysis of Rule 19(b).

# ■ DAYNARD v. NESS, MOTLEY, LOADHOLDT, RICHARDSON & POOLE, P.A.
### *184 F. Supp. 2d 55 (D. Mass. 2001)*

YOUNG, Chief Judge:
. . . The plaintiff, Professor Richard A. Daynard ("Daynard") of Northeastern University School of Law, has spent much of his academic career studying

how to defeat the tobacco industry in court. The defendants—the Ness, Motley, Loadholt, Richardson & Poole, P.A. law firm and one of its partners, Mr. Motley (together "the South Carolina defendants"), and the Scruggs, Milette, Bozeman & Dent, P.A. law firm and one of its partners, Mr. Scruggs (together "the Mississippi defendants")—were among the many law firms representing state governments in the titanic battle against the tobacco industry ("the State Tobacco Litigation").

Between 1993 and 1997, Daynard provided advice to the defendants. No written contract detailed how Daynard would be compensated, but Daynard alleges that he and one of the Mississippi defendants shook hands in Chicago, Illinois in 1996 on an agreement whereby he would receive 5% of any attorneys' fees paid to the defendants as a result of the State Tobacco Litigation. In 1997 and 1998, the tobacco industry agreed to settle the State Tobacco Litigation for billions of dollars. Since then, the defendants have received millions of dollars in attorneys' fees and Daynard has received nothing.

[The plaintiff brought suit against both the South Carolina defendants and the Mississippi defendants. Upon a successful motion by the latter to dismiss for lack of personal jurisdiction, the South Carolina defendants then moved to dismiss the case under Fed. R. Civ. P. 12(b)(7) for failure to join an indispensable party. The dismissal on grounds of lack of personal jurisdiction was on appeal at the time of this opinion; the order of dismissal ultimately was reversed. *See Daynard v. Ness, Motley, Loadholdt, Richardson & Poole, P.A.*, 290 F.3d 42 (1st Cir. 2002).]

The South Carolina defendants argue that the case should not proceed without the Mississippi defendants because it was Mr. Scruggs who allegedly shook hands with Daynard in Chicago, so any lawsuit without Mr. Scruggs would be incomplete and only spawn subsequent lawsuits that do include Mr. Scruggs. Daynard, in response, argues that the handshake in Chicago was merely the culmination of many assurances from both the South Carolina defendants and the Mississippi defendants that he would receive attorneys' fees. In other words, Daynard argues that the defendants together agreed to pay him 5% of their attorneys' fees from the State Tobacco Litigation, so under a theory of joint and several liability, only one defendant need be named in the complaint.

## 1. PROCEDURAL POSTURE

A defense of failure to join an indispensable party, Fed. R. Civ. P. 12(b)(7), may be made at any time before the end of trial. Fed. R. Civ. P. 12(h)(2). The defense turns on Rule 19, which implicitly distinguishes "necessary" parties from "indispensable" parties. A "necessary" party under Rule 19(a) is one that should be joined to effect a just adjudication, while an "indispensable" party under Rule 19(b) is simply a "necessary" party under Rule 19(a) who, for one reason or another, cannot be made a party and without whom the court determines the action cannot proceed. The important point to note is that "indispensable" is a subset of "necessary," not a mutually exclusive category.

Thus, determination of whether a party is "indispensable" requires two steps: First, is the party "necessary" under Rule 19(a)? Second, if the party is "necessary," is it also "indispensable" under Rule 19(b)? . . .

As the moving party, the South Carolina defendants bear the burden of showing why the Mississippi defendants are indispensable and dismissal is proper under Rule 12(b)(7). In meeting its burden, the moving party may present, and the court may consider, evidence outside of the pleadings. . . . Fed. R. Civ. P. 19 advisory committee's note (1966 amendment) (noting decision may "properly be deferred if adequate information is not available at the time").

## 2. DISCUSSION

### A. RULE 19(A)—"NECESSARY"?

#### (1) Some rules of thumb

Over the years, several rules of thumb have developed under Rule 19:

- Joint tortfeasors are not necessary parties. Thus, by definition, they may not be indispensable.
- Co-obligors [to a contract] may be necessary parties, but generally are not indispensable.
- As a general rule, an action to set aside a contract requires the joinder of all parties to the contract.

*Moore's Federal Practice* § 19.06[1]. . . .

The South Carolina defendants cite several decisions for the proposition that, generally speaking, all parties to a contract must be joined. The South Carolina defendants apparently advocate a rule of thumb in contravention to the rules of thumb recognized by the Supreme Court and the commentators, but regardless, the proper approach today is to examine each case in light of the factors mentioned in Rules 19(a) and 19(b).

#### (2) First circuit caselaw

In *Acton* [*Co. v. Bachman Foods, Inc.*, 668 F.2d 76 (1st Cir. 1982)], the First Circuit affirmed the dismissal of a contract action for failure to join an indispensable party. The facts are as follows: A parent corporation and its subsidiary agreed to purchase the assets of another company. When the deal fell through, two lawsuits arose: (i) the seller sued both the parent and the sub in New York state court for breach of contract, and (ii) the sub—without joining the parent—sued the seller in the District of Massachusetts seeking a declaration that the contract was void as a result of the seller's misrepresentations. The district court dismissed the sub's lawsuit for failure to join the parent. The First Circuit affirmed:

There is little doubt that [the parent], as a party to the letter of intent and to the purchase agreement, should be joined to this action if feasible. . . . To begin, [the parent] played a substantial role in negotiating both agreements; indeed, [the sub] did not even exist in April 1979 when the letter of intent was signed. Thus [the parent] may have rights under this preliminary agreement not shared by [the sub]. Moreover, according to the express terms of the purchase agreement, [the parent] and not [the sub] would be entitled to refund of the $250,000 deposit. Unless [the parent] were bound by the results of [the sub's] suit, it would remain free to commence a new action on its claims. [The parent's] presence is therefore desirable not only to avoid piecemeal and duplicative litigation, but also to provide complete relief to the [seller]. *See* Rule 19(a)(1).

In addition, [the parent], as [the sub's] parent corporation and as [the sub's] guarantor, might be bound by [the sub's] suit under the doctrine that *res judicata* applies not only to the actual parties but also to those in privity with the parties. If so, to proceed in [the parent's] absence might impair [the parent's] interest in the controversy very significantly. Even if [the parent] would not be legally bound, an adverse ruling would be a persuasive precedent in a subsequent proceeding, and would weaken [the parent's] bargaining position for settlement purposes. In either case, to proceed without [the parent] might "as a practical matter impair or impede" [the parent's] ability to protect its interest in this matter. Rule 19(a)(2)(i).* [The parent] is therefore a ["necessary" party].

668 F.2d at 78-79 (citations omitted). The facts of *Acton* are distinguishable from the case at bar in two notable respects: (i) the absent party in *Acton* was a co-obligee, not a co-obligor, and (ii) any judgment in *Acton* likely would have been binding against the absent defendant because it was in privity with the co-obligee.

In *H.D. Corp.* [*v. Ford Motor Co.*, 791 F.2d 987 (1st Cir. 1986)], several automobile dealerships brought a breach of contract action in the District of Puerto Rico against Ford Motor Company and its local subsidiary. The dealerships and Ford were all Delaware corporations, so the district court dismissed Ford from the action to preserve diversity, leaving only its local subsidiary as a defendant. The district court went on to dismiss the action entirely, however, because it concluded that Ford was an indispensable party. The First Circuit affirmed. The holding of *H.D. Corp.* is not instructive, though, for two reasons. First, the court held that Ford was "indispensable" without considering whether it was "necessary." Second, given the case-specific inquiry required by Rule 19(b), an opinion affirming a finding that a party is "indispensable" does not provide useful guidance far beyond its particular facts.

Finally, in *Pujol* [*v. Shearson/American Express, Inc.*, 877 F.2d 132 (1st Cir. 1989)], the First Circuit noted with approval the distinction traditionally drawn between joint tortfeasors and persons jointly liable on a contract:

> [I]f one thing is clear in respect to Rule 19, it is that, unlike a person vicariously liable in tort, a person potentially liable as a joint tortfeasor is not a

---

*Eds.' Note:* This case is interpreting an earlier version of Fed. R. Civ. P. 19. The language that appeared at 19(a)(2)(i) at the time of this case now appears (with slightly different language) at Fed. R. Civ. P. 19(a)(1)(B)(i).

necessary or indispensable party, but merely a permissive party subject to joinder under Rule 20. . . .

Of course, one might wonder why Rule 19 would treat "joint tortfeasors" differently in this respect than, say, persons jointly liable under a contract. *See Acton*, 688 F.2d at 81-82 ("an action seeking rescission of a contract must be dismissed unless all parties to the contract, and others having a substantial interest in it, can be joined"); *see also H.D. Corp.*, 791 F.2d at 993. The reason for the difference may lie in the history of joinder doctrine, or it may reflect a compromise between the interests served by Rule 19 and the policies of tort law. But, regardless of the reasons, this case presents no basis for ignoring such well established precedent [concerning jointly and severally liable tortfeasors].

877 F.2d at 137 (citations omitted). The quotation above, however, is dictum and adds nothing to the holdings of *Acton* and *H.D. Corp.*

### (3) *Janney*

In *Janney* [*Montgomery Scott, Inc. v. Shepard Niles, Inc.*, 11 F.3d 399 (3d Cir. 1993)], an investment bank agreed to be the exclusive advisor to a parent corporation and its subsidiaries. Later, the investment bank sued one of the subs—but not the parent—for failing to pay the fees contemplated by the agreement. Both the parent and the sub were co-obligors, but only the parent had signed the contract. The Third Circuit carefully analyzed each provision of Rule 19(a) and concluded that the parent was not a "necessary" party:

Rule 19(a)(1)—"in the person's absence complete relief cannot be accorded among those already parties." The court held that this factor did not apply because the defendants could be jointly and severally liable under the contract. The court noted that it was possible that the contract, in fact, did not impose joint and several liability on the defendants, but the court held that all inferences had to be drawn in the plaintiff's favor on a motion to dismiss, so the court assumed joint and several liability.

Rule 19(a)(2)(i)—"the person claims an interest relating to the subject of the action and is so situated that the disposition of the action in the person's absence may as a practical matter impair or impede the person's ability to protect that interest." The court held that this factor did not apply because any judgment against the defendants would not bind the absent defendant. The court also rejected the argument that any such judgment would nevertheless act as "persuasive precedent" and thus impair the absent defendant's ability to protect its interests:

> We are not sure what the district court means by the phrase "persuasive precedent." To the extent it involves the doctrine of *stare decisis*, we are not inclined to hold that any potential effect the doctrine may have on an absent party's rights makes the absent party's joinder compulsory under Rule 19(a) whenever "feasible." Such a holding would greatly expand the class of "necessary" or compulsory parties Rule 19(a) creates. Moreover, to whatever extent the rule's phrase "as a practical matter impair or impede" has broader

meaning than that given by principles of issue preclusion, we think the effect of the federal decision must be more direct and immediate than the effect a judgment in [the defendant's] favor would have on [the absent defendant] here. They are, after all, separate corporate entities. In any event, we do not believe any possibility of a "persuasive precedent" requires joinder under subsection 19(a)(2)(i). . . .

[The defendant] cites [*Acton Co. v. Bachman Foods, Inc.*, 668 F.2d 76 (1st Cir. 1982)] to support its argument that the potentially persuasive effect of the federal action on any related litigation justifies the district court's conclusion that the absent party's joinder is compulsory under Rule 19(a)(i). That argument ignores the United States Court of Appeals for the First Circuit's refusal to adopt a persuasive precedent standard for a Rule 19(a) determination that all tortfeasors who could be jointly and severally liable should be joined if feasible. *See Pujol v. Shearson/American Express, Inc.*, 877 F.2d 132, 136 (1st Cir. 1989) ("The mere fact, however, that Party A, in a suit against Party B, intends to introduce evidence that will indicate that a non-party, C, behaved improperly does not, by itself, make C a necessary party."). Though we recognize that the *Pujol* court distinguished joint tortfeasors from joint obligors and stated that *Acton* was still good law as applied to contract liability, we see no logical distinction that would justify treating contract actions differently than tort actions for purposes of compulsory joinder. Instead, we believe the distinction made by the Court of Appeals for the First Circuit is based on authority, not logic. Thus, to the extent *Pujol* goes beyond a panel's recognition of the need to accept controlling circuit precedent, it does not persuade us. For the reasons already stated, we hold instead that [the absent defendant], a co-obligor, is not a party whose joinder Rule 19(a)(2)(i) requires because continuation of the federal litigation in [a co-obligor's] absence will not create a precedent that might persuade another court to rule against [the co-obligor] on principles of *stare decisis*, or some other unidentified basis not encompassed by the rules of collateral estoppel or issue preclusion.

*Id.* at 407, 408-09 (citations and footnotes omitted).

Rule 19(a)(2)(ii)*—"the person claims an interest relating to the subject of the action and is so situated that the disposition of the action in the person's absence may leave any of the persons already parties subject to a substantial risk of incurring double, multiple, or otherwise inconsistent obligations by reason of the claimed interest." The court held that this factor did not apply because the risk of inconsistent *adjudications* is not the same thing as inconsistent *obligations*.

The possibility that [the defendant] may bear the whole loss if it is found liable [and the absent defendant later is found not liable] is not the equivalent of double liability. It is instead a common result of joint and several liability and should not be equated with prejudice. Inherent in the concept of joint and several liability is the right of a plaintiff to satisfy its whole judgment by execution against any one of the multiple defendants who are liable to him,

---

*Eds.' Note:* The corresponding provision in the current rule appears at Fed. R. Civ. P. 19(a)(1)(B)(ii).

thereby forcing the debtor who has paid the whole debt to protect itself by an action for contribution against the other joint obligors.

*Id.* at 412.

Thus, the Court in *Janney* held that the absent co-obligor was not even a "necessary" party under Rule 19(a), let alone an "indispensable" party under Rule 19(b).

### (4) The parties' arguments

First, pointing to subsection (a)(1), the South Carolina defendants argue that Daynard cannot get complete relief in this Court because he will not be able to recover the money owed by the Mississippi defendants. This argument assumes that Daynard entered into separate contracts with the South Carolina and Mississippi defendants, an assumption the Court cannot make on a motion to dismiss. To the contrary, the South Carolina defendants bear the burden of persuasion, so the Court must draw inferences in Daynard's favor and assume that the defendants are jointly and severally liable.

Second, pointing to subsection (a)(2)(i), the South Carolina defendants argue that because they likely will pursue the "empty chair" defense—in particular, that Daynard made a contract only with Mr. Scruggs—a judgment in favor of the South Carolina defendants would be "persuasive precedent" against the Mississippi defendants, thus impairing the Mississippi defendants' ability to defend themselves as a practical matter. As discussed above, both the First Circuit and *Janney* have rejected this very argument, and so must this Court.[5]

Third, pointing to subsection (a)(2)(ii), the South Carolina defendants argue that there is the possibility that they alone will end up footing the entire bill when, in fact, the Mississippi defendants are entirely or partly responsible. As discussed above, both the First Circuit and *Janney* have rejected this very argument, and so must this Court.

Fourth, recognizing the traditional rule of thumb that co-obligees are "indispensable" parties while co-obligors might not even be "necessary," the South Carolina defendants try to cast themselves as co-obligees under the alleged contract. In other words, the South Carolina defendants argue that Daynard still owes legal research and advice to the defendants—even though the State Tobacco Litigation settled years ago. This argument is as silly as it is belated. The only question before the Court is whether the defendants owe Daynard money; there has never been any suggestion that Daynard still owes services to the defendants. The Court rejects the notion that the South Carolina defendants are co-obligees and instead recognizes them for what they really are—co-obligors.

Finally, recognizing the traditional rule of thumb that an action to set aside a contract requires the joinder of all parties to the contract, the South

---

5. Similarly, the Mississippi defendants cannot be "necessary" merely because the South Carolina defendants need to obtain evidence from them. *E.g., Johnson v. Smithsonian Inst.*, 189 F.3d 180, 188-89 (2d Cir. 1999) (citing *Costello Publ'g Co. v. Rotelle*, 670 F.2d 1035, 1044-45 (D.C. Cir. 1981)).

Carolina defendants argue that a mutual release to which Daynard allegedly agreed puts the validity and enforceability of the alleged contract into question and thus requires joinder of all parties to the alleged contract. This argument twists the traditional rule of thumb, which is that an action in equity to determine the rights under a contract requires joinder of all the parties to the contract. The case at bar concerns only money damages (legal relief) and does not concern rescission or specific performance (equitable relief). Accordingly, the traditional rule of thumb that rescission requires joinder of all parties must give way to the traditional rule of thumb that a plaintiff need not name all co-obligors as defendants.

In short, the Court holds that it is not necessary for Daynard to join the Mississippi defendants in this action because they are (or, drawing inferences in Daynard's favor, could be) jointly and severally liable co-obligors.

### B. RULE 19(B)—"INDISPENSABLE"?

If the Mississippi defendants are not "necessary" under Rule 19(a), then by definition they cannot be "indispensable" under Rule 19(b). Nevertheless, the Court will consider the South Carolina defendants' arguments under Rule 19(b) for the sake of completeness.

If a "necessary" party cannot be joined (*e.g.*, because of a lack of personal jurisdiction), "the court shall determine whether in equity and good conscience the action should proceed among the parties before it, or should be dismissed, the absent person being thus regarded as indispensable." Fed. R. Civ. P. 19(b). The factors to be considered by the court include:

> [F]irst, to what extent a judgment rendered in the person's absence might be prejudicial to the person or those already parties; second, the extent to which, by protective provisions in the judgment, by the shaping of relief, or other measures, the prejudice can be lessened or avoided; third, whether a judgment rendered in the person's absence will be adequate; fourth, whether the plaintiff will have an adequate remedy if the action is dismissed for nonjoinder.

*Id.* The Supreme Court has identified four corresponding interests a court might want to consider:

> (1) the interest of the outsider whom it would have been desirable to join; (2) the defendant's interest in avoiding multiple litigation, inconsistent relief, or sole responsibility for a liability it shares with another; (3) the interest of the courts and the public in complete, consistent, and efficient settlement of controversies; and (4) the plaintiff's interest in having a forum.

*H.D. Corp.*, 791 F.2d at 992 (citing *Provident Tradesmens Bank & Trust Co. v. Patterson*, 390 U.S. 102, 108-111 (1968)).

. . . [T]he First Circuit will review this Court's determination under Rule 19(b) for an abuse of discretion. Accordingly, precedent provides little guidance. "Whether a person is 'indispensable,' that is, whether a particular lawsuit must be dismissed in the absence of that person, can only be determined in the context of particular litigation." *Provident Tradesmens*, 390 U.S. at 118. With this in mind, the Court turns to the four factors enumerated in Rule 19(b), which substantially overlap with the factors enumerated in Rule 19(a).

First, to what extent might a judgment rendered in the person's absence be prejudicial to the person or those already parties? This factor tends to favor Daynard. The South Carolina defendants argue that (i) there is the possibility that they alone will end up footing the entire bill, which would prejudice them; (ii) there is the possibility that a successful "empty chair" defense would result in "persuasive precedent," which would prejudice the Mississippi defendants; and (iii) there is the possibility of an inconsistent adjudication in a later lawsuit, which could prejudice any of the parties. The Court rejects these arguments for the same reasons given before, namely (i) joint and several liability by definition includes the possibility that one defendant ends up footing the entire bill, (ii) "persuasive precedent" alone cannot, as a practical matter, impair or impede the Mississippi defendants' ability to defend themselves, and (iii) Rule 19 is concerned with the risk of inconsistent obligations, not inconsistent adjudications.

Second, to what extent can the prejudice be lessened or avoided by protective provisions in the judgment, by the shaping of relief, or other measures? This factor does not seem relevant to this dispute. According to the advisory committee's note, "protective provisions" includes requiring a defendant to set aside money in case absent plaintiffs later obtain judgments, and the "shaping of relief" includes awarding money damages in lieu of specific performance where the latter might affect an absentee adversely.

Third, would a judgment rendered in the person's absence be adequate? This factor clearly favors Daynard. The South Carolina defendants are (or, drawing inferences in Daynard's favor, could be) jointly and severally liable. The South Carolina defendants complain that allowing Daynard to obtain complete relief from them will result in a second lawsuit between the defendants, but that is their problem, not Daynard's. Obviously a single lawsuit would be more efficient than multiple lawsuits, but this factor only concerns whether the judgment would be adequate to Daynard.

Fourth, would the plaintiff have an adequate remedy if the action is dismissed for nonjoinder? This factor clearly favors the South Carolina defendants. Daynard could bring suit against all the defendants in Mississippi.

In sum, the first and third factors favor Daynard, the second factor is not relevant, and the fourth factor favors the South Carolina defendants. The question is not simply how many factors point in one direction, of course, but "whether in equity and good conscience the action should proceed among the parties before [the court], or should be dismissed, the absent person being thus regarded as indispensable." Fed. R. Civ. P. 19(b). To this question the Court answers that it would allow the action to proceed against the South Carolina defendants even if the Mississippi defendants properly were regarded as "necessary" parties.

## Comments and Questions

1. Carefully consider each case that Judge Young describes (i.e., *Acton Co.*, *H.D. Corp.*, *Pujol*, and *Janney*), and be prepared to explain the result in each and why it is like or distinguishable from *Daynard*.

2. Put yourself in Judge Young's shoes. Why did he write "Part 2b" of his opinion regarding Rule 19(b)? Wasn't this unnecessary given his decision in "Part 2a"? Had the First Circuit decided, as it ultimately did, that the Mississippi defendants should not have been dismissed for lack of personal jurisdiction, what effect would that have had on the South Carolina defendants' Rule 12(b)(7) motion to dismiss?

3. What types of considerations might have convinced Professor Daynard and his lawyers not to file suit in Mississippi? What other techniques might these defendants have employed to get the case into Mississippi?

4. Is mandatory joinder disfavored? If so, why?

5. It should be apparent that there is considerable overlap between the four factors in parts (a) and (b) of Fed. R. Civ. P. 19. What is the difference, then, between "necessary" and "indispensable" parties?

6. Why does Fed. R. Civ. P. 12(h)(2) add "a defense of failure to join a party indispensable under Rule 19" to those which can be made as late as "at the trial on the merits"?

7. For a critical look at English and American antecedents to "necessary and indispensable party" doctrine, see Geoffrey C. Hazard, Jr., *Indispensable Party: The Historical Origin of a Procedural Phantom*, 61 Colum. L. Rev. 1254 (1961).

8. According to Fed. R. Civ. P. 19(c), the plaintiff is supposed to advise the court of any parties that should be joined if feasible, as well as the reasons that they have not been joined. The failure to advise the court of such persons might result in dismissal of the case or the establishment of facts against the plaintiff. According to the advisory committee notes to Rule 19(c), the court can notify such a person about the existence of the case and provide the person with an opportunity to intervene (unless, of course, the person's intervention would create jurisdictional difficulties, in which case a Rule 19(b) analysis must be performed). If the person declines to intervene, or if the court otherwise becomes aware of the presence of such a necessary party, the court may have the power under Rule 21 to order the joinder of such a person (at least as long as there are no jurisdiction, venue, or other barriers to joinder).

# K. INTERPLEADER

An individual or corporation who is or may be exposed to double or multiple liability may also initiate the joinder of the parties who have asserted or could assert such claims. This joinder device is called *interpleader*, and many of these cases involve insurance disputes. For example, a life insurance company may have issued a policy payable to the beneficiary "Roy Adams" upon the death of the insured. But when two persons named "Roy Adams" claim to be the beneficiaries entitled to the proceeds of the policy, the insurance company may be uncertain as to which of the two it should pay. Under these circumstances, the life insurance company can *interplead* those alleging rights to the proceeds. By doing so, the company seeks a determination of whom to pay and avoids the risk that it will have to pay the policy amount twice. Consequently, the insurance company, which ordinarily would be the defendant in a case in which a beneficiary makes a claim, becomes the plaintiff in an interpleader. In the terminology of interpleaders, the insurance company is the *stakeholder*. The *stake* is subject to the claims of the *adverse claimants*, who in this hypothetical would be the two persons named Roy Adams.

The words *stake* and *adverse claimants* convey an important restriction about the utility of the interpleader device: The claims must be demanding the same thing or obligation—that is, a piece of property, a prize, or, most commonly, the proceeds of an insurance policy. Importantly, Ultimate Auto could *not* interplead some other putative plaintiff who was injured by a suspension lift kit that Ultimate Auto sold; that putative plaintiff and Charles Carpenter's estate would not be asserting claims that compete for the same thing. Understand the important difference: The insurance company promised to pay one person named Roy Adams—the only question is *which* Roy Adams.

The Roy Adams hypothetical can be complicated still further if the insurance company is not only the stakeholder but also one of the adverse claimants. This could occur in our hypothetical if the insurance company claims that the premium was not timely paid and, thus, no payout is necessary. The insurance company would interplead both of the individuals named Roy Adams to avoid paying twice, but it would also be an adverse claimant and would argue that it should not have to pay even once.

Interpleader is also available to a stakeholder who is sued by one of the claimants, allowing it to interplead the other claimants by way of a third-party claim, cross-claim, or counterclaim. A trial court deciding an interpleader action first considers whether there is real potential for exposure to multiple liability for a single "claim." If so, then a court will proceed to address the merits of the interpleader action. Two types of interpleader are available in federal court: Rule 22 and 28 U.S.C. § 1335. (Regarding the latter, *see also* 28 U.S.C. §§ 1397 and 2361.) The major differences between the rule and the statute pertain to jurisdictional and venue requirements, which are the subject of Chapter 7.

## L. INTERVENTION

Federal Rule 24 allows nonparties to join ongoing litigation either as a matter of right or in the discretion of the court. Intervenors can protect their interests against the possible adverse effects of a judgment. The criteria for intervention as a matter of right differ in degree rather than in kind from those governing permissive or discretionary intervention.

## ■ UNITED STATES v. NORTHERN INDIANA PUBLIC SERVICE CO., ET AL.
### *100 F.R.D. 78 (N.D. Ind. 1983)*

SHARP, Chief Judge:

### I.

This case is presently before the court on the motion to intervene of the petitioner, Save the Dunes Council (Council) under Rule 24 Fed. R. Civ. P. The following facts are not disputed. On August 7, 1978, plaintiff, United States of America (United States) filed its "Notice of Condemnation" affecting 36.95 acres of land owned by Northern Indiana Public Service Company (NIPSCO) adjacent to its Michigan City Generating Station. NIPSCO filed its answer, objections to condemnation and motion to sustain objections on September 25, 1978. Subsequently, a request for a hearing on NIPSCO's legal objections was filed on October 26, 1981. A trial date of February 8, 1982 was set by order of the court October 9, 1981. That trial setting was vacated by order of January 22, 1982. On April 4, 1982, the Council filed a motion to intervene as a plaintiff under Rule 24. NIPSCO's response to the motion to intervene and a motion to strike were docketed April 8, 1982. Council then filed a memorandum in support of its motion to intervene and an answer to NIPSCO's motion to strike on April 20, 1982.

On September 7, 1983, the United States and NIPSCO entered into a stipulation and joint motion to dismiss. A pretrial conference was held in Lafayette, Indiana on October 20, 1983 where oral argument was heard on the intervention issue and the parties were instructed to file supplementary briefs by October 31, 1983. In addition, the Council filed, in open court, a copy of a pleading related to the subject matter of this case, a complaint for mandamus under 28 U.S.C. § 361, which had been filed on October 19, 1983 in the United States District Court for the District of Columbia. In compliance with this court's directive, supplemental briefs were filed by the Council on October 31, 1983 and by NIPSCO on November 1, 1983. To date, the United States had made no independent response to the Council's motion to intervene.

### II.

To intervene as of right under Fed. R. Civ. P. 24(a)(2), a proposed intervenor must show: (1) timely application; (2) an interest relating to the property or transaction which is the subject of the action; (3) that the disposition of the action may as a practical matter impair or impede his ability to protect that interest; and (4) that the interest is not adequately represented by existing parties.

Timeliness is a threshold question in a Rule 24(a) application and is determined by the court from all the circumstances in the exercise of its sound discretion. As soon as a prospective intervenor knows or has reason to know his interest may be adversely affected by the outcome of the litigation, he must move promptly to intervene. NIPSCO contends that the Council should not be allowed to intervene at this time because the Council had ample opportunity to petition the court prior to the time of the original parties' settlement. A careful review of the court record in this action indicates that the first reference to a possible settlement was alluded to in the joint motion for extension of time filed by the United States and NIPSCO on January 12, 1982. The Council filed its motion to intervene on April 2, 1982 while the parties' joint motion for dismissal was not filed until more than a year later on September 7, 1983. From the commencement of this action to the early months of 1982, the Council had no reason to believe that intervention would be required to protect its alleged interest in the tract of land since condemnation of the NIPSCO property would seem to effectuate the intent of Congress as manifested in a series of National Lakeshore expansion bills, all of which included the area at issue in this case. Moreover, there has been neither a trial nor an extensive exchange of pleadings. Thus, the first requirement—timeliness—has been met by the Council.

The second test the Council must meet concerns a determination as to whether or not it has an interest relating to the property or transaction which is the subject of the action. Council alleges that it has an environmental interest in that for the past 30 years it has been actively engaged in, and, has been at the forefront of, the campaign to preserve and protect the Indiana Dunes for public use and enjoyment.

There is as yet no consensus of what constitutes a litigable interest for purposes of standing and intervention under Rule 24(a). C.A. Wright, *Law of Federal Courts*, at 503 (4th ed. 1983). The more liberal view is set forth in *Cascade Natural Gas Corp. v. El Paso Natural Gas Co.*, 386 U.S. 129 (1967). That case expanded the application of "interest" by holding that a state, a customer, and a competitor all have a sufficient interest to intervene in a government antitrust divestiture proceeding. Cascade gives a decidedly broad interpretation to Rule 24 while noting that intervention of right is:

> . . . a kind of counterpart to Rule 19(a)(2)(i) on joinder of persons needed for just adjudication: where, upon motion of a party in an action, an absentee should be joined so that he may protect his interest which as a practical matter may be substantially impaired by the disposition of the action, he ought to have a right to intervene in the action on his own motion. *Id.* at 134 n.3.

However, the most recent interpretation of Rule 24(a)(2) by the Supreme Court has added a gloss that the rule is referring to a direct, "significantly protectable" interest in the property or transaction subject to the action.

*Donaldson v. United States*, 400 U.S. 517, 531 (1971). Cases in this circuit construing a Rule 24(a) interest also emphasize an interest which is legally protectable. In *Wade v. Goodschmidt*, 673 F.2d 182 (7th Cir. 1982), the court relied on this definition of "interest":

> [A]n interest, to satisfy the requirements of Rule 24(a)(2) must be significant, must be direct rather than contingent, and must be based on a right which belongs to the proposed intervenor rather than to an existing party to the suit.

*Id.* at 185-86 n. 5.

Clearly, the party with the paramount interest, indeed, the only legal interest, in the land at issue is NIPSCO. While the Council has played a laudatory role in the development of the Indiana Dunes National Lake Shore, with respect to this tract of land, it is essentially a private citizen with no interest in the property sought to be condemned to warrant intervention as a right.

Because the Council does not assert an interest in the property subject to this action, it has no protectable interest that can be impaired or impeded. Nor does it have the right to assert that its interest is being inadequately represented by the existing parties.

Moreover, the Council cannot avail itself of the permissive intervention allowed by Fed. R. Civ. P. 24(b). . . . While the Council's claim and this action center on the same factual basis, *i.e.*, the condemnation of the same tract of land, this court concludes that permissive intervention should be denied in order to avoid the likelihood of undue delay and prejudice to the rights of the original parties.

Four years have elapsed since the institution of this suit and the original parties have submitted a stipulated judgment for the court's approval. To allow intervention at this point in time to a party with no legal interest in the private property which is the subject of the proceeding and whose position is contrary to that of both the original parties, would serve no viable purpose except to prolong an already lengthy and tired lawsuit. Accordingly, it is ordered that the Council's motion for intervention under Rule 24 be and hereby is denied.

## Comments and Questions

1. What language do Fed. R. Civ. P. 19 and 24(a) have in common? What situation is each trying to address? Does it make sense to you that there would be two rules with such similar language? Consider that the rules are not identical—either in language or in usage. Further, while Rule 19 typically is used by a defendant to force the plaintiff to add a party, Rule 24 is used by an absentee party to become a party. Also, Fed. R. Civ. P. 24(a) contains the additional clause, "unless existing parties adequately

represent that interest." Moreover, since there is a more lenient test for intervention under Fed. R. Civ. P. 24(b), a judge may permit an absentee to intervene without having to justify fulfillment of the more stringent requirements of Fed. R. Civ. P. 24(a)(2). Some judges have been extremely lenient in permitting a wide range of intervening parties, yet have severely curtailed independent participation.

2. Federal statutes may also grant absentees the right of intervention, and Federal Rule 24 contemplates these rights. The Clean Air Act, for example, provides that in any government action brought to enforce compliance with the Act's standards "any person may intervene *as a matter of right.*" 42 U.S.C. § 7064(b)(1)(B) (emphasis added).

# Review Exercise No. 2

In this problem you must complete the opinion of the trial court. The factual background and procedural posture are already completed, and you are expected to write the portion that integrates the facts provided with the governing law. This exercise is drawn from *Rannels v. S.E. Nichols, Inc.*, 591 F.2d 242 (3d Cir. 1979).

Be a careful judge, who explains her or his actions. It should take you at least ninety minutes to answer this question fully.

JUSTICE, J.:

The facts that underlie this lawsuit for $2.8 million are traceable to a dispute over $2.00 between a customer and the management of a retail store. Ms. Flannel seeks to "make a federal case"—as certainly is her right under the existing statutes—out of the circumstances that befell her after she purchased a pair of blue jeans for eight dollars at the J.C. Penney store in Capital City, Northeastern. The following facts are alleged in her complaint filed in district court.

The day after she purchased the jeans, she discovered that the jeans were defective and returned them to the store. She requested that they give her a new pair or that they refund her the purchase price, which she had paid by personal check. The store refused. Ms. Flannel left the store with the jeans and then did two things: she stopped payment on her check and went and had the zipper replaced at the local cleaners at a cost of $2.00. With the repair bill in hand, she then returned to the store and demanded that the store pay her back for the cost of the repair. The customer-returns employee, Isabel Duffey, refused. Instead she made an oral demand of Ms. Flannel for $13.25 representing the original purchase price and the bank service handling charge for the stopped check. Ms. Flannel refused to honor this demand for payment in rather colorful language. The next day, the store's assistant manager,

Douglas A. Stauffer, filed a criminal complaint against her, charging her with a violation of the bad check statute. 18 N.G.L. § 4195.11.*

After the criminal complaint was filed, Ms. Flannel returned to the store and offered to pay the eight dollars; the offer was refused. Ms. Flannel went to see the store manager, Robert Boyd, who told Ms. Flannel that he had authorized the complaint because "you attempted fraud on my store." He also stated that he would not drop the complaint because "then the store would have to pay court costs and we want to make an example of you so that people don't try to stop checks on us and keep the goods." These remarks were made in the presence of Ms. Flannel, her son and other customers.

Ms. Flannel then wrote to the corporate president, Manfred Brecker, at the head office in New Jersey, explaining the history of the transaction and asking him to intervene and order his subordinates to drop the criminal complaint. She also told him that she was concerned about the defamation to her character and good standing in the community as she was the local PTA president and an elder in her church. His letter in response, as described in her complaint, shows that he was informed as to the facts of the transaction and that he supported the actions of his employees at the Capital City store in filing the criminal charges against her.

Ms. Flannel was tried and acquitted of the bad check charge and later voluntarily paid the Capital City store $6.00 "in full satisfaction and settlement of her debt."

Ms. Flannel then filed suit in this court for $2.8 million in damages for malicious prosecution. The elements of the relevant Northeastern law on malicious prosecution are: (1) the termination in the complainant's favor of the criminal proceedings; (2) want of probable cause for the criminal proceedings; and (3) malice. Probable cause has been defined as "a reasonable ground of suspicion supported by circumstances sufficiently strong in themselves as to make a cautious person believe that the person accused is guilty of the charged offense." Malice has been defined as "the intentional doing of a wrongful act without just cause or excuse, with an intent to inflict an injury or under circumstances that the law will imply an evil intent."

The defendants have filed a 12(b)(6) motion to dismiss, claiming that the allegations in the plaintiff's complaint fall short of making out a claim for relief under Northeastern law. We rule that . . .

[Students: Complete the opinion, giving your ruling and your reasoning.]

---

*18 N.G.L., § 4195.11 provides:

(a) Offense defined. A person commits an offense if s/he issues or passes a check or similar order for the payment of money, knowing that it will not be honored by the drawee.

(b) Presumption. For the purposes of this section as well as in any prosecution for theft committed by means of a bad check, an issuer is presumed to know that the check or order (other than a postdated check or order) would not be paid, if (1) the issuer had no account with the drawee at the time the check or order was issued; or (2) payment was refused by the drawee for lack of funds, upon presentation within thirty days after issue, and the issuer failed to make good within ten days after receiving notice of that refusal.

(c) Grading. An offense under this section is a misdemeanor of the second degree if the amount of the check or order exceeds $200.00; otherwise it is a summary offense.

# Review Exercise No. 3

You have ninety minutes to answer the following question. Your rules supplement is the only source you should require (though you may cite to cases we have studied).

To: Judicial Clerk
From: Judge L. Lapardo, Central Superior Court
Re: *Bentham et al. v. Delivery*
Date: June 25, 2012

Assume that Central is a state that has adopted the Fed. R. Civ. P. in all relevant parts. There is a two-year statute of limitations for torts cases. I have four motions pending before me in the above entitled case. *Please help me anticipate arguments on all sides, to the extent there are any, and tell me how to rule and why. Please include as much of your reasoning processes as you are able.*

Robert and Elisabeth Bentham, and Sally Schoose (hereafter called "Benthams" and "Schoose" or "plaintiffs") served one complaint with a summons on Home Delivery, Inc. ("Delivery" or "defendant") on January 5, 2012. "Delivery," in the complaint, is defined to mean the "corporation, and its servants, agents, and employees." The plaintiffs allege that the Benthams at all relevant times have lived on Elm Street, Capitol, Central, on the same block and five doors away from Schoose, who has lived at her home on Elm Street at all relevant times; that the Benthams retained Delivery in January 2010 to deliver groceries to their house once a week under an agreement that the Benthams had with Delivery whereby the plaintiffs would order groceries by phone on or before Tuesday of each week, and Delivery would deliver them to the Bentham house on Friday. The Benthams provided Delivery with a key to their house. The complaint further alleges that Schoose had the same deal with Delivery, beginning in February 2010, and that Schoose gave Delivery a key to her house. The complaint further alleges that on Friday, March 8, 2010, the Bentham house was negligently left unlocked by Delivery, and that as a result thereof, their house was burglarized that day, and $15,000 worth of property was stolen. The complaint also alleges that on Friday, April 12, 2010, the Schoose house was negligently left unlocked by Delivery, and that as a result thereof, her house was burglarized that day, and $9,000 worth of property was stolen. The plaintiffs seek damages in these amounts, plus interest, and demand a jury trial.

Delivery, in its answer, adopted the plaintiffs' definition of "Delivery." It admitted all allegations but the following: It denied that Delivery left either house unlocked, it denied any negligence, and it said it was without knowledge or information sufficient to form a belief as to whether the burglaries took place or as to the value of what was allegedly stolen.

No discovery has taken place as yet. Under Central law, if an employer is held responsible because of an employee's negligence (*respondeat superior*), the employer has a cause of action for indemnification from the employee.

(1) Defendant has moved to dismiss or to sever on the grounds of misjoinder of plaintiffs.

(2) A week ago, the Benthams moved to amend the complaint to add a count against Delivery for negligently delivering rotten food. Robert Bentham claims that on March 8, 2010, he ate sliced turkey that had been delivered by Delivery on that same day and was supposed to be fresh; that he became extremely ill from the bad turkey; and that he told Delivery of his illness the next day, at the same time he told them they were liable for the burglary.

(3) Delivery moves to implead Worker, whom they allege was their driver at all times and places in question. They seek indemnification from him. Central has no joint tortfeasor contribution statute.

(4) Notwithstanding your answer to the previous question, assume that Worker was not added as a third party defendant. Is s/he a Rule 19 party? Also, if there is a *Mr.* Schoose, is he a Rule 19 party?

# 4

# *Discovery*

## A. INTRODUCTION

As you saw in Chapter 3, the drafters of the Federal Rules of Civil Procedure had a vision of what an enlightened procedural regime would look like. Eschewing the technicalities of previous systems, they would make procedure simpler yet also more comprehensive. More specifically, this meant simplified nontechnical pleadings and enlarged joinder. It may be obvious, though, that if the parties are not going to be required to tell each other the specifics of their cases through the pleadings, some other mechanism would be needed, to convey that information. Thus we ended up with the multiple, expansive, and flexible discovery provisions found in the Federal Rules. Most important, the discovery rules revolutionized American procedure by establishing a broad scope for what may be obtained through discovery.

At common law, discovery was virtually nonexistent. The federal courts had no general inherent power to order discovery and were only invested with that power by two statutes allowing the taking of statements under oath, but only under very limited conditions. Trial by surprise was the norm because at the time of trial many litigants did not know what their adversary's position or evidence would be. The adoption of the discovery provisions of the Federal Rules transformed the practice of law in the United States. The Federal Rules made discovery a vital part of the litigation process.

Among the many benefits [the drafters] saw for expanded discovery were the following: the elimination of surprise; preserving testimony so it will be available in case of the death or other unavailability of witness; diminishing the importance of pleadings; increasing the effectiveness of the summary judgment; focusing the trial on the main points in controversy; and permitting each side to assess the strengths and weaknesses of their cases in advance, frequently making trials unnecessary because of informed settlement.

Stephen N. Subrin, *Fishing Expeditions Allowed: The Historical Background of the 1938 Federal Discovery Rules*, 39 B.C. L. Rev. 691, 716 (1998). These purposes remain the principal virtues of discovery in civil litigation today. But there is also vice.

Before we explore the major issues underlying the discovery rules and the specific wording of several of them, you should be aware of three critical points of orientation that will emerge repeatedly in this chapter. First, it is important to know that the American system is unique in its embrace (or reliance) upon expansive discovery. Indeed, we have been criticized in most other countries for the delays and expense created by our discovery system, as well as its intrusions upon privacy. Second, it is important to appreciate the unique role that civil litigation plays in the fabric of American society. Derivative of our historical distrust of government power and of our belief in individual responsibility, we rely heavily on private civil litigation to enforce norms of safety, to provide recompense for individual harms, and to vindicate individual rights. Put another way, our social safety net is much more porous than those common to most Western democracies; in the United States, private civil litigation carries much of that burden. And third, we want to emphasize early in this chapter the practical realities of today's "litigators" (yesterday's "trial lawyers") in large law firms: discovery will predominate your practice. As an editorial in the American Bar Association's *Litigation* magazine described in 1997: "[I]t is Discovery which we do. The motions, the papers, the depositions. This is the numbing, ditch digging work that determines the winner." But the study or practice of discovery should not be as tedious as the quote might suggest. Indeed, discovery is about gathering facts and developing a strategy—tools very familiar and essential to effective advocacy.

We start with a very short history of modern discovery in the United States. The story begins with broad attorney latitude and very little restraint imposed upon the parties by the original Federal Rules. In the next phase of the story, complaints abound about excesses—of attorney zealousness and abuse, of time and delay, and excessive cost. To be sure, liberalized rules of discovery stimulated explosive growth in the size and complexity of litigation. Judge Selya of the U.S. Court of Appeals for the First Circuit described the historical impact of liberal rules of discovery in very colorful terms: "A herd of bulls had been set loose in the decorous confines of the judge's lobby—and the china shop would never be the same." *In re San Juan Dupont Plaza Hotel Fire Litig.*, 859 F.2d 1007 (1st Cir. 1988). Indeed, the pretrial phase of litigation in some cases has taken on a nightmarish quality and has become prohibitively expensive.

The past three decades have witnessed repeated attempts by the rule-makers to rein in these alleged abuses. (We say *alleged* because, as you will see, although there are many instances of disgusting abuse, there is also evidence that, in the typical case, there is very little or no discovery at all.) In 1980, the Rules were amended to require discovery conferences early in the litigation. The year 1983 brought amendments that made the reduction of discovery explicitly part of pretrial conferences and introduced mandatory Rule 11 sanctions for discovery as well as pleading practice. Also in 1983, judges were invited to limit the extent and use of discovery in order to make it commensurate with the stakes of the litigation. In 1993 the drafters introduced limits on the number of interrogatories and depositions and a new regime requiring mandatory initial disclosures by both parties of certain essential information. The year 2000 brought yet another wave of discovery reforms: a narrower definition of the permissible scope of discovery, a presumptive time limit for depositions, and greater uniformity in enforcing the mandatory disclosures. And in the past decade, the phenomenon of electronically stored information has precipitated many questions, fewer answers, and some reforms.

As we begin this new chapter and examine a new phase of litigation, appreciate that and how all of the phases of litigation are conceptually intertwined. With regard to the conceptual link between pleadings and discovery, for example, remember that Justice Breyer's dissent in *Iqbal* suggested that the majority's concern about unwarranted litigation against government officials did not require a heightened pleading standard but rather could be addressed by "structur[ing] discovery in ways that diminish the risk of imposing unwarranted burdens upon public officials." But the majority was unpersuaded, given the (perceived or real) magnitude and inconvenience of discovery. After *Iqbal*, the conceptual link between pleadings and discovery continues to be a subject of discussion: how is a plaintiff with a meritorious claim supposed to obtain the detailed facts that *Iqbal* demands? Although some facts can be obtained through publically available resources and diligent investigation (which costs money), it may often be the case that defendant has exclusive access to relevant information and evidence. How can plaintiffs assert facts that cannot be known prior to discovery? Haven't *Twombly* and *Iqbal* materially diminished the liberal discovery regime in those cases in which previously a 12(b)(6) motion would have been denied? (Where could/should Iqbal have found the additional detail demanded of him?) Recognizing the close link between pleading and discovery, some scholars have suggested that *Iqbal* necessitates a mechanism for pre-filing discovery. *See, e.g.*, Scott Dodson, *New Pleading, New Discovery*, 109 Mich. L. Rev. 53 (2010).

The most effective way to understand and apply the rules and mechanics of discovery is, first, to appreciate the role of discovery in the jurisprudence of procedure. Accordingly, in Part B, we start by exploring in greater depth the tensions that explain this continuous cycle of criticism and reform. Then, in

Part C, we turn to the mechanics of the discovery process: the scope of permissible discovery, mandatory initial disclosure obligations, and the formal techniques (depositions, interrogatories, requests for admissions, document requests, and physical and mental examinations). This part concludes with a unit on the phenomenon of electronic discovery. Next, in Part D, we will consider issues pertaining to transnational discovery. And throughout this chapter you will find a number of practice exercises that challenge you to confront the ethical dilemmas and the practical applications of the subtleties of the rules. With this knowledge of the burdens and benefits of discovery, you will then be in a position to consider, in Part E, whether the current rulemaking process makes sense.

## B. DISCOVERY AND ITS TENSIONS

The primary function of the discovery process is to provide litigants with an opportunity to review all of the pertinent evidence prior to trial. This function is thought to be consistent with the pursuit of justice for at least three reasons. First, it reduces the chance of trial by ambush and facilitates determination upon the merits of the case. Second, it promotes settlement because it enables parties to assess the merits of their case well before trial. And third, it reduces the drain on the resources of the court because discovery educates the parties and often narrows the scope of issues in dispute.

Perhaps you associate the discovery process, however, not with the pursuit of justice, but rather with its notorious reputation for cost and abuse. Indeed, the discovery process has become a focal point of considerable criticism in the popular media. And to be sure, some litigants impose onerous burdens upon their adversaries, whether through excessive discovery requests to the other side or through production of an avalanche of documents to hide the proverbial needle in a haystack. In these circumstances, instead of being an essential element in the pursuit of justice, discovery proves to be a crippling obstacle. As you proceed through this chapter, think about the incentives that lead discovery *use* to become discovery *abuse*. When does it happen, and why?

Any study of the rules of discovery must begin with Rule 26. Generally speaking, a party is *entitled* to demand the discovery of any matter that:

- is relevant to the claim or defense of any party;
- is not unreasonably cumulative, burdensome, or disproportionate; and
- is not privileged.

*See* Fed. R. Civ. P. 26(b). Let's examine each of these three criteria in turn.

Given the capacity of the human imagination, the relevancy criterion is virtually without boundary. Moreover, a party is entitled to discovery not only of material that is relevant and admissible at trial, but also of information that "appears reasonably calculated to lead to the discovery of admissible evidence." Fed. R. Civ. P. 26(b)(1). Accordingly, it is an uphill battle to convince a court that discovery sought by opposing counsel is so unrelated to any claim or defense of any party that it cannot be said to be "relevant" within the expansive meaning of that term in Rule 26. We will revisit the scope of discovery in subsequent parts of this chapter.

The second discovery criterion is the product of a 1983 amendment to Rule 26. Prior to the amendment, Rule 26 provided for unlimited discovery "[u]nless the court orders otherwise." As amended, the Rule now provides that the court may limit the frequency of discovery when the information sought is unreasonably cumulative or duplicative, or can be obtained from another source, and also when the benefit to the requesting party is disproportionate to the burden of producing it. Naturally, good lawyers will usually have an argument why even multiple identical versions of a document need to be produced in order for them to prepare their case. These arguments are especially complex in the context of electronically stored records, which we will also consider later in this chapter.

The third discovery criterion exempts privileged material from discovery—even if it is "relevant." The most frequently invoked privilege is the attorney-client privilege, which precludes the discovery of confidential communications between an attorney and her client. By virtue of a 1970 amendment to Rule 26, limitations were placed on the discovery of trial preparation materials and on the methods for obtaining information about experts and their opinions.

Before delving any further into the mechanics of discovery, which we will address in Part C later in this chapter, we think it important to address explicitly three overlapping sources of tension that lurk within (and contribute to the formation of) our discovery rules: (1) the uncomfortable fit between the ideal that litigation is adversarial and the notion that discovery can require one side to help the other side prove its case; (2) whatever the grand intentions of discovery, those processes can be abused, can create inefficiencies, and can alter the outcomes of cases (including discouraging people from even filing a lawsuit); and (3) discovery obligations can work significant invasions of privacy.

## 1. Discovery in an Adversary System

The following is an excerpt from a 1947 Supreme Court decision that deals with the issue of an attorney's trial preparation and the protection of his work product. The excerpt is included here primarily because it outlines the Court's general attitude toward the purpose of the new paradigm of open-handed, party-controlled discovery. This was the Court's first major decision discussing discovery following the 1938 enactment of the Federal Rules. You will see how important discovery is, but you will also notice that we have known—from the beginning—that there will need to be some limitations.

# ■ HICKMAN v. TAYLOR

### 329 U.S. 495 (1947)

Justice MURPHY delivered the opinion of the Court:

This case presents an important problem under the Federal Rules of Civil Procedure . . . the extent to which a party may inquire into oral and written statements of witnesses, or other information, secured by an adverse party's counsel in the course of preparation for possible litigation after a claim has arisen. Examination into a person's files and records, including those resulting from the professional activities of an attorney, must be judged with care. It is not without reason that various safeguards have been established to preclude unwarranted excursions into the privacy of a man's work. At the same time, public policy supports reasonable and necessary inquiries. Properly to balance these competing interests is a delicate and difficult task. . . .

[The facts of the case are summarized as follows: The *J. M. Taylor* tug sank while towing a Baltimore & Ohio Railroad car float across the Delaware River. Five crew members drowned; four survived. Two months after the accident, the United States Steamboat Inspectors held a public hearing in which the four survivors were examined. Shortly thereafter, counsel for the tug owners, Fortenbaugh, took statements privately from survivors and witnesses in anticipation of possible litigation from the families of the deceased. Eventually, families of each of the deceased brought claims against the tug owners. All but one of the claims settled without litigation. About nine months after the accident, the fifth claimant (Petitioner) brought suit in the federal district court suing the tug owners and the railroad (Defendants).]

One year later, petitioner filed 39 interrogatories directed to the tug owners. The 38th interrogatory read:

> State whether any statements of the members of the crews of the Tugs *J. M. Taylor* and *Philadelphia* or of any other vessel were taken in connection with the towing of the car float and the sinking of the Tug *John M. Taylor.*
>
> Attach hereto exact copies of all such statements if in writing, and if oral, set forth in detail the exact provisions of any such oral statements or reports.

Supplemental interrogatories asked whether any oral or written statements, records, reports or other memoranda had been made concerning any matter relative to the towing operation, the sinking of the tug, the salvaging and repair of the tug, and the death of the deceased. If the answer was in the affirmative, the tug owners were then requested to set forth the nature of all such records, reports, statements or other memoranda.

The tug owners, through Fortenbaugh, answered all of the interrogatories except No. 38 and the supplemental ones just described. While admitting that statements of the survivors had been taken, they declined to summarize or set forth the contents. They did so on the ground that such requests called "for privileged matter obtained in preparation for litigation" and constituted "an attempt to obtain indirectly counsel's private files." It was claimed that answering these requests "would involve practically turning over not only the complete files, but also the telephone records and, almost, the thoughts of counsel."

In connection with the hearing on these objections, Fortenbaugh made a written statement and gave an informal oral deposition explaining the circumstances under which he had taken the statements. But he was not expressly asked in the deposition to produce the statements. . . . [The District Court held that the subjects of the petitioner's requests were not privileged and ordered counsel to answer the interrogatory and the supplemental interrogatories, produce all of the witnesses' statements, and state any facts concerning the case that Defendants learned through the witnesses, and to] produce Mr. Fortenbaugh's memoranda containing statements of fact by witnesses or to submit these memoranda to the Court for determination of those portions which should be revealed to Plaintiff. Upon their refusal, the court adjudged them in contempt and ordered them imprisoned until they complied.

The Third Circuit Court of Appeals, also sitting *en banc*, reversed the judgment of the District Court. It held that the information here sought was part of the "work product of the lawyer" and hence privileged from discovery under the Federal Rules of Civil Procedure. The importance of the problem, which has engendered a great divergence of views among district courts, led us to grant certiorari. . . .

The pre-trial deposition-discovery mechanism established by Rules 26 to 37 is one of the most significant innovations of the Federal Rules of Civil Procedure. Under the prior federal practice, the pre-trial functions of notice-giving, issue-formulation, and fact-revelation were performed primarily and inadequately by the pleadings. Inquiry into the issues and the facts before trial was narrowly confined and was often cumbersome in method. The new rules, however, restrict the pleadings to the task of general notice-giving and invest the deposition-discovery process with a vital role in the preparation for trial. The various instruments of discovery now serve (1) as a device, along with the pre-trial hearing under Rule 16, to narrow and clarify the basic issues between the parties, and (2) as a device for ascertaining the facts, or information as to the existence or whereabouts of facts, relative to those issues. Thus civil trials in the federal courts no longer need be carried on in the dark. The way is now clear, consistent with recognized privileges, for the parties to obtain the fullest possible knowledge of the issues and facts before trial. . . .

[T]he basic question at stake is whether [discovery] may be used to inquire into materials collected by an adverse party's counsel in the course of preparing for possible litigation. . . .

In urging that he has a right to inquire into the materials secured and prepared by Fortenbaugh, petitioner emphasizes that the deposition-discovery portions of the Federal Rules of Civil Procedure are designed to enable the parties to discover the true facts and to compel their disclosure wherever they

may be found. It is said that inquiry may be made under these rules, epitomized by Rule 26[b], as to any relevant matter which is not privileged; and
since the discovery provisions are to be applied as broadly and liberally as
possible, the privilege limitation must be restricted to its narrowest bounds.
On the premise that the attorney-client privilege is the one involved in this
case, petitioner argues that it must be strictly confined to confidential communications made by a client to his attorney. And since the materials here in
issue were secured by Fortenbaugh from third persons rather than from his
clients, the tug owners, the conclusion is reached that these materials are
proper subjects for discovery under Rule 26[b].

As additional support for this result, petitioner claims that to prohibit
discovery under these circumstances would give a corporate defendant a
tremendous advantage in a suit by an individual plaintiff. Thus in a suit
by an injured employee against a railroad or in a suit by an insured person
against an insurance company the corporate defendant could pull a dark veil
of secrecy over all the pertinent facts it can collect after the claim arises
merely on the assertion that such facts were gathered by its large staff of
attorneys and claim agents. At the same time, the individual plaintiff, who
often has direct knowledge of the matter in issue and has no counsel until
some time after his claim arises could be compelled to disclose all the intimate
details of his case. By endowing with immunity from disclosure all that a
lawyer discovers in the course of his duties, it is said, the rights of individual
litigants in such cases are drained of vitality and the lawsuit becomes more of
a battle of deception than a search for truth.

But framing the problem in terms of assisting individual plaintiffs in their
suits against corporate defendants is unsatisfactory. Discovery concededly
may work to the disadvantage as well as to the advantage of individual
plaintiffs. Discovery, in other words, is not a one-way proposition. It is available in all types of cases at the behest of any party, individual or corporate,
plaintiff or defendant. The problem thus far transcends the situation confronting this petitioner. And we must view that problem in light of the limitless situations where the particular kind of discovery sought by petitioner
might be used.

We agree, of course, that the deposition-discovery rules are to be accorded
a broad and liberal treatment. No longer can the time-honored cry of 'fishing
expedition' serve to preclude a party from inquiring into the facts underlying
his opponent's case. Mutual knowledge of all the relevant facts gathered by
both parties is essential to proper litigation. To that end, either party may
compel the other to disgorge whatever facts he has in his possession. The
deposition-discovery procedure simply advances the stage at which the disclosure can be compelled from the time of trial to the period preceding it, thus
reducing the possibility of surprise. But discovery, like all matters of procedure, has ultimate and necessary boundaries. . . .

Petitioner has made more than an ordinary request for relevant, nonprivileged facts in the possession of his adversaries or their counsel. He
has sought discovery as of right of oral and written statements of witnesses

whose identity is well known and whose availability to petitioner appears unimpaired. He has sought production of these matters after making the most searching inquiries of his opponents as to the circumstances surrounding the fatal accident, which inquiries were sworn to have been answered to the best of their information and belief. Interrogatories were directed toward all the events prior to, during and subsequent to the sinking of the tug. Full and honest answers to such broad inquiries would necessarily have included all pertinent information gleaned by Fortenbaugh through his interviews with the witnesses. Petitioner makes no suggestion, and we cannot assume, that the tug owners or Fortenbaugh were incomplete or dishonest in the framing of their answers. In addition, petitioner was free to examine the public testimony of the witnesses taken before the United States Steamboat Inspectors. We are thus dealing with an attempt to secure the production of written statements and mental impressions contained in the files and the mind of the attorney Fortenbaugh without any showing of necessity or any indication or claim that denial of such production would unduly prejudice the preparation of petitioner's case or cause him any hardship or injustice. For aught that appears, the essence of what petitioner seeks either has been revealed to him already through the interrogatories or is readily available to him direct from the witnesses for the asking. . . .

In our opinion, neither Rule 26 nor any other rule dealing with discovery contemplates production under such circumstances. That is not because the subject matter is privileged or irrelevant, as those concepts are used in these rules. Here is simply an attempt, without purported necessity or justification, to secure written statements, private memoranda and personal recollections prepared or formed by an adverse party's counsel in the course of his legal duties. As such, it falls outside the arena of discovery and contravenes the public policy underlying the orderly prosecution and defense of legal claims. Not even the most liberal of discovery theories can justify unwarranted inquiries into the files and the mental impressions of an attorney.

Historically, a lawyer is an officer of the court and is bound to work for the advancement of justice while faithfully protecting the rightful interests of his clients. In performing his various duties, however, it is essential that a lawyer work with a certain degree of privacy, free from unnecessary intrusion by opposing parties and their counsel. Proper preparation of a client's case demands that he assemble information, sift what he considers to be the relevant from the irrelevant facts, prepare his legal theories and plan his strategy without undue and needless interference. That is the historical and the necessary way in which lawyers act within the framework of our system of jurisprudence to promote justice and to protect their clients' interests. This work is reflected, of course, in interviews, statements, memoranda, correspondence, briefs, mental impressions, personal beliefs, and countless other tangible and intangible ways—aptly though roughly termed by the Circuit Court of Appeals in this case as the "Work product of the lawyer." Were such materials open to opposing counsel on mere demand, much of what is now put down in writing would remain unwritten. An attorney's thoughts, heretofore inviolate, would not be his own. Inefficiency, unfairness and sharp practices would inevitably develop in the giving of legal advice and in the preparation of cases for trial. The effect on the legal profession would be demoralizing. And the interests of the clients and the cause of justice would be poorly served.

We do not mean to say that all written materials obtained or prepared by an adversary's counsel with an eye toward litigation are necessarily free from discovery in all cases. Where relevant and non-privileged facts remain hidden in an attorney's file and where production of those facts is essential to the preparation of one's case, discovery may properly be had. Such written statements and documents might, under certain circumstances, be admissible in evidence or give clues as to the existence or location of relevant facts. Or they might be useful for purposes of impeachment or corroboration. And production might be justified where the witnesses are no longer available or can be reached only with difficulty. Were production of written statements and documents to be precluded under such circumstances, the liberal ideals of the deposition-discovery portions of the Federal Rules of Civil Procedure would be stripped of much of their meaning. But the general policy against invading the privacy of an attorney's course of preparation is so well recognized and so essential to an orderly working of our system of legal procedure that a burden rests on the one who would invade that privacy to establish adequate reasons to justify production through a subpoena or court order. That burden, we believe, is necessarily implicit in the rules as now constituted.

Rule 30(b), as presently written, gives the trial judge the requisite discretion to make a judgment as to whether discovery should be allowed as to written statements secured from witnesses. But in the instant case there was no room for that discretion to operate in favor of the petitioner. No attempt was made to establish any reason why Fortenbaugh should be forced to produce the written statements. There was only a naked, general demand for these materials as of right and a finding by the District Court that no recognizable privilege was involved. That was insufficient to justify discovery under these circumstances and the court should have sustained the refusal of the tug owners and Fortenbaugh to produce.

But as to oral statements made by witnesses to Fortenbaugh, whether presently in the form of his mental impressions or memoranda, we do not believe that any showing of necessity can be made under the circumstances of this case so as to justify production. Under ordinary conditions, forcing an attorney to repeat or write out all that witnesses have told him and to deliver the account to his adversary gives rise to grave dangers of inaccuracy and untrustworthiness. No legitimate purpose is served by such production. The practice forces the attorney to testify as to what he remembers or what he saw fit to write down regarding witnesses' remarks. Such testimony could not qualify as evidence; and to use it for impeachment or corroborative purposes would make the attorney much less an officer of the court and much more an ordinary witness. The standards of the profession would thereby suffer.

Denial of production of this nature does not mean that any material, non-privileged facts can be hidden from the petitioner in this case. He need not be unduly hindered in the preparation of his case, in the discovery of facts or in his anticipation of his opponents' position. Searching interrogatories directed to Fortenbaugh and the tug owners, production of written documents and statements upon a proper showing and direct interviews with the witnesses themselves all serve to reveal the facts in Fortenbaugh's possession to the fullest possible extent consistent with public policy. Petitioner's counsel frankly admits that he wants the oral statements only to help prepare himself to examine witnesses and to make sure that he has overlooked nothing. That is insufficient under the circumstances to permit him an exception to the policy underlying the privacy of Fortenbaugh's professional activities. If there should be a rare situation justifying production of these matters, petitioner's case is not of that type.

We fully appreciate the widespread controversy among the members of the legal profession over the problem raised by this case. It is a problem that rests on what has been one of the most hazy frontiers of the discovery process. But until some rule or statute definitely prescribes otherwise, we are not justified in permitting discovery in a situation of this nature as a matter of unqualified right. When Rule 26 and the other discovery rules were adopted, this Court and the members of the bar in general certainly did not believe or contemplate that all the files and mental processes of lawyers were thereby opened to the free scrutiny of their adversaries. And we refuse to interpret the rules at this time so as to reach so harsh and unwarranted a result.

We therefore affirm the judgment of the Circuit Court of Appeals.

Justice JACKSON, concurring:

. . . Counsel for the petitioner candidly said on argument that he wanted this information to help prepare himself to examine witnesses, to make sure he overlooked nothing. He bases his claim to it in his brief on the view that the Rules were to do away with the old situation where a law suit developed into "a battle of wits between counsel." But a common law trial is and always should be an adversary proceeding. Discovery was hardly intended to enable a learned profession to perform its functions either without wits or on wits borrowed from the adversary.

The real purpose and the probable effect of the practice ordered by the district court would be to put trials on a level even lower than a "battle of wits." I can conceive of no practice more demoralizing to the Bar than to require a lawyer to write out and deliver to his adversary an account of what witnesses have told him. Even if his recollection were perfect, the statement would be his language permeated with his inferences. Every one who has tried it knows that it is almost impossible so fairly to record the expressions and emphasis of a witness that when he testifies in the environment of the court and under the influence of the leading question there will not be departures in some respects. Whenever the testimony of the witness would

differ from the "exact" statement the lawyer had delivered, the lawyer's statement would be whipped out to impeach the witness. Counsel producing his
adversary's "inexact" statement could lose nothing by saying, "Here is a contradiction, gentlemen of the jury. I do not know whether it is my adversary or
his witness who is not telling the truth, but one is not." Of course, if this
practice were adopted, that scene would be repeated over and over again.
The lawyer who delivers such statements often would find himself branded
a deceiver afraid to take the stand to support his own version of the witness'
conversation with him, or else he will have to go on the stand to defend his
own credibility—perhaps against that of his chief witness, or possibly even
his client.

Every lawyer dislikes to take the witness stand and will do so only
for grave reasons. This is partly because it is not his role; he is almost invariably a poor witness. But he steps out of professional character to do it. He
regrets it; the profession discourages it. But the practice advocated here
is one which would force him to be a witness, not as to what he has seen or
done but as to other witnesses' stories, and not because he wants to do so but
in self-defense. . . .

## Comments and Questions

1. An important theme in this case is contained in the Court's statement:
"No longer can the time-honored cry of 'fishing expedition' serve to preclude a
party from inquiring into the facts underlying his opponent's case. Mutual
knowledge of all the relevant facts gathered by both parties is essential to
proper litigation. To that end, either party may compel the other to disgorge
whatever facts he has in his possession. The deposition-discovery procedure
simply advances the stage at which the disclosure can be compelled from the
time of trial to the period preceding it, thus reducing the possibility of
surprise." Does *Iqbal* undermine the notion that fishing expeditions are
allowed? To which "stage" of litigation does *Iqbal* move the moment "at
which . . . disclosure can be compelled"?

2. Does the element of surprise necessarily run counter to the pursuit of
justice? As one federal judge puts it, "A certain amount of surprise is often a
catalyst which precipitates the truth." *Margeson v. Boston & Maine R.R*, 16
F.R.D. 200, 201 (D. Mass. 1954). When does "surprise" become, instead, "trial
by ambush"?

3. The drafters of the Federal Rules thought that broad discovery would
help get the relevant facts into the open before trial, thereby reducing the
possibility of surprise and producing a more just result. Why, then, offer
protection to an attorney's work product? Put another way, why preserve
this particular element of surprise?

4. Of course, a system that allows broad and virtually unlimited access to
information is not without vice. Scholars of the law and economics movement
have described the basic incentives that lead to extraordinarily high

discovery costs. That model assumes that parties have the incentive to increase their opponent's legal costs. The greater the anticipated or actual legal expense, the more attractive that settlement becomes. And because it costs less to prepare a discovery request than to answer one, parties can inflict costs on their opponents with broad discovery requests, regardless of the value of the information to the requesting party.

5. Accounts of the elephantine mass of discovery in contemporary cases are quite familiar. In the *Exxon Valdez* oil spill cases, for example, "discovery took almost five years; the defendants were required to produce millions of pages of materials; the plaintiff took over one thousand depositions; Exxon deposed thousands of individuals and required them to produce tax records and other business records; and Exxon employed hundreds of expert witnesses, most of whom produced expert reports and most of whom were deposed by the plaintiffs." Keith E. Sealing, *Civil Procedure in Substantive Context: The Exxon-Valdez Cases*, 47 St. L. U. L.J. 63, 77 (2003). *See also In re Vioxx Products Liab. Litig.*, 760 F. Supp. 2d 640 (E.D. La. 2010) ("Millions of documents were discovered and collated. Thousands of depositions were taken and at least 1,000 discovery motions were argued."); *In re Digitek Products Liab. Litig.*, 264 F.R.D. 249 (S.D. W. Va. 2010) ("Merck has produced over 22 million pages of documents. Hundreds of depositions have taken place. This court has ruled on approximately one thousand pre-trial motions and has reviewed over 500,000 pages of documents.").

Extensive discovery can also be a problem in more traditional, simpler litigation. In an action by a physician against a county medical center for employment discrimination, the plaintiff's lawyer invested more than 4800 hours in three years of litigation that included the production of tens of thousands of documents and more than fifty depositions. *See Jadwin v. County of Kern*, 610 F. Supp. 2d 1129 (E.D. Cal. 2009). Does this amount of discovery appear reasonable and proportionate to you?

In each of these cases, of course, the lawyers for both sides must review—perhaps even scrutinize—every piece of paper. Indeed, in an article recounting her role in the tobacco litigation, attorney Martha Wivell, a partner in the law firm of Robins, Kaplan, Miller & Ciresi, L.L.P., answered the question how her firm reviewed the 30 million documents that were produced in her case. Her answer: "One at a time." *See* Martha Wivell, *Key to the Tobacco Fortress*, 38 Trial 45, 45 (Dec. 2002).

6. The following excerpt was authored by a litigator in New Jersey. The article is titled *Why I Love Document Reviews*.

> Before I became a lawyer, I was both a law secretary and a paralegal. In each of these roles, I loved doing document reviews. I have now been practicing law for more than 25 years. I still enjoy poring over documents, those of both my opponents and my clients. I cannot imagine a better way of getting the feel of a case—the good, the bad, and the ugly—than actually getting my hands dirty handling documents. . . .

Why . . . do young associates lament that they have been assigned to review documents . . . ? "It's boring," they say. "This is not why I became a lawyer." The only positive thing new associates say about document review: great billables!

What they don't realize is that reviewing documents produced in discovery is the equivalent of poking around in a friend's medicine cabinet or closet. The rules of civil procedure are license to snoop. If you have an interest in people— and you must to be a good litigator—document review is an opportunity to find out the intimate thoughts of the people involved in your case, whether they are acting as employees of corporations or as individuals. Documents also, of course, help explain your story of what happened in the case and why your client is the good guy. . . .

Another huge benefit of document review is that it is educational. Every litigator worth her salt becomes an expert in the subject matter of her case—at least for the time the case goes on—particularly if the subject matter is new to her. I have always enjoyed being a litigator for this reason. I get to learn about the ins and outs of welding, for example, or my client's corporate structure. For the life span of the case, I know more about the subject than most people except the experts (and sometimes even more than they do). And it is the documents I review that give me this knowledge.

Janet S. Kole, *Why I Love Document Reviews*, 33 Litig. 53, 53 (Winter 2007).

7. But the perception of laypersons and of many lawyers is that the discovery process has truly run amok. Consider the following excerpt written by the author of the 1991 bestseller *The Litigation Explosion*:

The current unpopularity of lawyers has been the subject of much hand-wringing, and no little indignation, on the part of such groups as the American Bar Association (ABA). . . . According to the ABA view, the prevailing low regard for lawyers has nothing whatsoever to do with the public's having noticed and reacted against any misconduct or hubris or overreaching by the legal profession or the legal system itself. Certainly not. Lawyers have plummeted in the occupational-esteem standing not because lawyers do more destructive or useless things than they used to, not because people think they've nosed into too many areas of American life, not because the system gives attorneys too much power to inflict on their opponents, their clients and third parties. No it's that the public has been terribly misled. If it only knew more about how the American legal system worked, it would not be so upset with lawyers. Its unfavorable view of lawyers arises from misunderstanding or, if you will, false consciousness. . . .

[L]awyers, I submit are so widely disliked in this country because they are so very widely, and correctly, feared for the power without responsibility they wield. . . . Nowhere else can a lawyer show up, dump a pile of papers on your front lawn, tie you up for years, responding to untold damage to your business and reputation, and then walk away with so few consequences if he is proven wrong. . . .

So the question I leave for the bar associations is: is your profession mistrusted because it's not understood? Or because it's understood too well?

Walter Olson, *Dentists, Bartenders and Lawyer Unpopularity*, Manhattan Instit., Civil Justice Memo No. 37 (Apr. 1999), available at *www.manhattan -institute.org/html/cjm_37.htm*. Why does American society give litigators so much power yet provide so little control over how they use it?

8. As Olson suggests, not only is the system to blame, but also the lawyers within it. Indeed, there are many instances demonstrating a lack of civility in the discovery process. In the following excerpt, Judge Marvin E. Aspen, a U.S. District Judge in the Northern District of Illinois, describes some of these problems:

> These are troubled times for lawyers. Not only is the practice of law suffering from the current economic malaise, but lawyer bashing has become our new national pastime. . . . Most of this public derision and media abuse is, of course, unjustified. But is some of it self-inflicted? Just how much has the legal profession contributed to the public's misperception of lawyers as heartless, self-interested parasites, flourishing only by virtue of others' misery and misfortune?
>
> Let us, for example, look at the following exchange during a deposition taken in Madison, Wisconsin, this year by two veteran Chicago trial lawyers. Attorney *V* had just asked Attorney *A* for a copy of a document he was using to question the witness:

> *Mr. V.:*  Please don't throw it at me.
> *Mr. A.:*  Take it.
> *Mr. V.:*  Don't throw it at me.
> *Mr. A.:*  Don't be a child, Mr. V. You look like a slob the way you're dressed, but you don't have to act like a slob.
> *Mr. V.:*  Stop yelling at me. Let's get on with it.
> *Mr. A.:*  Have you not? You deny I have given you a copy of every document?
> *Mr. V.:*  You just refused to give it to me.
> *Mr. A.:*  Do you deny it?
> *Mr. V.:*  Eventually you threw it at me.
> *Mr. A.:*  Oh, Mr. V., you're about as childish as you can get. You look like a slob, you act like a slob.
> *Mr. V.:*  Keep it up.
> *Mr. A.:*  Your mind belongs in the gutter.

> Although obviously an extreme incident of lawyer incivility, this interaction of attorneys during a multi-billion dollar case nonetheless exemplifies the erosion of professionalism in attorney relationships. . . .

Marvin E. Aspen, *The Search of Renewed Civility in Litigation*, 28 Val. U. L. Rev. 513, 513-514 (1994). Unfortunately, there are many additional examples of discovery squabbles that are viewable on the Internet. *See, e.g., http:// www.youtube.com/watch?v=td-KKmcYtrM* (last visited July 15, 2011).

9. One might argue that the specter of massive and invasive discovery creates the right incentives by discouraging litigation. The perils of discovery undoubtedly contribute to the current environment in which over 95 percent of all cases settle or are otherwise disposed of without a full-scale trial. Is that not a good thing?

## ■ WAYNE BRAZIL, THE ADVERSARY CHARACTER OF CIVIL DISCOVERY
### *31 Vand. L. Rev. 1295 (1978)*

[W]e need to study whether our elaborate struggles over discovery . . . may be incurable symptoms of pathology inherent in our rigid insistence that the parties control the evidence until it is all "prepared" and packaged for competitive manipulation at the eventual continuous trial.*

### [I]. THE PURPOSES OF DISCOVERY

The purposes that modern civil discovery is designed to accomplish are crucial to a system of dispute resolution committed to justice. In its seminal opinion about the scope of discovery, the United States Supreme Court declared that "[m]utual knowledge of all the relevant facts gathered by both parties is essential to proper litigation." Discovery is designed to serve as the principal mechanism by which such "[m]utual knowledge of all the relevant facts" will be achieved. As the Supreme Court of Illinois forthrightly stated, the overriding purpose of discovery is nothing less than to promote "the ascertainment of the truth and ultimate disposition of the lawsuit in accordance therewith. . . ."

Minimal reflection reveals a fundamental antagonism between the goal of truth through disclosure and the protective and competitive impulses that are at the center of the traditional adversary system of dispute resolution. While drafters and early proponents of the rules of discovery were not oblivious to that antagonism, they seem to have assumed that the rules themselves would reduce the size of the litigation arena in which adversary pressures and tactics in the pretrial process of gathering relevant evidentiary data.

The literature that emanated from the academic and Judicial proponents of discovery during the decades surrounding the 1938 adoption of the Federal Rules of Civil Procedure is replete with optimistic forecasts about the beneficial changes discovery would bring to the adversary system. Edson R. Sunderland, who is credited with drafting the discovery components of the 1938 Federal Rules, wrote that the new procedural rules: "mark the highest point so far reached in the English speaking world in the elimination of secrecy in the preparation for trial. Each party may in effect be called upon by his adversary or by the judge to lay all his cards upon the table, the important consideration being who has the stronger hand, not who can play the cleverer game."

Six years earlier, while advocating the discovery reforms that culminated in the Federal Rules, Sunderland had declared that:

Lawyers who constantly employ [discovery] in their practice find it an exceedingly valuable aid in promoting justice. Discovery procedure serves much the same function in the field of law as the x-ray in the field of medicine and

*Marvin E. Frankel, *The Search for Truth: An Umpireal View*, 123 U. Pa. L. Rev. 1031, 1054 (1975).

surgery; and if its use can be sufficiently extended and its methods simplified, litigation will largely cease to be a game of chance. . . .

[T]he primary purpose of the modern rules of discovery was to secure complete disclosure of all relevant evidentiary information and to do so by altering the nature of the relationship between the parties during the trial preparation period. . . . The unarticulated premise that seems to underlie much of the work of discovery's most vocal proponents is that the process of gathering, organizing, and sharing evidentiary information should take place in an essentially nonadversarial context. . . .

## [II]. ADVERSARY INSTINCTS AND THE UNDOING OF THE NONADVERSARIAL ASSUMPTION

The academic and judicial proponents of the modern rules of discovery apparently failed to appreciate how tenaciously litigators would hold to their adversarial ways and the magnitude of the antagonism between the principal purpose of discovery (the ascertainment of truth through disclosure) and the protective and competitive instincts that dominate adversary litigation. . . .

Instead of reducing the sway of adversary forces in litigation and confining them to the trial stage, discovery has greatly expanded the arenas in which those forces can operate. It also has provided attorneys with new weapons, devices, and incentives for the adversary gamesmanship that discovery was designed to curtail. Rather than discourage "the sporting or game theory of justice," discovery has expanded both the scope and the complexity of the sport. Modern discovery also has removed most of the decisive plays from the scrutiny of the court. Because so many civil cases are settled before trial and because the conduct of attorneys is subject only to fitful and superficial judicial review during the discovery stage, much of the decisive gamesmanship of modern litigation takes place in private settings.

Such factors as traditional professional loyalties, deeply ingrained lawyering instincts, and competitive economic pressures assured that the process of gathering and organizing evidence would not take place in an essentially nonadversarial context. Escape from this outcome would have required substantial changes in the institutional context within which discovery is conducted. However, no such changes have been made. Attorneys conducting discovery still are commanded by the rules of professional responsibility and by their own economic self-interest to commit their highest loyalty to their client's best interests. By contrast, there is generally no ethical pressure or financial incentive for attorneys voluntarily to disclose the fruits of their investigations or in any way make ascertainment of the truth easier for opposing counsel or the trier of fact. In short, all the well-established institutional pressures that for generations have operated to make attorneys partisan advocates and to make them view each other as committed adversaries have remained intact. In this context, it is indeed naive to expect that discovery, armed only with its own executional rules, could somehow resist the inroads of the adversarial and competitive pressures that dominate its surroundings. . . .

## [III]. DISCOVERY'S PSYCHOLOGICAL
## AND INSTITUTIONAL ENVIRONMENT

An appropriate way to begin an examination of the psychological and institutional environment within which discovery is conducted is by identifying the goals that motivate the attorneys who use discovery procedures. The process of identifying those goals must begin with acknowledgment of one controlling fact: attorneys who use discovery procedures are attorneys engaged in litigation. Discovery is a tool whose purposes are fixed by the purposes of the larger process of which it is a part. That larger process is litigation. Attorneys in litigation have five primary objectives: (1) to win; (2) to make money; (3) to avoid being sued for malpractice; (4) to earn the admiration of the professional community; and (5) to develop self-esteem for the quality of their performances. These objectives are not born simply of cynicism and selfishness. They are institutionalized commands that emanate from a system of combat within a competitive economic structure. It is not difficult to perceive that these goals make the purposes of discovery for individual litigators quite different from the purposes which the architects of the discovery system contemplated. . . .

[A]dversary litigation and competitive economics offer no institutionalized rewards for disclosure of potentially relevant data. They instead offer many institutional deterrents to full disclosure. Review of the primary means by which litigators seek to earn the rewards of the legal system graphically illustrates this generalization. Litigators generally believe they will win the primary forms of recognition our system offers not through full disclosure, not through relentless efforts to secure just results, not through honesty, openness, and uncalculating cooperation, nor even necessarily through efficiency and superior work quality, but rather by tailoring the most clever package of tactics and stratagems to fit the needs of a given case.

The means employed by litigators to achieve victory for their clients regularly involve manipulating people and the flow of information in order to present their client's positions as persuasively and favorably as possible. This manipulation may involve any or all of the following general techniques: not disclosing evidence that could be damaging to the client or helpful to an opposing party; not disclosing persuasive legal precedents that could be damaging to the client; undermining or deflating persuasive evidence and precedents that are damaging to the client and are introduced by opposing counsel, by such means as upsetting or discrediting honest and reliable witnesses or by burying adverse evidence under mounds of obfuscating evidentiary debris; overemphasizing and presenting out of context evidence and precedents that appear favorable to the client; pressuring or cajoling witnesses, jurors, and judges into adopting views that support the client's position; deceiving opposing counsel and parties about the weaknesses of the client's case and the strengths of opposing cases; aggravating and exploiting to the fullest extent possible vulnerabilities of the opposing party and counsel that have nothing to do with the merits of a given dispute by such means as intimidating an anxious opponent, spending a poor opponent into submission, or "soaking" in settlement an opponent who has public image problems or who for other reasons cannot endure the risk and public exposure of a trial. None of these techniques is illegal or violates the letter of the ethical rules of the profession. Indeed, the refusal to resort to at least some of these devices may be construed as a breach of an attorney's obligation "to represent his client zealously within the bounds of the law." . . .

## ■ STEPHEN LANDSMAN, DEFENSE OF THE ADVERSARIAL PROCESS
*Readings on Adversarial Justice: The American Approach to Adjudication 33-39 (1988)*

A fundamental lesson of Anglo-American legal history is that traditional methods of resolving disputes have served as a rampart against government tyranny. In light of this insight, reform of the judicial machinery should be approached with caution. The historical evidence will not support a flat refusal to change (innovation has been an important element in English and American law since the medieval period), but it does counsel caution where significant departures from previous practices are contemplated. Therefore, even if there were little good to say about the adversary system, those who argue for change would still face a significant burden of persuasion.

### BENEFITS OF PARTY CONTROL OF LITIGATION

A number of reasons, apart from the historical, warrant reliance on adversarial methods. The adversary process provides litigants with the means to control their lawsuits. The parties are preeminent in choosing the forum, designating the proofs, and running the process. The courts, as a general rule, pursue the questions the parties propound. Ultimately, the whole procedure yields results tailored to the litigants' needs and in this way reinforces individual rights. As already noted, this sort of procedure also enhances the economic efficiency of adjudication by sharply reducing impositional costs.

Party control yields other benefits as well. Perhaps most important, it promotes litigant and societal acceptance of decisions rendered by the courts. Adversary theory holds that if a party is intimately involved in the adjudicatory process and feels that he has been given a fair opportunity to present his case, he is likely to accept the results whether favorable or not. Assuming this theory is correct, the adversary process will serve to reduce post-litigation friction and to increase compliance with judicial mandates.

Adversary theory identifies litigant control as important to satisfy not only the parties but society as well. When litigants direct the proceedings, there is little opportunity for the judge to pursue her own agenda or to act on her biases. Because the judge seldom takes the lead in conducting the proceedings, she is unlikely to appear to be partisan or to become embroiled in the contest. Her detachment preserves the appearance of fairness as well as fairness itself. In legal proceedings, as the United States Supreme Court stated in *Offutt v. United States* [384 U.S. 11, 14 (1954)], "justice must satisfy the appearance of justice." When it fails to do so, social credibility is eroded and distrust introduced. There is little direct evidence of the extent of personal or societal acceptance of adversarial processes as contrasted with other adjudicatory methodologies. A number of multinational surveys, however, including those conducted by Professors John Thibaut and Laurens Walker, have found that a majority of subjects will designate adversary procedure as the fairest for resolving disputes. This finding lends support to the argument that adversary procedures are perceived as fairest and are more likely to satisfy litigants and onlookers than non-adversary alternatives.

Thibaut and Walker have provided empirical evidence that litigant control produces other sorts of benefits. First, it tends to encourage desirable conduct on the part of litigants and their counsel. Psychological experimentation has shown that an advocate working in an adversarial context who finds his client at a factual disadvantage will expend significant effort to improve his client's position. This is to be contrasted with the behavior of the advocate working in an inquisitorial setting who will seldom undertake an extensive search for better evidence to bolster a weak case. The adversary process appears to encourage advocates to protect parties facing an initial disadvantage and hence to improve the overall quality of the evidence upon which adjudication will be based.

Thibaut and Walker have also found that adversarial emphasis on party presentation tends to counteract the bias of the decision maker more effectively than does an approach requiring the active participation of the trier in marshaling the proof. This finding provides tangible support for the theoretical assertion that the best decision maker is one whose sole function is adjudication. Because the adversary process assigns the prosecutorial function to the parties, it serves to increase the likelihood that the trier will be able to devote her full attention to the neutral adjudication of the case.

The adversary process assigns each participant a single function. The judge is to serve as neutral and passive arbiter. Counsel are to act as zealous advocates. According to adversary theory, when each actor performs only a single function the dispute before the court will be resolved in the fairest and most efficient way. The strength of such a division of labor is that individual responsibilities are clear. The possibility that a participant in the system will face conflicting responsibility is minimized. Each knows what is expected of him and can work conscientiously to achieve a specifically defined goal. When participants in the judicial process are confronted with conflicting obligations, it becomes difficult for them to discharge any of their duties satisfactorily. The more frequently they face conflict, the more likely it is that they will not perform their assigned part or will not perform it in a way that minimizes conflict rather than fully discharging their responsibilities. Among the greatest dangers in this regard are that the judge will abandon neutrality if encouraged to search for material truth and that the attorney will compromise his client's interests if compelled to serve as an officer of the court rather than as an advocate. In either case the probity of the process is seriously undermined.

Party control has another beneficial effect as well. It affirms human individuality.  It mandates respect for the opinions of each party rather than those of his attorney, of the court, or of society at large. It provides the litigant a neutral forum in which to air his views and promises that those views will be heard and considered. The individualizing effect of adversary procedure has important implications besides those involving individual satisfaction. The receptiveness of adversary procedure to individual claims implies that an adversarial court will take a sympathetic view of the claims of individuals against the state. The prospects for sympathetic hearing are increased because the judge and, to an even greater extent, the jury are beyond governmental control and cannot be taken to task for their decisions.

These propositions concerning the receptiveness of adversarial courts to the claims of individual citizens are, at least in part, borne out by historical evidence. For centuries adversarial courts have served as a counterbalance to official tyranny and have worked to broaden the scope of individual rights. The steady expansion of doctrines protecting minorities both in England and in the United States reflects this fact. When adversarial process has been ignored in the operation of the courts, as in the days of the Star Chamber, human rights diminished and governmental repression increased.

We live in an era of expanding government power. The urgency of social problems, including the scarcity of resources and the exigencies of national defense, tends to lead the government to exert pressure on the citizenry to cooperate in ensuring the efficient operation of society as a whole. This pressure poses a keen threat to the maintenance of individual rights. In these circumstances, there is a need to preserve the kind of institution that will sympathetically review claims based on individual rights rather than on governmental necessity or the common good. Because the adversarial courts are primarily committed to hearing and to upholding the claims of individuals, they are most likely to be capable of handling this task.

## Comments and Questions

1. Professor Landsman offers a persuasive apology for the adversary process. Does it follow that each segment of the litigation process—such as discovery—should likewise be founded on these time-tested precepts?

2. Would the adversarial nature of adjudication be compromised if fact development were left to the judge?

3. Landsman speaks eloquently in defense of the adversary process as a guarantor of individual rights. What "rights," loosely defined, should an individual have (or expect) in discovery in the course of litigation?

4. Landsman has compiled a number of excerpts from writings that criticize or defend the adversary system. The preceding portion is from his introductory essay to the readings, which is largely laudatory of the adversary system. The book was produced under the sponsorship of the American Bar Association's Litigation Section. Decades of tension between adversarialism and the purposes of discovery have fomented much criticism and reform effort. Indeed, since 1938, the discovery rules have been amended substantially many times. Yet criticism persists.

5. You might be thinking that the ethical obligations of lawyers, if not the discovery rules themselves, might preclude abuse of the discovery process by lawyers. Currently in the United States, disciplinary rules are embodied in two "model" forms. The Model Code of Professional Responsibility and the Model Rules of Professional Conduct. The Model Code of Professional Responsibility was created in 1969, when the American Bar Association (ABA) grouped and adopted nearly fifty canons from various state bar associations. In 1983, the ABA adopted the Model Rules of Professional Conduct to replace the Model Code. In general, the Model Rules are more confining and less abstract than the Model Code. Nearly all of the states have moved from the Model Code to the Model Rules. We excerpt portions of the Model Code and the Model Rules here for you to consider the ethical obligations of lawyers in the context of discovery.

# ■ ABA MODEL CODE OF PROFESSIONAL RESPONSIBILITY

## CANON 7

### A Lawyer Should Represent a Client Zealously Within the Bounds of the Law

#### DISCIPLINARY RULE 7-101. REPRESENTING A CLIENT ZEALOUSLY

(A) A lawyer shall not intentionally:

(1) Fail to seek the lawful objectives of his client through reasonably available means permitted by law and the Disciplinary Rules, except as provided by DR 7-101(B). A lawyer does not violate this Disciplinary Rule, however, by acceding to reasonable requests of opposing counsel which do not prejudice the rights of his client, by being punctual to fulfilling all professional commitments, by avoiding offensive tactics, or by treating with courtesy and consideration all persons involved in the legal process.

(2) Fail to carry out a contract of employment entered into with a client for professional services, but he may withdraw as permitted under DR 2-110, DR 5-102, and DR 5-105.

(3) Prejudice or damage his client during the course of the professional relationship, except as required under DR 7-102(B).

(B) In his representation of a client, a lawyer may:

(1) Where permissible, exercise his professional judgment to waive or fail to assert a right or position of his client.

(2) Refuse to aid or participate in conduct that he believes to be unlawful, even though there is some support for an argument that the conduct is legal.

#### DISCIPLINARY RULE 7-102. REPRESENTING A CLIENT WITHIN THE BOUNDS OF THE LAW

(A) In his representation of a client, a lawyer shall not:

(1) File a suit, assert a position, conduct a defense, delay a trial, or take other action on behalf of his client when he knows or when it is obvious that such action would serve merely to harass or maliciously injure another.

(2) Knowingly advance a claim or defense that is unwarranted under existing law, except that he may advance such claim or defense if it can be supported by good faith argument for an extension, modification, or reversal of existing law.

(3) Conceal or knowingly fail to disclose that which he is required by law to reveal.

(4) Knowingly use perjured testimony or false evidence.

(5) Knowingly make a false statement of law or fact.

(6) Participate in the creation or preservation of evidence when he knows or it is obvious that the evidence is false.

(7) Counsel or assist his client in conduct that the lawyer knows to be illegal or fraudulent.

(8) Knowingly engage in other illegal conduct or conduct contrary to a Disciplinary Rule.

(B) A lawyer who receives information clearly established that:

(1) His client has, in the course of the representation, perpetrated a fraud upon a person or tribunal shall promptly call upon his client to rectify the same, and if his client refuses or is unable to do so, he shall reveal the fraud to the affected person or tribunal, except when the information is protected as a privileged communication.

(2) A person other than his client has perpetrated a fraud upon a tribunal shall promptly reveal the fraud to the tribunal.

# ■ ABA MODEL RULES OF PROFESSIONAL CONDUCT*

## RULE 1.1 COMPETENCE

**A lawyer shall provide competent representation to a client. Competent representation requires the legal knowledge, skill, thoroughness and preparation reasonably necessary for the representation.**

COMMENT:

*Legal Knowledge and Skill.* In determining whether a lawyer employs the requisite knowledge and skill in a particular matter, relevant factors include the relative complexity and specialized nature of the matter, the lawyer's general experience, the lawyer's training and experience in the field in question, the preparation and study the lawyer is able to give the matter and whether it is feasible to refer the matter to, or associate or consult with, a lawyer of established competence in the field in question. In many instances, the required proficiency is that of a general practitioner. Expertise in a particular field of law may be required in some circumstances. . . .

*ABA Model Rules of Professional Conduct, 2011 Edition. Copyright ©2011 by the American Bar Association. Reprinted with permission. Copies of ABA Model Rules of Professional Conduct 2008 Edition are available from Service Center, American Bar Association, 321 North Clark Street, Chicago, IL 60654, 1-800-285-2221. This information or any portion thereof may not be copied or disseminated in any form or by any means or stored in an electronic database or retrieval system without the express written consent of the American Bar Association.

*Thoroughness and Preparation.* Competent handling of a particular matter includes inquiry into and analysis of the factual and legal elements of the problem, and use of methods and procedures meeting the standards of competent practitioners. It also includes adequate preparation. The required attention and preparation are determined in part by what is at stake; major litigation and complex transactions ordinarily require more extensive treatment than matters of lesser complexity and consequence. . . .

### RULE 1.3 DILIGENCE

**A lawyer shall act with reasonable diligence and promptness in representing a client.**

#### COMMENT:

A lawyer should pursue a matter on behalf of a client despite opposition, obstruction or personal inconvenience to the lawyer, and take whatever lawful and ethical measures are required to vindicate a client's cause or endeavor. A lawyer must also act with commitment and dedication to the interests of the client and with zeal in advocacy upon the client's behalf. A lawyer is not bound, however, to press for every advantage that might be realized for a client. For example, a lawyer may have authority to exercise professional discretion in determining the means by which a matter should be pursued. *See* Rule 1.2. The lawyer's duty to act with reasonable diligence does not require the use of offensive tactics or preclude the treating of all persons involved in the legal process with courtesy and respect. . . .

### RULE 3.2 EXPEDITING LITIGATION

**A lawyer shall make reasonable efforts to expedite litigation consistent with the interests of the client.**

#### COMMENT:

Dilatory practices bring the administration of justice into disrepute. Although there will be occasions when a lawyer may properly seek a postponement for personal reasons, it is not proper for a lawyer to routinely fail to expedite litigation solely for the convenience of the advocates. Nor will a failure to expedite be reasonable if done for the purpose of frustrating an opposing party's attempt to obtain rightful redress or repose. It is not a justification that similar conduct is often tolerated by the bench and bar. The question is whether a competent lawyer acting in good faith would regard the course of action as having some substantial purpose other than delay. Realizing financial or other benefit from otherwise improper delay in litigation is not a legitimate interest of the client.

## Comments and Questions

1. Do these rules of professional responsibility establish meaningful parameters for determining what is ethical conduct in the context of discovery?

Is it unethical to use discovery primarily for the purpose of increasing your opponent's litigation expenses? Is it unethical to use discovery primarily for the purpose of delay or to gain some tactical advantage? Is it unethical to seek, through discovery, information, or documents that are not necessary for the prosecution or defense of your action? Is it unethical to respond to inquiries for discovery in a very restrictive manner to avoid the disclosure of relevant nonprivileged information?

2. Do you have any suggestions for improving the civility of lawyers in the legal profession? What effect is your legal education having on your civility in law school or in daily life? What effect do you think your legal education will have on your civility in practicing law? What do you think the causes are of a lack of civility in litigation?

3. For a very readable firsthand account of one young public-interest lawyer's struggle against a high-priced law firm and an overloaded judicial system, we highly recommend Philip G. Schrag, *Bleak House 1968: A Report on Consumer Test Litigation*, 44 N.Y.U. L. Rev. 115 (1969). As a twelve-month discovery process lumbers along, Professor Schrag highlights some of the practical considerations he faced as a litigator, such as when to object to an obviously improper deposition question. What if you know a court will not resolve such an objection for months, and even then, perhaps ambiguously so? Such questions further explore this basic tension between a lawyer's ethical responsibilities and the realities of the adversarial system.

## 2. *Efficiency and Effectuation Values in Discovery*

In the popular press—and in much of the discourse of procedural reform—the escalating expense of litigation and the increase in arduous, abusive, and acrimonious discovery is thought to be understood and obvious (and unnecessary even to prove). We want you to develop a more nuanced understanding of the problem.

We begin with an article by Loren Kieve, an accomplished litigator who now manages his own firm in San Francisco. Mr. Kieve made the provocative suggestion that we might consider getting rid of discovery altogether.

## ■ LOREN KIEVE, DISCOVERY REFORM
### *A.B.A. J. 81-86 (Dec. 1991)*

There has been almost universal agreement that discovery has become a nightmare. . . . Our legal system is predicated on the curious notion that a lawyer can file a lawsuit with only a bare idea of what the case—much less the trial—will look like, and then require the opposition and its lawyers to go through the cumbersome, expensive procedure of sifting through its files to turn over a vast array of material that is not merely relevant but that may "lead to the discovery" of relevant evidence. . . . The current discovery practice is a monster out of control. . . . [D]iscovery devours millions of dollars and countless hours of a lawyer's time in cases that would be better settled or tried with far less ado. . . .

Some have suggested cynically that lawyers have glommed onto discovery because it has become the ideal way to rack up billable hours . . . like the multi-headed Hydra of mythology. As soon as one discovery head is cut off, two more appear in its place. . . . The truth is that the system itself is the root evil. Like Mount Everest, a lawyer uses discovery "because it is there." It is one of the tools (choose your own metaphor—chainsaw, axe) the rules give us.

The obvious solution is one the rest of the civilized world (or at least the English and civil law system) has long used: no discovery. Lawyers in England and on the Continent investigate the case before it is filed (presumably trying all the while to settle it), obtain the documents and witnesses they need to try it, and, only then, file a lawsuit. At that point they are ready to try it.

Once the suit is filed, preliminary pleadings are filed to see if the case has legal merit. If it passes this test, a trial date is set. Before trial, the parties exchange lists of witnesses and a short statement of what they will say, and turn over copies of the exhibits they plan to use. Then they go to trial. If a witness is unavailable because he is in another jurisdiction or on his death-bed, then his deposition can be taken, but this is the only exception.

Not only do lawyers in England and Europe do this every day, so do U.S. criminal defense lawyers. . . . I know of no empirical study or scientific proof that suggests that this produces a result that is less fair. Nor do I know of any study or proof to indicate that our unique, over-burdened system is better.

## Comments and Questions

1. What is the role or roles of discovery in the dispute resolution process? What other mechanisms could fulfill these roles? For example, if discovery were eliminated, how, if at all, would issues be identified and framed for trial? With pleading requirements demanding greater particularity? And how, without access to discovery, would plaintiffs meet their burdens of production and persuasion? Would/could the elements of substantive law be rewritten to account for the fact that discovery was unavailable (or less available)?

2. One must also consider discovery in its broader social context. In the United States we rely heavily on private litigation to enforce our shared norms; these norms include laws regarding the environment, antitrust, banking, securities, consumer safety, employment discrimination, worker safety, civil rights, and so forth. In *The Litigation State* (Princeton Univ. Pr. 2010), Sean Farhang explains the magnitude of and the reasons for this uniquely American phenomenon. He writes that, in the past decade, an average of about 165,000 lawsuits are filed each year in federal district courts to enforce federal statutes. And more than 97 percent of these suits were filed by private litigants (as opposed to federal enforcement agencies). (This result is a product of several forces, including distrust of the government generally and the

executive branch in particular, confidence in the private sector and market incentives, the cost of public enforcement, and lawyers' interest in the availability of profitable litigation.) In this vein, discovery appears to be linked with the enforcement of our substantive norms.

> [D]iscovery is the American alternative to the administrative state. . . . Every day, hundreds of American lawyers caution their clients that an unlawful course of conduct will be accompanied by serious risk of exposure at the hands of some hundreds of thousands of lawyers, each armed with a subpoena power by which misdeeds can be uncovered. Unless corresponding new powers are conferred on public officers, constricting discovery would diminish the disincentives for lawless behavior across a wide spectrum of forbidden conduct.

Paul D. Carrington, *Renovating Discovery*, 49 Ala. L. Rev. 51, 54 (1997).

> Our discovery mechanisms are not so irrational when seen in context. Let me sketch out some examples. Consider our historic distrust of concentrated power. Our doctrines of federalism and separation of powers, the right to a jury trial, and the adversary system, including party control, reflect our historic distrust of residing power in one person or limited groups. We do not think that judges would ferret out negative aspects of our opponent's case and positive information to prove our own claims or defenses with the same motivation and intensity that self-interest propels. Perhaps if we had more experience with career judges, elevated as the result of performance based on objective criteria, as opposed to politically-appointed or elected judges, we would have more confidence in turning over discovery to the judiciary. . . . [I]t would be difficult to eliminate extensive discovery in United States civil litigation without also changing the relative places of civil litigation, lawyers, judges, and juries in our culture and the relative roles of pleading, discovery, summary judgment, and other elements of procedure. The rules and the culture are interrelated in complex ways that would be very difficult to disentangle, even if such rearrangements were deemed desirable.

Stephen N. Subrin, *Discovery in Global Perspective: Are We Nuts?*, 52 DePaul L. Rev. 299, 309 (2002).

Is broad discovery therefore an essential component of the American social, economic, and political milieu? Do restrictions on discovery lead to the under-enforcement of our substantive laws? What about the separation of powers; would this be an example of activist judging?

3. Consider what the combination of pleading reform and discovery practice means for you as a lawyer—and as a law student. If the pleading requirement demands details that can be obtained only through discovery, how will you get details regarding, say, the defendant's state of mind for the many causes of action that include intent as an essential element? Does the evolving nature of technology offer a solution? Should you learn a little less about formal discovery in a civil procedure course and a little more about private investigators and laws (like the Freedom of Information Act (FOIA)) that ensure access to certain government documents?

4. Although it is incontrovertible that discovery can be problematic, it is important to understand exactly where those problems surface. Useful empirical data is presented in the following article.

## ■ ELIZABETH G. THORNBURG, GIVING THE "HAVES" A LITTLE MORE
### 52 SMU L. Rev. 229, 246-249 (1999)

. . . Outcry about the cost and abuses of discovery is intimately connected with outcry about the "litigation explosion." The notion that we are experiencing a crisis in civil caseload was popularized by Walter K. Olson's 1991 [*The Litigation Explosion*], politicized by the President's Council on Competitiveness and fed by the media and by lawyers themselves. Careful empirical analysis, particularly that of professor Marc Gallanter, has demonstrated that no such crisis exists.[107] This scholarly rebuttal, however, does not seem to have made a dent in public perception. The same seems to be true of concerns about problems with discovery. Public outcry and media coverage continue to send the message that discovery is a gigantic and pervasive problem. This . . . Article examines what empirical research in fact indicates about discovery and the need, if any, for rule changes.

The most recent study by the Federal Judicial Center succinctly summarizes the findings of empirical researchers: "[T]he typical case has relatively little discovery, conducted at costs that are proportionate to the stakes of the litigation, and . . . discovery generally—but with notable exceptions—yields information that aids in the just disposition of cases."[108] This conclusion is supported by numerous studies going back thirty years. The Columbia Project for Effective Justice, working in the 1960s, deliberately chose cases to maximize the likelihood of finding discovery activity. Even within this group, only two-thirds of attorneys reported using formal discovery. The researchers further concluded that "the costs of discovery were not oppressive, either in relation to ability to pay or to the stakes of litigaiton."[110] Ten years later, the Federal Judicial Center (FJC) completed a significant study of discovery practices. This project studied 3,000 federal civil cases from six metropolitan districts.[111] The FJC found that in 52% of the cases, there was *no discovery at all*. In 72% of the cases, there were no more than *two* discovery events. At

107. *See generally* Marc S. Galanter, *Real World Torts: An Antidote to Anecdote*, 55 Md. L. Rev. 1093 (1996); Marc S. Galanter, *News from Nowhere: The Debased Debate on Civil Justice*, 71 Denv. U. L. Rev. 77 (1993); Marc S. Galanter, *The Day After the Litigation Explosion*, 46 Md. L. Rev. 3 (1986); Marc S. Galanter, *Reading the Landscape of Disputes: What We Know and Don't Know (and Think We Know) About Our Allegedly Contentious and Litigious Society*, 31 UCLA L. Rev. 2 (1983).

108. Thomas E. Willging et al., *An Empirical Study of Discovery and Disclosure Practice Under the 1993 Federal Rule Amendments*, 39 B.C. L. Rev. 525, 527 (1998).

110. Judith A. McKenna & Elizabeth C. Wiggins, *Empirical Research on Civil Discovery*, 39 B.C. L. Rev. 785, 787 (citing Columbia Project for Effective Justice).

111. *See generally* Paul R. Connolly et al., *Federal Judicial Center, Judicial Controls and the Civil Litigative Process: Discovery* (1978).

about the same time, the Civil Litigation Research Project (CLRP) at the University of Wisconsin studied "ordinary litigation": cases in which more than $1,000 is in controversy but excluding "mega" cases. The CLRP found that "relatively little discovery occurs in the ordinary lawsuit. We found no evidence of discovery in over half our cases. Rarely did the records reveal more than five separate discovery events."[113]

These studies were consistent but dated. The Advisory Committee therefore wisely looked to the RAND Institute for Civil Justice[114] and the Federal Judicial Center[115] for information about the current discovery environment. The findings of both groups were consistent with the older studies. The RAND study was based on 5,222 cases filed in 1992-1993 in twenty federal districts. RAND excluded from its sample cases that usually involve little or no discovery or management.[117] In cases that closed before issue was joined (28% of the sample), there was no discovery at all. In cases that closed after issue was joined but in 270 days or less (27% of the sample), the median lawyer work hours on discovery per litigant was a whopping three hours. Even in cases that closed more than 270 days after filing (45% of the sample), lawyers worked a median of twenty hours on discovery per litigant. Fifty-five percent of the RAND sample, then, involved little or no discovery. For 38% of general civil cases, lawyer work hours for discovery were zero.

The FJC studied 1000 cases closed in the last quarter of 1996 and strove to sample cases likely to involve discovery. The FJC focused on costs as reported by the attorneys in the cases studied. They found that the median cost of discovery was about $6,500 per client (about half of median litigation costs). Relative to stakes, the FJC found that discovery expenses were quite low. The median percentage was 3% of the stakes.

Despite consistent findings of low discovery cost and a functioning system, however, the studies are also consistent in finding a small percentage of cases in which there is a larger volume of discovery activity and discovery disputes. The 1978 FJC study concluded that a few cases—less than five percent—had more than ten discovery requests. The two modern studies also discovered a large amount of discovery concentrated in a small number of cases. For example, in the RAND study, the median number of discovery hours in the top 10% of cases was 300—fifteen times the median for discovery of the active cases. In the FJC study, while the median percentage of discovery expenses to stakes was quite low (3%), about 5% of attorneys estimated discovery expenses at 32% or more of the amount at stake. As the Director of the American Bar Foundation reminds us, "[a] rather small number of cases thus generated a very large amount of discovery."[125]

---

113. David M. Trubek et al., *The Costs of Ordinary Litigation*, 31 UCLA L. Rev. 72, 90 (1983).

114. *See* James S. Kakalik et al., *Discovery Management: Further Analysis of the Civil Justice Reform Act Evaluation Data*, 39 B.C. L. Rev. 613, 615 (1998).

115. *See* Willging, *supra* note 108 (reporting the FJC findings).

117. They excluded prisoner cases, administrative review of social security cases, bankruptcy appeals, foreclosures, forfeiture and penalty cases, and debt recovery. . . .

125. Bryant G. Garth, *Two Worlds of Civil Discovery: From Studies of Cost and Delay to the Markets in Legal Services and Legal Reform*, 39 B.C. L. Rev. 597, 600 (1998).

At least at a level of generality, the research has also identified character-istics that tend to be associated with this small percentage of problematic cases. These include amount at stake, case complexity, case contentiousness, subject matter of the lawsuit, size of law firm, number of parties, and number of claims, with the amount at stake having the strongest correlation with discov-ery problems. The consistency of these findings led the RAND researchers to recommend special attention to the small number of problem cases. . . .

These findings suggest that policymakers should consider focusing dis-covery rule changes and discovery management on the types of cases likely to have high discovery costs, and the discovery practices that are likely to gen-erate those high costs. More attention and research is clearly needed on how to identify those high discovery cost cases early in their life, and how best to manage discovery on those cases.

Similarly, the FJC researchers were led by their data to theorize that "there may be problem cases rather than isolated problems with each sepa-rate form of discovery."

What we do *not* know is why these particular cases generate a large volume of discovery and discovery disputes. What exactly are the problems? And are the problems caused by the rules or by forces outside the rules? What are the incentives for lawyers, clients, and judges that cause problems to arise and to have persisted over time? Can these situations be addressed by rule changes? . . .

## Comments and Questions

1. Despite the criticisms you have read about wide-open discovery, it is important to remember that discovery seems to work as intended in most cases and that discovery has become important in ferreting out illegal behav-ior through private litigation. The alternative would probably be substan-tially expanded government regulation and government prosecution. Would this be an improvement? In summarizing what he distilled from a conference of experts on discovery rules, the then Chair of the Civil Rules Advisory Committee started with these three conclusions:

(i) The desire for information in connection with the resolution of civil dis-putes was nearly universal. No one at the Conference seemed to advocate the elimination of requiring full disclosure of relevant information.

(ii) Discovery is now working effectively and efficiently in a majority of the cases, which represent "routine" cases.

(iii) In cases where discovery was actively used, it was thought to be unnec-essarily expensive and burdensome. . . .

Paul V. Niemeyer, *Here We Go Again: Are the Federal Discovery Rules Really in Need of Amendment?* 39 B.C. L. Rev. 517 (1998). Are these observations encouraging? Why or why not?

2. When Paul Niemeyer convened the Civil Rules Advisory Committee in the mid-1990s, he focused the committee's attention on the discovery rules by posing three questions:

(a) When fully used, is the discovery process too expensive for what it contributes to the dispute resolution process?

(b) Are there rule changes that can be made which might reduce the cost and delay of discovery without undermining a policy of full disclosure?

(c) Should the federal rules for discovery, applying to cases involving national substantive law and procedure, as well as to cases involving state law, be made uniform throughout the United States?

What are your answers to these questions? What three questions would you pose to frame a discussion on discovery reform?

3. If discovery is not a systemic problem for the ordinary lawyer with the ordinary case, as the empirical data suggests, why isn't the existing large group of ordinary lawyers trying this large majority of ordinary cases? Why, in light of the empirical data suggesting a relative normalcy of discovery, do so many attorneys nevertheless want significant changes made to the discovery process?

4. One inherent tension in American discovery practice is between the goal of seeking full disclosure and the importance in a democracy of protecting privacy. Professor Geoffrey Hazard focuses on privacy interests, especially in document discovery, in his article *From Whom No Secrets Are Hid*, 76 Tex. L. Rev. 1665 (1999). The following excerpt from that article is illustrative of Hazard's concern:

> [D]iscovery of documents in American litigation often is wide-ranging, with intrusion on the discovered party and expense to both parties. In high stakes litigation, discovery usually occurs on a massive scale, the sheer volume of documents going far beyond that produced in civil litigation in any other country. The targets of this document discovery regard it as particularly invasive. Managerial-level employees in public and private organizations feel more or less able to hold their own in deposition interrogation and recognize that everyone has a duty to give testimony about what he knows. But discovery of the documents goes after what public and private officials regard as their most private thoughts, such that this kind of discovery, to them, resembles self-incrimination. Discovery of documents is especially sensitive in international litigation. Put bluntly, the impression of American discovery in most foreign countries is that of an alien legal regime conducting a warrantless search in someone else's domestic territory. The scope the American system affords to private litigants for compulsory production of documents is ordinarily afforded in other countries only to prosecutorial criminal investigations by government agencies.

Why should a private individual and his or her lawyer be able to search the innermost thoughts of private and public officials? Such privacy invasions, when permitted at all, are usually thought to be the province of government—and are typically circumscribed by the protections of criminal procedure. Moreover, the government can be held accountable for excesses through elections.

5. Discovery rules can require parties to produce the "smoking gun" document that dooms their case. Discovery rules can require individuals to admit their failures, confront their misconduct, and otherwise tell the truth. Describe the dividing line between, on one hand, the need for an honest and forthright surrender of information essential to ensure a fair and accurate application of law to facts and, on the other hand, an unjustified and unnecessary interference with legitimate privacy interests.

6. Is it your sense that privacy expectations and interests are more passionately held today than they were in the first half of the twentieth century when the Federal Rules were promulgated and when *Hickman* was decided? To what extent is resistance to and suspicion of broad discovery about protecting privacy interests, and to what extent is it about something else? And what is the something else?

7. Has technology made it too easy for the techniques of discovery to invade another's privacy? Or has technology fundamentally transformed our understanding of what information is private? Either way, consider the information individuals share on social networks. One article—written for practitioners—referred to social networks as "a virtual information bonanza about a litigant's private life and state of mind." Ronald J. Levine and Susan L. Swatski-Lebson, *Whose Space? Discovery of Social Networking Web Sites*, Prod. Liab. L. & Strategy (L.J. Newsl., New York, N.Y.), Nov. 2008, at 11.

8. Some scholars have argued that discovery reforms are targeted almost exclusively at over-discovery—that is, parties trying to extract from their opponents more than that to which they are entitled (and more than a cost/benefit analysis could justify). Indeed, few proposals are instead targeted at abusive resistance to discovery. What are possible explanations for this difference? Consider also that empirical research commissioned by the Advisory Committee and done by the Federal Judicial Center suggests that the most common problems in document production are failure to respond adequately and failure to respond in a timely fashion. *See* Thomas E. Willging et al., *An Empirical Study of Discovery and Disclosure Practice Under the 1993 Federal Rule Amendments*, 39 B.C. L. Rev. 525, 540 (1998).

## C. THE MECHANICS OF DISCOVERY

We have now looked at some of the general tensions and problems inherent in the liberal wide-open discovery regime. You have seen the clash of, on one hand, the need for broad discovery within a society that places a heavy responsibility on private civil litigation; and, on the other, a deep resentment of the abuses that seem inevitably to plague a system in which lawyers are handsomely paid to aggressively represent their clients. In this part we review the mechanics of the discovery process. You will need to read carefully Federal Rules 26-37 in preparation for study of this part. We look, first, at

Fed. R. Civ. P. 26(b), which governs the permissible scope of *all* formal discovery under the Federal Rules. Next, we turn to the mandatory initial disclosures that parties, in most cases, are required to make within the first months of the commencement of the litigation. Thereafter, we discuss the most popular tools of discovery—depositions, written interrogatories, production of documents and things, physical and mental examinations, requests for admissions, and informal discovery. This discussion also includes a very basic introduction to the rules of evidence. Finally, we look at e-discovery.

## 1. The Scope of Discovery

As mentioned at the start of this chapter, the scope of discovery is intentionally broad. For litigators, of course, the appetite for discovery can be insatiable—discovery provides the facts and evidence that you may need to prove the elements of your causes of action. And who is to know whether the subject of any particular request is or is not *relevant* until you have had the opportunity to review the document requested or hear the answer to the interrogatory posed?

Many discovery motions are referred by federal district judges to magistrate judges. Magistrates are appointed by judges of federal district courts and possess many, but not all, of the powers of a federal judge. *See* 28 U.S.C. §§ 631-639. In the following case, Magistrate Judge Sebelius must identify and police the outer boundaries of discovery in a case brought under the Family and Medical Leave Act. Plaintiff is asking the court to compel the defendant to produce certain documents and to answer certain interrogatories. We will learn more about these and other formal discovery techniques later in this chapter. At this point, focus only on the scope of the requests and form your own conclusions about whether the requests fall inside or outside the scope of permissible discovery under Rule 26.

## ■ MOSS v. BLUE CROSS AND BLUE SHIELD OF KANSAS, INC.
*241 F.R.D. 683 (D. Kan. 2007)*

SEBELIUS, Magistrate Judge:

### I. BACKGROUND

Plaintiff has brought her claims under the Family and Medical Leave Act ("FMLA"), 29 U.S.C. § 2601 et seq. Specifically, plaintiff contends that defendant "violat[ed] the FMLA [by] interfering with, restraining and denying the Plaintiff's exercise or attempt to exercise her right to use protected leave." For the purposes of the present motion, the court will construe plaintiff's pleadings as also claiming FMLA retaliation against defendant. . . .

## II. INTERROGATORIES

### A. INTERROGATORY NOS. 8 AND 9

*Interrogatory No. 8.* List any and all employees in the last 10 years who have been terminated or disciplined, reprimanded, or suffered any type of adverse employment action whatsoever, for violating Blue Cross and Blue Shield of Kansas's ("BCBSKS") FMLA leave policy and in relation to the employees' identity provide the following:

—Any documents evidencing or supporting the terminations, discipline, reprimand or adverse employment action
—The date of such action
—The supervisors, management, or any person in a position of authority who participated in such action
—The personnel file of the employee involved in such action

*Response*: Defendant objects to this interrogatory as being overly broad, unduly burdensome, and not reasonably calculated to lead to the discovery of admissible evidence. There is no way to identify the designated employees other than by reviewing the personnel files of every person who worked for the defendant during the past ten years. That would include thousands of employees, and the time commitment necessary to review of the personnel files would be quite burdensome.

*Interrogatory No. 9.* List any and all employees who have been terminated, disciplined, reprimanded, or have been subject to any type of adverse employment action for failing to call in for two consecutive days pursuant to document BCBSKS000025, second paragraph that provides for this policy according to documents produced by BCBSKS.

—Any documents evidencing or supporting the termination, discipline, reprimand or adverse employment action.
—The date of such action
—The supervisors, management, or any person in a position of authority who participated in such action.
—The personnel file of the employee involved in such action

*Response*: Defendant objects to this interrogatory as being overly broad, unduly burdensome, and not reasonably calculated to lead to the discovery of admissible evidence. The interrogatory is unlimited by any date range, and thus calls for information throughout the years that defendant has utilized the referenced policy, or one with similar requirements. Furthermore, the only way to identify the employees is by reviewing the personnel files of all current and former employees who worked for defendant while such a policy was in effect. The time commitment to review all such personnel files would be quite burdensome.

### 1. Relevancy Objection

Generally, "a request for discovery should be considered relevant if there is 'any possibility' that the information sought may be relevant to the claim or defense of any party."[3] "When the discovery sought appears relevant, the party

---

3. Sheldon v. Vermonty, 204 F.R.D. 679, 689-90 (D. Kan. 2001). See also Fed. Rule Civ. P. 26(b)(1).

resisting the discovery has the burden to establish the lack of relevance by demonstrating that the requested discovery (1) does not come within the scope of relevance as defined under Fed. R. Civ. P. 26(b)(1), or (2) is of such marginal relevance that the potential harm occasioned by discovery would outweigh the ordinary presumption in favor of broad discovery."[4] When relevancy is not readily apparent, however, the party seeking discovery has the burden of showing the relevancy of the discovery request.

Plaintiff argues that Interrogatory Nos. 8 and 9 are "clearly relevant on [their] face, as [they] seek[] information to determine if BCBS is a continuous violator of federal law." However, proving that BCBS is a "continuous violator of federal law" does not appear relevant to any of the FMLA claims or defenses of the parties. Thus, plaintiff bears the burden of demonstrating the relevancy of Interrogatory Nos. 8 and 9.

Plaintiff offers two reasons why these Interrogatories are relevant. First, plaintiff argues that "[i]n employment cases, like this case, the scope of discovery is particularly broad and an employer's general practices and operations are relevant even if the plaintiff is asserting an individual employment violation, like the FMLA." Plaintiff is correct in that the Tenth Circuit has stated that discovery in employment discrimination claims should not be narrowly circumscribed. Indeed, such information is relevant in employment discrimination cases because the testimony of other employees about their treatment by the defendant is relevant to the issue of the employer's discriminatory intent.

Second, plaintiff argues, and the court agrees, that answers to Interrogatory Nos. 8 and 9 could lead to evidence as to whether BCBSKS uniformly applied its FMLA or its attendance "call in" policies. BCBSKS argues that its legitimate non-discriminatory reason for terminating plaintiff stems from her failure to meet its call in policy.[10] As part of a FMLA retaliation claim, plaintiff could prove this reason was a pretext. As "[a] plaintiff can demonstrate pretext by showing weaknesses, implausibilities, inconsistencies, incoherencies, or contradictions in the employer's reasons for its action . . ."[11] information regarding BCBSKS' application of its FMLA or its "call in" policies could lead to relevant evidence. Thus, the court finds that plaintiff has met her burden of establishing relevancy, and the court overrules defendant's objection.

### 2. Overly Broad and Unduly Burdensome

As the party objecting to discovery, defendant has "the burden of showing facts justifying their objection by demonstrating that the time or expense involved in responding to requested discovery is unduly burdensome."[14] Defendant has failed to provide an "affidavit or specific supporting information" to substantiate its overly broad and unduly burdensome objections to Interrogatory Nos. 8 and 9. Thus, defendant has not met its obligation to provide sufficient detail and explanation about the nature of the burden in terms of time, money, and procedure required to produce the requested documents.

---

4. Gen. Elec. Capital Corp. v. Lear Corp., 215 F.R.D. 637, 640 (D. Kan. 2003).

10. See Answer (Doc. 8) at p. 3-4; Response (Doc. 48) ("Plaintiff was terminated . . . because she failed to adhere to the company's policy requiring employees to contact their supervisor each day they are absent, unless leave has been approved.")

11. Richmond v. ONEOK, Inc., 120 F.3d 205, 209 (10th Cir. 1997).

14. Horizon Holdings, L.L.C. v. Genmar Holdings, Inc., 209 F.R.D. 208, 213 (D. Kan. 2002) (citing Snowden v. Connaught Lab., Inc., 137 F.R.D. 325, 326 (D. Kan. 1991)).

Further, the "mere fact that compliance with an inspection order will cause great labor and expense or even considerable hardship and the possibility of injury to the business of the party from whom discovery is sought does not itself require denial of the motion."[16]

### 3. Overly Broad and Unduly Burdensome on Their Face

However, defendant's failure to specify its potential burden is not dispositive of its objection. As defendant points out, an objecting party's "failure to meet its evidentiary burden is not necessarily fatal to its claim that the requests are unduly burdensome" because "an exception . . . applies when the discovery request is unduly burdensome on its face."[17] Courts in the District of Kansas have "held on numerous occasions that a request or interrogatory is unduly burdensome on its face if it used the omnibus term 'relating to' or 'regarding' with respect to a general category or group of documents."[18] Yet the request need not use "relating to" or "regarding" because the request's "overall wording" can make the request facially unduly burdensome and overly broad. Courts often ask whether the request's wording "requires the answering party to 'engage in mental gymnastics to determine what information may or may not be remotely responsive.'"[20]

Defendant chiefly argues that to locate any employee who has suffered "any type of adverse employment action" due to either violation of defendant's FMLA policy or defendant's "call in" attendance policy would require review of more than 1,800 personnel files. Moreover, defendant argues that determining "any type of adverse employment action" would include undocumented incidents of employees who had received verbal warnings or counseling. Consequently, collection of such "anecdotal evidence would require interviewing every current and former supervisor who worked for the company in the past five years." Defendant also argues Interrogatory No. 9 is not narrowed as to temporal scope and that even to limit Interrogatory No. 9 to the past five years, as suggested by defendant, would still require reviewing 1,800 personnel files.

The court agrees that to determine "any type of adverse employment action" would require defendant to engage in mental gymnastics in order to determine what might be remotely responsive as to Interrogatory Nos. 8 and 9. Moreover, the court finds the lack of temporal scope of Interrogatory No. 9 is facially over broad.

However, the court also finds that a review of 1,800 files is not necessarily overly broad or unduly burdensome on its face. Plaintiff argues that FMLA leave and termination for attendance is specifically coded by BCBSKS. Plaintiff concludes, and defendant does not refute, that such coding could easily be searched by computer. As plaintiff suggests, a simple computer search could produce information sufficient to respond to both Interrogatories or, at a minimum, guide defendant's further searches. Consequently, the court finds that a review of 1,800 files is not in and of itself overly broad and unduly burdensome on its face.

---

16. Snowden v. Connaught Lab., Inc., 137 F.R.D. 325, 332-33 (D. Kan. 1991).
17. Aikens v. Deluxe Fin. Servs., 217 F.R.D. 533, 537-38 (D. Kan. 2003).
18. *Id.*
20. Aikens, 217 F.R.D. at 538. . . .

### a. Adequate Guidance Exists

That the court has found in some respects Interrogatory Nos. 8 and 9 to be overly broad and unduly burdensome, "does not automatically relieve [the objecting party] of its obligation to provide responses . . . to the extent the request is not objectionable."[26] However, the court will not require a party "to respond to an overly broad discovery request unless adequate guidance exists as to what extent the request is not objectionable."

In establishing guidance and to avoid crafting an arbitrary order, "the court must define the extent to which the interrogatory is reasonably answerable and not objectionable."[27] To this end, the court may use "other matters of record [to] define the discoverability of certain information encompassed by the interrogatory."[28]

Consequently, the court directs defendant to respond to Interrogatory No. 8 to the extent it seeks to obtain information regarding only those employees who have been terminated or disciplined in writing (including reprimands) for violating BCBSKS' FMLA policy. As to Interrogatory No. 9, plaintiff proposes that defendant "could at least provide . . . all employees terminated for attendance." Thus, the court further directs defendant to respond to Interrogatory No. 9 to the extent it seeks information regarding documented instances of employee termination for attendance within the last five years. . . .

## II. DOCUMENT REQUESTS

Plaintiff seeks to compel production of documents responsive to Document Request Nos. 2, 3, 7, 8, 13-18, and 20. As discussed below, plaintiff's motion is granted as to Request Nos. 8, and 13-18.

### A. DOCUMENT REQUESTS NOS. 2 AND 3

*Document Request No. 2.* Any and all correspondence of any kind either to or from Michele Moss that is in the possession of BCBSKS.

*Response*: Defendant objects to the request as overly broad, unduly burdensome, and not reasonably calculated to lead to the discovery of admissible evidence. The request is so broad that it would conceivably include proprietary and confidential correspondence of various kinds between plaintiff and the health care providers that are in defendant's network, email messages between plaintiff and her non-supervisory co-workers that happen to reside on defendant's computer system, and the like. All nonprivileged correspondence regarding plaintiff's absences in May of 2006 and plaintiff's termination have previously been produced herein.

*Document Request No. 3.* Any documents bearing Michele Moss' name that you have in your possession or control.

*Response*: Defendant objects to the request as being overly broad, unduly burdensome, and not reasonably calculated to lead to the discovery of admissible

---

26. Aikens, 217 F.R.D. at 538 . . . See also Fed. R. Civ. P. 33(b)(1). . . .
27. Aikens, 217 F.R.D. at 538-39. . . .
28. *Id.* at 539. . . .

evidence. Plaintiff's name could appear in the company newsletter, birthday lists, lists of employees who subscribed to certain benefits, and other documents which have nothing to do with the claims plaintiff asserts in this case. To search through every document in defendant's possession to determine whether it lists plaintiff's name would be extraordinarily burdensome and time-consuming. Defendant has previously produced plaintiff's personnel file, FMLA file, workers compensation file, and unemployment claim file.

### 1. Overly Broad and Unduly Burdensome

Defendant argues that both Request No. 2 and 3 are overly burdensome and unduly burdensome on their face, and the court agrees. An objecting party's "failure to meet its evidentiary burden is not necessarily fatal to its claim that the requests are unduly burdensome" because "an exception . . . applies when the discovery request is unduly burdensome on its face."[36] Courts often ask whether the request's wording "requires the answering party to 'engage in mental gymnastics to determine what information may or may not be remotely responsive.'"[37]

Here, the court finds that requesting defendant to supply plaintiff with all correspondence of any kind sent either to or from plaintiff, as sought in Request No. 2, is overly broad on its face. As both parties note, plaintiff's five years of employment at BCBSKS required her to extensively communicate with the providers in BCBSKS' network. Further, defendant would have to search through every other employee's correspondence to determine what had been sent from other employees to plaintiff.

As to Request No. 3, in plaintiff's motion to compel, plaintiff agrees that "Request No. 3 is probably too broad." Thus, plaintiff "withdraw[s]" this request "and substitute[s] the following: Any document bearing Michele Moss' name that is either from or to Moss and another supervisor, manager, or anyone holding a higher position within the company unrelated to insurance benefits or servicing customer service requests from outside individuals." Defendant responds that the Federal Rules do not allow the court to "approve" a document request prior to the service of such request. The court does note that defendant apparently has provided plaintiff with "[a]ll nonprivileged correspondence regarding plaintiff's absences in May of 2006" and plaintiff's "termination" and "plaintiff's personnel file, FMLA file, workers compensation file and unemployment claim file."

The fact that the Request Nos. 2 and 3 are facially overly broad, however, "does not automatically relieve [the objecting party] of its obligation to provide responses . . . to the extent the request is not objectionable."[42] While the court agrees with defendant that it cannot "approve" of a substituted Request for Production, courts in the District of Kansas have used suggestions made by parties to craft guidance as to how the request at issue is not objectionable. However, to that end, the court finds plaintiff's strangely worded "substituted

---

36. Aikens, 217 F.R.D. at 537-38.
37. *Id.* at 538. . . .
42. Aikens, 217 F.R.D. at 538. . . .

request" insufficient guidance.[43] There may very well be documents in defendant's possession which are relevant or contain information which reasonably could lead to the discovery of admissible evidence regarding plaintiff's claims or defendant's defenses. But, plaintiff's suggestion to narrow the request to excluding from production only those documents involving "insurance benefits or serving customer service requests from outside individuals"[44] does not sufficiently provide guidance to resolve the problems presented by plaintiff's overly broad requests.

Moreover, the court can fashion no reasonable guidance on its own to define the extent to which either Request No. 2 or 3 are not objectionable. Because the court will not require a party "to respond to an overly broad discovery request unless adequate guidance exists as to what extent the request is not objectionable" defendant's overly broad and unduly burdensome objections are sustained.

### B. DOCUMENT REQUEST NOS. 7 AND 20

*Document Request No. 7.* Any and all documents from the previous 5 years to the present date relating to any legal action, civil or criminal, in which defendant has been involved either as a party, a witness, a plaintiff, a defendant or otherwise, pertaining to violations of Title VII, the ADEA, ADA, racial discrimination, sex discrimination, or violating the FMLA of 1993.

*Response*: Defendant objects to the request as being overly broad, unduly burdensome, and not reasonably calculated to lead to the discovery of admissible evidence.[45]

*Document Request No. 20.* Any and all confidential settlement agreements arising out of relating to claims of sex, race, or age discrimination, violations of ADA, ADEA, Title VII or the FMLA by any former employee, officer, agent, contractor, or vendor of Blue Cross Blue Shield of Kansas Inc. [sic].

*Response*: Defendant objects to the request as being overly broad, unduly burdensome, and not reasonably calculated to lead to the discovery of admissible evidence. Plaintiff does not assert any claims of sex discrimination (under Title VII or otherwise), age discrimination (under ADEA or otherwise), disability discrimination (under the ADA or otherwise), or any other violation of Title VII. The time for amendment of the pleading has passed. Furthermore, response to the request would require defendant to violate binding contractual confidentiality.

### 1. Overly Broad and Unduly Burdensome

The court finds that Request No. 7 is overly broad and unduly burdensome on its face. Courts in the District of Kansas routinely find "a request . . . unduly burdensome on its face if it use[s] the omnibus term 'relating to' or 'regarding' with respect to a general category or group of documents."[46] Here, Request No. 7 seeks "[a]ny and all documents . . . relating to any legal action in which defendant has been involved" regarding the general category of all forms of employment discrimination. To answer this request would require defendant

---

43. *Id.* at 539. . . .
44. Memorandum in Support (Doc. 30) at p. 14.
45. Defendant also notes that it has provided information regarding suits filed against it claiming violations of FMLA.
46. Aikens, 217 F.R.D. at 537.

to "'engage in mental gymnastics to determine what information may or may not be remotely responsive.'"[47] Because the court can determine no reasonable guidance to define the extent to which either Request No. 7 is not objectionable, defendant's overly broad and unduly burdensome objections are sustained.

### 2. Relevancy Objection

The court incorporates its analysis of the similarly worded Interrogatory No. 10 here and sustains defendant's relevancy objections as to Request Nos. 7 and 20. Just as plaintiff failed to demonstrate the relevancy of Interrogatory Nos. 10 (with the exception of that portion directed to discovery of claims regarding FMLA violations), so too plaintiff fails to meet her burden to prove the relevancy of Request Nos. 7 and 20.

To the extent that Request No. 20 seeks information regarding confidential settlement agreements involving FMLA claims, the court still finds Request No. 20 is not reasonably calculated to lead to the discovery of admissible evidence in this case. As discussed in *DIRECTV, Inc. v. Puccinelli*,[48] three potential standards exist regarding the discoverability of confidential settlement agreements. In deference to the strong public policy encouraging settlement, some courts have required a party seeking disclosure of confidential settlement agreements to meet a heightened standard in order to discover information related to or contained in the requested settlement agreements. Other courts, including courts in the District of Kansas, have refused to apply such a heightened standard. Rather, these courts apply only the general Fed. R. Civ. P. 26 standard, requiring the party opposing the discovery request to demonstrate that it is not relevant to a claim or defense or not reasonably calculated to lead to the discovery of admissible evidence. Still other courts adopt a compromise approach, requiring the party seeking discovery to demonstrate the relevance of the request. The court in *DIRECTV* determined that it need not choose which standard to follow because under any standard the production of confidential settlement agreements was warranted.

Defendant argues, and the court agrees, that the present case is distinguishable from *DIRECTV*. In *DIRECTV* defendants sought various settlement agreements between the plaintiff and persons who would be witnesses in the case. Here, plaintiff seeks settlement agreements between defendant and persons who have no interest in this proceeding.

Moreover, even under the general requirement of Rule 26, the least stringent standard, Request No. 20 is not reasonably calculated to lead to the discovery of admissible evidence regarding plaintiff's claims or defendant's defenses. Defendant argues that the settlement agreements, even those pertaining to the FMLA, are not relevant and the court agrees. Interrogatory No. 8 gives plaintiff the names of BCBSKS employees who were terminated or otherwise disciplined for violating defendant's FMLA policy and documents evidencing such termination or discipline. This would include those who reached confidential settlement agreements with defendant. In light of this grant, the court can find no discernable reason as to why the confidential settlement agreements themselves would be relevant to plaintiff's claim. Therefore, the court sustains defendant's relevancy objection.

---

47. Aikens, 217 F.R.D. at 538. . . .
48. 224 F.R.D. 677, 686-87 (D. Kan. 2004).

# Comments and Questions

1. Should discovery facilitate or promote fishing for new claims or defenses? Was Moss engaged in a fishing expedition with these requests?

2. Most judges detest hearing or resolving discovery disputes. Why would you suppose that this is the nearly universal reaction of judges? Are the issues in *Moss* any less meaningful or less desirable to resolve than, say, a motion to amend or a motion to dismiss?

3. The permissible scope of discovery was modified by amendment to the Federal Rules in the year 2000. Prior to that amendment, the scope of discovery under Rule 26 had extended to "any matter, not privileged, which is relevant to the subject matter involved in the pending action." The 2000 amendment narrowed that scope to any nonprivileged matter that is relevant to the "claim or defense" of any party. However, for "good cause, the court may order discovery of any matter relevant to the subject matter involved in the action." What constituencies benefit when the scope of discovery is broadened or narrowed? Professor Jeffrey Stempel has documented in great detail the extent to which proponents of the change tended to represent pro-defendant, pro-business interests. *See* Jeffrey W. Stempel, *Politics and Sociology in Federal Civil Rulemaking: Errors of Scope*, 52 Ala. L. Rev. 529, 530, 629 (2001). Would the analysis in *Moss* have been any different (or easier) under the previous rule?

4. Parties who receive discovery requests with which they do not want to comply can either object to the request or file a protective order under Fed. R. Civ. P. 26(c).

   If the responding party objects, the requesting party, in turn, has at least a couple of options: (1) The requesting party can abandon or reframe the request, or (2) can bring the dispute to the attention of the court by filing a motion to compel. With regard to the latter, read Fed. R. Civ. P. 37(a). What are the issues an attorney might consider before bringing a discovery dispute to the court's attention?

   By filing a motion for a protective order, the responding party brings the dispute to the attention of the court. Why would the party responding to document requests or interrogatories with any plausible objection to the request seek a protective order instead of simply objecting? Read Fed. R. Civ. P. 37(a)(4).

## Practice Exercise No. 15: Analyzing the Scope of Discovery in *City of Cleveland*

Imagine that all discovery matters in the *City of Cleveland* case have been referred to Judge Chrys, a magistrate judge in the Eastern Division of the Northern District of Ohio. The parties have asked for a discovery conference with the judge concerning the fundamental question whether the plaintiffs should be entitled to any discovery regarding written tests and the physical agility tests administered by the City of Cleveland prior to the year of the tests administered to the named plaintiffs. And if so, how far back—two years, five years, ten years? Maybe "it depends," but depends on *what*?

We know that some circuits have expressly held that discovery in employment discrimination suits is especially broad. But assume that the U.S. Court of Appeals for the Fifth Circuit, in which this court sits, has not taken a position. In other (nondiscrimination) cases, the court has taken a rather hard line against "fishing expeditions, discovery abuse, and inordinate expenses involved in overbroad and far-ranging discovery requests."

Judge Chrys has called the parties and their lawyers into her chambers for this conference, and has provided the following introduction: "The problem of setting a time period for the discovery ordered is a perplexing one because it does not admit of a lapidary solution. Life is often messy and cannot be divided into neat chronological segments. In this case the plaintiffs claim that they were discriminated against by the defendants. Some of these claims will require proof of intentional conduct by the defendants, and their case will be strengthened by circumstantial evidence that the defendants treated women a certain way because of their gender. Given the nature of the showing required, we must strike the balance between the need of the plaintiffs to have access to the evidence needed to prove their case and the defendant's burden in defending the action. You have asked for some direction from me, and I shall seek to find the golden mean between unduly restrictive and overbroad production. There may ultimately be many discovery disputes in this case, but I accept your invitation to determine, first, what should the beginning and end of the relevant period of discoverable information be. Of course, I would appreciate your input before I make this determination."

She then turns to you. Persons with last names beginning with the letters C-N represent the plaintiffs; persons with last names beginning with the letters O-Z represent the defendant City. Persons with last names beginning with the letters A and B shall be prepared to serve as law clerks to the judge.

## 2. *Mandatory Initial Disclosures*

Save certain exceptions, parties are required to disclose some information as a matter of course upon the commencement of the litigation. Fed. R. Civ. P. 26(a)(1) provides for the prompt and mandatory disclosure by both parties of the following information:

- the name, address, and telephone numbers of individuals "likely to have discoverable information—along with the subjects of that information—that the disclosing party may use to support its claims or defenses";

- a copy or description of "all documents, electronically stored information, and tangible things that the disclosing party has in its possession, custody, or control and may use to support its claims or defenses";
- a computation of damages claimed by the disclosing party, together with supporting materials; and
- insurance agreements under which an insurance business may be liable to satisfy all or part of a possible judgment.

These disclosures must be made within two weeks of the conference required by Fed. R. Civ. P. 26(f). That conference must occur at least twenty-one days prior to the Rule 16(b) conference, which, in turn, typically occurs within the first several months of the litigation. *See* Fed. R. Civ. P. 16(b). A party must make these disclosures based upon the information then reasonably available.

As an important practice note, Fed. R. Civ. P. 26(e) requires *supplementation* of any information that would have been subject to the mandatory disclosure requirement. Further, that obligation to disclose information the party may use connects directly to the exclusion sanction of Fed. R. Civ. P. 37(c)(1). Rule 37(c) provides an almost automatic sanction for a failure to disclose under Rule 26(a).

## Comments and Questions

1. Why would a party be obliged to disclose only that information that *supports* its claims or defenses? Wouldn't an obligation to disclose all information *relevant* to the subject matter of the action cast a wider and better net? This latter phraseology was the standard when mandatory disclosures were first adopted in 1993. Consider the following excerpt from Justice Scalia's dissent to the Court's transmittal to Congress of the 1993 discovery amendments:

. . . The proposed radical reforms to the discovery process are potentially disastrous and certainly premature—particularly the imposition on litigants of a continuing duty to disclose to opposing counsel. . . .

The proposed new regime does not fit comfortably within the American judicial system, which relies on adversarial litigation to develop the facts before a neutral decisionmaker. By placing upon lawyers the obligation to disclose information damaging to their clients—on their own initiative, and in a context where the lines between what must be disclosed and what need not be disclosed are not clear but require the exercise of considerable judgment—the new Rule would place intolerable strain upon lawyers' ethical duty to represent their clients and not to assist the opposing side. . . .

It seems to me most imprudent to embrace such a radical alteration that has not, as the advisory committee notes, been subjected to any significant testing on a local level. . . . Any major reform of the discovery rules should await completion of the pilot programs authorized by Congress, especially since courts already have substantial discretion to control discovery.

I am also concerned that this revision has been recommended in the face of nearly universal criticism from every conceivable sector of our judicial system, including judges, practitioners, litigants, academics, public interest groups, and national, state and local bar and professional associations. . . . Indeed, after the proposed rule in essentially its present form was published to comply with the notice-and-comment requirements of 28 U.S.C. § 2071(b), public criticism was so severe that the advisory committee announced abandonment of its duty-to-disclose regime (in favor of limited pilot experiments), but then, without further public comment or explanation, decided six weeks later to recommend the rule. . . .

Of course the mandatory initial disclosure obligation was later narrowed to its present form. Does the current (amended) scope of Fed. R. Civ. P. 26(a)(1) address Justice Scalia's concerns?

2. What survey or study would you design to ascertain whether the mandatory disclosure rule is working? Of the various interest groups identified by Justice Scalia as critical of the reform, whose satisfaction should we most care about?

3. With regard to the scope of the mandatory disclosure obligation, "use" is broadly defined in the Advisory Committee Notes to include "any use at a pretrial conference, to support a motion, or at trial."

4. You should also be familiar with two additional stages of mandatory disclosures. Fed. R. Civ. P. 26(a)(2)(D) requires certain disclosures of expert testimony at least ninety days before the trial date. A third stage requiring disclosures of the identities of witnesses and documents to be used at trial is to occur at least thirty days prior to trial. *See* Fed. R. Civ. P. 26(a)(3).

## 3. *Discovery Techniques*

The federal discovery rules outline the formal techniques by which parties may obtain discovery. These techniques include depositions (*see* Rules 27-32); interrogatories (*see* Rule 33); requests for production of documents (*see* Rule 34); physical and mental examinations (*see* Rule 35); and requests for admissions (*see* Rule 36). The permissible scope of discovery for all of these formal mechanisms, of course, is defined by Rule 26, which permits the discovery of any unprivileged matter that is relevant to the claim or defense of any party, and is not unreasonably cumulative or burdensome. Of course, upon a showing to the court of good cause, that scope may be expanded to include anything within the "subject matter of the action." In this part we identify certain advantages and disadvantages of the various formal as well as informal discovery techniques. We also discuss the increasingly important role of experts.

### a. A Brief Introduction to the Rules of Evidence

Although the scope of discovery is much broader than the scope of evidence that would be admissible at trial, the latter is also important at the discovery stage. First, if the evidence sought in discovery *would* be admissible at trial, then it most certainly should also be within the scope of permissible discovery. Second, if the discovery sought "appears reasonably calculated to *lead to* the discovery of admissible evidence," then it may be relevant under Fed. R. Civ. P. 26(b)(1). And third, remember that the parties are using discovery to acquire evidence that will be admissible at trial; if plaintiff's only evidence with regard to a particular element of a certain cause of action is not admissible at trial, then that plaintiff must use discovery to acquire evidence of that element that will be admissible. Accordingly, some basics about the law of evidence may be helpful to you as you contemplate the mechanics of discovery. Evidence itself is a complex subject and will be covered in a separate course; this is but an overview.

It is important to realize, in the words of one trial lawyer, that "the courtroom is its own reality": if evidence is not admitted into the record of that case by one of the established techniques, then it cannot be considered by the fact finder. Put another way, the evidence necessary to support a verdict must be *on the record*; the attorney thus must ensure that all pieces of the evidence that she wants the fact finder to consider are properly admitted lest they be ignored. Importantly, facts alleged in a pleading, discovery materials produced or held, and statements or arguments made in pretrial proceedings are not evidence and cannot support a verdict. Evidence is only that information that was introduced by the parties at trial (whether through testimony or documents or things) and was admitted by the court onto the record.* The rules of evidence govern what evidence is admissible for parties to submit for the record.

Most cases are not proved with "the smoking gun," that is, *direct evidence* of an issue. Direct evidence is evidence that is precisely on point. For example, in *Carpenter*, a witness on the stand can testify that she saw the jeep tip over to prove that it in fact tipped. Why it tipped will probably require *circumstantial evidence*, which is evidence relating to a series of facts other than those directly at issue in order to prove a fact at issue. An expert may take the stand in order to testify as to how raising a vehicle will alter its center of gravity and destabilize it when it turns a corner. This, along with other evidence, may permit an *inference* that the sale of the oversize tires and elevation kit without a warning was (1) negligent, (2) the cause in fact, and/or (3) the proximate cause of the death of Charlie Carpenter. A good deal of the civil litigator's skill and art relates to creatively getting facts into evidence that will later permit the drawing of desired inferences.

---

*There are a few methods of providing evidence that are often overlooked, such as asking the court to take judicial notice of a particular fact or by the submission of facts stipulated by the parties.

*[handwritten in margin: Fed & State Codes. Dig for evidence]*

When one is in federal court, the admissibility of evidence is governed by the Federal Rules of Evidence. In state court, admissibility is governed by either a written code or statute of evidence rules, often patterned after the federal rules, or common law rules of evidence, often supplemented by statutes. For purposes of our exercises in *Carpenter* and *City of Cleveland*, assume that the Federal Rules are the operative evidence rules. They are usually fairly representative of the common law of evidence, although in many instances they are weighted more toward admitting evidence than the corresponding common law rule.

*Relevant evidence*, according to Rule 401, "means evidence having any tendency to make the existence of any fact that is of consequence to the determination of the action more probable or less probable than it would be without the evidence." Fed. R. Evid. 401. In order to make a relevancy argument, one must usually turn to the concepts that you learned early in the course: causes of action and elements. After all, how does one know whether a fact is "of consequence to the determination of the action" unless one knows the cause of action relied upon, its elements, defenses and their elements, and the theories propounded by each side?

Consider *Carpenter v. Dee* again. If the sole theory in a negligence case was that the driver failed to wear his prescription glasses and therefore didn't see the pedestrian whom he hit, then evidence of unusually large tires on the vehicle would probably be irrelevant. (We say "probably" because maybe the high tires are relevant to line of vision, and perhaps you can come up with another "relevancy" argument.) But when the theories against a driver are that it was negligent to alter a jeep by lifting it with unusually large tires and a suspension kit (plus hockey pucks!) and to drive the jeep in that condition, otherwise irrelevant evidence suddenly becomes relevant.

The more remote the relationship between the proffered evidence and the issue in question, the less likely the judge will be to find it relevant. In our firefighters case, maybe it's a little relevant that in Paris ten years ago one engine company had a woman driver for one day, but it seems quite remote from the issues in the *Cleveland* case, and in all likelihood would be excluded on an evidence objection. In evidence parlance, the party trying to exclude evidence makes an *objection*. If the judge agrees with the objection, she *sustains* it. If the judge decides it's a bad objection, she *overrules* it. If the objection is overruled, that means that the witness at a trial will be ordered to answer the question or, if pertaining to physical evidence, the proffered exhibit will be admitted.

A witness's credibility is always relevant. The evidence rules permit a number of ways to *impeach* credibility, such as through *bias*, a *contradictory statement*, what is called *bad reputation for truth and veracity*, or documentation of a *conviction for a felony or for a crime involving dishonesty or false statement*. In unusual cases, otherwise relevant evidence might be excluded because it is *prejudicial* (*see* Rule 403). For instance, if the deceased in the *Carpenter* case was under indictment for burglary at the time of the accident, one could argue that the deceased was distracted at the time, and therefore consented to accompany Randall Dee in the jeep when he should have refused because of its altered construction. One might also argue that this testimony is relevant to the deceased's earning capacity. Whether or not this information is slightly probative of comparative negligence (assuming Charles Carpenter's negligence is relevant in the wrongful death action brought by his widow) or somewhat relevant to damage issues, some judges would consider the relevancy of such information to be sufficiently attenuated and thus outweighed by the potential prejudice.

*Hearsay* according to Rule 801(c) is "a statement, other than one made by the declarant [the person who makes a statement] at the trial or hearing, offered in evidence to prove the truth of the matter asserted." Fed. R. Evid. 801(c). Hearsay includes both oral and written statements. In general, even if an out-of-court statement introduced to prove the truth of its contents is signed or under oath, it is still hearsay. Hearsay is perhaps the most elusive of evidentiary concepts and takes many forms. Hearsay is generally inadmissible, unless one can find an exception to the hearsay rule.

Some hearsay examples are relatively easy. In *Carpenter*, if Melissa takes the stand in order to testify to what Lee told her about the jeep accident he witnessed, such testimony would ordinarily be hearsay. The fact finder would have to determine whether Lee's rendition of the accident were true, yet Lee would not be on the stand to be cross-examined. If Melissa were asked where Lee was standing at the time he allegedly saw the accident, she would probably answer "I don't know." She might say, "Ask Lee." That's the point; it is the person who actually witnessed the event who should testify, instead of the person to whom he or she told the story.

Sometimes an out-of-court statement is not being introduced for a hearsay purpose (that is, the truth of the matter asserted), and therefore it is admissible. In an oral contract case in which *A* says that *B* made an oral promise, the words of the contract are themselves relevant and admissible over a hearsay objection. If *C* takes the stand and says that he heard "*A* tell *B* that he would take care of her mother for $500 a week, and *B* said she'd pay that amount," then that is not hearsay in a lawsuit based on that contract. The words spoken are themselves relevant, and one doesn't need to cross-examine the speakers (*A* and *B*). It is enough that *C* can be cross-examined about where *C* was standing, and about *C*'s ability to hear or *C*'s bias. Indeed, for the same reasons, *A* and *B* could also testify to the words of contract which were spoken between them. The concept of "nonhearsay purpose" is tricky, and it takes many students enrolled in an evidence course (and many practicing attorneys) time to catch on.

Even if offered testimony is hearsay, it may be subject to an exception and thus admissible as evidence in court. Probably the most common way of getting around what would otherwise be hearsay is through what historically was called the *admissions* exception. Fed. R. Evid. 801(d)(2). For evidence purposes, an "admission" is any statement made by the party-opponent. It doesn't matter whether the opponent is in fact admitting anything. If your opponent said it or wrote it, it will not be excluded on hearsay grounds.

In other words, if in a motor vehicle personal injury negligence case the defendant said that "the roads were slippery the night of the accident," the plaintiff could put a witness on the stand to testify she heard what the defendant had said. It will be admitted against the defendant without any analysis of whether defendant thought he was admitting anything. If your opponent (the opposing party) said it or wrote it, and it's relevant, it normally will be admitted. For a very sophisticated reason, which we won't consider here, the drafters of the federal rules made "admissions" nonhearsay, rather than an exception (*see* Rule 801(d)(2)). But the result is the same: Statements of a party-opponent will be admitted over a hearsay objection.

The many hearsay exceptions are divided among those in which it matters whether or not the out-of-court declarant is available to testify because of reasons such as death, illness, refusal, or memory problems. Rule 804 lists the exceptions that require the proponent of what would otherwise be hearsay to show that the declarant is unavailable.

The *opinion* rule normally makes opinions by laypersons inadmissible. *See* Fed. R. Evid. 701. In a discrimination case, the plaintiff could not ordinarily say that in her opinion she was discriminated against. She would be permitted to describe how she was treated by the defendant-employer so that the fact finder can conclude whether there was discrimination in violation of the law. If a witness is shown through questions (or by stipulation of the parties) to be an expert (this is often called *qualification*) and seeks to give an opinion in her field of expertise that will aid the fact finder on a relevant point, then such *expert opinion* is normally admissible (*see* Fed. R. Evid. 702). There are occasions when a party needs experts in order to meet the production burden. For example, in a medical malpractice case the plaintiff will usually have trouble surviving a directed verdict without evidence from at least one expert on the standard of medical care that was allegedly breached and on the question of whether the alleged negligence was the cause of the alleged injury.

Another group of evidence rules relate to *privileges*. You have probably heard of the Fifth Amendment constitutional privilege against "self-incrimination." But several other privileges, frequently statutory, identify and protect confidential communications between certain people. Perhaps the most frequently used in litigation is the *attorney-client* privilege, which was developed at common law, but is now statutory in many states. If a protected professional relationship exists, such as that between attorney and client, it is the client who controls the privilege. The client, not the attorney, can waive the right to exclude oral and written communications between them that are related to their professional relationship. The rationale here is that without such a privilege, clients would not reveal information that their lawyers need to know in order to give good sound legal advice.

Many states also have some combination of the following privileges: *priest-penitent, doctor-patient, spousal (husband-wife), psychotherapist-patient*. Various rationales support these and other privileges that you will read about in your evidence class. The drafters of the Federal Rules were unable to reach agreement on privileges that would also satisfy Congress. This was particularly true with privileges relating to state secrets. Consequently, Fed. R. Evid. 501 is the only portion of the Federal Rules of Evidence on privileges in federal courts. Thus, the federal courts look to other sources (such as the Constitution, congressional statutes, and the common law developed in the federal courts or state evidence law, especially in diversity of citizenship cases) for the applicable evidence rules.

When lawyers need more guidance in evidence matters, they often look to a treatise called *McCormick on Evidence.* Lawyers also refer to Wright, Miller, and Kane's treatise, which covers the Federal Rules of Evidence as well as the Federal Rules of Civil Procedure. In addition, the annotated version of the Federal Rules of Evidence provides relevant case law after every rule. Lawyers often use this case law to supplement their arguments regarding the admissibility of a particular piece of evidence. The Advisory Committee Notes to the Federal Rules of Evidence are also quite helpful in this respect. There also exist Uniform Rules of Evidence, which some states have adopted in whole or in part. Lawyers in state court often use a handbook on the rules of evidence in their state. For direction with respect to a particular state evidence issue, lawyers often refer to state treatises that specifically discuss the particular state's evidence law.

### b. Depositions

Depositions are used by attorneys to question potential witnesses (both parties and nonparties) under oath about their knowledge of and participation in certain events or circumstances concerning the underlying action. Depositions typically are conducted orally, and every word that is spoken is recorded *verbatim* by a court reporter (or by mechanical means) and is transcribed. The witness (called the *deponent*) is given an opportunity to review the transcript and make technical corrections. Fed. R. Civ. P. 30(e).

Depositions are widely thought to be the most important step of the formal discovery process. It is perhaps no surprise, then, that half of the twelve discovery rules pertain solely to deposition practice. Read Fed. R. Civ. P. 27 through 32, which address a range of technicalities, including how depositions should be noticed, under what circumstances a witness may be deposed, before whom a deposition may be taken, and how a deposition transcript may be used.

A deposition may be scheduled on "reasonable notice" in writing. The noticing party may ask the witness to bring documents along, but that invokes the time limits of Fed. R. Civ. P. 34. *See* Fed. R. Civ. P. 30(b)(2). If the deponent is a nonparty, the noticing party must also provide for the attendance of the witness, usually by serving him with a subpoena. *See* Fed. R. Civ. P. 45. If a witness (whether a party or nonparty) fails to show up for the deposition, she may be assessed to pay the expenses and fees of the noticing party under Rule 30(g).

The noticing party schedules the location of the deposition and usually identifies her own law office as the situs. Depositions typically resemble a business meeting, with the deponent and his counsel on one side of the table and opposing counsel on the other side. Parties are entitled to attend any depositions taken in their case, and it is often a matter of strategy who, from each side, appears to observe a given deposition. Deponent's counsel may object to questions during the deposition, but the only objections that may preclude the deponent from answering the question posed are an objection as to the form of the question and an objection that to answer would reveal privileged information. All other answers are required and recorded, but remain "subject to the objection." Fed. R. Civ. P. 30(c).

There are at least five fundamental advantages to oral depositions. First, an oral deposition gives an attorney a chance to question potential witnesses under oath, in a manner similar to trial. This may be particularly useful as a means of assessing the demeanor of a witness under a variety of questioning styles. Second, while it is true that nearly all deponents will have been coached by an attorney prior to a deposition, responses to questions will have a degree of spontaneity unavailable under other discovery methods. Third, in a deposition an attorney has the opportunity to follow up on information revealed in answers and to take the questioning in any new direction that may reveal itself. Fourth, subject to the rules of evidence, anything recorded in a deposition is available for use at trial. Portions of depositions are often used to impeach a witness's testimony and can substitute for live testimony in cases where a witness is unavailable for trial. Fifth, nonparties may be deposed. Indeed, nonparties may also be subpoenaed to bring documents or other tangible items to the deposition and, thus, otherwise undiscoverable evidence may be obtained through questioning regarding those documents or items.

The most significant disadvantage to taking depositions is the expense. The party requesting the deposition must spend a significant amount of time preparing for each deposition. And at hourly billing rates of several hundred dollars an hour, this adds up quickly. Moreover, the counsel that notices the deposition must also hire a court reporter. The bill for a court reporter is the sum of two numbers: (1) an appearance fee of approximately $100 or an hourly rate of approximately $25, plus (2) a transcription fee of $3.50-$5.00 per page. Depending on the pace of the deposition, court reporters usually generate 45-55 pages per hour. Thus even excluding the expense associated with the lawyers' time, one seven-hour deposition will cost the requesting party approximately $2,000. In addition to these expenses, parties must also pay travel expenses when the deponent is not local. Deponents also suffer costs, including preparation time spent with their counsel and, often, lost time from work. Since 1993, there has been a limitation on the number of depositions parties may take as a matter of right (see Fed. R. Civ. P. 30(a)(2)(A)(i)); a 2000 amendment to Rule 30 requires that depositions be completed in the equivalent of one seven-hour day (see Fed. R. Civ P. 30(d)(1)); and courts may order even further limits (see Fed. R. Civ. P. 26(b)(2)). Lawyers, by agreement, can agree to waive the Federal Rules' numeric restrictions on depositions and other discovery mechanisms. (*See* Fed. R. Civ. P. 29.) Such stipulations are commonplace in complex matters.

Of course, in some cases, a lawyer contemplating the taking of a deposition may decide not to do so because she does not want the deponent (or the deponent's lawyer) to be able to infer anything about her theories of the case; similarly, she may not want the putative deponent to be confronted until the trial.

### c. Written Interrogatories

Under Fed. R. Civ. P. 33, written questions may be submitted to an opposing party and must be answered in writing, under oath, and returned within the specified time period. Read Fed. R. Civ. P. 33. Notice that Rule 33(b) specifies agency concepts for interrogating corporations and partnerships. Questions may seek any information discoverable under the scope of discovery standard of Rule 26(b)(1).

There are at least three advantages to using written interrogatories. First, interrogatories are usually the most useful mechanism for obtaining detailed and/or noncontroversial information from an adversary. If served early in the case, interrogatories can be very useful in obtaining names, addresses, dates, employers, relationships, histories, lists, numbers, or other technical information that a party may be required to assemble. Second, interrogatories are inexpensive to prepare and serve (or "propound") upon the opposing party. In fact, most lawyers (and many practice books) have pattern interrogatories for specific types of cases. Third, interrogatories are available for use at trial. Interrogatory answers are statements of an opposing party, and thus may be admitted as an admission under the Rules of Evidence over a hearsay objection.

The unfortunate downside to interrogatories, however, is that the answers are almost always drafted by lawyers and, thus, typically are crafted to contain as little useful information as possible. The answers are not spontaneously offered, and there is no opportunity for a timely follow-up question for clarification. Moreover, some lawyers delay the answering of interrogatories until their client is compelled to answer by the judge or will make every conceivable objection to the wording and scope of the interrogatories. As with depositions, there is a limit on the numbers of interrogatories that parties may serve as a matter of right. Fed. R. Civ. P. 33(a) now has a presumptive limit of twenty-five, and local rules may limit still further. *See* Fed. R. Civ. P. 26(b)(2).

An important strategic consideration that is part of both drafting and answering interrogatories is the extent to which you choose to inform the party of your theories of the case. On the one hand, the interrogatory is a subtle rhetorical device, an opportunity for advocacy; on the other hand, detail sufficient to persuade will necessarily inform the other party of your line of thinking and may give your opponent ample time to formulate a responsive theory.

Once again, remember that Fed. R. Civ. P. 26(e) imposes a continuing duty to supplement your discovery responses.

### d. Production of Documents and Things

Under Fed. R. Civ. P. 34, any party may request another party to produce documents and things and may then inspect and copy those documents and things before returning them to the producing party. Read Fed. R. Civ. P. 34. "Production" can include turning over a copy of the requested information or making it available at a specified time and place.

One advantage of what commonly is referred to as a *document request* is that the term "documents" is construed widely (as the listed items in the rule itself imply) to mean almost any type of written or electronically stored item of information. A document request may also include a request for things, which may include the physical inspection of real or personal property, including equipment, devices, vehicles, and the like. The broad scope of the definition of *document* works in tandem with the broad scope of discovery under Fed. R. Civ. P. 26(b).

One primary disadvantage of a document request is that it is difficult to strike a balance between over- and under-inclusiveness. On the one hand, a certain level of specificity is required, because a requesting party must request with specificity sufficient to ensure that the opposing party will deliver the sought documents. However, casting the request too broadly can result in an avalanche of documents that are responsive to the request but will bury the desired document(s).

One historical disadvantage to use of a discovery request was that Rule 34 was limited to parties and, even as to parties, to items only within their "possession, custody, or control." Later amendments to the Federal Rules, however, relaxed the requirement that the request be directed to a party. Part (c) of Rule 34 permits a party to subpoena documents even from a non-party in conformity with the requirements for a subpoena in Rule 45.

Again, remember that Fed. R. Civ. P. 26(e) imposes a continuing duty to supplement your discovery responses.

### e. Physical and Mental Examinations

Under Fed. R. Civ. P. 35, a physical and/or mental examination of a person may be requested when the person's condition is in controversy and the person to be examined is given proper notice. Read Fed. R. Civ. P. 35. Medical examinations are the only discovery tools for which advance court approval is required, and the court requires a showing of "good cause" for the examination.

This device applies only to a relatively narrow subset of cases, where the condition of the putative examinee is truly "in controversy." The Supreme Court has made clear that the Rule requires more than "mere conclusory allegations of the pleadings" or even "mere relevance to the case." Instead, there must be "an affirmative showing by the movant that each condition as to which examination is sought is really and genuinely in controversy." *Schlagenhauf v. Holder*, 379 U.S. 104 (1964).

When an examination is permitted, the court orders the time and place. Counsel for the party being examined typically is not permitted to attend. Re-read Fed. R. Civ. P. 35(b)(1), and you will see what, in addition to expense, may be viewed as a disadvantage of this device.

### f. Requests for Admissions

Under Fed. R. Civ. P. 36, a party may serve upon any other party a request for admission of any matter within the scope of discovery. Read Fed. R. Civ. P. 36. Requests for admissions typically are "question and answer" statements that are used by either party to further explore specific contentions. The requesting party formulates a "question" in the form of a statement, which the answering party is requested to admit or deny. For example, a defense attorney may incorporate a request such as "Admit or deny: Randall Dee was not wearing a seat belt at the time of the fatal accident." This type of request may be intended to determine whether certain affirmative defenses will be available at trial.

The primary benefit of requests for admission is that they provide an opportunity to "lock in" particular admissions or denials of fact. Unlike evidence at trial, which may be rebutted and refuted, once admitted, the fact must be taken as true in the pending action, unless the court permits the admission to be "withdrawn or amended." Fed. R. Civ. P. 36(b). Importantly, under the Federal Rules, there is no limit on the number of allowable requests a party can make. Accordingly, the device may be especially helpful as a pretrial device to obviate the need for certain presentations of proof, including, for example, establishing the foundations for the admissibility of documents.

### g. Informal Discovery

The Federal Rules do not discuss what are perhaps the most commonly used methods for discovering information. Informal discovery techniques include (1) nonparty interviews; (2) site visits; (3) exchange of information (for instance, cooperation with other attorneys who have handled cases against the same defendants or regarding similar events); (4) requests for information from government agencies (under the Freedom of Information Act, for example); (5) review of publicly available records; (6) private investigation; and (7) Internet research. Informal discovery thus refers to any form of extrajudicial research or inquiry that attempts to obtain facts relevant to the case.

There are two primary advantages to informal discovery techniques. First, informal discovery may cost less. Indeed, in certain circumstances the party may be able to perform the discovery for or in concert with the attorney, and thereby dramatically limit the fees incurred. Second, informal discovery often provides no notice to (nor requires any cooperation with) opposing parties. This may be particularly useful to an attorney who wishes to develop elements of her case without alerting her opponents to theories she may pursue (or to evidence that she already has).

It bears mentioning that informal discovery, such as information obtained from the Internet, may be inaccurate. Some informal discovery, such as the use of private investigators or the contact of nonparty witnesses, can—at some point—violate rules of professional ethics. And of course certain sources of informal discovery, such as hospitals or employers, will not release confidential information without the authorization of the party about whom information is sought. Nevertheless, informal discovery remains a valuable discovery tool for the effective litigator.

### h. Experts

In the past two decades, expert witnesses have performed an increasingly important role in the process of developing and, ultimately, presenting a case. It is now generally accepted that expert testimony is necessary to aid a jury, especially when scientific, medical, technological, or statistical information is presented. A study conducted by the Federal Judicial Center, for example, suggests that tort plaintiffs will, on average, use at least three experts; and defendants will use at least two. Yet experts typically are involved long before trial. Experts are routinely consulted to assist in the process of framing the pleadings, preparing discovery requests, responding to discovery, and when developing a strategy for pretrial motions.

The use of experts in presenting and interpreting evidence is not unique to the American system of jurisprudence. Civil law systems also use experts to aid in the interpretation of complicated evidence. However, where the American system allows the parties to choose, prepare, and groom their experts, most civil law systems put these decisions solely in the hands of the judge. That difference has a marked effect on the role of the expert in each instance. American experts are increasingly criticized for their biased opinions, offered as "expert testimony" to support the case for the hand that feeds them. In contrast, the judge-selected experts in the civil law system are viewed as neutral witnesses able to provide factual assertions regarding the evidence, not based upon the party that hired them.

Note that although there is not a specific discovery rule governing the involvement of experts, their participation is contemplated by the rules. When are you obliged to disclose the identity of your experts? Can experts be deposed?

## Comments and Questions

1. Could the petitioner in *Hickman v. Taylor* have noticed the deposition of Attorney Fortenbaugh? Could the petitioner force Fortenbaugh to answer interrogatories?

2. Understand how the discovery system requires cooperation between the parties. Lawyers may have very different impressions about the scope of permissible discovery under Rule 26(b)(1); what constitutes reasonable notice under Rule 30(b)(1) or reasonable particularity under Rule 34(b); how one counts twenty-five interrogatories under Rule 33(a); or whether the mental condition of a person is in controversy under Rule 35. Now armed with a better understanding of the particulars of the discovery rules, you may wish to revisit the uneasy placement of discovery within the broader context of our adversarial system. Would more specific discovery rules solve the problems created by adversarialism? Would it create new problems?

3. Start your own list of ways to defend against discovery. By creating such a list, neither you nor we are endorsing all of these techniques. Indeed, some lawyers engage in dubious behavior in discovery even though unethical methods should never be utilized. But here are some of the methods you might include in a list: objections to answering (such as objections to interrogatories or instructing a witness at a deposition not to answer); seeking continuances; restricting an answer or compliance with a request to the most narrow possible reading of the question or request; seeking a limiting order or a protective order; moving to quash; reading a request in the broadest possible light and thereby providing so much information that the most relevant information may become lost in the shuffle; claiming that the opponent has not complied with the required disclosure, meeting, planning, and certification requirements prior to commencing additional discovery. Find the corresponding Federal Rules that authorize each of these techniques (and for any additional techniques that you add to this list). When and how might a practice be authorized by rule yet unethical to use?

4. Start your own list of ways to compel discovery. Begin with the following and, again, find the corresponding Federal Rules that authorize them: seeking an order to compel; seeking the assistance of the court through case management; moving for sanctions; moving for a contempt order; defending and then trying to reach a voluntary and explicit agreement with opposing counsel on how discovery will be sensibly and fairly conducted, with very precise commitments. You can also move to force your opponent to comply with required disclosures, supplemental disclosures, or a discovery plan.

## Practice Exercise No. 16: Drafting Interrogatories in *City of Cleveland*

Imagine that you are an associate in a law firm representing the plaintiffs in the *City of Cleveland* case. A team of associates is working on discovery matters, and it is your responsibility to focus on developing interrogatories regarding the conspiracy claim under 42 U.S.C. § 1985(3), Count Three. (Other associates will be focusing on other claims and other discovery mechanisms.) Given the limit on the number of allowable interrogatories under Fed. R. Civ. P. 33, effective use of each interrogatory is a must. Draft (only) three interrogatories to be propounded to the defendants.

Now imagine that you are an associate in a law firm representing the defendants in the *City of Cleveland* case. Perform the same task for them, drafting (only) three interrogatories regarding the conspiracy claim to be propounded to the plaintiffs.

## Practice Exercise No. 17: Ethical Issues in Discovery

The following two fact patterns present issues that may arise in the context of discovery. We are interested in finding out how you would respond under each of these circumstances. (Assume that you are an attorney with the authority to make these choices.) Remember that you have a duty both to zealously (or "competently" and "diligently," under the Model Rules) represent your clients and to behave ethically. You may want to consider the potential effect your decision will have on your clients and their case, on the opposing party and its case, on your practice, and on the legal system generally. You may, of course, consider other factors as you see fit.

### *Scenario No. 1*

Your clients, the City Police Department, its Chief, and members of the Department, are defendants in a civil rights case. Plaintiff claims that two policemen stood by and watched her husband brutally beat her, and that their failure to stop the beating was part of a pattern and practice of refusing to come to the aid of victims of domestic violence. Plaintiff is represented by a solo practitioner who recently graduated from law school and (you know from a friend) has lots of debt and almost no assets. She is representing the plaintiff on a pro bono basis and (you have heard) has volunteered to front the costs for her client, pending settlement or a favorable verdict. You are a third-year associate in a successful, respected firm. Defendants pay (through the City) $250 per hour for your services, plus costs.

Plaintiff has sent you a request for production of the following documents and things, *inter alia:*

1. Any and all records from the period commencing five (5) years prior to the date of the incidents giving rise to the lawsuit of or pertaining

to any and all complaints, formal and/or informal, made by women to the City Police Department, regarding violence, abuse, forced sexual relations, and/or any other injury, act, or practice perpetrated upon them by a present or past husband, a present or past "boyfriend," and/or a present or past lover, and/or any other person known to them.

2. Any and all statements, memoranda, reports, or internal policy guidelines, pertaining to the period commencing five (5) years prior to the date of the incident giving rise to the lawsuit of or pertaining to the handling of complaints formal and/or informal, made by women to the City Police Department, regarding violence, abuse, forced sexual relations, and/or any other injury, act, or practice perpetrated upon them by a present or past husband, a present or past "boyfriend," and/or a present or past lover, and/or any other person known to them.

With no further investigation (based on conversations you have had with some of the defendants), you know that some items exist that arguably would fit into each category requested by the plaintiff. You also know that considerable time and expense (on the part of the Police Department) would be involved in fairly compiling all of the materials requested. From what you know so far, it could go a long way toward proving Plaintiff's claims if the request is read with any liberality. You also have reason to believe that there may even be some particularly damaging correspondence authored by the Chief and others in the department calling domestic violence cases "a real waste of time" and "none of our damn business."

You consider the following responses to the request (or any others that make sense to you):

(a) Produce nothing and respond that these "requests are overly broad, unduly burdensome, and request materials beyond the scope of discovery."

(b) Respond by offering the plaintiff access to the documents and records "as they are kept." This option would likely force you to review, for privileged documents, more than 3,000 boxes of stored complaints, memoranda, etc., in the City Police Department basement.

(c) Review all of your clients' files and produce what you understand to be the spirit of the request in as direct a manner as possible. Will you include documents and records pertaining to complaints made by women regarding matters unrelated to domestic violence?

(d) Ask the Chief to provide you with whatever he thinks fits the request. With this approach you're pretty sure that his "eyesight is poor."

Prepare, first, to explain to the clients your strategic options and recommendation(s). How is he (and/or "the City") likely to respond to your recommendation? Then, assume that your clients have concurred with your decision, but the opposing counsel calls you to complain. How will you respond to this? And finally, assume that the opposing counsel brings this dispute before a judge, and you are called upon to explain your approach. Can you defend your tactics?

*Scenario No. 2*

Continuing with the same facts as in Scenario 1, the Chief comes to your office to prepare for his deposition, which is to occur next week. Upon his arrival, he says, "Hey, I know I told you I hadn't exactly established a firm policy for how to handle domestic violence cases, but you know what? I forgot about this memo I sent around a couple of years ago. One of my best officers just gave me his copy this morning. I'm sure you'll love it because I took all of the ideas from a great civil rights lawyer on how police departments ought to handle these cases. Before I left the station this morning, I talked with a bunch of my veteran cops, and they all said they had seen copies of this; they distinctly remember my long lecture to them on handling these cases seriously. I can't believe that this slipped my mind earlier, but I've been under a lot of pressure, you know. I'm really feeling better about my deposition testimony already."

What are you going to ask or say to the Chief? And what will you do at the deposition if he has the opportunity to testify according to what you have just heard?

## 4. The Phenomenon of Electronic Discovery

We know that at least 95 percent of the documents generated today are electronic. Nearly 10 billion electronic documents are created each year. And according to the Radicati Group, nearly 300 billion e-mail messages are sent each day—that's 90 trillion messages per year or 2.8 million per second. Moreover, the production and storage of e-mails and other electronic information happen in multiple locations: servers, smartphones, tablets, home computers, thumb drives, and elsewhere, including "the cloud." With the complexity and number of systems, applications, and devices, most users cannot even fathom where all of the messages and documents are nor how long they survive. Electronic discovery has undoubtedly transformed the *quantity* of discoverable information that exists; one unanswered question is whether electronic discovery poses a challenge that is *qualitatively* different.

Approximately 70 percent of documents that are produced electronically are never printed. This means that anyone engaged in document discovery will necessarily need to understand the basics of how electronically stored information is retained and accessed. Accessing this information—which might be stored on back-up tapes and legacy technologies—will often require technical expertise But electronic information also will contain useful "metadata" that printed documents seldom have. For example, an electronic copy of an e-mail message would reveal not only the contents of the message, but the date and time that the recipient received the message, whether the recipient actually opened the message, to whom (if anyone) the recipient forwarded the message, and how or whether the recipient saved and stored the message.

Similarly, how a document was edited, and by whom, and when, is information that can often be extracted from an electronic file.

The explosive growth of technology has enormous implications for how discovery is conducted. The rules of electronic discovery are still in their relative infancy, but as a practical matter it is undeniably necessary to be familiar with electronic discovery so that you are able to frame requests, to respond to (and to resist) requests, and also to counsel clients with respect to the use, preservation, and retrieval of such information.

Let us explore, first, the mandatory initial disclosure obligation in the context of electronically stored information. Re-read Fed. R. Civ. P. 26(a)(1)(A)(ii). Consider the amount of work that will be necessary for you to produce or to describe in detail the "electronically stored information . . . that the disclosing party may use to support its claims or defenses." In order to comply (and to avoid the potentially dire consequences of failing to comply), you will need to have a very sophisticated understanding of your client's electronic records. You must know how and where your clients store electronic records and for how long, and how difficult it will be to retrieve those records. E-mail may be the most obvious such category of records, but consider the innumerable sources of "electronically stored information."

Next, notice the specific limitations on the scope of electronically stored information in Fed. R. Civ. P. 26(b)(2)(B).

> A party need not provide discovery of electronically stored information from sources that the party identifies as not reasonably accessible because of undue burden or cost. On motion to compel discovery or for a protective order, the party from whom discovery is sought must show that the information is not reasonably accessible because of undue burden or cost. If that showing is not made, the court may nonetheless order discovery from such sources if the requesting party shows good cause, considering the limitations of Rule 26(b)(2)(C). The court may specify conditions for the discovery.

The limitations of Rule 26(b)(2)(C), which apply to electronic and any other discovery, provide that:

> [T]he court must limit the frequency or extent of discovery otherwise allowed by these rules or by local rule if it determines that (i) the discovery sought is unreasonably cumulative or duplicative, or can be obtained from some other source that is more convenient, less burdensome, or less expensive; (ii) the party seeking discovery has had ample opportunity to obtain the information by discovery in the action; or (iii) the burden or expense of the proposed discovery outweighs its likely benefit, considering the needs of the case, the amount in controversy, the parties' resources, the importance of the issues at stake in the action, and the importance of the discovery in resolving the issues.

Of course the presumption in the United States is that each party will bear its own litigation expense, including the costs of responding to discovery requests. But the volume and expense of producing electronic information has caused some to revisit that premise. Neither of the preceding clauses of Federal Rule 26(b) explicitly mentions the possibility of *cost-shifting*. But the Advisory Committee's Note to the 2006 amendment that introduced that language is more explicit:

> The good-cause inquiry [of Rule 26(b)(2)(B)] and consideration of the Rule 26(b)(2)(C) limitation are coupled with the authority to set conditions for discovery. The conditions may take the form of limits on the amount, type, or sources of information required to be accessed and produced. The conditions may also include payment by the requesting party of part or all of the reasonable costs of obtaining information from sources that are not reasonably accessible. A requesting party's willingness to share or bear the access costs may be weighed by the court in determining whether there is good cause. But the producing party's burdens in reviewing the information for relevance and privilege may weigh against permitting the requested discovery.

Next, revisit Fed. R. Civ. P. 26(f). Pursuant to this rule, the parties must discuss the preservation of electronic documents at the early discovery conference and must also develop a discovery plan that addresses "any issues about disclosure or discovery of electronically stored information, including the form or forms in which it should be produced."

> The areas of discussion likely to arise are what information has been preserved to date, how much information is expected to be produced, what the form of production will be, whether cost-shifting or cost-sharing of the production is necessary, and how the parties should handle privileged materials. . . . Parties will need to know what sources of electronic evidence exist and will have to take a position on what evidence should and should not be produced.

Paul D. Weiner and Mary Kay Brown, *Navigating the New E-Discovery Rules*, 33 Litig. 29, 31 (Winter 2007). Issues pertaining to preservation and production each deserve further attention.

With regard to preservation, it is important to note that there is a duty as soon as litigation becomes "reasonably foreseeable." Although reasonable minds differ on exactly when that moment occurs, it is very critical that you (and in-house counsel and outside counsel advising companies) appreciate that this is (usually) well before the lawsuit is filed. This duty to preserve extends to both electronic and paper discovery, and it is essential that clients know when they must suspend any ordinary or extraordinary practices that could destroy evidence. Electronic discovery is different from paper discovery because doing "nothing" with regard to electronic data may result in its destruction due to deletion, overwriting, upgrading, or recycling.

> Given the lawyer's paramount role in preserving evidence, asking the client for detailed systems information such as the following is essential:
>
> • What relevant electronic evidence is in danger of being lost by deletion, overwriting, or recycling?

- Are the firm's backup tapes recycled; if so, how often?
- Are mass amounts of old information routinely purged from the system to create space for new files on the system?
- Are e-mails and other electronically stored information automatically deleted after they reside on the system or individual computers, including ISP accounts, for a set period of time (e.g., 30 days)?
- Are e-mails stored on a central server or individual desktop or laptop computers?
- Are computers ever wiped clean and reformatted, such as when an employee leaves the company?
- Are any IT infrastructure changes, modifications, or upgrades planned for the near future; if so, how will archival data be migrated to the new system?

The next step is to ensure such practices are immediately suspended and to document the steps the client takes in doing so.

Weiner & Brown, *supra*, at 33. The duty to preserve electronically stored information (and all other evidence) arises from many sources, including common law, statutes, regulations, or court order.

However, Rule 37(e) provides a safe harbor that, under certain conditions, insulates a party from sanctions for failing to preserve certain evidence. The safe harbor applies provided the electronically stored information is lost as a result of the routine, good-faith operation of an electronic information system. The rule is intended to capture those situations where the system itself, usually without input from or the awareness of the operator, deletes the data. And notice that the routine operation must have been performed in good faith. "An analysis of good faith will include a review of the steps the party took to comply with its preservation obligation." *Id.*

The duty to preserve evidence (electronic or otherwise) and the consequences of its destruction are explored in the following case.

## ■ TEAGUE v. TARGET CORP.
### *2007 WL 1041191 (W.D.N.C. 2007)*

MULLEN, United States District Judge:

This matter is before the court upon Defendant's Motion for Sanctions. Defendant seeks to have the court dismiss Plaintiff's claim for back pay due to spoliation of material evidence.

Plaintiff, a former employee of the Defendant Target, was terminated from her job on February 17, 2003. She filed this action alleging that she was wrongfully terminated on the basis of her gender in violation of public policy articulated in N.C. Gen. Stat. § 143.422.2. She also asserts a claim for intentional infliction of emotional distress. Plaintiff seeks to recover lost wages and benefits, compensatory, and punitive damages. Target has asserted various affirmative defenses to Plaintiff's claims, including failure to mitigate.

During discovery in this case, it was revealed that Plaintiff owned a home computer from December 1995 until August of 2004, on which she conducted her entire on-line job search after leaving Target, including researching job opportunities on the internet, submitting on-line employment applications, and exchanging emails with prospective employers. Plaintiff also used this computer to send and receive emails regarding her termination from Target and her claims of gender discrimination. Plaintiff claims that she discarded this computer because it "crashed" and her brother, who "dabbles" with computers, was unable to get the hard drive to work. Plaintiff claims she decided to buy a new computer during the tax-free weekend in August of 2004. Plaintiff admits she never took the computer to any type of computer professional to determine if it could be repaired. The computer was discarded approximately one year after she had retained counsel regarding her prospective claims against Target and after she filed her charge of discrimination with the EEOC. Since the home computer was discarded, the only documented evidence of Teague's post-termination job search is the work search records she submitted to the North Carolina Employment Security Commission ("ESC") to substantiate her claim for unemployment benefits. Teague has testified in her deposition that the ESC work search records are not necessarily complete, since she only recorded the two job applications she was required to make each week in order to qualify for benefits. Moreover, there are contradictions between the ESC records and Teague's interrogatory answers regarding her job search.

Defendant alleges that Plaintiff engaged in the spoliation of electronic evidence. "Spoliation refers to the destruction or material alteration of evidence or to the failure to preserve property for another's use as evidence in pending or reasonably foreseeable litigation." *Silvestri v. General Motors Corp.*, 271 F.3d 583, 590 (4th Cir. 2001). Parties have an affirmative duty to preserve material evidence. This duty arises long before the filing of an initial pleading in litigation. The Fourth Circuit states that the duty extends to that period prior to litigation "when a party reasonably should know that the evidence may be relevant to anticipated litigation." *Id.* at 591. In this case, Plaintiff discarded the computer well after she had retained counsel and filed her EEOC charge. Moreover, the computer contained evidence directly related to her lawsuit against Target.

While courts have broad discretion to sanction a party for spoliation, "the applicable sanction should be molded to serve the prophylactic, punitive, and remedial rationales underlying the spoliation doctrine." *Id.* at 590. Target seeks to have the court sanction Plaintiff by dismissing her claim for back pay. However, utilizing a sanction of dismissal for spoliation is generally not authorized absent bad faith conduct.

Another available sanction for spoliation is the issuance of jury instructions permitting the jurors to draw an adverse inference from a party's destruction of evidence. *Thompson v. U.S. Dept. of Housing and Urban Dev.*, 219 F.R.D. 93, 100-01 (D. Md. 2003). Evidence of bad faith or fraudulent intent is not required to obtain this instruction. Courts have held that three elements should be shown to warrant an adverse inference instruction for spoliation: (1) the party having control over the evidence had an obligation to preserve it when it was destroyed; (2) the destruction or loss was accompanied by a "culpable state of mind;" and (3) the evidence that was destroyed was relevant to the claims or defenses of the party that sought discovery of the spoliated evidence, to the extent that a reasonable factfinder could conclude that the lost evidence would have supported the claims or defenses of the party that sought it. *Residential Funding Corp. v. Degeorge Financial Corp.*, 306 F.3d 99, 107-08 (2d Cir. 2002). A "culpable state of mind" could include bad faith/knowing destruction; gross negligence; and ordinary negligence. *Id.* at 108. The court finds each of these three elements present in this case. Plaintiff clearly had an obligation to preserve her computer because it contained electronic evidence relating to her claims against Target and her efforts to mitigate her damages. As noted earlier, she had already hired counsel and filed an EEOC charge. Under the circumstances the court concludes that there is enough evidence that Plaintiff discarded the computer with a "culpable state of mind." The electronic information contained on the computer was clearly relevant to her claims and to the defenses of the Defendant. Accordingly, the court finds that an adverse inference instruction to the jury is warranted and appropriate.

It is therefore ordered that Defendant's Motion for Sanctions is hereby granted in part and denied in part. The court will sanction the Plaintiff for spoliation of evidence by giving an adverse inference jury instruction at trial.

## Comments and Questions

1. In light of the opinion, precisely how should the jury be instructed?

2. Would it have been an abuse of discretion for a district judge to sanction plaintiff by dismissing the claim for back pay?

3. The issue of when litigation becomes reasonably foreseeable (thereby triggering the duty to preserve) can be contentious and unpredictable. Rambus Inc., is a company founded to commercialize inventions related to DRAM computer memory, including its RDRAM product. Most companies have document retention policies, and Rambus had a "shred day" during which thousands of documents were destroyed. Thereafter, it was engaged in patent suits against manufacturers of SDRAM, an alternate type of memory technology. After the lawsuits were filed, the plaintiffs suing Rambus argued spoliation of evidence. Addressing the same legal issue and core facts, federal district judges on opposite coasts reached opposite conclusions. Because these were patent suits, the Federal Circuit heard both appeals. Rambus argued that "to be reasonably foreseeable, the litigation must be imminent, at least in the sense that it is probable and free of significant contingencies." The plaintiffs argued that reasonable foreseeability did not incorporate a requirement of imminence. The Federal Circuit held that the standard does not carry an independent requirement of imminence: while "[t]his standard does not trigger the duty to preserve documents from the mere existence of a potential claim or the distant possibility of litigation . . . it is not so inflexible as to require that litigation be imminent, or probable without significant contingencies." *See Micron Technology, Inc. v. Rambus Inc.*, 645 F.3d 1311 (Fed. Cir. 2011);

*Hynix Semiconductor Inc. v. Rambus Inc.*, 645 F.3d 1336 (Fed. Cir. 2011). This note was drawn from a May 5, 2011, entry on the Patently-O blog, one of the many excellent blogs that digest and analyze recent court opinions.

4. When litigation is reasonably foreseeable, an organization's general counsel will typically issue a "litigation hold notice" to all of the custodians of the organization's records. Paper or electronically stored information that would otherwise be destroyed by document retention policies (that shred paper, erase backup tapes, etc.) is to be preserved.

5. The *production* of electronically stored information raises a set of issues quite apart from those pertaining to *preservation*. For example, can a responding party simply print thousands of e-mail messages and produce the paper? Contrast this approach with production that is in some form that can be easily searched and catalogued by the requesting party. Of course these issues become ever magnified with the existence of complex interactive databases containing millions of electronic records—and circumstances where the data are stored on a system customized for the exclusive use and unique purposes of its host. Federal Rule 34 now contemplates that responses and objections will state the form of production. What does Rule 34 allow or command? And to the extent that the obligation to produce is expensive, how likely is the court to shift the costs of making the electronically stored information available?

# ■ HELMERT v. BUTTERBALL, LLC
## *2010 WL 2179180 (E.D. Ark. 2010)*

J. Leon HOLMES, District Judge.

This is a collective action brought by Sheila Helmert, Wilma Brown, and Lori West, on behalf of themselves and others similarly situated, against their former employer, Butterball, LLC, under the Fair Labor Standards Act ("FLSA"). The plaintiffs have filed a motion to compel pursuant to Federal Rule of Civil Procedure 37(a) in which they assert that the defendant's response to their first set of requests for production of documents is inadequate because the defendant has refused to conduct a meaningful search of its electronically stored information ("ESI"). Butterball has responded and argues that, while it agrees that the plaintiffs are entitled to more documents than those it has received thus far, the scope of the plaintiffs' request is much too broad. Butterball also argues that, because of the burdensome nature of the discovery, cost should be shifted to the plaintiffs. For the following reasons, the plaintiffs' motion to compel is granted in part and denied in part.

## I.

On April 18, 2008, the plaintiffs commenced this against Butterball, their former employer, for alleged violations of the FLSA and Arkansas law. The complaint alleges that the plaintiffs and other hourly production employees at its Huntsville, Ozark, and Jonesboro plants were not fully compensated for time spent donning, doffing, and sanitizing protective gear and equipment. . . .

On September 29, 2008, the plaintiffs served their first set of requests for production of documents. Included in this set was a request for "[a]ll documents, correspondence, e-mail, or other written materials related to employee donning and doffing of personal protective equipment, safety equipment, tools, uniforms, and/or other gear or clothing." The plaintiffs also requested "[a]ll documents evidencing communications amongst and between employees, management or otherwise, that concern payment of wages for time spent donning, doffing, walking, sanitizing, or waiting in any production facility" and "[a]ll documents related to Butterball's payroll procedures" and "punch-clock procedures." In response to the plaintiffs' request, Butterball produced 800 documents. In addition, it conducted a search for the phrase "donning and doffing" in the active and archived email boxes of 22 Butterball custodians—every custodian who had received a litigation hold notice in May 2007. Butterball did not limit the search by date. Based on that search, Butterball produced 87 emails. Butterball asked the plaintiffs to submit a list of other search terms or custodians if they did not feel that Butterball's search was sufficient. However, Butterball maintained that "it has produced all e-mail communications relevant to the subject matter of these [sic] lawsuit." The plaintiffs note that, on March 9, 2010, they received three additional email communications relevant to their case that should have been retrieved in the initial search.

On April 17, 2009, the plaintiffs requested that Butterball conduct another ESI search with an expanded list of eleven additional custodians and 52 additional search terms. The plaintiffs also asked Butterball about its email retention policies, server locations, and email backup and storage policies. On April 24, 2009, Butterball responded with a letter explaining that it would not "conduct additional e-discovery of either the additional custodians or search terms outlined in your April 17 letter" because it believed the requests were unduly burdensome and "would not lead to the discovery of any additional admissible evidence." In an effort to demonstrate how burdensome such a search would be, Butterball conducted the proposed search on the emails of Gary Lenaghan, the individual Butterball believed was "most likely to have additional discoverable emails." The search terms returned a total of 11,713 emails from Lenaghan's active and archived folders. Butterball reported, "It took 2.5 hours simply to retrieve the emails, almost none of which related to donning and doffing. Those that did relate to donning and doffing have already been produced." Again, Butterball reiterated that it had already "conducted a complete, diligent search of e-mails designed to discover all relevant, admissible communications."

After another request by the plaintiffs for additional e-discovery, Butterball agreed to "work with Plaintiffs on narrowing the list of additional custodians and search terms" under two conditions: the plaintiffs allow Butterball two months to conduct the search, and the plaintiffs refuse to

ask for any further electronic discovery.[2] Although the parties held a meet-
and-confer conference on June 5, 2009, it appears that nothing was resolved:
the plaintiffs would not agree to Butterball's two conditions for conducting
additional searches, and Butterball would not perform the searches without
the conditions being agreed upon.

   Counsel for the parties engaged in two more meet-and-confer conferences
on January 4, 2010, and January 12, 2010. On January 27, 2010, Butterball
submitted a proposal to the plaintiffs, offering to search the email folders and
inboxes of 29 custodians for the 12 previously proposed terms from May 10,
2007, to the present. The plaintiffs responded that they would not agree to a
discovery plan that allowed Butterball to fulfill its discovery obligations by
conducting a single ESI search for the remainder of the case. Plaintiffs'
counsel proposed an ESI search of 43 custodians for 70 separate terms dating
back to 2000. In addition to Butterball email accounts, the plaintiffs proposed
searching all sources of ESI, including computer hard drives, databases,
backup tapes, and non-Butterball email accounts to which Butterball had
access. Butterball responded that it would only be able to search active
and archived email back to May 10, 2007, the date the litigation hold notice
was issued, and it objected to the plaintiffs' proposed terms and custodians.
Butterball also opined that its email system would not allow for searches for
terms within the same sentence or within a certain number of words as
another term. On March 11, 2010, the plaintiffs filed this motion to compel
discovery of ESI.

## II.

Here, the plaintiffs move to compel the production of discoverable information resulting from a search of 70 separate terms from all possible sources
of ESI belonging to 43 Butterball custodians dating back to 2000. The plaintiffs claim that such a search will uncover nonprivileged information relevant
to the plaintiffs' claims. In its response, Butterball consents to search the
active and archived email folders of all but 10 of the 43 custodians identified
by the plaintiffs for the 12 terms it has already proposed dating back to
November 8, 2005. Butterball argues that a search of ESI beyond that
which the defendant proposes will be unreasonably duplicative of the information that has already been provided to the plaintiffs and will impose a
significant burden and expense upon Butterball. Butterball also contends
that some of the ESI that the plaintiffs want searched is not reasonably
accessible and that the plaintiffs have failed to meet their burden of showing
good cause for conducting a search of that information.

---

   2. Specifically, Butterball agreed to search the email folders and inboxes of the 22 custodians already
named, as well as five additional custodians . . . . Butterball agreed to search for the terms: "time-stud!,"
"time-motion stud!," "Alvarez," "de minimis," "gang time," "line time," "plug time," "preliminary activit!,"
"postliminary activit!," "Fair Labor Standards Act," "FLSA," and "don! and doff!"

Federal Rule of Civil Procedure 26(b) governs the scope and limits of the discovery of ESI. As an initial matter, parties may obtain discovery regarding any nonprivileged matter that is relevant to any party's claim or defense. Fed.R.Civ.P. 26(b)(1). "Relevancy is broadly construed, and a request for discovery should be considered relevant if there is 'any possibility' that the information sought may be relevant to the claim or defense of any party. A request for discovery should be allowed 'unless it is clear that the information sought can have no possible bearing' on the claim or defense of a party." *Moses v. Halstead*, 236 F.R.D. 667, 671 (D.Kan.2006). The materials need not be admissible at the trial if they are reasonably calculated to lead to the discovery of admissible evidence. Fed. R. Civ. P. 26(b)(1). Discovery of relevant, nonprivileged ESI is limited if the party from whom discovery is sought establishes that it is unreasonably cumulative or duplicative or that the burden or expense of the proposed discovery outweighs its likely benefit. *See* Fed. R. Civ. P. 26(b)(2)(B). "If the ESI is not reasonably accessible, it is only discoverable upon a showing of good cause by the requesting party, taking into consideration the limitations of Rule 26(b)(2)(C)." *Best Buy Stores, L.P. v. Developers Diversified Realty Corp.*, 247 F.R.D. 567, 569 (D. Minn. 2007); *see also* Fed. R. Civ. P. 26(b)(2)(C).

### A. PROPOSED SEARCH TERMS

The plaintiffs have divided their proposed search terms into four categories: (1) terms related to donning and doffing cases against Smithfield Foods and its subsidiaries; (2) terms related to Supreme Court and other seminal donning and doffing cases; (3) terms related to individuals, law firms, and industry organizations, and (4) terms related to Butterball's compensation practices.

#### 1. TERMS RELATED TO DONNING AND DOFFING CASES AGAINST SMITHFIELD FOODS AND ITS SUBSIDIARIES

First, the plaintiffs ask the Court to compel Butterball to search terms and phrases that correspond to the names of named plaintiffs from 17 donning and doffing cases filed against one of Butterball's owners, Smithfield Foods, Inc., and its operating companies and joint ventures. They argue that ESI that references any of these cases is "highly relevant to Butterball's alleged 'good faith' compliance with, and non-'willful' violation of, the FLSA." Under the FLSA, "[a]n award of liquidated damages . . . is mandatory unless the employer can show good faith and reasonable grounds for believing that it was not in violation of the FLSA." *Braswell v. City of El Dorado, Ark.*, 187 F.3d 954, 957 (8th Cir. 1999); *see* 29 U.S.C. § 216(b) (2006). The good faith defense requires the employer to establish "an honest intention to ascertain and follow the dictates of the FLSA." *Chao v. Barbeque Ventures, LLC*, 547 F.3d 938, 942 (8th Cir. 2008). Butterball asserts that it acted in good faith in its attempt to follow the FLSA. (Am.Ans. ¶¶ 20-22, 39, 48-49, 55-56, 60, 62.) Thus, the plaintiffs allege that they "are entitled to explore what research . . . Butterball may have engaged in (if any) as part of its alleged 'good faith' effort to ascertain the FLSA's requirements." Butterball argues that these terms will not reveal relevant information because neither Maxwell Farms, LLC, (51 percent owner of Butterball) nor Smithfield Foods (49 percent owner), who were involved in these cases, are involved in decisionmaking for Butterball. Even so, whether Butterball decisionmakers were aware of and engaged in correspondence about prior donning and doffing cases—even those involving other companies—is relevant to Butterball's good faith defense.

Butterball also contends that the burden of conducting a search with these terms outweighs the benefits. *See* Fed. R. Civ. P. 26(b)(2)(B). Specifically, Butterball suggests that a search of these terms will result in a number of documents and emails through which Butterball will have to comb for privilege, and Butterball attests that it is impossible to search emails for one word within the same sentence as another word, as some of the plaintiffs' search terms require, because Butterball's email system does not have that search capability. Butterball offers no cost estimate, however, to support its assertion that a search for the proposed terms would be overly burdensome. The terms the plaintiffs propose are, in fact, unique names of specific donning and doffing cases, and to the extent that these names are found in emails of Butterball custodians, it is likely that some of them will pertain to donning and doffing. In any discovery request, relevant documents must be combed for privilege, and the defendant offers no evidence as to why this request should be any different. The Court does agree that, to the extent that it is impossible to conduct an electronic search of emails for one term within the same sentence as another term, requiring Butterball to do so would be unduly burdensome. The plaintiffs offer no evidence that Butterball can, in fact, perform such a search electronically. Nor do they offer any alternative method for conducting such a search.[5]

Thus, the Court finds that the plaintiffs' proposed terms relating to prior donning and doffing cases involving Smithfield Foods and its subsidiaries are narrowly tailored to lead to the discovery of relevant information, with the exception of the terms that require Butterball to search for one term "within the same sentence as" another term.

## 2. TERMS RELATED TO SUPREME COURT AND SEMINAL DONNING AND DOFFING CASES

Likewise, the Court finds that the seven proposed search terms relating to Supreme Court and other seminal donning and doffing cases is likely to lead to the discovery of relevant emails and documents. Butterball does not deny that such terms may yield relevant information; rather it contends that "whatever emails searches for these terms would yield would already be

---

5. They do suggest that Butterball can search for the first term, and then search the document for the second term where the search term requires two or more words in the same document. Even this alternative, however, will not necessarily find words within the same sentence as other words.

captured in searches for 'donning and doffing' or 'don* and doff*.'" The Court finds that argument unpersuasive. It is quite possible, if not likely, that a custodian could refer to the "*Alvarez*" decision in an email, for instance, without ever mentioning the phrase "donning and doffing." In fact, when Butterball searched Lenaghan's active and archived emails for the term "Alvarez," the search returned 453 emails. After searching for the phrase "donning and doffing" in the active and archived email boxes of 22 Butterball custodians, Butterball produced only 87 total emails. Although Butterball did not search all 453 emails to determine which of those emails are discoverable, it is likely that some of the emails contain relevant, nonprivileged information not covered by the "donning and doffing" search. The Court finds that these search terms are narrowly tailored to lead to the discovery of relevant information.

### 3. TERMS RELATED TO INDIVIDUALS, LAW FIRMS, AND INDUSTRY ORGANIZATIONS

The plaintiffs also propose searching for terms and phrases that correspond to the names of individuals, law firms, and industry organizations documented in relevant ESI and documents that have been produced so far.[7] However, the plaintiffs offer no indication as to why these particular terms are likely to lead to the discovery of more relevant information. Simply because the terms were found in relevant documents and emails does not necessarily mean that a search of the terms will lead to other relevant documents or emails. In fact, there are probably many terms and phrases in the discovered documents a search of which would not lead to the discovery of other relevant information. Butterball also points out that, even if a search of these terms might produce some relevant, nonprivileged information, that information could be obtained in other ways. This Court agrees. While a search of terms like "Department of Labor," "Chicken Council," and "Jackson Lewis" (Butterball's counsel), may lead to the discovery of some relevant information, any relevant document or email that names the Department of Labor, the National Chicken Council, or Jackson Lewis is likely to include a word or phrase that is more specific to donning and doffing than simply the organization or firm name. To the extent that these terms are likely to lead to the production of relevant information, that information will merely duplicate information that could be produced by searching other, more specific terms.

---

7. The proposed terms are: (46) "Wylie," (47) "Wimberly" and "Lawson," (48) "Jackson Lewis," (49) "Chicken Council," (50) "Turkey Federation," (51) "Poultry and Egg Association," "Poultry & Egg Association," "Poultry and Egg," "Poultry & Egg," (52) "Poultry Federation," (53) "Marr," (54) "George" within the same sentence as "Watts," (55) "Pretanik," (56) "Brandenberger," (57) "Rybolt," (58) "Dorinda" within the same sentence as "Peacock," (59) "Michael" within the same sentence as "McCann," (60) "Templeton," (61) "Haygood," (62) "Lisa" within the same sentence as "Dixon," (63) "Joyner," (64) "Randy" or "Randolph" within the same sentence as "Sullivan," (65) "Roger" within the same sentence as "Miller," (66) "thowell@gmcom.net," (67) "Department of Labor," "USDOL," "DOL," "Labor Department," (68) "Labor Standards Division," "Division of Labor," "Wage and Hour Bureau," (69) "ARDOL," "NCDOL," "MODOL," "MODOL," "CODOL," and (70) "Kronos."

#### 4. TERMS RELATED TO BUTTERBALL COMPENSATION PRACTICES

Finally, the plaintiffs propose searching for terms related to donning and doffing compensation practices at Butterball.[8] According to the plaintiffs, some of these terms are designed to unveil discoverable ESI related to expert and non-expert liability analyses concerning potential damage estimates that are commonly conducted by donning and doffing defendants. Others are designed to capture ESI relevant to Butterball's compensation practices that are being challenged. Still others are designed to capture ESI relevant to the parties' legal claims and defenses as well as Butterball's knowledge of wage and hour laws. Butterball argues again that a search of these terms is overly burdensome and will exact "an enormous cost on Butterball." Yet Butterball offers no evidence of the estimated cost of conducting such a search. In the sample search of Lenaghan's active and archived emails, the term "back pay" returned 792 emails; the term "Kronos" returned 297 emails. While some of these emails may not be discoverable, the plaintiffs should have the opportunity to review any relevant, nonprivileged emails that the search uncovers to the extent that Butterball can perform the search.[9]

### B. PROPOSED CUSTODIANS

The plaintiffs ask the Court to compel Butterball to search the ESI of ten custodians that Butterball does not consent to search. Those custodians include (1) three owners and executives of Butterball's majority owner Maxwell Farms; (2) five current and former employees at Butterball's Longmont, Colorado, facility; and (3) two other former Butterball employees.

#### 1. THE MAXWELLS

The plaintiffs contend that a search of ESI belonging to Gordon and Louis Maxwell will lead to the discovery of relevant information. Specifically, the

---

8. These terms include: (1) "time" and "study," (2) "time" and "motion," (3) "travel time," "walk time," "walking time," (4) "off the clock," (5) "on the clock," (29) "continuous workday," "continuous work day," "continuous" within the same sentence as "day" or "work," (30) "back pay," "backpay," "back wage," "back-wages," (31) "6 minutes," "six minutes," (32) "2 minutes," "two minutes," (33) "de minimis," "deminimis," "deminimus," "de minimus," (34) "gang time," (35) "line time," (36) "plug time," (37) "Fair Labor Standards Act," "FLSA," (38) "Minimum Wage Act," "Minimum Wage Order," "Wage and Hour Act," "Minimum Wage Law," "wage act," "wage law," "wage regulation," "wage order," "AMWA," "CMWO," "NCWHA," "MMWL," (39) "doff," (40) "D & D," "D & D," "DandD," "D and D," (41) "overtime" and all possible variants, (42) "time and one half," "time and a half," "1.5," and "time" in the same sentence as "half," (43) "time clock," (44) "swipe in," (45) "swipe out," and (70) "Kronos." (Pls.' Ex. A.)

9. Butterball contends that it cannot search for terms within the same sentence as another term. Thus, terms that call for searches for words within the same sentence as another term should be excluded. Butterball also contends that it cannot search for two separate terms within the same document except by conducting a search for one term and then, from the documents containing that term, search for the second term. Because this process is more tedious than a single-term search, and the search phrases that require searching for two separate terms in the same document are not likely to lead to the discovery of relevant information, the Court will not require Butterball to conduct a search for two separate terms in the same document.

plaintiffs rely on the deposition testimony of Butterball's corporate designee Karen Ingram, which suggests that Gordon and Louis Maxwell, as part of Butterball's ownership, made the ultimate decision about compensation for time spent donning and doffing. Since Ingram's deposition was taken, both Gordon and Louis Maxwell have been deposed, and both have denied any involvement in Butterball's decisionmaking. While they concede that they have attended meetings two to three times each year held by Butterball management, they state that they attended the meetings as observers only. Thus, even if a search of their emails revealed information pertaining to donning and doffing, such information would not be relevant to any specific claim or defense presented in this case. Therefore, Butterball will not be compelled to conduct those searches and produce those emails.

The plaintiffs also contend that Jim Maxwell should be a subject of discovery because he and Walter Pelletier manage Maxwell Farms and make decisions for Butterball. In his deposition, Gordon Maxwell stated that Jim Maxwell, Walter Pelletier, Keith Shoemaker, and Jerry Godwin form Butterball's upper management group and probably made the ultimate decisions concerning whether Butterball should or should not pay employees for donning and doffing activities. Butterball points out that Gordon Maxwell did not know for sure whether or not donning-and-doffing-related decisions were decisions for upper management. Furthermore, Butterball states that Jim Maxwell is not a Butterball employee and does not have a Butterball email account and that any email exchanges in which he was included would be discoverable by searching the emails of Walter Pelletier (Maxwell Farris's representative to Butterball who was involved in approving Butterball's donning and doffing decisions) and Keith Shoemaker (Butterball's CEO). The Court agrees that any emails to which Jim Maxwell was a party almost surely would have included Pelletier, Shoemaker, or others whose emails will be searched, so a search of Jim Maxwell's emails would be duplicative. Butterball will not be required to search Jim Maxwell's emails.

### 2. LONGMONT EMPLOYEES

Butterball contends that searching the ESI of Rich Chosich, Robert Salcido, John Quarles, Shawn McFarland, and Miguel Ramirez, is not reasonably calculated to lead to the discovery of admissible evidence because each of these individuals are employees at Butterball's Longmont, Colorado, facility, which is not involved in this lawsuit. Butterball points out that, unlike the Arkansas facilities, the Longmont facility has never paid donning and doffing time, and donning and doffing is a subject of a mandatory collective bargaining between the company and the United Food and Commercial Workers Union. According to the plaintiffs, Butterball's argument "ignores the more pertinent fact that these individuals may have been the Butterball employees most knowledgeable of the legal requirements of the FLSA as it relates to donning and doffing compensation." Thus, a search of their emails is likely to lead to the discovery of evidence related to Butterball's knowledge of the

FLSA and, thereby, its good faith defense. The Longmont employees may very well have ESI containing relevant, nonprivileged information.

Butterball next contends that, even if a search of their ESI may lead to discoverable information, it should not be required to search the ESI of Rich Chosich, Robert Salcido, John Quarles, or Shawn McFarland because their emails are only available on backup tapes, and the burden of searching those tapes outweighs any possible discovery benefits. The Court will address the plaintiffs' proposed sources of ESI in Subsection C below. Here, it is sufficient to say that ESI belonging to the above-named employees is likely to lead to the discovery of relevant information.

### 3. TWO FORMER BUTTERBALL EMPLOYEES

The plaintiffs also seek to discover the ESI of two other former employees: Dan Blackshear, the former President of Sales, Marketing, Research and Development at Butterball; and Joe Adrian, the former Human Resources Manager at Butterball's Huntsville plant. Butterball does not deny that these former employees are legitimate sources of discovery. Rather, it contends that, because their emails are only available on backup tapes, their emails are not readily accessible and the burden of searching their emails outweighs the benefits of discovery. The Court will address this issue below.

### C. PROPOSED SOURCES OF ESI IN ADDITION TO ACTIVE AND ARCHIVED BUTTERBALL EMAILS

The plaintiffs have asked Butterball to search not only active and archived emails stored in Butterball email accounts, but also backup tapes where emails of former employees are kept, work laptops and hard drives of Butterball employees, and, where appropriate, outside email accounts. Butterball argues that a search of these additional sources of ESI would impose an undue hardship and would merely duplicate the search results of active and archived emails. This Court is not persuaded that a search of laptop or computer hard drives would duplicate the email search. A computer's hard drive could contain a number of relevant documents that were never sent by email. Likewise, this Court is unpersuaded that exploring Butterball's own hard drives would impose an unreasonable burden on Butterball, and Butterball makes no effort to explain why these sources would not be reasonably accessible.

Butterball does, however, make a showing that its backup tapes are not reasonably accessible. Reasonable accessibility is best understood in terms of whether the ESI "is kept in an accessible or inaccessible format (a distinction that corresponds closely to the expense of production)." *Zubulake v. UBS Warburg LLC*, 217 F.R.D. 309, 318 (S.D.N.Y. 2003). This distinction largely depends on the media on which the ESI is stored. *Id.* Requested data maintained on backup tapes is typically classified as inaccessible. *Id.* at 319-20. Here, "[t]o recover the emails stored on backup tapes to the point of being able to search them, a Novell server must be built, GroupWise installed, and then the entire post office restored, a process which takes several days. The hardware needed to restore a post office would cost approximately $10,000. In addition to this cost would be "the time [for] the network team to construct a Netware server, install the group wise software, find the appropriate backup tape and restore that tape." Only then could Butterball search the email accounts of former employees for particular terms. Based on these facts, the backup tapes are in fact inaccessible.

The plaintiffs argue that, even if the backup tapes are inaccessible, they have good cause for obtaining discovery from the tapes. The Federal Rules of Civil Procedure advisory committee's notes list seven factors to inform the "good cause" inquiry: (1) the specificity of the discovery request; (2) the quantity of information available from other and more easily accessed sources; (3) the failure to produce relevant information that seems likely to have existed but is no longer available on more easily accessed sources; (4) the likelihood of finding relevant responsive information that cannot be obtained from other, more easily accessed sources; (5) predictions as to the importance and usefulness of the further information; (6) the importance of the issues at stake in the litigation; and (7) the parties' resources. Fed.R.Civ.P. 26(b)(2) advisory committee's notes (2006 Amendment). Ultimately, "[t]he decision whether to require a responding party to search for and produce information that is not reasonably accessible depends not only on the burdens and costs of doing so, but also on whether those burdens and costs can be justified in the circumstances of the case." *Id.* "Whether good cause exists depends upon a weighing of the relevant considerations already identified." *Major Tours, Inc. v. Colorel*, Civil No. 05-3091(JBS/JS), 2009 WL 3446761, at *3 (D.N.J. Oct. 20, 2009).

As to the first factor, the plaintiffs have specifically identified the terms for which they would like to search, and their request is reasonably specific. *See id.* The second factor weighs in favor of the defendant. In response to the plaintiffs first request for documents, Butterball produced nearly 800 documents. Throughout the course of discovery, the plaintiffs will take a number of depositions and have access to countless documents and emails that are more readily accessible than the backup tapes. Third, this Court finds no evidence of spoliation. "The obligation to preserve evidence arises when the party has notice that the evidence is relevant to litigation or when a party should have known that the evidence may be relevant to future litigation." *Zubulake v. UBS Warburg, LLC*, 220 F.R.D. 212, 216 (S.D.N.Y. 2003). The plaintiffs argue that, because Butterball has documents in its privilege log dating back to 1999, it has anticipated litigation since then and should have kept all of its emails in an accessible format rather than transferring them to backup tapes. Butterball denies that assertion and points out that most of the documents on its privilege log do not belong to Butterball but to ConAgra, its predecessor. Even if ConAgra may have anticipated litigation as early as 1999, there is no evidence that Butterball or its employees had an obligation to preserve emails in a format other than as backup tapes. The fourth and fifth factors also weigh in favor of Butterball. Even though the backup tapes contain emails of persons who no longer work for Butterball, the plaintiffs offer no evidence to suggest that they will be unable to find or depose those persons or obtain the relevant information in another way. Furthermore, the plaintiffs cannot predict with any certainty whether a search of the backup tapes will yield relevant, useful information or how much information will be produced. The sixth and seventh factors weigh in favor of the plaintiffs: important issues of good faith are at stake here, and Butterball, as the largest producer of turkey products in the United States, has the resources available to conduct a search of its backup tapes.

A court should not treat the "good cause" factors as a checklist; rather, the factors should be weighed by importance. *Zubulake*, 217 F.R.D. at 322. Here, the Court finds it most significant that the plaintiffs have no idea what, if any, discoverable information may be obtained by rebuilding a server post office and searching the emails of the above-listed persons that are stored on the backup tapes. Thus, the Court concludes that the slim likelihood that new and relevant information may be discovered does not outweigh the substantial burden and expense required to retrieve the information from the backup tapes.

Finally, the plaintiffs seek to compel Butterball to search "non-Butterball ESI sources" in its possession and control, including the personal and professional email accounts of Jim Maxwell, Walter Pelletier, and Keith Shoemaker, who were not on Butterball's email system until mid-2008. The plaintiffs point out that these custodians are part of the upper management group of Butterball and would make ultimate decisions concerning whether Butterball should pay or not pay for donning and doffing activities. They also opine that Butterball has failed adequately to describe the ESI over which it and its custodians have possession and control. Although Butterball cursorily mentions that it does not have access to personal email accounts, it does not explain why these accounts are not reasonably accessible or unlikely to lead to the disclosure of relevant information. Active, online data is generally considered accessible. *Zubulake*, 217 F.R.D. at 318-20. Thus, in addition to conducting a search of active and archived emails in Butterball accounts, the defendant should also search hard drives, laptops, and the personal email accounts of Walter Pelletier and Keith Shoemaker for the search terms described above. To the extent that it has not yet done so, Butterball also should disclose all of the sources of ESI within its possession and control.

## D. PROPOSED TIME PERIOD TO SEARCH

The plaintiffs seek to compel Butterball to search ESI obtained since 2000. Butterball argues that a search for information prior to November 8, 2005, when the Supreme Court decided *IBP, Inc. v. Alvarez*, 546 U.S. 21 (2005), is not likely to lead to the discovery of relevant, nonprivileged information because (a) any electronic communications regarding donning and doffing would have occurred after the *Alvarez* decision and (b) Butterball did not acquire the facilities at issue in this lawsuit until October 2, 2006. The plaintiffs contend that they need ESI dating back to 2000 to determine whether Butterball was a part of any donning and doffing discussions, and in particular, a United States Department of Labor survey or investigation into FLSA compliance with respect to payment for donning and doffing activities.

The Court is not persuaded that a search of ESI prior to 2005 will result in the discovery of information relevant to a claim or defense that has been presented. Ultimately, the plaintiffs seek to determine whether or not Butterball has a good faith or non-willful defense under the FLSA, and for that reason, it is important to discover what Butterball, its employees, and its management knew or believed about donning-and-doffing-related compensation. The plaintiffs suggest that, if Butterball participated in the USDOL's surveys and investigations into FLSA compliance, then it might have believed that it was in violation of the FLSA and lack a good faith defense. The plaintiffs offer no evidence at this point, however, that Butterball participated in a USDOL survey or investigation or any other discussions regarding donning and doffing prior to 2005. Without evidence of such participation, the Court finds that a search of ESI prior to 2005 is not likely to lead to the discovery of relevant information.

## III.

Butterball proposes splitting the cost of the electronic discovery. However, a court should consider cost-shifting only when digital data is relatively inaccessible, such as in backup tapes. *See Opennheimer Fund, Inc. v. Sanders*, 437 U.S. 340, 358 (1978) ("[T]he presumption is that the responding party must bear the expense of complying with discovery requests, but he may invoke the district court's discretion . . . to grant orders protecting him from 'undue burden or expense . . . .'") In those cases, the court should consider: (1) the extent to which the request is specifically tailored to discover relevant information; (2) the availability of such information from other sources; (3) the total cost of production, compared to the amount in controversy; (4) the total cost of production, compared to the resources available to each party; (5) the relative ability of each party to control costs and its incentive to do so; (6) the importance of the issues at stake; and (7) the relative benefits to the parties of obtaining the information. *Zubulake*, 217 F.R.D. at 322. Courts should not consider cost shifting when ESI is kept in an accessible format. *Id.* at 318. Here, the Court has not compelled the discovery of any ESI that is not readily accessible. As a result, cost-shifting is inappropriate.

### CONCLUSION

For the reasons stated above, plaintiffs' motion to compel is granted in part and denied in part.

## Comments and Questions

1. Butterball argued (i) it would be too burdensome to perform the search that plaintiffs requested, and (ii) its system did not allow for word searches for terms within the same sentence or within a certain number of words as another term. Yet Butterball also contended that it had already "conducted a complete, diligent search of e-mails designed to discover all relevant, admissible communications." Is that reconcilable?

2. Are you sympathetic to Butterball's position? Would you have counseled them similarly or differently?

3. Electronic discovery requires counsel to be savvy about technology. Obtaining technical expertise costs more money than simply reviewing paper documents. How else does it fundamentally change discovery practice?

4. For online secondary sources on electronic discovery, visit the Digital Discovery Web site maintained by the Berkman Center for Internet & Society at Harvard Law School, *http://cyber.law.harvard.edu/digitaldiscovery/*. See also *www.kenwithers.com*.

5. The *Hellmert v. Butterball* case discussed cost-shifting only briefly. The following excerpt written for practitioners by practitioners offers a useful overview of the prevailing law on this point.

## ■ THOMAS Y. ALLMAN ET AL., COST-SHIFTING IN E-DISCOVERY
### *Practicing Law Institute, Electronic Discovery Deskbook § 7:5 (2011)*

[W]hile it is generally true that the responding party must bear the expense of complying with discovery requests, the . . . rules allow a responding party to seek cost-shifting once the requesting party shows good cause for the production of electronically-stored information (ESI) that is not reasonably accessible. The rules may also, as discussed below, allow cost-shifting in other cases, such as when the sheer amount of reasonably accessible ESI creates an undue burden on the responding party. In any case, cost-shifting may be partial or complete, depending on the specific facts of the controversy, although some courts will not shift more than one-half of the costs because of the producer-pays presumption.

### THE *ZUBULAKE* AND *MCPEEK* TESTS

The courts have not reached an entirely uniform framework for deciding when shifting the costs of producing inaccessible ESI is appropriate. Prior to the promulgation of the 2006 amendments, the leading tests were drawn from *McPeek v. Ashcroft*, 202 F.R.D. 31 (D.D.C. 2001), and *Zubulake v. UBS Warburg LLC*, 217 F.R.D. 309 (S.D.N.Y. 2003) (*Zubulake I*). *McPeek* enunciated the principle that "[t]he more likely it is that the [ESI] contains information that is relevant to a claim or defense, the fairer it is that" the responding party pay production or search costs. To inform the court on these issues, the magistrate judge ordered a small sample of the data to be produced.

*Zubulake I*, meanwhile, held that cost-shifting is potentially appropriate where the material requested is in an "inaccessible format," including data kept on backup tapes and data that has been "[e]rased, fragmented, or damaged" and so is "not readily usable." In such cases, *Zubulake I* counseled consideration of the following seven factors: (1) whether the ESI request is "specifically tailored to discover relevant information," (2) whether the information is otherwise available, (3) the cost of producing the ESI as compared to the amount in controversy, (4) the cost of producing the ESI as compared to the parties' resources, (5) the ability and incentive of each party to control costs, (6) the importance of the litigated issues, and (7) the benefits each party would receive from production of the information. The court cautioned, however, that consideration of the factors should not be a simple additive exercise; instead, the ultimate balance must be between the cost of production and the importance of the request to the case. As such, the first two factors, which the court saw as closely related to the *McPeek* test, are given the most weight, while the benefit to the parties is given the least, and the issue-importance variable is influential only in cases of extraordinary importance. As in *McPeek*, the *Zubulake I* court ordered a sampling of the inaccessible ESI to be selected by the requesting party for production. Using this sample, the court later shifted a percentage of the costs to the requesting party.

*Zubulake I*'s seven-factor list and *McPeek*'s marginal utility test were not the only analyses of cost-shifting propounded. . . . They were, however, the most persistently influential. . . . Since the 2006 amendments, however, judicial emphasis has shifted to a consideration of the factors made explicit in Rule 26(b)(2)(C)(i)-(iii). Nevertheless, while the Rules are now the focus, the extensive overlap between the *Zubulake* factors and Rule 26 considerations means that courts continue to consider the same kinds of factors as they did under the prior regime.

### COST-SHIFTING TRENDS

Several trends spanning the adoption of the 2006 amendments are identifiable. First, courts frequently allocate costs to any party that arguably acted in bad faith or in contradiction of a prior agreement between the parties, a technique that echoes the use of cost-shifting as a discovery sanction.[152] For example, if a responding party could foresee that material would be discoverable in a given suit but nevertheless chose to store it in an inaccessible format, cost-shifting will not be ordered. On the other hand, if information is inaccessible but stored in a particular format related to the

---

152. *See, e.g.*, . . . Peskoff v. Faber, 251 F.R.D. 59, 62-63 (D.D.C. 2008). . . .

normal use of the information as a matter of course, cost-shifting may occur.[154] Further, where the responding party unilaterally demands extra ESI-related work after the parties had agreed to particular protocol, the costs of the extra searches will not be shifted, and producing parties who fail to follow explicit court instructions will perform further discovery at their own cost.[156] Dilatory production or production of ESI in a sufficiently garbled format can also forestall cost-shifting. Even inflated cost estimates or simple negligence can underpin cost-shifting decisions.

Second, as the advisory committee note to the 2006 amendments makes clear, the requesting party's willingness to incur the cost of production is a factor that courts assess in determining whether there is good cause to produce inaccessible material, as often happens in cases where outside experts are hired to image computer hard drives or otherwise physically access the computers of a party. Volunteering to bear the cost, however, is no guarantee that a motion to compel will succeed, because cost-shifting is not a pure substitute for limits on discoverable material. Nevertheless, courts sometimes cite their power to allocate costs as a reason in favor of production or even mandate cost-shifting in lieu of forestalling further discovery.[164]

Third, even when parties do not volunteer to pay for special masters or ESI experts, shifting of their costs is likely.[165] This may be because experts and masters are used in cases where ESI discovery is particularly burdensome from practical or privilege standpoints, prominently including inspection or imaging of a party's computer. However, when the cost of hard-drive backup or a similar procedure is a preventive or preservative step, the responding party bears the cost.

Fourth, consistent with Rule 26's concerns about duplicative discovery, cost-shifting may be more frequent when previously produced information is sought in a second format. Where produced paper documents already exist in a quintessentially accessible ESI form without the knowledge of the requesting party, however, only the costs of *re*-producing the ESI are likely to shift.

Fifth, as in *Zubulake* and *McPeek*, courts still sometimes issue orders for small samples of ESI to gauge relevance and importance when it is possible to take such a sample, as with data stored on multiple backup tapes.[170] In such cases, authoritative allocations of cost may be delayed until the court understands how relevant or irrelevant ESI will be.

Sixth and finally, cost-shifting is more frequent when ESI is requested from a third party.

The question of cost-shifting for reasonably accessible ESI is more unsettled. One district court's local guidelines theoretically allow cost-shifting for both

---

154. *See, e.g.*, Semsroth v. City of Wichita, 239 F.R.D. 630, 634-635 (D. Kan. 2006).

156. *See* . . . Wactel v. Guardian Life Ins. Co., 239 F.R.D. 376, 385-388 (D.N.J. 2006).

164. *See* Self v. Equilon Enters., LLC, No. 4:00CV1903, 2007 WL 427964, at *3-*4 (E.D. Mo. Feb. 2, 2007).

165. *See, e.g.*, Xpel Techs. Corp. v. Am. Filter Film Distribs., No. SA-08-CV-0175, 2008 WL 744837 at *1 (W.D. Tex. Mar. 17, 2008). . . .

170. *See* Haka v. Lincoln County, 246 F.R.D. 577, 579 (W.D. Wis. 2007). . . .

accessible and inaccessible ESI while imposing a presumption that costs will be shifted for the latter but not for the former.[173] The author of *McPeek* has even argued that while the 2006 advisory committee note allows for consideration of the Rule 26(b)(ii)(C) factors where inaccessible ESI is concerned, "[t]he obvious negative corollary of this rule is that *accessible* [ESI] *must* be produced at the cost of the producing party."[174] While this view comports with *Zubulake*'s finding that cost-shifting should be considered only for ESI stored in an inaccessible format, it has been rejected by several courts and commentators, including the chair of the 2006 advisory committee.[176] Moreover, in some cases, disputes arise over whether or not the ESI is accessible. Thus, the same considerations may continue to inform cost-shifting decisions regarding both accessible and inaccessible ESI, though the presumption that costs fall on the responding party may prove harder to overcome in cases of accessible information.

### BEST PRACTICES

The following are best practices with respect to requests for cost-shifting:

- As with production requests generally, parties involved in cost-shifting disputes should present the court with specific requests and objections, because cost-shifting inquiries are highly fact-sensitive and courts consequently possess a great deal of discretion in deciding them. Where economic and practical details such as the cost of ESI discovery, the amount at stake, the resources of the parties, or the recovery methods to be used go unspecified, the court may make a determination adverse to the party failing to provide the requisite information.
- Information given to the court should also include the costs of attorney review of ESI as part of the production process, as these costs are generally not shifted to the requesting party.
- Information underpinning a magistrate judge's decision should be retained in case of further review, and requesting parties should note when shared-cost ESI production overlaps with producer-financed ESI production, as courts may relieve requesting parties of the cost for the overlapping materials.
- Parties seeking ESI discovery should also make precise requests with a focus on information near the heart of the issues in the case. The presentation of evidence to the court that such searches are likely to be fruitful will be especially helpful.

---

173. *See* O'Bar v. Lowe's Home Ctrs., Inc., No. 5:04CV00019-W, 2007 WL 1299180, at *6 (W.D.N.C. May 2, 2007). . . .

174. . . . IO Group, Inc. v. Veoh Networks, Inc., No. C06-03926, 2007 WL 1113800, at *7 (N.D. Cal. Apr. 13, 2007). . . .

176. *See* Fed. R. Civ. P. 26(b)(2) 2000 advisory committee note (noting comments to the effect that "courts have not implemented the [] limitations [of 26(b)(ii)(C)] with the vigor that was contemplated"); Parkdale Am., LLC v. Travelers Cas. & Sur. Co. of Am., No. 3:06CV789, 2007 WL 4165247, at *14 (W.D.N.C. Nov. 19, 2007) . . . . Lee H. Rosenthal, *A Few Thoughts on Electronic Discovery After December, 2006*, 116 Yale L.J. Pocket Part 167 (2006). . . .

• Requesting parties should, for the purpose of Rule 26(b)(2)(C)(i), make clear that inaccessible ESI is not attainable in any other manner.
• Parties should be attentive to both the expense of ESI discovery and potential alternative methods and should confer about potential cost-shifting as part of their early ESI discussions.

## Comments and Questions

1. The exorbitant cost of discovery has been criticized for decades. During those years, cost-shifting was discussed, but no serious proposals ever found traction. Electronic discovery, however, has changed that discourse. Does the discovery of electronic information present new issues and problems that are not adequately addressed in the rules? Does electronic discovery present some exigency that threatens the basic tenets of trust and integrity that form the foundation of discovery? Does (should) each generation of technology require a new set of rules?

2. Ordinarily, the voluntary disclosure of privileged information constitutes a waiver of any privilege that the disclosing party could otherwise have claimed (to avoid disclosure). But the volume of discovery—including, but certainly not limited to, electronic discovery—makes such disclosures almost unavoidable. Read Fed. R. Civ. P. 26(b)(5)(B). This provision requires a party who receives allegedly privileged or work product information to return, sequester, or destroy it upon notification.

This provision must be read within the context of Rule 26(f)(3)(D), which contemplates that the parties' discovery plan must address the procedure for dealing with claims of privilege that arise *after* production. The advisory committee notes to the 2006 rule contemplate two kinds of agreements. The first (the "quick peek") allows the requesting party to have unfettered access to the documents and files; and once the requesting party identifies those documents of interest to it, the producing party reviews that subset and asserts the privilege as to those documents to which it applies. The second type of agreement (the "claw back") allows one party to request that inadvertently produced privileged documents be returned to the disclosing party. The latter of these agreements is also codified in Federal Rule 26(b)(5)(B).

## Practice Exercise No. 18: E-Discovery in *City of Cleveland*

### Scenario No. 1

Your firm represents Sheldon Marshall in the *City of Cleveland* action. The senior partner asks you for help with respect to several issues regarding ongoing discovery. Dr. Marshall has explained to us that he typically deletes from his computer all prior drafts of exams and all e-mail correspondence with clients or employees of clients in preparation for creating the exams. But he also admits that this is not always true.

There is a Rule 34 document request from the plaintiffs to Marshall seeking, among other things, a printed copy of all e-mails, whether deleted or retained, from any agent, officer, or employee of the City of Cleveland to Marshall during the five years prior to the giving of the 2010 written and physical tests. Further, the request demands production of all drafts of prior exams, whether deleted or retained, drafted by or otherwise involving Dr. Marshall.

Marshall was first contacted by the City to create the tests in question five years ago. During this five-year period, Marshall has had two computers: a three-year-old Dell laptop operating on standard Windows software and, for a decade before the Dell, a 3-C-S Victoria Sunshine computer, manufactured by a now-defunct company, operating on Xyrite software.

Marshall does not know how to retrieve deleted e-mails or documents from either computer. But as he explained in an e-mail to the senior partner, he assumes (because techie friends have told him) that the hard drives may have deleted material somewhere. There may be some saved documents on the Sunshine computer, but he hasn't used that computer for years and he doesn't even know where its power cord is.

Your senior partner wants to know what her options are in responding to the request and what the federal judge, who is a reasonable judge, is likely to order.

### Scenario No. 2

Assume instead that you are in a firm that represents the City of Cleveland. The City of Cleveland, which is frequently sued on many matters, like all cities, has had a policy for the last ten years to purchase new computers every three years and to discard in the city dump all old computers and any backup drives. The triennial purge is now two weeks away. Assume that they have not yet been sued for the most recent exam, but there are still no women in the department and letters to the editor and editorials in the Cleveland Plain Dealer bemoan "this sorry state." The City's General Counsel and the Senior Partner meet regularly on the many legal issues confronting the City. The Senior Partner wants to know whether she should confront the General Counsel regarding this retention issue. She wants to know the potential risks and what specific rule language she should have in mind.

### Practice Exercise No. 19: Evaluating Discovery in *Carpenter v. Dee*

Carol Coblentz is the senior partner in the plaintiff's firm that represents Nancy Carpenter. She has just informed you that she thinks it is highly unlikely that this case will settle. You are her primary associate on the case. She thinks that her best shot in the case is against Ultimate Auto on a negligence theory of failure to warn. The insurance company for Randall Dee has already agreed to settle for the policy limit, and, as you know, Dee doesn't have a lot of assets. She has become convinced that the City of Lowell is judgment-proof, and she has her doubts on the case against the inspection garage. She wants to meet with you to discuss whatever further potential evidence she needs prior to trial on this one theory of liability against Ultimate Auto. You will find the discovery to date in the Case Files. Remember, this is a death action.

You have discussed preparation of cases for trial with Carol in the past. She always emphasizes two things: production burden (summary judgment and directed verdict are always on her mind) and persuasion burden (can she convince the fact finder, in this case a jury). She gets very upset with generalities when she is preparing for trial. She'll want to know: how she should set up her trial notebook, what evidence we have already under each major category, what additional evidence is needed, where that needed evidence resides, and how we will get it. She usually ends her preparation session in cases like this with two additional questions: Do you think we can meet our production burden? And do you think we can convince a jury (persuasion burden)? She'll also want to know what the odds of our prevailing are as to each burden, and why you think so.

## D. TRANSNATIONAL DISCOVERY*

National approaches to discovery can vary widely—even among neighboring countries that are derivative of the same legal tradition. Explanations for these variations include politics, culture, perceptions about the purposes of litigation, and, given the interrelatedness of procedure, other rules and doctrines. Systems can be differentiated by examining their approach to each of the following protocols: (i) the available mechanisms; (ii) the scope of inquiry; (iii) timing; (iv) the extent of judicial involvement; and (v) the participation of experts.

*Discovery Mechanisms.* American litigators have at their disposal a number of formal discovery techniques, including document requests, interrogatories, depositions, requests for admissions, and physical examinations. This list is unusually broad. Other common law systems—including Australia, England, Hong Kong, India, the Philippines, and Singapore—offer only a subset of this list. In particular, no common law countries other than the

---

*Much of the discussion in this section borrows from Thomas O. Main, *Global Issues in Civil Procedure* 33-54 (2006), and from Stephen McCaffrey and Thomas Main, *Transnational Litigation in Comparative Perspective: Theory and Application* (2008).

United States and (parts of) Canada liberally allow pre-trial depositions for the purpose of gathering evidence.

The civil law countries tend to maintain a still narrower set of pre-trial discovery mechanisms. In many countries, only documents are exchanged in advance of trial. Pre-trial discovery in Japan is limited primarily to document requests and interrogatories. In Belgium, other than receiving documents, the most a party can do to elicit detail from their opponent is to use their written submissions to the court to ask questions challenging the other party openly to respond. Many civil and common law countries have other discovery mechanisms (including depositions) available, but these techniques are for the limited use of preserving testimony that might be impossible to obtain at trial.

Among the discovery tools of almost all systems are automatic disclosure requirements. Either with the pleadings or at some later point, parties typically are obliged to disclose documents. Some require the disclosure only of documents that support the disclosing party's position; many others require the disclosure of all relevant documents.

*Scope of Inquiry.* A system's philosophy toward the gathering of evidence is also reflected in the permissible scope of discovery. We have already seen one end of the spectrum: The Federal Rules permit the discovery of any unprivileged matter that is relevant to the claim or defense of any party (provided the request is not unreasonably cumulative or burdensome). Under this regime, litigants tend to make broad requests, seeking unspecified information for the purpose of turning up anything that might be (or become) relevant to the case. These are the sort of "fishing expeditions" that are frequently derided by other systems. In other systems—whether of the common law or the civil law tradition—discovery requests must be more narrowly tailored and must correspond to the allegations and theories in the pleadings. These constraints are especially significant since, in other systems, the pleadings are both fixed and more precise. Whether a particular request is sufficiently specific depends upon the circumstances leading to the request and the system's tolerance for discovery.

*Timing.* The timing and sequence of gathering evidence are fundamentally different in the common law and civil law traditions. In the common law tradition, the discovery stage occurs in preparation for trial, when the evidence is then presented in full. In the civil law tradition, certain documents and evidence may be disclosed early in the action, but otherwise the evidence is simultaneously gathered and evaluated by the judge in a series of hearings. In Italy, for example, the discovery of evidence occurs over the course of a number of separate hearings spanning months or years. The purpose of the earlier hearings is to determine which mechanisms of evidence will be used; the latter hearings involve the "taking" of evidence.

*Judicial Involvement.* In most common law systems, certain initial disclosures may be required by procedural rule, but discovery otherwise is largely party-controlled. Under the Federal Rules, discovery requests and responses ordinarily are not filed with the court, and only if there is some dispute between the parties is the judge likely even to know whether or what discovery is under way.

In most civil law systems, however, the parties may not compel one another to produce evidence without the participation of the court. Because of the interrelatedness of discovery and trial, civil law systems view evidence gathering as a judicial function. While the parties may offer the names of witnesses, and will suggest questions to be put to the witnesses, the civil law judge typically decides which witnesses to summon, conducts the questioning, and records the evidence. The gathering and evaluation of the evidence are intertwined, and both tasks are undertaken as an exercise of the judicial function.

*Expert Evidence.* Under the Federal Rules, the use and selection of experts are largely within the control of the parties. It is not uncommon, then, for so-called hired guns to engage in a "battle of the experts." Not all common law systems, however, follow this model. In England, the new Civil Practice Rules restrict the use of expert witnesses "to that which is reasonably required to resolve the proceedings."* In particular, no expert witness can be used in any civil proceeding without the court's permission.

The civil law countries tend to be even more restrictive. Parties ordinarily cannot bring their own expert witnesses or present reports from their own experts. Instead, the court, upon acknowledging the need for expert testimony, appoints a neutral expert who submits a report answering the parties' questions and appears for questioning at trial. In Belgium, for example, the judge determines both the need for and the tasks of any expert. At a meeting with the expert, the parties give an overview of their respective positions and the evidence necessary for the expert to offer her opinion. The expert prepares a preliminary report upon which the parties are permitted to comment. The expert then prepares a final report that incorporates and responds to the parties' comments. The court is not bound by the conclusions of the expert, although, in practice, most courts follow the findings.

National differences in discovery practice present circumstances ripe not only for comparative study, but also for transnational conflict. Indeed "no aspect of international litigation has caused as much friction as the issue of discovery."† Most of these conflicts tend to develop when documents or other evidence is located in a foreign country that has a more restrictive approach to discovery.

It is a basic principle of international law that each state has sovereignty over all activities taking place within its territory. No state may perform an act in the territory of a foreign state without the latter state's consent. Many countries are uncomfortable with—even incensed by—the unilateral export of American-style discovery. From their perspective, American courts act outside their territorial boundaries and flout the rights and protections granted by the foreign law. Moreover, American discovery essentially

---

*Civil Procedure Rule 35.1.
†Andreas Lowenfeld, *International Litigation and the Quest for Reasonableness* 137 (1996).

privatizes the gathering of evidence, which in the civil law tradition is an act of the judicial sovereign.

A number of countries have adopted statutes to address the extraterritorial application of U.S. laws generally, and, in particular, discovery procedures, against foreign persons. To protect their citizens and information within their territories, if not also to defend the integrity of their court system, many countries prohibit the disclosure of such information. For example, in 1980 France added to its Penal Code, at No. 80-538, the following offense:

> [I]t is prohibited for any party to request, seek or disclose, in writing, orally or otherwise, economic, commercial, industrial, financial or technical documents or information leading to the constitution of evidence with a view to foreign judicial or administrative proceedings or in connection therewith.

These "blocking statutes" have taken various forms, including the constructive "seizure" by the (foreign) government of documents otherwise subject to discovery. By invoking these statutes, foreign litigants in American courts could thus argue that they could not perform their discovery obligations without violating the law of their own country. Through the wonder of globalization, then, a discovery dispute becomes a question of international relations and diplomacy: Which country's laws and values should prevail?

> Blocking statutes generally take one of three basic forms. First . . . there are older laws like the Swiss banking secrecy statutes. . . . Second, the most comprehensive foreign laws create blanket protection for large categories of documents and/or vest relatively broad discretion over disclosure issues in some government official. Especially around 1980 some of our most important trading partners attempted to cut back on the extraterritorial application of American laws by enacting broad nondisclosure statutes. For instance, the British Protection of Trading Interests Act of 1980 (PTIA) gives the British government the power to block most types of discovery. . . . Finally, a third type of law, such as Canada's Uranium Information Security Regulations has been aimed directly at frustrating specific American claims. The Canadian law arose out of the attempt by the Canadian government, along with several other foreign sovereigns, to quash American antitrust litigation concerning a worldwide uranium cartel. This was done by forbidding the production of any information relating to "conversations, discussions or meetings that took place between January 1, 1972 and December 31, 1975 . . . in respect of the production, import, export . . . use or sale of uranium."

David E. Teitelbaum, *Strict Enforcement of Extraterritorial Discovery*, 38 Stan. L. Rev. 841, 847-849 (1986).

Courts have balanced the interests and, in many respects, the blocking statutes have worked. Judges recognize that litigants are faced with the choice of violating either forum or foreign law. The blocking statutes have created enough friction to moderate the application abroad of discovery techniques, "consistent with the overall principle of reasonableness in the exercise of jurisdiction." Restatement of Foreign Relations Law of the United States § 437, Reporter's Note 5, p. 42.

Foreign resistance to discovery prompted the United States to propose the adoption of a convention on transnational discovery. The Hague Convention on the Taking of Evidence Abroad in Civil or Commercial Matters was intended to establish a system that would be tolerable to the state executing the request yet useful to the requesting state. The United States ratified the Convention by a unanimous vote of the Senate in 1972. Dozens of other countries have since joined.*

There are three alternative methods for obtaining evidence abroad under the Convention, but the most popular and useful is the Letter of Request. A litigant may request the court where the action is pending to transmit a *Letter of Request* to the *Central Authority* in the country where the evidence is to be obtained. The Central Authority transmits the request to the appropriate foreign court, which conducts an evidentiary proceeding under procedures of the foreign country. Importantly, Article 23 of the Convention authorizes a contracting state to declare that it will not execute any letter of request in aid of pretrial discovery of *documents*.

The Convention outlines a scope and procedure for foreign discovery that, although narrow and administratively cumbersome in comparison with the Federal Rules, identifies important common ground. But this common ground confines American litigators familiar with American discovery, who "need" broader discovery in order to meet their burdens of proof. Those litigators test the limits and durability of the Convention.

Product liability cases—especially cases in which a plaintiff seeks to show that an automobile, an airplane, a machine, a pharmaceutical product, or a gun could have been made safer but defendant made a deliberate decision to omit a protective device, to employ a part known to be hazardous, or to rush to market without adequate testing—are won or lost in very large measure depending on the outcome of discovery. It is no coincidence, then, that the major (and continuing) conflict over the Hague Evidence Convention has revolved around a series of accident cases. In each instance, the case involved an American injured party and a European manufacturer defending its product and production facilities from American discovery efforts.

The Court's decision in *Société Nationale Industrielle Aérospatiale*, which follows, addressed the extent to which litigants and courts were obliged to follow the Convention when engaged in transnational discovery. The petitioners to the Court (SNIA) were corporations, owned by the Republic of France, engaged in the business of designing, manufacturing, and marketing aircraft. One of their planes, the "Rallye," was allegedly advertised in American aviation publications as "the World's safest and most economical

---

*The Hague Conference on Private International Law maintains an excellent Web site, including the text of the Convention on the Taking of Evidence Abroad and a list of the contracting states. *See http://hcch.e-vision.nl/index_en.php?act=conventions.text&cid=82* (last visited July 1, 2005).

STOL plane." STOL was an acronym for "short takeoff and landing," and it referred to a fixed-wing aircraft that either takes off or lands with only a short horizontal run of the aircraft. On August 19, 1980, a Rallye crashed in Iowa, injuring the pilot and a passenger.

The plaintiffs (later the respondents in the Supreme Court action) brought separate suits based upon this accident in the U.S. District Court for the Southern District of Iowa, alleging that petitioners had manufactured and sold a defective plane and were thus liable under theories of negligence and breach of warranty. Plaintiffs sought discovery under the Federal Rules, and SNIA filed a motion for a protective order. SNIA argued that, because they were a French corporation, the Hague Evidence Convention was the only means through which the plaintiffs could conduct discovery. After all, defendants argued, the Hague Evidence Convention had been adopted by the U.S. Senate and thus was the law of the land. The plaintiffs argued, however, that compliance with the Convention was not mandatory. The district court agreed with the plaintiffs and denied the motion for a protective order. The case ultimately found its way to the Supreme Court.

## ■ SOCIÉTÉ NATIONALE INDUSTRIELLE AÉROSPATIALE v. UNITED STATES DISTRICT COURT
### *482 U.S. 522 (1987)*

Justice STEVENS delivered the opinion of the Court:

### [I]

. . . In arguing their entitlement to a protective order, petitioners correctly assert that both the discovery rules set forth in the Federal Rules of Civil Procedure and the Hague Convention are the law of the United States. This observation, however, does not dispose of the question before us; we must analyze the interaction between these two bodies of federal law. Initially, we note that at least four different interpretations of the relationship between the federal discovery rules and the Hague Convention are possible. Two of these interpretations assume that the Hague Convention by its terms dictates the extent to which it supplants normal discovery rules. First, the Hague Convention might be read as requiring its use to the exclusion of any other discovery procedures whenever evidence located abroad is sought for use in an American court. Second, the Hague Convention might be interpreted to require first, but not exclusive, use of its procedures. Two other interpretations assume that international comity, rather than the obligations created by the treaty, should guide judicial resort to the Hague Convention. Third, then, the Convention might be viewed as establishing a supplemental set of discovery procedures, strictly optional under treaty law, to which concerns of comity nevertheless require first resort by American courts in all cases. Fourth, the treaty may be viewed as an undertaking among sovereigns to facilitate discovery to which an American court should resort when it deems that course of action appropriate, after considering the situations of the parties before it as well as the interests of the concerned foreign state. . . .

We reject the first two of the possible interpretations as inconsistent with the language and negotiating history of the Hague Convention. The preamble of the Convention specifies its purpose "to facilitate the transmission and execution of Letters of Request" and to "improve mutual judicial co-operation in civil or commercial matters." 23 U.S.T., at 2557, T.I.A.S. No. 7444. The preamble does not speak in mandatory terms which would purport to describe the procedures for all permissible transnational discovery and exclude all other existing practices.[15] The text of the Evidence Convention itself does not modify the law of any contracting state, require any contracting state to use the Convention procedures, either in requesting evidence or in responding to such requests, or compel any contracting state to change its own evidence-gathering procedures.

The Convention contains three chapters. Chapter I, entitled "Letters of Requests," and chapter II, entitled "Taking of Evidence by Diplomatic Officers, Consular Agents and Commissioners," both use permissive rather than mandatory language. Thus, Article 1 provides that a judicial authority in one contracting state "may" forward a letter of request to the competent authority in another contracting state for the purpose of obtaining evidence. Similarly, Articles 15, 16, and 17 provide that diplomatic officers, consular agents, and commissioners "may . . . without compulsion," take evidence under certain conditions. The absence of any command that a contracting state must use Convention procedures when they are not needed is conspicuous.

Two of the Articles in chapter III, entitled "General Clauses," buttress our conclusion that the Convention was intended as a permissive supplement, not a pre-emptive replacement, for other means of obtaining evidence located abroad. Article 23 expressly authorizes a contracting state to declare that it will not execute any letter of request in aid of pretrial discovery of documents in a common-law country. Surely, if the Convention had been intended to replace completely the broad discovery powers that the common-law courts in the United States previously exercised over foreign litigants subject to their jurisdiction, it would have been most anomalous for the common-law contracting parties to agree to Article 23, which enables a contracting party to revoke its

---

15. The Hague Conference on Private International Law's omission of mandatory language in the preamble is particularly significant in light of the same body's use of mandatory language in the preamble to the Hague Service Convention, 20 U.S.T. 361, T.I.A.S. No. 6638. Article 1 of the Service Convention provides: "The present Convention shall apply in all cases, in civil or commercial matters, where there is occasion to transmit a judicial or extrajudicial document for service abroad." . . . [T]he Service Convention was drafted before the Evidence Convention, and its language provided a model exclusivity provision that the drafters of the Evidence Convention could easily have followed had they been so inclined. Given this background, the drafters' election to use permissive language instead is strong evidence of their intent.

consent to the treaty's procedures for pretrial discovery.[22] In the absence of explicit textual support, we are unable to accept the hypothesis that the common-law contracting states abjured recourse to all pre-existing discovery procedures at the same time that they accepted the possibility that a contracting party could unilaterally abrogate even the Convention's procedures. Moreover, Article 27 plainly states that the Convention does not prevent a contracting state from using more liberal methods of rendering evidence than those authorized by the Convention. Thus, the text of the Evidence Convention, as well as the history of its proposal and ratification by the United States, unambiguously supports the conclusion that it was intended to establish optional procedures that would facilitate the taking of evidence abroad.

An interpretation of the Hague Convention as the exclusive means for obtaining evidence located abroad would effectively subject every American court hearing a case involving a national of a contracting state to the internal laws of that state. Interrogatories and document requests are staples of international commercial litigation, no less than of other suits, yet a rule of exclusivity would subordinate the court's supervision of even the most routine of these pretrial proceedings to the actions or, equally, to the inactions of foreign judicial authorities. . . .

We conclude accordingly that the Hague Convention did not deprive the District Court of the jurisdiction it otherwise possessed to order a foreign national party before it to produce evidence physically located within a signatory nation.[25] . . .

## [II]

Petitioners contend that even if the Hague Convention's procedures are not mandatory, this Court should adopt a rule requiring that American litigants first resort to those procedures before initiating any discovery pursuant to the normal methods of the Federal Rules of Civil Procedure. The Court of

---

22. Thirteen of the seventeen signatory states have made declarations under Article 23 of the Convention that restrict pretrial discovery of documents.

25. The opposite conclusion of exclusivity would create three unacceptable asymmetries. First, within any lawsuit between a national of the United States and a national of another contracting party, the foreign party could obtain discovery under the Federal Rules of Civil Procedure, while the domestic party would be required to resort first to the procedures of the Hague Convention. This imbalance would run counter to the fundamental maxim of discovery that "[m]utual knowledge of all the relevant facts gathered by both parties is essential to proper litigation." *Hickman v. Taylor*, 329 U.S. 495, 507 (1947). Second, a rule of exclusivity would enable a company which is a citizen of another contracting state to compete with a domestic company on uneven terms, since the foreign company would be subject to less extensive discovery procedures in the event that both companies were sued in an American court. Petitioners made a voluntary decision to market their products in the United States. They are entitled to compete on equal terms with other companies operating in this market. But since the District Court unquestionably has personal jurisdiction over petitioners, they are subject to the same legal constraints, including the burdens associated with American judicial procedures, as their American competitors. A general rule according foreign nationals a preferred position in pretrial proceedings in our courts would conflict with the principle of equal opportunity that governs the market they elected to enter. Third, since a rule of first use of the Hague Convention would apply to cases in which a foreign party is a national of a contracting state, but not to cases in which a foreign party is a national of any other foreign state, the rule would confer an unwarranted advantage on some domestic litigants over others similarly situated.

Appeals rejected this argument because it was convinced that an American court's order ultimately requiring discovery that a foreign court had refused under Convention procedures would constitute "the greatest insult" to the sovereignty of that tribunal. We disagree with the Court of Appeals' view. It is well known that the scope of American discovery is often significantly broader than is permitted in other jurisdictions, and we are satisfied that foreign tribunals will recognize that the final decision on the evidence to be used in litigation conducted in American courts must be made by those courts. We therefore do not believe that an American court should refuse to make use of Convention procedures because of a concern that it may ultimately find it necessary to order the production of evidence that a foreign tribunal permitted a party to withhold.

Nevertheless, we cannot accept petitioners' invitation to announce a new rule of law that would require first resort to Convention procedures whenever discovery is sought from a foreign litigant. Assuming, without deciding, that we have the lawmaking power to do so, we are convinced that such a general rule would be unwise. In many situations the Letter of Request procedure authorized by the Convention would be unduly time consuming and expensive, as well as less certain to produce needed evidence than direct use of the Federal Rules. A rule of first resort in all cases would therefore be inconsistent with the overriding interest in the "just, speedy, and inexpensive determination" of litigation in our courts. *See* Fed. R. Civ. P. 1.

Petitioners argue that a rule of first resort is necessary to accord respect to the sovereignty of states in which evidence is located. It is true that the process of obtaining evidence in a civil-law jurisdiction is normally conducted by a judicial officer rather than by private attorneys. Petitioners contend that if performed on French soil, for example, by an unauthorized person, such evidence-gathering might violate the "judicial sovereignty" of the host nation. Because it is only through the Convention that civil-law nations have given their consent to evidence-gathering activities within their borders, petitioners argue, we have a duty to employ those procedures whenever they are available. We find that argument unpersuasive. If such a duty were to be inferred from the adoption of the Convention itself, we believe it would have been described in the text of that document. Moreover, the concept of international comity[27] requires in this context a more particularized analysis of the respective interests of the foreign nation and the requesting nation than petitioners' proposed general rule would generate. We therefore decline to hold as a blanket matter that comity requires resort to Hague Evidence Convention procedures without prior scrutiny in each case of the particular facts, sovereign interests, and likelihood that resort to those procedures will prove effective.[29]

---

27. Comity refers to the spirit of cooperation in which a domestic tribunal approaches the resolution of cases touching the laws and interests of sovereign states. . . .

29. The French "blocking statute" . . . does not alter our conclusion. It is well settled that such statutes do not deprive an American court of the power to order a party subject to its jurisdiction to produce evidence even though the act of production may violate that statute. *See Societe Internationale Pour Participations Industrielles et Commerciales, S.A. v. Rogers*, 357 U.S. 197, 204-06 (1958). Nor can the enactment of such a

Some discovery procedures are much more "intrusive" than others. In this case, for example, an interrogatory asking petitioners to identify the pilots who flew flight tests in the Rallye before it was certified for flight by the Federal Aviation Administration, or a request to admit that petitioners authorized certain advertising in a particular magazine, is certainly less intrusive than a request to produce all of the "design specifications, line drawings and engineering plans and all engineering change orders and plans and all drawings concerning the leading edge slats for the Rallye type aircraft manufactured by the Defendants." Even if a court might be persuaded that a particular document request was too burdensome or too "intrusive" to be granted in full, with or without an appropriate protective order, it might well refuse to insist upon the use of Convention procedures before requiring responses to simple interrogatories or requests for admissions. The exact line between reasonableness and unreasonableness in each case must be drawn by the trial court, based on its knowledge of the case and of the claims and interests of the parties and the governments whose statutes and policies they invoke.

American courts, in supervising pretrial proceedings, should exercise special vigilance to protect foreign litigants from the danger that unnecessary, or unduly burdensome, discovery may place them in a disadvantageous position. Judicial supervision of discovery should always seek to minimize its costs and inconvenience and to prevent improper uses of discovery requests. When it is necessary to seek evidence abroad, however, the district court must supervise pretrial proceedings particularly closely to prevent discovery abuses. For example, the additional cost of transportation of documents or witnesses to or from foreign locations may increase the danger that discovery may be sought for the improper purpose of motivating settlement, rather than finding relevant and probative evidence. Objections to "abusive" discovery that foreign litigants advance should therefore receive the most careful consideration. In addition, we have long recognized the demands of comity in suits involving foreign states, either as parties or as sovereigns with a coordinate interest in the litigation. American courts should therefore take care to demonstrate due respect for any special problem confronted by the foreign litigant on account of its nationality or the location of its operations, and for any sovereign interest expressed by a foreign state. We do not articulate specific rules to guide this delicate task of adjudication.

---

statute by a foreign nation require American courts to engraft a rule of first resort onto the Hague Convention, or otherwise to provide the nationals of such a country with a preferred status in our courts. It is clear that American courts are not required to adhere blindly to the directives of such a statute. Indeed, the language of the statute, if taken literally, would appear to represent an extraordinary exercise of legislative jurisdiction by the Republic of France over a United States district judge, forbidding him or her to order any discovery from a party of French nationality, even simple requests for admissions or interrogatories that the party could respond to on the basis of personal knowledge. It would be particularly incongruous to recognize such a preference for corporations that are wholly owned by the enacting nation. Extraterritorial assertions of jurisdiction are not one-sided. While the District Court's discovery orders arguably have some impact in France, the French blocking statute asserts similar authority over acts to take place in this country. The lesson of comity is that neither the discovery order nor the blocking statute can have the same omnipresent effect that it would have in a world of only one sovereign. The blocking statute thus is relevant to the court's particularized comity analysis only to the extent that its terms and its enforcement identify the nature of the sovereign interests in nondisclosure of specific kinds of material. . . .

# Comments and Questions

1. Although the Court's opinion announces that it would be within a trial court's discretion to require first resort to the Hague Evidence Convention, most judges have not done so. Why not?

2. Justice Blackmun's dissent noted that "it is the Executive that normally decides when a course of action is important enough to risk affronting a foreign nation or placing a strain on foreign commerce. It is the Executive, as well, that is best equipped to determine how to accommodate foreign interests along with our own." Is the question of foreign discovery more appropriately considered by the Executive and by Congress? But isn't the reasonableness of a particular discovery request more appropriately considered by a judge? How should these competing concerns be reconciled?

3. Does the enactment of a "blocking statute" disrespect the laws and institutions of other nations?

4. With the decision in *Aérospatiale* diluting the significance of the Hague Convention on the Taking of Evidence Abroad, the search for international common ground resumed. The ALI/UNIDROIT Transnational Rules mentioned in Chapter 3 include a proposed set of model discovery rules that reflect a compromise: They are based on a generalized version of a common law system outside the United States. If adopted, they would apply to transnational commercial disputes. These Rules strike a compromise between the regimes of broad and narrow discovery. As you read them, consider which of the two extremes is being asked to make the greater sacrifice.

# ∎ ALI/UNIDROIT, RULES OF TRANSNATIONAL CIVIL PROCEDURE*
### *128-134 (2005)*

### 21. DISCLOSURE

21.1 In accordance with the court's scheduling order, a party must identify to the court and other parties the evidence on which the party intends to rely, in addition to that provided in the pleading, including:

21.1.1 Copies of documents or other records, such as contracts and correspondence; and

21.1.2 Summaries of expected testimony of witnesses, including parties, witnesses, and experts, then known to the party. Witnesses must be identified, so far as practicable, by name, address, and telephone number. . . .

21.2 A party must amend the specification required in Rule 21.1 to include documents or witnesses not known when the list was originally prepared. Any change in the list of documents or witnesses must be immediately communicated in writing to the court and to all other parties, together with a justification for the amendment. . . .

### 22. EXCHANGE OF EVIDENCE

22.1 A party who has complied with disclosure duties prescribed in Rule 21, on notice to the other parties, may request the court to order production by any person of any evidentiary matter, not protected by confidentiality or privilege, that is relevant to the case and that may be admissible, including:

22.1.1 Documents and other records of information that are specifically identified or identified within specifically defined categories;

22.1.2 Identifying information, such as name and address, about specified persons having knowledge of a matter in issue; and

22.1.3 A copy of the report of any expert that another party intends to present.

22.2 The court must determine the request and order production accordingly. The court may order production of other evidence as necessary in the interest of justice. Such evidence must be produced within a reasonable time prior to the final hearing. . . .

### 23. DEPOSITION AND TESTIMONY BY AFFIDAVIT

23.1 A deposition of a party or other person may be taken by order of the court. Unless the court orders otherwise, a deposition may be presented as evidence in the record. . . .

23.4 With written permission of the court, a party may present a written statement of sworn testimony of any person, containing statements in their own words about relevant facts. . . .

———————————

5. Transnational judicial assistance is a two-way street. A number of cases have arisen in which foreign litigants have sought information from persons in the United States for use in actions pending abroad. Generally speaking, the Hague Evidence Convention has not played a significant role in these cases. Rather, litigants in foreign proceedings invoke 28 U.S.C. § 1782. Read that section in your rules supplement.

Notice that § 1782 does not require any showing of reciprocity and indeed does not require a request from the foreign court. The order may be made pursuant to a letter rogatory or request of the court or tribunal where the action is pending, "or upon the application of any interested person." Most of the cases under § 1782 involve applications to U.S. courts by litigants in foreign proceedings, in situations where it would be highly unlikely that the court where the action was pending would have made a corresponding request.

The statute provides that the U.S. court "may" provide judicial assistance, and a common defense to an application is the assertion that the foreign litigant was seeking discovery from an American court that it could never secure from the court where the action is being tried. A priori, should parties to foreign litigation be able to obtain discovery in the United States that they could not obtain in the courts where the action was being heard? Should it make any difference whether the person in the United States from whom information is sought is a party to the foreign proceeding? Why should the United States facilitate discovery against Americans for use in foreign litigation?

Is substantive law drafted with certain assumptions about the availability (or not) of discovery? Is § 1782, then, useful or destructive?

## E. PROCEDURAL RULEMAKING

At this point in the course you should be able to form an opinion about the wisdom of the current procedural rulemaking process. All of the Federal Rules are, of course, a product of the Rules Enabling Act, and you will certainly want to re-read 28 U.S.C. §§ 2072 and 2074 in preparation for this part. For an overview of the rulemaking process and an up-to-date status report of all current rulemaking efforts, we highly recommend that you click on the rulemaking link at *www.uscourts.gov.*

The questions you must face are: Who should make the rules? And by what process? To help you answer these questions, you will gain some perspective by reading differing views of procedural rulemaking. Professor Struve articulates the tenuous relationship between the Supreme Court's dual roles as both the maker and the arbiter of procedural rules. Professor Burbank concludes that the rulemaking process, bereft of a strong empirical foundation for formulating new policies, should be reconsidered. And Professor Walker defends the judiciary as the most effective rulemaking body among available options. As you read these articles, remember that the Rules and the rulemaking process affect the work of practitioners and their clients on a daily basis, and that frequent changes to the Rules have become an increasingly common feature of the current rulemaking process. In light of these concerns, who should be making procedural rules? The Supreme Court? The judiciary? The legislative branch? Practitioners? Academics? We are also including with these readings an excerpt of the Supreme Court's transmittal letter to Congress of the 1993 amendments (as well as Justice White's statement). These materials will give you some perspective of how the Court views its role in the rulemaking process.

## ■ CATHERINE T. STRUVE, THE PARADOX OF DELEGATION: INTERPRETING THE FEDERAL RULES OF CIVIL PROCEDURE
### *150 U. Pa. L. Rev. 1099, 1129-1131 (2002)*

. . . Should the Court wish to alter a Rule already in force, the Enabling Act does not contemplate that the Court could do so outside the rulemaking structure. Though the Court, like other entities, can suggest changes for the rulemakers' consideration, it cannot promulgate such changes against the wishes of the other participants in the rulemaking process.

Accordingly, since the Enabling Act conditions the delegation of rulemaking power on the Court's use of the prescribed procedures, it appears to require the Court to resort to those procedures when seeking to change a Rule. The matter is rendered somewhat more complex, however, by the question of the Court's inherent procedural authority. The Supreme Court has asserted that "certain implied powers must necessarily result" to the federal courts "from the nature of their institution," powers "which cannot be dispensed with . . . because they are necessary to the exercise of all others."

Advocates of judicial discretion thus might argue that, to the extent the Enabling Act's delegation merely duplicates the courts' inherent powers, courts should have greater latitude to interpret freely the Rules promulgated under the Act. Under this view, the Court can weigh policy considerations when exercising its inherent authority, and it should be accorded the same latitude when interpreting the Rules. This argument, however, overlooks the limits of such inherent powers. Although the question is murky . . . it is not at all clear that the federal courts' inherent powers include authority to promulgate rules of procedure. Rather, such inherent authority may be limited to powers necessary to the fulfillment of the courts' Article III responsibilities— a far narrower range than is covered by the current Federal Rules. Moreover, the courts' inherent powers—whatever their initial extent—are subject to Congress's separate authority to regulate federal court procedure. As the Court observed soon after the promulgation of the original Rules, "Congress has undoubted power to regulate the practice and procedure of federal courts, and may exercise that power by delegating to this or other federal courts authority to make rules not inconsistent with the statutes or constitution of the United States." So long as Congress's regulation of federal procedure does not "prevent[] a court from discharging its Article III duties," Congress's directives trump contrary principles adopted by the Supreme Court pursuant to its inherent authority. . . .

# ■ STEPHEN B. BURBANK, IGNORANCE AND PROCEDURAL LAW REFORM
### *59 Brook. L. Rev. 841, 841-842, 847, 854-855 (1993)*

In 1881, Oliver Wendell Holmes, Jr. observed that "ignorance is the best of law reformers. People are glad to discuss a question on general principles, when they have forgotten the special knowledge necessary for technical reasoning." . . .

I want to suggest that by failing to take seriously the task of defining limitations on the rulemaking power, the Supreme Court and those who assist it have encouraged Congress also to ignore the question of appropriate allocation rules. Similarly, by failing to seek empirical evidence on the operation of the Rules or proposed amendments, the rulemakers have both put their work product at risk of legislative override and encouraged Congress to initiate its own half-baked reforms. We need a moratorium on procedural law reform, whether by court rule or by statute, until such time as we know what we are doing. The knowledge needed concerns alternative reform strategies and their likely impacts, but we also need to know who is responsible for what.

If this sounds like crisis rhetoric . . . so be it. It is difficult, however, not to sense a crisis in federal procedural reform when the Chief Justice's letter transmitting the 1993 amendments to the Federal Rules disclaimed any implication "that the Court itself would have proposed these amendments in the form submitted," and when four other Justices indicated their agnosticism about, lack of competence to evaluate or disagreement with, one or more of the amendments. When a majority of the Supreme Court has washed its hands of proposed Federal Rules, and when some of the Justices have aired the dirty linen, what is it that should restrain Congress from responding to those who wish to do the same? . . .

If neutrality is not to be a prescription for ignorance, the rulemakers must have other sources of information about the likely impact of proposed Federal Rules or amendments that will serve as a surrogate for empirical work. Three possibilities come to mind: the collective experience and wisdom of the rulemakers, information provided through written comments and public hearings and the fruits of scholarly inquiry. It seems to me that the rulemakers' own knowledge base has been shrinking, or should I say narrowing, that their professed distaste for politics and unwillingness to share power have consequentially diminished the utility of public comment and that the nature of scholarship in the aid of legal reform has changed depressingly little since the days when Charles Clark was rewriting the Enabling Act as a scholar to suit his purposes as a rulemaker. . . .

It is time for a breather, for a group that includes rulemakers, members of Congress and members of the bar carefully to review where we have been, where we are going and where we should be going. It is time for a moratorium on ignorance and procedural law reform.

## ■ LAURENS WALKER, FEDERAL CIVIL RULEMAKING

*61 Geo. Wash. L. Rev. 455, 459-460 (1993)*

. . . The debate about the merits of judicial rulemaking is an old one, and I will not rehearse it, except to say that, in my view, the merits of judicial rulemaking far outweigh the demerits, largely because trial and appellate judges typically bring great expertise to the task. In the specific case of civil rulemaking, trial judges participate in far more trials than attorneys, and appellate judges review these same trials for error. This expertise is a sound starting point for the task of rulemaking. The chief alternative is legislative rulemaking, an alternative that diminishes the pertinent knowledge of the rulemaker. At best, the initial work might be done by legislators who are also attorneys, but enactment would almost certainly be left to a majority of legislators with no expertise at all. Executive participation in rulemaking has essentially the same shortcoming: Judicial expertise will be diminished or lost as an asset. By passing the Rules Enabling Act of 1934, Congress correctly determined that judicial expertise should be the foundation of civil rulemaking in federal courts.

# ■ LETTER OF TRANSMITTAL FROM CHIEF JUSTICE REHNQUIST

*Supreme Court of the United States Washington, D.C. 20543*

Chambers of
The CHIEF JUSTICE

April 22, 1993

Dear Mr. Speaker [of the House of Representatives]:

By direction of the Supreme Court of the United States, I have the honor to submit to the Congress amendments to the Federal Rules of Civil Procedure that have been adopted by the Supreme Court pursuant to Section 2072 of Title 28, United States Code. While the Court is satisfied that the required procedures have been observed, this transmittal does not necessarily indicate that the Court itself would have proposed these amendments in the form submitted.

Justice White has issued a separate statement. Justice Scalia has issued a dissenting statement, which Justice Thomas joins and Justice Souter joins in part. . . .

Sincerely,
/s/
William H. Rehnquist

[The Order transmitting the amendments has been omitted.]

## SUPREME COURT OF THE UNITED STATES AMENDMENTS TO THE FEDERAL RULES OF CIVIL PROCEDURE [APRIL 22, 1993]

Statement of Justice WHITE.

28 U.S.C. § 2072 empowers the Supreme Court to prescribe general rules of practice and procedure and rules of evidence for cases in the federal courts,

including proceedings before magistrates and courts of appeals. But the Court does not itself draft and initially propose these rules. Section 2073 directs the Judicial Conference to prescribe the procedures for proposing the rules mentioned in § 2072. The Conference is authorized to appoint committees to propose such rules. These rules advisory committees are to be made up of members of the professional bar and trial and appellate judges. The Conference is also to appoint a standing committee on rules of practice and evidence to review the recommendations of the advisory committees and to recommend to the Conference such rules and amendments to those rules "as may be necessary to maintain consistency and otherwise promote the interest of justice." § 2073(b). Any rules approved by the Conference are transmitted to the Supreme Court, which in turn transmits any rules "prescribed" pursuant to § 2072 to the Congress. Except as provided in § 2074(b), such rules become effective at a specified time unless Congress otherwise provides.

The members of the advisory and standing committees are carefully named by The Chief Justice, and I am quite sure that these experienced judges and lawyers take their work very seriously. It is also quite evident that neither the standing committee nor the Judicial Conference merely rubber stamps the proposals recommended to it. It is not at all rare that advisory committee proposals are returned to the originating committee for further study.

During my 31 years on the Court, the number of advisory committees has grown as necessitated by statutory changes. During that time, by my count at least, on some 64 occasions we have "prescribed" and transmitted to Congress a new set of rules or amendments to certain rules. Some of the transmissions have been minor, but many of them have been extensive. Over this time, Justices Black and Douglas, either together or separately, dissented 13 times on the ground that it was inappropriate for the Court to pass on the merits of the rules before it. Aside from those two Justices, Justices Powell, Stewart and then Justice Rehnquist dissented on one occasion and Justice O'Connor on another as to the substance of proposed rules. . . . Only once in my memory did the court refuse to transmit some of the rule changes proposed by the Judicial Conference. . . .

That the Justices have hardly ever refused to transmit the rules submitted by the Judicial Conference and the fact that, aside from Justices Black and Douglas, it has been quite rare for any Justice to dissent from transmitting any such rule, suggest that a sizable majority of the 21 Justices who sat during this period concluded that Congress intended them to have a rather limited role in the rulemaking process. The vast majority (including myself) obviously have not explicitly subscribed to the Black-Douglas view that many of the rules proposed dealt with substantive matters that the Constitution reserved to Congress and that in any event were prohibited by § 2072's injunction against abridging, enlarging or modifying substantive rights.

Some of us, however, have silently shared Justice Black's and Justice Douglas' suggestion that the enabling statutes be amended to place the responsibility upon the Judicial Conference rather than upon this Court. Since the statute was first enacted in 1934, 48 Stat. 1064, the Judicial Conference has been enlarged and improved and is now very active in its surveillance of the work of the federal courts and in recommending appropriate legislation to Congress. The present rules produced under 28 U.S.C. § 2072 are not prepared by us but by Committees of the Judicial Conference designated by The Chief Justice, and before coming to us they are approved by the Judicial Conference pursuant to 28 U.S.C. § 331. The Committees and the Conference are composed of able and distinguished members and they render a high public service. It is they, however, who do the work, not we, and the rules have only our imprimatur. The only contribution that we actually make is an occasional exercise of a veto power. If the rule-making for Federal District Courts is to continue under the present plan, we believe that the Supreme Court should not have any part in the task; rather, the statute should be amended to substitute the Judicial Conference. The Judicial Conference can participate more actively in fashioning the rules and affirmatively contribute to their content and design better than we can. Transfer of the function to the Judicial Conference would relieve us of the embarrassment of having to sit in judgment on the constitutionality of rules which we have approved and which as applied in given situations might have to be declared invalid.

374 U. S. 865, 869-870 (1963) (footnote omitted).

Despite the repeated protestations of both or one of those Justices, Congress did not eliminate our participation in the rulemaking process. Indeed, our statutory role was continued as the coverage of § 2072 was extended to the rules of evidence and to proceedings before magistrates. Congress clearly continued to direct us to "prescribe" specified rules. But most of us concluded that for at least two reasons Congress could not have intended us to provide another layer of review equivalent to that of the standing committee and the Judicial Conference. First, to perform such a function would take an inordinate amount of time, the expenditure of which would be inconsistent with the demands of a growing caseload. Second, some [of] us, and I remain of this view, were quite sure that the Judicial Conference and its committees, "being in large part judges of the lower courts and attorneys who are using the Rules day in and day out, are in a far better position to make a practical judgment upon their utility or inutility than we." 383 U. S. 1089, 1090 (1966) (Douglas, J., dissenting).

I did my share of litigating when in practice and once served on the Advisory Committee for the Civil Rules, but the trial practice is a dynamic profession, and the longer one is away from it the less likely it is that he or she should presume to second-guess the careful work of the active professionals manning the rulemaking committees, work that the Judicial Conference has approved. At the very least, we should not perform a de novo review and should defer to the Judicial Conference and its committees as long as they have some rational basis for their proposed amendments.

Hence, as I have seen the Court's role over the years, it is to transmit the Judicial Conference's recommendations without change and without careful study, as long as there is no suggestion that the committee system has not operated with integrity. If it has not, such a fact, or even such a claim, about a body so open to public inspection would inevitably surface. This has been my practice, even though on several occasions, based perhaps on out-of-date conceptions, I had serious questions about the wisdom of particular proposals to amend certain rules.

In connection with the proposed rule changes now before us, there is no suggestion that the rulemaking process has failed to function properly. No doubt the proposed changes do not please everyone, as letters I have received indicate. But I assume that such opposing views have been before the committees and have been rejected on the merits. That is enough for me.

Justice Douglas thought that the Court should be taken out of the rulemaking process entirely, but as long as Congress insisted on our "prescribing" rules, he refused to be a mere conduit and would dissent to forwarding rule changes with which he disagreed. I note that Justice Scalia seems to follow that example. But I also note that as time went on, Justice Douglas confessed to insufficient familiarity with the context in which new rules would operate to pass judgment on their merits.

In conclusion, I suggest that it would be a mistake for the bench, the bar, or the Congress to assume that we are duplicating the function performed by the standing committee or the Judicial Conference with respect to changes in the various rules which come to us for transmittal. As I have said, over the years our role has been a much more limited one.

## Practice Exercise No. 20: Assessing the Rulemaking Process

You have been asked to testify before the Senate Committee on the Judiciary regarding a proposal to revisit the rulemaking process contemplated by the current Rules Enabling Act. You may assume that Professors Struve, Burbank, and Walker have already testified before this Committee. The senators have asked you for your comments regarding the prior testimony. And they have identified several specific questions as possible lines of inquiry, including:

(1) Are there any separation of powers issues here? If there were no Rules Enabling Act, who would have the responsibility for drafting procedural rules—Congress or the Judiciary?

(2) We have seen throughout this chapter and others the politicization of procedure or, put another way, the ability of procedure to alter or mask substantive intentions. Does the Rules Enabling Act make sense in light of what we now know about the false dichotomy between substance and procedure? What or where is the dividing line between substance and procedure? *See generally* Thomas O. Main, *The Procedural Foundation of Substantive Law*, 87 Wash. U. L. Rev. 801 (2010); Stephen B. Burbank, *The Rules Enabling Act of 1934*, 130 U. Pa. L. Rev. 1015, 1127-1131 (1981).

(3) Constitutional issues aside, who is most competent to draft procedural rules? Lawyers? Judges? Academics? Congress? How should that process be designed?

(4) The shelf life of a Federal Rule of Civil Procedure seems to be on a steep decline. Where amendments to Federal Rules used to be relatively few and far between, they are now routine. "Only ten of the original Federal Rules of Civil Procedure have never been amended. Twenty six of the original rules—nearly one-third of the original 1938 set—have been amended at least five times. Fifty-one rules—approaching two-thirds of the original 1938 set—have been amended at least three times." Thomas O. Main, *Traditional Equity and Contemporary Procedure*, 78 Wash. L. Rev. 429, 481 (2003). Does this pace suggest to you that the rulemaking process is working or, rather, that it is not working?

(5) What rulemaking process would be called for if *efficiency* in the judicial system were the sole or at least a primary criterion?

(6) Does the philosophy (or philosophies) underlying the Federal Rules lead us to prefer one rulemaking process or another? For example, does our commitment to transsubstantive procedure require "an apolitical rulemaking process to ensure that rule amendments do not compromise the primary principles of transsubstantiality, generality, and flexibility"? Linda S. Mullenix, *Hope over Experience: Mandatory Informal Disclosure and the Politics of Rulemaking*, 69 N.C. L. Rev. 795, 841 (1991).

Prepare to be called upon to share your thoughts with regard to the Federal Rules of Civil Procedure. Naturally, you should prepare to explain and defend any reforms suggested in your remarks.

# 5

## The Right to Jury Trial and Judicial Control of Results

This chapter explores the debate over the civil jury, as well as the doctrine of the right to jury trial and the many methods for controlling the jury or preventing cases from reaching a trial, such as summary judgment, judgment as a matter of law (directed verdict and JNOV), jury instructions, motions for new trial, motions to vacate judgment, special verdicts, bifurcation, and remittitur and additur. The chapter ends with sections on closing arguments and appeals.

## A. VALUES AND HISTORICAL BACKGROUND

### 1. Introduction

When the Federal Rules of Civil Procedure were enacted, about 18 percent of civil cases in federal court were resolved by trial.* That percentage eroded to about 12 percent in 1962 and is now somewhere around 2 percent. (In fact, the number fluctuates considerably. For the years 2007-2010, the percentage of cases reaching a trial were 1.4 percent, 4.1 percent, 2.0 percent, and 1.2 percent, respectively.**) Tort cases such as *Carpenter v. Dee* had a 1-in-4 chance of reaching trial in 1938, but today have approximately a 1-in-50 chance. And of that narrow slice of cases that reach a trial, approximately

---

*Marc Galanter, *A World Without Trials?*, 2006 J. Disp. Resol. 7, 12-13 (2006).
**See Federal Judicial Caseload Statistics, *http://www.uscourts.gov/Statistics/FederalJudicial Caseload Statistics.aspx.*

two-thirds of those will be tried to a jury.* Why, then, would a course in Civil Procedure have a whole chapter on "The Right to Jury Trial and Judicial Control of Results"? Despite the relative paucity of actual civil jury trials, or of civil trials of any kind, the right to jury trial is claimed in a substantial percentage of cases, and the filing, preparation, and settlement of lawsuits is often done "in the shadow" of educated guesses about what a jury would ultimately decide if a jury trial did take place. Moreover, it is difficult to understand much of current civil procedure, and of the development of American law generally (and particularly in the field of evidence), without taking account of the historical ambivalence in our country about juries. You will see as this chapter unfolds, that there is a good deal of procedural doctrine defining and protecting the right to civil jury trial, accompanied by many different procedures to control juries and their verdicts, developed as a result of judicial distrust of laypeople's ability to act without prejudice and to deal with complexity.

Major tensions in American civil procedure emerge in debates about the civil jury and in the doctrine that has developed both to protect and to control the jury: formalism and definition versus narrative and less constraint; experts versus laypeople. Heated disputes in our society on issues of race and gender come to the fore in doctrinal battles about the selection and composition of juries. Political views influence whether one reads the right to jury trial more or less broadly and whether one would restrict or liberate the jury in the evidence they hear, the manner in which they are instructed, and the deference given to their decisions.

This chapter begins with two orientation sections, the first providing excerpts from the ongoing debate about the American civil jury and the second outlining a brief history of the development of the jury. You will then read about the constitutional right to trial by jury in civil cases and the quite complicated case law that has attempted to define that right. The Seventh Amendment to the U.S. Constitution states:

> In Suits at common law, where the value in controversy shall exceed twenty dollars, the right of trial by jury shall be preserved, and no fact tried by a jury shall be otherwise re-examined in any Court of the United States, than according to the rules of the common law.

The language "shall be preserved" has caused the Supreme Court to consider the extent to which one had the right to a civil jury as of 1791, when the Bill of Rights became part of the Constitution. Consequently, history is important not only to understand the context of another element of civil procedure, the jury, but also because courts turn to history in attempting to define the right.

Part C of this chapter covers the doctrine and practice that have developed around jury selection. You will see once again how a procedural issue becomes a lightning rod for ongoing cultural arguments about race and gender.

---

*This number likewise fluctuates considerably. For the years 2007-2010, the percentage of cases reaching a trial that were resolved by juries were 69 percent, 88 percent, 48 percent, and 68 percent, respectively.

The remainder of the chapter covers many different ways that have developed to influence, control, and overturn jury verdicts. Issues that you have previously heard about, such as summary judgment and directed verdict (now called judgment as a matter of law), will now be covered in more detail. And you will learn that some of this doctrine, such as ending a case early because there is insufficient evidence to permit the plaintiff to win, also governs cases in which the judge—not the jury—is the trier of fact, with permutations to take account of that difference.

As you read the following passages favoring or opposing the American civil jury, along with the remainder of the chapter, which explores jury composition and jury control, try to formulate and defend your own opinions about the continued utility (or lack thereof) of the civil jury. What are the most compelling arguments, pro and con?

## 2. *The Debate over the American Civil Jury*

What do modern juries do in the United States? In civil cases, they are instructed to impartially weigh the evidence, to decide what actually happened in the dispute ("the facts"), and to apply the law (as given by the judge) to those facts. The strategic importance of the jury in modern legal practice, then, is unquestioned, both in those cases actually decided by a jury and those settled in their "shadow." But the jury as an institution has been a target of sustained criticism for centuries. At the present time, about 80 percent of the jury trials in the world are conducted in the United States, a fact not lost on opponents of the jury concept: "Some opponents of the civil jury cite its abolition in other legal systems as evidence that civil juries are outmoded. Indeed, the use of civil juries has declined significantly in Canada and Australia and has effectively disappeared in England, their country of origin." *Developments in the Law— The Civil Jury*, 110 Harv. L. Rev. 1408, 1411 (1997). But the reforms are not unidirectional: there are also countries such as Japan, Russia, South Korea, and Spain that are introducing (or re-introducing) juries into their legal systems, although primarily for criminal cases. *See* Nancy S. Marder, *An Introduction to Comparative Jury Systems*, 86 Chi.-Kent L. Rev. 453 (2011) (suggesting that the jury may be "experiencing a renaissance" worldwide).

Those who oppose the use of the civil jury usually make efficiency arguments, emphasize the amateurish nature of lay jurors, and aver that jurors are influenced by prejudice and passion. Supporters, increasingly relying on empirical data, dispute such assumptions about inefficiency and incompetence. Moreover, they argue that the civil jury plays critical roles in a democracy—legitimizing the process, curbing arbitrary judicial behavior, inculcating community values, and permitting citizen participation and education, in addition to providing neutral, fair, and accurate dispute resolution. Consider the following voices from the debate, past and present, and draw your own conclusions:

Mark Twain said, "The jury system puts a ban upon intelligence and honesty, and a premium upon ignorance, stupidity, and perjury. It is a shame that we must continue to use a worthless system because it was good a thousand years ago." Mark Twain, *Roughing It* 309 (1872).

Dean Erwin Griswold of Harvard Law School said, "Even in the best of cases trial by jury is the apotheosis of amateurs. How can anyone think that 12 people selected at random in twelve different ways with the only criterion being a complete lack of general qualification, would have special ability to decide on disputes between people?" Erwin N. Griswold, Harvard Law School, Dean's Report 5-6 (1962-1963).

And Edward J. Devitt, a statesman who served in the U.S. House of Representatives and was later appointed to the federal bench, wrote:

> [W]e live in a different age now and our society has grown increasingly complex, as has our legal system. In earlier times, a jury might have been called upon to sit for a day or two to consider a simple dispute between neighbors. Today, however, a jury often finds itself sitting for many months, attempting to assimilate mountains of evidence in controversies pitting large corporations against each other in complicated cases involving antitrust, securities, tax, patent, and similar business related issues. . . .
>
> A lengthy trial . . . may make it impossible to impanel a jury of impartial minds of diverse backgrounds. It is unrealistic to suppose that employed persons, who compose the group most likely to have any familiarity with business matters of the type frequently at issue in lengthy litigation, would be available for jury service in lengthy trials. Judge Charles L. Brieant of the Southern District of New York aptly put it: "[M]ust litigants be left with a panel consisting solely of retired people, the idle rich, those on welfare, and housewives whose children are grown? Hardly a 'fair cross section of the community wherein the court convenes.'" . . .
>
> Studies of this subject suggest that factual issues presented in a case can be considered complex, either when the facts needing resolution are conceptually difficult for a non-specialist to understand, or when the facts are made difficult by the volume of evidentiary material needed to establish them. It also has been suggested that legal issues can be considered complex when they are multiple, overlapping, ambiguous, or pose issues requiring instructions on close questions of statutory interpretation. Even with instructions carefully crafted with an eye toward clarity and simplicity, it is practically impossible in some specialized fields of law to guide a jury through the awesome job of rationally applying complex instructions to a huge volume of technical evidence.

Edward J. Devitt, *Should Jury Trial Be Required in Civil Cases? A Challenge to the Seventh Amendment*, 47 J. Air L. & Comm. 495, 497, 498, 500 (1982).

## ■ JEROME T. FRANK, COURTS ON TRIAL
### *110-111, 129-130 (1949)*

. . . There are three theories of the jury's function:

(1) The naive theory is that the jury merely finds the facts; that it must not, and does not, concern itself with the legal rules, but faithfully accepts the rules as stated to them by the trial judge.

(2) A more sophisticated theory has it that the jury not only finds the facts but, in its deliberation in the jury-room, uses legal reasoning to apply to those facts the legal rules it learned from the judge. . . .

This theory ascribes to jurors a serpentine wisdom. It assumes that they thoroughly understand what the judge tells them about the rules, and that they circumvent the rules by falsely contriving—with consummate skill and cunning—the exact findings of fact which, correlated with those rules, will logically compel the result they desire.

(3) We come now to a third theory which may be called the "realistic" theory. It is based on what anyone can discover by questioning the average person who has served as a juror—namely that often the jury are neither able to, nor do they attempt to, apply the instructions of the court. The jury are more brutally direct. They determine that they want Jones to collect $5,000 from the railroad company, or that they don't want pretty Nellie Brown to go to jail for killing her husband; and they bring in their general verdict accordingly. Often, to all practical intents and purposes, the judge's statement of the legal rules might just as well never have been expressed. . . .

The "realistic" theory, then, is that, in many cases, the jury, often without heeding the legal rules, determine, not the "facts," but the respective legal rights and duties of the parties to the suit. For the judgment of the court usually follows the general verdict of the jury, so that the verdict results in a decision which determines those rights and duties. . . .

The [pro-jury] argument that juries make better rules than judges do has at least the virtue of honestly admitting the realities—of conceding that jurors often disregard what the trial judge tells the jurors about the [rules]. But as a rational defense of the jury system, it is surely curious. It asserts that, desirably, each jury is a twelve-man ephemeral legislature, not elected by the voters, but empowered to destroy what the elected legislators have enacted or authorized. Each jury is thus a legislative assembly, legislating independently of all others. For even if a jury does no more than nullify a legal rule by refusing to apply it in a particular lawsuit, yet it is legislating, since the power to destroy legal rules is legislative power. This argument for the jury should lead to a revised description of our legislative system to show that it consists, in the case of our federal government for instance, of (1) a Senate, (2) a House of Representatives, and (3) a multitude of juries.

I have one objection to such a description: I think it too sophisticated. It implies that the members of the ordinary jury say to themselves, "We don't like this legal rule of which the judge told us, and we won't apply it but will apply one of our own making." But when, as often happens, juries do not understand what the judge said to them about the applicable rule, it simply is not true that they refuse to follow it because they dislike it. Many juries in reaching their verdicts act on their emotional responses to the lawyers and the witnesses; they like or dislike, not any legal rule, but they do like an artful lawyer for the plaintiff, the poor widow, the brunette with the soulful eyes, and they do dislike the big corporation, the Italian with the thick, foreign accent. We do not have uniform jury nullification of harsh rules; we have juries avoiding—often in ignorance that they are so doing—excellent as well as bad rules, and in capricious fashion.

## ■ HARRY KALVEN, THE DIGNITY OF THE CIVIL JURY
### 50 U. Va. L. Rev. 1055, 1059-1067 (1964)

How much longer is a jury trial than a bench trial? . . . By using a series of estimates, we reached the conclusion that on the average a bench trial would be 40 percent less time consuming than a jury trial of the same case. . . .

As we come to the merits of the institution, it may be useful to sketch three main heads under which criticism and defense of the jury have fallen.

First, there is a series of collateral advantages and disadvantages such as the fact that the jury provides an important civic experience for the citizen; that, because of popular participation the jury makes tolerable the stringency of certain decisions; or that because of its transient personnel the jury acts as a lightning rod for animosity and suspicion which might otherwise center on the more exposed judge; or that the jury is a guarantor of integrity since it is said to be more difficult to reach twelve men than one. On the negative side it is urged that jury fees are an added expense to the administration of justice; that jury service often imposes an unfair economic and social burden on those forced to serve; and that exposure to jury service disenchants the citizen and leads him to lose confidence in the administration of justice.

Although many of these considerations loom large in the tradition of jury debate, they are unamenable to research and will not concern us here. We have, however, collected considerable data bearing on the reaction of jurors to service. It will suffice for present purposes simply to state that there is much evidence that most people, once actually serving in a trial, become highly serious and responsible toward their task and toward the joint effort to deliberate to a verdict. . . . The heart of the matter, the trial itself and deliberation, is very often a major and moving experience in the life of the citizen-juror.

The second cluster of issues goes to the competence of the jury. Can it follow and remember the presentation of the facts and weigh the conflicting evidence? Can it follow and remember the law? Can it deliberate effectively?

The third cluster of issues goes to the adherence of the jury to the law, to what its admirers call its sense of equity and what its detractors view as its taste for anarchy.

The latter two issues go to the heart of the debate and have long been the occasion for a heated exchange of proverbs. Further, they may seem so heavily enmeshed in difficult value judgments as to make further discussion unpromising. Yet it is precisely here that our empirical studies can offer some insight, although they too cannot fully dispose of the issues.

When one asserts that jury adjudication is of low quality, he must be asserting that jury decisions vary in some significant degree from those a judge would have made in the same cases.

[The University of Chicago Jury Project found that, in a study of several thousand personal injury cases, judges and juries agreed on liability in 79 percent of cases. "The judge disagrees with the jury because he is more pro-plaintiff about as often as the jury disagrees with him because it is more pro-plaintiff." In awarding damages, there is more disagreement. Of the 44 percent of cases where both judge and jury agreed, the jury gave the higher award in 23 percent, the judge gave a higher award in 17 percent, and the awards were approximately equal in 4 percent of cases. Jury awards averaged about 20 percent higher than those of the judge.]

There are . . . some further observations about the issue of jury competence. We have been told often enough that the jury trial is a process whereby twelve inexperienced laymen, who are probably strangers to each other, are invited to apply law which they will not understand to facts which they will not get straight and by secret deliberation arrive at a group decision. We are told also that heroic feats of learning law, remembering facts, and running an orderly discussion as a group are called for in every jury trial. . . .

In the judge-jury survey the trial judge, among other things, classified each case as to whether it was "difficult to understand" or "easy." We can therefore spell out the following hypothesis to test against the judge-jury data. If the jury has a propensity not to understand, that propensity should be more evident in the cases rated by the judges as difficult than in those rated as easy. Further, disagreement should be higher in cases which the jury does not understand than in cases which they do understand since, where the jury misunderstands the case, it must be deciding on a different basis than the judge. We reach, then, the decisive hypothesis to test, namely, that the jury should disagree more often with the judges in difficult cases than in easy ones. However, when we compare the decision patterns in easy cases with those in difficult cases we find that the level of disagreement remains the same. . . .

Any mystery as to why the plausible *a priori* surmises of jury incompetence should prove so wrong is considerably reduced when we take a closer look at the dynamics of the jury process, a look we have been able to take as a result of intensive and extensive post-trial juror interviews in actual cases and as a result of complete observation of jury deliberations in mock experimental cases, a technique used widely in the project. We observed that the trial had structured the communication to the jury far more than the usual comment recognizes and had made certain points quite salient. A more important point is that the jury can operate by *collective* recall. Different jurors remember, and make available to all, different items of the trial so that the jury as a group remembers far more than most of its members could as individuals. It tends, in this connection, to be as strong as its strongest link. The conclusion, therefore, is that the jury understands well enough for its purposes and that its intellectual incompetence has been vastly exaggerated. . . .

## ■ VALERIE P. HANS AND NEIL VIDMAR, JUDGING THE JURY*
### *247-249 (1986)*

In judging the jury there are some other issues to consider. The first concerns the alternatives to the jury. In France, West Germany, and some other European countries, mixed tribunals composed of a judge and prominent laypersons decide legal cases. In Britain, minor crimes are tried in a magistrate's courts by tribunals of laypersons. However, in most instances those who advocate abolition of the jury propose that the jury's work should be done by a judge. The question then becomes, are judges really superior to juries? Unfortunately, we have little data about the competency of judges, though . . . we know that the jury would agree with their decisions in four cases out of five. To be sure, judges have training in law, and perhaps, as Judge Frank claimed, they attempt to be more scientific in their approach to the evidence. On the other hand, many knowledgeable legal commentators have argued that judges are not necessarily better triers of fact. A jury which contains one or more persons proficient in automobile repair might be far better at assessing evidence in a products liability case involving a car manufacturer than a judge whose experience with things mechanical is limited to changing a spare tire. Even if one argues that the average judge is smarter in discerning legal facts than the average juror, is the judge as smart as twelve jurors?

We must also consider the fact that trials are about justice as well as law. The inescapable fact is that despite attempts in recent years to recruit minority group members and women into the judiciary, the overwhelming majority of judges are still white males who come from a privileged sector of our society. Often their views of the world reflect their backgrounds. Some rather rigidly adhere to a narrow perspective of justice and fairness that is not consistent with that of the general community. . . .

There are two other aspects to the political side of the jury. One is its "legitimating" function. In a democracy the average citizen obeys the law not so much because of its threat but because he or she grants it legitimacy, that is, accepts it as a body of rules to be followed. It may be true that democracies can survive without juries. Many Western democracies do not have juries and seem to function quite well. Yet, in the United States, Canada and Great Britain, the jury is an important symbol that helps to confer legitimacy to law.

The remaining political aspect of the jury concerns its socializing function. Not only does the jury system allow the people to contribute to the legal system, but the legal system, through the jury, contributes to the education of the people.

# Comments and Questions

1. There is widespread agreement that jury verdicts help lawyers and their clients assess the value of cases for settlement purposes. Moreover, jury verdicts influence behavior, particularly when the parties are informed professionals or employed in a business in which profit is influenced by financial losses, real or potential. Indeed, one purpose of the tort liability system is to deter unreasonable behavior, and the jury often determines what is reasonable. There are, though, fewer jury trials than one might expect.

In the courts of general jurisdiction of 22 states (and the District of Columbia) that contain 58 percent of the U.S. population, the portion of cases reaching jury trial declined from 1.8 percent of dispositions in 1976 to 0.6 percent in 2002; bench trials fell from 34.3 to 15.2 percent. The absolute number of jury trials is down by one-third and the absolute number of bench trials is down 6.6 percent.

Marc Galanter, *A World Without Trials?*, 2006 J. Disp. Resol. 7, 9 (2006) (citing Brian J. Ostrom et al., *Examining Trial Trends in the State Courts*, 1 J. Empirical Legal Stud. 755, 768-769 (2004)). Is it possible that the demand for jury input on such matters as reasonableness has declined?

The shrinking of trials is particularly striking because virtually everything else in the legal world is growing. There is more law. The amount of regulation continues to grow. The volume of authoritative legal material continues to expand. For example, the annual increment of published federal cases increased from 5,782 pages in 1962 to 13,490 pages in 2002, an increase of 133 percent. . . . In 1960 there were 385,933 lawyers in the United States; in 2000 there were 1,066,328. . . . [And] for the last third of the twentieth century the legal business grew several times as fast as the overall economy. Amid all this growth, the place of law, lawyers and courts in public consciousness continues to expand. And in that consciousness, the image of the trial remains central. The decline of trials remains a well-kept secret.

*Id.* at 11-12 (citations omitted). The secret is no longer as well kept. For articles denouncing the disappearance of jury trials, *see, e.g.*, Stephen B. Burbank and Stephen N. Subrin, *Litigation and Democracy: Restoring a Realistic Prospect of Trial*, 46 Harv. C.R.-C.L. L. Rev. 399 (2011); William G. Young, *Vanishing Trials, Vanishing Juries, Vanishing Constitution*, 40 Suffolk U. L. Rev. 67 (2006); Arthur R. Miller, *The Pretrial Rush to Judgment: Are the "Litigation Explosion," "Liability Crisis," and Efficiency Cliches Eroding Our Day in Court and Jury Trial Commitments?*, 78 N.Y.U. L. Rev. 982 (2003).

2. Still, many Americans participate each year in the jury process. The National Center for State Courts reports that more than 32 million citizens are summoned to serve as jurors every year to partake in over 150,000 jury trials in U.S. state and federal courts. According to one survey, approximately 24 percent of Americans report having served on a jury at least once. Ryan Y. Park, *The Globalizing Jury Trial: Lessons and Insights from Korea*, 58 Am. J.

Comp. L. 525, 575-576 (2010). *See also* Karen A. Berris, *Appearance Rates of Potential Jurors Who Confirm, Postpone, or Fail to Respond to the Jury Summons: Are Postponed Jurors Saying "No" or "Not Now"?*, 59 Drake L. Rev. 649 (2011). Those who serve on juries usually find it a positive and important experience:

> [F]or many of the millions of Americans who have exercised the power and experienced the responsibility, jury service turns out to be an unforgettable, even transforming experience. Although a majority of people try to avoid service, nearly three quarters of those who do serve come away with a more favorable view of the system than they had before. They eagerly tell war stories from the jury room: many decide to write about what they saw and accomplished. Nearly every juror interviewed for this book is proud of the job he or she did, proud of the seriousness of deliberations, proud of having exercised power soberly, proud—rightly or wrongly—of the verdicts that were reached. More than when they vote, or pay taxes, or attend a parade, they are realizing the democratic vision that still sustains our nation: They are governing themselves.
>
> There's disorder in the court but not despair. The jury system can be saved and is, for all our disappointments, well worth saving.

Stephen J. Adler, *Trial and Error in the American Courtroom* 242 (1994).

3. You have read about the famous Kalven and Zeisel University of Chicago Jury Project, conducted in the 1950s, which found that judges and juries agreed on liability approximately 80 percent of the time in personal injury cases. More recent studies continue to find that by any measure, juries appear to act competently most of the time. In 1986, Valerie P. Hans and Neil Vidmar published *Judging the Jury*, which analyzes empirical data about juries. Here are some of their conclusions:

> Based on the various studies examining different aspects of the jury, we can conclude that the jury has not been shown, as a general matter, to be incompetent. . . . No doubt some juries are. Yet, the data from studies of hundreds of jury trials and jury simulations suggest that actual incompetence is a rare phenomenon. Juries do differ sometimes from the way judges would have decided, but it is on grounds other than incompetence.
>
> . . . Sometimes the jury is at war with the law, but for the most part it is, in Kalven and Zeisel's phrase, a "modest war." There are very few instances in which the jury rejects the law outright. Rather it sometimes bends the law to comport with its own sense of what is just, fair, and equitable. Some will argue that this is still wrong; the law should always be followed. Others will say that the jury is doing exactly what it was intended that it should do. Regardless, the hard facts indicate that on the whole the jury behaves responsibly and rationally.

*Id.* at 120 and 163. And a more recent study by the National Center for State Courts and the Bureau of Justice Standards reached these conclusions about state court civil jury litigation:

> Overall, plaintiffs are successful in 49% of tort jury trials. . . . The distribution of successful plaintiffs in medical malpractice cases . . . is concentrated around

the national average of 30 percent. The median jury award is $52,000, a relatively modest sum in light of the estimated legal costs of taking a case through to a jury verdict. . . . Punitive damages are included in 6 percent of all general civil cases with a monetary award. . . . For all cases with a punitive award, the median is $50,000, but the mean is 17 times larger ($859,000). . . . During 1992 state court juries in the 75 most populous counties awarded an estimated $327,300,000 in punitive damages. Overall, tort cases account for just over a third of all dollars awarded as punitive damages, while contract-related cases account for 63 percent. Employment cases with punitive damages, most of which are employment discrimination cases, account for 40 percent of all the money awarded in punitive damages. . . . None of the punitive damages awards in medical malpractice or product liability cases (excluding toxic substance cases) were more than twice the compensatory damages (citations omitted). . . .

Brian J. Ostrom, David B. Rottman, and John A. Goerdt, *A Step Above Anecdote: A Profile of the Civil Jury in the 1990s*, 79 Judicature 233, 235-240 (Mar.-Apr. 1996).

A 1998 symposium focused on *The American Civil Jury: Illusion and Reality*. The papers, many of which were empirical studies, are printed in 48 DePaul L. Rev. No. 2 (Winter 1998). Most of the articles stress data similar to that described here and conclude that attacks on the American jury—allegations of exorbitant and irrational verdicts and jury prejudice, particularly against business or corporations—are largely mythology, unsupported by the data.

Yet the attacks on jury incompetence and jury unpredictability persist. And so do the empirical studies suggesting otherwise.

Taken as a whole, the [empirical] work reveals that there are substantial relationships between the strength of the trial evidence and jury verdicts, powerful linear relationships between the severity of a plaintiff's injury and the eventual jury award, and strong, predominantly linear (in logs) relationships between compensatory damage awards and punitive damage awards. Furthermore, when scholars have compared the decision-making of juries, judges, and other decision makers, the overall patterns appear more similar than different. That is, the same models and similar key variables account for both judge and jury decision making.

Valerie P. Hans and Theodore Eisenberg, *The Predictability of Juries*, 60 DePaul L. Rev. 375, 379 (2011) (summarizing findings of collected research on civil juries).

4. One of the major battlegrounds in the debate over the positive and negative aspects of the American jury is punitive damages. There are at least three major empirical and normative questions involved in the debate, and none of them yield clear-cut answers: (1) Do juries award punitive damages more frequently and in larger amounts than judges? (2) Are jury verdicts, and particularly punitive damages, and the threat thereof, an effective means of deterring undesirable, and in some cases dangerous,

behavior? (3) When juries award huge punitive damages, way out of proportion to a particular plaintiff's loss, does this constitute good evidence of jury irrationality and undesirable emotionality?

With respect to the first question, regarding the frequency and amounts of jury-awarded punitive damages, two recent studies give diametrically opposed results (and in some instances, they analyze the same data). In a 2002 Cornell Law Review article, five co-authors examine 1996 data covering one year of judge-and-jury trial outcomes from forty-five trial courts, comprising nearly 9,000 trials. Their conclusion: "[S]ubstantial change in punitive award patterns would not result from shifting greater responsibility to judges. Juries and judges award punitive damages at about the same rate, and their punitive awards bear about the same relation to their compensatory awards. Jury punitive damages have a bit more spread than judge awards, but the effect is not robust and leads to few jury punitive awards outside the range of what judges are expected to award." Theodore Eisenberg, Neil LaFountain, Brian Ostrom, David Rottman, and Martin T. Wells, *Juries, Judges, and Punitive Damages: An Empirical Study*, 87 Cornell L. Rev. 743 (2002).

Vanderbilt Law professors Joni Hersch and W. Kip Viscusi refute the Eisenberg study on just about every major point. In addition to examining the same data as the Eisenberg group, they sought to find every punitive damage award of at least $100 million over the period 1985-2002. Of the sixty-three such "blockbuster" awards that they found, 95 percent were awarded by juries. And the jury awards were highly unpredictable and not significantly correlated with compensatory damages. Joni Hersch and W. Kip Viscusi, *Punitive Damages: How Judges and Juries Perform*, 33 J. Legal Stud. 1 (2004).

The second question, whether large jury awards, including huge punitive damage verdicts, have a deterrent effect on future illegal behavior is also contentious. A recent *ABA Journal* article gives both sides. Here is an excerpt:

> In a recent study funded by Exxon, Viscusi found no safety or environmental differences between states that allow punitive damages and states that don't.
>
> "Thus, there is no deterrence benefit that justifies the chaos and economic disruption inflicted by punitive damages," he wrote.
>
> However, the [Dallas] *Morning News* and the *SMU Law Review* study identified more than 250 cases in which jury verdicts led to some change.
>
> Those changes ranged from corporations recalling potentially dangerous products and manufacturers modifying how they dispose of waste, to businesses reforming how they treat their employees and police departments rewriting rules on car chases and excessive force.

Mark Curriden, *Power of 12—Jurors increasingly are sending loud messages of censure with megabuck verdicts. But critics charge that a jury is the least qualified body to decide public policy*, 87 A.B.A. J. 36, 39 (2001).

Perhaps the hardest question to get a handle on is whether the large punitive damage verdicts meted out by juries are frequently irrational or the result of irresponsible, unchecked emotions. This may well be a case in which the picture is in the eyes of the beholder. Probably the most cited example of allegedly irresponsible jury behavior is the famous (or infamous) McDonald's spilt hot coffee case in which the jury awarded the plaintiff huge punitive damages, resulting in a torrent of jury-bashing at what was called the "outrageous" behavior of a typical "runaway" jury. But there is another view of the case:

> When a jury awarded Stella Liebeck $2.7 million in punitive damages after she had suffered third-degree burns from a spilled cup of McDonald's coffee, many members of the public and press denigrated the result, describing it as "outrageous" and the jury as "running away." What was often ignored in these accounts of the case was that the eighty-one-year-old woman's injuries were very serious, that McDonald's had known about the problem of its exceptionally hot coffee, but had declined to warn consumers or to change the temperature at which it served its coffee, and the trial judge subsequently reduced the $2.7 million punitive damage award to $480,000.

Nancy S. Marder, *Juries and Damages: A Commentary*, 48 DePaul L. Rev. 427, 428 (1998) (citations omitted).

It turns out that Mrs. Liebeck was hospitalized for eight days and required skin grafts. McDonald's policy was to serve coffee 15 to 20 degrees hotter than its competitors, and had in fact received 700 complaints about its hot coffee during the previous five years ("some involving serious burns"), but did not change its policy. "[In] the aftermath of the case, McDonald's lowered the temperature of its coffee." The "$2,700,000 punitive damage award was chosen by the jury to be equal to two days worth of coffee revenue for McDonald's." Samuel R. Gross and Kent D. Syverud, *Don't Try: Civil Jury Verdicts in a System Geared to Settlement*, 44 UCLA L. Rev. 1, 5 (1996) (citations omitted). Although there are undoubtedly cases in which punitive damages awarded by juries are exorbitant and unfair (a topic discussed in Chapter 2), perhaps the McDonald's case and others like it show that the jury, the jury trial, and the punitive damages worked exactly as they should. One group of scholars, however, using simulations to discern how diverse groups of people would assess punitive damages, found that jurors were likely to be very predictable and sound in determining the degree of outrageousness in behavior, but that they would be highly arbitrary and unpredictable in placing a dollar amount on that behavior. Cass R. Sunstein, Daniel Kahneman, and David Schkade, *Assessing Punitive Damages (With Notes on Cognition and Valuation in Law)*, 107 Yale L.J. 2071 (1998).

5. Consider again the tiny fraction of cases that reach a jury trial. Describe the profile of cases that are most likely to reach that stage of litigation. For example, would it be the cases where compensatory and punitive damages are high (or low)? Would it be cases where liability and/or damages are more

ambiguous (or more certain)? Do you think that *Carpenter v. Dee* has characteristics that would make it a case likely to reach a trial?

6. One consequence of the perception that juries are incompetent and/or unpredictable is the growth of a new profession of jury consultants. Many jury consultants emphasize the ways in which their services can leverage jurors' incompetence and/or predict jury trial outcomes.

7. The Arizona Jury Filming Project provides useful insight into the jury deliberation process. The Arizona Supreme Court, in conjunction with the American Bar Foundation (and with the consent of all of the participants), videotaped fifty actual civil jury deliberations. Results from this project paint a very positive picture of juries—suggesting that jurors are, on the whole, competent, unbiased, and diligent. American Bar Foundation, *How Civil Juries Really Decide Cases*, 18 Researching L., No. 2 (Spring 2007).

8. In thinking about the burdens and benefits of the American jury, punitive damages, and civil litigation in America generally, there is one other critical consideration. The United States relies less on government for the enforcement of social norms and also supplies less of a safety net for its citizens than many other countries. Much of the task of the enforcement of safety standards falls on the civil litigation system, and in turn on juries. One wanting to dramatically alter our heavy reliance on civil litigation and juries would, to act sensibly, have to consider whether to forgo whatever deterrence and compensation the current private civil litigation system provides or whether to replace it with governmental activity of a different and more substantial nature. *See generally* Sean Farhang, *The Litigation State* (Princeton 2010).

9. Detractors of the jury system must also defend the baggage that attends the alternative: judicial determination. Are judges immune from the criticism that, like juries, some may be ignorant, emotional, prejudiced, or unpredictable? In fact, judges are subject to many of the same psychological tendencies that influence laypeople. Chris Guthrie et al., *Blinking on the Bench: How Judges Decide Cases*, 93 Cornell L. Rev. 1, 43 (2007); Jeffrey J. Rachlinski et al., *Does Unconscious Race Bias Affect Trial Judges?*, 84 Notre Dame L. Rev. 1195 (2008).

In state courts many state judges are now elected to the bench. Two excellent articles discussing the untoward effects of elected judges are Madhavi M. McCall and Michael A. McCall, *Campaign Contributions, Judicial Decisions, and the Texas Supreme Court*, 90 Judicature 214 (Mar.-Apr. 2007), and Rachel Caulfield, *Judicial Elections: Today's Trends and Tomorrow's Forecast*, Judges' J. 6 (Winter 2007). Another very accessible discussion of these issues appears in *The Debate over Judicial Elections and State Court Judicial Selection*, 21 Geo. J. Legal Ethics 1347 (2008).

10. Which pro-jury arguments do you find the strongest? Which anti-jury arguments are most persuasive? What other arguments can you imagine for and against the use of juries in particular cases?

11. Three current debates about the jury are especially worth noting:

a. *Size.* "In a series of decisions in the 1970s [*Williams v. Florida*, 399 U.S. 78 (1970); *Colgrove v. Battin*, 413 U.S. 149 (1973); *Ballew v. Georgia*, 435 U.S.

223 (1978)], the U.S. Supreme Court set aside 600 years of settled common law tradition and two centuries of constitutional history, including the reversal of its own precedents to the contrary, in holding that both criminal and civil juries smaller than 12 do not violate constitutional requirements. Many states and federal districts took advantage of the permission that the Court, in effect, granted them to reduce the size of their juries. . . . [T]he majority of justices concluded that the size of the jury made no difference, at least down to sizes as small as six." (Footnotes omitted.) Michael J. Saks, *The Smaller the Jury, the Greater the Unpredictability*, 79 Judicature 263 (Mar.-Apr. 1996).

There is now a great deal of theory and empirical data suggesting that the Supreme Court was mistaken and that in fact the reduction of the size of the jury to six increases the unpredictability of verdicts and awards, reduces the likelihood of representation on the jury by minority groups, makes it more difficult for a dissenting member of the jury to argue her position (because of the reduced chance of having an ally), and reduces the collective memory and experience of the group. Thomas Gilovich et al., Social Psychology 555-566 (2d ed. 2011); Valerie P. Hans, *The Power of Twelve: The Impact of Jury Size and Unanimity on Civil Jury Decision Making*, 4 Del. L. Rev. 1, 8 (2001); *see also* Shari Seidman Diamond et al., *Achieving Diversity on the Jury: Jury Size and the Peremptory Challenge*, 6 J. Empirical Legal Stud. 425 (2009). In 1996, the Judicial Conference's Standing Committee on Rules of Practice and Procedure voted overwhelmingly to submit a proposal to amend Fed. R. Civ. P. 48 to restore twelve-member juries, but the recommendation was not adopted by the Judicial Conference. *See The Civil Jury (Developments in the Law)*, 110 Harv. L. Rev. 1408, 1487 (1997).

b. *Unanimity*. "The Seventh Amendment was held to require a unanimous verdict in *American Pub. Co. v. Fisher*, 1897, 166 U.S. 464. More recently the Court has held that the Fourteenth Amendment does not require a unanimous verdict in a state criminal case. *Apodaca v. Oregon*, 1972, 406 U.S. 404, but that the Sixth Amendment requires a unanimous verdict in a federal prosecution. 406 U.S. at 366 (Powell, J., concurring). There are no recent opinions on the requirement of unanimity in civil cases, but if the issue should arise, it seems very likely that the Court would hold that unanimity is not required." Charles A. Wright and Mary Kay Kane, *Law of Federal Courts* § 94, at 670-671 n.5 (7th ed. 2011). Fed. R. Civ. P. 48 requires a unanimous verdict "[u]nless the parties otherwise stipulate." Some jury simulation studies suggest that moving to non-unanimity in jury verdicts may have some unfortunate consequences. For example, when unanimity, is required, deliberations may last longer, but evaluation of the evidence and the law may be more thorough, jurors in the minority may participate more actively in the discussion and be more listened to, and jurors may be more satisfied with the final verdict. Valerie P. Hans and Neil Vidmar, *Judging the Jury* 175 (1986). In *Apodaca*, Justice Douglas vigorously argued that "human experience teaches that polite and academic conversation is no substitute for the earnest and robust argument necessary to reach unanimity." *Johnson v. Louisiana*, 406 U.S. 380, 389 (1972) (Douglas, J.) (dissenting).

In a fire insurance case in which the insurance company's only defense was an affirmative one—that the plaintiff had committed arson—the Ninth Circuit held that the jury had to unanimously agree that the insured was not the arsonist before it could award the insured damages under the insurance contract. *Jazzabi v. Allstate Ins. Co.*, 278 F.3d 979 (9th Cir. 2002). Does this make sense? Maybe the jury should instead be charged that the plaintiff wins if the jury unanimously finds that the defendant did not persuade them by a preponderance of the evidence that the plaintiff committed arson.

Understand also that eliminating the unanimity requirement—especially in combination with smaller juries—makes jury awards less predictable. Michael J. Saks, *The Smaller the Jury, the Greater the Unpredictability*, 79 Judicature 263 (1996); Nicole L. Waters, *Does Jury Size Matter?: A Review of the Literature* 4 (report prepared for the Administrative Office of the Courts by the National Center for State Courts) (2004).

c. *Complexity*. Some argue that in complex civil cases that are apt to last a long time, the Constitution does not require a jury trial. In an enigmatic footnote in *Ross v. Bernard*, 396 U.S. 531, 538 n.10 (1970), the Supreme Court mentioned a new factor, in addition to custom and remedy sought, as relevant to whether a party is entitled to a jury trial under the Seventh Amendment: "the practical abilities and limitations of juries." Some have also argued that there exist English precedents before 1791 for an exception to the Seventh Amendment for complex cases. Others have made a similar argument, relying on the Due Process Clause of the Fifth Amendment. However, "[t]he Ninth Circuit has rejected all of these arguments and held that there is no complexity exception. The Third Circuit rejected the historical argument and the argument from the *Ross* footnote, but accepted, in guarded form, a complexity exception based on the due-process argument. Finally, the Fifth Circuit has expressed no opinion on whether there can be a complexity exception, but has held that if such an exception exists, it cannot reach a case where the trial court finds only that 'it would be most difficult, if not impossible, for a jury to reach a rational decision (citations omitted).'" Charles A. Wright and Mary Kay Kane, *Law of Federal Courts* § 92 at 658 (7th ed. 2011). You may recall from the famous Kalven Chicago jury study that juries do not disagree with judges more in difficult cases than they do in easier ones.

Professor Graham Lilly of the University of Virginia Law School has argued that the increasing complexity of contemporary litigation, and particularly the central role played by expert testimony, science, and statistics in today's cases, make the jury—as currently selected—an inappropriate body to decide complex cases. One of his examples of how misguided it is to use jurors in complex cases is *Brooke Group Ltd. v. Brown Williamson Tobacco Corp.*, 509 U.S. 209 (1993), a 115-day trial, which involved an alleged predatory pricing scheme in the domestic cigarette market. Lilly cites to two researchers who conducted post-trial juror interviews, and found that "the jurors were overwhelmed, frustrated, and confused by testimony well beyond their comprehension." In the article that Lilly relies upon for his information about jurors in the *Brooke Group* case (Arthur Austin, *The Jury System at*

*Risk from Complexity, the New Media, and Deviancy*, 73 Denv. U. L. Rev. 51 (1995)), Austin concluded that "at no time did any juror grasp—even at the margins—the law, the economics, or any other testimony relating to the allegations or defense."

Professor Lilly urges the courts, including the Supreme Court, to revisit Justice White's suggestion in *Ross v. Bernard* that "the practical abilities and limitations of juries" is one appropriate criterion for determining the scope of the right to a jury under the Seventh Amendment. He also suggests requiring jurors to have a certain level of formal education, or equivalent training or experience, for specific types of cases, and the use of expert jury panels depending on the type of case, as means of retaining the benefits of jury trial, while at the same time achieving more suitable jurors. Finally, he proposes the increased use of court-appointed experts to assist jurors in complex cases. Graham C. Lilly, *The Decline of the American Jury*, 72 U. Colo. L. Rev. 53 (2001). For a comprehensive account of questions and cases regarding the complexity exception, see James Oldham, *On the Question of a Complexity Exception to the Seventh Amendment Guarantee of Trial by Jury*, 71 Ohio St. L.J. 1031 (2010).

12. The modern jury debate has revolved less around abolishing the jury altogether than around possible modifications of the jury system. Consider the following proposed modifications in light of the values discussed in the preceding text, as well as the "notice and the right to be heard" values discussed earlier in the book:

(i) allowing jurors to take notes during all or parts of the trial;
(ii) allowing jurors to ask questions of the witnesses;
(iii) rewriting jury instructions in simpler language (jury instructions ordinarily are given only orally, can be several hours long, and are often complex);
(iv) giving legal instructions to the jury before the evidence is heard;
(v) allowing interim summation by counsel and discussion by jurors;
(vi) permitting jurors to have written copies of the instructions;
(vii) increasing juror fees;
(viii) reducing juror "down time" by scheduling attorney-judge conferences when jurors are not present; and/or
(ix) special verdicts (which we will discuss later in this chapter).

Many of these modifications are already present in some jurisdictions, and researchers are beginning to assess their impact. *See, e.g.*, Lynne Forster Lee and Irwin A. Horowitz, *The Effects of Jury-Aid Innovations on Juror Performance in Complex Civil Trials*, 86 Judicature 184 (2003). "Although justice and fairness cannot be measured by an objective standard, [there is evidence that such innovations can enhance] the jury trial process and jurors' understanding during the trials' various phases." James F. Holderman, *Trying the ABA's Principles for Juries and Jury Trial*, 33 A.B.A. Litig. No. 33, at 9 (Spring 2007).

13. Do *Twombly* and *Iqbal* offer any hint as to how the Court perceives the importance and centrality of juries?

### 3. *The Historical Background of the Modern American Civil Jury*

While some historians trace the modern American civil jury back to the ancient civilizations of Greece and Rome or to the Scandinavians who settled England before A.D. 1000, most modern scholars begin the story of the jury at the time of the Norman Conquest of England in 1066. Those early juries were committees assembled by William the Conqueror to determine who owned the various tracts of land in a given area. Later, trial by jury became an alternative to the other forms of trial available, which involved various forms of battle or ordeal, or compurgation, and in which each side would bring forth friends to swear to the truth of his position. Jurors were selected from the local community where the dispute arose and were required to have some familiarity with the facts of the case. In a sense, then, the earliest juries were groups of witnesses, who discussed the case among themselves and arrived at a verdict. The judge's role in such a case was to tell the jurors the law that applied to the dispute. *See* Lloyd E. Moore, *The Jury: Tool of Kings, Palladium of Liberty* (2d ed. 1985).

In the centuries that followed, the distinction between juror and witness became more pronounced. In one intermediary phase, jurors who had personal knowledge of the case were required to testify in open court as witnesses and then to return to the jury box. Gradually, courts recognized the need for jurors who based their verdict not on personal knowledge, but only on the evidence presented in court. Elaborate procedures developed to ensure that only disinterested persons sat on juries. *See* John Marshall Mitnick, *From Neighbor-Witness to Judge of Proofs: The Transformation of the English Civil Juror*, 32 Am. J. Legal Hist. 201 (1988).

When the first English colonists brought trial by jury to America, it was still in flux. As late as 1670, in *Bushell's Case*, 124 Eng. Rep. 1006 (C.P), an English judge declared that jurors had the right to use their personal knowledge to decide the verdict. In colonial America, jurors often heard three different versions of the law from three different judges. In such cases, the jury could decide both fact and law, a situation that prevailed in some colonies, such as Massachusetts, until the Revolution. *See* William E. Nelson, *Americanization of the Common Law* (1975).

During the colonial period, juries were perceived to be guardians of local community values against outsider judges appointed by the royal governor. They were also seen as bulwarks of integrity against corrupt public officials, and, finally, as revolution drew near, as wellsprings of patriotism in the fight against imperialist injustices. British attempts to constrain the use of jury trial were among the foremost complaints of the founders of the movement for American independence and were mentioned in the Declaration of Independence.

When the British presence was eradicated and American judges were placed at the head of the various courts, some leaders of the new nation sought to restrain the influence of juries, who, they believed, were thwarting creditors from collecting on their debts and jeopardizing the economic stability of the new nation. At the Constitutional Convention, which was dominated by pro-creditor Federalists, no provision for civil jury trial was adopted in the original document. Indeed, in Federalist No. 83, Alexander Hamilton argued that the right to civil jury trial was not fundamental to liberty and that, given the diversity of practice throughout the states, it would be impossible to draft a provision that would satisfy all factions.

The omission of a right to jury trial in civil cases, as well as a provision that would have allowed the Supreme Court to reconsider factual issues decided by a jury, were among the chief rallying cries of the pro-debtor Anti-Federalists, whose impassioned pleas in state legislatures' ratification debates called for a guarantee of civil jury trial in all common law cases. In the end, the Anti-Federalists won the debate. The Seventh Amendment to the Constitution, adopted in 1791, provides that "[i]n suits at common law, where the amount in controversy exceeds twenty dollars, the right to trial by jury shall be preserved. . . ." For a complete discussion of the Federalist/Anti-Federalist debate over the Seventh Amendment, see Charles W. Wolfram, *The Constitutional History of the Seventh Amendment*, 57 Minn. L. Rev. 639 (1973). When all thirteen colonies became states, they, too, ensured the right to trial by jury in both criminal and civil cases. *Id.* at 655-656.

## B. THE RIGHT TO JURY TRIAL IN CIVIL CASES IN FEDERAL COURT

Read the language of the Seventh Amendment. In its earliest review of the Seventh Amendment, the Supreme Court, under Justice Story, declared that the "common law" referred to in the Constitution should be determined by looking at the common law of England. *United States v. Wonson*, 28 F. Cas. 745. Later courts refined the analysis, focusing on the historical implications of the word "preserved" to require looking at the common law of England in 1791—when the Seventh Amendment was adopted.

Two complications arose, one almost immediately and the other after the merger of law and equity in federal practice. First, what about civil causes of action created by statute after 1791? Were these actions automatically exempted from the Seventh Amendment because they were not part of the "common law"? Second, after the merger of law and equity, what are the rights of parties who raise both equitable and legal (or common law) claims? Justice Story began to answer these questions in the 1830 Supreme Court case *Parsons v. Bedford*, 28 U.S. 433, 447:

> By *common law*, [the framers of the Seventh Amendment] meant . . . not merely suits, which the *common* law recognized among its old and settled proceedings, but suits, in which *legal* rights were to be ascertained and determined, in contradistinction to those where equitable rights alone were recognized, and equitable remedies were administered.

In recent history, beginning with *Beacon Theaters v. Westover*, 359 U.S. 500 (1959), and continuing until the present day, the Supreme Court has continued to wrestle with the answers to these questions.

# ■ CHAUFFEURS, TEAMSTERS AND HELPERS, LOCAL NO. 391 v. TERRY
### *494 U.S. 558 (1990)*

Justice MARSHALL delivered the opinion of the Court, except as to Part III-A:

This case presents the question whether an employee who seeks relief in the form of back pay for a union's alleged breach of its duty of fair representation has a right to trial by jury. We hold that the Seventh Amendment entitles such a plaintiff to a jury trial.

## I

McLean Trucking Company and the Chauffeurs, Teamsters and Helpers Local Union No. 391 were parties to a collective-bargaining agreement that governed the terms and conditions of employment at McLean's terminals. The 27 respondents were employed by McLean as truckdrivers in bargaining units covered by the agreement, and all were members of the Union. In 1982 McLean implemented a change in operations that resulted in the elimination of some of its terminals and the reorganization of others. As part of that change, McLean transferred respondents to the terminal located in Winston-Salem and agreed to give them special seniority rights in relation to "inactive" employees in Winston-Salem who had been laid off temporarily.

After working in Winston-Salem for approximately six weeks, respondents were alternately laid off and recalled several times. Respondents filed a grievance with the Union, contesting the order of the layoffs and recalls. Respondents also challenged McLean's policy of stripping any driver who was laid off of his special seniority rights. Respondents claimed that McLean breached the collective-bargaining agreement by giving inactive drivers preference over respondents. After these proceedings, the grievance committee ordered McLean to recall any respondent who was then laid off and to lay off any inactive driver who had been recalled; in addition, the committee ordered McLean to recognize respondents' special seniority rights until the inactive employees were properly recalled.

On the basis of this decision, McLean recalled respondents and laid off the drivers who had been on the inactive list when respondents transferred to Winston-Salem. Soon after this, though, McLean recalled the inactive employees, thereby allowing them to regain seniority rights over respondents. In the next round of layoffs, then, respondents had lower priority than inactive drivers and were laid off first. Accordingly, respondents filed another grievance, alleging that McLean's actions were designed to circumvent the initial decision of the grievance committee. The Union representative appeared before the grievance committee and presented the contentions of respondents and those of the inactive truckdrivers. At the conclusion of the hearing, the committee held that McLean had not violated the committee's first decision.

McLean continued to engage in periodic layoffs and recalls of the workers at the Winston-Salem terminal. Respondents filed a third grievance with the Union, but the Union declined to refer the charges to a grievance committee on the ground that the relevant issues had been determined in the prior proceedings.

In July 1983, respondents filed an action in District Court, alleging that McLean had breached the collective-bargaining agreement in violation of § 301 of the Labor Management Relations Act, 1947, 61 Stat. 156, 29 U.S.C. § 185 (1982 ed.) and that the Union had violated its duty of fair representation. [Section 301(a) of the Labor Management Relations Act, 1947, provides for suits by and against labor unions: "Suits for violation of contracts between an employer and a labor organization representing employees in an industry affecting commerce as defined in this chapter, or between any such labor organizations, may be brought in any district court of the United States having jurisdiction of the parties, without respect to the amount in controversy or without regard to the citizenship of the parties." 61 Stat. 156, 29 U.S.C. § 185 (a) (1982).] Respondents requested a permanent injunction requiring the defendants to cease their illegal acts and to reinstate them to their proper seniority status; in addition, they sought, inter alia, compensatory damages for lost wages and health benefits. In 1986 McLean filed for bankruptcy; subsequently, the action against it was voluntarily dismissed, along with all claims for injunctive relief.

Respondents had requested a jury trial in their pleadings. The Union moved to strike the jury demand on the ground that no right to a jury trial exists in a duty of fair representation suit. The District Court denied the motion to strike. After an interlocutory appeal, the Fourth Circuit affirmed the trial court, holding that the Seventh Amendment entitled respondents to a jury trial of their claim for monetary relief. We granted the petition for certiorari to resolve a circuit conflict on this issue, and now affirm the judgment of the Fourth Circuit.

## II

... [Employees] must prove the same two facts to recover money damages: that the employer's action violated the terms of the collective-bargaining agreement and that the union breached its duty of fair representation.

## III

We turn now to the constitutional issue presented in this case—whether respondents are entitled to a jury trial. The Seventh Amendment provides that "[i]n Suits at common law, where the value in controversy shall exceed twenty dollars, the right of trial by jury shall be preserved." The right to a jury trial includes more than the common-law forms of action recognized in 1791; the phrase "Suits at common law" refers to "suits in which legal rights [are] to be ascertained and determined, in contradistinction to those where equitable rights alone [are] recognized, and equitable remedies [are] administered." *Parsons v. Bedford*, 3 Pet. 433, 447, 7 L. Ed. 732 (1830) ("[T]he amendment then may well be construed to embrace all suits which are not of equity and admiralty jurisdiction, whatever may be the peculiar form which they may assume to settle legal rights"). The right extends to causes of action created by Congress. Since the merger of the systems of law and equity, *see* Fed. R. Civ. P. 2, this Court has carefully preserved the right to trial by jury where legal rights are at stake. As the Court noted in *Beacon Theatres, Inc. v. Westover*, "Maintenance of the jury as a fact-finding body is of such importance and occupies so firm a place in our history and jurisprudence that any seeming curtailment of the right to a jury trial should be scrutinized with the utmost care." 359 U.S. 500, 501 (1959).

To determine whether a particular action will resolve legal rights, we examine both the nature of the issues involved and the remedy sought. "First, we compare the statutory action to 18th-century actions brought in the courts of England prior to the merger of the courts of law and equity. Second, we examine the remedy sought and determine whether it is legal or equitable in nature." 481 U.S., at 417-418. The second inquiry is the more important in our analysis.

**A**

An action for breach of a union's duty of fair representation was unknown in 18th-century England; in fact, collective-bargaining was unlawful. We must therefore look for an analogous cause of action that existed in the 18th century to determine whether the nature of this duty of fair representation suit is legal or equitable.

The Union contends that this duty of fair representation action resembles a suit brought to vacate an arbitration award because respondents seek to set aside the result of the grievance process. In the 18th century, an action to set aside an arbitration award was considered equitable. 2 Joseph Story, *Commentaries on Equity Jurisprudence* § 1452, pp. 789-790 (13th ed. 1886) (equity courts had jurisdiction over claims that an award should be set aside on the ground of "mistake of the arbitrators"). . . .

The arbitration analogy is inapposite, however, to the Seventh Amendment question posed in this case. No grievance committee has considered respondents' claim that the Union violated its duty of fair representation; the grievance process was concerned only with the employer's alleged breach of the collective-bargaining agreement. Thus, respondents' claim against the Union cannot be characterized as an action to vacate an arbitration award. . . .

The Union next argues that respondents' duty of fair representation action is comparable to an action by a trust beneficiary against a trustee for breach of fiduciary duty. Such actions were within the exclusive jurisdiction of courts of equity. This analogy is far more persuasive than the arbitration analogy. Just as a trustee must act in the best interests of the beneficiaries, a union, as the exclusive representative of the workers, must exercise its power to act on behalf of the employees in good faith, *Vaca v. Sipes*, [386 U.S., 171, 177 (1967)]. Moreover, just as a beneficiary does not directly control the actions of a trustee, an individual employee lacks direct control over a union's actions taken on his behalf. . . .

Respondents contend that their duty of fair representation suit is less like a trust action than an attorney malpractice action, which was historically an action at law. . . . [W]e find that, in the context of the Seventh Amendment inquiry, the attorney malpractice analogy does not capture the relationship between the union and the represented employees as fully as the trust analogy does.

The attorney malpractice analogy is inadequate in several respects. Although an attorney malpractice suit is in some ways similar to a suit alleging a union's breach of its fiduciary duty, the two actions are fundamentally different. The nature of an action is in large part controlled by the nature of the underlying relationship between the parties. Unlike employees represented by a union, a client controls the significant decisions concerning his representation. Moreover, a client can fire his attorney if he is dissatisfied with his attorney's performance. . . . Thus, we find the malpractice analogy less convincing than the trust analogy.

Nevertheless, the trust analogy does not persuade us to characterize respondents' claim as wholly equitable. The Union's argument mischaracterizes the nature of our comparison of the action before us to 18th-century forms of action. As we observed in *Ross v. Bernhard*, 396 U.S. 531 (1970), "The Seventh Amendment question depends on the nature of the issue to be tried rather than the character of the overall action." *Id.*, at 538 (finding a right to jury trial in a shareholder's derivative suit, a type of suit traditionally brought in courts of equity, because plaintiffs' case presented legal issues of breach of contract and negligence). As discussed above, . . . to recover from the Union here, respondents must prove both that McLean violated § 301 by breaching the collective-bargaining agreement and that the Union breached its duty of fair representation. When viewed in isolation, the duty of fair representation issue is analogous to a claim against a trustee for breach of fiduciary duty. The § 301 issue, however, is comparable to a breach of contract claim—a legal issue.

Respondents' action against the Union thus encompasses both equitable and legal issues. The first part of our Seventh Amendment inquiry, then, leaves us in equipoise as to whether respondents are entitled to a jury trial.

**B**

Our determination under the first part of the Seventh Amendment analysis is only preliminary. In this case, the only remedy sought is a request for compensatory damages representing back pay and benefits. Generally, an action for money damages was "the traditional form of relief offered in the courts of law." *Curtis v. Loether*, 415 U.S. 189, 196 (1974). This Court has not, however, held that "any award of monetary relief must necessarily be 'legal' relief." *Ibid.* Nonetheless, because we conclude that the remedy respondents seek has none of the attributes that must be present before we will find an exception to the general rule and characterize damages as equitable, we find that the remedy sought by respondents is legal.

First, we have characterized damages as equitable where they are restitutionary, such as in "action[s] for disgorgement of improper profits," *Tull* [*v. United States*, 481 U.S. 412, 424 (1987)]. The back pay sought by respondents is not money wrongfully held by the Union, but wages and benefits they would have received from McLean had the Union processed the employees' grievances properly. Such relief is not restitutionary.

Second, a monetary award "incidental to or intertwined with injunctive relief" may be equitable. *Tull*, 481 U.S. at 424. *See, e.g., Mitchell v. DeMario Jewelry, Inc.*, 361 U.S. 288, 291-292 (1960) (district court had power, incident to its injunctive powers, to award back pay under the Fair Labor Standards Act; also back pay in that case was restitutionary). Because respondents seek only money damages, this characteristic is clearly absent from the case.

The Union argues that the back pay relief sought here must nonetheless be considered equitable because this Court has labeled back pay awarded under Title VII, 42 U.S.C. § 2000e et seq. (1982 ed.), as equitable. *See Albemarle Paper Co. v. Moody*, 422 U.S. 405, 415-418 (1975) (characterizing back pay awarded against employer under Title VII as equitable in context of assessing whether judge erred in refusing to award such relief). It contends that the Title VII analogy is compelling in the context of the duty of fair representation because its back pay provision was based on the NLRA provision governing back pay awards for unfair labor practices, 29 U.S.C. § 160(c) (1982 ed.). ("[W]here an order directs reinstatement of an employee, back pay may be required of the employer or labor organization"). We are not convinced.

The Court has never held that a plaintiff seeking back pay under Title VII has a right to a jury trial. *See Lorillard v. Pons*, 434 U.S. 575, 581-582 (1978). Assuming, without deciding, that such a Title VII plaintiff has no right to a jury trial, the Union's argument does not persuade us that respondents are not entitled to a jury trial here. Congress specifically characterized back pay under Title VII as a form of "equitable relief." 42 U.S.C. § 2000e-5(g) (1982 ed.). . . . Congress made no similar pronouncement regarding the duty of fair representation. Furthermore, the Court has noted that back pay sought from an employer under Title VII would generally be restitutionary in nature, *see Curtis v. Loether*, at 197, in contrast to the damages sought here from the Union. Thus, the remedy sought in this duty of fair representation case is clearly different from back pay sought for violations of Title VII. . . .

We hold, then, that the remedy of back pay sought in this duty of fair representation action is legal in nature. Considering both parts of the Seventh Amendment inquiry, we find that respondents are entitled to a jury trial on all issues presented in their suit.

## IV

On balance, our analysis of the nature of respondents' duty of fair representation action and the remedy they seek convinces us that this action is a legal one. Although the search for an adequate 18th-century analog revealed that the claim includes both legal and equitable issues, the money damages respondents seek are the type of relief traditionally awarded by courts of law. Thus, the Seventh Amendment entitles respondents to a jury trial, and we therefore affirm the judgment of the Court of Appeals.

Justice BRENNAN, concurring in part and concurring in the judgment:

I agree with the Court that respondents seek a remedy that is legal in nature and that the Seventh Amendment entitles respondents to a jury trial on their duty of fair representation claims. I therefore join Parts I, II, III-B, and IV of the Court's opinion. I do not join that part of the opinion which reprises the particular historical analysis this Court has employed to determine whether a claim is a "Suit at common law" under the Seventh Amendment, . . . because I believe the historical test can and should be simplified. . . .

I believe that our insistence that the jury trial right hinges in part on a comparison of the substantive right at issue to forms of action used in English courts 200 years ago needlessly convolutes our Seventh Amendment jurisprudence. For the past decade and a half, this Court has explained that the two parts of the historical test are not equal in weight, that the nature of the remedy is more important than the nature of the right. Since the existence of a right to jury trial therefore turns on the nature of the remedy, absent congressional delegation to a specialized decisionmaker, there remains little purpose to our rattling through dusty attics of ancient writs. The time has come to borrow William of Occam's razor and sever this portion of our analysis. . . .

Requiring judges, with neither the training nor time necessary for reputable historical scholarship, to root through the tangle of primary and secondary sources to determine which of a hundred or so writs is analogous to the right at issue has embroiled courts in recondite controversies better left to legal historians. . . .

Furthermore, inquiries into the appropriate historical analogs for the rights at issue are not necessarily susceptible of sound resolution under the best of circumstances. . . .

In addition, modern statutory rights did not exist in the 18th-century and even the most exacting historical research may not elicit a clear historical analog. The right at issue here, for example, is a creature of modern labor law quite foreign to Georgian England. . . .

To rest the historical test required by the Seventh Amendment solely on the nature of the relief sought would not, of course, offer the federal courts a rule that is in all cases self-executing. Courts will still be required to ask which remedies were traditionally available at law and which only in equity. But this inquiry involves fewer variables and simpler choices, on the whole, and is far more manageable than the scholasticist debates in which we have been engaged. Moreover, the rule I propose would remain true to the Seventh Amendment, as it is undisputed that, historically, "[j]urisdictional lines [between law and equity] were primarily a matter of remedy." John C. McCoid, II, *Procedural Reform and the Right to Jury Trial: A Study of Beacon Theatres, Inc. v. Westover*, 116 U. Pa. L. Rev. 1 (1967). . . .

The encroachment on civil jury trial by colonial administrators was a "deeply divisive issue in the years just preceding the outbreak of hostilities between the colonies and England," and all thirteen States reinstituted the right after hostilities ensued. Charles W. Wolfram, *The Constitutional History of the Seventh Amendment*, 57 Minn. L. Rev. 639, 654-655 (1973). . . .

We can guard this right and save our courts from needless and intractable excursions into increasingly unfamiliar territory simply by retiring that prong of our Seventh Amendment test which we have already cast into a certain doubt. If we are not prepared to accord the nature of the historical analog sufficient weight for this factor to affect the outcome of our inquiry, except in the rarest of hypothetical cases, what reason do we have for insisting that federal judges proceed with this arduous inquiry? It is time we read the writing on the wall, especially as we ourselves put it there.

[The opinion of Justice STEVENS, concurring in part and concurring in the judgment, is omitted.]

Justice KENNEDY, with whom Justice O'CONNOR and Justice SCALIA join, dissenting:

. . . To determine whether rights and remedies in a duty of fair representation action are legal in character, we must compare the action to the 18th-century cases permitted in the law courts of England, and we must examine the nature of the relief sought. I agree also with those Members of the Court who find that the duty of fair representation action resembles an equitable trust action more than a suit for malpractice.

I disagree with the analytic innovation of the Court that identification of the trust action as a model for modern duty of fair representation actions is insufficient to decide the case. The Seventh Amendment requires us to determine whether the duty of fair representation action "is more similar to cases that were tried in courts of law than to suits tried in courts of equity." *Tull v. United States*, 481 U.S. 412, 417 (1987). Having made this decision in favor of an equitable action, our inquiry should end. Because the Court disagrees with this proposition, I dissent.

## I

[Justice Kennedy explains that he finds the analogy to an equitable suit by a beneficiary against a trustee more persuasive, largely because a trustee is required to serve all beneficiaries with impartiality and may not ordinarily be directed to act by a beneficiary. He notes that this is unlike an action by a client against an attorney because the attorney is entrusted with representing the sole interests of the client and acts as an agent on the client's behalf. Moreover, Justice Kennedy states that the remedies available to employees in claims for breach of the duty of fair representation are equitable in nature and are therefore more like the remedies available in an action against a trustee. On the other hand, in an action by a client against an attorney, compensatory damages are often the appropriate remedy.]

## II

The Court relies on two lines of precedents to overcome the conclusion that the trust action should serve as the controlling model. The first consists of cases in which the Court has considered simplifications in litigation resulting from modern procedural reforms in the federal courts. Justice Marshall asserts that these cases show that the Court must look at the character of individual issues rather than claims as a whole. The second line addresses the significance of the remedy in determining the equitable or legal nature of an action for the purpose of choosing the most appropriate analogy. Under these cases, the Court decides that the respondents have a right to a jury because they seek money damages. These authorities do not support the Court's holding.

### A

In three cases we have found a right to trial by jury where there are legal claims that, for procedural reasons, a plaintiff could have or must have raised in the courts of equity before the systems merged. In *Beacon Theatres, Inc. v. Westover*, 359 U.S. 500 (1959), Fox, a potential defendant threatened with legal antitrust claims, brought an action for declaratory and injunctive relief against Beacon, the likely plaintiff. Because only the courts of equity had offered such relief prior to the merger of the two court systems, Fox had thought that it could deprive Beacon of a jury trial. Beacon, however, raised the antitrust issues as counterclaims and sought a jury. We ruled that, because Beacon would have had a right to a jury trial on its antitrust claims, Fox could not deprive it of a jury merely by taking advantage of modern declaratory procedures to sue first. The result was consistent with the spirit of the Federal Rules of Civil Procedure, which allow liberal joinder of legal and equitable actions, and the Declaratory Judgment Act, 28 U.S.C. §§ 2201, 2202 (1982 ed.), which preserves the right to jury trial to both parties. *See* 359 U.S., at 509-510.

In *Dairy Queen, Inc. v. Wood*, 369 U.S. 469 (1962), we held, in a similar manner, that a plaintiff, by asking in his complaint for an equitable accounting for trademark infringement, could not deprive the defendant of a jury trial on contract claims subsumed within the accounting. Although a court of equity would have heard the contract claims as part of the accounting suit, we found them severable under modern procedure. *See id.*, at 477-479.

In *Ross v. Bernhard*, 396 U.S. 531 (1970), a shareholder-plaintiff demanded a jury trial in a derivative action asserting a legal claim on behalf of his corporation. The defendant opposed a jury trial. In deciding the case, we recognized that only the courts of equity had procedural devices allowing shareholders to raise a corporation's claims. We nonetheless again ruled that modern procedure allowed trial of the legal claim to a jury. *See id.* at 542.

These three cases responded to the difficulties created by a merged court system. *See* John C. McCoid, II, *Procedural Reform and the Right to Jury Trial: A Study of Beacon Theatres, Inc. v. Westover*, 116 U. Pa. L. Rev. 1 (1967). They stand for the proposition that, because distinct courts of equity no longer exist, the possibility or necessity of using former equitable procedures to press a legal claim no longer will determine the right to a jury. Justice Marshall reads these cases to require a jury trial whenever a cause of action contains legal issues and would require a jury trial in this case because the respondents must prove a breach of the collective-bargaining agreement as one element of their claim.

I disagree. The respondents, as shown above, are asserting an equitable claim. Having reached this conclusion, the *Beacon, Dairy Queen*, and *Ross* cases are inapplicable. . . .

**B**

The Court also rules that, despite the appropriateness of the trust analogy as a whole, the respondents have a right to a jury trial because they seek money damages. The nature of the remedy remains a factor of considerable importance in determining whether a statutory action had a legal or equitable analog in 1791, but we have not adopted a rule that a statutory action permitting damages is by definition more analogous to a legal action than to any equitable suit. In each case, we look to the remedy to determine whether, taken with other factors, it places an action within the definition of "suits at common law." . . .

**III**

The Court must adhere to the historical test in determining the right to a jury because the language of the Constitution requires it. The Seventh Amendment "preserves" the right to jury trial in civil cases. We cannot preserve a right existing in 1791 unless we look to history to identify it. Our precedents are in full agreement with this reasoning and insist on adherence to the historical test. No alternatives short of rewriting the Constitution exist. . . .

If Congress has not provided for a jury trial, we are confined to the Seventh Amendment to determine whether one is required. Our own views respecting the wisdom of using a jury should be put aside. Like Justice Brennan, I admire the jury process. Other judges have taken the opposite view. *See, e.g.*, Jerome Frank, *Law and the Modern Mind* 170-185 (1931). But the judgment of our own times is not always preferable to the lessons of history. Our whole constitutional experience teaches that history must inform the judicial inquiry. Our obligation to the Constitution and its Bill of Rights, no less than the compact we have with the generation that wrote them for us, do not permit us to disregard provisions that some may think to be mere matters of historical form. . . .

## Comments and Questions

1. Articulate the current test as interpreted by Justice Marshall writing for the majority. For an excellent example of a lower court applying this test, see *Pereira v. Farace*, 413 F.3d 330 (2nd Cir. 2005).

2. Justice Brennan and Justice Kennedy would each apply a different test. How do their approaches differ from each other, and from Justice Marshall's?

3. Although the Supreme Court continues to apply the historical test, it made room for consideration of functional criteria and policy in a 1996 Seventh Amendment case. In *Markman v. Westview Instruments, Inc.*, 517 U.S. 370 (1996), a unanimous Court agreed that in a patent infringement claim the interpretation of terms in a patent is a matter of law to be decided by the court, not a jury. After finding the historical evidence equivocal, the Court took into consideration "the relative interpretative skills of judges and juries and the statutory policies that ought to be furthered" in allocating the interpretation to either judge or jury.

4. As you have learned, modern procedure has merged law and equity into one court. A single judge wears both hats. One treatise puts the ensuing jury right problem this way: "What is the scope of the jury trial right when the right is 'preserved' in terms of a distinction (between law and equity) that has been abolished (by merger)? The problem is unsolvable." Fleming James, Jr., Geoffrey C. Hazard, Jr., and John Leubsdorf, *Civil Procedure* 508 (5th ed. 2001). This treatise has a comprehensive description of the case law concerning the right to a civil jury trial (pp. 491-533). *See also* Charles W. Wolfram, *The Constitutional History of the Seventh Amendment*, 57 Minn. L. Rev. 639, 744-747 (1973); Martin Redish, *Seventh Amendment Right to Jury Trial: A Study in the Irrationality of Decision Making*, 70 Nw. U. L. Rev. 486, 530-531 (1975).

5. Remember that the constitutional analysis is unnecessary if the statute itself provides litigants the right to jury trial. In these circumstances, the right to jury trial would be premised on the statute, regardless of whether the Constitution would also require a jury. When statutes are silent on the issue, the parties may argue about congressional intent. *See, e.g., NLRB v. Jones & Laughlin*, 301 U.S. 1 (1937) (jury trial would subvert purpose of Congress in creating separate administrative agency for labor disputes); *Katchen v. Landy*, 382 U.S. 323 (1966) (Bankruptcy Court is special, Chancery-like court for resolving complex disputes; jury trial would subvert Congress's intent as expressed by Bankruptcy Act).

Now consider one other possibility. Can a statute create a cause of action and expressly deny litigants the right to a jury trial thereunder? The quick answer would be no—because the Seventh Amendment is a *constitutional* right that no statute could abridge. But what is the counter-argument?

6. Regarding discrimination suits under the Civil Rights Acts, the Court has split its decisions. In *Curtis v. Loether*, 415 U.S. 189 (1974), it held that litigants in a Title VIII housing discrimination lawsuit were entitled to trial by jury. In cases of intentional discrimination on the basis of race, the Court has provided trial by jury in suits brought under § 1981, but it did not for those under Title VII. The 1991 Civil Rights Act, however, specifically provides for trial by jury in intentional employment discrimination cases on the basis of race, gender, and religion. The Supreme Court has not specifically

ruled on the issue, but most lower courts have agreed that there is no right to jury trial for nonintentional, or "disparate impact," discrimination cases under Title VII.

7. In *Beacon Theatres, Inc. v. Westover*, 359 U.S. 500 (1959); *Dairy Queen, Inc. v. Wood*, 369 U.S. 469 (1962); and *Ross v. Bernhard*, 396 U.S. 531 (1970), the Supreme Court said unequivocally that, where equitable and legal claims are joined in the same action, the legal claims must be tried to a jury before the court resolves any equitable issues. These cases involved legal and equitable claims originally joined in the same civil lawsuit. At least one federal circuit court has ruled that a judge may determine an issue common to equitable and legal claims prior to a jury trial when the claims were originally brought separately and have since been consolidated under Fed. R. Civ. P. 42(a). *Newfound Management Corp. v. Lewis*, 131 F.3d 108 (3d Cir. 1997). Why should consolidated claims be treated differently?

8. As you will learn in Constitutional Law, the Seventh Amendment is one of the few Bill of Rights guarantees that has not been applied to the states through the Fourteenth Amendment's Due Process Clause. Most state constitutions provide a right to trial by jury, although the form of the right varies from state to state, with some providing greater right to jury trial than the federal courts, and others providing a restricted right. How would you write a constitutional amendment to guarantee the right to trial by jury? Would you seek to expand or constrict the right as currently provided at the federal level? What other purposes would your amendment serve?

## Practice Exercise No. 21: Legislative Exercise Regarding Right to Jury Trial

You are a politician assigned to a legislative committee that is deciding whether to allow jury trials for Title VII disparate impact discrimination suits, such as the Cleveland Firefighters lawsuit. Using *Terry* and the other materials in this section, try to decide whether the Seventh Amendment requires (or should require) the right to trial by jury in such cases. Regardless of whether the Seventh Amendment requires it, should Congress provide for juries as a matter of right in Title VII disparate impact cases?

## Practice Exercise No. 22: Law Firm Strategy Session Regarding Jury Trial in *City of Cleveland*

You are an associate at a staff meeting of the attorneys in the *City of Cleveland* case. The task of this meeting is limited to one question: whether or not to demand a jury trial. If your last name begins with the letters A-L, you are counsel for the plaintiffs; all others represent the defendants.

# C. JURY SELECTION: TECHNIQUES AND PURPOSES, INCLUDING PEREMPTORY CHALLENGES

In this section, you will learn the basic premises and techniques of modern jury selection, explore the need for a fair representation of the community in the jury pool, and examine current attempts to curb discrimination in jury selection. You begin with an orientation essay, followed by the federal jury statutes and an overview of the case law.

## 1. Attorney Behavior

In most courts a "pool" or "panel" of potential jurors has been selected by lottery in advance. In some instances, prior to their encounter with any attorneys, the jurors are shown a film or are simply told about the duties of a juror. Prospective jurors are often given a pamphlet describing the obligations of jurors and detailing what will go on in the courtroom. In most courts, the lawyers are given a list of basic information about who is in the pool. In federal court, the lawyers are given a list that contains the pool members' names, addresses, occupations, and spouses' occupations. Normally, lawyers would not see the list of who is in the pool until right before the jury is selected.

Next, there is what is called a voir dire examination of the prospective jurors as part of the selection process. The stated purpose is to disqualify jurors who cannot be impartial and fair. For instance, a prospective juror may know one of the parties or lawyers, or have previous information about the lawsuit. But lawyers also use the process to begin establishing a rapport with the jury and advocating their view of the case through the questions that they ask.

Depending on the section of the country and the particular court, the voir dire is conducted in different ways. It used to be that the voir dire was conducted primarily by the lawyers, who asked the potential jurors a number of questions. It is probably more typical today, particularly in federal court, for the judge to do the bulk of the questioning. In some courts, the judge asks preliminary questions, and the attorneys are permitted to add a few questions of their own.

Of course, good lawyering calls for finding out in advance how the voir dire will be conducted in your particular case. In some courts, the entire panel is questioned. In others, a smaller number of potential jurors are randomly picked from the panel to be questioned. Sometimes, the whole panel gets general questions, with more particular questions reserved for the chosen portion of the pool.

Most young lawyers spend a lot of time seeking information about local practices and customs from older lawyers and clerks. One needs to know how many jurors will hear the case and how many alternates. Who asks the questions at voir dire? Who picks the jury foreperson, and where will she be seated? Must the jury return a unanimous vote? Can they ask questions or take notes? It may be important for the lawyers to read any pamphlet and view any instructional film that is given or shown to the jurors. The jurors are the audience, and it is crucial for the advocate to know the common information base.

Lawyers can challenge jurors either for cause or with peremptory challenges, for which a cause is not given. The number of challenges for cause is unlimited; sometimes statutes list the "for cause" reasons. Statutes normally also list the number of permitted peremptory challenges. Some statutes permit the judge to add to the number of peremptory challenges. You will also want to know in advance such things as whether you have a second chance to strike jurors once a full jury has been selected and whether you will have to state in open court the name of the juror you have challenged, as well as the reason for the strike.

Lawyers vary on their theories of jury selection; naturally, the court, locale, jury pool, type of case, local customs, and similar matters are relevant. For instance, in some courts the panel sits for an entire month. If it is nearer to the end of the month, some lawyers are reluctant to ever strike a potential juror, except for obvious and noncontroversial cause. The person one strikes may have become a luncheon companion of a juror—now resentful—who later sits on the jury. This concern is heightened if the lawyer has had to publicly challenge or strike a juror; but even if the process is secret, some lawyers are hesitant to have the jurors guessing about who made the challenge. Some lawyers, if permitted, like to say in open court: "No challenges; I am content." Perhaps they believe that this advertises that they have such a strong case that it does not matter which jurors are selected.

As you think about the jurors whom you would challenge or strike, probe your own reasoning and prejudices. Some lawyers seek jurors who have certain ethnic or professional characteristics. Some very good lawyers doubt their own ability—or anyone's ability—to strike jurors rationally, and they very rarely challenge a juror. For instance, it used to be folklore that employees of insurance companies were defense-prone in civil cases; some attorneys now think that it is equally likely that an employee of a large company could be hostile to other large entities. One's sense of such matters may change from decade to decade. It has remained a constant, however, that lawyers are reluctant to use up their peremptory challenges unless they absolutely have to; they are afraid that a subsequently selected juror may be worse than the one they already "bumped."

Regardless of the philosophy that you develop for jury selection, remember that every time you appear before a judge or jury, you too are on trial. The judge and jurors who will sit in your case are watching and listening. This does not mean that you should change your personality for the voir dire or trial; often who we really are comes out during the pressure of a trial anyway.

It does mean you should consider how best to present the "you" who you are during each stage of litigation.

## Comments and Questions

1. What assumptions, if any, do you have about potential jurors? How would you go about testing whether they are true or false?

2. How do attorneys know when their jury selection techniques have worked? How do they know if they have failed? What other factors might influence the outcome of a case? In Great Britain, attorneys have extremely limited rights to challenge jurors and have little or no opportunity to ask them questions. Are you inclined to think that their system is better or worse? In federal court, Fed. R. Civ. P. 47(a) leaves to the judge's discretion whether to conduct examination of potential jurors herself or permit the parties or their attorneys to conduct the examination. Consider the results of at least one study, which indicates that the verdicts of juries selected according to the current procedure and those selected at random with no attorney input do not differ significantly. Valerie P. Hans and Neil Vidmar, *Judging the Jury* 90 (1986) (citing Hans Zeisel and Shari S. Diamond, *The Effect of Peremptory Challenges on Jury and Verdict: An Experiment in a Federal District Court*, 30 Stan. L. Rev. 491 (1978).)

3. Techniques for selecting jurors have become increasingly complex in the past decade or so, with an entire cottage industry of jury consultants available to clients with adequate means to pay for their services. Consider the following account, taken from Valerie P. Hans and Neil Vidmar's *Judging the Jury* and based on contemporary newspaper accounts. As you read it, think about the techniques M.C.I. used. Would justice be served by widespread use of such methods? What are the potential drawbacks, if any?

## ■VALERIE P. HANS AND NEIL VIDMAR, JUDGING THE JURY
### 79-80 (1986)

In June of 1980, after 15 weeks of testimony, a federal jury deciding an antitrust suit awarded M.C.I. Communications Corporation $600 million, to be paid by the American Telephone and Telegraph Company. Antitrust awards are automatically tripled for punitive purposes, which meant that M.C.I. was to receive the largest antitrust judgment ever—the stunning amount of $1.8 billion. Although the attorneys for the winning side were jubilant, they were not really surprised by the decision. Before the trial, they had engaged jury researchers who used sophisticated social science techniques to determine which jurors would be most favorable to M.C.I., and to predict how jurors would react to the evidence.

A Chicago research firm conducted a telephone poll of local residents and supplemented it by personal interviews. In their interview they asked questions designed to reveal whether the respondents, if they were jurors, would be likely to side with M.C.I. or AT&T. They also obtained the demographic characteristics of these individuals. With computer analyses of these responses, the researchers developed demographic profiles of people who were favorable and unfavorable to M.C.I.'s case, knowledge that would later be of benefit in selecting jurors for the trial.

Next, the firm paid individuals of varying sympathy toward M.C.I. to meet on three successive evenings. On each evening, a mock jury composed of eight of these individuals listened to M.C.I.'s attorneys present abbreviated versions of both M.C.I.'s and AT&T's sides of the dispute in a minitrial. The researchers and attorneys then watched the mock jurors deliberate on the case through a one-way mirror. What they learned from behind the one-way mirror affected how the attorneys presented their side before the real jury.

M.C.I. was suing AT&T for damages they alleged were due to AT&T's monopolistic practices. By law, AT&T was required to share its long lines with other communication companies, and this information was presented to the simulated juries. The first evening, from behind the one-way mirror, the observers watched while the mock jurors debated heatedly about the fairness of this law. After all, some jurors argued, why should AT&T have to share its lines with competitors if it owned the lines? The attorneys learned from their experiences. The next evening, they emphasized to the mock jury that they were to decide the M.C.I.-AT&T case according to the letter of the law, regardless of their personal views about its fairness. That night, the jurors did not have much trouble accepting the law.

Another lesson from the observations may have played a role in netting M.C.I. the largest antitrust award in history. In the first evening's presentation, the attorney representing M.C.I.'s side argued that M.C.I. had suffered $100 million in lost profit from AT&T's monopolistic behavior. The first mock jury decided in M.C.I.'s favor and awarded it exactly $100 million. Noting the similarity, the attorneys wondered what would happen if they avoided mentioning a specific figure. The next night they experimented, and left it to the jury's speculation how much AT&T had cost M.C.I. With no exact dollar amounts to guide or constrain them, the second mock jury's award was $900 million.

Thus, from the community surveys and the mock juries, the M.C.I. attorneys learned what kinds of jurors to look for and to eliminate during the selection process. They also obtained tactical clues about how to present their case to different types of individuals. Morton Hunt, a journalist who has written about the M.C.I. case, likened it to "putting juries on the couch." In a sense, though, in M.C.I.'s attempt to put its jury on the couch, the M.C.I. team was doing more precisely and with scientific assistance what lawyers have tried to do for centuries: stack the jury in their favor. The M.C.I. team may have been *too* successful. The jury award was judged to be excessive and on appeal it was overturned. A second jury evaluating the damages awarded M.C.I. only $37.8 million.

# ■ FEDERAL JURY SELECTION STATUTES

### 28 U.S.C. § 1861 Declaration of Policy

It is the policy of the United States that all litigants in Federal courts entitled to trial by jury shall have the right to grand and petit juries selected at random from a fair cross section of the community in the district or division wherein the court convenes. It is further the policy of the United States that all citizens shall have the opportunity to be considered for service on grand and petit juries in the district courts of the United States, and shall have an obligation to serve as jurors when summoned for that purpose.

### 28 U.S.C. § 1862 Exemptions

No citizen shall be excluded from service as a grand or petit juror in the district courts of the United States or in the Court of International Trade on account of race, color, religion, sex, national origin, or economic status.

### 28 U.S.C. § 1865 Qualification for Jury Service

(a) The chief judge of the district court, or such other district court judge as the plan may provide, on his initiative or upon recommendation of the clerk or jury commission, shall determine solely on the basis of information provided on the juror qualification form and other competent evidence whether a person is unqualified for, or exempt, or to be excused from jury service. The clerk shall enter such determination in the space provided on the juror qualification form and in any alphabetical list of names drawn from the master jury wheel. If a person did not appear in response to a summons, such fact shall be noted on said list.

(b) In making such determination the chief judge of the district court, or such other district court judge as the plan may provide, shall deem any person qualified to serve on grand and petit juries in the district court unless he—

(1) is not a citizen of the United States eighteen years old who has resided for a period of one year within the judicial district;

(2) is unable to read, write, and understand the English language with a degree of proficiency sufficient to fill out satisfactorily the juror qualification form;

(3) is unable to speak the English language;

(4) is incapable, by reason of mental or physical infirmity, to render satisfactory jury service; or

(5) has a charge pending against him for the commission of, or has been convicted in a State or Federal court of record of, a crime punishable by imprisonment for more than one year and his civil rights have not been restored.

## Comments and Questions

1. What is a "fair cross section of the community"? Should diversity be based on race and ethnicity, religion, age, gender, political views, or some other criteria? The most common method of juror selection is the use of voter registration lists covering the district or division in which the court resides. Does a collection of registered voters represent a "fair cross section of the community"? What groups might be excluded or underrepresented when jurors are drawn solely from voter registration lists?

2. The Supreme Court has ruled that the requirement of a "fair cross section of the community" applies only to the jury pool or panel as a whole, not to any one particular jury. What are the practical and philosophical reasons for such a distinction? What are its likely results?

## 2. Peremptory Challenges and Discrimination

Traditionally, attorneys have used their peremptory challenges to remove jurors on grounds that did not amount to "cause." These grounds range from "gut" feelings to the systematic exclusion of certain types of people. Clarence Darrow advised criminal defense lawyers to exclude women from juries; Melvin Belli, in contrast, suggests in his books on trial technique that the defense should seek to include women, because of their alleged "sympathy" for defendants. The most notorious uses of peremptories—to exclude members of a single race, ethnic group, or gender on the basis of often unproved assumptions and beliefs—have been under attack in recent years.

In *Batson v. Kentucky*, 476 U.S. 79 (1986), a criminal case, the Supreme Court ruled that the use of peremptory challenges by the government to systematically exclude black jurors violated the Fourteenth Amendment Equal Protection rights of a black defendant. Under *Batson* and its progeny, once the defendant makes a *prima facie* showing that the prosecution used peremptory challenges to exclude members of a particular racial or ethnic group from the jury, the burden shifts to the government to come forward with a race-neutral explanation for challenging the jurors.

In *Powers v. Ohio*, 499 U.S. 400 (1991), the Court extended the right to a white criminal defendant who protested the prosecution's exclusion of blacks from the jury. Several questions remained, however. One of the most pressing questions was, did the *Batson* rule apply to civil cases, where the government was not a litigant? The key doctrinal question revolved around the constitutional law concept of "state action." Under the Fourteenth Amendment, from which *Batson* and *Powers* rights are derived, only the government is prohibited from taking away an individual's equal protection of the law. Can private plaintiffs and defendants be characterized as "state actors" when they challenge jurors?

The *Batson* holding has been expanded by subsequent cases to include peremptory strikes in civil actions, *see, e.g., Edmonson v. Leesville Concrete*

*Co., Inc.*, 500 U.S. 614, 616, 618 (1991), and peremptory challenges based on gender, *see, e.g., J.E.B. v. Alabama ex rel. T.B.*, 511 U.S. 127, 128-129 (1994). In *Edmonson*, the majority found "state action" because peremptory challenges are sanctioned and administered by the courts. And in *J.E.B.*, Justice Blackmun held that gender discrimination in jury selection violates the Fourteenth Amendment and "causes harm to litigants, the community, and the individual jurors who are wrongfully excluded from participation in the judicial process." *Id.*, 511 U.S. at 140.

## Comments and Questions

1. Even in cases where the Seventh Amendment (or a state constitution) guarantees the right to jury trial in a particular case, both parties may waive the right and choose instead to try the case before a single judge. Fed. R. Civ. P. 38(b) requires a party with the right to try an issue to a jury to serve upon the other parties a written jury demand "no later than 10 days after the last pleading directed to the issue is served," and to file the demand in court in accordance with Rule 5(d). Otherwise, the right is waived. Fed. R. Civ. P. 38(d). (Recall that many lawyers put their demand in their complaint or answer in order not to waive their right by inadvertence.) In other words, the Seventh Amendment does not *require* jury trial in any civil case. Should it? Why or why not? Put another way: Whose right is it?

2. Although the Court in *Batson* relied on the rights of the criminal defendant to forbid racially based challenges, the *Edmonson* Court locates the rights in a different player. Whose rights are being protected in *Edmonson*? The results of the Court's *Batson* decision influenced the criminal arena as well. In *Georgia v. McCollum*, 505 U.S. 42 (1992), the Court extended *Batson* to allow the prosecution to assert the Equal Protection rights of the jurors against a criminal defendant who has excluded black jurors.

3. *Batson* articulated a three-part test to detect race-based uses of peremptory strikes; that test continues to be used today. First, the party opposing the strike must show that circumstances surrounding a particular strike permit an inference that the peremptory challenge was race-based. For instance, a party may satisfy the first part of the test by proving that the opposing party excluded all members of a cognizable racial group. Second, the burden shifts to the proponent of the challenge to provide a race-neutral reason for exercising the strike. If the prosecution satisfies this burden of production, third, it is then incumbent upon the party opposing the strike to prove to the court that use of the strike was motivated by purposeful discrimination. If the race-neutral reason for the striking of a juror applies equally to a juror who was impaneled, then this evidence of pretext can support a conclusion of purposeful discrimination. *See, e.g., Turner v. Marshall*, 121 F.3d 1248, 1251-1252 (9th Cir. 1997) (race-neutral reasons are pretextual when impaneled nonminority juror shared characteristics of struck minority juror).

4. In *Purkett v. Elem*, 514 U.S. 765 (1995), the majority held in a *per curiam* opinion (Justice Stevens, joined by Justice Breyer, dissenting) that a race-neutral explanation tendered by the proponent of a peremptory challenge need not be "persuasive, or even plausible." In this case, the prosecutor said that he challenged one black male because he "'had long curly hair, . . . the longest hair on anybody on the panel by far'" and "'he had a mustache and goatee type beard.'" He challenged a second black male because he "'also has a mustache and goatee type beard. Those are the only two people on the jury . . . with facial hair. . . . And I don't like the way they looked, with the way the hair is cut, both of them. And the mustaches and the beards look suspicious to me.'" He added that he feared that the second struck juror, who had had a sawed-off shotgun pointed at him during a supermarket robbery, would believe that "'to have a robbery you have to have a gun, and there is no gun in this case.'" The Supreme Court upheld the challenges, reversing the Court of Appeals for the Eighth Circuit, which had found that the prosecution's explanation for striking the first of the two black males was "pretextual." The Court stated that all that is required under the second step in *Batson* is a "legitimate reason . . . not a reason that makes sense, but a reason that does not deny equal protection."

Many have argued that *Batson*'s framework is fundamentally flawed—manifest in a lingering and tragic legacy that the courts almost never find purposeful discrimination. "[T]he *Batson* challenge process may allow the implicit biases of the judges and attorneys to go unchecked during jury selection. Thus, while judge-dominated voir dire may result in implicitly biased jurors deciding cases, the *Batson* challenge process may result in implicitly biased courtroom actors selecting jurors. In his concurring opinion in *Batson*, Justice Marshall foreshadowed the discovery of implicit bias, stating: 'A prosecutor's own conscious or unconscious racism may lead him easily to the conclusion that a prospective black juror is "sullen," or "distant," a characterization that would not have come to his mind if a white juror had acted identically. A judge's own conscious or unconscious racism may lead him to accept such an explanation as well supported. . . . Even if all parties approach the Court's mandate with the best of conscious intentions, that mandate requires them to confront and overcome their own racism on all levels—a challenge I doubt all of them can meet.' The promise of *Batson* remains illusory for two reasons in particular: trial judges are reluctant to doubt prosecutors' proffered reasons for their challenged strikes, and appellate courts are highly deferential to the trial courts' decisions on these matters. . . . Batson and its progeny appear to remain ineffective, despite the fact that other members of the Court have recognized the role of implicit bias in the legal system." Judge Mark W. Bennett, *Unraveling the Gordian Knot of Implicit Bias in Jury Selection: The Problems of Judge-Dominated Voir Dire, The Failed Promise of* Batson, *and Proposed Solutions*, 4 Harv. L. & Pol'y Rev. 149 (2010). Put more bluntly, "*Batson* is either a disingenuous charade or an ill-conceived sinkhole." Anthony Page, Batson's *Blind-Spot: Unconscious Stereotyping and the Peremptory Challenge*, 85 B.U. L. Rev. 155, 178-179 (2005).

5. Notwithstanding the Supreme Court's holding that racially based challenges are unconstitutional, empirical data indicate that people of color are underrepresented in both the jury pool and in the jury as finally constituted. Professor Deborah Ramirez has summarized the data and explained why it is disturbing:

> In judicial districts in which minorities comprise a relatively small percentage of the population, even a jury venire that fairly reflects the population of the district would produce some juries that contain no minority jurors. Furthermore, jury venires often do not fairly reflect the percentage of minorities in the general population, thereby exacerbating the problem. In both federal and state courts, in cities and towns across the nation, the percentage of minority jurors remains significantly lower than the percentage of minority adults living in the communities from which these jurors are selected.
>
> When a jury that is not racially mixed must pass judgment in a case involving minority defendants or victims, the fairness of its judgment is often met with skepticism, rightly or wrongly. Both minority defendants and victims, having experienced prejudice among citizens outside the courts, fear that prejudice may be carried into the jury room. They believe that some minority representation on the jury is critical to a fair outcome. As a result, the failure to secure a multiracial jury may diminish the credibility and legitimacy of the jury's verdict and, in certain highly publicized cases, shatter the public confidence needed to preserve peace following the verdict [citations omitted].

Deborah Ramirez, *The Mixed Jury and the Ancient Custom of Trial by Jury de Linguae: A History and a Proposal for Change*, 74 B.U. L. Rev. 777, 780-781 (1994).

There are many reasons why minorities are frequently underrepresented in both the jury pool and the jury. Local residency requirements and standards requiring the ability to read, write, speak, and understand English, or excluding members of the court or a law enforcement agency, can all be factors. The source lists, often reliant on voting lists, tip prospective jurors to the elderly, the relatively affluent, the self-employed, and government workers, and away from minorities, including blacks, Hispanics, and women. Those who frequently change residence, who often happen to be citizens of color, are less likely to register to vote. Even when other lists are used, such as driver's registration lists, the manner in which duplicate names remain can lead to underrepresentation. Some states have subjective tests, such as "good character," "sound judgment," "mentally sound," and "intelligence," that can result in discriminatory exclusion. Language requirements, lack of follow-up of qualification questionnaires sent to prospective jurors, and excuses from jury duty based on travel difficulties and the loss of wages are additional factors. Hiroshi Fukurai and Edgar W. Butler, *Sources of Racial Disenfranchisement in the Jury and Jury Selection System*, 13 Nat'l Black L.J. 238 (1994). The use of race-based peremptory challenges, hiding under the pretense of "neutral reasons," also may be a critical factor: "[A] statistical analysis of the results of federal lower court decisions . . . reveals that the federal courts rarely find *Batson* violations and overwhelmingly accept proffered 'neutral reasons.'" Jeffrey Brand, *The Supreme Court, Equal Protection, and Jury Selection: Denying That Race Still Matters*, 1994 Wis. L. Rev. 511, 584.

6. Professor Ramirez has explained that the problem of achieving juries with a diverse mix of participants is by no means a new one, and that "for 600 years English law used quotas to create mixed juries. Beginning in the Twelfth Century, the legal principle called *de medietate linguae* or 'the jury of the half tongue' guaranteed Jewish civil and criminal defendants in England that one-half of their jurors would be fellow Jews." Deborah Ramirez, *Affirmative Jury Selection: A Proposal to Advance Both the Deliberative Ideal and Jury Diversity*, 1998 U. Chi. Legal F. 161, 167-168 (citations omitted). Later, the same right was extended to alien merchants, "eventually becoming a right enjoyed by all aliens to a jury divided equally between English nationals and fellow countrymen. When the English colonized the New World, they brought with them this principle." *Id.* (Ramirez does not, however, propose quotas as a solution for achieving more diverse juries.)

7. Some suggestions to achieve interracial juries, especially when people of color are parties, are to (1) eliminate peremptory challenges; (2) treat challenges differently when they operate to the detriment of a minority group; (3) affirmatively add a quota of minorities to the jury pool or the jury; and (4) allow peremptory additions of each party's choice to the qualified jury pool from which the ultimate jury will be picked. In addition to the previously cited articles by Jeffrey Brand and Deborah Ramirez, see Albert W. Alschuler, *Racial Quotas and the Jury*, 44 Duke L.J. 704 (1995).

8. As mentioned above, judges can also have biases and prejudices that may be difficult or impossible to set aside. Justice Cardozo put it this way: "[E]very day there is borne in on me a new conviction of the inescapable relation between the truth without us and the truth within. The spirit of the age, as it is to each of us, is too often only the spirit of the group in which the accidents of birth or education or occupation or fellowship have given us a place. No effort or revolution of the mind will overthrow utterly and at all times the empire of these subconscious loyalties." Benjamin N. Cardozo, *The Nature of the Judicial Process* 174-175 (1921). Justice Holmes made a similar point: "What we most love and revere generally is determined by early associations. I love granite rocks and barberry bushes, no doubt because with them were my earliest joys that reach back through the past eternity of my life. But while one's experience thus makes certain preferences dogmatic for oneself, recognition of how they came to be so leaves one able to see that others, poor souls, may be equally dogmatic about something else. And this again means skepticism." Oliver Wendell Holmes, *Natural Law*, 32 Harv. L. Rev. 40, 41 (1918). The possibility that judges may be prone to outside pressures and inner prejudice may have become more pronounced in recent years as the judiciary has become noticeably polarized politically and as judicial elections have become more heated and expensive. *See, e.g., Fierce Campaigns Signal a New Era for State Courts—Escalating Cost of Races—Battles*

*for Ideological Control That Critics Call Damaging to Judges' Impartiality*, N.Y. Times, June 5, 2000, at A1, col. 3; and David Barnhizer, *"On the Make": Campaign Funding and the Corrupting of the American Judiciary*, 50 Cath. U. L. Rev. 361 (2001). Of course the politicization of the federal judicial appointments process is not a new phenomenon. Michael J. Gerhardt, *The Federal Appointments Process: A Constitutional and Historical Analysis* (2001). *See also* John S. Baker, Jr., *Ideology and the Confirmation of Federal Judges*, 43 S. Tex. L. Rev. 177 (2001).

That judges and other court personnel, let alone other lawyers, may be unable to put aside their prejudices with respect to race and gender is the topic of numerous state and federal court race and gender bias studies. *See, e.g.*, Todd D. Peterson, *Studying the Impact of Race and Ethnicity in the Federal Courts*, 64 Geo. Wash. L. Rev. 173, 178 (1996): "Forty-three percent of minority lawyers reported that they had been ignored or not listened to by a federal judge because of gender, race, or ethnicity, while only seven percent of white lawyers reported such experiences. Female minority litigators reported such experiences in even higher numbers. . . . Forty percent of African American respondents believed that they were at a disadvantage compared to white attorneys in a bench trial, while only two percent of white attorneys believed that African American litigators suffer such a disadvantage." (Citations omitted.) (This article describes a Federal D.C. Circuit Study and Report on Race and Ethnicity (which is reprinted in the same issue of the George Washington Law Review), and in note 4, page 174, lists a number of other court bias studies.) Here are conclusions of Massachusetts state court studies: "Minority attorneys often receive poor treatment from other attorneys, courtroom personnel and some judges because of their race and ethnicity. Such conduct ranges from a negative perception of the attorneys' professionalism to discourteous and discriminatory comments and actions." Commission to Study Racial and Ethnic Bias in the Courts, Massachusetts Supreme Judicial Court, Final Report, Equal Justice 117 (Sept. 1994): "Gender bias exists in many forms throughout the Massachusetts court system. Sexist language and behavior are still common. Beyond these overt signs of bias, many practices and procedures exist that may not appear motivated by bias but nonetheless produce biased results." *Report of the Gender Bias Study of The Supreme Judicial Court, Commonwealth of Massachusetts* 1 (1989).

9. *J.E.B. v. Alabama* prompts the question of what other groups should be entitled to *Batson* protection. In *Hernandez v. New York*, 500 U.S. 352 (1991), the Supreme Court found that peremptory challenges based on ethnic origin (the struck jurors were Hispanic) were illegal, but upheld challenges based on the prospective Spanish-speaking jurors' inability to reassure the prosecutor that they would rely solely on the English translations of testimony given in Spanish. A number of states have indicated that religion-based peremptories would violate state law. Some commentators (and at least one court) have taken the position that peremptory challenges based on disability also are illegal. *See* Andrew Weis, *Peremptory Challenges: The Last Barrier to Jury Service for People with Disabilities*, 33 Willamette L. Rev. 1 (Winter 1997);

and *People v. Green*, 561 N.Y.S.2d 130 (N.Y. Co. Ct. 1990) (involving challenges to deaf jurors). For contrary analyses, see *U.S. v. Harris*, 197 F.3d 870 (7th Cir. 1999) (peremptory challenge based on disability does not violate equal protection); *State v. Davis*, 504 N.W.2d 767 (Minn. 1993) (refusing to extend *Batson* to peremptory strikes based on religion).

One Florida judge warned that such inroads on the peremptory challenge mark "the beginning of the end of the unfettered use of the peremptory challenge. . . ." *Alen v. State*, 596 So. 2d 1083, 1086 (Fla. Dist. Ct. App. 1992). This judge predicted that the court's decision, which forbade discriminatory peremptory strikes against African Americans, would eventually extend to ban all forms of peremptory challenges, "whether based on race, ethnic origin, nationality, gender, religion, wealth, or age." *Id.* "[I]t seems obvious that the peremptory challenge system, as we know it, is totally doomed." *Id.* at 1087.

10. Perhaps the system is "doomed," but is it worth preserving? Perhaps we should "invent ways to achieve governmental purposes that do not deploy the group-based identities yet again." Martha Minow, *Not Only for Myself—Identity, Politics and the Law* (1997). One of Professor Minow's three examples is the elimination of peremptory challenges. Consider whether you are convinced by her argument, which follows:

> Several benefits could emerge from this elimination of the peremptory challenge. The messy administration of the Equal Protection challenges and the strategic gamesmanship surrounding jury selection would end, or at least be forced into the "for cause" exclusions, which require reasons and judicial approval. Eliminating peremptory challenges would reduce the parties' (and lawyers') abilities to shape the jury and seek to influence their results, which could both help but also significantly hurt members of disadvantaged groups. The very practice of trying to shape the jury through peremptory challenges has been deeply characterized by stereotypic predictions about how members of particular groups would respond to the topics on trial. Ending the peremptory challenge would, at least symbolically, rule all such thinking out of bounds, at least in this setting.
>
> Indeed, parties, and lawyers, commonly seek to remove jurors based on their group characteristics because they load many presumptions—and prejudices—onto those identities. The prosecution tries to exclude people who look like the defendant on the assumption of undue sympathy; the defense tries to exclude those whose racial and ethnic membership differs from that of the defendant. Why permit peremptory challenges that presume that people *cannot* empathize across lines of difference? Not only is such a rule untrue to human possibilities, it might also be a self-fulfilling prophecy.
>
> Eliminating peremptory challenges would not halt attention to group-based categories, for aggressive anti-discrimination enforcement would still be needed at the systemic levels defining the pool of available jurors and calling specific people to serve. Eliminating peremptory challenges would afford one way to restrict the use of governmentally imposed group-based categories while still achieving the underlying governmental purpose. It would send a signal that a practice must end if it plays into or reinforces group stereotyping.

*Id.* at 99-100.

11. What effect(s), if any, do you think the elimination of peremptory challenges would have on the behavior of lawyers, judges, and prospective jurors?

———————————————

Take a moment to assess your feelings about juries. The next subjects you will learn include the mechanisms by which a judge can take cases away from the jury at various points before, during, and after the trial. Try to evaluate these powerful jury-controlling tools in light of what you believe about the jury.

# D. SUMMARY JUDGMENT

The discussion in this chapter thus far has been about the role and composition of the American jury. The remainder of the chapter covers several judicial methods for controlling and limiting the power of the jury. Throughout this chapter, you will want to consider the advantages and disadvantages of each method and the extent to which they improve or hinder the benefits of jury trial.

Although our focus will frequently be on the relationship of these procedural steps to the right and substance of jury trial, you should keep in mind that some of the procedural incidents we discuss also apply to nonjury cases. For instance, summary judgment applies both to jury and nonjury cases. A motion for summary judgment is typically made after discovery and before trial. It might be helpful for you to familiarize yourself now with the rule governing summary judgment. *See* Fed. R. Civ. P. 56.

You can probably figure out on your own why the drafters of the Federal Rules made available a motion for summary judgment at a point after discovery and before trial.* Bear in mind that as originally construed, Rules 8(a) and 12(b)(6) made it relatively easy for a plaintiff to survive to the discovery stage. Charles Clark and his colleagues on the Advisory Committee did not think it made much sense to try to weed out many cases at the pleading stage. But since the pleadings alone would strain out few meritless cases, some mechanism was needed after discovery to weed out cases in which it was clear what the result at trial would be. It does not make sense to force the parties to try a case in which the result is a foregone conclusion. For instance, if you as a judge knew in a negligence case that the plaintiff was incapable of producing evidence at trial of unreasonable care, why put the parties and the

———————————————

*But the drafters probably did not think that summary judgment would be used frequently and in all types of cases. They were thinking in terms of the English experience in which summary judgment was used, in the words of Charles Clark, "as a simple and quick way of disposing of routine matters. Typically these are cases of debts or liquidated demands." *See* Stephen B. Burbank, *Vanishing Trials and Summary Judgment in Federal Civil Cases: Drifting Toward Bethlehem or Gomorrah,* 1 J. Emp. L. Stud. 591, 602 n.48 (2004).

court system to the expense of a trial? To put it another way, assume that you as a judge could predict with certainty that at the trial in a given case, a directed verdict (now called "judgment as a matter of law," Fed. R. Civ. P. 50(a)) would have to be granted in favor of the defendant because the plaintiff had not entered sufficient evidence to permit the jury to find one or more elements of the plaintiff's cause of action. Wouldn't it be both fair and efficient to enter a judgment prior to trial, rather than go through the time, expense, and anguish to the parties and witnesses (and the jurors) of a futile jury trial? (Rule 50(a), Judgment as a Matter of Law, is discussed in detail in a later section.)

But, as is typical in devising and interpreting procedures, there are dangers in whatever tack one takes. If it is too easy for a moving party to gain a judgment on what, after all, is only a prediction of what the evidence will be at trial, then the right to jury trial can be seriously impaired. If, on the other hand, courts are too reluctant to grant a summary judgment in cases that will later be determined by the granting of a directed verdict, it is wasteful to the parties and the public, and unfair to the party who ultimately wins. Even when there will be no jury, the judge considering a summary judgment motion must be careful not to deprive a party of what might have been a different result if witnesses had to appear before the judge in person, with the added formality of a full trial, cross-examination, and opening and closing arguments.

Four additional points bear mention. First, keep in mind the differences that a judge must consider among a 12(b)(6) motion, a motion for summary judgment, and a motion for a directed verdict. In a 12(b)(6), there exist only the *allegations* in the complaint. In summary judgment, the judge, in trying to predict what the *evidence* will be at trial, can consider the pleadings, affidavits, and discovery. (The mention of pleadings in Rule 56(c) is a bit misleading. Since, as you will see, the judge is trying to predict at the summary judgment stage what evidence will have been admitted by the time of a motion for directed verdict, a mere allegation in an unverified pleading would not aid a party trying to show that she will adduce evidence at the trial.) Unlike the 12(b)(6) motion (based on allegations alone) or the summary judgment motion (primarily based on affidavits and discovery), the directed verdict motion will be based on the evidence actually admitted at the trial (plus evidence taken to be true by virtue of admissions, stipulations, or otherwise).

Second, most motions for summary judgment or directed verdict that result in a final judgment for the moving party are motions made by the defendant. Can you see why? For a plaintiff to win at summary judgment, she would have to convince the judge that she will have admissible, persuasive, noncontroverted evidence to prove every element of her cause of action. In a negligence case, for example, a plaintiff moving for a summary judgment would have to persuade the judge through affidavits and discovery (and facts admitted by the defendant to be true) that reasonable people would have to believe that there was a duty, a breach of duty or unreasonable care, cause in

*[handwritten margin note: All the elements to prove negligence case]*

fact, proximate cause, and a certain amount of damages. The plaintiff moving for summary judgment would have to convince the judge that there was no credibility issue and no task to be performed by the jury on *any* of the elements. In short, the moving plaintiff would have to convince the judge that she has met both her production and persuasion burdens in a manner permitting no reasonable argument to the contrary. On the other hand, the defendant in a negligence case who seeks a summary judgment (or directed verdict) would have to poke a hole in only one of the elements, and as to that, she would have to show only that the plaintiff's production burden cannot be met. It is considerably easier to show a lack of potential evidence as to one element than to convince a judge that all elements must be taken as true.

Third, study the critical language in Rule 56(a), which states that the moving party is entitled to a summary judgment if the "movant shows that there is no genuine dispute as to any material fact and the movant is entitled to a judgment as a matter of law." The term *material fact* has a rather specialized meaning in this context—a meaning that embodies some notion of relevance, but goes beyond merely that. Let's say in the *Carpenter* case that genuine disputes exist as to unreasonable care, causation, and the amount of damages. But assume further that there is uncontroverted evidence leading to the inescapable conclusion that the statute of limitations has already run. If the defendant can persuade the judge at the summary judgment stage that, at a trial, it (the defendant) necessarily would win on this affirmative defense (in effect, a verdict would have to be directed on the statute of limitations in favor of the defendant), then this would render the issues of unreasonable care, causation, and the amount of damages "immaterial." Similarly, if a defendant convinces a judge that at trial the plaintiff will have no admissible evidence to permit a finding as to any one of the plaintiff's elements, that would render dispute as to facts with respect to any other element "immaterial."

*[handwritten margin note: If statute of lim wins & judge can give verdict then others are immaterial]*

Put another way, a judge could believe at the summary judgment stage that there are loads of disputed facts (as to the color of the jeep, the sobriety of the driver, the amount of damages), but if the plaintiff still will have to lose because of a failure of evidence as to one element (or if an affirmative defense must be taken as true), that renders all other disputes immaterial. In these instances, summary judgment should be granted even though there are disputes of fact; summary judgment would be appropriate because there is no genuine dispute as to any *material* fact.

Fourth, it is a bit awkward conceptually when the moving party at summary judgment is not the party with the burden of production and persuasion at the trial. Regrettably, this is in fact the typical situation: The defendant has the burden of convincing the judge to grant a summary judgment motion based on the argument that the plaintiff will have an insufficiency of evidence to meet its production burden on at least one element at the trial. In these cases, the moving party (the defendant) has a positive burden to do something to win on the motion, but it is with respect to a negative, to wit: that the plaintiff lacks the evidence to survive a directed verdict. What *exactly* the movant-defendant must show has been the subject of much litigation. For example, if there has been no discovery at all, can the defendant merely move for summary judgment (and do nothing more), thus forcing the plaintiff to reveal the supporting evidence for each element of plaintiff's case? Or, at the other extreme, must the defendant demonstrate not only that the plaintiff has no evidence of a particular element but also that such evidence could not exist? The significance of these two different interpretations is evident in the fact patterns of the *Adickes* and *Celotex* cases that follow: does the absence of evidence to support one of the elements of the plaintiff's case necessarily mean that summary judgment should enter? Since *Adickes* and *Celotex*, Rule 56 was amended to address this issue—at least in part. Read 56(c)(1)(A) & (B).

## 1. An Extraordinary Remedy

The first case you will read is *Adickes v. S.H. Kress & Co.* Note that there is historical background on this case following the opinion. Some students may prefer to read the history first.

## ■ADICKES v. S. H. KRESS & CO.
### 398 U.S. 144 (1970)

Justice HARLAN delivered the opinion of the Court:
Petitioner, Sandra Adickes, a white school teacher from New York, brought this suit in the United States District Court for the Southern District of New York against respondent S. H. Kress & Co. ("Kress") to recover damages under 42 U.S.C. § 1983 for an alleged violation of her constitutional rights under the Equal Protection Clause of the Fourteenth Amendment. The suit arises out of Kress' refusal to serve lunch to Miss Adickes at its restaurant facilities in its Hattiesburg, Mississippi, store on August 14, 1964, and Miss Adickes' subsequent arrest upon her departure from the store by the Hattiesburg police on a charge of vagrancy. At the time of both the refusal to serve and the arrest, Miss Adickes was with six young people, all Negroes, who were her students in a Mississippi "Freedom School" where she was teaching that summer. Unlike Miss Adickes, the students were offered service, and were not arrested.

Petitioner's complaint had two counts, each bottomed on § 1983, and each alleging that Kress had deprived her of the right under the Equal Protection Clause of the Fourteenth Amendment not to be discriminated against on the basis of race. The first count charged that Miss Adickes had been refused service by Kress because she was a "Caucasian in the company of Negroes." Petitioner sought, inter alia, to prove that the refusal to serve her was pursuant to a "custom of the community to segregate the races in public eating places." However, in a pretrial decision, 252 F. Supp. 140 (1966), the District Court ruled that to recover under this court, Miss Adickes would have to prove that at the time she was refused service, there was a specific "custom ... of refusing service to whites in the company of Negroes" and that this custom was "enforced by the State" under Mississippi's criminal trespass statute. Because petitioner was unable to prove at the trial that there were other instances in Hattiesburg of a white person having been refused service while in the company of Negroes, the District Court directed a verdict in favor of respondent. A divided panel of the Court of Appeals affirmed on this ground, also holding that § 1983 "requires that the discriminatory custom or usage be proved to exist in the locale where the discrimination took place, and in the State generally," and that petitioner's "proof on both points was deficient."

The second count of her complaint, alleging that both the refusal of service and her subsequent arrest were the product of a conspiracy between Kress and the Hattiesburg police, was dismissed before trial on a motion for summary judgment. The District Court ruled that petitioner had "failed to allege any facts from which a conspiracy might be inferred." 252 F. Supp., at 144. This determination was unanimously affirmed by the Court of Appeals, 409 F.2d, at 126-127.

Miss Adickes, in seeking review here, claims that the District Court erred both in directing a verdict on the substantive count, and in granting summary judgment on the conspiracy count. Last Term we granted certiorari, 394 U.S. 1011 (1969), and we now reverse and remand for further proceedings on each of the two counts.

As explained in Part I, because the respondent failed to show the absence of any disputed material fact, we think the District Court erred in granting summary judgment. With respect to the substantive count, for reasons explained in Part II, we think petitioner will have made out a claim under § 1983 for violation of her equal protection rights if she proves that she was refused service by Kress because of a state-enforced custom requiring racial segregation in Hattiesburg restaurants. We think the courts below erred (1) in assuming that the only proof relevant to showing that a custom was state-enforced related to the Mississippi criminal trespass statute; (2) in defining the relevant state-enforced custom as requiring proof of a practice both in Hattiesburg and throughout Mississippi, of refusing to serve white persons in the company of Negroes rather than simply proof of state-enforced segregation of the races in Hattiesburg restaurants.

## I

Briefly stated, the conspiracy count of petitioner's complaint made the following allegations: While serving as a volunteer teacher at a "Freedom School" for Negro children in Hattiesburg, Mississippi, petitioner went with six of her students to the Hattiesburg Public Library at about noon on August 14, 1964. The librarian refused to allow the Negro students to use the library, and asked them to leave. Because they did not leave, the librarian called the Hattiesburg chief of police who told petitioner and her students that the library was closed, and ordered them to leave. From the library, petitioner and the students proceeded to respondent's store where they wished to eat lunch. According to the complaint, after the group sat down to eat, a policeman came into the store "and observed [Miss Adickes] in the company of the Negro students." A waitress then came to the booth where petitioner was sitting, took the orders of the Negro students, but refused to serve petitioner because she was a white person "in the company of Negroes." The complaint goes on to allege that after this refusal of service, petitioner and her students left the Kress store. When the group reached the sidewalk outside the store, "the Officer of the Law who had previously entered [the] store" arrested petitioner on a groundless charge of vagrancy and took her into custody.

On the basis of these underlying facts petitioner alleged that Kress and the Hattiesburg police had conspired (1) "to deprive [her] of her right to enjoy equal treatment and service in a place of public accommodation"; and (2) to cause her arrest "on the false charge of vagrancy."

## A. CONSPIRACIES BETWEEN PUBLIC OFFICIALS AND PRIVATE PERSONS—GOVERNING PRINCIPLES

The terms of § 1983 make plain two elements that are necessary for recovery. First, the plaintiff must prove that the defendant has deprived him of a right secured by the "Constitution and laws" of the United States. Second, the plaintiff must show that the defendant deprived him of this constitutional right "under color of any statute, ordinance, regulation, custom, or usage, of any State or Territory." This second element requires that the plaintiff show that the defendant acted "under color of law."

As noted earlier we read both counts of petitioner's complaint to allege discrimination based on race in violation of petitioner's equal protection rights. Few principles of law are more firmly stitched into our constitutional fabric than the proposition that a State must not discriminate against a person because of his race or the race of his companions, or in any way act to compel or encourage racial segregation. Although this is a lawsuit against a private party, not the State or one of its officials, our cases make clear that petitioner will have made out a violation of her Fourteenth Amendment rights and will be entitled to relief under § 1983 if she can prove that a Kress employee, in the course of employment, and a Hattiesburg policeman somehow reached an understanding to deny Miss Adickes service in the Kress store, or to cause her subsequent arrest because she was a white person in the company of Negroes.

The involvement of a state official in such a conspiracy plainly provides the state action essential to show a direct violation of petitioner's Fourteenth Amendment equal protection rights, whether or not the actions of the police were officially authorized, or lawful; [citations omitted]. Moreover, a private party involved in such a conspiracy, even though not an official of the State, can be liable under § 1983. "Private persons, jointly engaged with state officials in the prohibited action, are acting 'under color' of law for purposes of the statute. To act 'under color' of law does not require that the accused be an officer of the State. It is enough that he is a willful participant in joint activity with the State or its agents," *United States v. Price*, 383 U.S. 787, 794 (1966).

## B. SUMMARY JUDGMENT

We now proceed to consider whether the District Court erred in granting summary judgment on the conspiracy count. In granting respondent's motion, the District Court simply stated that there was "no evidence in the complaint or in the affidavits and other papers from which a 'reasonably-minded person' might draw an inference of conspiracy," 252 F. Supp., at 144, *aff'd*, 409 F.2d at 126-127. Our own scrutiny of the factual allegations of petitioner's complaint, as well as the material found in the affidavits and depositions presented by Kress to the District Court, however, convinces us that summary judgment was improper here, for we think respondent failed to carry its burden of showing the absence of any genuine issue of fact. Before explaining why this is so, it is useful to state the factual arguments, made by the parties concerning summary judgment, and the reasoning of the courts below.

In moving for summary judgment, Kress argued that "uncontested facts" established that no conspiracy existed between any Kress employee and the police. To support this assertion, Kress pointed first to the statements in the deposition of the store manager (Mr. Powell) that (a) he had not communicated with the police,[8] and that (b) he had, by a prearranged tacit signal,[9] ordered the food counter supervisor to see that Miss Adickes was refused service only because he was fearful of a riot in the store by customers angered at seeing a "mixed group" of whites and blacks eating together.[10] Kress also

8. In his deposition, Powell admitted knowing Hugh Herring, chief of police of Hattiesburg, and said that he had seen and talked to him on two occasions in 1964 prior to the incident with Miss Adickes. (App. 123-126). When asked how often the arresting officer, Ralph Hillman, came into the store, Powell stated that he didn't know precisely but "Maybe every day." However, Powell said that on August 14 he didn't recall seeing any policemen either inside or outside the store (App. 136), and he denied (1) that he had called the police, (2) that he had agreed with any public official to deny Miss Adickes the use of the library, (3) that he had agreed with any public official to refuse Miss Adickes service in the Kress store on the day in question, or (4) that he had asked any public official to have Miss Adickes arrested. App. 154-155.

9. The signal, according to Powell, was a nod of his head. Powell claimed that at a meeting about a month earlier with Miss Baggett, the food counter supervisor, he "told her not to serve the white person in the group if I . . . shook my head no. But, if I didn't give her any sign, to go ahead and serve anybody." App. 135. Powell stated that he had prearranged this tacit signal with Miss Baggett because "there was quite a lot of violence . . . in Hattiesburg" directed towards whites "with colored people, in what you call a mixed group." App. 131.

10. Powell described the circumstances of his refusal as follows: "On this particular day, just shortly after 12 o'clock, I estimate there was 75 to 100 people in the store, and the lunch counter was pretty—was pretty well to capacity there, full, and I was going up towards the front of the store in one of the aisles, and looking towards the front of the store, and there was a group of colored girls, and a white woman who came into the north door, which was next to the lunch counter. And the one thing that really stopped me and called my attention to this group, was the fact that they were dressed alike. They all had on, what looked like a light blue denim skirt. And the best I can remember is that they were—they were almost identical, all of them. And they came into the door, and people coming in stopped to look, and they went on to the booths. And there happened to be two empty there. And one group of them and the white woman sat down in one, and the rest of them sat in the second group. And, almost immediately there—I mean this, it didn't take just a few seconds from the time they came into the door to sit down, but, already the people began to mill around the store and started coming over towards the lunch counter. And, by that time I was up close to the

relied on affidavits from the Hattiesburg chief of police,[11] and the two arresting officers,[12] to the effect that store manager Powell had not requested that petitioner be arrested. Finally, Kress pointed to the statements in petitioner's own deposition that she had no knowledge of any communication between any Kress employee and any member of the Hattiesburg police, and was relying on circumstantial evidence to support her contention that there was an arrangement between Kress and the police.

Petitioner, in opposing summary judgment, pointed out that respondent had failed in its moving papers to dispute the allegation in petitioner's complaint, a statement at her deposition,[13] and an unsworn statement by a Kress employee,[14] all to the effect that there was a policeman in the store at the time of the refusal to serve her, and that this was the policeman who subsequently arrested her. Petitioner argued that although she had no knowledge of an agreement between Kress and the police, the sequence of events created a

---

candy counter, and I had a wide open view there. And the people had real sour looks on their faces, nobody was joking, or being corny, or carrying on. They looked like a frightened mob. They really did. I have seen mobs before. I was in Korea during the riots in 1954 and 1955. And I know what they are. And this actually got me. I looked out towards the front, and we have what they call see-through windows. There is no backs to them. You can look out of the store right into the street. And the north window, it looks right into the lunch counter. 25 or 30 people were standing there looking in, and across the street even, in a jewelry store, people were standing there, and it looked really bad to me. It looked like one person could have yelled 'Let's get them,' which has happened before, and cause this group to turn into a mob. And, so, quickly I just made up my mind to avoid the riot, and protect the people that were in the store, and my employees, as far as the people in the mob who were going to get hurt themselves. I just knew that something was going to break loose there." App. 133-134.

11. The affidavit of the chief of police, who it appears was not present at the arrest, states in relevant part: "Mr. Powell had made no request of me to arrest Miss Sandra Adickes or any other person, in fact, I did not know Mr. Powell personally until the day of this statement. (*But cf.* Powell's statement at his deposition, n.8, *supra.*) Mr. Powell and I had not discussed the arrest of this person until the day of this statement and we had never previously discussed her in any way." (App. 107.)

12. The affidavits of Sergeant Boone and Officer Hillman each state, in identical language: "I was contacted on this date by Mr. John H. Williams, Jr., a representative of Genesco, owners of S. H. Kress and Company, who requested that I make a statement concerning alleged conspiracy in connection with the aforesaid arrest. This arrest was made on the public streets of Hattiesburg, Mississippi, and was an officers discretion arrest. I had not consulted with Mr. G. T. Powell, Manager of S. H. Kress and Company in Hattiesburg, and did not know his name until this date. No one at the Kress store asked that the arrest be made and I did not consult with anyone prior to the arrest." (App. 110, 112.)

13. When asked whether she saw any policeman in the store up to the time of the refusal of service, Miss Adickes answered: "My back was to the door, but one of my students saw a policeman come in." (App. 75.) She went on to identify the student as "Carolyn." At the trial, Carolyn Moncure, one of the students who was with petitioner, testified that "about five minutes" after the group had sat down and while they were still waiting for service, she saw a policeman come in the store. She stated: "(H)e came in the store, my face was facing the front of the store, and he came in the store and he passed, and he stopped right at the end of our booth, and he stood up and he looked around and he smiled, and he went to the back of the store, he came right back and he left out." (App. 302.) This testimony was corroborated by that of Dianne Moncure, Carolyn's sister, who was also part of the group. She testified that while the group was waiting for service, a policeman entered the store, stood "for awhile" looking at the group, and then "walked to the back of the store." (App. 291.)

14. During discovery, respondent gave to petitioner an <u>unsworn</u> statement by Miss Irene Sullivan, a check-out girl. In this statement Miss Sullivan said that she had seen Patrolman Hillman come into the store "(s)hortly after 12:00 noon," while petitioner's group was in the store. She said that he had traded a "hello greeting" with her, and then walked past her check-out counter toward the back of the store "out of (her) line of vision." She went on: "A few minutes later Patrolman Hillman left our store by the northerly front door just slightly ahead of a group composed of several Negroes accompanied by a white woman. As Hillman stepped onto the sidewalk outside our store the police car pulled across the street and into an alley that is alongside our store. The police car stopped and Patrolman Hillman escorted the white woman away from the Negroes and into the police car." (App. 178.)

substantial enough possibility of a conspiracy to allow her to proceed to trial, especially given the fact that the noncircumstantial evidence of the conspiracy could only come from adverse witnesses. Further, she submitted an affidavit specifically disputing the manager's assertion that the situation in the store at the time of the refusal was "explosive," thus creating an issue of fact as to what his motives might have been in ordering the refusal of service.

We think that on the basis of this record, it was error to grant summary judgment. As the moving party, respondent had the burden of showing the absence of a genuine issue as to any material fact, and for these purposes the material it lodged must be viewed in the light most favorable to the opposing party. Respondent here did not carry its burden because of its failure to foreclose the possibility that there was a policeman in the Kress store while petitioner was awaiting service, and that this policeman reached an understanding with some Kress employee that petitioner not be served.

It is true that Mr. Powell, the store manager, claimed in his deposition that he had not seen or communicated with a policeman prior to his tacit signal to Miss Baggett, the supervisor of the food counter. But respondent did not submit any affidavits from Miss Baggett,[16] or from Miss Freeman,[17] the waitress who actually refused petitioner service, either of whom might well have seen and communicated with a policeman in the store. Further, we find it particularly noteworthy that the two officers involved in the arrest each failed in his affidavit to foreclose the possibility (1) that he was in the store while petitioner was there; and (2) that, upon seeing petitioner with Negroes, he communicated his disapproval to a Kress employee, thereby influencing the decision not to serve petitioner.

Given these unexplained gaps in the materials submitted by respondent, we conclude that respondent failed to fulfill its initial burden of demonstrating what is a critical element in this aspect of the case—that there was no policeman in the store. If a policeman were present, we think it would be open to a jury, in light of the sequence that followed, to infer from the circumstances that the policeman and a Kress employee had a "meeting of the minds" and thus reached an understanding that petitioner should be refused service. Because "[o]n summary judgment the inferences to be drawn from the underlying facts contained in [the moving party's] materials must be viewed in the light most favorable to the party opposing the motion," *United*

---

16. In a supplemental brief filed in this Court respondent lodged a copy of an unsworn statement by Miss Baggett denying any contact with the police on the day in question. Apart from the fact that the statement is unsworn, *see* Fed. R. Civ. P. 56(e), the statement itself is not in the record of the proceedings below and therefore could not have been considered by the trial court. Manifestly, it cannot be properly considered by us in the disposition of the case. During discovery, petitioner attempted to depose Miss Baggett. However, Kress successfully resisted this by convincing the District Court that Miss Baggett was not a "managing agent," and "was without power to make managerial decisions."

17. The record does contain an unsworn statement by Miss Freeman in which she states that she "did not contact the police or ask anyone else to contact the police to make the arrest which subsequently occurred." (App. 177.) (Emphasis added.) This statement, being unsworn, does not meet the requirements of Fed. R. Civ. P. 56(e), and was not relied on by respondent in moving for summary judgment. Moreover, it does not foreclose the possibility that Miss Freeman was influenced in her refusal to serve Miss Adickes by some contact with a policeman present in the store.

*States v. Diebold, Inc.*, 369 U.S. 654, 655 (1962), we think respondent's failure to show there was no policeman in the store requires reversal.

Pointing to Rule 56(e),* as amended in 1963,[18] respondent argues that it was incumbent on petitioner to come forward with an affidavit properly asserting the presence of the policeman in the store, if she were to rely on that fact to avoid summary judgment. Respondent notes in this regard that none of the materials upon which petitioner relied met the requirements of Rule 56(e).

This argument does not withstand scrutiny, however, for both the commentary on and background of the 1963 amendment conclusively show that it was not intended to modify the burden of the moving party under Rule 56(c) to show initially the absence of a genuine issue concerning any material fact. The Advisory Committee note on the amendment states that the changes were not designed to "affect the ordinary standards applicable to the summary judgment." And, in a comment directed specifically to a contention like respondent's, the Committee stated that "[w]here the evidentiary matter in support of the motion does not establish the absence of a genuine issue, summary judgment must be denied even if no opposing evidentiary matter is presented." Because respondent did not meet its initial burden of establishing the absence of a policeman in the store, petitioner here was not required to come forward with suitable opposing affidavits.

If respondent had met its initial burden by, for example, submitting affidavits from the policemen denying their presence in the store at the time in question, Rule 56(e) would then have required petitioner to have done more than simply rely on the contrary allegation in her complaint. To have avoided conceding this fact for purposes of summary judgment, petitioner would have had to come forward with either (1) the affidavit of someone who saw the policeman in the store or (2) an affidavit under Rule 56(f) explaining why at that time it was impractical to do so. Even though not essential here to defeat respondent's motion, the submission of such an affidavit would have been the preferable course for petitioner's counsel to have followed. As one commentator has said: "It has always been perilous for the opposing party neither to proffer any countering evidentiary materials nor file a 56(f) affidavit. And the peril rightly continues (after the amendment to Rule 56(e)). Yet the party moving for summary judgment has the burden to show that he is entitled to judgment under established principles; and if he does not discharge that burden then he is not entitled to judgment. No defense to an insufficient showing is required." 6 James Moore, *Federal Practice*, 6.22(2), pp. 2824-2825 (2d ed. 1966). . . .

---

*Eds.' Note:* Rule 56 has been amended slightly and restyled considerably since 1970. Much of what was once in 56(c) and (e) is in the contemporary 56(a) and (c). And the contemporary 56(d) includes much of the prior 56(f).

18. The amendment added the following to Rule 56(e): "When a motion for summary judgment is made and supported as provided in this rule, an adverse party may not rest upon the mere allegations or denials of his pleading, but his response, by affidavits or as otherwise provided in this rule, must set forth specific facts showing that there is a genuine issue for trial. If he does not so respond, summary judgment, if appropriate, shall be entered against him."

[We have omitted Part II of Justice Harlan's opinion, which addresses the meaning of "custom" for purposes of § 1983 and the substance of the alleged Fourteenth Amendment violation. We also have omitted Justice Black's concurring opinion; the opinion of Justice Douglas, dissenting in part; and the opinion of Justice Brennan, concurring in part and dissenting in part.]

---

As you read the historical background that follows, consider whether it helps explain this case. This background may also be relevant in helping you reconcile *Adickes* with *Celotex*, which follows this historical account.

## Background of Adickes v. S. H. Kress & Co.*

In Mississippi in 1964, no one could have foreseen that this story—among all that was happening—would have such a profound effect. Mississippi was a state at war with itself. In the four months after Sandra Adickes arrived in Mississippi, three persons would be killed, "80 beaten, three wounded by gunfire in 35 shootings, more than 1,000 arrested, 35 Negro churches burned . . . and 31 homes and other buildings bombed. In addition [there would be] several unsolved murders of Negroes that may have been connected with the racial conflict." John Herbers, *Communique from the Mississippi Front*, N.Y. Times Mag., Oct. 8, 1964, at 34.

Barely a year before, federal troops had faced down a mob of armed whites as James Meredith became the first black to register at the University of Mississippi. In the ensuing disturbance, two journalists were killed.

Black rhetoric, though mild compared to what would follow in the late 1960s, had taken on an undertone of violence. Pulitzer Prize winner Hodding Carter wrote, "Attitudes on both sides have been hardening. A fatalistic belief in an eventual and inevitable showdown has animated many members of both races. . . . The hatred of the Negro for the white man is stark, naked and openly expressed to anyone to whom a Negro is willing to talk." Hodding Carter, *Mississippi Now—Hate and Fear*, N.Y. Times Mag., June 23, 1963, at 11, 24. Mississippians feared race riots like those that had occurred in Washington, New York, Chicago, and Detroit.

Frightened by unprecedented black militancy, whites girded themselves for war. Rumors flew. It was said that black men, designated with white Band-Aids on their throats, had been assigned to rape white women; black cooks were poisoning the food at local restaurants; black maids had been instructed to harass their white mistresses by hiding valuables so that their owners would briefly be terrified that they had been stolen.

*Thanks to Joel Rosen, a 1994 graduate of Northeastern University School of Law, for research and writing. Mr. Rosen was an editor at *Boston Magazine* and a columnist for the *Lawrence Eagle Tribune*. Mr. Rosen was a partner at Metaxas, Norman & Pidgeon, before starting his own firm in 2007, Rosen Law Office, in Andover, Massachusetts.

The whites' response was terrible. Medgar Evers, the Mississippi-born field secretary for the National Association for the Advancement of Colored People (NAACP) was shot to death in an ambush. The Ku Klux Klan "airforce" used light planes to drop bombs on black churches and meeting places. Others drove by in cars, spraying community centers with a hail of bullets. In the arrest of men accused of bombing black homes in southwestern Mississippi, police uncovered a cache of high-powered rifles, carbines and pistols, dynamite bombs, several thousand rounds of ammunition, hand grenades, clubs, and blackjacks.

Northern liberals, seeking to help African Americans join the mainstream of the country, concentrated on two areas. One was the overthrow of segregation imposed by Mississippi law. The other was to get blacks to vote.

Voter registration was the most obvious and immediate means of power sharing. The 900,000 blacks in Mississippi made up 42 percent of the state's population; their potential political power was enormous. Getting them to seize that power, however, was difficult in the face of white resistance. Blacks, dependent on whites for jobs, were afraid to risk their survival by antagonizing the power structure. Behind the threat of starvation loomed that of violence.

As if these barriers to participation were not enough, the state required that prospective voters be of "good moral character," pass a literacy test, and interpret two sections of the state constitution. Robert Kennedy's Justice Department challenged these arbitrary testing procedures as discriminatory, particularly as applied to uneducated blacks. But in March, 1964, a federal court upheld the constitutionality of those laws. Clearly, then, if black voters were to be registered, they must first be educated.

The two-tiered program of education and registration was the goal of the Freedom Schools, a project underwritten by the Council of Federated Organizations (COFO) and run by a Yale historian named Staughton Lynd. COFO set up forty-seven schools throughout Mississippi in churches, dance halls, and panel trucks. They were a welcome supplement to the sixth-grade education of the average Mississippi black. The black schools were typically underfunded, and black children were expected to help pay for their education by spending one day a year picking cotton.

The Freedom Schools were ad hoc gatherings that specialized in African-American history and American government. They allowed a free range of ideas, and classes discussed topics like skepticism, power sharing, and the right to vote. Teachers and students canvassed the black neighborhoods, signing up voters and talking about new ideas. Predictably, the white reaction to these schools was sometimes deprecatory, sometimes violent. *See* Pat Waters, *Their Text Is a Civil Rights Primer*, N.Y. Times Mag., Dec. 20, 1964, at 44.

In the early months of 1964, Sandra Adickes was in New York, training for her work at the Freedom Schools. She learned that she would not be merely making lesson plans and teaching classes. Rather, she would live among the poor blacks and participate in the life of their community. "If we were called upon to chop cotton, if that is the thing people did in the community, and we wanted to be good Freedom School teachers, that . . . is what we would do." Brief for Petitioner (*Adickes v. Kress*) at 44. The trainees were instructed never to resist arrest, never to provoke incidents. "If we were insulted we were . . . not to respond to abuse. . . . We were advised not to travel alone, so in case one of us is arrested, the other could at least report, or if we were both arrested . . . we would offer some sort of comfort to each other." *Id.* at 50. Adickes had no illusions about how white Mississippians would see the Freedom School teachers. "They think of themselves as God-fearing, law-abiding, good citizens, and you are atheists and communists, and you are there to . . . destroy their way of life." *Id.* at 51.

On July 4, two days after Congress passed the Civil Rights Act of 1964, Sandra Adickes left New York for a Freedom School in Hattiesburg, Mississippi.

Hattiesburg, the seat of Forrest County, was a city of 35,000, largely black. Civil rights leaders had targeted the city for voter-registration efforts. The city stepped up harassment of the Northern agitators. In March, ten clergymen were arrested and fined in the registration drive. In May, another seven demonstrators were arrested for unlawful picketing. On July 10, a rabbi and two other whites were beaten by segregationists. By then, Sandra Adickes had finished her orientation and begun teaching at the local Freedom School.

Adickes lived with a black family in Palmer's Crossing, a rural, black community on the outskirts of Hattiesburg. She joined approximately seven other teachers at the Priest Creek Baptist Church, instructing eighty African-American students in The History of the American Negro, American Social Ideals, and Current Events, including the passage of the 1964 Civil Rights Act.

In early August, the class was discussing what new freedoms the Civil Rights Act provided. The conversation turned to immediate, simple freedoms. What the students really wanted was to go to the Holiday Inn, the white schools, the public library, and the movies. Only one movie theater had admitted blacks until that time, and that was in a small roped-off section. Some of the students said that since the Civil Rights Act had passed, they had eaten at lunch counters at local Woolworth and Kress department stores but that service had been deliberately slow and other customers had insulted them while they were eating. The class was determined to go on a simple field trip, to a place to which they had never been admitted, although their parents paid taxes to support it: the Hattiesburg Public Library. Then they would have lunch.

Adickes, along with five black girls and one boy, took the bus from Palmer's Crossing into the white section of town and walked to the library. A young woman at the desk was on the phone when the group walked in. She hung up, buzzed her supervisor, and then turned to the members of the group, who were asking for library cards. "We are not giving any cards right now," she said.

The supervisor arrived and suggested that the children try a branch of the library that served blacks. The students replied that they had been there, but the branch did not have the books they wanted. The supervisor told the students that she was a Yankee and was sympathetic to their cause; in fact she had tried to get the trustees to integrate the library. The trustees, she said, had told her they would close the library if that were to happen. Didn't the students agree that a segregated library was better than no library at all?

When it turned out that the students did not agree, the librarian said, "Close your mouths and open your minds." Finally, this sympathetic Yankee threw up her hands. "I can't make you go," she said, "but if you insist on staying, I will have to close the library and call the police."

The party refused. In several minutes the chief of police arrived and closed the library.

Following this object lesson on the effect of federal law on their everyday civil rights, the party decided to have lunch. They started for the lunch counter at Woolworth's, but when that was crowded, they decided on the nearby S. H. Kress store. While the group waited for a table, Hattiesburg patrolman Ralph Hillman entered the store and then left. A waitress then took the students' orders for hamburgers and Cokes. Adickes asked if the waitress had forgotten about her.

"No," the waitress said, "I am not serving you."

Adickes asked why.

"We have to serve Negroes," the waitress said, "but we are not serving whites who come in with them."

"Do you realize," asked Adickes, continuing the civics lesson, "this is a violation of the Civil Rights Bill [sic]?"

The waitress said she was acting under orders from her manager, Mr. G. T. Powell, who later testified that he gave those orders because he feared the "explosive situation" in the store.

The group left without eating. As Adickes stepped out onto the sidewalk, a police car pulled out of an alley and stopped on the street in front of her. In it were patrolman Hillman and a sergeant. They arrested her on a charge of vagrancy. Adickes had over fifty dollars with her and had a job making $2,200 a year as a New York City schoolteacher. She did not fit the definition of a vagrant who is "without regular employment or any visible means of support," and told the officers so. One replied, "We have orders to pick you up." Then he took her arm, saying, "Don't resist," and she got into the back of the cruiser.

On the way down, one of the officers taunted her, asking repeatedly, "Are you a nigger? You with the Liberace glasses, are you a nigger?"

The ride took five minutes, after which she was booked, fingerprinted, and placed in a cell. After about an hour, three lawyers came down to bail her out.

Adickes did not take the case to trial again after the Supreme Court decision in her favor.

Sandra Adickes did not drop out of the legal limelight, though. She turned up again in federal court against New York City in 1969. The suit involved a scuffle during a teachers' strike in which she allegedly kicked a policeman in the groin. When she was arrested for interfering with the arrest of another teacher, she sued the city, also under 42 U.S.C. § 1983, for depriving her of her constitutional provision for such a right. Adickes did not win.

## Comments and Questions

1. During the era of *Adickes*, summary judgment was often referred to as an "extraordinary remedy"—one that should be granted only when there was not the "slightest doubt" as to the actual facts. *See, e.g., Tomalewski v. State Farm Life Ins. Co.*, 494 F.2d 882 (3d Cir. 1974); *Clausen & Sons, Inc. v. Hamm Brewing Co.*, 395 F.2d 388 (8th Cir. 1968). It was extraordinary because the court was taking a case away from the jury.

2. Consider the questions presented in *Adickes* from a normative perspective. *Should* Adickes be able to present her claim to a jury? *Should* a jury be able to find that there existed a conspiracy based upon the evidence described?

3. Assume that all of the evidence in the *Adickes* case was presented in the form of factual allegations in Adickes's complaint. Would that complaint survive a 12(b)(6) motion to dismiss for failure to state a claim after *Twombly*, which likewise involved an element of conspiracy or agreement?

4. Sandra Adickes recently gave a speech about her involvement in the case and her perspective on developments since. Her remarks are available at the Web site of the Civil Procedure Section of the Association of American Law Schools; *see http://nathenson.org/aalscivpro/files/docs/Adickes_Remarks.pdf*. She lauds the role of courageous lawyers, such as Eleanor Jackson Piel, who are willing to offer legal representation in cases like her own.

### 2. A Focal Point of Litigation

As you have seen, by the mid-1980s there had been a good deal of criticism about alleged abuses of the wide-open, permissive Federal Rules. Amendments to the discovery rules and Rule 11 were one reaction. *Twombly* and *Iqbal* are more recent reactions in the pleading arena. Allegations about frivolous lawsuits also brought demands for more judicial responsiveness to summary judgment motions. *Celotex* and two other cases decided in the same term (*see* the notes following *Celotex*) were read by most commentators as an attempt to dissuade and terminate what the majority of the Supreme Court thought was a growing number of meritless lawsuits.

### ■ CELOTEX CORP. v. CATRETT
*477 U.S. 317 (1986)*

Justice REHNQUIST delivered the opinion of the Court:

The United States District Court for the District of Columbia granted the motion of petitioner Celotex Corporation for summary judgment against respondent Catrett because the latter was unable to produce evidence in support of her allegation in her wrongful-death complaint that the decedent had been exposed to petitioner's asbestos products. A divided panel of the

Court of Appeals for the District of Columbia Circuit reversed, however, holding that petitioner's failure to support its motion with evidence tending to negate such exposure precluded the entry of summary judgment in its favor. *Catrett v. Johns-Manville Sales Corp.*, 244 U.S. App. D.C. 160, 756 F.2d 181 (1985). This view conflicted with that of the Third Circuit in *In re Japanese Electronic Products*, 723 F.2d 238 (1983), *rev'd on other grounds sub nom. Matsushita Electric Industrial Co. v. Zenith Radio Corp.*, 475 U.S. 574 (1986). We granted certiorari to resolve the conflict, and now reverse the decision of the District of Columbia Circuit.

Respondent commenced this lawsuit in September 1980, alleging that the death in 1979 of her husband, Louis H. Catrett, resulted from his exposure to products containing asbestos manufactured or distributed by 15 named corporations. Respondent's complaint sounded in negligence, breach of warranty, and strict liability. Two of the defendants filed motions challenging the District Court's in personam jurisdiction, and the remaining 13, including petitioner, filed motions for summary judgment. Petitioner's motion, which was first filed in September 1981, argued that summary judgment was proper because respondent had "failed to produce evidence that any [Celotex] product . . . was the proximate cause of the injuries alleged within the jurisdictional limits of [the District] Court." In particular, petitioner noted that respondent had failed to identify, in answering interrogatories specifically requesting such information, any witnesses who could testify about the decedent's exposure to petitioner's asbestos products. In response to petitioner's summary judgment motion, respondent then produced three documents which she claimed "demonstrate that there is a genuine material factual dispute" as to whether the decedent had ever been exposed to petitioner's asbestos products. The three documents included a transcript of a deposition of the decedent, a letter from an official of one of the decedent's former employers whom petitioner planned to call as a trial witness, and a letter from an insurance company to respondent's attorney, all tending to establish that the decedent had been exposed to petitioner's asbestos products in Chicago during 1970-1971. Petitioner, in turn, argued that the three documents were inadmissible hearsay and thus could not be considered in opposition to the summary judgment motion.

In July 1982, almost two years after the commencement of the lawsuit, the District Court granted all of the motions filed by the various defendants. The court explained that it was granting petitioner's summary judgment motion because "there [was] no showing that the plaintiff was exposed to the defendant Celotex's product in the District of Columbia or elsewhere within the statutory period." Respondent appealed only the grant of summary judgment in favor of petitioner, and a divided panel of the District of Columbia Circuit reversed. The majority of the Court of Appeals held that petitioner's summary judgment motion was rendered "fatally defective" by the fact that petitioner "made no effort to adduce *any evidence*, in the form of affidavits or otherwise, to support its motion." 244 U.S. App. D.C., at 163, 756 F.2d, at 184 (emphasis in original). According to the majority, Rule 56(e) of the Federal Rules of Civil Procedure, and this Court's decision in *Adickes v. S. H. Kress & Co.*, 398 U.S. 144, 159 (1970), establish that "the party opposing the motion for summary judgment bears the burden of responding only after the moving party has met its burden of coming forward with proof of the absence of any genuine issues of material fact." The majority therefore declined to consider petitioner's argument that none of the evidence produced by respondent in opposition to the motion for summary judgment would have been admissible at trial. *Ibid.* The dissenting judge argued that "[t]he majority errs in supposing that a party seeking summary judgment must always make an affirmative evidentiary showing, even in cases where there is not a triable, factual dispute." According to the dissenting judge, the majority's decision "undermines the traditional authority of trial judges to grant summary judgment in meritless cases."

We think that the position taken by the majority of the Court of Appeals is inconsistent with the standard for summary judgment set forth in Rule 56(c) of the Federal Rules of Civil Procedure. Under Rule 56(c), summary judgment is proper "if the pleadings, depositions, answers to interrogatories, and admissions on file, together with the affidavits, if any, show that there is no genuine issue as to any material fact and that the moving party is entitled to a judgment as a matter of law." In our view, the plain language of Rule 56(c) mandates the entry of summary judgment, after adequate time for discovery and upon motion, against a party who fails to make a showing sufficient to establish the existence of an element essential to that party's case, and on which that party will bear the burden of proof at trial. In such a situation, there can be "no genuine issue as to any material fact," since a complete failure of proof concerning an essential element of the nonmoving party's case necessarily renders all other facts immaterial. The moving party is "entitled to a judgment as a matter of law" because the nonmoving party has failed to make a sufficient showing on an essential element of her case with respect to which she has the burden of proof. "[T]h[e] standard [for granting summary judgment] mirrors the standard for a directed verdict under Federal Rule of Civil Procedure 50(a). . . ." *Anderson v. Liberty Lobby, Inc.*, 477 U.S. 242, 250 (1986).

Of course, a party seeking summary judgment always bears the initial responsibility of informing the district court of the basis for its motion, and identifying those portions of "the pleadings, depositions, answers to interrogatories, and admissions on file, together with the affidavits, if any," which it believes demonstrate the absence of a genuine issue of material fact. But unlike the Court of Appeals, we find no express or implied requirement in Rule 56 that the moving party support its motion with affidavits or other similar materials negating the opponent's claim. On the contrary, Rule 56(c), which refers to *"the affidavits, if any* . . ." (emphasis added), suggests the absence of such a requirement. And if there were any doubt about the meaning of Rule 56(c) in this regard, such doubt is clearly removed by Rules 56(a) and (b), which provide that claimants and defendants, respectively, may move for summary judgment "with or without supporting affidavits." . . .

Respondent argues, however, that Rule 56(e), by its terms, places on the nonmoving party the burden of coming forward with rebuttal affidavits, or other specified kinds of materials, only in response to a motion for summary judgment "made and supported as provided in this rule." According to respondent's argument, since petitioner did not "support" its motion with affidavits, summary judgment was improper in this case. But as we have already explained, a motion for summary judgment may be made pursuant to Rule 56 "with or without supporting affidavits." In cases like the instant one, where the nonmoving party will bear the burden of proof at trial on a dispositive issue, a summary judgment motion may properly be made in reliance solely on the "pleadings, depositions, answers to interrogatories, and admissions on file." Such a motion, whether or not accompanied by affidavits, will be "made and supported as provided in this rule," and Rule 56(e) therefore requires the nonmoving party to go beyond the pleadings and by her own affidavits, or by the "depositions, answers to interrogatories, and admissions on file," designate "specific facts showing that there is a genuine issue for trial."

We do not mean that the nonmoving party must produce evidence in a form that would be admissible at trial in order to avoid summary judgment. Obviously, Rule 56 does not require the nonmoving party to depose her own witnesses. Rule 56(e) permits a proper summary judgment motion to be opposed by any of the kinds of evidentiary materials listed in Rule 56(c), except the mere pleadings themselves, and it is from this list that one would normally expect the nonmoving party to make the showing to which we have referred.

The Court of Appeals in this case felt itself constrained, however, by language in our decision in *Adickes v. S. H. Kress & Co.*, 398 U.S. 144 (1970). There we held that summary judgment had been improperly entered in favor of the defendant restaurant in an action brought under 42 U.S.C. § 1983. In the course of its opinion, the *Adickes* Court said that "both the commentary on and the background of the 1963 amendment conclusively show that it was not intended to modify the burden of the moving party . . . to show initially the absence of a genuine issue concerning any material fact." *Id.* at 159. We think that this statement is accurate in a literal sense, since we fully agree with the *Adickes* Court that the 1963 amendment to Rule 56(e) was not designed to modify the burden of making the showing generally required by Rule 56(c). It also appears to us that, on the basis of the showing before the Court in *Adickes*, the motion for summary judgment in that case should have been denied. But we do not think the *Adickes* language quoted above should be construed to mean that the burden is on the party moving for summary judgment to produce evidence showing the absence of a genuine issue of material fact, even with respect to an issue on which the nonmoving party bears the burden of proof. Instead, as we have explained, the burden on the moving party may be discharged by "showing"—that is, pointing out to the district court—that there is an absence of evidence to support the non-moving party's case.

The last two sentences of Rule 56(e) were added, as this Court indicated in *Adickes*, to disapprove a line of cases allowing a party opposing summary judgment to resist a properly made motion by reference only to its pleadings. While the *Adickes* Court was undoubtedly correct in concluding that these two sentences were not intended to reduce the burden of the moving party, it is also obvious that they were not adopted to add to that burden. . . .

In this Court, respondent's brief and oral argument have been devoted as much to the proposition that an adequate showing of exposure to petitioner's asbestos products was made as to the proposition that no such showing should have been required. But the Court of Appeals declined to address either the adequacy of the showing made by respondent in opposition to petitioner's motion for summary judgment, or the question whether such a showing, if reduced to admissible evidence, would be sufficient to carry respondent's burden of proof at trial. We think the Court of Appeals with its superior knowledge of local law is better suited than we are to make these determinations in the first instance.

The Federal Rules of Civil Procedure have for almost 50 years authorized motions for summary judgment upon proper showings of the lack of a genuine, triable issue of material fact. Summary judgment procedure is properly regarded not as a disfavored procedural shortcut, but rather as an integral part of the Federal Rules as a whole, which are designed "to secure the just, speedy and inexpensive determination of every action." Fed. R. Civ. Proc. 1; *see* William Schwarzer, *Summary Judgment Under the Federal Rules: Defining Genuine Issues of Material Fact*, 99 F.R.D. 465, 467 (1984). Before the shift to "notice pleading" accomplished by the Federal Rules, motions to dismiss a complaint or to strike a defense were the principal tools by which factually insufficient claims or defenses could be isolated and prevented from going to trial with the attendant unwarranted consumption of public and private resources. But with the advent of "notice pleading," the motion to dismiss seldom fulfills this function anymore, and its place has been taken by the motion for summary judgment. Rule 56 must be construed with due regard not only for the rights of persons asserting claims and defenses that are adequately based in fact to have those claims and defenses tried to a jury, but also for the rights of persons opposing such claims and defenses to demonstrate in the manner provided by the Rule, prior to trial, that the claims and defenses have no factual basis.

The judgment of the Court of Appeals is accordingly reversed, and the case is remanded for further proceedings consistent with this opinion.

Justice WHITE, concurring:

I agree that the Court of Appeals was wrong in holding that the moving defendant must always support his motion with evidence or affidavits showing the absence of a genuine dispute about a material fact. I also agree that the movant may rely on depositions, answers to interrogatories, and the like, to demonstrate that the plaintiff has no evidence to prove his case and hence that there can be no factual dispute. But the movant must discharge the burden the Rules place upon him: It is not enough to move for summary judgment without supporting the motion in any way or with a conclusory assertion that the plaintiff has no evidence to prove his case.

A plaintiff need not initiate any discovery or reveal his witnesses or evidence unless required to do so under the discovery Rules or by court order. Of course, he must respond if required to do so; but he need not also depose his witnesses or obtain their affidavits to defeat a summary judgment motion asserting only that he has failed to produce any support for his case. It is the defendant's task to negate, if he can, the claimed basis for the suit. . . .

Justice BRENNAN, with whom the CHIEF JUSTICE and Justice BLACKMUN join, dissenting:

This case requires the Court to determine whether Celotex satisfied its initial burden of production in moving for summary judgment on the ground that the plaintiff lacked evidence to establish an essential element of her case at trial. I do not disagree with the Court's legal analysis. The Court clearly rejects the ruling of the Court of Appeals that the defendant must provide affirmative evidence disproving the plaintiff's case. Beyond this, however, the Court has not clearly explained what is required of a moving party seeking summary judgment on the ground that the nonmoving party cannot prove its case. This lack of clarity is unfortunate: district courts must routinely decide summary judgment motions, and the Court's opinion will very likely create confusion. For this reason, even if I agreed with the Court's result, I would have written separately to explain more clearly the law in this area. However, because I believe that Celotex did not meet its burden of production under Federal Rule of Civil Procedure 56, I respectfully dissent from the Court's judgment.

## I

Summary judgment is appropriate where the Court is satisfied "that there is no genuine issue as to any material fact and that the moving party is entitled to a judgment as a matter of law." Fed. R. Civ. P. 56(c). The burden of establishing the nonexistence of a "genuine issue" is on the party moving for summary judgment. This burden has two distinct components: an initial burden of production, which shifts to the nonmoving party if satisfied by the moving party; and an ultimate burden of persuasion, which always remains on the moving party. The court need not decide whether the moving party has satisfied its ultimate burden of persuasion unless and until the Court finds that the moving party has discharged its initial burden of production. *Adickes v. S. H. Kress & Co.*, 398 U.S. 144, 157-161 (1970); 1963 Advisory Committee's Notes on Fed. R. Civ. P. 56(e).

The burden of production imposed by Rule 56 requires the moving party to make a prima facie showing that it is entitled to summary judgment. The manner in which this showing can be made depends upon which party will bear the burden of persuasion on the challenged claim at trial. If the moving party will bear the burden of persuasion at trial, that party must support its motion with credible evidence—using any of the materials specified in Rule 56(c)—that would entitle it to a directed verdict if not controverted at trial. *Ibid.* Such an affirmative showing shifts the burden of production to the party opposing the motion and requires that party either to produce evidentiary materials that demonstrate the existence of a "genuine issue" for trial or to submit an affidavit requesting additional time for discovery. *Ibid.;* Fed. R. Civ. P. 56(e), (f).

If the burden of persuasion at trial would be on the nonmoving party, the party moving for summary judgment may satisfy Rule 56's burden of production in either of two ways. First, the moving party may submit affirmative evidence that negates an essential element of the nonmoving party's claim. Second, the moving party may demonstrate to the Court that the nonmoving party's evidence is insufficient to establish an essential element of the nonmoving party's claim. If the nonmoving party cannot muster sufficient evidence to make out its claim, a trial would be useless and the moving party is entitled to summary judgment as a matter of law. *Anderson v. Liberty Lobby, Inc.*, 477 U.S. 242, 249 (1986).

Where the moving party adopts this second option and seeks summary judgment on the ground that the nonmoving party—who will bear the burden of persuasion at trial—has no evidence, the mechanics of discharging Rule 56's burden of production are somewhat trickier. Plainly, a conclusory assertion that the nonmoving party has no evidence is insufficient. Such a "burden" of production is no burden at all and would simply permit summary judgment procedure to be converted into a tool for harassment. Rather, as the Court confirms, a party who moves for summary judgment on the ground that the nonmoving party has no evidence must affirmatively show the absence of evidence in the record. This may require the moving party to depose the nonmoving party's witnesses or to establish the inadequacy of documentary evidence. If there is literally no evidence in the record, the moving party may demonstrate this by reviewing for the court the admissions, interrogatories, and other exchanges between the parties that are in the record. Either way, however, the moving party must affirmatively demonstrate that there is no evidence in the record to support a judgment for the nonmoving party.

If the moving party has not fully discharged this initial burden of production, its motion for summary judgment must be denied, and the Court need not consider whether the moving party has met its ultimate burden of persuasion. Accordingly, the nonmoving party may defeat a motion for summary judgment that asserts that the nonmoving party has no evidence by calling the Court's attention to supporting evidence already in the record that was overlooked or ignored by the moving party. In that event, the moving party must respond by making an attempt to demonstrate the inadequacy of this evidence, for it is only by attacking all the record evidence allegedly supporting the nonmoving party that a party seeking summary judgment satisfies Rule 56's burden of production. Thus, if the record disclosed that the moving party had overlooked a witness who would provide relevant testimony for the nonmoving party at trial, the Court could not find that the moving party had discharged its initial burden of production unless the moving party sought to demonstrate the inadequacy of this witness' testimony. Absent such a demonstration, summary judgment would have to be denied on the ground that the moving party had failed to meet its burden of production under Rule 56.

The result in *Adickes v. S. H. Kress & Co., supra,* is fully consistent with these principles. In that case, petitioner was refused service in respondent's lunchroom and then was arrested for vagrancy by a local policeman as she left. Petitioner brought an action under 42 U.S.C. § 1983 claiming that the refusal of service and subsequent arrest were the product of a conspiracy between respondent and the police; as proof of this conspiracy, petitioner's complaint alleged that the arresting officer was in respondent's store at the time service was refused. Respondent subsequently moved for summary judgment on the ground that there was no actual evidence in the record from which a jury could draw an inference of conspiracy. In response, petitioner pointed to a statement from her own deposition and an unsworn statement by a Kress employee, both already in the record and both ignored by respondent, that the policeman who arrested petitioner was in the store at the time she was refused service. We agreed that "[i]f a policeman were present, . . . it would be open to a jury, in light of the sequence that followed, to infer from the circumstances that the policeman and Kress employee had a 'meeting of the minds' and thus reached an understanding that petitioner should be refused service." 398 U.S., at 158. Consequently, we held that it was error to grant summary judgment "on the basis of this record" because respondent had "failed to fulfill its initial burden" of demonstrating that there was no evidence that there was a policeman in the store. *Id.*, at 157-158.

The opinion in *Adickes* has sometimes been read to hold that summary judgment was inappropriate because the respondent had not submitted affirmative evidence to negate the possibility that there was a policeman in the store. The Court of Appeals apparently read *Adickes* this way and therefore required Celotex to submit evidence establishing that plaintiff's decedent had not been exposed to Celotex asbestos. I agree with the Court that this reading of *Adickes* was erroneous and that Celotex could seek summary judgment on the ground that plaintiff could not prove exposure to Celotex asbestos at trial. However, Celotex was still required to satisfy its initial burden of production.

## II

I do not read the Court's opinion to say anything inconsistent with or different than the preceding discussion. My disagreement with the Court concerns the application of these principles to the facts of this case.

Defendant Celotex sought summary judgment on the ground that plaintiff had "failed to produce" any evidence that her decedent had ever been exposed to Celotex asbestos. Celotex supported this motion with a two-page "Statement of Material Facts as to Which There is No Genuine Issue" and a three-page "Memorandum of Points and Authorities" which asserted that the plaintiff had failed to identify any evidence in responding to two sets of interrogatories propounded by Celotex and that therefore the record was "totally devoid" of evidence to support plaintiff's claim.

Approximately three months earlier, Celotex had filed an essentially identical motion. Plaintiff responded to this earlier motion by producing three pieces of evidence which she claimed "[a]t the very least . . . demonstrate that there is a genuine factual dispute for trial,": (1) a letter from an insurance representative of another defendant describing asbestos products to which plaintiff's decedent had been exposed; (2) a letter from T. R. Hoff, a former supervisor of decedent, describing asbestos products to which decedent had been exposed; and (3) a copy of decedent's deposition from earlier workmen's compensation proceedings. Plaintiff also apparently indicated at that time that she intended to call Mr. Hoff as a witness at trial.

Celotex subsequently withdrew its first motion for summary judgment. However, as a result of this motion, when Celotex filed its second summary judgment motion, the record did contain evidence—including at least one witness—supporting plaintiff's claim. Indeed, counsel for Celotex admitted to this Court at oral argument that Celotex was aware of this evidence and of plaintiff's intention to call Mr. Hoff as a witness at trial when the second summary judgment motion was filed. Moreover, plaintiff's response to Celotex' second motion pointed to this evidence—noting that it had already been provided to counsel for Celotex in connection with the first motion—and argued that Celotex had failed to "meet its burden of proving that there is no genuine factual dispute for trial."

On these facts, there is simply no question that Celotex failed to discharge its initial burden of production. Having chosen to base its motion on the argument that there was no evidence in the record to support plaintiff's claim, Celotex was not free to ignore supporting evidence that the record clearly contained. Rather, Celotex was required, as an initial matter, to attack the adequacy of this evidence. Celotex' failure to fulfill this simple requirement constituted a failure to discharge its initial burden of production under Rule 56, and thereby rendered summary judgment improper. This case [therefore] is indistinguishable from *Adickes*. . . .

[The dissenting opinion of Justice STEVENS is omitted.]

## Comments and Questions

1. In *Celotex*, the plaintiff defeated the summary judgment motion on remand to the appeals court that had earlier heard the case. Judge Kenneth Starr, a judge on that appeals court, wrote an opinion denying defendant's summary judgment motion. *Catrett v. Johns-Mansville*, 826 F.2d 33 (D.C. Cir. 1987).

2. Do you agree with Justice Brennan that *Adickes* and *Celotex* are reconcilable? For further discussion on this point, we highly recommend Adam

N. Steinman, *The Irrepressible Myth of* Celotex: *Reconsidering Summary Judgment Burdens Twenty Years After the Trilogy*, 63 Wash. & Lee L. Rev. 81 (2006).

3. The Supreme Court ruled on two other summary judgment cases during the same term as *Celotex*; the three cases are frequently referred to as the "trilogy" of summary judgment cases. Most commentators at the time read the trilogy as signaling that the federal courts would be more favorably disposed to summary judgment motions than before. For instance, a partner at Skadden, Arps, Slate, Meagher & Flom, a large New York City law firm, already noted this tendency a year after the trilogy: "There is no question that the courts are more hospitable toward summary judgment. The attitude throughout the country has been changing toward them. Judges want more than ever to dispose of cases if they can at an early stage." Stephen Labaton, *The Summary Judgment Rule*, N.Y. Times, Aug. 17, 1987, at 22.

For a more recent assessment of summary judgment practice subsequent to the 1986 trilogy of cases, see Stephen B. Burbank, *Vanishing Trials and Summary Judgment in Federal Civil Cases: Drifting Toward Bethlehem or Gomorrah?*, 1 J. Emp. Legal Stud. 591 (2004). Professor Burbank's evaluation of the available empirical information suggests "there is a reasonable basis to conclude that the rate of case termination by summary judgment in federal civil cases nationwide increased substantially in the period between 1960 and 2000, with one plausible (and perhaps conservative) range being from approximately 1.8 percent to approximately 7.7 percent. There is evidence, however, that the termination rate—indeed, the rate of activity more generally—under this supposedly uniform rule varies substantially in different parts of the country and in different types of cases." *Id.* at 592-593. In an examination of 1996 data from the U.S. District Court for the District of Columbia, Judge Patricia Wald reported that 22 percent of the terminations were by summary judgment, and only 3 percent by trial. Patricia M. Wald, *Summary Judgment at Sixty*, 76 Tex. L. Rev. 1897 (1998). "We are approaching a time when a civil trial will be thought of as a 'pathological event.'" *Id.* at 1915. "While judges appear to be requiring plaintiffs to plead facts with ever greater detail in order to survive motions to dismiss, they also seem reluctant to find genuine issues of material fact meriting a trial, often declaring that the factual issues are immaterial, or requiring a higher standard of proof at summary judgment that a fact [is] in dispute than had traditionally been thought necessary." *Id.* at 1942. Interestingly, Professor Burbank's review of the data suggests that the effect of summary judgment on the decline of trials actually began in the 1970s, before *Celotex*. Burbank, *supra*, 1 J. Emp. Legal Stud. at 620-621.

4. The second case in the trilogy was *Anderson v. Liberty Lobby, Inc.*, 477 U.S. 242 (1986). In *Liberty Lobby*, the district court had granted summary judgment on the grounds that in libel suits of this nature, the plaintiff needed to prove actual malice, and the plaintiff did not show that it would have evidence at the trial permitting such a finding. The appellate court reversed, saying that the plaintiff's obligation to prove actual malice at the trial by clear

and convincing evidence did not apply at the summary judgment stage. Justice White, writing for the majority, is explicit that the summary judgment motion requires the court to predict what would happen to the case at the directed verdict stage: "The petitioners suggest, and we agree, that this standard [for summary judgment under Rule 56(c)] mirrors the standard for a directed verdict under Federal Rules of Civil Procedure 50(a), which is that the trial judge must direct a verdict if, under the governing law, there can be but one reasonable conclusion as to the verdict." *Id.* at 250.

Justice White further stated, "Our holding that the clear-and-convincing standard of proof should be taken into account in ruling on summary judgment motions does not denigrate the role of the jury." *Id.* at 255. But Justice Brennan argued in dissent that when trial judges try to apply a "clear-and-convincing" standard at the summary judgment stage, they cannot avoid weighing evidence, and thus improperly infringing on the province of the jury. Justice Brennan complained that the Court's opinion did not explain how a judge should "assess how one-sided evidence is, or what a 'fair-minded' jury could 'reasonably' decide. . . . I simply cannot square the direction that the judge 'is not himself to weigh the evidence' with the direction that the judge also bear in mind the 'quantum' of proof required and consider whether the evidence is of sufficient 'caliber or quantity' to meet that 'quantum.' I would have thought that a determination of the 'caliber and quantity,' i.e., the importance and value, of the evidence in light of the 'quantum,' i.e., amount 'required,' could *only* be performed by weighing the evidence." *Id.* at 265, 266 (emphasis in original).

Justice Rehnquist, joined by Chief Justice Burger, argued in dissent that the majority's test would be difficult to apply. If the plaintiff could show that it had evidence of malice at the summary judgment stage, Justice Rehnquist did not see how a judge ruling on a summary judgment motion could determine that it would be insufficient evidence for the jury to find malice at the trial itself, unless the judge made a credibility determination. Justice Rehnquist concluded: "The primary effect of the Court's opinion today will likely be to cause the decisions of trial judges on summary judgment motions in libel cases to be more erratic and inconsistent than before. This is largely because the Court has created a standard that is different from the standard traditionally applied in summary judgment motions without even hinting as to how its new standard will be applied to particular cases." *Id.* at 272-273.

On remand, the federal district court applied the "clear and convincing evidence of actual malice" standard and granted summary judgment on seven of the nine counts remanded. *Liberty Lobby v. Anderson*, 1991 WL 186998 (D.D.C. May 1, 1991).

5. The third case of the trilogy, *Matsushita Elec. Industrial Co. v. Zenith Radio Corp.*, 475 U.S. 574 (1986), dealt with a claim by Zenith Co. against twenty-one Japanese companies manufacturing or selling consumer electronics products in America or controlling American firms that sell the products. Zenith alleged that the Japanese companies had conspired, in violation of the Sherman Antitrust Act and other statutes, to keep prices artificially

high in Japan in order to subsidize artificially low prices in the United States, in order to push American companies out of the market. The case focused on a "Five Company Rule"—an agreement that defendants had made with each other that no one company would have more than five distributors.

The district court, finding that Zenith's theory did not make economic sense, granted summary judgment to the defendants. The appeals court reversed summary judgment with respect to some of the defendants, finding sufficient evidence from which a jury could infer a conspiracy. The Supreme Court reversed and remanded, with Justice Powell writing the majority opinion, in which Justices Burger, Marshall, Rehnquist, and O'Connor joined.

The Court ruled that "where the record taken as a whole could not lead a rational trier of fact to find for the nonmoving party, there is no genuine issue for trial." *Id.* at 587. On the facts of the *Matsushita* case, the Court held that Zenith, the nonmover with the burden of proof at trial, had failed to present evidence at the summary judgment stage that "tends to exclude the possibility that the alleged conspirators acted independently." *Id.* at 588. The Court reasoned that the plaintiff's theory did not make economic sense and that the Five Company Rule would tend to raise, not lower, prices. Nor would the court allow the plaintiff to survive summary judgment based on the proposed testimony of plaintiff's expert that there was a conspiracy; the Court found that the expert's opinion was "implausible" and inconsistent with other evidence in the record.

Justice White, joined by Justices Brennan, Blackmun, and Stevens, dissented, arguing that the majority had disregarded traditional summary judgment doctrine. They found the majority's disregard for the expert's proposed testimony a clear violation of the judicial obligation not to weigh evidence and assess credibility when ruling on a summary judgment motion: "If the Court intends to give every judge hearing a motion for summary judgment in an antitrust case the job of determining if the evidence makes the inference of conspiracy more probable than not, it is overturning settled law. If the Court does not intend such a pronouncement, it should refrain from using unnecessarily broad and confusing language." *Id.* at 598, 601. With respect to the majority's rejection of the opinion of the plaintiff's proposed expert, the dissent concluded: "No doubt the Court prefers its own economic theorizing to Dr. DePodwin's, but that is not a reason to deny the fact finder an opportunity to consider Dr. DePodwin's views on how petitioners' alleged collusion harmed respondents." *Id.* at 598, 603. Indeed, from our current knowledge of how Japanese electronics firms have employed long-term pricing strategies to maximize efficiency, we may wonder whether DePodwin's testimony would have struck fact finders as unbelievable. Isn't a court's judgment that there is no evidence different from its refusal to believe evidence that will be presented?

6. Summary judgment has become a focal point of litigation, with very high stakes. As a result, parties are inclined to invest in discovery earlier and more fervently to ensure that their case will survive this critical stage. *See* Hon. Diane P. Wood, *Summary Judgment and the Law of Unintended Consequences*, 36 Okla. City U. L. Rev. 231 (2011).

7. Since a summary judgment motion can dispose of an entire case (or an important issue in a case) without there being a trial, the courts have developed a number of means to protect the parties, particularly the nonmoving party. For example, even courts that normally do not permit oral argument on motions usually do permit such argument on summary judgment motions. You have already read how the trial court is to give the nonmoving party the benefit of accepting its potential admissible evidence as true at the summary judgment stage, and also to give the nonmoving party the benefit of permissible inferences.

Further, you will recall from the opinion in *Adickes* that the Rules allow a nonmovant to postpone consideration of a summary judgment motion when it is impractical for them to present facts to defeat that motion. See Rule 56(d). Although the nonmovant is by no means entitled to additional time, this is the Rule and tack you should consider as a plaintiff whenever a defendant moves for summary judgment while discovery is still underway.

8. Notice that Rule 56(a) contemplates that a summary judgment may be entered on "part of [a] claim or defense." This is commonly referred to as a *partial* summary judgment. After a partial summary judgment, some facts or some elements will be treated as true at trial, leaving the fact finder with only the remaining facts and elements to consider. Understand, then, that a summary judgment could resolve just one element of a cause of action, or a whole cause of action, or even an entire case.

9. The Supreme Court found summary adjudication to be constitutional in *Fidelity & Deposit Co. v. United States*, 187 U.S. 315, 318-322 (1902). But the transformation of the summary judgment device over the course of the past century may raise new problems with the Seventh Amendment. *See* Suja Thomas, *Why Summary Judgment Is Unconstitutional*, 93 Va. L. Rev. 139, 144 (2007). Professor Thomas has also discussed how the *Twombly* and *Iqbal* decisions have, in certain respects, moved the summary judgment standard into the pleading phase. *See* Suja A. Thomas, *The New Summary Judgment Motion: The Motion to Dismiss Under Iqbal and Twombly*, 14 Lewis & Clark L. Rev. 15 (2010).

10. The following opinion is a much more recent opinion from the Supreme Court on the issue of summary judgment. As you read it, consider whether this case gives defendants any additional ammunition at the summary judgment stage that the trilogy generally or *Matsushita* in particular hadn't already provided.

## ■ SCOTT v. HARRIS
*127 S. Ct. 1769 (2007)*

Justice SCALIA delivered the opinion of the Court:
We consider whether a law enforcement official can, consistent with the Fourth Amendment, attempt to stop a fleeing motorist from continuing his public-endangering flight by ramming the motorist's car from behind.

Put another way: Can an officer take actions that place a fleeing motorist at risk of serious injury or death in order to stop the motorist's flight from endangering the lives of innocent bystanders?

### I

In March 2001, a Georgia county deputy clocked respondent's vehicle traveling at 73 miles per hour on a road with a 55-mile-per-hour speed limit. The deputy activated his blue flashing lights indicating that respondent should pull over. Instead, respondent sped away, initiating a chase down what is in most portions a two-lane road, at speeds exceeding 85 miles per hour. The deputy radioed his dispatch to report that he was pursuing a fleeing vehicle, and broadcast its license plate number. Petitioner, Deputy Timothy Scott, heard the radio communication and joined the pursuit along with other officers. In the midst of the chase, respondent pulled into the parking lot of a shopping center and was nearly boxed in by the various police vehicles. Respondent evaded the trap by making a sharp turn, colliding with Scott's police car, exiting the parking lot, and speeding off once again down a two-lane highway.

Following respondent's shopping center maneuvering, which resulted in slight damage to Scott's police car, Scott took over as the lead pursuit vehicle. Six minutes and nearly 10 miles after the chase had begun, Scott decided to attempt to terminate the episode by employing a "Precision Intervention Technique ('PIT') maneuver, which causes the fleeing vehicle to spin to a stop." Brief for Petitioner 4. Having radioed his supervisor for permission, Scott was told to "'[g]o ahead and take him out.'" *Harris v. Coweta County*, 433 F.3d 807, 811 (11th Cir. 2005). Instead, Scott applied his push bumper to the rear of respondent's vehicle.[1] As a result, respondent lost control of his vehicle, which left the roadway, ran down an embankment, overturned, and crashed. Respondent was badly injured and was rendered a quadriplegic.

Respondent filed suit against Deputy Scott and others under Rev. Stat. § 1979, 42 U.S.C. § 1983, alleging, inter alia, a violation of his federal constitutional rights, viz. use of excessive force resulting in an unreasonable seizure under the Fourth Amendment. In response, Scott filed a motion for summary judgment based on an assertion of qualified immunity. The District Court denied the motion, finding that "there are material issues of fact on which the issue of qualified immunity turns which present sufficient disagreement to require submission to a jury." On interlocutory appeal, the United States Court of Appeals for the Eleventh Circuit affirmed the District Court's decision to allow respondent's Fourth Amendment claim against Scott to proceed to trial. Taking respondent's view of the facts as given, the

---

1. Scott says he decided not to employ the PIT maneuver because he was "concerned that the vehicles were moving too quickly to safely execute the maneuver." Brief for Petitioner 4. Respondent agrees that the PIT maneuver could not have been safely employed. See Brief for Respondent 9. It is irrelevant to our analysis whether Scott had permission to take the precise actions he took.

Court of Appeals concluded that Scott's actions could constitute "deadly force" under *Tennessee v. Garner*, 471 U.S. 1 (1985), and that the use of such force in this context "would violate [respondent's] constitutional right to be free from excessive force during a seizure. Accordingly, a reasonable jury could find that Scott violated [respondent's] Fourth Amendment rights."

## II

In resolving questions of qualified immunity, courts are required to resolve a "threshold question: Taken in the light most favorable to the party asserting the injury, do the facts alleged show the officer's conduct violated a constitutional right? This must be the initial inquiry." *Saucier v. Katz*, 533 U.S. 194, 201 (2001). If, and only if, the court finds a violation of a constitutional right, "the next, sequential step is to ask whether the right was clearly established ... in light of the specific context of the case." *Ibid.* ....[4] We therefore turn to the threshold inquiry: whether Deputy Scott's actions violated the Fourth Amendment.

## III

### A

The first step in assessing the constitutionality of Scott's actions is to determine the relevant facts. As this case was decided on summary judgment, there have not yet been factual findings by a judge or jury, and respondent's version of events (unsurprisingly) differs substantially from Scott's version. When things are in such a posture, courts are required to view the facts and draw reasonable inferences "in the light most favorable to the party opposing the [summary judgment] motion." ...

There is, however, an added wrinkle in this case: existence in the record of a videotape capturing the events in question. There are no allegations or indications that this videotape was doctored or altered in any way, nor any contention that what it depicts differs from what actually happened. The videotape quite clearly contradicts the version of the story told by respondent and adopted by the Court of Appeals. For example, the Court of Appeals adopted respondent's assertions that, during the chase, "there was little, if any, actual threat to pedestrians or other motorists, as the roads were mostly empty and [respondent] remained in control of his vehicle." Indeed, reading the lower court's opinion, one gets the impression that respondent, rather than fleeing from police, was attempting to pass his driving test:

> [T]aking the facts from the non-movant's viewpoint, [respondent] remained in control of his vehicle, slowed for turns and intersections, and typically used his

---

4. We need not address the wisdom of *Saucier* in this case, however, because the constitutional question with which we are presented is, as discussed in Part III-B, *infra*, easily decided. Deciding that question first is thus the "better approach," *County of Sacramento v. Lewis*, 523 U.S. 833, 841, n.5 (1998), regardless of whether it is required.

indicators for turns. He did not run any motorists off the road. Nor was he a threat to pedestrians in the shopping center parking lot, which was free from pedestrian and vehicular traffic as the center was closed. Significantly, by the time the parties were back on the highway and Scott rammed [respondent], the motorway had been cleared of motorists and pedestrians allegedly because of police blockades of the nearby intersections. 433 F.3d 807, 815-816 (citations omitted).

The videotape tells quite a different story. There we see respondent's vehicle racing down narrow, two-lane roads in the dead of night at speeds that are shockingly fast. We see it swerve around more than a dozen other cars, cross the double-yellow line, and force cars traveling in both directions to their respective shoulders to avoid being hit. We see it run multiple red lights and travel for considerable periods of time in the occasional center left-turn-only lane, chased by numerous police cars forced to engage in the same hazardous maneuvers just to keep up. Far from being the cautious and controlled driver the lower court depicts, what we see on the video more closely resembles a Hollywood-style car chase of the most frightening sort, placing police officers and innocent bystanders alike at great risk of serious injury.

At the summary judgment stage, facts must be viewed in the light most favorable to the nonmoving party only if there is a "genuine" dispute as to those facts. Fed. Rule Civ. Proc. 56(c). As we have emphasized, "[w]hen the moving party has carried its burden under Rule 56(c), its opponent must do more than simply show that there is some metaphysical doubt as to the material facts. . . . Where the record taken as a whole could not lead a rational trier of fact to find for the nonmoving party, there is no 'genuine issue for trial.'" *Matsushita Elec. Industrial Co. v. Zenith Radio Corp.*, 475 U.S. 574, 586-587 (1986) (footnote omitted). "[T]he mere existence of some alleged factual dispute between the parties will not defeat an otherwise properly supported motion for summary judgment; the requirement is that there be no genuine issue of material fact." *Anderson v. Liberty Lobby, Inc.*, 477 U.S. 242, 247-248 (1986). When opposing parties tell two different stories, one of which is blatantly contradicted by the record, so that no reasonable jury could believe it, a court should not adopt that version of the facts for purposes of ruling on a motion for summary judgment.

That was the case here with regard to the factual issue whether respondent was driving in such fashion as to endanger human life. Respondent's version of events is so utterly discredited by the record that no reasonable jury could have believed him. The Court of Appeals should not have relied on such visible fiction; it should have viewed the facts in the light depicted by the videotape.

**B**

Judging the matter on that basis, we think it is quite clear that Deputy Scott did not violate the Fourth Amendment. Scott does not contest that his decision to terminate the car chase by ramming his bumper into respondent's vehicle constituted a "seizure." . . . It is also conceded, by both sides, that a claim of "excessive force in the course of making [a] . . . 'seizure' of [the] person . . . [is] properly analyzed under the Fourth Amendment's 'objective reasonableness' standard." *Graham v. Connor*, 490 U.S. 386, 388 (1989). The question we need to answer is whether Scott's actions were objectively reasonable.[8] . . .

In determining the reasonableness of the manner in which a seizure is effected, "[w]e must balance the nature and quality of the intrusion on the individual's Fourth Amendment interests against the importance of the governmental interests alleged to justify the intrusion." *United States v. Place*, 462 U.S. 696, 703 (1983). Scott defends his actions by pointing to the paramount governmental interest in ensuring public safety, and respondent nowhere suggests this was not the purpose motivating Scott's behavior. Thus, in judging whether Scott's actions were reasonable, we must consider the risk of bodily harm that Scott's actions posed to respondent in light of the threat to the public that Scott was trying to eliminate. Although there is no obvious way to quantify the risks on either side, it is clear from the videotape that respondent posed an actual and imminent threat to the lives of any pedestrians who might have been present, to other civilian motorists, and to the officers involved in the chase. *See* Part III-A, *supra*. It is equally clear that Scott's actions posed a high likelihood of serious injury or death to respondent-though not the near certainty of death posed by, say, shooting a fleeing felon in the back of the head, *see Garner, supra*, at 4, or pulling alongside a fleeing motorist's car and shooting the motorist, *cf. Vaughan v. Cox*, 343 F.3d 1323, 1326-1327 (11th Cir. 2003). So how does a court go about weighing the perhaps lesser probability of injuring or killing numerous bystanders against the perhaps larger probability of injuring or killing a single person? We think it appropriate in this process to take into account not only the number of lives at risk, but also their relative culpability. It was respondent, after all, who intentionally placed himself and the public in danger by unlawfully engaging in the reckless, high-speed flight that ultimately produced the choice between two evils that Scott confronted. Multiple police cars, with blue lights flashing and sirens blaring, had been chasing respondent for nearly 10 miles, but he ignored their warning to stop. By contrast, those who might have been harmed had Scott not taken the action he did were entirely innocent. We have little difficulty in concluding it was reasonable for Scott to take the action that he did.[10]

---

8. Justice Stevens incorrectly declares this to be "a question of fact best reserved for a jury," and complains we are "usurp[ing] the jury's factfinding function." At the summary judgment stage, however, once we have determined the relevant set of facts and drawn all inferences in favor of the nonmoving party to the extent supportable by the record, *see* Part III-A, *supra*, the reasonableness of Scott's actions—or, in Justice Stevens' parlance, "[w]hether [respondent's] actions have risen to a level warranting deadly force,"—is a pure question of law.

10. The Court of Appeals cites *Brower v. County of Inyo*, 489 U.S. 593, 595 (1989), for its refusal to "countenance the argument that by continuing to flee, a suspect absolves a pursuing police officer of any possible liability for all ensuing actions during the chase," 433 F.3d, at 816. The only question in Brower was whether a police roadblock constituted a seizure under the Fourth Amendment. In deciding that question, the relative culpability of the parties is, of course, irrelevant; a seizure occurs whenever the police are "responsib[le] for the termination of [a person's] movement," 433 F.3d, at 816, regardless of the

But wait, says respondent: Couldn't the innocent public equally have been protected, and the tragic accident entirely avoided, if the police had simply ceased their pursuit? We think the police need not have taken that chance and hoped for the best. Whereas Scott's action-ramming respondent off the road-was certain to eliminate the risk that respondent posed to the public, ceasing pursuit was not. First of all, there would have been no way to convey convincingly to respondent that the chase was off, and that he was free to go. Had respondent looked in his rear-view mirror and seen the police cars deactivate their flashing lights and turn around, he would have had no idea whether they were truly letting him get away, or simply devising a new strategy for capture. Perhaps the police knew a shortcut he didn't know, and would reappear down the road to intercept him; or perhaps they were setting up a roadblock in his path. Given such uncertainty, respondent might have been just as likely to respond by continuing to drive recklessly as by slowing down and wiping his brow.[11]

Second, we are loath to lay down a rule requiring the police to allow fleeing suspects to get away whenever they drive so recklessly that they put other people's lives in danger. It is obvious the perverse incentives such a rule would create: Every fleeing motorist would know that escape is within his grasp, if only he accelerates to 90 miles per hour, crosses the double-yellow line a few times, and runs a few red lights. The Constitution assuredly does not impose this invitation to impunity-earned-by-recklessness. Instead, we lay down a more sensible rule: A police officer's attempt to terminate a dangerous high-speed car chase that threatens the lives of innocent bystanders does not violate the Fourth Amendment, even when it places the fleeing motorist at risk of serious injury or death. . . .

The car chase that respondent initiated in this case posed a substantial and immediate risk of serious physical injury to others; no reasonable jury could conclude otherwise. Scott's attempt to terminate the chase by forcing respondent off the road was reasonable, and Scott is entitled to summary judgment. The Court of Appeals' decision to the contrary is reversed.

[The concurring opinions of Justice GINSBURG and Justice BREYER are omitted.]

Justice STEVENS, dissenting:

Today, the Court asks whether an officer may "take actions that place a fleeing motorist at risk of serious injury or death in order to stop the motorist's flight from endangering the lives of innocent bystanders." Depending on

---

reason for the termination. Culpability is relevant, however, to the reasonableness of the seizure—to whether preventing possible harm to the innocent justifies exposing to possible harm the person threatening them.

11. Contrary to Justice Stevens' assertions, we do not "assum[e] that dangers caused by flight from a police pursuit will continue after the pursuit ends," nor do we make any "factual assumptions," with respect to what would have happened if the police had gone home. We simply point out the uncertainties regarding what would have happened, in response to respondent's factual assumption that the high-speed flight would have ended.

the circumstances, the answer may be an obvious "yes," an obvious "no," or sufficiently doubtful that the question of the reasonableness of the officer's actions should be decided by a jury, after a review of the degree of danger and the alternatives available to the officer. A high speed chase in a desert in Nevada is, after all, quite different from one that travels through the heart of Las Vegas.

Relying on a de novo review of a videotape of a portion of a nighttime chase on a lightly traveled road in Georgia where no pedestrians or other "bystanders" were present, buttressed by uninformed speculation about the possible consequences of discontinuing the chase, eight of the jurors on this Court reach a verdict that differs from the views of the judges on both the District Court and the Court of Appeals who are surely more familiar with the hazards of driving on Georgia roads than we are. The Court's justification for this unprecedented departure from our well-settled standard of review of factual determinations made by a district court and affirmed by a court of appeals is based on its mistaken view that the Court of Appeals' description of the facts was "blatantly contradicted by the record" and that respondent's version of the events was "so utterly discredited by the record that no reasonable jury could have believed him."

Rather than supporting the conclusion that what we see on the video "resembles a Hollywood-style car chase of the most frightening sort,"[1] the tape actually confirms, rather than contradicts, the lower courts' appraisal of the factual questions at issue. More important, it surely does not provide a principled basis for depriving the respondent of his right to have a jury evaluate the question whether the police officers' decision to use deadly force to bring the chase to an end was reasonable.

Omitted from the Court's description of the initial speeding violation is the fact that respondent was on a four-lane portion of Highway 34 when the officer clocked his speed at 73 miles per hour and initiated the chase. More significant—and contrary to the Court's assumption that respondent's vehicle "force[d] cars traveling in both directions to their respective shoulders to avoid being hit"—a fact unmentioned in the text of the opinion explains why those cars pulled over prior to being passed by respondent. The sirens and flashing lights on the police cars following respondent gave the same warning that a speeding ambulance or fire engine would have provided.[3] The 13 cars that respondent passed on his side of the road before entering the shopping center, and both of the cars that he passed on the right after leaving the

---

1. I can only conclude that my colleagues were unduly frightened by two or three images on the tape that looked like bursts of lightning or explosions, but were in fact merely the headlights of vehicles zooming by in the opposite lane. Had they learned to drive when most high-speed driving took place on two-lane roads rather than on superhighways—when split-second judgments about the risk of passing a slow-poke in the face of oncoming traffic were routine—they might well have reacted to the videotape more dispassionately.

3. While still on the four-lane portion of Highway 34, the deputy who had clocked respondent's speed turned on his blue light and siren in an attempt to get respondent to pull over. It was when the deputy turned on his blue light that the dash-mounted video camera was activated and began to record the pursuit.

center, no doubt had already pulled to the side of the road or were driving along the shoulder because they heard the police sirens or saw the flashing lights before respondent or the police cruisers approached.[4] A jury could certainly conclude that those motorists were exposed to no greater risk than persons who take the same action in response to a speeding ambulance, and that their reactions were fully consistent with the evidence that respondent, though speeding, retained full control of his vehicle.

The police sirens also minimized any risk that may have arisen from running "multiple red lights," *ibid.* In fact, respondent and his pursuers went through only two intersections with stop lights and in both cases all other vehicles in sight were stationary, presumably because they had been warned of the approaching speeders. Incidentally, the videos do show that the lights were red when the police cars passed through them but, because the cameras were farther away when respondent did so and it is difficult to discern the color of the signal at that point, it is not entirely clear that he ran either or both of the red lights. In any event, the risk of harm to the stationary vehicles was minimized by the sirens, and there is no reason to believe that respondent would have disobeyed the signals if he were not being pursued.

My colleagues on the jury saw respondent "swerve around more than a dozen other cars," and "force cars traveling in both directions to their respective shoulders," but they apparently discounted the possibility that those cars were already out of the pursuit's path as a result of hearing the sirens. Even if that were not so, passing a slower vehicle on a two-lane road always involves some degree of swerving and is not especially dangerous if there are no cars coming from the opposite direction. At no point during the chase did respondent pull into the opposite lane other than to pass a car in front of him; he did the latter no more than five times and, on most of those occasions, used his turn signal. On none of these occasions was there a car traveling in the opposite direction. In fact, at one point, when respondent found himself behind a car in his own lane and there were cars traveling in the other direction, he slowed and waited for the cars traveling in the other direction to pass before overtaking the car in front of him while using his turn signal to do so. This is hardly the stuff of Hollywood. To the contrary, the video does not reveal any incidents that could even be remotely characterized as "close calls."

In sum, the factual statements by the Court of Appeals quoted by the Court were entirely accurate. That court did not describe respondent as a "cautious" driver as my colleagues imply, but it did correctly conclude that there is no evidence that he ever lost control of his vehicle. That court also correctly pointed out that the incident in the shopping center parking lot did not create any risk to pedestrians or other vehicles because the chase occurred just before 11 p.m. on a weekday night and the center was closed. It is apparent from the record (including the videotape) that local police had

---

4. Although perhaps understandable, because their volume on the sound recording is low (possibly due to sound proofing in the officer's vehicle), the Court appears to minimize the significance of the sirens audible throughout the tape recording of the pursuit.

blocked off intersections to keep respondent from entering residential neigh-borhoods and possibly endangering other motorists. I would add that the videos also show that no pedestrians, parked cars, sidewalks, or residences were visible at any time during the chase. The only "innocent bystanders" who were placed "at great risk of serious injury," were the drivers who either pulled off the road in response to the sirens or passed respondent in the opposite direction when he was driving on his side of the road.

I recognize, of course, that even though respondent's original speeding violation on a four-lane highway was rather ordinary, his refusal to stop and subsequent flight was a serious offense that merited severe punishment. It was not, however, a capital offense, or even an offense that justified the use of deadly force rather than an abandonment of the chase. The Court's concern about the "imminent threat to the lives of any pedestrians who might have been present," while surely valid in an appropriate case, should be discounted in a case involving a nighttime chase in an area where no pedestrians were present.

What would have happened if the police had decided to abandon the chase? We now know that they could have apprehended respondent later because they had his license plate number. Even if that were not true, and even if he would have escaped any punishment at all, the use of deadly force in this case was no more appropriate than the use of a deadly weapon against a fleeing felon in *Tennessee v. Garner*, 471 U.S. 1 (1985). In any event, any uncertainty about the result of abandoning the pursuit has not prevented the Court from basing its conclusions on its own factual assumptions.[5] The Court attempts to avoid the conclusion that deadly force was unnecessary by spec-ulating that if the officers had let him go, respondent might have been "just as likely" to continue to drive recklessly as to slow down and wipe his brow. That speculation is unconvincing as a matter of common sense and improper as a matter of law. Our duty to view the evidence in the light most favorable to the nonmoving party would foreclose such speculation if the Court had not used its observation of the video as an excuse for replacing the rule of law with its ad hoc judgment. There is no evidentiary basis for an assumption that dan-gers caused by flight from a police pursuit will continue after the pursuit ends. Indeed, rules adopted by countless police departments throughout the country are based on a judgment that differs from the Court's. *See,* e.g., App. to Brief for Georgia Association of Chiefs of Police, Inc., as Amicus Curiae A-52 ("During a pursuit, the need to apprehend the suspect should always outweigh the level of danger created by the pursuit. When the

5. In noting that Scott's action "was certain to eliminate the risk that respondent posed to the public" while "ceasing pursuit was not," the Court prioritizes total elimination of the risk of harm to the public over the risk that respondent may be seriously injured or even killed. The Court is only able to make such a statement by assuming, based on its interpretation of events on the videotape, that the risk of harm posed in this case, and the type of harm involved, rose to a level warranting deadly force. These are the same types of questions that, when disputed, are typically resolved by a jury; this is why both the District Court and the Court of Appeals saw fit to have them so decided. Although the Court claims only to have drawn factual inferences in respondent's favor "to the extent supportable by the record," its own view of the record has clearly precluded it from doing so to the same extent as the two courts through which this case has already traveled.

immediate danger to the public created by the pursuit is greater than the immediate or potential danger to the public should the suspect remain at large, then the pursuit should be discontinued or terminated. . . . [P]ursuits should usually be discontinued when the violator's identity has been established to the point that later apprehension can be accomplished without danger to the public").

Although *Garner* may not, as the Court suggests, "establish a magical on/off switch that triggers rigid preconditions" for the use of deadly force, it did set a threshold under which the use of deadly force would be considered constitutionally unreasonable:

> Where the officer has probable cause to believe that the suspect poses a threat of serious physical harm, either to the officer or to others, it is not constitutionally unreasonable to prevent escape by using deadly force. Thus, if the suspect threatens the officer with a weapon or there is probable cause to believe that he has committed a crime involving the infliction or threatened infliction of serious physical harm, deadly force may be used if necessary to prevent escape, and if, where feasible, some warning has been given. 471 U.S., at 11-12.

Whether a person's actions have risen to a level warranting deadly force is a question of fact best reserved for a jury. Here, the Court has usurped the jury's factfinding function and, in doing so, implicitly labeled the four other judges to review the case unreasonable. It chastises the Court of Appeals for failing to "vie[w] the facts in the light depicted by the videotape" and implies that no reasonable person could view the videotape and come to the conclusion that deadly force was unjustified. However, the three judges on the Court of Appeals panel apparently did view the videotapes entered into evidence and described a very different version of events:

> At the time of the ramming, apart from speeding and running two red lights, Harris was driving in a non-aggressive fashion (i.e., without trying to ram or run into the officers). Moreover, . . . Scott's path on the open highway was largely clear. The videos introduced into evidence show little to no vehicular (or pedestrian) traffic, allegedly because of the late hour and the police blockade of the nearby intersections. Finally, Scott issued absolutely no warning (e.g., over the loudspeaker or otherwise) prior to using deadly force. *Harris v. Coweta County*, 433 F.3d 807, 819, n. 14 (11th Cir. 2005).

If two groups of judges can disagree so vehemently about the nature of the pursuit and the circumstances surrounding that pursuit, it seems eminently likely that a reasonable juror could disagree with this Court's characterization of events. Moreover, under the standard set forth in *Garner*, it is certainly possible that "a jury could conclude that Scott unreasonably used deadly force to seize Harris by ramming him off the road under the instant circumstances." 433 F.3d, at 821.

The Court today sets forth a per se rule that presumes its own version of the facts: "A police officer's attempt to terminate a dangerous high-speed car chase that threatens the lives of innocent bystanders does not violate the

Fourth Amendment, even when it places the fleeing motorist at risk of serious injury or death." Not only does that rule fly in the face of the flexible and case-by-case "reasonableness" approach applied in *Garner* and *Graham v. Connor*, 490 U.S. 386 (1989), but it is also arguably inapplicable to the case at hand, given that it is not clear that this chase threatened the life of any "innocent bystande[r]."[8] In my view, the risks inherent in justifying unwarranted police conduct on the basis of unfounded assumptions are unacceptable, particularly when less drastic measures—in this case, the use of stop sticks[9] or a simple warning issued from a loudspeaker—could have avoided such a tragic result. In my judgment, jurors in Georgia should be allowed to evaluate the reasonableness of the decision to ram respondent's speeding vehicle in a manner that created an obvious risk of death and has in fact made him a quadriplegic at the age of 19.

## Comments and Questions

1. Is the Court's viewing of the videotape appropriate? Is it engaged in impermissible fact finding or has it properly undertaken a *de novo* review of defendant's summary judgment motion?

2. Three law professors conducted a study that showed the video of the high-speed chase to a diverse sample of 1350 Americans. Although a majority of those surveyed agreed with the majority's conclusion on the key issues, there were sharp differences of opinion along cultural, ideological, and other lines. The professors attributed the divisions to the psychological disposition of individuals to resolve disputed facts in a manner supportive of their group identities. The article criticizes the Court's suggestion that there was only one "reasonable" view of the facts, suggesting that this reflects a form of bias—cognitive liberalism—that consists in the failure to recognize the connection perceptions of societal risk and contested visions of the ideal society. And when courts fail to take steps to counteract that bias, they needlessly invest the law with culturally partisan overtones that detract from the law's legitimacy. *See* Dan M. Kahan, David A. Hoffman, and Donal Braman, *Whose Eyes Are You Going to Believe?* Scott v. Harris *and the Perils of Cognitive Illiberalism*, 122 Harv. L. Rev. 837 (2009).

3. Justice Stevens writes that the Court has "implicitly labeled the four other judges to review the case unreasonable." Is this criticism compelling, or is it unfair?

4. The purpose of the doctrine of qualified immunity is to ensure that insubstantial lawsuits are terminated quickly. How meaningful is the substantive doctrine of qualified immunity if plaintiffs can survive the pleading stage with mere notice pleading and can defeat a summary judgment motion

8. It is unclear whether, in referring to "innocent bystanders," the Court is referring to the motorists driving unfazed in the opposite direction or to the drivers who pulled over to the side of the road, safely out of respondent's and petitioner's path.

9. "Stop sticks" are a device which can be placed across the roadway and used to flatten a vehicle's tires slowly to safely terminate a pursuit.

with flimsy evidence? Should the pleading standard, the summary judgment standard, or both be modified in these cases? Should that modification be undertaken by amending the text of the rule(s) or by tailoring their application?

## 3. The Fact-Law Distinction

During your law career, you will hear many times that issues of fact are for the jury and issues of law are for the judge. And yet, the very notion of summary judgment and directed verdict presupposes that judges are permitted to enter the domain of factual issues. Hence, this can be confusing. In order to ensure that juries do not act irrationally, the theory goes, judges must be certain that before the jury can decide a factual issue on behalf of the party with the burden of production, there is sufficient evidence to permit reasonable people to make such a finding. Thus, the judiciary has created a threshold legal issue in order to decide the factual issue: It is deemed a legal question whether there is sufficient evidence to make a rational factual determination.

When a judge says that something is a question of law, this is a shorthand for saying, "I have determined that the jury should not hear the issue." When a judge grants a summary judgment motion on behalf of a defendant because of a failure in the plaintiff's prima facie case, she is saying, "As a matter of law, I have determined that the plaintiff has not shown it will have sufficient evidence at the trial to permit a jury to find for the plaintiff on all of its elements."

It is by no means written in concrete which issues the judge will turn into "law" questions, and which will be treated as "factual" issues for the jury. Perhaps it is best to see "as a matter of law" as shorthand for saying that, based on policy considerations, a judge thinks the judiciary is better at deciding the question than a jury of laypeople.

William Schwarzer, a Senior U.S. District Judge for the Northern District of California and a former Director of the Federal Judicial Center, has pointed out that the fact/law distinction takes place at another level as well: The initial question of whether the issue to be decided, often a mixed question of law and fact, should be decided by the jury at all. In the following article, Senior Judge Schwarzer explains this level of decision and gives examples.

## ■ WILLIAM SCHWARZER, SUMMARY JUDGMENT UNDER THE FEDERAL RULES: DEFINING GENUINE ISSUES OF MATERIAL FACT
### 99 F.R.D. 465, 471-474 (1984)

Thus the court should first consider whether the disputed issue, as a matter of precedent or policy, should be decided by the jury or by the court. That approach should present no difficulty with respect to a large category of issues traditionally tried to juries. Whether a defendant has failed to use due care in the operation of his vehicle, whether he was driving in the course of his employment, and whether the injuries suffered by plaintiff were proximately caused by the defendant's operation of the vehicle are issues of ultimate fact for the jury. Similarly, whether a person had reasonable cause, acted within a reasonable time or can be charged with notice are jury issues. All are ultimate facts turning on examination and assessment of human behavior within the common experience of jurors. Concerning issues of this sort, "[i]t is assumed that twelve men know more of the common affairs of life than does one man, that they can draw wiser and safer conclusions from admitted facts thus occurring than can a single judge." Decisions of such issues, moreover, are generally ad hoc, with little resort to policy, with precedent playing a minor part, and with no compelling need for uniform or predictable outcomes. Of such mixed issues of fact and law, one can say that their law content is relatively low.

This does not mean that every such issue must be submitted to the jury, i.e. that summary judgment is precluded. That will turn on the second prong of the test—whether the motion or the opposition is sufficient to establish that the proponent of the issue could survive a motion for directed verdict or for judgment n.o.v. . . .

A second category of ultimate fact issues consists of those which involve the application of predominantly legal standards to undisputed historical facts. The decision here turns not so much on factors within the common experience of jurors as on matters of law and policy and on technical questions underlying the particular legal scheme. It should not be made ad hoc; consistency, uniformity and predictability here are important to the administration of the underlying laws. Issues of this sort arise most frequently in the application of legislation or of public policies. Examples include whether a union breached its duty of fair representation, whether a controlling person acted in good faith within the meaning of the securities laws, whether location restrictions in a dealer agreement were an unreasonable restraint in violation of the antitrust laws. . . . Of mixed questions such as these, it is fair to say that their law content predominates.

Ultimate fact issues of this sort are properly decided by the court and are therefore appropriate for summary judgment if the underlying historical facts are not disputed. That is true even though the process of decision requires the trial court to "weigh the evidence" on both sides of the argument in deciding what ultimate fact to derive. . . .

A third category consists of those issues of ultimate fact which may be appropriate for jury determination in some cases but not in others. One example of such a variable issue is the existence of a conspiracy under the antitrust laws. In certain conspiracy cases the lawfulness of joint conduct of defendants can turn on their purpose and intent, a question of fact usually disputed and well within the conventional sphere of the jury. In other cases, the conspiracy issue may turn on whether, as a matter of law and policy, a particular relationship among parties, the historical facts of which are not disputed, should be treated as an unlawful conspiracy. . . .

## 4. Strategic Considerations

Like all motions, there are strategic matters to consider before filing a summary judgment motion. This is not just a matter of avoiding sanctions or avoiding a likely waste of time and money, although these are important considerations. To file a summary judgment motion and memorandum or brief in support thereof means educating opposing counsel about your view of their case and, in some instances, of your own case. On the other hand, it may be a way of smoking out opposing counsel's best case in advance of trial. But even this is more complicated. If a party against whom the motion is brought thinks she can easily defeat it without revealing all of her cards, she may do so. For instance, a plaintiff may have many theories of recovery or cumulative potential evidence, but reveal at the summary judgment stage only enough to survive the motion. This, too, is complex. It would be embarrassing—if not malpractice—for counsel defending against a summary judgment to hold back in order not to educate an opponent, only to find out that her client loses at the summary judgment stage.

Bear in mind that winning or losing the motion is not the only issue and that there are audiences other than opposing counsel. One must consider who the judge is likely to be and whether the summary judgment motion is a good means of early education for the judge. Will the judge who hears the motion be the same judge who sits at trial? There also looms the question of settlement. Will it be easier or harder to settle the case once the motion is filed and after each side files memoranda in support of or opposing the motion, or once the outcome of your motion is known? Do you want to run that risk?

Some cases look stronger or weaker depending on whether they are decided on a written record or with live testimony. Some cases simply look different when you consider whether a judge or a jury will be the fact finder. Even though a summary judgment motion is in large measure a prediction of what would happen at the directed verdict stage at trial, the situations are different psychologically. Many cases demand the drawing of inferences, for example, and sympathetic testimony for one side or another may contract or expand the inferences that a judge is willing to draw or to permit a jury to draw.

Finally, consider these questions. Will the filing of a summary judgment motion delay your trial date? Is delay good or bad for your client? Is a swift decision—even if it is a negative one—a priority for your client? Perhaps you and your client are trying to establish a new cause of action in your jurisdiction, and you want an appellate court to hear the question as soon as possible. But, then again, you may want to attempt to convince appellate judges to stretch current precedent with the aid of an entire trial record.

Litigation is a human enterprise in which experience means a great deal; lawyers tend to become more valuable with age and practice. If you choose to do trial work, over time you will work out your own sense of litigation strategy. You will become more skilled at deciding which variables are most important to you and your client—and, if your client is lucky, your mind will remain open to new variables and new assessments of the old variables.

## Practice Exercise No. 23: Summary Judgment
## Motion Session in *Carpenter*

This practice exercise has two parts. You may be assigned either or
both. For each part, read the summary judgment motion of the third-
party defendants, the memorandum in support of the motion, the Regulations, the stipulation of all parties, and the Restatement excerpts, which are
in the Case Files, as well as any other materials in the *Carpenter v. Dee* case
that you feel are relevant to the exercise. (Assume that the Massachusetts
summary judgment rule is identical to Fed. R. Civ. P. 56. Moreover, in
recent years, the Massachusetts Supreme Judicial Court, when interpreting
Mass. R. Civ. P. 56, has cited and followed the reasoning of the U.S.
Supreme Court's trilogy cases. There is absolutely no need to go beyond
the pages of this textbook, including the Case Files, in order to do a first-
rate job on these exercises.) As you read the materials, consider how, if you
represented Dale McGill and McGill's Garage, you would attempt to convince a judge that there is no material issue of fact for the jury to decide and
that this is a case that can be decided at summary judgment as a matter of
law. Is it your position that the issue to be decided at summary judgment is
for the court and not the jury or that, as to one or more elements, Ultimate
Auto will have insufficient evidence for the court to find for it—or that both
are true?

For purposes of both the written and oral portion of the exercise, assume
that this is the structure of the case. Nancy Carpenter sued the Dees. She then
amended to add Ultimate Auto and the City as defendants. Ultimate Auto
impleaded McGill and his Garage. The Dees, Ultimate Auto, and the City
each filed cross-claims against each other. After discovery, and before any
amendment by Carpenter to claim against McGill and his Garage, McGill
and his Garage moved for summary judgment against Ultimate Auto, and
Ultimate Auto opposed this motion. It is the McGill and McGill Garage summary judgment motion against Ultimate Auto that you will address in both the
written and oral portions of the Exercise.

In the actual case, the City also moved for summary judgment, and that
motion was denied. As a matter of trial strategy, however, the plaintiff's
counsel later dropped the allegations against the City, because of (a) concern
for the feelings a jury might have about blaming police officers for failing to
get the jeep off the road (or otherwise warn), which might in turn prejudice a
jury against the plaintiff's strong claim against Ultimate Auto; (b) concern
about the reaction of jurors as taxpayers who might not want to cost the City
money which, in turn, might somehow poison them against the plaintiff generally; (c) concern that juries think a plaintiff's case is weaker when a shotgun
approach is used of suing everyone in sight; (d) belief that the City was largely
judgment-proof; and (e) belief that the case against the City was not very
strong anyway. In fact, after the actual lawsuit, the Massachusetts legislature passed a statute making it very unlikely that a case such as this could be
successfully sustained against a Massachusetts municipality.

A. Written Exercise. *As counsel for Ultimate Auto, prepare a Memorandum for the Court in Opposition to the Third-Party Motion for Summary Judgment.* The memorandum cannot exceed four double-spaced pages (including the caption). The memoranda will be collected at the end of class. Before you prepare your memorandum, make sure you are clear on how many arguments you have. You may wish first to make an outline. For instance, are you arguing that the law requires a broader duty than the third-party defendants suggest, or that there are underlying factual disputes, or both? Or do you have other arguments? As to each argument, make sub-arguments or a list of reasons. Definition and clarity are essential in constructing effective legal arguments.

B. Oral Exercise. *As counsel for Ultimate Auto or the Garage, prepare an oral argument for or against the summary judgment motion.* A motion session judge will hear argument from both sides on the summary judgment motion of McGill and the Garage against Ultimate Auto. If your last name begins with any letter from H through T, be prepared to argue orally on behalf of Ultimate Auto. If your last name begins with any other letter, be prepared to argue for Dale McGill and McGill's Garage in favor of the summary judgment motion. Assume that the judge will ask to hear first from the moving party. Also assume that the judge was recently appointed to the bench, and is unfamiliar with the details of your case.

# E.  DISMISSAL, DIRECTED VERDICTS, JUDGMENTS NOTWITHSTANDING THE VERDICT, NEW TRIAL MOTIONS, AND MOTIONS TO VACATE JUDGMENT

You have now studied summary judgment, which takes place prior to trials. We next want to teach you about three jury-control mechanisms—directed verdict, judgment notwithstanding the verdict (JNOV), and new trial motions—and about methods for dismissing cases and having judgments vacated. If we were going in chronological order, a timeline for a typical federal jury case might look something like the following. Don't take the timeline too literally; not every step must take place, and many steps overlap or could happen in a different order for any of a number of good reasons.

Complaint

12(b) motions

Answer

Motions for voluntary or involuntary dismissal

Rule 16 scheduling conference and order (*see* Chapter 6)

Discovery

Motions to amend

Settlement discussion

Motions for summary judgment

Rule 16 pretrial conference

Trial

Motions for directed verdict/judgment as a matter of law

Verdict

Entry of judgment

Motions for JNOV/judgment as a matter of law

Motions for new trial

Appeals

Motions to vacate judgment

Execution of judgment

You should also have some picture in your mind of what goes on at a trial. A jury trial begins with impaneling a jury, including voir dire and challenges of jurors for cause and peremptory challenges, topics that we have already covered. Whether there is a jury or not, the next stage is for the plaintiff and the defendant to give opening statements, with the plaintiff ordinarily going first. The parties then present their evidence through witnesses and exhibits. As each party presents its evidence, the opposing parties may object on the grounds that the evidence is inadmissible. The defendant's lawyer has an opportunity to cross-examine each of the plaintiff's witnesses, usually followed by re-direct and re-cross. After the plaintiff rests, and assuming that there is not a directed verdict motion or that such a motion has been denied, the defendant presents its case in the same manner that the plaintiff did (with direct and cross-examination). The plaintiff can then present rebuttal evidence, and then the defendant can do the same. Assuming that the case is not disposed of by directed verdict motions after all parties have rested, there are then final arguments by each side. In many courts, the defendant closes first, followed by the plaintiff. In others, the plaintiff is permitted to have the first and final closing arguments, with the defendant's closing argument in between. If there is a jury, the judge will usually instruct it on the law after all of the closing arguments. Some judges choose to instruct at the beginning of the case and at the end, while others instruct the jury immediately before the lawyers give their closing arguments. The jury then deliberates and returns a verdict, filling in the verdict slip or answering the questions presented by the judge, sometimes both. (*See* Fed. R. Civ. P. 49.)

We next discuss the current ground rules on dismissals, directed verdict motions, judgment notwithstanding the verdict, and motions for new trial.

## 1. Voluntary Dismissal

Fed. R. Civ. P. 41(a)(1) prescribes when a plaintiff has a right to dismiss a case voluntarily, and 41(a)(2) describes the court's power to permit a plaintiff to dismiss a case voluntarily. Note that in the normal case, the plaintiff has an absolute right to dismiss voluntarily prior to the adverse party's filing an answer or a motion for summary judgment. Unless otherwise stated in the court's notice of dismissal or in a stipulation of dismissal signed by all parties who have appeared in the action, or unless the plaintiff has previously filed and dismissed the same claim in a state or federal court, then such voluntary dismissal will be *without prejudice*. That means the plaintiff can bring the claim again; put another way, it means the dismissal will *not* have a *res judicata* effect.

Under Fed. R. Civ. P. 41(a)(2), the plaintiff, in situations not covered by 41(a)(1), can apply to the court for a voluntary dismissal, and the court, upon "terms that the court considers proper," has the power to grant it. Unless the court otherwise states, this dismissal will also be "without prejudice." The reference to "terms" is an invitation to the court to condition the dismissal on the plaintiff's paying all or part of the defendant's expenses to date in defending the suit. The court can also decide to permit the voluntary dismissal only with prejudice. If the case has proceeded very far, and the court and the other party have already expended significant resources and time on the case, the court will likely dismiss with prejudice or dismiss without prejudice on the condition that plaintiff pay defendant's expenses to defend to date. Fed. R. Civ. P. 41(d) covers a lacuna in 41(a)(1), to wit: situations in which the plaintiff has an absolute right to voluntarily dismiss "without prejudice," but this is not the first time the plaintiff has had the same claim dismissed. In this situation, the court can award the costs of the action previously dismissed to the opposing party and "may stay the proceedings until the plaintiff has complied." There is a circuit conflict over whether federal district courts may award attorneys' fees under Rule 41(d)'s use of the word "costs" of the previously dismissed claim, and if so, whether the district court must first give notice of the approximate costs and/or an opportunity to withdraw the motion to dismiss. *See* Michael E. Solimine and Amy E. Lippert, *Deregulating Voluntary Dismissals*, 36 U. Mich. J.L. Ref. 367 (2003).

Notice that Fed. R. Civ. P. 41(c) permits claimants other than plaintiffs to seek dismissals. This is because counterclaims, cross-claims, and third-party claims put the defendant in a plaintiff's posture for those aspects of the case.

## 2. Involuntary Dismissal

Often a court orders a case dismissed even though the plaintiff would very much like it to continue. For instance, you have already seen dismissals for failure to state a claim or for failure to survive a summary judgment motion. Pursuant to Fed. R. Civ. P. 41(b), unless the court otherwise orders, these and other involuntary dismissals operate "as an adjudication on the merits," which is another way of saying the dismissal has a *res judicata* effect. When we reach Chapters 7 and 8 we will consider in more detail why dismissals for lack of subject matter jurisdiction, personal jurisdiction, and venue do not have *res judicata* effect; a 12(b)(7) dismissal for failure to join a Rule 19 (necessary and indispensable) party also does not have *res judicata* effect. Involuntary dismissals for failing to comply with a court order operate "as an adjudication on the merits." It would be a very inefficient system, if not an unfair one, that permitted a plaintiff or its attorney to fail to comply with a discovery order, an order relating to pre-trial conferences, or other orders of the court, without the ultimate available sanction of dismissal with prejudice.

### 3. *Directed Verdict (Judgment as a Matter of Law)*

We have been anticipating this device ever since Chapter 3, when you were first exposed to the burden of production, and you have met the concept again in our classes on summary judgment. To refresh your recollection, the party with the burden of production on an issue (we have been using the word *element* previously, instead of *issue*, for that is usually what is at stake) has the obligation to enter sufficient evidence on that issue to permit a reasonable fact finder to find for that party. Otherwise, as to that issue, and upon proper motion by the opposition, the party with the production burden will lose. If losing on that issue means the party cannot win on the claim, it will lose the case.

Just as in summary judgment, the judge deciding a directed verdict motion is obligated to consider the evidence of the nonmoving party in the light most favorable to that party, taking the nonmover's conceivably believable evidence as true and giving the nonmover the benefit of all reasonable inferences. This procedural mechanism is usually used by a defendant to defeat a plaintiff, before the fact finder even deliberates on the evidence, on the ground that, on at least one element of the plaintiff's cause of action, no reasonable fact finder could find for the plaintiff. We will consider after *Galloway* the less typical situation of a plaintiff's seeking and receiving a directed verdict or "judgment as a matter of law."

As the new version of Fed. R. Civ. P. 50 puts it, in cases tried before a jury, if a claim cannot be maintained without a party's having "a legally sufficient evidentiary basis to find for the party on that issue," and if such evidence was not presented—and if the party has been fully heard with respect to that issue—then the court "[may] grant a motion for judgment as a matter of law" on that claim. Fed. R. Civ. P. 50(a)(1)(B). Read Federal Rule 50 with particular care, as it contains complexity and nuance.

As the new rule is worded, a party may move for judgment as a matter of law at any time before submission to the jury. Fed. R. Civ. P. 50(a)(2). According to the Advisory Committee Notes on the amendment, this means that a judge could, for instance, require a plaintiff to introduce all of her evidence on a necessary element early in a case (such as duty or unreasonable care in a negligence case) and then, prior to the plaintiff's resting on the entire case, permit the defendant to move for judgment as a matter of law on the grounds of insufficient evidence on the one element. Please read the Advisory Committee Notes on the 1991 amendments to the Federal Rules to discover why the language was changed from "directed verdict" to "judgment as a matter of law," even though the Advisory Committee hastened to add that the new rule "effects no change in the existing standard" that has been "articulated in long-standing case law."

As you think about the dissenters' position in *Galloway*, that there has been a gradual erosion in civil cases involving the Seventh Amendment right to jury trial, consider whether the amendments to Rule 50 continue that erosion. For instance, what effect does the parties' ability to move for "judgment as a matter of law" any time before submission to the jury have on the right to (or quality of) jury trial? Compare the language to the previous rendition of Fed. R. Civ. P. 50(a).

The concept of "sufficiency of evidence to permit a finding on an element of the case" (put another way, the idea of a "production burden") is also applicable in cases without a jury. For instance, if in a Title VII case without a jury the plaintiff had no evidence of discrimination (either through adverse impact or adverse treatment), then it would not make sense to force the defendant to present evidence or for the judge to hear it. Rule 52(c) covers this situation, and permits the judge to enter judgment as a matter of law against a party on a claim that the party cannot win, so long as that party "has been fully heard on an issue," the court finds against the party on that issue, and it is dispositive of the case.

Notice that Rule 52(c), which deals with actions without a jury, does not use the Rule 50(a) language about "legally sufficient evidentiary basis." Can you see why? Assume in *Carpenter*, for example, that the parties chose to try the case on a jury-waived basis. Assume further that the plaintiff introduced evidence that would be sufficient to permit a finding of unreasonable care against Ultimate Auto, the retailer, but that the judge does not believe the plaintiff's evidence, and the judge knows this even before the defendant has put on any evidence of its own. Could the judge enter judgment as a matter of law against the plaintiff, even though she could not have done so had there been a jury? Does the difference in language between Rules 50(a) and 52(c) make sense? In both jury cases and nonjury cases, could the plaintiff achieve a judgment as a matter of law prior to the defendant's having an opportunity to put on its case?

## 4. Judgment Notwithstanding the Verdict (JNOV/Renewed Judgment as a Matter of Law)

Even after the jury has rendered a verdict, a judge—having previously denied a directed verdict motion on the same grounds—can grant the party against whom the judgment was rendered a judgment notwithstanding the verdict. The test is identical to that of directed verdict (or the test for judgment as a matter of law, under Fed. R. Civ. P. 50(a)). For the federal rendition of this concept, see Fed. R. Civ. P. 50(b)—the *renewed* motion for judgment as a matter of law.

Consider a simple motor vehicle negligence case. Assume the plaintiff, a pedestrian, has introduced its evidence, and rested. The defendant, driver of a car, moves for directed verdict on the ground that there is insufficient evidence for the jury to find for the plaintiff on the element of unreasonable care. The judge may think the defendant is correct about the insufficiency of evidence, and be tempted to grant the motion, but remain uncertain. Since it is a close question—for example, one based on the inferences that can be drawn from a skid mark—the judge thinks that an appellate court may disagree. Can you see two reasons why it may make sense for the judge to deny the initial motion for directed verdict, and then, if the jury finds for the plaintiff, grant the motion for JNOV? If you need help, or just want to check your instincts, the Advisory Committee Notes to the 1991 amendments to Fed. R. Civ. P. 50(b) discuss this issue.

Re-read the Seventh Amendment to the U.S. Constitution carefully, concentrating on the language about "no fact tried by a jury," and you will see why JNOV was constitutionally problematic. (*JNOV* is shorthand for a somewhat different common law motion which, using Latin, was called *judgment non obstante veredicto.*) The motion was held unconstitutional by a bare majority in *Slocum v. New York Life Insurance Co.*, 228 U.S. 364 (1913). In *Baltimore & Carolina Line, Inc. v. Redman*, 295 U.S. 654 (1935), the Court allowed such a motion in a case in which the trial judge had reserved decision on the directed verdict motion until after the verdict was rendered. The Court seized upon the "reservation" to distinguish *Slocum*. The original drafters of the Federal Rules went one step further in Fed. R. Civ. P. 50(b) and said that if a party seeks directed verdict at the close of *all* of the evidence and it is denied or not granted, "the court is deemed to have submitted the action to the jury subject to a later determination of the legal questions raised by the motion." This fiction, which also remains in the current version of Rule 50(b), has been held sufficient to render the Rule and the practice constitutional. *Neely v. Martin K. Eby Construction Co.*, 386 U.S. 317, 321 (1967).

Courts have affirmed the requirement that a party move for directed verdict at the close of all of the evidence in order to bring a motion for JNOV. *See* 9A Charles A. Wright, Arthur R. Miller, and Mary Kay Kane, *Federal Practice and Procedure* § 2537. When such motions are plausible (remembering the applicability of Rule 11 to motions), defense counsel normally moves for directed verdict after the plaintiff rests, and then, if denied, again after all parties rest. In all motions under Fed. R. Civ. P. 50, Rule 50(a)(2) requires the moving party to "specify the judgment sought and the law and facts that entitle the movant to the judgment." (Does Federal Rule 7(b)(1)(A) require that this motion be made in writing?)

The failure to file a renewed motion for judgment as a matter of law may constitute a waiver of the opportunity to challenge the sufficiency of the evidence on appeal. In *Unitherm Food Systems, Inc. v. Swift-Eckrich, Inc.*, 546 U.S. 394 (2006), the defendant properly filed its Rule 50(a) motion, and this motion was denied by the court. After the jury returned a verdict for plaintiff, the defendant neglected to file its renewed motion under Rule 50(b). On appeal, defendant argued the insufficiency of plaintiff's evidence and sought a *new trial*. Importantly, the defendant did not argue on the appeal that it was entitled to judgment as a matter of law. To be sure, defendant inadvertently waived the ability to challenge the sufficiency of evidence under Rule 50(b) by failing to raise that motion. But the Court also would not allow defendant to challenge the sufficiency of evidence under Rule 50(a)—even though defendant had properly asserted it. Compare the options available to the district judge under Rule 50(a)(1) and under Rule 50(b). Can you explain why the Court concluded that neither the district court nor the appellate courts would have the authority to grant a new trial under these circumstances?

## 5. *Motions for New Trial*

Even after the jury renders its verdict (or a judge without a jury, for that matter), the losing side can still move for a new trial. *See* Fed. R. Civ. P. 59(a)(1) and (a)(2). In fact, in federal court, pursuant to Rule 59(d), the judge is explicitly empowered to grant a new trial on the judge's own initiative. Students often find the notion of new trial motions the "straw that breaks the camel's back" when it comes to judicial control of juries. But before you draw that conclusion, give it some thought.

Consider first the language of the Rule itself, which says that a new trial may be granted in jury cases "for any reason for which a new trial has heretofore been granted in an action at law in federal court." Fed. R. Civ. P. 59(a)(1)(A). Many states have similar language, although the state rule would instead look to the historical practice in the courts of the state in question. Other states, by statute or rule, list the grounds for new trial motions, but these are often quite similar to the grounds that would be permissible in federal court or in a state that merely looks to precedents.

One type of new trial motion should not be problematic at all. Assume that after the jury has rendered its verdict (or even during a case), a judge becomes convinced that she has made a mistake that would be reversible error if considered by an appellate court, and that there is no way to correct the error. Say, for instance, the judge realizes after the jury has rendered its verdict and has been released that she mistakenly admitted evidence over correct objection, and that this was not "harmless" within the meaning of Fed. R. Civ. P. 61. Or assume that she was incorrect in her charge to the jury in a material way, even though the losing party had tried to save the court from error by complying with Fed. R. Civ. P. 51 ("Instructions to the Jury; Objections"). If the losing party moves for a new trial on grounds for which an appellate court would grant a new trial on appeal, then surely it makes sense for the new trial to be granted by the trial judge if she is now aware of the reversible error. Would not any other solution be wasteful, if not cruel, because it would force parties into the time, expense, and anxiety of an appeal in which the result is known? We realize that it is rare that a trial judge will be sure she has committed reversible error, but, nonetheless, trial judges should (and thus likely do) try to do justice by granting new trials when they are fairly certain an appellate court would do the same.

Perhaps a bit more problematic, but nonetheless well-established law in many jurisdictions, is the granting of new trial motions on grounds that the jury verdict is so excessive or inadequate as to demonstrate that the jury has misunderstood its duty or acted with extreme prejudice. The situation is most clear when the damages are liquidated, as in a written contract case with a specified monetary amount, and the jury finds for the plaintiff in an amount unrelated to the contractual provision. A tort verdict that contains an amount for "pain and suffering" or "disfigurement" is by its very nature discretionary. Consequently, the grant of a new trial because of the excessiveness or inadequacy of the award has a discretionary element. But even here, some awards would to most reasonable people seem "unsupported by the evidence." Consider a negligently caused scratch, without any sign of malice or realistically increased risk to the plaintiff, which results in a multimillion dollar award. Shouldn't a trial judge, who, like the jury, has taken an oath to do justice, grant a new trial? The courts are not in agreement on how far appellate courts should exercise authority over trial courts in granting or denying motions for a new trial based on the amount of damages.

Later, we will take up other questions related to damages and jury control, such as whether a judge can threaten to grant a new trial unless the plaintiff agrees to take less money (*remittitur*) or unless the defendant agrees to pay more (*additur*). Also can a trial, or a new trial, appropriately be held on only damages, if the judge believes the jury was right on liability but wrong on damages? We will also consider new trial motions on the grounds of "jury misconduct." Here again, even the most enthusiastic proponent of civil juries would want some judicial control. Thus, "[b]ribery, private communication with a party, improper remarks made in the jury's presence by a court officer or other outsider, consulting documents not in evidence, and the like, are sufficient grounds for setting aside a verdict (citations omitted)." Fleming James, Jr., Geoffrey C. Hazard, Jr., and John Leubsdorf, *Civil Procedure* § 7.27, at 470 (5th ed. 2001).

More difficult questions arise when the alleged jury misconduct relates to the deliberative process of the jury. For example, should a verdict be set aside because a juror incorrectly remembered the testimony of a witness or misinterpreted the judge's instructions, although one could not infer these mistakes by examining the verdict? Such examples, which reflect the imperfection of human beings and social structures rather than perversion of the entire process, are usually handled by evidentiary rules that protect against intrusion into the jury's deliberations while at the same time admitting evidence of gross misconduct.

Let's consider several compelling policy issues. If lawyers, and then judges, were permitted to delve frequently and deeply into the deliberation of jurors, then perhaps few jury verdicts could stand. It is unlikely that twelve or six people could behave perfectly, hard as they might try. (Of course, the same could be said of a judge acting alone.) Indeed, if it were easy to attack jury verdicts because of faults in the deliberations, and if all that is said in the jury room were made admissible through the testimony of jurors, then (1) an attorney who has lost a case would feel obligated to question each juror at length, and (2) some jurors would not want to speak (or at least not say what they think) during deliberations. This would create real potential for juror silence during deliberations, and for juror harassment after verdict. (This leaves aside those intrusions on the jury, such as bribery or private conversations with one of the parties, that already are clearly forbidden and certainly should be.)

The Federal Rules of Evidence provide one attempt to find a healthy balance on this issue. This federal solution incorporates much of the common law rule that a jury verdict cannot be impeached by the testimony of the jurors themselves, but tries to draw a line between the normal deliberative process and unfair external intrusions upon it:

Fed. R. Evid. 606(b) *Inquiry into the validity of verdict or indictment.* Upon an inquiry into the validity of a verdict or indictment, a juror may not testify as to any matter or statement occurring during the course of the jury's deliberations or to the effect of anything upon that or any other juror's mind or emotions as influencing the juror to assent to or dissent from the verdict or indictment or concerning the juror's mental processes in connection therewith, except that a juror may testify on the question whether extraneous prejudicial information was improperly brought to the jury's attention or whether any outside influence was improperly brought to bear upon any juror. Nor may a juror's affidavit or evidence of any statement by the juror concerning a matter about which the juror be precluded from testifying be received for these purposes.

Sometimes, behavior by the jury as a whole seems reprehensible but does not involve external influence. For example, Professors James, Hazard, and Leubsdorf describe the cases of "reaching a verdict by flipping a coin, agreeing to abide by the vote of a majority when a unanimous verdict is required, and determining damages by averaging the sums put down by each juror (the quotient verdict)." Fleming James, Jr., Geoffrey Hazard, Jr., and John Leubsdorf, *Civil Procedure* § 7.27 at 470 (5th ed. 2001). Courts disagree about how to handle these improprieties. One solution is to treat the behavior as substantive grounds for a new trial, but, in keeping with Fed. R. Evid. 606(b), to permit the behavior to be proved only by competent evidence other than the testimony of the jurors themselves. Such testimony might be given by an eavesdropper or a court official who finds a document in the jury room that indicates a quotient verdict.

Finally, we have arrived at the motion for new trial that you may find the most problematic: a motion for a new trial on the grounds that the verdict "is against the weight of the evidence." In federal courts, and in most state courts, the losing attorney can appeal to the discretion of the trial judge to grant a new trial motion, *not* because there is insufficient evidence to support the jury verdict (that is, the directed verdict or JNOV standard), but because the verdict is clearly wrong: The jury made a horrible mistake; there has been a gross miscarriage of justice. We will later raise issues about this motion after you have read *Galloway*, but before forming your opinion, consider the words of one state supreme court judge:

> The authority of the common pleas in the control and revision of excessive verdicts through the means of new trials was firmly settled in England before the foundation of this colony, and has always existed here without challenge under any of our constitutions. It is a power to examine the whole case on the law and the evidence, with a view to securing a result, not merely legal, but also not manifestly against justice, without which the jury system would be a capricious and intolerable tyranny, which no people could long endure. This court has had occasion more than once recently to say that it was a power the courts ought to exercise unflinchingly.

*Smith v. Times Publishing Co.*, 178 Pa. 481 (1897).

In *Aetna Casualty & Surety Co. v. Yeatts*, 122 F.2d 350 (4th Cir. 1941), which relies on the above quote, Judge Parker stated the position of most state and federal courts on the motion for a new trial on the ground that the verdict is *against the weight of the evidence:*

> On such a motion it is the duty of the trial judge to set aside the verdict and grant a new trial, if he is of the opinion that the verdict is against the clear weight of the evidence, or is based upon evidence that is false, or will result in a miscarriage of justice, even though there may be substantial evidence which would prevent the direction of a verdict.

Most appellate courts, including the federal, tend to leave this motion to the discretion of the trial judge, and almost always refuse to upset either the grant or the denial of the motion. It seems clear that the motion is brought far more often than it is granted. Moreover, it is rare that a party loses the same jury case twice and is granted yet a third jury trial on successive motions that call upon the judge to exercise this discretionary power.

If you were a judge, under what circumstances would you grant a motion for a new trial on the ground that the verdict is against the weight of the evidence? Do you think the judge should be required to state the reasons for granting such a motion? When denying such a motion? (Judges frequently deny or grant these motions, like other motions, without explanation.)

This would be a logical place to introduce you to motions to *vacate judgment* (Fed. R. Civ. P. 60), for such motions permit the correction of error in much the same way as motions for a new trial, except they usually are filed later. For pedagogical reasons, however, it makes more sense for you to now read *Galloway*, which is more directly related to directed verdict and the common law motion for a new trial. We will cover Rule 60 at the end of the comments.

## 6. *Judgments as a Matter of Law and New Trial Motions in More Detail*

### ■ GALLOWAY v. UNITED STATES
### *319 U.S. 372 (1943)*

Justice RUTLEDGE delivered the opinion of the Court:

Petitioner seeks benefits for total and permanent disability by reason of insanity he claims existed May 31, 1919. On that day his policy of yearly renewable term insurance lapsed for nonpayment of premium.

The suit was filed June 15, 1938. At the close of all the evidence the District Court granted the Government's motion for a directed verdict. Judgment was entered accordingly. The Circuit Court of Appeals affirmed. Both courts held the evidence legally insufficient to sustain a verdict for petitioner. He says this was erroneous and, in effect, deprived him of trial by jury, contrary to the Seventh Amendment.

The constitutional argument, as petitioner has made it, does not challenge generally the power of federal courts to withhold or withdraw from the jury cases in which the claimant puts forward insufficient evidence to support a verdict. The contention is merely that his case as made was substantial, the courts' decisions to the contrary were wrong, and therefore their effect has been to deprive him of a jury trial. . . . [T]he only question is whether the evidence was sufficient to sustain a verdict for petitioner. On that basis, we think the judgments must be affirmed.

### I

Certain facts are undisputed. Petitioner worked as a longshoreman in Philadelphia and elsewhere prior to enlistment in the Army November 1, 1917. [The record does not show whether this employment was steady and continuous or was spotty and erratic. But there is no contention that petitioner's behavior was abnormal before he arrived in France in April, 1918.] He became a cook in a machine gun battalion. His unit arrived in France in April, 1918. He served actively until September 24. From then to the following January he was in a hospital with influenza. He then returned to active duty. He came back to the United States, and received honorable discharge April 29, 1919. He enlisted in the Navy January 15, 1920, and was discharged for bad conduct in July. The following December he again enlisted in the Army and served until May, 1922, when he deserted. Thereafter he was carried on the Army records as a deserter.

In 1930 began a series of medical examinations by Veterans' Bureau physicians. On May 19 that year his condition was diagnosed as "Moron, low grade;

observation, dementia praecox, simple type." In November, 1931, further examination gave the diagnosis, "Psychosis with other diseases or conditions (organic disease of the central nervous system—type undetermined)." In July, 1934, still another examination was made, with diagnosis: "Psychosis manic and depressive insanity incompetent; hypertension, moderate; otitis media, chronic, left; varicose veins left, mild; abscessed teeth roots; myocarditis, mild."

Petitioner's wife, the nominal party in this suit, was appointed guardian of his person and estate in February, 1932. Claim for insurance benefits was made in June, 1934, and was finally denied by the Board of Veterans' Appeals in January, 1936. This suit followed two and a half years later.

Petitioner concededly is now totally and permanently disabled by reason of insanity and has been for some time prior to institution of this suit. It is conceded also that he was sound in mind and body until he arrived in France in April, 1918.

The theory of his case is that the strain of active service abroad brought on an immediate change, which was the beginning of a mental breakdown that has grown worse continuously through all the later years. Essential in this is the view it had become a total and permanent disability not later than May 31, 1919.

The evidence to support this theory falls naturally into three periods, namely, that prior to 1923; the interval from then to 1930; and that following 1930. It consists in proof of incidents occurring in France to show the beginnings of change; testimony of changed appearance and behavior in the years immediately following petitioner's return to the United States as compared with those prior to his departure; the medical evidence of insanity accumulated in the years following 1930; and finally the evidence of a physician, given largely as medical opinion, which seeks to tie all the other evidence together as foundation for the conclusion, expressed as of 1941, that petitioner's disability was total and permanent as of a time not later than May of 1919.

Documentary exhibits included military, naval and Veterans' Bureau records. Testimony was given by deposition or at the trial chiefly by five witnesses. One, O'Neill, was a fellow worker and friend from boyhood; two, Wells and Tanikawa, served with petitioner overseas; Lt. Col. Albert K. Mathews, who was an Army chaplain, observed him or another person of the same name at an Army hospital in California during early 1920; and Dr. Wilder, a physician, examined him shortly before the trial and supplied the only expert testimony in his behalf. The petitioner also put into evidence the depositions of Commander Platt and Lt. Col. James E. Matthews, his superior officers in the Navy and the Army, respectively, during 1920-22.

What happened in France during 1918-19 is shown chiefly by Wells and Tanikawa. Wells testified to an incident at Aisonville, where the unit was billeted shortly after reaching France and before going into action. Late at night petitioner created a disturbance, "hollering, screeching, swearing. . . . The men poured out from the whole section." Wells did not see the incident, but heard petitioner swearing at his superior officers and saw "the result, a black eye for Lt. Warner." However, he did not see "who gave it to him." Wells personally observed no infraction of discipline except this incident, and did not know what brought it on. Petitioner's physical appearance was good, he "carried on his duties as a cook all right," and the witness did not see him after June 1, except for about three days in July when he observed petitioner several times at work feeding stragglers.

Tanikawa, Hawaiian-born citizen, served with petitioner from the latter's enlistment until September, 1918, when Galloway was hospitalized, although the witness thought they had fought together and petitioner was "acting queer" at the Battle of the Argonne in October. At Camp Greene, North Carolina, petitioner was "just a regular soldier, very normal, . . . pretty neat." After reaching France "he was getting nervous . . . , kind of irritable, always picking a fight with other soldier." This began at Aisonville. Tanikawa saw Galloway in jail, apparently before June. It is not clear whether these are references to the incident Wells described.

Tanikawa described another incident in June "when we were on the Marne," the Germans "were on the other side and we were on this side." It was a new front, without trenches. The witness and petitioner were on guard duty with others. Tanikawa understood the Germans were getting ready for a big drive. "One night he (petitioner) screamed. He said, 'The Germans are coming' and we all gagged him." There was no shooting, the Germans were not coming, and there was nothing to lead the witness to believe they were. Petitioner was court martialed for the matter, but Tanikawa did not know "what they did with him." He did not talk with Galloway that night, because "he was out of his mind" and appeared insane. Tanikawa did not know when petitioner left the battalion or what happened to him after (as the witness put it) the Argonne fight, but heard he went to the hospital, "just dressing station I guess." The witness next saw Galloway in 1936, at a disabled veterans' post meeting in Sacramento, California. Petitioner then "looked to me like he wasn't all there. Insane. About the same . . . as compared to the way he acted in France, particularly when they gagged him. . . ."

O'Neill was "born and raised with" petitioner, worked with him as a longshoreman, and knew him "from when he come out of the army for seven years, . . . I would say five or six years." When petitioner returned in April or May, 1919, "he was a wreck compared to what he was when he went away. The fellow's mind was evidently unbalanced." Symptoms specified were withdrawing to himself; crying spells; alternate periods of normal behavior and nonsensical talk; expression of fears that good friends wanted "to beat him up"; spitting blood and remarking about it in vulgar terms. Once petitioner said, "G—d—it, I must be a Doctor Jekyll and Mr. Hyde."

O'Neill testified these symptoms and this condition continued practically the same for about five years. In his opinion petitioner was "competent at times and others was incompetent." The intervals might be "a couple of days, a couple of months." In his normal periods Galloway "would be his old self . . . absolutely O.K."

O'Neill was definite in recalling petitioner's condition and having seen him frequently in 1919, chiefly however, and briefly, on the street during lunch hour. He was not sure Galloway was working and was "surprised he got in the Navy, I think in the Navy or in the Government service."

O'Neill maintained he saw petitioner "right on from that (1920) at times." But his recollection of dates, number of opportunities for observation, and concrete events was wholly indefinite. He would fix no estimate for the number of times he had seen petitioner: "In 1920 I couldn't recall whether it was one or a thousand." For later years he would not say whether it was "five times or more or less." When he was pinned down by cross-examination, the effect of his testimony was that he recalled petitioner clearly in 1919 "because there was such a vast contrast in the man," but for later years he could give little or no definite information.

[The Court reprinted the following excerpt from the testimony in a footnote:

"X Can you tell us approximately how many times you saw him in 1919?"
"A. No; I seen him so often that it would be hard to give any estimate."
"X And the same goes for 1920?"
"A. I wouldn't be sure about 1920. I remember him more when he first came home because there was such a vast contrast in the man. Otherwise, if nothing unusual happened, I wouldn't probably recall him at all, you know, that is, recall the particular time and all."
"X Well, do you recall him at all in 1920?"
"A. I can't say."
"X And could you swear whether or not you ever saw him in 1921?"
"A. I think I seen him both in 1921 and 1920 and 1921 and right on. I might not see him for a few weeks or months at a time, but I think I saw him a few times in all the years right up to, as I say, at least five years after."
"X Can you give us an estimate as to the number of times you saw him in 1920?"
"A. No, I would not."
"X Was it more than five times or less?"
"A. In 1920 I couldn't recall whether it was one or a thousand. The time I recall him well is when he first come home, but I know that I seen him right on from that at times."
"X And the same goes for 1921, 1922, 1923 and 1924?"
"A. I would say for five years afterwards, but I don't know just when or how often I seen him except when he first come home for the first couple of months."
"X But for years after his return you couldn't say definitely whether you saw him five times or more or less, could you?"
"A. No, because it was a thing that there was a vast contrast when he first come home and everybody noticed it and remarked about it and it was more liable to be remembered. You could ask me about some more friends I knew during those years and I wouldn't know except there was something unusual."

The Court further noted that "[p]etitioner's own evidence shows without dispute he was on active duty in the Navy from January 15, 1920, to July of that year and in the Army from December, 1920, to May 6, 1922. As is noted in the text, O'Neill was not sure he was working and 'was surprised he got in the

Navy, I think in the Navy or in the Government service.' He only 'heard some talk' of petitioner's having reenlisted in the Army, but 'if it was the fact, I would be surprised that he could do it owing to his mental condition.' O'Neill was not certain that he saw Galloway in uniform after the first week of his return to Philadelphia from overseas, although he said he saw petitioner during 'the periods of those reenlistments . . . but I can't recall about it.'"]

O'Neill recalled one specific occasion after 1919 when petitioner returned to Philadelphia, "around 1920 or 1921, but I couldn't be sure," to testify in a criminal proceeding. He also said, "After he was away for five or six years, he came back to Philadelphia, but I wouldn't know nothing about dates on that. He was back in Philadelphia for five or six months or so, and he was still just evidently all right, and then he would be off."

Lt. Col. (Chaplain) Mathews said he observed a Private Joseph Galloway, who was a prisoner for desertion and a patient in the mental ward at Fort MacArthur Station Hospital, California, during a six weeks period early in 1920. The chaplain's testimony gives strong evidence the man he observed was insane. However, there is a fatal weakness in this evidence. In his direct testimony, which was taken by deposition, the chaplain said he was certain that the soldier was petitioner. When confronted with the undisputed fact that petitioner was on active duty in the Navy during the first half of 1920, the witness at first stated that he might have been mistaken as to the time of his observation. Subsequently he reasserted the accuracy of his original statement as to the time of observation, but admitted that he might have been mistaken in believing that the patient-prisoner was petitioner. In this connection he volunteered the statement, "Might I add, sir, that I could not now identify that soldier if I were to meet him face to face, and that is because of the long lapse of time." The patient whom the witness saw was confined to his bed. The record is barren of other evidence, whether by the hospital's or the Army's records or otherwise, to show that petitioner was either patient or prisoner at Fort MacArthur in 1920 or at any other time.

Commander Platt testified that petitioner caused considerable trouble by disobedience and leaving ship without permission during his naval service in the first half of 1920. After "repeated warnings and punishments, leading to court martials," he was sentenced to a bad conduct discharge.

Lt. Col. James E. Matthews (not the chaplain) testified by deposition which petitioner's attorney interrupted Dr. Wilder's testimony to read into evidence. The witness was Galloway's commanding officer from early 1921 to the summer of that year, when petitioner was transferred with other soldiers to another unit. At first Colonel Matthews considered making petitioner a corporal, but found him unreliable and had to discipline him. Petitioner "drank considerably," was "what we called a bolshevik," did not seem loyal, and "acted as if he was not getting a square deal." The officer concluded "he was a moral pervert and probably used narcotics," but could not secure proof of this. Galloway was court martialed for public drunkenness and disorderly conduct, served a month at hard labor, and returned to active duty. At times he "was one of the very best soldiers I had," at others undependable. He was physically sound, able to do his work, perform close order drill, etc., "very well." He had alternate periods of gaiety and depression, talked incoherently at times, gave the impression he would fight readily, but did not resent orders and seemed to get along well with other soldiers. The officer attributed petitioner's behavior to alcohol and narcotics and it occurred to him at no time to question his sanity.

Dr. Wilder was the key witness. He disclaimed specializing in mental disease, but qualified as having given it "special attention." He first saw petitioner shortly before the trial, examined him "several times." He concluded petitioner's ailment "is a schizophrenic branch or form of praecox." Dr. Wilder heard the testimony and read the depositions of the other witnesses, and examined the documentary evidence. Basing his judgment upon this material, with inferences drawn from it, he concluded petitioner was born with "an inherent instability," though he remained normal until he went to France; began there "to be subjected to the strain of military life, then he began to go to pieces." In May, 1919, petitioner "was still suffering from the acuteness of the breakdown. . . . He is going down hill still, but the thing began with the breakdown. . . ." Petitioner was "definitely insane, yes, sir," in 1920 and "has been insane at all times, at least since July, 1918, the time of this episode on the Marne"; that is, "to the point that he was unable to adapt himself. I don't mean he has not had moments when he could not perform some routine tasks," but "from an occupational standpoint . . . he has been insane." He could follow "a mere matter of routine," but would have no incentive, would not keep a steady job, come to work on time, or do anything he didn't want to do. Dr. Wilder pointed to petitioner's work record before he entered the service and observed: "At no time after he went into the war do we find him able to hold any kind of a job. He broke right down." He explained petitioner's enlistment in the Navy and later in the Army by saying, "It would have been no trick at all *for a man who was reasonably conforming* to get into the Service." (Emphasis added.)

However, the witness knew "nothing whatever except his getting married" about petitioner's activities between 1925 and 1930, and what he knew of them between 1922 and 1925 was based entirely on O'Neill's testimony and a paper not of record here. Dr. Wilder at first regarded knowledge concerning what petitioner was doing between 1925 and 1930 as not essential. "We have a continuing disease, quite obviously beginning during his military service, and quite obviously continuing in 1930, and the minor incidents don't seem to me. . . ." Counsel for the government interrupted to inquire, "Well, if he was continuously employed for eight hours a day from 1925 to 1930 would that have any bearing?" The witness replied, "It would have a great deal." Upon further questioning, however, he reverted to his first position, stating it would not be necessary or helpful for him to know what petitioner was doing from 1925 to 1930: "I testified from the information I had."

## II

This, we think, is the crux of the case and distinguishes it from the cases on which petitioner has relied. His burden was to prove total and permanent disability as of a date not later than May 31, 1919. He has undertaken to do this by showing incipience of mental disability shortly before that time and its continuance and progression throughout the succeeding years. He has clearly established incidence of total and permanent disability as of some period prior to 1938, when he began this suit. For our purposes this may be taken as medically established by the Veterans' Bureau examination and diagnosis of July, 1934.

But if the record is taken to show that some form of mental disability existed in 1930, which later became total and permanent, petitioner's problem remains to demonstrate by more than speculative inference that this condition itself began on or before May 31, 1919 and continuously existed or progressed through the intervening years to 1930.

To show origin before the crucial date, he gives evidence of two abnormal incidents occurring while he was in France, one creating the disturbance before he came near the fighting front, the other yelling that the Germans were coming when he was on guard duty at the Marne. There is no other evidence of abnormal behavior during his entire service of more than a year abroad.

That he was court martialed for these sporadic acts and bound and gagged for one does not prove he was insane or had then a general breakdown in "an already fragile mental constitution," which the vicissitudes of a longshoreman's life had not been able to crack.

To these two incidents petitioner adds the testimony of O'Neill that he looked and acted like a wreck, compared with his former self, when he returned from France about a month before the crucial date, and O'Neill's vague recollections that this condition continued through the next two, three, four or five years.

O'Neill's testimony apparently takes no account of petitioner's having spent 101 days in a hospital in France with influenza just before he came home. But, given the utmost credence, as is required, it does no more than show that petitioner was subject to alternating periods of gaiety and depression for some indefinite period after his return, extending perhaps as late as 1922. But because of its vagueness as to time, dates, frequency of opportunity for observation, and specific incident, O'Neill's testimony concerning the period from 1922 to 1925 is hardly more than speculative.

We have then the two incidents in France followed by O'Neill's testimony of petitioner's changed condition in 1919 and its continuance to 1922. There is also the testimony of Commander Platt and Lt. Col. James E. Matthews as to his service in the Navy and the Army, respectively, during 1920-1922. Neither thought petitioner was insane or that his conduct indicated insanity. Then follows a chasm of eight years. The only evidence we have concerning this period is the fact that petitioner married his present guardian at some time within it, an act from which in the legal sense no inference of insanity can be drawn.

This period was eight years of continuous insanity, according to the inference petitioner would be allowed to have drawn. If so, he should have no need of inference. Insanity so long and continuously sustained does not hide itself from the eyes and ears of witnesses. The assiduity which produced the evidence of two "crazy" incidents during a year and a half in France should produce one during eight years or, for that matter, five years in the United States.

Inference is capable of bridging many gaps. But not, in these circumstances, one so wide and deep as this. Knowledge of petitioner's activities and behavior from 1922 or 1925 to 1930 was peculiarly within his ken and that of his wife, who has litigated this cause in his and presumably, though indirectly, in her own behalf. His was the burden to show continuous disability. What he did in this time, or did not do, was vital to his case. Apart from the mere fact of his marriage, the record is blank for five years and almost blank for eight. For all that appears, he may have worked full time and continuously for five and perhaps for eight, with only a possible single interruption.

No favorable inference can be drawn from the omission. It was not one of oversight or inability to secure proof. That is shown by the thoroughness with which the record was prepared for all other periods, before and after this one, and by the fact petitioner's wife, though she married him during the period and was available, did not testify. The only reasonable conclusion is that petitioner, or those who acted for him, deliberately chose, for reasons no doubt considered sufficient (and which we do not criticize, since such matters including tactical ones, are for the judgment of counsel) to present no evidence or perhaps to withhold evidence readily available concerning this long interval, and to trust to the genius of expert medical inference and judicial laxity to bridge this canyon.

In the circumstances exhibited, the former is not equal to the feat, and the latter will not permit it. No case has been cited and none has been found in which inference, however expert, has been permitted to make so broad a leap and take the place of evidence which, according to all reason, must have been at hand. To allow this would permit the substitution of inference, tenuous at best, not merely for evidence absent because impossible or difficult to secure, but for evidence disclosed to be available and not produced. This would substitute speculation for proof. Furthermore, the inference would be more plausible perhaps if the evidence of insanity as of May, 1919, were stronger than it is, such for instance as Chaplain Mathews' testimony would have furnished if it could be taken as applying to petitioner. But, on this record, the evidence of insanity as of that time is thin at best, if it can be regarded as at all more than speculative.

Beyond this, there is nothing to show totality or permanence. These come only by what the Circuit Court of Appeals rightly characterized as "long-range retroactive diagnosis." That might suffice, notwithstanding this crucial inference was a matter of opinion, if there were factual evidence over which the medical eye could travel and find continuity through the intervening years. . . . But eight years are too many to permit it to skip, when the bridge-heads (if the figure may be changed) at each end are no stronger than they are here, and when the seer first denies, then admits, then denies again, that what took place in this time would make "a great deal" of difference in what he saw. Expert medical inference rightly can do much. But we think the feat attempted here too large for its accomplishment. . . .

## III

What has been said disposes of the case as the parties have made it. For that reason perhaps nothing more need be said. But objection has been advanced that, in some manner not wholly clear, the directed verdict practice offends the Seventh Amendment.

It may be noted, first, that the Amendment has no application of its own force to this case. The suit is one to enforce a monetary claim against the United States. It hardly can be maintained that under the common law in 1791 jury trial was a matter of right for persons asserting claims against the sovereign. Whatever force the Amendment has therefore is derived because Congress in the legislation cited, has made it applicable. Even so, the objection made on the score of its requirements is untenable.

If the intention is to claim generally that the Amendment deprives the federal courts of power to direct a verdict for insufficiency of evidence, the short answer is the contention has been foreclosed by repeated decisions made here consistently for nearly a century. More recently the practice has been approved explicitly in the promulgation of the Federal Rules of Civil Procedure. *Cf.* Rule 50. The objection therefore comes too late.

Furthermore, the argument from history is not convincing. It is not that "the rules of the common law" in 1791 deprived trial courts of power to withdraw cases from the jury, because not made out, or appellate courts of power to review such determinations. The jury was not absolute master of fact in 1791. Then as now courts excluded evidence for irrelevancy and relevant proof for other reasons. The argument concedes they weighed the evidence, not only piecemeal but in toto for submission to the jury, by at least two procedures, the demurrer to the evidence and the motion for a new trial. The objection is not therefore to the basic thing, which is the power of the court to withhold cases from the jury or set aside the verdict for insufficiency of the evidence. It is rather to incidental or collateral effects, namely, that the directed verdict as now administered differs from both those procedures because, on the one hand, allegedly higher standards of proof are required and, on the other, different consequences follow as to further maintenance of the litigation. Apart from the standards of proof, the argument appears to urge that in 1791, a litigant could challenge his opponent's evidence, either by the demurrer, which when determined ended the litigation, or by motion for a new trial which if successful, gave the adversary another chance to prove his case; and therefore the Amendment excluded any challenge to which one or the other of these consequences does not attach.

The Amendment did not bind the federal courts to the exact procedural incidents or details of jury trial according to the common law in 1791, any more than it tied them to the common-law system of pleading or the specific rules of evidence then prevailing. . . .

Each of the classical modes of challenge [that is, demurrer to the evidence and new trial motions] disproves the notion that the characteristic feature of the other, for effect upon continuing the litigation, became a part of the Seventh Amendment's guaranty to the exclusion of all others. That guaranty did not incorporate conflicting constitutional policies, that challenge to an opposing case must be made with the effect of terminating the litigation finally and, at the same time, with the opposite effect of requiring another trial. Alternatives so contradictory give room, not for the inference that one or the other is required, but rather for the view that neither is essential.

Finally, the objection appears to be directed generally at the standards of proof judges have required for submission of evidence to the jury. . . . Whatever may be the general formulation, the essential requirement is that mere speculation be not allowed to do duty for probative facts, after making due allowance for all reasonably possible inferences favoring the party whose case is attacked. . . .

Judged by this requirement, or by any standard other than sheer speculation, we are unable to conclude that one whose burden, by the nature of his claim, is to show continuing and total disability for nearly twenty years supplies the essential proof of continuity when he wholly omits to show his whereabouts, activities or condition for five years, although the record discloses evidence must have been available, and, further, throws no light upon three additional years, except for one vaguely described and dated visit to his former home. . . . The words "total and permanent" are the statute's, not our own. They mean something more than incipient or occasional disability. We hardly need add that we give full credence to all of the testimony. But that cannot cure its inherent vagueness or supply essential elements omitted or withheld.

Accordingly, the judgment is Affirmed.

Justice BLACK, with whom Justice DOUGLAS and Justice MURPHY concur, dissenting:

The Seventh Amendment to the Constitution provides:

In suits at common law, where the value in controversy shall exceed twenty dollars, the right of trial by jury shall be preserved, and no fact tried by a jury shall be otherwise re-examined in any Court of the United States, than according to the rules of the common law.

The Court here re-examines testimony offered in a common law suit, weighs conflicting evidence, and holds that the litigant may never take this case to a jury. The founders of our government thought that trial of fact by juries rather than by judges was an essential bulwark of civil liberty. For this reason, among others, they adopted Article III, § 2 of the Constitution, and the Sixth and Seventh Amendments. Today's decision marks a continuation of the gradual process of judicial erosion which in one hundred fifty years has slowly worn away a major portion of the essential guarantee of the Seventh Amendment.

## I

. . . In 1789, juries occupied the principal place in the administration of justice. They were frequently in both criminal and civil cases the arbiters not only of fact but of law. Less than three years after the ratification of the Seventh Amendment, this Court called a jury in a civil case brought under our original jurisdiction. There was no disagreement as to the facts of the case. Chief Justice Jay, charging the jury for a unanimous Court, three of whose members had sat in the Constitutional Convention, said: "For as, on the one hand, it is presumed, that juries are the best judges of facts; it is, on the other hand, presumable, that the court[s] are the best judges of law. But still, both objects are lawfully within your power of decision." *State of Georgia v. Brailsford*, 3 Dall. 1, 4, 1 L. Ed. 483. Similar views were held by state courts in Connecticut, Massachusetts, Illinois, Louisiana and presumably elsewhere. . . .

As Hamilton had declared in The Federalist, the basic judicial control of the jury function was in the court's power to order a new trial. In 1830, this Court said: "The only modes known to the common law to re-examine such facts, are the granting of a new trial by the court where the issue was tried, or to which the record was properly returnable; or the award of a venire facias de novo, by an appellate court, for some error of law which intervened in the proceedings." *Parsons v. Bedford*, [4 Pet. 433, 448 (1830)]. That retrial by a new jury rather than factual reevaluation by a court is a constitutional right of genuine value was restated as recently as *Slocum v. New York Life Insurance Co.*, 228 U.S. 364.

A long step toward the determination of fact by judges instead of by juries was the invention of the directed verdict. In 1850, what seems to have been the first directed verdict case considered by this Court, *Parks v. Ross*, 11 How. 362, 374, was presented for decision. The Court held that the directed verdict serves the same purpose as the demurrer to the evidence, and that since there was "no evidence whatever" on the critical issue in the case, the directed verdict was approved. The decision was an innovation, a departure from the traditional rule restated only fifteen years before in *Greenleaf v. Birth*, 1835, 9 Pet. 292, 299, in which this Court had said: "Where there is no evidence tending to prove a particular fact, the court[s] are bound so to instruct the jury, when requested; but they cannot legally give any instruction which shall take from the jury the right of weighing the evidence and determining what effect it shall have."

This new device contained potentialities for judicial control of the jury which had not existed in the demurrer to the evidence. In the first place, demurring to the evidence was risky business, for in so doing the party not only admitted the truth of all the testimony against him but also all reasonable inferences which might be drawn from it; and upon joinder in demurrer the case was withdrawn from the jury while the court proceeded to give final judgment either for or against the demurrant. Imposition of this risk was no mere technicality; for by making withdrawal of a case from the jury dangerous to the moving litigant's cause, the early law went far to assure that facts would never be examined except by a jury. Under the directed verdict practice the moving party takes no such chance, for if his motion is denied, instead of suffering a directed verdict against him, his case merely continues into the hands of the jury. The litigant not only takes no risk by a motion for a directed verdict, but in making such a motion gives himself two opportunities to avoid the jury's decision; for under the federal variant of judgment notwithstanding the verdict, the judge may reserve opinion on the motion for a directed verdict and then give judgment for the moving party after the jury was formally found against him. In the second place, under the directed verdict practice the courts soon abandoned the "admission of all facts and reasonable inferences" standard referred to, and created the so-called "substantial evidence" rule which permitted directed verdicts even though there was far more evidence in the case than a plaintiff would have needed to withstand a demurrer.

The substantial evidence rule did not spring into existence immediately upon the adoption of the directed verdict device. For a few more years federal judges held to the traditional rule that juries might pass finally on facts if there was "any evidence" to support a party's contention. The rule that a case must go to the jury unless there was "no evidence" was completely repudiated in *Schuylkill and Dauphin Improvement Co. v. Munson*, 14 Wall. 442, 447, 448 (1871), upon which the Court today relies in part. There the Court declared that "some" evidence was not enough—there must be evidence sufficiently persuasive to the judge so that he thinks "a jury can properly proceed." The traditional rule was given an ugly name, "the scintilla rule," to hasten its demise.

Later cases permitted the development of added judicial control. New and totally unwarranted formulas, which should surely be eradicated from the law at the first opportunity, were added as recently as 1929 in *Gunning v. Cooley*, 281 U.S. 90, which, by sheerest dictum, made new encroachments on the jury's constitutional functions. There it was announced that a judge might weigh the evidence to determine whether he, and not the jury, thought it was "overwhelming" for either party, and then direct a verdict. [The case] also suggests quite unnecessarily for its decision, that "When a plaintiff produces evidence that is consistent with an hypothesis that the defendant is not negligent, and also with one that he is, his proof tends to establish neither." This dictum . . . assumes that a judge can weigh conflicting evidence with mathematical precision and which wholly deprives the jury of the right to resolve that conflict. . . . With it, and other tools, jury verdicts on disputed facts have been set aside or directed verdicts authorized so regularly as to make the practice commonplace while the motion for directed verdict itself has become routine. . . .

Even *Gunning v. Cooley*, 281 U.S. at page 94, acknowledged that "issues that depend on the credibility of witnesses . . . are to be decided by the jury." Today the Court comes dangerously close to weighing the credibility of a witness and rejecting his testimony because the majority do not believe it.

The story thus briefly told depicts the constriction of a constitutional civil right and should not be continued. . . .

The language of the Seventh Amendment cannot easily be improved by formulas. The statement of a district judge in *Tarter v. United States*, D.C., 17 F. Supp. 691, 692, 693, represents, in my opinion, the minimum meaning of the Seventh Amendment:

> The Seventh Amendment to the Constitution guarantees a jury trial in law cases, where there is substantial evidence to support the claim of the plaintiff in an action. If a single witness testifies to a fact sustaining the issue between the parties, or if reasoning minds might reach different conclusions from the testimony of a single witness, one of which would substantially support the issue of the contending party, the issue must be left to the jury. Trial by jury is a fundamental guaranty of the rights of the people, and judges should not search the evidence with meticulous care to deprive litigants of jury trials.

The call for the true application of the Seventh Amendment is not to words, but to the spirit of honest desire to see that Constitutional right preserved. Either the judge or the jury must decide facts and to the extent that we take this responsibility, we lessen the jury function. Our duty to preserve this one of the Bill of Rights may be peculiarly difficult, for here it is our own power which we must restrain. . . . As for myself, I believe that a verdict should be directed, if at all, only when, without weighing the credibility of the witnesses, there is in the evidence no room whatever for honest difference of opinion over the factual issue in controversy. . . .

## II

The factual issue for determination here is whether the petitioner incurred a total and permanent disability not later than May 31, 1919. It is undisputed that the petitioner's health was sound in 1918, and it is evidently conceded that he was disabled at least since 1930. When in the intervening period, did the disability take place?

A doctor who testified diagnosed the petitioner's case as a schizophrenic form of dementia praecox. He declared it to be sound medical theory that while a normal man can retain his sanity in the face of severe mental or physical shock, some persons are born with an inherent instability so that they are mentally unable to stand sudden and severe strain. The medical testimony was that this petitioner belongs to the latter class and that the shock of actual conflict on the battle front brought on the incurable affliction from which he now suffers. The medical witness testified that the dominant symptoms of the condition are extreme introversion and preoccupation with personal interests, a persecution complex, and an emotional instability which may be manifested by extreme exhilaration alternating with unusual depression or irrational outbursts. Persons suffering from this disease are therefore unable to engage in continuous employment.

The petitioner relies on the testimony of wartime and post war companions and superiors to show that his present mental condition existed on the crucial date. There is substantial testimony from which reasonable men might conclude that the petitioner was insane from the date claimed. [Justice Black then summarized that testimony.]

. . . All of this evidence, if believed, showed a man healthy and normal before he went to the war suffering for several years after he came back from a disease which had the symptoms attributed to schizophrenia and who was insane from 1930 until his trial. Under these circumstances, I think that the physician's testimony of total and permanent disability by reason of continuous insanity from 1918 to 1938 was reasonable. The fact that there was no direct testimony for a period of five years, while it might be the basis of fair argument to the jury by the government, does not, as the Court seems to believe, create a presumption against the petitioner so strong that his case must be excluded from the jury entirely. Even if during these five years the petitioner was spasmodically employed, we could not conclude that he was not totally and permanently disabled. . . . It is not doubted that schizophrenia is permanent even though there may be a momentary appearance of recovery. . . .

This case graphically illustrates the injustice resulting from permitting judges to direct verdicts instead of requiring them to await a jury decision and then, if necessary, allow a new trial. The chief reason given for approving a directed verdict against this petitioner is that no evidence except expert medical testimony was offered for a five to eight year period. Perhaps, now that the petitioner knows he has insufficient evidence to satisfy a judge even though he may have enough to satisfy a jury, he would be able to fill this time gap to meet any judge's demand. If a court would point out on a motion for new trial that the evidence as to this particular period was too weak, the petitioner would be given an opportunity to buttress the physician's evidence. If, as the Court believes, insufficient evidence has been offered to sustain a jury verdict for the petitioner, we should at least authorize a new trial. . . .

I believe that there is a reasonable difference of opinion as to whether the petitioner was totally and permanently disabled by reason of insanity on May 31, 1919, and that his case therefore should have been allowed to go to the jury. The testimony of fellow soldiers, friends, supervisors, and of a medical expert whose integrity and ability is not challenged cannot be rejected by any process available to me as a judge.

## Comments and Questions

1. For class, please be prepared to answer these questions about *Galloway*:

(a) What is the cause of action and its elements?

(b) Which of the elements are not disputed? Explain how you know this.

(c) In advance of trial, what methods could Galloway's lawyer have used to make certain that the points of common agreement were taken as true at the trial? (Do not yet consider Rule 16 or case management. We will do that later.) Could either side have gained a victory using Fed. R. Civ. P. 12(b)(6) or 12(c)?

(d) Assume that you are Galloway's lawyer and that after you, representing the plaintiff, have rested, defense counsel moves for directed verdict (or "judgment as a matter of law" under Rule 50). The judge will call on you to explain precisely how you have met your production burden as to each disputed element. Be precise with the evidence. The judge will also ask you: "To what extent can I use the fact that you did not put plaintiff's wife on the stand? Do you have any reasons for not doing so other than the risk that her evidence would destroy your case? Tell me honestly, do I have a right to ask you that question?"

(e) Assume that you represent the government. Explain the failure of evidence as to any element for which you think there is an insufficiency of evidence to permit a plaintiff's verdict. Among other questions, the trial judge will ask you: "Are you not asking me to engage in assessing credibility and weighing the evidence? I'm not allowed to do that, am I?"

(f) Assume now that you are a clerk to the trial judge, who turns to you: "Clerk, I think the plaintiff's evidence is extremely weak and perhaps even nonexistent as to one element. Would this be a good case for me to let the case go to the jury, and then to grant a JNOV, rather than granting the directed verdict motion?" Why and why not? Consider the strategic considerations for the lawyers, their clients, the jurors, and the court system. What are the consequences if the judge goes the JNOV route as opposed to the directed verdict? Which method is more efficient? Are you sure? Explain.

(g) You represent the defendant. Assume that on February 1, a Thursday, the jury comes in with a plaintiff's verdict in *Galloway* and judgment is entered the same day. You wish to move for a JNOV and a new trial. You are awaiting a copy of the transcript, and therefore want the most time possible. Absent a snowstorm, when is the latest you can file your motions? Can you get an enlargement of time under Rule 6? Do the lengths of time for the making of such motions make sense?

(h) You are a member of a new organization ("S.A.J."—Save American Juries—pronounced "SAGE") of lawyers, judges, and legal scholars who have organized to find ways to engender new respect for the right to jury trial in civil cases and to lobby state and federal legislators to invigorate that right. Take realistic positions on the motions for directed verdict, for JNOV, and for a new trial because the verdict is against the weight of the evidence, and be prepared to defend those positions. You should know that not everyone agrees with the history given in Justice Black's dissent about the modern instruments of control over juries. In Woolhandler and Collins, *The Article III Jury*, 87 Va. L. Rev. 587, at 591-592 (2001), the authors argue that premodern federal control of juries "likely exceeded the level of modern judicial controls."

2. Defendants make motions for directed verdict based on many different theories. Many of the arguments overlap. Here are some:

(a) There is insufficient evidence of one or more elements to permit reasonable people to find that it is true. This is often a matter of arguing that inferences do not stretch so far as the plaintiff claims. You have seen the argument in *Galloway*. If you have occasion to do research on directed verdict cases in federal court, particularly those in which it matters how little evidence can suffice in order for a plaintiff to survive a directed verdict motion and how far inferences can be stretched, you should appraise the case law with caution. The many Supreme Court Federal Employment Liability Act (FELA) cases supporting plaintiffs' verdicts may be idiosyncratic to that field for a number of historical and policy reasons. *See, e.g.,* 9A Charles A. Wright, Arthur R. Miller, and Mary Kay Kane, *Federal Practice and Procedure* § 2526.

(b) The facts are in a "fog." No one knows what happened. Therefore, the plaintiff cannot make out a prima facie case. Sometimes, this is a literal argument, as in the motor vehicle accident in which both drivers are killed, no witnesses exist (perhaps because it happened in a fog), and no reconstruction is possible, based on the remaining physical evidence. In these and similar circumstances, defendants argue that a jury would have to engage in "mere speculation" or that a plaintiff's finding would be only "guesswork."

(c) We know what happened, but reasonable people cannot find that it meets the legal standard. For instance, the plaintiff might describe the defendant's activity in great detail, but as a matter of law there was "no duty" or the activity does not add up to negligence or whatever wrongdoing is alleged. In a contract case, the defendant may ask the court to interpret a written contract such that the plaintiff's rendition of factual events, even if believed, cannot rationally be found to be a breach of anything the defendant promised to do.

(d) The defendant may concede that the plaintiff has presented evidence of an element, but argues that no reasonable person could believe that evidence because it is not credible on its face. This is one way to read *Galloway*, or the *Matsushita* case, which we addressed in our discussion of summary judgment.

(e) There may be another kind of case in which the evidence seems to permit two equal but inconsistent inferences, and the defendant argues that the jury would only be guessing which one is true. The classic example of this in federal court is *Pennsylvania Railroad Co. v. Chamberlain*, 288 U.S. 333 (1933), but that case is probably no longer the rule in federal court. "The courts recognize that they lack the ability to say whether two or more inferences are equal." 9A Charles A. Wright, Arthur R. Miller, and Mary Kay Kane, *Federal Practice and Procedure* § 2528 (citation omitted).

(f) Sometimes plaintiffs try to survive a directed verdict motion by arguing that the evidence is in the defendant's hands and that the jury, in judging the demeanor of the defendant or another witness, should find that the defendant or the witness is so unbelievable that the opposite is true: "Since the defendant denies he did it, and you can see what a rascal and liar he is, you should believe the opposite." This argument will not usually wash. Indeed, if it did, it would be difficult for defendants ever to win a directed verdict or for appellate courts to know whether a motion for directed verdict was incorrectly denied, for the jury might always believe the opposite of what they heard. If you want to research this issue, find where *Dyer v. MacDougall*, 201 F.2d 265 (2d Cir. 1952), is included in the procedural treatise or hornbook of your choice, for that is the opinion (rendered by Justice Learned Hand) that scholars frequently invoke when discussing this topic. We put the issue here because once a defendant defeats the plaintiff's argument to draw the positive inference from disbelief of a denial, the plaintiff may be left with no evidence of a particular element.

(g) A defendant can seek a directed verdict by using evidence that must be believed. This could help a defendant in two ways. Perhaps evidence that must be believed will defeat one of plaintiff's necessary elements. Or perhaps an affirmative defense that must be taken as true will defeat the plaintiff "as a matter of law." Some courts say that whenever the testimony of a witness is involved, the issue must go to the jury, for the jury might disbelieve the testimony based on credibility. The prevailing view, however, regards the clear, uncontradicted, consistent, unimpeached testimony of even interested witnesses as evidence that must be taken as true, and therefore as sufficient basis for a directed verdict in favor of the party having the persuasion burden as well as the initial production burden. This amounts to a holding that reasonable people could not disbelieve such testimony on the basis of demeanor evidence.

3. The Federal Rules of Evidence play an important role in directed verdict, and consequently, in summary judgment. As the federal courts have taken a more active role in excluding expert testimony that they believe is unreliable (*see Daubert v. Merrill Dow Pharmaceuticals, Inc.*, 509 U.S. 579 (1993), and *Kumho Tire Co. Ltd. v. Carmichael*, 526 U.S. 137 (1999)), this in turn has led to increased restriction of what cases are permitted to reach a jury, and, if they do survive a directed verdict motion, what testimony the jury can consider.

4. Plaintiffs do, on occasion, win directed verdicts, even though they have the burden of both production and persuasion. We have discussed this possibility previously, and it should now be clear to you why it is usually more unlikely for a plaintiff to win a directed verdict than for a defendant. Still, some cases are ripe for a plaintiff's directed verdict, such as a promissory note case in which the defendant has no defense and the damages are liquidated. Bear in mind also that a plaintiff can frequently win on some of its elements "as a matter of law." For example, if a defendant admits an element in the pleading, or through answering positively or neglecting to answer a request for an admission (Fed. R. Civ. P. 36), or through stipulation or a blanket admission on the stand, the judge can instruct the jury that the element

must be believed. In the alternative, the judge can just omit such an element from those that the jury is instructed to consider.

5. You should understand that it is a question of law whether or not to grant a directed verdict—even though that determination necessarily involves factual issues. Another way to think of this is that a judge must decide the legal question of whether or not there are facts sufficient to let the jury deliberate on the matter.

6. The Supreme Court continues to try to clarify what the trial court should examine in deciding motions for judgment as a matter of law. In a unanimous opinion, the Supreme Court dealt with what constitutes a sufficiency of evidence to permit a plaintiff to survive a directed verdict motion in a disparate treatment age discrimination case in which the discharged plaintiff employee put in evidence of a prima facie case (he was a member of a protected class—over forty years of age, qualified for the position in question, discharged by the employer, and replaced by younger people), and also put in evidence refuting the nondiscriminatory reason proffered for his discharge. *Reeves v. Sanderson Plumbing Products, Inc.*, 530 U.S. 133 (2000). The plaintiff also had evidence of some discriminatory statements made by a supervisor concerning his age. Justice O'Connor, writing for the court, explained that although *St. Mary's Honor Center v. Hicks*, 509 U.S. 502 (1993), held that the fact finder's disbelief of the nondiscriminatory reason put forth by the employer-defendant, coupled with the plaintiff's initial prima facie case, did not mean automatic victory for the plaintiff, for the fact finder must still find discriminatory intent in order for the plaintiff to win, "[i]n appropriate circumstances, the trier of fact can reasonably infer from the falsity of the explanation that the employer is dissembling to cover up the discriminatory purpose." The Supreme Court reversed the Fifth Circuit's reversal of the jury verdict because the Circuit Court "misapplied the standard of review dictated by Rule 50. The court disregarded evidence favorable to Reeves [the plaintiff]—the evidence supporting his prima facie case and undermining respondent's nondiscriminatory explanation—and failed to draw all reasonable inferences in his favor." In a concurring opinion, Justice Ginsburg reiterated the principle of evidence law stated by Justice O'Connor, that "the jury is entitled to treat a party's dishonesty about a material fact as evidence of culpability," and expressed her opinion that when a plaintiff in a disparate treatment discrimination suit introduces both types of evidence—a prima facie case and a sufficiency of evidence to permit the fact finder to "conclude that the employer's proffered explanation for its actions was false"—this will typically permit the case to go to the jury in order to decide whether it draws the permissible inference of discriminatory intent. In her view, the permissible inference remains unless the defendant can "conclusively" demonstrate (which she suspects is atypical) "that discrimination could not have been the defendant's true motivation"; under those circumstances, according to Justice Ginsburg, the defendant would be entitled to judgment as a matter of law.

7. Shortly after the Federal Rules of Civil Procedure became law, the Supreme Court, in *Montgomery Ward & Co. v. Duncan*, 311 U.S. 243

(1940), was called upon to interpret the relationship between a motion for JNOV and a motion for new trial (Fed. R. Civ. P. 59). An amendment to Rule 50 in 1963 sought to clarify what a trial judge should do when confronted with both motions, and subsequent amendments have attempted to give further guidance. What is the trial judge now obligated to do when she grants a JNOV and has also been requested to grant a new trial? Consider why, from the defendant's point of view, it may be important to have an opportunity to argue the JNOV motion for a new trial in front of the same judge who heard argument for the motion for JNOV. Under what circumstances would it become relevant whether the trial judge decides both the JNOV and new trial motions? Does this suggest potential unfairness to the nonmoving party, normally the plaintiff?

The Supreme Court has interpreted Rule 50 to allow a circuit court, upon finding some of plaintiff's evidence admitted at the trial to be inadmissible, and further finding that the defendant, absent that evidence, was entitled to judgment as a matter of law, to enter final judgment for the defendant. Although this denies the plaintiff the opportunity to now present its new trial motion to the trial judge, the court thought it was not unfair because the plaintiff has had a full opportunity to enter its best case. *Weisgram v. Marley Co.*, 528 U.S. 440 (2000).

## Practice Exercise No. 24: Ruling upon a Motion for Directed Verdict in *City of Cleveland*

You are a law clerk in a judge's chambers discussing the *City of Cleveland* case. Read the judge's memorandum on directed verdict and the portions of the judge's Trial Notebook, which are in the Case Files. Assume that the plaintiffs' counsel have now rested and that the defendant has moved for a directed verdict on all four counts. The defendant's counsel must be told on which counts the case will proceed. The judge is in a hurry, not wanting to leave the jury out for an extended recess. Although the judge will hear argument by counsel, the judge wants your advice as to whether you would grant directed verdict on any of the counts. As you will see from the memorandum, the judge is sure how to rule on one of the counts. Of course, the judge may also consider whether to go the JNOV route. The memorandum will tell you which count you should be most prepared on. Prepare to give informed advice.

## Review Exercise No. 4

You will benefit most from the quiz if you follow the directions: Set aside at least ninety minutes to answer this question; if you finish early this is an indication that you are not wrestling sufficiently with the facts. Use only your rule book. Answer the question yourself before discussing it with your study group. The question involves a one-count complaint for injurious falsehood, and the elements of that cause of action appear at the end of the question.

Pristine Linear Technologies ("PLT") is the United States' largest manufacturer and seller of automatic car wash systems. Theresa Dupont ("Dupont") owns several gas stations in the Sacramento, California area. On August 1, 2009, Dupont ordered three automatic car wash systems from PLT. Dupont informed PLT that she planned to install these car wash systems in three of her new Sacramento area gas stations. Dupont promptly paid $500,000 for the three systems, and PLT shipped the systems from their facility in Miami, Florida. Because construction of the three gas stations was not completed at the time that Dupont ordered the car wash systems, she requested that delivery of those systems be delayed until the construction projects were completed; and PLT agreed to do so. PLT then contacted a business associate in Sacramento named Stan Pembroke, and paid him to store the three car wash systems in one of his warehouses. Pembroke owns dozens of gas stations and related enterprises throughout the Sacramento area and is a competitor of Dupont's.

On February 1, 2010, Dupont called PLT to arrange for the delivery of two of the three car wash systems. Two of the systems were delivered as requested; the third system remained in storage with Pembroke.

On May 1, 2010, Dupont contacted the Sacramento Police Department and told them that Pembroke possessed and was attempting to sell an automatic car wash system that belonged to her (Dupont). Dupont supplied the police with documentation that she had ordered and paid PLT for the automatic car wash system. Pembroke was immediately arrested and indicted on charges of theft. On July 1, 2010, the prosecutors abandoned the prosecution and dropped all of the charges. Around this same time, upon Dupont's request, the third car wash system was delivered to her.

On November 24, 2010, lawyers for PLT and Pembroke filed a lawsuit against Dupont in a federal district court in California. Dupont was properly served with a summons and a copy of the complaint later that same day. The complaint alleged each of the factual details specified in the preceding paragraphs, and claimed that "as a result of Dupont's unsubstantiated accusation of theft, the plaintiffs incurred substantial damages." The defendant moved to dismiss for failure to state a claim; that motion was denied. After discovery, defendant's motion for summary judgment also was denied.

At trial, a jury found in favor of Pembroke (but not in favor of PLT), and awarded Pembroke $250,000 in damages. The defendant's timely motion for a directed verdict (judgment as a matter of law) was denied. Now pending before the judge is Dupont's renewed motion for judgment as a matter of law (JNOV). The evidence of record includes the facts that are reported in this question, all of which were supported by evidence presented at trial. Additional evidence offered by the parties is included below:

Winkler, a gas station owner unaffiliated with the parties, testified that he had been asked by Pembroke on March 30, 2010, whether he (Winkler) wanted to buy a car wash system "quickly and discreetly." Winkler declined the offer and knew none of the details about which car system Pembroke was offering to sell. Winkler testified that he immediately made Dupont aware of this conversation because he knew that Dupont had been adding car wash systems to some of her gas stations.

Whitford, another gas station owner unaffiliated with the parties, testified that he had been asked by Pembroke in the middle of March 2010 whether he (Whitford) was in the market for a car wash system. When Whitford declined, Pembroke said that that was unfortunate since he had a "freebie that he needed to unload." Whiftford further testified that he told Dupont about this conversation a week or so later because he had heard from someone else that Pembroke had been storing Dupont's car wash systems as a favor to Dupont.

Dupont testified that a few days after she had heard from both Winkler and Whitford she called Pembroke to ask whether and why he had her car wash system. Dupont testified that Pembroke denied storing or even knowing anything about her car wash systems. According to Dupont, in that telephone conversation Pembroke denied that he had even spoken with the folks at PLT within the last couple of years.

Dupont testified that she called PLT the same day that she called Pembroke, and that when she didn't hear back from the PLT folks within twenty-four hours, she "panicked." That's why she called the police the very next day.

Dupont testified that in early 2010 her businesses were in financial crisis, and that her competititors were well aware of her tenuous situation. "I had to fend off the vultures," she said.

Dupont testified that the first two car wash systems were delivered promptly after she had requested delivery. Dupont admitted that she had not asked PLT to deliver the third car wash system before she called the police.

Dupont testified that she was not ready for the third car wash system to be delivered because the gas station had not been constructed, and delivery of the system would have interfered with that construction. Dupont testified that when she ultimately asked for the car wash system to be delivered, she received it the next day.

Pembroke testified that he never offered to sell Dupont's car wash system to anyone. He testified: "How could I sell it when she had already paid PLT for it?"

Pembroke admitted that he knew Dupont was financially vulnerable and had joked to Dupont and to others that he would be buying her assets in a "ladies-only garage sale" sometime very soon.

Pembroke testified that he used an independent trucking company to deliver the first two car wash systems to Dupont. His own employees delivered the third system.

The chief executive officer of PLT testified that he never instructed Pembroke to do anything with Dupont's car wash systems other than to store them and to send him the bill for storage. He testified: "Of course, we weren't trying to sell that car wash system. I don't need to sell the same machine twice when I have others in manufacture."

The chief executive officer of PLT also testified that he never told Dupont that he was using Pembroke to store her car wash systems because he knew that would make her nervous since he was a competitor. "But it was just storage. There was no reason for her to worry about it, so I didn't tell her."

The police and prosecutor testified that, after Dupont notified the police department that her property was in Pembroke's possession, she did not "push the case." Dupont played no role in the decision to indict. They called Dupont from time to time, and she simply answered their questions. When asked whether she ever made any false statements to them, the police and the prosecutor both testified "No. It was her property, not Pembroke's."

PLT submitted legal bills indicating an expense of $85,000 attributable to the criminal investigation into the theft. Someone from the PLT public relations department testified that PLT also suffered "serious reputational harm from this. A conservative estimate would put that loss at $150,000."

Pembroke submitted bills from a criminal lawyer indicating a balance owing in the amount of $115,000 for legal services associated with the theft indictment. A local business school professor who had reviewed Pembroke's business records testified that Pembroke had suffered lost wages and lost profits because of the distraction and reputational loss associated with the theft charges that had damaged Pembroke in amounts that exceeded $550,000.

Assume that the only law under which PLT and Pembroke could possibly recover in this jurisdiction is a claim for injurious falsehood, which provides that one who (i) makes a false statement (ii) with intent to harm the interests of another (iii) is liable for any provable loss. The statute of limitations on all claims is two years.

What arguments will the defendant make to support her renewed motion for judgment as a matter of law (JNOV)? What will Pembroke argue? And how should the court rule?


## 7. Motion to Vacate Judgment

Re-read Fed. R. Civ. P. 60, which gives the ground rules for moving to vacate a judgment in federal court. These rules are typical of what applies in most states as well. Rule 60 is mostly used subsequent to the time period that is permitted for making motions for JNOV or for new trial motions, but nothing prevents a losing party from making all three motions together if the time periods permit.

Fed. R. Civ. P. 60 requires the lawyer to do additional research before relying upon it. For example, many of the categories in Rule 60(b) have been interpreted in ways that one would be unlikely to infer by only reading the rule; the interpretations generally narrow the application of the Rule. The following list of examples is by no means exhaustive:

(1) The "mistake, inadvertence, surprise, or excusable neglect" language in Rule 60(b)(1) has been severely limited by case law. In most of the cases in

which a judgment is vacated under this provision, the losing party is unable to have any trial because of a default judgment or similar reason.

(2) The "newly discovered evidence" cases (60(b)(2)) tend to tack on a number of additional requirements. Some cases say, for example, that the evidence must not be merely cumulative or impeaching, and that such evidence must relate to facts that were in existence at the time of trial. The provision itself requires that the matter could not have been discovered "by reasonable diligence" in time to move for a Rule 59(b) new trial, which is a difficult condition to meet, given the many discovery devices.

(3) Cases applying the "fraud . . . , misrepresentation, or misconduct by an opposing party" category in Rule 60(b)(3) tend to consider a number of factors, such as the opportunities for detection of the misconduct, before or during trial, and the strength of the proof of the misconduct. These interpretive factors are complicated by the fact that fraud can also be a reason for voiding a judgment under 60(b)(4) and that the Rule explicitly "does not limit a court's power to . . . set aside a judgment for fraud on the court" through an independent action. Fed. R. Civ. P. 60(d). That there are several subcategories of fraud cases under Rule 60(b) is not merely a matter of academic concern, for the motions under 60(b)(1), (2), and (3) must be made within a year, and other motions must be made "within a reasonable time." Since the independent action is not a motion, it may have a different time period.

(4) Rule 60(b)(6) establishes the category "any other reason that justifies relief." Since this category is not subject to the one-year limitation set forth in Fed. R. Civ. P. 60(c)(1), lawyers frequently try to recast a motion that would ordinarily be brought under (b)(1), (2), and (3) into a reason not covered by those provisions. The courts tend to rule, however, that if the case could have been covered by the 60(b)(1) through (3) categories, then litigants cannot avoid the one-year limitation by seeking refuge in the catchall language of 60(b)(6).

———————————

The following case considers the application of the language of Fed. R. Civ. P. 60(a), (b)(1), and (b)(6). As you read the case, ask yourself how you would have decided it. Are you surprised by the court's result? Be prepared to explain the court's reasoning as to all three applicable provisions. Could you write an equally persuasive opinion reaching a different conclusion?

## ■ BRANDON v. CHICAGO BOARD OF EDUCATION
### 143 F.3d 293 (7th Cir. 1998)

ROVNER, Circuit Judge:

Lorenzo Brandon sought Rule 60 relief from a judgment entered against him for failure to prosecute his case. The district court denied relief and Brandon now appeals. The facts are unusual. Indeed, Brandon claims they are unique. Brandon filed his Americans with Disabilities action against the Chicago Board of Education on August 2, 1995. His attorneys, Paul F. Peters and James C. Reho, entered appearances in the case, listing as their address the Law Offices of Paul F. Peters, One North LaSalle Street, Chicago. It is undisputed that in docketing the case, the Clerk of the United States District Court erroneously entered, Paul A. Peters, another Chicago attorney, who is located at 10 South LaSalle Street, Chicago, as attorney for the plaintiff. As a result of this error, subsequent mailings from the court were directed to the wrong attorney at the wrong address. Admirably, Paul A. Peters actually took the time to write to the Clerk of the district court, informing the Clerk that he was not counsel of record in the case, had no connection to the case, and was returning any materials sent to him.

Unfortunately, the Clerk's office still did not understand the nature of its error, and continued to send all minute orders and other mailings to the wrong address. As a result, Brandon's counsel never received notice of two different status hearings, and failed to appear. After failing to appear for the second status hearing, the court dismissed the case for want of prosecution on December 13, 1995. The order dismissing the case was also sent to the wrong address. A little more than a year passed before plaintiff's counsel began to wonder what happened to the case. Upon visiting the Clerk's office in late 1996, he discovered his case had been quite active without him. Included in the court's file was the letter from Paul A. Peters, orders setting status hearings, and the order dismissing the case for want of prosecution.[1]

On December 16, 1996, one year and three days after the dismissal, Paul F. Peters filed a Rule 60 motion to vacate the judgment. Astonishingly, yet another clerical error, this one caused by plaintiff's counsel, caused the motion to be spindled under the wrong case number. When plaintiff's counsel noticed this error on the day the motion was to be heard, he pointed it out to the Clerk's office. The Clerk's office told him the motion would not be heard that day, and would have to be re-noticed. Plaintiff's counsel then refiled the motion under the correct case number. Before the new date for the hearing, however, plaintiff's counsel received a minute order from the court, granting the motion. As a courtesy, plaintiff's counsel sent a letter to defendant's counsel, stating that the motion had been granted and no appearance was necessary on the date set for hearing the motion. Nevertheless, defendant's counsel appeared in court on the day of the hearing and persuaded the court to vacate its order granting Rule 60 relief. After briefing on the motion, the court ultimately denied Rule 60 relief.

On appeal, Brandon argues that he cannot be faulted for a lack of diligence when he was never notified by the court that there was anything he was supposed to be doing. He never ignored a court order, he contends, because he

---

1. The Board of Education filed two motions early in the case, one to extend the time to answer, and the other to file the answer *instanter*. Brandon received a notice for each of these motions, and opposed neither. The court entered minute orders granting the motions and, as before, the Clerk mailed the minute orders to the wrong attorney. The Board rightly points out that Brandon should have known something was amiss when he failed to receive either order.

never knew about any orders. Rather, the clerical error in the Clerk's office was the source of the problem, and the district court abused its discretion in refusing to grant Rule 60 relief. Although Brandon initially moved for relief under Rule 60(a), he subsequently argued (and argues on appeal) that he is entitled to relief under Rule 60(b)(6). He admitted at oral argument that he is abandoning any claim to relief under Rule 60(a), which by its own terms applies only to clerical mistakes in "judgments, orders or other parts of the record and errors therein arising from oversight or omission."[2] The Chicago Board of Education focuses its response on Brandon's lack of entitlement to relief under Rule 60(b)(1), stating that it is the only conceivably relevant subsection.

We begin by examining, Rule 60(b), which provides, in relevant part, as follows:

> On motion and upon such terms as are just, the court may relieve a party or a party's legal representative from a final judgment, order, or proceeding for the following reasons: (1) mistake, inadvertence, surprise, or excusable neglect; (2) newly discovered evidence which by due diligence could not have been discovered in time to move for a new trial under Rule 59(b); (3) fraud (whether heretofore denominated intrinsic or extrinsic), misrepresentation, or other misconduct of an adverse party; (4) the judgment is void; (5) the judgment has been satisfied, released, or discharged, or a prior judgment upon which it is based has been reversed or otherwise vacated, or it is no longer equitable that the judgment should have prospective application; or (6) any other reason justifying relief from the operation of the judgment. The motion shall be made within a reasonable time, and for reasons (1), (2), and (3) not more than one year after the judgment, order, or proceeding was entered or taken.

Neither side argues that subsections (2) through (5) are applicable. Instead, Brandon argues that he is entitled to relief under subsection (b)(6), the catchall section. The Board contends that subsection (b)(1) is the only applicable section. The parties agree that we may not reverse a trial court's denial of a Rule 60(b) motion absent an abuse of discretion. *See Dickerson v. Board of Education of Ford Heights, Illinois,* 32 F.3d 1114, 1116 (7th Cir.1994) (trial court's denial of Rule 60(b) motion reviewed under a highly deferential standard, and reversed only for abuse of discretion). Moreover, because a court's dismissal for failure to prosecute is itself

---

2. Brandon is correct to abandon his Rule 60(a) argument. *See Wesco Products Co. v. Alloy Automotive Co.,* 880 F.2d 981, 984 (7th Cir. 1989). We noted there that district courts often have difficulty determining whether motions are brought to correct a clerical error (as opposed to some other kind of error). "In this circuit, we have identified the relevant distinction as being between changes that implement the result intended by the court at the time the order was entered and changes that alter the original meaning to correct a legal or factual error. Thus, '[i]f the flaw lies in the translation of the original meaning to the judgement, then Rule 60(a) allows a correction; if the judgement captures the original meaning but is infected by error, [] the parties must seek another source of authority to correct the mistake.'" *Id.* (citing *United States v. Griffin,* 782 F.2d 1393, 1396-97 (7th Cir. 1986)) (internal citations omitted). In the instant case, as in *Wesco,* the dismissal for want of prosecution accurately reflected the court's intention at the time it was entered. Thus, the error, to the extent there was one, was not in the transcription, but in the court's decision, a ground for relief not contained in Rule 60(a).

reviewed only for abuse of discretion, "a court's decision under Rule 60(b) not to reinstate a case dismissed for want of prosecution has been described as 'discretion piled on discretion.'" *Id.*, 32 F. 3d at 1117.

"Inherent in the structure of Rule 60(b) is the principle that the first three clauses and the catchall clause are mutually exclusive. Thus, if the asserted grounds for relief fall within the terms of the first three clauses of Rule 60(b), relief under the catchall provision is not available." *Wesco Products Co. v. Alloy Automotive Co.*, 880 F.2d 981, 983 (7th Cir.1989) (internal citations omitted). Therefore, we must first determine if the relief sought falls within Rule 60(b)(1). We noted in *Wesco* that Rule 60(b)(1) applies to errors by judicial officers as well as parties. 880 F.2d at 984-985. The district court here appeared to be analyzing the motion pursuant to Rule 60(b)(1), finding that "[t]here was a lack of diligence," and that this was "certainly not excusable neglect." *See* Transcript of Proceedings before the Honorable George W. Lindberg, Feb. 11, 1997, at p. 8. The district court also acknowledged that Rule 60(b)(1) applies to errors by the court, stating that "if the rules mean anything, and the Seventh Circuit jurisprudence means anything, it means that lawyers must follow their cases. They cannot rely on the Judge, the law clerks or the courtroom deputies or the Clerk's office. They must follow their case." *Id.*

We agree with the district court that Rule 60(b)(1) is the appropriate mechanism for analyzing Brandon's request for relief. Indeed, the facts here demonstrate an unusual combination of error by the Clerk's office and neglect by the attorney.[3] Rule 60(b)(1) covers both. Having found that Rule 60(b)(1) applies, we must necessarily find that Rule 60(b)(6) does not apply. *Wesco*, 880 F.2d at 983. By its own terms, a motion brought pursuant to Rule 60(b)(1) must be made within one year of the date the judgment was entered. "[T]he one year time limit is jurisdictional and may not be extended in any event...." *Wesco*, 880 F.2d at 985. No one disputes that Brandon brought his motion one year and three days after judgment was entered against him. We therefore conclude that the district court did not abuse its discretion in denying relief.

# F. TYPES OF VERDICTS, BIFURCATION, TRIFURCATION, INSTRUCTIONS, REMITTITUR, AND ADDITUR

In this section we introduce the rationale, doctrine, and strategic concerns of jury instructions, bifurcation and trifurcation, types of verdict, and remittitur and additur. Are these ways of helping the jury to be just and rational, or do they invade the jury's fact-finding province?

---

3. The instant case is distinguishable from the cases cited in the *Wesco* dissent, where various court clerks affirmatively misled parties as to the status of their cases. *See* 880 F.2d at 986-87 (Ripple, J. dissenting Here, the Clerk did not affirmatively mislead plaintiff's counsel in any way. Indeed, when plaintiff's counsel finally went to the Clerk's office to determine the status of the case, the Clerk provided a complete and accurate record of the proceedings.

## 1. Types of Verdicts

Traditionally, juries rendered general verdicts. In civil cases, juries were asked only to find for the plaintiff or for the defendant, and if for the plaintiff, to state the amount of monetary damages. One procedural device already available in federal and state courts is the *special verdict*, which provides means by which trial judges can structure a jury's reasoning process. Under the Federal Rules of Civil Procedure, the trial judge can submit written questions to the jury, and the jury returns a special verdict in the form of written findings of fact. Alternatively, the judge can have the jury return a general verdict, but answer interrogatories that have been posed to it by the judge. With either method, the judge is outlining the way the jury should approach the issue, step by step. Read Fed. R. Civ. P. 49.

Some of the traditional arguments for special verdicts are that restricting the decision-making functions of the jury would "improve the deliberation process by packaging the dispute in distinct, manageable components," "concentrat[e] juror attention on certain matters," "aid the jurors in sorting out the facts and avoiding confusion," "ensure a truly unanimous decision," "facilitate the appellate process by spelling out the premises underlying the jury's ultimate conclusions," and "[be] extremely helpful in the application of collateral estoppel (issue preclusion)." *See* Mark Brodin, *Accuracy, Efficiency, and Accountability in the Litigation Process—The Case for the Fact Verdict*, 59 U. Cin. L. Rev. 15 (1990). These arguments all imply that the jury could use some help in structuring their deliberations and decisions. What do you think?

## 2. Bifurcation and Trifurcation

Another reform is splitting trials into stages. "Bifurcation" typically separates a case into two potential trials, usually liability and causation first. If the defendant wins, that ends the matter. If the plaintiff wins on liability and causation, and the case does not settle at that point, there is then a trial on damages. Of course, judicial separation can happen in many ways, although the term "bifurcation" is usually used to denote the separation of elements into two trials. A judge can also try parties separately or separate out different causes of action for trial. Fed. R. Civ. P. 42(b) is usually the authorization relied upon in federal court for such judicial dividing. "Trifurcation" divides a case into three parts for purposes of trial, usually separating out causation, liability (fault), and damages. Once again, if the plaintiff loses on one element, like causation, that obviates the need for a trial on the other elements. If the plaintiff wins on the first element, that may well lead to settlement.

The arguments in favor of bifurcation and trifurcation fall into three spheres. First, there is efficiency. You have already read how the determination of one portion of a case for the defendant will eliminate the need to go further. What is perhaps less obvious is that even if the plaintiff wins the first portion, say on liability, this will frequently lead to settlement, resulting in further efficiency and money-saving for the court and the parties. Second, by severing damages from liability, or causation from both, this eliminates some of the emotional element from jury consideration. For instance, if the injuries to the plaintiff are extensive and heart-rending, and those injuries are tried as part of a unitary case, this may cause a jury to find for the plaintiff on liability when otherwise they might not find the defendant at fault. Similarly, if causation is tried first in a trifurcated case, this can decrease the possibility that the horrendous injuries or untoward conduct of the defendant will magnetically draw a jury to a jury verdict on all elements, even though the conduct has not caused the harm.

In an interesting article in the *Columbia Business Law Review,* Meiring de Villiers analyzes experimental and trial data, as well as relying on theories of group deliberation, and makes comparisons between unitary trials in product liability cases and bifurcated trials, with liability being tried prior to damages. His conclusions seem very plausible: (1) When all elements are tried together, there will be some cases in which the jury might not have otherwise found liability, but instead will compromise by giving diminished damages; (2) when cases are bifurcated, there will be some cases in which the jury will not find liability, because they are unable to achieve a compromise verdict on the damage portion, which is not before them, and yet do not want to be a hung jury; and (3) once the plaintiff in a bifurcated case wins on the first stage, liability, there will be instances when the plaintiff achieves a higher damage settlement or a higher jury verdict than he or she would have had the case been tried in a unitary fashion (once again, this is because the jury cannot readily make the compromise they sometimes made in example "1" of finding liability, but giving lesser damages, because liability has already been found).

This leads de Villiers to a third sphere of argument in favor of bifurcation in products liability cases. Here is his conclusion:

> The theoretical analysis presented in the article has important public policy implications. Trial bifurcation will encourage plaintiffs to file suit in cases where evidence of liability is strong, and discourage marginal cases. Bifurcated litigation will provide clearer guidance to manufacturers of the product safety standard they will be expected to achieve, promote the achievement of deterrence, compensation and product safety, and reduce the likelihood that a high-risk/high-utility product, that is valued by consumers, will be driven out of the market on the whim of a minority of extremely risk-averse jurors [i.e., jurors who force the majority of jurors in a given case to find liability in exchange for reduced damages].

Meiring de Villiers, *A Legal and Policy Analysis of Bifurcated Litigation,* 2000 Colum. Bus. L. Rev. 153, 197. Other articles support the de Villiers pro-bifurcation view. *See, e.g.,* Steven S. Gensler, *Bifurcation Unbound,* 75 Wash. L. Rev. 705 (2000) (arguing that if trials were bifurcated between liability and damages stages, perhaps 70 percent would end without reaching the damages phase).

As you might expect, there are a group of counterarguments made by those who prefer a unitary, nonsplit trial. Throughout this book, we have presented the position that litigation generally, and jury trials in particular, are by no means merely a mechanical method of applying law to facts. Rather, we have suggested that there is a lot more going on, and that concepts of citizen participation, legitimization of results, community values, and the importance and power of narrative are critical parts of the mix.

## ■ ED SHERMAN, SEGMENTING AGGREGATE LITIGATION
### 25 Rev. Litig. 691, 704-706 (2006)

Courts have differed on their willingness to find that such methods comport with standards of efficiency and fairness. One of the most serious challenges is whether use of different juries violates the Reexamination Clause of the Seventh Amendment. Bifurcation has been said to be limited in "recognition of the fact that inherent in the Seventh Amendment guarantee of a trial by jury is the general right of a litigant to have only one jury pass on a common issue of fact."[48] The test, based on a 1931 case concerning a partial new trial, is that an issue may only be separated if so distinct and separable from others that a trial of it alone may be had without injustice.[49] Although there may be some overlapping of evidence in different segments of a bifurcated case, courts have generally found that such issues as liability, damages, causation, and affirmative defenses satisfy the "distinct and separable" test, and there is no violation of the Seventh Amendment. "[The] Seventh Amendment prohibition is not against having two juries review the same evidence, but rather against having two juries decide the same essential issues."[50]

Cases in two circuits have found a Seventh Amendment violation in the use of bifurcation. In *In re Rhone-Poulenc Rorer, Inc.*,[51] the trial court certified a class action and ordered an initial trial limited to the question of the negligence of the defendant manufacturers of blood solids for hemophiliacs that resulted in their being infected with AIDS. If negligence were found, the class members could file individual suits which would use special verdicts and the preclusion doctrine to avoid relitigation of the issue of negligence. In finding the court exceeded its authority, Judge Posner stated that issues of comparative negligence and proximate cause which would arise in the individual suits overlapped the issue of negligence and thus improperly allowed reexamination by different juries. The Fifth Circuit, in *Castano v.*

48. *Alabama v. Blue Bird Body Co.*, 573 F.2d 309, 318 (5th Cir. 1978).
49. *Gasoline Prods. Co. v. Champlin Ref. Co.*, 283 U.S. 494, 500 (1971).
50. *In re Paoli R.R. Yard PCB Litig.*, 113 F.3d 444, 452 n.5 (3d Cir. 1997).
51. 51 F.3d 1293 (7th Cir. 1995).

*American Tobacco Co.*,[54] adopted this analysis. Rejecting a proposed class-wide trial of "core liability" issues relating to defendant tobacco companies' conduct concerning "nicotine addiction," which was to be followed by trials of the individual issues of class members, Judge Smith found a risk of reexamination. Comparative fault was a central issue, given the long-time warnings on tobacco packages and general recognition of health risks in smoking. He reasoned:

> There is a risk that in apportioning fault, the second jury could reevaluate the defendant's fault, determine that the defendant was not at fault, and apportion 100% of the fault to the plaintiff. In such a situation, the second jury would be impermissibly reconsidering the findings of a first jury.

Undoubtedly issues that are not sufficiently free-standing to warrant separate trial should not be the subject of bifurcation. But presumably a second jury would be instructed that it had to accept the first jury's findings. Judge Rovner, dissenting in *Rhone-Poulenc*, noted that the trial judge could modify severance orders, procedural decisions, and certification rulings to avoid any Seventh Amendment problems. Judge Weinstein commented in *Simon v. Philip Morris* that "there is some doubt about whether a second jury would be reexamining the first jury's findings of the defendant's negligence when it found the plaintiff also contributorily liable to some percentage (assuming that the first jury did not put an end to the case by finding no negligence)."[59] But he also found that reexamination could be avoided in bifurcation by appropriate judicial supervision. *Rhone-Poulenc* and *Castano* have not been followed by most courts which have continued to order bifurcation in appropriate cases, finding no Seventh Amendment problem even as to issues like comparative fault and proximate cause.

Bifurcation may have an effect on the outcome of the case. In routine personal injury cases it has been reported that the defense wins almost twice as frequently when the liability issues are tried separately.[61] This experience with routine cases has also been found in research on mass torts.[62] An economic analysis concluded that:

> [A] sequential trial lowers the expected cost of litigation compared to a unitary trial for both the plaintiff and defendant because it holds out the prospect of avoiding litigation on subsequent issues if the defendant wins the current

---

54. 84 F.3d 734 (5th Cir. 1996).

59. *Simon v. Philips, Inc.*, 200 F.R.D. 21, 48 (E.D.N.Y. 2001).

61. *See* Warren F. Schwartz, *Severance—A Means of Minimizing the Role of Burden and Expense in Determining the Outcome of Litigation*, 20 Vand. L. Rev. 1197 (1967); Jack B. Weinstein, *Routine Bifurcation of Jury Negligence Trials: An Example of the Questionable Use of Rule Making Power*, 14 Vand. L. Rev. 831 (1961).

62. Kenneth S. Bordens & Irwin A. Horowitz, *Mass Tort Civil Litigation: The Impact of Procedural Changes on Jury Decisions*, 73 Judicature 22, 25-26 (1989) (empirical experiments using sixty-six juries showed that plaintiffs received favorable verdicts significantly more often in unitary trials than in bifurcated trials, although the damages awarded were significantly lower).

issue or the parties settle the remaining issues after the current one is decided.[63]

It has also been found that "the bifurcation of general causation in the separated trial condition produces greater disbelief about causation yielding fewer verdicts for the plaintiffs."[64] There are thus many strategic considerations for courts and counsel in the use of bifurcation, but it has become a significant device for the segmenting and ultimate disposition of aggregate litigation.

## Comments and Questions

1. Understand the *fairness* arguments that can be made in favor of bifurcation as well as the *fairness* arguments that can be made in opposition to bifurcation. Similarly, understand the *efficiency* arguments that can be made both in favor of and in opposition to bifurcation.

2. One of the more famous instances of bifurcation appeared in the *Bendectin* case, where many deformed children were among the plaintiffs. Not only was causation tried first (resulting in a defense verdict that ended the case), but "[f]earing undue prejudice to the defendant, the trial court also excluded from the courtroom all visibly deformed plaintiffs and all plaintiffs under the age of ten." *In re Bendectin Litigation*, 857 F.2d 290 (6th Cir. 1988). Presumably, the order excluding some of the plaintiffs was part of defendant's motivation for seeking to bifurcate. Was this a positive or negative consequence of bifurcation?

3. Although defendants are typically the party that can most benefit from bifurcation, consider circumstances where it would be in the plaintiff's interest to bifurcate.

## Practice Exercise No. 25: Motion to Bifurcate in *City of Cleveland*

Review the motion to bifurcate and the accompanying brief in the *City of Cleveland* Case Files. In the actual firefighters litigation, two companion cases had been consolidated for trial. One was brought by the United States of America, solely on the Title VII cause of action. The other is the private class action that you have been following in the Case Files. Assume that the motion to bifurcate and the accompanying memorandum were filed about halfway through the discovery process and that the United States of America is correct in its assertion that little or no discovery on individualized damages

---

63. William M. Landes, *Sequential Versus Unitary Trials: An Economic Analysis*, 22 J. Legal Stud. 99, 100-01 (1993).

64. Bordens & Horowitz, supra note 62, at 27.

has taken place at this point. If you represented the plaintiffs in the private class action, would you oppose the motion? Why or why not? As a judicial clerk, how would you advise a judge to rule on the motion?

## 3. *Jury Instructions*

If you are more pro-jury than skeptical of the jury process, we want your honest opinion on the practice of instructing juries. In the *City of Cleveland* Case Files, you will find the judge's instructions on the § 1983 count of the class action plaintiffs against the city. As you read those instructions, consider whether you agree that a jury should be instructed at all. If you are generally wary of the court's controlling the jury, are you willing to concede that instructions of some kind are necessary? Be prepared to defend your opinion.

If you generally think juries need a good deal of guidance, be prepared to give your assessment of the judge's instructions in this case. Are they helpful to the jurors in making a rational, law-based decision? In what ways, if any, would you have framed the instructions differently? We are not asking you at this time to comment on the correctness of the law stated, but to consider such matters as the tone, clarity, and degree of specificity of the instructions. Was there too much "legalese"? Would commenting on the evidence itself, or describing some of the evidence, have been helpful to the jury?

It is common in federal courts, and in some states, for judges to comment on the evidence. It is improper for a judge, of course, to actually tell a jury who should win, but when commenting on the evidence is allowed, the trial judge can summarize particular evidence, or inform the jury of the types of things they may wish to consider. Naturally, sometimes the summary or comment is not as neutral as one party or the other would like.

## Comments and Questions

1. Assume that the judge showed you the instructions, which are in the Case Files, before giving them to the jury. The judge has asked for your comments, if any.

(a) Assume that you represent the City of Cleveland. Do you approve of the type of verdict that the judge has chosen, of the judge's language in the question he posed, and of his explanation of what the jury should do with the question and the verdict slips? (Does the judge have authority in the Rules to use this method? Which method is it?) What changes would you suggest, especially on the verdict method and on the judge's instructions about that method?

(b) Assume that you represent the plaintiffs. Answer the same questions in item (a), making concrete suggestions for changes if you want them.

2. Assume now that the defendant City in the *City of Cleveland* case has rested much sooner than either side actually expected, because its evidence

went in smoothly and quickly. The judge turns to both sides, tells them generally what the charge will cover, and tells them to make their closing arguments. After closing arguments, and before either side has given the judge any written requests for instructions, the judge instructs the jury in the words that have been printed in the Case Files. (Most federal judges actually would ask for your written requested instructions well before this point in the trial and would probably tell you in a final pre-trial conference order when your written requests should be filed. Frequently, the time would be several days prior to the commencement of trial, with the right to make further requests if they were necessitated by surprise occurrences at the trial.) After giving the instructions, and before the jury retires to deliberate, the judge turns to you, representing the City. Would you have a right to ask for clarifying or additional instructions? Be prepared to tell the judge under the applicable provisions of the Rules what, if anything, you want the judge now to instruct the jury prior to their deliberations.

3. Federal Rule 51 emphasizes that the trial judge is authorized to require attorneys to submit proposed jury instructions prior to trial. The rule also requires the judge, before instructing the jury and before closing arguments, to inform the attorneys of the jury instructions that will be given. If a judge definitively decides on the record to not read a proposed jury instruction, the proposing party need not make a later objection in order to preserve the issue for appeal; otherwise, both the initial request and the objection are needed to preserve the point on appeal.

4. As you continue to consider your views about the civil jury and about the many methods that have developed both to guide and control it, consider an example of what we know about an actual case. Our sources are an article by Steven Brill, the editor-in-chief of *American Lawyer* (Steven Brill, *Inside the Jury Room at the Washington Post Libel Trial*, Amer. Law., 937 (Nov. 1982)), and the Order and Memorandum dated May 2, 1983, of Judge Oliver Gasch of the U.S. District Court, District of Columbia, in *Tavoulareas v. The Washington Post Company, et al.*, C.A. No. 80-3032. The additional defendants included *Post* editors Ben Bradlee and Bob Woodward. Tavoulareas was the president of Mobil Oil, and his son, Peter, was in the oil tanker business. In 1979, the *Post* published two articles about the father, a famous self-made man, and his son. The headline of the story, which appeared on the front page, was "Mobil Chief Sets Up Son in Venture." The lead paragraph stated: "Mobil Oil Corp. president William P. Tavoulareas set up his son five years ago as a partner in a London-based shipping management firm that has since done millions of dollars in business operating Mobil-owned ships under exclusive, no-bid contracts." The father, who claimed that he helped his son only when an opportunity arose, was upset that his "unblemished reputation" (Brill's words) had been sullied. He talked with Ben Bradlee four days after the first story, seeking a retraction, and only got a brief subsequent story adding a little information.

Tavoulareas said he tried to get the *Post* to admit their mistakes for a year, "[b]ut they're so damn arrogant. I kept telling them I'd sue." The lawsuit alleged libel. The plaintiffs were represented by John Walsh, a trial lawyer at the well-known Wall Street firm of Cadwallader, Wickersham & Taft (Taft was President William Howard Taft's brother and Wickersham was appointed to the initial Advisory Committee that drafted the Federal Rules of Civil Procedure). The *Post* and its staff were represented by the legendary Washington, D.C., firm of Williams & Connolly (the Williams, of course, was Edward Bennett Williams). Irving Younger, who at the time was probably the country's most famous lecturer on evidence and jury strategy (although he "insists he always prefers a judge to a jury"), was chosen to be lead counsel for the *Post*. Prior to Younger's involvement, Williams & Connolly insisted on a jury trial.

The trial lasted nineteen days. The judge instructed the jury:

> It is not the defendants' burden to prove that the articles are true. The burden is upon the plaintiffs to prove to you that are they are substantially false. . . . It is not enough for William Tavoulareas to prove the defendants did not conduct a thorough investigation of the facts or that they were negligent in the way they wrote or edited the articles. To recover, William Tavoulareas must prove the defendants had a high degree of awareness that the articles were false or probably false and that they were recklessly disregarded, whether the articles were false or not. If you find the defendants believed the sources of information in the story to be reliable and believed the story to be accurate when published, you must find the defendants have not acted with actual malice as to William Tavoulareas.

Brill reports that the jury foreman, who was going to attend law school the next fall, and the five other jurors, under his insistent lead, "operated as if these instructions had not been given." The jury foreman insisted that it was the obligation of the *Post* to prove in the article itself that the headline that the father had "set up his son" was accurate. In fact, Irving Younger had pitched his defense, which Brill thought was a mistake, on the ground that the article was accurate. Younger's experience had taught him that stressing burden of proof was not a good way to argue or win a lawsuit when one's client is accused of wrongdoing; instead, you should argue and prove that your client is in the right.

One of the jurors told the judge that a written copy of the instructions would be helpful, but the judge, with the agreement of counsel, did not allow that out of fear that "the instructions might be read piecemeal instead of taken as a whole." Brill reports: "[F]our jurors would later volunteer to me that, as one put it, 'we never understood the instructions and never pretended to.'" Although the first vote of the jury was 4-2 in favor of the *Post* on all counts, the young jury foreman kept "yelling," according to one juror, "where's the set-up?" By the third day of deliberations, the last of the six jurors gave in and compromised on a $250,000 verdict for compensatory damages for the father, William Tavoulareas, against the *Post*, an investigative reporter, and a freelance reporter. After a brief trial for the jury to consider punitive damages, at which the *Post* conceded its healthy financial condition and William Tavoulareas testified to a legal bill of about $1.8 million, the jury awarded the father an additional $1.8 million in punitive damages.

In later discussing the case and what prompted their decision, "[s]everal jurors . . . mentioned the judge's vacation plans and the humiliation of a hung jury." The final juror to relent, several recalled, told the others "that the pressure was too much for her, that she felt sick, and that this case was why, in her view, that there should be 12 jurors as there had been when she's served on jury panels in the past." When asked what would have happened if the jury had just been asked to decide "whether the Post had been recklessly or deliberately inaccurate or unfair," a juror answered: "Oh, in that case, there's no way the plaintiff would have won. We all, even . . . [the foreman], I think, conceded they hadn't done anything careless or on purpose."

Both sides appealed, the plaintiffs' counsel arguing that if the *Post* was liable to the father, then the son should have also won, and the defendants' counsel continuing to insist that there was no evidence to support the verdict, and seeking a JNOV or a reduction of damages. Months later, in a nine-page single-spaced memorandum opinion, the bulk of which meticulously reviewed the evidence in the light most favorable to plaintiff, the judge concluded: "Under the standards enunciated by the Supreme Court, . . . the jury verdict in this case will withstand the motions for JNOV only if there is sufficient evidence in the record from which a jury could reasonably find, by clear and convincing proof,* that the defendants published the November 30 article with actual malice. The article in question falls far short of being a model of fair, unbiased, investigative journalism. There is no evidence in the record, however, to show that it contained knowing lies or statements made in reckless disregard of the truth. Reviewed under the stringent test set forth by the Supreme Court in *New York Times Co. v. Sullivan*, the verdict in plaintiff's favor must be set aside." Consequently, the judge granted the defendants' motions for JNOV.

So, that's the story. Does this change your mind about jury cases? What lessons about civil litigation and jury trials do you draw from it?

## 4. Remittitur and Additur

We have now considered bifurcation, different types of jury verdicts, and jury instructions. The remaining "jury control" doctrine relates to what are called *remittitur* and *additur*. To understand these concepts, you will have to recall what you learned about motions for a new trial based on the contention, in whole or in part, that the monetary amount of the jury verdict was too large or too small "as a matter of law." Given the time and expense to society and the parties resulting from the grant of a new trial, some courts devised the practice of conditioning the grant of a new trial (when damages were excessive) on the plaintiff's refusal to consent to a reduction of damages to a specific amount

---

*\* Eds.' Note:* This is not the burden in the ordinary civil case; in the typical case, the plaintiff does not have to adduce "clear and convincing proof," but must merely convince the jury on the evidence (including all reasonable inferences) that it is more likely than not that all elements of the prima facie case are true.

(called *nisi remittitur damna*). Put another way, the judge is either explicitly or implicitly saying to plaintiff's counsel: "I agree with the defendant that the damages are excessive, and will grant defendant's motion for a new trial, unless your client agrees to reduce the verdict by X amount of dollars."

There are additional, longer-standing precedents for the remittitur, which reduces damages, than for the additur, which increases them. In the additur situation, the judge is either explicitly or implicitly saying to the defendant's counsel: "The plaintiff, although winning the case, has moved for a new trial on the grounds that the damages given in the verdict are inadequate. I agree with the plaintiff, and intend to grant the plaintiff's motion for a new trial unless your client agrees to increase the damages by X dollars. It is your client's choice."

Before considering what you think of these devices, you should be aware of both constitutional and practical considerations. In *Dimick v. Schiedt*, 293 U.S. 474 (1935), the Supreme Court considered the constitutionality of additur and, in a 5-4 decision, found it unconstitutional for federal courts to use the device. The Court distinguished remittitur and implied, in dicta, that it would permit that device to stand. The points of distinction, according to the majority, were some evidence of the practice of remittitur in England prior to 1791 and that in the case of remittitur "what remains is included in the verdict along with the unlawful excess—in that sense it has been found by the jury—and the remittitur has the effect of merely lopping off the excrescence." The additur, according to the majority, is a "bald addition of something which in no sense can be said to be included in the verdict." *Id.* at 486. The Supreme Court has since given mixed signals about whether it would continue to hold additur unconstitutional. In *Tull v. United States*, 481 U.S. 412, 533 n.16 (1996), the Court implied that *Dimick* was an anomaly and hinted that the Court may "rethink" the additur question "on a later day." But more recently, in *Feltner v. Columbia Pictures Television, Inc.*, 523 U.S. 340 (1998), the Supreme Court found a jury trial right in assessing damages under the federal copyright statute and suggested that *Tull* was "at least in tension with" prior Supreme Court precedent, including *Dimick*, 523 U.S. at 355 n.9. Additur, and more frequently remittitur, have been permitted by the highest court of some states. State courts have been more willing to permit additur in cases where the amount to be added is a liquidated amount, such as a fixed financial amount in a contract, or readily calculable interest.

Assuming that a court is permitted to grant the motion for a new trial unless the nonmoving party agrees to lesser or greater damages, the question remains how a court should set the amount to be remitted or added. Consider these three possibilities in remittitur. The judge will grant defendant's motion for a new trial unless the plaintiff agrees to (1) remit the least amount possible that will bring the verdict into the range of what the judge believes is a permissible verdict; (2) remit the amount that will make the verdict what the judge believes a reasonable jury should have awarded; (3) remit the greatest amount possible that will bring the verdict to the smallest award that the judge believes to be rational, given the evidence.

If the plaintiff refuses to remit (or the defendant refuses to add) and the judge, therefore, decides to grant the motion for a new trial, the judge may also consider whether to grant a total new trial, or only a new trial on damages. To grant a new trial only on damages, of course, raises many of the same issues as bifurcation.

Some evidence suggests that plaintiffs in the United States often collect considerably less than the total amounts of their verdicts and the accrued interest. The widespread use of remittitur is one reason; another is settlement pending new trials or appeals, or during the period that plaintiffs try to collect on their judgments. Perhaps most important, the financial straits of defendants (such as bankruptcy or a lack of funds or property to pay the award) may result in plaintiffs' taking a good deal less than the damages award plus interest.

Although there are few empirical studies on the post-verdict adjustment of jury awards, one such study demonstrated that, at least in larger cases, plaintiffs ultimately recover substantially less than the jury award:

> Ivy Broder reviewed a sample of 198 jury awards of $1 million or more that occurred between 1984 and 1985. Plaintiffs received the original jury award in just slightly more than a quarter of the cases. On average, the final aggregate disbursement to plaintiffs was 57% lower than the original verdict. The amount of the reduction varied by case type. Medical malpractice awards, for example, were reduced by 27% on average. However, the average statistic obscures the fact that larger awards were reduced more than smaller awards. Broder's report did not indicate whether the reduction was made by the trial judge or an appeal court or whether it resulted from post-verdict settlements or inability to collect from the defendant.

Neil Vidmar, Felicia Gross, and Mary Rose, *Jury Awards for Medical Malpractice and Post-Verdict Adjustments of Those Awards*, 48 DePaul L. Rev. 265, 279-280 (1998) (summarizing Ivy E. Broder, *Characteristics of Million Dollar Awards: Jury Verdicts and Final Disbursements*, 11 Just. Sys. J. 349, 350 (1986)).

## Comments and Questions

1. What is the specific constitutional problem raised by remittitur or additur? Scrutinize the language of the Seventh Amendment to the U.S. Constitution. Does the majority's constitutional distinction in *Dimick* make sense to you? Why might a state constitutional decision on additur come out differently from the *Dimick* case? When a defendant moves for a new trial based on excessive damages and the plaintiff remits the amount suggested by the judge so that the new trial motion is denied, should the defendant still be able to appeal the case? Can the defendant's appeal, if allowed at all, include the excessiveness of damages even after the remittitur? Can it include the excessiveness of damages before the remittitur? When a remittitur has been

made, what risks does the defendant's counsel run if he or she decides to appeal the verdict?

In addition to checking the Seventh Amendment, please apply your common sense to all of these questions. There is no need for you to do additional research on them at this time, but when you determine where you are going to practice, you will want to acquaint yourself with both the law and the custom.

Consider the options provided in the immediately preceding question on the test that the judge should use in determining the amount of remittitur. What are the pros and cons of each test? Which would you choose? In granting a motion for new trial based on excessive or inadequate damages, should the new trial be on all issues, or on damages only? What are the pros and cons of each? In this regard, would you treat some types of cases differently from others?

2. Review the methods of jury control we have considered: rules of evidence, summary judgment, directed verdict, JNOV, instructions, new-trial motions because the verdict is against the weight of the evidence, new-trial motions based on excessive or inadequate damages, specialized types of verdicts or interrogatories for the jury, bifurcation and trifurcation, and remittitur and additur and judicial control of punitive damages. Which, if any, offend your sense of how juries should work? Which methods seem most sensible and fair to you?

### Practice Exercise No. 26: Motions to Challenge a Jury Verdict

John Dinkins, a successful 32-year-old black male, has just won a malpractice claim against Forsyth Laboratories in state court in the State of Crabtree. The jury came in with a general verdict for Mr. Dinkins for $100,000. Forsyth Laboratories misread a laboratory test that would have diagnosed stomach cancer in its early stages. As a result of the lab's error, Mr. Dinkins's cancer was not detected until it had spread to other organs. Had the test been read accurately by the lab, Mr. Dinkins would have had a 90-95 percent survival chance after prompt removal of the cancer. Because of the delayed diagnosis, Mr. Dinkins had to endure two major operations, and is currently undergoing chemotherapy. His likelihood of survival has decreased to 50-60 percent.

In the past eighteen months in the State of Crabtree, four similar cases have been successfully tried by plaintiffs similarly situated as to age (pre- and post-incident), earning capacity, estimated life expectancy prior to the cancer, and survival rate after the misdiagnosis. These four jury verdicts averaged exactly $400,000. All plaintiffs in these four cases were white males.

The plaintiff believes that the low jury verdict was due to racial prejudice and stereotyping by jurors, as well as social devaluation of black males generally. During the trial, the defendants introduced medical evidence that black males have a higher rate of heart disease—both hereditarily and as a result of their dietary and lifestyle choices—than males of other races. The defendants also introduced evidence that Mr. Dinkins, although financially stable, chose to live in the inner city and to drive a fast, fancy sports car.

**Question:** If you represented Dinkins, what motions would you bring to challenge this verdict? What arguments would you make? Anticipate Forsyth's justifications and strategies.

## G. CLOSING ARGUMENTS

One of the most exciting moments in a trial lawyer's life is standing up to give a closing argument. Some lawyers start thinking about their closing arguments early in their analysis and preparation of a case, as a means of focusing their case preparation on what aspects of the case will eventually provide their most persuasive advocacy. Before moving on to other aspects of procedure, we want you to read about some of that sense of exhilaration.

### ■ LLOYD PAUL STRYKER, THE ART OF ADVOCACY
*111-112, 125-129 (1954)*

. . . The summation is the high point in the art of advocacy; it is the combination and the culmination of all of its many elements. It is the climax of the case. It is the opportunity to rescue a cause until that time perhaps seemingly lost. It calls for every skill the advocate possesses. It calls for more than skill—it is a summons to his courage, a testing ground of his character, a trial of his logic and reasoning powers, his memory, his patience and his tact, his ability to express himself in convincing words; in short, it is an assay of every power of persuasion he possesses. Small wonder, then, that there have been few great summations. . . .

An advocate is one who has been called to the aid of a fellow citizen in deep trouble. You are that advocate, and your one, sole and single aim is to aid that fellow citizen with all your heart and soul and mind.

The jury is watching you with an even greater scrutiny than that with which they looked at you while you were making, now so long ago, your opening address. They remember what you promised them; they have a good recollection of the evidence that followed and they are challenging you to persuade them that you have proved all that you promised them you would prove.

But if they have been studying you, your scrutiny of them has been no less intense. You will remember how they looked when certain evidence was introduced, how they reacted to your cross-examinations. Some one or more of them may have asked questions of a witness on the stand, and you will be thinking now, as you thought then, of the significance of those questions and the way in which the questioner received the answers. If you have succeeded thus far in the trial in establishing some credit with the jury, if your firmness, your good manners, and your complete integrity have won you some measure of approval in the jury box, you will strain now to avoid everything that may forfeit that good will and you will do all within your power to strengthen it. . . .

For each new case the lawyer has a special problem. He alone has seen and heard the witnesses. He, not some master of the past, has divined the feeling of his judge and jury; he alone has felt the atmosphere of his own courtroom and is, therefore, in a better position to decide upon his course of action than all the silent mentors of the printed page.

Imagination is of incalculable aid. An illustration of how it can be used was once given by a great Chicago lawyer, Weymouth Kirkland. He had been called upon to defend a group of insurance companies which were resisting claims based on the alleged death of an engineer named Peck. The plaintiff contended that Peck had fallen overboard from a steamer while crossing Lake Michigan. The defendants, on the other hand, were seeking to establish that Peck had never fallen overboard, that he had left his coat in his stateroom as a ruse, and that when the boat docked in the early morning, he had quietly slipped down the gangplank.

Much evidence was adduced by the plaintiff for the purpose of establishing that if Peck had in fact fallen overboard, the current and the prevailing winds would have carried his body to a particular spot. One of the plaintiff's witnesses was a cook on another steamer whose ship, three days after Peck's disappearance, sailed past the exact spot where other witnesses had said the currents would have carried Peck's body. On his direct examination, the cook said that exactly at that spot he happened to glance out from his locker, saw the body, and recognized it as that of his old friend, Peck.

It was a nice opportunity for cross-examination, and Mr. Kirkland used it in this way:

*Q.* How long had you known Peck?
*A.* Fifteen years.
*Q.* You knew him well?
*A.* Yes, sir.
*Q.* How did you happen to see his body?
*A.* I looked out of the porthole.
*Q.* You recognized it beyond doubt as the body of Peck?
*A.* Yes, sir.
*Q.* Did you make any outcry when you saw the body?
*A.* No, sir.
*Q.* Did you ask the captain to stop the ship?
*A.* No, sir.
*Q.* What were you doing when you happened to look out of the window and saw the body?
*A.* I was peeling potatoes.
*Q.* And when the body of your old friend, Peck, floated by, you just kept on peeling potatoes?
*A.* Yes, sir.

It was a bit of cross-examination well done. And how was it used in the summing up? Did Mr. Kirkland tell the jury that the cook's testimony was palpably untrue? Did he denounce the absurdity of the answers? He handled it far more adroitly. As he stood before the jury for his final appeal, he produced a potato from one pocket and a knife from another. Thus equipped, he rested one foot on a chair and proceeded to peel the potato, saying: "What ho? What have we here? Who is this floating past? As I live and breathe, if it isn't my old friend Peck! I shall tell the captain about this in the morning. In the meantime, I must go right on peeling my potatoes."

By innuendo he had destroyed all the cook's testimony. A little wit had accomplished far more than the finest rhetoric or the fiercest denunciation of this perjurer.

If I were asked to name the prerequisites of an advocate, I would mention imagination among the first. One seeking to persuade a court or jury which does not possess that quality would be a man impervious to all the overtones and subtle possibilities presented by the facts. Imagination for the trial lawyer is as essential as for the novelist, the artist, or the poet. Poetry and literature and painting are the products of a mental synthesis of ideas fused from many elements; and so it is that by the formation and expression of mental images that your true advocate brings before the jury [the] essence of his contention. In a single flood he dramatizes the real point and makes his hearers see a picture which their untrained senses had not yet dismissed.

Whatever means you employ, you must lift your jury from mere logic to the springs of action that transcend cold reasoning, to the feelings and the emotions that govern, inspire, and produce the verdict. Never for an instant forget that it is a favorable verdict you are seeking.

The most impregnable of syllogisms will not secure it for you. Nothing will do it but the hearts and wills of twelve men whom you must capture. You must find a way to reach those hearts. How better can you do this than by such a systematic arrangement and presentation of the facts that each bit of evidence fits into the pattern of your theory and every circumstance advances your contention. But persuasion is far more than that—persuasion is effected only when you make those who hear you want to follow you, only when you have, as it were, so proselytized your listeners as to turn them into zealots for your cause.

If you had the Stradivarius, you would not possess a more glorious instrument than the hearts and souls of twelve men. And if you had all the skill of Paganini, Ysaye, or Zimbalist, if you had all of Mischa Elman's magic, you would not have too much with which to make your jurors' heartstrings vibrate. There ranged before you they court the inspired touch of a master's hand.

And yet all your artistry will fail if your listeners who hear and feel your art suspect that it is nothing else. Plain men like to think themselves above emotion, impervious to rhetoric and susceptible only to cold reason. Knowing this, it will be yours somehow to disguise your highest flights so that Pegasus seems only a rather well-built and serviceable draft horse.

You must not be only a musician but an actor. You must have studied your client so perceptively that you can understudy him. You must be him. You must not merely play Hamlet, you must be Hamlet himself. More than a musician or an actor, you must be a soldier and a leader. You must be a general and a humble platoon leader who knows how to gain compliance with the most potent of all military orders: "Follow me!" You must make your jury follow you even as they follow your eyes that search them through and through. The true advocate is even more than that; he is a conqueror whose will has brought about subjection and surrender. Is advocacy an art? Is there anywhere a greater one? . . .

## Practice Exercise No. 27: Analyzing Closing Arguments in *City of Cleveland*

Edited portions of the three closing arguments in the firefighters case are in the Case Files. The case was a bit unusual in that initially the § 1983 cause of action was to be decided by a jury, and the Title VII cause of action was to be tried solely to the judge. The judge permitted the evidence on both counts to come in at the same time and to be heard both by him and the jury. By the end of the case, however, the § 1983 cause of action had been eliminated at the directed verdict stage. Consequently, the portions of the final arguments you are about to read were presented to the judge, without a jury, and were solely on the count under Title VII.

Mr. Calipari represented the U.S. government as plaintiff against the defendants in a case that had been consolidated with the class action against the defendants. Ms. Jennifer represented the plaintiffs in the class action. Mr. Solimine represented the City of Cleveland and the other defendants in both cases.

Consider these questions as you read the final arguments:

(1) How does the speaker perceive his or her audience? What types of arguments does the speaker think will be most persuasive?

(2) What are the relative importance of facts, law, emotions, and morality to the arguments?

(3) In what ways do the speakers' own personalities and views of the litigation process inform their closing arguments?

(4) Can you outline each argument, and is it an outline that makes sense to you, given the purpose or purposes of the closing argument?

(5) Does the speaker have a major theory of the case or a major focus for his or her argument? If so, what is it?

(6) In what ways, if any, would the arguments have differed if they were made to a jury?

(7) What arguments do you think were most persuasive? Would they have influenced or persuaded you if you were the judge or a member of a jury?

(8) What would you have done differently?

## Practice Exercise No. 28: Preparing and Delivering Closing Arguments in *City of Cleveland*

With this exercise, we hope to provide you with an opportunity (1) to prepare and perhaps present a closing argument in a case that you know in great detail; (2) to help you experience how the formal litigation process (elements, causes of action, burdens of proof) and the passion, morality, and common sense of a real life story come together in creative advocacy; and (3) to help you see an important aspect of the near-end of a process so that you can better understand the relationships among several parts of the process (complaint, discovery, motions, trial).

Accordingly, prepare a closing argument to a jury for the plaintiffs or the City of Cleveland on the § 1983 cause of action in the *City of Cleveland* case. Prepare a typed outline of your closing argument (not more than three pages double-spaced) and hand it in at the end of class. Along with your name, please put at the top of the page the side you represent. The choice of client is up to you. Do not concern yourself with the class action aspects of the case. Assume that the directed verdict motion on § 1983 was denied and that the City of Cleveland is the only remaining defendant. The case will go to the jury only on liability issues (including causation), not on damages. The judge will instruct the jury after both closing arguments with the same instructions you have in your Case Files, except there will only be a general verdict. Assume that the City's counsel will argue first and the plaintiffs' lawyer second. Assume that the jury will be given only general verdict slips. You should be able to make a credible argument that lasts no more than fifteen minutes.

You may argue using any evidence that appears anywhere in the *City of Cleveland* Case Files, including even (for this purpose only) allegations in the complaint, the initial plaintiffs' memorandum, and the closing arguments. Most importantly, you may use any of the evidence noted in the Judge's Trial Notebook (in the Case Files). Feel free to consult anyone. You may use the library, but you need not. Regardless of what help you get, your written outline should be your own. And, of course, your oral argument, if you are called upon, should be your own.

## Note: Tips on Making a Closing Argument

Most lawyers making a closing argument have a very good idea of what they are going to say; they have an outline, but they do not read the argument. They want to make eye contact with the judge or jury, and, if they are not arguing first, they want to adjust their argument to what the other lawyers have already argued.

Closing arguments to a jury usually state in general form the major instructions that the judge will give (if she hasn't already given them). The lawyer wants the jury to consider the law that they have to apply as they listen to the closing argument. Closing arguments usually rely heavily on the evidence that has come in during the trial, and they suggest how that evidence and natural inferences drawn therefrom support the conclusion. A good closing is not simply a summary of the testimony of the witnesses and other evidence; instead, a good argument uses select pieces to advance an argument. Often, closing arguments will address the motivation of important parties and witnesses, focusing on the credibility of certain so-called evidence. Closing arguments try to tell a story—to give a picture in words—that draws the jury to the desired conclusion and leaves a mark that jurors will remember throughout their deliberations.

Closing arguments may not include references to evidence that is not in the record. Also, as in most legal arguments, it is important not to ignore your opponents' strongest points. Rather, you must address them and undermine them—whether through evidence, logic, legal doctrine, morality, or otherwise. Explain to the jury why the picture painted by the opponent is inaccurate or at least incomplete.

If there are important exhibits, remember that the jury will usually have them in the jury room during their deliberations. Some lawyers like to weave the exhibits into their closing argument, so that the jury will be reminded of their argument as they review the exhibits.

It is unethical for a lawyer to say who or what they believe during a closing argument. Instead, you will use phrases like "The evidence suggests . . ." or "The evidence permits only one sound conclusion . . ." Be sure to tell the fact finder exactly what you want them to do. For example, it is not patronizing and, in fact, is helpful to be as direct as, "If you agree with me, ladies and gentlemen of the jury, you should put an 'x' on the line on the jury slip that says 'for the defendant.'" When damages are involved in a matter, you will need to check with local law and custom to ascertain to what extent you may discuss particular sums of money. In many, if not most, jurisdictions you are not allowed in closing argument to ask the jury to "be in the plaintiff's shoes," nor are you allowed to suggest that they consider the value of having one day without the plaintiff's injury and multiplying that by life expectancy.

Most important, realize that there is no single right—or even best—way to make a closing. The effectiveness of the closing arguments depends on your personality, the type of case, the evidence, your witnesses, the jury, the judge, the ambience of the courtroom, and your ability to process each of these influences. Rhetoric—the art of persuasion—is an ancient and admirable enterprise. Enjoy.

## H. APPEALS

The value of a favorable trial verdict is materially diminished if it cannot survive appellate review. Winners can quickly become losers, and losers have a second chance to convince the court that a verdict in their favor is the just result or that a new trial is necessary.

The appellate process differs from the trial proceedings in the lower courts in both its procedure and its purpose. The attorneys do not try their case as if the first trial had never happened, but rather present alleged errors of the trial judge for the appellate court to review. The appellate court serves the purpose of supervising the trial judge's decisions and establishing uniformity of the law within its jurisdiction. During the proceedings below, the trial judge may not have the time to consider the issues with the care and reflection afforded to appellate judges. Furthermore, the perspective of the appellate court offers a check on the potential arbitrariness of the trial judge and may instill confidence in the trial process by reaffirming the judge's decisions.

Unlike a trial court, an appellate court looks somewhat beyond the rights of the parties in the specific case before them. The appellate courts are the voice of authority on the law in their jurisdiction and thus attempt to create a uniform body of law for predicting the outcome of future cases. Procedures for achieving these goals may vary, but the Federal Rules of Appellate Procedure establish mechanisms for the federal courts, and substantially similar rules have been adopted in many state courts.

The Judiciary Act of 1789 established three levels of courts in the federal system: the Supreme Court, circuit courts, and district courts. There are currently thirteen courts of appeals—eleven for numbered circuits, one for the District of Columbia, and the Court of Appeals for the Federal Circuit, established in 1982. The U.S. Courts of Appeals may hear the decisions of the federal district courts of the states and territories in their regions. For practical purposes, the right to appeal is statutory, not constitutional.

The appellate courts will hear only alleged errors that are revealed in the trial record, and ordinarily no new factual findings will be taken into consideration. The trial record must also reveal that the aggrieved party made a timely objection to the alleged error. The alleged error must have materially affected the outcome of the case and must be necessary to the decree in order to be reviewable. If the party does not raise an error that is found in the trial record, the appellate court will usually consider it waived.

Federal courts and most state courts require finality in the trial court as a basis for appellate jurisdiction. This requirement, known as the final judgment rule, ensures that the proceedings below are completed before the review process begins. The timing of an appeal usually requires notice within thirty days after the final judgment is rendered.

The main principle behind this final judgment rule is the conservation of judicial resources. Finality requires that the trial below end on the merits and "leave nothing for the court to do but execute the judgment." *Catlin v. United States*, 324 U.S. 229, 233 (1945). If finality is not present, the appeal may be unnecessary. The pending proceedings may settle, or the issue may have become moot as a result of the trial. Also, denying immediate review prevents the use of expensive delaying tactics and harassment of opposing parties.

Not all requests for immediate appeal are denied. Immediate review can be important in providing guidance to the trial court and in preventing hardship. Exceptions to the final judgment rule include the collateral order doctrine, interlocutory appeals, and writs of mandamus and prohibition.

The collateral order doctrine is a judicial exception to the final judgment rule and exempts only a small number of cases—those in which there is an order that is an offshoot of the principal litigation, and where the appeal does not require delving into the merits of the case: "[T]he order must conclusively determine the disputed question, resolve an important issue completely separate from the merits of the action, and be effectively unreviewable on appeal from a final judgment." *Coopers & Lybrand v. Livesay*, 437 U.S. 463, 468 (1978).

An interlocutory decision is made while the case is pending in the trial court, but prior to the final determination of the merits. Under 28 U.S.C. § 1292, an interlocutory appeal may be taken from interlocutory orders with respect to injunctions, receiverships, and the rights and liabilities of parties to admiralty cases. Also, district court judges can, under limited circumstances, state in an interlocutory order that they think an immediate appeal would "materially advance the ultimate termination of the litigation," and the court of appeals, upon application, has discretion to permit such on appeal. Similarly, Federal Rule 23(f) states that "[a] court of appeals may permit an appeal from an order granting or denying class-action certification under this rule if a petition for permission to appeal is filed with the circuit clerk within fourteen days after the order is entered."

Writs of mandamus and prohibition seek an order from the appellate court to order a requirement or a prohibition of a certain action by a public official. The public official may be a judge of a lower court, making the procedure similar to interlocutory orders. In *Kerr v. United States District Court*, 426 U.S. 394 (1976), the U.S. Supreme Court stated, "[T]he remedy of mandamus is a drastic one" and "only exceptional circumstances amounting to judicial 'usurpation of power' will justify the invocation of this extraordinary remedy." *Kerr* also set forth various conditions for which the court would issue a writ, including if the party seeking the writ has no other adequate means to attain the desired relief, and if the party is able to establish that the need for the issuance is "clear and indisputable."

In the courts of appeals, ordinarily a panel of three judges reaches its decision by a majority vote. (On occasion, all of the judges of a court of appeals will hear an appeal.) Even though the panel may decide that the trial court erred in its decision, not all errors at trial are grounds for reversal. The likelihood of reversal depends on the standard of review. In reviewing the district court's finding of fact, the appellate court normally will defer to the authority of the trial judge, who has greater familiarity with the entire case and has observed the demeanor evidence at trial. Under Fed. R. Civ. P. 52(a), the appellate court will set aside findings of fact only if they are "clearly erroneous." In *United States v. U.S. Gypsum Co.*, 333 U.S. 364, 395 (1948), the Court defined the clearly erroneous standard as "when the reviewing court on the entire evidence is left with definite and firm conviction that a mistake has been committed." The trial judge must have misunderstood the law or made a finding without adequate evidentiary support. However, if the case below was a jury trial, the appellate court gives even greater deference to the findings of fact.

In *Cooper Indus., Inc. v. Leatherman Tool Group, Inc.*, 532 U.S. 424 (2001) (discussed in Chapter 2), the court held that while a jury's determination of compensatory damages is "essentially a factual determination," and thus reviewed only for clear error, a jury's award of punitive damages should be reviewed *de novo* since it is but "an expression of [the jury's] moral condemnation."

Fed. R. App. P. 52(a) does not require a "clearly erroneous" standard for reviewing conclusions of law. The absence of a standard for conclusions of law in the Federal Rules of Appellate Procedure has left the appellate courts with complete authority to freely consider conclusions of law. However, the appellate court will reverse only if it thinks the trial court, more likely than not, erred in its decision. The standard to be applied in cases of mixed fact and law is generally the same standard as that applied to questions of pure law, although the courts have determined which standard to use in certain cases, like contract cases. Where a trial court judge makes a conclusion of law based on the four corners of the document, the appellate court will review the appeal *de novo*. But where the trial court considers extrinsic evidence to make a conclusion, the conclusion rests on findings of fact and, therefore, may be reviewable by the "clearly erroneous" standard.

Finally, when a trial judge makes a discretionary ruling, the standard for review is "abuse of discretion." Since the trial judge is in the best position to make discretionary rulings, the ruling will be overturned only if the appellate court is convinced that the judge was clearly wrong.

After a court of appeals renders its decision, an aggrieved party may seek an appeal at the next level of review. Seeking review from a U.S. Court of Appeals to the Supreme Court of the United States is almost always done through the discretionary writ of certiorari. Whether the Supreme Court grants the writ depends on such criteria as conflicts among circuits, the general importance of the legal questions involved, and the public importance of the case.

If the case originated in a state court, the party ordinarily has the right of appeal to the state's intermediate appellate court. As in the federal court system, most states require a petition to the state's highest court, which is granted only by the discretion of that court. Under 28 U.S.C. § 1257, if a question of federal law exists, and a final judgment or decree has been "rendered by the highest court of a State in which a decision could be had . . ." then the decision "may be reviewed by the [United States] Supreme Court by writ of certiorari. . . ."

Only a small percentage of the cases in which review is sought by the Supreme Court of the United States are granted certiorari and disposed of by a written opinion. In fact, the number of Supreme Court written opinions has steadily declined. For example, in 1980, 4,174 cases were docketed and 159 were disposed of by written opinion. While the number of docketed cases each year now typically exceeds 10,000 cases, the number of cases disposed by written opinion is consistently less than 100—recently as few as 68.

## Review Exercise No. 5

This question is designed to help you determine how much you have learned in the course to date, to help you review and learn some more, and to practice tackling typical law school exam questions.

You will benefit most from the quiz if you follow the directions: Put aside at least two hours to take this quiz; if you finish early, you should assume that you did not use sufficient precision and detail in your answer. Use only your rule book. Try the exam on your own before discussing it with your study group.

### *Memorandum*

To: Summer Judicial Intern
From: Judge Moran, State Trial Court Judge
Date: November 10, 2012

In March 2012 Wayne Earnest and Cleveland Grover (hereafter, "Earnest" and "Grover," respectively) filed one complaint in my trial court and requested a jury. The statute of limitations for all cases in this jurisdiction is two years. Our state has adopted the Federal Rules of Civil Procedure in all relevant respects.* Our state does not have a contribution statute.

The complaint alleges: the plaintiffs' names and the names of Jill Joke and Sally Sales, as defendants (hereafter, "Joke" and "Sales," respectively); that on Halloween, October 31, 2010, at 9:15 A.M., Earnest entered The Joke Shop, owned and managed by Joke; at 3:30 P.M. Grover did the same; at about the time each opened the door, a ghost suddenly appeared, and then there was the sound of a loud explosion; as a result, each plaintiff was greatly scared; Earnest required seven weeks of medical care for his resulting fright, and Grover, as a result, did and still does require and receive medical care for his resulting fright; as a result each has incurred large medical expenses, missed several months of work, has severe anxiety and headaches, and has difficulty sleeping; wherefore each demands $200,000 in damages. The complaint is signed by a lawyer.

Joke filed a timely answer, in which she (1) admitted ownership and general management of The Joke Shop, denied all other allegations, and alleged that on October 31, 2010, she was not working in The Joke Shop; nor was it supposed to be open; nor was Sales an employee of hers at the

---

* In this state, however, the complaint does not have to allege subject matter jurisdiction because the trial courts are courts of general jurisdiction and can hear almost all types of cases.

time; (2) raised a 12(b)(6) defense; and (3) counterclaimed against Grover for failing to pay for $2,500 of goods purchased from The Joke Shop between January 1 and October 31, 2010, under terms that the price of each purchase was due at the time of purchase. Joke also filed an impleader claim against Sales stating that "Sales had been fired on October 15, 2010, and had no right being in The Joke Shop on October 31, 2010; that she, Joke, had intended and ordered that the Shop be closed that day; and that if she, Joke, is held liable, it would be as a result of Sales' negligence and trespass, and that Sales should therefore indemnify her." Joke also filed an impleader claim against Carl Cap alleging that if "on October 31, 2010, Carl Cap caused an explosion, I had nothing to do with it, since I was not there and knew nothing about it; that Grover alleges said explosion scared him; if it did, and if I am held liable, then Cap must indemnify me."

After discovery, Joke filed an affidavit that restates under oath everything alleged in her answer, counterclaim, and two impleaders. Joke also submitted a portion of deposition taken of Grover's doctor, which says "Grover was anxious and had all the same symptoms before October 31, 2010, as he had after. I do not believe that the October 31st incident, if it happened at all, caused him any harm." Joke also filed interrogatory answers of Sales in which she states, among other things, that "I was working in the Joke Shop with permission on October 31, 2010, but by noon I had discontinued all pranks. Carl Cap, whom both Joke and I had forbidden to come in the store, played a loud recording of an explosion outside the store window, which may have surprised Earnest. I only saw Cap after it happened." Grover filed an affidavit that states "Although I was anxious before the October 31, 2010, negligence of Joke and Sales, I felt much worse afterwards and probably would have gone back to work sooner and required less medical help, had the ghost and loud explosion noise not frightened me."

Although there was extensive discovery in which every party sought all relevant information, I have provided you (in this memo) all relevant portions of pleadings, affidavits, and discovery that you need to help me decide the motions before me.

I have to rule on:

1. Joke's 12(b)(6);
2. A motion for summary judgment by Joke against Grover;
3. A motion by Joke to dismiss against Grover for misjoinder, or, in the alternative, to sever the two plaintiffs' cases;
4. Motions by Sales and Cap to dismiss each respective impleader as improper;
5. A motion by Grover to dismiss Joke's counterclaim against him as improper;
6. A motion filed two weeks ago by Grover to amend his complaint by adding: "In addition, when I came back the next day to complain to Joke, Joke intentionally punched me in the nose, broke it, and caused me to incur headaches, medical expense, and lose additional work."

How should I rule on each of the above motions? *(Notice the date of this memorandum and assume that you are responding on this date.)* Please give me your analysis and reasons. Rule on all of the motions, even if one or more rulings might render others moot. There are, of course, additional pleadings and motions in the Earnest and Sales portions of the case, but I do not have to decide those yet.

# 6

![black square graphic]

# *Questioning and Taming the Current System*

Critics of the American federal and state civil justice systems cite costs and delays as serious, chronic problems. The special problems of delay and cost associated with pre-trial discovery constitute only part of the problem produced by explosive numbers of court filings, lawyer-driven pleadings, and conventional judicial passivity. For those who are litigants and those who cannot afford to be, the quality of justice is reduced when it is delayed and expensive. A separate line of criticism points to the assumptions and effects of the adversary system. Adversarial process is supposed to promote truth-telling, fairness, and the enforcement of rights. Critics allege that instead, as actually operated, the adversarial system promotes nondisclosure, manipulation, and winner-take-all solutions, rather than promoting constructive problem solving.

Others focus on the capacity—or incapacity—of courts to deal with law-suits crafted under liberal pleading rules that permit multiparty, multiclaim suits involving complex social and economic problems. Some emphasize the need for sharp limits on adjudication, while others defend the creative responses of judges to the contemporary shape of litigation, including litigation involving public institutions and public values.

This chapter examines the premises and criticisms of the adversary system, their relationship to the judges' role, the debates over the capacity of courts to address complex litigation, the controversy over whether there indeed is a crisis of litigation in the United States, and descriptions and evaluations of alternatives developed both within the context of litigation and beyond the courts. Given the fact that most cases filed in the federal and state courts never reach trial, the options of settlement, negotiation, arbitration, and mediation are crucial to every piece of litigation.

Chapter 4, Discovery, considered the effect of the adversarial system on the search for truth. This chapter draws on that introduction to the adversarial system and considers two areas of doctrine and practice that also raise questions about the role of the adversary system in modern litigation: the structural injunction and alternative dispute resolution (ADR). The first area expresses the pinnacle of court power in the form of commands to the state to act. The second area expresses a retreat of the courts from a public law mode to a more private mode. In ADR, courts become a space for individuals to solve their problems, rather than a forum of law declaration. In some forms of ADR, such as arbitration, courts have been replaced by private adjudication. In both contexts, judges are asked to take on roles that are different from the traditional neutral role associated with judging. The final section of this chapter weaves together the two issues and considers to what extent judges should adopt a more proactive approach to "managing" cases.

## A. WHAT ARE THE STRENGTHS AND LIMITATIONS OF COURTS?

Some kinds of disputes may not lend themselves to the adversarial process. Professors Lon Fuller and Abram Chayes explore the debate over the capacity of courts to address complex social and economic problems. As you read, keep in mind lawsuits over segregated schools, violent prisons, and failing economic entities, such as railroads, as well as your own views about the debate. Consider Lon Fuller's discussion of the limits of adjudication; what kinds of legal disputes do you think fit his notion of a "polycentric task"? Should they be sent out of courts to some other settings for dispute resolution, or is there a way that the adversarial process can be modified to meet them? The case that follows these excerpts, *Brown v. Plata*, concerns the imposition of a structural injunction to address prison overcrowding in California. This case demonstrates how the disagreement over the role of the judge plays out in practice and illustrates one way that procedures have been altered in prison reform litigation to address the issues Fuller raises.

## ■ LON FULLER, THE FORMS AND LIMITS OF ADJUDICATION
### *92 Harv. L. Rev. 353 (1978)*

Attention is now directed to the question, What kinds of tasks are inherently unsuited to adjudication? The test here will be that used throughout. If a given task is assigned to adjudicative treatment, will it be possible to preserve the meaning of the affected party's participation through proofs and arguments?

[For purposes of addressing the question of limits, t]his section introduces a concept—that of the "polycentric task"—which has been derived from Michael Polanyi's book *The Logic of Liberty* (1951). In approaching that concept it will be well to begin with a few examples.

Some months ago a wealthy lady by the name of Timken died in New York leaving a valuable, but somewhat miscellaneous, collection of paintings to the Metropolitan Museum and the National Gallery "in equal shares," her will indicating no particular apportionment. When the will was probated the judge remarked something to the effect that the parties seemed to be confronted with a real problem. The attorney for one of the museums spoke up and said, "We are good friends. We will work it out somehow or other." What makes this problem of effecting an equal division of the paintings a polycentric task? It lies in the fact that the disposition of any single painting has implications for the proper disposition of every other painting. If it gets the Renoir, the Gallery may be less eager for the Cézanne but all the more eager for the Bellows, etc. If the proper apportionment were set for argument, there would be no clear issue to which either side could direct its proofs and contentions. Any judge assigned to hear such an argument would be tempted to assume the role of mediator or to adopt the classical solution: Let the older brother (here the Metropolitan) divide the estate into what he regards as equal shares, let the younger brother (the National Gallery) take his pick.

As a second illustration suppose in a socialist regime it were decided to have all wages and prices set by courts which would proceed after the usual forms of adjudication. It is, I assume, obvious that here is a task that could not successfully be undertaken by the adjudicative method. . . .

We may visualize this kind of situation by thinking of a spider web. A pull on one strand will distribute tensions after a complicated pattern throughout the web as a whole. Doubling the original pull will, in all likelihood, not simply double each of the resulting tensions but will create a different complicated pattern of tensions. This would certainly occur, for example, if the doubled pull caused one or more of the weaker strands to snap. This is a "polycentric" situation because it is "many centered"—each crossing of strands is a distinct center for distributing tensions. . . .

It should be carefully noted that a multiplicity of affected persons is not an invariable characteristic of polycentric problems. This is sufficiently illustrated in the case of Mrs. Timken's will. That case also illustrated the fact that rapid changes with time are not an invariable characteristic of such problems. On the other hand, in practice polycentric problems of possible concern to adjudication will normally involve many affected parties and a somewhat fluid state of affairs. Indeed, the last characteristic follows from the simple fact that the more interacting centers there are, the more the likelihood that one of them will be affected by a change in circumstances, and, if the situation is polycentric, this change will communicate itself after a complex pattern to other centers. . . .

Now, if it is important to see clearly what a polycentric problem is, it is equally important to realize that the distinction involved is often a matter of degree. There are polycentric elements in almost all problems submitted to adjudication. A decision may act as a precedent, often an awkward one, in some situation not foreseen by the arbiter. Again, suppose a court in a suit between one litigant and a railway holds that it is an act of negligence for the railway not to construct an underpass at a particular crossing. There may be nothing to distinguish this crossing from other crossings on the line. As a matter of statistical probability it may be clear that constructing underpasses along the whole line would cost more lives (through accidents in blasting, for example) than would be lost if the only safety measure were the familiar "Stop, Look & Listen" sign. If so, then what seems to be a decision simply declaring the rights and duties of two parties is in fact an inept solution for a polycentric problem, some elements of which cannot be brought before the court in a simple suit by one injured party against a defendant railway. In lesser measure, concealed polycentric elements are probably present in almost all problems resolved by adjudication. It is not, then, a question of distinguishing black from white. It is a question of knowing when the polycentric elements have become so significant and predominant that the proper limits of adjudication have been reached. . . .

The final question to be addressed is this: When an attempt is made to deal by adjudicative forms with a problem that is essentially polycentric, what happens? As I see it, three things can happen, sometimes all at once. *First*, the adjudicative solution may fail. Unexpected repercussions make the decision unworkable; it is ignored or modified, sometimes repeatedly. *Second*, the purported arbiter ignores judicial proprieties—he "tries out" various solutions in posthearing conferences, consults parties not represented at the hearings, guesses at facts not proved and not properly matters for anything like judicial notice. *Third*, instead of accommodating his procedures to the nature of the problem he confronts, he may reformulate the problem so as to make it amenable to solution through adjudicative procedures.

Only the last of these needs illustration. Suppose it is agreed that an employer's control over promotions shall be subject to review through arbitration. Now obviously an arbiter cannot decide whether when Jones was made a Machinist Class A there was someone else more deserving in the plant, or whether, in view of Jones' age, it would have been better to put him in another job with comparable pay. This is the kind of allocative problem for which adjudication is utterly unsuited. There are, however, two ways of obtaining a workable control over promotions through arbitration. One of these is through the posting of jobs; when a job is vacant, interested parties may apply for promotion into it. At the hearing, only those who have made application are entitled to be considered, and of course only the posted job is in issue. Here the problem is simplified in advance to the point where it can be arbitrated, though not without difficulty, particularly in the form of endless arguments as to whether there was in fact a vacancy that ought to have been posted, and whether a claimant filed his application on time and in the proper form, etc. The other way of accommodating the problem to arbitration is for the arbiter to determine not who should be promoted but who *has* been promoted. That is, the contract contains certain "job descriptions" with the appropriate rate for each; the claimant asserts that he is in fact doing the work of a Machinist A, though he is still assigned the pay and title of a Machinist B. The controversy has two parties—the company and the claimant as represented by the union—and a single factual issue, is the claimant in fact doing the work of a Machinist A?

In practice the procedure of applying for appointment to posted jobs will normally be prescribed in the contract itself, so that the terms of the agreement keep the arbitrator's function with respect to promotions within manageable limits. The other method of making feasible a control of promotions through arbitration will normally result from the arbitrator's own perception of the limitations of his role. The contract may simply contain a schedule of job rates and job classifications and a general clause stating that "discharges, promotions, and layoffs shall be subject to the grievance procedure." If the arbitrator were to construe such a contract to give him general supervision over promotions, he would embark himself upon managerial tasks wholly unsuited to solution by any arbitrative procedure. An instinct toward preserving the integrity of his role will move him, therefore, to construe the contract in the manner already indicated, so that he avoids any responsibility with respect to the assignment of duties and merely decides whether the duties actually assigned make appropriate the classification assigned by the company to the complaining employee. . . .

In closing this discussion of polycentricity, it will be well to caution against two possible misunderstandings. The suggestion that polycentric problems are often solved by a kind of "managerial intuition" should not be taken to imply that it is an invariable characteristic of polycentric problems that they resist rational solution. There are rational principles for building bridges of structural steel. But there is no rational principle which states, for example, that the angle between girder A and girder B must always be 45 degrees. This depends on the bridge as a whole. One cannot construct a bridge by conducting successive separate arguments concerning the proper angle for every pair of intersecting girders. One must deal with the whole structure.

Finally, the fact that an adjudicative decision affects and enters into a polycentric relationship does not of itself mean that the adjudicative tribunal is moving out of its proper sphere. On the contrary, there is no better illustration of a polycentric relationship than an economic market, and yet the laying down of rules that will make a market function properly is one for which adjudication is generally well suited. The working out of our common law of contracts case by case has proceeded through adjudication, yet the basic principle underlying the rules thus developed is that they should promote the free exchange of goods in a polycentric market. The court gets into difficulty, not when it lays down rules about contracting, but when it attempts to write contracts. . . .

# ■ ABRAM CHAYES, THE ROLE OF THE JUDGE IN PUBLIC LAW LITIGATION
*89 Harv. L. Rev. 1281 (1976)*

. . . We are witnessing the emergence of a new model of civil litigation and, I believe, our traditional conception of adjudication and the assumptions upon which it is based provide an increasingly unhelpful, indeed misleading framework for assessing either the workability or the legitimacy of the roles of judge and court within this model.

In our received tradition, the lawsuit is a vehicle for settling disputes between private parties about private rights. The defining features of this conception of civil adjudication are:

1. The lawsuit is *bipolar*. Litigation is organized as a contest between two individuals or at least two unitary interests, diametrically opposed, to be decided on a winner-take-all basis.
2. Litigation is *retrospective*. The controversy is about an identified set of completed events: whether they occurred, and if so with what consequences for the legal relations of the parties.
3. *Right and remedy are interdependent*. The scope of the relief is derived more or less logically from the substantive violation under the general theory that the plaintiff will get compensation measured by the harm caused by the defendant's breach of duty—in contract by giving plaintiff the money he would have had absent the breach; in tort by paying the value of the damage caused.
4. The lawsuit is a *self-contained* episode. The impact of the judgment is confined to the parties. If plaintiff prevails there is a simple compensatory transfer, usually of money, but occasionally the return of a thing or the performance of a definite act. If defendant prevails, a loss lies where it has fallen. In either case, entry of judgment ends the court's involvement.
5. The process is *party-initiated* and *party-controlled*. The case is organized and the issues defined by exchanges between the parties. Responsibility for fact development is theirs. The trial judge is a neutral arbiter of their interactions who decides questions of law only if they are put in issue by an appropriate move of a party. . . .

Whatever its historical validity, the traditional model is clearly invalid as a description of much current civil litigation in the federal district courts. Perhaps the dominating characteristic of modern federal litigation is that lawsuits do not arise out of disputes between private parties about private rights. Instead, the object of litigation is the vindication of constitutional or statutory policies. The shift in the legal basis of the lawsuit explains many, but not all, facets of what is going on "in fact" in federal trial courts. For this reason, although the label is not wholly satisfactory, I shall call the emerging model "public law litigation."

The characteristic features of the public law model are very different from those of the traditional model. The party structure is sprawling and amorphous, subject to change over the course of the litigation. The traditional adversary relationship is suffused and intermixed with negotiating and mediating processes at every point. The judge is the dominant figure in organizing and guiding the case, and he draws for support not only on the parties and their counsel, but on a wide range of outsiders—masters, experts, and oversight personnel. Most important, the trial judge has increasingly become the creator and manager of complex forms of ongoing relief, which have widespread effects on persons not before the court and require the judge's continuing involvement in administration and implementation. School desegregation, employment discrimination, and prisoners' or inmates' rights cases come readily to mind as avatars of this new form of litigation. But it would be mistaken to suppose that it is confined to these areas. Antitrust, securities fraud and other aspects of the conduct of corporate business, bankruptcy and reorganizations, union governance, consumer fraud, housing discrimination, electoral reapportionment, environmental management—cases in all these fields display in varying degrees the features of public law litigation. . . .

## II. The Public Law Litigation Model

Sometime after 1875, the private law theory of civil adjudication became increasingly precarious in the face of a growing body of legislation designed explicitly to modify and regulate basic social and economic arrangements. At the same time, the scientific and deductive character of judicial lawmaking came under attack, as the political consequences of judicial review of that legislation became urgent.

These developments are well known and have become an accepted part of our political and intellectual history. I want to address in somewhat greater detail the correlative changes that have occurred in the procedural structure of the lawsuit. Most discussion of these procedural developments, while recognizing that change has been far-reaching, proceeds on the assumption that the new devices are no more than piecemeal "reforms" aimed at improving the functional characteristics or the efficacy of litigation conducted essentially in the traditional mode. I suggest, however, that these developments are interrelated as members of a recognizable, if changing, system and that taken together they display a new model of judicial action and the judicial role, both of which depart sharply from received conceptions.

### A. The Demise of Bipolar Structure

Joinder of parties, which was strictly limited at common law, was very liberalized under the codes to conform with the approach of equity calling for joinder of all parties having an "interest" in the controversy. The codes, however, did not at first produce much freedom of joinder. Instead, the courts defined the concept of "interest" narrowly to exclude those without an independent legal right to the remedy to be given in the main dispute. . . .

. . . Today, the Supreme Court is struggling manfully, but with questionable success, to establish a formula for delimiting who may sue that stops short of "anybody who might be significantly affected by the situation he seeks to litigate."

"Anybody"—even "almost anybody"—can be a lot of people, particularly where the matters in issue are not relatively individualized private transactions or encounters. Thus, the stage is set for the class action. . . . Whatever the resolution of the current controversies surrounding class actions, I think it unlikely that the class action will ever be taught to behave in accordance with the precepts of the traditional model of adjudication. The class suit is a reflection of our growing awareness that a host of important public and private interactions—perhaps the most important in defining the conditions and opportunities of life for most people—are conducted on a routine or bureaucratized basis and can no longer be visualized as bilateral transactions between private individuals. From another angle, the class action responds to the proliferation of more or less well-organized groups in our society and the tendency to perceive interests as group interests, at least in very important aspects. . . .

## B. THE TRIUMPH OF EQUITY

One of the most striking procedural developments of this century is the increasing importance of equitable relief. It is perhaps too soon to reverse the traditional maxim to read that money damages will be awarded only when no suitable form of specific relief can be devised. But surely, the old sense of equitable remedies as "extraordinary" has faded.

I am not concerned here with specific performance—the compelled transfer of a piece of land or a unique thing. This remedy is structurally little different from traditional money-damages. It is a one-time, one-way transfer requiring for its enforcement no continuing involvement of the court. Injunctive relief, however, is different in kind, even when it takes the form of a simple negative order. Such an order is a presently operative prohibition, enforceable by contempt, and it is a much greater constraint on activity than the risk of future liability implicit in the damage remedy. Moreover, the injunction is continuing. Over time, the parties may resort to the court for enforcement or modification of the original order in light of changing circumstances. Finally, by issuing the injunction, the court takes public responsibility for any consequences of its decree that may adversely affect strangers to the action.

Beyond these differences, the prospective character of the relief introduces large elements of contingency and prediction into the proceedings. Instead of a dispute retrospectively oriented toward the consequences of a closed set of events, the court has a controversy about future probabilities. Equitable doctrine, naturally enough, given the intrusiveness of the injunction and the contingent nature of the harm, calls for a balancing of the interests of the parties. And if the immediate parties' interests were to be weighed and evaluated, it was not too difficult to proceed to a consideration of other interests that might be affected by the order. . . .

## C. THE CHANGING CHARACTER OF FACTFINDING

The traditional model of adjudication was primarily concerned with assessing the consequences for the parties of specific past instances of conduct. This retrospective orientation is often inapposite in public law litigation, where the lawsuit generally seeks to enjoin future or threatened action, or to modify a course of conduct presently in train or a condition presently existing. In the former situation the question whether threatened action will materialize, in what circumstances, and with what consequences can, in the nature of things, be answered only by an educated guess. In the latter case, the inquiry is only secondarily concerned with how the condition came about, and even less with the subjective attitudes of the actors, since positive regulatory goals are ordinarily defined without reference to such matters. Indeed, in dealing with the actions of large political or corporate aggregates, notions of will, intention, or fault increasingly become only metaphors.

In the remedial phases of public law litigation, factfinding is even more clearly prospective. . . . [T]he contours of relief are not derived logically from the substantive wrong adjudged, as in the traditional model. The elaboration of a decree is largely a discretionary process within which the trial judge is called upon to assess and appraise the consequences of alternative programs that might correct the substantive fault. In both the liability and remedial phases, the relevant inquiry is largely the same: How can the policies of a public law best be served in a concrete case?

In public law litigation, then, factfinding is principally concerned with "legislative" rather than "adjudicative" fact. And "fact evaluation" is perhaps a more accurate term than "factfinding." The whole process begins to look like the traditional description of legislation: Attention is drawn to a "mischief," existing or threatened, and the activity of the parties and court is directed to the development of on-going measures designed to cure that mischief. Indeed, if, as is often the case, the decree sets up an affirmative regime governing the activities in controversy for the indefinite future and having binding force for persons within its ambit, then it is not very much of a stretch to see it as, pro tanto, a legislative act. . . .

The courts, it seems, continue to rely primarily on the litigants to produce and develop factual materials, but a number of factors make it impossible to leave the organization of the trial exclusively in their hands. With the diffusion of the party structure, fact issues are no longer sharply drawn in a confrontation between two adversaries, one asserting the affirmative and the other the negative. The litigation is often extraordinarily complex and extended in time, with a continuous and intricate interplay between factual and legal elements. It is hardly feasible and, absent a jury, unnecessary to set aside a contiguous block of time for a "trial stage" at which all significant factual issues will be presented. The scope of the fact investigation and the sheer volume of factual material that can be exhumed by the discovery process pose enormous problems of organization and assimilation. All these factors thrust the trial judge into an active role in shaping, organizing and facilitating the litigation. We may not yet have reached the investigative judge of the continental systems, but we have left the passive arbiter of the traditional model a long way behind.

### D. THE DECREE

The centerpiece of the emerging public law model is the decree. It differs in almost every relevant characteristic from relief in the traditional model of adjudication, not the least in that it is the centerpiece. The decree seeks to adjust future behavior, not to compensate for past wrong. It is deliberately fashioned rather than logically deduced from the nature of the legal harm suffered. It provides for a complex, on-going regime of performance rather than a simple, one-shot, one-way transfer. Finally, it prolongs and deepens, rather than terminates, the court's involvement with the dispute. . . .

I suggested above that a judicial decree establishing an ongoing regime of conduct is pro tanto a legislative act. But in actively shaping and monitoring the decree, mediating between the parties, developing his own sources of expertise and information, the trial judge has passed beyond even the role of legislator and has become a policy planner and manager.

### E. A MORPHOLOGY OF PUBLIC LAW LITIGATION

The public law litigation model portrayed in this paper reverses many of the crucial characteristics and assumptions of the traditional concept of adjudication:

1. The scope of the lawsuit is not exogenously given but is shaped primarily by the court and parties.
2. The party structure is not rigidly bilateral but sprawling and amorphous.
3. The fact inquiry is not historical and adjudicative but predictive and legislative.
4. Relief is not conceived as compensation for past wrong in a form logically derived from the substantive liability and confined in its impact to the immediate parties; instead, it is forward looking, fashioned ad hoc on flexible and broadly remedial lines, often having important consequences for many persons including absentees.
5. The remedy is not imposed but negotiated.
6. The decree does not terminate judicial involvement in the affair: its administration requires the continuing participation of the court.
7. The judge is not passive, his function limited to analysis and statement of governing rules; he is active, with responsibility not only for credible fact evaluation but for organizing and shaping the litigation to ensure a just and viable outcome.

8. The subject matter of the lawsuit is not a dispute between private individuals about private rights, but a grievance about the operation of public policy.

In fact, one might say that, from the perspective of the traditional model, the proceeding is recognizable as a lawsuit only because it takes place in a courtroom before an official called a judge. But that is surely too sensational in tone. All of the procedural mechanisms outlined above were historically familiar in equity practice. It is not surprising that they should be adopted and strengthened as the importance of equity has grown in modern times. . . .

## IV. SOME THOUGHTS ON LEGITIMACY

. . . As the traditional model has been displaced in recent years, . . . questions of judicial legitimacy and accountability have reasserted themselves. . . .

In my view, judicial action only achieves such legitimacy by responding to, indeed by stirring, the deep and durable demand for justice in our society. I confess some difficulty in seeing how this is to be accomplished by erecting the barriers of the traditional conception to turn aside, for example, attacks on exclusionary zoning and police violence, two of the ugliest remaining manifestations of official racism in American life. In practice, if not in words, the American legal tradition has always acknowledged the importance of substantive results for the legitimacy and accountability of judicial action. . . .

## Comments and Questions

1. What are the sources for the criteria and judgments used by Fuller and Chayes in the debate over the function and capacities of courts? Fuller relies on a notion of rationality at the core of the judicial process. Is this notion intrinsic to due process? Is it intrinsic to the ideal of a court or to the reality of courts as operated in the contemporary United States? Chayes relies on examples of courts engaged in innovative practices. Do such examples give hope for the capacity of all courts, or do they merely illuminate the abilities of extraordinary judges? Where, if at all, do commitments to democratic participation and accountability to the broad public fit in his scheme?

2. In the debate over the role of courts in addressing complex or "polycentric" disputes (in Fuller's terms), what concerns emerge about judicial legitimacy and the efficacy of the courts' actions?

3. Do the public law courts described by Chayes abandon the premises of adversarial justice? How important are those premises to the tasks of fact finding, judgment, and enforcement? Can those tasks be accomplished as well, and as legitimately, through party collaboration and negotiation?

## ■ BROWN v. PLATA
### 131 S. Ct. 1910 (2011)

Justice KENNEDY delivered the opinion of the Court.

This case arises from serious constitutional violations in California's prison system. The violations have persisted for years. They remain uncorrected. The appeal comes to this Court from a three-judge District Court order directing California to remedy two ongoing violations of the Cruel and Unusual Punishments Clause, a guarantee binding on the States by the Due Process Clause of the Fourteenth Amendment. The violations are the subject of two class actions in two Federal District Courts. The first involves the class of prisoners with serious mental disorders. That case is *Coleman v. Brown*. The second involves prisoners with serious medical conditions. That case is *Plata v. Brown*. The order of the three-judge District Court is applicable to both cases. . . .

The appeal presents the question whether the remedial order issued by the three-judge court is consistent with requirements and procedures set forth in a congressional statute, the Prison Litigation Reform Act of 1995 (PLRA). 18 U.S.C. § 3626. The order leaves the choice of means to reduce overcrowding to the discretion of state officials. But absent compliance through new construction, out-of-state transfers, or other means—or modification of the order upon a further showing by the State—the State will be required to release some number of prisoners before their full sentences have been served. High recidivism rates must serve as a warning that mistaken or premature release of even one prisoner can cause injury and harm. The release of prisoners in large numbers—assuming the State finds no other way to comply with the order—is a matter of undoubted, grave concern.

At the time of trial, California's correctional facilities held some 156,000 persons. This is nearly double the number that California's prisons were designed to hold, and California has been ordered to reduce its prison population to 137.5% of design capacity. By the three-judge court's own estimate, the required population reduction could be as high as 46,000 persons. Although the State has reduced the population by at least 9,000 persons during the pendency of this appeal, this means a further reduction of 37,000 persons could be required. As will be noted, the reduction need not be accomplished in an indiscriminate manner or in these substantial numbers if satisfactory, alternate remedies or means for compliance are devised. The State may employ measures, including good-time credits and diversion of low-risk offenders and technical parole violators to community-based programs, that will mitigate the order's impact. The population reduction potentially required is nevertheless of unprecedented sweep and extent.

Yet so too is the continuing injury and harm resulting from these serious constitutional violations. For years the medical and mental health care provided by California's prisons has fallen short of minimum constitutional requirements and has failed to meet prisoners' basic health needs. Needless suffering and death have been the well-documented result. Over the whole course of years during which this litigation has been pending, no other remedies have been found to be sufficient. Efforts to remedy the violation have been frustrated by severe overcrowding in California's prison system. Short term gains in the provision of care have been eroded by the long-term effects of severe and pervasive overcrowding.

Overcrowding has overtaken the limited resources of prison staff; imposed demands well beyond the capacity of medical and mental health facilities; and created unsanitary and unsafe conditions that make progress in the provision of care difficult or impossible to achieve. The overcrowding is the "primary cause of the violation of a Federal right," 18 U.S.C. § 3626(a)(3)(E)(i), specifically the severe and unlawful mistreatment of prisoners through grossly inadequate provision of medical and mental health care.

This Court now holds that the PLRA does authorize the relief afforded in this case and that the court-mandated population limit is necessary to remedy the violation of prisoners' constitutional rights. The order of the three-judge court, subject to the right of the State to seek its modification in appropriate circumstances, must be affirmed.

## I

### A

The degree of overcrowding in California's prisons is exceptional. California's prisons are designed to house a population just under 80,000, but at the time of the three-judge court's decision the population was almost double that. The State's prisons had operated at around 200% of design capacity for at least 11 years. Prisoners are crammed into spaces neither designed nor intended to house inmates. As many as 200 prisoners may live in a gymnasium, monitored by as few as two or three correctional officers. As many as 54 prisoners may share a single toilet.

. . . In 2006, then-Governor Schwarzenegger declared a state of emergency in the prisons, as "'immediate action is necessary to prevent death and harm caused by California's severe prison overcrowding.'" The consequences of overcrowding identified by the Governor include "'increased, substantial risk for transmission of infectious illness'" and a suicide rate "'approaching an average of one per week.'"

Prisoners in California with serious mental illness do not receive minimal, adequate care. Because of a shortage of treatment beds, suicidal inmates may be held for prolonged periods in telephone-booth sized cages without toilets. . . . Wait times for mental health care range as high as 12 months. In 2006, the suicide rate in California's prisons was nearly 80% higher than the national average for prison populations; and a court-appointed Special Master found that 72.1% of suicides involved "some measure of inadequate assessment, treatment, or intervention, and were therefore most probably foreseeable and/or preventable."

Prisoners suffering from physical illness also receive severely deficient care. California's prisons . . . have only half the clinical space needed to treat the current population. . . . The number of staff is inadequate, and prisoners face significant delays in access to care. A prisoner with severe abdominal pain died after a 5-week delay in referral to a specialist; a prisoner with "constant and extreme" chest pain died after an 8-hour delay in evaluation by a doctor; and a prisoner died of testicular cancer after a "failure of MDs to work up for cancer in a young man with 17 months of testicular pain." California Prison Health Care Receivership Corp., K. Imai, Analysis of CDCR Death Reviews 2006, pp. 6-7 (Aug. 2007). . . . Many more prisoners, suffering from severe but not life-threatening conditions, experience prolonged illness and unnecessary pain.

### B

These conditions are the subject of two federal cases. The first to commence, *Coleman v. Brown*, was filed in 1990. *Coleman* involves the class of seriously mentally ill persons in California prisons. Over 15 years ago, in 1995, after a 39-day trial, the *Coleman* District Court found "overwhelming evidence of the systematic failure to deliver necessary care to mentally ill inmates" in California prisons. *Coleman v. Wilson*, 912 F.Supp. 1282, 1316 (E.D.Cal.). The court appointed a Special Master to oversee development and implementation of a remedial plan of action.

In 2007, 12 years after his appointment, the Special Master in *Coleman* filed a report stating that, after years of slow improvement, the state of mental health care in California's prisons was deteriorating. The Special Master ascribed this change to increased overcrowding. . . . Prisons had retained more mental health staff, but the "growth of the resource [had] not matched the rise in demand." . . . The Special Master concluded that many early "achievements have succumbed to the inexorably rising tide of population, leaving behind growing frustration and despair."

### C

The second action, *Plata v. Brown*, involves the class of state prisoners with serious medical conditions. After this action commenced in 2001, the State conceded that deficiencies in prison medical care violated prisoners' Eighth Amendment rights. The State stipulated to a remedial injunction. The State failed to comply with that injunction, and in 2005 the court appointed a Receiver to oversee remedial efforts. The court found that "the California prison medical care system is broken beyond repair," resulting in an "unconscionable degree of suffering and death." . . .

Prisons were unable to retain sufficient numbers of competent medical staff, and would "hire any doctor who had 'a license, a pulse and a pair of shoes.'" Medical facilities lacked "necessary medical equipment" and did "not meet basic sanitation standards." "Exam tables and counter tops, where prisoners with . . . communicable diseases are treated, [were] not routinely disinfected."

In 2008, three years after the District Court's decision, the Receiver described continuing deficiencies in the health care provided by California prisons. . . .

A report by the Receiver detailed the impact of overcrowding on efforts to remedy the violation. Overcrowding had increased the incidence of infectious disease, and had led to rising prison violence and greater reliance by custodial staff on lockdowns, which "inhibit the delivery of medical care and increase the staffing necessary for such care." . . .

**D**

The *Coleman* and *Plata* plaintiffs, believing that a remedy for unconstitutional medical and mental health care could not be achieved without reducing overcrowding, moved their respective District Courts to convene a three-judge court empowered under the PLRA to order reductions in the prison population. . . .

The three-judge court heard 14 days of testimony and issued a 184-page opinion, making extensive findings of fact. The court ordered California to reduce its prison population to 137.5% of the prisons' design capacity within two years. Assuming the State does not increase capacity through new construction, the order requires a population reduction of 38,000 to 46,000 persons. Because it appears all but certain that the State cannot complete sufficient construction to comply fully with the order, the prison population will have to be reduced to at least some extent. The court did not order the State to achieve this reduction in any particular manner. Instead, the court ordered the State to formulate a plan for compliance and submit its plan for approval by the court. . . .

The State appealed. . . .

**II**

As a consequence of their own actions, prisoners may be deprived of rights that are fundamental to liberty. Yet the law and the Constitution demand recognition of certain other rights. Prisoners retain the essence of human dignity inherent in all persons. Respect for that dignity animates the Eighth Amendment prohibition against cruel and unusual punishment. . . .

To incarcerate, society takes from prisoners the means to provide for their own needs. Prisoners are dependent on the State for food, clothing, and necessary medical care. . . . A prison that deprives prisoners of basic sustenance, including adequate medical care, is incompatible with the concept of human dignity and has no place in civilized society.

If government fails to fulfill this obligation, the courts have a responsibility to remedy the resulting Eighth Amendment violation. Courts must be sensitive to the State's interest in punishment, deterrence, and rehabilitation, as well as the need for deference to experienced and expert prison administrators faced with the difficult and dangerous task of housing large numbers of convicted criminals. Courts nevertheless must not shrink from their obligation to "enforce the constitutional rights of all 'persons,' including prisoners." *Cruz v. Beto*, 405 U.S. 319, 321 (1972) *(per curiam)*. Courts may not allow constitutional violations to continue simply because a remedy would involve intrusion into the realm of prison administration.

Courts faced with the sensitive task of remedying unconstitutional prison conditions must consider a range of available options, including appointment of special masters or receivers and the possibility of consent decrees. When necessary to ensure compliance with a constitutional mandate, courts may enter orders placing limits on a prison's population. By its terms, the PLRA restricts the circumstances in which a court may enter an order "that has the purpose or effect of reducing or limiting the prison population." 18 U.S.C. § 3626(g)(4). The order in this case does not necessarily require the State to release any prisoners. The State may comply by raising the design capacity of its prisons or by transferring prisoners to county facilities or facilities in other States. Because the order limits the prison population as a percentage of design capacity, it nonetheless has the "effect of reducing or limiting the prison population." *Ibid.*

Under the PLRA, only a three-judge court may enter an order limiting a prison population. § 3626(a)(3)(B). [Before such a three-judge court may be convened, the PLRA requires that the court have "previously entered an order for less intrusive relief that has failed to remedy" the deprivation of the federal right. 18 U.S.C. § 3626(a)(3)(A)(i). To issue an order limiting the prison population, the three-judge court must find (1) "crowding is the primary cause" of the deprivation of a federal right, (2) "no other relief will remedy the violation," (3) the relief must "extend no further than necessary to correct the violation, and in making the determination the court must (4) "give substantial weight to any adverse impact on public safety or the operation of the criminal justice system caused by the relief." § 3626(a)(1)(A). The standard of review is deferential.] . . .

### 3

The three-judge court acknowledged that the violations were caused by factors in addition to overcrowding and that reducing crowding in the prisons would not entirely cure the violations. . . .

As this case illustrates, constitutional violations in conditions of confinement are rarely susceptible of simple or straightforward solutions. In addition to overcrowding the failure of California's prisons to provide adequate medical and mental health care may be ascribed to chronic and worsening budget shortfalls, a lack of political will in favor of reform, inadequate facilities, and systemic administrative failures. The *Plata* District Judge, in his order appointing the Receiver, compared the problem to "'a spider web, in which the tension of the various strands is determined by the relationship among all the parts of the web, so that if one pulls on a single strand, the tension of the entire web is redistributed in a new and complex pattern.'" (quoting Fletcher, *The Discretionary Constitution: Institutional Remedies and Judicial Legitimacy*, 91 Yale L.J. 635, 645 (1982)). Only a multifaceted approach aimed at many causes, including overcrowding, will yield a solution.

The PLRA should not be interpreted to place undue restrictions on the authority of federal courts to fashion practical remedies when confronted with complex and intractable constitutional violations. Congress limited the availability of limits on prison populations, but it did not forbid these measures altogether. See 18 U.S.C. § 3626. . . .

Courts should presume that Congress was sensitive to the real-world problems faced by those who would remedy constitutional violations in the prisons and that Congress did not leave prisoners without a remedy for violations of their constitutional rights. . . . A finding that overcrowding is the "primary cause" of a violation is therefore permissible, despite the fact that additional steps will be required to remedy the violation.

### C

The three-judge court was also required to find by clear and convincing evidence that "no other relief will remedy the violation of the Federal right." § 3626(a)(3)(E)(ii).

The State argues that the violation could have been remedied through a combination of new construction, transfers of prisoners out of State, hiring of medical personnel, and continued efforts by the *Plata* Receiver and *Coleman* Special Master. The order in fact permits the State to comply with the population limit by transferring prisoners to county facilities or facilities in other States, or by constructing new facilities to raise the prisons' design capacity. And the three-judge court's order does not bar the State from undertaking any other remedial efforts. If the State does find an adequate remedy other than a population limit, it may seek modification or termination of the three-judge court's order on that basis. The evidence at trial, however, supports the three-judge court's conclusion that an order limited to other remedies would not provide effective relief. . . .

The State claims that, even if each of these measures were unlikely to remedy the violation, they would succeed in doing so if combined together. Aside from asserting this proposition, the State offers no reason to believe it is so. Attempts to remedy the violations in *Plata* have been ongoing for 9 years. In *Coleman*, remedial efforts have been ongoing for 16. At one time, it may have been possible to hope that these violations would be cured without a reduction in overcrowding. A long history of failed remedial orders, together with substantial evidence of overcrowding's deleterious effects on the provision of care, compels a different conclusion today.

The common thread connecting the State's proposed remedial efforts is that they would require the State to expend large amounts of money absent a reduction in overcrowding. The Court cannot ignore the political and fiscal reality behind this case. California's Legislature has not been willing or able to allocate the resources necessary to meet this crisis absent a reduction in overcrowding. There is no reason to believe it will begin to do so now, when the State of California is facing an unprecedented budgetary shortfall. As noted above, the legislature recently failed to allocate funds for planned new construction. Without a reduction in overcrowding, there will be no efficacious remedy for the unconstitutional care of the sick and mentally ill in California's prisons.

**D**

The PLRA states that no prospective relief shall issue with respect to prison conditions unless it is narrowly drawn, extends no further than necessary to correct the violation of a federal right, and is the least intrusive means necessary to correct the violation. 18 U.S.C. § 3626(a). When determining whether these requirements are met, courts must "give substantial weight to any adverse impact on public safety or the operation of a criminal justice system." *Ibid.*

**1**

The three-judge court acknowledged that its order "is likely to affect inmates without medical conditions or serious mental illness." . . .

The population limit imposed by the three-judge court does not fail narrow tailoring simply because it will have positive effects beyond the plaintiff class. Narrow tailoring requires a " " "fit" between the [remedy's] ends and the means chosen to accomplish those ends.' " The scope of the remedy must be proportional to the scope of the violation, and the order must extend no further than necessary to remedy the violation. . . .

This case is unlike cases where courts have impermissibly reached out to control the treatment of persons or institutions beyond the scope of the violation. Even prisoners with no present physical or mental illness may become afflicted, and all prisoners in California are at risk so long as the State continues to provide inadequate care. . . . Prisoners who are not sick or mentally ill do not yet have a claim that they have been subjected to care that violates the Eighth Amendment, but in no sense are they remote bystanders in California's medical care system. They are that system's next potential victims.

A release order limited to prisoners within the plaintiff classes would, if anything, unduly limit the ability of State officials to determine which prisoners should be released. As the State acknowledges in its brief, "release of seriously mentally ill inmates [would be] likely to create special dangers because of their recidivism rates." The order of the three-judge court gives the State substantial flexibility to determine who should be released. If the State truly believes that a release order limited to sick and mentally ill inmates would be preferable to the order entered by the three-judge court, the State can move the three-judge court for modification of the order on that basis. The State has not requested this relief from this Court. . . .

Although the three-judge court's order addresses the entire California prison system, it affords the State flexibility to accommodate differences between institutions. There is no requirement that every facility comply with the 137.5% limit. Assuming no constitutional violation results, some facilities may retain populations in excess of the limit provided other facilities fall sufficiently below it so the system as a whole remains in compliance with the order. . . . The alternative—a series of institution-specific population limits—would require federal judges to make these choices. . . .

Nor is the order overbroad because it limits the State's authority to run its prisons, as the State urges in its brief. . . . The State may choose how to allocate prisoners between institutions; it may choose whether to increase the prisons' capacity through construction or reduce the population; and, if it does reduce the population, it may decide what steps to take to achieve the necessary reduction. . . .

. . . The State's desire to avoid a population limit, justified as according respect to state authority, creates a certain and unacceptable risk of continuing violations of the rights of sick and mentally ill prisoners, with the result that many more will die or needlessly suffer. The Constitution does not permit this wrong.

**2**

In reaching its decision, the three-judge court gave "substantial weight" to any potential adverse impact on public safety from its order. The court devoted nearly 10 days of trial to the issue of public safety, and it gave the question extensive attention in its opinion. Ultimately, the court concluded that it would be possible to reduce the prison population "in a manner that preserves public safety and the operation of the criminal justice system."

The PLRA's requirement that a court give "substantial weight" to public safety does not require the court to certify that its order has no possible adverse impact on the public. A contrary reading would depart from the statute's text by replacing the word "substantial" with "conclusive." Whenever a court issues an order requiring the State to adjust its incarceration and criminal justice policy, there is a risk that the order will have some adverse impact on public safety in some sectors. . . .

This inquiry necessarily involves difficult predictive judgments regarding the likely effects of court orders. Although these judgments are normally made by state officials, they necessarily must be made by courts when those courts fashion injunctive relief to remedy serious constitutional violations in the prisons. These questions are difficult and sensitive, but they are factual questions and should be treated as such. Courts can, and should, rely on relevant and informed expert testimony when making factual findings. . . .

The three-judge court credited substantial evidence that prison populations can be reduced in a manner that does not increase crime to a significant degree. Some evidence indicated that reducing overcrowding in California's prisons could even improve public safety. Then-Governor Schwarzenegger, in his emergency proclamation on overcrowding, acknowledged that "'overcrowding causes harm to people and property, leads to inmate unrest and misconduct, . . . and increases recidivism as shown within this state and in others.'" . . .

Expert witnesses produced statistical evidence that prison populations had been lowered without adversely affecting public safety in a number of jurisdictions, including certain counties in California, as well as Wisconsin, Illinois, Texas, Colorado, Montana, Michigan, Florida, and Canada.

The court found that various available methods of reducing overcrowding would have little or no impact on public safety. Expansion of good-time credits would allow the State to give early release to only those prisoners who pose the least risk of reoffending. Diverting low-risk offenders to community programs such as drug treatment, day reporting centers, and electronic monitoring would likewise lower the prison population without releasing violent convicts. The State now sends large numbers of persons to prison for violating a technical term or condition of their parole, and it could reduce the prison population by punishing technical parole violations through community-based programs. This last measure would be particularly beneficial as it would reduce crowding in the reception centers, which are especially hard hit by overcrowding. The court's order took account of public safety concerns by giving the State substantial flexibility to select among these and other means of reducing overcrowding.

The State submitted a plan to reduce its prison population in accordance with the three-judge court's order, and it complains that the three-judge court approved that plan without considering whether the specific measures contained within it would substantially threaten public safety . . . Courts should presume that state officials are in a better position to gauge how best to preserve public safety and balance competing correctional and law enforcement concerns. The decision to leave details of implementation to the State's discretion protected public safety by leaving sensitive policy decisions to responsible and competent state officials. . . .

## III

Establishing the population at which the State could begin to provide constitutionally adequate medical and mental health care, and the appropriate time frame within which to achieve the necessary reduction, requires a degree of judgment. . . . Courts have substantial flexibility when making these judgments. . . .

Nevertheless, the PLRA requires a court to adopt a remedy that is "narrowly tailored" to the constitutional violation and that gives "substantial weight" to public safety. 18 U.S.C. § 3626(a). When a court is imposing a population limit, this means the court must set the limit at the highest population consistent with an efficacious remedy. The court must also order the population reduction achieved in the shortest period of time reasonably consistent with public safety.

### A

The three-judge court concluded that the population of California's prisons should be capped at 137.5% of design capacity. This conclusion is supported by the record. Indeed, some evidence supported a limit as low as 100% of design capacity. . . .

Although the three-judge court concluded that the "evidence in support of a 130% limit is strong," it found that some upward adjustment was warranted in light of "the caution and restraint required by the PLRA." The three-judge court noted evidence supporting a higher limit. In particular, the State's Corrections Independent Review Panel had found that 145% was the maximum "operable capacity" of California's prisons, although the relevance of that determination was undermined by the fact that the panel had not considered the need to provide constitutionally adequate medical and mental health care, as the State itself concedes. . . . After considering, but discounting, this evidence, the three-judge court concluded that the evidence supported a limit lower than 145%, but higher than 130%. It therefore imposed a limit of 137.5%.

This weighing of the evidence was not clearly erroneous. . . . In light of substantial evidence supporting an even more drastic remedy, the three-judge court complied with the requirement of the PLRA in this case.

**B**

The three-judge court ordered the State to achieve this reduction within two years. At trial and closing argument before the three-judge court, the State did not argue that reductions should occur over a longer period of time. The State later submitted a plan for court approval that would achieve the required reduction within five years, and that would reduce the prison population to 151% of design capacity in two years. The State represented that this plan would "safely reach a population level of 137.5% over time." The three-judge court rejected this plan because it did not comply with the deadline set by its order. . . .

The three-judge court, however, retains the authority, and the responsibility, to make further amendments to the existing order or any modified decree it may enter as warranted by the exercise of its sound discretion. . . . A court that invokes equity's power to remedy a constitutional violation by an injunction mandating systemic changes to an institution has the continuing duty and responsibility to assess the efficacy and consequences of its order. . . .

These observations reflect the fact that the three-judge court's order, like all continuing equitable decrees, must remain open to appropriate modification. They are not intended to cast doubt on the validity of the basic premise of the existing order. The medical and mental health care provided by California's prisons falls below the standard of decency that inheres in the Eighth Amendment. This extensive and ongoing constitutional violation requires a remedy, and a remedy will not be achieved without a reduction in overcrowding. The relief ordered by the three-judge court is required by the Constitution and was authorized by Congress in the PLRA. The State shall implement the order without further delay.

The judgment of the three-judge court is affirmed.

*It is so ordered.*

**APPENDIX A**

Mule Creek State Prison
Aug. 1, 2008

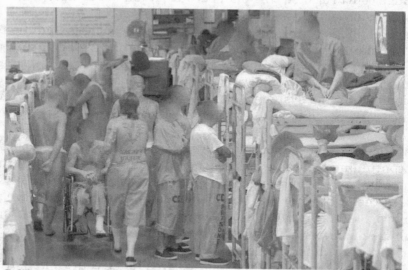

California Institution for Men
Aug. 7, 2006

Salinas Valley State Prison
July 29, 2008
Correctional Treatment Center (dry cages/holding cells for people wait-
ing for mental health crisis bed)

Justice SCALIA, with whom Justice THOMAS joins, dissenting.

Today the Court affirms what is perhaps the most radical injunction issued by a court in our Nation's history: an order requiring California to release the staggering number of 46,000 convicted criminals.

There comes before us, now and then, a case whose proper outcome is so clearly indicated by tradition and common sense, that its decision ought to shape the law, rather than vice versa. One would think that, before allowing the decree of a federal district court to release 46,000 convicted felons, this Court would bend every effort to read the law in such a way as to avoid that outrageous result. Today, quite to the contrary, the Court disregards stringently drawn provisions of the governing statute, and traditional constitutional limitations upon the power of a federal judge, in order to uphold the absurd.

The proceedings that led to this result were a judicial travesty. I dissent because the institutional reform the District Court has undertaken violates the terms of the governing statute, ignores bedrock limitations on the power of Article III judges, and takes federal courts wildly beyond their institutional capacity.

## I

### A

. . . [I]t is inconceivable that anything more than a small proportion of prisoners in the plaintiff classes have personally received sufficiently atrocious treatment that their Eighth Amendment right was violated—which, as the Court recognizes, is why the plaintiffs do not premise their claim on "deficiencies in care provided on any one occasion." Rather, the plaintiffs' claim is that they are all part of a medical system so defective that some number of prisoners will inevitably be injured by incompetent medical care, and that this number is sufficiently high so as to render the system, as a whole, unconstitutional.

But what procedural principle justifies certifying a class of plaintiffs so they may assert a claim of systemic unconstitutionality? I can think of two possibilities, both of which are untenable. The first is that although some or most plaintiffs in the class do not *individually* have viable Eighth Amendment claims, the class as a whole has collectively suffered an Eighth Amendment violation. That theory is contrary to the bedrock rule that the sole purpose of classwide adjudication is to aggregate claims that are individually viable. . . .

The second possibility is that every member of the plaintiff class *has* suffered an Eighth Amendment violation merely by virtue of being a patient in a poorly-run prison system, and the purpose of the class is merely to aggregate all those individually viable claims. This theory has the virtue of being consistent with procedural principles, but at the cost of a gross substantive departure from our case law. Under this theory, each and every prisoner who happens to be a patient in a system that has systemic weaknesses . . . has suffered cruel or unusual punishment, even if that person cannot make an individualized showing of mistreatment. Such a theory of the Eighth Amendment is preposterous. . . .

Whether procedurally wrong or substantively wrong, the notion that the plaintiff class can allege an Eighth Amendment violation based on "system-wide deficiencies" is assuredly wrong. It follows that the remedy decreed here is also contrary to law, since the theory of systemic unconstitutionality is central to the plaintiffs' case. . . .

It is also worth noting the peculiarity that the vast majority of inmates most generously rewarded by the re-lease order—the 46,000 whose incarceration will be ended—do not form part of any aggrieved class even under the Court's expansive notion of constitutional violation. Most of them will not be prisoners with medical conditions or severe mental illness; and many will undoubtedly be fine physical specimens who have developed intimidating muscles pumping iron in the prison gym.

**B**

Even if I accepted the implausible premise that the plaintiffs have established a systemwide violation of the Eighth Amendment, I would dissent from the Court's endorsement of a decrowding order. That order is an example of what has become known as a "structural injunction." As I have previously explained, structural injunctions are radically different from the injunctions traditionally issued by courts of equity, and presumably part of "the judicial Power" conferred on federal courts by Article III:

> The mandatory injunctions issued upon termination of litigation usually required 'a single simple act.' H. McClintock, Principles of Equity § 15, pp. 32-33 (2d ed.1948). Indeed, there was a 'historical prejudice of the court of chancery against rendering decrees which called for more than a single affirmative act.' *Id.*, § 61, at 160. And where specific performance of contracts was sought, it was the categorical rule that no decree would issue that required ongoing supervision. . . . Compliance with these 'single act' mandates could, in addition to being simple, be quick; and once it was achieved the contemnor's relationship with the court came to an end, at least insofar as the subject of the order was concerned. . . . [*Mine Workers v. Bagwell*, 512 U.S. 821, 841-842 (1994) (Scalia, J., concurring).]

Structural injunctions depart from that historical practice, turning judges into long-term administrators of complex social institutions such as schools, prisons, and police departments. Indeed, they require judges to play a role essentially indistinguishable from the role ordinarily played by executive officials. Today's decision not only affirms the structural injunction but vastly expands its use, by holding that an entire system is unconstitutional because it *may produce* constitutional violations.

The drawbacks of structural injunctions have been described at great length elsewhere. This case illustrates one of their most pernicious aspects: that they force judges to engage in a form of factfinding-as-policymaking that is outside the traditional judicial role. The factfinding judges traditionally engage in involves the determination of past or present facts based (except for a limited set of materials of which courts may take "judicial notice") exclusively upon a closed trial record. That is one reason why a district judge's factual findings are entitled to plain-error review: because having viewed the trial first hand he is in a better position to evaluate the evidence than a judge reviewing a cold record. In a very limited category of cases, judges have also traditionally been called upon to make some predictive judgments: which custody will best serve the interests of the child, for example, or whether a particular one-shot injunction will remedy the plaintiff's grievance. When a judge manages a structural injunction, however, he will inevitably be required to make very broad empirical predictions necessarily based in large part upon policy views—the sort of predictions regularly made by legislators and executive officials, but inappropriate for the Third Branch.

This feature of structural injunctions is superbly illustrated by the District Court's proceeding concerning the decrowding order's effect on public safety. The PLRA requires that, before granting "[p]rospective relief in [a] civil action with respect to prison conditions," a court must "give substantial weight to any adverse impact on public safety or the operation of a criminal justice system caused by the relief." 18 U.S.C. § 3626(a)(1)(A). Here, the District Court discharged that requirement by making the "factual finding" that "the state has available methods by which it could readily reduce the prison population to 137.5% design capacity or less without an adverse impact on public safety or the operation of the criminal justice system." It found the evidence "clear" that prison overcrowding would "perpetuate a criminogenic prison system that itself threatens public safety," and volunteered its opinion that "[t]he population could be reduced even further with the reform of California's antiquated sentencing policies and other related changes to the laws." It "reject[ed] the testimony that inmates released early from prison would commit additional new crimes," finding that "shortening the length of stay through earned credits would give inmates incentives to participate in programming designed to lower recidivism," and that "slowing the flow of technical parole violators to prison, thereby substantially reducing the churning of parolees, would by itself improve both the prison and parole systems, and public safety." . . .

The District Court cast these predictions (and the Court today accepts them) as "factual findings," made in reliance on the procession of expert witnesses that testified at trial. Because these "findings" have support in the record, it is difficult to reverse them under a plain-error standard of review. And given that the District Court devoted nearly 10 days of trial and 70 pages of its opinion to this issue, it is difficult to dispute that the District Court has discharged its statutory obligation to give "substantial weight to any adverse impact on public safety."

But the idea that the three District Judges in this case relied solely on the credibility of the testifying expert witnesses is fanciful. *Of course* they were relying largely on their own beliefs about penology and recidivism. And *of course* different district judges, of different policy views, would have "found" that rehabilitation would not work and that releasing prisoners would increase the crime rate. I am not saying that the District Judges rendered their factual findings in bad faith. I am saying that it is impossible for judges to make "factual findings" without inserting their own policy judgments, when the factual findings *are* policy judgments. What occurred here is no more judicial factfinding in the ordinary sense than would be the factual findings that deficit spending will not lower the unemployment rate, or that the continued occupation of Iraq will decrease the risk of terrorism. Yet, because they have been branded "factual findings" entitled to deferential review, the policy preferences of three District Judges now govern the operation of California's penal system.

It is important to recognize that the dressing-up of policy judgments as factual findings is not an error peculiar to this case. It is an unavoidable concomitant of institutional-reform litigation. When a district court issues an injunction, it must make a factual assessment of the anticipated consequences of the injunction. And when the injunction undertakes to restructure a social institution, assessing the factual consequences of the injunction is necessarily the sort of predictive judgment that our system of government allocates to other government officials.

But structural injunctions do not simply invite judges to indulge policy preferences. They invite judges to indulge *incompetent* policy preferences. Three years of law school and familiarity with pertinent Supreme Court precedents give no insight whatsoever into the management of social institutions. Thus, in the proceeding below the District Court determined that constitutionally adequate medical services could be provided if the prison population was 137.5% of design capacity. This was an empirical finding it was utterly unqualified to make. Admittedly, the court did not generate that number entirely on its own; it heard the numbers 130% and 145% bandied about by various witnesses and decided to split the difference. But the ability of judges to spit back or even average-out numbers spoon-fed to them by expert witnesses does not render them competent decisionmakers in areas in which they are otherwise unqualified. . . .

### C

My general concerns associated with judges' running social institutions are magnified when they run prison systems, and doubly magnified when they force prison officials to release convicted criminals. . . .

### II

The Court's opinion includes a bizarre coda noting that "[t]he State may wish to move for modification of the three-judge court's order to extend the deadline for the required reduction to five years." *Ante*, at 1947. . . . It also invites the District Court to "consider whether it is appropriate to order the State to begin without delay to develop a system to identify prisoners who are unlikely to reoffend," and informs the State that it "should devise systems to select those prisoners least likely to jeopardize public safety." *Ibid.* (What a good idea!)

The legal effect of this passage is unclear—I suspect intentionally so. If it is nothing but a polite remainder to the State and to the District Court that the injunction is subject to modification, then it is entirely unnecessary. . . .

I suspect, however, that this passage is a warning shot across the bow, telling the District Court that it had *better* modify the injunction if the State requests what we invite it to request. Such a warning, if successful, would achieve the benefit of a marginal reduction in the inevitable murders, robberies, and rapes to be committed by the released inmates. But it would achieve that at the expense of intellectual bankruptcy, as the Court's "warning" is entirely alien to ordinary principles of appellate review of injunctions. . . .

Of course what is really happening here is that the Court, overcome by common sense, disapproves of the results reached by the District Court, but cannot remedy them (it thinks) by applying ordinary standards of appellate review. It has therefore selected a solution unknown in our legal system: A deliberately ambiguous set of suggestions on how to modify the injunction, just deferential enough so that it can say with a straight face that it is "affirming," just stern enough to put the District Court on notice that it will likely get reversed if it does not follow them. . . . That we are driven to engage in these extralegal activities should be a sign that the entire project of permitting district courts to run prison systems is misbegotten.

But perhaps I am being too unkind. The Court, or at least a majority of the Court's majority, must be aware that the judges of the District Court are likely to call its bluff, since they know full well it cannot possibly be an abuse of discretion to refuse to accept the State's proposed modifications in an injunction that has just been approved (*affirmed*) in its present form. An injunction, after all, does not have to be perfect; only good enough for government work, which the Court today says this *is*. So perhaps the coda is nothing more than a ceremonial washing of the hands—making it clear for all to see, that if the terrible things sure to happen as a consequence of this outrageous order do happen, they will be none of this Court's responsibility. After all, did we not want, and indeed even suggest, something better? . . .

[Dissent of Justice Alito, with whom The Chief Justice joins, omitted].

## Comments and Questions

1. What role does the standard of review play in the majority and dissenting opinions? To what extent ought the Supreme Court revisit the findings of the lower courts? Justice Scalia argues that the lower courts' conclusions were not factual findings at all. What are the different views articulated in the case as to what factual findings are?

2. What is the argument that the courts in the California prison overcrowding litigation overstepped the bounds set by Article III? Does this argument hang on one's interpretation of the language of the Prison Litigation Reform Act or of the constitutional limitations on the role of the judge? (You may want to reread Article III at this point.)

3. How would you describe the relationship between the majority and dissent in *Brown* and the views articulated by Fuller and Chayes in the preceding excerpts?

4. Underlying the disagreement expressed by the Court is an empirical question: what is the effect of incarceration on the crime rate? If incarceration reduces the crime rate, it may be because of its deterrent effect or the incapacitation effect. The debate in *Plata* is largely framed in terms of incapacitation rather than deterrence. But differentiating between the two effects of incarceration is very difficult, as they are closely related. The extent to which incarceration and increasingly stiff penalties reduce the crime rate because of a deterrence effect is contested. *See* Steven N. Durlaf and Daniel S. Nagin, *Imprisonment and Crime: Can Both Be Reduced?* 10 Criminology & Pub. Pol. 1, 9 (2011). The incapacitation effect is also contested. There is strong empirical evidence that there is a negative relationship between crime and age. *See* David P. Farrington, *Age and Crime*, in *Crime and Justice: An Annual Review of Research* (Michael H. Tonry and Norval Morris, eds. 1986); Travis Hirschi and Michael R. Gottfredson. *Age and the Explanation of Crime*, 89 Am. J. Soc. 552-584 (1983). For at least that set of older prisoners, incarceration may have a deterrent effect on younger prisoners but not an incapacitation effect.

# B. ALTERNATIVE DISPUTE RESOLUTION

Critics of the adversary system and the burgeoning workload of the courts often advocate alternative procedures for resolving human problems with greater use of negotiation, compromise, and direct involvement of the parties in problem solving. The adversary system tends to translate tensions and conflicts into a dualist pattern of win-or-lose and all-or-nothing frameworks; it also tends to emphasize the sole goal of individual gain for each party. Professor Carrie Menkel-Meadow contrasts the adversary framework with a problem-solving focus. "Instead of 'maximizing individual gain,' we can be focused on 'solving the problem,' 'creating the transaction,' 'planning for the future,' 'improving relationships,' and perhaps even seeking 'joint gain' and 'achieving justice.' Thus, a good legal problem solver needs a greater repertoire of intellectual choices or 'tropes' as well as a much broader and deeper set of behaviors." Carrie J. Menkel-Meadow, *When Winning Isn't Everything: The Lawyer as Problem Solver*, 28 Hofstra L. Rev. 905, 910 (2000). A broader repertoire of options should place litigation within a larger toolbox among a variety of other problem-solving and dispute-resolving techniques. This section describes varying techniques, identifies contemporary debates and issues arising with them, and points to resources for learning more.

Alternatives to adjudication may improve party and public satisfaction and voluntary compliance with resolutions. The two most basic alternatives to litigation, of course, are "lumping it," in which an injured or unhappy party decides to live with the harm or dissatisfaction without pursuing a complaint or seeking redress, and negotiation, used by a dissatisfied or harmed party to pursue an informal accommodation or settlement by directly discussing it with the other party. Yet negotiation between the parties or even between their lawyers may not be sufficient where there is little trust, shared experience, or civility. Even when they prefer informal nonjudicial approaches, parties and lawyers increasingly turn to third parties to help resolve their disputes because they lack trust, experience, or mores that would permit them to reach a satisfactory result without help.

Alternative dispute resolution (ADR) is a general term referring to alternatives to the formal adversarial process that offer more guidance and support than simple negotiation between the parties or their representatives. ADR supporters champion its potential for circumventing the cost and delay of litigation and for generating flexible and creative solutions to disputes. Its critics charge that these methods compromise parties' rights through unequal bargaining power and encourage secrecy. Both of these results undermine public values.

## 1. Introduction to Mediation and Arbitration

Two basic ADR methods are mediation and arbitration.

*Mediation:* A neutral actor facilitates an agreement that is negotiated between the disputants. Mediation can be especially constructive where the disputing parties have ongoing relationships, as with divorcing parents facing issues of child custody and visitation. Observers identify two types of mediators: facilitative and evaluative. In neither instance does the mediator make a decision. A facilitative mediator works to improve communication, elicit mutual understandings of each side's underlying needs and goals, and encourage parties to generate options in order to help them find a solution they can jointly embrace. Evaluative mediators, in contrast, elicit strengths and weaknesses on each side of the dispute and then offer estimates of what would happen if the dispute ends up before a judge in terms of legal or factual determinations or economic valuations of disputed issues. *See* Leonard L. Riskin, *Understanding Mediators' Orientations, Strategies, and Techniques: A Grid for the Perplexed,* 1 Harv. Negot. L. Rev. 7 (1996).

*Arbitration:* The disputing parties agree upon the selection of a neutral and skilled decisionmaker who is entrusted with making a final, binding, and nonappealable judgment based on presentations by the parties. Although in the past, the scope of issues open to arbitration was confined to those over which the parties contracted, increasingly the scope of arbitration has been expanded. The procedure can be quite informal or it can mirror courtroom practices, including rules governing evidence and motions. The arbitrator's ability to fashion remedies is broad, given historical limitations on judicial review of arbitration, although courts may be involved in enforcing arbitrated solutions as the product of contractual agreements. Ever since Congress adopted the Federal Arbitration Act of 1925, courts have enforced the agreement to arbitrate as well as the results of arbitration.

Arbitration has its roots in resolving disputes between organized labor and management. It has spread in recent years to disputes between non-unionized employees and their employers, consumers and retailers, physicians and patients, physicians and health care provider organizations, and international commercial transactions. A notable difference between arbitration and trials is the absence of a right to a jury in arbitration.

## 2. What Advocates Say About ADR

When should ADR be pursued, and what sort is appropriate—a new innovation, arbitration, or mediation? If mediation is chosen, should it be facilitative or evaluative? In this context, consider how a range of scholars and practitioners describe the strengths and limitations of the alternatives in comparison with litigation and with one another in theory and in practice.

a. Unlike the tension, hairsplitting, and hostility promoted by the adversary system, mediation and arbitration can build trust between the parties. As an initial matter, the parties negotiate common ground rules to mediate or agree upon a shared decisionmaker to arbitrate—and thereby start the process of resolving their dispute with agreement rather than further conflict. *See* Jethro K. Lieberman and James F. Henry, *Lessons from the Alternative Dispute Resolution Movement*, 53 Chi. L. Rev. 424 (1986).

b. The results of ADR are superior to the results of adjudication because they require less time and expense, generate flexibility, and allow people to deal with the emotional as well as financial features of disputes. ADR also permits creative solutions such as renegotiating an entire contract rather than pursuing a breach of contract and antitrust claims. An ADR solution in a child custody dispute can arrange a weekly parental visitation schedule to accommodate the desires of the two children to spend some time apart and some time together, as well as with the divorced parents, rather than a rigid schedule moving the children together to one parent for the week and the other for the weekend. *See* Frank E. A. Sander, *Dispute Resolution Within and Outside the Courts* (National Association of Attorneys General and ABA 1990); *The Paths of Civil Litigation*, 113 Harv. L. Rev. 1851, 1852-1853 (2000); Jonathan R. Harkavy, *Privatizing Workplace Justice: The Advent of Mediation in Resolving Sexual Harassment Disputes*, 34 Wake Forest L. Rev. 135 (1999).

c. Use of ADR promotes party control, self-determination, and satisfaction—even across cultural differences—while lowering court caseloads and expenses. Leonard Riskin and James E. Westbrook, *Dispute Resolution and Lawyers* 5 (2d ed. 1997); Cynthia A. Savage, *Culture and Mediation: A Red Herring*, 5 Am. U. J. Gender & Law 269 (1996).

## 3. What Critics Say About ADR

a. Because of its greater informality, ADR does not guard against the imbalances in power between disputing parties and instead allows more powerful parties to take advantage of less powerful parties. Mediation programs within courts may pressure parties into accepting settlements that reflect the agendas of the mediator, or the party with more political or economic power. *See* Richard Delgado et al., *Fairness and Formality: Minimizing the Risk of Prejudice in Alternative Dispute Resolution*, 1985 Wis. L. Rev. 1359 (1985).

b. By focusing on individuals and typically operating in sessions closed to public view, ADR veils the public implications of private settlements and derails the collective action that litigation can help mobilize. Carrie Menkel-Meadow, *Pursuing Settlement in an Adversary Culture: A Tale of Innovation Co-opted or "The Law of ADR,"* 19 Fla. St. U. L. Rev. 1 (1991).

c. ADR undermines or waters down rights and justice by generating private compromises acceded to by parties lacking full autonomy or control, which creates special dangers to constitutional rights, civil rights, and environmental law. Owen M. Fiss, *Against Settlement*, 93 Yale L.J. 1073 (1984).

d. ADR often does not save costs or time, especially when the parties continue to retain separate legal representation and when the process is prolonged. Lisa Bernstein, *Understanding the Limits of Court-Connected ADR: A Critique of Federal Court-Annexed Arbitration Programs*, 141 U. Pa. L. Rev. 2169 (1993); James S. Kakalik et al., *An Evaluation of Mediation and Early Evaluation Under the Civil Justice Reform Act* (1996). *But see* Michael Heise, *Justice Delayed? An Empirical Analysis of Civil Case Disposition Time*, 50 Case W. Res. L. Rev. 813 (2000) for more positive results.

---

The arguments in favor of ADR have contributed to a massive increase during the 1980s and 1990s in the use of mediation, arbitration, and other variations both by private initiative and through court-connected programs. The arguments against ADR reflect a more recent backlash that has triggered the development of due process protocols within the American Arbitration Association's own guidelines for employment and consumer disputes. Legislative reforms have also put a brake on court-mandated ADR.

## 4. The Contemporary Discourse

Four specific issues raised by the increasing use of ADR offer a window into debates over when and what kind of ADR should be pursued: (1) What degree of participation mandated by the government is consistent with ADR and procedural justice? (2) When should courts decline to enforce contractual clauses mandating ADR on the theory that consumers or employees lacked sufficient bargaining power or concerns about how much of the justice business is becoming controlled by private actors, secluded from public view? (3) When public rights or resources are at issue, is ADR appropriate? (4) Should parties be able to privately negotiate access to judicial review of resolutions reached through ADR? Each question exposes aspects of the comparison between public procedures and private compromises in the resolutions of disputes.

a. *Mandatory participation.* When people have a right to go to court, they may always choose not to go, either by settling privately or by agreeing to pursue mediation, arbitration, or some other alternative process. When, if ever, should a court direct the parties to pursue an alternative dispute process and preclude access to litigation, at least until such alternatives have been explored? The Society of Professionals in Dispute Resolution has recommended mandatory participation in nonbinding dispute resolution processes but only where such compulsory process is more likely to serve the interests of the parties, protection of historically disadvantaged groups, the needs of the courts to function effectively, and public trust in the system. *Report 1 of the Law and Public Policy Committee of the Society of Professionals in Dispute Resolution* (1990). According to the Alternative Dispute Resolution Act of 1998, 28 U.S.C. § 652(a), federal courts can mandate participation in ADR in certain cases—often as a precondition to access to adjudication—but "only with respect to mediation, early neutral evaluation, and if the parties consent, arbitration." Federal courts have construed this law to preempt state legislation meant to ensure party access to courts. *Allied Bruce Terminix Cos., Inc. v. Dobson*, 513 U.S. 265 (1995); *Perry v. Thomas*, 482 U.S. 483 (1987); *Southland Corp. v. Keating*, 465 U.S. 1 (1984).

b. *Judicial enforcement of contracts mandating ADR.* The Supreme Court has ruled that securities customers must use arbitration rather than bringing fraud claims to court because they signed a customer agreement accepting arbitration. *Rodriguez de Quijas v. Shearson/American Express, Inc.*, 490 U.S. 477 (1989). The Supreme Court has also upheld binding arbitration agreements in employment contracts. *See, e.g., 14 Penn Plaza LLC v. Pyett*, 556 U.S. 247 (2009); *Circuit City Stores, Inc. v. Adams*, 532 U.S. 105 (2001).

Courts have not been sympathetic to claims of duress or unequal bargaining power when consumers challenge contractual terms mandating arbitration— even when the consumers include minors and persons who do not speak English. *See* Jean R. Sternlight, *Panacea or Corporate Tool? Debunking the Supreme Court's Preference for Binding Arbitration*, 74 Wash. U. L.Q. 637, 709 (1996).

The Federal Arbitration Act (FAA) limits states' power to protect consumers, employees, and other individuals from binding arbitration imposed by contracts that they may not have understood nor had sufficient ability to alter. The ability of states to regulate arbitration context has been limited using the doctrine of federal preemption—by which federal law, under the Supremacy Clause of Article IV of the Constitution, prevents the states from interfering with the application of federal law. For example, the Supreme Court of California had held that consumer contracts that did not include a provision for classwide arbitration (to permit small claims to be aggregated together before the arbitrator) were unconscionable. The Supreme Court pre-empted California's rule under the FAA. *See AT&T v. Concepcion*, 131 S. Ct. 1740 (2011). This decision indicates that it will be very difficult for states to regulate arbitration agreements in adhesion contracts. Arbitration clauses are common in financial transactions governing credit cards, banking, investment, accounting, and increasingly also present in employment and consumer agreements. Should state—and federal—courts do more to protect ordinary people's access to court to resolve disputes arising in these settings or instead advance the trend of enforcement of waivers of court access in adhesion contracts? Should this be treated as a question of procedure, or contract, or federal and state relations?

c. *ADR and the public sector*. Rooted initially in private sector labor rela-tions and then in resolving family and neighborhood disputes, mediation and arbitration are now commonly used in public sector disputes, including the enforcement of the Clean Air Act, oil spill clean-up, conflicts over zoning and land use, and employment discrimination claims. *See* Philip J. Harter, *Nego-tiating Regulations: A Cure for Malaise*, 71 Geo. L.J. 1 (1982). The Supreme Court has enforced agreements to arbitrate discrimination claims in work-places lacking collective bargaining agreements, *Gilmer v. Interstate/ Johnson Lane Corp.*, 500 U.S. 20 (1991), while also allowing the Equal Employment Opportunity Commission itself to proceed with enforcement actions seeking back pay remedies even for specific employees who have signed arbitration agreements. *EEOC v. Waffle House, Inc.*, 534 U.S. 279 (2002). In *Waffle House*, the Court protected the arbitration alternative but also preserved a role for the public agency to pursue administrative and judicial enforcement on behalf of a particular employee bound by an arbitra-tion agreement but unable to recover relief in that process. One way to under-stand the decision is to note that only the employer and employee—not the EEOC—are parties to the contract establishing arbitration for disputes. Yet courts on other occasions have concluded that nonsignatories can be com-pelled to arbitrate. *See* Jaime Dodge Byrnes and Elizabeth Pollman, *Arbitra-tion, Consent and Contractual Theory: The Implications of* EEOC v. Waffle House, 8 Harv. Negot. L. Rev. 289 (2003). What values are served by barring the individual employee from litigating, due to predispute arbitration agree-ment, but not barring the federal agency from litigating on behalf of that same individual?

Given the potential benefits of mediation, why should it not be used to resolve disputes over racial discrimination or restraints on freedom of expres-sion? Observers assert that constitutional and fundamental moral issues cannot be mediated, but allocation and distribution questions can. Why would this be the case? Do you disagree? In any use of nonjudicial dispute resolution that implicates public rights and interests—such as disputes over rights to water or minerals, use of coastal zones or tribal lands, or risks to endangered species—what groups should take part, and who should repre-sent the public interest?

d. *Judicial review of arbitration*. Federal law allows judicial review of arbitration decisions if the award "was procured by corruption, fraud, or undue means," or where the arbitrators misbehaved in ways that prejudiced the rights of a party or that exceeded the arbitrators' power. 9 U.S.C. § 10(a). Judicial revision of arbitration awards under this provision has been limited and rare, and courts have declined to ask whether an arbitration award was correct or even reasonable. *See IDS Life Ins. Co. v. Royal Alliance Assoc., Inc.*, 266 F.3d 645 (7th Cir. 2001). But in *Cole v. Burns*, the court offered review where an arbitrator displayed "manifest disregard of the law." *Cole v. Burns International Security Services*, 105 F.3d 1465, 1486 (D.C. Cir. 1997). What power ought the courts be given to monitor and alter the results of dispute processes entered into by private parties?

Importantly, private parties cannot contract *for* judicial review for errors of law or fact by the arbitrator. The Supreme Court has held that parties cannot enforce a contract expanding judicial review once the arbitration is over. The Court explained that the FAA embodied "a national policy favoring arbitration with just the limited review needed to maintain arbitration's essential virtue of resolving disputes straightaway." *Hall Street Associates L.L.C. v. Mattel, Inc.*, 552 U.S. 576, 588 (2008). This approach is not universal. Under English law, for example, courts can review arbitration decisions for legal errors unless the parties explicitly contract to preclude such judicial review. Arbitration Act of 1996 (1996 c.23), § 69.

## Practice Exercise No. 29: Alternative Dispute Resolution Under Local Rule

Here is a local rule for the U.S. District Court for the District of Massachusetts on Alternative Dispute Resolution, and a letter that one judge in the district requires lawyers to mail to their clients. These local rules responded initially to the Civil Justice Reform Act of 1990 and then to the Alternative Dispute Resolution Act of 1998, requiring each district court to authorize the use of ADR in all civil actions. 28 U.S.C. § 651 et seq.

Assume that an identical local rule is in effect for the *City of Cleveland* case. Your clients have received a form letter identical to the one that follows, and you have told them that you will discuss the letter with them. (If your last name begins with letter *A* through *J*, you represent the City; and if your last name begins with letter *K* through *Z*, you represent the plaintiffs.) In class, you will engage in a strategy session discussing what you should recommend to your client about ADR and the letter's options in their case. Your instructor is an older lawyer in your office. Most people use the terms "mediation" and "conciliation" interchangeably. This technique employs a third party to help the litigants reach a resolution of the dispute on their own agreed-upon terms. In arbitration, a third party (or group of people) hears evidence, usually at a formal hearing, and gives a formal decision, in much the same way a judge would. The litigants can agree, or a previous contract can compel, that the arbitration decision be binding, enforceable, and have a claim-preclusion effect. Many, if not most, arbitrators would say that they are applying the applicable law to the facts that they believe to be true after hearing and weighing the evidence.

The descriptions of mini-trial, summary jury trial, and early neutral evaluation in the Local Rule and judge's letter are rather straightforward.

### Rule 16.4 Alternative Dispute Resolution

(a) The judicial officer shall encourage the resolution of disputes by settlement or other alternative dispute resolution programs.

(b) **Settlement.** At every conference conducted under these rules, the judicial officer shall inquire as to the utility of the parties conducting settlement negotiations, explore means of facilitating those negotiations, and offer whatever assistance may be appropriate in the circumstances. Assistance may include a reference of the case to another judicial officer for settlement purposes. Whenever a settlement conference is held, a representative of each party who has settlement authority shall attend or be available by telephone.

(c) **Other Alternative Dispute Resolution Programs.**

(1) Discretion of Judicial Officer. The judicial officer, following an exploration of the matter with all counsel, may refer appropriate cases to alternative dispute resolution programs that have been designated for use in the district court or that the judicial officer may make available. The dispute resolution programs described in subdivisions (2) through (4) are illustrative, not exclusive.

(2) Mini-trial.

(a) The judicial officer may convene a mini-trial upon the agreement of all parties, either by written motion or their oral motion in open court entered upon the record.

(b) Each party, with or without the assistance of counsel, shall present his or her position before:

(1) selected representatives for each party, or

(2) an impartial third party, or

(3) both selected representatives for each party and an impartial third party.

(c) An impartial third party may issue an advisory opinion regarding the merits of the case.

(d) Unless the parties agree otherwise, the advisory opinion of the impartial third party is not binding.

(e) The impartial third party's advisory opinion is not appealable.

(f) Neither the advisory opinion of an impartial third party nor the presentations of the parties shall be admissible as evidence in any subsequent proceeding, unless otherwise admissible under the rules of evidence. Also, the occurrence of the mini-trial shall not be admissible.

(3) Summary jury trial.

(a) The judicial officer may convene a summary jury trial:

(1) with the agreement of all parties, either by written motion or their oral motion in court entered upon the record, or

(2) upon the judicial officer's determination that a summary jury trial would be appropriate, even in the absence of the agreement of all the parties.

(b) There shall be six (6) jurors on the panel, unless the parties agree otherwise.

(c) The panel may issue an advisory opinion regarding:

(1) the respective liability of the parties, or

(2) the damages of the parties, or

(3) both the respective liability and the damages of the parties.

(d) Unless the parties agree otherwise, the advisory opinion is not binding and it shall not be appealable.

(e) Neither the panel's advisory opinion nor its verdict, nor the presentations of the parties shall be admissible as evidence in any subsequent proceeding, unless otherwise admissible under the rules of evidence. Also, the occurrence of the summary jury trial shall not be admissible.

(4) Mediation.

(a) The judicial officer may grant mediation upon the agreement of all parties.

(b) The mediator selected may be an individual, group of individuals or institution. The mediator shall be compensated as agreed by the parties.

(c) The mediator shall meet, either jointly or separately, with each party and counsel for each party and shall take any steps that may appear appropriate in order to assist the parties to resolve the impasse or controversy.

(d) If mediation does not result in a resolution of the dispute, the parties shall promptly report the termination of mediation to the judicial officer.

(e) If an agreement is reached between the parties on any issues, the mediator shall make appropriate note of that agreement and shall refer the parties to the judicial officer for entry of a court order.

(f) Any communication related to the subject matter of the dispute made during the mediation by any participant, mediator, or any other person present at the mediation shall be a confidential communication to the full extent contemplated by Fed. R. Evid. 408. No admission, representation, statement, or other confidential communication made in setting up or conducting the proceedings not otherwise discoverable or obtainable shall be admissible as evidence or subject to discovery.

Adopted effective, October 1, 1992.

## UNITED STATES DISTRICT COURT DISTRICT
## OF MASSACHUSETTS BOSTON, 02109

William G. Young
District Judge

Date: _____

Dear Litigant:

Your case has been assigned to this session of the U.S. District Court for all pretrial proceedings and trial. I assure you that our goal is to give your case a fair, impartial, and just trial as soon as possible. To that end, I have today met with the attorneys and placed your case on the running trial list in this session as of _____.

As you may appreciate, full-scale trials are expensive, and the time spent awaiting trial is frequently lengthy. Therefore, I want you to be aware of various other programs we offer that may possibly resolve your case to your satisfaction with less expense and delay. Each of these programs is voluntary, and all parties to the lawsuit must agree before implementing any such program in your case. I list these programs in the order that they most resemble a trial in this Court.

1. *Trial before a Magistrate Judge:* You may agree to try your case, with or without a jury, before a U.S. Magistrate Judge. A Magistrate Judge is a judicial officer appointed by the judges of this Court for this purpose. The trial takes place in this courthouse and, if a jury has been claimed, before a federal jury. The advantage of this program is its speed—cases can usually be reached for trial before a Magistrate Judge within a few months. Moreover, the parties can usually agree with the Magistrate Judge upon a specific day to begin the trial. There is no charge for this service.

2. *Trial before a retired Superior Court Justice:* You may agree to try your case to a federal jury before a distinguished retired justice of the Massachusetts Superior Court. The Superior Court is "the great trial court of the Commonwealth," and its justices are experts on jury trials and issues of Massachusetts law. The advantages are the same as for trials before Magistrate Judges—a speedy hearing and definite trial date. The cost of this program to you will be $250 per trial day plus sharing the per trial day cost of a court reporter. The trial will take place in this courthouse before a federal jury.

3. *Arbitration:* You may agree to resolve your case by submitting it to a skilled neutral arbitrator or group of arbitrators. You will have a chance to participate in the choice of arbitrators. Advantages of this program are that prompt arbitration hearings may be scheduled and the arbitrators may be technically skilled in the issues raised in this lawsuit. You and the other parties will share the costs of the arbitrators and the administration of the arbitration program.

4. *Summary jury trial:* You may agree to a summary jury trial. This is an advisory one-day proceeding before a federal jury. Each party will have the chance to make a brief presentation of its position, and, properly charged as to the law, the jury will render a nonbinding advisory verdict. I will meet with the attorneys that same day to discuss whether a settlement of the case is possible and proper. It may be helpful to you and the other parties to obtain the views of the summary jury in order to better evaluate your position. There is no cost for this program.

5. *Mediation:* You may agree to voluntary mediation. If you agree, I will appoint a skilled, neutral, and experienced mediator promptly to explore with all parties and their attorneys whether a settlement of this case may be reached that will satisfy your basic concerns. Unlike the previous options, mediation never imposes a result on the parties. Rather, it seeks to reach agreement. Prompt mediation may minimize your overall litigation costs.

6. *Early neutral evaluation:* You may agree to have your case evaluated by a neutral attorney skilled in the issues raised in this case. This may assist you in evaluating your position and may aid you in deciding whether to settle, press on to trial, or avail yourself of one or more of these other options.

Your attorney is familiar with each of these options and can advise you in detail concerning what advantages they may offer you. If the parties can agree, you may pursue variations on these options with the support of this Court.

Should you wish further information on any of these points or should all parties agree to pursue any one or a variant of any of them, your attorney should feel free to consult with Courtroom Deputy Clerk Kate Myrick, Esq., or Docket Clerk Elizabeth Smith.

## Practice Exercise No. 30: Alternative Dispute Resolution in *Carpenter*

For the purpose of this exercise (only), assume the following facts and circumstances for the *Carpenter* case. A firm trial date has been set for the case, and that date is exactly two months away. Ultimate Auto, which is represented by a lawyer from its insurance company ("Commercial"), and the lawyer for Nancy Carpenter have agreed to attempt to settle the case through a facilitated (and nonbinding) mediation. A second insurance company, the insurer of the jeep, has already offered $10,000 (the maximum payable under the policy) to Carpenter; the Dees, however, are still in the case. The Dees' lawyer has declined the invitation to mediate. Assume that summary judgment was entered in favor of McGill and McGill's Garage, and thus they are out of the case. Assume that the City is still in the case, but the City has recently filed for bankruptcy and is judgment-proof. The City's general counsel refuses to show up for the mediation; she insists that the case against the City is spurious.

Ultimate Auto had a liability insurance policy with Commercial. Under these liability policies, insurance companies will typically assume the obligation of defending the insured. Naturally, this makes the insured somewhat dependent on the acts of the insurers, because the insurers typically have the power to settle the case up to the policy limit (and thereby foreclose an insured's exposure) or may instead refuse to settle the case and expose the insured to liability for any amounts in excess of the "policy limit." State laws typically impose some obligation on insurers to make good-faith efforts to compromise claims where the recovery may exceed the policy limits of the insured's protections. The policy issued by Commercial to Ultimate Auto has a policy limit of $500,000.

The mediator in this case insists that clients attend with their attorneys. The mediator's general practice is to first meet with the parties and their counsel together, and to tell them his or her ground rules for the mediation. Often, the mediator will give a short speech about the importance of civility, the advantages of a mediated settlement (including cost savings and the possibility of creative solutions), the cloak of confidentiality, and some insight into the mediator's views about his or her role in the process of the mediation. The mediator then typically asks the parties to sign various documents including, among other things, confidentiality agreements and promises to pay the mediator's fees. (Mediators will typically charge approximately $2,000 for a full day of mediation, and $1,000 for any portion of a half day. The parties usually share the expense equally.) The mediation in this case is scheduled for four hours. The mediator will answer any questions about the mediation process, and will then ask to hear opening statements from the lawyers about their views of the case and about previous negotiations, if any. The mediator is usually also very willing to hear any statements that the clients may wish to make. Most mediators will also ask for a written statement from each side; the mediator may even ask for a submission in advance of the mediation session. (The mediator will usually ask for you to identify any information that you expect the mediator to keep confidential.)

After both sides have had the opportunity to make their opening statements, the mediator typically will separate the parties, with the plaintiff's team in one conference room and the defendant's team in another. The mediator then performs a sort of "shuttle diplomacy" going back and forth between the two rooms with demands and counter-offers. Occasionally the mediator may bring everyone back together; and if there is a settlement, the mediator will meet with everyone to summarize and, ultimately, to memorialize the settlement in writing.

Assume in this case that Carpenter's lawyer and Commercial's lawyer have met briefly previously. Plaintiff's lawyer made a demand of $1.5 million and the defendant's lawyer offered $25,000. In this brief negotiation, plaintiff's lawyer shared with defense counsel the major economic information contained in the letter from Economics Specialists of Boston, Inc. that is in the Case Files. Defense counsel was (or at least appeared) unimpressed. The parties were so far apart that they then thought that an exchange of further offers and counter-offers was unlikely to lead to an agreement. Commercial's lawyer then wrote the president of Ultimate Auto that he should consider getting his own lawyer in order to protect Ultimate Auto against a judgment that could be greater than the policy limit. Ultimate Auto has declined to retain an additional lawyer. Assume that the plaintiff's lawyer has taken the case on a contingency basis: one-third of the recovery, plus out-of-pocket disbursements. The defense's lawyer is paid $140 an hour by Commercial. Discovery has been completed. The lawyers agree that it would probably take between three and five days to try the case.

This practice has four potential parts. Your professor may wish to do any of them.

A. *Demand Letter.* Each of you should write a three-page double-spaced demand letter, on behalf of Nancy Carpenter, addressed to Ultimate Auto. You may wish to review the essentials of writing a demand letter, introduced in Practice Exercise No. 9, in Chapter 3.

B. *Writing Assignment.* Each of you should write a three-page, double-spaced opening statement to the mediator. If your last name begins with the letter A through M, you represent Nancy Carpenter and her son; if N through Z, you are the lawyer representing Ultimate Auto (and Commercial).

C. *Oral Statement.* Each of you should prepare an opening statement to the mediator of approximately five to ten minutes in length. If your last name begins with the letter A through M, you represent Nancy Carpenter and her son; if N through Z, you are the lawyer representing Ultimate Auto (and Commercial).

D. *Mediation.* Each of you should prepare to participate in a mediation session. If your last name begins with the letter A through C, you should prepare to play the role of Nancy Carpenter. The *lawyer* for Nancy Carpenter will be selected from persons with last names beginning with the letters H through L. If your last name begins with the letter D through G, you should prepare to play the role of Adam Jenkins, the president of Ultimate Auto. The *lawyer* for Ultimate Auto (selected and paid for by Commercial) will be selected from persons with last names beginning with the letters M through Q. Persons with last names beginning with the letters R and S should prepare to serve as the mediator. And persons with last names beginning with the letters T through Z should prepare to play the role of an assistant vice president of Commercial with authority to settle the case. The mediation may be conducted inside or outside the class. There may also be individual instructions for particular roles to accompany these general instructions.

## 5. An Alternative to ADR

As advocated by ADR visionaries, such as Frank Sander, many courts brought mediation, arbitration, settlement conferences, and other ADR programs into the courthouse. Congress adopted the federal Alternative Dispute Resolution Act of 1998, which requires each federal district court to adopt a dispute resolution program and many states have incorporated mediation and other ADR techniques within their court systems. The conjunction of ADR and courts has produced institutional innovations, such as the summary jury trial, invented by Judge Thomas Lambros. The summary jury trial is a court-initiated and supervised voluntary and nonbinding settlement process intended to offer each party a chance to present its factual case before a jury. The jury then reports its reaction to the conflicting evidence and thereby offers the settlement process outside information about the weaknesses in each party's case. *See* Thomas D. Lambros, *The Summary Jury Trial: An Effective Aid to Settlement*, 77 Judicature 6 (1993). Other innovations include the case-screening conference, designed to elicit facts and details surrounding cases in order to match the parties with a particular dispute process and a specific neutral third party to assist in the resolution. *See* Ericka B. Gray, *One Approach to Diagnostic Assessment of Civil Cases: The Individual Case-Screening Conference*, The Court Manager 21 (Summer 1992).

Once incorporated into the judicial process, however, ADR may decline in quality or even depart from its own preconditions. Nancy Welsh warns that civil nonfamily "mediation" in courts often devolves into traditional settlement conferences, dominated by lawyers, and leads to compromised monetary settlements. These procedures fail to empower parties, promote communication and mutual understanding, or develop creative solutions. Nancy A. Welsh, *Making Deals in Court-Connected Mediation: What's Justice Got to Do with It?*, 79 Wash. U. L.Q. 787 (2001). To the extent that ADR suffers from reduced quality, it jeopardizes the perceived fairness of the court-sponsored process, which has historically rested on procedures allowing parties to tell their stories to a neutral and even-handed third party. *Id.* at 820-822. If the parties develop strong relationships with their lawyers and are able to observe their lawyers' presentations, Welsh suggests that court-connected ADR can comport with procedural justice. But lawyers who do not understand or do not appropriately tell their clients' stories and mediators who exclude the parties from discussions or pressure parties into settlements risk undermining procedural justice. *Id.* at 857. In light of these concerns, consider the reforms for a "simple track" proposed next. If you were charged with creating such a system, what would it look like?

# ■ STEPHEN B. BURBANK AND STEPHEN N. SUBRIN, LITIGATION AND DEMOCRACY: RESTORING A REALISTIC PROSPECT OF TRIAL

*46 Harv. C.R.-C.L. L. Rev. 399, 409-412 (Summer 2011)*

Our first proposal advocates categorical restrictions on discovery as part of a separate set of rules for "simple" cases. A number of states have such separate tracks, as do England and Wales. We are not prepared to specify all the details of such a track, an effort that should be informed by experience in jurisdictions that already employ tracking. We can, however, set forth a few central features of the proposal.

We would retain notice pleading as the norm, mindful that the claim to effective court access of those initiating simple cases is as strong as that of those initiating complex cases. But we share the view, which animates recent reforms in England and Wales, that proportionality should be a foundational principle underlying procedural rules. For many simple cases, discovery of the breadth permitted by the existing Federal Rules is not proportional, and its availability is an invitation to economic oppression. Moreover, many observers of current federal practice have asserted that it is more expensive to litigate the same case in federal court than state court. If true (and we believe it is), this is in part due not just to the many opportunities for extensive discovery but also to the multiple required steps that have been introduced to try to obviate the need for such discovery: mandatory disclosure, discovery conferences, pretrial conferences, and lists of witnesses and their expected testimony. The high cost of litigation dissuades some potential litigants with meritorious claims from commencing suit and forces some of those who do sue, and some defendants, into settlements that do not truly reflect the merits.

Less discovery for simple cases thus does not mean second-class justice for those cases. Rather, by reducing the breadth of discovery, we effectively reduce transaction costs and force lawyers to focus on the heart of the dispute. This and other features of the simple case track we advocate should enhance the realistic prospects of a trial and thus the possibility that settlements will do justice to the parties—in short, that the law will actually be enforced.

The rule makers have appeared to heed, even if faint-heartedly, the lessons of empirical studies that suggest the value of bright-line rules. In a series of amendments, they have introduced presumptive limits on the number of interrogatories and depositions and on the length of depositions. We say "faint-heartedly" because such limits can be avoided by stipulation and court order. Moreover, the limits are so high (i.e., ten depositions per side) that they are either irrelevant or an invitation to economic oppression in many lawsuits. This suggests to us that, in addition to tolerating very little pretrial case management and mandating virtually unchangeable discovery and trial schedules, the rules for a simple case track should include non-negotiable limits on the number of interrogatories and depositions and on the length of depositions. Dispensation from these rules should be available only by court order to prevent manifest injustice (or some similarly daunting standard). Some of those numbers might vary within the simple case track depending on whether the case is subject to mandatory disclosure.

The rule makers have not attempted any limit on document discovery presumably because they could not come up with any limiting principles that did not seem insupportably arbitrary. We acknowledge that document discovery is the hardest nut to crack. Progress should be possible, however, so long as we are guided by the proportionality principle, have the comfort of knowing that "simple" cases do not include those implicating the private enforcement of federal statutory norms (see below), and remember that broad discovery can be an instrument of economic oppression and a perverse incentive for lawyers billing by the hour. Document discovery under the Federal Rules required court approval (for good cause shown) prior to 1970. In other common law countries that require disclosure or permit discovery of documents, but generally do not view private litigation as an enforcement tool, "the scope of discovery or disclosure is specified and limited." Precedent for requiring such specificity exists in this country in cases permitting direct discovery from abroad.

From a narrow efficiency perspective, a rule requiring that document requests in simple track cases be specific may help to solve the problem of the cost of searching for responsive documents, but it may not be adequate for that purpose. One additional area that might be explored, but that we do not now advocate, is a time window keyed to an objective characteristic of the litigation (such as a designated number of years from the date when the allegedly harm-producing conduct took place). In addition, since the search costs in question may be most burdensome for electronic documents (particularly e-mail), unlike the Court in *Twombly*, which relied heavily on a twenty-year-old theoretical article on discovery that antedated three sets of amendments to the discovery rules, we would acknowledge the e-discovery amendments recently made and seek empirical evidence concerning their effectiveness.

Objections often made to tracking proposals include the difficulty of drawing the lines necessary to sort cases into tracks and the likelihood of costly satellite litigation over decisions made. The answer to the latter, we believe, is to provide sufficiently objective and determinate criteria for the initial decision and not to permit any appeal. In addition, we would give exclusive responsibility for case assignment to federal judges who are dedicated (in part) to the task. Because there would be no appeal, magistrate judges probably could not be used for this purpose, but district judges serving in senior status might be ideal.

The task of defining "simple" cases is, to be sure, not simple. As indicated above, however, we conclude that cases implicating the private enforcement of public law should not be included because, among other things, broader discovery than that available in the simple case track may be necessary for adequate enforcement. Fortunately, some objective criteria for implementing this exclusion from the simple case track are to be found in statutory provisions for multiple damages and one-way pro-plaintiff fee-shifting. For more than a century Congress has used both of these kinds of provisions to promote private enforcement of federal statutes. Assuming that private enforcement cases are protected, it may be sufficient to define the rest of the landscape in terms of the amount in controversy. Any such amount—for instance, cases involving less than $500,000 are assigned to the simple case track—is arbitrary, but the line must be drawn somewhere. In order to prevent costly satellite litigation, the judge with responsibility for case assignment should have unreviewable discretion to determine whether the case as pleaded realistically exceeds the limit.

Congressional action will probably be necessary to overcome the traditional judicial hostility to a simple case track. Creation of such a track would almost certainly lead to more litigation in federal court—the so-called highway effect. Congress should ensure that the federal judiciary has resources that are adequate to the task, with "adequate" defined in a fashion that honors the best traditions of the federal courts rather than the bare minimum.

## C. MANAGERIAL JUDGING AND THE ROLE OF COURTS IN AN ERA OF ALTERNATIVE DISPUTE RESOLUTION

Echoing concerns first expressed by Dean Roscoe Pound in 1909, Simon Rifkind observed in 1979 that "there is a growing—and justified—apprehension that (1) [q]uantitatively, the courts are carrying too heavy a burden—and probably a burden beyond the capability of mitigation by merely increasing the number of judges; and (2) [q]ualitatively, the courts are being asked to solve problems for which they are not institutionally equipped, or not as well equipped as are other available agencies." Simon H. Rifkind, *Are We Asking Too Much of Our Courts?*, in *The Pound Conference: Perspectives on Justice in the Future* (1979).

To deal with complex court cases and heavy dockets, many judges have experimented with managerial techniques such as using their role as judge to promote settlement, directing cases to mediation or other alternative dispute resolution methods, and employing court-appointed assistants to create claims-processing mechanisms. One prominent lawyer, who has served as a court-appointed master establishing claims-processing mechanisms in several contexts, explains, "What I do is not really ADR. It is CJM—creative judicial management of a very serious problem that inundates the courts." Kenneth R. Feinberg, *Response to Deborah Hensler, A Glass Half Full, a Glass Half Empty: The Use of Alternative Dispute Resolution in Mass Personal Injury Litigation*, 73 Tex. L. Rev. 1647 (1995).

The legal profession has conflicting views on these issues. Consider the arguments offered in two relatively early articles on case management, one by an enthusiast (Judge William W. Schwarzer), and one by a critic (Professor Judith Resnik, who coined the term "managerial judging" in a longer, influential article entitled *Managerial Judges*, 96 Harv. L. Rev. 374 (1982)).

## ■ WILLIAM W. SCHWARZER, MANAGING CIVIL LITIGATION: THE TRIAL JUDGE'S ROLE
### *61 Judicature 400 (1978)*

My concern here is less with the judge's role at trial than before trial. Most civil cases are terminated before trial: in the federal system, less than 10 percent of the cases filed go to trial. Most judicial and private effort is expended on litigation that never reaches trial, through discovery, motions and other formal and informal interlocutory proceedings. It is a frequent complaint that costs incurred even before trial make litigation uneconomical. In addition, what is done in proceedings before trial tends to determine the scope and dimensions of the trial itself. The role of the judge in the pretrial stage of litigation is therefore of sufficient importance to warrant consideration.

Because of the great impact of pretrial activity and proceedings on the magnitude of the burden imposed by litigation on the courts and parties, and because there is room for improvement in the disposition of litigation, whether or not it is eventually tried, I urge that judges intervene in civil litigation and take an appropriately active part in its management from the beginning. If that role is discharged in a fair, informed and sensitive manner, it should aid greatly in achieving these objectives:

1. Define the issues to be litigated and limit pretrial activity to relevant matters;
2. Control pretrial discovery and other activity to avoid unnecessary expense and burden;
3. Arrive at a settlement of the controversy as early as possible or attempt to discover methods for resolving it as expeditiously and economically as possible; and
4. Insure that any trial will be well prepared and limited strictly to matters that cannot be otherwise disposed of.

### JUDICIAL MANAGEMENT POWER

No reform of the judicial system is needed to enable the trial judge to perform these kinds of litigation management functions on his own motion, as many judges already do. In the federal system, the Federal Rules of Civil Procedure, particularly Rule 16, give the judge sufficient authority and discretion to intervene sua sponte in pretrial proceedings. Moreover, the U.S. Supreme Court has recognized "the power inherent in every court to control the disposition of the causes on its docket with economy of time and effort for itself, for counsel and for litigants."

Neither the court's inherent management power nor its power under Rule 16 is unlimited. Parties cannot be compelled to litigate the case according to the court's discretion. They can, however, be compelled to comply with pretrial procedures reasonably necessary to implement Rule 1 of the Federal Rules of Civil Procedure to assure the "just, speedy and inexpensive determination of every action." While the courts appear not to be wholly in agreement on where to draw the line, judges clearly have the power to require that cases be fully and adequately prepared before they go to trial and that pretrial activity be conducted economically and efficiently.

Although adequate power exists for judicial intervention, the concept of judicial intervention runs counter to accepted notions. The first of these . . . is the traditional conception of the judge's role in the adversary process: that the judge is supposed to be passive and let lawyers litigate without interference except when one side or the other calls upon him. As Justice David W. Peck has put it, lawyers and judges "are apt to think of themselves as representing opposite poles and exercising divergent functions. The lawyer partisan, the judge reflective."

Judge Frankel, in his recent Cardozo lecture, "The Search for Truth—An Umpireal View," argued that

> [o]ur system does not allow much room for effective or just intervention by the trial judge in the adversary fight about the facts. The judge views the case from a peak of Olympian ignorance. His intrusion will in too many cases result from partial or skewed insights. . . .

Marvin E. Frankel, *The Search for Truth—An Umpireal View*, 123 U. Pa. L. Rev. 1031, 1042 (1975). Later in the lecture, he stressed that

> [t]he ignorance and unpreparedness of the judge are intended axioms of the system. . . . The judge is not to have investigated or explored the evidence before trial . . . without an investigative file, the American trial judge is a blind and blundering intruder, acting in spasms as sudden flashes of seeming light may lead or mislead him at odd times.

*Id.* Though each of these observers was discussing the judge's role at trial, rather than before trial, they reflect an attitude to which pretrial intervention would be foreign. It somehow equates ignorance with impartiality, and it fails to take into account the extent to which even the passive judge must in the normal course intervene in the fight about the facts and make rulings regardless of any ignorance or lack of preparation. In every interlocutory dispute about discovery, amendments, joinder, class action determination and pretrial relief, the judge must make decisions which (1) are made without the benefit of a full and complete record, and (2) have a direct impact on the fight about facts by aiding one party and hampering the other. Similarly, rulings at the trial on the admissibility of evidence and the scope of examination must be based on the judge's current appraisal of the facts of the case and his judgment concerning the course the trial should follow.

### THE NEED FOR INTERVENTION

The judge is, of course, not to become a third party in a general search for the truth. But ignorance and lack of preparation do not insulate him from having direct control over how counsel conduct the litigation, whether he acts sua sponte or only when called upon by the parties. His rulings through the litigation, even procedural ones, implicate the merits and affect the outcome, yet must be made on the strength of whatever knowledge of the case the judge is able to acquire along the way. In any case, therefore, the cause of justice would seem to be better served by an informed and prepared judge capable of making sound rulings than by Judge Frankel's model of "the ignorant and unprepared judge [who] is, ideally, the properly bland figurehead in the adversary scheme of things." . . .

The reform of pretrial discovery under the Federal Rules of Civil Procedure, it is true, was intended to minimize judicial intervention. But, that philosophy, though still widely held, is giving way to a growing recognition that it imposes unacceptable costs. For complex litigation, for example, courts have adopted procedures under the Manual for Complex Litigation premised on active judicial management of the litigation from the outset. The time has come to consider a similar approach for civil litigation generally.

The present crisis might well be relieved by revised or new rules of procedure in such areas as discovery and class actions. But the utility of rules is directly proportional to the wisdom and firmness with which they are administered. Because each case is unique in its facts, personalities and needs, general rules do not obviate the need for individualized judicial management.

### No Threat to Fairness

It may be argued that intervention sua sponte jeopardizes the judge's appearance of impartiality. Inasmuch as action resulting from intervention may be interpreted as favoring one party at the expense of the other, the fact that the action was taken on the initiative of the judge, not in response to one party's application, may give rise to suspicions of bias. The argument lacks force, however, where the judge acts in a reasoned and fair manner after having heard the parties and having considered their views.

Moreover, justice is not better served by the passive judge who by inaction permits litigation to blunder along its costly way toward exhaustion of the litigants, when it might have long been settled or at least controlled to everyone's benefit. One may fairly ask whether the parties left to themselves can always be depended on to prosecute litigation diligently, economically and in good faith; to avoid wars of attrition and harassment, obstruction and delay; and to exclude extraneous personal considerations from the conduct of the litigation. . . .

Judges must appear, as well as be, fair in their conduct, but they ought not to be hobbled by the fear that entirely proper actions might arouse suspicion. . . .

### The Efficiency Issue

Finally, judicial intervention is met by contradictory arguments from opposing camps. First, some criticize preoccupation with efficiency, placing quantity above quality in dispensing justice. Implying judges are becoming subservient to computers and productivity statistics, they argue "slow justice is always preferable to speedy injustice."

That argument, however, does not undercut the case for judicial management of litigation when the purpose is to achieve the optimum allocation of resources, judicial and private. If by judicial intervention, discovery burdens are lightened, the interests of justice are served for litigants directly involved and for others whose cases are pending.

Then there are those who argue that judicial intervention is an inefficient use of the judge's limited time, and that judges should "minimize . . . [their] investment of time through the early stages of a case." Statistics have been offered to prove that pretrial conferences resulted in a net loss of judicial time, but many judges disagree. An hour or less spent reviewing the case file and meeting with lawyers may often produce substantial time savings by, for example, obviating future discovery disputes and motions, disclosing areas of factual or legal agreement, eliminating issues from trial, bringing about an earlier settlement, or reducing the time required for trial.

As we will discuss later, the controversy is likely to assume more modest dimensions and more manageable shape after the judge, with his knowledge and experience, has discussed the case with the parties and directs them to talk to each other. And as cases are brought to a more rapid conclusion than under the traditional "laissez-faire" system, the quality of justice improves because judges will have more time to devote to the cases remaining on their docket. It seems, therefore, that the busier the judge and the heavier his case load, the more urgent the need for intervention early in civil cases, especially when calendars are burdened with criminal cases entitled to priority. . . .

The time has come to discard the stereotype of "the ignorant and unprepared judge [as] the properly bland figurehead in the adversary scheme of things," the fear that the interests of justice will be compromised by judicial intervention, and the assumption that judges are too busy to use their time wisely. It is time to clear the way for active judicial participation in the management of civil litigation.

## THE PROCESS OF INTERVENTION

The purpose of judicial intervention is to promote the "just, speedy, and inexpensive determination to every action." It contemplates that the judge, having familiarized himself with the file and the controlling law and discussed the case informally with counsel, will then supply the appropriate degree of guidance based on his judgment and experience.

Probably the most effective setting is an informal conference in chambers with both counsel and, where appropriate, the clients. The formality of the courtroom, with its trappings of adversary confrontation, hardly promotes the reasoned dialogue, flexibility and accommodation to which the judge's intervention should lead.

Discovery disputes, for example, generally are more readily and constructively resolved by in-chambers discussion moderated by the judge than by formal motion. Similarly, a determination of whether or not a particular issue is in dispute and requires trial may be better made in chambers. Settlement conferences certainly belong in chambers, not in the courtroom. And settlement negotiations are often the next logical step after informal discussion has revealed that the differences between the parties are not as great as conventional litigation posturing had indicated.

As early in the litigation as possible, the judge should urge counsel to define the factual and legal issues, to develop an appropriate discovery program, and to lay out a schedule for motions, pretrial and trial. Working with the judge on these matters, counsel are likely to be more reasonable than if left to themselves. The mere expectation of intervention—the knowledge that the judge is watching or at least available to intervene—is likely to moderate the litigation tactics of the parties, minimizing the need for actual intervention.

Defining and specifying issues at an early conference between court and counsel is of great importance. Rule 8 of the Federal Rules of Civil Procedure requires that the complaint contain "a short and plain statement of the claim showing that the pleader is entitled to relief." Pleadings rarely meet that test. A conference will help disclose just what claim plaintiff asserts to obtain relief and what is in issue. This will narrow the scope of the controversy and focus discovery on essentials. It may reveal areas of agreement and issues that can be disposed of by motion in advance of trial; the judge may call for the filing of motions which appear to him to have possible merit and which a party may have overlooked. It may also indicate that motions contemplated by a party would be futile, thus saving time and expense for everyone. . . .

### THE JUDGE'S APPROACH

By participating in a settlement conference, the judge must not, and need not, create doubts in the minds of parties about their ability to obtain a fair trial. He may well determine that a settlement conference should be held before another judge who will not try the case or, if he himself has participated in discussions, that another judge should try the case. But a judge need not jeopardize the appearance of impartiality if he simply suggests to the parties how an objective observer might react to some of the evidence and contentions of the parties.

Judicial intervention to promote the settlement of cases should be an exercise in tact and understanding, not coercion. The judge who can listen with a third ear may well receive subliminal messages pointing the way to settlement. And having won the confidence and respect of the parties, a sympathetic and knowledgeable judge will be in a better position to discuss the strengths and weaknesses of the case with each side, perhaps separately, to persuade them of the benefits of settlement and to suggest means to narrow differences. Once the conference procedure has become known to the bar, moreover, counsel, aware of what is expected, will tend to begin negotiations on their own sooner and more seriously.

The passive judge who, conforming to the traditional role model, passes up the opportunity to serve as a catalyst for settlement, will probably try many cases that could have been settled and, in doing so, will render no particular benefit to the administration of justice.

If the case must go to trial, judicial intervention can help assure that it has been thoroughly prepared. Merely holding a pretrial conference, however, accomplishes little. The benefits of pretrial are directly proportional to the amount of effort invested by court and counsel.

At the pretrial conference, the judge, having prepared himself by review of the file, should require each side to specify the disputed legal and factual issues, to identify the proposed witnesses in the order they will appear, to summarize each witness's testimony, and to identify and exchange each proposed exhibit and state its foundation. This process will produce many, sometimes surprising benefits:

1. It will expose the unprepared lawyer and prevent the wasteful charades that pass for trials when lawyers are unprepared;
2. It will enable the judge to spot undisputed issues (which can be disposed of by stipulation) and redundant or unnecessary evidence;
3. It will disclose evidence problems which can be resolved in advance, rather than in time-consuming and disruptive side-bar conferences at trial;
4. It will permit resolution of foundation and authenticity issues concerning exhibits, further saving trial time; and
5. It may indicate the possibility of deciding some issues on motion.

Intervention at this point means that no case goes to trial until the shape and content of the trial have been thoroughly discussed by court and counsel. Experience has shown that the trial time saved as a result of thorough pretrial far exceeds the time required for pretrial. Pretrial should, however, be tailored to the needs of the particular case to spare the parties the expense and burden of complying with boilerplate pretrial orders that impose requirements disproportionate to the case.

Finally, the education the judge receives in the process will enable him to try the case in more informed and effective fashion, perhaps even reducing risk of reversible error. . . .

# ■ JUDITH RESNIK, MANAGERIAL JUDGES AND COURT DELAY: THE UNPROVEN ASSUMPTIONS
*23 Judge's J. 8 (1984)*

In growing numbers, federal judges are adopting an increasingly managerial stance. Judges not only adjudicate the merits of issues presented to them by litigants but also meet with parties in chambers to encourage settlement of disputes and to supervise case preparation. As managers, judges learn about cases much earlier than they have in the past, and they negotiate with parties about the course, timing, and scope of pretrial activities.

When acting as pretrial managers, judges typically initiate contact with the parties to a lawsuit. In federal courts, under the new amendments to Rule 16 of the Federal Rules of Civil Procedure, within 120 days of the filing of a complaint, judges are obliged to issue scheduling orders, detailing the timing for pretrial motions, amendment of pleadings, and discovery. Nearly all cases receive pretrial attention under Rule 16, and some judges have already adopted the supervisory stance contemplated by the recent amendments.

Managerial meetings are usually informal and contrast sharply with the highly stylized structure of the courtroom. Pretrial conferences often occur in chambers; the participants may sit around tables, and the judge may wear business dress. The informal judge-litigant contact provides judges with information beyond that traditionally within their ken. Conference topics are wide-ranging, the judges' concerns broad. The supposedly rigid structure of evidentiary rules, designed to insulate decision-makers from extraneous or impermissible information, is not relevant to case management. Managerial judges are not silent auditors of retrospective events told by witnesses; judges instead become part of the tales.

Pretrial supervision is also relatively private. . . . Many judges conduct pretrials in chambers; generally, neither court reporters nor the public attend. Finally, the decisions reached at pretrial conferences are rarely reviewable until after (and if) a final judgment on the merits is rendered.

Federal judges' new managerial role has emerged for several reasons. The creation in 1938 of pretrial discovery rights generated some disputes that parties brought to court; trial judges undertook the task of resolving discovery disputes and, in the process, became mediators and negotiators. Once involved in pretrial discovery, many judges became convinced that their presence at other points in lawsuits' development would be beneficial; supervision of discovery became a conduit for judicial control over all phases of litigation and thus infused lawsuits with the continual presence of the judge-overseer.

In part because of their new oversight role, and in part because of increasing caseloads, many judges became concerned about the volume of their work. To reduce the pressure, judges turned to efficiency experts, who suggested judicial management as an important technique of calendar control. Under the experts' guidance, judges have increasingly experimented with schemes for speeding the resolution of cases and for persuading litigants whenever possible to settle rather than try cases. During the past decade, enthusiasm for the managerial movement has become widespread. What began as an experiment has become obligatory in virtually all cases in federal courts and is increasingly common in state courts as well.

In the rush to conquer the mountain of work, few have considered whether reliance upon trial judges for informal dispute resolution and for case management is a positive step, and whether judicial management can accomplish the many goals set for it. Little empirical evidence exists to support the claim that judicial management works—either to settle cases or to provide cheaper, quicker, or fairer dispositions.

Proponents of judicial management have also failed to consider the systemic effects of the shift in the judicial role. Management is a new form of judicial activism, a behavior that usually attracts substantial criticism. Judicial management may be teaching judges to value their statistics, such as the number of case dispositions, more than they value the quality of those dispositions. Further, because managerial judging is less visible than traditional adjudication and is usually unreviewable until after final judgments have been rendered, managerial judging gives trial courts more authority and at the same time provides litigants with fewer procedural safeguards to protect them from abuse of that authority. In sum, judicial management merits our close attention and our study before we embrace it as the slogan for the courts of the 1980s.

### QUESTIONABLE BENEFITS

Managerial judging's proponents believe that their system of management improves the use of judicial resources. They argue that, with judges in charge of the litigation system, court resources are better allocated, case dispositions speeded and delay reduced while the quality of judicial decision-making is unimpaired. No one can oppose efforts to curtail exploitation of the judicial system and make dispute resolution quick and inexpensive. I do, however, question the extent to which managerial judging contributes to these worthy aims and whether it is wise to rely upon judges to achieve these goals.

Proponents of managerial judging typically assume that management enhances efficiency in three respects. They claim that case management decreases delay, produces more dispositions, and reduces litigation costs. But close examination of the currently available information reveals little support for a firm conclusion that judicial management is responsible for efficiency gains in federal district courts.

*Delay Reduction.* The first step is assessing the question of delay reduction to decide whether there is a "problem" of delay in federal trial courts. This assessment is not simple to make. In appellate courts, we have shared perception in the amount of time it "should" take to prepare a brief, or the amount of time it "should" take to decide an appeal. In contrast, when we turn to trial courts, it is more difficult to determine the amount of time that "should" be spent to prepare a case for trial. The scope of issues and the number of actors vary greatly among cases as well as throughout the evolution of a single case. Case complexity at the trial level can reasonably require postponement of deadlines not merely by days or weeks (as in the appellate courts) but by months or years. As of yet, we do not have a substantive theory about the proper interval at which cases should proceed through the trial courts.

Moreover, in 1980, the median time for a case to move from filing to disposition in federal district court was only eight months. For cases that were tried, the interval was 20 months. I cannot with confidence assert that such data reveals "delay" in the federal courts. Illustrative of the difficulty in deciding that question is a change in nomenclature. Many researchers who have studied "delay" now address the question of "pace." Such researchers are unable to agree on how to explain why some courts process cases more quickly than others.

But if we were to assume that the pace of some civil litigation had been unduly delayed, we would still encounter problems in assessing the claim that judicial management speeds case processing. Even when we find that some courts with managerial judges have faster disposition rates than some other courts without managerial judges, we have great difficulty identifying the causes for the differences. Cases are filed, withdrawn, settled, or dismissed for a variety of reasons, including changes in legislation, new appellate decisions, shifts in business practices, and fluctuations in the availability of attorneys. Although it is theoretically possible to control for such variables, researchers are hampered by the absence of firsthand, unfiltered information about why cases conclude when they do.... Management advocates rely instead on anecdote and intuition to support their claims.

*Increasing the Number of Dispositions.* In addition to not knowing what impact judicial management has on delay, we also do not know what impact judicial management has on settlement rates. While proponents often claim increased settlement rates as a result of judicial management, most researchers have concluded that intensive judicial settlement efforts do not lead to more dispositions than would have otherwise occurred.

The claim of "the more dispositions the better" raises difficult valuation tasks; decision making must be assessed qualitatively as well as quantitatively. On any given day, are four judges, who speak with parties to 16 lawsuits and report that 12 of those cases ended without trial, more "productive" than four judges who preside at four trials? Is it relevant to an assessment of "productivity" that three of those four trials are settled after ten days of testimony. Or that, in the one case tried to conclusion, the judge writes a 40-page opinion on a novel point of law that is subsequently affirmed by the Supreme Court and thereafter affects thousands of litigants? Measuring judicial accomplishments is complex. Scales designed to measure achievement in other institutions cannot simply be imported into the courtroom.

*Reducing Costs.* Management advocates assume that judicial supervision not only saves time and produces more dispositions but also limits the ability of litigants to impose unfair financial pressure on their opponents and limits the ability of attorneys to justify excessive billing. Proponents therefore conclude that managerial judges reduce courts' and litigants' costs. But no data exist to support this conclusion. And, if we rely instead on intuition, it is not obvious that judicial supervision averts costly adversarial decisions or attorney misconduct. First, some lawyers use every occasion for contact with judges to argue their clients' cases. Thus, supervision itself can present further opportunities for vigorous adversarial encounters and for more billable hours. Second, the line between attorney misconduct and aggressive but ethical representation is often difficult to discern. Third, even with judicial oversight, lawyers may be able to hide their misconduct; procedural innovations may simply force attorneys to develop new techniques of obfuscation and avoidance.

Moreover, judicial management itself imposes costs. Judges' time is one of the most expensive resources in the courthouse. Rather than concentrate all of their energies on deciding motions, charging juries, and drafting opinions, managerial judges must meet with parties, develop litigation plans, and compel obedience to their new management rules. Managerial judges have more data sheets to complete, more conferences to attend, and ever more elaborate local procedural rules to draft and debate. Even when some of these tasks are delegated to staff, administrative structures must be put into place and then supervised. Although litigants and judges can contain some costs by relying on conference calls, and written exchanges, they still must spend substantial amounts of time and money. Further, because many cases settle without judicial intervention, management may require judges to supervise lawsuits that would not have consumed any judicial resources.

We are not yet able to reach any firm conclusions on whether and how management reduces costs. Until we have data on the number of judge-hours that management consumes and on its costs to the parties, we cannot calculate the net costs of managerial judging and thereby learn whether we have conserved resources. And, if we include in our equation the additional costs discussed below—of the possible increase in erroneous decisions and the loss of public participation—our calculation becomes even more complex.

In sum, I am skeptical of claims that judicial management increases court productivity at reduced costs. Data are not available to support most of these conclusions, and intuition does not compel them. Moreover, managerial proponents have rarely addressed or included in their assessments the effects of judicial management on the nature of adjudication.

## POSSIBLE RISKS

Transforming the judge from adjudicator to manager substantially expands the opportunities for judges to use—or to abuse—their powers. When deciding how much time to allow parties to prepare their cases, when running settlement conferences, when insisting, as some judges do, on ex parte meetings with each side, the trial judge sits unsupervised, virtually beyond review. Judges can create rules for the pretrial phase of lawsuits that parties have no way of challenging; with the individual calendar system in the federal courts, parties must be careful not to offend the one judge who is assigned a case at filing and presides over it until its disposition.

In addition to enhancing the power of judges, management tends to undermine traditional constraints on the use of that power. Judges, when creating management rules, need not submit their ideas to the discipline of written justification or to outside scrutiny. Many decisions are made privately; some are off the record; virtually all are beyond appellate review.

Furthermore, no explicit norms or standards guide judges in their decisions about what to demand of litigants. What does "good," "skilled," or "judicious" management entail? Other than their own intuitions, judges have little to inform them. Few institutional constraints inhibit judges during the informal pretrial phase. During pretrial management, judges are restrained only by personal beliefs about the proper role of judge-managers. . . .

*The Threat to Impartiality.* A major technique of management is to rely on the private, informal meetings between judges and lawyers to discuss discovery schedules and to explore settlement proposals—meetings beyond the constraints of the formal courtroom setting. But substantial risks inhere in the informality. The extensive information that judges receive during pretrial conferences is not filtered by the rules of evidence. Some of the information is received ex parte, a process that deprives the opposing party of the opportunity to contest the validity of the information received. Moreover, judges are often in close contact with attorneys during the course of management. Such interactions may become occasions for the development of intense feelings about the case or the parties—feelings of admiration, kinship, or antipathy. Management may be a fertile field for the growth of personal bias.

Moreover, judges with supervisory obligations may gain stakes in the case they manage. Their prestige may ride on "efficient" management, as calculated by the speed and number of dispositions. Competition and peer pressure may tempt judges to rush litigants because of reasons unrelated to the merits of the disputes. Reported opinions, as well as attorneys' anecdotes, substantiate the fact that some judges have elevated efficiency and management goals over considerations of fairness.

Unreviewable power, casual contact, and interest in outcome (or in aggregate outcomes) have not traditionally been associated with the "due process" decision-making model. These features do not evoke images of reasoned adjudication, images that form the very basis of both our faith in the judicial process and our enormous grant of power to judges. . . .

Case processing is no longer viewed as a means to an end; instead, it appears to have become the desired goal. Quantity has become all important; quality is occasionally mentioned and then ignored. . . .

## CONCLUSION

I argue for reflection before we plunge headlong into judicial management. I do not mean to suggest that adjudication must be frozen into earlier forms or that more efficient decision making is an unworthy aim. Rather, as we reorient the judicial system to accommodate contemporary demands, I believe that we should preserve the core of adjudication.

To help judges remain impartial, we should design rules to limit the flow of untested information to them. To ensure that judges have the patience for deliberation, we should refrain from giving them too many distracting new responsibilities. To hold judges accountable for the quality—not merely the quantity—of their actions, we should require them to act in public and to state reasons for their decisions. In sum we should not simply embrace the new management ethic; we must think carefully about what role judges should take and then craft rules to enable judges to act accordingly.

## Practice Exercise No. 31: Review of Settlement and Consideration of Judicial Case Management

Approximately 9,900 plaintiffs filed lawsuits against nearly 200 defendants alleging injuries arising out of their exposure to harmful chemicals in the aftermath of the tragedy of September 11, 2001. The plaintiffs include New York City employees such as firefighters and police officers, as well as civilian volunteers and others. Judge Alvin Hellerstein, United States District Judge for the Southern District of New York, appointed two special masters, both law professors, to set up a sampling procedure to encourage settlement. They developed a method for allocating the plaintiffs into groups. Sample cases from each group would go forward as "bellwether trials." The results of these trials would be used to help the parties reach a settlement for the remaining cases.

Under the experts' plan, plaintiffs were required to fill out questionnaires regarding types of diseases they suffered and the severity of their injury. The information was entered into a database. The groups were then organized based on type of illness and severity of the alleged harm. Out of the first group of 2,000 cases, the special masters collected 200 of those alleging the most severe injuries, 25 additional cases of other diseases that had not been included in the severity chart, and 400 cases chosen at random. Of these, the judge picked two cases, the defense lawyers picked two cases, and the plaintiffs' lawyers picked two cases, for a total of six cases (ultimately increased to twelve) set to proceed through pre-trial and trial. Judge Hellerstein explained that this "allows the parties to get a good sense of the strengths and weaknesses of all the cases" and presumably would lead to settlement. *See* Mark Hamblett, *Plan Implemented to Resolve Suits in World Trade Center Cleanup*, N.Y. L.J. (Feb. 25, 2009).

Before any trials were scheduled, the parties arrived at a settlement which they presented to the judge. The settlement required that 95 percent of the plaintiffs agree to it before it would become binding on the defendants, but provided little information as to what each plaintiff would ultimately receive. The judge expressed concerns about the fairness of the settlement and its complexity and scheduled a fairness hearing. The fairness hearing is a procedural protection made available in class actions. *See* Fed. R. Civ. P. 23(e). In a fairness hearing, the parties and anyone else with an interest in the litigation come before the court and present their perspective on the settlement. In a class action, the judge must approve the settlement for it to go forward. In an individual litigation, such as the many lawsuits making up the litigation here, parties decide whether or not to settle and do not need judicial approval. There is no federal rule providing for fairness hearings in cases that are not class actions.

The parties were concerned that the judge would disapprove of the settlement and appealed to the Second Circuit.* They argued that the judge had overreached his power by ordering a fairness hearing. Imagine that you are clerk to a member of the appellate court hearing this case. Your judge is concerned that the proceeding will not be sufficiently adversarial because no one is presenting Judge Hellerstein's point of view. The judge has asked you and another clerk to present the arguments for each side. Be prepared to make the best arguments for each side and to recommend an ultimate conclusion to the judge.

---

*In the real case, *In re World Trade Center Disaster Site Litigation*, the parties withdrew their appeal and presented a revised settlement to the court. The court ultimately held a fairness hearing and approved the settlement. You can find the documents, including Judge Hellerstein's orders, on the Southern District website: *http://www.nysd.uscourts.gov/sept11*.

# 7

The Choice of an
Appropriate Court:
Personal Jurisdiction,
Notice, and Venue

## A. INTRODUCTION AND OVERVIEW

In addition to the issues we have already explored concerning the viability of the claim for relief and the availability of a meaningful remedy, a plaintiff's lawyer contemplating a lawsuit must also choose an appropriate court to hear the case. In order to entertain an action and enter a valid and enforceable judgment, that court must have adjudicatory power consisting of (1) *personal jurisdiction* over the defendant, and (2) *subject matter jurisdiction* over the case. A third requirement is that adequate *notice* be sent apprising the defendant of the action.

*Personal* (sometimes referred to as *territorial*) *jurisdiction* is a reflection of the geographic limitations on the judicial power of the sovereign states within our federal system. Assume that Nancy Carpenter had moved to Florida following her husband's tragic death and decided to bring suit against Randall Dee in the courts of that state. Intuitively it seems unfair to require Dee to defend a lawsuit in a distant state when all the events giving rise to the claim occurred in Massachusetts. We may also question the authority of a Florida court to adjudicate a matter when that state has no connection to the lawsuit other than being the recently adopted residence of the plaintiff. Both concerns—fairness and power—play a role in the doctrine of personal jurisdiction. Over time (and what could fairly be called a long and winding road), the Supreme Court has developed an elaborate constitutional calculus for determining when a court has power to summon a defendant from beyond its borders.

While the concept of personal jurisdiction allocates judicial power among the states, *subject matter jurisdiction* (the topic of Chapter 8) allocates power between the federal and state court systems. Federal courts have *limited subject matter jurisdiction*. Constitutional and statutory provisions restrict their adjudicatory authority to certain types of cases, mainly disputes between citizens of different states ("diversity" cases) and disputes arising under federal law ("federal question" cases), such as patent, antitrust, and civil rights cases. In contrast, state courts have *general subject matter jurisdiction*—that is, they can hear and decide most categories of cases, including those that can be heard in federal court over which there is concurrent jurisdiction.

Once the principles of *personal* and *subject matter jurisdiction* identify those courts that have authority over both the defendant and the controversy, the administrative concept of *venue* further restricts the location of the lawsuit. Within the federal system, venue determines the appropriate judicial district(s) in which the case may be filed. The federal trial courts in New York State, for example, are divided into four districts: Eastern, Western, Northern, and Southern. Statutory provisions in the Judicial Code assign cases to particular districts based primarily on the residence of the parties, or the location of the events upon which the claim is based. State venue statutes assign cases to particular counties based on a variety of similar criteria.

As you recall from Chapter 1, notice and opportunity to defend a lawsuit are the core precepts of due process of law. Adequate *notice* to the defendant is thus the final prerequisite for a valid judgment, and is usually provided by serving the defendant (in hand or by postal delivery) with a copy of the complaint together with a summons.

## B. JURISDICTION OVER THE PERSON OR PROPERTY OF THE DEFENDANT

Perhaps the most familiar evolution of American case law (certainly to first-year law students) has occurred in the area of personal jurisdiction. Since the decision in *Pennoyer v. Neff* in 1877, the courts have struggled with the task of defining the conditions that must be met before a court may require a nonresident to appear and defend. The complexity of the problem stems in part from the very nature of our federal system of government.

Each state retains its own sovereignty, a significant aspect of which is the power to adjudicate disputes. Because a judgment may have consequences beyond the borders of the state that renders it, the adjudication of disputes unavoidably implicates the conflicting authorities of the separate sovereigns. A valid judgment entered by a court in *State A* is entitled under our Constitution (Art. IV, § 1) to "full faith and credit" in all other states. If the judgment is against a citizen of *State B*, that state must (when requested by the plaintiff) recognize and enforce it against the defendant and any assets found within *State B*. The Supreme Court has made clear that the full faith and credit command is "exacting," not discretionary, with respect to a judgment rendered by a court possessing adjudicatory authority over the subject matter and the persons governed by the judgment. *Franchise Tax Board of California v. Hyatt*, 538 U.S. 488, 494 (2003).*

*Pennoyer's* traditional conception of jurisdiction required the physical presence of the defendant or his property within the adjudicating state. In the years immediately following 1877—a time of tremendous expansion of interstate industry and commerce—the *Pennoyer* scheme proved too confining, as it frustrated the ability of states to offer a judicial forum to residents who had claims against nonresidents. Its demise was inevitable.

The process began subtly, with resort to legal fictions such as "constructive presence" and "implied consent" to be sued, but in 1945 gave way to a new framework for the analysis of personal jurisdiction—*International Shoe Co. v. Washington's* concept of "minimum contacts." Informed by notions of fair play as much as sovereign power, the modern formulation is highly contextual, and weighs many factors and policy concerns.

A word of warning about this chapter and the three that follow: We are leaving our focus on promulgated rules of procedure and entering an area of high-density judge-made legal doctrine.

# C. THE TRADITIONAL CONCEPTION OF PERSONAL JURISDICTION

*A Glossary of Terms.* Before turning to the *Pennoyer* opinion (which generations of law students have insisted is not written in the English language), it is helpful to define certain terms central to the traditional conception of personal jurisdiction.

*In personam* jurisdiction is the power of a court to enter a money judgment against the defendant; the judgment may, if necessary, be satisfied by seizing and liquidating the defendant's assets. An in personam judgment (rendered, for example, in a personal injury tort action) is said to follow the defendant, meaning that it must be given "full faith and credit" and be enforced by any state in which the defendant or his assets are found.

*In rem* jurisdiction is the power of a court to act with regard to property (such as real estate) within its borders. An in rem judgment affects the interests of persons in the property (and may indeed extinguish those interests) but, unlike an in personam judgment, does not create an obligation on the

---

* Foreign judgments are not covered by the Full Faith and Credit Clause, and the United States is not a party to any international treaty providing for their enforcement. Recognition is governed by the laws of the several states, either by common law or the Uniform Foreign Judgment Recognition Act. *See generally* Gary Born and Peter Rutledge, *International Civil Litigation in United States Courts* 1079-1081 (5th ed. 2011).

defendant's part to pay money to the plaintiff. An action to determine title to property among opposing claimants is an example of in rem jurisdiction.

*Quasi in rem* jurisdiction is a hybrid of the other two forms of adjudicatory power. It is based on the presence of the defendant's property (either real or personal) within the forum state, but it permits the court to enter a judgment for an amount of money not exceeding the value of the property, and which may be satisfied from the forced sale of the property. Unlike the "true" in rem action just described, the claim for relief in a quasi in rem action is unrelated to the property, which merely provides the basis for jurisdiction.

***

An example of litigation breeding litigation, *Pennoyer v. Neff* actually involved two successive lawsuits. Oregon attorney Mitchell sued nonresident Neff in state court in Oregon seeking $300 in legal fees allegedly due him. Neff's failure to appear led to a default judgment, which resulted in the forced sale of Neff's land in Oregon in order to satisfy the judgment. In the second suit, filed in federal court, Neff sought to recover his land from Pennoyer, who had purchased it at a sheriff's sale. The outcome of the second action turned upon the validity of the judgment entered in the first.

## ■ PENNOYER v. NEFF
### *95 U.S. 714 (1877)*

Justice FIELD delivered the opinion of the Court:

This is an action to recover the possession of a tract of land, of the alleged value of $15,000, situated in the State of Oregon. The plaintiff asserts title to the premises by a patent of the United States issued to him in 1866, under the act of Congress of Sept. 27, 1850, usually known as the Donation Law of Oregon. The defendant claims to have acquired the premises under a sheriff's deed, made upon a sale of the property on execution issued upon a judgment recovered against the plaintiff in one of the circuit courts of the State. The case turns upon the validity of this judgment.

It appears from the record that the judgment was rendered in February, 1866, in favor of J. H. Mitchell, for less than $300, including costs, in an action brought by him upon a demand for services as an attorney; that, at the time the action was commenced and the judgment rendered, the defendant therein, the plaintiff here, was a non-resident of the State that he was not personally served with process, and did not appear therein; and that the judgment was entered upon his default in not answering the complaint, upon a constructive service of summons by publication.

The Code of Oregon provides for such service when an action is brought against a non-resident and absent defendant, who has property within the State. It also provides, where the action is for the recovery of money or damages, for the attachment of the property of the non-resident. And it also declares that no natural person is subject to the jurisdiction of a court of the State, "unless he appear in the court, or be found within the State, or be a resident thereof, or have property therein; and, in the last case, only to the extent of such property at the time the jurisdiction attached." Construing this latter provision to mean, that, in an action for money or damages where a defendant does not appear in the court, and is not found within the State, and is not a resident thereof, but has property therein, the jurisdiction of the court extends only over such property, the declaration expresses a principle of general, if not universal, law. The authority of every tribunal is necessarily restricted by the territorial limits of the State in which it is established. Any attempt to exercise authority beyond those limits would be deemed in every other forum, as has been said by this court, an illegitimate assumption of power, and be resisted as mere abuse. In the case against the plaintiff, the property here in controversy sold under the judgment rendered was not attached, nor in any way brought under the jurisdiction of the court. Its first connection with the case was caused by a levy of the execution. It was not, therefore, disposed of pursuant to any adjudication, but only in enforcement of a personal judgment, having no relation to the property, rendered against a non-resident without service of process upon him in the action, or his appearance therein. The court below did not consider that an attachment of the property was essential to its jurisdiction or to the validity of the sale, but held that the judgment was invalid from defects in the affidavit upon which the order of publication was obtained, and in the affidavit by which the publication was proved.

There is some difference of opinion among the members of this court as to the rulings upon these alleged defects. . . .

If, therefore, we were confined to the rulings of the court below upon the defects in the affidavits mentioned, we should be unable to uphold its decision. But it was also contended in that court, and is insisted upon here, that the judgment in the State court against the plaintiff was void for want of personal service of process on him, or of his appearance in the action in which it was rendered and that the premises in controversy could not be subjected to the payment of the demand of a resident creditor except by a proceeding in rem; that is, by a direct proceeding against the property for that purpose. If these positions are sound, the ruling of the Circuit Court as to the invalidity of that judgment must be sustained, notwithstanding our dissent from the reasons upon which it was made. And that they are sound would seem to follow from two well-established principles of public law respecting the jurisdiction of an independent State over persons and property. The several States of the Union are not, it is true, in every respect independent, many of the rights and powers which originally belonged to them being now vested in the government created by the Constitution. But, except as restrained and limited by that instrument, they possess and exercise the authority of independent States, and the principles of public law to which we have referred are applicable to them. One of these principles is, that every State possesses exclusive jurisdiction and sovereignty over persons and property within its territory. . . . The other principle of public law referred to follows from the one mentioned; that is, that no State can exercise direct jurisdiction and authority over persons or property without its territory. The several States are of equal dignity and authority, and the independence of one implies the exclusion of power from all others. And so it is laid down by jurists, as an elementary principle, that the laws of one State have no operation outside of its territory, except so far as is allowed by comity; and that no tribunal established by it can extend its process beyond that territory so as to subject either persons or property to its decisions. "Any exertion of authority of this sort beyond this limit," says Story, "is a mere nullity, and incapable of binding such persons or property in any other tribunals."

But as contracts made in one State may be enforceable only in another State, and property may be held by non-residents, the exercise of the jurisdiction which every State is admitted to possess over persons and property within its own territory will often affect persons and property without it. To any influence exerted in this way by a State affecting persons resident or property situated elsewhere, no objection can be justly taken; while any direct exertion of authority upon them, in an attempt to give ex-territorial operation to its laws, or to enforce an ex-territorial jurisdiction by its tribunals, would be deemed an encroachment upon the independence of the State in which the persons are domiciled or the property is situated, and be resisted as usurpation. . . .

So the State, through its tribunals, may subject property situated within its limits owned by non-residents to the payment of the demand of its own citizens against them; and the exercise of this jurisdiction in no respect infringes upon the sovereignty of the State where the owners are domiciled. Every State owes protection to its own citizens; and, when non-residents deal with them, it is a legitimate and just exercise of authority to hold and appropriate any property owned by such non-residents to satisfy the claims of its citizens. It is in virtue of the State's jurisdiction over the property of the non-resident situated within its limits that its tribunals can inquire into that non-resident's obligations to its own citizens, and the inquiry can then be carried only to the extent necessary to control the disposition of the property. If the non-resident have no property in the State, there is nothing upon which the tribunals can adjudicate. . . .

Jurisdiction is acquired in one of two modes: first, as against the person of the defendant by the service of process; or, secondly, by a procedure against the property of the defendant within the jurisdiction of the court. In the latter case, the defendant is not personally bound by the judgment beyond the property in question. And it is immaterial whether the proceeding against the property be by an attachment or bill in chancery. It must be substantially a proceeding in rem. . . .

If, without personal service, judgments in personam, obtained ex parte against non-residents and absent parties, upon mere publication of process, which, in the great majority of cases, would never be seen by the parties interested, could be upheld and enforced, they would be the constant instruments of fraud and oppression. Judgments for all sorts of claims upon contracts and for torts, real or pretended, would be thus obtained, under which property would be seized, when the evidence of the transactions upon which they were founded, if they ever had any existence, had perished.

Substituted service by publication, or in any other authorized form, may be sufficient to inform parties of the object of proceedings taken where property is once brought under the control of the court by seizure or some equivalent act. The law assumes that property is always in the possession of its owner, in person or by agent; and it proceeds upon the theory that its seizure will inform him, not only that it is taken into the custody of the court, but that he must look to any proceedings authorized by law upon such seizure for its condemnation and sale. Such service may also be sufficient in cases where the object of the action is to reach and dispose of property in the State, or of some interest therein, by enforcing a contract or a lien respecting the same, or to partition it among different owners, or, when the public is a party, to condemn and appropriate it for a public purpose. In other words, such service may answer in all actions which are substantially proceedings in rem. But where the entire object of the action is to determine the personal rights and obligations of the defendants, that is, where the suit is merely in personam, constructive service in this form upon a non-resident is ineffectual for any purpose. Process from the tribunals of one State cannot run into another State, and summon parties there domiciled to leave its territory and respond to proceedings against them. Publication of process or notice within the State where the tribunal sits cannot create any greater obligation upon the non-resident to appear. Process sent to him out of the State, and process published within it, are equally unavailing in proceedings to establish his personal liability.

The want of authority of the tribunals of a State to adjudicate upon the obligations of non-residents, where they have no property within its limits, is not denied by the court below: but the position is assumed, that, where they have property within the State, it is immaterial whether the property is in the first instance brought under the control of the court by attachment or some other equivalent act, and afterwards applied by its judgment to the satisfaction of demands against its owner; or such demands be first established in a personal action, and the property of the nonresident be afterwards seized and sold on execution. But the answer to this position has already been given in the statement, that the jurisdiction of the court to inquire into and determine his obligations at all is only incidental to its jurisdiction over the property. Its jurisdiction in that respect cannot be made to depend upon facts to be ascertained after it has tried the cause and rendered the judgment. If the judgment be previously void, it will not become valid by the subsequent discovery of property of the defendant, or by his subsequent acquisition of it. The judgment, if void when rendered, will always remain void: it cannot occupy the doubtful position of being valid if property be found, and void if there be none. Even if the position assumed were confined to cases where the non-resident defendant possessed property in the State at the commencement of the action, it would still make the validity of the proceedings and judgment depend upon the question whether, before the levy of the execution, the defendant had or had not disposed of the property. If before the levy the property should be sold, then, according to this position, the judgment would not be binding. This doctrine would introduce a new element of uncertainty in judicial proceedings. The contrary is the law: the validity of every judgment depends upon the jurisdiction of the court before it is rendered, not upon what may occur subsequently. . . .

The force and effect of judgments rendered against non-residents without personal service of process upon them, or their voluntary appearance, have been the subject of frequent consideration in the courts of the United States and of the several States, as attempts have been made to enforce such judgments in States other than those in which they were rendered, under the provision of the Constitution requiring that "full faith and credit shall be given in each State to the public acts, records, and judicial proceedings of every other State"; and the act of Congress providing for the mode of authenticating such acts, records, and proceedings, and declaring that, when thus authenticated, "they shall have such faith and credit given to them in every court within the United States as they have by law or usage in the courts of the State from which they are or shall or taken." In the earlier cases, it was supposed that the act gave to all judgments the same effect in other States which they had by law in the State where rendered. But this view was afterwards qualified so as to make the act applicable only when the court rendering the judgment had jurisdiction of the parties and of the subject-matter, and not to preclude an inquiry into the jurisdiction of the court in which the judgment was rendered, or the right of the State itself to exercise authority over the person or the subject-matter. . . .

[T]he courts of the United States are not required to give effect to judgments of this character when any right is claimed under them. Whilst they are not foreign tribunals in their relations to the State courts, they are tribunals of a different sovereignty, exercising a distinct and independent jurisdiction, and are bound to give to the judgments of the State courts only the same faith and credit which the courts of another State are bound to give to them.

Since the adoption of the Fourteenth Amendment to the Federal Constitution, the validity of such judgments may be directly questioned, and their enforcement in the State resisted, on the ground that proceedings in a court of justice to determine the personal rights and obligations of parties over whom that court has no jurisdiction do not constitute due process of law. Whatever difficulty may be experienced in giving to those terms a definition which will embrace every permissible exertion of power affecting private rights, and exclude such as is forbidden, there can be no doubt of their meaning when applied to judicial proceedings. They then mean a course of legal proceedings according to those rules and principles which have been established in our systems of jurisprudence for the protection and enforcement of private rights. To give such proceedings any validity, there must be a tribunal competent by its constitution—that is, by the law of its creation—to pass upon the subject-matter of the suit; and, if that involves merely a determination of the personal liability of the defendant, he must be brought within its jurisdiction by service of process within the State, or his voluntary appearance.

Except in cases affecting the personal status of the plaintiff, and cases in which that mode of service may be considered to have been assented to in advance, as hereinafter mentioned, the substituted service of process by publication, allowed by the law of Oregon and by similar laws in other States, where actions are brought against non-residents, is effectual only where, in connection with process against the person for commencing the action, property in the State is brought under the control of the court, and subjected to its disposition by process adapted to that purpose, or where the judgment is sought as a means of reaching such property or affecting some interest therein; in other words, where the action is in the nature of a proceeding in rem. As stated by Cooley in his *Treatise on Constitutional Limitations*, 405, for any other purpose than to subject the property of a non-resident to valid claims against him in the State, "due process of law would require appearance or personal service before the defendant could be personally bound by any judgment rendered."

It is true that, in a strict sense, a proceeding in rem is one taken directly against property, and has for its object the disposition of the property, without reference to the title of individual claimants; but, in a larger and more general sense, the terms are applied to actions between parties, where the direct object is to reach and dispose of property owned by them, or of some interest therein. Such are cases commenced by attachment against the property of debtors, or instituted to partition real estate, foreclose a mortgage, or enforce a lien. So far as they affect property in the State, they are substantially proceedings in rem in the broader sense which we have mentioned. . . .

It follows from the views expressed that the personal judgment recovered in the State court of Oregon against the plaintiff herein, then a non-resident of the State, was without any validity, and did not authorize a sale of the property in controversy.

To prevent any misapplication of the views expressed in this opinion, it is proper to observe that we do not mean to assert, by anything we have said, that a State may not authorize proceedings to determine the status of one of its citizens towards a non-resident, which would be binding within the State, though made without service of process or personal notice to the non-resident. The jurisdiction which every State possesses to determine the civil status and capacities of all its inhabitants involves authority to prescribe the conditions on which proceedings affecting them may be commenced and carried on within its territory. The State, for example, has absolute right to prescribe the conditions upon which the marriage relation between its own citizens shall be created, and the causes for which it may be dissolved. One of the parties guilty of acts for which, by the law of the State, a dissolution may be granted, may have removed to a State where no dissolution is permitted. The complaining party would, therefore, fail if a divorce were sought in the

State of the defendant; and if application could not be made to the tribunals of the complainant's domicile in such case, and proceedings be there instituted without personal service of process or personal notice to the offending party, the injured citizen would be without redress.

Neither do we mean to assert that a State may not require a non-resident entering into a partnership or association within its limits, or making contracts enforceable there, to appoint an agent or representative in the State to receive service of process and notice in legal proceedings instituted with respect to such partnership, association, or contracts, or to designate a place where such service may be made and notice given, and provide, upon their failure, to make such appointment or to designate such place that service may be made upon a public officer designated for that purpose, or in some other prescribed way, and that judgments rendered upon such service may not be binding upon the non-residents both within and without the State. . . . Nor do we doubt that a State, on creating corporations or other institutions for pecuniary or charitable purposes, may provide a mode in which their conduct may be investigated, their obligations enforced, or their charters revoked, which shall require other than personal service upon their officers or members. Parties becoming members of such corporations or institutions would hold their interest subject to the conditions prescribed by law.

In the present case, there is no feature of this kind, and, consequently, no consideration of what would be the effect of such legislation in enforcing the contract of a non-resident can arise. The question here respects only the validity of a money judgment rendered in one State, in an action upon a simple contract against the resident of another, without service of process upon him, or his appearance therein.

Judgment affirmed.

[The dissenting opinion of Justice HUNT is omitted.]

## Comments and Questions

1. For the story behind the story in *Pennoyer,* as well as its colorful cast of characters, see Wendy Collins Perdue, *Sin, Scandal, and Substantive Due Process: Personal Jurisdiction and* Pennoyer *Reconsidered*, 62 Wash. L. Rev. 479 (1987).

2. Was the jurisdiction in the first case, *Mitchell v. Neff*, in personam or in rem (or something in between)? What about the second case, *Neff v. Pennoyer?*

3. Try to reconstruct the opposing arguments presented by the parties before the Supreme Court in *Pennoyer v. Neff.*

4. What were the several bases for the exercise of jurisdiction provided in the Code of Oregon? Did the Supreme Court decision in *Pennoyer* modify any of these?

5. Why should the then newly adopted Due Process Clause of the Fourteenth Amendment set the outer limits of state court power? What values are protected by the clause in this context? Why are geographic boundaries so important to the Supreme Court's conception of adjudicatory authority?

Regarding Justice Field's invocation of the Due Process Clause, Professor Perdue writes:

> Field's final and most startling step was to introduce the due process clause of the fourteenth amendment into his jurisdictional analysis. This step was unnecessary and surprising for several reasons. First, that clause had not been raised or argued by either party or by the court below. Second, Field had already concluded that the federal courts were not required to (and hence would not) enforce the prior Oregon judgment. Third, the due process discussion was dictum for the additional reason that the fourteenth amendment did not exist at the relevant time. Finally, the specific due process "holding" of the case—that a judgment rendered without personal jurisdiction is unenforceable even in the rendering forum—has been viewed by at least some courts and commentators as itself quite novel.

Perdue, *supra*, 62 Wash. L. Rev. at 499-500.

As you read the post-*Pennoyer* cases that follow, consider Professor Perdue's further observation: "[Justice] Field's approach to personal jurisdiction continues to dominate modern personal jurisdiction doctrine. His opinion in *Pennoyer* not only laid the foundation for treating personal jurisdiction as a substantive liberty interest, but also established that geographic boundaries are central in the protection of that interest." 62 Wash. L. Rev. at 480.

6. How do the Due Process and Full Faith and Credit Clauses interact on the matter of adjudicatory power?

7. What part does *notice* play in the Court's decision in *Pennoyer*? Was Neff actually notified of the pendency of *Mitchell v. Neff*? If not, why was the absence of notice not *itself* a constitutional due process defect in the prior proceedings? What is the "substituted service by publication" referred to by the Court, and how could such dubious notice possibly be deemed constitutionally sufficient?

8. What does *Pennoyer v. Neff* hold? Contrast the much narrower ruling of the lower court, which reached the same result—invalidating the sheriff's deed that had conveyed Neff's land to Pennoyer—but for different reasons involving defects in the affidavit of service.

9. If you were representing Mitchell in a replay of *Mitchell v. Neff* after the Supreme Court's decision, what procedural steps would you follow to ensure proper adjudicatory power over defendant Neff? Would bringing the suit in federal court overcome the personal jurisdiction problem? The answer, we will see in Part G later in this chapter, is no.

10. What openings are suggested in the last three paragraphs of *Pennoyer* that may allow expansion of the confining *Jurisdiction = Physical Presence* equation? In what situations, for example, may a nonresident be required to

appoint an agent to receive process within the forum state? Is this not a stretched version of consent?

Note the reference to a type of jurisdiction that permits a court to decide matters concerning the *civil status* of the litigants regarding marriage or the custody of children. A court, it is suggested, may entertain a divorce action brought by a resident even though the other spouse is beyond the usual reach of in personam power. Entry of an order to pay alimony or child support, however, may require the court to have in personam power over the defendant spouse. Compare NYCPLR § 302(b) with *Burnett v. Burnett*, 208 W. Va. 748, 755 (2000).

The civil status language in *Pennoyer* has been relied upon to hold that a court need not have in personam power over an abusive nonresident husband in order to issue a domestic protection order against him. *See Hemenway v. Hemenway*, 159 N.H. 680, 687 (Sup. Ct. 2010); *Caplan v. Donovan*, 450 Mass 463, 468-470 (Sup. Jud. Ct. 2008).

11. *When and how should the issue of personal jurisdiction be raised?* How did Neff go about procedurally challenging the exercise of jurisdiction over him in *Mitchell v. Neff*? Why is this approach called a *collateral attack?* (Hint: Did Neff raise the objection in the original proceeding, or later in a different proceeding?)

A more typical collateral challenge occurs when a nonresident defendant who is aware of the lawsuit fails to show up in court, deliberately suffering a default judgment with the intention of challenging jurisdiction when the plaintiff later sues to enforce the judgment in the defendant's home state. The risk of this approach is that the only basis left for opposing the judgment, once it becomes final in the original lawsuit, is the jurisdictional challenge—the defendant can no longer defend on the merits in the subsequent enforcement suit. This strategy places all the defendant's eggs in the jurisdictional basket. If the court rejects the challenge, the judgment will be enforced no matter what the merits of the claim. Under what circumstances might such a risky defense strategy make sense? What if defendant has no real defense on the merits?

Assuming that Neff had been aware of Mitchell's lawsuit against him at the time it was still pending, what other options would have been available to challenge the court's power? In a *direct attack*, defendant files a motion to dismiss for lack of personal jurisdiction in the original proceeding (pursuant to Fed. R. Civ. P. 12(b)(2) in modern practice). If the court rules against the defendant and a final judgment is entered upholding jurisdiction, that determination is binding and forecloses any collateral challenge to jurisdiction. *See Baldwin v. Iowa State Traveling Men's Assn.*, 283 U.S. 522 (1931), and Chapter 10.

Could Neff have appeared in the Oregon state court action and successfully argued that the court had no adjudicatory power over him? Note that *appearance* in court is itself one of the traditional bases for exercising power over the defendant, and is expressly set out in the Code of Oregon. The modern device of a "special appearance" now saves the objecting defendant from this Catch-22 dilemma, as we will see in the cases that follow.

If Neff appeared today in a federal action brought against him by Mitchell, and filed an answer merely denying that he owed Mitchell any legal fees, could he assert the defense of lack of personal jurisdiction later in the proceeding? Look at Fed. R. Civ. P. 12(h)(1). The so-called fragile defenses, including lack of personal jurisdiction, are *waived* if not raised at the outset. Compare Fed. R. Civ. P. 12(h)(3): "If the court determines at any time that it lacks *subject matter jurisdiction*, the court must dismiss the action." Why is the objection to subject matter jurisdiction immune from waiver, and moreover the responsibility of the judge *in the absence of any objection from the parties*? We will come back to this point in the next chapter.

Could Neff raise his objection to personal jurisdiction in his first filing *together with* a 12(b)(6) motion to dismiss for failure to state a claim? *See* Fed. R. Civ. P. 12(b) and (g).

12. *Why do litigants and their lawyers care so much about personal jurisdiction?* By the end of this chapter we will have read more than a dozen cases in which the parties fight vigorously—all the way to the Supreme Court—over the issue of personal jurisdiction. Like all such procedural disputes, these are not abstract or philosophical conflicts but, rather, are firmly rooted in competing strategic and practical concerns.

Plaintiffs choose the forum in which the lawsuit is initially filed, usually (although not always) their home state, for reasons of convenience and familiarity as well as in the hope that they will somehow benefit from a home court advantage. Where the defendant is from a distant state, the inconvenience and expense of litigation may translate into a more favorable settlement of the case for plaintiffs. The nonresident defendant can (and often does) challenge the plaintiff's choice of forum with a motion to dismiss for lack of personal jurisdiction, which, if successful, may mean the plaintiff has to bear the expense of pursuing the litigation in the defendant's home state. In certain situations (discussed in Chapter 9) a litigant's choice of forum may reflect an effort to shop for more favorable law.

---

Would strict application of *Pennoyer*'s conception of adjudicatory authority permit the exercise of jurisdiction over the defendants in our next two cases, *Harris v. Balk* and *Hess v. Pawloski*?

# ■ HARRIS v. BALK
### *198 U.S. 215 (1905)*

Statement by Justice PECKHAM:

The plaintiff in error brings the case here in order to review the judgment of the supreme court of North Carolina, affirming a judgment of a lower court against him for $180, with interest, as stated therein. . . .

The facts are as follows: The plaintiff in error, Harris, was a resident of North Carolina at the time of the commencement of this action, in 1896, and prior to that time was indebted to the defendant in error, Balk, also a resident of North Carolina, in the sum of $180, for money borrowed from Balk by

Harris during the year 1896, which Harris verbally promised to repay, but there was no written evidence of the obligation. During the year above mentioned one Jacob Epstein, a resident of Baltimore, in the state of Maryland, asserted that Balk was indebted to him in the sum of over $300. In August, 1896, Harris visited Baltimore for the purpose of purchasing merchandise, and while he was in that city temporarily on August 6, 1896, Epstein caused to be issued out of a proper court in Baltimore a foreign or nonresident writ of attachment against Balk, attaching the debt due Balk from Harris, which writ the sheriff at Baltimore laid in the hands of Harris, with a summons to appear in the court at a day named. With that attachment, a writ of summons and a short declaration against Balk (as provided by the Maryland statute) were also delivered to the sheriff, and by him set up at the courthouse door, as required by the law of Maryland. Before the return day of the attachment writ Harris left Baltimore, and returned to his home in North Carolina. He did not contest the garnishee process, which was issued to garnish the debt which Harris owed Balk. After his return Harris made an affidavit on August 11, 1896, that he owed Balk $180, and stated that the amount had been attached by Epstein, of Baltimore, and by his counsel in the Maryland proceeding Harris consented therein to an order of condemnation against him as such garnishee for $180, the amount of his debt to Balk. Judgment was thereafter entered against the garnishee, and in favor of the plaintiff, Epstein, for $180. After the entry of the garnishee judgment, condemning the $180 in the hands of the garnishee, Harris paid the amount of the judgment to one Warren, an attorney of Epstein, residing in North Carolina. On August 11, 1896, Balk commenced an action against Harris before a justice of the peace in North Carolina, to recover the $180 which he averred Harris owed him. The plaintiff in error, by way of answer to the suit, pleaded in bar the recovery of the Maryland judgment and his payment thereof, and contended that it was conclusive against the defendant in error in this action, because that judgment was a valid judgment in Maryland, and was therefore entitled to full faith and credit in the courts of North Carolina. This contention was not allowed by the trial court, and judgment was accordingly entered against Harris for the amount of his indebtedness to Balk, and that judgment was affirmed by the supreme court of North Carolina. The ground of such judgment was that the Maryland court obtained no jurisdiction to attach or garnish the debt due from Harris to Balk, because Harris was but temporarily in the state, and the situs of the debt was in North Carolina.

Justice PECKHAM, after making the foregoing statement, delivered the opinion of the Court:

The state court of North Carolina has refused to give any effect in this action to the Maryland judgment; and the Federal question is whether it did not thereby refuse the full faith and credit to such judgment which is required by the Federal Constitution. If the Maryland court had jurisdiction to award it, the judgment is valid and entitled to the same full faith and credit in North Carolina that it has in Maryland as a valid domestic judgment.

The defendant in error contends that the Maryland court obtained no jurisdiction to award the judgment of condemnation, because the garnishee, although at the time in the state of Maryland, and personally served with process therein, was a nonresident of that state, only casually or temporarily within its boundaries; that the situs of the debt due from Harris, the garnishee, to the defendant in error herein, was in North Carolina, and did not accompany Harris to Maryland; that, consequently, Harris, though within the state of Maryland, had not possession of any property of Balk, and the Maryland state court therefore obtained no jurisdiction over any property of Balk in the attachment proceedings, and the consent of Harris to the entry of the judgment was immaterial. The plaintiff in error, on the contrary, insists that, though the garnishee were but temporarily in Maryland, yet the laws of that state provide for an attachment of this nature if the debtor, the garnishee, is found in the state, and the court obtains jurisdiction over him by the service of process therein; that the judgment, condemning the debt from Harris to Balk, was a valid judgment, provided Balk could himself have sued Harris for the debt in Maryland. This, it is asserted, he could have done, and the judgment was therefore entitled to full faith and credit in the courts of North Carolina.

The cases holding that the state court obtains no jurisdiction over the garnishee if he be but temporarily within the state proceed upon the theory that the situs of the debt is at the domicil either of the creditor or of the debtor, and that it does not follow the debtor in his casual or temporary journey into another state, and the garnishee has no possession of any property or credit of the principal debtor in the foreign state.

We regard the contention of the plaintiff in error as the correct one. . . .

There can be no doubt that Balk, as a citizen of the state of North Carolina, had the right to sue Harris in Maryland to recover the debt which Harris owed him. Being a citizen of North Carolina, he was entitled to all the privileges and immunities of citizens of the several states, one of which is the right to institute actions in the courts of another state. The law of Maryland provides for the attachment of credits in a case like this. . . .

It thus appears that Balk could have sued Harris in Maryland to recover his debt, notwithstanding the temporary character of Harris' stay there; it also appears that the municipal law of Maryland permits the debtor of the principal debtor to be garnished, and therefore if the court of the state where the garnishee is found obtains jurisdiction over him, through the service of process upon him within the state, then the judgment entered is a valid judgment. . . .

It seems to us, therefore, that the judgment against Harris in Maryland, condemning the $180 which he owed to Balk, was a valid judgment, because the court had jurisdiction over the garnishee by personal service of process within the state of Maryland. . . . The defendant in error, Balk, had notice of this attachment, certainly within a few days after the issuing thereof and the entry of judgment thereon, because he sued the plaintiff in error to recover his debt within a few days after his (Harris') return to North Carolina, in which suit the judgment in Maryland was set up by Harris as a plea in bar to Balk's claim. . . .

The judgment of the Supreme Court of North Carolina must be reversed, and the cause remanded for further proceedings not inconsistent with the opinion of this court.

Reversed.

Justice HARLAN and Justice DAY dissented.

## Comments and Questions

1. What was the basis for the exercise of jurisdiction by the Maryland court over Balk in *Epstein v. Balk*? Is this consistent with *Pennoyer*? What language in *Pennoyer* permits this exercise of judicial power? What type of jurisdiction is this?

2. Why would the Supreme Court uphold a procedure as dubious as this: basing jurisdiction over a creditor on "attachment" of the debt by seizing the debtor? Can you think of other intangibles that might serve this function in future cases?

3. What notice did Balk have of the proceeding in Maryland?

▪ **HESS v. PAWLOSKI**
*274 U.S. 352 (1927)*

Justice BUTLER delivered the opinion of the Court:

This action was brought by defendant in error to recover damages for personal injuries. The declaration alleged that plaintiff in error negligently and wantonly drove a motor vehicle on a public highway in Massachusetts, and that by reason thereof the vehicle struck and injured defendant in error. Plaintiff in error is a resident of Pennsylvania. No personal service was made on him, and no property belonging to him was attached. The service of process was made in compliance with chapter 90, General Laws of Massachusetts, as amended by Stat. 1923, c. 431, § 2, the material parts of which follow:

The acceptance by a nonresident of the rights and privileges conferred by section three or four, as evidence by his operating a motor vehicle thereunder, or the operation by a nonresident of a motor vehicle on a public way in the commonwealth other than under said sections, shall be deemed equivalent to an appointment by such nonresident of the registrar or his successor in office, to be his true and lawful attorney upon whom may be served all lawful processes in any action or proceeding against him, growing out of any accident or collision in which said nonresident may be involved while operating a motor vehicle on such a way, and said acceptance or operation shall be a signification of his agreement that any such process against him which is so served shall be of the same legal force and validity as if served on him personally. Service of such process shall be made by leaving a copy of the process with a fee of two dollars in the hands of the registrar, or in his office, and such service shall be sufficient service upon the said nonresident: Provided, that notice of such service and a copy of the process are forthwith sent by registered mail by the plaintiff to the defendant, and the defendant's return receipt and the plaintiff's affidavit of compliance herewith are appended to the writ and entered with the declaration. The court in which the action is pending may order such continuances as may be necessary to afford the defendant reasonable opportunity to defend the action.

Plaintiff in error appeared specially for the purpose of contesting jurisdiction, and filed an answer in abatement and moved to dismiss on the ground that the service of process, if sustained, would deprive him of his property without due process of law, in violation of the Fourteenth Amendment. The court overruled the answer in abatement and denied the motion. The Supreme Judicial Court held the statute to be a valid exercise of the police power, and affirmed the order. . . .

The question is whether the Massachusetts enactment contravenes the due process clause of the Fourteenth Amendment.

The process of a court of one state cannot run into another and summon a party there domiciled to respond to proceedings against him. Notice sent outside the state to a nonresident is unavailing to give jurisdiction in an action against him personally for money recovery. *Pennoyer v. Neff*, 95 U.S. 741. There must be actual service within the state of notice upon him or upon someone authorized to accept service for him. A personal judgment rendered against a nonresident, who has neither been served with process nor appeared in the suit, is without validity. The mere transaction of business in a state by nonresident natural persons does not imply consent to be bound by the process of its courts. The power of a state to exclude foreign corporations, although not absolute, but qualified, is the ground on which such an implication is supported as to them. But a state may not withhold from nonresident individuals the right of doing business therein. The privileges and immunities clause of the Constitution (Section 2, Art. 4), safeguards to the citizens of one state the right "to pass through, or to reside in any other state for purposes of trade, agriculture, professional pursuits, or otherwise." And it prohibits state legislation discriminating against citizens of other states. Motor vehicles are dangerous machines, and, even when skillfully and carefully operated, their use is attended by serious dangers to persons and property. In the public interest the state may make and enforce regulations reasonably calculated to promote care on the part of all, residents and nonresidents alike, who use its highways. The measure in question operates to require a nonresident to answer for his conduct in the state where arise causes of action alleged against him, as well as to provide for a claimant a convenient method by which he may sue to enforce his rights. Under the statute the implied consent is limited to proceedings growing out of accidents or collisions on a highway in which the nonresident may be involved. It is required that he shall actually receive and receipt for notice of the service and a copy of the process. And it contemplates such continuances as may be found necessary to give reasonable time and opportunity for defense. It makes no hostile discrimination against nonresidents, but tends to put them on the same footing as residents. Literal and precise equality in respect of this matter is not attainable; it is not required. The state's power to regulate the use of its highways extends to their use by nonresidents as well as by residents. And, in advance of the operation of a motor vehicle on its highway by a nonresident, the state may require him to appoint one of its officials as his agent on whom process may be served in proceedings growing out of such use. . . . [H]aving the power so to exclude, the state may declare that the use of the highway by the nonresident is the equivalent of the appointment of the registrar as agent on whom process may be served. The difference between the formal and implied appointment is not substantial, so far as concerns the application of the due process clause of the Fourteenth Amendment.

Judgment affirmed.

## Comments and Questions

1. What is the basis for the exercise of jurisdiction over the nonresident motorist? Is this consistent with *Pennoyer*? What language in *Pennoyer* permits this?

2. Why would the Supreme Court condone so dubious a fiction as "implied consent to suit"? What is the relevance of the Court's assertion that "motor vehicles are dangerous machines" to the issue of jurisdiction? Are policy concerns beginning to enter the jurisdictional analysis?

3. Note that both the Massachusetts nonresident motorist statute and the Supreme Court decision upholding it treat the matter of notice (i.e., registered mail to the defendant in Pennsylvania) as separate and apart from the issue of adjudicatory power, which is based on service of process in Massachusetts on Hess's "appointed" representative, the Registrar of Motor Vehicles. The Court recognizes that the "process of one state cannot run into another and summon a party there domiciled to respond to proceedings against him. Notice sent outside the state to a nonresident is unavailing to give jurisdiction in an action against him personally for money recovery. There must be actual service within the state of notice upon him or upon someone authorized to accept service for him."

Within the traditional *Pennoyer* scheme, notice and jurisdiction were virtually inseparable because the primary basis for establishing in personam jurisdiction, namely, service of process on defendant within the state, simultaneously provided notice of the lawsuit. Now, with the change in focus from in-state service on defendant to in-state *activities* by the defendant (a move finally accomplished in *International Shoe, infra*), jurisdiction and notice begin to travel divergent paths.

4. Note that Balk's challenge to jurisdiction in the previous case, *Harris v. Balk*, was a collateral attack. Contrast it with the direct attack mounted by Hess, who "appeared specially for the purpose of contesting jurisdiction."

5. Lest you think these implied consent statutes are a relic of a distant past, Massachusetts still has a nonresident motorist statute, see Mass. Gen. Laws ch. 90, § 3A. Florida has one for out-of-state operators of aircraft and watercraft, see Fla. Stat. Ann. § 48.19. But South Dakota, a favorite of pheasant hunters, may take the prize:

> The hunting of game birds or animals in this state by a nonresident shall be deemed an appointment by such nonresident of the secretary of state of South Dakota to be his true and lawful attorney upon whom may be served legal process in any action or proceeding against such nonresident or his personal representative growing out of such hunting which results in damages or loss to person or property, and said hunting shall be a signification of such nonresident's agreement that any such process in any action against him or his personal representative which is so served shall be of the same legal force and validity as if served upon him, or his personal representative, personally. S.D. Cod. Laws § 15-7-13.

## D. THE MODERN CONCEPTION OF PERSONAL JURISDICTION

Under pressure from an ever-expanding interstate economy, the rigid *Pennoyer* framework was stretched to the breaking point to accommodate the aggressive reach of states seeking to provide local forums for citizens litigating claims against nonresident persons and corporations. In 1945, the Supreme Court finally discarded the outdated structure and, with it, such fictions as implied consent and "presence," in favor of a revised theory of personal jurisdiction premised on actual connections between the defendant and forum state. The vehicle was the following landmark case.

## ■ INTERNATIONAL SHOE CO. v. STATE OF WASHINGTON
### *326 U.S. 310 (1945)*

Chief Justice STONE delivered the opinion of the Court:

The questions for decision are (1) whether, within the limitations of the due process clause of the Fourteenth Amendment, appellant, a Delaware corporation, has by its activities in the State of Washington rendered itself amenable to proceedings in the courts of that state to recover unpaid contributions to the state unemployment compensation fund exacted by [the] Washington Unemployment Compensation Act, . . . , and (2) whether the state can exact those contributions consistently with the due process clause of the Fourteenth Amendment.

The statutes in question set up a comprehensive scheme of unemployment compensation, the costs of which are defrayed by contributions required to be made by employers to a state unemployment compensation fund. The contributions are a specified percentage of the wages payable annually by each employer for his employees' services in the state. The assessment and collection of the contributions and the fund are administered by respondents. Section 14(c) of the Act authorizes respondent Commissioner to issue an order and notice of assessment of delinquent contributions upon prescribed personal service of the notice upon the employer if found within the state, or, if not so found, by mailing the notice to the employer by registered mail at his last known address. . . .

In this case notice of assessment for the years in question was personally served upon a sales solicitor employed by appellant in the State of Washington, and a copy of the notice was mailed by registered mail to appellant at its address in St. Louis, Missouri. Appellant appeared specially before the office of unemployment and moved to set aside the order and notice of assessment on the ground that the service upon appellant's salesman was not proper service upon appellant; that appellant was not a corporation of the State of Washington and was not doing business within the state; that it had no agent within the state upon whom service could be made; and that appellant is not an employer and does not furnish employment within the meaning of the statute.

The motion was heard on evidence and a stipulation of facts by the appeal tribunal which denied the motion and ruled that respondent Commissioner was entitled to recover the unpaid contributions. That action was affirmed by the Commissioner; both the Superior Court and the [state] Supreme Court affirmed. Appellant in each of these courts assailed the statute as applied, as a violation of the due process clause of the Fourteenth Amendment. . . .

The facts as found by the appeal tribunal and accepted by the state Superior Court and Supreme Court, are not in dispute. Appellant is a Delaware corporation, having its principal place of business in St. Louis, Missouri, and is engaged in the manufacture and sale of shoes and other footwear. It maintains places of business in several states, other than Washington, at which its manufacturing is carried on and from which its merchandise is distributed interstate through several sales units or branches located outside the State of Washington.

Appellant has no office in Washington and makes no contracts either for sale or purchase of merchandise there. It maintains no stock of merchandise in that state and makes there no deliveries of goods in intrastate commerce. During the years from 1937 to 1940, now in question, appellant employed eleven to thirteen salesmen under direct supervision and control of sales managers located in St. Louis. These salesmen resided in Washington; their principal activities were confined to that state; and they were compensated by commissions based upon the amount of their sales. The commissions for each year totaled more than $31,000. Appellant supplies its salesmen with a line of samples, each consisting of one shoe of a pair, which they display to prospective purchasers. On occasion they rent permanent sample rooms, for exhibiting samples, in business buildings, or rent rooms in hotels or business buildings temporarily for that purpose. The cost of such rentals is reimbursed by appellant.

The authority of the salesmen is limited to exhibiting their samples and soliciting orders from prospective buyers, at prices and on terms fixed by appellant. The salesmen transmit the orders to appellant's office in St. Louis for acceptance or rejection, and when accepted the merchandise for filling the orders is shipped f.o.b. from points outside Washington to the purchasers within the state. All the merchandise shipped into Washington is invoiced at the place of shipment from which collections are made. No salesman has authority to enter into contracts or to make collections.

The Supreme Court of Washington was of opinion that the regular and systematic solicitation of orders in the state by appellant's salesmen, resulting in a continuous flow of appellant's product into the state, was sufficient to constitute doing business in the state so as to make appellant amenable to suit in its courts. But it was also of opinion that there were sufficient additional activities shown to bring the case within the rule frequently stated, that solicitation within a state by the agents of a foreign corporation plus some additional activities there are sufficient to render the corporation amenable to suit brought in the courts of the state to enforce an obligation arising out of its activities there. The court found such additional activities in the salesmen's display of samples sometimes in permanent display rooms, and the salesmen's residence within the state, continued over a period of years, all resulting in a substantial volume of merchandise regularly shipped by appellant to purchasers within the state. . . .

Appellant . . . insists that its activities within the state were not sufficient to manifest its "presence" there and that in its absence the state courts were without jurisdiction, that consequently it was a denial of due process for the state to subject appellant to suit. It refers to those cases in which it was said that the mere solicitation of orders for the purchase of goods within a state, to be accepted without the state and filled by shipment of the purchased goods interstate, does not render the corporation seller amenable to suit within the state. And appellant further argues that since it was not present within the state, it is a denial of due process to subject it to taxation or other money exaction. It thus denies the power of the state to lay the tax or to subject appellant to a suit for its collection.

Historically the jurisdiction of courts to render judgment in personam is grounded on their de facto power over the defendant's person. Hence his presence within the territorial jurisdiction of the court was prerequisite to its rendition of a judgment personally binding him. *Pennoyer v. Neff*, 95 U.S. 714, 733. But now that the *capias ad respondendum* has given way to personal service of summons or other form of notice, due process requires only that in order to subject a defendant to a judgment in personam, if he be not present within the territory of the forum, he have certain minimum contacts with it such that the maintenance of the suit does not offend "traditional notions of fair play and substantial justice."

Since the corporate personality is a fiction, although a fiction intended to be acted upon as though it were a fact, it is clear that unlike an individual its "presence" without, as well as within, the state of its origin can be manifested only by activities carried on in its behalf by those who are authorized to act for it. To say that the corporation is so far "present" there as to satisfy due process requirements, for purposes of taxation or the maintenance of suits against it in the courts of the state, is to beg the question to be decided. For the terms "present" or "presence" are used merely to symbolize those activities of the corporation's agent within the state which courts will deem to be sufficient to satisfy the demands of due process. Those demands may be met by such contacts of the corporation with the state of the forum as make it reasonable, in the context of our federal system of government, to require the corporation to defend the particular suit which is brought there. An "estimate of the inconveniences" which would result to the corporation from a trial away from its "home" or principal place of business is relevant in this connection.

"Presence" in the state in this sense has never been doubted when the activities of the corporation there have not only been continuous and systematic, but also give rise to the liabilities sued on, even though no consent to be sued or authorization to an agent to accept service of process has been given. Conversely it has been generally recognized that the casual presence of the corporate agent or even his conduct of single or isolated items of activities in a state in the corporation's behalf are not enough to subject it to suit on causes of action unconnected with the activities there. To require the corporation in such circumstances to defend the suit away from its home or other jurisdiction where it carries on more substantial activities has been thought to lay too great and unreasonable a burden on the corporation to comport with due process.

While it has been held in cases on which appellant relies that continuous activity of some sorts within a state is not enough to support the demand that the corporation be amenable to suits unrelated to that activity, there have been instances in which the continuous corporate operations within a state were thought so substantial and of such a nature as to justify suit against it on causes of action arising from dealings entirely distinct from those activities.

Finally, although the commission of some single or occasional acts of the corporate agent in a state sufficient to impose an obligation or liability on the corporation has not been thought to confer upon the state authority to enforce it, other such acts, because of their nature and quality and the circumstances of their commission, may be deemed sufficient to render the corporation liable to suit. True, some of the decisions holding the corporation amenable to suit have been supported by resort to the legal fiction that it has given its consent to service and suit, consent being implied from its presence in the state through the acts of its authorized agents. But more realistically it may be said that those authorized acts were of such a nature as to justify the fiction.

It is evident that the criteria by which we mark the boundary line between those activities which justify the subjection of a corporation to suit, and those which do not, cannot be simply mechanical or quantitative. The test is not merely, as has sometimes been suggested, whether the activity, which the corporation has seen fit to procure through its agents in another state, is a little more or a little less. Whether due process is satisfied must depend rather upon the quality and nature of the activity in relation to the fair and orderly administration of the laws which it was the purpose of the due process clause to insure. That clause does not contemplate that a state may make binding a judgment in personam against an individual or corporate defendant with which the state has no contacts, ties, or relations. *Cf. Pennoyer v. Neff, supra.*

But to the extent that a corporation exercises the privilege of conducting activities within a state, it enjoys the benefits and protection of the laws of that state. The exercise of that privilege may give rise to obligations; and, so far as those obligations arise out of or are connected with the activities within the state, a procedure which requires the corporation to respond to a suit brought to enforce them can, in most instances, hardly be said to be undue.

Applying these standards, the activities carried on in behalf of appellant in the State of Washington were neither irregular nor casual. They were systematic and continuous throughout the years in question. They resulted in a large volume of interstate business, in the course of which appellant received the benefits and protection of the laws of the state, including the right to resort to the courts for the enforcement of its rights. The obligation which is here sued upon arose out of those very activities. It is evident that these operations establish sufficient contacts or ties with the state of the forum to make it reasonable and just according to our traditional conception of fair play and substantial justice to permit the state to enforce the obligations which appellant has incurred there. Hence we cannot say that the maintenance of the present suit in the State of Washington involves an unreasonable or undue procedure.

We are likewise unable to conclude that the service of the process within the state upon an agent whose activities establish appellant's "presence" there was not sufficient notice of the suit, or that the suit was so unrelated to those activities as to make the agent an inappropriate vehicle for communicating the notice. It is enough that appellant has established such contacts with the state that the particular form of substituted service adopted there gives reasonable assurance that the notice will be actual. Nor can we say that the mailing of the notice of suit to appellant by registered mail at its home office was not reasonably calculated to apprise appellant of the suit. . . .

Appellant having rendered itself amenable to suit upon obligations arising out of the activities of its salesmen in Washington, the state may maintain the present suit in personam to collect the tax laid upon the exercise of the privilege of employing appellant's salesmen within the state. . . .

Affirmed.

Justice JACKSON took no part in the consideration of the case.

Justice BLACK delivered the following opinion:

. . . I believe that the Federal Constitution leaves to each State, without any "ifs" or "buts," a power to tax and to open the doors of its courts for its citizens to sue corporations whose agents do business in those States. Believing that the Constitution gave the States that power, I think it a judicial deprivation to condition its exercise upon this Court's notion of "fair play," however appealing that term may be. Nor can I stretch the meaning of due process so far as to authorize this Court to deprive a State of the right to afford judicial protection to its citizens on the ground that it would be more "convenient" for the corporation to be sued somewhere else.

There is a strong emotional appeal in the words "fair play," "justice," and "reasonableness." But they were not chosen by those who wrote the original Constitution or the Fourteenth Amendment as a measuring rod for this Court to use in invalidating State or Federal laws passed by elected legislative representatives. No one, not even those who most feared a democratic government, ever formally proposed that courts should be given power to invalidate legislation under any such elastic standards. . . . For application of this natural law concept, whether under the terms "reasonableness," "justice," or "fair play," makes judges the supreme arbiters of the country's laws and practices. This result, I believe, alters the form of government our Constitution provides. I cannot agree.

## Comments and Questions

1. Consider how International Shoe Co. had structured its business practices. No offices or inventory were maintained outside its home state of Missouri. Sales representatives had no authority to enter into contracts in the states in which they worked—they merely solicited orders and transmitted them back to headquarters in St. Louis. Product was sent "F.O.B. St. Louis," which meant that customers legally took possession at the point of shipment, thus avoiding the appearance that deliveries were being made beyond the borders of Missouri. The only items belonging to International Shoe that could be found in Washington were the single-shoe samples that the sales representatives displayed to potential purchasers, obviously lacking market value that could be attached. Given the doctrine regarding the exercise of jurisdiction prior to the *International Shoe* decision, can you see why the company did business this way? Would you also have advised them to choose another name?

2. Reconstruct the opposing arguments presented by the parties before the Supreme Court in *International Shoe*.

3. What is the basis set forth by the Court for the exercise of jurisdiction over the nonresident corporation? How would you articulate the revised framework of personal jurisdiction? What is left of *Pennoyer*? Note that *International Shoe* leaves intact the traditional bases for the exercise of jurisdiction: residence/domicile in the forum state, appearance in the action,

service on defendant within the forum state, in rem power over claimants in a dispute over land, and quasi in rem power over nonresidents who have property in the state (but any judgment is limited to the value of the property). *International Shoe* supplements, but does not supplant, these methods of obtaining adjudicatory power.

4. Chief Justice Stone observes that the "obligation which is here sued upon [contributions to the unemployment compensation fund] arose out of [International Shoe's] very activities [in Washington]." Within the Court's formulation, what is the link between the nonresident's *level of activity* in the forum state and the *relation of the plaintiff's claim to that activity*?

Consider the following spectrum, ranging from merely causing injury in the forum state (which we will explore in several cases that follow, beginning with *World-Wide Volkswagen*), to major involvement such as "doing business" (which we will see in Part F, *infra*, gives rise to "general jurisdiction," meaning amenability to suit on any claim even if it arose in another state):

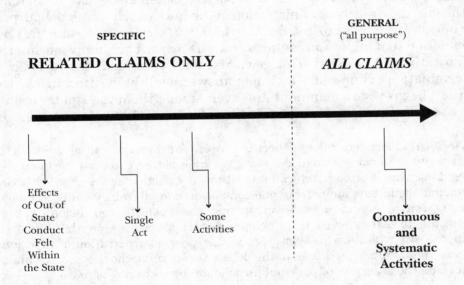

SPECIFIC                                        GENERAL
("all purpose")

**RELATED CLAIMS ONLY**          *ALL CLAIMS*

Effects
of Out of
State          Single          Some                  **Continuous
Conduct          Act          Activities                 and
Felt                                            Systematic
Within                                          Activities**
the State

What policy considerations would draw the Court to focus on these two variables—the nonresident's *level of activity* in the forum state and the *relation of the plaintiff's claim to that activity*? Can you articulate the benefit/burden rationale that underlies Stone's theory of personal jurisdiction? Subsequent decisions will return to this rationale more explicitly.

5. In which forum activity category did Chief Justice Stone place International Shoe Co.? Was it necessary to decide, given that the claim clearly arose out of the company's activities in Washington? Where would you place the defendant in *Hess v. Pawloski*? What about defendant Balk in *Harris*? Or does that latter exercise of jurisdiction fall outside Stone's in personam categories?

6. If the claim asserted against International Shoe had arisen from a collision between a company truck and a citizen of Washington vacationing in San Diego, California, would the state court in Washington have jurisdiction over Interational Shoe when the plaintiff returned home and filed a tort suit? (Assume the company has the same contacts with Washington as in the original case.) If not, where could plaintiff obtain adjudicatory power over International Shoe?

7. Employing between eleven and thirteen sales representatives who together generated total commissions of $31,000 per year was deemed sufficient "minimum contacts" with the state for suit against the employer on the related unemployment fund claim. Would six sales reps have sufficed? Three? What if there were *no* reps, but instead a catalogue operation run completely out-of-state, and a dissatisfied Seattle customer sued for breach of contract after delivery of the wrong items?

8. Whether due process standards are met, *International Shoe* teaches, depends "upon the quality and nature of the [defendant's] activity in relation to the fair and orderly administration of the laws which it was the purpose of the due process clause to insure." What kind of "test" is this? Note the Court's admonition that minimum contacts analysis "cannot be simply mechanical or quantitative." As Justice Thurgood Marshall once said, the jurisdictional determination "is one in which few answers will be written in black and white. The greys are dominant and even among them the shades are innumerable." *Kulko v. Superior Court*, 436 U.S. 84, 92 (1978). On a similar note:

> The idea of black letter law seduces us. We crave coherence and certainty in the law as we do in many areas of our lives. We know better, of course. We know that legal doctrine is often indeterminate—that in a particular case, perfectly convincing arguments supporting one conclusion can often be countered by perfectly convincing arguments supporting the opposite conclusion. Yet we continue to search for rules, principles, tests, approaches—anything that will impose order on doctrine. Nowhere is the inherent frustration of this quest more vividly illustrated than in the debates concerning the due process limitations on the assertion of personal jurisdiction by state courts.

Richard K. Greenstein, *The Nature of Legal Argument: The Personal Jurisdiction Paradigm*, 38 Hastings. L.J. 855 (1987).

9. What does Justice Hugo Black think of terms like "fair play" and "reasonableness" as the measuring rods for adjudicatory power? What standard would he substitute?

10. One court has admonished regarding the *International Shoe* standard:

> This rule of law has been truncated in the minds and jargon of lawyers to "minimum contact"; however, minimum contact does not mean "minimum" or "slight" contact. Minimum contact requires that a foreign defendant have at least enough contact with [the forum] to satisfy minimum standards of due process.

*Leonard v. USA Petroleum Corp.*, 829 F. Supp. 882 (S.D. Tex. 1993).

# E. NOTE ON LONG-ARM STATUTES

*International Shoe* established a constitutional basis for the exercise of personal jurisdiction that focused on the nonresident's* activities or contacts within the forum state. Constitutional power is not, however, self-executing. A court must first be authorized by appropriate legislation or otherwise to assert jurisdiction (look back at the Code of Oregon in *Pennoyer*, at Mass. Gen. Laws ch. 90 in *Hess*, and at § 14(c) of the Washington Statutes in *International Shoe*). Only then is the minimum-contacts analysis employed to determine whether the particular assertion is within the permissible boundaries of due process.

In the years following the Court's decision in *International Shoe*, states enacted "long-arm" statutes that authorized their courts to exercise jurisdiction over nonresidents who engaged in certain enumerated acts within the state. Typical among them is New York's CPLR § 302:

Personal jurisdiction by acts of non-domiciliaries.

(a) Acts which are the basis of jurisdiction. As to a cause of action arising from any of the acts enumerated in this section, a court may exercise personal jurisdiction over any non-domiciliary, or his executor or administrator, who in person or through an agent:

(1) transacts any business within the state or contracts anywhere to supply goods or services in the state; or

(2) commits a tortious act within the state, except as to a cause of action for defamation of character arising from the act; or

(3) commits a tortious act without the state causing injury to person or property within the state, except as to a cause of action for defamation of character arising from the act, if he

(i) regularly does or solicits business, or engages in any other persistent course of conduct, or derives substantial revenue from goods used or consumed or services rendered, in the state, or

(ii) expects or should reasonably expect the act to have consequences in the state and derives substantial revenue from interstate or international commerce; or

(4) owns, uses or possesses any real property situated within the state. . . .

*The Nexus Requirement.* Note that the jurisdiction authorized by the long-arm statute is limited to claims *"arising from"* the enumerated act. (Look back at Chief Justice Stone's constitutional analysis of single-act jurisdiction in *International Shoe* to see why this is so.) In *Crocker v. Hilton International Barbados, Ltd.*, 976 F.2d 797 (1st Cir. 1992), for example, where the plaintiff alleged that her rape while a guest at the Barbados hotel resulted from lax security, the court affirmed dismissal of the complaint

---

* Although *International Shoe* involved a corporate defendant, we will see that the minimum contacts analysis was soon applied to individual defendants as well.

for lack of personal jurisdiction in Massachusetts. The plaintiff premised jurisdiction on the facts that she had booked the room through a travel agency in Massachusetts and that the parent company, Hilton International, had advertised the Barbados hotel in Massachusetts. The First Circuit observed, however, that it is not enough that a defendant "transact business" in the forum state within the meaning of the long-arm statute; the crucial question is whether plaintiff's claim *arose out of* this activity, and the court held here that it did not—that the booking and advertising were too remote from the events on the island to satisfy the "arising from" requirement.

A similar result followed in *Bell v. Imperial Palace Hotel/Casino, Inc.*, 200 F. Supp. 2d 1082 (E.D. Mo. 2001), where plaintiffs sought damages for personal injuries suffered at the defendant hotel in Las Vegas, Nevada. The Bells' effort to base jurisdiction in their home state on defendant's only contact with the forum, a Web site maintained by Imperial Palace and accessible to residents in Missouri, failed because neither plaintiffs nor their travel agent booked the reservation on the Web site, or even claimed to have ever viewed it. "The Court can see no causal link or relationship between Mr. Bell's accident and the sole forum contact by Imperial Palace, its Web site. Without such a connection, specific personal jurisdiction does not exist." 200 F. Supp. 2d at 1088.

Other courts have applied a more relaxed standard for the nexus between the defendant's activity and the claim. The California Supreme Court requires only that there be "a substantial nexus or connection between the defendant's forum activities and the plaintiff's claim. . . . Thus, a claim need not arise directly from the defendant's forum contacts in order to be sufficiently related to the contact to warrant the exercise of specific jurisdiction." *Snowney v. Harrah's Entertainment, Inc.*, 35 Cal. 4th 1054, 1068, 112 P.3d 28, 43 (2005). The California resident's consumer class action against the Nevada hotel claimed it had failed to notify guests that an energy surcharge would be imposed on them at checkout. The hotel advertised heavily in California and maintained a Web site that quoted room rates and permitted visitors to make reservations by credit card. Although plaintiff made his reservations by phone, and there was no indication he had accessed the Web site or been induced by the ads, the court affirmed the exercise of specific jurisdiction over the defendant.

Similarly, in *Nowak v. Tak How Investments, Ltd.*, 94 F.3d 708 (1st Cir. 1996), the Hong Kong hotel was held subject to jurisdiction in Massachusetts in wrongful death action by the family of the victim who drowned in defendant's pool while accompanying her husband on a business trip, because the hotel had solicited the business in Massachusetts that brought her to the hotel. And in *Shoppers Food Warehouse v. Mopreno*, 746 A.2d 320, 332-336 (D.C. Ct. App. 2000), the District of Columbia Court of Appeals articulated a "related to or discernible relationship" standard, which permitted the exercise of jurisdiction over the Maryland supermarket in a slip and fall case brought by a District resident, based on defendant's weekly ads in District newspapers, even though plaintiff did not contend that the ads had brought her to the store.

For more on the concept of "relatedness" between the claim and defendant's activities, see Lea Brilmayer, *Related Contacts and Personal Jurisdiction*, 101 Harv. L. Rev. 1444 (1988), and Mary Twitchell, *A Rejoinder to Professor Brilmayer*, 101 Harv. L. Rev. 1465 (1988).

*Long-Arm Statute Analysis.* Determining whether a court may assert jurisdiction over a nonresident pursuant to a long-arm statute requires a two-step inquiry:

1. Does the plaintiff's claim arise from activity of the defendant that fits within an enumerated category?
2. If so, would application of the statute nonetheless reach beyond the constitutional constraints of *International Shoe*'s minimum-contacts test?

The first question is one of statutory construction; the second involves the substantial body of constitutional case law that has been developed since 1945, to be explored in the pages that follow.

Rather than spelling out specific acts, as New York's CPLR § 302 does, some states have opted for an open-ended approach. California, for example, provides: "A court of this state may exercise jurisdiction on any basis not inconsistent with the Constitution of this state or of the United States." Cal. Code Civ. Proc. § 410.10. This scheme collapses the usual two-step inquiry (statutory authority and constitutionality of application) into one.

For a history of long-arm legislation and a current survey of the state statutes, see Douglas D. McFarland, *Dictim Run Wild: How Long-Arm Statutes Extended to the Limits of Due Process*, 84 B.U. L. Rev. 491 (2004).

# F. NOTE ON SPECIFIC AS COMPARED TO GENERAL JURISDICTION

As previously noted, long-arm statutes do not replace the traditional grounds for in personam jurisdiction, namely domicile or citizenship, incorporation in the forum state, service of process on the defendant in the state, appearance in court, and consent. Rather, they implement the constitutional authority to reach nonresidents who, though falling outside these categories, engage in certain activities in the state that give rise to the plaintiff's claim.

The *specific jurisdiction* authorized by long-arm statutes must be compared with *general jurisdiction*, which is power over *all* claims, whether related to defendant's activities within the forum state or not. General jurisdiction derives from the traditional bases of jurisdiction listed above. Thus for example an individual or corporate citizen may be sued in its home state on claims arising there *or elsewhere*.

*International Shoe* held that a corporate nonresident's conduct of continuous, systematic, and substantial business in the forum would also subject that defendant to general jurisdiction over any claim, regardless of where it arose. In *Perkins v. Benguet Consolidated Mining Co.*, 342 U.S. 437 (1952), the Court ruled that an Ohio state court could properly exercise jurisdiction over a Philippine corporation on a stockholder's claim even though it did not arise from anything the defendant did in the state. The mining company had halted operations and temporarily relocated its president to Ohio for the duration of the Japanese military occupation of the Philippine Islands. At his office in Ohio the president maintained the company files, carried on correspondence, drew salary checks, maintained a bank account, and held directors' meetings—in short, he carried on "a continuous and systematic supervision of the necessarily limited wartime activities of the company." Given this high level of activity (which would place it at the right of our spectrum set out in Note 4 following *International Shoe*), it would not violate due process for Ohio to assert jurisdiction over the company on the plaintiff's claim for dividends despite the fact that the claim arose from transactions conducted outside the forum state.

We will have more to say about general jurisdiction later in this chapter.

Toward the lower end of the activity spectrum is *McGee v. International Life Insurance Co.*, 355 U.S. 220 (1957), a suit by the beneficiary on a life insurance policy owned by her deceased son. The insurance company had no office or agent in the forum state of California and, indeed, had not, as far as the record indicated, ever solicited or conducted any business there except for the *one* policy sold through the mail that was sued upon. The California court exercised specific jurisdiction based on a statute subjecting nonresident corporations to suit on insurance contracts entered into with residents of the state.

Mrs. McGee recovered a default judgment for the death benefit, which she sought to enforce in defendant's home state of Texas (as the company had no assets to seize in California). The Texas courts refused, holding that the judgment was not entitled to full faith and credit because the California court lacked jurisdiction over International Life Insurance Co.

The Supreme Court reversed in a decision authored by Justice Black, who noted a "clearly discernible trend" toward expanding the scope of jurisdiction over nonresidents. Given "the fundamental transformation of our national economy over the years," he wrote, "today many commercial transactions touch two or more States and may involve parties separated by the full continent. With this increasing nationalization of commerce has come a great increase in the amount of business conducted by mail across state lines. At the same time modern transportation and communication have made it much less burdensome for a party sued to defend himself in a State where he engages in economic activity." 355 U.S. at 222-223.

Reflecting the high-water mark of specific jurisdiction, *McGee* concluded that the Due Process Clause allowed the California court to enter a judgment binding on the Texas company, notwithstanding its scant contacts with the forum state:

It is sufficient for purposes of due process that the suit was based on a contract that had substantial connection with that state. The contract was delivered in

California, the premiums were mailed from there, and the insured was a resident of that state when he died. It cannot be denied that California has a manifest interest in providing effective means of redress for its residents when their insurers refuse to pay claims. These residents would be at a severe disadvantage if they were forced to follow the insurance company to a distant state in order to hold it legally accountable. When claims were small or moderate, individual claimants frequently could not afford the cost of bringing an action in a foreign forum—thus in effect making the company judgment-proof. Often the crucial witnesses—as here on the company's defense of suicide—will be found in the insured's locality. Of course, there may be inconvenience to the insurer if it is held amenable to suit in California, where it had this contract, but certainly nothing that amounts to a denial of due process. There is no contention that respondent did not have adequate notice or sufficient time to prepare its defenses and appear.

355 U.S. at 222-224.

Can you find a foreshadowing of this expansive approach to personal jurisdiction in Justice Black's separate opinion in *International Shoe*? What social policy considerations entered into Black's elaboration of due process doctrine? As you read the cases to follow, consider the accuracy of Black's perception of a "clearly discernible trend" toward expanding specific jurisdiction.

As noted previously, remember that the proper exercise of specific jurisdiction requires that plaintiff's claim *arise out of* the particular act performed by the defendant within the forum state.

# G. NOTE ON PERSONAL JURISDICTION IN FEDERAL COURT

A common source of confusion for students is the issue of personal jurisdiction in federal court. Given the focus on *state* sovereignty and *state* boundaries in *Pennoyer* and *International Shoe*, together with the fact that the Fourteenth Amendment Due Process Clause limits only *state* power, one might assume that a *federal* trial court would not be limited by state geography in its jurisdictional reach. This assumption would, however, be wrong. Although the constitutional constraints on a federal court's exercise of jurisdiction (found in the Fifth Amendment's Due Process Clause) are defined by the national boundaries of the United States, the federal courts have not been given the full extent of their potential adjudicatory power.

The vehicle controlling personal jurisdiction in federal court is Fed. R. Civ. P. 4, which on its face seems only to deal with service of process. But look at 4(k)(1)(A), which incorporates the local state long-arm statute as a constraint on federal court jurisdiction. The jurisdictional reach of a federal district court in Illinois is consequently determined by, and equivalent to, the reach of the state trial courts there. (If federal courts offered plaintiffs a longer reach than state courts, consider the considerable incentive for forum-shopping that would be created.)

There are some notable exceptions to the equation of federal and state long-arm jurisdiction. Fed. R. Civ. P. 4(k)(1)(B), the so-called 100-mile bulge rule, authorizes jurisdiction over an impleaded party not otherwise within the district court's reach if service was effected within 100 miles of the court. Subsection (C) provides for nationwide service when authorized by a federal statute; an interpleader action under 28 U.S.C. § 1335, for example, would implicate this provision. And, more dramatically, Fed. R. Civ. P. 4(k)(2) extends federal power to its outermost constitutional limits in federal claims (28 U.S.C. § 1331) cases.

*Fed. R. Civ. P. 4(k)(2)—The "Federal Long-Arm Statute" and Jurisdiction over Foreign Corporations*

With an increasingly global economy, it becomes more and more common for plaintiffs in U.S. courts to seek recovery against foreign corporate defendants. As we will see, the constraints of minimum-contacts analysis can make obtaining personal jurisdiction over such entities in state courts difficult.

It was in this context that Fed. R. Civ. P. 4(k)(2) was added in 1993 to allow federal courts to exercise personal jurisdiction "over the person of any defendant who is not subject to the jurisdiction of the courts of general jurisdiction of any state" when sued on claims arising under federal law, and where "the exercise of jurisdiction is consistent with the Constitution and laws of the United States." The Advisory Committee Note explains:

> The paragraph corrects a gap in the enforcement of federal law. Under the former rule, a problem was presented when the defendant was a non-resident of the United States having contacts with the United States sufficient to justify the application of United States law and to satisfy federal standards for forum selection, but having insufficient contact with any single state to support jurisdiction under state long-arm legislation or meet the requirements of the Fourteenth Amendment limitation on state court territorial jurisdiction. In such cases, the defendant was shielded from the enforcement of federal law by the fortuity of a favorable limitation on the power of state courts, which was incorporated into federal practice by the former rule.

Three elements are required for the exercise of jurisdiction under 4(k)(2): (1) the claim must arise under federal law; (2) the defendant must be beyond the jurisdictional reach of any state court; and (3) the exercise of jurisdiction must not violate the defendant's rights under the Constitution, meaning that even though defendant's contacts are so scattered that no one state has jurisdiction, there are *sufficient aggregate contacts* with the United States as a whole to satisfy the Fifth Amendment's Due Process Clause.

The first two elements were made out in *United States v. Swiss American Bank, Ltd*, 274 F.3d 610 (1st Cir. 2001), in which the government sued under the RICO (Racketeer Influenced and Corrupt Organizations) Act to recover illegal drug proceeds that had been forfeited by a depositor in the foreign bank incorporated and located in Antigua. But the third requirement was held lacking, the Court of Appeals finding insufficient ties to the United States because the Bank had no physical presence and only intermittent contacts (such as the placing of advertisements in an airline magazine). Moreover, the Bank had not solicited the depositor's business in the United States; rather, he had opened the accounts in Antigua with moneys from outside the United States. *See also BP Chemicals Ltd. v. Formosa Chemical & Fibre Corp.*, 229 F.3d 254 (3d Cir. 2000) (defendant had insufficient purposeful contacts with United States).

For cases that did exercise jurisdiction over foreign defendants pursuant to 4(k)(2), see *ISI International, Inc. v. Borden Ladner Gervais LLP*, 256 F.3d 548 (7th Cir. 2001) (Canadian law firm, sued under federal law that forbids making false or deceptive statements in connection with commercial activities in interstate commerce, had sufficient aggregate contacts with several states to be sued in federal court in Illinois), and *Graduate Management Admission Council v. Raju*, 241 F. Supp. 2d 589 (E.D. Va. 2003) (Indian Internet Web site operator who specifically targeted U.S. customers was suable for copyright and trademark infringement). In *Mwani v. Osama bin Laden*, 417 F.3d 1 (D.C. Cir. 2005), the provision was invoked to assert jurisdiction over defendant in an Alien Tort Claims action, finding he had "engaged in unabashedly malignant actions directed at and felt in this forum" by purposefully directing his terror at the United States.

For further discussion of Fed. R. Civ. P. 4(k)(2) as well as other bases for the exercise of federal adjudicatory authority in international disputes, see Stephen B. Burbank, *The United States' Approach to International Civil Litigation: Recent Developments in Forum Selection*, 19 U. Pa. J. Intl. Econ. L. 1 (1998); Thomas Main, *Global Issues in Civil Procedure* 63-74 (2006).

# H. NOTE ON PERSONAL JURISDICTION UNDER INTERNATIONAL LAW

The *Restatement (Third) of Foreign Relations Law*, which purports to set forth the general consensus on principles of international law, provides in § 421:

> (1) A state may exercise jurisdiction through its courts to adjudicate with respect to a person or thing if the relationship of the state to the person or thing is such as to make the exercise of jurisdiction reasonable.
>
> (2) In general, a state's exercise of jurisdiction to adjudicate with respect to a person or thing is reasonable if, at the time jurisdiction is asserted:
>
> > (a) the person or thing is present in the territory of the state, other than transitorily;
> >
> > (b) the person, if a natural person, is domiciled in the state;
> >
> > (c) the person, if a natural person, is resident in the state;
> >
> > (d) the person, if a natural person, is a national of the state;

(e) the person, if a corporation or comparable juridical person, is organized pursuant to the law of the state;

(f) a ship, aircraft or other vehicle to which the adjudication relates is registered under the laws of the state;

(g) the person, whether natural or juridical, has consented to the exercise of jurisdiction;

(h) the person, whether natural or juridical, regularly carries on business in the state;

(i) the person, whether natural or juridical, had carried on activity in the state, but only in respect of such activity;

(j) the person, whether natural or juridical, had carried on outside the state an activity having a substantial, direct, and foreseeable effect within the state, but only in respect of such activity; or

(k) the thing that is the subject of adjudication is owned, possessed, or used in the state, but only in respect of a claim reasonably connected with that thing.

(3) A defense of lack of jurisdiction is generally waived by any appearance by or on behalf of a person or thing (whether as plaintiff, defendant, or third party), if the appearance is for a purpose that does not include a challenge to the exercise of jurisdiction.

***

Does this formulation sound familiar? Compare the expansive authority asserted in the French Civil Code Article 14:

An alien, even not residing in France, may be summoned before the French courts for fulfillment of obligations contracted by him in France toward a French person; he may be brought before French courts for obligations contracted by him in a foreign country toward French persons.

[Now that's truly *long-arm* jurisdiction.]

# I. MINIMUM-CONTACTS ANALYSIS IN OPERATION

The *International Shoe* formulation of the minimum-contacts test, like most legal doctrine in its initial stages, left many unanswered questions and considerable room for analytical development by courts in the face of live cases.

One of the early and most important elaborations came in *Hanson v. Denckla*, 357 U.S. 235 (1958). While residing in Pennsylvania, Dora Donner established a trust with the Wilmington Trust Co. of Delaware as trustee. She retained the right to receive the income until her death and to designate the beneficiaries who would ultimately get her substantial assets. Donner later moved to Florida, where she designated the children of one of her three daughters to receive $400,000 from the trust upon her death. She died a resident of Florida.

The two daughters whose children were not provided for filed suit in Florida state court challenging the disposition of the trust. The court exercised jurisdiction over the Delaware trustee, and invalidated the trust on technical grounds. When the daughters sought to enforce this decree against the trustee in its home state of Delaware, however, the courts ruled that it was not entitled to full faith and credit because the Florida court possessed neither in personam jurisdiction over the Wilmington Trust Co., nor in rem jurisdiction over the assets of the trust located in Delaware. The U.S. Supreme Court agreed:

> [The parties seeking to enforce the Florida decree] urge that the circumstances of this case amount to sufficient affiliation with the State of Florida to empower its courts to exercise personal jurisdiction over this nonresident defendant. Principal reliance is placed upon *McGee v. International Life Ins. Co.* In *McGee* the Court noted the trend of expanding personal jurisdiction over nonresidents. As technological progress has increased the flow of commerce between States, the need for jurisdiction over nonresidents has undergone a similar increase. At the same time, progress in communications and transportation has made the defense of a suit in a foreign tribunal less burdensome. In response to these changes, the requirements for personal jurisdiction over nonresidents have evolved from the rigid rule of *Pennoyer v. Neff* to the flexible standard of *International Shoe Co. v. State of Washington.* But it is a mistake to assume that this trend heralds the eventual demise of all restrictions on the personal jurisdiction of state courts. Those restrictions are more than a guarantee of immunity from inconvenient or distant litigation. They are a consequence of territorial limitations on the power of the respective States. However minimal the burden of defending in a foreign tribunal, a defendant may not be called upon to do so unless he has had the "minimal contacts" with that State that are a prerequisite to its exercise of power over him.
>
> We fail to find such contacts in the circumstances of this case. The defendant trust company has no office in Florida, and transacts no business there. None of the trust assets has ever been held or administered in Florida, and the record discloses no solicitation of business in that State either in person or by mail.
>
> The cause of action in this case is not one that arises out of an act done or transaction consummated in the forum State. In that respect, it differs from *McGee v. International Life Ins. Co.* In *McGee*, the nonresident defendant solicited a reinsurance agreement with a resident of California. The offer was accepted in that State, and the insurance premiums were mailed from there until the insured's death. Noting the interest California has in providing effective redress for its residents when nonresident insurers refuse to pay claims on insurance they have solicited in that State, the Court upheld jurisdiction because the suit was based on a contract which had substantial connection with that State. In contrast, this action involves the validity of an agreement that was entered without any connection with the forum State.

The agreement was executed in Delaware by a trust company incorporated in that State and a settlor domiciled in Pennsylvania. The first relationship Florida had to the agreement was years later when the settlor became domiciled there, and the trustee remitted the trust income to her in that State. From Florida Mrs. Donner carried on several bits of trust administration that may be compared to the mailing of premiums in *McGee*. But the record discloses no instance in which the trustee performed any acts in Florida that bear the same relationship to the agreement as the solicitation in *McGee*. Consequently, this suit cannot be said to be one to enforce an obligation that arose from a privilege the defendant exercised in Florida.

357 U.S. at 250-252.

Significantly, the Court went on to emphasize that the "unilateral activity of those who claim some relationship with a nonresident defendant cannot satisfy the requirement of contact with the forum State. The application of that rule will vary with the quality and nature of the defendant's activity, but it is essential in each case that there be *some act by which the defendant purposefully avails itself of the privilege of conducting activities within the forum State*, thus invoking the benefits and protections of its laws." 357 U.S. at 253 (emphasis added).

This "purposeful availment" gloss on the minimum-contacts test proved to be a crucial constraint on the exercise of jurisdiction, as we will see in the case that immediately follows. *See also Leonard v. USA Petroleum Corp.*, 829 F. Supp. 882 (S.D. Tex. 1993) ("It is USA Petroleum's own acts, not the acts of [plaintiff, a Texas resident who claimed he was owed a commission on an oral contract because while in Texas he located and produced a buyer for defendant's service stations in Puerto Rico], that establish the jurisdictional minimum contact with a state. To be subject to jurisdiction in Texas, USA Petroleum must itself have acted to establish meaningful contact with the state. . . . [A]ll of the acts [plaintiff] describes were done on his own initiative.").

What is happening to the trend, observed by Justice Black just one year before in *McGee*, toward liberalizing the restrictions on personal jurisdiction?

## ■ WORLD-WIDE VOLKSWAGEN CORP.
## v. WOODSON
*444 U.S. 286 (1980)*

Justice WHITE delivered the opinion of the Court:

The issue before us is whether, consistently with the Due Process Clause of the Fourteenth Amendment, an Oklahoma court may exercise in personam jurisdiction over a nonresident automobile retailer and its wholesale distributor in a products-liability action, when the defendants' only connection with Oklahoma is the fact that an automobile sold in New York to New York residents became involved in an accident in Oklahoma.

## I

Respondents Harry and Kay Robinson purchased a new Audi automobile from petitioner Seaway Volkswagen, Inc. (Seaway), in Massena, N.Y., in 1976. The following year the Robinson family, who resided in New York, left that State for a new home in Arizona. As they passed through the State of Oklahoma, another car struck their Audi in the rear, causing a fire which severely burned Kay Robinson and her two children.[1]

The Robinsons subsequently brought a products-liability action in the District Court for Creek County, Okla., claiming that their injuries resulted from defective design and placement of the Audi's gas tank and fuel system. They joined as defendants the automobile's manufacturer, Audi NSU Auto Union Aktiengesellschaft (Audi); its importer Volkswagen of America, Inc. (Volkswagen); its regional distributor, petitioner World-Wide Volkswagen Corp. (World-Wide); and its retail dealer, petitioner Seaway. Seaway and World-Wide entered special appearances,[3] claiming that Oklahoma's exercise of jurisdiction over them would offend the limitations on the State's jurisdiction imposed by the Due Process Clause of the Fourteenth Amendment.

The facts presented to the District Court showed that World-Wide is incorporated and has its business office in New York. It distributes vehicles, parts, and accessories, under contract with Volkswagen, to retail dealers in New York, New Jersey, and Connecticut. Seaway, one of these retail dealers, is incorporated and has its place of business in New York. Insofar as the record reveals, Seaway and World-Wide are fully independent corporations whose relations with each other and with Volkswagen and Audi are contractual only. Respondents adduced no evidence that either World-Wide or Seaway does any business in Oklahoma, ships or sells any products to or in that State, has an agent to receive process there, or purchases advertisements in any media calculated to reach Oklahoma. In fact, as respondents' counsel conceded at oral argument, there was no showing that any automobile sold by World-Wide or Seaway has ever entered Oklahoma with the single exception of the vehicle involved in the present case.

Despite the apparent paucity of contacts between petitioners and Oklahoma, the District Court rejected their constitutional claim and reaffirmed that ruling in denying petitioners' motion for reconsideration. Petitioners then sought a writ of prohibition* in the Supreme Court of Oklahoma to restrain the District Judge, respondent Charles S. Woodson, from exercising in personam jurisdiction over them. They renewed their contention that, because they had no "minimal contacts," with the State of Oklahoma, the

---

1. The driver of the other automobile does not figure in the present litigation.

3. Volkswagen also entered a special appearance in the District Court, but unlike World-Wide and Seaway did not seek review in the Supreme Court of Oklahoma and is not a petitioner here. Both Volkswagen and Audi remain as defendants in the litigation pending before the District Court in Oklahoma.

*Eds.' Note:* This writ was the best available means for an immediate appeal of the trial judge's ruling refusing to dismiss the action.

actions of the District Judge were in violation of their rights under the Due Process Clause.

The Supreme Court of Oklahoma denied the writ, holding that personal jurisdiction over petitioners was authorized by Oklahoma's "long-arm" statute, Okla. Stat., Tit. 12, § 1701.03(a)(4) (1971).[7] Although the court noted that the proper approach was to test jurisdiction against both statutory and constitutional standards, its analysis did not distinguish these questions, probably because § 1701.03(a)(4) has been interpreted as conferring jurisdiction to the limits permitted by the U.S. Constitution. The court's rationale was contained in the following paragraph:

> In the case before us, the product being sold and distributed by the petitioners is by its very design and purpose so mobile that petitioners can foresee its possible use in Oklahoma. This is especially true of the distributor, who has the exclusive right to distribute such automobile in New York, New Jersey and Connecticut. The evidence presented below demonstrated that goods sold and distributed by the petitioners were used in the State of Oklahoma, and under the facts we believe it reasonable to infer, given the retail value of the automobile, that the petitioners derive substantial income from automobiles which from time to time are used in the State of Oklahoma. This being the case, we hold that under the facts presented, the trial court was justified in concluding that the petitioners derive substantial revenue from goods used or consumed in this State.

We granted certiorari to consider an important constitutional question with respect to state-court jurisdiction and to resolve a conflict between the Supreme Court of Oklahoma and the highest courts of at least four other States. We reverse.

## II

The Due Process Clause of the Fourteenth Amendment limits the power of a state court to render a valid personal judgment against a nonresident defendant. A judgment rendered in violation of due process is void in the rendering State and is not entitled to full faith and credit elsewhere. *Pennoyer v. Neff*, 95 U.S. 714, 732-733 (1877). Due process requires that the defendant be given adequate notice of the suit, *Mullane v. Central Hanover Trust Co.*, 339 U.S. 306, 313-314 (1950), and be subject to the personal jurisdiction of the court, *International Shoe Co. v. Washington*, 326 U.S. 310 (1945). In the present case, it is not contended that notice was inadequate; the

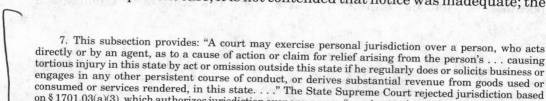

7. This subsection provides: "A court may exercise personal jurisdiction over a person, who acts directly or by an agent, as to a cause of action or claim for relief arising from the person's . . . causing tortious injury in this state by act or omission outside this state if he regularly does or solicits business or engages in any other persistent course of conduct, or derives substantial revenue from goods used or consumed or services rendered, in this state. . . ." The State Supreme Court rejected jurisdiction based on § 1701.03(a)(3), which authorizes jurisdiction over any person "causing tortious injury in this state by an act or omission in this state." Something in addition to the infliction of tortious injury was required.

only question is whether these particular petitioners were subject to the jurisdiction of the Oklahoma courts.

As has long been settled, and as we reaffirm today, a state court may exercise personal jurisdiction over a nonresident defendant only so long as there exist "minimum contacts" between the defendant and the forum State. *International Shoe Co. v. Washington, supra*, at 316. The concept of minimum contacts, in turn, can be seen to perform two related, but distinguishable, functions. It protects the defendant against the burdens of litigating in a distant or inconvenient forum. And it acts to ensure that the States through their courts, do not reach out beyond the limits imposed on them by their status as coequal sovereigns in a federal system.

The protection against inconvenient litigation is typically described in terms of "reasonableness" or "fairness." We have said that the defendant's contacts with the forum State must be such that maintenance of the suit "does not offend 'traditional notions of fair play and substantial justice.'" *International Shoe Co. v. Washington.* The relationship between the defendant and the forum must be such that it is "reasonable . . . to require the corporation to defend the particular suit which is brought there." Implicit in this emphasis on reasonableness is the understanding that the burden on the defendant, while always a primary concern, will in an appropriate case be considered in light of other relevant factors, including the forum State's interest in adjudicating the dispute; the plaintiff's interest in obtaining convenient and effective relief, at least when that interest is not adequately protected by the plaintiff's power to choose the forum; the interstate judicial system's interest in obtaining the most efficient resolution of controversies; and the shared interest of the several States in furthering fundamental substantive social policies.

The limits imposed on state jurisdiction by the Due Process Clause, in its role as a guarantor against inconvenient litigation, have been substantially relaxed over the years. As we noted in *McGee v. International Life Ins. Co.*, this trend is largely attributable to a fundamental transformation in the American economy: "Today many commercial transactions touch two or more States and may involve parties separated by the full continent. With this increasing nationalization of commerce has come a great increase in the amount of business conducted by mail across state lines. At the same time modern transportation and communication have made it much less burdensome for a party sued to defend himself in a State where he engages in economic activity." The historical developments noted in *McGee*, of course, have only accelerated in the generation since that case was decided.

Nevertheless, we have never accepted the proposition that state lines are irrelevant for jurisdictional purposes, nor could we, and remain faithful to the principles of interstate federalism embodied in the Constitution. The economic interdependence of the States was foreseen and desired by the Framers. In the Commerce Clause, they provided that the Nation was to be a common market, a "free trade unit" in which the States are debarred from acting as separable economic entities. But the Framers also intended that the

States retain many essential attributes of sovereignty, including, in particular, the sovereign power to try causes in their courts. The sovereignty of each State, in turn, implied a limitation on the sovereignty of all of its sister States—a limitation express or implicit in both the original scheme of the Constitution and the Fourteenth Amendment.

Hence, even while abandoning the shibboleth that "[t]he authority of every tribunal is necessarily restricted by the territorial limits of the State in which it is established," *Pennoyer v. Neff*, we emphasized that the reasonableness of asserting jurisdiction over the defendant must be assessed "in the context of our federal system of government," *International Shoe Co. v. Washington*, and stressed that the Due Process Clause ensures not only fairness, but also the "orderly administration of the laws." As we noted in *Hanson v. Denckla*: "As technological progress has increased the flow of commerce between the States, the need for jurisdiction over nonresidents has undergone a similar increase. At the same time, progress in communications and transportation has made the defense of a suit in a foreign tribunal less burdensome. In response to these changes, the requirements for personal jurisdiction over nonresidents have evolved from the rigid rule of *Pennoyer v. Neff*, to the flexible standard of *International Shoe Co. v. Washington*. But it is a mistake to assume that this trend heralds the eventual demise of all restrictions on the personal jurisdiction of state courts. Those restrictions are more than a guarantee of immunity from inconvenient or distant litigation. They are a consequence of territorial limitations on the power of the respective States."

Thus, the Due Process Clause "does not contemplate that a state may make binding a judgment in personam against an individual or corporate defendant with which the state has no contacts, ties, or relations." *International Shoe Co. v. Washington*. Even if the defendant would suffer minimal or no inconvenience from being forced to litigate before the tribunals of another State; even if the forum State has a strong interest in applying its law to the controversy; even if the forum State is the most convenient location for litigation, the Due Process Clause, acting as an instrument of interstate federalism, may sometimes act to divest the State of its power to render a valid judgment. *Hanson v. Denckla*.

## III

Applying these principles to the case at hand, we find in the record before us a total absence of those affiliating circumstances that are a necessary predicate to any exercise of state-court jurisdiction. Petitioners carry on no activity whatsoever in Oklahoma. They close no sales and perform no services there. They avail themselves of none of the privileges and benefits of Oklahoma law. They solicit no business there either through salespersons or through advertising reasonably calculated to reach the State. Nor does the record show that they regularly sell cars at wholesale or retail to Oklahoma customers or residents or that they indirectly, through others, serve or seek to serve the Oklahoma market. In short, respondents seek to base jurisdiction on one, isolated occurrence and whatever inferences can be drawn therefrom: the fortuitous circumstance that a single Audi automobile, sold in New York to New York residents, happened to suffer an accident while passing through Oklahoma.

It is argued, however, that because an automobile is mobile by its very design and purpose it was "foreseeable" that the Robinsons' Audi would cause injury in Oklahoma. Yet "foreseeability" alone has never been a sufficient benchmark for personal jurisdiction under the Due Process Clause. In *Hanson v. Denckla*, it was no doubt foreseeable that the settlor of a Delaware trust would subsequently move to Florida and seek to exercise a power of appointment there; yet we held that Florida courts could not constitutionally exercise jurisdiction over a Delaware trustee that had no other contacts with the forum State. In *Kulko v. California Superior Court*, 436 U.S. 84 (1978), it was surely "foreseeable" that a divorced wife would move to California from New York, the domicile of the marriage, and that a minor daughter would live with the mother. Yet we held that California could not exercise jurisdiction in a child-support action over the former husband who had remained in New York.

If foreseeability were the criterion, a local California tire retailer could be forced to defend in Pennsylvania when a blowout occurs there, *see Erlanger Mills, Inc. v. Cohoes Fibre Mills, Inc.*, 239 F.2d 502, 507 (4th Cir. 1956); a Wisconsin seller of a defective automobile jack could be haled before a distant court for damage caused in New Jersey, *Reilly v. Phil Tolkan Pontiac, Inc.*, 372 F. Supp. 1205 (N.J. 1974); or a Florida soft-drink concessionaire could be summoned to Alaska to account for injuries happening there, *see Uppgren v. Executive Aviation Services, Inc.*, 304 F. Supp. 165, 170-171 (Minn. 1969). Every seller of chattels would in effect appoint the chattel his agent for service of process. His amenability to suit would travel with the chattel. We recently abandoned the outworn rule of *Harris v. Balk*, that the interest of a creditor in a debt could be extinguished or otherwise affected by any State having transitory jurisdiction over the debtor. *Shaffer v. Heitner*, 433 U.S. 186 (1977). Having [interred] the mechanical rule that a creditor's amenability to a *quasi in rem* action travels with his debtor, we are unwilling to endorse an analogous principle in the present case.

This is not to say, of course, that foreseeability is wholly irrelevant. But the foreseeability that is critical to due process analysis is not the mere likelihood that a product will find its way into the forum State. Rather, it is that the defendant's conduct and connection with the forum State are such that he should reasonably anticipate being haled into court there. The Due Process Clause, by ensuring the "orderly administration of the laws," *International Shoe Co. v. Washington*, gives a degree of predictability to the legal system that allows potential defendants to structure their primary conduct with some minimum assurance as to where that conduct will and will not render them liable to suit.

When a corporation "purposefully avails itself of the privilege of conducting activities within the forum State," *Hanson v. Denckla*, it has clear notice that it is subject to suit there, and can act to alleviate the risk of burdensome litigation by procuring insurance, passing the expected costs on to customers, or, if the risks are too great, severing its connection with the State. Hence if the sale of a product of a manufacturer or distributor such as Audi or Volkswagen is not simply an isolated occurrence, but arises from the efforts of the manufacturer or distributor to serve directly or indirectly, the market for its product in other States, it is not unreasonable to subject it to suit in one of those States if its allegedly defective merchandise has there been the source of injury to its owner or to others. The forum State does not exceed its powers under the Due Process Clause if it asserts personal jurisdiction over a corporation that delivers its products into the stream of commerce with the expectation that they will be purchased by consumers in the forum State. *Cf. Gray v. American Radiator & Standard Sanitary Corp.*, 22 Ill. 2d 432 (1961).

But there is no such or similar basis for Oklahoma jurisdiction over World-Wide or Seaway in this case. Seaway's sales are made in Massena, N.Y. World-Wide's market, although substantially larger, is limited to dealers in New York, New Jersey, and Connecticut. There is no evidence of record that any automobiles distributed by World-Wide are sold to retail customers outside this tristate area. It is foreseeable that the purchasers of automobiles sold by World-Wide and Seaway may take them to Oklahoma. But the mere "unilateral activity of those who claim some relationship with a nonresident defendant cannot satisfy the requirement of contact with the forum State." *Hanson v. Denckla.*

In a variant on the previous argument, it is contended that jurisdiction can be supported by the fact that petitioners earn substantial revenue from goods used in Oklahoma. The Oklahoma Supreme Court so found drawing the inference that because one automobile sold by petitioners had been used in Oklahoma, others might have been used there also. While this inference seems less than compelling on the facts of the instant case, we need not question the court's factual findings in order to reject its reasoning.

This argument seems to make the point that the purchase of automobiles in New York, from which the petitioners earn substantial revenue, would not occur but for the fact that the automobiles are capable of use in distant States like Oklahoma. Respondents observe that the very purpose of an automobile is to travel, and that travel of automobiles sold by petitioners is facilitated by an extensive chain of Volkswagen service centers throughout the country, including some in Oklahoma. However, financial benefits accruing to the defendant from a collateral relation to the forum State will not support jurisdiction if they do not stem from a constitutionally cognizable contact with that State. In our view, whatever marginal revenues petitioners may receive by virtue of the fact that their products are capable of use in Oklahoma is far too attenuated a contact to justify that State's exercise of in personam jurisdiction over them.

Because we find that petitioners have no "contacts, ties, or relations" with the State of Oklahoma, the judgment of the Supreme Court of Oklahoma is Reversed.

Justice BRENNAN, dissenting:

. . . Because I believe that the Court reads *International Shoe* and its progeny too narrowly, and because I believe that the standards enunciated by those cases may already be obsolete as constitutional boundaries, I dissent.

. . . In [this case], I would find that the forum State has an interest in permitting the litigation to go forward, the litigation is connected to the forum, the defendant is linked to the forum, and the burden of defending is not unreasonable. Accordingly, I would hold that it is neither unfair nor unreasonable to require these defendants to defend in the forum State. . . .

The interest of the forum State and its connection to the litigation is strong. The automobile accident underlying the litigation occurred in Oklahoma. The plaintiffs were hospitalized in Oklahoma when they brought suit. Essential witnesses and evidence were in Oklahoma. The State has a legitimate interest in enforcing its laws designed to keep its highway system safe, and the trial can proceed at least as efficiently in Oklahoma as anywhere else.

The petitioners are not unconnected with the forum. Although both sell automobiles within limited sales territories, each sold the automobile which in fact was driven to Oklahoma where it was involved in an accident. It may be true, as the Court suggests, that each sincerely intended to limit its commercial impact to the limited territory, and that each intended to accept the benefits and protection of the laws only of those States within the territory. But obviously these were unrealistic hopes that cannot be treated as an automatic constitutional shield.

An automobile simply is not a stationary item or one designed to be used in one place. An automobile is intended to be moved around. Someone in the business of selling large numbers of automobiles can hardly plead ignorance of their mobility or pretend that the automobiles stay put after they are sold. It is not merely that a dealer in automobiles foresees that they will move. The dealer actually intends that the purchasers will use the automobiles to travel to distant States where the dealer does not directly "do business." The sale of an automobile does purposefully inject the vehicle into the stream of interstate commerce so that it can travel to distant States.

. . . The Court accepts that a State may exercise jurisdiction over a distributor which "serves" that State "indirectly" by "deliver[ing] its products into the stream of commerce with the expectation that they will be purchased by consumers in the forum State." It is difficult to see why the Constitution should distinguish between a case involving goods which reach a distant State through a chain of distribution and a case involving goods which reach the same State because a consumer, using them as the dealer knew the customer would, took them there. In each case the seller purposefully injects the goods into the stream of commerce and those goods predictably are used in the forum State.

Furthermore, an automobile seller derives substantial benefits from States other than its own. A large part of the value of automobiles is the extensive, nationwide network of highways. Significant portions of that network have been constructed by and are maintained by the individual States, including Oklahoma. The States, through their highway programs, contribute in a very direct and important way to the value of petitioners' businesses. Additionally, a network of other related dealerships with their service departments operates throughout the country under the protection of the laws of the various States, including Oklahoma, and enhances the value of petitioners' businesses by facilitating their customers' traveling.

Thus, the Court errs in its conclusion that "petitioners have no 'contacts, ties, or relations'" with Oklahoma. There obviously are contacts, and, given Oklahoma's connection to the litigation, the contacts are sufficiently significant to make it fair and reasonable for the petitioners to submit to Oklahoma's jurisdiction. . . .

The plaintiffs in [this] case brought suit in a forum with which they had significant contacts and which had significant contacts with the litigation. I am not convinced that the defendants would suffer any "heavy and disproportionate burden" in defending the suits. Accordingly, I would hold that the Constitution should not shield the defendants from appearing and defending in the plaintiffs' chosen fora.

Justice MARSHALL, with whom Justice BLACKMUN joins, dissenting:
. . .

This is a difficult case, and reasonable minds may differ as to whether respondents have alleged a sufficient "relationship among the defendant[s], the forum, and the litigation," to satisfy the requirements of *International Shoe.* I am concerned, however, that the majority has reached its result by taking an unnecessarily narrow view of petitioners' forum-related conduct. The majority asserts that "respondents seek to base jurisdiction on one, isolated occurrence and whatever inferences can be drawn therefrom: the fortuitous circumstance that a single Audi automobile, sold in New York to New York residents, happened to suffer an accident while passing through Oklahoma." If that were the case, I would readily agree that the minimum contacts necessary to sustain jurisdiction are not present. But the basis for the assertion of jurisdiction is not the happenstance that an individual over whom petitioner had no control made a unilateral decision to take a chattel with him to a distant State. Rather, jurisdiction is premised on the deliberate and purposeful actions of the defendants themselves in choosing to become part of a nationwide, indeed a global, network for marketing and servicing automobiles.

Petitioners are sellers of a product whose utility derives from its mobility. The unique importance of the automobile in today's society, which is discussed in Mr. Justice Blackmun's dissenting opinion, needs no further elaboration. Petitioners know that their customers buy cars not only to make short trips, but also to travel long distances. In fact, the nationwide service network with which they are affiliated was designed to facilitate and encourage such travel. Seaway would be unlikely to sell many cars if authorized service were available only in Massena, N.Y. Moreover, local dealers normally derive a substantial portion of their revenues from their service operations and thereby obtain a further economic benefit from the opportunity to service cars which were sold in other States. It is apparent that petitioners have not attempted to minimize the chance that their activities will have effects in other States; on the contrary, they have chosen to do business in a way that increases that chance, because it is to their economic advantage to do so.

To be sure, petitioners could not know in advance that this particular automobile would be driven to Oklahoma. They must have anticipated, however, that a substantial portion of the cars they sold would travel out of New York. Seaway, a local dealer in the second most populous State, and World-Wide, one of only seven regional Audi distributors in the entire country, would scarcely have been surprised to learn that a car sold by them had been driven in Oklahoma on Interstate 44, a heavily traveled transcontinental highway. In the case of the distributor, in particular, the probability that some of the cars it sells will be driven in every one of the contiguous States must amount to a virtual certainty. This knowledge should alert a reasonable businessman to the likelihood that a defect in the product might manifest itself in the forum State—not because of some unpredictable, aberrant, unilateral action by a single buyer, but in the normal course of the operation of the vehicles for their intended purpose.

. . .

I sympathize with the majority's concern that the persons ought to be able to structure their conduct so as not to be subject to suit in distant forums. But that may not always be possible. Some activities by their very nature may foreclose the option of conducting them in such away as to avoid subjecting oneself to jurisdiction in multiple forums. This is by no means to say that all sellers of automobiles should be subject to suit everywhere; but a distributor of automobiles to a multistate market and a local automobile dealer who makes himself part of a nationwide network of dealerships can fairly expect that the cars they sell may cause injury in distant States and that they may be called on to defend a resulting lawsuit there. . . .

. . . Accordingly, I dissent.

Justice BLACKMUN, dissenting:

I confess that I am somewhat puzzled why the plaintiffs in this litigation are so insistent that the regional distributor and the retail dealer, the petitioners here, who handled the ill-fated Audi automobile involved in this litigation, be named defendants. It would appear that the manufacturer and the importer, whose subjectability to Oklahoma jurisdiction is not challenged before this Court, ought not to be judgment-proof. It may, of course, ultimately amount to a contest between insurance companies that, once begun, is not easily brought to a termination. Having made this much of an observation, I pursue it no further.

For me, a critical factor in the disposition of the litigation is the nature of the instrumentality under consideration. It has been said that we are a nation on wheels. What we are concerned with here is the automobile and its peripatetic character. One need only examine our national network of interstate highways, or make an appearance on one of them, or observe the variety of license plates present not only on those highways but in any metropolitan area, to realize that any automobile is likely to wander far from its place of licensure or from its place of distribution and retail sale. . . .

It therefore seems to me not unreasonable—and certainly not unconstitutional and beyond the reach of the principles laid down in *International Shoe Co. v. Washington*, and its progeny—to uphold Oklahoma jurisdiction over this New York distributor and this New York dealer when the accident happened in Oklahoma. I see nothing more unfair for them than for the manufacturer and the importer. All are in the business of providing vehicles that spread out over the highways of our several States. It is not too much to anticipate at the time of distribution and at the time of retail sale that this Audi would be in Oklahoma. . . .

My position need not now take me beyond the automobile and the professional who does business by way of distributing and retailing automobiles. Cases concerning other instrumentalities will be dealt with as they arise and in their own contexts.

. . .

## Comments and Questions

1. By the time *World-Wide Volkswagen* was decided, it was well settled that the commission of a tort *within* a state established jurisdiction over the nonresident tortfeasor for a claim arising from the conduct. Had the Robinsons collided on the Oklahoma highway with a car driven by a Texas citizen, for example, that person could have been sued in Oklahoma on a negligence claim arising from the accident even if he had left the state immediately afterward (as in *Hess v. Pawloski, supra*). The actual lawsuit filed by the Robinsons fell in a murkier area—the plaintiffs were seeking recovery for something that happened *outside* the state (the design and manufacture of the Audi with a rear gas tank) that merely had *effects* within the state (the explosion and consequent injuries). On the activity spectrum diagram in Note 4 following *International Shoe*, this falls on the far left.

In an influential case cited in *World-Wide Volkswagen*, the Illinois Supreme Court had held an out-of-state component manufacturer amenable to suit on just such an "effects" theory. *See Gray v. American Radiator & Standard Sanitary Corp.*, 22 Ill. 2d 432 (1961). Defendant Titan had manufactured its allegedly defective safety valve in Ohio and sold it to American Radiator, which incorporated the valve into a water heater at its plant in Pennsylvania. The heater was then sold to plaintiff Phyllis Gray in Illinois, where it exploded. Titan was held subject to jurisdiction because its alleged negligence caused injurious effects in the forum state.

The issue of whether the mere fact that the allegedly defective product ended up in the forum state, where it caused injury, should subject the manufacturer to suit there, has sharply divided the Supreme Court, first in *World-Wide Volkswagen,* then in *Asahi Metal Industry Co. v. Superior Court*, and most recently in *J. McIntyre Machinery, Ltd. v. Nicastro*, which follow below. The prevailing view in each is that *purposeful action* on the part of the defendant, such as its distribution of the product in the state, is the prerequisite to adjudicatory power, thereby reaffirming *Hanson v. Denkla*. World-Wide VW and the Seaway dealership were connected to Oklahoma only through the unilateral act of their customers, the Robinsons, much as the Delaware trust company was connected to Florida solely by virtue of its client's decision to move there.

2. The justices in *World-Wide Volkswagen* all agree that *foreseeability of suit* is an important ingredient of due process analysis, as it allows potential defendants to predict where they are subject to suit and thus structure their business accordingly. But they strongly disagree about what it means. Justice White's opinion for the Court states: "[T]he foreseeability that is critical to due process analysis is not the mere likelihood that a product will find its way into the forum State. Rather, it is that the defendant's conduct and connection with the forum State are such that he should reasonably anticipate being haled into court there."

Is White suggesting that a defendant can reasonably foresee suit *only where* it has established minimum contacts? When foreseeability is equated with the existence of minimum contacts, does it not wash out as an independent factor in the analysis? Do you sense some circular reasoning here? Justice Brennan, in an omitted section of his dissent, complains: "A defendant cannot know if his actions will subject him to jurisdiction in another State until we have declared what the law of jurisdiction is." 444 U.S. at 311 n.18.

How do the dissenters define *foreseeability*? What is the significance to them of the fact that defendants' product is highly mobile, and could foreseeably travel to any state?

Note Justice Blackmun's pitch for a categorical rule permitting dealers to be sued wherever their defective automobiles allegedly cause injury, so as to avoid "parsing every variant in the myriad of motor vehicles fact situations that present themselves."

3. On the issue of foreseeability of suit in Oklahoma, would it have made a difference if the Robinsons had *actually told* their salesperson at the Seaway dealership that they would be taking their Audi through Oklahoma on their way to Arizona? What might the dissenters have done with this information? Should amenability to suit turn on the fortuitous nature of such conversations?

4. What role should geographic proximity play in the analysis of jurisdiction? What if the Robinsons' accident had occurred in Connecticut, within an hour's drive of the dealership? Shouldn't Seaway have reasonably anticipated the Audi ending up there? Justice Brennan reads the majority opinion as

"exclud[ing] jurisdiction in a contiguous State such as Pennsylvania as surely as in more distant States such as Oklahoma." 444 U.S. at 306 n.10.

For the majority, it is the crossing of state boundaries, not distance, that counts, because in their view personal jurisdiction is a matter of state sovereign power. Thus Justice White asserts that "the Due Process Clause, acting as an instrument of interstate federalism, may sometimes act to divest the State of its power to render a valid judgment" even if the defendant would suffer "minimal or no inconvenience."

In sharp contrast, the minority justices treat the matter more as one of convenience to the parties, and interest of the forum state in litigating the case. Brennan (in an omitted section of his dissent) observes ironically that "a courtroom just across the state line from a defendant may often be far more convenient for the defendant than a court-room in a distant corner of his own State." 444 U.S. at 301 n.1.

5. Justice White concedes that a "forum State does not exceed its powers under the Due Process Clause if it asserts personal jurisdiction over a corporation that delivers its products into the stream of commerce with the expectation that they will be purchased by consumers in the forum State." The disagreement on the Court seems to focus on the nature and extent of the *expectation*, which gets us back to the split on the "foreseeability" issue. The Court will further elaborate on this "stream of commerce" concept in *Asahi Metal Industry Co.* and *J. McIntyre Machinery, Ltd. v. Nicastro*, set out below.

6. The Court clearly resists an interpretation of "minimum contacts" that would subject local retailers to suit in any distant location where their product happens to end up. Can you see why this conjures up the specter of *Harris v. Balk* (the debt travels with the debtor) for the majority?

If you think *World-Wide Volkswagen* was wrongly decided, how would you feel if the Robinsons filed suit in Oklahoma against Mom & Pop's grocery store (located in Brooklyn, New York) when a can of cola they had purchased for their trip exploded en route? Should amenability to suit follow that soda can? Are there sufficient distinctions between the two scenarios that should make a difference on the jurisdictional question?

7. Are you as "puzzled" as Justice Blackmun about why the Robinsons were so intent on keeping World-Wide and Seaway in the lawsuit when "deep pockets" Audi and VW were no longer contesting jurisdiction (probably because they were conducting a substantial level of activities in Oklahoma) and could certainly pay any judgment rendered?

In *World-Wide Volkswagen v. Woodson—The Rest of the Story*, 72 Neb. L. Rev. 1122 (1993), Professor Charles W. Adams reveals that the Robinsons' lawyer, believing a state court jury would be more generous to his clients than a federal jury, sought to prevent removal of the case to federal court. (We will explore removal procedure in Chapter 8.) It was therefore necessary to maintain non-diverse parties on each side of the litigation (to defeat § 1332 diversity jurisdiction). Since the Robinsons were still citizens of New York, maintaining World-Wide and Seaway (also New York entities) as defendants would block removal.

Following the Supreme Court decision releasing these defendants, complete diversity of citizenship existed and the case was removed and tried in federal district court. The federal jury rendered a verdict for the defendants, as the Robinson's lawyer had feared.

8. In what ways does Justice Brennan's dissent reflect the same expansive philosophy of personal jurisdiction expressed by Justice Black in *International Shoe* and *McGee*? Note Brennan's explicit reliance on the *McGee* factors: the forum state's interest; the plaintiff's interest; the actual burden on defendant; the location of witnesses and evidence.

9. If personal jurisdiction is a function of state sovereignty, how can it be that a defendant may *consent to* jurisdiction, or inadvertently *waive* the objection? *See* Fed. R. Civ. P. 12(h)(1). As we have seen, the lack of subject matter jurisdiction *cannot* be cured by consent or waiver of the parties, and may even be raised by the court on its own initiative, because it goes to the core authority of the court to proceed with the case. *See* Fed. R. Civ. P. 12(h)(3) and Advisory Committee Note.

10. Only two years after *World-Wide Volkswagen Corp. v. Woodson*, the Court shifted its emphasis away from the state sovereignty rationale of personal jurisdiction. In *Insurance Corp. of Ireland, Ltd. v. Compagnie des Bauxites de Guinee*, 456 U.S. 694 (1982), it explained:

> The personal jurisdiction requirement recognizes and protects an individual liberty interest. It represents a restriction on judicial power *not as a matter of sovereignty*, but as a matter of individual liberty. . . . It is true that we have stated that the requirement of personal jurisdiction, as applied to state courts, reflects an element of federalism and the character of state sovereignty vis-a-vis other States [citing *World-Wide Volkswagen Corp. v. Woodson*]. . . . The restriction on state sovereign power described in *World-Wide Volkswagen Corp.*, however, must be seen as ultimately a function of the individual liberty interest preserved by the Due Process Clause. That Clause is the only source of the personal jurisdiction requirement and the Clause itself makes no mention of federalism concerns. Furthermore, if the federalism concept operated as an independent restriction on the sovereign power of the court, it would not be possible to waive the personal jurisdiction requirement: Individual actions cannot change the powers of sovereignty, although the individual can subject himself to powers from which he may otherwise be protected.
>
> Because the requirement of personal jurisdiction represents first of all an individual right, it can, like other such rights, be waived.

If the Court cannot settle on the rationale underlying the concept of personal jurisdiction, is it any wonder the doctrine surrounding it often appears to be in flux? For a fundamental reconceptualization of that doctrine that rejects the *International Shoe* focus on fairness to the parties in favor of an approach founded on a state's "legitimate interest in the dispute," *see*

A. Benjamin Spencer, *Jurisdiction to Adjudicate: A Revised Analysis*, 73 U. Chi. L. Rev. 617 (2006).

11. *World-Wide Volkswagen* roundly rejects the position that merely causing an effect or injury in a state is a sufficient basis for the exercise of personal jurisdiction over the actor. How then can we explain the result in the next case?

## ■ CALDER v. JONES
### 465 U.S. 783 (1984)

*[handwritten: defamation = intentional tort*
*v.*
*negligence = no intent., lack of care]*

Justice REHNQUIST delivered the opinion of the Court:

Respondent Shirley Jones brought suit in California Superior Court claiming that she had been libeled in an article written and edited by petitioners in Florida. The article was published in a national magazine with a large circulation in California. Petitioners were served with process by mail in Florida and caused special appearances to be entered on their behalf, moving to quash the service of process for lack of personal jurisdiction. The superior court granted the motion on the ground that First Amendment concerns weighed against an assertion of jurisdiction otherwise proper under the Due Process Clause. The California Court of Appeal reversed, rejecting the suggestion that First Amendment considerations enter into the jurisdictional analysis. We now affirm.

Respondent lives and works in California. She and her husband brought this suit against the National Enquirer, Inc., its local distributing company, and petitioners for libel, invasion of privacy, and intentional infliction of emotional harm. The Enquirer is a Florida corporation with its principal place of business in Florida. It publishes a national weekly newspaper with a total circulation of over 5 million. About 600,000 of those copies, almost twice the level of the next highest State, are sold in California. Respondent's and her husband's claims were based on an article that appeared in the Enquirer's October 9, 1979 issue. Both the Enquirer and the distributing company answered the complaint and made no objection to the jurisdiction of the California court.

Petitioner South is a reporter employed by the Enquirer. He is a resident of Florida, though he frequently travels to California on business. South wrote the first draft of the challenged article, and his byline appeared on it. He did most of his research in Florida, relying on phone calls to sources in California for the information contained in the article.[4] Shortly before publication, South called respondent's home and read to her husband a

---

4. The superior court found that South made at least one trip to California in connection with the article. South hotly disputes this finding, claiming that an uncontroverted affidavit shows that he never visited California to research the article. Since we do not rely for our holding on the alleged visit, . . . we find it unnecessary to consider the contention.

draft of the article so as to elicit his comments upon it. Aside from his frequent trips and phone calls, South has no other relevant contacts with California.

Petitioner Calder is also a Florida resident. He has been to California only twice—once, on a pleasure trip, prior to the publication of the article and once after to testify in an unrelated trial. Calder is president and editor of the Enquirer. He "oversee[s] just about every function of the Enquirer." He reviewed and approved the initial evaluation of the subject of the article and edited it in its final form. He also declined to print a retraction requested by respondent. Calder has no other relevant contacts with California. . . .

The Due Process Clause of the Fourteenth Amendment to the United States Constitution permits personal jurisdiction over a defendant in any State with which the defendant has "certain minimum contacts . . . such that the maintenance of the suit does not offend 'traditional notions of fair play and substantial justice.'" In judging minimum contacts, a court properly focuses on "the relationship among the defendant, the forum, and the litigation." The plaintiff's lack of "contacts" will not defeat otherwise proper jurisdiction, but they may be so manifold as to permit jurisdiction when it would not exist in their absence. Here, the plaintiff is the focus of the activities of the defendants out of which the suit arises.

The allegedly libelous story concerned the California activities of a California resident. It impugned the professionalism of an entertainer whose television career was centered in California. [The article alleged that respondent drank so heavily as to prevent her from fulfilling her professional obligations.] The article was drawn from California sources, and the brunt of the harm, in terms both of respondent's emotional distress and the injury to her professional reputation, was suffered in California. In sum, California is the focal point both of the story and of the harm suffered. Jurisdiction over petitioners is therefore proper in California based on the "effects" of their Florida conduct in California. *World-Wide Volkswagen Corp. v. Woodson*, 444 U.S. 286, 297-298 (1980).

Petitioners argue that they are not responsible for the circulation of the article in California. A reporter and an editor, they claim, have no direct economic stake in their employer's sales in a distant State. Nor are ordinary employees able to control their employer's marketing activity. The mere fact that they can "foresee" that the article will be circulated and have an effect in California is not sufficient for an assertion of jurisdiction. *World-Wide Volkswagen Corp. v. Woodson*, 444 U.S. at 295. They do not "in effect appoint the [article their] agent for service of process." *World-Wide Volkswagen Corp. v. Woodson*, 444 U.S. at 296. . . .

[But] petitioners are not charged with mere untargeted negligence. Rather, their intentional, and allegedly tortious, actions were expressly aimed at California. Petitioner South wrote and petitioner Calder edited an article that they knew would have a potentially devastating impact upon respondent. And they knew that the brunt of that injury would be felt by respondent in the State in which she lives and works and in which the National Enquirer has its largest circulation. Under the circumstances, petitioners must "reasonably anticipate being haled into court there" to answer for the truth of the statements made in their article. *World-Wide Volkswagen Corp. v. Woodson*, 444 U.S. at 297. An individual injured in California need not go to Florida to seek redress from persons who, though remaining in Florida, knowingly cause the injury in California.

Petitioners are correct that their contacts with California are not to be judged according to their employer's activities there. On the other hand, their status as employees does not somehow insulate them from jurisdiction. Each defendant's contacts with the forum State must be assessed individually. In this case, petitioners are primary participants in an alleged wrongdoing intentionally directed at a California resident, and jurisdiction over them is proper on that basis. . . .

We hold that jurisdiction over petitioners in California is proper because of their intentional conduct in Florida calculated to cause injury to respondent in California. The judgment of the California Court of Appeal is affirmed.

## Comments and Questions

1. Why did the *National Enquirer* file an answer without raising an objection to personal jurisdiction, as Calder and South did? (Hint: There are many inquiring minds in the Golden State.)

2. Note the Court's effort to distinguish *World-Wide Volkswagen*, in which defendants were charged "with mere untargeted negligence," and the instant case, where defendants' "intentional, and allegedly tortious, actions were expressly aimed at California." Are you persuaded? Does this emphasis on intentional conduct toward the forum state harken back to *Hanson v. Denkla*?

3. In *Keeton v. Hustler Magazine, Inc.*, 465 U.S. 770 (1984), decided the same day as *Calder*, a New York resident alleging defamation brought suit in the corporate defendant's home state of Ohio. When the case was dismissed because that state's statute of limitations had run, she filed in New Hampshire, which had a longer limitations period. *Hustler* objected that jurisdiction was lacking. The Court ultimately ruled that the sale in New Hampshire of 10,000 to 15,000 copies of the magazine each month, even though its only contact with the forum, was sufficient to justify the exercise of jurisdiction over defendant on this claim. "Where *Hustler Magazine* has continuously and deliberately exploited the New Hampshire market, it must reasonably anticipate being haled into court there in a libel action based on the contents of its magazine."

4. In yet another example of the expansive reach of jurisdiction in defamation cases, the Ninth Circuit Court of Appeals held that there was jurisdiction in California over the *New York Daily News* and its columnist in an action brought by a California resident, even though the newspaper sold only thirteen daily editions and eighteen Sunday editions to subscribers in

California. *See Gordy v. Daily News*, 95 F.3d 829 (9th Cir. 1996). In contrast to *Keeton*, where the rationale for the exercise of jurisdiction derived from the substantial number of magazines sold in the forum state, the court here (as in *Calder*) found determinative that the plaintiff lived in California and the column "was of a nature that would clearly have a severe impact on Gordy as an individual. It is reasonable to expect the bulk of the harm from defamation of an individual to be felt in his domicile." 95 F.3d at 833.

5. Do *Calder*, *Keeton*, and *Gordy* create a special rule of personal jurisdiction for defamation actions?

These three precedents were distinguished in *Noonan v. Winston Company*, 135 F.3d 85 (1st Cir. 1998). The plaintiff, George Noonan, was a Boston police detective actively involved in the campaign against smoking. To his chagrin, he became aware of a magazine advertisement for Winston cigarettes appearing in several magazines in France that featured his photograph. He brought a lawsuit against the tobacco company and the French advertising agency for defamation and unauthorized use of the photo in federal district court in Massachusetts. The First Circuit affirmed dismissal pursuant to Fed. R. Civ. P. 12(b)(2):

> Plaintiffs do not allege, and the record does not suggest, that any acts by [the French advertising agency] were committed with sufficient purpose to satisfy [*Calder*'s] intent requirement. The defendants did not direct their actions toward Massachusetts. That the advertisement contains French text and a French phone number suggests [it was] created for a French audience. This interpretation is corroborated, without contradiction, by [its] representative who stated that "[t]he advertisement was aimed solely at the French consumer market." Furthermore, [defendant] "was not aware that some copies of the magazines bearing the advertisement" would reach Massachusetts.
>
> In *Calder*, because the libelous story was generated from California sources, concerned a California celebrity, and appeared in a newspaper with a forum circulation of 600,000 copies, the Court found that California was the focal point of both the effect and the story. Here, however, plaintiffs' claims rest on an advertisement which appeared in 305 individual magazines circulated in Massachusetts. This small distribution, by itself, does not merit a finding that Massachusetts was the focal point of the events in question, or that [defendant] aimed the advertisements toward Massachusetts. The size of a distribution of offending material helps determine whether a defendant acted intentionally. The Supreme Court has held that a publisher's regular circulation of a large number of magazines containing allegedly libelous content in a forum state indicated deliberate and continuous exploitation of a market and, therefore, was sufficient to support jurisdiction. *See Keeton v. Hustler Magazine, Inc.*, 465 U.S. 770, 781 (1984). . . .
>
> Plaintiffs urge us to rely on *Gordy v. The Daily News*, 95 F.3d 829 (9th Cir. 1996), a case in which the Ninth Circuit found that the distribution of under twenty newspapers was sufficient to confer jurisdiction over a foreign newspaper and its reporter. Unlike [the French defendant], however, the *Gordy* defendants targeted the forum state by distributing newspapers via regular customer subscriptions to forum addresses. Here, as noted, [defendant]

denies knowing the ultimate destination of the magazines that reached Massachusetts, and plaintiffs have not alleged otherwise. While we sympathize with George Noonan's distress at seeing his image used to promote a product he despises, his Massachusetts-based injury is not enough to support jurisdiction over the defendants. To find otherwise would inappropriately credit random, isolated, or fortuitous contacts and negate the reason for the purposeful availment requirement. Without finding minimum contacts, we need not, and do not, proceed to the reasonableness analysis.

135 F.3d at 90-92.

6. What if the alleged defamatory material appears on the Internet rather than in print? Katherine Griffis brought a defamation action against Marianne Luban based on messages Luban posted on *sci.archaeology*, an Internet newsgroup, challenging Griffis's credentials as an Egyptologist and accusing her of getting her degree from a "box of Cracker Jacks." Griffis, who taught courses in ancient Egyptian history at the University of Alabama, filed suit in Alabama state court. Luban, a Minnesota resident, defaulted on advice of counsel, who believed the Alabama courts did not have jurisdiction over her.

Griffis then sued to enforce the Alabama judgment in Minnesota. Defendant answered that it was not entitled to full faith and credit because the Alabama court lacked personal jurisdiction. The Minnesota Supreme Court agreed: The mere fact that Luban had known that the subject of her criticisms lived in Alabama and that the Internet postings would affect her there was not sufficient to establish jurisdiction in that state, given the universal reach of the Internet. *Griffis v. Luban*, 646 N.W.2d 527 (Minn. 2002):

> While the record supports the conclusion that Luban's statements were intentionally directed at Griffis, whom she knew to be an Alabama resident, we conclude that the evidence does not demonstrate that Luban's statements were "expressly aimed" at the state of Alabama. The parties agree that Luban published the allegedly defamatory statements on an internet newsgroup accessible to the public, but nothing in the record indicates that the statements were targeted at the state of Alabama or at an Alabama audience beyond Griffis herself. The newsgroup on which Luban posted her statements was organized around the subjects of archeology and Egyptology, not Alabama or the University of Alabama academic community. According to Griffis, Luban's messages were widely read by her colleagues—the other amateur Egyptologists who participated in the *sci.archaeology* newsgroup. But Griffis has not presented evidence that any other person in Alabama read the statements. Nor has she asserted that Alabama has a unique relationship with the field of Egyptology, like the close relationship between the plaintiff's profession and the forum state that the Supreme Court found relevant in *Calder*. Therefore, even if we assume Luban's statements were widely read by followers of the *sci.archaeology* newsgroup, the readers most likely would be spread all around the country—maybe even around the world—and not necessarily in the Alabama forum. The fact that messages posted to the newsgroup *could* have been read in Alabama, just as they *could* have been read anywhere in the world, cannot suffice to establish Alabama as the focal point of the defendant's conduct.

646 N.W.2d 536.

The opposite conclusion was reached in *Abiomed, Inc. v. Turnbull*, 379 F. Supp. 2d 90 (D. Ma. 2005), in which the Massachusetts corporate plaintiff alleged that an Ohio resident and employee of a competitor had engaged in a protracted campaign of defamation on the Internet. Turnbull allegedly posted several hundred anonymous messages on a *Yahoo.com* message board dedicated to discussion of Abiomed and frequented by Massachusetts residents. Concluding that "the hailing of the defendant into a Massachusetts court to answer for his actions was foreseeable, if not inevitable," the 12(b)(2) motion to dismiss was denied.

We will return to the intriguing question of jurisdiction based on Internet connections, and defamation on the Internet, in Section K, later in this chapter.

7. *Calder* allowed suit against the *Enquirer*'s editor and reporter because each knew the major impact of the story would be felt in California, thus establishing a purposeful connection to the forum. Could that theory justify exercising jurisdiction over *the source* of a story as well? In *Hugel v. McNell*, 886 F.2d 1 (1st Cir. 1989), *cert. denied*, 494 U.S. 1079 (1990), the First Circuit answered in the affirmative. Defendants were the sources of information leading to publication of a *Washington Post* article entitled "CIA Spymaster Accused of Improper Stock Practices." The story forced Hugel to resign his post as deputy director of the Central Intelligence Agency, and he filed a defamation action against the nonresident McNells in the federal district court in New Hampshire.

Defendants challenged jurisdiction, but the First Circuit Court of Appeals disagreed:

> The McNells knew that release of the allegedly false information would have a devastating impact on Hugel, and it can be fairly inferred that they intended the brunt of the injury to be felt in New Hampshire where Hugel had an established reputation as a businessman and public servant. . . . The McNells could reasonably expect to be haled into a New Hampshire court to answer for their conduct, and thus the assertion of *in personam* jurisdiction over the McNells satisfies the dictates of due process.

But compare *National Association of Real Estate Appraisers, Inc. v. Schaeffer*, 1989 WL 267762 (C.D. Cal. 1989). After Schaeffer (a Rhode Island resident) obtained certification from the plaintiff association (an Arizona corporation) for his pet cat Tobias to be an appraiser, he publicized the incident to show the lax licensing standards in the real estate industry. The *Orange County Register* (a California newspaper) telephoned Schaeffer in Rhode Island, and he responded to questions and the reporter's request for a photo of Tobias. The *Register* ran the story, which was disseminated nationwide.

The California federal district court granted Schaeffer's motion to dismiss for lack of personal jurisdiction, concluding that his response to an unsolicited phone call was insufficient to constitute purposeful minimum contacts with California. Unlike *Calder*, where the defendants knew that Shirley Jones would bear the brunt of her injury in her home state of California, the plaintiff association here was not located in California and thus it could not be said that defendant's conduct was calculated to cause injury in the state.

Jurisdiction was similarly found lacking in *Madara v. Hall*, 916 F.2d 1510 (11th Cir. 1990), a libel action arising from unflattering comments made by entertainer Daryl Hall while interviewed by telephone in New York. The action was filed by the California plaintiff in Florida, which had a generous statute of limitations and where a small number of copies of the magazine in which the story appeared were sold. Defendant had also performed occasional concerts in Florida and his records were sold there, but these activities were unrelated to the allegedly libelous interview, and the court concluded that Hall had not established purposeful minimum contacts with Florida:

> Simply giving an interview to a reporter is not enough to cause Hall to anticipate being haled into court in Florida. Hall was not the magazine's publisher and did not control its circulation and distribution; thus, he is in a qualitatively different position than the defendant [magazine] in *Keeton*. . . . By giving the interview, Hall did not appoint copies of the magazine as his agent for service of process wherever a third party, the publisher, might choose to send these magazines.

916 F.2d at 1519.

---

We now return to the product liability area. What do the next two cases teach us about the outer boundaries of personal jurisdiction based on the global commerce in goods, and the viability of the "stream of commerce" theory discussed in *World-Wide Volkswagen?*

# ■ ASAHI METAL INDUSTRY CO., LTD. v. SUPERIOR COURT OF CALIFORNIA, SOLANO COUNTY
*480 U.S. 102 (1987)*

Justice O'CONNOR announced the judgment of the Court and delivered the unanimous opinion of the Court with respect to Part I, the opinion of the Court with respect to Part II-B, in which the CHIEF JUSTICE, Justice BRENNAN, Justice WHITE, Justice MARSHALL, Justice BLACKMUN, Justice POWELL, and Justice STEVENS join, and an opinion with respect to Parts II-A and III, in which the CHIEF JUSTICE, Justice POWELL, and Justice SCALIA join:

This case presents the question whether the mere awareness on the part of a foreign defendant that the components it manufactured, sold, and delivered outside the United States would reach the forum State in the stream of commerce constitutes "minimum contacts" between the defendant and the forum State such that the exercise of jurisdiction "does not offend 'traditional notions of fair play and substantial justice.'" *International Shoe Co. v. Washington*, 326 U.S. 310, 316 (1945).

*[handwritten marginalia: Zurcher → Cheng Shin (Taiwan) ↓ Rule 14 Asahi (Japan)]*

## I

On September 23, 1978, on Interstate Highway 80 in Solano County, California, Gary Zurcher lost control of his Honda motorcycle and collided with a tractor. Zurcher was severely injured, and his passenger and wife, Ruth Ann Moreno, was killed. In September 1979, Zurcher filed a product liability action in the Superior Court of the State of California in and for the County of Solano. Zurcher alleged that the 1978 accident was caused by a sudden loss of air and an explosion in the rear tire of the motorcycle, and alleged that the motorcycle tire, tube, and sealant were defective. Zurcher's complaint named, inter alia, Cheng Shin Rubber Industrial Co., Ltd. (Cheng Shin), the Taiwanese manufacturer of the tube. Cheng Shin in turn filed a cross-complaint seeking indemnification from its codefendants and from petitioner, Asahi Metal Industry Co., Ltd. (Asahi), the manufacturer of the tube's valve assembly. Zurcher's claims against Cheng Shin and the other defendants were eventually settled and dismissed, leaving only Cheng Shin's indemnity action against Asahi.

California's long-arm statute authorizes the exercise of jurisdiction "on any basis not inconsistent with the Constitution of this state or of the United States." Asahi moved to quash Cheng Shin's service of summons, arguing the State could not exert jurisdiction over it consistent with the Due Process Clause of the Fourteenth Amendment.

In relation to the motion, the following information was submitted by Asahi and Cheng Shin. Asahi is a Japanese corporation. It manufactures tire valve assemblies in Japan and sells the assemblies to Cheng Shin, and to several other tire manufacturers, for use as components in finished tire tubes. Asahi's sales to Cheng Shin took place in Taiwan. The shipments from Asahi to Cheng Shin were sent from Japan to Taiwan. Cheng Shin bought and incorporated into its tire tubes 150,000 Asahi valve assemblies in 1978; 500,000 in 1979; 500,000 in 1980; 100,000 in 1981; and 100,000 in 1982. Sales to Cheng Shin accounted for 1.24 percent of Asahi's income in 1981 and 0.44 percent in 1982. Cheng Shin alleged that approximately 20 percent of its sales in the United States are in California. Cheng Shin purchases valve assemblies from other suppliers as well, and sells finished tubes throughout the world.

In 1983 an attorney for Cheng Shin conducted an informal examination of the valve stems of the tire tubes sold in one cycle store in Solano County. The attorney declared that of the approximately 115 tire tubes in the store, 97 were purportedly manufactured in Japan or Taiwan, and of those 97, 21 valve stems were marked with the circled letter "A", apparently Asahi's trademark. Of the 21 Asahi valve stems, 12 were incorporated into Cheng Shin tire tubes. The store contained 41 other Cheng Shin tubes that incorporated the valve assemblies of other manufacturers. An affidavit of a manager of Cheng Shin whose duties included the purchasing of component parts stated: "'In discussions with Asahi regarding the purchase of valve stem assemblies the fact that my Company sells tubes throughout the world and specifically the United States has been discussed. I am informed and believe that Asahi was fully aware that valve stem assemblies sold to my Company and to others would end up throughout the United States and in California.'" An affidavit of the president of Asahi, on the other hand, declared that Asahi "'has never contemplated that its limited sales of tire valves to Cheng Shin in Taiwan would subject it to lawsuits in California.'" The record does not include any contract between Cheng Shin and Asahi.

Primarily on the basis of the above information, the Superior Court denied the motion to quash summons, stating: "Asahi obviously does business on an international scale. It is not unreasonable that they defend claims of defect in their product on an international scale."

The Court of Appeal of the State of California issued a peremptory writ of mandate commanding the Superior Court to quash service of summons. The court concluded that "it would be unreasonable to require Asahi to respond in California solely on the basis of ultimately realized foreseeability that the product into which its component was embodied would be sold all over the world including California."

The Supreme Court of the State of California reversed and discharged the writ issued by the Court of Appeal. The court observed: "Asahi has no offices, property or agents in California. It solicits no business in California and has made no direct sales [in California]." Moreover, "Asahi did not design or control the system of distribution that carried its valve assemblies into California." Nevertheless, the court found the exercise of jurisdiction over Asahi to be consistent with the Due Process Clause. It concluded that Asahi knew that some of the valve assemblies sold to Cheng Shin would be incorporated into tire tubes sold in California, and that Asahi benefited indirectly from the sale in California of products incorporating its components. The court considered Asahi's intentional act of placing its components into the stream of commerce—that is, by delivering the components to Cheng Shin in Taiwan—coupled with Asahi's awareness that some of the components would eventually find their way into California, sufficient to form the basis for state court jurisdiction under the Due Process Clause.

We granted certiorari, and now reverse.

## II

### A

The Due Process Clause of the Fourteenth Amendment limits the power of a state court to exert personal jurisdiction over a nonresident defendant. "[T]he constitutional touchstone" of the determination whether an exercise of personal jurisdiction comports with due process "remains whether the defendant purposefully established 'minimum contacts' in the forum State." *Burger King Corp. v. Rudzewicz*, 471 U.S. 462, 474 (1985). Most recently we have reaffirmed the oft-quoted reasoning of *Hanson v. Denckla* that minimum contacts must have a basis in "some act by which the defendant purposefully avails itself of the privilege of conducting activities within the forum State, thus invoking the benefits and protections of its laws." *Burger King*, 471 U.S. at 475. "Jurisdiction is proper . . . where the contacts proximately result from actions by the defendant himself that create a 'substantial connection' with the forum State."

Applying the principle that minimum contacts must be based on an act of the defendant, the Court in *World-Wide Volkswagen Corp. v. Woodson* rejected the assertion that a consumer's unilateral act of bringing the defendant's product into the forum State was a sufficient constitutional basis for personal jurisdiction over the defendant. It had been argued in *World-Wide Volkswagen* that because an automobile retailer and its wholesale distributor sold a product mobile by design and purpose, they could foresee being haled into court in the distant States into which their customers might drive. The Court rejected this concept of foreseeability as an insufficient basis for jurisdiction under the Due Process Clause. The Court disclaimed, however, the idea that "foreseeability is wholly irrelevant" to personal jurisdiction, concluding that "[t]he forum State does not exceed its powers under the Due Process Clause if it asserts personal jurisdiction over a corporation that delivers its products into the stream of commerce with the expectation that they will be purchased by consumers in the forum State." The Court reasoned: "When a corporation 'purposefully avails itself of the privilege of conducting activities within the forum State,' *Hanson v. Denckla*, it has clear notice that it is subject to suit there, and can act to alleviate the risk of burdensome litigation by procuring insurance, passing the expected costs on to customers, or, if the risks are too great, severing its connection with the State. Hence if the sale of a product of a manufacturer or distributor . . . is not simply an isolated occurrence, but arises from the efforts of the manufacturer or distributor to serve, directly or indirectly, the market for its product in other States, it is not unreasonable to subject it to suit in one of those States if its allegedly defective merchandise has there been the source of injury to its owners or to others."

In *World-Wide Volkswagen* itself, the state court sought to base jurisdiction not on any act of the defendant, but on the foreseeable unilateral actions of the consumer. Since *World-Wide Volkswagen*, lower courts have been confronted with cases in which the defendant acted by placing a product in the stream of commerce, and the stream eventually swept defendant's product into the forum State, but the defendant did nothing else to purposefully avail itself of the market in the forum State. Some courts have understood the Due Process Clause, as interpreted in *World-Wide Volkswagen*, to allow an exercise of personal jurisdiction to be based on no more than the defendant's act of placing the product in the stream of commerce. Other courts have understood the Due Process Clause and the above-quoted language in

*World-Wide Volkswagen* to require the action of the defendant to be more purposefully directed at the forum State than the mere act of placing a product in the stream of commerce.

The reasoning of the Supreme Court of California in the present case illustrates the former interpretation of *World-Wide Volkswagen*. The Supreme Court of California held that, because the stream of commerce eventually brought some valves Asahi sold Cheng Shin into California, Asahi's awareness that its valves would be sold in California was sufficient to permit California to exercise jurisdiction over Asahi consistent with the requirements of the Due Process Clause. The Supreme Court of California's position was consistent with those courts that have held that mere foreseeability or awareness was a constitutionally sufficient basis for personal jurisdiction if the defendant's product made its way into the forum State while still in the stream of commerce.

Other courts, however, have understood the Due Process Clause to require something more than that the defendant was aware of its product's entry into the forum State through the stream of commerce in order for the State to exert jurisdiction over the defendant. In the present case, for example, the State Court of Appeal did not read the Due Process Clause, as interpreted by *World-Wide Volkswagen*, to allow "mere foreseeability that the product will enter the forum state [to] be enough by itself to establish jurisdiction over the distributor and retailer." . . .

We now find this latter position to be consonant with the requirements of due process. The "substantial connection" between the defendant and the forum State necessary for a finding of minimum contacts must come about by an action of the defendant purposefully directed toward the forum State. The placement of a product into the stream of commerce, without more, is not an act of the defendant purposefully directed toward the forum State. Additional conduct of the defendant may indicate an intent or purpose to serve the market in the forum State, for example, designing the product for the market in the forum State, advertising in the forum State, establishing channels for providing regular advice to customers in the forum State, or marketing the product through a distributor who has agreed to serve as the sales agent in the forum State. But a defendant's awareness that the stream of commerce may or will sweep the product into the forum State does not convert the mere act of placing the product into the stream into an act purposefully directed toward the forum State.

Assuming, *arguendo*, that respondents have established Asahi's awareness that some of the valves sold to Cheng Shin would be incorporated into tire tubes sold in California, respondents have not demonstrated any action by Asahi to purposefully avail itself of the California market. Asahi does not do business in California. It has no office, agents, employees, or property in California. It does not advertise or otherwise solicit business in California. It did not create, control, or employ the distribution system that brought its valves to California. There is no evidence that Asahi designed its product in anticipation of sales in California. On the basis of these facts, the exertion of personal jurisdiction over Asahi by the Superior Court of California* exceeds the limits of due process.

**B**

The strictures of the Due Process Clause forbid a state court to exercise personal jurisdiction over Asahi under circumstances that would offend " 'traditional notions of fair play and substantial justice.' " *International Shoe Co. v. Washington.*

We have previously explained that the determination of the reasonableness of the exercise of jurisdiction in each case will depend on an evaluation of several factors. A court must consider the burden on the defendant, the interests of the forum State, and the plaintiff's interest in obtaining relief. It must also weigh in its determination "the interstate judicial system's interest in obtaining the most efficient resolution of controversies; and the shared interest of the several States in furthering fundamental substantive social policies." *World-Wide Volkswagen.*

A consideration of these factors in the present case clearly reveals the unreasonableness of the assertion of jurisdiction over Asahi, even apart from the question of the placement of goods in the stream of commerce.

Certainly the burden on the defendant in this case is severe. Asahi has been commanded by the Supreme Court of California not only to traverse the distance between Asahi's headquarters in Japan and the Superior Court of California in and for the County of Solano, but also to submit its dispute with Cheng Shin to a foreign nation's judicial system. The unique burdens placed upon one who must defend oneself in a foreign legal system should have significant weight in assessing the reasonableness of stretching the long arm of personal jurisdiction over national borders.

When minimum contacts have been established, often the interests of the plaintiff and the forum in the exercise of jurisdiction will justify even the serious burdens placed on the alien defendant. In the present case, however, the interests of the plaintiff and the forum in California's assertion of jurisdiction over Asahi are slight. All that remains is a claim for indemnification asserted by Cheng Shin, a Taiwanese corporation, against Asahi. The transaction on which the indemnification claim is based took place in Taiwan; Asahi's components were shipped from Japan to Taiwan. Cheng Shin has not demonstrated that it is more convenient for it to litigate its indemnification claim against Asahi in California rather than in Taiwan or Japan.

Because the plaintiff is not a California resident, California's legitimate interests in the dispute have considerably diminished. The Supreme Court of California argued that the State had an interest in "protecting its consumers by ensuring that foreign manufacturers comply with the state's safety

---

*We have no occasion here to determine whether Congress could, consistent with the Due Process Clause of the Fifth Amendment, authorize federal court personal jurisdiction over alien defendants based on the aggregate of national contacts, rather than on the contacts between the defendant and the State in which the federal court sits. [*Eds.' Note:* Six years later, Fed. R. Civ. P. 4(k)(2) was adopted, as discussed in Part G, *supra.*]

standards." The State Supreme Court's definition of California's interest, however, was overly broad. The dispute between Cheng Shin and Asahi is primarily about indemnification rather than safety standards. Moreover, it is not at all clear at this point that California law should govern the question whether a Japanese corporation should indemnify a Taiwanese corporation on the basis of a sale made in Taiwan and a shipment of goods from Japan to Taiwan. The possibility of being haled into a California court as a result of an accident involving Asahi's components undoubtedly creates an additional deterrent to the manufacture of unsafe components; however, similar pressures will be placed on Asahi by the purchasers of its components as long as those who use Asahi components in their final products, and sell those products in California, are subject to the application of California tort law.

*World-Wide Volkswagen* also admonished courts to take into consideration the interests of the "several States," in addition to the forum State, in the efficient judicial resolution of the dispute and the advancement of substantive policies. In the present case, this advice calls for a court to consider the procedural and substantive policies of other nations whose interests are affected by the assertion of jurisdiction by the California court. The procedural and substantive interests of other nations in a state court's assertion of jurisdiction over an alien defendant will differ from case to case. In every case, however, those interests, as well as the Federal interest in Government's foreign relations policies, will be best served by a careful inquiry into the reasonableness of the assertion of jurisdiction in the particular case, and an unwillingness to find the serious burdens on an alien defendant outweighed by minimal interests on the part of the plaintiff or the forum State. "Great care and reserve should be exercised when extending our notions of personal jurisdiction into the international field." *United States v. First National City Bank*, 379 U.S. 378, 404 (1965) (Harlan, J., dissenting).

Considering the international context, the heavy burden on the alien defendant, and the slight interests of the plaintiff and the forum State, the exercise of personal jurisdiction by a California court over Asahi in this instance would be unreasonable and unfair.

## III

Because the facts of this case do not establish minimum contacts such that the exercise of personal jurisdiction is consistent with fair play and substantial justice, the judgment of the Supreme Court of California is reversed, and the case is remanded for further proceedings not inconsistent with this opinion.

It is so ordered.

Justice BRENNAN, with whom Justice WHITE, Justice MARSHALL, and Justice BLACKMUN join, concurring in part and concurring in the judgment:

I do not agree with the interpretation in Part II-A of the stream-of-commerce theory, nor with the conclusion that Asahi did not "purposely avail itself of the California market." I do agree, however, with the Court's conclusion in Part II-B that the exercise of personal jurisdiction over Asahi in this case would not comport with "fair play and substantial justice," *International Shoe Co. v. Washington*. This is one of those rare cases in which "minimum requirements inherent in the concept of 'fair play and substantial justice' . . . defeat the reasonableness of jurisdiction even [though] the defendant has purposefully engaged in forum activities." *Burger King Corp. v. Rudzewicz*, 471 U.S. 462, 477-478 (1985). I therefore join Parts I and II-B of the Court's opinion, and write separately to explain my disagreement with Part II-A.

Part II-A states that "a defendant's awareness that the stream of commerce may or will sweep the product into the forum State does not convert the mere act of placing the product into the stream into an act purposefully directed toward the forum State." Under this view, a plaintiff would be required to show "[a]dditional conduct" directed toward the forum before finding the exercise of jurisdiction over the defendant to be consistent with the Due Process Clause. I see no need for such a showing, however. The stream of commerce refers not to unpredictable currents or eddies, but to the regular and anticipated flow of products from manufacture to distribution to retail sale. As long as a participant in this process is aware that the final product is being marketed in the forum State, the possibility of a lawsuit there cannot come as a surprise. Nor will the litigation present a burden for which there is no corresponding benefit. A defendant who has placed goods in the stream of commerce benefits economically from the retail sale of the final product in the forum State, and indirectly benefits from the State's laws that regulate and facilitate commercial activity. These benefits accrue regardless of whether that participant directly conducts business in the forum State, or engages in additional conduct directed toward that State. Accordingly, most courts and commentators have found that jurisdiction premised on the placement of a product into the stream of commerce is consistent with the Due Process Clause, and have not required a showing of additional conduct.

The endorsement in Part II-A of what appears to be the minority view among Federal Courts of Appeals represents a marked retreat from the analysis in *World-Wide Volkswagen v. Woodson*. In that case, "respondents [sought] to base jurisdiction on one, isolated occurrence and whatever inferences can be drawn therefrom: the fortuitous circumstance that a single Audi automobile, sold in New York to New York residents, happened to suffer an accident while passing through Oklahoma." The Court held that the possibility of an accident in Oklahoma, while to some extent foreseeable in light of the inherent mobility of the automobile, was not enough to establish minimum contacts between the forum State and the retailer or distributor. The Court then carefully explained:

> [T]his is not to say, of course, that foreseeability is wholly irrelevant. But the foreseeability that is critical to due process analysis is not the mere likelihood that a product will find its way into the forum State. Rather, it is that the

defendant's conduct and connection with the forum State are such that he should reasonably anticipate being haled into Court there.

The Court reasoned that when a corporation may reasonably anticipate litigation in a particular forum, it cannot claim that such litigation is unjust or unfair, because it "can act to alleviate the risk of burdensome litigation by procuring insurance, passing the expected costs on to consumers, or, if the risks are too great, severing its connection with the State." . . .

In this case, the facts found by the California Supreme Court support its finding of minimum contacts. The court found that "[a]lthough Asahi did not design or control the system of distribution that carried its valve assemblies into California, Asahi was aware of the distribution system's operation, and it knew that it would benefit economically from the sale in California of products incorporating its components."[4] Accordingly, I cannot join the determination in Part II-A that Asahi's regular and extensive sales of component parts to a manufacturer it knew was making regular sales of the final product in California is insufficient to establish minimum contacts with California.

Justice STEVENS, with whom Justice WHITE and Justice BLACKMUN join, concurring in part and concurring in the judgment:

The judgment of the Supreme Court of California should be reversed for the reasons stated in Part II-B of the Court's opinion. While I join Parts I and II-B, I do not join Part II-A for two reasons. First, it is not necessary to the Court's decision. An examination of minimum contacts is not always necessary to determine whether a state court's assertion of personal jurisdiction is constitutional. Part II-B establishes, after considering the factors set forth in *World-Wide Volkswagen Corp. v. Woodson*, that California's exercise of jurisdiction over Asahi in this case would be "unreasonable and unfair." This finding alone requires reversal; this case fits within the rule that "minimum requirements inherent in the concept of 'fair play and substantial justice' may defeat the reasonableness of jurisdiction even if the defendant has purposefully engaged in forum activities." *Burger King*, 471 U.S. at 477-478. Accordingly, I see no reason in this case for the plurality to articulate "purposeful direction" or any other test as the nexus between an act of a defendant and the forum State that is necessary to establish minimum contacts.

Second, even assuming that the test ought to be formulated here, Part II-A misapplies it to the facts of this case. The plurality seems to assume that an unwavering line can be drawn between "mere awareness" that a component will find its way into the forum State and "purposeful availment" of the forum's market. Over the course of its dealings with Cheng Shin, Asahi has arguably engaged in a higher quantum of conduct than "[t]he placement

---

4. Moreover, the Court found that "at least 18 percent of the tubes sold in a particular California motorcycle supply shop contained Asahi valve assemblies," and that Asahi had an ongoing business relationship with Cheng Shin involving average annual sales of hundreds of thousands of valve assemblies.

of a product into the stream of commerce, without more. . . ." Whether or not this conduct rises to the level of purposeful availment requires a constitutional determination that is affected by the volume, the value, and the hazardous character of the components. In most circumstances I would be inclined to conclude that a regular course of dealing that results in deliveries of over 100,000 units annually over a period of several years would constitute "purposeful availment" even though the item delivered to the forum State was a standard product marketed throughout the world.

## Comments and Questions

1. Identify the facts pertinent to the jurisdictional issue in *Asahi*, as well as the gaps in what is known about Asahi's connections to California.

2. How is the issue of foreseeability raised by the conflicting affidavits submitted by Cheng Shin and Asahi? What does *Asahi* add to our understanding of the interplay among the concepts of foreseeability, purposeful availment, and minimum contacts?

3. What does *Asahi* actually hold? Answering this question requires a close reading of the opinion of the Court authored by Justice O'Connor (the critical section IIA of which is joined only by Rehnquist, Powell, and Scalia) as well as the separate opinions of Justice Brennan (joined by three colleagues) and Justice Stevens. Sketch out the areas of agreement and disagreement among the O'Connor group, the Brennan group, and Justice Stevens. Which group is Stevens closest to? Although all agree on the end result—that jurisdiction cannot be exercised over Asahi—they travel quite distinct paths to reach that point.

4. What role do the "fair play and substantial justice" factors play in the *Asahi* decision? Consider the significance of these facts: (1) Asahi was a foreign corporation, and would have been subjected to the unfamiliar American legal system if compelled to defend in California; (2) the only remaining claim against Asahi was a third-party claim for indemnification asserted by another foreign corporation (the original plaintiff Zurcher having settled and left the litigation); (3) the valves in question traveled a circuitous route—Asahi manufactured the valve assemblies in Japan, then shipped them to Taiwan, where they were incorporated into Cheng Shin's tire tubes, and they ended up on a motorcycle in California.

What is the relationship between the "fair play" factors and the "minimum-contacts" test after *Asahi*? Have the former been elevated to co-equal status with the latter? This matter is explored in more depth in *Burger King Corp. v. Rudzewicz*, set out later in this chapter.

5. Note Justice O'Connor's heavy emphasis on the factor of purposeful conduct directed toward the forum:

The placement of a product into the stream of commerce, without more, is not an act of the defendant purposefully directed toward the forum State. *Additional conduct* of the defendant may indicate an intent or purpose to serve the market in the forum State, for example, designing the product for the market in the forum State, advertising in the forum State, establishing channels for providing regular advice to customers in the forum State, or marketing the product through a distributor who has agreed to serve as the sales agent in the forum State (emphasis added).

Such "additional conduct" was found in the case of the French corporation Perrier, sued in two states on claims arising from its startling admission that benzene was found in its "naturally pure" water. *In re Perrier Bottled Water Litigation*, 754 F. Supp. 264 (D. Conn. 1990). The district court found that Perrier had designed its containers specifically for U.S. markets, as its bottles were labeled in ounces rather than metric measures. *See also State of New Hampshire v. North Atlantic Refining Ltd.*, 160 N.H. 275, 284-285 (2010) (defendant in groundwater contamination action formulated its gasoline specifically for the northeastern U.S. market, including New Hampshire).

Similarly in *Vermeulen v. Renault*, 985 F.2d 1534, 1550 (11th Cir. 1993), the court found jurisdiction over the French auto manufacturer in a design defect action brought by an accident victim in Georgia. The Eleventh Circuit concluded that Renault had delivered its cars into the stream of commerce with the expectation that they would be purchased by consumers in the United States, and found "additional conduct" of the type Justice O'Connor referred to in *Asahi*: "[Defendant] designed the Renault LeCar for the American market, advertised the LeCar in the United States, established channels for customers in the United States to seek advice about the LeCar, and maintained a distribution network by which LeCars were imported into the United States." 985 F.2d at 1550.

Distinguishing *Asahi*, the *Vermeulen* court wrote:

First, the plaintiff in this case is not a foreign corporation seeking indemnification from another foreign corporation, as in *Asahi*, but rather a United States citizen who seeks relief for the crippling injuries she suffered as a result of an alleged defect in her Renault LeCar. Her interest in having her case adjudicated in this country is manifest.

Second, this case, unlike *Asahi*, is not about indemnification but rather about product safety. The interest of the United States in adjudicating this dispute is also manifest, given that it has a compelling interest in protecting persons within its borders from unsafe products that find their way into the country.

985 F.2d at 1551.

6. If you are frustrated by *Asahi*'s lack of clarity, you are not alone. The Fifth Circuit Court of Appeals expressed it this way: "Because the [Supreme] Court's splintered view of minimum contacts in *Asahi* provides no clear guidance on this issue, we continue to gauge [the nonresident defendant's] contacts with Texas by the stream of commerce standard as described in *World-Wide Volkswagen* and embraced in this circuit." *Ruston Gas Turbines, Inc. v. Donaldson Company, Inc.*, 9 F.3d 415, 420 (5th Cir. 1993).

The federal circuits were understandably split on the proper reading of *Asahi*. For a case siding with the Brennan group, see *Barone v. Rich Bros. Interstate Display Fireworks Co.*, 25 F.3d 610 (8th Cir. 1994), holding a Japanese manufacturer subject to jurisdiction in a personal injury action in Nebraska pursuant to a liberal stream of commerce analysis. The Eighth Circuit noted that "a plurality of the Court in *Asahi* indicated its desire to limit this line of cases, but Justice O'Connor failed to muster a majority on that issue. . . . Five justices agreed that continuous placement of a significant number of products into the stream of commerce with knowledge that the product would be distributed into the forum state represents sufficient minimum contacts to satisfy due process."

Contrast that with *Bridgeport Music, Inc. v. Still N The Water Pub*, 327 F.3d 472 (6th Cir. 2003), dismissing a copyright infringement action against a music publisher based on Justice O'Connor's narrower "stream of commerce *plus*" approach, which the Sixth Circuit found controlling: "The placement of a product into the stream of commerce, without more, is *not* an act of the defendant purposefully directed toward the forum State."

To read more about the application of stream of commerce theory in international product liability cases in the years following *Asahi*, see Gary Born and Peter Rutledge, *International Civil Litigation in United States Courts* 137-162 (5th ed. 2011).

7. Does *Asahi* permit a manufacturer to insulate itself from suit merely by using an intermediary distributor, even when it is aware that its products are being sold and used in the forum state? If so, isn't this a big "escape clause" for corporate wrongdoers? We'll come back to this matter again in the next case.

8. What result if the tire valve had been manufactured by an Ohio corporation at a factory in Cleveland, shipped to a Pennsylvania company for assembly into a tube in Pittsburgh, and then ended up in a tire that exploded in California? (In other words, remove the international dimension.) What additional information would you need to decide if the California court would have jurisdiction over the domestic Ohio company in an action brought by the accident victim?

9. The issues raised by *Asahi* divided the business community as sharply as the Court. The Chamber of Commerce of the United Kingdom submitted an *amicus* brief in support of Asahi Metal Industry Co., Ltd., arguing that "a rule of U.S. law that a foreign component part manufacturer is subject to the personal jurisdiction of any U.S. court in the territory in which it may be aware its foreign customer's products might come to rest, would substantially increase the costs and uncertainties of international trade for British manufacturers," and could lead to retaliatory measures adversely affecting free trade.

The California Manufacturers Association (CMA) countered in its *amicus* brief that the assertion of jurisdiction in such cases would protect California consumers from "duplicative and costly litigation which would otherwise be made necessary but for the granting of jurisdiction; and the manufacturer doing business in California, subjected to the sword of myriad state laws, rules and regulations, should be entitled to seek a shield of protection from those same laws when faced with defending an action in court commenced as a result of the use of a faulty foreign or alien component." The CMA further asserted that a "reversal of the California court's holding [asserting jurisdiction] may jeopardize the lives, safety and health of California consumers, businesses and manufacturers, by providing another barrier which increases the difficulty an individual or company presently confronts when seeking a legitimate and lawful solution to the assignment of responsibility."

---

Given the importance of the jurisdictional issue in global trade contexts like *Asahi*, and the inconclusiveness of the Court's split resolution, it was inevitable that the matter would be revisited. It just took the Court twenty-four years to do so.

## ■ J. MCINTYRE MACHINERY, LTD. v. NICASTRO
### *131 S. Ct. 2780 (2011)*

JUSTICE KENNEDY announced the judgment of the Court and delivered an opinion, in which The CHIEF JUSTICE, Justice SCALIA, and Justice THOMAS join.

Whether a person or entity is subject to the jurisdiction of a state court despite not having been present in the State either at the time of suit or at the time of the alleged injury, and despite not having consented to the exercise of jurisdiction, is a question that arises with great frequency in the routine course of litigation. The rules and standards for determining when a State does or does not have jurisdiction over an absent party have been unclear because of decades-old questions left open in *Asahi Metal Industry Co. v. Superior Court of Cal., Solano Cty.*, 480 U.S. 102 (1987).

Here, the Supreme Court of New Jersey, relying in part on *Asahi*, held that New Jersey's courts can exercise jurisdiction over a foreign manufacturer of a product so long as the manufacturer "knows or reasonably should know that its products are distributed through a nationwide distribution system that might lead to those products being sold in any of the fifty states." *Nicastro v. McIntyre Machinery America, Ltd.*, 201 N. J. 48, 76, 77, 987 A. 2d 575, 591, 592 (2010). Applying that test, the court concluded that a British manufacturer of scrap metal machines was subject to jurisdiction in New Jersey, even though at no time had it advertised in, sent goods to, or in any relevant sense targeted the State.

That decision cannot be sustained. Although the New Jersey Supreme Court issued an extensive opinion with careful attention to this Court's cases and to its own precedent, the "stream of commerce" metaphor carried the decision far afield. Due process protects the defendant's right not to be coerced except by lawful judicial power. As a general rule, the exercise of judicial power is not lawful unless the defendant "purposefully avails itself of the privilege of conducting activities within the forum State, thus invoking the benefits and protections of its laws." *Hanson v. Denckla*. There may be exceptions, say, for instance, in cases involving an intentional tort. But the general rule is applicable in this products-liability case, and the so-called "stream-of-commerce" doctrine cannot displace it.

*Nicastro → McIntyre(UK)*
*NJ             ↓*
*Distribution*
*| nat'l solicitation*

## I

This case arises from a products-liability suit filed in New Jersey state court. Robert Nicastro seriously injured his hand while using a metal-shearing machine manufactured by J. McIntyre Machinery, Ltd. (J. McIntyre). The accident occurred in New Jersey, but the machine was manufactured in England, where J. McIntyre is incorporated and operates. The question here is whether the New Jersey courts have jurisdiction over J. McIntyre, notwithstanding the fact that the company at no time either marketed goods in the State or shipped them there. Nicastro was a plaintiff in the New Jersey trial court and is the respondent here; J. McIntyre was a defendant and is now the petitioner.

At oral argument in this Court, Nicastro's counsel stressed three primary facts in defense of New Jersey's assertion of jurisdiction over J. McIntyre. See Tr. of Oral Arg. 29-30.

First, an independent company agreed to sell J. McIntyre's machines in the United States. J. McIntyre itself did not sell its machines to buyers in this country beyond the U.S. distributor, and there is no allegation that the distributor was under J. McIntyre's control.

Second, J. McIntyre officials attended annual conventions for the scrap recycling industry to advertise J. McIntyre's machines alongside the distributor. The conventions took place in various States, but never in New Jersey.

Third, no more than four machines (the record suggests only one), including the machine that caused the injuries that are the basis for this suit, ended up in New Jersey.

In addition to these facts emphasized by respondent, the New Jersey Supreme Court noted that J. McIntyre held both United States and European patents on its recycling technology. It also noted that the U.S. distributor "structured [its] advertising and sales efforts in accordance with" J. McIntyre's "direction and guidance whenever possible," and that "at least some of the machines were sold on consignment to" the distributor.

In light of these facts, the New Jersey Supreme Court concluded that New Jersey courts could exercise jurisdiction over petitioner without contravention of the Due Process Clause. Jurisdiction was proper, in that court's view, because the injury occurred in New Jersey; because petitioner knew or reasonably should have known "that its products are distributed through a nationwide distribution system that might lead to those products being sold in any of the fifty states"; and because petitioner failed to "take some reasonable step to prevent the distribution of its products in this State."

Both the New Jersey Supreme Court's holding and its account of what it called "[t]he stream-of-commerce doctrine of jurisdiction" were incorrect, however. This Court's *Asahi* decision may be responsible in part for that court's error regarding the stream of commerce, and this case presents an opportunity to provide greater clarity.

## II

The Due Process Clause protects an individual's right to be deprived of life, liberty, or property only by the exercise of lawful power. . . . A court may subject a defendant to judgment only when the defendant has sufficient contacts with the sovereign "such that the maintenance of the suit does not offend 'traditional notions of fair play and substantial justice.'" *International Shoe Co. v. Washington*. . . . As a general rule, the sovereign's exercise of power requires some act by which the defendant "purposefully avails itself of the privilege of conducting activities within the forum State, thus invoking the benefits and protections of its laws," *Hanson*, though in some cases, as with an intentional tort, the defendant might well fall within the State's authority by reason of his attempt to obstruct its laws. In products-liability cases like this one, it is the defendant's purposeful availment that makes jurisdiction consistent with "traditional notions of fair play and substantial justice."

A person may submit to a State's authority in a number of ways. There is, of course, explicit consent. Presence within a State at the time suit commences through service of process is another example. Citizenship or domicile—or, by analogy, incorporation or principal place of business for corporations—also indicates general submission to a State's powers. *Goodyear Dunlop Tires Operations, S. A. v. Brown.* Each of these examples reveals circumstances, or a course of conduct, from which it is proper to infer an intention to benefit from and thus an intention to submit to the laws of the forum State. These examples support exercise of the general jurisdiction of the State's courts and allow the State to resolve both matters that originate within the State and those based on activities and events elsewhere. By contrast, those who live or operate primarily outside a State have a due process right not to be subjected to judgment in its courts as a general matter.

There is also a more limited form of submission to a State's authority for disputes that "arise out of or are connected with the activities within the state." *International Shoe Co.* Where a defendant "purposefully avails itself of the privilege of conducting activities within the forum State, thus invoking the benefits and protections of its laws," *Hanson*, it submits to the judicial power of an otherwise foreign sovereign to the extent that power is exercised in connection with the defendant's activities touching on the State. In other words, submission through contact with and activity directed at a sovereign may justify specific jurisdiction "in a suit arising out of or related to the defendant's contacts with the forum."

The imprecision arising from *Asahi*, for the most part, results from its statement of the relation between jurisdiction and the "stream of commerce." The stream of commerce, like other metaphors, has its deficiencies as well as its utility. It refers to the movement of goods from manufacturers through distributors to consumers, yet beyond that descriptive purpose its meaning is far from exact. This Court has stated that a defendant's placing goods into the stream of commerce "with the expectation that they will be purchased by consumers within the forum State" may indicate purposeful availment. *World-Wide Volkswagen Corp. v. Woodson* (finding that expectation lacking). But that statement does not amend the general rule of personal jurisdiction. It merely observes that a defendant may in an appropriate case be subject to jurisdiction without entering the forum—itself an unexceptional proposition—as where manufacturers or distributors "seek to serve" a given State's market. The principal inquiry in cases of this sort is whether the defendant's activities manifest an intention to submit to the power of a sovereign. In other words, the defendant must "purposefully avai[l] itself of the privilege of conducting activities within the forum State, thus invoking the benefits and protections of its laws." *Hanson*. Sometimes a defendant does so by sending its goods rather than its agents. The defendant's transmission of goods permits the exercise of jurisdiction only where the defendant can be said to have targeted the forum; as a general rule, it is not enough that the defendant might have predicted that its goods will reach the forum State.

In *Asahi*, an opinion by Justice Brennan for four Justices outlined a different approach. It discarded the central concept of sovereign authority in favor of considerations of fairness and foreseeability. As that concurrence contended, "jurisdiction premised on the placement of a product into the stream of commerce [without more] is consistent with the Due Process Clause," for "[a]s long as a participant in this process is aware that the final product is being marketed in the forum State, the possibility of a lawsuit there cannot come as a surprise" (opinion concurring in part and concurring in judgment). It was the premise of the concurring opinion that the defendant's ability to anticipate suit renders the assertion of jurisdiction fair. In this way, the opinion made foreseeability the touchstone of jurisdiction.

The standard set forth in Justice Brennan's concurrence was rejected in an opinion written by Justice O'Connor; but the relevant part of that opinion, too, commanded the assent of only four Justices, not a majority of the Court. That opinion stated: "The 'substantial connection' between the defendant and the forum State necessary for a finding of minimum contacts must come about by an action of the defendant purposefully directed toward the forum State. The placement of a product into the stream of commerce, without more, is not an act of the defendant purposefully directed toward the forum State."

Since *Asahi* was decided, the courts have sought to reconcile the competing opinions. But Justice Brennan's concurrence, advocating a rule based on general notions of fairness and foreseeability, is inconsistent with the premises of lawful judicial power. This Court's precedents make clear that it is the defendant's actions, not his expectations, that empower a State's courts to subject him to judgment.

The conclusion that jurisdiction is in the first instance a question of authority rather than fairness explains, for example, why the principal opinion in *Burnham* [*infra*] "conducted no independent inquiry into the desirability or fairness" of the rule that service of process within a State suffices to establish jurisdiction over an otherwise foreign defendant. As that opinion explained, "[t]he view developed early that each State had the power to hale before its courts any individual who could be found within its borders." Furthermore, were general fairness considerations the touchstone of jurisdiction, a lack of purposeful availment might be excused where carefully crafted judicial procedures could otherwise protect the defendant's interests, or where the plaintiff would suffer substantial hardship if forced to litigate in a foreign forum. That such considerations have not been deemed controllings is instructive. See, e.g., *World-Wide Volkswagen*.

. . .

[A]lthough this case and *Asahi* both involve foreign manufacturers, the undesirable consequences of Justice Brennan's approach are no less significant for domestic producers. The owner of a small Florida farm might sell crops to a large nearby distributor, for example, who might then distribute them to grocers across the country. If foreseeability were the controlling criterion, the farmer could be sued in Alaska or any number of other States' courts without ever leaving town. And the issue of foreseeability may itself be contested so that significant expenses are incurred just on the preliminary issue of jurisdiction. Jurisdictional rules should avoid these costs whenever possible.

The conclusion that the authority to subject a defendant to judgment depends on purposeful availment, consistent with Justice O'Connor's opinion in Asahi, does not by itself resolve many difficult questions of jurisdiction that will arise in particular cases. The defendant's conduct and the economic realities of the market the defendant seeks to serve will differ across cases, and judicial exposition will, in common-law fashion, clarify the contours of that principle.

## III

In this case, petitioner directed marketing and sales efforts at the United States. It may be that, assuming it were otherwise empowered to legislate on the subject, the Congress could authorize the exercise of jurisdiction in appropriate courts. That circumstance is not presented in this case, however, and it is neither necessary nor appropriate to address here any constitutional concerns that might be attendant to that exercise of power. Nor is it necessary to determine what substantive law might apply were Congress to authorize jurisdiction in a federal court in New Jersey. A sovereign's legislative authority to regulate conduct may present considerations different from those presented by its authority to subject a defendant to judgment in its courts. Here the question concerns the authority of a New Jersey state court to exercise jurisdiction, so it is petitioner's purposeful contacts with New Jersey, not with the United States, that alone are relevant.

Respondent has not established that J. McIntyre engaged in conduct purposefully directed at New Jersey. Recall that respondent's claim of jurisdiction centers on three facts: The distributor agreed to sell J. McIntyre's machines in the United States; J. McIntyre officials attended trade shows in several States but not in New Jersey; and up to four machines ended up in New Jersey. The British manufacturer had no office in New Jersey; it neither paid taxes nor owned property there; and it neither advertised in, nor sent any employees to, the State. Indeed, after discovery the trial court found that the "defendant does not have a single contact with New Jersey short of the machine in question ending up in this state." These facts may reveal an intent to serve the U.S. market, but they do not show that J. McIntyre purposefully availed itself of the New Jersey market.

It is notable that the New Jersey Supreme Court appears to agree, for it could "not find that J. McIntyre had a presence or minimum contacts in this State—in any jurisprudential sense—that would justify a New Jersey court to exercise jurisdiction in this case." The court nonetheless held that petitioner could be sued in New Jersey based on a "stream-of-commerce theory of jurisdiction." As discussed, however, the stream-of-commerce metaphor cannot supersede either the mandate of the Due Process Clause or the limits on judicial authority that Clause ensures. The New Jersey Supreme Court also cited "significant policy reasons" to justify its holding, including the State's "strong interest in protecting its citizens from defective products." That interest is doubtless strong, but the Constitution commands restraint before discarding liberty in the name of expediency. . . .

Due process protects petitioner's right to be subject only to lawful authority. At no time did petitioner engage in any activities in New Jersey that reveal an intent to invoke or benefit from the protection of its laws. New Jersey is without power to adjudge the rights and liabilities of J. McIntyre, and its exercise of jurisdiction would violate due process. The contrary judgment of the New Jersey Supreme Court is

Reversed.

Justice BREYER, with whom Justice ALITO joins, concurring in the judgment.

The Supreme Court of New Jersey adopted a broad understanding of the scope of personal jurisdiction based on its view that "[t]he increasingly fast-paced globalization of the world economy has removed national borders as barriers to trade." I do not doubt that there have been many recent changes in commerce and communication, many of which are not anticipated by our precedents. But this case does not present any of those issues. So I think it unwise to announce a rule of broad applicability without full consideration of the modern-day consequences.

In my view, the outcome of this case is determined by our precedents. Based on the facts found by the New Jersey courts, respondent Robert Nicastro failed to meet his burden to demonstrate that it was constitutionally proper to exercise jurisdiction over petitioner J. McIntyre Machinery, Ltd. (British Manufacturer), a British firm that manufactures scrap-metal machines in Great Britain and sells them through an independent distributor in the United States (American Distributor). On that basis, I agree with the plurality that the contrary judgment of the Supreme Court of New Jersey should be reversed.

### I

In asserting jurisdiction over the British Manufacturer, the Supreme Court of New Jersey relied most heavily on three primary facts as providing constitutionally sufficient "contacts" with New Jersey, thereby making it fundamentally fair to hale the British Manufacturer before its courts: (1) The American Distributor on one occasion sold and shipped one machine to a New Jersey customer, namely, Mr. Nicastro's employer, Mr. Curcio; (2) the British Manufacturer permitted, indeed wanted, its independent American Distributor to sell its machines to anyone in America willing to buy them; and (3) representatives of the British Manufacturer attended trade shows in "such cities as Chicago, Las Vegas, New Orleans, Orlando, San Diego, and San Francisco." In my view, these facts do not provide contacts between the British firm and the State of New Jersey constitutionally sufficient to support New Jersey's assertion of jurisdiction in this case.

None of our precedents finds that a single isolated sale, even if accompanied by the kind of sales effort indicated here, is sufficient. Rather, this Court's previous holdings suggest the contrary. The Court has held that a single sale to a customer who takes an accident-causing product to a different State (where the accident takes place) is not a sufficient basis for asserting jurisdiction. See *World-Wide Volkswagen Corp. v. Woodson*, 444 U.S. 286 (1980). And the Court, in separate opinions, has strongly suggested that a single sale of a product in a State does not constitute an adequate basis for asserting jurisdiction over an out-of-state defendant, even if that defendant places his goods in the stream of commerce, fully aware (and hoping) that such a sale will take place. See *Asahi Metal Industry Co. v. Superior Court of Cal., Solano Cty.*, 480 U.S. 102, 111 (1987) (opinion of O'Connor, J.) (requiring "something more" than simply placing "a product into the stream of commerce," even if defendant is "awar[e]" that the stream "may or will sweep the product into the forum State"); (Brennan, J., concurring in part and concurring in judgment) (jurisdiction should lie where a sale in a State is part of "the regular and anticipated flow" of commerce into the State, but not where that sale is only an "edd[y]," *i.e.*, an isolated occurrence); (Stevens, J., concurring in part and concurring in judgment) (indicating that "the volume, the value, and the hazardous character" of a good may affect the jurisdictional inquiry and emphasizing Asahi's "regular course of dealing").

Here, the relevant facts found by the New Jersey Supreme Court show no "regular . . . flow" or "regular course" of sales in New Jersey; and there is no "something more," such as special state-related design, advertising, advice, marketing, or anything else. Mr. Nicastro, who here bears the burden of proving jurisdiction, has shown no specific effort by the British Manufacturer to sell in New Jersey. He has introduced no list of potential New Jersey customers who might, for example, have regularly attended trade shows. And he has not otherwise shown that the British Manufacturer "purposefully avail[ed] itself of the privilege of conducting activities" within New Jersey, or that it delivered its goods in the stream of commerce "with the expectation that they will be purchased" by New Jersey users. *World-Wide Volkswagen, supra,* at 297-298, 100 S.Ct. 559 (internal quotation marks omitted).

There may well have been other facts that Mr. Nicastro could have demonstrated in support of jurisdiction. And the dissent considers some of those facts. But the plaintiff bears the burden of establishing jurisdiction, and here I would take the facts precisely as the New Jersey Supreme Court stated them.

Accordingly, on the record present here, resolving this case requires no more than adhering to our precedents.

## II

I would not go further. Because the incident at issue in this case does not implicate modern concerns, and because the factual record leaves many open questions, this is an unsuitable vehicle for making broad pronouncements that refashion basic jurisdictional rules.

### A

The plurality seems to state strict rules that limit jurisdiction where a defendant does not "inten[d] to submit to the power of a sovereign" and cannot "be said to have targeted the forum." But what do those standards mean when a company targets the world by selling products from its Web site? And does it matter if, instead of shipping the products directly, a company consigns the products through an intermediary (say, Amazon.com) who then receives and fulfills the orders? And what if the company markets its products through popup advertisements that it knows will be viewed in a forum? Those issues have serious commercial consequences but are totally absent in this case.

### B

But though I do not agree with the plurality's seemingly strict no-jurisdiction rule, I am not persuaded by the absolute approach adopted by the New Jersey Supreme Court and urged by respondent and his amici. Under that view, a producer is subject to jurisdiction for a products-liability action so long as it "knows or reasonably should know that its products are distributed through a nation-wide distribution system that might lead to those products being sold in any of the fifty states." In the context of this case, I cannot agree.

For one thing, to adopt this view would abandon the heretofore accepted inquiry of whether, focusing upon the relationship between "the defendant, the *forum,* and the litigation," it is fair, in light of the defendant's contacts *with that forum*, to subject the defendant to suit there. *Shaffer v. Heitner,* 433 U.S. 186, 204 (1977) (emphasis added). It would ordinarily rest jurisdiction instead upon no more than the occurrence of a product-based accident in the forum State. But this Court has rejected the notion that a defendant's amenability to suit "travel[s] with the chattel." *World-Wide Volkswagen,* 444 U.S., at 296, 100 S.Ct. 559.

For another, I cannot reconcile so automatic a rule with the constitutional demand for "minimum contacts" and "purposefu[l] avail[ment]," each of which rest upon a particular notion of defendant-focused fairness. A rule like the New Jersey Supreme Court's would permit every State to assert jurisdiction in a products-liability suit against any domestic manufacturer who sells its products (made anywhere in the United States) to a national distributor, no matter how large or small the manufacturer, no matter how distant the forum, and no matter how few the number of items that end up in the particular forum at issue. What might appear fair in the case of a large manufacturer which specifically seeks, or expects, an equal-sized distributor to sell its product in a distant State might seem unfair in the case of a small manufacturer (say, an Appalachian potter) who sells his product (cups and saucers) exclusively to a large distributor, who resells a single item (a coffee mug) to a buyer from a distant State (Hawaii). I know too little about the range of these or in-between possibilities to abandon in favor of the more absolute rule what has previously been this Court's less absolute approach.

Further, the fact that the defendant is a foreign, rather than a domestic, manufacturer makes the basic fairness of an absolute rule yet more uncertain. I am again less certain than is the New Jersey Supreme Court that the nature of international commerce has changed so significantly as to require a new approach to personal jurisdiction.

It may be that a larger firm can readily "alleviate the risk of burdensome litigation by procuring insurance, passing the expected costs on to customers, or, if the risks are too great, severing its connection with the State." *World-Wide Volkswagen, supra,* at 297, 100 S.Ct. 559. But manufacturers come in many shapes and sizes. It may be fundamentally unfair to require a small Egyptian shirt maker, a Brazilian manufacturing cooperative, or a Kenyan coffee farmer, selling its products through international distributors, to respond to products-liability tort suits in virtually every State in the United States, even those in respect to which the foreign firm has no connection at all but the sale of a single (allegedly defective) good. And a rule like the New Jersey Supreme Court suggests would require every product manufacturer, large or small, selling to American distributors to understand not only the tort law of every State, but also the wide variance in the way courts within different States apply that law. See, *e.g.,* Dept. of Justice, Bureau of Justice Statistics

Bulletin, Tort Trials and Verdicts in Large Counties, 2001, p. 11 (reporting percentage of plaintiff winners in tort trials among 46 populous counties, ranging from 17.9% (Worcester, Mass.) to 69.1% (Milwaukee, Wis.)).

At a minimum, I would not work such a change to the law in the way either the plurality or the New Jersey Supreme Court suggests without a better understanding of the relevant contemporary commercial circumstances.

This case presents no such occasion, and so I again reiterate that I would adhere strictly to our precedents and the limited facts found by the New Jersey Supreme Court. And on those grounds, I do not think we can find jurisdiction in this case. Accordingly, though I agree with the plurality as to the outcome of this case, I concur only in the judgment of that opinion and not its reasoning.

Justice GINSBURG, with whom Justice SOTOMAYOR and Justice KAGAN join, dissenting.

A foreign industrialist seeks to develop a market in the United States for machines it manufactures. It hopes to derive substantial revenue from sales it makes to United States purchasers. Where in the United States buyers reside does not matter to this manufacturer. Its goal is simply to sell as much as it can, wherever it can. It excludes no region or State from the market it wishes to reach. But, all things considered, it prefers to avoid products liability litigation in the United States. To that end, it engages a U.S. distributor to ship its machines state-side. Has it succeeded in escaping personal jurisdiction in a State where one of its products is sold and causes injury or even death to a local user?

Under this Court's pathmarking precedent in *International Shoe Co. v. Washington*, and subsequent decisions, one would expect the answer to be unequivocally, "No." But instead, six Justices of this Court, in divergent opinions, tell us that the manufacturer has avoided the jurisdiction of our state courts, except perhaps in States where its products are sold in sizeable quantities. Inconceivable as it may have seemed yesterday, the splintered majority today "turn[s] the clock back to the days before modern long-arm statutes when a manufacturer, to avoid being haled into court where a user is injured, need only Pilate-like wash its hands of a product by having independent distributors market it."

## I

On October 11, 2001, a three-ton metal shearing machine severed four fingers on Robert Nicastro's right hand. Alleging that the machine was a dangerous product defectively made, Nicastro sought compensation from the machine's manufacturer, J. McIntyre Machinery Ltd. (McIntyre UK). Established in 1872 as a United Kingdom corporation, and headquartered in Nottingham, England, McIntyre UK "designs, develops and manufactures a complete range of equipment for metal recycling." The company's product line, as advertised on McIntyre UK's Web site, includes "metal shears, balers, cable and can recycling equipment, furnaces, casting equipment and . . . the world's best aluminium dross processing and cooling system." McIntyre UK holds both United States and European patents on its technology.

The machine that injured Nicastro, a "McIntyre Model640 Shear," sold in the United States for $24,900 in 1995, and features a "massive cutting capacity." According to McIntyre UK's product brochure, the machine is "use[d] throughout the [w]orld." McIntyre UK represented in the brochure that, by "incorporat[ing] off-the-shelf hydraulic parts from suppliers with international sales outlets," the 640 Shear's design guarantees serviceability "wherever [its customers] may be based." Ibid. The instruction manual advises "owner[s] and operators of a 640 Shear [to] make themselves aware of [applicable health and safety regulations]," including "the American National Standards Institute Regulations (USA) for the use of Scrap Metal Processing Equipment."

Nicastro operated the 640 Shear in the course of his employment at Curcio Scrap Metal (CSM) in Saddle Brook, New Jersey. "New Jersey has long been a hotbed of scrap-metal businesses. . . ." New Jersey recycling facilities processed 2,013,730 tons of scrap iron, steel, aluminum, and other metals—more than any other State—outpacing Kentucky, its nearest competitor, by nearly 30 percent.

CSM's owner, Frank Curcio, "first heard of [McIntyre UK's] machine while attending an Institute of Scrap Metal Industries [(ISRI)] convention in Las Vegas in 1994 or1995, where [McIntyre UK] was an exhibitor." ISRI "presents the world's largest scrap recycling industry trade show each year." The event attracts "owners [and] managers of scrap processing companies" and others "interested in seeing—and purchasing—new equipment." According to ISRI, more than 3,000 potential buyers of scrap processing and recycling equipment attend its annual conventions, "primarily because th[e] exposition provides them with the most comprehensive industry-related shopping experience concentrated in a single, convenient location." Exhibitors who are ISRI members pay $3,000 for 10′ × 10′ booth space.

McIntyre UK representatives attended every ISRI convention from 1990 through 2005. These annual expositions were held in diverse venues across the United States; in addition to Las Vegas, conventions were held 1990-2005 in New Orleans, Orlando, San Antonio, and San Francisco. McIntyre UK's president, Michael Pownall, regularly attended ISRI conventions. He attended ISRI's Las Vegas convention the year CSM's owner first learned of, and saw, the 640 Shear. McIntyre UK exhibited its products at ISRI trade shows, the company acknowledged, hoping to reach "anyone interested in the machine from anywhere in the United States."

Although McIntyre UK's U.S. sales figures are not in the record, it appears that for several years in the 1990's, earnings from sales of McIntyre UK products in the United States "ha[d] been good" in comparison to "the rest of the world." In response to interrogatories, McIntyre UK stated that its commissioning engineer had installed the company's equipment in several States—Illinois, Iowa, Kentucky, Virginia, and Washington.

From at least 1995 until 2001, McIntyre UK retained an Ohio-based company, McIntyre Machinery America, Ltd. (McIntyre America), "as its exclusive distributor for the entire United States." Though similarly named, the two companies were separate and independent entities with "no commonality of ownership or management." In invoices and other written communications, McIntyre America described itself as McIntyre UK's national distributor, "America's Link" to "Quality Metal Processing Equipment" from England.

In a November 23, 1999 letter to McIntyre America, McIntyre UK's president spoke plainly about the manufacturer's objective in authorizing the exclusive distributorship: "All we wish to do is sell our products in the [United] States—and get paid!" Notably, McIntyre America was concerned about U.S. litigation involving McIntyre UK products, in which the distributor had been named as a defendant. McIntyre UK counseled McIntyre America to respond personally to the litigation, but reassured its distributor that "the product was built and designed by McIntyre Machinery in the UK and the buck stops here—if there's something wrong with the machine." Answering jurisdictional interrogatories, McIntyre UK stated that it had been named as a defendant in lawsuits in Illinois, Kentucky, Massachusetts, and West Virginia. And in correspondence with McIntyre America, McIntyre UK noted that the manufacturer had products liability insurance coverage.

Over the years, McIntyre America distributed several McIntyre UK products to U.S. customers. . . . To achieve McIntyre UK's objective, i.e., "to sell [its] machines to customers throughout the United States, the two companies [were acting] closely in concert with each other." McIntyre UK never instructed its distributor to avoid certain States or regions of the country; rather, as just noted, the manufacturer engaged McIntyre America to attract customers "from anywhere in the United States."

In sum, McIntyre UK's regular attendance and exhibitions at ISRI conventions was surely a purposeful step to reach customers for its products "anywhere in the United States." At least as purposeful was McIntyre UK's engagement of McIntyre America as the conduit for sales of McIntyre UK's machines to buyers "throughout the United States." Given McIntyre UK's endeavors to reach and profit from the United States market as a whole, Nicastro's suit, I would hold, has been brought in a forum entirely appropriate for the adjudication of his claim. He alleges that McIntyre UK's shear machine was defectively designed or manufactured and, as a result, caused injury to him at his workplace. The machine arrived in Nicastro's New Jersey workplace not randomly or fortuitously, but as a result of the U.S. connections and distribution system that McIntyre UK deliberately arranged.[5]

---

5. McIntyre UK resisted Nicastro's efforts to determine whether other McIntyre machines had been sold to New Jersey customers. McIntyre did allow that McIntyre America "may have resold products it purchased from [McIntyre UK] to a buyer in New Jersey," but said it kept no record of the ultimate destination of machines it shipped to its distributor. A private investigator engaged by Nicastro found at least one McIntyre UK machine, of unspecified type, in use in New Jersey. But McIntyre UK objected that the investigator's report was "unsworn and based upon hearsay." Moreover, McIntyre UK

On what sensible view of the allocation of adjudicatory authority could the place of Nicastro's injury within the United States be deemed off limits for his products liability claim against a foreign manufacturer who targeted the United States (including all the States that constitute the Nation) as the territory it sought to develop?

## II

A few points on which there should be no genuine debate bear statement at the outset. First, all agree, McIntyre UK surely is not subject to general (all-purpose) jurisdiction in New Jersey courts, for that foreign-country corporation is hardly "at home" in New Jersey. See *Goodyear Dunlop Tires Operations, S.A. v. Brown.* The question, rather, is one of specific jurisdiction, which turns on an "affiliatio[n] between the forum and the underlying controversy." *Goodyear Dunlop.*

Second, no issue of the fair and reasonable allocation of adjudicatory authority among States of the United States is present in this case. New Jersey's exercise of personal jurisdiction over a foreign manufacturer whose dangerous product caused a workplace injury in New Jersey does not tread on the domain, or diminish the sovereignty, of any sister State. Indeed, among States of the United States, the State in which the injury occurred would seem most suitable for litigation of a products liability tort claim. See *World-Wide Volkswagen Corp. v. Woodson,* 444 U.S. 286, 297 (1980) (if a manufacturer or distributor endeavors to develop a market for a product in several States, it is reasonable "to subject it to suit in one of those States if its allegedly defective [product] has there been the source of injury"); 28 U.S.C. § 1391(a)-(b) (in federal-court suits, whether resting on diversity or federal-question jurisdiction, venue is proper in the judicial district "in which a substantial part of the events or omissions giving rise to the claim occurred").

Third, the constitutional limits on a state court's adjudicatory authority derive from considerations of due process, not state sovereignty. . . . "The restriction on state sovereign power described in *World-Wide Volkswagen Corp.* . . . must be seen as ultimately a function of the individual liberty interest preserved by the Due Process Clause. That Clause is the only source of the personal jurisdiction requirement and the Clause itself makes no mention of federalism concerns. Furthermore, if the federalism concept operated as an independent restriction on the sovereign power of the court, it would not be possible to waive the personal jurisdiction requirement: Individual actions cannot change the powers of sovereignty, although the individual can subject himself to powers from which he may otherwise be protected." . . .

Finally, in *International Shoe* itself, and decisions thereafter, the Court has made plain that legal fictions, notably "presence" and "implied consent,"

---

maintained, no evidence showed that the machine the investigator found in New Jersey had been "sold into [that State]."

should be discarded, for they conceal the actual bases on which jurisdiction rests. "[T]he relationship among the defendant, the forum, and the litigation" determines whether due process permits the exercise of personal jurisdiction over a defendant, and "fictions of implied consent" or "corporate presence" do not advance the proper inquiry.

Whatever the state of academic debate over the role of consent in modern jurisdictional doctrines, the plurality's notion that consent is the animating concept draws no support from controlling decisions of this Court. Quite the contrary, the Court has explained, a forum can exercise jurisdiction when its contacts with the controversy are sufficient; invocation of a fictitious consent, the Court has repeatedly said, is unnecessary and unhelpful. See, e.g., *Burger King Corp. v. Rudzewicz*, 471 U.S. 462, 472 (1985) (Due Process Clause permits "forum . . . to assert specific jurisdiction over an out-of-state defenzdant who has not consented to suit there"); *McGee v. International Life Ins. Co.*, 355 U.S. 220, 222 (1957) ("[T]his Court [has] abandoned 'consent,' 'doing business,' and 'presence' as the standard for measuring the extent of state judicial power over [out-of-state] corporations.").[6]

## III

This case is illustrative of marketing arrangements for sales in the United States common in today's commercial world.[7] A foreign-country manufacturer engages a U.S. company to promote and distribute the manufacturer's products, not in any particular State, but anywhere and everywhere in the United States the distributor can attract purchasers. The product proves defective and injures a user in the State where the user lives or works. Often, as here, the manufacturer will have liability insurance covering personal injuries caused by its products.

When industrial accidents happen, a long-arm statute in the State where the injury occurs generally permits assertion of jurisdiction, upon giving proper notice, over the foreign manufacturer. For example, the State's statute might provide, as does New York's long-arm statute, for the "exercise [of] personal jurisdiction over any non-domiciliary . . . who . . . "commits a tortious act without the state causing injury to person or property within the state, . . . if he . . . expects or should reasonably expect the act to have consequences in the state and derives substantial revenue from interstate or international commerce." N. Y. Civ. Prac. Law Ann. § 302(a)(3)(ii) (West

---

6. But see ante, at 4-8 (plurality opinion) (maintaining that a forum may be fair and reasonable, based on its links to the episode in suit, yet off limits because the defendant has not submitted to the State's authority). The plurality's notion that jurisdiction over foreign corporations depends upon the defendant's "submission," ante, at 6, seems scarcely different from the long-discredited fiction of implied consent. It bears emphasis that a majority of this Court's members do not share the plurality's view.

7. Last year, the United States imported nearly 2 trillion dollars in foreign goods. Census Bureau, U.S. International Trade in Goods and Services (Apr. 2011). Capital goods, such as the metal shear machine that injured Nicastro, accounted for almost 450 billion dollars in imports for 2010. New Jersey is the fourth-largest destination for manufactured commodities imported into the United States, after California, Texas, and New York.

2008). Or, the State might simply provide, as New Jersey does, for the exercise of jurisdiction "consistent with due process of law." N. J. Ct. Rule 4:4-4(b)(1) (2011).

The modern approach to jurisdiction over corporations and other legal entities, ushered in by *International Shoe*, gave prime place to reason and fairness. Is it not fair and reasonable, given the mode of trading of which this case is an example, to require the international seller to defend at the place its products cause injury? Do not litigational convenience and choice-of-law considerations point in that direction? On what measure of reason and fairness can it be considered undue to require McIntyre UK to defend in New Jersey as an incident of its efforts to develop a market for its industrial machines anywhere and everywhere in the United States?[8] Is not the burden on McIntyre UK to defend in New Jersey fair, i.e., a reasonable cost of transacting business internationally, in comparison to the burden on Nicastro to go to Nottingham, England to gain recompense for an injury he sustained using McIntyre's product at his workplace in Saddle Brook, New Jersey?

McIntyre UK dealt with the United States as a single market. Like most foreign manufacturers, it was concerned not with the prospect of suit in State X as opposed to State Y, but rather with its subjection to suit anywhere in the United States. As a McIntyre UK officer wrote in an e-mail to McIntyre America: "American law—who needs it?!" If McIntyre UK is answerable in the United States at all, is it not "perfectly appropriate to permit the exercise of that jurisdiction . . . at the place of injury"?

In sum, McIntyre UK, by engaging McIntyre America to promote and sell its machines in the United States, "purposefully availed itself" of the United States market nationwide, not a market in a single State or a discrete collection of States. (For purposes of international law and foreign relations, the separate identities of individual states of the Union are generally irrelevant.) McIntyre UK thereby availed itself of the market of all States in which its products were sold by its exclusive distributor. "Th[e] 'purposeful availment' requirement," this Court has explained, simply "ensures that a defendant will not be haled into a jurisdiction solely as a result of 'random,' 'fortuitous,' or 'attenuated' contacts." Adjudicatory authority is appropriately exercised where "actions by the defendant himself" give rise to the affiliation with the forum. How could McIntyre UK not have intended, by its actions targeting a national market, to sell products in the fourth largest destination for imports among all States of the United States and the largest scrap metal market?

Courts, both state and federal, confronting facts similar to those here, have rightly rejected the conclusion that a manufacturer selling its products across the USA may evade jurisdiction in any and all States, including the

---

8. The plurality suggests that the Due Process Clause might permit a federal district court in New Jersey, sitting in diversity and applying New Jersey law, to adjudicate McIntyre UK's liability to Nicastro. See ante, at 10-11. In other words, McIntyre UK might be compelled to bear the burden of traveling to New Jersey and defending itself there under New Jersey's products liability law, but would be entitled to federal adjudication of Nicastro's state-law claim. I see no basis in the Due Process Clause for such a curious limitation.

State where its defective product is distributed and causes injury. They have held, instead, that it would undermine principles of fundamental fairness to insulate the foreign manufacturer from accountability in court at the place within the United States where the manufacturer's products caused injury.

## IV

### A

While this Court has not considered in any prior case the now-prevalent pattern presented here—a foreign-country manufacturer enlisting a U.S. distributor to develop a market in the United States for the manufacturer's products—none of the Court's decisions tug against the judgment made by the New Jersey Supreme Court. McIntyre contends otherwise, citing *World-Wide Volkswagen*, and *Asahi Metal Industry Co. v. Superior Court of Cal., Solano Cty*.

*World-Wide Volkswagen* concerned a New York car dealership that sold solely in the New York market, and a New York distributor who supplied retailers in three States only: New York, Connecticut, and New Jersey. New York residents had purchased an Audi from the New York dealer and were driving the new vehicle through Oklahoma en route to Arizona. On the road in Oklahoma, another car struck the Audi in the rear, causing a fire which severely burned the Audi's occupants. Rejecting the Oklahoma courts' assertion of jurisdiction over the New York dealer and distributor, this Court observed that the defendants had done nothing to serve the market for cars in Oklahoma. Jurisdiction, the Court held, could not be based on the customer's unilateral act of driving the vehicle to Oklahoma.

Notably, the foreign manufacturer of the Audi in *World-Wide Volkswagen* did not object to the jurisdiction of the Oklahoma courts and the U.S. importer abandoned its initially stated objection. And most relevant here, the Court's opinion indicates that an objection to jurisdiction by the manufacturer or national distributor would have been unavailing. To reiterate, the Court said in *World-Wide Volkswagen* that, when a manufacturer or distributor aims to sell its product to customers in several States, it is reasonable "to subject it to suit in [any] one of those States if its allegedly defective [product] has there been the source of injury."

*Asahi* arose out of a motorcycle accident in California. Plaintiff, a California resident injured in the accident, sued the Taiwanese manufacturer of the motorcycle's tire tubes, claiming that defects in its product caused the accident. The tube manufacturer cross-claimed against Asahi, the Japanese maker of the valve assembly, and Asahi contested the California courts' jurisdiction. By the time the case reached this Court, the injured plaintiff had settled his case and only the indemnity claim by the Taiwanese company against the Japanese valve-assembly manufacturer remained.

The decision was not a close call. The Court had before it a foreign plaintiff, the Taiwanese manufacturer, and a foreign defendant, the Japanese valve-assembly maker, and the indemnification dispute concerned a transaction between those parties that occurred abroad. All agreed on the bottom line: The Japanese valve-assembly manufacturer was not reasonably brought into the California courts to litigate a dispute with another foreign party over a transaction that took place outside the United States.

Given the confines of the controversy, the dueling opinions of Justice Brennan and Justice O'Connor were hardly necessary. How the Court would have "estimate[d] . . . the inconveniences," see *International Shoe*, had the injured Californian originally sued Asahi is a debatable question. Would this Court have given the same weight to the burdens on the foreign defendant had those been counterbalanced by the burdens litigating in Japan imposed on the local California plaintiff? Cf. *Calder v. Jones*, 465 U.S. 783, 788 (1984) (a plaintiff's contacts with the forum "may be so manifold as to permit jurisdiction when it would not exist in their absence").

In any event, Asahi, unlike McIntyre UK, did not itself seek out customers in the United States, it engaged no distributor to promote its wares here, it appeared at no tradeshows in the United States, and, of course, it had no Web site advertising its products to the world. Moreover, Asahi was a component-part manufacturer with "little control over the final destination of its products once they were delivered into the stream of commerce." It was important to the Court in *Asahi* that "those who use Asahi components in their final products, and sell those products in California, [would be] subject to the application of California tort law." To hold that *Asahi* controls this case would, to put it bluntly, be dead wrong.[9]

**B**

The Court's judgment also puts United States plaintiffs at a disadvantage in comparison to similarly situated complainants elsewhere in the world. Of particular note, within the European Union, in which the United Kingdom is a participant, the jurisdiction New Jersey would have exercised is not at all exceptional. The European Regulation on Jurisdiction and the Recognition and Enforcement of Judgments provides for the exercise of specific jurisdiction "in matters relating to tort . . . in the courts for the place where the harmful event occurred." Council Reg. 44/2001, Art. 5, 2001 O. J. (L. 12) 4. The European Court of Justice has interpreted this prescription to authorize jurisdiction either where the harmful act occurred or at the place of injury.

**V**

[C]onsiderations of litigational convenience and the respective situations of the parties [should] determine when it is appropriate to subject a defendant

---

9. The plurality notes the low volume of sales in New Jersey. A $24,900 shearing machine, however, is unlikely to sell in bulk worldwide, much less in any given State. By dollar value, the price of a single machine represents a significant sale. Had a manufacturer sold in New Jersey $24,900 worth of flannel shirts, cigarette lighters, or wire-rope splices, the Court would presumably find the defendant amenable to suit in that State.

to trial in the plaintiff's community. Litigational considerations include "the convenience of witnesses and the ease of ascertaining the governing law." As to the parties, courts would differently appraise two situations: (1) cases involving a substantially local plaintiff, like Nicastro, injured by the activity of a defendant engaged in interstate or international trade; and (2) cases in which the defendant is a natural or legal person whose economic activities and legal involvements are largely home-based, i.e., entities without designs to gain substantial revenue from sales in distant markets. . . . Courts presented with [the] first scenario—a local plaintiff injured by the activity of a manufacturer seeking to exploit a multistate or global market—have repeatedly confirmed that jurisdiction is appropriately exercised by courts of the place where the product was sold and caused injury. [Appendix of cases omitted.]

For the reasons stated, I would hold McIntyre UK answerable in New Jersey for the harm Nicastro suffered at his workplace in that State using McIntyre UK's shearing machine. While I dissent from the Court's judgment, I take heart that the plurality opinion does not speak for the Court, for that opinion would take a giant step away from the "notions of fair play and substantial justice" underlying *International Shoe*.

## Comments and Questions

1. Having stated the obvious, that "[t]he rules and standards for determining when a State does or does not have jurisdiction over an absent party have been unclear because of decades-old questions left open in *Asahi Metal Industry Co. v. Superior Court of Cal., Solano Cty.*," Justice Kennedy sees *Nicastro* as "an opportunity to provide greater clarity." Has he achieved that objective? Does the Court adopt Justice O'Connor's "additional conduct" test? Or some variation on it? Have we merely moved from the murkiness of *Asahi*'s 4:4:1 split to the ambiguity of 4:2:3?

2. In the continuing debate about whether personal jurisdiction is a matter of sovereign power or individual liberty, where does Kennedy come out? Note Justice Ginsburg's (joined by Sotomayor and Kagan) clear answer in her dissent:

[T]he constitutional limits on a state court's adjudicatory authority derive from considerations of due process, not state sovereignty. . . . "The restriction on state sovereign power described in *World-Wide Volkswagen Corp.* . . . must be seen as ultimately a function of the individual liberty interest preserved by the Due Process Clause. That Clause is the only source of the personal jurisdiction requirement and the Clause itself makes no mention of federalism concerns. Furthermore, if the federalism concept operated as an independent restriction on the sovereign power of the court, it would not be possible to waive the personal jurisdiction requirement: Individual actions cannot change the powers of sovereignty, although the individual can subject himself to powers from which he may otherwise be protected." 131 S. Ct. at 2798 [citation omitted].

Can there be "greater clarity" of the personal jurisdiction question absent agreement on the Court about its fundamental premise?

3. Basing adjudicatory authority on implied consent has long been discredited, going back to *International Shoe*. Were you surprised to see Justice Kennedy revive it with his transformation of the minimum-contacts concept into the question of whether the defendant exhibited an "intention to submit to the laws of the forum State"? Note the following passage from the plurality opinion:

> There is also a more limited form [as compared to general jurisdiction] of submission to a State's authority for disputes that "arise out of or are connected with the activities within the state." *International Shoe Co.* Where a defendant "purposefully avails itself of the privilege of conducting activities within the forum State, thus invoking the benefits and protections of its laws," *Hanson*, it submits to the judicial power of an otherwise foreign sovereign to the extent that power is exercised in connection with the defendant's activities touching on the State. In other words, submission through contact with and activity directed at a sovereign may justify specific jurisdiction "in a suit arising out of or related to the defendant's contacts with the forum."

Note Justice Ginsburg's surprise:

> Whatever the state of academic debate over the role of consent in modern jurisdictional doctrines, the plurality's notion that consent is the animating concept draws no support from controlling decisions of this Court. Quite the contrary, the Court has explained, a forum can exercise jurisdiction when its contacts with the controversy are sufficient; invocation of a fictitious consent, the Court has repeatedly said, is unnecessary and unhelpful.

131 S. Ct. at 2799.

4. What do you make of the unlikely pairing of Justices Breyer and Alito, concurring? For an opinion that purports to "not go further [than resting on past precedent]" (131 S. Ct. at 2792), does it nonetheless go further? What kind of case does Breyer envision would raise "the relevant contemporary commercial circumstances" meriting a rethinking of personal jurisdiction doctrine?

Throughout the oral argument, Breyer expressed concern for any rule that would subject every small business, like a women's pottery cooperative in India or goat herders in Ethiopa, to suit wherever a buyer distributes its product. Transcript, Oral Argument, pp. 30-34, 50-51. Is that analogous to *Nicastro*? Could the little-guy defendant not be protected in such cases through weighing of the fair play factors?

5. Had you been an observer in court during the first minutes of the oral argument in *Nicastro*, could you have predicted where at least two of the justices would come out?

*Mr. Fergenson:*   Mr. Chief Justice, and may it please the Court: Because J. McIntyre did not direct any activity at residents of New Jersey either itself or by directing its distributor MMA to do so and had no awareness or knowledge that the distributor took the action that it did toward New Jersey, New Jersey lacked adjudicative jurisdiction.

*Justice Scalia:* When you say "its distributor," was this distributor at all controlled by the defendant?

*Mr. Fergenson:* No, Your Honor. It was not. And both under Ohio law and under the Restatement (Second) Agency, section 1-1, the right to control is essential to ascribe actions to create an agency, and it's on a per-purpose basis.

*Justice Scalia:* It might be better to refer to it as the company that distributed its product, rather than calling it "its distributor."

*Mr. Fergenson:* Very good, Your Honor.

*Justice Scalia:* It's loaded, it seems to me.

*Justice Kagan:* Mr. Fergenson, in your question presented to this court, you asked whether there's personal jurisdiction—and I'm quoting here— "solely because the manufacturer targets the United States market for the sale of the product."

So I'm taking from that, that you acknowledge that this manufacturer, McIntyre, a British manufacturer, targeted the United States market for the sale of its product. That's correct, yes?

*Mr. Fergenson:* Yes.

Transcript, Oral Argument, pp. 3-5.

6. Look back at Part G, "Note on Personal Jurisdiction in Federal Court." Justice Kennedy makes the intriguing suggestion in Part III of the plurality opinion (repeating an earlier one by Justice O'Connor in *Asahi*, 480 U.S. at 113 n.*) that Congress could resolve the *Nicastro* problem by simply expanding federal district court authority to the limits of the nation's borders, creating nationwide jurisdiction and thus presumably requiring only sufficient contacts with the United States itself, not any particular state, to satisfy constitutional concerns. Fed. R. Civ. P. 4(k)(2) does this, *but only for federal claims* (28 U.S.C. § 1331). As there is no federal statute providing a claim for defective product liability, Congress would have to expand 4(k)(2) to state law claims entertained through diversity jurisdiction to follow Kennedy's suggestion. Politically, is this a realistic possibility?

Note that the highly influential U.S. Chamber of Commerce filed an *amicus* brief in support of petitioner J. McIntyre Machinery, Ltd., citing the "vital concerns" for the nation's business community that were at stake, and raising the possibility of federal legislation of the type Kennedy ponders. The *amicus* brief filed by a group of law professors (and who knows more about personal jurisdiction?) in support of Nicastro responds that such legislation is unnecessary, and urges the Court to adopt "a clear rule that a manufacturer establishes minimum contacts with the forum state when it purposefully endeavors to access the U.S. market generally and its product is thereby distributed to and causes injury in the forum state" (at pp. 25-26).

7. *Nicastro* allows a foreign manufacturer to insulate itself from suit in any state by careful arrangement through an independent distributor, even as it directs the latter to sell anywhere it can. J. McIntyre's stated objective was "All we wish to do is sell our products in the States and get paid." Transcript, Oral Argument, p. 26. But it also wanted to avoid being subject to U.S. litigation; as a McIntyre UK officer said in an e-mail to the American distributor: "American law—who needs it?" 131 S. Ct., at 2801 (Ginsburg, dissenting).

Could a domestic corporation follow the same game plan, and so easily avoid suit in any state but its home?

8. How would you describe the current state of "stream of commerce" theory? You will have a chance to apply it in the practice exercise that follows.

## Practice Exercise No. 32: Applying a Long-Arm Statute in *Carpenter v. Dee*

### *Memorandum*

To: Associates
From: Carol Coblentz
Re: Jurisdiction Issue in *Carpenter v. Dee*

As you know, this case is pending in Massachusetts Superior Court, and we have been permitted to amend to join Ultimate Auto, Inc. as a party defendant. One of our theories is that Dee should have been warned about the use of the oversized tires he purchased there. Ultimate is incorporated in New Hampshire and has its only place of business (the retail parts store) in Nashua, New Hampshire. Not surprisingly, Ultimate has moved to dismiss for lack of personal jurisdiction, and I would like some help preparing for the hearing.

I sent an initial set of interrogatories to Ultimate Auto and gained the following pertinent information. Its corporate officers all live in Nashua, NH (approximately ten miles from the Massachusetts border), except for the Vice President, William Q. Manconi, who lives in Lawrence, MA. Manconi commutes to work, but sometimes does paperwork for the company in his office at home.

Ultimate advertises in several southern New Hampshire newspapers and on two Nashua radio stations. The advertising copy states: "Buy Ultimate, the ultimate in tires. Our tires will take you safely from the streets of Nashua through the White and Green Mountains, to the Berkshires and the Alleghenies, in cities as tough on tires as Boston, New York, and Chicago, prairies as beautiful as North Dakota, and farms as rolling as Nebraska. Our expertise and prices will not be beat throughout New England. We are the Ultimate in tires." When I drive in Lawrence, Massachusetts, which is about thirty miles from Nashua, I can pick up one of the two radio stations that Ultimate Auto advertises on. And a Nashua newspaper that carries the Ultimate ads can be purchased at some newsstands in Lawrence.

Ultimate Auto keeps no records of what percentage of its sales are to people who, like Randall Dee, reside outside New Hampshire. Its manager says that "lots of people come from Massachusetts to buy from us. We are particularly well known by hunters, sportsmen, and car buffs. And there's no sales tax!" Most years Ultimate sets up a booth to promote its store at the Auto Show in Boston. ③ *auto show in boston*

I'd like you to brief me on the current state of personal jurisdiction law. Regarding the significance of Ultimate's advertising, take a look at a case I came across, *Shoppers Food Warehouse v. Mopreno*, 746 A.2d 320 (D.C. App. Ct. 2000), where the District of Columbia court placed great stock in the fact that the Maryland defendant placed ads in the *Washington Post* soliciting customers in bold letters: "No Matter Where You Live, It's Worth the Drive!" 746 A.2d at 330-331. *nexus*

Please think about what further factual information we might need to get, and how we should structure our legal argument. You will need the Massachusetts Long-Arm statute, which I have attached below.

***Now assume the following different scenario.*** Carpenter's attorney has identified the suspension lift kit as the culprit in causing the Jeep CJ7 to roll over. Discovery has revealed that the defective kit was manufactured by China Specialty Auto-Parts, Ltd., at its plant in Wuhan. China Specialty uses a number of distributors to sell its products in the United States, and the one covering the eastern states is USA Specialty Auto-Parts, Inc., of Baltimore, MD., a domestic corporation wholly separate from China Specialty. USA Specialty sells hundreds of China Specialty lift kits per year to Massachusetts retailers, including the one in Lowell where Randall bought the kit he installed in the Jeep CJ7.

*China ↓ USA (cust) ↓ Baltimore MD.*

USA Specialty Auto-Parts has just declared bankruptcy, leaving China Specialty Auto-Parts, Ltd., as Nancy Carpenter's only hope for recovery. Construct an argument that the Massachusetts Superior Court can assert adjudicatory power over the Chinese corporation. How do you assess your chances of success after *Nicastro*?

*Nicastro - con. not non juris. over Chinese*

[Justice Ginsburg posed a similar scenario at the oral argument in *Nicastro*, and raised the question of whether a plaintiff should be forced to sue a manufacturer in its home country if that venue does not provide "a trusted legal system." Transcript, Oral Argument, pp. 24-25.]

### *Massachusetts General Laws Jurisdiction of Courts over Persons in Other States and Countries*

Mass. Gen. Laws ch. 223A § 3. Transactions or conduct for personal jurisdiction

*• find the provision in the LA statute • then nake argument*

A court may exercise personal jurisdiction over a person, who acts directly or by an agent, as to a cause of action in law or equity arising from the person's

    (a) transacting any business in this commonwealth;

    (b) contracting to supply services or things in this commonwealth;

    (c) causing tortious injury by an act or omission in this commonwealth;

    (d) causing tortious injury in this commonwealth by an act or omission outside this commonwealth if he regularly does or solicits business, or engages in any other persistent course of conduct, or derives substantial revenue from goods used or consumed or services rendered, in this commonwealth;

(e) having an interest in, using or possessing real property in this common wealth;

(f) contracting to insure any person, property or risk located within this commonwealth at the time of contracting;

(g) maintaining a domicile in this commonwealth while a party to a personal or marital relationship out of which arises a claim for divorce, alimony, property settlement, parentage of a child, child support or child custody; or the commission of any act giving rise to such a claim; or

(h) having been subject to the exercise of personal jurisdiction of a court of the commonwealth which has resulted in an order of alimony, custody, child support or property settlement, notwithstanding the subsequent departure of one of the original parties from the commonwealth, if the action involves modification of such order or orders and the moving party resides in the commonwealth, or if the action involves enforcement of such order notwithstanding the domicile of the moving party.

---

In our next case, we shift from the tort to the commercial context, where the parties have chosen to enter into structured relationships. How—if at all—should this change the personal jurisdiction calculus?

## ■ BURGER KING CORP. v. RUDZEWICZ
### 471 U.S. 462 (1985)

Justice BRENNAN delivered the opinion of the Court:

The State of Florida's long-arm statute extends jurisdiction to "[a]ny person, whether or not a citizen or resident of this state," who, *inter alia*, "[b]reach[es] a contract in this state by failing to perform acts required by the contract to be performed in this state," so long as the cause of action arises from the alleged contractual breach. Fla. Stat. § 48.193(1)(g) (Supp. 1984). The United States District Court for the Southern District of Florida, sitting in diversity, relied on this provision in exercising personal jurisdiction over a Michigan resident who allegedly had breached a franchise agreement with a Florida corporation by failing to make required payments in Florida. The question presented is whether this exercise of longarm jurisdiction offended "traditional conception[s] of fair play and substantial justice" embodied in the Due Process Clause of the Fourteenth Amendment. *International Shoe Co. v. Washington*, 326 U.S. 310, 320 (1945).

## I

### A

Burger King Corporation is a Florida corporation whose principal offices are in Miami. It is one of the world's largest restaurant organizations, with over 3,000 outlets in the 50 States, the Commonwealth of Puerto Rico, and 8 foreign nations. Burger King conducts approximately 80% of its business through a franchise operation that the company styles the "Burger King System"—"a comprehensive restaurant format and operating system for the sale of uniform and quality food products." Burger King licenses its franchisees to use its trademarks and service marks for a period of 20 years and leases standardized restaurant facilities to them for the same term. In addition, franchisees acquire a variety of proprietary information concerning the "standards, specifications, procedures and methods for operating a Burger King Restaurant." They also receive market research and advertising assistance; ongoing training in restaurant management;[2] and accounting, cost-control, and inventory-control guidance. By permitting franchisees to tap into Burger King's established national reputation and to benefit from proven procedures for dispensing standardized fare, this system enables them to go into the restaurant business with significantly lowered barriers to entry.

In exchange for these benefits, franchisees pay Burger King an initial $40,000 franchise fee and commit themselves to payment of monthly royalties, advertising and sales promotion fees, and rent computed in part from monthly gross sales. Franchisees also agree to submit to the national organization's exacting regulation of virtually every conceivable aspect of their operations. Burger King imposes these standards and undertakes its rigid regulation out of conviction that "[u]niformity of service, appearance, and quality of product is essential to the preservation of the Burger King image and the benefits accruing therefrom to both Franchisee and Franchisor."

Burger King oversees its franchise system through a two-tiered administrative structure. The governing contracts provide that the franchise relationship is established in Miami and governed by Florida law, and call for payment of all required fees and forwarding of all relevant notices to the Miami headquarters. The Miami headquarters sets policy and works directly with its franchisees in attempting to resolve major problems. Day-to-day monitoring of franchisees, however, is conducted through a network of 10 district offices which in turn report to the Miami headquarters.

The instant litigation grows out of Burger King's termination of one of its franchisees, and is aptly described by the franchisee as "a divorce proceeding among commercial partners." The appellee John Rudzewicz, a Michigan citizen and resident, is the senior partner in a Detroit accounting firm. In 1978, he was approached by Brian MacShara, the son of a business acquaintance,

---

2. Mandatory training seminars are conducted at Burger King University in Miami and at Whopper College Regional Training Centers around the country.

who suggested that they jointly apply to Burger King for a franchise in the Detroit area. MacShara proposed to serve as the manager of the restaurant if Rudzewicz would put up the investment capital; in exchange, the two would evenly share the profits. Believing that MacShara's idea offered attractive investment and tax-deferral opportunities, Rudzewicz agreed to the venture.

Rudzewicz and MacShara jointly applied for a franchise to Burger King's Birmingham, Michigan, district office in the autumn of 1978. Their application was forwarded to Burger King's Miami headquarters, which entered into a preliminary agreement with them in February 1979. During the ensuing four months it was agreed that Rudzewicz and MacShara would assume operation of an existing facility in Drayton Plains, Michigan. MacShara attended the prescribed management courses in Miami during this period, and the franchisees purchased $165,000 worth of restaurant equipment from Burger King's Davmor Industries division in Miami. Even before the final agreements were signed, however, the parties began to disagree over site-development fees, building design, computation of monthly rent, and whether the franchisees would be able to assign their liabilities to a corporation they had formed. During these disputes Rudzewicz and MacShara negotiated both with the Birmingham district office and with the Miami headquarters.[7] With some misgivings, Rudzewicz and MacShara finally obtained limited concessions from the Miami headquarters, signed the final agreements, and commenced operations in June 1979. By signing the final agreements, Rudzewicz obligated himself personally to payments exceeding $1 million over the 20-year franchise relationship.

The Drayton Plains facility apparently enjoyed steady business during the summer of 1979, but patronage declined after a recession began later that year. Rudzewicz and MacShara soon fell far behind in their monthly payments to Miami. Headquarters sent notices of default, and an extended period of negotiations began among the franchisees, the Birmingham district office, and the Miami headquarters. After several Burger King officials in Miami had engaged in prolonged but ultimately unsuccessful negotiations with the franchisees by mail and by telephone,[9] headquarters terminated the franchise and ordered Rudzewicz and MacShara to vacate the premises. They refused and continued to occupy and operate the facility as a Burger King restaurant.

---

7. Although Rudzewicz and MacShara dealt with the Birmingham district office on a regular basis, they communicated directly with the Miami headquarters in forming the contracts; moreover, they learned that the district office had "very little" decisionmaking authority and accordingly turned directly to headquarters in seeking to resolve their disputes.

9. Miami's policy was to "deal directly" with franchisees when they began to encounter financial difficulties, and to involve district office personnel only when necessary. In the instant case, for example, the Miami office handled all credit problems, ordered cost-cutting measures, negotiated for a partial refinancing of the franchisees' debts, communicated directly with the franchisees in attempting to resolve the dispute, and was responsible for all termination matters.

B

Burger King commenced the instant action in the United States District Court for the Southern District of Florida in May 1981, invoking that court's diversity jurisdiction pursuant to 28 U.S.C. § 1332(a) and its original jurisdiction over federal trademark disputes pursuant to § 1338 (a).[10] Burger King alleged that Rudzewicz and MacShara had breached their franchise obligations "within [the jurisdiction of] this district court" by failing to make the required payments "at plaintiff's place of business in Miami, Dade County, Florida," and also charged that they were tortiously infringing its trademarks and service marks through their continued, unauthorized operation as a Burger King restaurant. Burger King sought damages, injunctive relief, and costs and attorney's fees. Rudzewicz and MacShara entered special appearances and argued, inter alia, that because they were Michigan residents and because Burger King's claim did not "arise" within the Southern District of Florida, the District Court lacked personal jurisdiction over them. The District Court denied their motions after a hearing, holding that, pursuant to Florida's long-arm statute, "a non-resident Burger King franchisee is subject to the personal jurisdiction of this Court in actions arising out of its franchise agreements." Rudzewicz and MacShara then filed an answer and a counterclaim seeking damages for alleged violations by Burger King of Michigan's Franchise Investment Law.

After a 3-day bench trial, the court again concluded that it had "jurisdiction over the subject matter and the parties to this cause." Finding that Rudzewicz and MacShara had breached their franchise agreements with Burger King and had infringed Burger King's trademarks and service marks, the court entered judgment against them, jointly and severally, for $228,875 in contract damages. The court also ordered them "to immediately close Burger King Restaurant Number 775 from continued operation or to immediately give the keys and possession of said restaurant to Burger King Corporation," found that they had failed to prove any of the required elements of their counterclaim, and awarded costs and attorney's fees to Burger King.

Rudzewicz appealed to the Court of Appeals for the Eleventh Circuit.[11] A divided panel of that Circuit reversed the judgment, concluding that the District Court could not properly exercise personal jurisdiction over Rudzewicz pursuant to Fla. Stat. § 48.193(1)(g) (Supp. 1984) because "the circumstances of the Drayton Plains franchise and the negotiations which led to it left Rudzewicz bereft of reasonable notice and financially unprepared for the prospect of franchise litigation in Florida." *Burger King Corp. v. MacShara,*

---

10. Rudzewicz and MacShara were served in Michigan with summonses and copies of the complaint pursuant to Federal Rule of Civil Procedure 4.

11. MacShara did not appeal his judgment. In addition, Rudzewicz entered into a compromise with Burger King and waived his right to appeal the District Court's finding of trademark infringement and its entry of injunctive relief. Accordingly, we need not address the extent to which the tortious act provisions of Florida's long-arm statute, *see* Fla. Stat. § 48.193(1)(b) (Supp. 1984), may constitutionally extend to out-of-state trademark infringement. *Cf. Calder v. Jones*, 465 U.S. 783, 788-789 (1984) (tortious out-of-state conduct); *Keeton v. Hustler Magazine, Inc.*, 465 U.S. 770, 776 (1984) (same).

724 F.2d 1505, 1513 (1984). Accordingly, the panel majority concluded that "[j]urisdiction under these circumstances would offend the fundamental fairness which is the touchstone of due process." *Ibid.*

Burger King appealed the Eleventh Circuit's judgment to this Court. . . . We now reverse.

## II

### A

The Due Process Clause protects an individual's liberty interest in not being subject to the binding judgments of a forum with which he has established no meaningful "contacts, ties, or relations." *International Shoe Co. v. Washington*, 326 U.S. at 319.[13] By requiring that individuals have "fair warning that a particular activity may subject [them] to the jurisdiction of a foreign sovereign," the Due Process Clause "gives a degree of predictability to the legal system that allows potential defendants to structure their primary conduct with some minimum assurance as to where that conduct will and will not render them liable to suit."

Where a forum seeks to assert specific jurisdiction over an out-of-state defendant who has not consented to suit there,[14] this "fair warning" requirement is satisfied if the defendant has "purposefully directed" his activities at residents of the forum, and the litigation results from alleged injuries that "arise out of or relate to" those activities.[15] Thus "[t]he forum State does not exceed its powers under the Due Process Clause if it asserts personal jurisdiction over a corporation that delivers its products into the stream of commerce with the expectation that they will be purchased by consumers in the forum State" and those products subsequently injure forum consumers. *World-Wide Volkswagen Corp. v. Woodson, supra*, 444 U.S. at 297-298. Similarly, a publisher who distributes magazines in a distant State may fairly be held accountable in that forum for damages resulting there from an allegedly defamatory story. *Keeton v. Hustler Magazine, Inc., supra; see also Calder v. Jones*, 465 U.S. 783 (1984) (suit against author and editor). And with respect to interstate contractual obligations, we have emphasized that parties who

---

13. Although this protection operates to restrict state power, it "must be seen as ultimately a function of the individual liberty interest preserved by the Due Process Clause" rather than as a function "of federalism concerns." *Insurance Corp. of Ireland v. Compagnie des Bauxites de Guiné*, 456 U.S. 694 (1982).

14. We have noted that, because the personal jurisdiction requirement is a waivable right, there are a "variety of legal arrangements" by which a litigant may give "express or implied consent to the personal jurisdiction of the court." *Insurance Corp. of Ireland v. Compagnie des Bauxites de Guiné, supra*, at 703. For example, particularly in the commercial context, parties frequently stipulate in advance to submit their controversies for resolution within a particular jurisdiction. *See National Equipment Rental, Ltd. v. Szukhent*, 375 U.S. 311 (1964). Where such forum-selection provisions have been obtained through "freely negotiated" agreements and are not "unreasonable and unjust," *The Bremen v. Zapata Off-Shore Co.*, 407 U.S. 1, 15 (1972), their enforcement does not offend due process. [*Eds.' Note:* We will take up the topic of forum selection clauses in Part L.]

15. "Specific" jurisdiction contrasts with "general" jurisdiction, pursuant to which "a State exercises personal jurisdiction over a defendant in a suit not arising out of or related to the defendant's contacts with the forum." *Perkins v. Benguet Consolidated Mining Co.*, 342 U.S. 437 (1952).

"reach out beyond one state and create continuing relationships and obligations with citizens of another state" are subject to regulation and sanctions in the other State for the consequences of their activities.

We have noted several reasons why a forum legitimately may exercise personal jurisdiction over a nonresident who "purposefully directs" his activities toward forum residents. A State generally has a "manifest interest" in providing its residents with a convenient forum for redressing injuries inflicted by out-of-state actors. Moreover, where individuals "purposefully derive benefit" from their interstate activities, it may well be unfair to allow them to escape having to account in other States for consequences that arise proximately from such activities; the Due Process Clause may not readily be wielded as a territorial shield to avoid interstate obligations that have been voluntarily assumed. And because "modern transportation and communications have made it much less burdensome for a party sued to defend himself in a State where he engages in economic activity," it usually will not be unfair to subject him to the burdens of litigating in another forum for disputes relating to such activity.

Notwithstanding these considerations, the constitutional touchstone remains whether the defendant purposefully established "minimum contacts" in the forum State. *International Shoe Co. v. Washington, supra*, 326 U.S. at 316. Although it has been argued that foreseeability of causing injury in another State should be sufficient to establish such contacts there when policy considerations so require, the Court has consistently held that this kind of foreseeability is not a "sufficient benchmark" for exercising personal jurisdiction. *World-Wide Volkswagen Corp. v. Woodson*, 444 U.S. at 295. Instead, "the foreseeability that is critical to due process analysis . . . is that the defendant's conduct and connection with the forum State are such that he should reasonably anticipate being haled into court there." *Id.*, at 297. In defining when it is that a potential defendant should "reasonably anticipate" out-of-state litigation, the Court frequently has drawn from the reasoning of *Hanson v. Denckla*, 357 U.S. 235, 253 (1958):

> The unilateral activity of those who claim some relationship with a nonresident defendant cannot satisfy the requirement of contact with the forum State. The application of that rule will vary with the quality and nature of the defendant's activity, but it is essential in each case that there be some act by which the defendant purposefully avails itself of the privilege of conducting activities within the forum State, thus invoking the benefits and protections of its laws.

This "purposeful availment" requirement ensures that a defendant will not be haled into a jurisdiction solely as a result of "random," "fortuitous," or "attenuated" contacts, or of the "unilateral activity of another party or a third person,"[17] Jurisdiction is proper, however, where the contacts proximately

---

17. Applying this principle, the Court has held that the Due Process Clause forbids the exercise of personal jurisdiction over an out-of-state automobile distributor whose only tie to the forum resulted from

result from actions by the defendant himself that create a "substantial connection" with the forum State.[18] Thus where the defendant "deliberately" has engaged in significant activities within a State, or has created "continuing obligations" between himself and residents of the forum, he manifestly has availed himself of the privilege of conducting business there, and because his activities are shielded by "the benefits and protections" of the forum's laws it is presumptively not unreasonable to require him to submit to the burdens of litigation in that forum as well.

Jurisdiction in these circumstances may not be avoided merely because the defendant did not physically enter the forum State. Although territorial presence frequently will enhance a potential defendant's affiliation with a State and reinforce the reasonable foreseeability of suit there, it is an inescapable fact of modern commercial life that a substantial amount of business is transacted solely by mail and wire communications across state lines, thus obviating the need for physical presence within a State in which business is conducted. So long as a commercial actor's efforts are "purposefully directed" toward residents of another State, we have consistently rejected the notion that an absence of physical contacts can defeat personal jurisdiction there.

Once it has been decided that a defendant purposefully established minimum contacts within the forum State, these contacts may be considered in light of other factors to determine whether the assertion of personal jurisdiction would comport with "fair play and substantial justice." *International Shoe Co. v. Washington*, 326 U.S. at 320. Thus courts in "appropriate case[s]" may evaluate "the burden on the defendant," "the forum State's interest in adjudicating the dispute," "the plaintiff's interest in obtaining convenient and effective relief," "the interstate judicial system's interest in obtaining the most efficient resolution of controversies," and the "shared interest of the several States in furthering fundamental substantive social policies." *World-Wide Volkswagen Corp. v. Woodson, supra*, 444 U.S. at 292. These considerations sometimes serve to establish the reasonableness of jurisdiction upon a lesser showing of minimum contacts than would otherwise be required. *See, e.g., Keeton v. Hustler Magazine, Inc., supra*, 465 U.S. at 780; *Calder v. Jones, supra*, 465 U.S. at 788-789; *McGee v. International Life Insurance Co., supra*, 355 U.S. at 223-224. On the other hand, where a

---

a customer's decision to drive there, *World-Wide Volkswagen Corp. v. Woodson, supra*; over a divorced husband sued for child-support payments whose only affiliation with the forum was created by his former spouse's decision to settle there, *Kulko v. California Superior Court*, 436 U.S. 84 (1978); and over a trustee whose only connection with the forum resulted from the settlor's decision to exercise her power of appointment there, *Hanson v. Denckla*, 357 U.S. 235 (1958). In such instances, the defendant has had no "clear notice that it is subject to suit" in the forum and thus no opportunity to "alleviate the risk of burdensome litigation" there. *World-Wide Volkswagen Corp. v. Woodson, supra*, 444 U.S. at 297.

18. So long as it creates a "substantial connection" with the forum, even a single act can support jurisdiction. *McGee v. International Life Insurance Co.*, 355 U.S. at 223. The Court has noted, however, that "some single or occasional acts" related to the forum may not be sufficient to establish jurisdiction if "their nature and quality and the circumstances of their commission" create only an "attenuated" affiliation with the forum. *International Shoe Co. v. Washington*, 326 U.S. 310, 318 (1945); *World-Wide Volkswagen Corp. v. Woodson*, 444 U.S. at 299. This distinction derives from the belief that, with respect to this category of "isolated" acts, *id.* at 297, the reasonable foreseeability of litigation in the forum is substantially diminished.

defendant who purposefully has directed his activities at forum residents seeks to defeat jurisdiction, he must present a compelling case that the presence of some other considerations would render jurisdiction unreasonable. Most such considerations usually may be accommodated through means short of finding jurisdiction unconstitutional. For example, the potential clash of the forum's law with the "fundamental substantive social policies" of another State may be accommodated through application of the forum's choice-of-law rules. Similarly, a defendant claiming substantial inconvenience may seek a change of venue. Nevertheless, minimum requirements inherent in the concept of "fair play and substantial justice" may defeat the reasonableness of jurisdiction even if the defendant has purposefully engaged in forum activities. *World-Wide Volkswagen Corp. v. Woodson*, *supra*, 444 U.S. at 292. As we previously have noted, jurisdictional rules may not be employed in such a way as to make litigation "so gravely difficult and inconvenient" that a party unfairly is at a "severe disadvantage" in comparison to his opponent. *The Bremen v. Zapata Off-Shore Co.*, 407 U.S. 1, 18 (1972) (re forum-selection provisions); *McGee v. International Life Insurance Co.*, *supra*, 355 U.S. at 223-224.

## B

### (1)

Applying these principles to the case at hand, we believe there is substantial record evidence supporting the District Court's conclusion that the assertion of personal jurisdiction over Rudzewicz in Florida for the alleged breach of his franchise agreement did not offend due process. At the outset, we note a continued division among lower courts respecting whether and to what extent a contract can constitute a "contact" for purposes of due process analysis. If the question is whether an individual's contract with an out-of-state party alone can automatically establish sufficient minimum contacts in the other party's home forum, we believe the answer clearly is that it cannot. The Court long ago rejected the notion that personal jurisdiction might turn on "mechanical" tests, *International Shoe Co. v. Washington*, *supra*, 326 U.S. at 319, or on "conceptualistic . . . theories of the place of contracting or of performance." Instead, we have emphasized the need for a "highly realistic" approach that recognizes that a "contract" is "ordinarily but an intermediate step serving to tie up prior business negotiations with future consequences which themselves are the real object of the business transaction." It is these factors—prior negotiations and contemplated future consequences, along with the terms of the contract and the parties' actual course of dealing—that must be evaluated in determining whether the defendant purposefully established minimum contacts within the forum.

In this case, no physical ties to Florida can be attributed to Rudzewicz other than MacShara's brief training course in Miami. Rudzewicz did not maintain offices in Florida and, for all that appears from the record, has never even visited there. Yet this franchise dispute grew directly out of "a contract which had a substantial connection with that State." *McGee v. International Life Insurance Co.*, 355 U.S. at 223. Eschewing the option of operating an independent local enterprise, Rudzewicz deliberately "reach[ed] out beyond" Michigan and negotiated with a Florida corporation for the purchase of a long-term franchise and the manifold benefits that would derive from affiliation with a nationwide organization. Upon approval, he entered into a carefully structured 20-year relationship that envisioned continuing and wide-reaching contacts with Burger King in Florida. In light of Rudzewicz' voluntary acceptance of the long-term and exacting regulation of his business from Burger King's Miami headquarters, the "quality and nature" of his relationship to the company in Florida can in no sense be viewed as "random," "fortuitous," or "attenuated." Rudzewicz' refusal to make the contractually required payments in Miami, and his continued use of Burger King's trademarks and confidential business information after his termination, caused foreseeable injuries to the corporation in Florida. For these reasons it was, at the very least, presumptively reasonable for Rudzewicz to be called to account there for such injuries.

The Court of Appeals concluded, however, that in light of the supervision emanating from Burger King's district office in Birmingham, Rudzewicz reasonably believed that "the Michigan office was for all intents and purposes the embodiment of Burger King" and that he therefore had no "reason to anticipate a Burger King suit outside of Michigan." This reasoning overlooks substantial record evidence indicating that Rudzewicz most certainly knew that he was affiliating himself with an enterprise based primarily in Florida. The contract documents themselves emphasize that Burger King's operations are conducted and supervised from the Miami headquarters, that all relevant notices and payments must be sent there, and that the agreements were made in and enforced from Miami. Moreover, the parties' actual course of dealing repeatedly confirmed that decisionmaking authority was vested in the Miami headquarters and that the district office served largely as an intermediate link between the headquarters and the franchisees. When problems arose over building design, site-development fees, rent computation, and the defaulted payments, Rudzewicz and MacShara learned that the Michigan office was powerless to resolve their disputes and could only channel their communications to Miami. Throughout these disputes, the Miami headquarters and the Michigan franchisees carried on a continuous course of direct communications by mail and by telephone, and it was the Miami headquarters that made the key negotiating decisions out of which the instant litigation arose.

Moreover, we believe the Court of Appeals gave insufficient weight to provisions in the various franchise documents providing that all disputes would be governed by Florida law. The franchise agreement, for example, stated: "This Agreement shall become valid when executed and accepted by BKC at Miami, Florida; it shall be deemed made and entered into in the State of Florida and shall be governed and construed under and in accordance with the laws of the State of Florida. The choice of law designation does not require that all suits concerning this Agreement be filed in Florida." The Court of Appeals reasoned that choice-of-law provisions are irrelevant to the question of personal jurisdiction, relying on *Hanson v. Denckla* for the proposition that "the center of gravity for choice-of-law purposes does not necessarily confer the sovereign prerogative to assert jurisdiction." This reasoning misperceives the import of the quoted proposition. The Court in *Hanson* and subsequent cases has emphasized that choice-of-law analysis—which focuses on all elements of a transaction, and not simply on the defendant's conduct—is distinct from minimum-contacts jurisdictional analysis—which focuses at the threshold solely on the defendant's purposeful connection to the forum. Nothing in our cases, however, suggests that a choice-of-law provision should be ignored in considering whether a defendant has "purposefully invoked the benefits and protections of a State's laws" for jurisdictional purposes. Although such a provision standing alone would be insufficient to confer jurisdiction, we believe that, when combined with the 20-year interdependent relationship Rudzewicz established with Burger King's Miami headquarters, it reinforced his deliberate affiliation with the forum State and the reasonable foreseeability of possible litigation there. As Judge Johnson argued in his dissent below, Rudzewicz "purposefully availed himself of the benefits and protections of Florida's laws" by entering into contracts expressly providing that those laws would govern franchise disputes.[24]

**(2)**

Nor has Rudzewicz pointed to other factors that can be said persuasively to outweigh the considerations discussed above and to establish the unconstitutionality of Florida's assertion of jurisdiction. We cannot conclude that Florida had no "legitimate interest in holding [Rudzewicz] answerable on a claim related to" the contacts he had established in that State.[25] Moreover, although Rudzewicz has argued at some length that Michigan's Franchise Investment Law governs many aspects of this franchise relationship, he has not demonstrated how Michigan's acknowledged interest might possibly render jurisdiction in Florida unconstitutional.[26] Finally, the Court of Appeals' assertion that the Florida litigation "severely impaired [Rudzewicz']

24. In addition, the franchise agreement's disclaimer that the "choice of law designation does not require that all suits concerning this Agreement be filed in Florida," reasonably should have suggested to Rudzewicz that by negative implication such suits could be filed there. The lease also provided for binding arbitration in Miami of certain condemnation disputes, and Rudzewicz conceded the validity of this provision at oral argument. Although it does not govern the instant dispute, this provision also should have made it apparent to the franchisees that they were dealing directly with the Miami headquarters and that the Birmingham district office was not "for all intents and purposes the embodiment of Burger King."

25. Complaining that "when Burger King is the plaintiff, you won't 'have it your way' because it sues all franchisees in Miami," Brief for Appellee 19, Rudzewicz contends that Florida's interest in providing a convenient forum is negligible given the company's size and ability to conduct litigation anywhere in the country. We disagree. Absent compelling considerations, *cf. McGee v. International Life Insurance Co.*, 355 U.S. at 223, a defendant who has purposefully derived commercial benefit from his affiliations in a forum may not defeat jurisdiction there simply because of his adversary's greater net wealth.

26. Rudzewicz has failed to show how the District Court's exercise of jurisdiction in this case might have been at all inconsistent with Michigan's interests. To the contrary, the court found that Burger King had fully complied with Michigan law, and there is nothing in Michigan's franchise Act suggesting that

ability to call Michigan witnesses who might be essential to his defense and counterclaim," is wholly without support in the record. And even to the extent that it is inconvenient for a party who has minimum contacts with a forum to litigate there, such considerations most frequently can be accommodated through a change of venue. Although the Court has suggested that inconvenience may at some point become so substantial as to achieve constitutional magnitude, *McGee v. International Life Insurance Co.*, *supra*, 355 U.S. at 223, this is not such a case.

The Court of Appeals also concluded, however, that the parties' dealings involved "a characteristic disparity of bargaining power" and "elements of surprise," and that Rudzewicz "lacked fair notice" of the potential for litigation in Florida because the contractual provisions suggesting to the contrary were merely "boilerplate declarations in a lengthy printed contract." Rudzewicz presented many of these arguments to the District Court, contending that Burger King was guilty of misrepresentation, fraud, and duress; that it gave insufficient notice in its dealings with him; and that the contract was one of adhesion. After a 3-day bench trial, the District Court found that Burger King had made no misrepresentations, that Rudzewicz and Mac-Shara "were and are experienced and sophisticated businessmen," and that "at no time" did they "ac[t] under economic duress or disadvantage imposed by" Burger King. Federal Rule of Civil Procedure 52(a) requires that "[f]indings of fact shall not be set aside unless clearly erroneous," and neither Rudzewicz nor the Court of Appeals has pointed to record evidence that would support a "definite and firm conviction" that the District Court's findings are mistaken. To the contrary, Rudzewicz was represented by counsel throughout these complex transactions and, as Judge Johnson observed in dissent below, was himself an experienced accountant "who for five months conducted negotiations with Burger King over the terms of the franchise and lease agreements, and who obligated himself personally to contracts requiring over time payments that exceeded $1 million." Rudzewicz was able to secure a modest reduction in rent and other concessions from Miami headquarters; moreover, to the extent that Burger King's terms were inflexible, Rudzewicz presumably decided that the advantages of affiliating with a national organization provided sufficient commercial benefits to offset the detriments.[28]

---

Michigan would attempt to assert exclusive jurisdiction to resolve franchise disputes affecting its residents. In any event, minimum-contacts analysis presupposes that two or more States may be interested in the outcome of a dispute, and the process of resolving potentially conflicting "fundamental substantive social policies," *World-Wide Volkswagen Corp. v. Woodson*, 444 U.S. at 292, can usually be accommodated through choice-of-law rules rather than through outright preclusion of jurisdiction in one forum.

28. We do not mean to suggest that the jurisdictional outcome will always be the same in franchise cases. Some franchises may be primarily intrastate in character or involve different decisionmaking structures, such that a franchisee should not reasonably anticipate out-of-state litigation. Moreover, commentators have argued that franchise relationships may sometimes involve unfair business practices in their inception and operation. *See* H. Brown, *Franchising Realities and Remedies* 4-5 (2d ed. 1978). For these reasons, we reject Burger King's suggestion for "a general rule, or at least a presumption, that participation in an interstate franchise relationship" represents consent to the jurisdiction of the franchisor's principal place of business.

## III

Notwithstanding these considerations, the Court of Appeals apparently believed that it was necessary to reject jurisdiction in this case as a prophylactic measure, reasoning that an affirmance of the District Court's judgment would result in the exercise of jurisdiction over "out-of-state consumers to collect payments due on modest personal purchases" and would "sow the seeds of default judgments against franchisees owing smaller debts." 724 F.2d at 1511. We share the Court of Appeals' broader concerns and therefore reject any talismanic jurisdictional formulas; "the facts of each case must [always] be weighed" in determining whether personal jurisdiction would comport with "fair play and substantial justice."[29] The "quality and nature" of an interstate transaction may sometimes be so "random," "fortuitous," or "attenuated"[30] that it cannot fairly be said that the potential defendant "should reasonably anticipate being haled into court" in another jurisdiction. We also have emphasized that jurisdiction may not be grounded on a contract whose terms have been obtained through "fraud, undue influence, or overweening bargaining power" and whose application would render litigation "so gravely difficult and inconvenient that [a party] will for all practical purposes be deprived of his day in court." Just as the Due Process Clause allows flexibility in ensuring that commercial actors are not effectively "judgment proof" for the consequences of obligations they voluntarily assume in other States, so too does it prevent rules that would unfairly enable them to obtain default judgments against unwitting customers.

For the reasons set forth above, however, these dangers are not present in the instant case. Because Rudzewicz established a substantial and continuing relationship with Burger King's Miami headquarters, received fair notice from the contract documents and the course of dealing that he might be subject to suit in Florida, and has failed to demonstrate how jurisdiction in that forum would otherwise be fundamentally unfair, we conclude that the District Court's exercise of jurisdiction pursuant to Fla. Stat. § 48.193(1)(g) (Supp. 1984) did not offend due process. The judgment of the Court of Appeals is accordingly reversed, and the case is remanded for further proceedings consistent with this opinion.

Justice POWELL took no part in the consideration or decision of this case.

Justice STEVENS, with whom Justice WHITE joins, dissenting:

In my opinion there is a significant element of unfairness in requiring a franchisee to defend a case of this kind in the forum chosen by the franchisor. It is undisputed that appellee maintained no place of business in Florida, that he

---

29. This approach does, of course, preclude clear-cut jurisdictional rules. But any inquiry into "fair play and substantial justice" necessarily requires determinations "in which few answers will be written 'in black and white. The greys are dominant and even among them the shades are innumerable.'" *Kulko v. California Superior Court*, 436 U.S. at 92.

30. *Hanson v. Denckla*, 357 U.S. at 253; *Keeton v. Hustler Magazine, Inc.*, 465 U.S. at 774; *World-Wide Volkswagen Corp. v. Woodson*, 444 U.S. at 299.

had no employees in that State, and that he was not licensed to do business there. Appellee did not prepare his French fries, shakes, and hamburgers in Michigan, and then deliver them into the stream of commerce "with the expectation that they [would] be purchased by consumers in" Florida. To the contrary, appellee did business only in Michigan, his business, property, and payroll taxes were payable in that State, and he sold all of his products there.

Throughout the business relationship, appellee's principal contacts with appellant were with its Michigan office. Notwithstanding its disclaimer, the Court seems ultimately to rely on nothing more than standard boilerplate language contained in various documents to establish that appellee "'purposefully availed himself of the benefits and protections of Florida's laws.'" Such superficial analysis creates a potential for unfairness not only in negotiations between franchisors and their franchisees but, more significantly, in the resolution of the disputes that inevitably arise from time to time in such relationships. . . .

## Comments and Questions

1. Note that in its first paragraph, the Court confirms that the jurisdictional reach of the federal district court in Florida where Burger King filed the case is the same as that of the state courts there—that is, controlled in the first instance by the Florida long-arm statute, and then measured against the due process standards of *International Shoe*. This is a consequence of Fed. R. Civ. P. 4(k)(1)(A).

2. For dissenter Stevens, there is no jurisdiction because Rudzewicz "did not prepare his French fries, shakes and hamburgers in Michigan, and then deliver them into the stream of commerce with the expectation that they would be purchased by customers in Florida." Does Brennan's opinion for the Court treat this as a "stream of commerce" case? How does the Court distinguish *World-Wide Volkswagen*?

3. What does *Burger King* teach us about the relationship between the "fair play" factors and the "minimum-contacts" test? Look at the final paragraph of section IIA in the decision. The First Circuit has summed up the three questions that now must be asked to determine whether jurisdiction exists:

(1) whether the state long-arm statute authorizes jurisdiction; (2) whether defendant has sufficient minimum contacts so that exercise of jurisdiction does not offend due process; and (3) whether exercise of jurisdiction is reasonable, and therefore does not offend due process.

*Noonan v. Winston Company*, 135 F.3d 85, 89 (1st Cir. 1998).

4. Consider the significance of the provision in the franchise agreements quoted by the Court in section IIB(1): "This agreement shall become valid when executed and accepted by BKC at Miami, Florida; it shall be deemed made and entered into in the State of Florida and shall be governed and construed under and in accordance with the laws of the State of Florida. The choice of law designation does not require that all suits concerning

this Agreement be filed in Florida." In Part O, later in this chapter, we will explore forum selection clauses that go the next step—that is, that actually designate a particular forum before any dispute arises.

5. Suppose Rudzewicz had been a management consultant retained by Burger King to evaluate its operations in Michigan. After a brief phone conversation, his contract for the project was sent from the Miami headquarters to his office in Michigan, where he signed and returned it by mail. The contract called for the work to be completed within three months. Dissatisfied with his work product, Burger King files a breach of contract action in Florida. Is there jurisdiction over Rudzewicz for this claim? What distinguishes this case from the actual *Burger King Corp. v. Rudzewicz*?

6. Suppose Rudzewicz had clipped a mail order form from a magazine and sent it to the Sunshine Fitness Company in Miami, and the company in response shipped its Sweat-Your-Pounds-Away Exerciser to his home in Michigan. If Rudzewicz fails to pay the bill, can Sunshine sue him in Florida? What distinguishes this case from the actual *Burger King Corp. v. Rudzewicz*? Note Justice Brennan's reference at the beginning of section III to the concern the Eleventh Circuit had about jurisdiction over "out-of-state consumers to collect payments due on modest personal purchases," which would "sow the seeds of default judgments." How does Brennan attempt to alleviate this concern?

7. Suppose Rudzewicz is injured on the Exerciser and files a product liability action against Sunshine in his home state of Michigan. Is there jurisdiction over the Florida company on his tort claim? What distinguishes this case from the actual *Burger King Corp. v. Rudzewicz*?

8. Although Burger King prevailed, the Court refused its request to create a general rule that participation in an interstate franchise relationship would *always* constitute consent to jurisdiction in the state of the franchiser's principal place of business, opting instead for an *ad hoc* approach. Look at the Court's footnote 28. Was counsel for Burger King wise in basing the proposed rule on a *consent* theory? Ironically, such a theory is back in vogue. See note 3 following *Nicastro*, above.

Why do you think the Court is so hesitant to adopt categorical rules (e.g., for automobile product defect cases, for franchise arrangements) in the area of personal jurisdiction?

## Practice Exercise No. 33: Ruling on a Rule 12(b)(2) Motion to Dismiss in a Contract Action

### *Memorandum*

To: Law Clerk
From: U.S. District Judge, District of Massachusetts
Re: Recommendation on 12(b)(2) Motion in *Shaw v. Northern Law School*

Norris Shaw, a Massachusetts citizen, has filed a diversity action against Northern Law School of Vermont (NLS) and one of its faculty, Albert Gloss. In a two-count complaint, Shaw seeks damages against the school for breach of contract and against Gloss for intentional infliction of emotional distress.

After reading an article about NLS in the *Boston Globe*'s Education Section (and intrigued by the prospect of learning law amidst the beauty of the Green Mountains and Ben & Jerry's Ice Cream), Shaw wrote the school and expressed interest. NLS responded by mailing its catalogue and application form to Shaw's home in Massachusetts. He filled out the application, mailed it back to NLS, and in the spring received an acceptance letter. Shaw sent in his $500 deposit and enrolled as a law student in the fall.

In his second year at NLS, Shaw took "Extremely Complex Litigation" from Professor Gloss (a lifelong Vermonter). Although he thought he had mastered the materials, Shaw received a failing grade and as a result was dismissed from the school. After attempting unsuccessfully to have the grade changed through the school's appeals procedure, he returned to Massachusetts and filed the instant lawsuit in federal court in Boston.

In his complaint, Shaw alleges that he regularly disagreed with Professor Gloss in class and that Gloss failed him in retaliation, thus intentionally inflicting emotional distress upon him. In a second count, he asserts that the school's refusal to reverse the failing grade constitutes a breach of its implied contractual obligation to deal fairly with him.

Defendants NLS and Gloss have both moved to dismiss the complaint pursuant to Fed. R. Civ. P. 12(b)(2). The school has filed an affidavit asserting that its only place of business is in Vermont, that it has never maintained any office, mailing address, or telephone listing in Massachusetts, and that it has never done business or advertised there. The affidavit does concede that NLS regularly sends recruiters to Massachusetts to inform pre-law advisors and undergraduates about the school. Gloss has submitted an affidavit asserting that he has never set foot in Massachusetts, and has no connection whatever with the state.

I need a memorandum from you recommending how I should rule on these two motions. (The Massachusetts long-arm statute is reprinted in Practice Exercise No. 32.)

## J. PERSONAL JURISDICTION IN CYBERSPACE

How can a theory of jurisdiction so rooted in territorial notions and land borders adapt itself to the Internet Age, when business and communication are conducted in cyberspace?

## ■ ALS SCAN, INC. v. DIGITAL SERVICE CONSULTANTS, INC.
### 293 F.3d 707 (4th Cir. 2002)

NIEMEYER, Circuit Judge:

The question presented in this appeal is whether a Georgia-based Internet Service Provider subjected itself to personal jurisdiction in Maryland by enabling a website owner to publish photographs on the Internet, in violation of a Maryland corporation's copyrights. Adapting the traditional due process principles used to determine a State's authority to exercise personal jurisdiction over out-of-state persons to the Internet context, we hold that in the circumstances of this case, a Maryland court cannot constitutionally exercise jurisdiction over the Georgia Internet Service Provider. Accordingly, we affirm the district court's order dismissing the complaint against the Internet Service Provider for lack of personal jurisdiction.

ALS Scan, Inc., a Maryland corporation with its place of business in Columbia, Maryland, commenced this action for copyright infringement against Digital Service Consultants, Inc. ("Digital"), and Digital's customers, Robert Wilkins and Alternative Products, Inc. (collectively, "Alternative Products"). ALS Scan, which creates and markets adult photographs of female models for distribution over the Internet, claims that Alternative Products appropriated copies of hundreds of ALS Scan's copyrighted photographs and placed them on its websites, *www.abpefarc.net* and *www.abpeuarc.com*, thereby gaining revenue from them through membership fees and advertising. ALS Scan further alleges that Digital, as the Internet Service Provider ("ISP") for Alternative Products, "enabled" Alternative Products to publish ALS Scan's copyrighted photographs on the Internet by providing Alternative Products with the bandwidth service needed to maintain its websites. ALS Scan thus alleges that all of the defendants have infringed and are infringing its copyrights within Maryland and elsewhere by selling, publishing, and displaying its copyrighted photographs.

Digital filed a motion to dismiss the complaint against it under Federal Rule of Civil Procedure 12(b)(2), asserting that the district court lacked personal jurisdiction over it. In support of its motion, Digital provided affidavits demonstrating that Digital is a Georgia corporation with its only place of business in Atlanta. Digital asserts that it is an ISP which provided bandwidth service to Alternative Products as a customer but that it is not affiliated in any way with Alternative Products except through an arms-length customer relationship. In addition, Digital states that it did not select the infringing photographs for publication; it did not have knowledge that they were posted on Alternative Products' web site; and it received no income from Alternative Products' subscribers. Digital acknowledges that it does maintain its own web site, *www.dscga.com*, but asserts that its web site "contains no means for any person to enter into a contract with, transfer funds to, or otherwise transact business with, Digital."

Digital also states that, other than through the Internet, it has no contacts with the State of Maryland. It avers that it conducts no business and has no offices in Maryland; that it has no contracts with any persons or entities in Maryland; that it derives no income from any clients or business in Maryland; that it does not advertise in Maryland (other than through its website); and that it owns no property in Maryland.

In a responding affidavit, ALS Scan asserts that copies of its copyrighted photographs have appeared on Alternative Products' two websites, *www.abpefarc.net* and *www.abpeuarc.com*. It also alleges that one of its employees in Maryland purchased an "on-line" membership to *www.abpefarc.net*, using a credit card, and, by obtaining that membership, the employee received a "user name" and a "password" to access the website. That website, it asserts, displayed ALS Scan's copyrighted photographs, allegedly in violation of the Copyright Act.

The district court granted Digital's motion to dismiss for lack of personal jurisdiction. The court found that it had neither specific nor general jurisdiction over Digital because "Digital does not engage in any continuous and systematic activities within Maryland, and there is no evidence that [ALS Scan's] claim arises out of any contacts which Digital may have with Maryland." From the district court's ruling, ALS Scan filed this interlocutory appeal.

## II

. . . Under Federal Rule of Civil Procedure 4(k)(1)(A), a federal court may exercise personal jurisdiction over a defendant in the manner provided by state law. Maryland courts have concluded that the State's longarm statute, Md. Code Ann., Courts & Jud. Proc. § 6-103, expands Maryland's exercise of personal jurisdiction to the extent allowed by the Due Process Clause of the Fourteenth Amendment. "Because the limits of Maryland's statutory authorization for the exercise of personal jurisdiction are coterminous with the limits of the Due Process Clause, the statutory inquiry necessarily merges with the constitutional inquiry, and the two inquiries essentially become one." Thus, we apply the constitutional limitations on state service of process incorporated in Rule 4(k)(1)(A), and our inquiry coalesces into the question of whether Digital has sufficient minimum contacts with Maryland.

. . . "Due process requires only that in order to subject a defendant to a judgment *in personam*, if he be not present within the territory of the forum, he have certain minimum contacts with it such that the maintenance of the suit does not offend 'traditional notions of fair play and substantial justice.'" *Int'l Shoe*. With respect to corporations, the Court has recognized that "unlike an individual, its 'presence' without, as well as within, the state of its origin can be manifested only by activities carried on in its behalf by those who are authorized to act for it." *Id.* Thus, "the terms 'present' or 'presence' are used merely to symbolize those activities of the corporation's agent within the state which courts will deem to be sufficient to satisfy the demands of due process." *Id.*

Although the courts have recognized that the standards used to determine the proper exercise of personal jurisdiction may evolve as technological progress occurs, it nonetheless has remained clear that technology cannot eviscerate the constitutional limits on a State's power to exercise jurisdiction over a defendant. In *Hanson v. Denckla*, 357 U.S. 235 (1958), the Court explored the problem of reconciling technological advances with the limits of personal jurisdiction and stated:

As technological progress has increased the flow of commerce between States, the need for jurisdiction over nonresidents has undergone a similar increase. At the same time, progress in communications and transportation has made the defense of a suit in a foreign tribunal less burdensome. In response to these changes, the requirements for personal jurisdiction over nonresidents have evolved from the rigid rule of *Pennoyer v. Neff* to the flexible standard of *International Shoe Co. v. State of Washington*. But it is a mistake to assume that this trend heralds the eventual demise of all restrictions on the personal jurisdiction of state courts. Those restrictions are more than a guarantee of immunity from inconvenient or distant litigation. They are a consequence of territorial limitations on the power of the respective States. However minimal the burden of defending in a foreign tribunal, a defendant may not be called upon to do so unless he has had the "minimal contacts" with that State that are a prerequisite to its exercise of power over him.

The Court has thus mandated that limits on the states' power to exercise personal jurisdiction over nonresidents must be maintained, despite the growing ease with which business is conducted across state lines.

Determining the extent of a State's judicial power over persons outside of its borders under the *International Shoe* standard can be undertaken through two different approaches—by finding specific jurisdiction based on conduct connected to the suit or by finding general jurisdiction. If the defendant's contacts with the State are also the basis for the suit, those contacts may establish specific jurisdiction. In determining specific jurisdiction, we consider (1) the extent to which the defendant "purposefully avail[ed]" itself of the privilege of conducting activities in the State; (2) whether the plaintiffs' claims arise out of those activities directed at the State; and (3) whether the exercise of personal jurisdiction would be constitutionally "reasonable."

On the other hand, if the defendant's contacts with the State are not also the basis for suit, then jurisdiction over the defendant must arise from the defendant's general, more persistent, but unrelated contacts with the State. To establish general jurisdiction over the defendant, the defendant's activities in the State must have been "continuous and systematic," a more demanding standard than is necessary for establishing specific jurisdiction.

## III

In this case, ALS Scan argues that Digital's activity in enabling Alternative Products' publication of the infringing photographs on the Internet, thereby causing ALS Scan injury in Maryland, forms a proper basis for the district court's specific jurisdiction over Digital. The question thus becomes whether a person electronically transmitting or enabling the transmission of information via the Internet to Maryland, causing injury there, subjects the person to the jurisdiction of a court in Maryland, a question of first impression in the Fourth Circuit.

Applying the traditional due process principles governing a State's jurisdiction over persons outside of the State based on Internet activity requires some adaptation of those principles because the Internet is omnipresent—when a person places information on the Internet, he can communicate with persons in virtually every jurisdiction. If we were to conclude as a general principle that a person's act of placing information on the Internet subjects that person to personal jurisdiction in each State in which the information is accessed, then the defense of personal jurisdiction, in the sense that a State has geographically limited judicial power, would no longer exist. The person placing information on the Internet would be subject to personal jurisdiction in every State.

[T]he argument could be made that the Internet's electronic signals are surrogates for the person and that Internet users conceptually enter a State to the extent that they send their electronic signals into the State, establishing those minimum contacts sufficient to subject the sending person to personal jurisdiction in the State where the signals are received. Under this argument, the electronic transmissions "symbolize those activities . . . within the state which courts will deem to be sufficient to satisfy the demands of due process." *Int'l Shoe*. But if that broad interpretation of minimum contacts were adopted, State jurisdiction over persons would be universal, and notions of limited State sovereignty and personal jurisdiction would be eviscerated.

[I]t would be difficult to accept a structural arrangement in which each State has unlimited judicial power over every citizen in each other State who uses the Internet. That thought certainly would have been considered outrageous in the past when interconnections were made only by telephones. But now . . . the breadth and frequency of electronic contacts through computers has resulted in billions of interstate connections and millions of interstate transactions entered into solely through the vehicle of the Internet. . . . [W]e must develop, under existing principles, the more limited circumstances when it can be deemed that an out-of-state citizen, through electronic contacts, has conceptually "entered" the State via the Internet for jurisdictional purposes. Such principles are necessary to recognize that a State does have limited judicial authority over out-of-state persons who use the Internet to contact persons within the State. Drawing on the requirements for establishing specific jurisdiction, which requires *purposeful* conduct directed at the State and that the plaintiff's claims arise from the purposeful conduct, we adopt today the model developed in *Zippo Manufacturing Co. v. Zippo Dot Com, Inc.*, 952 F. Supp. 1119 (W.D. Pa. 1997).

In *Zippo*, the court concluded that "the likelihood that personal jurisdiction can be constitutionally exercised is directly proportionate to the nature and quality of commercial activity that an entity conducts over the Internet." Recognizing a "sliding scale" for defining when electronic contacts with a State are sufficient, the court elaborated:

> At one end of the spectrum are situations where a defendant clearly does business over the Internet. If the defendant enters into contracts with residents of a foreign jurisdiction that involve the knowing and repeated transmission of computer files over the Internet, personal jurisdiction is proper. At the opposite end are situations where a defendant has simply posted information on an Internet Web site which is accessible to users in foreign jurisdictions. A passive Web site that does little more than make information available to those who are

interested in it is not grounds for the exercise [of] personal jurisdiction. The middle ground is occupied by interactive Web sites where a user can exchange information with the host computer. In these cases, the exercise of jurisdiction is determined by examining the level of interactivity and commercial nature of the exchange of information that occurs on the Web site.

Thus, adopting and adapting the *Zippo* model, we conclude that a State may, consistent with due process, exercise judicial power over a person outside of the State when that person (1) directs electronic activity into the State, (2) with the manifested intent of engaging in business or other interactions within the State, and (3) that activity creates, in a person within the State, a potential cause of action cognizable in the State's courts. Under this standard, a person who simply places information on the Internet does not subject himself to jurisdiction in each State into which the electronic signal is transmitted and received. Such passive Internet activity does not generally include directing electronic activity into the State with the manifested intent of engaging business or other interactions in the State thus creating in a person within the State a potential cause of action cognizable in courts located in the State.

This standard for reconciling contacts through electronic media with standard due process principles is not dissimilar to that applied by the Supreme Court in *Calder v. Jones*, 465 U.S. 783 (1984). In *Calder*, the Court held that a California court could constitutionally exercise personal jurisdiction over a Florida citizen whose only material contact with California was to write a libelous story in Florida, directed at a California citizen, for a publication circulated in California, knowing that the "injury would be felt by [the Californian] in the State in which she lives and works." Analogously, under the standard we adopt and apply today, specific jurisdiction in the Internet context may be based only on an out-of-state person's Internet activity directed at Maryland and causing injury that gives rise to a potential claim cognizable in Maryland.

Applying this standard to the present case, we conclude that Digital's activity was, at most, passive and therefore does not subject it to the judicial power of a Maryland court even though electronic signals from Digital's facility were concededly received in Maryland. Digital functioned from Georgia as an ISP, and in that role provided bandwidth to Alternative Products, also located in Georgia, to enable Alternative Products to create a website and send information over the Internet. It did not select or knowingly transmit infringing photographs specifically to Maryland with the intent of engaging in business or any other transaction in Maryland. Rather, its role as an ISP was at most passive. Surely, it cannot be said that Digital "purposefully availed" itself of the privilege of conducting business or other transactions in Maryland.

Indeed, the only *direct* contact that Digital had with Maryland was through the general publication of its website on the Internet. But that website is unrelated to ALS Scan's claim in this case because Digital's website was not involved in the publication of any infringing photographs.

Thus, under the standard articulated in this case, Digital did not direct its electronic activity specifically at any target in Maryland; it did not manifest an intent to engage in a business or some other interaction in Maryland; and none of its conduct in enabling a website created a cause of action in Maryland. . . .

Accordingly, we agree with the district court that Digital's contacts in Maryland do not justify a Maryland court's exercise of specific jurisdiction over Digital.

## IV

. . . We are not prepared at this time to recognize that a State may obtain general jurisdiction over out-of-state persons who regularly and systematically transmit electronic signals into the State via the Internet based solely on those transmissions. Something more would have to be demonstrated. And we need not decide today what that "something more" is because ALS Scan has shown no more.

## V

For the foregoing reasons, we affirm the order of the district court dismissing the complaint against Digital for lack of personal jurisdiction.

## Comments and Questions

1. Look back at *Griffis v. Luban*, discussed in note 6 following *Calder v. Jones*, above. These Internet cases raise what Justice Breyer refers to in *Nicastro* as the "many recent changes in commerce and communication, many of which are not anticipated by our precedents." How does the Fourth Circuit translate past precedent into the new age?

2. The U.S. Chamber of Commerce urged the Court in *Nicastro* to "make clear that certain forms of internet advertising do not satisfy the 'additional conduct' requirement of *Asahi*." See Brief of the Chamber of Commerce of the USA as *Amicus Curiae* in Support of Petitioner, pp. 24-25. The Court has yet to tackle the issue.

3. Unlike defendant Digital in the case above, Harrah's Hotel in Las Vegas maintained an interactive Web site that permitted visitors to make reservations, and "by touting the proximity of their hotels to California and providing driving directions from California to their hotels, defendants' Web site specifically targeted residents of California." *See Snowney v. Harrah's Entertainment, Inc.*, 35 Cal. 4th 1054, 1068, 112 P.3d 28, 43 (2005). This purposeful availment rendered the Nevada hotel subject to specific jurisdiction in an action in California by a resident unhappy about an energy surcharge imposed by the hotel when he checked out.

But other courts have insisted on "something more" in the way of targeting the forum state, examining for example the number of hits and actual transactions consummated from residents. See, e.g., *iAccess, Inc. v. Webcard Technologies, Inc.*, 182 F. Supp. 1183 (D. Utah 2002).

What is clear is that "the mere existence of a website that is visible in a forum and that gives information about a company and its products is not enough, by itself, to subject a defendant to personal jurisdiction in that forum." *Cossaboon v. Me. Med. Ctr.*, 600 F.3d 25, 35 (1st Cir. 2010). See also *Bensusan Restaurant Corp. v. King*, 126 F.3d 25 (2d Cir. 1997) (rejecting jurisdiction over "The Blue Note" jazz club in Columbia, Missouri, sued in New York by the Blue Note club in lower Manhattan for trademark infringement based on the defendant's expropriation of the plaintiff's famous name on its Web site); *Roberts v. Legendary Marine Sales*, 447 Mass. 860, 864-865 (Sup. Jud. Ct. 2006) (rejecting argument that defendant's advertisement on its passive Web site, which induced plaintiff to purchase an allegedly defective boat, was sufficient to establish jurisdiction).

4. *Zippo Manufacturing Co.*'s sliding scale analysis has not met with universal approval. One court has observed:

> [I]t is not clear why a website's level of interactivity should be determinative on the issue of personal jurisdiction. As even courts adopting the *Zippo* test have recognized, a court cannot determine whether personal jurisdiction is appropriate simply by deciding whether a website is "passive" or "interactive" (assuming that websites can be readily classified into one category or the other). Even a "passive" website may support a finding of jurisdiction if the defendant used its website intentionally to harm the plaintiff in the forum state. *See Panavision International, LP v. Toeppen*, 141 F.3d 1316, 1322 (9th Cir.1998). Similarly, an "interactive" or commercial website may not be sufficient to support jurisdiction if it is not aimed at residents in the forum state. *See GTE New Media Services, Inc. v. BellSouth Corp.*, 199 F.3d 1343, 1349-50 (D.C.Cir.2000). Moreover, regardless how interactive a website is, it cannot form the basis for personal jurisdiction unless a nexus exists between the website and the cause of action or unless the contacts through the website are so substantial that they may be considered "systematic and continuous" for the purpose of general jurisdiction. Thus, a rigid adherence to the *Zippo* test is likely to lead to erroneous results.

*Hy Cite Corp. v. Badbusinessbureau.com. LLC*, 297 F. Supp. 2d 1154, 1169 (W.D. Wis. 2004).

5. To read more about the topic of Internet jurisdiction, see Greg Lastowka, *Virtual Justice: The New Laws of Online Worlds* 75-101 (2010); Joel R. Reidenberg, *Technology and Internet Jurisdiction*, 153 U. Pa. L. Rev. 1951 (2005); A. Benjamin Spencer, *Jurisdiction and the Internet: Returning to Traditional Principles to Analyze Network-Mediated Contacts*, 2006 U. Ill. L. Rev. 71 (2006); C. Douglas Floyd and Shima Baradaran-Robison, *Toward a Unified Test of Personal Jurisdiction in an Era of Widely Diffused Wrongs: The Relevance of Purpose and Effects*, 81 Ind. L.J. 601 (2006); Danielle Keats

Citron, *Minimum Contacts in a Borderless World: Voiceover Internet Protocol and the Coming Implosion of Personal Jurisdiction Theory*, 39 U.C. Davis. L. Rev. 1481 (2006). For a collection of cases to date, see Richard E. Kaye, *Internet Web Site Activities of Nonresident Person or Corporation as Conferring Personal Jurisdiction Under Long-Arm Statutes and Due Process Clause*, 81 A.L.R. 5th 41 (2010).

6. The Communications Decency Act, 42 U.S.C. § 230, shields Internet service providers from defamation liability for merely conveying content obtained from a third party. § 230(c)(1) provides that "[n]o provider or user of an interactive computer service shall be treated as the publisher or speaker of any information provided by another information content provider." And "[n]o cause of action may be brought and no liability imposed under any State or local law that is inconsistent with this section." § 230(e)(3). *See Doe v. Friendfinder Network, Inc.*, 540 F. Supp. 2d 288 (D.N.H. 2008) (and cases cited). The Act does not, however, affect claims pertaining to intellectual property or privacy, § 230(e)(2), (4), and thus is not applicable in cases such as *ALS Scan*.

## Practice Exercise No. 34: Electronic Contacts and Virtual Presence

### *Memorandum*

To: Associate
From: Partner
Re: Advice on *Nancy Nickels v. David Dimes*

Our client David Dimes, a coin collector who resides in California, has been sued in the U.S. District Court in New Jersey in a defamation action. Dimes agreed to purchase a rare coin from Nickels, a resident of New Jersey who operates a coin business on the Internet auction site *eBay*, the leading online marketplace. Upon seeing the coin advertised, Dimes e-mailed Nickels for further information before placing his successful bid on *eBay*. Dimes paid for his purchase through an online payment service that withdrew the money from his checking account.

When he received the Fed Ex package from Nickels, Dimes was aghast to see that it was empty. He immediately e-mailed Nickels and requested a refund, which was not forthcoming. After several follow-up e-mails to Nickels, to which he received no response, Dimes posted very negative comments on *eBay*'s customer feedback page, accusing Nickels of being a fraud and a cheat, which became part of Nickels's seller profile.

Nickels filed the defamation action in the U.S. District Court in her home state alleging economic injury to her *eBay* coin business, and harm to her personal reputation. It strikes me that jurisdiction over our client in New Jersey is highly questionable given that his only ties to that state are electronic. He has never been to the Garden State, nor has he had any other dealings with it.

Please prepare a memorandum in support of our motion to dismiss. (Assume New Jersey has the same long-arm statute as Massachusetts, set out in Practice Exercise 32.)

*Now assume instead* that Dimes reacts to the empty package by filing a civil action in federal district court in California, alleging state law claims of breach of contract and fraud. Nickels files a motion to dismiss for lack of personal jurisdiction. As law clerk to the U.S. District Judge, prepare a memo advising on the motion. Recall that California's long-arm statute is open-ended, and extends power to the limits of the Due Process Clause.

## K. JURISDICTION BASED ON THE PRESENCE OF DEFENDANT'S PROPERTY

Would it have made any difference on the issue of adjudicatory power over Professor Gloss in Practice Exercise 33 if he owned a vacation home on Martha's Vineyard in Massachusetts? If Gloss had graded Shaw's examination there, arguably that might provide specific jurisdiction over Shaw's claim for intentional infliction of emotional distress.

Ownership of the home in the forum state also raises two other possible bases of jurisdiction that go back to the original *Pennoyer* formulation. First, Shaw could try to have the professor served with process at or en route to the home—service within the state constitutes physical "presence." We will have more to say about so-called tag jurisdiction in the next section. Second, Shaw could cause the home to be attached and assert quasi in rem jurisdiction— under the *Pennoyer* scheme the presence of Gloss's property in Massachusetts creates jurisdiction on the unrelated tort claim, permitting entry of a judgment up to the value of the property. The Court's 1977 decision in the case that follows, however, radically altered this category of adjudicatory power.

*Shaffer v. Heitner* involves a type of lawsuit we have not yet encountered. In a shareholder derivative action, stockholders sue on behalf of the corporation to enforce rights and obligations that the corporation itself has failed to act upon. Defendants are the officers and directors accused of mismanagement, or worse. Any recovery is (at least theoretically) for the benefit of the corporation.

┌ Appellants          ┌ as Custodian for Mark Andrew
                                                 Heitner

## ■ SHAFFER v. HEITNER
### 433 U.S. 186 (1977)

Justice MARSHALL delivered the opinion of the Court:
The controversy in this case concerns the constitutionality of a Delaware statute that allows a court of that State to take jurisdiction of a lawsuit by

sequestering any property of the defendant that happens to be located in Delaware. Appellants contend that the sequestration statute as applied in this case violates the Due Process Clause of the Fourteenth Amendment both because it permits the state courts to exercise jurisdiction despite the absence of sufficient contacts among the defendants, the litigation, and the State of Delaware and because it authorizes the deprivation of defendants' property without providing adequate procedural safeguards. We find it necessary to consider only the first of these contentions.

### I

Appellee Heitner, a nonresident of Delaware, is the owner of one share of stock in the Greyhound Corp., a business incorporated under the laws of Delaware with its principal place of business in Phoenix, Ariz. On May 22, 1974, he filed a shareholder's derivative suit in the Court of Chancery for New Castle County, Del., in which he named as defendants Greyhound, its wholly owned subsidiary Greyhound Lines, Inc.,[1] and 28 present or former officers or directors of one or both of the corporations. In essence, Heitner alleged that the individual defendants had violated their duties to Greyhound by causing it and its subsidiary to engage in actions that resulted in the corporation's being held liable for substantial damages in a private antitrust suit[2] and a large fine in a criminal contempt action.[3] The activities which led to these penalties took place in Oregon.

Simultaneously with his complaint, Heitner filed a motion for an order of sequestration of the Delaware property of the individual defendants pursuant to Del. Code Ann., Tit. 10, § 366 (1975).[4] This motion was accompanied

---

1. Greyhound Lines, Inc., is incorporated in California and has its principal place of business in Phoenix, Ariz.

2. A judgment of $13,146,090 plus attorneys' fees was entered against Greyhound in *Mt. Hood Stages, Inc. v. Greyhound Corp.*, 1972-3 Trade Cas. P 74,824, *aff'd*, 555 F.2d 687 (9th Cir. 1977).

3. *See United States v. Greyhound Corp.*, 363 F. Supp. 525 (N.D. Ill. 1973) and 370 F. Supp. 881 (N.D. Ill.), *aff'd*, 508 F.2d 529 (7th Cir. 1974). Greyhound was fined $100,000 and Greyhound Lines $500,000.

4. Section 366 provides:

(a) If it appears in any complaint filed in the Court of Chancery that the defendant or any one or more of the defendants is a nonresident of the State, the Court may make an order directing such nonresident defendant or defendants to appear by a day certain to be designated. Such order shall be served on such nonresident defendant or defendants by mail or otherwise, if practicable, and shall be published in such manner as the Court directs, not less than once a week for 3 consecutive weeks. The Court may compel the appearance of the defendant by the seizure of all or any part of his property, which property may be sold under the order of the Court to pay the demand of the plaintiff, if the defendant does not appear, or otherwise defaults. Any defendant whose property shall have been so seized and who shall have entered a general appearance in the cause may, upon notice to the plaintiff, petition the Court for an order releasing such property or any part thereof from the seizure. The Court shall release such property unless the plaintiff shall satisfy the Court that because of other circumstances there is a reasonable possibility that such release may render it substantially less likely that plaintiff will obtain satisfaction of any judgment secured. If such petition shall not be granted, or if no such petition shall be filed, such property shall remain subject to seizure and may be sold to satisfy any judgment entered in the case. The Court may at any time release such property or any part thereof upon the giving of sufficient security.

(b) The Court may make all necessary rules respecting the form of process, the manner of issuance and return thereof, the release of such property from seizure and for the sale of the

by a supporting affidavit of counsel which stated that the individual defendants were nonresidents of Delaware. The affidavit identified the property to be sequestered as

> common stock, 3% Second Cumulative Preferred Stock and stock unit credits of the Defendant Greyhound Corporation, a Delaware corporation, as well as all options and all warrants to purchase said stock issued to said individual Defendants and all contractural [*sic*] obligations, all rights, debts or credits due or accrued to or for the benefit of any of the said Defendants under any type of written agreement, contract or other legal instrument of any kind whatever between any of the individual Defendants and said corporation.

The requested sequestration order was signed the day the motion was filed. Pursuant to that order, the sequestrator "seized" approximately 82,000 shares of Greyhound common stock belonging to 19 of the defendants,[7] and options belonging to another 2 defendants. These seizures were accomplished by placing "stop transfer" orders or their equivalents on the books of the Greyhound Corp. So far as the record shows, none of the certificates representing the seized property was physically present in Delaware. The stock was considered to be in Delaware, and so subject to seizure, by virtue of Del. Code Ann., Tit. 8, § 169 (1975), which makes Delaware the situs of ownership of all stock in Delaware corporations.[9]

All 28 defendants were notified of the initiation of the suit by certified mail directed to their last known addresses and by publication in a New Castle County newspaper. The 21 defendants whose property was seized (hereafter referred to as appellants) responded by entering a special appearance for the purpose of moving to quash service of process and to vacate the sequestration order. They contended that the ex parte sequestration procedure did not accord them due process of law and that the property seized was not capable of attachment in Delaware. In addition, appellants asserted that under the rule of *International Shoe Co. v. Washington*, 326 U.S. 310 (1945), they did not have sufficient contacts with Delaware to sustain the jurisdiction of that State's courts.

---

property so seized, and may require the plaintiff to give approved security to abide any order of the Court respecting the property.

(c) Any transfer or assignment of the property so seized after the seizure thereof shall be void and after the sale of the property is made and confirmed, the purchaser shall be entitled to and have all the right, title and interest of the defendant in and to the property so seized and sold and such sale and confirmation shall transfer to the purchaser all the right, title and interest of the defendant in and to the property as fully as if the defendant had transferred the same to the purchaser in accordance with law.

7. The closing price of Greyhound stock on the day the sequestration order was issued was $14 3/8. New York Times, May 23, 1974, p. 62. Thus, the value of the sequestered stock was approximately $1.2 million.

9. Section 169 provides: "For all purposes of title, action, attachment, garnishment and jurisdiction of all courts held in this State, but not for the purpose of taxation, the situs of the ownership of the capital stock of all corporations existing under the laws of this State, whether organized under this chapter or otherwise, shall be regarded as in this State."

The Court of Chancery rejected these arguments in a letter opinion which emphasized the purpose of the Delaware sequestration procedure:

> The primary purpose of "sequestration" as authorized by 10 Del. C. § 366 is not to secure possession of property pending a trial between resident debtors and creditors on the issue of who has the right to retain it. On the contrary, as here employed, "sequestration" is a process used to compel the personal appearance of a nonresident defendant to answer and defend a suit brought against him in a court of equity. It is accomplished by the appointment of a sequestrator by this Court to seize and hold property of the nonresident located in this State subject to further Court order. If the defendant enters a general appearance, the sequestered property is routinely released, unless the plaintiff makes special application to continue its seizure, in which event the plaintiff has the burden of proof and persuasion.

This limitation on the purpose and length of time for which sequestered property is held, the court concluded, rendered inapplicable the due process requirements enunciated in *Sniadach v. Family Finance Corp.*, 395 U.S. 337 (1969); *Fuentes v. Shevin*, 407 U.S. 67 (1972); and *Mitchell v. W. T. Grant Co.*, 416 U.S. 600 (1974). The court also found no state law or federal constitutional barrier to the sequestrator's reliance on Del. Code Ann., Tit. 8, § 169 (1975). Finally, the court held that the statutory Delaware situs of the stock provided a sufficient basis for the exercise of quasi in rem jurisdiction by a Delaware court.

On appeal, the Delaware Supreme Court affirmed the judgment of the Court of Chancery. Most of the Supreme Court's opinion was devoted to rejecting appellants' contention that the sequestration procedure is inconsistent with the due process analysis developed in the *Sniadach* line of cases. The court based its rejection of that argument in part on its agreement with the Court of Chancery that the purpose of the sequestration procedure is to compel the appearance of the defendant, a purpose not involved in the *Sniadach* cases. The court also relied on what it considered the ancient origins of the sequestration procedure and approval of that procedure in the opinions of this Court, Delaware's interest in asserting jurisdiction to adjudicate claims of mismanagement of a Delaware corporation, and the safeguards for defendants that it found in the Delaware statute.

Appellants' claim that the Delaware courts did not have jurisdiction to adjudicate this action received much more cursory treatment. The court's analysis of the jurisdictional issue is contained in two paragraphs: "There are significant constitutional questions at issue here but we say at once that we do not deem the rule of *International Shoe* to be one of them. . . . The reason of course, is that jurisdiction under § 366 remains . . . *quasi in rem* founded on the presence of capital stock here, not on prior contact by defendants with this forum. Under 8 Del. C. § 169 the "'situs of the ownership of the capital stock of all corporations existing under the laws of this State . . . [is] in this State,' and that provides the initial basis for jurisdiction. Delaware may constitutionally establish situs of such shares here, . . . it has done so and the presence thereof provides the foundation for § 366 in this case. . . ."

We reverse.

## II

The Delaware courts rejected appellants' jurisdictional challenge by noting that this suit was brought as a quasi in rem proceeding. Since quasi in rem jurisdiction is traditionally based on attachment or seizure of property present in the jurisdiction, not on contacts between the defendant and the State, the courts considered appellants' claimed lack of contacts with Delaware to be unimportant. This categorical analysis assumes the continued soundness of the conceptual structure founded on the century-old case of *Pennoyer v. Neff*, 95 U.S. 714 (1878). . . .

[U]nder *Pennoyer* state authority to adjudicate was based on the jurisdiction's power over either persons or property. This fundamental concept is embodied in the very vocabulary which we use to describe judgments. If a court's jurisdiction is based on its authority over the defendant's person, the action and judgment are denominated "in personam" and can impose a personal obligation on the defendant in favor of the plaintiff. If jurisdiction is based on the court's power over property within its territory, the action is called "in rem" or "quasi in rem." The effect of a judgment in such a case is limited to the property that supports jurisdiction and does not impose a personal liability on the property owner, since he is not before the court. In *Pennoyer*'s terms, the owner is affected only "indirectly" by an in rem judgment adverse to his interest in the property subject to the court's disposition.

By concluding that "[t]he authority of every tribunal is necessarily restricted by the territorial limits of the State in which it is established," *Pennoyer* sharply limited the availability of in personam jurisdiction over defendants not resident in the forum State. If a nonresident defendant could not be found in a State, he could not be sued there. On the other hand, since the State in which property was located was considered to have exclusive sovereignty over that property, in rem actions could proceed regardless of the owner's location.

The *Pennoyer* rules generally favored nonresident defendants by making them harder to sue. This advantage was reduced, however, by the ability of a resident plaintiff to satisfy a claim against a nonresident defendant by bringing into court any property of the defendant located in the plaintiff's State. . . .

[In *International Shoe*] the relationship among the defendant, the forum, and the litigation, rather than the mutually exclusive sovereignty of the States on which the rules of *Pennoyer* rest, became the central concern of the inquiry into personal jurisdiction. The immediate effect of this departure from *Pennoyer*'s conceptual apparatus was to increase the ability of the state courts to obtain personal jurisdiction over nonresident defendants.

No equally dramatic change has occurred in the law governing jurisdiction in rem. There have, however, been intimations that the collapse of the *in personam* wing of *Pennoyer* has not left that decision unweakened as a foundation for in rem jurisdiction. Well-reasoned lower court opinions have questioned the proposition that the presence of property in a State gives that State jurisdiction to adjudicate rights to the property regardless of the relationship of the underlying dispute and the property owner to the forum. The overwhelming majority of commentators have also rejected *Pennoyer's* premise that a proceeding "against" property is not a proceeding against the owners of that property. Accordingly, they urge that the "traditional notions of fair play and substantial justice" that govern a State's power to adjudicate in personam should also govern its power to adjudicate personal rights to property located in the State. . . .

It is clear, therefore, that the law of state-court jurisdiction no longer stands securely on the foundation established in *Pennoyer*. We think that the time is ripe to consider whether the standard of fairness and substantial justice set forth in *International Shoe* should be held to govern actions in rem as well as in personam.

## III

The case for applying to jurisdiction *in rem* the same test of "fair play and substantial justice" as governs assertions of jurisdiction in personam is simple and straightforward. It is premised on recognition that "[t]he phrase, 'judicial jurisdiction over a thing,' is a customary elliptical way of referring to jurisdiction over the interests of persons in a thing." *Restatement (Second) of Conflict of Laws* § 56, This recognition leads to the conclusion that in order to justify an exercise of jurisdiction *in rem*, the basis for jurisdiction must be sufficient to justify exercising "jurisdiction over the interests of persons in a thing."[23] The standard for determining whether an exercise of jurisdiction over the interests of persons is consistent with the Due Process Clause is the minimum-contacts standard elucidated in *International Shoe*.

This argument, of course, does not ignore the fact that the presence of property in a State may bear on the existence of jurisdiction by providing contacts among the forum State, the defendant, and the litigation. For example, when claims to the property itself are the source of the underlying controversy between the plaintiff and the defendant, it would be unusual for the State where the property is located not to have jurisdiction. In such cases, the defendant's claim to property located in the State would normally indicate that he expected to benefit from the State's protection of his interest. The State's strong interests in assuring the marketability of property within its borders and in providing a procedure for peaceful resolution of disputes about

---

23. It is true that the potential liability of a defendant in an *in rem* action is limited by the value of the property, but that limitation does not affect the argument. The fairness of subjecting a defendant to state-court jurisdiction does not depend on the size of the claim being litigated.

the possession of that property would also support jurisdiction, as would the likelihood that important records and witnesses will be found in the State. The presence of property may also favor jurisdiction in cases such as suits for injury suffered on the land of an absentee owner, where the defendant's ownership of the property is conceded but the cause of action is otherwise related to rights and duties growing out of that ownership.[29]

It appears, therefore, that jurisdiction over many types of actions which now are or might be brought *in rem* would not be affected by a holding that any assertion of state-court jurisdiction must satisfy the *International Shoe* standard. For the type of *quasi in rem* action typified by *Harris v. Balk* and the present case, however, accepting the proposed analysis would result in significant change. These are cases where the property which now serves as the basis for state-court jurisdiction is completely unrelated to the plaintiff's cause of action. Thus, although the presence of the defendant's property in a State might suggest the existence of other ties among the defendant, the State, and the litigation, the presence of the property alone would not support the State's jurisdiction. If those other ties did not exist, cases over which the State is now thought to have jurisdiction could not be brought in that forum.

Since acceptance of the *International Shoe* test would most affect this class of cases, we examine the arguments against adopting that standard as they relate to this category of litigation. Before doing so, however, we note that this type of case also presents the clearest illustration of the argument in favor of assessing assertions of jurisdiction by a single standard. For in cases such as *Harris* and this one, the only role played by the property is to provide the basis for bringing the defendant into court. Indeed, the express purpose of the Delaware sequestration procedure is to compel the defendant to enter a personal appearance.[33] In such cases, if a direct assertion of personal jurisdiction over the defendant would violate the Constitution, it would seem that an indirect assertion of that jurisdiction should be equally impermissible.

The primary rationale for treating the presence of property as a sufficient basis for jurisdiction to adjudicate claims over which the State would not have jurisdiction if *International Shoe* applied is that a wrongdoer "should not be able to avoid payment of his obligations by the expedient of removing his assets to a place where he is not subject to an in personam suit." *Restatement* § 66, Comment a. *Accord*, Developments 955. This justification, however, does not explain why jurisdiction should be recognized without regard to whether the property is present in the State because of an effort to avoid the owner's obligations. Nor does it support jurisdiction to adjudicate the underlying claim. At most, it suggests that a State in which property is located should have jurisdiction to attach that property, by use of proper

29. If such an action were brought under the *in rem* jurisdiction rather than under a long-arm statute, it would be a *quasi in rem* action. . . .

33. This purpose is emphasized by Delaware's refusal to allow any defense on the merits unless the defendant enters a general appearance, thus submitting to full in personam liability.

procedures,[34] as security for a judgment being sought in a forum where the litigation can be maintained consistently with *International Shoe*. Moreover, we know of nothing to justify the assumption that a debtor can avoid paying his obligations by removing his property to a State in which his creditor cannot obtain personal jurisdiction over him. The Full Faith and Credit Clause, after all, makes the valid in personam judgment of one State enforceable in all other States.[36]

It might also be suggested that allowing *in rem* jurisdiction avoids the uncertainty inherent in the *International Shoe* standard and assures a plaintiff of a forum.[37] We believe, however, that the fairness standard of *International Shoe* can be easily applied in the vast majority of cases. Moreover, when the existence of jurisdiction in a particular forum under *International Shoe* is unclear, the cost of simplifying the litigation by avoiding the jurisdictional question may be the sacrifice of "fair play and substantial justice." That cost is too high.

We are left, then, to consider the significance of the long history of jurisdiction based solely on the presence of property in a State. Although the theory that territorial power is both essential to and sufficient for jurisdiction has been undermined, we have never held that the presence of property in a State does not automatically confer jurisdiction over the owner's interest in that property. [But] "traditional notions of fair play and substantial justice" can be as readily offended by the perpetuation of ancient forms that are no longer justified as by the adoption of new procedures that are inconsistent with the basic values of our constitutional heritage. The fiction that an assertion of jurisdiction over property is anything but an assertion of jurisdiction over the owner of the property supports an ancient form without substantial modern justification. Its continued acceptance would serve only to allow state-court jurisdiction that is fundamentally unfair to the defendant.

We therefore conclude that all assertions of state-court jurisdiction must be evaluated according to the standards set forth in *International Shoe* and its progeny.[39]

---

34. *See North Georgia Finishing, Inc. v. Di-Chem, Inc.* 419 U.S. 601 (1975); *Mitchell v. W. T. Grant Co.*, 416 U.S. 600 (1974); *Fuentes v. Shevin*, 407 U.S. 67 (1972); *Sniadach v. Family Finance Corp.*, 395 U.S. 337 (1969).

36. Once it has been determined by a court of competent jurisdiction that the defendant is a debtor of the plaintiff, there would seem to be no unfairness in allowing an action to realize on that debt in a State where the defendant has property, whether or not that State would have jurisdiction to determine the existence of the debt as an original matter.

37. This case does not raise, and we therefore do not consider, the question whether the presence of a defendant's property in a State is a sufficient basis for jurisdiction when no other forum is available to the plaintiff.

39. It would not be fruitful for us to re-examine the facts of cases decided on the rationales of *Pennoyer* and *Harris* to determine whether jurisdiction might have been sustained under the standard we adopt today. To the extent that prior decisions are inconsistent with this standard, they are overruled.

## IV

The Delaware courts based their assertion of jurisdiction in this case solely on the statutory presence of appellants' property in Delaware. Yet that property is not the subject matter of this litigation, nor is the underlying cause of action related to the property. Appellants' holdings in Greyhound do not, therefore, provide contacts with Delaware sufficient to support the jurisdiction of that State's courts over appellants. If it exists, that jurisdiction must have some other foundation.

Appellee Heitner did not allege and does not now claim that appellants have ever set foot in Delaware. Nor does he identify any act related to his cause of action as having taken place in Delaware. Nevertheless, he contends that appellants' positions as directors and officers of a corporation chartered in Delaware provide sufficient "contacts, ties, or relations," *International Shoe Co. v. Washington*, 326 U.S. at 319, with that State to give its courts jurisdiction over appellants in this stockholder's derivative action. This argument is based primarily on what Heitner asserts to be the strong interest of Delaware in supervising the management of a Delaware corporation. That interest is said to derive from the role of Delaware law in establishing the corporation and defining the obligations owed to it by its officers and directors. In order to protect this interest, appellee concludes, Delaware's courts must have jurisdiction over corporate fiduciaries such as appellants.

This argument is undercut by the failure of the Delaware Legislature to assert the state interest appellee finds so compelling. Delaware law bases jurisdiction, not on appellants' status as corporate fiduciaries, but rather on the presence of their property in the State. Although the sequestration procedure used here may be most frequently used in derivative suits against officers and directors, the authorizing statute evinces no specific concern with such actions. Sequestration can be used in any suit against a nonresident, and reaches corporate fiduciaries only if they happen to own interests in a Delaware corporation, or other property in the State. But as Heitner's failure to secure jurisdiction over seven of the defendants named in his complaint demonstrates, there is no necessary relationship between holding a position as a corporate fiduciary and owning stock or other interests in the corporation. If Delaware perceived its interest in securing jurisdiction over corporate fiduciaries to be as great as Heitner suggests, we would expect it to have enacted a statute more clearly designed to protect that interest.

Moreover, even if Heitner's assessment of the importance of Delaware's interest is accepted, his argument fails to demonstrate that Delaware is a fair forum for this litigation. The interest appellee has identified may support the application of Delaware law to resolve any controversy over appellants' actions in their capacities as officers and directors. But we have rejected the argument that if a State's law can properly be applied to a dispute, its courts necessarily have jurisdiction over the parties to that dispute.

[The State] does not acquire . . . jurisdiction by being the "center of gravity" of the controversy, or the most convenient location for litigation. The issue is personal jurisdiction, not choice of law. It is resolved in this case by considering the acts of the (appellants).

*Hanson v. Denckla*, 357 U.S. 235, 254 (1958).

Appellee suggests that by accepting positions as officers or directors of a Delaware corporation, appellants performed the acts required by *Hanson v. Denckla*. He notes that Delaware law provides substantial benefits to corporate officers and directors, and that these benefits were at least in part the incentive for appellants to assume their positions. It is, he says, "only fair and just" to require appellants, in return for these benefits, to respond in the State of Delaware when they are accused of misusing their power.

But like Heitner's first argument, this line of reasoning establishes only that it is appropriate for Delaware law to govern the obligations of appellants to Greyhound and its stockholders. It does not demonstrate that appellants have "purposefully avail[ed themselves] of the privilege of conducting activities within the forum State," *Hanson v. Denckla, supra*, at 253, in a way that would justify bringing them before a Delaware tribunal. Appellants have simply had nothing to do with the State of Delaware. Moreover, appellants had no reason to expect to be haled before a Delaware court. Delaware, unlike some States, has not enacted a statute that treats acceptance of a directorship as consent to jurisdiction in the State. And "(i)t strains reason . . . to suggest that anyone buying securities in a corporation formed in Delaware 'impliedly consents' to subject himself to Delaware's . . . jurisdiction on any cause of action." Appellants, who were not required to acquire interests in Greyhound in order to hold their positions, did not by acquiring those interests surrender their right to be brought to judgment only in States with which they had had "minimum contacts."

Delaware's assertion of jurisdiction over appellants in this case is inconsistent with that constitutional limitation on state power. The judgment of the Delaware Supreme Court must, therefore, be reversed. It is so ordered.

Justice REHNQUIST took no part in the consideration or decision of this case.

Justice POWELL, concurring:
I agree that the principles of *International Shoe Co. v. Washington* should be extended to govern assertions of in rem as well as in personam jurisdiction in a state court. I also agree that neither the statutory presence of appellants' stock in Delaware nor their positions as directors and officers of a Delaware corporation can provide sufficient contacts to support the Delaware courts' assertion of jurisdiction in this case.

I would explicitly reserve judgment, however, on whether the ownership of some forms of property whose situs is indisputably and permanently located within a State may, without more, provide the contacts necessary to subject a defendant to jurisdiction within the State to the extent of the value of the property. In the case of real property, in particular, preservation of the common-law concept of *quasi in rem* jurisdiction arguably would avoid the uncertainty of the general *International Shoe* standard without significant cost to "'traditional notions of fair play and substantial justice.'"

Subject to the foregoing reservation, I join the opinion of the Court.

Justice STEVENS, concurring in the judgment:

The Due Process Clause affords protection against "judgments without notice." *International Shoe Co. v. Washington*, 326 U.S. 310, 324 (opinion of Black, J.). Throughout our history the acceptable exercise of *in rem* and *quasi in rem* jurisdiction has included a procedure giving reasonable assurance that actual notice of the particular claim will be conveyed to the defendant. Thus, publication, notice by registered mail, or extraterritorial personal service has been an essential ingredient of any procedure that serves as a substitute for personal service within the jurisdiction.

The requirement of fair notice also, I believe, includes fair warning that a particular activity may subject a person to the jurisdiction of a foreign sovereign. If I visit another State, or acquire real estate or open a bank account in it, I knowingly assume some risk that the State will exercise its power over my property or my person while there. My contact with the State, though minimal, gives rise to predictable risks.

Perhaps the same consequences should flow from the purchase of stock of a corporation organized under the laws of a foreign nation, because to some limited extent one's property and affairs then become subject to the laws of the nation of domicile of the corporation. As a matter of international law, that suggestion might be acceptable because a foreign investment is sufficiently unusual to make it appropriate to require the investor to study the ramifications of his decision. But a purchase of securities in the domestic market is an entirely different matter.

One who purchases shares of stock on the open market can hardly be expected to know that he has thereby become subject to suit in a forum remote from his residence and unrelated to the transaction. As a practical matter, the Delaware sequestration statute creates an unacceptable risk of judgment without notice. Unlike the 49 other States, Delaware treats the place of incorporation as the situs of the stock, even though both the owner and the custodian of the shares are elsewhere. Moreover, Delaware denies the defendant the opportunity to defend the merits of the suit unless he subjects himself to the unlimited jurisdiction of the court. Thus, it coerces a defendant either to submit to personal jurisdiction in a forum which could not otherwise obtain such jurisdiction or to lose the securities which have been attached. If its procedure were upheld, Delaware would, in effect, impose a duty of inquiry on every purchaser of securities in the national market. For unless the purchaser ascertains both the State of incorporation of the company whose shares he is buying, and also the idiosyncrasies of its law, he may be assuming an unknown risk of litigation. I therefore agree with the Court that on the record before us no adequate basis for jurisdiction exists and that the Delaware statute is unconstitutional on its face.

How the Court's opinion may be applied in other contexts is not entirely clear to me. I agree with Mr. Justice Powell that it should not be read to invalidate quasi in rem jurisdiction where real estate is involved. I would also not read it as invalidating other long-accepted methods of acquiring jurisdiction over persons with adequate notice of both the particular controversy and the fact that their local activities might subject them to suit. My uncertainty as to the reach of the opinion, and my fear that it purports to decide a great deal more than is necessary to dispose of this case, persuade me merely to concur in the judgment.

Justice BRENNAN, concurring in part and dissenting in part:

I join Parts I-III of the Court's opinion. I fully agree that the minimum-contacts analysis developed in *International Shoe Co. v. Washington* represents a far more sensible construct for the exercise of state-court jurisdiction than the patchwork of legal and factual fictions that has been generated from the decision in *Pennoyer v. Neff*. It is precisely because the inquiry into minimum contacts is now of such overriding importance, however, that I must respectfully dissent from Part IV of the Court's opinion.

## I

The primary teaching of Parts I-III of today's decision is that a State, in seeking to assert jurisdiction over a person located outside its borders, may only do so on the basis of minimum contacts among the parties, the contested transaction, and the forum State. The Delaware Supreme Court could not have made plainer, however, that its sequestration statute, Del. Code Ann., Tit. 10, § 366 (1975), does not operate on this basis, but instead is strictly an embodiment of quasi in rem jurisdiction, a jurisdictional predicate no longer constitutionally viable: "[J]urisdiction under § 366 remains . . . *quasi in rem* founded on the presence of capital stock here, not on prior contact by defendants with this forum." *Greyhound Corp. v. Heitner*, 361 A.2d 225, 229 (1976). This state-court ruling obviously comports with the understanding of the parties, for the issue of the existence of minimum contacts was never pleaded by appellee, made the subject of discovery, or ruled upon by the Delaware courts. These facts notwithstanding, the Court in Part IV reaches the minimum contacts question and finds such contacts lacking as applied to appellants. Succinctly stated, once having properly and persuasively decided that the quasi in rem statute that Delaware admits to having enacted is invalid, the Court then proceeds to find that a minimum-contacts law that Delaware expressly denies having enacted also could not be constitutionally applied in this case.

In my view, a purer example of an advisory opinion is not to be found. . . .

My concern with the inappropriateness of the Court's action is highlighted by two other considerations. First, an inquiry into minimum contacts inevitably is highly dependent on creating a proper factual foundation detailing the contacts between the forum State and the controversy in question. Because neither the plaintiff-appellee nor the state courts viewed such an inquiry as germane in this instance, the Court today is unable to draw upon a proper factual record in reaching its conclusion; moreover, its disposition denies appellee the normal opportunity to seek discovery on the contacts issue. Second, it must be remembered that the Court's ruling is a constitutional one and necessarily will affect the reach of the jurisdictional laws of all 50 States. Ordinarily this would counsel restraint in constitutional pronouncements. Certainly it should have cautioned the Court against reaching out to decide a question that, as here, has yet to emerge from the state courts ripened for review on the federal issue.

## II

Nonetheless, because the Court rules on the minimum-contacts question, I feel impelled to express my view. While evidence derived through discovery might satisfy me that minimum contacts are lacking in a given case, I am convinced that as a general rule a state forum has jurisdiction to adjudicate a shareholder derivative action centering on the conduct and policies of the directors and officers of a corporation chartered by that State. Unlike the Court, I therefore would not foreclose Delaware from asserting jurisdiction over appellants were it persuaded to do so on the basis of minimum contacts.

It is well settled that a derivative lawsuit as presented here does not inure primarily to the benefit of the named plaintiff. Rather, the primary beneficiaries are the corporation and its owners, the shareholders. "The cause of action which such a plaintiff brings before the court is not his own but the corporation's. . . . Such a plaintiff often may represent an important public and stockholder interest in bringing faithless managers to book."

Viewed in this light, the chartering State has an unusually powerful interest in insuring the availability of a convenient forum for litigating claims involving a possible multiplicity of defendant fiduciaries and for vindicating the State's substantive policies regarding the management of its domestic corporations. I believe that our cases fairly establish that the State's valid substantive interests are important considerations in assessing whether it constitutionally may claim jurisdiction over a given cause of action.

In this instance, Delaware can point to at least three interrelated public policies that are furthered by its assertion of jurisdiction. First, the State has a substantial interest in providing restitution for its local corporations that allegedly have been victimized by fiduciary misconduct, even if the managerial decisions occurred outside the State. The importance of this general state interest in assuring restitution for its own residents previously found expression in cases that went outside the then-prevailing due process framework to authorize state-court jurisdiction over nonresident motorists who injure others within the State. *Hess v. Pawloski*, 274 U.S. 352 (1927). More recently, it has led States to seek and to acquire jurisdiction over nonresident tortfeasors whose purely out-of-state activities produce domestic conse-quences. *E.g., Gray v. American Radiator & Standard Sanitary Corp.*, 22 Ill. 2d 432 (1961). Second, state courts have legitimately read their jurisdic-tion expansively when a cause of action centers in an area in which the forum State possesses a manifest regulatory interest. *E.g., McGee v. International Life Ins. Co.*, 355 U.S. 220 (1957) (insurance regulation). Finally, a State like Delaware has a recognized interest in affording a convenient forum for super-vising and overseeing the affairs of an entity that is purely the creation of that State's law. For example, even following our decision in *International Shoe*, New York courts were permitted to exercise complete judicial authority over nonresident beneficiaries of a trust created under state law, even though, unlike appellants here, the beneficiaries personally entered into no associa-tion whatsoever with New York. *Mullane v. Central Hanover Bank & Trust Co.*, 339 U.S. 306, 313 (1950). I, of course, am not suggesting that Delaware's varied interests would justify its acceptance of jurisdiction over any transac-tion touching upon the affairs of its domestic corporations. But a derivative action which raises allegations of abuses of the basic management of an insti-tution whose existence is created by the State and whose powers and duties are defined by state law fundamentally implicates the public policies of that forum. . . .

I, therefore, would approach the minimum-contacts analysis differently than does the Court. Crucial to me is the fact that appellants voluntarily associated themselves with the State of Delaware, "invoking the benefits and protections of its laws," by entering into a long-term and fragile rela-tionship with one of its domestic corporations. They thereby elected to assume powers and to undertake responsibilities wholly derived from that State's rules and regulations, and to become eligible for those benefits that Delaware law makes available to its corporations' officials. While it is possible that countervailing issues of judicial efficiency and the like might clearly favor a different forum, they do not appear on the meager record before us and, of course, we are concerned solely with "minimum" contacts, not the "best" contacts. I thus do not believe that it is unfair to insist that appellants make themselves available to suit in a competent forum that Delaware might create for vindication of its important public policies directly pertaining to appellants' fiduciary associations with the State.

## Comments and Questions

1. What does *Shaffer* hold? How would you state the broadest version of the holding? The narrowest?

2. What in rem and quasi in rem cases remain viable after *Shaffer*? Does Professor Gloss's vacation home in Practice Exercise 33 provide a basis for exercising jurisdiction over him after this decision? What if Gloss is an absentee owner, who never comes to Massachusetts, and the claim is for

an injury suffered by a passer-by who falls into a hole negligently left in the sidewalk in front of the house? What if an adjacent neighbor seeks to legally settle the boundary between her property and Gloss's?

3. What are the points of disagreement that Justices Powell and Stevens have with the Court's opinion? How would they treat Professor Gloss's vacation home as an asserted basis for adjudicatory power over him? What role does predictability of outcomes (as compared to the uncertainty of minimum-contacts analysis) play in their reasoning?

4. What is the basis for Justice Brennan's accusation that the Court overstepped its authority by rendering "an advisory opinion" on the minimum-contacts issue?

5. Trace Justice Brennan's argument that, measured against the *International Shoe* standard, the Delaware courts *did have* constitutional power over the defendants? Does Brennan anticipate the importance the "fair play" factors would assume a decade later in *Burger King* and *Asahi*?

6. If Delaware had had an open-ended long-arm statute like California's (e.g., "A court of this state may exercise jurisdiction on any basis not inconsistent with the Constitution of this state or of the United States"), would *Shaffer* have come out differently? Was the Court's problem with Delaware's exercise of jurisdiction prompted by constitutional concerns, or by the *particular statutory basis* asserted? It did not help Heitner's case that the Delaware scheme allowed its courts to hold a nonresident's property hostage unless and until the defendant entered a general appearance. *See* § 366(a), set out in the Court's footnote 4.

7. In response to *Shaffer*, Delaware did expand its long-arm reach when it enacted Del. Code Ann. tit. 10, § 3114:

> Every nonresident of this State who after September 1, 1977, accepts election or appointment as a director, trustee or member of the governing body of a corporation organized under the laws of this State or who after June 30, 1978, serves in such capacity and every resident of this State who so accepts election or appointment or serves in such capacity and thereafter removes residence from this State shall, by such acceptance or by such service, be deemed thereby to have consented to the appointment of the registered agent of such corporation (or, if there is none, the Secretary of State) as an agent upon whom service of process may be made in all civil actions or proceedings brought in this State, by or on behalf of, or against such corporation, in which such director, trustee or member is a necessary or proper party, or in any action or proceeding against such director, trustee or member for violation of a duty in such capacity, whether or not the person continues to serve as such director, trustee or member at the time suit is commenced. Such acceptance or service as such director, trustee or member shall be a signification of the consent of such director, trustee or member that any process when so served shall be of the same legal force and validity as if served upon such director, trustee or member within this State and such appointment of the registered agent (or, if there is none, the Secretary of State) shall be irrevocable.

The Delaware Supreme Court upheld the statute in *Armstrong v. Pomerance*, 423 A.2d 174 (1980), ruling that the state has a substantial interest in overseeing the conduct of those owing fiduciary duties to shareholders of Delaware corporations. The court reasoned that such interest far outweighs any burden to defendants (who have voluntarily associated themselves with such corporations by accepting directorships) in being required to submit to the jurisdiction of the courts.

8. Note the *Shaffer* Court's distinction between a state's power to attach property located within its borders to enforce a valid judgment entered in another state, and jurisdiction to adjudicate the underlying claim. *See* the Court's footnote 36 and accompanying text.

9. The Federal Rules of Civil Procedure limit the use of attachment jurisdiction to situations where the defendant cannot be reached through other means. *See* Fed. R. Civ. P. 4(n). The Advisory Committee Note to the 1993 amendment explains: "Given the liberal availability of long-arm jurisdiction, the exercise of power *quasi-in-rem* has become almost an anachronism. Circumstances too spare to affiliate the defendant to the forum state sufficiently to support long-arm jurisdiction over the defendant's person are also inadequate to support seizure of the defendant's assets fortuitously found within the state (citing *Shaffer*)." Would Justices Powell and Stevens agree with that statement?

10. In 1999 Congress passed the Anti-Cybersquatting Consumer Protection Act (ACPA), 15 U.S.C. § 1125(d), to address situations in which someone would register a domain name (such as Coke.com) that included a trademark (such as "Coke") held by another person. A domain name is the device allowing a person to use their computer to locate an Internet Web site. A portion of the ACPA provides that a person claiming that their trademark is being violated as part of a domain name may, so long as the person claimed to have violated the trademark is not subject to personal jurisdiction anywhere in the United States, bring an in rem action directly against the domain name "in the judicial district in which the . . . domain name registry . . . is located." 15 U.S.C. § 1125(d)(2). The registry is the entity that maintains the computer equipment on which domain names are listed, thus enabling the Internet to function. Thus, in simple terms, the ACPA operates on the principle that a domain name is property that is located where the registry is located. For all names ending in .com and .net the location of the registry is in the Eastern District of Virginia.

Are the ACPA's in rem provisions consistent with the Court's decision in *Shaffer v. Heitner*? Consider the case of a person from Germany, with no contacts to the United States, who registers a .com domain name in Germany. That name is then entered on a computer in Virginia where all .com names are entered. Assuming that line of computer code is property and that the German registrant is not subject to personal jurisdiction anywhere in the United States, is the ACPA constitutional in its attempt to obtain jurisdiction over the absent registrant solely by attaching the domain name?

The Fourth Circuit Court of Appeals has held that the ACPA's in rem provisions are constitutional. In a pair of decisions issued on the same day, two different panels of the court sustained the ACPA on two quite different, and inconsistent, grounds. First, in *Porsche Cars N. Am. Inc. v. Porsche.net*, 302 F.3d 248, 259-260 (4th Cir. 2003), the court held that *Shaffer* did not even apply to the ACPA because the domain name situation involved a true in rem action. *Shaffer*, the court reasoned, dealt only with quasi in rem cases and had no application to true in rem cases. Thus, the court upheld the in rem provisions under the logic of *Pennoyer*.

In the second case, *Harrods Ltd. v. Sixty Internet Domain Names*, 302 F.3d 214, 224 (4th Cir. 2003), a separate panel of the court held that *Shaffer* did require that a minimum-contacts analysis apply to every assertion of personal jurisdiction whether denominated as true in rem or not. However, the court held that one was to judge the minimum contacts not in terms of the absent defendant, but rather in terms of the property at issue. Thus, because the domain name had minimum contacts with the location of the registry (regardless of the situation with the absent citizen of Germany), the ACPA passed muster.

Which of the Fourth Circuit cases is a better reading of *Shaffer*? Are they both wrong? For a thorough and insightful discussion of the ACPA arguing that the in rem provisions are in fact unconstitutional under *Shaffer* and that the Fourth Circuit is incorrect in both *Harrods* and *Porsche*, see Michael P. Allen, *In Rem Jurisdiction from* Pennoyer *to* Shaffer *to the Anti-Cybersquatting Consumer Protection Act*, 11 George Mason L. Rev. 245 (2002).

11. Justice Marshall's opinion for the Court in *Shaffer* holds that "*all* assertions of state-court jurisdiction must be evaluated according to the standards set forth in *International Shoe* and its progeny." 433 U.S. at 212 (emphasis added). As you read the next case, consider the risks of such broad categorical pronouncements.

# L. JURISDICTION BASED SOLELY ON PERSONAL SERVICE WITHIN THE FORUM STATE

## ■ BURNHAM v. SUPERIOR COURT OF CALIFORNIA

*495 U.S. 604 (1990)*

> 1) NON-R personally served w/ process while temporarily in forum state
>
> 2) Suit is unrelated to his activities in the forum state

Justice SCALIA announced the judgment of the Court and delivered an opinion in which the CHIEF JUSTICE and Justice KENNEDY join, and in which Justice WHITE joins with respect to Parts I, II-A, II-B, and II-C:

The question presented is whether the Due Process Clause of the Fourteenth Amendment denies California courts jurisdiction over a nonresident, who was personally served with process while temporarily in that State, in a suit unrelated to his activities in the State.

## I

Petitioner Dennis Burnham married Francie Burnham in 1976 in West Virginia. In 1977 the couple moved to New Jersey, where their two children were born. In July 1987 the Burnhams decided to separate. They agreed that Mrs. Burnham, who intended to move to California, would take custody of the children. Shortly before Mrs. Burnham departed for California that same month, she and petitioner agreed that she would file for divorce on grounds of "irreconcilable differences."

In October 1987, petitioner filed for divorce in New Jersey state court on grounds of "desertion." Petitioner did not, however, obtain an issuance of summons against his wife and did not attempt to serve her with process. Mrs. Burnham, after unsuccessfully demanding that petitioner adhere to their prior agreement to submit to an "irreconcilable differences" divorce, brought suit for divorce in California state court in early January 1988.

In late January, petitioner visited southern California on business, after which he went north to visit his children in the San Francisco Bay area, where his wife resided. He took the older child to San Francisco for the weekend. Upon returning the child to Mrs. Burnham's home on January 24, 1988, petitioner was served with a California court summons and a copy of Mrs. Burnham's divorce petition. He then returned to New Jersey.

Later that year, petitioner made a special appearance in the California Superior Court, moving to quash the service of process, on the ground that the court lacked personal jurisdiction over him because his only contacts with California were a few short visits to the State for the purposes of conducting business and visiting his children. The Superior Court denied the motion, and the California Court of Appeal denied mandamus relief, rejecting petitioner's contention that the Due Process Clause prohibited California courts from asserting jurisdiction over him because he lacked "minimum contacts" with the State. The court held it to be "a valid jurisdictional predicate for in personam jurisdiction" that the "defendant [was] present in the forum state and personally served with process." We granted certiorari.

## II

### A

The proposition that the judgment of a court lacking jurisdiction is void traces back to the English Year Books, and was made settled law by Lord Coke in *Case of the Marshalsea* (K.B. 1612). Traditionally that proposition was embodied in the phrase *coram non judice*, "before a person not a judge"— meaning, in effect, that the proceeding in question was not a judicial proceeding because lawful judicial authority was not present, and could therefore not yield a judgment. American courts invalidated, or denied recognition to, judgments that violated this common-law principle long before the Fourteenth Amendment was adopted. In *Pennoyer v. Neff*, we announced that the judgment of a court lacking personal jurisdiction violated the Due Process Clause of the Fourteenth Amendment as well.

To determine whether the assertion of personal jurisdiction is consistent with due process, we have long relied on the principles traditionally followed by American courts in marking out the territorial limits of each State's authority. That criterion was first announced in *Pennoyer v. Neff, supra,* in which we stated that due process "mean[s] a course of legal proceedings according to those rules and principles which have been established in our systems of jurisprudence for the protection and enforcement of private rights," including the "well-established principles of public law respecting the jurisdiction of an independent State over persons and property." In what has become the classic expression of the criterion, we said in *International Shoe Co. v. Washington* that a state court's assertion of personal jurisdiction satisfies the Due Process Clause if it does not violate "'traditional notions of fair play and substantial justice.'" Since *International Shoe,* we have only been called upon to decide whether these "traditional notions" permit States to exercise jurisdiction over absent defendants in a manner that deviates from the rules of jurisdiction applied in the 19th century. We have held such deviations permissible, but only with respect to suits arising out of the absent defendant's contacts with the State.[1] The question we must decide today is whether due process requires a similar connection between the litigation and the defendant's contacts with the State in cases where the defendant is physically present in the State at the time process is served upon him.

**B**

Among the most firmly established principles of personal jurisdiction in American tradition is that the courts of a State have jurisdiction over nonresidents who are physically present in the State. The view developed early that each State had the power to hale before its courts any individual who could be found within its borders, and that once having acquired jurisdiction over such a person by properly serving him with process, the State could retain jurisdiction to enter judgment against him, no matter how fleeting his visit. That view had antecedents in English common-law practice, which sometimes allowed "transitory" actions, arising out of events outside the country, to be maintained against seemingly nonresident defendants who were present in England. Justice Story believed the principle, which he

---

1. We have said that "[e]ven when the cause of action does not arise out of or relate to the foreign corporation's activities in the forum State, due process is not offended by a State's subjecting the corporation to its in personam jurisdiction when there are sufficient contacts between the State and the foreign corporation." Our only holding supporting that statement, however, involved "regular service of summons upon [the corporation's] president while he was in [the forum State] acting in that capacity." *See Perkins v. Benguet Consolidated Mining Co.,* 342 U.S. 437, 440 (1952). It may be that whatever special rule exists permitting "continuous and systematic" contacts to support jurisdiction with respect to matters unrelated to activity in the forum applies only to corporations, which have never fitted comfortably in a jurisdictional regime based primarily upon *"de facto* power over the defendant's person." *International Shoe Co. v. Washington.* We express no views on these matters—and, for simplicity's sake, omit reference to this aspect of "contacts"-based jurisdiction in our discussion.

traced to Roman origins, to be firmly grounded in English tradition: "[B]y the common law[,] personal actions, being transitory, may be brought in any place, where the party defendant may be found," for "every nation may . . . rightfully exercise jurisdiction over all persons within its domains."

. . .

Decisions in the courts of many States in the 19th and early 20th centuries held that personal service upon a physically present defendant sufficed to confer jurisdiction, without regard to whether the defendant was only briefly in the State or whether the cause of action was related to his activities there. . . . Most States, moreover, had statutes or common-law rules that exempted from service of process individuals who were brought into the forum by force or fraud, or who were there as a party or witness in unrelated judicial proceedings. These exceptions obviously rested upon the premise that service of process conferred jurisdiction. Particularly striking is the fact that, as far as we have been able to determine, not one American case from the period (or, for that matter, not one American case until 1978) held, or even suggested, that in-state personal service on an individual was insufficient to confer personal jurisdiction.

This American jurisdictional practice is, moreover, not merely old; it is continuing. . . . We do not know of a single state or federal statute, or a single judicial decision resting upon state law, that has abandoned in-state service as a basis of jurisdiction. Many recent cases reaffirm it.

### C

Despite this formidable body of precedent, petitioner contends, in reliance on our decisions applying the *International Shoe* standard, that in the absence of "continuous and systematic" contacts with the forum, a nonresident defendant can be subjected to judgment only as to matters that arise out of or relate to his contacts with the forum. This argument rests on a thorough misunderstanding of our cases.

The view of most courts in the 19th century was that a court simply could not exercise *in personam* jurisdiction over a nonresident who had not been personally served with process in the forum. *Pennoyer v. Neff*, while renowned for its statement of the principle that the Fourteenth Amendment prohibits such an exercise of jurisdiction, in fact set that forth only as dictum and decided the case (which involved a judgment rendered more than two years before the Fourteenth Amendment's ratification) under "well-established principles of public law." Those principles, embodied in the Due Process Clause, required (we said) that when proceedings "involv[e] merely a determination of the personal liability of the defendant, he must be brought within [the court's] jurisdiction by service of process within the State, or his voluntary appearance." We invoked that rule in a series of subsequent cases, as either a matter of due process or a "fundamental principl[e] of jurisprudence."

Later years, however, saw the weakening of the *Pennoyer* rule. In the late 19th and early 20th centuries, changes in the technology of transportation and communication, and the tremendous growth of interstate business activity, led to an "inevitable relaxation of the strict limits on state jurisdiction" over nonresident individuals and corporations. *Hanson v. Denckla*, 357 U.S. 235, 260 (1958) (Black, J., dissenting). States required, for example, that nonresident corporations appoint an in-state agent upon whom process could be served as a condition of transacting business within their borders, and provided in-state "substituted service" for nonresident motorists who caused injury in the State and left before personal service could be accomplished. We initially upheld these laws under the Due Process Clause on grounds that they complied with *Pennoyer*'s rigid requirement of either "consent," *see, e.g., Hess v. Pawloski, supra,* or "presence." As many observed, however, the consent and presence were purely fictional. Our opinion in *International Shoe* cast those fictions aside and made explicit the underlying basis of these decisions: Due process does not necessarily require the States to adhere to the unbending territorial limits on jurisdiction set forth in *Pennoyer.* The validity of assertion of jurisdiction over a non-consenting defendant who is not present in the forum depends upon whether "the quality and nature of [his] activity" in relation to the forum renders such jurisdiction consistent with "'traditional notions of fair play and substantial justice.'" Subsequent cases have derived from the *International Shoe* standard the general rule that a State may dispense with in-forum personal service on nonresident defendants in suits arising out of their activities in the State. As *International Shoe* suggests, the defendant's litigation-related "minimum contacts" may take the place of physical presence as the basis for jurisdiction: "Historically the jurisdiction of courts to render judgment *in personam* is grounded on their de facto power over the defendant's person. Hence his presence within the territorial jurisdiction of a court was prerequisite to its rendition of a judgment personally binding on him. *Pennoyer v. Neff.* But now that the *capias ad respondendum* has given way to personal service of summons or other form of notice, due process requires only that in order to subject a defendant to a judgment *in personam*, if he be not present within the territory of the forum, he have certain minimum contacts with it such that the maintenance of the suit does not offend 'traditional notions of fair play and substantial justice.'"

Nothing in *International Shoe* or the cases that have followed it, however, offers support for the very different proposition petitioner seeks to establish today: that a defendant's presence in the forum is not only unnecessary to validate novel, nontraditional assertions of jurisdiction, but is itself no longer sufficient to establish jurisdiction. That proposition is unfaithful to both elementary logic and the foundations of our due process jurisprudence. The distinction between what is needed to support novel procedures and what is needed to sustain traditional ones is fundamental. . . .

The short of the matter is that jurisdiction based on physical presence alone constitutes due process because it is one of the continuing traditions of our legal system that define the due process standard of "traditional notions of fair play and substantial justice." That standard was developed by analogy to "physical presence," and it would be perverse to say it could now be turned against that touchstone of jurisdiction.

**D**

Petitioner's strongest argument, though we ultimately reject it, relies upon our decision in *Shaffer v. Heitner*. In that case, a Delaware court hearing a shareholder's derivative suit against a corporation's directors secured jurisdiction quasi in rem by sequestering the out-of-state defendants' stock in the company, the situs of which was Delaware under Delaware law. Reasoning that Delaware's sequestration procedure was simply a mechanism to compel the absent defendants to appear in a suit to determine their personal rights and obligations, we concluded that the normal rules we had developed under *International Shoe* for jurisdiction over suits against absent defendants should apply—*viz.*, Delaware could not hear the suit because the defendants' sole contact with the State (ownership of property there) was unrelated to the lawsuit.

It goes too far to say, as petitioner contends, that *Shaffer* compels the conclusion that a State lacks jurisdiction over an individual unless the litigation arises out of his activities in the State. *Shaffer*, like *International Shoe*, involved jurisdiction over an absent defendant, and it stands for nothing more than the proposition that when the "minimum contact" that is a substitute for physical presence consists of property ownership it must, like other minimum contacts, be related to the litigation. Petitioner wrenches out of its context our statement in *Shaffer* that "all assertions of state-court jurisdiction must be evaluated according to the standards set forth in *International Shoe* and its progeny." When read together with the two sentences that preceded it, the meaning of this statement becomes clear:

> The fiction that an assertion of jurisdiction over property is anything but an assertion of jurisdiction over the owner of the property supports an ancient form without substantial modern justification. Its continued acceptance would serve only to allow state-court jurisdiction that is fundamentally unfair to the defendant.
>
> We therefore conclude that all assertions of state-court jurisdiction must be evaluated according to the standards set forth in *International Shoe* and its progeny.

*Ibid. Shaffer* was saying, in other words, not that all bases for the assertion of *in personam* jurisdiction (including, presumably, in-state service) must be treated alike and subjected to the "minimum contacts" analysis of *International Shoe*, but rather that *quasi in rem* jurisdiction, that fictional "ancient form," and *in personam* jurisdiction, are really one and the same and must be treated alike—leading to the conclusion that *quasi in rem* jurisdiction, i.e., that form of in personam jurisdiction based upon a "property ownership" contact and by definition unaccompanied by personal, instate service, must satisfy the litigation-relatedness requirement of *International Shoe*.

The logic of *Shaffer's* holding—which places all suits against absent non-residents on the same constitutional footing, regardless of whether a separate Latin label is attached to one particular basis of contact—does not compel the conclusion that physically present defendants must be treated identically to absent ones. As we have demonstrated at length, our tradition has treated the two classes of defendants quite differently, and it is unreasonable to read *Shaffer* as casually obliterating that distinction. *International Shoe* confined its "minimum contacts" requirement to situations in which the defendant "be not present within the territory of the forum," and nothing in *Shaffer* expands that requirement beyond that.

It is fair to say, however, that while our holding today does not contradict *Shaffer*, our basic approach to the due process question is different. We have conducted no independent inquiry into the desirability or fairness of the prevailing in-state service rule, leaving that judgment to the legislatures that are free to amend it; for our purposes, its validation is its pedigree, as the phrase "traditional notions of fair play and substantial justice" makes clear. *Shaffer* did conduct such an independent inquiry, asserting that "'traditional notions of fair play and substantial justice' can be as readily offended by the perpetuation of ancient forms that are no longer justified as by the adoption of new procedures that are inconsistent with the basic values of our constitutional heritage." Perhaps that assertion can be sustained when the "perpetuation of ancient forms" is engaged in by only a very small minority of the States. Where, however, as in the present case, a jurisdictional principle is both firmly approved by tradition and still favored, it is impossible to imagine what standard we could appeal to for the judgment that it is "no longer justified." While in no way receding from or casting doubt upon the holding of *Shaffer* or any other case, we reaffirm today our time-honored approach. For new procedures, hitherto unknown, the Due Process Clause requires analysis to determine whether "traditional notions of fair play and substantial justice" have been offended. But a doctrine of personal jurisdiction that dates back to the adoption of the Fourteenth Amendment and is still generally observed unquestionably meets that standard.

### III

A few words in response to Justice Brennan's opinion concurring in the judgment: It insists that we apply "contemporary notions of due process" to determine the constitutionality of California's assertion of jurisdiction. But our analysis today comports with that prescription, at least if we give it the only sense allowed by our precedents. The "contemporary notions of due process" applicable to personal jurisdiction are the enduring "traditional notions of fair play and substantial justice" established as the test by *International Shoe*. By its very language, that test is satisfied if a state court adheres to jurisdictional rules that are generally applied and have always been applied in the United States.

But the concurrence's proposed standard of "contemporary notions of due process" requires more: It measures state-court jurisdiction not only against traditional doctrines in this country, including current state-court practice, but also against each Justice's subjective assessment of what is fair and just. Authority for that seductive standard is not to be found in any of our personal jurisdiction cases. It is, indeed, an outright break with the test of "traditional notions of fair play and substantial justice," which would have to be reformulated "our notions of fair play and substantial justice."

The subjectivity, and hence inadequacy, of this approach becomes apparent when the concurrence tries to explain why the assertion of jurisdiction in the present case meets its standard of continuing-American-tradition-plus-innate-fairness. Justice Brennan lists the "benefits" Mr. Burnham derived from the State of California—the fact that, during the few days he was there, "[h]is health and safety [were] guaranteed by the State's police, fire, and emergency medical services; he [was] free to travel on the State's roads and waterways; he likely enjoy[ed] the fruits of the State's economy." Three days' worth of these benefits strike us as powerfully inadequate to establish, as an abstract matter, that it is "fair" for California to decree the ownership of all Mr. Burnham's worldly goods acquired during the 10 years of his marriage, and the custody over his children. We daresay a contractual exchange swapping those benefits for that power would not survive the "unconscionability" provision of the Uniform Commercial Code. Even less persuasive are the other "fairness" factors alluded to by Justice Brennan. It would create "an asymmetry," we are told, if Burnham were permitted (as he is) to appear in California courts as a plaintiff, but were not compelled to appear in California courts as defendant; and travel being as easy as it is nowadays, and modern procedural devices being so convenient, it is no great hardship to appear in California courts. The problem with these assertions is that they justify the exercise of jurisdiction over everyone, whether or not he ever comes to California. The only "fairness" elements setting Mr. Burnham apart from the rest of the world are the three days' "benefits" referred to above—and even those do not set him apart from many other people who have enjoyed three days in the Golden State (savoring the fruits of its economy, the availability of its roads and police services) but who were fortunate enough not to be served with process while they were there and thus are not (simply by reason of that savoring) subject to the general jurisdiction of California's courts. In other words, even if one agreed with Justice Brennan's conception of an equitable bargain, the "benefits" we have been discussing would explain why it is "fair" to assert general jurisdiction over Burnham-returned-to-New-Jersey-after-service only at the expense of proving that it is also "fair" to assert general jurisdiction over Burnham-returned-to-New-Jersey-without-service—which we know does not conform with "contemporary notions of due process."

There is, we must acknowledge, one factor mentioned by Justice Brennan that both relates distinctively to the assertion of jurisdiction on the basis of personal instate service and is fully persuasive—namely, the fact that a defendant voluntarily present in a particular State has a "reasonable expectatio[n]" that he is subject to suit there. By formulating it as a "reasonable expectation" Justice Brennan makes that seem like a "fairness" factor; but in reality, of course, it is just tradition masquerading as "fairness." The only reason for charging Mr. Burnham with the reasonable expectation of being subject to suit is that the States of the Union assert adjudicatory jurisdiction over the person, and have always asserted adjudicatory jurisdiction over the person, by serving him with process during his temporary physical presence in their territory. That continuing tradition, which anyone entering California should have known about, renders it "fair" for Mr. Burnham, who voluntarily entered California, to be sued there for divorce—at least "fair" in the limited sense that he has no one but himself to blame. Justice Brennan's long journey is a circular one, leaving him, at the end of the day, in complete reliance upon the very factor he sought to avoid: The existence of a continuing tradition is not enough, fairness also must be considered; fairness exists here because there is a continuing tradition.

While Justice Brennan's concurrence is unwilling to confess that the Justices of this Court can possibly be bound by a continuing American tradition that a particular procedure is fair, neither is it willing to embrace the logical consequences of that refusal—or even to be clear about what consequences (logical or otherwise) it does embrace. Justice Brennan says that "[f]or these reasons [i.e., because of the reasonableness factors enumerated above], as a rule the exercise of personal jurisdiction over a defendant based on his voluntary presence in the forum will satisfy the requirements of due process." The use of the word "rule" conveys the reassuring feeling that he is establishing a principle of law one can rely upon—but of course he is not. Since Justice Brennan's only criterion of constitutionality is "fairness," the phrase "as a rule" represents nothing more than his estimation that, usually, all the elements of "fairness" he discusses in the present case will exist. But what if they do not? Suppose, for example, that a defendant in Mr. Burnham's situation enjoys not three days worth of California's "benefits," but 15 minutes' worth. Or suppose we remove one of those "benefits"—"enjoy[ment of] the fruits of the State's economy"—by positing that Mr. Burnham had not come to California on business, but only to visit his children. Or suppose that Mr. Burnham were demonstrably so impecunious as to be unable to take advantage of the modern means of transportation and communication that Justice Brennan finds so relevant. Or suppose, finally, that the California courts lacked the "variety of procedural devices" that Justice Brennan says can reduce the burden upon out-of-state litigants. One may also make additional suppositions, relating not to the absence of the factors that Justice Brennan discusses, but to the presence of additional factors bearing upon the ultimate criterion of "fairness." What if, for example, Mr. Burnham were visiting a sick child? Or a dying child? Cf. *Kulko v. Superior Court of California, City and County of San Francisco*, 436 U.S. 84, 93 (1978) (finding the exercise of long-arm jurisdiction over an absent parent unreasonable because it would "discourage parents from entering into reasonable visitation agreements"). Since, so far as one can tell, Justice Brennan's approval of applying the in-state service rule in the present case rests on the presence of all the factors he lists, and on the absence of any others, every different case will present a different litigable issue. Thus, despite the fact that he manages to work the word "rule" into his formulation, Justice Brennan's approach does not establish a rule of law at all, but only a "totality of the circumstances" test, guaranteeing what traditional territorial rules of jurisdiction were designed precisely to avoid: uncertainty and litigation over the preliminary issue of the forum's competence. It may be that those evils, necessarily accompanying a freestanding "reasonableness" inquiry, must be accepted at the margins, when we evaluate nontraditional forms of jurisdiction newly adopted by the States, *see, e.g., Asahi Metal Industry Co. v. Superior Court of California, Solano County*, 480 U.S. 102, 115 (1987). But that is no reason for injecting them into the core of our American practice, exposing to such a "reasonableness" inquiry the ground of jurisdiction that has hitherto been considered the very baseline of reasonableness, physical presence.

The difference between us and Justice Brennan has nothing to do with whether "further progress [is] to be made" in the "evolution of our legal system." It has to do with whether changes are to be adopted as progressive by the American people or decreed as progressive by the Justices of this Court. Nothing we say today prevents individual States from limiting or entirely abandoning the in-state-service basis of jurisdiction. And nothing prevents an overwhelming majority of them from doing so, with the consequence that the "traditional notions of fairness" that this Court applies may change. But the States have overwhelmingly declined to adopt such limitation or abandonment, evidently not considering it to be progress.[5] The question is whether, armed with no authority other than individual Justices' perceptions of fairness that conflict with both past and current practice, this Court can compel the States to make such a change on the ground that "due process" requires it. We hold that it cannot.

Because the Due Process Clause does not prohibit the California courts from exercising jurisdiction over petitioner based on the fact of in-state service of process, the judgment is Affirmed.

Justice WHITE, concurring in part and concurring in the judgment:
I join Parts I, II-A, II-B, and II-C of Justice Scalia's opinion and concur in the judgment of affirmance. The rule allowing jurisdiction to be obtained over

---

5. I find quite unacceptable as a basis for this Court's decisions Justice Brennan's view that "the raison d'être of various constitutional doctrines designed to protect out-of-staters, such as the Art. IV Privileges and Immunities Clause and the Commerce Clause," entitles this Court to brand as "unfair," and hence unconstitutional, the refusal of all 50 States "to limit or abandon bases of jurisdiction that have become obsolete," *ibid.* "Due process" (which is the constitutional text at issue here) does not mean that process which shifting majorities of this Court feel to be "due"; but that process which American society—self-interested American society, which expresses its judgments in the laws of self-interested States—has traditionally considered "due." The notion that the Constitution, through some penumbra emanating from the Privileges and Immunities Clause and the Commerce Clause, establishes this Court as a Platonic check upon the society's greedy adherence to its traditions can only be described as imperious.

a nonresident by personal service in the forum State, without more, has been and is so widely accepted throughout this country that I could not possibly strike it down, either on its face or as applied in this case, on the ground that it denies due process of law guaranteed by the Fourteenth Amendment. Although the Court has the authority under the Amendment to examine even traditionally accepted procedures and declare them invalid, *e.g.*, *Shaffer v. Heitner*, there has been no showing here or elsewhere that as a general proposition the rule is so arbitrary and lacking in common sense in so many instances that it should be held violative of due process in every case. Furthermore, until such a showing is made, which would be difficult indeed, claims in individual cases that the rule would operate unfairly as applied to the particular nonresident involved need not be entertained. At least this would be the case where presence in the forum State is intentional, which would almost always be the fact. Otherwise, there would be endless, fact-specific litigation in the trial and appellate courts, including this one. Here, personal service in California, without more, is enough, and I agree that the judgment should be affirmed.

Justice BRENNAN, with whom Justice MARSHALL, Justice BLACKMUN, and Justice O'CONNOR join, concurring in the judgment:

I agree with Justice Scalia that the Due Process Clause of the Fourteenth Amendment generally permits a state court to exercise jurisdiction over a defendant if he is served with process while voluntarily present in the forum State.[1] I do not perceive the need, however, to decide that a jurisdictional rule that "'has been immemorially the actual law of the land,'" automatically comports with due process simply by virtue of its "pedigree." Although I agree that history is an important factor in establishing whether a jurisdictional rule satisfies due process requirements, I cannot agree that it is the only factor such that all traditional rules of jurisdiction are, ipso facto, forever constitutional. Unlike Justice Scalia, I would undertake an "independent inquiry into the . . . fairness of the prevailing in-state service rule." I therefore concur only in the judgment.

**I**

I believe that the approach adopted by Justice Scalia's opinion today—reliance solely on historical pedigree—is foreclosed by our decisions in *International Shoe Co. v. Washington*, and *Shaffer v. Heitner*. In *International Shoe*, we held that a state court's assertion of personal jurisdiction does not violate the Due Process Clause if it is consistent with "'traditional notions of fair play and substantial justice.'"[2] In *Shaffer*,

---

1. I use the term "transient jurisdiction" to refer to jurisdiction premised solely on the fact that a person is served with process while physically present in the forum State.

2. Our reference in *International Shoe* to "'traditional notions of fair play and substantial justice,'" meant simply that those concepts are indeed traditional ones, not that, as Justice Scalia's opinion suggests, their specific content was to be determined by tradition alone. We recognized that contemporary societal norms must play a role in our analysis.

we stated that "all assertions of state-court jurisdiction must be evaluated according to the standards set forth in *International Shoe* and its progeny." 433 U.S. at 212 (emphasis added). The critical insight of *Shaffer* is that all rules of jurisdiction, even ancient ones, must satisfy contemporary notions of due process. No longer were we content to limit our jurisdictional analysis to pronouncements that "[t]he foundation of jurisdiction is physical power," and that "every State possesses exclusive jurisdiction and sovereignty over persons and property within its territory." *Pennoyer v. Neff.* 95 U.S. 714, 722 (1878). While acknowledging that "history must be considered as supporting the proposition that jurisdiction based solely on the presence of property satisfie[d] the demands of due process," we found that this factor could not be "decisive." 433 U.S. at 211-212. We recognized that "'[t]raditional notions of fair play and substantial justice' can be as readily offended by the perpetuation of ancient forms that are no longer justified as by the adoption of new procedures that are inconsistent with the basic values of our constitutional heritage." I agree with this approach and continue to believe that "the minimum-contacts analysis developed in *International Shoe* . . . represents a far more sensible construct for the exercise of state-court jurisdiction than the patchwork of legal and factual fictions that has been generated from the decision in *Pennoyer v. Neff.*" *Id.*, at 219 (Brennan, J., concurring in part and dissenting in part) (citation omitted).

While our holding in *Shaffer* may have been limited to quasi in rem jurisdiction, our mode of analysis was not. Indeed, that we were willing in *Shaffer* to examine anew the appropriateness of the quasi in rem rule—until that time dutifully accepted by American courts for at least a century—demonstrates that we did not believe that the "pedigree" of a jurisdictional practice was dispositive in deciding whether it was consistent with due process. We later characterized *Shaffer* as "abandon[ing] the outworn rule of *Harris v. Balk*, 198 U.S. 215 (1905), that the interest of a creditor in a debt could be extinguished or otherwise affected by any State having transitory jurisdiction over the debtor." *World-Wide Volkswagen Corp. v. Woodson*, 444 U.S. 286, 296 (1980); *see also Rush v. Savchuk*, 444 U.S. 320, 325-326 (1980). If we could discard an "ancient form without substantial modern justification" in *Shaffer*, we can do so again. Lower courts, commentators, and the American Law Institute all have interpreted *International Shoe* and *Shaffer* to mean that every assertion of state-court jurisdiction, even one pursuant to a "traditional" rule such as transient jurisdiction, must comport with contemporary notions of due process. Notwithstanding the nimble gymnastics of Justice Scalia's opinion today, it is not faithful to our decision in *Shaffer*.

## II

Tradition, though alone not dispositive, is of course relevant to the question whether the rule of transient jurisdiction is consistent with due process.[7] Tradition is salient not in the sense that practices of the past are automatically reasonable today; indeed, under such a standard, the legitimacy of transient jurisdiction would be called into question because the rule's historical "pedigree" is a matter of intense debate. The rule was a stranger to the common law and was rather weakly implanted in American jurisprudence "at the crucial time for present purposes: 1868, when the Fourteenth Amendment was adopted." For much of the 19th century, American courts did not uniformly recognize the concept of transient jurisdiction, and it appears that the transient rule did not receive wide currency until well after our decision in *Pennoyer v. Neff*, 95 U.S. 714 (1878).

Rather, I find the historical background relevant because, however murky the jurisprudential origins of transient jurisdiction, the fact that American courts have announced the rule for perhaps a century (first in dicta, more recently in holdings) provides a defendant voluntarily present in a particular State today "clear notice that [he] is subject to suit" in the forum. *World-Wide Volkswagen Corp. v. Woodson*, 444 U.S. at 297. Regardless of whether Justice Story's account of the rule's genesis is mythical, our common understanding now, fortified by a century of judicial practice, is that jurisdiction is often a function of geography. The transient rule is consistent with reasonable expectations and is entitled to a strong presumption that it comports with due process. "If I visit another State, . . . I knowingly assume some risk that the State will exercise its power over my property or my person while there. My contact with the State, though minimal, gives rise to predictable risks." . . .

By visiting the forum State, a transient defendant actually "avail[s]" himself of significant benefits provided by the State. His health and safety are guaranteed by the State's police, fire, and emergency medical services; he is free to travel on the State's roads and waterways; he likely enjoys the fruits of the State's economy as well. Moreover, the Privileges and Immunities Clause of Article IV prevents a state government from discriminating against a transient defendant by denying him the protections of its law or the right of access to its courts. Subject only to the doctrine of *forum non conveniens*, an out-of-state plaintiff may use state courts in all circumstances in which those courts would be available to state citizens. Without transient jurisdiction, an asymmetry would arise: A transient would have the full benefit of the power of the forum State's courts as a plaintiff while retaining immunity from their authority as a defendant.

---

7. I do not propose that the "contemporary notions of due process" to be applied are no more than "each Justice's subjective assessment of what is fair and just." Rather, the inquiry is guided by our decisions beginning with *International Shoe Co. v. Washington*, and the specific factors that we have developed to ascertain whether a jurisdictional rule comports with "traditional notions of fair play and substantial justice." *See, e.g., Asahi Metal Industry Co. v. Superior Court of California, Solano County* (noting "several factors," including "the burden on the defendant, the interests of the forum State, and the plaintiff's interest in obtaining relief"). This analysis may not be "mechanical or quantitative," *International Shoe*, but neither is it "freestanding" or dependent on personal whim. Our experience with this approach demonstrates that it is well within our competence to employ.

The potential burdens on a transient defendant are slight. "[M]odern transportation and communications have made it much less burdensome for a party sued to defend himself" in a State outside his place of residence. That the defendant has already journeyed at least once before to the forum— as evidenced by the fact that he was served with process there—is an indication that suit in the forum likely would not be prohibitively inconvenient. Finally, any burdens that do arise can be ameliorated by a variety of procedural devices.[13] For these reasons, as a rule the exercise of personal jurisdiction over a defendant based on his voluntary presence in the forum will satisfy the requirements of due process.[14]

In this case, it is undisputed that petitioner was served with process while voluntarily and knowingly in the State of California. I therefore concur in the judgment.

Justice STEVENS, concurring in the judgment:

As I explained in my separate writing, I did not join the Court's opinion in *Shaffer v. Heitner*, because I was concerned by its unnecessarily broad reach. The same concern prevents me from joining either Justice Scalia's or Justice Brennan's opinion in this case. For me, it is sufficient to note that the historical evidence and consensus identified by Justice Scalia, the considerations of fairness identified by Justice Brennan, and the common sense displayed by Justice White, all combine to demonstrate that this is, indeed, a very easy case. Accordingly, I agree that the judgment should be affirmed.

---

13. For example, in the federal system, a transient defendant can avoid protracted litigation of a spurious suit through a motion to dismiss for failure to state a claim or though a motion for summary judgment. Fed. Rules Civ. Proc. 12(b)(6) and 56. He can use relatively inexpensive methods of discovery, such as oral deposition by telephone (Rule 30(b)(7)), deposition upon written questions (Rule 31), interrogatories (Rule 33), and requests for admission (Rule 36), while enjoying protection from harassment (Rule 26(c)), and possibly obtaining costs and attorney's fees for some of the work involved (Rules 37(a)(4), (b)-(d)). Moreover, a change of venue may be possible. 28 U.S.C. § 1404. In state court, many of the same procedural protections are available, as is the doctrine of *forum non conveniens*, under which the suit may be dismissed. *See generally* Abrams, *Power, Convenience, and the Elimination of Personal Jurisdiction in the Federal Courts*, 58 Ind. L.J. 1, 23-25 (1982).

14. Justice Scalia . . . insists that because of its historical "pedigree," the rule is "the very baseline of reasonableness." Thus is revealed Justice Scalia's belief that tradition alone is completely dispositive and that no showing of unfairness can ever serve to invalidate a traditional jurisdictional practice. I disagree both with this belief and with Justice Scalia's assessment of the fairness of the transient jurisdiction bargain. I note, moreover, that the dual conclusions of Justice Scalia's opinion create a singularly unattractive result. Justice Scalia suggests that when and if a jurisdictional rule becomes substantively unfair or even "unconscionable," this Court is powerless to alter it. Instead, he is willing to rely on individual States to limit or abandon bases of jurisdiction that have become obsolete. This reliance is misplaced, for States have little incentive to limit rules such as transient jurisdiction that make it easier for their own citizens to sue out-of-state defendants. That States are more likely to expand their jurisdiction is illustrated by the adoption by many States of long-arm statutes extending the reach of personal jurisdiction to the limits established by the Federal Constitution. Out-of-staters do not vote in state elections or have a voice in state government. We should not assume, therefore, that States will be motivated by "notions of fairness" to curb jurisdictional rules like the one at issue here. The reasoning of Justice Scalia's opinion today is strikingly oblivious to the raison d'être of various constitutional doctrines designed to protect out-of-staters, such as the Art. IV Privileges and Immunities Clause and the Commerce Clause.

## Comments and Questions

1. Keep in mind that the controversy in *Burnham* concerns whether personal service within the forum is *itself* sufficient to establish jurisdiction over a nonresident. In such situations, service of process serves the dual purpose of establishing adjudicatory power *and* providing notice of the litigation, just as in the good old days of *Pennoyer*.

2. Justice Marshall's opinion in *Shaffer*, which invalidated quasi in rem jurisdiction despite its "long history," observed that due process "can be as readily offended by the perpetuation of ancient forms that are no longer justified as by the adoption of new procedures." Contrast Justice Scalia's virtual equation of tradition with due process while upholding transient jurisdiction in *Burnham*. What arguments favor each position? How should one weigh predictability and certainty against flexibility and discretion regarding legal standards?

3. Contrast the very different readings of the same short phrase. For Scalia, the operative word is "*traditional* notions of fair play and substantial justice." For Brennan, the emphasis is on the latter two concepts.

4. Note Justice White's condemnation of the ad hoc approach to in-state service that Brennan advocates in his concurrence, because it would require "endless, fact-specific litigation." Can you sympathize with White's frustration regarding the minimum-contacts/fundamental fairness calculus?

5. As in *Asahi*, the Justices in *Burnham* agree on the end result, but not on the path leading to it. What does *Burnham* actually hold?

6. What do you make of Sandra Day O'Connor joining the Court's liberals?

7. Does Brennan really make a persuasive case that Mr. Burnham had sufficient minimum contacts by virtue of his three days in the Golden State?

8. After *Burnham*, would service on Professor Gloss in Massachusetts in our Practice Exercise 33 establish adjudicatory power over him, even absent any other connection to the forum? Or would we need to know more about his relationship to the state?

9. In the legendary case of *Grace v. MacArthur*, 170 F. Supp. 442 (E.D. Ark. 1959), a citizen of Tennessee contested the exercise of jurisdiction over him in Arkansas. A U.S. marshall had personally served defendant while he was a passenger on a nonstop flight from Memphis to Dallas, when "said airplane was in the Eastern District of Arkansas and directly above Pine Bluff, Arkansas, in said District." Without addressing the *International Shoe* issue, the court upheld jurisdiction based solely on service at 35,000 feet altitude. Do you see why some have dubbed this "tag jurisdiction"? Would a court reach the same result after *Burnham*?

10. Does in-state service work on corporate defendants? Wenche Siemer v. Learjet Acquisition Corp., 966 F.2d 179 (5th Cir. 1992), held that service in Texas on the designated corporate agent of Learjet did not satisfy the requirements of due process so as to permit suit in Texas. The air crash out of which the lawsuit arose occurred in Egypt on a flight from Greece to Saudi Arabia. Decedents and the plaintiff-survivors were all residents of Greece or other

European countries. The plane had been based in Greece and operated by a Greek company. It was not designed, manufactured, or serviced in Texas; nor had it ever been owned by a Texas resident.

The court rejected plaintiffs' assertion that jurisdiction could be based solely on in-state service on the corporate agent, finding their reliance on *Burnham* "puzzling": "*Burnham* did not involve a corporation and did not decide any jurisdictional issue pertaining to corporations." 966 F.2d at 182. The court quoted Justice Scalia's observation in his footnote 1 in *Burnham* that corporations "have never fitted comfortably in a jurisdictional regime based primarily upon de facto power over the defendant's person."

Judicial power over corporations must thus be based, the Fifth Circuit held, on either one of the two constitutionally permissible bases—specific act jurisdiction over claims related to in-state activities, or such continuous and systematic conduct in the forum as to justify general jurisdiction over any claim.

For more on this topic, see 4A Charles A. Wright, Arthur R. Miller, Mary Kay Kane, and R. Marcus, *Federal Practice and Procedure* § 1069.4 (3d ed.).

11. What if a defendant is served after being tricked into visiting the state, or while there to testify as a witness or appear as a party in another matter? A generally recognized immunity protects nonresidents in such situations. *See* Fleming James, Jr., Geoffrey C. Hazard, Jr., and John Leubsdorf, *Civil Procedure* §§ 2.15, 2.17 at 104-106, 111 (5th ed. 2001). In *Voice Systems Marketing Co. v. Appropriate Technology Corp.*, 153 F.R.D. 117 (E.D. Mich. 1994), for example, the court granted a motion to dismiss for insufficiency of service after finding that plaintiff had induced the corporate president to travel from California to Michigan, ostensibly to correct problems with security products sold to the plaintiff, but actually to serve him with process.

12. *A Domestic Forum for International Human Rights Cases.* Transient jurisdiction has played a critical role in civil actions against high-ranking foreign nationals accused of violations of international law. *Xuncax v. Gramajo*, 886 F. Supp. 162 (D. Mass. 1995), was brought by nine expatriate citizens of Guatemala against the former defense minister of that country, seeking damages under the Torture Victim Protection Act. Gramajo was served with process while attending his commencement at Harvard's Kennedy School of Government in Cambridge, Massachusetts, thus establishing adjudicatory power over him. A default judgment for $47 million was entered after he returned to Guatemala.

Bosnian leader Radovan Karadzic was similarly held subject to personal jurisdiction in an action brought by victims of alleged atrocities in the Balkans, based on service of process in a Manhattan hotel. *Kadic v. Karadzic*, 70 F.3d 232 (2d Cir. 1995). When Karadzic was approached by process servers in the hotel lobby, his security guards knocked the papers to the floor. The court nonetheless ruled that the service was effective, and rejected Karadzic's argument that he was immune from service because he was in New York on official United Nations business.

An earlier influential decision by the Second Circuit Court of Appeals had established that the federal courts have jurisdiction in such cases whenever the alleged torturer is found and served within the United States. The defendant in *Filartiga v. Pena-Irala*, 630 F.2d 876 (2d Cir. 1980), was served while being detained at the Brooklyn Navy Yard pending deportation back to Paraguay, where as Inspector General of the Police he allegedly had plaintiff's son kidnapped and tortured to death in retaliation for his father's political activities.

For a case asserting general jurisdiction over foreign companies in an action accusing them of complicity in human rights abuses abroad, see *Wiwa v. Royal Dutch Petroleum Co.*, 226 F.3d 88 (2d Cir. 2000), *cert. denied*, 532 U.S. 941, discussed in Part M, below.

Subject matter jurisdiction (discussed in Chapter 8) in these international human rights cases is based upon the Alien Tort Statute (ATS), which was part of the Judiciary Act of 1789, and is now codified at 28 U.S.C. § 1350. It provides federal district courts with jurisdiction over civil actions brought by aliens alleging torts committed in violation of the "law of nations or a treaty of the United States."

Arguing that ATS cases interfere with the conduct of foreign policy and the "war on terrorism," the Bush Administration sought to put an end to such litigation. *See* Brief of the United States of America as Amicus Curiae, *John Doe 1 v. Unocal Corp.*, 2002 WL 31063976 (9th Cir. Sept. 18, 2002), *reh'g en banc granted*, 2003 WL 359787 (9th Cir. Feb. 14, 2003). The case, alleging that multinational oil companies subjected Burmese villagers to systematic human rights abuses including forced labor, murder, rape, and torture during construction of a gas pipeline, was dismissed by agreement of all the parties in 2005.

In 2004, the U.S. Supreme Court gave the ATS a narrow reading, granting the federal courts subject matter jurisdiction only over cases asserting violations of norms of customary international law of the type recognized in 1789. *Sosa v. Alvarez-Machain*, 542 U.S. 692 (2004). For more on the ATS, see Kristin Myles and Daniel Collins, *The Future of International Rights Litigation*, 32 Litigation 40 (2006).

## M. GENERAL JURISDICTION

Although the main focus of the Supreme Court's considerable output on the topic of personal jurisdiction has concerned specific jurisdiction, you will recall that Chief Justice Stone described a broader form of adjudicatory power as well in *International Shoe*. When the forum activities of a corporate defendant are sufficiently continuous, systematic, and substantial, it may be sued there even on claims unrelated to those activities, as in *Perkins v. Benguet Consolidated Mining Co.*, 342 U.S. 437 (1957) (Part F, above).

It has long been recognized that a state has such plenary jurisdiction over its natural and corporate citizens—they are subject to suit on any claim, whether arising from events that occurred in the state or not. *See* Jack H. Friedenthal, Mary Kay Kane, and Arthur R. Miller, *Civil Procedure* § 3.6 (4th ed. 2005). A state may enter a personal judgment against a domiciliary even if he is absent from the state and cannot be served with process there. General jurisdiction exists over a corporation that is incorporated in the forum state, or whose headquarters or principal place of business is located there. Thus there will always be *at least one forum* in which a defendant may be sued.

Short of corporate citizenship, what level of activity is necessary to assert general jurisdiction? Consider the following case.

## ■ GOODYEAR DUNLOP TIRES OPERATIONS, S. A., ET AL. v. BROWN ET UX., CO-ADMINISTRATORS OF THE ESTATE OF BROWN, ET AL.
*131 S. Ct. 2846 (2011)*

Justice GINSBURG delivered the opinion of the Court.

This case concerns the jurisdiction of state courts over corporations organized and operating abroad. We address, in particular, this question: Are foreign subsidiaries of a United States parent corporation amenable to suit in state court on claims unrelated to any activity of the subsidiaries in the forum State?

A bus accident outside Paris that took the lives of two 13-year-old boys from North Carolina gave rise to the litigation we here consider. Attributing the accident to a defective tire manufactured in Turkey at the plant of a foreign subsidiary of The Goodyear Tire and Rubber Company (Goodyear USA), the boys' parents commenced an action for damages in a North Carolina state court; they named as defendants Goodyear USA, an Ohio corporation, and three of its subsidiaries, organized and operating, respectively, in Turkey, France, and Luxembourg. Goodyear USA, which had plants in North Carolina and regularly engaged in commercial activity there, did not contest the North Carolina court's jurisdiction over it; Goodyear USA's foreign subsidiaries, however, maintained that North Carolina lacked adjudicatory authority over them.

A state court's assertion of jurisdiction exposes defendants to the State's coercive power, and is therefore subject to review for compatibility with the Fourteenth Amendment's Due Process Clause. *International Shoe Co. v. Washington.* Opinions in the wake of the pathmarking *International Shoe* decision have differentiated between general or all-purpose jurisdiction, and specific or case-linked jurisdiction. A court may assert general jurisdiction over foreign (sister-state or foreign-country) corporations to hear any and all claims against them when their

*General – continuous and systematic*

affiliations with the State are so "continuous and systematic" as to render them essentially at home in the forum State. Specific jurisdiction, on the other hand, depends on an "affiliatio[n] between the forum and the underlying controversy," principally, activity or an occurrence that takes place in the forum State and is therefore subject to the State's regulation. In contrast to general, all-purpose jurisdiction, specific jurisdiction is confined to adjudication of "issues deriving from, or connected with, the very controversy that establishes jurisdiction."

*Specific*

Because the episode-in-suit, the bus accident, occurred in France, and the tire alleged to have caused the accident was manufactured and sold abroad, North Carolina courts lacked specific jurisdiction to adjudicate the controversy. Were the foreign subsidiaries nonetheless amenable to general jurisdiction in North Carolina courts? Confusing or blending general and specific jurisdictional inquiries, the North Carolina courts answered yes. Some of the tires made abroad by Goodyear's foreign subsidiaries, the North Carolina Court of Appeals stressed, had reached North Carolina through "the stream of commerce"; that connection, the Court of Appeals believed, gave North Carolina courts the handle needed for the exercise of general jurisdiction over the foreign corporations.

A connection so limited between the forum and the foreign corporation, we hold, is an inadequate basis for the exercise of general jurisdiction. Such a connection does not establish the "continuous and systematic" affiliation necessary to empower North Carolina courts to entertain claims unrelated to the foreign corporation's contacts with the State.

*HOLDING*

*no general jurisdiction*

## I

On April 18, 2004, a bus destined for Charles de Gaulle Airport overturned on a road outside Paris, France. Passengers on the bus were young soccer players from North Carolina beginning their journey home. Two 13-year-olds, Julian Brown and Matthew Helms, sustained fatal injuries. The boys' parents, respondents in this Court, filed a suit for wrongful-death damages in the Superior Court of Onslow County, North Carolina, in their capacity as administrators of the boys' estates. Attributing the accident to a tire that failed when its plies separated, the parents alleged negligence in the "design, construction, testing, and inspection" of the tire.

Goodyear Luxembourg Tires, SA (Goodyear Luxembourg), Goodyear Lastikleri T. A. S. (Goodyear Turkey), and Goodyear Dunlop Tires France, SA (Goodyear France), petitioners here, were named as defendants. Incorporated in Luxembourg, Turkey, and France, respectively, petitioners are indirect subsidiaries of Goodyear USA, an Ohio corporation also named as a defendant in the suit. Petitioners manufacture tires primarily for sale in European and Asian markets. Their tires differ in size and construction from tires ordinarily sold in the United States. They are designed to carry significantly heavier loads, and to serve under road conditions and speed limits in the manufacturers' primary markets.

In contrast to the parent company, Goodyear USA, which does not contest the North Carolina courts' personal jurisdiction over it, petitioners are not registered to do business in North Carolina. They have no place of business, employees, or bank accounts in North Carolina. They do not design, manufacture, or advertise their products in North Carolina. And they do not solicit business in North Carolina or themselves sell or ship tires to North Carolina customers. Even so, a small percentage of petitioners' tires (tens of thousands out of tens of millions manufactured between 2004 and 2007) were distributed within North Carolina by other Goodyear USA affiliates. These tires were typically custom ordered to equip specialized vehicles such as cement mixers, waste haulers, and boat and horse trailers. Petitioners state, and respondents do not here deny, that the type of tire involved in the accident, a Goodyear Regional RHS tire manufactured by Goodyear Turkey, was never distributed in North Carolina.

Petitioners moved to dismiss the claims against them for want of personal jurisdiction. The trial court denied the motion, and the North Carolina Court of Appeals affirmed. Acknowledging that the claims neither "related to, nor . . . ar[o]se from, [petitioners'] contacts with North Carolina," the Court of Appeals confined its analysis to "general rather than specific jurisdiction," which the court recognized required a "higher threshold" showing: A defendant must have "continuous and systematic contacts" with the forum. That threshold was crossed, the court determined, when petitioners placed their tires "in the stream of interstate commerce without any limitation on the extent to which those tires could be sold in North Carolina."

Nothing in the record, the court observed, indicated that petitioners "took any affirmative action to cause tires which they had manufactured to be shipped into North Carolina." The court found, however, that tires made by petitioners reached North Carolina as a consequence of a "highly-organized distribution process" involving other Goodyear USA subsidiaries. Petitioners, the court noted, made "no attempt to keep these tires from reaching the North Carolina market." Indeed, the very tire involved in the accident, the court observed, conformed to tire standards established by the U.S. Department of Transportation and bore markings required for sale in the United States. As further support, the court invoked North Carolina's "interest in providing a forum in which its citizens are able to seek redress for [their] injuries," and noted the hardship North Carolina plaintiffs would experience "[were they] required to litigate their claims in France," a country to which they have no ties. The North Carolina Supreme Court denied discretionary review.

We granted certiorari to decide whether the general jurisdiction the North Carolina courts asserted over petitioners is consistent with the Due Process Clause of the Fourteenth Amendment.

*[handwritten margin notes: "General - all purpose", "Specific - case linked (minimum)"]*

## II

### A

The Due Process Clause of the Fourteenth Amendment sets the outer boundaries of a state tribunal's authority to proceed against a defendant. The canonical opinion in this area remains *International Shoe*, in which we held that a State may authorize its courts to exercise personal jurisdiction over an out-of-state defendant if the defendant has "certain minimum contacts with [the State] such that the maintenance of the suit does not offend 'traditional notions of fair play and substantial justice.'"

*[handwritten margin note: "Specific Jurisdiction"]*

Endeavoring to give specific content to the "fair play and substantial justice" concept, the Court in *International Shoe* classified cases involving out-of-state corporate defendants. First, as in *International Shoe* itself, jurisdiction unquestionably could be asserted where the corporation's in-state activity is "continuous and systematic" and that activity gave rise to the episode-in-suit. Further, the Court observed, the commission of certain "single or occasional acts" in a State may be sufficient to render a corporation answerable in that State with respect to those acts, though not with respect to matters unrelated to the forum connections. The heading courts today use to encompass these two *International Shoe* categories is "specific jurisdiction." Adjudicatory authority is "specific" when the suit "aris[es] out of or relate[s] to the defendant's contacts with the forum."

*International Shoe* distinguished from cases that fit within the "specific jurisdiction" categories, "instances in which the continuous corporate operations within a state [are] so substantial and of such a nature as to justify suit against it on causes of action arising from dealings entirely distinct from those activities." Adjudicatory authority so grounded is today called "general jurisdiction." For an individual, the paradigm forum for the exercise of general jurisdiction is the individual's domicile; for a corporation, it is an equivalent place, one in which the corporation is fairly regarded as at home (domicile, place of incorporation, and principal place of business are paradigm bases for the exercise of general jurisdiction).

Since *International Shoe*, this Court's decisions have elaborated primarily on circumstances that warrant the exercise of specific jurisdiction, particularly in cases involving "single or occasional acts" occurring or having their impact within the forum State. As a rule in these cases, this Court has inquired whether there was "some act by which the defendant purposefully avail[ed] itself of the privilege of conducting activities within the forum State, thus invoking the benefits and protections of its laws." *Hanson v. Denckla.* See, e.g., *World-Wide Volkswagen Corp. v. Woodson*, 444 U.S. 286, 287, 297 (1980) (Oklahoma court may not exercise personal jurisdiction "over a nonresident automobile retailer and its wholesale distributor in a products-liability action, when the defendants' only connection with Oklahoma is the fact that an automobile sold in New York to New York residents became involved in an accident in Oklahoma"); *Burger King Corp. v. Rudzewicz*, 471 U.S. 462, 474-475 (1985) (franchisor headquartered in Florida may maintain

*[handwritten margin note: "for Specific"]*

breach-of-contract action in Florida against Michigan franchisees, where agreement contemplated on-going interactions between franchisees and franchisor's headquarters); *Asahi Metal Industry Co. v. Superior Court of Cal., Solano Cty.*, 480 U.S. 102, 105 (1987) (Taiwanese tire manufacturer settled product liability action brought in California and sought indemnification there from Japanese valve assembly manufacturer; Japanese company's "mere awareness . . . that the components it manufactured, sold, and delivered outside the United States would reach the forum State in the stream of commerce" held insufficient to permit California court's adjudication of Taiwanese company's cross-complaint).

In only two decisions postdating *International Shoe* has this Court considered whether an out-of-state corporate defendant's in-state contacts were sufficiently "continuous and systematic" to justify the exercise of general jurisdiction over claims unrelated to those contacts: *Perkins v. Benguet Consol. Mining Co.*, 342 U.S. 437 (1952) (general jurisdiction appropriately exercised over Philippine corporation sued in Ohio, where the company's affairs were overseen during World War II); and *Helicopteros*, 466 U.S. 408 (helicopter owned by Colombian corporation crashed in Peru; survivors of U.S. citizens who died in the crash, the Court held, could not maintain wrongful-death actions against the Colombian corporation in Texas, for the corporation's helicopter purchases and purchase-linked activity in Texas were insufficient to subject it to Texas court's general jurisdiction).

**B**

To justify the exercise of general jurisdiction over petitioners, the North Carolina courts relied on the petitioners' placement of their tires in the "stream of commerce." The stream-of-commerce metaphor has been invoked frequently in lower court decisions permitting "jurisdiction in products liability cases in which the product has traveled through an extensive chain of distribution before reaching the ultimate consumer." Typically, in such cases, a nonresident defendant, acting outside the forum, places in the stream of commerce a product that ultimately causes harm inside the forum.

Many States have enacted long-arm statutes authorizing courts to exercise specific jurisdiction over manufacturers when the events in suit, or some of them, occurred within the forum state. For example, the "Local Injury; Foreign Act" subsection of North Carolina's long-arm statute authorizes North Carolina courts to exercise personal jurisdiction in "any action claiming injury to person or property within this State arising out of [the defendant's] act or omission outside this State," if, "in addition[,] at or about the time of the injury," "[p]roducts . . . manufactured by the defendant were used or consumed, within this State in the ordinary course of trade." As the North Carolina Court of Appeals recognized, this provision of the State's long-arm statute "does not apply to this case," for both the act alleged to have caused injury (the fabrication of the allegedly defective tire) and its impact (the accident) occurred outside the forum. [The court instead relied on N.C. Gen. Stat. Ann. § 1-75.4(1)(d), which provides for jurisdiction, "whether the claim arises within or without [the] State," when the defendant "[i]s engaged in substantial activity within this State, whether such activity is wholly interstate, intrastate, or otherwise." This provision, the North Carolina Supreme Court has held, was "intended to make available to the North Carolina courts the full jurisdictional powers permissible under federal due process."]

The North Carolina court's stream-of-commerce analysis elided the essential difference between case-specific and all-purpose (general) jurisdiction. Flow of a manufacturer's products into the forum, we have explained, may bolster an affiliation germane to specific jurisdiction. See, e.g., *World-Wide Volkswagen* (where "the sale of a product . . . is not simply an isolated occurrence, but arises from the efforts of the manufacturer or distributor to serve . . . the market for its product in [several] States, it is not unreasonable to subject it to suit in one of those States if its allegedly defective merchandise *has there been the source of injury to its owner or to others*" (emphasis added)). But ties serving to bolster the exercise of specific jurisdiction do not warrant a determination that, based on those ties, the forum has general jurisdiction over a defendant.

A corporation's "continuous activity of some sorts within a state," *International Shoe* instructed, "is not enough to support the demand that the corporation be amenable to suits unrelated to that activity." Our 1952 decision in *Perkins v. Benguet Consol. Mining Co.* remains "[t]he textbook case of general jurisdiction appropriately exercised over a foreign corporation that has not consented to suit in the forum."

Sued in Ohio, the defendant in *Perkins* was a Philippine mining corporation that had ceased activities in the Philippines during World War II. To the extent that the company was conducting any business during and immediately after the Japanese occupation of the Philippines, it was doing so in Ohio: the corporation's president maintained his office there, kept the company files in that office, and supervised from the Ohio office "the necessarily limited wartime activities of the company." Although the claim-in-suit did not arise in Ohio, this Court ruled that it would not violate due process for Ohio to adjudicate the controversy.

We next addressed the exercise of general jurisdiction over an out-of-state corporation over three decades later, in *Helicopteros*. In that case, survivors of United States citizens who died in a helicopter crash in Peru instituted wrongful-death actions in a Texas state court against the owner and operator of the helicopter, a Colombian corporation. The Colombian corporation had no place of business in Texas and was not licensed to do business there. "Basically, [the company's] contacts with Texas consisted of sending its chief executive officer to Houston for a contract-negotiation session; accepting into its New York bank account checks drawn on a Houston bank; purchasing helicopters, equipment, and training services from [a Texas enterprise] for substantial sums; and sending personnel to [Texas] for training." These links to Texas, we determined, did not "constitute the kind of continuous and systematic general business contacts . . . found to exist in Perkins," and were insufficient to support the exercise of jurisdiction over a claim that neither "ar[o]se out of . . . no[r] related to" the defendant's activities in Texas.

*Helicopteros* concluded that "mere purchases [made in the forum State], even if occurring at regular intervals, are not enough to warrant a State's assertion of [general] jurisdiction over a nonresident corporation in a cause of action not related to those purchase transactions." We see no reason to differentiate from the ties to Texas held insufficient in *Helicopteros*, the sales of petitioners' tires sporadically made in North Carolina through intermediaries. Under the sprawling view of general jurisdiction urged by respondents and embraced by the North Carolina Court of Appeals, any substantial manufacturer or seller of goods would be amenable to suit, on any claim for relief, wherever its products are distributed. But cf. *World-Wide Volkswagen*, 444 U.S., at 296 (every seller of chattels does not, by virtue of the sale, "appoint the chattel his agent for service of process").

Measured against *Helicopteros* and *Perkins*, North Carolina is not a forum in which it would be permissible to subject petitioners to general jurisdiction. Unlike the defendant in *Perkins*, whose sole wartime business activity was conducted in Ohio, petitioners are in no sense at home in North Carolina. Their attenuated connections to the State fall far short of "the continuous and systematic general business contacts" necessary to empower North Carolina to entertain suit against them on claims unrelated to anything that connects them to the State.[10]

### C

Respondents belatedly assert a "single enterprise" theory, asking us to consolidate petitioners' ties to North Carolina with those of Goodyear USA and other Goodyear entities. In effect, respondents would have us pierce Goodyear corporate veils, at least for jurisdictional purposes. Neither below nor in their brief in opposition to the petition for certiorari did respondents urge disregard of petitioners' discrete status as subsidiaries and treatment of all Goodyear entities as a "unitary business," so that jurisdiction over the parent would draw in the subsidiaries as well. Respondents have therefore forfeited this contention, and we do not address it.

For the reasons stated, the judgment of the North Carolina Court of Appeals is

Reversed.

---

10. The North Carolina Court of Appeals invoked the State's "well-recognized interest in providing a forum in which its citizens are able to seek redress for injuries that they have sustained." But "[g]eneral jurisdiction to adjudicate has in [United States] practice never been based on the plaintiff's relationship to the forum. There is nothing in [our] law comparable to . . . article 14 of the Civil Code of France (1804) under which the French nationality of the plaintiff is a sufficient ground for jurisdiction." (French law permitting plaintiff-based jurisdiction is rarely invoked in the absence of other supporting factors). When a defendant's act outside the forum causes injury in the forum, by contrast, a plaintiff's residence in the forum may strengthen the case for the exercise of specific jurisdiction. See Calder v. Jones, 465 U.S. 783, 788 (1984).

## Comments and Questions

1. It appears that the only consensus on the Court in the realm of personal jurisdiction lies in this area of general jurisdiction. But does Justice Ginsburg take this rare opportunity of a *unanimous* decision to spell out the contours of this plenary authority, or does she stop at telling us what level of activity is *insufficient* to support it? Short of being incorporated in the forum state or having a principal place of business there (we will explore the concept of principal place of business for diversity purposes in Chapter 8), what level of "doing business" or "continuous and systematic" activities gives rise to power over all claims, related to forum activity or not? Or to use her phrase, when can it be said that a defendant is "at home" in the forum? 131 S. Ct., at 2857.

Note Justice Ginsburg's helpful contribution to the vocabulary: general *or all-purpose jurisdiction*, and specific or *case-linked jurisdiction*.

2. The Court's two earlier precedents on this topic were seemingly easy cases. The Benguet Consolidated Mining Co. conducted its only wartime activities from its relocated office in Ohio; had the Court not rendered the company subject to general jurisdiction, one wonders where else Perkins could have brought her suit. *Perkins v. Benguet Consolidated Mining Co.*, 342 U.S. 437 (1952).

In *Helicopteros Nacionales de Colombia v. Hall*, 466 U.S. 408 (1984), on the other hand, defendant's ties to Texas were far too tenuous, as described by Justice Blackmun:

Petitioner Helicopteros Nacionales de Colombia, S.A. (Helicol), is a Colombian corporation with its principal place of business in the city of Bogota in that country. It is engaged in the business of providing helicopter transportation for oil and construction companies in South America. On January 26, 1976, a helicopter owned by Helicol crashed in Peru. Four United States citizens were among those who lost their lives in the accident. Respondents are the survivors and representatives of the four decedents.

At the time of the crash, respondents' decedents were employed by Consorcio, a Peruvian consortium, and were working on a pipeline in Peru. Consorcio is the alter ego of a joint venture named Williams-Sedco-Horn (WSH). The venture had its headquarters in Houston, Tex. Consorcio had been formed to enable the venturers to enter into a contract with Petro Peru, the Peruvian state-owned oil company. Consorcio was to construct a pipeline for Petro Peru running from the interior of Peru westward to the Pacific Ocean. Peruvian law forbade construction of the pipeline by any non-Peruvian entity.

Consorcio/WSH needed helicopters to move personnel, materials, and equipment into and out of the construction area. In 1974, upon request of Consorcio/WSH, the chief executive officer of Helicol, Francisco Restrepo, flew to the United States and conferred in Houston with representatives of the three joint venturers. At that meeting, there was a discussion of prices, availability, working conditions, fuel, supplies, and housing. Restrepo represented that Helicol could have the first helicopter on the job in 15 days. The Consorcio/WSH representatives decided to accept the contract proposed by Restrepo. Helicol began performing before the agreement was formally signed in Peru on

November 11, 1974. (Respondents acknowledge that the contract was executed in Peru and not in the United States.) The contract was written in Spanish on official government stationery and provided that the residence of all the parties would be Lima, Peru. It further stated that controversies arising out of the contract would be submitted to the jurisdiction of Peruvian courts. In addition, it provided that Consorcio/WSH would make payments to Helicol's account with the Bank of America in New York City.

Aside from the negotiation session in Houston between Restrepo and the representatives of Consorcio/WSH, Helicol had other contacts with Texas. During the years 1970-1977, it purchased helicopters (approximately 80% of its fleet), spare parts, and accessories for more than $4 million from Bell Helicopter Company in Fort Worth. In that period, Helicol sent prospective pilots to Fort Worth for training and to ferry the aircraft to South America. It also sent management and maintenance personnel to visit Bell Helicopter in Fort Worth during the same period in order to receive "plant familiarization" and for technical consultation. Helicol received into its New York City and Panama City, Fla., bank accounts over $5 million in payments from Consorcio/WSH drawn upon First City National Bank of Houston.

Beyond the foregoing, there have been no other business contacts between Helicol and the State of Texas. Helicol never has been authorized to do business in Texas and never has had an agent for the service of process within the State. It never has performed helicopter operations in Texas or sold any product that reached Texas, never solicited business in Texas, never signed any contract in Texas, never had any employee based there, and never recruited an employee in Texas. In addition, Helicol never has owned real or personal property in Texas and never has maintained an office or establishment there. Helicol has maintained no records in Texas and has no shareholders in that State. None of the respondents or their decedents were domiciled in Texas, but all of the decedents were hired in Houston by Consorcio/WSH to work on the Petro Peru pipeline project. (Respondents' lack of residential or other contacts with Texas of itself does not defeat otherwise proper jurisdiction. *Keeton v. Hustler Magazine, Inc.*, 465 U.S. 770, 780 (1984). We mention respondents' lack of contacts merely to show that nothing in the nature of the relationship between respondents and Helicol could possibly enhance Helicol's contacts with Texas. The harm suffered by respondents did not occur in Texas. Nor is it alleged that any negligence on the part of Helicol took place in Texas.)

Where would you place the Goodyear European subsidiaries on the activity spectrum calibrated by these two earlier cases?

3. Interestingly, Justice Brennan (who seems never to have encountered an exercise of jurisdiction he did not like) concluded that there was specific jurisdiction over Helicol, a matter the majority found had been waived by failure of the parties to raise it (see 466 U.S., at 415 n.10):

[T]he Court refuses to consider any distinction between contacts that are "related to" the underlying cause of action and contacts that "give rise" to the underlying cause of action. In my view, however, there is a substantial difference between these two standards for asserting specific jurisdiction. Thus, although I agree that the respondents' cause of action did not formally "arise out of" specific activities initiated by Helicol in the State of Texas, I believe that the wrongful-death claim filed by the respondents is significantly related to the undisputed contacts between Helicol and the forum. On that basis, I would conclude that the Due Process Clause allows the Texas courts to assert specific jurisdiction over this particular action.

. . . [T]he contacts between Helicol and the State of Texas are directly and significantly related to the underlying claim filed by the respondents. The negotiations that took place in Texas led to the contract in which Helicol agreed to provide the precise transportation services that were being used at the time of the crash. Moreover, the helicopter involved in the crash was purchased by Helicol in Texas, and the pilot whose negligence was alleged to have caused the crash was actually trained in Texas. This is simply not a case, therefore, in which a state court has asserted jurisdiction over a nonresident defendant on the basis of wholly unrelated contacts with the forum. Rather, the contacts between Helicol and the forum are directly related to the negligence that was alleged in the respondent Hall's original complaint. Because Helicol should have expected to be amenable to suit in the Texas courts for claims directly related to these contacts, it is fair and reasonable to allow the assertion of jurisdiction in this case.

466 U.S., at 425-426.

What is the difference between a claim *arising out of*, and one *relating to*, defendant's contacts within the forum? *See* Lea Brilmayer, *Related Contacts and Personal Jurisdiction*, 101 Harv. L. Rev. 1444 (1988). Would Brennan's broader definition change the result in any of the cases we have read? Look back at *Crocker v. Hilton International Barbados, Ltd.* in Part E of this chapter.

In rejecting a broad "but-for" standard of relation in favor of a requirement that defendant's in-state activity must form a material element of the plaintiff's claim, the First Circuit explained:

At heart, these concepts are all designed to ensure that exercises of jurisdiction comport with due process. The Due Process Clause requires fair warning as to where individuals' conduct will subject them to suit, and for purposes of specific jurisdiction, this "fair warning" requirement is satisfied if the defendant has purposefully directed his activities at residents of the forum, *and the litigation results from alleged injuries that arise out of or relate to those activities*.

*Harlow v. Children's Hospital*, 432 F.3d 50, 61 (1st Cir. 2005) (emphasis added).

4. Note Justice Ginsburg's concern in *Goodyear* that the lower court decision finding jurisdiction over the out-of-state claims based on stream-of-commerce theory both blurred the important distinction between general and specific jurisdiction, and amounted to a "sprawling view of general jurisdiction" that would subject "any substantial manufacturer or seller" to suit "on any claim for relief, wherever its products are distributed," a result already foreclosed in *World-Wide Volkswagen. See* 131 S. Ct., at 2856-2857.

5. In *Nichols v. G. D. Searle & Co.*, 991 F.2d 1195 (4th Cir. 1993), plaintiffs brought a product liability diversity action directed at defendant's intrauterine device (IUD). Even though the claims arose elsewhere and the plaintiffs were nonresidents of Maryland, they argued that G. D. Searle was subject to general jurisdiction in that state because it employed seventeen to twenty-one marketing representatives there (together with company automobiles, samples, and promotional materials) and generated annual sales between $9 and $13 million (approximately 2 percent of its total). The Fourth Circuit disagreed, observing: "[B]ecause specific jurisdiction has expanded tremendously, plaintiffs now may generally bring their claims in the forum in which they arose. As a result, obsolescing notions of general jurisdiction, which functioned primarily to ensure that a forum was available for plaintiffs to bring their claims, have been rendered largely unnecessary. Thus broad constructions of general jurisdiction should be generally disfavored." 991 F.2d at 1200 (citations omitted).

In a similar vein, the Maryland Court of Appeals adopted a sliding-scale scheme when it noted that in cases where it is not clear whether general or specific jurisdiction is applicable, "the proper approach is to identify the approximate position of the case on the continuum that exists between the two extremes, and apply the corresponding standard, recognizing that the quantum of required contacts increases as the nexus between the contacts and the cause of action decreases." *Camelback Ski Corp. v. Behning*, 539 A.2d 1107, 1111 (1988).

6. For a case asserting general jurisdiction over two foreign multinational corporations on human rights claims, see *Wiwa v. Royal Dutch Petroleum Co.*, 226 F.3d 88 (2d Cir. 2000), *cert. denied*, 532 U.S. 941 (2001). Nigerian émigrés sued under the Alien Tort Statute, alleging that the defendant companies (one incorporated in the Netherlands and the other in the United Kingdom) had participated in human rights abuses against them in Nigeria because of their opposition to oil exploration there. The Second Circuit concluded that defendants were subject to general jurisdiction because they were "doing business" in New York through a small investor-relations office operated by a subsidiary in Manhattan. Thus, even though plaintiffs' claims did not arise in or relate to activities in New York, they could be heard in federal district court in New York. Despite arguments from *amici curiae* (including the New York Stock Exchange) contending that the ruling could damage American business interests abroad, the Supreme Court refused to review the decision. Query: Is this decision still good law after *Goodyear*?

7. *Timing of Contacts.* Should a corporation's contacts with the forum be measured at the time the claim arose, or when the complaint is filed? Courts have distinguished between assertions of general jurisdiction, in which contacts are measured up to the time the complaint is filed, and specific jurisdiction, in which the focus is limited to contacts leading up to and surrounding the claimed injury. The First Circuit has explained:

The reason for this approach stems from the basic distinction between specific and general jurisdiction. . . . Unlike the specific jurisdiction analysis, which focuses on the cause of action, the defendant and the forum, a general jurisdiction inquiry is dispute blind, the sole focus being on whether there are continuous and systematic contacts between the defendant and the forum. Accordingly, [for general jurisdiction] a court should consider all of a defendant's contacts with the forum state prior to the filing of the lawsuit, rather than just those contacts that are related to the particular cause of action the plaintiff asserts.

*Harlow v. Children's Hospital, supra*, 432 F.3d at 65. Contacts arising *after* the filing of the complaint are irrelevant to either inquiry. *See generally* Todd David Peterson, *The Timing of Minimum Contacts*, 79 Geo. Wash. L. Rev. 101 (2010).

## N. CONSENT

As we have seen, consent is one of the traditional bases for the exercise of adjudicatory power. A defendant can voluntarily appear in court and thereby submit to jurisdiction. A defendant who appears and fails to assert a timely objection to personal jurisdiction thereby waives that objection—a form of involuntary consent. *See* Fed. R. Civ. P. 12(h)(1).

*Pennoyer* suggested that states could require nonresidents conducting certain activities within the state to "consent" to the appointment of an agent to receive service of process for actions arising out of those activities. In the post-*Pennoyer* years, courts even resorted to the fiction of *implied* consent to justify the exercise of jurisdiction over nonresidents, as in *Hess v. Pawloski, supra.*

By operation of a "forum-selection clause," consent to jurisdiction can take place *before* the dispute even arises, as illustrated by the next case.

■ **CARNIVAL CRUISE LINES, INC. v. SHUTE**
*499 U.S. 585 (1991)*

Justice BLACKMUN delivered the opinion of the Court:
In this admiralty case we primarily consider whether the United States Court of Appeals for the Ninth Circuit correctly refused to enforce a forum-selection clause contained in tickets issued by petitioner Carnival Cruise Lines, Inc., to respondents Eulala and Russel Shute.

### I

The Shutes, through an Arlington, Wash., travel agent, purchased passage for a 7-day cruise on petitioner's ship, the Tropicale. Respondents paid the fare to the agent who forwarded the payment to petitioner's headquarters in Miami, Fla. Petitioner then prepared the tickets and sent them to respondents in the State of Washington. The face of each ticket, at its left-hand lower corner, contained this admonition: "SUBJECT TO CONDITIONS

OF CONTRACT ON LAST PAGES IMPORTANT! PLEASE READ CON-
TRACT—ON LAST PAGES 1, 2, 3" App. 15.

The following appeared on "contract page 1" of each ticket:

TERMS AND CONDITIONS OF PASSAGE CONTRACT TICKET

. . . 3. (a) The acceptance of this ticket by the person or persons named
hereon as passengers shall be deemed to be an acceptance and agreement by
each of them of all of the terms and conditions of this Passage Contract Ticket.

. . . 8. It is agreed by and between the passenger and the Carrier that all
disputes and matters whatsoever arising under, in connection with or incident
to this Contract shall be litigated, if at all, in and before a Court located in the
State of Florida, U.S.A., to the exclusion of the Courts of any other state or country.

The last quoted paragraph is the forum-selection clause at issue.

## II

Respondents boarded the Tropicale in Los Angeles, Cal. The ship sailed to
Puerto Vallarta, Mexico, and then returned to Los Angeles. While the ship
was in international waters off the Mexican coast, respondent Eulala Shute
was injured when she slipped on a deck mat during a guided tour of the ship's
galley. Respondents filed suit against petitioner in the United States District
Court for the Western District of Washington, claiming that Mrs. Shute's
injuries had been caused by the negligence of Carnival Cruise Lines and
its employees.

Petitioner moved for summary judgment, contending that the forum
clause in respondents' tickets required the Shutes to bring their suit against
petitioner in a court in the State of Florida. Petitioner contended, alternatively, that the District Court lacked personal jurisdiction over petitioner
because petitioner's contacts with the State of Washington were insubstantial. The District Court granted the motion, holding that petitioner's contacts
with Washington were constitutionally insufficient to support the exercise of
personal jurisdiction.

The Court of Appeals reversed . . . [concluding] that the forum clause
should not be enforced because it "was not freely bargained for." As an
"independent justification" for refusing to enforce the clause, the Court of
Appeals noted that there was evidence in the record to indicate that "the
Shutes are physically and financially incapable of pursuing this litigation
in Florida" and that the enforcement of the clause would operate to deprive
them of their day in court. . . .

In evaluating the reasonableness of the forum clause at issue in this case,
[a]s an initial matter, we do not adopt the Court of Appeals' determination
that a nonnegotiated forum-selection clause in a form ticket contract is never
enforceable simply because it is not the subject of bargaining. Including a
reasonable forum clause in a form contract of this kind well may be permissible for several reasons. First, a cruise line has a special interest in limiting
the fora in which it potentially could be subject to suit. Because a cruise ship
typically carries passengers from many locales, it is not unlikely that a

mishap on a cruise could subject the cruise line to litigation in several different fora. Additionally, a clause establishing ex ante the forum for dispute resolution has the salutary effect of dispelling any confusion about where suits arising from the contract must be brought and defended, sparing litigants the time and expense of pretrial motions to determine the correct forum and conserving judicial resources that otherwise would be devoted to deciding those motions. Finally, it stands to reason that passengers who purchase tickets containing a forum clause like that at issue in this case benefit in the form of reduced fares reflecting the savings that the cruise line enjoys by limiting the fora in which it may be sued.

We also do not accept the Court of Appeals' "independent justification" for its conclusion that . . . the clause should not be enforced because "[t]here is evidence in the record to indicate that the Shutes are physically and financially incapable of pursuing this litigation in Florida." . . . In dismissing the case for lack of personal jurisdiction over petitioner, the District Court made no finding regarding the physical and financial impediments to the Shutes' pursuing their case in Florida. . . . In the present case, Florida is not a "remote alien forum," nor—given the fact that Mrs. Shute's accident occurred off the coast of Mexico—is this dispute an essentially local one inherently more suited to resolution in the State of Washington than in Florida. [W]e conclude that they have not satisfied the "heavy burden of proof" required to set aside the clause on grounds of inconvenience.

It bears emphasis that forum-selection clauses contained in form passage contracts are subject to judicial scrutiny for fundamental fairness. In this case, there is no indication that petitioner set Florida as the forum in which disputes were to be resolved as a means of discouraging cruise passengers from pursuing legitimate claims. Any suggestion of such a bad-faith motive is belied by two facts: Petitioner has its principal place of business in Florida, and many of its cruises depart from and return to Florida ports. Similarly, there is no evidence that petitioner obtained respondents' accession to the forum clause by fraud or overreaching. Finally, respondents have conceded that they were given notice of the forum provision and, therefore, presumably retained the option of rejecting the contract with impunity. In the case before us, therefore, we conclude that the Court of Appeals erred in refusing to enforce the forum-selection clause.

The judgment of the Court of Appeals is reversed. It is so ordered.

Justice STEVENS, with whom Justice MARSHALL joins, dissenting:
The Court prefaces its legal analysis with a factual statement that implies that a purchaser of a Carnival Cruise Lines passenger ticket is fully and fairly notified about the existence of the choice of forum clause in the fine print on the back of the ticket. Even if this implication were accurate, I would disagree with the Court's analysis. But, given the Court's preface, I begin my dissent by noting that only the most meticulous passenger is likely to become aware of the forum-selection provision. I have therefore appended to this opinion a facsimile of the relevant text, using the type size that actually appears in the ticket itself. A careful reader will find the forum-selection clause in the 8th of the 25 numbered paragraphs. [See Figure 7.1.]

Of course, many passengers, like the respondents in this case, will not have an opportunity to read paragraph 8 until they have actually purchased their tickets. By this point, the passengers will already have accepted the condition set forth in paragraph 16(a), which provides that "[t]he Carrier shall not be liable to make any refund to passengers in respect of . . . tickets wholly or partly not used by a passenger." Not knowing whether or not that provision is legally enforceable, I assume that the average passenger would accept the risk of having to file suit in Florida in the event of an injury, rather than canceling—without a refund—a planned vacation at the last minute. The fact that the cruise line can reduce its litigation costs, and therefore its liability insurance premiums, by forcing this choice on its passengers does not, in my opinion, suffice to render the provision reasonable.

Even if passengers received prominent notice of the forum-selection clause before they committed the cost of the cruise, I would remain persuaded that the clause was unenforceable. . . . These clauses are typically the product of disparate bargaining power between the carrier and the passenger, and they undermine the strong public interest in deterring negligent conduct. . . .

Forum-selection clauses in passenger tickets involve the intersection of two strands of traditional contract law that qualify the general rule that courts will enforce the terms of a contract as written. Pursuant to the first strand, courts traditionally have reviewed with heightened scrutiny the terms of contracts of adhesion, form contracts offered on a take-or-leave basis by a party with stronger bargaining power to a party with weaker power. Some commentators have questioned whether contracts of adhesion can justifiably be enforced at all under traditional contract theory because the adhering party generally enters into them without manifesting knowing and voluntary consent to all their terms.

The common law, recognizing that standardized form contracts account for a significant portion of all commercial agreements, has taken a less extreme position and instead subjects terms in contracts of adhesion to scrutiny for reasonableness. . . .

The stipulation in the ticket that Carnival Cruise sold to respondents certainly lessens or weakens their ability to recover for the slip and fall incident that occurred off the west coast of Mexico during the cruise that originated and terminated in Los Angeles, California. It is safe to assume that the witnesses—whether other passengers or members of the crew—can be assembled with less expense and inconvenience at a west coast forum than in a Florida court several thousand miles from the scene of the accident. . . .

Under these circumstances, the general prohibition against stipulations purporting "to lessen, weaken, or avoid" the passenger's right to a trial certainly should be construed to apply to the manifestly unreasonable stipulation in these passengers' tickets. . . .

I respectfully dissent.

---

The following ticket was appended at the end of the case as Figure 7.1.

## TERMS AND CONDITIONS OF PASSAGE CONTRACT TICKET

1. (a) Whenever the word "Carrier" is used in this Contract it shall mean and include, jointly and severally, the Vessel, its owners, operators, characters and lenders. The term "Passenger" shall include, the plural where appropriate, and all persons engaging to and/or traveling under this Contract the masculine includes the feminine.

(b) The Master, Officers and Crew of the Vessel shall have the benefit of all of the terms and conditions of this contract.

2. This ticket is valid only for the person or persons named hereon as the passenger or passengers and cannot be transferred without the Carrier's consent written hereon. Passage money shall be deemed to be earned when paid and not refundable.

3. (a) The acceptance of this ticket by the person or persons named hereon as passengers shall be deemed to be an acceptance and agreement by each of them of all of the terms and conditions of this Passage Contract Ticket.

(b) The passenger admits a full understanding of the character of the Vessel and assumes all risk incident to travel and transportation and handling of passengers and cargo. The Vessel may or may not carry a ship's physician at the election of the Carrier. The fare includes full board, ordinary ship's food during the voyage, but no spirits, wine, beer or mineral waters.

4. The Carrier shall not be liable for any loss of life or personal injury or delay whatsoever wheresoever arising and howsoever caused even though the same may have been caused by the negligence or default of the Carrier or its servants or agents. No undertaking or warranty is given or shall be implied respecting the seaworthiness, fitness or condition of the Vessel. This exemption from liability shall extend to the employees, servants and agents of the Carrier and for this purpose this exemption shall be deemed to constitute a Contract entered into between the passenger and the Carrier on behalf of all persons who are or become from time to time its employees servants or agents and all such persons shall to this extent be deemed to be parties to this Contract.

5. The Carrier shall not be liable for losses of valuables unless stored in the Vessel's safety depository and then not exceeding $500 in any event.

6. If the Vessel carries a surgeon, physician, masseuse, barber, hair dresser or manicurist, it is done solely for the convenience of the passenger and any such person in dealing with the passenger is not and shall not be considered in any respect whatsoever, as the employee, servant or agent of the Carrier and the Carrier shall not be liable for any act or omission of such person or those under his orders or assisting him with respect to treatment, advice or care of any kind given to any passenger.

The surgeon, physician, masseuse, barber, hair dresser or manicurist shall be entitled to make a proper charge for any service performed with respect to a passenger and the Carrier shall not be concerned in any way whatsoever in any such arrangement.

7. The Carrier shall not be liable for any claims whatsoever of the passenger unless full particulars thereof in writing be given to the Carrier of their agents within 185 days after the passenger shall be landed from the Vessel or in the case the voyage is abondoned within 185 days thereafter. Suit to recover any claim shall not be maintainable in any event unless commenced within one year after the date of the loss, injury or death.

8. It is agreed by and between the passenger and the Carrier that all disputes and matters whatsoever arising under, in connection with or incident to this Contract whall be litigated, if at all, in and before a Court located in the State of Florida U.S.A. to the exclusion of the Courts of any other state or country.

9. The Carrier in arranging for the service called for by all shore feature coupons or shore excursion tickets, acts only as agent for the holder thereof and assumes no responsibility and in no event shall be liable for any loss, damage, injury or delay to or of said person and/or baggage. property or effects in connection with said services, nor does Carrier guarantee the performance of any such service.

CONTRACT PAGE 1

## Figure 7.1

## Comments and Questions

1. *Carnival Cruise Lines* aptly illustrates the strategic importance of the matter of personal jurisdiction. The Ninth Circuit Court of Appeals, in refusing to enforce the clause, had concluded that "the Shutes are physically and financially incapable of pursuing this litigation in Florida" and that the enforcement of the clause would operate to deprive them of their day in court. In an article critical of the Supreme Court's decision to the contrary, Professor Linda Mullenix writes that "[a]s a practical matter, these [forum selection] clauses cause unwitting plaintiffs to forfeit legitimate legal claims due to the plaintiff's frequent inability to mount a case in a distant, inconvenient forum," and tip "the procedural balance in favor of well-heeled, savvy defendants." She accuses the Court of "tacitly encouraging highly-skilled, high-stakes forum shopping." Linda Mullenix, *Another Easy Case, Some More Bad Law:* Carnival Cruise Lines *and Contractual Personal Jurisdiction*, 27 Tex. Intl. L.J. 323 (1992).

2. Why would the Court "sell out" consumers in these situations with such apparent indifference? Did Justice Blackmun really believe Carnival would pass its savings in litigation costs along to its passengers? Is *Carnival Cruise Lines* simply a reflection of pro-business bias, or a preference for private ordering? Or might it reflect a desire (as in *Burnham*) to preserve some basis for adjudicatory authority that is free from the complexity of due process analysis?

One commentator complains that "by neglecting contract law dealing with adhesion and ignoring principles of due process, the *Shute* Court abandoned the consumer's rights in an age of form contracts and in a legal system that prefers the efficiency of justice rather than its equity." John McKinley Kirby, *Consumer's Right to Sue at Home Jeopardized Through Forum Selection Clause in* Carnival Cruise Lines v. Shute, 70 N.C. L. Rev. 888 (1992). Kirby fears that

> a patron who slips and falls in a movie theater may be required to litigate her claim, if at all, in the home forum of the corporation due to a clause on her ticket. A consumer injured by a defective automobile could be limited to filing suit in the remote forum of the manufacturer due to a forum clause on the sales form, while the dealer that sold the automobile might be protected from suit in the purchaser's forum by notice on the doors that entering the premises signifies acceptance of a specified forum for all claims. The gains that *International Shoe* and its progeny made toward allowing plaintiffs to sue in their home jurisdictions will be largely recaptured by corporations in a frenzy to lower legal costs.

*Id.*, at 914-915.

Should there be different rules here for consumers and commercial actors? For plaintiffs and defendants?

3. Would the Court have enforced a "no-liability clause" disclaiming any responsibility for injuries suffered during the cruise if one had been inserted into the passage contract? Doesn't the forum selection clause amount to the

same thing for passengers like the Shutes who lack the wherewithal to litigate in the distant forum?

4. How strict is the Court's "judicial scrutiny for fundamental fairness" here? What would "a bad-faith motive" behind insisting on the clause look like?

5. Under what circumstances would a court refuse to enforce a forum selection clause? In *Walker v. Carnival Cruise Lines*, 107 F. Supp. 2d 1135 (N.D. Cal. 2000), plaintiffs were severely disabled passengers suing for violations of the Americans with Disabilities Act. The court declined to hold the plaintiffs to the forum selection clause in their ticket requiring suit in Florida because "plaintiffs' physical disabilities and economic constraints are so severe that, in combination, they would preclude plaintiffs from having their day in court and, second, the fact that plaintiffs are seeking to vindicate important civil rights." 107 F. Supp. 2d at 1138.

*Casavant v. Norwegian Cruise Line, Ltd.*, 63 Mass. App. 785 (2005), *cert. denied*, 546 U.S. 1173 (2006), similarly declined to enforce a forum selection clause because the cruise passengers were not afforded a reasonable time to reject the contract without incurring unfair penalties. The plaintiffs were scheduled to depart Boston on September 16, 2001, but in the aftermath of the terrorist attacks days before, they sought to reschedule. The cruise line refused to refund their money and the plaintiffs brought suit in the Massachusetts Superior Court, which dismissed based on the forum selection clause requiring that all litigation be filed in Florida. The Appeals Court reversed, noting that the contract had not been sent to the Casavants until they had paid in full, and only two weeks before the sail date. "Because the manner and means of the delivery of the terms of the contract for passage did not fairly allow the Casavants the option of rejecting with impunity, the Florida-dictated forum selection clause is not enforceable." 63 Mass. App. at 788-789. The plaintiffs went on to prevail in their action at trial and on appeal. *Casavant v. Norwegian Cruise Line Ltd.*, 460 Mass. 500 (2011).

In the typical personal injury case, however, forum selection clauses have been enforced against cruise passengers even where they require suit in a foreign country. *See, e.g., Effron v. Sun Line Cruises, Inc.*, 67 F.3d 7 (2d Cir. 1995) (clause requiring suit in Athens, Greece, enforced against Florida resident in case arising out of South American cruise).

6. Congress overruled *Carnival Cruise Lines* by amending an admiralty statute in 1992 to provide that a vessel passenger leaving from or returning to a U.S. port has a statutory right to bring an action for personal injury in *any* court of competent jurisdiction, and that the right could not be limited by a forum selection clause in a passenger ticket. Subsequent changes to the statutory language, however, appear to have restored the *Carnival Cruise Lines* result. *See Smith v. Doe*, 991 F. Supp. 781 (E.D. La. 1998) (and citations). For a discussion of the unusual legislative route followed here, see Michael F. Sturley, *Congressional Action "Overruling" the Supreme Court*, 24 J. Mar. L. & Com. 399 (1993); Note *Dark of the Night Legislation Takes Aim at Forum*

*Selection Clauses: Statutory Revision to* Carnival Cruise Lines, Inc. v. Shute, 6 U.S.F. Mar. L.J. 259 (1993).

7. Does it make a difference when the forum selection clause forces a consumer to *defend* in a distant forum? What if Carnival Cruise Lines had sued the Shutes in Florida because the check they used to pay for the cruise was returned unpaid? Look back at clause 8 of the contract. Consider the following article which appeared in the *Massachusetts Lawyers Weekly*, April 14, 2003:

## Forum Selection Clause Upheld

The Appellate Division of the District Court recently reinstated three collection claims brought by Leasecomm Corp. that had previously been dismissed for lack of personal jurisdiction. The Appellate Division opinions are the latest in a series of decisions upholding the forum selection clause used by Leasecomm in its contracts, which requires that all legal disputes be settled in Massachusetts.

Leasecomm, an out-of-state financing company that lends money to small business owners, has come under fire for bringing thousands of claims in Massachusetts every year even though most of the claims are against non-Massachusetts defendants. The company receives thousands of default judgments each year as many of the out-of-state defendants cannot afford to travel to Massachusetts for their hearings.

The out-of-state defendants in each of the recent cases had argued that Massachusetts did not have any personal jurisdiction over them, or alternatively, that Massachusetts was forum non conveniens. While the District Court judges agreed in each case and granted the defendants' motions to dismiss, the Appellate Division panel reversed their decisions and upheld the forum selection clause in the Leasecomm contracts.

"A forum selection clause will be enforced by Massachusetts courts 'if it is fair and reasonable to do so,'" said Judge Brian R. Merrick, writing the majority opinion in *Leasecomm Corp. v. Crawford.* "We emphasize that economic hardship or geographical inconvenience are considered to have been contemplated by the parties when they entered into the contract with a forum selection clause and are not generally a reason to disregard a forum selection clause."

Similarly, the majority opinion rejected the challenges based on forum non conveniens.

One Appellate Division judge dissented, however, and said that the number of cases brought and the number of default judgments received by Leasecomm pointed to some unfairness. "Undoubtedly, there exists a risk in the extension of credit," said Judge Mark S. Coven. "But where a party's extension of credit results in the breach rate admitted herein, a judicial system cannot narrowly limit its focus by proceeding on a case-by-case basis, thereby overlooking the larger picture, the larger problem and the real issues of fairness and reasonableness." Coven added: "It is a perversion to say that the adjudication by default of nearly [55,000] cases through the use of a forum selection clause somehow measures up to the spirit and substance of fairness and reasonableness envisioned by the United States Supreme Court and our Supreme Judicial Court."

8. The following has appeared on the back of the monthly telephone bill from Sprint Communications: "Pursuant to K.S.A. 60-308(b)(11), as a business customer, you may be subject to jurisdiction in Kansas for any dispute relating to your telephone service with Sprint. This is because you have arranged for or continued to receive phone service managed, operated or monitored in the State of Kansas." Is this a forum-selection clause?

9. What about "click-wrap" and "browse-wrap" forum selection clauses, common when an Internet user clicks the "I agree" button. *See generally* Greg Lastowka, *Virtual Justice: The New Laws of Online Worlds* 92-96 (2010). The following is typical:

## END USER LICENSE AGREEMENT

PLEASE READ THIS AGREEMENT CAREFULLY. BY CLICKING THE "I AGREE" BUTTON AT THE TOP OF THIS PAGE, YOU AGREE TO BE BOUND BY THE TERMS AND CONDITIONS OF THIS AGREEMENT. THIS AGREEMENT IS ENFORCEABLE LIKE ANY WRITTEN NEGOTI-ATED AGREEMENT SIGNED BY YOU.

*\*\*\**

**11. Governing Law.** This Agreement will be governed by and construed in accordance with the substantive laws in force in the State of [X], and any disputes shall be subject to the exclusive jurisdiction of the courts of the State of [X].

"Click-wrap" forum selection clauses have met with mixed results in the courts. Compare *DeJohn v. The .TV Corp. Intern.*, 245 F. Supp. 2d 913 (N.D. Ill. 2003) (upholding clause) with *Specht v. Netscape Communications Corp.*, 306 F.3d 17 (2d Cir. 2002) (plaintiffs' downloading of software did not constitute acceptance of defendants' license terms).

10. The federal courts are in disagreement as to which of the Fed. R. Civ. P. 12(b) motions is the appropriate vehicle for a defendant seeking dismissal pursuant to a forum selection clause. *See Silva v. Encyclopedia Britannica Inc.*, 239 F.3d 385 (1st Cir. 2001). The answer determines whether the motion is waived if not filed initially [(12(b)2 and 12(b)(3)], or preserved for later filing [12(b)(1) and 12(b)(6)].

11. Contractual provisions can not only dictate the forum for any lawsuit, but take such suits out of the court system altogether by mandating arbitration. As you have seen in Chapter 6, agreements to arbitrate in consumer and employment contracts have largely been upheld by the Supreme Court.

## O. NOTICE

You will recall that within the *Pennoyer* framework, dominated by the concept of "presence," notice of the lawsuit occurred simultaneously with the act that gave rise to jurisdiction, namely personal service or attachment of property within the state. ("Substituted service by publication" was held to be inadequate absent attachment of Neff's land.) As the basis for adjudicatory power became divorced from service, however, notifying a defendant had to be accomplished through other means. In *Hess v. Pawloski*, for example, the Massachusetts nonresident motorist statute required that notice be sent by registered mail to the defendant's residence. The following case defined the constitutional parameters of adequate notice.

## ■ MULLANE v. CENTRAL HANOVER BANK & TRUST CO.
### *339 U.S. 306 (1950)*

Justice JACKSON delivered the opinion of the Court:

This controversy questions the constitutional sufficiency of notice to beneficiaries on judicial settlement of accounts by the trustee of a common trust fund established under the New York Banking Law, Consol. Laws, c. 2. The New York Court of Appeals considered and overruled objections that the statutory notice contravenes requirements of the Fourteenth Amendment and that by allowance of the account beneficiaries were deprived of property without due process of law. The case is here on appeal. . .

C of A

Common trust fund legislation is addressed to a problem appropriate for state action. Mounting overheads have made administration of small trusts undesirable to corporate trustees. In order that donors and testators of moderately sized trusts may not be denied the service of corporate fiduciaries, the District of Columbia and some thirty states other than New York have permitted pooling small trust estates into one fund for investment administration. The income, capital gains, losses and expenses of the collective trust are shared by the constituent trusts in proportion to their contribution. By this plan, diversification of risk and economy of management can be extended to those whose capital standing alone would not obtain such advantage.

Statutory authorization for the establishment of such common trust funds is provided in the New York Banking Law. Under this Act a trust company may, with approval of the State Banking Board, establish a common fund and, within prescribed limits, invest therein the assets of an unlimited number of estates, trusts or other funds of which it is trustee. Each participating trust shares ratably in the common fund, but exclusive management and control is in the trust company as trustee, and neither a fiduciary nor any beneficiary of a participating trust is deemed to have ownership in any particular asset or investment of this common fund. The trust company must keep fund assets separate from its own, and in its fiduciary capacity may not deal with itself or any affiliate. Provisions are made for accountings twelve to fifteen months after the establishment of a fund and triennially thereafter. The decree in each such judicial settlement of accounts is made binding and conclusive as to any matter set forth in the account upon everyone having any interest in the common fund or in any participating estate, trust or fund.

In January, 1946, Central Hanover Bank and Trust Company established a common trust fund in accordance with these provisions, and in March, 1947, it petitioned the Surrogate's Court for settlement of its first account as common trustee. During the accounting period a total of 113 trusts, approximately half inter vivos and half testamentary, participated in the common trust fund, the gross capital of which was nearly three million dollars. The record does not show the number or residence of the beneficiaries, but they were many and it is clear that some of them were not residents of the State of New York.

The only notice given beneficiaries of this specific application was by publication in a local newspaper in strict compliance with the minimum requirements of N.Y. Banking Law:

> After filing such petition (for judicial settlement of its account) the petitioner shall cause to be issued by the court in which the petition is filed and shall publish not less than once in each week for four successive weeks in a newspaper to be designated by the court a notice or citation addressed generally without naming them to all parties interested in such common trust fund and in such estates, trusts or funds mentioned in the petition, all of which may be described in the notice or citation only in the manner set forth in said petition and without setting forth the residence of any such decedent or donor of any such estate, trust or fund.

Thus the only notice required, and the only one given, was by newspaper publication setting forth merely the name and address of the trust company, the name and the date of establishment of the common trust fund, and a list of all participating estates, trusts or funds.

At the time the first investment in the common fund was made on behalf of each participating estate, however, the trust company, pursuant to the requirements of the Banking Law, had notified by mail each person of full age and sound mind whose name and address was then known to it and who was "entitled to share in the income therefrom . . . [or] . . . who would be entitled to share in the principal if the event upon which such estate, trust or fund will become distributable should have occurred at the time of sending such notice." Included in the notice was a copy of those provisions of the Act relating to the sending of the notice itself and to the judicial settlement of common trust fund accounts.

Upon the filing of the petition for the settlement of accounts, appellant was, by order of the court pursuant to the Banking Law, appointed special guardian and attorney for all persons known or unknown not otherwise appearing who had or might thereafter have any interest in the income of the common trust fund; and appellee Vaughan was appointed to represent those similarly interested in the principal. There were no other appearances on behalf of anyone interested in either interest or principal.

Appellant appeared specially, objecting that notice and the statutory provisions for notice to beneficiaries were inadequate to afford due process under the Fourteenth Amendment, and therefore that the court was without jurisdiction to render a final and binding decree. Appellant's objections were entertained and overruled, the Surrogate holding that the notice required and given was sufficient. A final decree accepting the accounts has been entered, affirmed by the Appellate Division of the Supreme Court.

The effect of this decree, as held below, is to settle "all questions respecting the management of the common fund." We understand that every right which beneficiaries would otherwise have against the trust company, either as trustee of the common fund or as trustee of any individual trust, for improper management of the common trust fund during the period covered by the accounting is sealed and wholly terminated by the decree.

We are met at the outset with a challenge to the power of the State—the right of its courts to adjudicate at all as against those beneficiaries who reside without the State of New York. It is contended that the proceeding is one *in personam* in that the decree affects neither title to nor possession of any *res*, but adjudges only personal rights of the beneficiaries to surcharge their trustee for negligence or breach of trust. Accordingly, it is said, under the strict doctrine of *Pennoyer v. Neff*, the Surrogate is without jurisdiction as to nonresidents upon whom personal service of process was not made.

Distinctions between actions *in rem* and those *in personam* are ancient and originally expressed in procedural terms what seems really to have been a distinction in the substantive law of property under a system quite unlike our own. The legal recognition and rise in economic importance of incorporeal or intangible forms of property have upset the ancient simplicity of property law and the clarity of its distinctions, while new forms of proceedings have confused the old procedural classification. American courts have sometimes classed certain actions as *in rem* because personal service of process was not required, and at other times have held personal service of process not required because the action was *in rem*.

Judicial proceedings to settle fiduciary accounts have been sometimes termed *in rem*, or more indefinitely *quasi in rem*, or more vaguely still, "in the nature of a proceeding *in rem*." It is not readily apparent how the courts of New York did or would classify the present proceeding, which has some characteristics and is wanting in some features of proceedings both in rem and in personam. But in any event we think that the requirements of the Fourteenth Amendment to the Federal Constitution do not depend upon a classification for which the standards are so elusive and confused generally and which, being primarily for state courts to define, may and do vary from state to state. Without disparaging the usefulness of distinctions between actions in rem and those in personam in many branches of law, or on other issues, or the reasoning which underlies them, we do not rest the power of the State to resort to constructive service in this proceeding upon how its courts or this Court may regard this historic antithesis. It is sufficient to observe that, whatever the technical definition of its chosen procedure, the interest of each state in providing means to close trusts that exist by the grace of its laws and are administered under the supervision of its courts is so insistent and rooted in custom as to establish beyond doubt the right of its courts to determine the interests of all claimants, resident or nonresident, provided its procedure accords full opportunity to appear and be heard.

Quite different from the question of a state's power to discharge trustees is that of the opportunity it must give beneficiaries to contest. Many controversies have raged about the cryptic and abstract words of the Due Process Clause but there can be no doubt that at a minimum they require that deprivation of life, liberty or property by adjudication be preceded by notice and opportunity for hearing appropriate to the nature of the case.

In two ways this proceeding does or may deprive beneficiaries of property. It may cut off their rights to have the trustee answer for negligent or illegal impairments of their interests. Also, their interests are presumably subject to diminution in the proceeding by allowance of fees and expenses to one who, in their names but without their knowledge, may conduct a fruitless or uncompensatory contest. Certainly the proceeding is one in which they may be deprived of property rights and hence notice and hearing must measure up to the standards of due process.

Personal service of written notice within the jurisdiction is the classic form of notice always adequate in any type of proceeding. But the vital interest of the State in bringing any issues as to its fiduciaries to a final settlement can be served only if interests or claims of individuals who are outside of the State can somehow be determined. A construction of the Due Process Clause which would place impossible or impractical obstacles in the way could not be justified.

Against this interest of the State we must balance the individual interest sought to be protected by the Fourteenth Amendment. This is defined by our holding that "the fundamental requisite of due process of law is the opportunity to be heard." This right to be heard has little reality or worth unless one is informed that the matter is pending and can choose for himself whether to appear or default, acquiesce or contest.

The Court has not committed itself to any formula achieving a balance between these interests in a particular proceeding or determining when constructive notice may be utilized or what test it must meet. Personal service has not in all circumstances been regarded as indispensable to the process due to residents, and it has more often been held unnecessary as to nonresidents. We disturb none of the established rules on these subjects. No decision constitutes a controlling or even a very illuminating precedent for the case before us. But a few general principles stand out in the books.

*due process.*

An elementary and fundamental requirement of due process in any proceeding which is to be accorded finality is notice reasonably calculated, under all the circumstances, to apprise interested parties of the pendency of the action and afford them an opportunity to present their objections. The notice must be of such nature as reasonably to convey the required information, and it must afford a reasonable time for those interested to make their appearance. But if with due regard for the practicalities and peculiarities of the case these conditions are reasonably met the constitutional requirements are satisfied. . . .

But when notice is a person's due, process which is a mere gesture is not due process. The means employed must be such as one desirous of actually informing the absentee might reasonably adopt to accomplish it. The reasonableness and hence the constitutional validity of any chosen method may be defended on the ground that it is in itself reasonably certain to inform those affected, or, where conditions do not reasonably permit such notice, that the form chosen is not substantially less likely to bring home notice than other of the feasible and customary substitutes.

It would be idle to pretend that publication alone, as prescribed here, is a reliable means of acquainting interested parties of the fact that their rights are before the courts. It is not an accident that the greater number of cases reaching this Court on the question of adequacy of notice have been concerned with actions founded on process constructively served through local newspapers. Chance alone brings to the attention of even a local resident an advertisement in small type inserted in the back pages of a newspaper, and if he makes his home outside the area of the newspaper's normal circulation the odds that the information will never reach him are large indeed. The chance of actual notice is further reduced when as here the notice required does not even name those whose attention it is supposed to attract, and does not inform acquaintances who might call it to attention. In weighing its sufficiency on the basis of equivalence with actual notice we are unable to regard this as more than a feint.

Nor is publication here reinforced by steps likely to attract the parties' attention to the proceeding. It is true that publication traditionally has been acceptable as notification supplemental to other action which in itself may reasonably be expected to convey a warning. The ways of an owner with tangible property are such that he usually arranges means to learn of any direct attack upon his possessory or proprietary rights. Hence, [seizure] of a ship, attachment of a chattel or entry upon real estate in the name of law may reasonably be expected to come promptly to the owner's attention. When the state within which the owner has located such property seizes it for some reason, publication or posting affords an additional measure of notification. A state may indulge the assumption that one who has left tangible property in the state either has abandoned it, in which case proceedings against it deprive him of nothing, or that he has left some caretaker under a duty to let him know that it is being jeopardized. . . .

In the case before us there is, of course, no abandonment. On the other hand these beneficiaries do have a resident fiduciary as caretaker of their interest in this property. But it is their caretaker who in the accounting becomes their adversary. Their trustee is released from giving notice of jeopardy, and no one else is expected to do so. Not even the special guardian is required or apparently expected to communicate with his ward and client, and, of course, if such a duty were merely transferred from the trustee to the guardian, economy would not be served and more likely the cost would be increased.

This Court has not hesitated to approve of resort to publication as a customary substitute in another class of cases where it is not reasonably possible or practicable to give more adequate warning. Thus it has been recognized that, in the case of persons missing or unknown, employment of an indirect and even a probably futile means of notification is all that the situation permits and creates no constitutional bar to a final decree foreclosing their rights.

Those beneficiaries represented by appellant whose interests or whereabouts could not with due diligence be ascertained come clearly within this category. As to them the statutory notice is sufficient. However great the odds that publication will never reach the eyes of such unknown parties, it is not in the typical case much more likely to fail than any of the choices open to legislators endeavoring to prescribe the best notice practicable.

Nor do we consider it unreasonable for the State to dispense with more certain notice to those beneficiaries whose interests are either conjectural or future or, although they could be discovered upon investigation, do not in due course of business come to knowledge of the common trustee. Whatever searches might be required in another situation under ordinary standards of diligence, in view of the character of the proceedings and the nature of the interests here involved we think them unnecessary. We recognize the practical difficulties and costs that would be attendant on frequent investigations into the status of great numbers of beneficiaries, many of whose interests in the common fund are so remote as to be ephemeral and we have no doubt that such impracticable and extended searches are not required in the name of due process. The expense of keeping informed from day to day of substitutions among even current income beneficiaries and presumptive remaindermen, to say nothing of the far greater number of contingent beneficiaries, would impose a severe burden on the plan, and would likely dissipate its advantages. These are practical matters in which we should be reluctant to disturb the judgment of the state authorities.

Accordingly we overrule appellant's constitutional objections to published notice insofar as they are urged on behalf of any beneficiaries whose interests or addresses are unknown to the trustee.

As to known present beneficiaries of known place of residence, however, notice by publication stands on a different footing. Exceptions in the name of necessity do not sweep away the rule that within the limits of practicability notice must be such as is reasonably calculated to reach interested parties. Where the names and post office addresses of those affected by a proceeding are at hand, the reasons disappear for resort to means less likely than the mails to apprise them of its pendency.

The trustee has on its books the names and addresses of the income beneficiaries represented by appellant, and we find no tenable ground for dispensing with a serious effort to inform them personally of the accounting, at least by ordinary mail to the record addresses. Certainly sending them a copy of the statute months and perhaps years in advance does not answer this purpose. The trustee periodically remits their income to them, and we think that they might reasonably expect that with or apart from their remittances word might come to them personally that steps were being taken affecting their interests.

We need not weigh contentions that a requirement of personal service of citation on even the large number of known resident or nonresident beneficiaries would, by reasons of delay if not of expense, seriously interfere with the proper administration of the fund. Of course personal service even without the jurisdiction of the issuing authority serves the end of actual and personal notice, whatever power of compulsion it might lack. However, no such service is required under the circumstances. This type of trust presupposes a large number of small interests. The individual interest does not stand alone but is identical with that of a class. The rights of each in the integrity of the fund and the fidelity of the trustee are shared by many other beneficiaries. Therefore notice reasonably certain to reach most of those interested in objecting is likely to safeguard the interests of all, since any objections sustained would inure to the benefit of all. We think that under such circumstances reasonable risks that notice might not actually reach every beneficiary are justifiable. "Now and then an extraordinary case may turn up, but constitutional law, like other mortal contrivances, has to take some chances, and in the great majority of instances, no doubt, justice will be done."

The statutory notice to known beneficiaries is inadequate, not because in fact it fails to reach everyone, but because under the circumstances it is not reasonably calculated to reach those who could easily be informed by other means at hand. However it may have been in former times, the mails today are recognized as an efficient and inexpensive means of communication. Moreover, the fact that the trust company has been able to give mailed notice to known beneficiaries at the time the common trust fund was established is persuasive that postal notification at the time of accounting would not seriously burden the plan.

In some situations the law requires greater precautions in its proceedings than the business world accepts for its own purposes. In few, if any, will it be satisfied with less. Certainly it is instructive, in determining the reasonableness of the impersonal broadcast notification here used, to ask whether it would satisfy a prudent man of business, counting his pennies but finding it in his interest to convey information to many persons whose names and addresses are in his files. We are not satisfied that it would. Publication may theoretically be available for all the world to see, but it is too much in our day to suppose that each or any individual beneficiary does or could examine all that is published to see if something may be tucked away in it that affects his property interests. We have before indicated in reference to notice by publication that, "Great caution should be used not to let fiction deny the fair play that can be secured only by a pretty close adhesion to fact."

We hold the notice of judicial settlement of accounts required by the New York Banking Law is incompatible with the requirements of the Fourteenth Amendment as a basis for adjudication depriving known persons whose whereabouts are also known of substantial property rights. Accordingly the judgment is reversed and the cause remanded for further proceedings not inconsistent with this opinion.

Reversed.

Justice DOUGLAS took no part in the consideration or decision of this case.

Justice BURTON, dissenting:

These common trusts are available only when the instruments creating the participating trusts permit participation in the common fund. Whether or not further notice to beneficiaries should supplement the notice and representation here provided is properly within the discretion of the State. The Federal Constitution does not require it here.

## Comments and Questions

1. Note how *Mullane* anticipates *Shaffer v. Heitner*'s later repudiation of the distinction between in rem and in personam power for purposes of due process analysis.

2. According to Justice Jackson (who had recently returned to the Court after his stint as chief U.S. prosecutor at the Nuremberg Trials following World War II), what is the basis for jurisdiction over the nonresident beneficiaries? Reread this passage:

It is sufficient to observe that, whatever the technical definition of its chosen procedure, the interest of each state in providing means to close trusts that exist by the grace of its laws and are administered under the supervision of its courts is so insistent and rooted in custom as to establish beyond doubt the right of its courts to determine the interests of all claimants, resident or nonresident, provided its procedure accords full opportunity to appear and be heard.

339 U.S. at 313. If not in rem or in personam, what type of jurisdiction is this? Can you see why it has been dubbed "jurisdiction by necessity"? *See* George B. Fraser, Jr., *Jurisdiction by Necessity—An Analysis of the* Mullane *Case*, 100 U. Pa. L. Rev. 305 (1951).

3. Why would the Court set so elastic a constitutional standard as "notice reasonably calculated, under all the circumstances [and with due regard for the practicalities and peculiarities of the case], to apprise interested parties of the pendency of the action and afford them an opportunity to present their objections"? Doesn't such a "test" virtually ensure "endless litigation" on the adequacy of notice in particular cases? What is the alternative?

4. Note how pragmatic Justice Jackson is in distinguishing between beneficiaries whose interests or addresses are unknown, and those for whom the bank has addresses. Each is entitled to the "best notice practicable" under the circumstances. That means the latter group must receive mail notice; the former have to settle for the "chance notice" of publication in a local newspaper. Neither gets personal in-hand service, the cost of which would significantly exhaust the trust funds.

5. Decisions since *Mullane* have set notice by U.S. mail as the constitutional minimum for defendants whose addresses can be ascertained by reasonably diligent efforts. *See Walker v. City of Hutchinson*, 352 U.S. 112 (1956) (where landowner's name was known to City, newspaper publication was inadequate notice of condemnation proceedings); *Greene v. Lindsey*, 456 U.S. 444 (1982) (posting notices of eviction proceedings on doors of public housing tenants violated due process where evidence indicated notices were often removed); *Mennonite Board of Missions v. Adams*, 462 U.S. 791 (1983) (notice by publication and posting was inadequate to notify a mortgagee of a pending tax sale).

For a case authorizing notice by publication because defendant's address was unknown and not ascertainable, see *Mwani v. Osama bin Laden*, 417 F.3d 1 (D.C. Cir. 2005). Plaintiffs, victims of the 1998 bombing of the American embassy in Kenya, were granted leave by the district court to serve bin Laden by publication in three newspapers, including the *International Herald Tribune* and *Al-Quds Al-Arabi*, an Arabic publication in which bin Laden had himself published at least one *fatwa* threatening the United States.

6. In *Dusenbery v. U.S.*, 534 U.S. 161 (2002), the Court emphasized that due process requires a reasonably calculated *attempt* to provide actual notice, *not actual notice itself.* The Court concluded that certified mail addressed to Dusenbery at the prison where he was incarcerated on federal drug charges was adequate notice of a procedure to forfeit the $22,000 in cash found at the time of his arrest, even though the authorities could not document that he had actually received the notice.

The means employed, however, "must be such as one desirous of actually informing the absentee might reasonably adopt to accomplish it." *Mullane*, 339 U.S. at 315. So when certified mail notice of an upcoming tax sale was returned marked "unclaimed," the state was constitutionally required to take additional practicable steps, such as resending the notice by regular mail, which requires no signature at time of delivery. *Jones v. Flowers*, 547 U.S. 220 (2006). "We do not think that a person who actually desired to inform a real property owner of an impending tax sale of a house he owns would do nothing when a certified letter sent to the owner is returned unclaimed." 547 U.S. at 229.

7. Fed. R. Civ. P. 4 controls notice (which is the responsibility of the plaintiff, see Fed. R. Civ. P. 4(c)(1)) in federal actions. The provisions for service of process (consisting of the complaint and a summons to appear in court, see Fed. R. Civ. P. 4(a)(1) and Form 3) on defendants, which traditionally required in-hand service by a U.S. marshal, have been considerably liberalized by amendments over the years designed to facilitate the initiation of litigation and reduce costs (as well as to foster cooperation among adversaries and counsel). Service can now be effected by "any person who is at least 18 years old and not a party," Fed. R. Civ. P. 4(c)(2); and process can be left at the defendant's "dwelling or usual place of abode with someone of suitable age and discretion who resides there," Fed. R. Civ. P. 4(e)(2)(B); in the alternative, state rules for process may be followed. Fed. R. Civ. P. 4(e)(1).

Most significantly, service by mail has been incorporated and expanded through provisions providing for waiver of service. *See* Fed. R. Civ. P. 4(d). The plaintiff mails (the Advisory Committee Note to the 1993 Amendment includes "electronic communications" as well) the complaint and request for waiver to defendant, who may sign and return it, thus accomplishing notice.

What is the incentive for defendant to sign and return the waiver of service? Look at Fed. R. Civ. P. 4(d)(3). What is the penalty for not waiving? *See* Fed. R. Civ. P. 4(a)(2). What is meant by "without good cause" in this provision? *See* Advisory Committee Note to the 1993 Amendment.

The waiver provisions are designed to enforce the defendant's "duty to avoid costs associated with the service of a summons not needed to inform the defendant regarding the commencement of the action." Advisory Committee Note to the 1993 Amendment.

Note as well the provisions for serving individuals in foreign countries, Fed. R. Civ. P. 4(f) (incorporating the Hague Convention on Service Abroad); for corporations, Fed. R. Civ. P. 4(h); and for the federal government and its officials, Fed. R. Civ. P. 4(i).

8. For an early case approving of service of process by e-mail, see *Rio Properties, Inc. v. Rio International Interlink*, 284 F.3d 1007 (9th Cir. 2002).

## P. VENUE AND *FORUM NON CONVENIENS*

Beyond the constraints of personal jurisdiction, venue requirements operate as a further geographical limitation on the plaintiff's choice of court. Venue serves as an administrative funnel to direct cases to those locales (within the states that have jurisdiction) that have a connection to either the parties or the events that gave rise to the litigation. State venue rules identify the counties in which an action may be brought,* while federal venue provisions identify particular federal judicial districts (e.g., the Southern District of New York, the Northern District of Michigan).

28 U.S.C. § 1391, the general federal venue statute (recently revised by the Jurisdiction and Venue Clarification Act of 2011), provides for both party-based and claim-based venue. Venue is proper in either (1) "a judicial district in which any defendant resides, if all defendants are residents of the state in which the district is located" [note that a corporate defendant is deemed to reside in any district where it is "subject to the court's personal jurisdiction with respect to the civil action in question," § 1391(c)(2)], or (2) "a judicial district in which a substantial part of the events or omissions giving rise to the claim occurred, or a substantial part of property that is the subject of the action is situated." (For a generous interpretation of this latter provision, see *Uffner v. La Reunion Francaise, S.A.*, 244 F.3d 38 (1st Cir. 2001)).

Under the so-called fallback provision, which is triggered only if neither the party-based nor claim-based provisions identify an appropriate district (as where, for example, the defendants are from different states, and the events giving rise to the claim occurred in a foreign country), the action may be brought in any judicial district "in which any defendant is subject to the court's personal jurisdiction with respect to such action."

The federal venue provisions apply to the original parties to the action, and are not affected by third parties added by impleader or otherwise.

For more on federal venue, consult Larry L. Teply and Ralph U. Whitten, *Civil Procedure* 348-407.

Like personal jurisdiction, an objection to venue must be raised in a timely manner or it is waived. Fed. R. Civ. P. 12(h)(1). But unlike personal jurisdiction, proper venue is *not* a constitutional requirement for a valid judgment, and thus cannot be raised by way of collateral attack.

If a case is filed in a district in which venue does not properly lie, the court may, as an alternative to dismissal pursuant to Fed. R. Civ. P. 12(b)(3), transfer the case "in the interest of justice" to a district "in which it could have been brought," i.e., in which the requirements of jurisdiction and venue are met. *See* 28 U.S.C. § 1406.

---

*The Massachusetts venue statute applicable in *Carpenter v. Dee*, for example, provides generally that a civil action shall be brought in the county where any resident party lives or has a usual place of business. Mass. Gen. Laws ch. 223, § 1. Other states have more elaborate rules. California for example provides:

> The superior court in the county where the defendants or some of them reside at the commencement of the action is the proper court for the trial of the action. If the action is for injury to person or personal property or for death from wrongful act or negligence, the superior court in either the county where the injury occurs or the injury causing death occurs or the county where the defendants, or some of them reside at the commencement of the action, is a proper court for the trial of the action. [I]f a defendant has contracted to perform an obligation in a particular county, the superior court in the county where the obligation is to be performed, where the contract in fact was entered into, or where the defendant or any defendant resides at the commencement of the action is a proper court for the trial of an action founded on that obligation. . . .

Cal. Code Civ. Proc. § 395

A second transfer provision applies where venue is proper, but the district court determines that "[f]or the convenience of the parties and witnesses, in the interest of justice," the case should be heard in another federal district "where it might have been brought" or "any district or division to which all parties have consented." 28 U.S.C. § 1404. This provision codifies, but does not displace, the common law doctrine of *forum non conveniens*, as discussed in the next case.

# ■ PIPER AIRCRAFT CO. v. REYNO
### *454 U.S. 235 (1981)*

Justice MARSHALL delivered the opinion of the Court:

These cases arise out of an air crash that took place in Scotland. Respondent, acting as representative of the estates of several Scottish citizens killed in the accident, brought wrongful-death actions against petitioners that were ultimately transferred to the United States District Court for the Middle District of Pennsylvania. Petitioners moved to dismiss on the ground of *forum non conveniens*. After noting that an alternative forum existed in Scotland, the District Court granted their motions. The United States Court of Appeals for the Third Circuit reversed. The Court of Appeals based its decision, at least in part, on the ground that dismissal is automatically barred where the law of the alternative forum is less favorable to the plaintiff than the law of the forum chosen by the plaintiff. Because we conclude that the possibility of an unfavorable change in law should not, by itself, bar dismissal, and because we conclude that the District Court did not otherwise abuse its discretion, we reverse.

## I

### A

In July 1976, a small commercial aircraft crashed in the Scottish highlands during the course of a charter flight from Blackpool to Perth. The pilot and five passengers were killed instantly. The decedents were all Scottish subjects and residents, as are their heirs and next of kin. There were no eyewitnesses to the accident. At the time of the crash the plane was subject to Scottish air traffic control.

The aircraft, a twin-engine Piper Aztec, was manufactured in Pennsylvania by petitioner Piper Aircraft Co. (Piper). The propellers were manufactured in Ohio by petitioner Hartzell Propeller, Inc. (Hartzell). At the time of the crash the aircraft was registered in Great Britain and was owned and maintained by Air Navigation and Trading Co., Ltd. (Air Navigation). It was operated by McDonald Aviation, Ltd. (McDonald), a Scottish air taxi service. Both Air Navigation and McDonald were organized in the United Kingdom. The wreckage of the plane is now in a hangar in Farnsborough, England.

The British Department of Trade investigated the accident shortly after it occurred. A preliminary report found that the plane crashed after developing a spin, and suggested that mechanical failure in the plane or the propeller was responsible. At Hartzell's request, this report was reviewed by a three-member Review Board, which held a 9-day adversary hearing attended by all interested parties. The Review Board found no evidence of defective equipment and indicated that pilot error may have contributed to the accident. The pilot, who had obtained his commercial pilot's license only three months earlier, was flying over high ground at an altitude considerably lower than the minimum height required by his company's operations manual.

In July 1977, a California probate court appointed respondent Gaynell Reyno administratrix of the estates of the five passengers. Reyno is not related to and does not know any of the decedents or their survivors; she was a legal secretary to the attorney who filed this lawsuit. Several days after her appointment, Reyno commenced separate wrongful-death actions against Piper and Hartzell in the Superior Court of California, claiming negligence and strict liability. Air Navigation, McDonald, and the estate of the pilot are not parties to this litigation. The survivors of the five passengers whose estates are represented by Reyno filed a separate action in the United Kingdom against Air Navigation, McDonald, and the pilot's estate. Reyno candidly admits that the action against Piper and Hartzell was filed in the United States because its laws regarding liability, capacity to sue, and damages are more favorable to her position than are those of Scotland. Scottish law does not recognize strict liability in tort. Moreover, it permits wrongful-death actions only when brought by a decedent's relatives. The relatives may sue only for "loss of support and society."

On petitioners' motion, the suit was removed to the United States District Court for the Central District of California. Piper then moved for transfer to the United States District Court for the Middle District of Pennsylvania, pursuant to 28 U.S.C. § 1404(a).[4] Hartzell moved to dismiss for lack of personal jurisdiction, or in the alternative, to transfer.[5] In December 1977, the District Court quashed service on Hartzell and transferred the case to the Middle District of Pennsylvania. Respondent then properly served process on Hartzell.

**B**

In May 1978, after the suit had been transferred, both Hartzell and Piper moved to dismiss the action on the ground of *forum non conveniens*. The District Court granted these motions in October 1979. It relied on the balancing test set forth by this Court in *Gulf Oil Corp. v. Gilbert*, 330 U.S. 501

---

4. Section 1404(a) provides: "For the convenience of parties and witnesses, in the interest of justice, a district court may transfer any civil action to any other district or division where it might have been brought."

5. The District Court concluded that it could not assert personal jurisdiction over Hartzell consistent with due process. However, it decided not to dismiss Hartzell because the corporation would be amenable to process in Pennsylvania.

(1947), and its companion case, *Koster v. Lumbermen's, Mut. Cas. Co.*, 330 U.S. 518 (1947). In those decisions, the Court stated that a plaintiff's choice of forum should rarely be disturbed. However, when an alternative forum has jurisdiction to hear the case, and when trial in the chosen forum would "establish . . . oppressiveness and vexation to a defendant . . . out of all proportion to plaintiff's convenience," or when the "chosen forum [is] inappropriate because of considerations affecting the court's own administrative and legal problems," the court may, in the exercise of its sound discretion, dismiss the case. *Koster, supra*, at 524. To guide trial court discretion, the Court provided a list of "private interest factors" affecting the convenience of the litigants, and a list of "public interest factors" affecting the convenience of the forum. *Gilbert, supra*, 330 U.S. at 508-509.[6]

After describing our decisions in *Gilbert* and *Koster*, the District Court analyzed the facts of these cases. It began by observing that an alternative forum existed in Scotland; Piper and Hartzell had agreed to submit to the jurisdiction of the Scottish courts and to waive any statute of limitations defense that might be available. It then stated that plaintiff's choice of forum was entitled to little weight. The court recognized that a plaintiff's choice ordinarily deserves substantial deference. It noted, however, that Reyno "is a representative of foreign citizens and residents seeking a forum in the United States because of the more liberal rules concerning products liability law," and that "the courts have been less solicitous when the plaintiff is not an American citizen or resident, and particularly when the foreign citizens seek to benefit from the more liberal tort rules provided for the protection of citizens and residents of the United States."

The District Court next examined several factors relating to the private interests of the litigants, and determined that these factors strongly pointed towards Scotland as the appropriate forum. Although evidence concerning the design, manufacture, and testing of the plane and propeller is located in the United States, the connections with Scotland are otherwise "overwhelming." The real parties in interest are citizens of Scotland, as were all the decedents. Witnesses who could testify regarding the maintenance of the aircraft, the training of the pilot, and the investigation of the accident—all essential to the defense—are in Great Britain. Moreover, all witnesses to damages are located in Scotland. Trial would be aided by familiarity with Scottish topography, and by easy access to the wreckage.

The District Court reasoned that because crucial witnesses and evidence were beyond the reach of compulsory process, and because the defendants

---

6. The factors pertaining to the private interests of the litigants included the "relative ease of access to sources of proof; availability of compulsory process for attendance of unwilling, and the cost of obtaining attendance of willing, witnesses; possibility of view of premises, if view would be appropriate to the action; and all other practical problems that make trial of a case easy, expeditious and inexpensive." The public factors bearing on the question included the administrative difficulties flowing from court congestion; the "local interest in having localized controversies decided at home"; the interest in having the trial of a diversity case in a forum that is at home with the law that must govern the action; the avoidance of unnecessary problems in conflict of laws, or in the application of foreign law; and the unfairness of burdening citizens in an unrelated forum with jury duty.

would not be able to implead potential Scottish third-party defendants, it would be "unfair to make Piper and Hartzell proceed to trial in this forum." The survivors had brought separate actions in Scotland against the pilot, McDonald, and Air Navigation. "[I]t would be fairer to all parties and less costly if the entire case was presented to one jury with available testimony from all relevant witnesses." Although the court recognized that if trial were held in the United States, Piper and Hartzell could file indemnity or contribution actions against the Scottish defendants, it believed that there was a significant risk of inconsistent verdicts.[7]

The District Court concluded that the relevant public interests also pointed strongly towards dismissal. The court determined that Pennsylvania law would apply to Piper and Scottish law to Hartzell if the case were tried in the Middle District of Pennsylvania. As a result, "trial in this forum would be hopelessly complex and confusing for a jury." In addition, the court noted that it was unfamiliar with Scottish law and thus would have to rely upon experts from that country. The court also found that the trial would be enormously costly and time-consuming; that it would be unfair to burden citizens with jury duty when the Middle District of Pennsylvania has little connection with the controversy; and that Scotland has a substantial interest in the outcome of the litigation.

In opposing the motions to dismiss, respondent contended that dismissal would be unfair because Scottish law was less favorable. The District Court explicitly rejected this claim. It reasoned that the possibility that dismissal might lead to an unfavorable change in the law did not deserve significant weight; any deficiency in the foreign law was a "matter to be dealt with in the foreign forum."

### C

On appeal, the United States Court of Appeals for the Third Circuit reversed and remanded for trial. The decision to reverse appears to be based on two alternative grounds. First, the Court held that the District Court abused its discretion in conducting the *Gilbert* analysis. Second, the Court held that dismissal is never appropriate where the law of the alternative forum is less favorable to the plaintiff. . . .

We granted certiorari in these cases to consider the questions they raise concerning the proper application of the doctrine of *forum non conveniens*.

### II

The Court of Appeals erred in holding that plaintiffs may defeat a motion to dismiss on the ground of *forum non conveniens* merely by showing that the

---

7. The District Court explained that inconsistent verdicts might result if petitioners were held liable on the basis of strict liability here, and then required to prove negligence in an indemnity action in Scotland. Moreover, even if the same standard of liability applied, there was a danger that different juries would find different facts and produce inconsistent results.

substantive law that would be applied in the alternative forum is less favorable to the plaintiffs than that of the present forum. The possibility of a change in substantive law should ordinarily not be given conclusive or even substantial weight in the *forum non conveniens* inquiry. . . .

[B]y holding that the central focus of the *forum non conveniens* inquiry is convenience, *Gilbert* implicitly recognized that dismissal may not be barred solely because of the possibility of an unfavorable change in law. Under *Gilbert*, dismissal will ordinarily be appropriate where trial in the plaintiff's chosen forum imposes a heavy burden on the defendant or the court, and where the plaintiff is unable to offer any specific reasons of convenience supporting his choice.[15] If substantial weight were given to the possibility of an unfavorable change in law, however, dismissal might be barred even where trial in the chosen forum was plainly inconvenient. . . .

In fact, if conclusive or substantial weight were given to the possibility of a change in law, the *forum non conveniens* doctrine would become virtually useless. Jurisdiction and venue requirements are often easily satisfied. As a result, many plaintiffs are able to choose from among several forums. Ordinarily, these plaintiffs will select that forum whose choice-of-law rules are most advantageous. Thus, if the possibility of an unfavorable change in substantive law is given substantial weight in the *forum non conveniens* inquiry, dismissal would rarely be proper. . . .

The Court of Appeals' approach is not only inconsistent with the purpose of the *forum non conveniens* doctrine, but also poses substantial practical problems. If the possibility of a change in law were given substantial weight, deciding motions to dismiss on the ground of *forum non conveniens* would become quite difficult. Choice-of-law analysis would become extremely important, and the courts would frequently be required to interpret the law of foreign jurisdictions. First, the trial court would have to determine what law would apply if the case were tried in the chosen forum, and what law would apply if the case were tried in the alternative forum. It would then have to compare the rights, remedies, and procedures available under the law that would be applied in each forum. Dismissal would be appropriate only if the court concluded that the law applied by the alternative forum is as favorable to the plaintiff as that of the chosen forum. The doctrine of *forum non conveniens*, however, is designed in part to help courts avoid conducting complex exercises in comparative law. As we stated in *Gilbert*, the public interest factors point towards dismissal where the court would be required to "untangle problems in conflict of laws, and in law foreign to itself."

Upholding the decision of the Court of Appeals would result in other practical problems. At least where the foreign plaintiff named an American

---

15. In other words, *Gilbert* held that dismissal may be warranted where a plaintiff chooses a particular forum, not because it is convenient, but solely in order to harass the defendant or take advantage of favorable law. This is precisely the situation in which the Court of Appeals' rule would bar dismissal.

manufacturer as defendant, a court could not dismiss the case on grounds of *forum non conveniens* where dismissal might lead to an unfavorable change in law. The American courts, which are already extremely attractive to foreign plaintiffs, would become even more attractive. The flow of litigation into the United States would increase and further congest already crowded courts.

The Court of Appeals based its decision, at least in part, on an analogy between dismissals on grounds of *forum non conveniens* and transfers between federal courts pursuant to § 1404(a). In *Van Dusen v. Barrack*, 376 U.S. 612 (1964), this Court ruled that a § 1404(a) transfer should not result in a change in the applicable law. . . .

[But] the reasoning employed in *Van Dusen v. Barrack* is simply inapplicable to dismissals on grounds of *forum non conveniens*. That case did not discuss the common-law doctrine. Rather, it focused on "the construction and application" of § 1404(a). Emphasizing the remedial purpose of the statute, *Barrack* concluded that Congress could not have intended a transfer to be accompanied by a change in law. The statute was designed as a "federal housekeeping measure," allowing easy change of venue within a unified federal system. The Court feared that if a change in venue were accompanied by a change in law, forum-shopping parties would take unfair advantage of the relaxed standards for transfer. . . .

We do not hold that the possibility of an unfavorable change in law should never be a relevant consideration in a *forum non conveniens* inquiry. Of course, if the remedy provided by the alternative forum is so clearly inadequate or unsatisfactory that it is no remedy at all, the unfavorable change in law may be given substantial weight; the district court may conclude that dismissal would not be in the interests of justice. In these cases, however, the remedies that would be provided by the Scottish courts do not fall within this category. Although the relatives of the decedents may not be able to rely on a strict liability theory, and although their potential damages award may be smaller, there is no danger that they will be deprived of any remedy or treated unfairly.

## III

The Court of Appeals also erred in rejecting the District Court's *Gilbert* analysis. The Court of Appeals stated that more weight should have been given to the plaintiff's choice of forum, and criticized the District Court's analysis of the private and public interests. However, the District Court's decision regarding the deference due plaintiff's choice of forum was appropriate. Furthermore, we do not believe that the District Court abused its discretion in weighing the private and public interests.

### A

The District Court acknowledged that there is ordinarily a strong presumption in favor of the plaintiff's choice of forum, which may be overcome only when the private and public interest factors clearly point towards trial in the alternative forum. It held, however, that the presumption applies with less force when the plaintiff or real parties in interest are foreign.

The District Court's distinction between resident or citizen plaintiffs and foreign plaintiffs is fully justified. In *Koster*, the Court indicated that a plaintiff's choice of forum is entitled to greater deference when the plaintiff has chosen the home forum. When the home forum has been chosen, it is reasonable to assume that this choice is convenient. When the plaintiff is foreign, however, this assumption is much less reasonable. Because the central purpose of any *forum non conveniens* inquiry is to ensure that the trial is convenient, a foreign plaintiff's choice deserves less deference.

**B**

The *forum non conveniens* determination is committed to the sound discretion of the trial court. It may be reversed only when there has been a clear abuse of discretion; where the court has considered all relevant public and private interest factors, and where its balancing of these factors is reasonable, its decision deserves substantial deference.... In examining the District Court's analysis of the public and private interests, however, the Court of Appeals seems to have lost sight of this rule, and substituted its own judgment for that of the District Court.

**(1)**

In analyzing the private interest factors, the District Court stated that the connections with Scotland are "overwhelming." This characterization may be somewhat exaggerated. Particularly with respect to the question of relative ease of access to sources of proof, the private interests point in both directions. As respondent emphasizes, records concerning the design, manufacture, and testing of the propeller and plane are located in the United States. She would have greater access to sources of proof relevant to her strict liability and negligence theories if trial were held here. However, the District Court did not act unreasonably in concluding that fewer evidentiary problems would be posed if the trial were held in Scotland. A large proportion of the relevant evidence is located in Great Britain....

The District Court correctly concluded that the problems posed by the inability to implead potential third-party defendants clearly supported holding the trial in Scotland. Joinder of the pilot's estate, Air Navigation, and McDonald is crucial to the presentation of petitioners' defense. If Piper and Hartzell can show that the accident was caused not by a design defect, but rather by the negligence of the pilot, the plane's owners, or the charter company, they will be relieved of all liability. It is true, of course, that if Hartzell and Piper were found liable after a trial in the United States, they could institute an action for indemnity or contribution against these parties in Scotland. It would be far more convenient, however, to resolve all claims in one trial....

**(2)**

The District Court's review of the factors relating to the public interest was also reasonable. On the basis of its choice-of-law analysis, it concluded that if the case were tried in the Middle District of Pennsylvania, Pennsylvania law would apply to Piper and Scottish law to Hartzell. It stated that a trial involving two sets of laws would be confusing to the jury. It also noted its own lack of familiarity with Scottish law. Consideration of these problems was clearly appropriate under *Gilbert;* in that case we explicitly held that the need to apply foreign law pointed towards dismissal. [Moreover] all other public interest factors favored trial in Scotland.

Scotland has a very strong interest in this litigation. The accident occurred in its airspace. All of the decedents were Scottish. Apart from Piper and Hartzell, all potential plaintiffs and defendants are either Scottish or English. As we stated in *Gilbert*, there is "a local interest in having localized controversies decided at home." Respondent argues that American citizens have an interest in ensuring that American manufacturers are deterred from producing defective products, and that additional deterrence might be obtained if Piper and Hartzell were tried in the United States, where they could be sued on the basis of both negligence and strict liability. However, the incremental deterrence that would be gained if this trial were held in an American court is likely to be insignificant. The American interest in this accident is simply not sufficient to justify the enormous commitment of judicial time and resources that would inevitably be required if the case were to be tried here.

**IV**

The Court of Appeals erred in holding that the possibility of an unfavorable change in law bars dismissal on the ground of *forum non conveniens*. It also erred in rejecting the District Court's *Gilbert* analysis. The District Court properly decided that the presumption in favor of the respondent's forum choice applied with less than maximum force because the real parties in interest are foreign. It did not act unreasonably in deciding that the private interests pointed towards trial in Scotland. Nor did it act unreasonably in deciding that the public interests favored trial in Scotland. Thus, the judgment of the Court of Appeals is

Reversed.

[The opinion of Justice WHITE, concurring in part and dissenting in part, has been omitted. The dissenting opinion of Justice STEVENS, joined by Justice BRENNAN, likewise has been omitted.]

## Comments and Questions

1. Be prepared to explain the strategies and procedural moves of the parties in this case. Why do you think the Scottish plaintiffs (through their

American representative) prefer an American forum, and the American defendants, Piper and Hartzell, a Scottish forum? How did the case make the reverse "Manifest Destiny" journey from the superior court in California to the federal district court in Pennsylvania, and then on to Scotland?

2. What are the differences between a change of venue under § 1404, a transfer under § 1406, and a dismissal for *forum non conveniens*? Given the first two statutory provisions, "the common-law doctrine of *forum non conveniens* has continuing application [in federal courts] only in cases where the alternative forum is abroad." *Sinochem International Co. Ltd. v. Malaysia International Shipping Co.*, 549 U.S. 422, 430 (2007). See also 28 U.S.C. § 1407, providing for transfer of actions raising common questions and pending in different districts to a single district for purposes of "coordinated or consolidated pretrial proceedings"—the multidistrict litigation procedure used in mass tort cases (e.g., asbestos, tobacco, and breast implant litigation).

3. With the vitality of transient presence as a basis for personal jurisdiction (*see Burnham v. Superior Court, supra*), *forum non conveniens* gives courts a discretionary fail-safe for avoiding litigation in a forum both inconvenient to defendants and far removed from the witnesses and evidence. In *MacLeod v. MacLeod*, 383 A.2d 39 (Me. 1978), a Virginia resident sued her former husband for breach of a French divorce decree. The couple having married in New York, the only basis for jurisdiction in Maine was service of process upon defendant—a CIA employee who lived abroad and had no permanent residence—while he happened to be in Maine to attend his parents' golden wedding anniversary party.

The Supreme Judicial Court of Maine affirmed dismissal of the action: "The present action concerns a nonresident plaintiff suing a nonresident defendant upon transitory causes of action which did not arise in the State of Maine. Given those facts, the trial court could rightly consider exercising its discretionary power, notwithstanding the existence of both subject matter and personal jurisdiction, to decline jurisdiction over the action." Noting that there can be no dismissal under *forum non conveniens* without an assurance that there is an alternative forum for plaintiff's action, the trial court's order was modified to condition dismissal on defendant's acceptance of service in Virginia, where plaintiff was residing and defendant held a driver's license.

4. When a multinational chemical company headquartered in New York was sued in federal district court there by victims of a devastating gas plant disaster in Bhopal, India, the Second Circuit Court of Appeals affirmed dismissal on grounds of *forum non conveniens* (conditioned upon defendant's agreement to submit to jurisdiction in India and to waive the statute of limitations defense). *See In Re Union Carbide Corporation Gas Plant Disaster*, 809 F.2d 195 (2d Cir. 1984), *cert. denied*, 484 U.S. 871:

> The vast majority of material witnesses and documentary proof bearing on causation of and liability for the accident is located in India, not the United States, and would be more accessible to an Indian court than to a United States court. The records are almost entirely in Hindi or other Indian languages,

understandable to an Indian court without translation. The witnesses for the most part do not speak English but Indian languages understood by an Indian court but not by an American court. These witnesses could be required to appear in an Indian court but not in a court of the United States. Although witnesses in the United States could not be subpoenaed to appear in India, they are comparatively few in number and most are employed by UCC which, as a party, would produce them in India, with lower overall transportation costs than if the parties were to attempt to bring hundreds of Indian witnesses to the United States. Lastly, Judge Keenan properly concluded that an Indian court would be in a better position to direct and supervise a viewing of the Bhopal plant, which was sealed after the accident. Such a viewing could be of help to a court in determining liability issues.

809 F.2d at 201.

5. The Second Circuit reached the opposite conclusion in *Wiwa v. Royal Dutch Petroleum Co.*, 226 F.3d 88 (2d Cir. 2000), *cert. denied*, 532 U.S. 941 (2001) [discussed previously in note 6 after *Goodyear*], where Nigerian émigrés sought to hold two foreign corporations accountable for human rights abuses committed upon them in Nigeria. Reversing the district court's dismissal on *forum non conveniens* grounds, the court noted the strong policy in favor of an American forum in actions brought under the Alien Tort Statute, which "convey[s] the message that torture committed under color of law of a foreign nation in violation of international law is 'our business,' as such conduct not only violates the standards of international law but also as a consequence violates our domestic law." 226 F.3d at 106. *See also* Kathryn Lee Boyd, *The Inconvenience of Victims: Abolishing* Forum Non Conveniens *in U.S. Human Rights Litigation*, 39 Va. J. Intl. L. 41 (1998).

6. Some states have a legislative formulation of *forum non conveniens* written into their long-arm statute. *See, e.g.*, Mass. Gen. Laws ch. 223A, § 5: "When the court finds that in the interest of substantial justice the action should be heard in another forum, the court may stay or dismiss the action in whole or in part on any conditions that may be just." A negligence action filed in Massachusetts against a New York college alleging that plaintiff was beaten by fellow students there was dismissed pursuant to this provision, conditioned on the school waiving the statute of limitations defense in New York. *Green v. Manhattanville College*, 40 Mass. App. 76, 661 N.E.2d 123 (1996).

7. The presence of a forum selection clause is an important (though not conclusive) factor to be weighed when a court rules on a motion for transfer of venue under § 1404 or 1406, as we will see in *Stewart Organization, Inc. v. Ricoh Corp.*, 487 U.S. 22 (1988), discussed in Chapter 9. *See also Detroit Coke Corp. v. NKK Chemical USA, Inc.*, 794 F. Supp. 214 (E.D. Mich. 1992) (granting defendants' motion to transfer pursuant to a forum selection clause in the purchase agreement); *Flake v. Medline Industries, Inc.*, 882 F. Supp. 947 (E.D. Cal. 1995) (age discrimination case transferred pursuant to a forum selection clause in the employment contract).

8. The Supreme Court has held (unanimously) that a district court has discretion to dismiss on *forum non conveniens* grounds even without resolving whether it has subject matter or personal jurisdiction (which, in that case, would have required considerable time and expense), if it determines that a foreign tribunal is a more suitable forum. *Sinochem International Co. Ltd. v. Malaysia International Shipping Co.*, 549 U.S. 422 (2007).

## Practice Exercise No. 35: Location, Location, Location

Las Vegas resident and small-time talent agent Danny Rose finally realized his lifelong dream of attending the Academy Awards ceremony at the Hollywood Bowl. But when the award for best actress in a low-budget horror movie went to Becky Roland, a former client who had rudely fired Rose some years before, he jumped from his seat in protest, ran wildly toward the stage screaming "She's a no-talent hack!!!" and, in front of 5,000 live witnesses and 50 million TV viewers, was physically removed by security. While being dragged out by LAPD officer Clint Westwood, moonlighting at the event, Rose allegedly suffered permanent and disabling injuries, as well as irreparable harm to his reputation.

Seeking legal advice, Rose was told no jury in LA would ever find against a member of its police force in such circumstances. But by luck, Rose found out that Westwood was flying to New York in a week to attend a family wedding. As Westwood walked through the terminal at LaGuardia Airport, a process server hired by Danny's lawyer handed him a summons and complaint in a civil action filed that day in the United States District Court for the Eastern District of New York (where the airport is located) seeking $150,000 in damages.

As an associate with the firm Westwood has retained to represent him, your supervising partner has asked you to prepare a memo discussing all the options, and chances of success, for getting the case out of New York (with its notoriously generous juries). Please advise her as well as to any other information you might need.

## Review Exercise No. 6

### *Assignment*

To: Summer Associate
From: Senior Partner
Re: Request for Memorandum in Monarch Insurance Matter

We represent Monarch of Maine Insurance Corp. ("Monarch"), a Maine corporation whose only place of business is in Portland, Maine. Shortly after Dr. Sheldon Marshall, test consultant to the City of Cleveland, was served with process as a defendant in the firefighter discrimination case pending in the U.S. District Court for the Northern District of Ohio, he moved to implead Monarch. The third-party complaint alleges that Monarch issued a policy to Marshall providing him with $1 million of liability coverage for "claims made during the policy period against the insured arising from the insured's preparation of civil service testing devices." The policy excludes coverage for intentional or deliberate wrongful acts; and Monarch, citing the plaintiffs' allegations that Marshall conspired with City officials to exclude females from the fire department, sent Marshall a letter denying coverage based on this exclusion.

I have interviewed Jan McNew, the president of Monarch. Jan tells me that Dr. Marshall came to her several years ago while he was vacationing in Maine. Marshall was looking for standard liability insurance for his consulting practice. He told Jan that he consulted on civil service exams for clients up and down the East Coast, and had recently received feelers from other parts of the country. Marshall was very excited about his expanding business, and approached Monarch because of its reputation for personalized service and competitive rates.

Dr. Marshall's policy includes the following provision, standard in Monarch contracts: "Suits arising from this policy must be filed in a court within the State of Maine." Marshall's attorney has informed us that they will contest this provision on the grounds that Marshall never saw it when he signed up for the insurance coverage. Rather, he claims, Jan McNew told him at the time "not to be concerned about all that small print stuff—it's just for the lawyers. We'll take good care of you, you'll see. Just sign on the bottom line."

Jan McNew believes that as a small insurance company, Monarch should not have to defend a suit like this so far from Maine, and expects us to vigorously contest the impleader in Ohio.

Together with a copy of the third-party complaint, Dr. Marshall's lawyer has mailed to our firm a "Request for Defendant Service Waiver" pursuant to Fed. R. Civ. P. 4(d). Please advise me how we should respond to that Request, as well as to the motion to implead our client. What are Monarch's procedural options to contest jurisdiction, the arguments in favor of dismissal, and the chances of success on each? If you think that further legal or factual research is needed, please let me know.

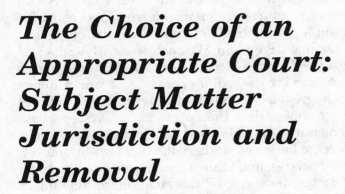

# 8

# *The Choice of an Appropriate Court: Subject Matter Jurisdiction and Removal*

## A. INTRODUCTION TO SUBJECT MATTER JURISDICTION

As noted in the previous chapter, subject matter jurisdiction is one of the three constitutional requirements for a valid and enforceable judgment, the other two being personal jurisdiction and notice. But unlike the other two, a defect in subject matter jurisdiction cannot generally be challenged in a collateral attack.*

The issue of subject matter jurisdiction—the power of a court to hear a particular type of case—focuses our attention on the choice between state courts, on one hand, and federal courts, on the other. State court systems vary by state, and each has its own terminology to describe its trial and appellate courts. States may have multiple layers of trial courts, allocating their judicial business to one layer or another based upon the amount of money in controversy; states also tend to use various specialized trial courts for certain matters (e.g., probate courts, juvenile courts, commercial courts). Appellate jurisdiction in state courts also varies.

---

*The Restatement (Second) of Judgments identifies only three narrow areas in which collateral attacks are appropriate: (1) where the lack of subject matter jurisdiction is so clear as to make application of res judicata manifestly unjust; (2) where the prior judgment would substantially infringe upon the authority of another tribunal or agency; and (3) where the court lacked the capability to make an adequately informed determination of its own jurisdiction and as a matter of procedural fairness a belated attack on jurisdiction should be allowed. Restatement (Second) of Judgments § 12 (1982). As with personal jurisdiction, a defendant who appears in the proceeding and unsuccessfully challenges subject matter authority is bound by that ruling in a collateral proceeding. *See* Chapter 10.

Lawyers routinely refer to state courts as having *general subject matter jurisdiction*. This can be confusing. As an initial matter, notwithstanding use of the words *general* and *jurisdiction*, this term has nothing to do with the concept of general jurisdiction in personal jurisdiction; this is completely different. Next, understand that within a particular state court system, the courts that are not specialized courts are often referred to as courts of *general jurisdiction*. For example, in the State of Ohio the court of general jurisdiction is the Court of Common Pleas (in Massachusetts, the Superior Court; in New York, the Supreme Court; in Texas, the District Court). In this sense, courts of general jurisdiction are the ordinary or general courts. References to state courts in the aggregate as courts of *general subject matter jurisdiction*, however, convey the notion that state court systems can (with only a few exceptions) hear *all* types of cases. This includes cases arising under federal, state, or foreign laws; cases where in-state citizens, out-of-state citizens, or foreigners are parties; and many other cases, no matter the complexity, the number of parties involved, or the small/large amount in controversy. Most importantly, the phrase *general subject matter jurisdiction* is intended to mark the contrast to federal courts, which are courts of *limited subject matter jurisdiction*.

A plaintiff may file in a federal court only if the case falls within the limited parameters of federal subject matter authority—mainly cases between citizens of different states and cases in which the claim arises from federal law.* As we will see, a defendant can also exercise the federal option when a case filed in state court falls within the scope of federal subject matter jurisdiction—such a case may be "removed" to federal court by the defendant.

The subject matter jurisdiction of federal courts is limited by the U.S. Constitution. Article III, § 2, sets the constitutional parameters of federal judicial power, extending it (most importantly for our purposes) to:

- "all Cases . . . arising under this Constitution, the Laws of the United States, and Treaties made," and
- "all Cases . . . between citizens of different States."

It was left to Congress to effectuate this grant of power, which it has done in the Judicial Code provisions 28 U.S.C. §§ 1331 and 1332 (among others) empowering the federal courts to hear "all civil actions arising under the Constitution, laws or treaties of the United States" and cases "between citizens of different States," but in the latter category, only where the amount in controversy exceeds $75,000.

In a very narrow subset of these cases where the federal courts have subject matter jurisdiction, the federal courts have *exclusive jurisdiction*. In these cases (which include patent, copyright, admiralty, and bankruptcy,

---

*Other cases enumerated within federal judicial authority include admiralty cases, controversies in which the United States is a party, and controversies between two or more states (such as border disputes).

for example), only the federal courts—and not the state courts—may assert jurisdiction. Understand, then, that in all other cases that fall within the federal courts' limited subject matter jurisdiction, the matter could be heard in either federal or state courts. This is usually described as the *concurrent subject matter jurisdiction* of federal and state courts.

In practice, where both the federal and state courts have authority to hear a case, the litigant's choice is usually dictated by strategic and pragmatic concerns. Wider availability of pre-trial discovery, for example, may attract plaintiff's counsel in a products liability case to a federal rather than state court. A plaintiff in a civil rights action may prefer a federal court judge to a state court judge in the belief that the former is more experienced in such matters. *See* Burt Neuborne, *The Myth of Parity*, 90 Harv. L. Rev. 1105 (1977). The prospect of more generous juries may, on the other hand, lead lawyers to file in state rather than federal court (as was apparently the case in *World-Wide Volkswagen Corp. v. Woodson*, in Chapter 7). Familiarity with the processes and rules of a particular system may incline lawyers to select it over another. While some commentators have viewed the parallel state and federal court systems as an historical anachronism and dysfunctional redundancy, the late Professor Robert Cover discerned distinct advantages, such as permitting jurisdictional choice (and thus a kind of fairness) to litigants while encouraging innovation among competing courts. *See* Robert Cover, *The Uses of Jurisdictional Redundancy: Interest, Ideology and Innovation*, 22 Wm. & Mary L. Rev. 639 (1981). The coexistence of the two sets of courts has also been the subject of intense political battles by those interests that have a stake in expanding or denying access to federal courts.

## B. FEDERAL QUESTION JURISDICTION

Consider, first, why the framers of the Constitution would contemplate that the limited subject matter jurisdiction of federal courts could include "all Cases . . . arising under this Constitution, the Laws of the United States, and Treaties made." Art. III, § 2. Is it the relative expertise of federal courts? Did the framers expect state courts to be hostile to federal rights? And/or would federal jurisdiction insulate state courts from the consequences of unpopular decisions?

The Constitution defines the permissible scope of the judicial Power (notice that the Constitution defines the term Power with a capital "P"), but it does not provide federal district courts with subject matter jurisdiction to hear these cases. Indeed, the Constitution does not even require that federal district courts exist. But the Constitution provides that Congress may ordain and establish inferior courts—such as federal district courts— to hear cases that fall within the scope of the judicial Power. Most of our attention in this unit will focus on 28 U.S.C. § 1331, the federal question statute. Read that code section now and notice the similarity of language between it and the corresponding language in Art. III, § 2. But as we will see later, these common words have different meanings.

To the extent that the federal question statute extends to "*all* civil actions arising under," it is a general provision. 28 U.S.C. § 1331 (emphasis added). For contrast, review a few code provisions that give the federal courts subject matter jurisdiction over specialized matters. *See, e.g.*, 28 U.S.C. §§ 1333-1340, 1343-1351, 1361-1364. Many of these specialized federal question statutes have been part of the federal courts' jurisdiction from the outset. It was not until 1875, however, that Congress passed Section 1331.

Section 1331 is brief yet opaque. Case law has exposed and explored the ambiguity of the words "civil actions arising under." Does a civil action "arise under" federal law if the defendant's affirmative defense (rather than the plaintiff's cause of action) invokes federal law? Do claims that turn on an interpretation or application of federal law "arise under" federal law? We begin with the seminal case on the scope of federal question jurisdiction.

## ■ LOUISVILLE & NASHVILLE RAILROAD COMPANY v. MOTTLEY ( appellees )
### *211 U.S. 149 (1908)*

Statement by Justice MOODY:

The appellees (husband and wife), being residents and citizens of Kentucky, brought this suit in equity in the circuit court of the United States for the western district of Kentucky against the appellant, a railroad company and a citizen of the same state. The object of the suit was to compel the specific performance of the following contract:

> Louisville, Ky., Oct. 2d, 1871. The Louisville & Nashville Railroad Company, in consideration that E. L. Mottley and wife, Annie E. Mottley, have this day released company from all damages or claims for damages for injuries received by them on the 7th of September, 1871, in consequence of a collision of trains on the railroad of said company at Randolph's Station, Jefferson County, Kentucky, hereby agrees to issue free passes on said railroad and branches now existing or to exist, to said E. L. & Annie E. Mottley for the remainder of the present year, and thereafter to renew said passes annually during the lives of said Mottley and wife or either of them.

The bill alleged that in September, 1871, plaintiffs, while passengers upon the defendant railroad, were injured by the defendant's negligence, and released their respective claims for damages in consideration of the agreement for transportation during their lives, expressed in the contract. It is alleged that the contract was performed by the defendant up to January 1, 1907, when the defendant declined to renew the passes. The bill then alleges that the refusal to comply with the contract was based solely upon that part of the act of Congress of June 29, 1906 which forbids the giving of free passes or free transportation. The bill further alleges: First, that the act of Congress referred to does not prohibit the giving of passes under the circumstances of this case; and, second, that, if the law is to be construed as prohibiting such passes, it is in conflict with the 5th Amendment of the Constitution, because it deprives the plaintiffs of their property without due process of law. The defendant demurred to the bill. The judge of the circuit court overruled the demurrer, entered a decree for the relief prayed for, and the defendant appealed directly to this court.

Justice MOODY, after making the foregoing statement, delivered the opinion of the court:

Two questions of law were raised by the demurrer to the bill, were brought here by appeal, and have been argued before us. They are, first, whether that part of the act of Congress of June 29, 1906 which forbids the giving of free passes or the collection of any different compensation for transportation of passengers than that specified in the tariff filed, makes it unlawful to perform a contract for transportation of persons who, in good faith, before the passage of the act, had accepted such contract in satisfaction of a valid cause of action against the railroad; and, second, whether the statute, if it should be construed to render such a contract unlawful, is in violation of the 5th Amendment of the Constitution of the United States. We do not deem it necessary, however, to consider either of these questions, because, in our opinion, the court below was without jurisdiction of the cause. Neither party has questioned that jurisdiction, but it is the duty of this court to see to it that the jurisdiction of the circuit court, which is defined and limited by statute, is not exceeded. This duty we have frequently performed of our own motion.

There was no diversity of citizenship, and it is not and cannot be suggested that there was any ground of jurisdiction, except that the case was a "suit . . . arising under the Constitution or laws of the United States." It is the settled interpretation of these words, as used in this statute, conferring jurisdiction, that a suit arises under the Constitution and laws of the United States only when the plaintiff's statement of his own cause of action shows that it is based upon those laws or that Constitution. It is not enough that the plaintiff alleges some anticipated defense to his cause of action, and asserts that the defense is invalidated by some provision of the Constitution of the United States. Although such allegations show that very likely, in the course of the litigation, a question under the Constitution would arise, they do not show that the suit, that is, the plaintiff's original cause of action, arises under the Constitution. In *Tennessee v. Union & Planters' Bank*, 152 U.S. 454, the plaintiff, the state of Tennessee, brought suit in the circuit court of the United States to recover from the defendant certain taxes alleged to be due under the laws of the state. The plaintiff alleged that the defendant claimed an immunity from the taxation by virtue of its charter, and that therefore the tax was void, because in violation of the provision of the Constitution of the United States, which forbids any state from passing a law impairing the obligation of contracts. The cause was held to be beyond the jurisdiction of the circuit court, the court saying, by Mr. Justice Gray (p. 464): "A suggestion of one party, that the other will or may set up a claim under the Constitution or laws of the United States, does not make the suit one arising under that Constitution or those laws." Again, in *Boston & M. Consol. Copper & S. Min. Co. v. Montana Ore Purchasing Co.*, 188 U.S. 632, the plaintiff brought suit in the circuit court of the United States for the conversion of copper ore and for an injunction against its continuance. The plaintiff then alleged, for the purpose of showing jurisdiction, in substance, that the defendant would set up in defense certain laws of the United States. The cause was held to be beyond the jurisdiction of the circuit court, the court saying, by Mr. Justice Peckham (pp. 638, 639):

It would be wholly unnecessary and improper, in order to prove complainant's cause of action, to go into any matters of defense which the defendants might possibly set up, and then attempt to reply to such defense, and thus, if possible, to show that a Federal question might or probably would arise in the course of the trial of the case. To allege such defense and then make an answer to it before the defendant has the opportunity to itself plead or prove its own defense is inconsistent with any known rule of pleading, so far as we are aware, and is improper.

The rule is a reasonable and just one that the complainant in the first instance shall be confined to a statement of its cause of action, leaving to the defendant to set up in his answer what his defense is, and, if anything more than a denial of complainant's cause of action, imposing upon the defendant the burden of proving such defense.

Conforming itself to that rule, the complainant would not, in the assertion or proof of its cause of action, bring up a single Federal question. The presentation of its cause of action would not show that it was one arising under the Constitution or laws of the United States.

The only way in which it might be claimed that a Federal question was presented would be in the complainant's statement of what the defense of defendants would be, and complainant's answer to such defense. Under these circumstances the case is brought within the rule laid down in *Tennessee v. Union & Planters' Bank, supra*. That case has been cited and approved many times since. . . . The application of this rule to the case at bar is decisive against the jurisdiction of the circuit court.

It is ordered that the judgment be reversed and the case remitted to the circuit court with instructions to dismiss the suit for want of jurisdiction.

## Comments and Questions

1. Although neither party questioned subject matter jurisdiction, the Court was obligated to raise the issue on its own. Would this be true if the question had been one of personal jurisdiction? Look back at Fed. R. Civ. P. 12(h) and compare subdivisions (1) and (3). Why the different treatment? Where defense counsel picks up on the issue of lack of subject matter

jurisdiction in the district court, a Fed. R. Civ. P. 12(b)(1) motion to dismiss is the device for challenging the court's authority to hear the case.

2. As subject matter jurisdiction is a defense that cannot be waived, understand that subject matter jurisdiction is also something that cannot be created by the parties' consent.

3. One corollary of the limited nature of federal subject matter jurisdiction is that there is something of a presumption against its existence that plaintiff must overcome. Reread Fed. R. Civ. P. 8(a)(1). If the defendant challenges subject matter jurisdiction by filing a motion to dismiss under Rule 12(b)(1), the plaintiff shoulders the burden of proof.

4. Can you articulate the Court's definition of when a lawsuit "arises under" the Constitution or laws of the United States? Why is this referred to by commentators as the "well-pleaded complaint" rule? (Hint: It has nothing to do with the clarity or precision of the complaint.) Would the Court have had subject matter jurisdiction if the Mottleys had filed a complaint alleging that a retroactive revoking of their free passage contract violated the Due Process Clause?

5. Is the *Mottley* result dictated by the language of Article III, § 2, or 28 U.S.C. § 1331? If not, why would the Court adopt a more restrictive view of federal question jurisdiction than either the Constitution or statutory provisions appear to require? In a case like *Mottley* where issues of federal law are likely to dominate the proceedings, why deny access to a federal forum simply because the source of the federal law is something other than the plaintiff's "well-pleaded" complaint?

6. Professor Charles Alan Wright has observed:

> Because of [the *Mottley*] rule, it does not suffice for jurisdiction that the answer raises a federal question. If the basis for original federal-question jurisdiction is that the federal courts have a special expertness in applying federal law, and that assertions of federal law will be received more hospitably in a federal court, it would seem that the courts should have jurisdiction where there is some federal issue regardless of which pleading raises it. The rule to the contrary probably stems from the conceptual notion that unless the initial pleading is sufficient to invoke the jurisdiction of the court, the court lacks power to require responsive pleadings or take any other act in the case.

Charles A. Wright and Mary Kay Kane, *Law of Federal Courts* § 18 at 111 (7th ed. 2011).

7. Despite acknowledging that the *Mottley* rule "may produce awkward results," the Supreme Court has concluded that it generally "makes sense as a quick rule of thumb" and continues to apply it. *See Franchise Tax Board v. Construction Laborers Vacation Trust*, 463 U.S. 1, 11 (1983). If not by focusing exclusively on those aspects of the complaint that are essential to the plaintiff's claim, how might the federal courts instead determine whether an action "arises under" federal law?

8. After their case was dismissed by the federal courts for lack of subject matter jurisdiction, the Mottleys refiled their action in a Kentucky state court

(since a dismissal for want of jurisdiction has no res judicata effect, as we will see in Chapter 10). The case proceeded through the state court system, where the Mottleys prevailed. But ultimately the Railroad appealed to the U.S. Supreme Court, which again denied the Mottleys recovery. On this second appeal, the Supreme Court addressed the constitutionality of the statute upon which the Railroad relied to defend against the breach of contract claim. In an opinion by the first Justice Harlan, the Court seemed to be begging the Mottleys' forgiveness for depriving them of a recovery of at least some free train rides from the railroad that nearly killed them:

> It may be, as suggested, that a refusal to enforce the agreement of 1871 will operate as a great hardship upon the defendants in error. But that consideration cannot control the determination of this controversy. Our duty is to ascertain the intention of Congress in passing the statute upon which the railroad company relies as prohibitive of the further enforcement of the agreement in suit. That intention is to be gathered from the words of the act, interpreted according to their ordinary acceptation, and, when it becomes necessary to do so, in the light of the circumstances as they existed when the statute was passed. The court cannot mold a statute simply to meet its views of justice in a particular case.

The Mottleys thus secured their place of prominence in the Litigation Losers Hall of Fame.

The appellate jurisdiction of the U.S. Supreme Court is determined by the scope of the judicial Power outlined in Art. III, § 2. Why, if the *Mottley* case did not arise under federal law (in the opinion you studied above), did the Supreme Court have subject matter jurisdiction to hear the *Mottley* case on this second appeal?

9. How would you redraft § 1331 to overturn *Mottley* and expand federal judicial power to its full constitutional limits?

10. *Declaratory Judgments*. What would happen if the litigation roles of the Mottleys and the Railroad were reversed? Assume that the Railroad had seized the initiative and brought a declaratory judgment action (now possible under 28 U.S.C. §§ 2201-2202, the Federal Declaratory Judgment Act) in federal court claiming that the Act of Congress invalidated the Mottleys' free pass and seeking a ruling that the consequent termination of the agreement was not in conflict with the Due Process Clause of the Fifth Amendment. Wouldn't the Railroad's complaint "arise under" the Constitution and laws of the United States—whether because the Due Process Clause is essentially the "cause of action" or because the suit arises under the Federal Declaratory Judgment Act, a federal law? Is the "well-pleaded complaint" rule so easily circumvented?

The answer is "no." In the context of a declaratory judgment action, courts essentially hypothesize the substance of the action that would be filed but for the availability of declaratory judgments. In other words, who would have brought a suit, and alleging what? If that hypothetical action could properly be filed in federal court, then the declaratory judgment action likewise falls within the scope of the court's subject matter jurisdiction. *See, e.g., Franchise Tax Board v. Construction Laborers Vacation Trust*, 463 U.S. 1 (1983), and *Skelly Oil Co. v. Phillips Petroleum Co.*, 339 U.S. 667 (1950). "To sanction suits for declaratory relief as within the jurisdiction of the District Courts merely because, as in this case, artful pleading anticipates a defense based on federal law would contravene the whole trend of jurisdictional legislation by Congress, disregard the effective functioning of the federal judicial system and distort the limited procedural purpose of the Declaratory Judgment Act." *Skelly Oil Co., supra*, 339 U.S. at 673-674.

11. Counterclaims have fared no better than anticipated defenses under the *Mottley* rule. Federal jurisdiction cannot be created by a defendant's pleading of a counterclaim arising under federal law. *See The Holmes Group, Inc. v. Vornado Air Circulation Systems, Inc.*, 535 U.S. 826 (2002). "[S]ince the plaintiff is 'the master of the complaint,' the well-pleaded-complaint rule enables him, by eschewing claims based on federal law, . . . to have the cause heard in state court." 535 U.S. at 831.

Although a defendant's counterclaim does not affect the analysis of whether the plaintiff's claim falls within the scope of federal subject matter jurisdiction, you should remember that counterclaims, third-party claims, and cross-claims each will require their own independent basis for federal subject matter jurisdiction if a party wishes to assert them in a pending federal court action. Indeed, federal subject matter jurisdiction is an inquiry that federal courts will entertain as to each and every claim against each and every defendant.

12. *Embedded Federal Issues.* A recurrent problem under § 1331 is whether there is jurisdiction over claims that arise from a mixture of federal and state law. A mixture occurs, for example, when a state law cause of action incorporates some element of federal law.

In *Merrell Dow Pharmaceuticals Inc. v. Thompson*, 478 U.S. 804 (1986), plaintiffs sought damages for birth deformities allegedly caused by the drug Bendectin. The complaint asserted state law claims of negligence and product liability; it also alleged violations of the Federal Food, Drug and Cosmetic Act, which, although not giving rise to an independent private right of action, nonetheless would constitute negligence per se under state law. Merrell Dow removed the case from state to federal court, arguing that it was founded in part on a claim arising under federal law. In a 5-4 decision the Supreme Court ruled that there was no federal question jurisdiction because "a complaint alleging a violation of a federal statute as an element of a state cause of action, when Congress has determined that there should be no private, federal cause of action for the violation, does not state a claim 'arising under the Constitution, laws or treaties of the United States.'" 478 U.S. at 817.

The holding in *Merrell Dow*, however, was not altogether clear as to whether a state law claim could ever invoke federal question jurisdiction. Specifically, it wasn't clear whether there was no federal question in

*Merrell Dow* because (i) the claim arose under state law; (ii) the embedded federal issue was not sufficiently substantial; or (iii) Congress had not created a private right of action.

Nearly twenty years later, the Court returned to the problem of embedded federal issues in *Grable & Sons Metal Products, Inc. v. Darue Engineering & Manufacturing*, 545 U.S. 308 (2005). The principal facts of this case began in 1994, when the Internal Revenue Service (I.R.S.) seized property from Grable & Sons to satisfy delinquent federal taxes. The company received notice of the seizure and of the sale by certified mail, but challenged neither. Darue Engineering & Manufacturing purchased the property at the sale. Several years later, Grable brought a state court action to quiet title—a state law claim. Grable argued that Darue Engineering & Manufacturing's title was invalid because the I.R.S. failed to provide them with the *personal* notice required by the statute. Defendant sought to remove the action to federal court, asserting federal question jurisdiction. The Supreme Court granted review "to resolve a split within the Court of Appeals on whether *Merrell Dow* always requires a federal cause of action as a condition for exercising federal question jurisdiction."

Affirming defendant's removal from state to federal court, Justice Souter wrote for the unanimous Court: "Whether Grable was given notice within the meaning of the federal statute is thus an essential element of its quiet title claim, and the meaning of the federal statute is actually in dispute; it appears to be the only legal or factual interest contested in the case. . . . [T]he national interest in providing a federal forum for federal tax litigation is sufficiently substantial to support the exercise of federal question jurisdiction." The Court invoked "the commonsense notion that a federal court ought to be able to hear claims recognized under state law that nonetheless turn on substantial questions of federal law, and thus justify resort to the experience, solicitude, and hope of uniformity that a federal forum offers on federal issues."

The Court thus rejected the view that a federal cause of action is a necessary condition for exercising federal question jurisdiction. The Court said that *Merrell Dow* should be read in its entirety as treating the absence of a federal statute as evidence relevant to, but not dispositive of, "the sensitive judgments about congressional intent that § 1331 requires." Jurisdiction turns on "whether the state-law claim necessarily stated a federal issue, actually disputed and substantial, which a federal forum may entertain without disturbing a congressionally approved balance of federal and state judicial responsibilities." 545 U.S. at 314. But Justice Souter also stressed the narrowness of the Court's holding. The Court stressed that instances where a state court cause of action turns on an issue of federal law and reflects an important national interest would be "rare."

What does *Grable* do to the following observation Justice Stevens made in *Merrell Dow Pharmaceuticals Inc. v. Thompson*?

There is no single, precise definition of that concept; rather, the phrase "arising under" masks a welter of issues regarding the interrelation of federal and state authority and the proper management of the federal judicial system. This much, however, is clear. The vast majority of cases that come within this grant of jurisdiction are covered by Justice Holmes' statement that a "suit arises under the law that creates the cause of action." Thus, the vast majority of cases brought under the general federal-question jurisdiction of the federal courts are those in which federal law creates the cause of action.

478 U.S. at 808.

For a critique of *Grable* arguing for a return to the "earlier understanding" of "arising under" in which a "claim created by state statute or state common law is not a federal question," see Douglas D. McFarland, *The True Compass: No Federal Question in a State Law Claim*, 55 Kan. L. Rev. 1 (2006). For a critique arguing that *Grable* is part of a disturbing pattern of federal usurpation of state court jurisdiction (also including *Bush v. Gore*, 531 U.S. 98 (2000) and the Class Action Fairness Act, discussed *infra*), see A. Benjamin Spencer, *Anti-Federalist Procedure*, 64 Wash. & Lee L. Rev. 233, 248-251 (2007).

12. It is interesting that Congress did not grant the lower federal courts generalized jurisdiction over federal question cases until 1875, although Art. III had authorized such subject matter authority in 1789. "In the early days of our republic, Congress was content to leave the task of interpreting and applying federal laws in the first instance to the state courts." *Merrell Dow Pharmaceuticals, Inc. v. Thompson*, 478 U.S. 804, 826 (1986) (Brennan, J., dissenting). Moreover, from 1875 until 1980, there was an amount in controversy requirement for federal question cases.

13. 28 U.S.C. § 1343(a)(3) grants jurisdiction over actions alleging the deprivation of rights secured by the Constitution or laws of the United States. Why was this grant of "special federal question jurisdiction" thought necessary, given its obvious overlap with the generalized statutory authority under § 1331?

14. Given that jurisdiction under 28 U.S.C. § 1331 is dependent upon plaintiff asserting a viable federal claim, how do courts distinguish between a dismissal for failure to state a claim under Fed. R. Civ. P 12(b)(6) and a dismissal for lack of subject matter jurisdiction under Fed. R. Civ. P 12(b)(1)? The implications of each are quite different, including that the latter motion may be made at any time, even after trial and entry of judgment.

In *Arbaugh v. Y & H Corporation*, 546 U.S. 500 (2006), a bartender/waitress sued her New Orleans employer for sexual harassment under Title VII and won a verdict for compensatory and punitive damages. Two weeks later the defendant restaurant filed a motion to dismiss for lack of subject matter jurisdiction, claiming for the first time that it did not employ the requisite fifteen or more employees and was thus not an "employer" for Title VII purposes. The trial court agreed and vacated the judgment.

The Court reversed in an opinion by Justice Ginsburg concluding that the defendant's challenge went to the merits of plaintiff's claim and thus could not be raised so late in the lawsuit. "A plaintiff properly invokes § 1331 jurisdiction when she pleads a colorable claim 'arising under' the Constitution or laws of the United States. . . . [T]he threshold number of employees for application of Title VII is an element of a plaintiff's claim for relief, not a jurisdictional issue." 546 U.S. at 501.

15. Strict limitations on federal subject matter jurisdiction can, when combined with other principles such as sovereignty, place certain disputes beyond the jurisdiction of any court. In *American-Style Justice in No Man's Land*, 36 Ga. L. Rev. 895 (2002), Professor Peter Nicolas chronicles congressional efforts over the past century to fill these gaps and also to provide "a federal forum where the existing fora, while theoretically available, were perceived by Congress as inadequate to protect the rights of particular parties either due to parochial bias or other actual or perceived deficiencies." The article exposes a universe of contemporary "no forum" and "biased forum" jurisdictional quagmires with respect to civil disputes arising in Indian Country or those arising elsewhere involving Indian tribes, tribal entities, and tribal members.

## C. DIVERSITY JURISDICTION

While it is understandable that the Framers would grant the federal courts authority to hear cases arising under federal law, it is harder to explain the provision of diversity jurisdiction, which provides for the adjudication of some *state law* claims in federal court. Indeed, assuming the requisite amount in controversy, a Virginia plaintiff may sue a Maryland citizen on a state law claim in federal court.

No doubt a major impetus for diversity jurisdiction was the concern in 1789 (when persons identified more with their locality than with the new national entity) that the state courts might not be level playing fields in cases pitting nonresident litigants against forum residents. Similarly, President and Chief Justice William Howard Taft said that diversity jurisdiction "was the single most important element in securing capital for the development of the southern and western United States." William Howard Taft, *Possible and Needed Reforms in Administration of Justice in Federal Courts*, 8 A.B.A. J. 601, 604 (1922).

Diversity jurisdiction has long been controversial. Judge Henry Friendly wrote a seminal article in 1928 documenting the debate over it at the time of the framing of the Constitution and persisting thereafter. Henry J. Friendly, *The Historic Basis of Diversity Jurisdiction*, 41 Harv. L. Rev. 483 (1928). Over the years there have been legislative efforts (so far unsuccessful) to eliminate it. A 1982 Report of the House Judiciary Committee submitted in support of one such attempt observed: "[T]he abolition of diversity jurisdiction is an important step in reducing endemic court congestion and its insidious effects on litigants. . . . [T]he original reasons for diversity jurisdiction have long since disappeared." Of course, others disagree. With regard to the need for a federal forum for some state law claims, consider these comments from a Justice of the West Virginia

Supreme Court: "As long as I am allowed to redistribute wealth from out-of-state companies to injured in-state plaintiffs, I shall continue to do so. Not only is my sleep enhanced when I give someone else's money away, but so is my job security, because the in-state plaintiffs, their families and their friends will re-elect me." Richard Neely, *The Product Liability Mess: How Business Can Be Rescued from the Politics of State Courts* 4 (1988). Do you think that bias against out-of-state litigants is a serious concern? To the extent that it is a concern, what is it about federal, as opposed to state, courts that prevents or minimizes such discrimination?

The vast majority of cases in federal court on diversity jurisdiction are based upon 28 U.S.C. § 1332(a)(1), which regards actions between and among U.S. citizens (including U.S. corporations). There are two essential prerequisites for this species of diversity jurisdiction: (1) complete diversity; and (2) a sufficient amount in controversy. We will consider each of these issues separately.

## 1. Complete Diversity

A very early Supreme Court opinion, *Strawbridge v. Curtiss*, 7 U.S. (3 Cranch) 267 (1806), imposed a significant limitation on diversity jurisdiction under 28 U.S.C. § 1332(a)(1) by requiring *complete* diversity. In *Strawbridge*, there were citizens from different states on both sides of the "v.," but there were also citizens from the same state on both sides of the "v." (e.g., Plaintiff from Massachusetts v. Defendant 1 from Vermont and Defendant 2 from Massachusetts). The Court required—and § 1332 still requires—"complete diversity," meaning every plaintiff must be a citizen of a different state than every defendant in the action. Shared citizenship between any two parties across the "v." destroys diversity jurisdiction. "[We] have adhered to the complete diversity rule in light of the purpose of the diversity requirement, which is to provide a federal forum for important disputes where state courts might favor, or be perceived as favoring, home-state litigants. The presence of parties from the same State on both sides of a case dispels this concern, eliminating a principal reason for conferring § 1332 jurisdiction over any of the claims in the action." *Exxon Mobil Corp. v. Allapattah Services, Inc.*, 545 U.S. 546, 553 (2005).

Especially because of the requirement of complete diversity, determining the citizenship of a party is critical. Is a student from Florida who is going to law school in Georgia a citizen of Florida or Georgia? What is the citizenship of a corporation that is incorporated in Delaware, has a principal place of business in Illinois, and does substantial business in all fifty states? And what is the citizenship of a partnership whose partners all work in New York, but who live in New Jersey, Connecticut, and New York? How does one determine the citizenship of a party—whether that party is a person, a corporation, or something else?

The citizenship of a natural person is determined for diversity purposes by the concept of *domicile. Mas v. Perry*, 489 F.2d 1396, 1399 (5th Cir. 1974).

One's domicile is determined by the last place where she was both present and intending to remain indefinitely. In other words, if a person's current residence is a place where she intends to remain indefinitely, the current residence would be her domicile—and, therefore, her state of citizenship for purposes of the diversity analysis. But if a person's current residence is not a place where she intends to remain indefinitely, then her domicile would be the place where she was last both present and intending to remain indefinitely. An individual always has only one domicile, and she keeps that domicile until she or he assumes a new domicile.

Whether one intends to remain somewhere indefinitely is a highly fact-specific inquiry. Sometimes people move to a different state without intending to remain there indefinitely (in which case, they maintain their previous domicile). Sometimes a person is displaced from a domicile by a natural disaster. What then? In the next case we see that courts may consider a number of factors to determine whether an individual possesses the intent to remain somewhere indefinitely.

## ■ OCHOA v. PV HOLDING CORP.
### 2007 WL 496612 (E.D. La. 2007)

FELDMAN, United States District Judge:
Before the Court is the plaintiff's motion to remand. For the reasons that follow, the plaintiff's motion is granted.

### I

Angela Ochoa was injured while riding in a Ford Explorer that was rear-ended by Paul Gulley, who was driving a Budget rental car. The accident happened on February 2, 2006 in New Orleans. Ms. Ochoa, a Louisiana citizen, sued Paul Gulley, Budget Rent A Car System, Inc., and PV Holding Corporation (the title holder of Budget rental cars) in state court on October 5, 2006. [Defendants] removed the suit to this Court on November 30, 2006, invoking the Court's diversity jurisdiction.

The plaintiff now moves to remand, contending that the Court lacks subject matter jurisdiction. Budget is a citizen of Delaware. Before his apartment was destroyed by Hurricane Katrina on August 29, 2005, Paul Gulley had lived in Orleans Parish, Louisiana. He evacuated to Arlington, Texas, where he has been living since the storm. The issue before the Court is the evacuee Paul Gulley's domicile at the time the state court petition was filed. . . .

[Defendants] removed this case on the basis of diversity jurisdiction. . . . The plaintiff contends that the Court lacks subject matter jurisdiction because Paul Gulley was a Louisiana domiciliary at the time the complaint and removal petition were filed.

The Court agrees that it lacks subject matter jurisdiction. . . .

## II

To exercise diversity jurisdiction, complete diversity must exist between the plaintiffs and all of the properly joined defendants, and the amount in controversy must exceed $75,000. *See* 28 U.S.C. § 1332.

By providing that the judicial power of the United States shall extend to controversies "between Citizens of Different States," Article III, § 2 of the United States Constitution vests diversity jurisdiction in federal courts. For a court to have subject matter jurisdiction over a case based upon 28 U.S.C. § 1332, *complete* diversity must exist between the plaintiff and the defendant (no plaintiff may be a citizen of the same state as any defendant). *Strawbridge v. Curtiss*, 7 U.S. (3 Cranch) 267 (1806); *Freeman v. Northwest Acceptance Corp.*, 754 F.2d 553, 555 (5th Cir. 1985); *Mas v. Perry*, 489 F.2d 1396, 1398-00 (5th Cir. 1974), *cert. denied*, 419 U.S. 842 (1974). The determination of state citizenship for diversity purposes is a matter of federal common law and is not determined by state law. *Mas v. Perry*, 489 F.2d at 1399; *Coury v. Prot*, 85 F.3d 244, 248 (5th Cir. 1996). Diversity of citizenship must be present at the time the complaint is filed; therefore, the Court examines a litigant's domicile at the time when the complaint was filed. *Mas*, 489 F.2d at 1399. . . .

In ascertaining domicile, the Court is not limited to the pleadings; rather, it may review record evidence, affidavits, and testimony concerning facts underlying the citizenship of the parties. *Coury v. Prot*, 85 F.3d at 249. While relevant to the determination of domicile, a statement of intent is "entitled to little weight if it conflicts with objective facts." *Freeman v. Northwest Acceptance Corp.*, 754 F.2d 553, 556 (5th Cir. 1985).

In determining one's domicile, the Court should address a variety of factors, none of which is itself determinative. *Coury v. Prot*, 85 F.3d at 251. In fact, "[t]he court should look to all evidence shedding light on the litigant's intention to establish domicile." *Id.* The actual fact of residence and the real intention of remaining there, as disclosed by a person's entire course of conduct, are the controlling factors. *See Freeman*, 754 F.2d at 555-56.[3]

## III

Federal subject matter jurisdiction here turns on where was Gulley's domicile on October 5, 2006 when this lawsuit was filed. The defendants have the burden of showing that removal was proper; thus, they must show that Gulley was a Texas domiciliary at the time the plaintiff filed her complaint. The Court finds that the defendants have not carried their burden.

---

3. Some factors the Court may examine include the places where the litigant exercises civil and political rights, pays taxes, owns real and personal property, has his drivers and other licenses, maintains bank accounts, belongs to clubs and churches, has places of business or employment, and maintains a home for his family. *Coury v. Prot*, 85 F.3d at 251 (citations omitted).

The parties agreed to limited discovery relating to the issue of Gulley's domicile and he was deposed in December 2006. Gulley testified that he was born in New Orleans and lived there until Hurricane Katrina. Though he was living in Texas, he was "visiting family" in New Orleans when the car accident giving rise to this lawsuit happened in February 2006.

The plaintiff characterizes Gulley as being domiciled in Louisiana in February 2006 when the accident happened and months later when she filed this lawsuit. She points to Gulley's Louisiana driver's license, which he presented at the time of the accident, and the fact that he did not have permanent employment in Texas until shortly before his deposition.

The defendants characterize Gulley as being domiciled in Texas, pointing to his deposition testimony that he has resided in Texas since he evacuated there shortly after the storm, does not intend to live in Louisiana, and recently got a job in Texas.

The Court notes that the record provides few objective facts concerning Gulley's domicile in October 2006; indeed, the record consists only of Gulley's deposition testimony, which is attached (albeit unauthenticated) to the defendants' opposition to the plaintiff's motion to remand. Accordingly, the defendants have not addressed many of the objective facts that typically aid the Court in ascertaining domicile, e.g., the places where the litigant exercises civil and political rights, pays taxes, owns real and personal property, has his drivers and other licenses, maintains bank accounts, belongs to clubs and churches, has places of business or employment, and maintains a home for his family. *See Coury v. Prot*, 85 F.3d at 151.

The record shows that Gulley works and resides in Texas. The defendants do not dispute that Gulley has a Louisiana driver's license. He has lived in New Orleans all of his life until he was forced to leave because Hurricane Katrina destroyed his home; he has family in New Orleans. He was in New Orleans at the time of the accident, though the record does not show the duration of his stay or how often he travels between Texas and Louisiana, nor when he developed his present intention to stay in Texas "indefinitely."

Gulley's recent employment in Texas and his subjective statement that he does not presently intend to live in New Orleans fall short of establishing that his domicile several months ago—at the time the complaint was filed—was Texas and not Louisiana. There is little objective evidence to corroborate his subjective present statement of intent. The defendants bear the burden of showing diverse citizenship because they are attempting to invoke this Court's subject matter jurisdiction. They have failed to carry that burden to show that Gulley was a citizen of Texas at the time the complaint was filed; thus, the Court lacks removal jurisdiction based on diversity of citizenship.

Accordingly, the plaintiff's motion to remand is granted. The case is hereby remanded to the Civil District Court for the Parish of Orleans.

## Comments and Questions

1. For diversity purposes, a U.S. corporation is deemed a citizen of both its state of incorporation and the state where it has its principal place of business. Read 28 U.S.C. § 1332(c)(1). Unlike a natural person, a corporation may thus be a citizen of more than one state if incorporated in a state different from where its principal place of business is located. If a corporation that is incorporated in Delaware with a principal place of business in Texas files a lawsuit against a corporation that is incorporated in Delaware with a principal place of business in Virginia, complete diversity is absent and 1332(a)(1) does not authorize jurisdiction.

A corporation's principal place of business is determined by the location of its "nerve center," meaning where the corporation has its headquarters—its "center of overall direction, control, and coordination." *Hertz Corp. v. Friend*, __ U.S. __, 130 S. Ct. 1181 (2010).

2. For diversity purposes, an unincorporated association (e.g., a limited liability company (LLC), a partnership, labor union, the governing board of an institution) usually is a citizen of the states of each of its members. Thus if a partnership wants to sue a California corporation that has its principal place of business in Nevada, there is no diversity jurisdiction if *any* member of the partnership-plaintiff is a citizen of either California or Nevada.

3. Actions that involve foreign citizens (or foreign corporations) do not fall within the scope of 28 U.S.C. § 1332(a)(1), which is limited to actions between "citizens of different States." The word "citizen" in that subsection means U.S. citizen. And use of the capital letter S on the word "State" means one of the United States. Accordingly, if the action involves a foreign citizen or a foreign corporation, diversity jurisdiction must be founded on one of the other subsections of § 1332.

Sections 1332(a)(2) and (a)(3) are often referred to as alienage jurisdiction. These sections authorize another type of diversity jurisdiction. If a California plaintiff wants to sue a Panamanian defendant, she would invoke § 1332(a)(2), which (assuming the requisite amount in controversy) extends jurisdiction to actions between "citizens of a State and citizens or subjects of a foreign state." A "citizen[ ] of a State" refers to a U.S. citizen that is domiciled in one of the United States. (In the hypothetical, for example, this is the "California plaintiff.") A "citizen[ ] or subject[ ] of a foreign state" refers to an alien citizen or alien corporation. (In the hypothetical, this is the "Panamanian defendant.") Notice, however, that if the Panamanian defendant has been admitted to the United States for permanent residence and is domiciled in California, the action no longer falls within the scope of § 1332(a)(2). Essentially, the Panamanian citizen is deemed a citizen of California, destroying diversity jurisdiction.

Section 1332(a)(3) provides jurisdiction when aliens are joined as additional parties in a lawsuit that would otherwise fall within the scope of § 1332(a)(1). If the California plaintiff wants to sue the Panamanian defendant *and a second defendant*, a U.S. citizen domiciled in Texas, this scenario is covered by § 1332(a)(3) because it is an action between "citizens of different states" (to wit, the California plaintiff and the Texas defendant) "in which citizens or subjects of a foreign state are additional parties" (to wit, the Panamanian defendant).

4. Assuming the requisite amount in controversy, under what provision of Section 1332 is there diversity jurisdiction over an action brought by a single plaintiff, a citizen of Austria, against a single defendant, a citizen of Mexico? To read more about federal diversity jurisdiction over cases involving aliens, see Thomas Main, *Global Issues in Civil Procedure* 148-165 (2006).

5. Generally speaking, jurisdictional statutes are construed narrowly. Such an approach can lead to unusual results. Consider this fact pattern, which is based on a real case:

In a highly publicized contract dispute arising from the epic film *Cleopatra*, the motion picture studio sought to recover $25 million in damages from Richard Burton and Elizabeth Taylor. These two great actors from Hollywood's Golden Age met on the set of *Cleopatra* and eventually married. Burton was a British subject. Elizabeth Taylor was a citizen of the United States who, at the relevant time, lived abroad and intended to remain there indefinitely. The plaintiff was a Delaware corporation with a principal place of business in California. Is there diversity jurisdiction? Try to answer this question yourself before reading any further.

Section 1332(a)(1) would not authorize jurisdiction because Burton was a foreign citizen.

Section 1332(a)(2) would not authorize jurisdiction because although Burton was a "citizen[ ] or subject[ ] of a foreign state," the other defendant, Taylor, was not. Indeed, Taylor was an American citizen.

Section 1332(a)(3) would not authorize jurisdiction because, as to the first part of this subsection, this was not an action between "citizens of different States." Although the plaintiff was a citizen of a state (two states, actually), neither of the defendants was a "citizen of [a] State." Burton was not a U.S. citizen. And Taylor, although a U.S. citizen, was not a citizen *of a State*. Instead she was a citizen domiciled abroad. Without a (United) "State" to which she could be attributed, the statute did not authorize diversity jurisdiction. This phenomenon is often referred to as "the Stateless citizen." *See Twentieth Century-Fox Film Corporation v. Taylor and Burton*, 239 F. Supp. 913 (S.D.N.Y. 1965).

Consider, then, the following hypothetical. Paz, who was born, raised, and has always lived in New Hampshire, sues Dietz, who was born and raised in Connecticut but recently moved to Paris with the dream of becoming a fashion designer there. Assuming an amount in controversy of $250,000 on a state law claim, would a U.S. district court in New Hampshire have diversity jurisdiction over the suit? How about a U.S. district court in Connecticut?

6. Diversity must exist at the time the complaint is filed, and jurisdiction is unaffected by subsequent changes in the citizenship of the parties. *See Dole Food Co. v. Patrickson*, 538 U.S. 468, 478 (2003); *Grupo Dataflux v. Atlas Global Group, L.P.*, 541 U.S. 567 (2004) (postfiling change in plaintiff's

citizenship could not cure defect in diversity jurisdiction). Imagine that a plaintiff with a $100,000 state law claim against a citizen of the same state moves to a neighboring state for the purpose of establishing diversity jurisdiction in federal court. Consider two possibilities: (1) What if the plaintiff "moved" to the neighboring state only for the day, and "moved" back the day after filing the suit? (2) What if the plaintiff "moved" to the neighboring state, genuinely intends to remain there indefinitely, but admits that the move was *solely* to establish diversity jurisdiction and not for any other reason?

7. *The Domestic Relations and Probate Exceptions.* Even when the parties are completely diverse, matters of domestic relations (divorce, alimony, and custody) and probate (wills, trusts, and estates) have long been considered outside the realm of diversity jurisdiction by virtue of judicially created exceptions. *See generally Marshall v. Marshall*, 547 U.S. 293 (2006) (Anna Nicole Smith's dispute with her stepson over her husband's estate), and *Ankenbrandt v. Richards*, 504 U.S. 689 (1992). What explains this carveout? Are these matters more "local" than other matters of state law (such as malpractice, fraud, battery, trespass)? Do they require expertise that only state judges possess? Is it sexism? *See* Judith Resnik, *"Naturally" Without Gender: Women, Jurisdiction, and the Federal Courts*, 66 N.Y.U. L. Rev. 1682 (1991).

8. Significantly, the complete diversity requirement is an interpretation of § 1332, and not an Article III requirement. This means that Congress is free to modify the complete diversity rule as it has to permit federal interpleader actions on "minimal diversity"—that is, as long as any two rival claimants are diverse. *See* 28 U.S.C. § 1335 and *State Farm Fire & Casualty Co. v. Tashire*, 386 U.S. 523 (1967). Federal actions where there is only minimal diversity have also been recently authorized by the Multiparty, Multiforum Trial Jurisdiction Act (MMTJA) and by the Class Action Fairness Act (CAFA); both of these acts are discussed in Chapter 11.

## 2. Amount in Controversy

The amount in controversy for purposes of diversity jurisdiction is determined by the sum claimed by the plaintiff in good faith, and the standard for dismissal for lack of the jurisdictional minimum is quite high: "It must appear to a legal certainty that the claim is really for less than the jurisdictional amount to justify dismissal." *St. Paul Mercury Indemnity Co. v. Red Cab Co.*, 303 U.S. 283 (1938). *See, e.g., Sellers v. O'Connell*, 701 F.2d 575 (6th Cir. 1983) (complaint dismissed where plaintiff was only entitled to recover maximum of $9,875 in pension benefits). Since January 1997, in order to assert jurisdiction the matter in controversy must "exceed[ ] the sum or value of $75,000, exclusive of interest and costs." 28 U.S.C. § 1332.

Federal jurisdiction is not lost retroactively because a judgment is ultimately entered for less than the jurisdictional minimum. *See Mas v. Perry*, *supra*, 489 F.2d at 1400 (the fact that plaintiff husband recovered only $5,000 does not deprive federal court of jurisdiction, as his claim was made in good faith based on the evidence presented). Federal judges do, however, have the authority to impose court costs on a plaintiff who recovers less than the requisite minimum. 28 U.S.C. § 1332(b).

Like the "well-pleaded complaint" rule for § 1331 jurisdiction, the aim here is to be able to determine § 1332 jurisdiction early in the litigation on the basis of the complaint. Once jurisdiction "attaches," subsequent events (like the award of less than the jurisdictional minimum or the relocation of a diverse party to a non-diverse state) do not deprive the court of power. Do you see how the interests of efficiency and certainty dictate this approach? What would happen if subject matter jurisdiction were contingent on the ultimate award of damages?

In order to reach the requisite amount in controversy, a plaintiff may aggregate all claims (related or not, see Fed. R. Civ. P. 18) brought against a single defendant in the complaint. For example, a plaintiff may join a $50,000 tort claim and a (related or unrelated) $40,000 contract claim against a diverse defendant and fall within the scope of the court's diversity subject matter jurisdiction.

A plaintiff may not, however, join *parties* to reach the amount in controversy. In other words, a plaintiff cannot satisfy the amount in controversy by joining a $50,000 claim against one defendant with a $40,000 claim against a second defendant.

But now consider an alternative scenario: what if plaintiff #1 has a $100,000 claim and plaintiff #2 has a related $30,000 claim against a single defendant? In *Exxon Mobil Corp. v. Allapattah Services, Inc.*, 545 U.S. 546 (2005), the Court held that the supplemental jurisdiction statute (discussed in Part D) overturned prior decisions to the contrary and permits the exercise of diversity jurisdiction even where some plaintiffs fail to satisfy the minimum amount in controversy, as long as (1) at least one plaintiff does meet it, (2) complete diversity exists among the parties, and (3) all the claims are part of the same case or controversy.

In actions seeking declaratory or injunctive relief, the general rule is that courts weigh the value of the right sought to be enforced (as, for example, the value to plaintiff of preventing infringement of its trade name) or the cost to the defendant. Charles Alan Wright and Mary Kay Kane, *Law of Federal Courts* § 33 at 204 (7th ed. 2011).

## Comments and Questions

1. You are now familiar with both federal question and diversity jurisdiction. In cases where the requirements of one or both of these jurisdictional bases are met, consider again how counsel chooses between federal or state court. Would you expect judges of the two systems to share the same sympathies, practice backgrounds, and philosophies? Do state judges and federal judges attend the same law schools, work at the same law firms, and navigate

the same social circles? The fraternity of federal district judges is rather small (about 700)—smaller than the size of many law firms; what effect does that have? What are the relative abilities of federal and state judges? Note that state court judges are elected in most states, while federal judges are appointed for life. Would you expect the relative accountability of state judges to have a discernible effect on the outcome of judicial rulings? Time-to-trial and backlogs are likely to differ in particular localities. Might the location of the court influence your decision, as between, for example, a federal court that will draw a mostly suburban jury and a state court in the inner city? What about cost differentials? Another question, which we will address in Chapter 9, is whether the same substantive laws and procedures would be applied in the state and federal courts in the diversity action.

2. Many of the restrictions on federal question and diversity jurisdiction are designed to ensure that federal courts are put to their best use. After all, the dispute resolution provided by federal courts is a limited, shared, public resource. How should this resource be allocated for maximum effect?

Which cases that arise under federal law "belong" in federal court, and which may be filed there? Which counterclaims that arise under federal law belong in federal court, and which may be filed there? Which cases that arise under state law whose outcomes will turn on a controlling issue of federal law belong in federal court, and which may be filed there?

Diversity jurisdiction accounts for about one-quarter to one-third of the cases in federal court. Do you find concerns about provincial bias persuasive? Should a resident plaintiff suing a nonresident defendant have the choice to file in her own state or federal court? (Does she have that choice, assuming the requisite amount in controversy?)

3. Although lawyers talk of separate state and federal court systems—and of cases arising under "federal law" or "state law"—it is important for you to appreciate the magnitude of "state law" that would apply in federal courts, and vice versa. We refer here not just to the law that gives rise to the cause of action, but also to hundreds of matters that arise throughout the course of litigation—in federal court, for example, statutes and rules of procedure often incorporate state law by reference. Similarly, in state court, the U.S. Constitution and the preemptive reach of federal statutes apply even if the cause of action arises under state law. Bottom line: federal courts are routinely considering and applying state law; and state courts are routinely considering and applying federal law.

## Review Exercise No. 7

Prem, a resident of California for the past twelve years, seeks your assistance. She has asked you to represent her in a lawsuit against her former employer, Def Engineering, Inc. (Def). Def is a Delaware corporation with a principal place of business in New York, NY. For many years, Def has maintained a large operation in Los Angeles, CA; the Los Angeles branch generates, on average, $55 million in annual revenues. Prem worked primarily with the Los Angeles branch, but also worked closely with the company's activities throughout the western United States.

Prem has shown you a copy of her contract with Def, and it appears that she has a strong claim for breach. The contract provides that during the term of the contract she can only be terminated for cause, and there is little or no evidence of a for-cause termination. Indeed, her letter of termination explains that the company is terminating her "with great regret" and the letter identifies the economic downturn as the reason for their decision. She was terminated one month ago, and she still has twenty-four months remaining on the consulting agreement, which pays her $40,000 per year.

Prem is despondent about the loss of her job even though she already has another job offer for similar work and for substantially the same salary in New York City. Prem lived in New York all her life before moving to California. She says she always planned to retire back in New York, but may need to move back there sooner than she had initially planned.

1. Assume a one-count complaint for breach of contract under state law. Would a federal court in California or in New York have subject matter jurisdiction? To the extent your answers are "it depends," identify the additional facts that you need, describe how you will obtain those facts, and explain how those facts would resolve the matter of federal subject matter jurisdiction.

2. As a matter of good public policy, does this case belong in federal court or state court? Explain your answer.

3. Prem is a fifty-seven-year-old woman and, therefore, a member of a protected class under the Age Discrimination in Employment Act (ADEA). Prem does not, however, believe that she was terminated because of her age. (Prem says, "Definitely not. They cut everyone in my job group, both young and old.") Preliminary research also suggests that Prem may have been an independent contractor (rather than an employee), and therefore would not covered by the ADEA. Assuming that you and your client would prefer to be in federal court, *should* you include a second cause of action under the ADEA just to establish or to strengthen the case for federal subject matter jurisdiction? Will that work?

# D. SUPPLEMENTAL JURISDICTION

Although the federal courts possess only limited subject matter jurisdiction, a small margin of "supplemental" jurisdiction has been recognized to encompass claims that do not fall within either the federal question or diversity categories but are closely connected to such claims already being entertained by the court. As you read the next cases, consider the policy and pragmatic considerations underlying this "stretch" jurisdiction.

## ■ UNITED MINE WORKERS OF AMERICA v. GIBBS
### 383 U.S. 715 (1966)

Justice BRENNAN delivered the opinion of the Court:

Respondent Paul Gibbs was awarded compensatory and punitive damages in this action against petitioner United Mine Workers of America (UMW) for alleged violations of § 303 of the Labor Management Relations Act, 1947, 61 Stat. 158, as amended, and of the common law of Tennessee. The case grew out of the rivalry between the United Mine Workers and the Southern Labor Union over representation of workers in the southern Appalachian coal fields. Tennessee Consolidated Coal Company, not a party here, laid off 100 miners of the UMW's Local 5881 when it closed one of its mines in southern Tennessee during the spring of 1960. Late that summer, Grundy Company, a wholly-owned subsidiary of Consolidated, hired respondent as mine superintendent to attempt to open a new mine on Consolidated's property at nearby Gray's Creek through use of members of the Southern Labor Union. As part of the arrangement, Grundy also gave respondent a contract to haul the mine's coal to the nearest railroad loading point.

On August 15 and 16, 1960, armed members of Local 5881 forcibly prevented the opening of the mine, threatening respondent and beating an organizer for the rival union. . . . [A] picket line was maintained there for nine months; and no further attempts were made to open the mine during that period.

Respondent lost his job as superintendent, and never entered into performance of his haulage contract. He testified that he soon began to lose other trucking contracts and mine leases he held in nearby areas. Claiming these effects to be the result of a concerted union plan against him, he sought recovery not against Local 5881 or its members, but only against petitioner, the international union. The suit was brought in the United States District Court for the Eastern District of Tennessee, and jurisdiction was premised on allegations of secondary boycotts under § 303. The state law claim, for which jurisdiction was based upon the doctrine of pendent jurisdiction, asserted "an unlawful conspiracy and an unlawful boycott aimed at him and (Grundy) to maliciously, wantonly and willfully interfere with his contract of employment and with his contract of haulage."

. . . The jury's verdict was that the UMW had violated both § 303 and state law. Gibbs was awarded $60,000 as damages under the employment contract and $14,500 under the haulage contract; he was also awarded $100,000 punitive damages. On motion, the trial court set aside the award of damages with respect to the haulage contract on the ground that damage was unproved. It also held that union pressure on Grundy to discharge respondent as supervisor would constitute only a primary dispute with Grundy, as respondent's employer, and hence was not cognizable as a claim under § 303. Interference with the employment relationship was cognizable as a state claim, however, and a remitted award was sustained on the state law claim. The Court of Appeals for the Sixth Circuit affirmed. We granted *certiorari*. We reverse.

## I

. . . With the adoption of the Federal Rules of Civil Procedure . . . the impulse is toward entertaining the broadest possible scope of action consistent with fairness to the parties; joinder of claims, parties and remedies is strongly encouraged. [*See, e.g.*, Fed. R. Civ. Proc. 2, 18-20, 42.] . . . Pendent jurisdiction, in the sense of judicial power, exists whenever there is a claim "arising under [the] Constitution, the Laws of the United States, and Treaties made, or which shall be made, under their Authority . . ." U.S. Const., Art. III, § 2, and the relationship between that claim and the state claim permits the conclusion that the entire action before the court comprises but one constitutional "case." The federal claim must have substance sufficient to confer subject matter jurisdiction on the court. The state and federal claims must derive from a common nucleus of operative fact. But if, considered without regard to their federal or state character, a plaintiff's claims are such that he would ordinarily be expected to try them all in one judicial proceeding, then, assuming substantiality of the federal issues, there is power in federal courts to hear the whole.

That power need not be exercised in every case in which it is found to exist. It has consistently been recognized that pendent jurisdiction is a doctrine of discretion, not of plaintiff's right. Its justification lies in considerations of judicial economy, convenience and fairness to litigants; if these are not present a federal court should hesitate to exercise jurisdiction over state claims, even though bound to apply state law to them, *Erie R. Co. v. Tompkins*, 304 U.S. 64. Needless decisions of state law should be avoided both as a matter of comity and to promote justice between the parties, by procuring for them a surer-footed reading of applicable law. Certainly, if the federal claims are dismissed before trial, even though not insubstantial in a jurisdictional sense, the state claims should be dismissed as well. Similarly, if it appears that the state issues substantially predominate, whether in terms of proof, of the scope of the issues raised, or of the comprehensiveness of the remedy sought, the state claims may be dismissed without prejudice and left for resolution to state tribunals. There may, on the other hand, be situations in which the state claim is so closely tied to questions of federal policy that the argument for exercise of pendent jurisdiction is particularly strong. In the present case, for example, the allowable scope of the state claim implicates the federal doctrine of pre-emption; while this interrelationship does not create statutory federal question jurisdiction, *Louisville & N. R. Co. v. Mottley*, 211 U.S. 149, its existence is relevant to the exercise of discretion.

Finally, there may be reasons independent of jurisdictional considerations, such as the likelihood of jury confusion in treating divergent legal theories of relief, that would justify separating state and federal claims for trial, Fed. Rule Civ. Proc. 42(b). If so, jurisdiction should ordinarily be refused.

The question of power will ordinarily be resolved on the pleadings. But the issue whether pendent jurisdiction has been properly assumed is one which remains open throughout the litigation. Pretrial procedures or even the trial itself may reveal a substantial hegemony of state law claims, or likelihood of jury confusion, which could not have been anticipated at the pleading stage. Although it will of course be appropriate to take account in this circumstance of the already completed course of the litigation, dismissal of the state claim might even then be merited. For example, it may appear that the plaintiff was well aware of the nature of his proofs and the relative importance of his claims; recognition of a federal court's wide latitude to decide ancillary questions of state law does not imply that it must tolerate a litigant's effort to impose upon it what is in effect only a state law case. Once it appears that a state claim constitutes the real body of a case, to which the federal claim is only an appendage, the state claim may fairly be dismissed.

We are not prepared to say that in the present case the District Court exceeded its discretion in proceeding to judgment on the state claim. We may assume for purposes of decision that the District Court was correct in its holding that the claim of pressure on Grundy to terminate the employment contract was outside the purview of § 303. Even so, the § 303 claims based on secondary pressures on Grundy relative to the haulage contract and on other coal operators generally were substantial. . . . The state and federal claims arose from the same nucleus of operative fact and reflected alternative remedies. Indeed, the verdict sheet sent in to the jury authorized only one award of damages, so that recovery could not be given separately on the federal and state claims.

It is true that the § 303 claims ultimately failed and that the only recovery allowed respondent was on the state claim. We cannot confidently say, however, that the federal issues were so remote or played such a minor role at the trial that in effect the state claim only was tried. Although the District Court dismissed as unproved the § 303 claims that petitioner's secondary activities included attempts to induce coal operators other than Grundy to cease doing business with respondent, the court submitted the § 303 claims relating to Grundy to the jury. The jury returned verdicts against petitioner on those § 303 claims, and it was only on petitioner's motion for a directed verdict and a judgment n.o.v. that the verdicts on those claims were set aside. . . . We thus conclude that although it may be that the District Court might, in its sound discretion, have dismissed the state claim, the circumstances show no error in refusing to do so.

[The Court went on to reverse the verdict of conspiracy under state law because Gibbs had not met his burden of proof.]

[The concurring opinion of Justice HARLAN is omitted.]

## Comments and Questions

1. Where does the Court find constitutional authority in Article III for "pendent jurisdiction"? Was there statutory authority at the time *Gibbs* was decided? 28 U.S.C. § 1367 (discussed later in this chapter) is of much more recent vintage.

2. What are the pragmatic and judicial efficiency arguments that underlie the Court's endorsement of pendent jurisdiction? Consider a plaintiff in Gibbs's situation, with an injury that he believes gives rise to claims under *both* federal and state law. This could be a citizen alleging a police officer used excessive force to restrain him in violation of his federal civil rights (§ 1983) and also seeking recovery under state tort claims for assault and battery, and so forth. Or it could be an employee alleging sexual harassment in violation of both Title VII and the state tort law of intentional infliction of emotional distress. Absent recognition of pendent jurisdiction (and without diversity of citizenship), what forum options would they have?

3. What is the standard for the exercise of pendent jurisdiction under *Gibbs*? If this test is met, *must* the federal court exercise pendent jurisdiction? If not, under what circumstances does Justice Brennan envision a court declining jurisdiction over state claims that arise out of the same nucleus of facts as the federal claim?

4. If the justification for exercise of federal adjudicatory power over a state law claim is that the latter is appended to a federal claim being entertained, how can the court resolve the state claim even *after* the federal claim has failed (as it did in *Gibbs*)? Does this mean a plaintiff can use pendent jurisdiction to gain access to the federal forum for state claims merely by asserting *any* federal claim, no matter how frivolous? What does Justice Brennan mean when he writes that "assuming *substantiality* of the federal issues, there is power in federal courts to hear the whole [case]" (emphasis added)?

5. In *Maguire v. Marquette University*, 814 F.2d 1213 (7th Cir. 1987), plaintiff brought a federal action under Title VII alleging she was denied appointment to the Jesuit school's theology department because of her gender. After discovery she amended her complaint to add a pendent claim asserting breach of Wisconsin's law of academic freedom, asserting she was rejected because of her views favoring abortion. Defendant's motion for summary judgment on the Title VII count was granted because plaintiff's own submissions indicated that the motivating factor behind her rejection was not gender but her public statements regarding abortion. The district court went on to decide the state law claim on the merits.

On appeal, the Seventh Circuit reversed. Citing *Gibbs*, the court ruled that "[w]hen, as here, the federal claim is dismissed *before* trial, the district court should relinquish jurisdiction of any pendent state law claim unless there is some independent basis of federal jurisdiction." 814 F.2d at 1218 (emphasis added). As another court put it, "[w]here the federal element which is the basis for jurisdiction is disposed of early in the case, as on the pleadings, it smacks of the tail wagging the dog to continue with a federal hearing of the state claim." *McFaddin Express, Inc. v. Adley Corp.*, 346 F.2d 424, 427 (2d Cir. 1965).

\* \* \*

Just as *pendent jurisdiction* stretches a federal court's authority over a federal claim to encompass a state law claim arising from the same facts, *ancillary jurisdiction* expands the authority of a federal court entertaining a diversity action, as explored in the next case.

## ■ OWEN EQUIPMENT AND ERECTION COMPANY v. KROGER
*437 U.S. 365 (1978)*

Justice STEWART delivered the opinion of the Court:

In an action in which federal jurisdiction is based on diversity of citizenship, may the plaintiff assert a claim against a third-party defendant when there is no independent basis for federal jurisdiction over that claim? The Court of Appeals for the Eighth Circuit held in this case that such a claim is within the ancillary jurisdiction of the federal courts. We granted *certiorari* because this decision conflicts with several recent decisions of other Courts of Appeals.

### I

On January 18, 1972, James Kroger was electrocuted when the boom of a steel crane next to which he was walking came too close to a high-tension electric power line. The respondent (his widow, who is the administratrix of his estate) filed a wrongful-death action in the United States District Court for the District of Nebraska against the Omaha Public Power District (OPPD). Her complaint alleged that OPPD's negligent construction, maintenance, and operation of the power line had caused Kroger's death. Federal jurisdiction was based on diversity of citizenship, since the respondent was a citizen of Iowa and OPPD was a Nebraska corporation.

OPPD then filed a third-party complaint pursuant to Fed. Rule Civ. Proc. 14(a) against the petitioner, Owen Equipment and Erection Co. (Owen), alleging that the crane was owned and operated by Owen, and that Owen's negligence had been the proximate cause of Kroger's death.[3] OPPD later moved for summary judgment on the respondent's complaint against it. While this motion was pending, the respondent was granted leave to file an amended complaint naming Owen as an additional defendant. Thereafter, the District Court granted OPPD's motion for summary judgment in an

---

3. Under Rule 14(a), a third-party defendant may not be impleaded merely because he may be liable to the plaintiff. While the third-party complaint in this case alleged merely that Owen's negligence caused Kroger's death, and the basis of Owen's alleged liability to OPPD is nowhere spelled out, OPPD evidently relied upon the state common-law right of contribution among joint tortfeasors. The petitioner has never challenged the propriety of the third-party complaint as such.

unreported opinion. The case thus went to trial between the respondent and the petitioner alone.

The respondent's amended complaint alleged that Owen was "a Nebraska corporation with its principal place of business in Nebraska." Owen's answer admitted that it was "a corporation organized and existing under the laws of the State of Nebraska," and denied every other allegation of the complaint. On the third day of trial, however, it was disclosed that the petitioner's principal place of business was in Iowa, not Nebraska,[5] and that the petitioner and the respondent were thus both citizens of Iowa.[6] The petitioner then moved to dismiss the complaint for lack of jurisdiction. The District Court reserved decision on the motion, and the jury thereafter returned a verdict in favor of the respondent. In an unreported opinion issued after the trial, the District Court denied the petitioner's motion to dismiss the complaint.

The judgment was affirmed on appeal. The Court of Appeals held that under this Court's decision in *Mine Workers v. Gibbs*, 383 U.S. 715, the District Court had jurisdictional power, in its discretion, to adjudicate the respondent's claim against the petitioner because that claim arose from the "core of 'operative facts' giving rise to both [respondent's] claim against OPPD and OPPD's claim against Owen." It further held that the District Court had properly exercised its discretion in proceeding to decide the case even after summary judgment had been granted to OPPD, because the petitioner had concealed its Iowa citizenship from the respondent. Rehearing en banc was denied by an equally divided court.

## II

It is undisputed that there was no independent basis of federal jurisdiction over the respondent's state-law tort action against the petitioner, since both are citizens of Iowa. And although Fed. Rule Civ. Proc. 14(a) permits a plaintiff to assert a claim against a third-party defendant, it does not purport to say whether or not such a claim requires an independent basis of federal jurisdiction. Indeed, it could not determine that question, since it is axiomatic that the Federal Rules of Civil Procedure do not create or withdraw federal jurisdiction. Fed. Rule Civ. Proc. 82.

In affirming the District Court's judgment, the Court of Appeals relied upon the doctrine of ancillary jurisdiction, whose contours it believed were defined by this Court's holding in *Mine Workers v. Gibbs*, *supra*. The *Gibbs* case differed from this one in that it involved pendent jurisdiction, which concerns the resolution of a plaintiff's federal- and state-law claims against a single defendant in one action. By contrast, in this case there was no claim based upon

5. The problem apparently was one of geography. Although the Missouri River generally marks the boundary between Iowa and Nebraska, Carter Lake, Iowa, where the accident occurred and where Owen had its main office, lies west of the river, adjacent to Omaha, Neb. Apparently the river once avulsed at one of its bends, cutting Carter Lake off from the rest of Iowa.

6. Title 28 U.S.C. § 1332(c) provides that "[f]or the purposes of [diversity jurisdiction] . . . , a corporation shall be deemed a citizen of any State by which it has been incorporated and of the State where it has its principal place of business."

substantive federal law, but rather state-law tort claims against two different defendants. Nonetheless, the Court of Appeals was correct in perceiving that *Gibbs* and this case are two species of the same generic problem: Under what circumstances may a federal court hear and decide a state-law claim arising between citizens of the same state? But we believe that the Court of Appeals failed to understand the scope of the doctrine of the *Gibbs* case.

The plaintiff in *Gibbs* alleged that the defendant union had violated the common law of Tennessee as well as the federal prohibition of secondary boycotts. This Court held that, although the parties were not of diverse citizenship, the District Court properly entertained the state-law claim as pendent to the federal claim. The crucial holding was stated as follows:

> Pendent jurisdiction, in the sense of judicial power, exists whenever there is a claim "arising under [the] Constitution, the Laws of the United States, and Treaties made, or which shall be made, under their Authority. . . ." U.S. Const., Art. III, § 2, and the relationship between that claim and the state claim permits the conclusion that the entire action before the court comprises but one constitutional "case." . . . The state and federal claims must derive from a common nucleus of operative fact. But if, considered without regard to their federal or state character, a plaintiff's claims are such that he would ordinarily be expected to try them all in one judicial proceeding, then, assuming substantiality of the federal issues, there is power in federal courts to hear the whole.

It is apparent that *Gibbs* delineated the constitutional limits of federal judicial power. But even if it be assumed that the District Court in the present case had constitutional power to decide the respondent's lawsuit against the petitioner,[10] it does not follow that the decision of the Court of Appeals was correct. Constitutional power is merely the first hurdle that must be overcome in determining that a federal court has jurisdiction over a particular controversy. For the jurisdiction of the federal courts is limited not only by the provisions of Art. III of the Constitution, but also by Acts of Congress.

[S]tatutory law as well as the Constitution may limit a federal court's jurisdiction over nonfederal claims. . . . [Thus] a finding that federal and nonfederal claims arise from a "common nucleus of operative fact," the test of *Gibbs*, does not end the inquiry into whether a federal court has power to hear the nonfederal claims along with the federal ones. Beyond this constitutional minimum, there must be an examination of the posture in which the nonfederal claim is asserted and of the specific statute that confers jurisdiction over the federal claim, in order to determine whether "Congress in [that statute] has . . . expressly or by implication negated" the exercise of jurisdiction over the particular nonfederal claim.

---

10. Federal jurisdiction in *Gibbs* was based upon the existence of a question of federal law. The Court of Appeals in the present case believed that the "common nucleus of operative fact" test also determines the outer boundaries of constitutionally permissible federal jurisdiction when that jurisdiction is based upon diversity of citizenship. We may assume without deciding that the Court of Appeals was correct in this regard.

## III

The relevant statute in this case, 28 U.S.C. § 1332(a)(1), confers upon federal courts jurisdiction over "civil actions where the matter in controversy exceeds the sum or value of $10,000* . . . and is between . . . citizens of different States." This statute and its predecessors have consistently been held to require complete diversity of citizenship.[13] That is, diversity jurisdiction does not exist unless each defendant is a citizen of a different state from each plaintiff. Over the years Congress has repeatedly re-enacted or amended the statute conferring diversity jurisdiction, leaving intact this rule of complete diversity. Whatever may have been the original purposes of diversity-of-citizenship jurisdiction, this subsequent history clearly demonstrates a congressional mandate that diversity jurisdiction is not to be available when any plaintiff is a citizen of the same state as any defendant.

Thus it is clear that the respondent could not originally have brought suit in federal court naming Owen and OPPD as co-defendants, since citizens of Iowa would have been on both sides of the litigation. Yet the identical lawsuit resulted when she amended her complaint. Complete diversity was destroyed just as surely as if she had sued Owen initially. In either situation, in the plain language of the statute, the "matter in controversy" could not be "between . . . citizens of different States."

It is a fundamental precept that federal courts are courts of limited jurisdiction. The limits upon federal jurisdiction, whether imposed by the Constitution or by Congress, must be neither disregarded nor evaded. Yet under the reasoning of the Court of Appeals in this case, a plaintiff could defeat the statutory requirement of complete diversity by the simple expedient of suing only those defendants who were of diverse citizenship and waiting for them to implead nondiverse defendants.[17] If, as the Court of Appeals thought, a "common nucleus of operative fact" were the only requirement for ancillary jurisdiction in a diversity case, there would be no principled reason why the respondent in this case could not have joined her cause of action against Owen in her original complaint as ancillary to her claim against OPPD. Congress' requirement of complete diversity would thus have been evaded completely.

It is true, as the Court of Appeals noted, that the exercise of ancillary jurisdiction over nonfederal claims has often been upheld in situations

---

*Eds. Note:* In the original Judiciary Act of 1789, the amount in controversy requirement was $500. It was raised to $2,000 in 1887, to $3,000 in 1911, to $10,000 in 1958, to $50,000 in 1988, and to the current $75,000 in 1996.

13. *E.g., Strawbridge v. Curtiss*, 3 Cranch 267. It is settled that complete diversity is not a constitutional requirement. *State Farm Fire & Cas. Co. v. Tashire*, 386 U.S. 523.

17. This is not an unlikely hypothesis, since a defendant in a tort suit such as this one would surely try to limit his liability by impleading any joint tortfeasors for indemnity or contribution. Some commentators have suggested that the possible abuse of third-party practice could be dealt with under 28 U.S.C. § 1359, which forbids collusive attempts to create federal jurisdiction. The dissenting opinion today also expresses this view. But there is nothing necessarily collusive about a plaintiff's selectively suing only those tortfeasors of diverse citizenship, or about the named defendants' desire to implead joint tortfeasors. Nonetheless, the requirement of complete diversity would be eviscerated by such a course of events.

involving impleader, cross-claims or counterclaims. But in determining whether jurisdiction over a nonfederal claim exists, the context in which the nonfederal claim is asserted is crucial. And the claim here arises in a setting quite different from the kinds of nonfederal claims that have been viewed in other cases as falling within the ancillary jurisdiction of the federal courts.

First, the nonfederal claim in this case was simply not ancillary to the federal one in the same sense that, for example, the impleader by a defendant of a third-party defendant always is. A third-party complaint depends at least in part upon the resolution of the primary lawsuit. Its relation to the original complaint is thus not mere factual similarity but logical dependence. The respondent's claim against the petitioner, however, was entirely separate from her original claim against OPPD, since the petitioner's liability to her depended not at all upon whether or not OPPD was also liable. Far from being an ancillary and dependent claim, it was a new and independent one.

Second, the nonfederal claim here was asserted by the plaintiff, who voluntarily chose to bring suit upon a state-law claim in a federal court. By contrast, ancillary jurisdiction typically involves claims by a defending party haled into court against his will, or by another person whose rights might be irretrievably lost unless he could assert them in an ongoing action in a federal court. A plaintiff cannot complain if ancillary jurisdiction does not encompass all of his possible claims in a case such as this one, since it is he who has chosen the federal rather than the state forum and must thus accept its limitations. "[T]he efficiency plaintiff seeks so avidly is available without question in the state courts."

It is not unreasonable to assume that, in generally requiring complete diversity, Congress did not intend to confine the jurisdiction of federal courts so inflexibly that they are unable to protect legal rights or effectively to resolve an entire, logically entwined lawsuit. Those practical needs are the basis of the doctrine of ancillary jurisdiction. But neither the convenience of litigants nor considerations of judicial economy can suffice to justify extension of the doctrine of ancillary jurisdiction to a plaintiff's cause of action against a citizen of the same State in a diversity case. Congress has established the basic rule that diversity jurisdiction exists under 28 U.S.C. § 1332 only when there is complete diversity of citizenship. The policy of the statute calls for its strict construction. To allow the requirement of complete diversity to be circumvented as it was in this case would simply flout the congressional command.

Accordingly, the judgment of the Court of Appeals is reversed.

[Dissenting opinion of Justices WHITE and BRENNAN omitted.]

## Comments and Questions

1. Under the doctrine of ancillary jurisdiction, it had long been recognized that a federal district court could entertain an impleader against a third-

party defendant even though addition of that party defeats complete diversity. In a products liability action against a dealership that allegedly sold a defective automobile to the injured plaintiff, the dealer may implead the manufacturer asserting a "claim over" ("is or may be liable" for all or part of plaintiff's claim against the original defendant) despite the fact that the third-party defendant shares citizenship with either defendant or plaintiff. The rationale is that consolidation of the main and ancillary claims fosters judicial efficiency and avoids inconsistent results. Otherwise, the original defendant would have to seek contribution in a separate state proceeding following the federal litigation.

Ancillary jurisdiction has been available as well to accommodate compulsory counterclaims (Fed. R. Civ. P. 13(a)), cross-claims (Fed. R. Civ. P. 13(g)), and interventions (Fed. R. Civ. P. 24(a)). Can you see why?

2. How does *Owen Equipment Co. v. Kroger* distinguish the assertion of jurisdiction over plaintiff's claim against Owen Equipment from the well-established authority to entertain the original defendant's (OPPD's) impleader against Owen? What is the rationale for drawing the line here?

3. Given the Court's logic, would it have made a difference to the result if Kroger's original claim against OPPD had *not* been dismissed on summary judgment?

\* \* \*

*Pendent jurisdiction* permits a federal court to entertain a related state law claim against a party already answering a federal claim. *Ancillary jurisdiction* permits the court to hear a related claim against a party impleaded by an original defendant. The following case involves a hybrid of the two, referred to as *pendent party* jurisdiction.

## ■ FINLEY v. UNITED STATES
### *490 U.S. 545 (1989)*

Justice SCALIA delivered the opinion of the Court:

On the night of November 11, 1983, a twin-engine plane carrying petitioner's husband and two of her children struck electric transmission lines during its approach to a San Diego, California, airfield. No one survived the resulting crash. Petitioner brought a tort action in state court, claiming that San Diego Gas and Electric Company had negligently positioned and inadequately illuminated the transmission lines, and that the city of San Diego's negligent maintenance of the airport's runway lights had rendered them inoperative the night of the crash. When she later discovered that the Federal Aviation Administration (FAA) was in fact the party responsible for the runway lights, petitioner filed the present action against the United States in the United States District Court for the Southern District of California. The complaint based jurisdiction upon the Federal Tort Claims Act (FTCA), 28 U.S.C. § 1346(b), alleging negligence in the FAA's operation and maintenance of the runway lights and performance of air traffic control functions. Almost a year later, she moved to amend the federal complaint to include claims against the original state-court defendants, as to which no independent basis for federal jurisdiction existed. The District Court granted petitioner's motion and asserted "pendent" jurisdiction under *Mine Workers v. Gibbs*, 383 U.S. 715 (1966), finding it "clear" that "judicial economy and efficiency" favored trying the actions together, and concluding that they arose "from a common nucleus of operative facts." The District Court certified an interlocutory appeal to the Court of Appeals for the Ninth Circuit under 28 U.S.C. § 1292(b). That court summarily reversed . . . , categorically reject[ing] pendent-party jurisdiction under the FTCA. We granted *certiorari* to resolve a split among the Circuits on whether the FTCA permits an assertion of pendent jurisdiction over additional parties.

The FTCA provides that "the district courts . . . shall have exclusive jurisdiction of civil actions on claims against the United States" for certain torts of federal employees acting within the scope of their employment. 28 U.S.C. § 1346(b). Petitioner seeks to append her claims against the city and the utility to her FTCA action against the United States, even though this would require the District Court to extend its authority to additional parties for whom an independent jurisdictional base—such as diversity of citizenship, 28 U.S.C. § 1332(a)(1)—is lacking.

In 1807 Chief Justice Marshall wrote for the Court that "courts which are created by written law, and whose jurisdiction is defined by written law, cannot transcend that jurisdiction." . . . It remains rudimentary law that "[a]s regards all courts of the United States inferior to this tribunal, two things are necessary to create jurisdiction, whether original or appellate. The Constitution must have given to the court the capacity to take it, and an act of Congress must have supplied it. . . . To the extent that such action is not taken, the power lies dormant."

Despite this principle, in a line of cases by now no less well established we have held, without specific examination of jurisdictional statutes, that federal courts have "pendent" claim jurisdiction—that is, jurisdiction over nonfederal claims between parties litigating other matters properly before the court—to the full extent permitted by the Constitution. *Mine Workers v. Gibbs*, which has come to stand for the principle in question, held that "[p]endent jurisdiction, in the sense of judicial power, exists whenever there is a claim 'arising under [the] Constitution, the Laws of the United States, and Treaties made, or which shall be made, under their Authority . . . ,' U.S. Const., Art. III, § 2, and the relationship between that claim and the state claim permits the conclusion that the entire action before the court comprises but one constitutional 'case.'" The requisite relationship exists, *Gibbs* said, when the federal and nonfederal claims "derive from a common nucleus of operative fact" and are such that a plaintiff "would ordinarily be expected to try them in one judicial proceeding." Petitioner contends that the same criterion applies here, leading to the result that her state-law claims against San Diego Gas and Electric Company and the city of San Diego may be heard in conjunction with her FTCA action against the United States.

Analytically, petitioner's case is fundamentally different from *Gibbs* in that it brings into question what has become known as pendent-party jurisdiction, that is, jurisdiction over parties not named in any claim that is independently cognizable by the federal court. We may assume, without deciding, that the constitutional criterion for pendent-party jurisdiction is analogous to the constitutional criterion for pendent-claim jurisdiction, and that petitioner's state-law claims pass that test. Our cases show, however, that with respect to the addition of parties, as opposed to the addition of only claims, we will not assume that the full constitutional power has been congressionally authorized, and will not read jurisdictional statutes broadly. . . .

[I]n *Owen Equipment & Erection Co. v. Kroger*, we held that the jurisdiction which § 1332(a)(1) confers over a "matter in controversy" between a plaintiff and defendant of diverse citizenship cannot be read to confer pendent jurisdiction over a different, nondiverse defendant, even if the claim involving that other defendant meets the *Gibbs* test. "*Gibbs*," we said, "does not end the inquiry into whether a federal court has power to hear the nonfederal claims along with the federal ones. Beyond this constitutional minimum, there must be an examination of the posture in which the non-federal claim is asserted and of the specific statute that confers jurisdiction over the federal claim."

The most significant element of "posture" or of "context" in the present case . . . is precisely that the added claims involve added parties over whom no independent basis of jurisdiction exists. While in a narrow class of cases a federal court may assert authority over such a claim "ancillary" to jurisdiction otherwise properly vested . . . we have never reached such a result solely on the basis that the *Gibbs* test has been met. And little more basis than that can be relied upon by petitioner here. As in *Kroger*, the relationship between petitioner's added claims and the original complaint is one of "mere factual similarity," which is of no consequence since "neither the convenience of the litigants nor considerations of judicial economy can suffice to justify extension of the doctrine of ancillary jurisdiction." It is true that here, unlike in *Kroger*, the party seeking to bring the added claims had little choice but to be in federal rather than state court, since the FTCA permits the Federal Government to be sued only there. But that alone is not enough. . . .

The second factor invoked by *Kroger*, the text of the jurisdictional statute at issue, likewise fails to establish petitioner's case. The FTCA, § 1346(b), confers jurisdiction over "civil actions on claims against the United States." It does not say "civil actions on claims that include requested relief against the United States," nor "civil actions in which there is a claim against the United States"—formulations one might expect if the presence of a claim against the United States constituted merely a minimum jurisdictional requirement, rather than a definition of the permissible scope of FTCA actions. Just as the statutory provision "between . . . citizens of different States" has been held to mean citizens of different states and no one else, so also here we conclude that "against the United States" means against the United States and no one else. "Due regard for the rightful independence of state governments . . . requires that [federal courts] scrupulously confine their own jurisdiction to the precise limits which the statute has defined." The statute here defines jurisdiction in a manner that does not reach defendants other than the United States. . . .

Because the FTCA permits the Government to be sued only in federal court, our holding that parties to related claims cannot necessarily be sued there means that the efficiency and convenience of a consolidated action will sometimes have to be forgone in favor of separate actions in state and federal courts. . . . [T]he present statute permits no other result. . . .

For the foregoing reasons, the judgment of the Court of Appeals is Affirmed.

Justice BLACKMUN, dissenting:

. . . Where, as here, Congress' preference for a federal forum for a certain category of claims makes the federal forum the only possible one in which the constitutional case may be heard as a whole, the sensible result is to permit the exercise of pendent-party jurisdiction. . . . I therefore dissent.

Justice STEVENS, with whom Justice BRENNAN and Justice MARSHALL join, dissenting:

The Court's holding is not faithful to our precedents and casually dismisses the accumulated wisdom of our best judges. As we observed more than 16 years ago, "numerous decisions throughout the courts of appeals since [*Mine Workers v. Gibbs*, 383 U.S. 715 (1966),] have recognized the existence of judicial power to hear pendent claims involving pendent parties where 'the entire action before the court comprises but one constitutional case' as defined in *Gibbs*." . . .

I would thus hold that the grant of jurisdiction to hear "civil actions on claims against the United States" authorizes the federal courts to hear state-law claims against a pendent party. [T]he fact that such claims are within the exclusive federal jurisdiction, together with the absence of any evidence of congressional disapproval of the exercise of pendent-party jurisdiction in FTCA cases, provides a fully sufficient justification for applying the holding in *Gibbs* to this case. . . .

The doctrine of pendent jurisdiction rests in part on a recognition that forcing a federal plaintiff to litigate his or her case in both federal and state courts impairs the ability of the federal court to grant full relief, and "imparts a fundamental bias against utilization of the federal forum owing to the deterrent effect imposed by the needless requirement of duplicate litigation if the federal forum is chosen." "The courts, by recognizing pendent jurisdiction, are effectuating Congress' decision to provide the plaintiff with a federal forum for litigating a jurisdictionally sufficient claim." This is especially the case when, by virtue of the grant of exclusive federal jurisdiction, "only in a federal court may all of the claims be tried together." In such circumstances, in which Congress has unequivocally indicated its intent that the federal right be litigated in a federal forum, there is reason to believe that Congress did not intend that the substance of the federal right be diminished by the increased costs in efficiency and convenience of litigation in two forums. No such special federal interest is present when federal jurisdiction is invoked on the basis of the diverse citizenship of the parties and the state-law claims may be litigated in a state forum.

I respectfully dissent.

\* \* \*

## The Supplemental Jurisdiction Statute:
## 28 U.S.C. § 1367

In response to *Finley*, Congress enacted 28 U.S.C. § 1367:

(a) Except as provided in subsections (b) and (c) or as expressly provided otherwise by Federal statute, in any civil action of which the district courts have original jurisdiction, the district courts shall have supplemental jurisdiction over all other claims that are so related to claims in the action within such original jurisdiction that they form part of the same case or controversy under Article III of the United States Constitution. Such supplemental jurisdiction shall include claims that involve the joinder or intervention of additional parties.

(b) In any civil action of which the district courts have original jurisdiction founded solely on section 1332 of this title, the district courts shall not have supplemental jurisdiction under subsection (a) over claims by plaintiffs against persons made parties under Rule 14, 19, 20, or 24 of the Federal Rules of Civil Procedure, or over claims by persons proposed to be joined as plaintiffs under Rule 19 of such rules, or seeking to intervene as plaintiffs under Rule 24 of such rules, when exercising supplemental jurisdiction over such claims would be inconsistent with the jurisdictional requirements of section 1332.

(c) The district courts may decline to exercise supplemental jurisdiction over a claim under subsection (a) if:

(1) the claim raises a novel or complex issue of State law,

(2) the claim substantially predominates over the claim or claims over which the district court has original jurisdiction,

(3) the district court has dismissed all claims over which it has original jurisdiction, or

(4) in exceptional circumstances, there are other compelling reasons for declining jurisdiction.

(d) The period of limitations for any claim asserted under subsection (a), and for any other claim in the same action that is voluntarily dismissed at the same time as or after the dismissal of the claim under subsection (a), shall be tolled while the claim is pending and for a period of 30 days after it is dismissed unless State law provides for a longer tolling period.

(e) As used in this section, the term "State" includes the District of Columbia, the Commonwealth of Puerto Rico, and any territory or possession of the United States.

The following are excerpts from the legislative history of § 1367.

# ■ HOUSE REPORT NO. 101-734

*1990 U.S. Code Congressional and Admin. News 6873*

... The doctrines of pendent and ancillary jurisdiction, in this section jointly labeled supplemental jurisdiction, refer to the authority of the federal courts to adjudicate, without an independent basis of subject matter jurisdiction, claims that are so related to other claims within the district courts' original jurisdiction that they form part of the same cases or controversy under Article III of the United States Constitution.

Supplemental jurisdiction has enabled federal courts and litigants to take advantage of the federal procedural rules on claim and party joinder to deal economically in single rather than multiple litigation with related matters, usually those arising from the same transaction, occurrence, or series of transactions or occurrences. Moreover, the district court's exercise of supplemental jurisdiction, by making federal court a practical arena for the resolution of an entire controversy, has effectuated Congress' intent in the jurisdictional statutes to provide plaintiffs with a federal forum for litigating claims within original federal jurisdiction.

Recently, however, in *Finley v. United States*, the Supreme Court cast substantial doubt on the authority of the federal courts to hear some claims within supplemental jurisdiction. In *Finley* the Court held that a district court, in a Federal Tort Claims Act suit against the United States, may not exercise supplemental jurisdiction over a related claim by the plaintiff against an additional, nondiverse defendant. The Court's rationale that "with respect to the addition of parties, as opposed to the addition of only claims, we will not assume that the full constitutional power has been congressionally authorized, and will not read jurisdictional statutes broadly," threatens to eliminate other previously accepted forms of supplemental jurisdiction. Already, for example, some lower courts have interpreted *Finley* to prohibit the exercise of supplemental jurisdiction in formerly unquestioned circumstances.

Legislation, therefore, is needed to provide the federal courts with statutory authority to hear supplemental claims. Indeed, the Supreme Court has virtually invited Congress to codify supplemental jurisdiction by commenting in *Finley*, "Whatever we say regarding the scope of jurisdiction ... can of course be changed by Congress. What is of paramount importance is that Congress be able to legislate against a background of clear interpretive rules, so that it may know the effect of the language it adopts." This section would authorize jurisdiction in a case like *Finley*, as well as essentially restore the pre-*Finley* understandings of the authorization for and limits on other forms of supplemental jurisdiction. In federal-question cases, it broadly authorizes the district courts to exercise supplemental jurisdiction over additional claims, including claims involving the joinder of additional parties. In diversity cases, the district courts may exercise supplemental jurisdiction, except when doing so would be inconsistent with the jurisdictional requirements of the diversity statute. In both cases, the district courts,

as under current law, would have discretion to decline supplemental jurisdiction in appropriate circumstances.

[Section 1367(a)] generally authorizes the district court to exercise jurisdiction over a supplemental claim whenever it forms part of the same
constitutional case or controversy as the claim or claims that provide the
basis of the district court's original jurisdiction. In providing for supplemental jurisdiction over claims involving the addition of parties, subsection
(a) explicitly fills the statutory gap noted in *Finley v. United States*.

[Section 1367(b)] prohibits a district court in a case over which it has
jurisdiction founded solely on the general diversity provision, 28 U.S.C.
§ 1332, from exercising supplemental jurisdiction in specified circumstances.
In diversity-only actions the district courts may not hear plaintiffs'
supplemental claims when exercising supplemental jurisdiction would
encourage plaintiffs to evade the jurisdictional requirement of 28 U.S.C.
§ 1332 by the simple expedient of naming initially only those defendants
whose joinder satisfies § 1332's requirements and later adding claims not
within original federal jurisdiction against other defendants who have intervened or been joined on a supplemental basis. In accord with case law, the
subsection also prohibits the joinder or intervention of persons and plaintiffs
if adding them is inconsistent with § 1332's requirements. . . .

[Section 1367(c)] codifies the factors that the Supreme Court has recognized as providing legitimate bases upon which a district court may decline
jurisdiction over a supplemental claim, even though it is empowered to hear
the claim. Subsection (c)(1)-(3) codifies the factors recognized as relevant
under current law. Subsection (c)(4) acknowledges that occasionally there
may exist other compelling reasons for a district court to decline
supplemental jurisdiction, which the subsection does not foreclose a court
from considering in exceptional circumstances. As under current law, subsection (c) requires the district court, in exercising its discretion, to undertake
a case-specific analysis. . . .

[Section 1367(d)] provides a period of tolling of statutes of limitations for
any supplemental claim that is dismissed under this section and for any other
claims in the same action voluntarily dismissed at the same time or after the
supplemental claim is dismissed. The purpose is to prevent the loss of claims
to statutes of limitations where state law might fail to toll the running of the
period of limitations while a supplemental claim was pending in federal
court. It also eliminates a possible disincentive from such a gap in tolling
when a plaintiff might wish to seek voluntary dismissal of other claims in
order to pursue an entire matter in state court when a federal court dismisses
a supplemental claim.

## Comments and Questions

1. House Report No. 101-734 notes elsewhere that "§ 1367 subsection (a)
codifies the scope of supplemental jurisdiction first articulated by the

Supreme Court in *United Mine Workers v. Gibbs*," and the "net effect of sub-section (b) is to implement the principal rationale of *Owen Equipment & Erection Co.*" Can you identify the precise language that accomplishes these results? What precise language overturns *Finley*? How might you improve the drafting of § 1367 to achieve its stated purposes more clearly?

2. David D. Siegel in a commentary on an earlier version of § 1367 observed that since pendent and ancillary jurisdiction "have been brought under the single caption of 'supplemental jurisdiction,' there is probably no need to draw a line between them at all." But are there not some significant lingering differences between the two in §§ 1367(a) and (b)?

3. The language in § 1367(a) referring to claims so related that "they form part of the same case or controversy under Article III" codifies the *Gibbs* concept of federal and nonfederal claims deriving from "a common nucleus of operative fact." How broad is this concept? Consider the following hypothetical offered by Professor Martin Redish in a related context:

> [A]ssume a traffic accident, followed by a fist fight between the drivers. Driver A sues driver B for negligence in causing the accident; driver B counterclaims for battery arising out of the postaccident fight. On a purely linguistic or con-ceptual level, these two incidents could be characterized as either being part of the same occurrence or not. Courts that define the phrase in terms of eviden-tiary overlap would probably decline to find these incidents to be part of the same occurrence, because there likely will be little, if any, evidentiary overlap. Yet courts that define the phrase in terms of the broader concept of "logical relationship" would quite probably find that the incidents are, in fact, part of the same occurrence.

Martin Redish, *Reassessing the Allocation of Judicial Business Between State and Federal Courts: Federal Jurisdiction and the "Martian Chronicles,"* 78 Va. L. Rev. 1769, 1822-1823 (1992). Given the policy underlying § 1367, which approach makes more sense? The problem of defining "same transaction or occurrence" is familiar to us from our look at joinder in Chapter 3, and will be encountered again with regard to the doctrine of finality in Chapter 10.

4. Plaintiffs in *Raygor v. Regents of University of Minnesota*, 534 U.S. 533 (2002), alleged in federal court that the state university had violated their rights under the Age Discrimination in Employment Act (ADEA) by forcing their early retirement. They also asserted a related state law claim under § 1367. The case was dismissed as barred by the Eleventh Amendment, which has been read to provide sovereign immunity to states from certain litigation in federal court. When plaintiffs refiled their state claims in state court, the statute of limitations had run and they sought to rely on § 1367(d), the so-called savings clause. The Court refused to apply that section to cases dis-missed on Eleventh Amendment grounds, as to do so would in its view intrude on the state's immunity. *But compare Jinks v. Richland County, South Caro-lina*, 538 U.S. 456 (2003) (holding that § 1367(d) can constitutionally be applied to lawsuits against a state's political subdivisions).

5. As noted earlier in Part C, § 1367 provides access to a federal forum for diversity cases in which joined plaintiffs lack the requisite amount-in-controversy provided *at least one plaintiff* satisfies it (and complete diversity is intact). *Exxon Mobil Corp. v. Allapattah Services, Inc.*, 545 U.S. 546 (2005).

## Practice Exercise No. 36: Challenging Subject Matter Jurisdiction in *City of Cleveland*

Review the complaint in the *City of Cleveland* case. Assume that the plaintiffs' case survived all pre-trial challenges and has gone to trial. At the close of the evidence the case went to the jury, which is in the midst of deliberating. Counsel for the City has now appeared in court with a motion to dismiss the Ohio civil service fraud count for lack of subject matter jurisdiction. Please prepare for an argument on the motion. Students with last names beginning with A-M represent the defendant City; all others represent the plaintiffs in opposition.

## Practice Exercise No. 37: Challenging Subject Matter Jurisdiction in *Carpenter*

Review the amended complaint and third-party complaints in the *Carpenter* case. Assume for purposes of this exercise that Nancy Carpenter has always resided in New Hampshire and that her action is filed in federal district court in Massachusetts. She sues Dee and Ultimate Auto, both Massachusetts citizens; Ultimate has impleaded McGill's Garage, also a Massachusetts corporation, and its sole owner, Dale McGill, a citizen of New Hampshire.

Nancy now seeks to amend her complaint to sue the Garage and McGill directly. The latter two parties have moved to dismiss both Ultimate's and Carpenter's claims for lack of subject matter jurisdiction. Students with last names beginning with A-F represent the Garage and McGill; G-M represent Ultimate Auto; and N-Z represent Nancy Carpenter in opposition to the motion.

## E. REMOVAL

As we have seen, federal and state courts overlap considerably in their jurisdictional authority. Plaintiffs have the initial choice of federal or state court in federal question and diversity cases. If a plaintiff with such a choice opts for the state court, defendant may usually remove to federal court under 28 U.S.C. § 1441. We say "usually" because the defendant's right to remove to federal court is not completely coextensive with the plaintiff's right to initially choose the federal forum. Read § 1441(b)(2). As the Supreme Court observed recently, the "scales are not evenly balanced" as an in-state plaintiff may invoke diversity jurisdiction but an in-state defendant may not. *Lincoln Property Co. v. Roche*, 546 U.S. 81 (2005). Why would Congress withhold the federal court option from a defendant sued in a diversity case in his home state? (Does Congress similarly withhold the federal court option from a plaintiff suing in a diversity case in her home state?)

A defendant who wants to remove an action from state to federal court does not make a motion. Rather, 28 U.S.C. § 1446(a) explains that the defendant simply files a notice of removal in the federal district embracing the place where the state action is pending. If removal is improper (i.e., if the federal court does not have jurisdiction), the plaintiff should file a motion to *remand* the case back to state court. 28 U.S.C. § 1447(c). Many of the cases discussed in the preceding federal question section arose in the context of removal. Sometimes plaintiffs are trying to establish federal subject matter jurisdiction; and sometimes they are trying to avoid it.

Next, notice the timing requirement for removal. 28 U.S.C. § 1446(b). Defendants must remove the action before the thirty-day window closes. In the ordinary case, the thirty days begins to run from service of the complaint. Accordingly, if there is federal question or diversity jurisdiction, the defendant must act promptly if he wishes to invoke the federal forum. Occasionally, a case that was not removable at the time that the complaint was served will become removable by subsequent events: a non-diverse party may be dropped or a federal cause of action may be added. 28 U.S.C. § 1446(b)(3). If the changed circumstance creates diversity jurisdiction, a thirty-day window opens, *provided* the removal occurs within one year of the commencement of the action; after one year, the action simply is not removable absent bad faith on the part of the plaintiff. See 28 U.S.C. § 1446(c)(1). If the changed circumstance creates federal question jurisdiction, however, a thirty-day window opens no matter how much time has passed since the commencement of the action.

Another important technical requirement of removal practice regards cases where there is more than one defendant. When more than one defendant is joined in the action, *all* must join in the notice of removal. 28 U.S.C. § 1446(b)(2)(A). Absent unanimity among the defendants about exercising the right to remove, then, the action will not be removed. There is one narrow exception to this rule about unanimity. 28 U.S.C. § 1441(c)(2). The exception regards situations where a civil action includes both removable and nonremovable claims. And that is a phenomenon that we still need to address.

Occasionally a case will include some claims that are removable and some that are not. Consider, for example, a Kansas plaintiff who has two causes of action against a Kansas defendant—the first cause of action is a federal claim, and the second cause of action is an unrelated state law claim. When plaintiff files this action in state court, defendant might, for strategic reasons, prefer that the action be litigated in a federal court. But is this lawsuit removable to federal court?

The analysis of removability begins with 28 U.S.C. § 1441(a). Could a federal court have exercised original subject matter jurisdiction over this action? Although a federal court would have federal question subject matter jurisdiction over the count that raises the federal cause of action, the court would not have subject matter jurisdiction over the state law claim. This second cause of action is not a federal question, and there is no diversity between the parties. Nor would there be supplemental jurisdiction over the state law claim under 28 U.S.C. § 1367, because we are told that this claim is *unrelated* to the federal question. (Remember 28 U.S.C. § 1367(a).) So a federal court would not have had original jurisdiction over the entire civil action.

But when a claim includes both a removable (federal question) claim and a non-removable (state law) claim, 28 U.S.C. § 1441(c) provides important guidance. The statutory schema contemplates that the entire action should be removed, the non-removable claims severed, and those non-removable claims remanded to the state court. In our hypothetical, then, if the Kansas defendant timely elects to remove the case, the federal question claim will be litigated in federal court, and the state law claim in state court.

Now consider two variations of that hypothetical. (1) Everything in the hypothetical stays the same except that the state law claim is *related* to the federal question claim. Is this removable? (2) Everything in the hypothetical stays the same (including that the state law claim is *unrelated* to the federal question) except that the state law claim is asserted against the Kansas defendant and also a Missouri defendant). Is this removable?

## Comments and Questions

1. Think about the strategy and ethics of drafting a complaint to invoke or to avoid federal jurisdiction. Occasionally state law will provide more protection in a particular context than will federal law. Imagine, for example, a state law that provides more protection than Title VII in the context of employment discrimination. Should you add a federal question under Title VII even when you don't need it just to get into federal court?

Or a plaintiff may structure her case to make it non-removable. Imagine your Texas client has a high-value products claim against a Delaware company, a manufacturer with a principal place of business in Florida. If this action is filed in state court, defendant may remove it: the amount in controversy is satisfied and there is complete diversity. Should you add a Texas defendant—say, the seller of the product—even though the substantive claim against the Texas defendant is weaker and even though you know that the Texas defendant is not able to pay any judgment even if you were able to recover?

Revisit the facts in *World-Wide Volkswagen* (from Chapter 7). What was the plaintiffs' domicile? And what were the states of citizenship of the various defendants? Were the plaintiffs pursuing federal or state law causes of action? Was the case removable? Would the case have been removable if World-Wide Volkswagen and Seaway were not named as additional defendants? Would the case have been removable if World-Wide Volkswagen and Seaway were dismissed for lack of personal jurisdiction?

2. We have focused only on the general removal provisions of the Code. We do not address specialized provisions for specific cases such as cases involving suits against federal officers, 28 U.S.C. § 1442, or torts by federal employees, 28 U.S.C. § 2679(d). Further, new removal provisions have been added by CAFA and MMTJA, which are mentioned again in Chapter 11.

3. The *Mottley* rule regarding what constitutes a federal question claim also controls in the context of removal jurisdiction. *See Oklahoma Tax Commission v. Graham*, 489 U.S. 838 (1989) (possible existence of tribal sovereign immunity defense did not convert state tax claims into federal questions). One exception applies when a federal statute completely preempts a state cause of action. *See Aetna Health Inc. v. Davila*, 542 U.S. 200 (2004) (state law action against HMOs [health maintenance organizations] was preempted by federal ERISA [Employee Retirement Income Security Act] law and thus removable to federal court); *Beneficial National Bank v. Anderson*, 539 U.S. 1 (2003) (defendants could remove action even though plaintiffs' complaint relied solely on state law because National Bank Act provided the exclusive remedy for their usury claims).

*[handwritten: Domicile — residency intention to remain indef.]*

### Review Exercise No. 8

*[handwritten: § 1332 • Comp. div. • + 75,000]*

You have been consulted by the Very-Clean Vacuum Company regarding the following matter. Very-Clean has been served with a summons and complaint at its headquarters in St. Louis, Missouri. The complaint reads as follows:

### UNITED STATES DISTRICT COURT
### FOR THE SOUTHERN DISTRICT OF NEW YORK

| | |
|---|---|
| Jane Whitecroft and John Whitecroft, Plaintiffs, *[handwritten: Connecticut]* v. *[handwritten: and maybe Missouri]* Very-Clean Vacuum Company, Inc., Defendants. *[handwritten: Missouri / Delaware?]* | Civil Action No. _____ COMPLAINT |

1. Plaintiffs are husband and wife and residents of the State of Connecticut. Defendant is incorporated in the State of Delaware and has its principal place of business in Missouri. The matter in controversy exceeds $75,000.

2. On April 1, 2010, plaintiffs purchased a Very-Clean Model 500V Vacuum at the Ace Discount Store in White Plains, New York.

3. Soon after purchasing the Model 500V, plaintiff John Whitecroft was vacuuming the living room in his house shared with plaintiff Jane Whitecroft. The machine suddenly emitted a large electrical spark and exploded in flames.

4. As a result, plaintiff John Whitecroft was severely burned, suffering permanent and disabling injuries. The plaintiffs' home was destroyed by fire and all their personal belongings lost in the blaze.

5. Plaintiffs allege, upon information and belief, that the fire resulted from the negligence of defendant Very-Clean Vacuum Company, Inc., in the manufacture of the Model 500V and the subsequent negligent failure to warn consumers who had purchased the machines of the immediate danger, and/or that the Model 500V was a product in a defective condition, which was unreasonably dangerous to the user.

WHEREFORE, plaintiffs pray that judgment be rendered against defendant in the amount of $6,000,000, with interest and costs, and for such other relief as may be appropriate.

/s/

Ina Jatoba
Attorney for Plaintiffs
1001 3rd Avenue
New York, New York 10022

* * *

Very-Clean's general counsel informs you that the Company is very nervous about this action, especially given the amount of damages sought. The Company has a great safety record, but he concedes there have been other reported problems with the Model 500V. Very-Clean has received letters from several other purchasers reporting electrical problems with the same model, although none has suffered the type of catastrophic injuries that the Whitecrofts allege. Several of these purchasers have also threatened suit.

Nonetheless, the Company stands behind its product. The people in engineering believe that the accidents with the Model 500V have likely resulted because the consumers have plugged the machines into two-pronged, ungrounded electrical sockets instead of the three-pronged grounded sockets recommended in the instructions.

Very-Clean has always relied upon Second-Guess Testing Labs, located nearby in St. Louis, to assure the quality of its products. Very-Clean has retained them to put each of its prospective products through a series of grueling tests prior to placing them on the market. Second-Guess reported that it had tested the Model 500V and certified its safety and dependability to Very-Clean. If there is a defect in the product, Second-Guess apparently failed to detect it.

Corporate counsel is quite surprised that the Company's products are being sold in New York, since Very-Clean distributes only to retailers in the Midwest. (At one time about fifteen years ago, when the Company was just getting started, it did ship products to stores in New York, New Jersey, and Connecticut, but discontinued such sales because they proved unprofitable, given the high transportation costs.) It appears that one of the retail stores Very-Clean distributes to in the Midwest went out of business and its inventory was acquired by Ace Discount, a national chain, which explains how the Model 500V ended up on sale in White Plains, New York.

Very-Clean has learned that Jane Whitecroft has been enrolled for the past two years as a doctoral student at Washington University in St. Louis, Missouri. She subleases an apartment near the university, which she lives in while school is in session, but spends the rest of the year with her husband in Connecticut, where she is writing her dissertation.

Corporate counsel reports that after the accident the Whitecrofts engaged in a vicious publicity campaign against Very-Clean, appearing on talk shows and news programs and characterizing the Company as recklessly disregarding the public's safety. This has significantly hurt Very-Clean's reputation and business.

The New York State long-arm statute appears in Chapter 7.

Prepare a memorandum discussing:

(1) How Very-Clean should respond to this complaint. Consider all possible procedural objections and defenses, including jurisdictional. For each, outline the manner in which it should be raised (by pleading or motion), the specific Federal Rule of Civil Procedure or other provision relied upon, and the likelihood of prevailing on the objection or defense in court. Include a list of any additional facts you may need to investigate to complete your analysis, and explain how the information would be used.

(2) What additional claims and parties should Very-Clean consider? For each, outline the manner in which it should be raised (by pleading or motion) and the specific provisions of the Federal Rules of Civil Procedure or Judicial Code relied upon. Include a discussion of the jurisdictional problems (if any) with each option.

# 9

Choice of Federal or
State Law—The Erie
Doctrine

We learned in Chapter 8 that a federal court has subject matter jurisdiction of a civil action if the claim arises under federal law (28 U.S.C. § 1331), or if the parties are of diverse citizenship (28 U.S.C. § 1332). In the former case, the law that controls the rights and obligations of the parties is obviously the federal law from which the claim arises. Thus in an action brought under the Fair Housing Act of 1968 (42 U.S.C. §§ 3601 et seq.) alleging discrimination in the rental of an apartment, the federal statute (and decisional law interpreting it) will determine the elements of the claim, the defenses available to defendant, and the remedies plaintiff may be awarded if successful in the action.

For federal diversity cases, however, the matter of what law applies perplexed the courts for many years. After all, these are state law claims being entertained by courts of a different sovereign. Does the federal district court apply state or federal law in a personal injury action between citizens of different states? Even after the Supreme Court settled this question in favor of state substantive law, it faced an even more elusive issue: Is the federal court required to conform to the *procedural* rules that the state court would apply as well?

Choice of law issues arise because a court with jurisdictional power over a case does not necessarily also have authority to apply its own law to resolve the matter. A California court may have jurisdiction over a contract action based solely on service of process on the defendant while present in that state (*see Burnham v. Superior Court* in Chapter 7). But if neither party is a forum resident and the events giving rise to the claim occurred elsewhere, would it be proper for the court to resolve the case by reference to California law of contract? What if plaintiff had "shopped" for the forum because its law is more favorable to him than the other jurisdictions more closely connected to the case?

The choice of law predicament has two dimensions in our federal system. The "vertical" choice, between federal and state law, raises fundamental issues of power-sharing and is the subject of this chapter. "Horizontal" choice issues arise when it is determined that state law applies, and the question becomes which state's law. This complex topic is covered in Conflict of Law courses and will not be treated at length here. (Note that similar choice of law problems arise in the international context, as for example between Member States in the European Union, and are often addressed by conventions and other agreements. *See* Thomas Main, *Global Issues in Civil Procedure* 166-174 (2006).)

---

As you read the landmark case below, consider how choice of law issues influenced the Pennsylvania plaintiff's strategic decision to file in federal district court in New York.

## ■ ERIE RAILROAD CO. v. TOMPKINS
### 304 U.S. 64 (1938)

Justice BRANDEIS delivered the opinion of the Court:

The question for decision is whether the oft-challenged doctrine of *Swift v. Tyson* shall now be disapproved.

Tompkins, a citizen of Pennsylvania, was injured on a dark night by a passing freight train of the Erie Railroad Company while walking along its right of way at Hughestown in that State. He claimed that the accident occurred through negligence in the operation, or maintenance, of the train; that he was rightfully on the premises as licensee because on a commonly used beaten footpath which ran for a short distance alongside the tracks; and that he was struck by something which looked like a door projecting from one of the moving cars. To enforce that claim he brought an action in the federal court for southern New York, which had jurisdiction because the company is a corporation of that State. It denied liability; and the case was tried by a jury.

The Erie insisted that its duty to Tompkins was no greater than that owed to a trespasser. It contended, among other things, that its duty to Tompkins, and hence its liability, should be determined in accordance with the Pennsylvania law; that under the law of Pennsylvania as declared by its highest court, persons who use pathways along the railroad right of way—that is a longitudinal pathway as distinguished from a crossing—are to be deemed trespassers; and that the railroad is not liable for injuries to undiscovered trespassers resulting from its negligence, unless it be wanton or wilful. Tompkins denied that any such rule had been established by the decisions of the

*Tompkins says*

Pennsylvania courts; and contended that, since there was no statute of the State on the subject, the railroad's duty and liability is to be determined in federal courts as a matter of general law.

The trial judge refused to rule that the applicable law precluded recovery. The jury brought in a verdict of $30,000; and the judgment entered thereon was affirmed by the Circuit Court of Appeals, which held that it was un- necessary to consider whether the law of Pennsylvania was as contended, because the question was one not of local, but of general, law and that "upon questions of general law the federal courts are free, in the absence of a local statute, to exercise their independent judgment as to what the law is; and it is well settled that the question of the responsibility of a railroad for injuries caused by its servants is one of general law. . . . Where the public has made open and notorious use of a railroad right of way for a long period of time and without objection, the company owes to persons on such permis- sive pathway a duty of care in the operation of its trains. . . . It is likewise generally recognized law that a jury may find that negligence exists toward a pedestrian using a permissive path on the railroad right of way if he is hit by some object projecting from the side of the train."

*NY — affirmed*

The Erie had contended that application of the Pennsylvania rule was required, among other things, by § 34 of the Federal Judiciary Act of September 24, 1789, which provides:

> The laws of the several States, except where the Constitution, treaties, or stat- utes of the United States otherwise require or provide, shall be regarded as rules of decision in trials at common law, in the courts of the United States, in cases where they apply.

*Certiori granted*

Because of the importance of the question whether the federal court was free to disregard the alleged rule of the Pennsylvania common law, we granted certiorari.

First. *Swift v. Tyson* held that federal courts exercising jurisdiction on the ground of diversity of citizenship need not, in matters of general jurispru- dence, apply the unwritten law of the State as declared by its highest court; that they are free to exercise an independent judgment as to what the common law of the State is—or should be; and that, as there stated by Mr. Justice Story:

> [T]he true interpretation of the thirty-fourth section limited its application to state laws strictly local, that is to say, to the positive statutes of the state, and the construction thereof adopted by the local tribunals, and to rights and titles to things having a permanent locality, such as the rights and titles to real estate, and other matters immovable and intraterritorial in their nature and character. It never has been supposed by us, that the section did apply, or was intended to apply, to questions of a more general nature, not at all dependent upon local statutes or local usages of a fixed and permanent operation, as, for example, to the construction of ordinary contracts or other written instruments,

and especially to questions of general commercial law, where the state tribunals are called upon to perform the like functions as ourselves, that is, to ascertain upon general reasoning and legal analogies, what is the true exposition of the contract or instrument, or what is the just rule furnished by the principles of commercial law to govern the case.

The Court in applying the rule of § 34 to equity cases, in *Mason v. United States*, said: "The statute, however, is merely declarative of the rule which would exist in the absence of the statute." The federal courts assumed, in the broad field of "general law," the power to declare rules of decision which Congress was confessedly without power to enact as statutes. Doubt was repeatedly expressed as to the correctness of the construction given § 34, and as to the soundness of the rule which it introduced. But it was the more recent research of a competent scholar, who examined the original document, which established that the construction given to it by the Court was erroneous; and that the purpose of the section was merely to make certain that, in all matters except those in which some federal law is controlling, the federal courts exercising jurisdiction in diversity of citizenship cases would apply as their rules of decision the law of the State, unwritten as well as written.[5]

Criticism of the doctrine became widespread after the decision of *Black & White Taxicab Co. v. Brown & Yellow Taxicab Co.*, 276 U.S. 518. There, Brown and Yellow, a Kentucky corporation owned by Kentuckians, and the Louisville and Nashville Railroad, also a Kentucky corporation, wished that the former should have the exclusive privilege of soliciting passenger and baggage transportation at the Bowling Green, Kentucky, railroad station; and that the Black and White, a competing Kentucky corporation, should be prevented from interfering with that privilege. Knowing that such a contract would be void under the common law of Kentucky, it was arranged that the Brown and Yellow reincorporate under the law of Tennessee, and that the contract with the railroad should be executed there. The suit was then brought by the Tennessee corporation in the federal court for western Kentucky to enjoin competition by the Black and White; an injunction issued by the District Court was sustained by the Court of Appeals; and this Court, citing many decisions in which the doctrine of *Swift v. Tyson* had been applied, affirmed the decree.

Second. Experience in applying the doctrine of *Swift v. Tyson* had revealed its defects, political and social; and the benefits expected to flow from the rule did not accrue. Persistence of state courts in their own opinions on questions of common law prevented uniformity; and the impossibility of discovering a satisfactory line of demarcation between the province of general law and that of local law developed a new well of uncertainties.

5. Charles Warren, *New Light on the History of the Federal Judiciary Act of 1789*, 37 Harv. L. Rev. 49, 51-52, 81-88, 108 (1923).

On the other hand, the mischievous results of the doctrine had become apparent. Diversity of citizenship jurisdiction was conferred in order to prevent apprehended discrimination in state courts against those not citizens of the State. *Swift v. Tyson* introduced grave discrimination by non-citizens against citizens. It made rights enjoyed under the unwritten "general law" vary according to whether enforcement was sought in the state or in the federal court; and the privilege of selecting the court in which the right should be determined was conferred upon the non-citizen. Thus, the doctrine rendered impossible equal protection of the law. In attempting to promote uniformity of law throughout the United States, the doctrine had prevented uniformity in the administration of the law of the State.

The discrimination resulting became in practice far-reaching. This resulted in part from the broad province accorded to the so-called "general law" as to which federal courts exercised an independent judgment. In addition to questions of purely commercial law, "general law" was held to include the obligations under contracts entered into and to be performed within the State, the extent to which a carrier operating within a State may stipulate for exemption from liability for his own negligence or that of his employee; the liability for torts committed within the State upon persons resident or property located there, even where the question of liability depended upon the scope of a property right conferred by the State; and the right to exemplary or punitive damages. Furthermore, state decisions construing local deeds, mineral conveyances, and even devises of real estate were disregarded.

In part the discrimination resulted from the wide range of persons held entitled to avail themselves of the federal rule by resort to the diversity of citizenship jurisdiction. Through this jurisdiction individual citizens willing to remove from their own State and become citizens of another might avail themselves of the federal rule. And, without even change of residence, a corporate citizen of the State could avail itself of the federal rule by re-incorporating under the laws of another State, as was done in the Taxicab case.

The injustice and confusion incident to the doctrine of *Swift v. Tyson* have been repeatedly urged as reasons for abolishing or limiting diversity of citizenship jurisdiction. Other legislative relief has been proposed. If only a question of statutory construction were involved, we should not be prepared to abandon a doctrine so widely applied throughout nearly a century. But the unconstitutionality of the course pursued has now been made clear and compels us to do so.

Third. Except in matters governed by the Federal Constitution or by Acts of Congress, the law to be applied in any case is the law of the State. And whether the law of the State shall be declared by its Legislature in a statute or by its highest court in a decision is not a matter of federal concern. There is no federal general common law. Congress has no power to declare substantive rules of common law applicable in a State whether they be local in their nature or "general," be they commercial law or a part of the law of torts. And no clause in the Constitution purports to confer such a power upon the federal courts. As stated by Mr. Justice Field when protesting in

*Baltimore & Ohio R. Co. v. Baugh*, against ignoring the Ohio common law of fellow servant liability:

> I am aware that what has been termed the general law of the country—which is often little less than what the judge advancing the doctrine thinks at the time should be the general law on a particular subject—has been often advanced in judicial opinions of this court to control a conflicting law of a State. I admit that learned judges have fallen into the habit of repeating this doctrine as a convenient mode of brushing aside the law of a State in conflict with their views. And I confess that, moved and governed by the authority of the great names of those judges, I have, myself, in many instances, unhesitatingly and confidently, but I think now erroneously, repeated the same doctrine. But, notwithstanding the great names which may be cited in favor of the doctrine, and notwithstanding the frequency with which the doctrine has been reiterated, there stands, as a perpetual protest against its repetition, the Constitution of the United States, which recognizes and preserves the autonomy and independence of the States—independence in their legislative and independence in their judicial departments. Supervision over either the legislative or the judicial action of the States is in no case permissible except as to matters by the Constitution specifically authorized or delegated to the United States. Any interference with either, except as thus permitted, is an invasion of the authority of the State and, to that extent, a denial of its independence.

The fallacy underlying the rule declared in *Swift v. Tyson* is made clear by Mr. Justice Holmes. The doctrine rests upon the assumption that there is "a transcendental body of law outside of any particular State but obligatory within it unless and until changed by statute," that federal courts have the power to use their judgment as to what the rules of common law are; and that in the federal courts "the parties are entitled to an independent judgment on matters of general law":

> [B]ut law in the sense in which courts speak of it today does not exist without some definite authority behind it. The common law so far as it is enforced in a State, whether called common law or not, is not the common law generally but the law of that State existing by the authority of that State without regard to what it may have been in England or anywhere else. . . . [T]he authority and only authority is the State, and if that be so, the voice adopted by the State as its own [whether it be of its Legislature or of its Supreme Court] should utter the last word.

Thus the doctrine of *Swift v. Tyson* is, as Mr. Justice Holmes said, "an unconstitutional assumption of powers by courts of the United States which no lapse of time or respectable array of opinion should make us hesitate to correct." In disapproving that doctrine we do not hold unconstitutional § 34 of the Federal Judiciary Act of 1789 or any other Act of Congress. We merely declare that in applying the doctrine this Court and the lower courts have invaded rights which in our opinion are reserved by the Constitution to the several States.

Fourth. The defendant contended that by the common law of Pennsylvania as declared by its highest court in *Falchetti v. Pennsylvania R. Co.*, the only duty owed to the plaintiff was to refrain from wilful or wanton injury. The plaintiff denied that such is the Pennsylvania law. In support of their respective contentions the parties discussed and cited many decisions of the Supreme Court of the State. The Circuit Court of Appeals ruled that the question of liability is one of general law; and on that ground declined to decide the issue of state law. As we hold this was error, the judgment is reversed and the case remanded to it for further proceedings in conformity with our opinion. Reversed.

Justice CARDOZO took no part in the consideration or decision of this case.

Justice REED, concurring:

I concur in the conclusion reached in this case, in the disapproval of the doctrine of *Swift v. Tyson*, and in the reasoning of the majority opinion except in so far as it relies upon the unconstitutionality of the "course pursued" by the federal courts.

The "doctrine of *Swift v. Tyson*," as I understand it, is that the words "the laws," as used in § 34, line one, of the Federal Judiciary Act of September 24, 1789, do not include in their meaning "the decisions of the local tribunals." Mr. Justice Story, in deciding that point, said:

> Undoubtedly, the decisions of the local tribunals upon such subjects are entitled to, and will receive, the most deliberate attention and respect of this Court; but they cannot furnish positive rules, or conclusive authority, by which our own judgments are to be bound up and governed.

To decide the case now before us and to "disapprove" the doctrine of *Swift v. Tyson* requires only that we say that the words "the laws" include in their meaning the decisions of the local tribunals. As the majority opinion shows, by its reference to Mr. Warren's researches and the first quotation from Mr. Justice Holmes, that this Court is now of the view that "laws" includes "decisions," it is unnecessary to go further and declare that the "course pursued" was "unconstitutional," instead of merely erroneous.

The "unconstitutional" course referred to in the majority opinion is apparently the ruling in *Swift v. Tyson* that the supposed omission of Congress to legislate as to the effect of decisions leaves federal courts free to interpret general law for themselves. I am not at all sure whether, in the absence of federal statutory direction, federal courts would be compelled to follow state decisions. There was sufficient doubt about the matter in 1789 to induce the first Congress to legislate. No former opinions of this Court have passed upon it. Mr. Justice Holmes evidently saw nothing "unconstitutional" which required the overruling of *Swift v. Tyson*, for he said in the very opinion quoted by the majority, "I should leave *Swift v. Tyson* undisturbed, . . . but I would not allow it to spread the assumed dominion into new fields." If the opinion commits this Court to the position that the Congress is without power to declare what rules of substantive law shall govern the federal courts, that conclusion also seems questionable. The line between procedural and substantive law is hazy but no one doubts federal power over procedure. The Judiciary Article and the "necessary and proper" clause of Article One may fully authorize legislation, such as this section of the Judiciary Act.

In this Court, *stare decisis*, in statutory construction, is a useful rule, not an inexorable command. It seems preferable to overturn an established construction of an Act of Congress, rather than, in the circumstances of this case, to interpret the Constitution. . . .

[In his dissenting opinion, Justice BUTLER, joined by Justice MCREYNOLDS, argued for adherence to the long-standing *Swift v. Tyson* precedent.]

## Comments and Questions

1. Identify the courts (with both subject matter and personal jurisdiction) in which Tomkins could have filed his action. Do you see why he chose the federal district in New York? Professor Edward A. Purcell, Jr., recounts the critical role Columbia Law student Aaron L. Danzig, as research assistant to Tomkins's lawyer, played in this choice of forum. *See* Edward A. Purcell, Jr., *The Story of* Erie: *How Litigants, Lawyers, Judges, Politics, and Social Change Reshape the Law*. In *Civil Procedure Stories*, Kevin M. Clermont, ed. (2d ed. 2008), at 39.

2. Justice Brandeis's critique of *Swift v. Tyson*, which had permitted the federal courts to apply (and indeed make up) their own "general common law" in cases like *Erie*, weaves several rhetorical threads. Identify the statutory, constitutional, and policy arguments Brandeis arrays against *Swift*.

3. What are the "mischievous results" of *Swift* referred to by Brandeis? How are these illustrated by the *Black & White Taxicab Co.* case?

4. Imagine that Tomkins was not walking alone on this fateful night, and that you are the personal injury attorney consulted by both Harry and his friend Jake (a citizen of New York) after they were severely injured along the tracks in Hughestown. *Before* the *Erie* decision, under the *Swift v. Tyson* regime, how would you assess Jake's chances of recovery against the Erie Railroad, as compared to Harry's? How would you explain this to Jake? Can you see what Brandeis meant when he wrote that *Swift* "rendered impossible equal protection of the law"? Would different standards of care apply to Jake's and Harry's civil actions *after* the *Erie* decision?

5. In *Swift*, how had Justice Story been able to construe § 34 of the Judiciary Act of 1789 (the Rules of Decision Act) in a manner that permitted federal courts to ignore state "laws" when they appeared in the form of *case*, as opposed to *statutory*, law? Is this consistent with the plain meaning of the statutory language? If not, what might have motivated the Court to stray so far from the ordinary meaning of "laws"?

Note that the first Judiciary Act had "the right answer" to the vertical choice of law quandary. It just took succeeding generations 150 years to rediscover it.

6. What specific provision (if any) of the Constitution does Brandeis rely upon for the conclusion that *Swift* represented "an unconstitutional assumption of powers by the Courts of the United States"? The Tenth Amendment would have been a likely choice, as it provides: "The powers not delegated to the United States by the Constitution, nor prohibited by it to the States, are reserved to the States respectively, or to the people."

For one noted legal scholar, "*Erie*'s ambiguities are several and obvious. If the decision rests on statutory grounds, the constitutional portion may be unnecessary *dictum*. Even if it is constitutionally based, the Court confused the matter by failing to cite directly any provision of the Constitution and by placing some of the apparent constitutional analysis in the portion of the opinion that rests on other grounds. One can find in the opinion possible invocations of the doctrines of due process, equal protection, separation of powers, and federalism." George D. Brown, *The Ideologies of Forum Shopping—Why Doesn't a Conservative Court Protect Defendants?*, 71 U.N.C. L. Rev. 649, 657 (1993).

Professor John Hart Ely finds no surprise in the Court's failure to indicate precisely what constitutional provision *Swift* had violated: "[T]he lack of a relevant provision was precisely the point. The [*Swift*] interpretation was unconstitutional, but not because the federal common law rules that had been developed under it were encroaching on areas of 'state substantive law.' . . . It was unconstitutional because nothing in the Constitution provided the central government with a general lawmaking authority of the sort the Court had been exercising under *Swift*." John Hart Ely, *The Irrepressible Myth of* Erie, 87 Harv. L. Rev. 693, 702-703 (1974).

*[handwritten margin note:* Swift uncot. *]*

7. Two distinctions made by Justice Reed in his concurrence play a very significant role in the post-*Erie* era. First, he reminds us that Congress may have the authority to declare substantive law that would govern in federal courts (as if, for example, it had enacted a Federal Railway Safety Act that applied to Tomkins's accident), even if a federal judge does not have this authority. Second, and more important from the perspective of the cases we take up next, Reed distinguishes between "substantive" and "procedural" law, observing that while the line between the two may be hazy, "no one doubts federal power over procedure." Indeed, under established principles, a forum follows its own rules of procedure even while applying the substantive law of another jurisdiction. *See Restatement (Second) Conflicts* § 122.

We will return to the elusive substance/procedure dichotomy shortly.

8. On Justice Reed's second point, note that the *Erie* decision and the adoption of the Federal Rules of Civil Procedure both occurred in the same momentous year of 1938. Prior to the FRCP, federal district courts were required by the Conformity Acts to follow the procedure of the state courts in the state in which they sat, creating what many federal court practitioners considered sheer chaos. In 1934 Congress, persuaded that a uniform body of

procedure was desirable, set the federal rulemaking process in motion with the Rules Enabling Act* authorizing the Supreme Court to "prescribe by general rules, the forms of process, writs, pleadings, and motions, and the practice and procedure of the district courts and courts of appeals in the United States in civil actions. . . ." Significantly, the Rules Enabling Act stipulated that "[s]uch rules shall not abridge, enlarge, or modify any substantive right. . . ."

As Professor Mary Kay Kane has observed: "The year 1938 thus began a new era in the balance of power between state and federal courts—one that was to be controlled by the wavering (sometimes almost evanescent) line between substance and procedure." Mary Kay Kane, *The Golden Wedding Years:* Erie Railroad Company v. Tompkins *and the Federal Rules*, 63 Notre Dame L. Rev. 671, 673 (1988).

9. When *Erie Railroad v. Tomkins* resolved the vertical choice of law issue in favor of state over federal substantive law, it opened a second, horizontal choice between the tort law of Pennsylvania (where Tomkins's accident occurred) and New York (where the Railroad was incorporated and the federal court hearing the case sat). Complex conflicts of laws principles now seek to identify the state with "the most significant relationship" to the issue in question, but at the time of the *Erie* decision categorical rules pointed to the law of the state in which the accident occurred. *See generally* Russell J. Weintraub, *Commentary on the Conflict of Laws* (6th ed. 2010). Thus the *Erie* Court assumed Pennsylvania law would control, and remanded for determination of what duty of care was owed Tomkins under that law.

10. *Klaxon Co. v. Stentor Electric Mfg. Co.*, 313 U.S. 487 (1941), required federal courts in diversity actions to apply the same conflicts rule that would be applied by courts of the state in which they sit. "Otherwise, the accident of diversity of citizenship would constantly disturb equal administration of justice in coordinate state and federal courts sitting side by side." 313 U.S. at 496. Thus in the *Klaxon* breach of contract action, the federal district court in Delaware was bound to apply the law of whatever state the Delaware state courts would look to if they were entertaining the action. As we will see in our next case, the goal was to conform results in federal diversity cases to those that would obtain if the case had been filed in state court.

11. What if *Erie* commands application of state law, but that state's highest court has not pronounced on the subject? The Second Circuit Court of Appeals has observed:

> Absent law from a state's highest court, a federal court sitting in diversity has to predict how the state court would resolve an ambiguity in state law. In predicting how a state's highest court would rule on an issue, it is helpful to consider the decisions of the state's trial and appellate courts. The holding of an intermediate appellate state court . . . is a datum for ascertaining state law which is

---

*The current version is at 28 U.S.C. § 2072. For a more in-depth history of the Rules Enabling Act, *see* Chapter 4, Part E(4).

not to be disregarded by a federal court unless it is convinced by other persuasive data that the highest court of the state would decide otherwise. Other data include relevant case law from other jurisdictions on the same or analogous issues, scholarly writings in the field, and any other resources available to the state's highest court.

*Fieger v. Pitney Bowes Credit Corp.*, 251 F.3d 386, 399 (2d Cir. 2001). *See also Werwinski v. Ford Motor Co.*, 286 F.3d 661, 670 (3d Cir. 2002); *Iodice v. United States*, 289 F.3d 270, 275 (4th Cir. 2002). *See generally* Erwin Chemerinsky, *Federal Jurisdiction* § 5.3, at 326-329 (4th ed. 2003).

Judge Henry Friendly put it more succinctly in *Nolan v. Transocean Air Lines*, 276 F.2d 280, 281 (2d Cir. 1960): "Our principal task, in this diversity of citizenship case, is to determine what the New York courts would think the California courts would think on an issue about which neither has thought."

12. Justice Brandeis's assertion that "there is no federal general common law" is a bit of an overstatement. Indeed, the lead sentence in that paragraph contains the important caveat: "Except in matters governed by the Federal Constitution or by Acts of Congress...." Federal courts have developed common law in such specialized areas as labor relations, antitrust, and maritime disputes. *See generally* Charles A. Wright and Mary Kay Kane, *Law of Federal Courts* § 60, at 413-424 (6th ed. 2002); Erwin Chemerinsky, *supra*, §§ 6.1-6.3, at 353-380.

13. One scholar's take on *Erie* and the overruling of *Swift v. Tyson* is that it was part of a reaction against the dramatic expansion of federal power in the New Deal era:

> Brandeis also detected unwanted centralization in another area, far less significant politically, but more immediately relevant to the judicial system. In 1934, the Rules Enabling Act which [Brandeis] opposed, had authorized the Supreme Court to promulgate rules of procedure for both legal and equitable actions, and in December, 1937 the newly drafted Federal Rules of Civil procedure came before the Court for review. Brandeis alone dissented from the Court's approval, and he cherished the hope that Congress might veto the new rules. He feared their potential rigidity; he felt that the Court should not take responsibility for a set of rules to which it could not give adequate consideration, and, likely most important, he believed that they represented yet another example of needless centralization. By overruling *Swift*, the Court would establish a new area of decentralized authority and counterbalance the new centralizing Federal Rules.

Edward A. Purcell, Jr., *Brandeis and the Progressive Constitution:* Erie, *the Judicial Power, and the Politics of the Federal Courts in Twentieth Century America* 135-136 (2000).

Another scholar suggests that Brandeis had become dismayed at the widespread tactic of corporate litigants removing personal injury cases to federal court in order to impose greater burdens on plaintiffs suing them: "*Erie* was a part of his overall campaign. Abolishing the general federal common law would eliminate a major incentive for intra-state forum shopping [to federal court] and reduce the utility of a variety of popular manipulative tactics." Stephen B. Burbank, *Semtek, Forum Shopping, and Federal Common Law*, 77 Notre Dame L. Rev. 1027, 1033 (2002) (citing Edward A. Purcell, Jr., *Brandeis,* Erie, *and the New Deal "Constitutional Revolution,"* 26 J. Sup. Ct. Hist. 257, 272-273 (2001)).

14. Soon after it was handed down, the usually reserved *New York Times* pronounced *Erie* a "transcendentally significant opinion." *N.Y. Times*, May 3, 1938, at 22, col. 5, as quoted in Irving Younger, *Observation: What Happened in* Erie, 56 Tex. L. Rev. 1011, 1029 (1978). It certainly had a devastating impact on Harry Tompkins, whose $30,000 jury verdict (a handsome sum at the time) was vacated. Tompkins died severely disabled and destitute. Bob Rizzi, Erie *Memoirs Reveal Drama, Tragedy*, 63 Harv. L. Rec. 2 (Sept. 24, 1976). For more of the story, and photographs of Tomkins before and after the accident, see *http://www.luzernecountybar.org/erie.pdf*.

Was "justice" done in *Erie*? How could one of the Court's great liberals, dubbed the "People's Attorney" for his earlier conscience-driven advocacy as a litigator, deliver this result?

15. How many civil procedure cases have their own official historical marker?

*Used with permission of the Pennsylvania Historical and Museum Commission.*

The challenge after *Erie Railroad Co. v. Tompkins* was distinguishing procedure from substance, as Justice Reed had perceptively foreseen. As you read the following case, compare your own intuitive characterizations with the Court's definitions. Is a statute of limitations procedural *or* substantive?

# ■ GUARANTY TRUST CO. v. YORK
### *326 U.S. 99 (1945)*

Justice FRANKFURTER delivered the opinion of the Court:

[Guaranty Trust Co., acting as trustee, agreed to a buy-out plan in which noteholders of the Corporation received only 50 percent of the face value of their notes. The disgruntled among them brought a class action in federal court alleging state law claims of breach of trust, and invoking diversity jurisdiction. Guaranty Trust moved for summary judgment, which was granted on the grounds the action was time-barred by the New York statute of limitations. The Second Circuit Court of Appeals reversed, holding that the federal district court was not required to apply the state statute of limitations, but could exercise its own judgment as to timeliness.]

The importance of the question for the disposition of litigation in the federal courts led us to bring the case here. . . . Our only concern is with the holding that the federal courts in a suit like this are not bound by local law.

We put to one side the considerations relevant in disposing of questions that arise when a federal court is adjudicating a claim based on a federal law. Our problem only touches transactions for which rights and obligations are created by one of the States, and for the assertion of which, in case of diversity of the citizenship of the parties, Congress has made a federal court another available forum.

Our starting point must be the policy of federal jurisdiction which *Erie R. Co. v. Tompkins* embodies. In overruling *Swift v. Tyson*, *Erie R. Co. v. Tompkins* did not merely overrule a venerable case. It overruled a particular way of looking at law which dominated the judicial process long after its inadequacies had been laid bare. Law was conceived as a "brooding omnipresence" of Reason, of which decisions were merely evidence and not themselves the controlling formulations. Accordingly, federal courts deemed themselves free to ascertain what Reason, and therefore Law, required wholly independent of authoritatively declared State law, even in cases where a legal right as the basis for relief was created by State authority and could not be created by federal authority and the case got into a federal court merely because it was "between Citizens of different States" under Art. III, § 2 of the Constitution of the United States.

This impulse to freedom from the rules that controlled State courts regarding State-created rights was so strongly rooted in the prevailing views concerning the nature of law, that the federal courts almost imperceptibly were led to mutilating construction even of the explicit command given to them by Congress to apply State law in cases purporting to enforce the law of a State. *See* § 34 of the Judiciary Act of 1789. The matter was fairly summarized by the statement that "During the period when *Swift v. Tyson* (1842-1938) ruled the decisions of the federal courts, its theory of their freedom in matters of general law from the authority of state courts pervaded opinions of this Court involving even state statutes or local law."

. . . Since it was conceived that there was "a transcendental body of law outside of any particular State but obligatory within it unless and until changed by statute," State court decisions were not "the law" but merely someone's opinion—to be sure an opinion to be respected—concerning the content of this all-pervading law. Not unnaturally, the federal courts assumed power to find for themselves the content of such a body of law. The notion was stimulated by the attractive vision of a uniform body of federal law. To such sentiments for uniformity of decision and freedom from diversity in State law the federal courts gave currency, particularly in cases where equitable remedies were sought, because equitable doctrines are so often cast in terms of universal applicability when close analysis of the source of legal enforceability is not demanded. . . .

And so this case reduces itself to the narrow question whether, when no recovery could be had in a State court because the action is barred by the statute of limitations, a federal court in equity can take cognizance of the suit because there is diversity of citizenship between the parties. Is the outlawry, according to State law, of a claim created by the States a matter of "substantive rights" to be respected by a federal court of equity when that court's jurisdiction is dependent on the fact that there is a State-created right, or is such statute of "a mere remedial character," which a federal court may disregard?

Matters of "substance" and matters of "procedure" are much talked about in the books as though they defined a great divide cutting across the whole domain of law. But, of course, "substance" and "procedure" are the same keywords to very different problems. Neither "substance" nor "procedure" represents the same invariants. Each implies different variables depending upon the particular problem for which it is used. And the different problems are only distantly related at best, for the terms are in common use in connection with situations turning on such different considerations as those that are relevant to questions pertaining to ex post facto legislation, the impairment of the obligations of contract, the enforcement of federal rights in the State courts and the multitudinous phases of the conflict of laws.

Here we are dealing with a right to recover derived not from the United States but from one of the States. When, because the plaintiff happens to be a non-resident, such a right is enforceable in a federal as well as in a State court, the forms and mode of enforcing the right may at times, naturally enough, vary because the two judicial systems are not identical. But since a federal court adjudicating a State-created right solely because of the diversity of citizenship of the parties is for that purpose, in effect, only another court of the State, it cannot afford recovery if the right to recover is made unavailable by the State nor can it substantially affect the enforcement of the right as given by the State.

And so the question is not whether a statute of limitations is deemed a matter of "procedure" in some sense. The question is whether such a statute concerns merely the manner and the means by which a right to recover, as recognized by the State, is enforced, or whether such statutory limitation is a matter of substance in the aspect that alone is relevant to our problem, namely, does it significantly affect the result of a litigation for a federal court to disregard a law of a State that would be controlling in an action upon the same claim by the same parties in a State court?

It is therefore immaterial whether statutes of limitation are characterized either as "substantive" or "procedural" in State court opinions in any use of those terms unrelated to the specific issue before us. *Erie R. Co. v. Tompkins* was not an endeavor to formulate scientific legal terminology. It expressed a policy that touches vitally the proper distribution of judicial power between State and federal courts. In essence, the intent of that decision was to insure that, in all cases where a federal court is exercising jurisdiction solely because of the diversity of citizenship of the parties, the outcome of the litigation in the federal court should be substantially the same, so far as legal rules determine the outcome of a litigation, as it would be if tried in a State court. The nub of the policy that underlies *Erie R. Co. v. Tompkins* is that for the same transaction the accident of a suit by a non-resident litigant in a federal court instead of in a State court a block away should not lead to a substantially different result. And so, putting to one side abstractions regarding "substance" and "procedure," we have held that in diversity cases the federal courts must follow the law of the State as to burden of proof, *Cities Service Co. v. Dunlap*, 308 U.S. 208, as to conflict of laws, *Klaxon Co. v. Stentor Co.*, 313 U.S. 487, as to contributory negligence, *Palmer v. Hoffman*, 318 U.S. 109, 117. *Erie R. Co. v. Tompkins* has been applied with an eye alert to essentials in avoiding disregard of State law in diversity cases in the federal courts. A policy so important to our federalism must be kept free from entanglements with analytical or terminological niceties.

Plainly enough, a statute that would completely bar recovery in a suit if brought in a State court bears on a State-created right vitally and not merely formally or negligibly. As to consequences that so intimately affect recovery or non-recovery a federal court in a diversity case should follow State law. . . . [I]f a plea of the statute of limitations would bar recovery in a State court, a federal court ought not to afford recovery. . . .

To make an exception to *Erie R. Co. v. Tompkins* on the equity side of a federal court is to reject the considerations of policy which, after long travail, led to that decision. Judge Augustus N. Hand thus summarized below the fatal objection to such inroad upon *Erie R. Co. v. Tompkins*:

> In my opinion it would be a mischievous practice to disregard state statutes of limitation whenever federal courts think that the result of adopting them may be inequitable. Such procedure would promote the choice of United States

rather than of state courts in order to gain the advantage of different laws. The main foundation for the criticism of *Swift v. Tyson* was that a litigant in cases where federal jurisdiction is based only on diverse citizenship may obtain a more favorable decision by suing in the United States courts.

143 F.2d 503, 529, 531.

Diversity jurisdiction is founded on assurance to nonresident litigants of courts free from susceptibility to potential local bias. The Framers of the Constitution, according to Marshall, entertained "apprehensions" lest distant suitors be subjected to local bias in State courts, or, at least, viewed with "indulgence the possible fears and apprehensions" of such suitors. *Bank of the United States v. Deveaux*, 5 Cranch 61, 87. And so Congress afforded out-of-State litigants another tribunal, not another body of law. The operation of a double system of conflicting laws in the same State is plainly hostile to the reign of law. Certainly, the fortuitous circumstance of residence out of a State of one of the parties to a litigation ought not to give rise to a discrimination against others equally concerned but locally resident. The source of substantive rights enforced by a federal court under diversity jurisdiction, it cannot be said too often, is the law of the States. Whenever that law is authoritatively declared by a State, whether its voice be the legislature or its highest court, such law ought to govern in litigation founded on that law, whether the forum of application is a State or a federal court and whether the remedies be sought at law or may be had in equity. . . .

The judgment is reversed and the case is remanded for proceedings not inconsistent with this opinion.

[The dissenting opinion of Justice RUTLEDGE is omitted.]

## Comments and Questions

1. How did operation of a statute of limitations become a "substantive" matter in *Guaranty Trust*? How did "substantive" become "outcome determinative"? What is Justice Frankfurter's reasoning behind these seemingly counterintuitive propositions? What lessons from *Erie* is he applying?

2. *Guaranty Trust* reads the intent of *Erie* "to insure that, in all cases where a federal court is exercising jurisdiction solely because of the diversity of citizenship of the parties, the outcome of the litigation in the federal court should be substantially the same, so far as legal rules determine the outcome of a litigation, as it would be if tried in a State court." What about Justice Reed's unrebutted assertion in *Erie* that "no one doubts federal power *over procedure*"?

3. What were the implications of the outcome test for the then newly adopted Federal Rules of Civil Procedure? After *Guaranty Trust*, the two pivotal civil procedure events of 1938—the *Erie* decision and the adoption of the Federal Rules—appeared to be on a collision course.

4. Do you see why Professor Charles E. Clark, principal draftsperson of the Federal Rules, remarked that *Guaranty Trust* reduced federal judges to

"ventriloquists' dummies" mouthing state law? Quoted in Daniel J. Meador, *Transformation of the American Judiciary*, 46 Ala. L. Rev. 763, 765 (1995). *See also Richardson v. C.I.R.*, 126 F.2d 562, 567 (2d Cir. 1942) (Judge Jerome Frank).

5. The *Guaranty Trust* Court was clearly troubled (as it was in *Erie*) by the operation of a "double system of conflicting laws in the same State." Plaintiff York, in the Court's view, must not be allowed to shop for a more favorable limitations rule merely because of the fortuity of diversity with his defendant. The outcome test certainly solved that problem, by requiring conformity to state law whenever application of conflicting federal law would significantly alter the result of the litigation.

But was the cure (outcome conformity) more harmful to the operation of the judicial system than the disease (different outcomes between federal and state courts)? One federal practice after another fell in the wake of the outcome-test juggernaut. *See, e.g., Ragan v. Merchants Transfer & Warehouse Co.*, 337 U.S. 530 (1949) (federal practice of deeming a case commenced for statute of limitations purposes upon filing of the complaint was displaced by state statute providing for tolling only upon service of process on defendant); *Cohen v. Beneficial Industrial Loan Corp.*, 337 U.S. 541 (1949) (state law requiring plaintiffs in shareholder derivative actions to post security to indemnify defendant for costs and attorneys' fees in event defendant prevails required dismissal of federal diversity action, even though the federal rule required no such security); *Bernhardt v. Polygraphic Co. of America*, 350 U.S. 198 (1956) (federal court could not enforce arbitration agreement contained in employment contract sued upon in diversity action in the face of state law rendering arbitration agreements revocable). *See also Palmer v. Hoffman*, 318 U.S. 109 (1943) (predating *Guaranty Trust*) (the question of who has the burden of proof on contributory negligence is a matter of state law, which in this case placed the burden on the plaintiff; thus federal courts in diversity cases must conform, notwithstanding that Fed. R. Civ. P. 8(c) makes it an affirmative defense).

Indeed, it is not hard to imagine virtually *any* conflict in rules having an outcome-determinative effect in the right circumstances. If a federal district court is hearing a diversity case arising from an accident in State *A*, and State *A*'s rules require that an answer be filed within ten days of service (rather than the twenty-one days allowed by Fed. R. Civ. P. 12(a)), must the federal court default the defendant on Day 11 if an answer has not been filed? If State *A* requires that pleadings be on 8½ × 14 paper, and plaintiff files in federal court on 8½ × 11 paper at 5 P.M. on the very last day before the statute of limitations runs, must the federal court dismiss, as the state court would? If the courts in State *A* close at 4 P.M., and a party in the diversity case files its brief on the day it is due at 4:45 P.M. in the federal court clerk's office, which is open until 5 P.M., must the clerk reject it?

Does it make sense to characterize paper size, days to file the answer, or courthouse hours as "substantive"? Are these matters of the same importance as the standard of care owed by the railroad in *Erie*? Do these matters turn on the constitutional allocation of powers between the two court systems?

It was left to the ingenuity of two renowned Supreme Court Justices to rescue federal procedure from the *Erie*-gone-wild slicing machine in the two cases that follow.

NC    SC

# ■ BYRD v. BLUE RIDGE RURAL ELECTRIC COOPERATIVE, INC.
*356 U.S. 525 (1958)*

Justice BRENNAN delivered the opinion of the Court:

This case was brought in the District Court for the Western District of South Carolina. Jurisdiction was based on diversity of citizenship. 28 U.S.C. § 1332. The petitioner, a resident of North Carolina, sued respondent, a South Carolina corporation, for damages for injuries allegedly caused by the respondent's negligence. He had judgment on a jury verdict. The Court of Appeals for the Fourth Circuit reversed and directed the entry of judgment for the respondent. We granted certiorari, and subsequently ordered reargument.

The respondent is in the business of selling electric power to subscribers in rural sections of South Carolina. The petitioner was employed as a lineman in the construction crew of a construction contractor. . . . The petitioner was injured while connecting power lines to one of the new substations.

One of respondent's affirmative defenses was that, under the South Carolina Workmen's Compensation Act,* the petitioner—because the work contracted to be done by his employer was work of the kind also done by the respondent's own construction and maintenance crews—had the status of a statutory employee of the respondent and was therefore barred from suing the respondent at law because obliged to accept statutory compensation benefits as the exclusive remedy for his injuries. Two questions concerning this defense are before us: (1) whether the Court of Appeals erred in directing judgment for respondent without a remand to give petitioner an opportunity to introduce further evidence; and (2) whether petitioner, state practice notwithstanding, is entitled to a jury determination of the factual issues raised by this defense.

[After deciding that a remand was necessary on the issue of whether Byrd was an "employee" within the meaning of the workers' compensation statute, the Court addressed the second question.]

A question is also presented as to whether on remand the factual issue is to be decided by the judge or by the jury. The respondent argues on the basis of the decision of the Supreme Court of South Carolina in *Adams v. Davison-Paxon Co.*, 230 S.C. 532, that the issue of immunity should be decided by the judge and not by the jury. That was a negligence action brought in the state

---

*\* Eds.' Note:* Workers compensation schemes, which date to the early twentieth century, operate as a kind of no-fault insurance: employees collect benefits for workplace injuries without having to prove their employer was negligent, and in return the employer is exempt from tort suits, which carry the potential for far larger recoveries in compensatory and punitive damages.

trial court against a store owner by an employee of an independent contractor who operated the store's millinery department. The trial judge denied the store owner's motion for a directed verdict made upon the ground that [the workers compensation statute] barred the plaintiff's action. The jury returned a verdict for the plaintiff. The South Carolina Supreme Court reversed, holding that it was for the judge and not the jury to decide on the evidence whether the owner was a statutory employer, and that the store owner had sustained his defense. . . .

The respondent argues that this state-court decision governs the present diversity case and "divests the jury of its normal function" to decide the disputed fact question of the respondent's immunity under [the statute]. This is to contend that the federal court is bound under *Erie R. Co. v. Tompkins* to follow the state court's holding to secure uniform enforcement of the immunity created by the State.

First. It was decided in *Erie R. Co. v. Tompkins* that the federal courts in diversity cases must respect the definition of state-created rights and obligations by the state courts. We must, therefore, first examine the rule in *Adams v. Davison-Paxon Co.* to determine whether it is bound up with these rights and obligations in such a way that its application in the federal court is required. The Workmen's Compensation Act is administered in South Carolina by its Industrial Commission. The South Carolina courts hold that, on judicial review of actions of the Commission, the question whether the claim of an injured workman is within the Commission's jurisdiction is a matter of law for decision by the court, which makes its own findings of fact relating to that jurisdiction. The South Carolina Supreme Court states no reasons in *Adams v. Davison-Paxon Co.* why, although the jury decides all other factual issues raised by the cause of action and defenses, the jury is displaced as to the factual issue raised by the affirmative defense under [the statute]. The decisions cited to support the holding are . . . concerned solely with defining the scope and method of judicial review of the Industrial Commission. A State may, of course, distribute the functions of its judicial machinery as it sees fit. The decisions relied upon, however, furnish no reason for selecting the judge rather than the jury to decide this single affirmative defense in the negligence action. They simply reflect a policy that administrative determination of "jurisdictional facts" should not be final but subject to judicial review. The conclusion is inescapable that the *Adams* holding is grounded in the practical consideration that the question had theretofore come before the South Carolina courts from the Industrial Commission and the courts had become accustomed to deciding the factual issue of immunity without the aid of juries. We find nothing to suggest that this rule was announced as an integral part of the special relationship created by the statute. Thus the requirement appears to be merely a form and mode of enforcing the immunity, *Guaranty Trust Co. v. York*, and not a rule intended to be bound up with the definition of the rights and obligations of the parties. . . .

Second. But cases following *Erie* have evinced a broader policy to the effect that the federal courts should conform as near as may be—in the absence of other considerations—to state rules even of form and mode where the state rules may bear substantially on the question whether the litigation would come out one way in the federal court and another way in the state court if the federal court failed to apply a particular local rule. *E.g., Guaranty Trust Co. v. York, supra; Bernhardt v. Polygraphic Co.* Concededly the nature of the tribunal which tries issues may be important in the enforcement of the parcel of rights making up a cause of action or defense, and bear significantly upon achievement of uniform enforcement of the right. It may well be that in the instant personal-injury case the outcome would be substantially affected by whether the issue of immunity is decided by a judge or a jury. Therefore, were "outcome" the only consideration, a strong case might appear for saying that the federal court should follow the state practice.

But there are affirmative countervailing considerations at work here. The federal system is an independent system for administering justice to litigants who properly invoke its jurisdiction. An essential characteristic of that system is the manner in which, in civil common-law actions, it distributes trial functions between judge and jury and, under the influence—if not the command[10]—of the Seventh Amendment, assigns the decisions of disputed questions of fact to the jury. The policy of uniform enforcement of state-created rights and obligations, *see, e.g., Guaranty Trust Co. v. York*, cannot in every case exact compliance with a state rule[12]—not bound up with rights and obligations—which disrupts the federal system of allocating functions between judge and jury. *Herron v. Southern Pacific Co.*, 283 U.S. 91. Thus the inquiry here is whether the federal policy favoring jury decisions of disputed fact questions should yield to the state rule in the interest of furthering the objective that the litigation should not come out one way in the federal court and another way in the state court.

We think that in the circumstances of this case the federal court should not follow the state rule. It cannot be gainsaid that there is a strong federal policy against allowing state rules to disrupt the judge-jury relationship in the federal courts. . . . "[S]tate laws cannot alter the essential character or function of a federal court" because that function "is not in any sense a local matter, and state statutes which would interfere with the appropriate performance of that function are not binding upon the federal court under either the Conformity Act or the 'rules of decision' Act." Perhaps even more clearly in light of the influence of the Seventh Amendment the function assigned to the jury "is an essential factor in the process for which the Federal Constitution provides." . . .

Third. We have discussed the problem upon the assumption that the outcome of the litigation may be substantially affected by whether the

---

10. Our conclusion makes unnecessary the consideration of—and we intimate no view upon—the constitutional question whether the right of jury trial protected in federal courts by the Seventh Amendment embraces the factual issue of statutory immunity when asserted, as here, as an affirmative defense in a common law negligence action.

12. This Court held in *Sibbach v. Wilson & Co.*, 312 U.S. 1, that Federal Rule of Civil Procedure 35 should prevail over a contrary state rule.

issue of immunity is decided by a judge or a jury. But clearly there is not present here the certainty that a different result would follow, *cf. Guaranty Trust Co. v. York, supra,* or even the strong possibility that this would be the case, *cf. Bernhardt v. Polygraphic Co., supra.* There are factors present here which might reduce that possibility. The trial judge in the federal system has powers denied the judges of many States to comment on the weight of evidence and credibility of witnesses, and discretion to grant a new trial if the verdict appears to him to be against the weight of the evidence. We do not think the likelihood of a different result is so strong as to require the federal practice of jury determination of disputed factual issues to yield to the state rule in the interest of uniformity of outcome.

. . .

Reversed and remanded.

[The concurring and dissenting opinions of Justices WHITTAKER, FRANKFURTER, and HARLAN are omitted. The persistence of outcome-determination analysis among some on the Court is reflected in the following excerpt from Justice WHITTAKER:

It thus seems to be settled under the South Carolina Workmen's Compensation Law, and the decisions of the highest court of that State construing it, that the question whether exclusive jurisdiction, in cases like this, is vested in its Industrial Commission or in its courts of general jurisdiction is one for decision by the court, not by a jury. The Federal District Court, in this diversity case, is bound to follow the substantive South Carolina law that would be applied if the trial were to be held in a South Carolina court, in which State the Federal District Court sits. *Erie R. Co. v. Tompkins,* 304 U.S. 64. A Federal District Court sitting in South Carolina may not legally reach a substantially different result than would have been reached upon a trial of the same case "in a State court a block away." *Guaranty Trust Co. v. York,* 326 U.S. 99, 109.]

## Comments and Questions

1. What are the strategic implications for the litigants here of having a jury instead of a judge decide whether Byrd was a statutory "employee" of the Cooperative? If you represented Byrd, which decision maker would you prefer? While the conventional wisdom is that individuals are usually better off in front of juries when suing corporate defendants, there is much contradictory data. *See, e.g.,* Jeffrey J. Rachlinski, *Evidence Based Law,* 96 Cornell L. Rev. 901, 914-917 (2011).

2. Why doesn't the Seventh Amendment, protecting the right to jury trial, provide a simple answer to the judge vs. jury issue in *Byrd*? Look at the Court's footnote 10. What does the Court mean by "under the influence—if not the command—of the Seventh Amendment"?

3. Compare the extent to which the outcome of the litigation might be affected by the conflict in *Byrd* with the extent of outcome-determination in *Guaranty Trust* and in *Erie.* What are the implications of this comparison for

the twin *Erie* concerns of discouraging forum shopping and avoiding inconsistent results? How does Justice Brennan utilize this comparison in his analysis?

4. How would you articulate the test adopted by the Court to determine which mode of practice will control in situations like *Byrd*, where the state rule vies with "affirmative [federal] countervailing considerations"? The federal practice at stake here, maximizing jury participation in decision making, is said to reflect "the essential character or function of a federal court." On the state practice side of the balance, what does Brennan mean by the phrase "bound up" with state-created rights and obligations "in such a way that its application in the federal court is required," which he does not find is the case with the South Carolina rule? Where does outcome determination fit into the analysis?

5. *Byrd* does not address the larger group of *Erie*-doctrine cases where the federal practice at stake does not embody the very character of federal litigation, like allocation of authority between judge and jury, but is far more mundane, such as the manner in which process is served on the defendant. What happens when such a practice, codified in the Fed. R. Civ. P., conflicts with state practice? The next case represented the second phase of the rescue of federal procedure.

## ■ HANNA v. PLUMER
### 380 U.S. 460 (1965)

Chief Justice WARREN delivered the opinion of the Court:

The question to be decided is whether, in a civil action where the jurisdiction of the United States district court is based upon diversity of citizenship between the parties, service of process shall be made in the manner prescribed by state law or that set forth in Rule 4(d)(1) of the Federal Rules of Civil Procedure.

On February 6, 1963, petitioner, a citizen of Ohio, filed her complaint in the District Court for the District of Massachusetts, claiming damages in excess of $10,000 for personal injuries resulting from an automobile accident in South Carolina, allegedly caused by the negligence of one Louise Plumer Osgood, a Massachusetts citizen deceased at the time of the filing of the complaint. Respondent, Mrs. Osgood's executor and also a Massachusetts citizen, was named as defendant. On February 8, service was made by leaving copies of the summons and the complaint with respondent's wife at his residence, concededly in compliance with Rule 4(d)(1),* which provides:

The summons and complaint shall be served together. The plaintiff shall furnish the person making service with such copies as are necessary. Service shall be made as follows:

---

*Eds.' Note:* The rule now appears as Fed. R. Civ. P. 4(e)(2).

(1) Upon an individual other than an infant or an incompetent person, by delivering a copy of the summons and of the complaint to him personally or by leaving copies thereof at his dwelling house or usual place of abode with some person of suitable age and discretion then residing therein. . . .

Respondent filed his answer on February 26, alleging, inter alia, that the action could not be maintained because it had been brought "contrary to and in violation of the provisions of Massachusetts General Laws Chapter 197, Section 9." That section provides:

Except as provided in this chapter, an executor or administrator shall not be held to answer to an action by a creditor of the deceased which is not commenced within one year from the time of his giving bond for the performance of his trust, or to such an action which is commenced within said year unless before the expiration thereof the writ in such action has been served by delivery in hand upon such executor or administrator or service thereof accepted by him or a notice stating the name of the estate, the name and address of the creditor, the amount of the claim and the court in which the action has been brought has been filed in the proper registry of probate. . . .

On October 17, 1963, the District Court granted respondent's motion for summary judgment, citing *Ragan v. Merchants Transfer Co.*, 337 U.S. 530, and *Guaranty Trust Co. v. York*, 326 U.S. 99, in support of its conclusion that the adequacy of the service was to be measured by § 9, with which, the court held, petitioner had not complied. On appeal, petitioner admitted non-compliance with § 9, but argued that Rule 4(d)(1) defines the method by which service of process is to be effected in diversity actions. The Court of Appeals for the First Circuit, finding that "relatively recent amendments [to § 9] evince a clear legislative purpose to require personal notification within the year,"[1] concluded that the conflict of state and federal rules was over "a substantive rather than a procedural matter," and unanimously affirmed. Because of the threat to the goal of uniformity of federal procedure posed by the decision below, we granted certiorari.

---

1. Section 9 is in part a statue of limitations, providing that an executor need not "answer to an action . . . which is not commenced within one year from the time of his giving bond. . . ." This part of the statute, the purpose of which is to speed the settlement of estates, is not involved in this case, since the action clearly was timely commenced. (Respondent filed bond on March 1, 1962; the complaint was filed February 6, 1963; and the service—the propriety of which is in dispute—was made on February 8, 1963.) 331 F.2d at 159. Cf. *Guaranty Trust Co. v. York, supra; Ragan v. Merchants Transfer Co., supra*. Section 9 also provides for the manner of service. Generally, service of process must be made by "delivery in hand," although there are two alternatives: acceptance of service by the executor, or filing of a notice of claim, the components of which are set out in the statute, in the appropriate probate court. The purpose of this part of the statute, which is involved here, is, as the court below noted, to insure that executors will receive actual notice of claims. *Parker v. Rich*, 297 Mass. 111, 113-114 (1937). Actual notice is of course also the goal of Rule 4(d)(1); however, the Federal Rule reflects a determination that this goal can be achieved by a method less cumbersome than that prescribed in § 9. In this case the goal seems to have been achieved; although the affidavit filed by respondent in the District Court asserts that he had not been served in hand nor had he accepted service, it does not allege lack of actual notice.

We conclude that the adoption of Rule 4(d)(1), designed to control service of process in diversity actions,[3] neither exceeded the congressional mandate embodied in the Rules Enabling Act nor transgressed constitutional bounds, and that the Rule is therefore the standard against which the District Court should have measured the adequacy of the service. Accordingly, we reverse the decision of the Court of Appeals.

The Rules Enabling Act, 28 U.S.C. § 2072 (1958 ed.), provides, in pertinent part:

> The Supreme Court shall have the power to prescribe, by general rules, the forms of process, writs, pleadings, and motions, and the practice and procedure of the district courts of the United States in civil actions.
>
> Such rules shall not abridge, enlarge or modify any substantive right and shall preserve the right of trial by jury. . . .

Under the cases construing the scope of the Enabling Act, Rule 4(d)(1) clearly passes muster. Prescribing the manner in which a defendant is to be notified that a suit has been instituted against him, it relates to the "practice and procedure of the district courts." "The test must be whether a rule really regulates procedure,—the judicial process for enforcing rights and duties recognized by substantive law and for justly administering remedy and redress for disregard or infraction of them." *Sibbach v. Wilson & Co.*, 312 U.S. 1, 14.

In *Mississippi Pub. Corp. v. Murphree*, 326 U.S. 438, this Court upheld Rule 4(f), which permits service of a summons anywhere within the State (and not merely the district) in which a district court sits:

> We think that Rule 4(f) is in harmony with the Enabling Act. . . . Undoubtedly most alterations of the rules of practice and procedure may and often do affect the rights of litigants. Congress' prohibition of any alteration of substantive rights of litigants was obviously not addressed to such incidental effects as necessarily attend the adoption of the prescribed new rules of procedure upon the rights of litigants who, agreeably to rules of practice and procedure, have been brought before a court authorized to determine their rights. *Sibbach v. Wilson & Co.*, 312 U.S. 1, 11-14. The fact that the application of Rule 4(f) will operate to subject petitioner's rights to adjudication by the district court for northern Mississippi will undoubtedly affect those rights. But it does not operate to abridge, enlarge or modify the rules of decision by which that court will adjudicate its rights.

Thus were there no conflicting state procedure, Rule 4(d)(1) would clearly control. However, respondent, focusing on the contrary Massachusetts rule, calls to the Court's attention another line of cases, a line which—like the Federal Rules—had its birth in 1938. *Erie R. Co. v. Tompkins*, overruling

---

3. "These rules govern the procedure in the United States district courts in all suits of a civil nature whether cognizable as cases at law or in equity, with the exceptions stated in Rule 81. . . ." Fed. R. Civ. P. 1.

*Swift v. Tyson*, held that federal courts sitting in diversity cases, when deciding questions of "substantive" law, are bound by state court decisions as well as state statutes. The broad command of *Erie* was therefore identical to that of the Enabling Act: federal courts are to apply state substantive law and federal procedural law. However, as subsequent cases sharpened the distinction between substance and procedure, the line of cases following *Erie* diverged markedly from the line construing the Enabling Act. *Guaranty Trust Co. v. York* made it clear that *Erie*-type problems were not to be solved by reference to any traditional or common-sense substance-procedure distinction:

> And so the question is not whether a statute of limitations is deemed a matter of "procedure" in some sense. The question is . . . does it significantly affect the result of a litigation for a federal court to disregard a law of a State that would be controlling in an action upon the same claim by the same parties in a State court?

Respondent, by placing primary reliance on *York* and *Ragan*, suggests that the *Erie* doctrine acts as a check on the Federal Rules of Civil Procedure, that despite the clear command of Rule 4(d)(1), *Erie* and its progeny demand the application of the Massachusetts rule. Reduced to essentials, the argument is: (1) *Erie*, as refined in *York*, demands that federal courts apply state law whenever application of federal law in its stead will alter the outcome of the case. (2) In this case, a determination that the Massachusetts service requirements obtain will result in immediate victory for respondent. If, on the other hand, it should be held that Rule 4(d)(1) is applicable, the litigation will continue, with possible victory for petitioner. (3) Therefore, *Erie* demands application of the Massachusetts rule. The syllogism possesses an appealing simplicity, but is for several reasons invalid.

In the first place, it is doubtful that, even if there were no Federal Rule making it clear that in-hand service is not required in diversity actions, the *Erie* rule would have obligated the District Court to follow the Massachusetts procedure. "Outcome-determination" analysis was never intended to serve as a talisman. *Byrd v. Blue Ridge Cooperative*. Indeed, the message of *York* itself is that choices between state and federal law are to be made not by application of any automatic, "litmus paper" criterion, but rather by reference to the policies underlying the *Erie* rule. *Guaranty Trust Co. v. York*.

The *Erie* rule is rooted in part in a realization that it would be unfair for the character or result of a litigation materially to differ because the suit had been brought in a federal court.

> Diversity of citizenship jurisdiction was conferred in order to prevent apprehended discrimination in state courts against those not citizens of the State. *Swift v. Tyson* introduced grave discrimination by non-citizens against citizens. It made rights enjoyed under the unwritten 'general law' vary according to whether enforcement was sought in the state or in the federal court; and the

privilege of selecting the court in which the right should be determined was conferred upon the non-citizen. Thus, the doctrine rendered impossible equal protection of the law.

*Erie R. Co. v. Tompkins, supra*, at 74-75.

The decision was also in part a reaction to the practice of "forum-shopping" which had grown up in response to the rule of *Swift v. Tyson.* That the *York* test was an attempt to effectuate these policies is demonstrated by the fact that the opinion framed the inquiry in terms of "substantial" variations between state and federal litigation. Not only are nonsubstantial, or trivial, variations not likely to raise the sort of equal protection problems which troubled the Court in *Erie;* they are also unlikely to influence the choice of a forum. The "outcome-determination" test therefore cannot be read without reference to the twin aims of the *Erie* rule: discouragement of forum-shopping and avoidance of inequitable administration of the laws.[9]

The difference between the conclusion that the Massachusetts rule is applicable, and the conclusion that it is not, is of course at this point "outcome-determinative" in the sense that if we hold the state rule to apply, respondent prevails, whereas if we hold that Rule 4(d)(1) governs, the litigation will continue. But in this sense every procedural variation is "outcome-determinative." For example, having brought suit in a federal court, a plaintiff cannot then insist on the right to file subsequent pleadings in accord with the time limits applicable in the state courts, even though enforcement of the federal timetable will, if he continues to insist that he must meet only the state time limit, result in determination of the controversy against him. So it is here. Though choice of the federal or state rule will at this point have a marked effect upon the outcome of the litigation, the difference between the two rules would be of scant, if any, relevance to the choice of a forum. Petitioner, in choosing her forum, was not presented with a situation where application of the state rule would wholly bar recovery; rather, adherence to the state rule would have resulted only in altering the way in which process was served.[11] Moreover, it is difficult to argue that permitting service of defendant's wife to take the place of in-hand service of defendant himself

9. The Court of Appeals seemed to frame the inquiry in terms of how "important" § 9 is to the State. In support of its suggestion that § 9 serves some interest the State regards as vital to its citizens, the court noted that something like § 9 has been on the books in Massachusetts a long time, that § 9 has been amended a number of times, and that § 9 [was] designed to make sure that executors receive actual notice. *See* note 1, *supra.* The apparent lack of relation among these three observations is not surprising, because it is not clear to what sort of question the Court of Appeals was addressing itself. One cannot meaningfully ask how important something is without first asking "important for what purpose?" *Erie* and its progeny make clear that when a federal court sitting in a diversity case is faced with a question of whether or not to apply state law, the importance of a state rule is indeed relevant, but only in the context of asking whether application of the rule would make so important a difference to the character or result of the litigation that failure to enforce it would unfairly discriminate against citizens of the forum State, or whether application of the rule would have so important an effect upon the fortunes of one or both of the litigants that failure to enforce it would be likely to cause a plaintiff to choose the federal court.

11. We cannot seriously entertain the thought that one suing an estate would be led to choose the federal court because of a belief that adherence to Rule 4(d)(1) is less likely to give the executor actual notice than § 9, and therefore, more likely to produce a default judgment. Rule 4(d)(1) is well designed to give actual notice, as it did in this case. *See* note 1, *supra.*

alters the mode of enforcement of state-created rights in a fashion sufficiently "substantial" to raise the sort of equal protection problems to which the *Erie* opinion alluded.

There is, however, a more fundamental flaw in respondent's syllogism: the incorrect assumption that the rule of *Erie R. Co. v. Tompkins* constitutes the appropriate test of the validity and therefore the applicability of a Federal Rule of Civil Procedure. The *Erie* rule has never been invoked to void a Federal Rule. It is true that there have been cases where this Court has held applicable a state rule in the face of an argument that the situation was governed by one of the Federal Rules. But the holding of each such case was not that *Erie* commanded displacement of a Federal Rule by an inconsistent state rule, but rather that the scope of the Federal Rule was not as broad as the losing party urged, and therefore, there being no Federal Rule which covered the point in dispute, *Erie* commanded the enforcement of state law. . . . (Here, of course, the clash is unavoidable; Rule 4(d)(1) says—implicitly, but with unmistakable clarity—that in-hand service is not required in federal courts.) At the same time, in cases adjudicating the validity of Federal Rules, we have not applied the *York* rule or other refinements of *Erie*, but have to this day continued to decide questions concerning the scope of the Enabling Act and the constitutionality of specific Federal Rules in light of the distinction set forth in *Sibbach. E.g., Schlagenhauf v. Holder*, 379 U.S. 104.

Nor has the development of two separate lines of cases been inadvertent. The line between "substance" and "procedure" shifts as the legal context changes. "Each implies different variables depending upon the particular problem for which it is used." *Guaranty Trust Co. v. York, supra*, at 108. It is true that both the Enabling Act and the *Erie* rule say, roughly, that federal courts are to apply state "substantive" law and federal "procedural" law, but from that it need not follow that the tests are identical. For they were designed to control very different sorts of decisions. When a situation is covered by one of the Federal Rules, the question facing the court is a far cry from the typical, relatively unguided *Erie* choice: the court has been instructed to apply the Federal Rule, and can refuse to do so only if the Advisory Committee, this Court, and Congress erred in their prima facie judgment that the Rule in question transgresses neither the terms of the Enabling Act nor constitutional restrictions.

We are reminded by the *Erie* opinion that neither Congress nor the federal courts can, under the guise of formulating rules of decision for federal courts, fashion rules which are not supported by a grant of federal authority contained in Article I or some other section of the Constitution; in such areas state law must govern because there can be no other law. But the opinion in *Erie*, which involved no Federal Rule and dealt with a question which was "substantive" in every traditional sense (whether the railroad owed a duty of care to Tompkins as a trespasser or a licensee), surely neither said nor implied that measures like Rule 4(d)(1) are unconstitutional. For the constitutional provision for a federal court system (augmented by the Necessary and Proper Clause) carries with it congressional power to make rules governing the practice and pleading in those courts, which in turn includes a power to regulate matters which, though falling within the uncertain area between substance and procedure, are rationally capable of classification as either. Neither *York* nor the cases following it ever suggested that the rule there laid down for coping with situations where no Federal Rule applies is coextensive with the limitation on Congress to which *Erie* had adverted. Although this Court has never before been confronted with a case where the applicable Federal Rule is in direct collision with the law of the relevant State, courts of appeals faced with such clashes have rightly discerned the implications of our decisions.

> One of the shaping purposes of the Federal Rules is to bring about uniformity in the federal courts by getting away from local rules. This is especially true of matters which relate to the administration of legal proceedings, an area in which federal courts have traditionally exerted strong inherent power, completely aside from the powers Congress expressly conferred in the Rules. The purpose of the *Erie* doctrine, even as extended in *York* and *Ragan*, was never to bottle up federal courts with "outcome-determinative" and "integral-relations" stoppers—when there are "affirmative countervailing [federal] considerations" and when there is a Congressional mandate (the Rules) supported by constitutional authority.

*Lumbermen's Mutual Casualty Co. v. Wright*, 322 F.2d 759, 764 (5th Cir. 1963).

*Erie* and its offspring cast no doubt on the long-recognized power of Congress to prescribe housekeeping rules for federal courts even though some of those rules will inevitably differ from comparable state rules. "When, because the plaintiff happens to be a non-resident, such a right is enforceable in a federal as well as in a State court, the forms and mode of enforcing the right may at times, naturally enough, vary because the two judicial systems are not identic." *Guaranty Trust Co. v. York, supra*. Thus, though a court, in measuring a Federal Rule against the standards contained in the Enabling Act and the Constitution, need not wholly blind itself to the degree to which the Rule makes the character and result of the federal litigation stray from the course it would follow in state courts, it cannot be forgotten that the *Erie* rule, and the guidelines suggested in *York*, were created to serve another purpose altogether. To hold that a Federal Rule of Civil Procedure must cease to function whenever it alters the mode of enforcing state-created rights would be to disembowel either the Constitution's grant of power over federal procedure or Congress' attempt to exercise that power in the Enabling Act. Rule 4(d)(1) is valid and controls the instant case.

Reversed.

Justice HARLAN, concurring:

It is unquestionably true that up to now *Erie* and the cases following it have not succeeded in articulating a workable doctrine governing choice of law in diversity actions. I respect the Court's effort to clarify the situation in today's opinion. However, in doing so I think it has misconceived the constitutional premises of *Erie* and has failed to deal adequately with those past decisions upon which the courts below relied.

*Erie* was something more than an opinion which worried about "forum-shopping and avoidance of inequitable administration of the laws," although to be sure these were important elements of the decision. I have always regarded that decision as one of the modern cornerstones of our federalism, expressing policies that profoundly touch the allocation of judicial power between the state and federal systems. *Erie* recognized that there should not be two conflicting systems of law controlling the primary activity of citizens, for such alternative governing authority must necessarily give rise to a debilitating uncertainty in the planning of everyday affairs.[1] And it recognized that the scheme of our Constitution envisions an allocation of law-making functions between state and federal legislative processes which is undercut if the federal judiciary can make substantive law affecting state affairs beyond the bounds of congressional legislative powers in this regard. Thus, in diversity cases *Erie* commands that it be the state law governing primary private activity which prevails.

The shorthand formulations which have appeared in some past decisions are prone to carry untoward results that frequently arise from oversimplification. The Court is quite right in stating that the "outcome-determinative" test of *Guaranty Trust Co. v. York*, if taken literally, proves too much, for any rule, no matter how clearly "procedural," can affect the outcome of litigation if it is not obeyed. In turning from the "outcome" test of *York* back to the unadorned forum-shopping rationale of *Erie*, however, the Court falls prey to like oversimplification, for a simple forum-shopping rule also proves too much; litigants often choose a federal forum merely to obtain what they consider the advantages of the Federal Rules of Civil Procedure or to try their cases before a supposedly more favorable judge. To my mind the proper line of approach in determining whether to apply a state or a federal rule, whether "substantive" or "procedural," is to stay close to basic principles by inquiring if the choice of rule would substantially affect those primary decisions respecting human conduct which our constitutional system leaves to state regulation. If so, *Erie* and the Constitution require that the state rule prevail, even in the face of a conflicting federal rule.

The Court weakens, if indeed it does not submerge, this basic principle by finding, in effect, a grant of substantive legislative power in the constitutional provision for a federal court system (*compare Swift v. Tyson*), and through it, setting up the Federal Rules as a body of law inviolate. "The constitutional provision for a federal court system . . . carries with it congressional power . . . to regulate matters which, though falling within the uncertain area between substance and procedure, are rationally capable of

---

1. Since the rules involved in the present case are parallel rather than conflicting, this rationale does not come into play here.

classification as either." So long as a reasonable man could characterize any duly adopted federal rule as "procedural," the Court, unless I misapprehend what is said, would have it apply no matter how seriously it frustrated a State's substantive regulation of the primary conduct and affairs of its citizens. Since the members of the Advisory Committee, the Judicial Conference, and this Court who formulated the Federal Rules are presumably reasonable men, it follows that the integrity of the Federal Rules is absolute. Whereas the unadulterated outcome and forum-shopping tests may err too far toward honoring state rules, I submit that the Court's "arguably procedural, ergo constitutional" test moves too fast and far in the other direction.

The courts below relied upon this Court's decisions in *Ragan v. Merchants Transfer Co.*, 337 U.S. 530, and *Cohen v. Beneficial Loan Corp.*, 337 U.S. 541. Those cases deserve more attention than this Court has given them, particularly *Ragan* which, if still good law, would in my opinion call for affirmance of the result reached by the Court of Appeals. Further, a discussion of these two cases will serve to illuminate the "diversity" thesis I am advocating.

In *Ragan* a Kansas statute of limitations provided that an action was deemed commenced when service was made on the defendant. Despite Federal Rule 3 which provides that an action commences with the filing of the complaint, the Court held that for purposes of the Kansas statute of limitations a diversity tort action commenced only when service was made upon the defendant. The effect of this holding was that although the plaintiff had filed his federal complaint within the state period of limitations, his action was barred because the federal marshal did not serve a summons on the defendant until after the limitations period had run. I think that the decision was wrong. At most, application of the Federal Rule would have meant that potential Kansas tort defendants would have to defer for a few days the satisfaction of knowing that they had not been sued within the limitations period. The choice of the Federal Rule would have had no effect on the primary stages of private activity from which torts arise, and only the most minimal effect on behavior following the commission of the tort. In such circumstances the interest of the federal system in proceeding under its own rules should have prevailed.

*Cohen v. Beneficial Loan Corp.* held that a federal diversity court must apply a state statute requiring a small stockholder in a stockholder derivative suit to post a bond securing payment of defense costs as a condition to prosecuting an action. Such a statute is not "outcome determinative"; the plaintiff can win with or without it. The Court now rationalizes the case on the ground that the statute might affect the plaintiff's choice of forum, but as has been pointed out, a simple forum-shopping test proves too much. The proper view of *Cohen* is, in my opinion, that the statute was meant to inhibit small stockholders from instituting "strike suits," and thus it was designed and could be expected to have a substantial impact on private primary activity. Anyone who was at the trial bar during the period when *Cohen* arose can appreciate the strong state policy reflected in the statute. I think it wholly legitimate to view Federal Rule 23 as not purporting to deal with the problem. But even had the Federal Rules purported to do so, and in so doing provided a substantially less effective deterrent to strike suits, I think the state rule should still have prevailed. That is where I believe the Court's view differs from mine; for the Court attributes such overriding force to the Federal Rules that it is hard to think of a case where a conflicting state rule would be allowed to operate, even though the state rule reflected policy considerations which, under *Erie*, would lie within the realm of state legislative authority.

It remains to apply what has been said to the present case. The Massachusetts rule provides that an executor need not answer suits unless in-hand service was made upon him or notice of the action was filed in the proper registry of probate within one year of his giving bond. The evident intent of this statute is to permit an executor to distribute the estate which he is administering without fear that further liabilities may be outstanding for which he could be held personally liable. If the Federal District Court in Massachusetts applies Rule 4(d)(1) of the Federal Rules of Civil Procedure instead of the Massachusetts service rule, what effect would that have on the speed and assurance with which estates are distributed? As I see it, the effect would not be substantial. It would mean simply that an executor would have to check at his own house or the federal courthouse as well as the registry of probate before he could distribute the estate with impunity. As this does not seem enough to give rise to any real impingement on the vitality of the state policy which the Massachusetts rule is intended to serve, I concur in the judgment of the Court.

## Comments and Questions

1. Note how Chief Justice Warren foreshadows the result early on in the *Hanna* decision when he observes: "Because of the threat to the goal of uniformity of federal procedure posed by the decision below, we granted certiorari."

2. Compare the extent to which the outcome of the litigation is affected by the rules conflict in *Hanna* with the extent of outcome-determination in (1) *Erie*; (2) *Guaranty Trust*; (3) *Byrd*. How does Chief Justice Warren use these comparisons to justify his decision in *Hanna*? What are the implications of this comparison for the "twin aims of *Erie*," i.e., discouraging forum shopping and avoiding inconsistent results?

3. What is the critical time juncture for assessing outcome determination—in *Hanna*, is it on the day the case was filed, or at the point where defendant's motion for summary judgment was decided (and the one-year statute of limitations had passed)? Do you see the difference between using these competing points of reference? Why does Warren choose the former, the day the suit was filed? (Hint: When does forum shopping by a plaintiff occur? Look at the Court's footnote 11.) Note Warren's observation that "petitioner, in choosing her forum, was not presented with a situation where application of the state rule would wholly bar recovery; rather, adherence to the state

rule would have resulted only in altering the way in which process was served."

4. Mass. Gen. Laws ch. 197, § 9, requires *both* that suit be filed against an executor within one year from his giving bond, *and* that suit be commenced by in-hand personal service. Regarding the one-year limitation, why was *Hanna* not controlled by the long-established rule of *Guaranty Trust* that a federal court sitting in diversity had to follow the statute of limitations of the state that created the claim? Look at the Court's footnote 1.

5. Can you see why the Court would grant more deference to a Federal Rule of Civil Procedure, which has the congressional imprimatur of the Rules Enabling Act and the elaborate rulemaking process behind it (look back at Chapter 4, Part E(4)), than to a practice lacking that pedigree, such as the judge-made custom of extending time for filing suits seeking equitable relief in *Guaranty Trust*? This renders defendant's syllogism—"(1) *Erie*, as refined in *York*, demands that federal courts apply state law whenever application of federal law in its stead will alter the outcome of the case. (2) In this case, a determination that the Massachusetts service requirements obtain will result in immediate victory for respondent. If, on the other hand, it should be held that Rule 4(d)(1) is applicable, the litigation will continue, with possible victory for petitioner. (3) Therefore, *Erie* demands application of the Massachusetts rule"—fundamentally flawed in the eyes of the *Hanna* Court. Do you see why a Court concerned about the uniformity of federal procedure, and the viability of the Fed. R. Civ. P., would have to reject this syllogism?

For reflections on *Hanna* by Chief Justice Warren's law clerk at the time it was decided, see John Hart Ely, *The Irrepressible Myth of* Erie, 87 Harv. L. Rev. 693 (1974).

6. ***Erie* cases after *Hanna*.** *Hanna* has added an important initial step to the analysis of conflicts between state and federal practice in federal diversity cases, namely identification of *the source* of the federal side of the conflict. Different tracks (what Chief Justice Warren refers to as "the development of two separate lines of cases") are followed, depending on whether there is a Fed. R. Civ. P. on point or not. What is the test for determining whether to apply a Fed. R. Civ. P. when it *directly conflicts* with state practice? Do you see why Justice Harlan characterizes this track as "the Court's 'arguably procedural, ergo constitutional' test"?

What is the test where the competing federal practice is *not* codified in the Fed. R. Civ. P., the so-called unguided *Erie* choice? Note that in the latter situation, the Rules of Decision Act (as construed in *Erie* and *Guaranty Trust*) is the controlling statute (usually pointing to the state's rule), while in the former it is the Rules Enabling Act (as construed in *Hanna*, and virtually assuring application of the Fed. R. Civ. P.). *See generally* John Hart Ely, *The Irrepressible Myth of* Erie, 87 Harv. L. Rev. 693 (1974).

7. The Rules Enabling Act authorizes the promulgation of rules of "practice and procedure." 28 U.S.C. § 2072. How does the Court read the proviso that "[s]uch rules shall not abridge, enlarge or modify any

substantive right"? Note that *Hanna* distinguishes the substance/procedure dichotomy drawn in the Rules Enabling Act from the same dichotomy in the "unguided" choice where the federal practice is not codified. Can you articulate this difference?

8. Was Justice Harlan correct in arguing that under the Court's test, "the integrity of the Federal Rules is absolute" and "it is hard to think of a case where a conflicting state rule would be allowed to operate, even though the state rule reflected policy considerations which, under *Erie*, would lie within the realm of state legislative authority"? Consider this prediction when you read *Walker v. ARMCO Steel Corp*, our next case.

9. What alternative test would Justice Harlan impose for resolving the choice of law issue? Is his "does-the-choice-of-rule-substantially-affect-those-primary-decisions-respecting-human-conduct-which-our-constitutional-system-leaves-to-state-regulation" test workable, or is it too fuzzy?

10. Given that the Supreme Court itself is the rule-making authority that ultimately adopts and amends the Federal Rules of Civil Procedure under the Rules Enabling Act, does the Court have a conflict of interest when it later judicially considers the validity of a rule? Justices Black and Douglas thought so. Dissenting from the adoption of proposed amendments to the Federal Rules of Civil Procedure in 1963, they suggested that the responsibility for drafting should be shifted: "Transfer of the function to the Judicial Conference would relieve us of the embarrassment of having to sit in judgment on the constitutionality of rules which we have approved and which in given circumstances might have to be declared invalid." 374 U.S. 865, 869-870 (1963).

Justice White joined this view in 1993, adding: "I did my share of litigating when in practice and once served on the Advisory Committee for the Civil Rules, but the trial practice is a dynamic profession, and the longer one is away from it the less likely it is that he or she should presume to second-guess the careful work of the active professionals manning the rulemaking committees, work that the Judicial Conference has approved." 146 F.R.D. 501, 504 (1993).

11. In his influential article *The Rules Enabling Act of 1934*, 130 U. Pa. L. Rev. 1015 (1982), Professor Stephen Burbank concludes that the second sentence of the Act has been misinterpreted by the courts. In his view, the proscription that the rules "shall neither abridge, enlarge nor modify the substantive rights of any litigant" was intended to allocate power between the Supreme Court and Congress as a matter of the separation of powers *within* the federal government, and is not directed at the relation *between* the federal government and the states. If Burbank is right, what are the implications for the analysis adopted by the Court in *Hanna*?

---

How invulnerable are the Federal Rules of Civil Procedure after *Hanna*? The following case may surprise you.

# ■ WALKER v. ARMCO STEEL CORP. — *foreign corp.*

### *446 U.S. 740 (1980)*

Justice MARSHALL delivered the opinion of the Court:

This case presents the issue whether in a diversity action the federal court should follow state law or, alternatively, Rule 3 of the Federal Rules of Civil Procedure in determining when an action is commenced for the purpose of tolling the state statute of limitations.

## I

According to the allegations of the complaint, petitioner, a carpenter, was injured on August 22, 1975, in Oklahoma City, Okla., while pounding a Shef-field nail into a cement wall. Respondent was the manufacturer of the nail. Petitioner claimed that the nail contained a defect which caused its head to shatter and strike him in the right eye, resulting in permanent injuries. The defect was allegedly caused by respondent's negligence in manufacture and design.

Petitioner is a resident of Oklahoma, and respondent is a foreign corporation having its principal place of business in a State other than Oklahoma. Since there was diversity of citizenship, petitioner brought suit in the United States District Court for the Western District of Oklahoma. The complaint was filed on August 19, 1977. Although summons was issued that same day, service of process was not made on respondent's authorized service agent until December 1, 1977.[2] On January 5, 1978, respondent filed a motion to dismiss the complaint on the ground that the action was barred by the applicable Oklahoma statute of limitations. Although the complaint had been filed within the 2-year statute of limitations, state law does not deem the action "commenced" for purposes of the statute of limitations until service of the summons on the defendant, Okla. Stat., Tit. 12, § 97 (1971). If the complaint is filed within the limitations period, however, the action is deemed to have commenced from that date of filing if the plaintiff serves the defendant within 60 days, even though that service may occur outside the limitations period. In this case, service was not effectuated until long after this 60-day period had expired. Petitioner in his reply brief to the motion to dismiss admitted that his case would be foreclosed in state court, but he argued that Rule 3 of the Federal Rules of Civil Procedure governs the manner in which an action is commenced in federal court for all purposes, including the tolling of the state statute of limitations.

---

2. The record does not indicate why this delay occurred. The face of the process record shows that the United States Marshal acknowledged receipt of the summons on December 1, 1977, and that service was effectuated that same day. At oral argument counsel for petitioner stated that the summons was found "in an unmarked folder in the filing cabinet" in counsel's office some 90 days after the complaint had been filed. Counsel conceded that the summons was not delivered to the Marshal until December 1. It is unclear why the summons was placed in the filing cabinet.

The District Court dismissed the complaint as barred by the Oklahoma statute of limitations. The court concluded that Okla. Stat., Tit. 12, § 97 (1971) was "an integral part of the Oklahoma statute of limitations," and therefore under *Ragan v. Merchants Transfer & Warehouse Co.*, 337 U.S. 530 (1949), state law applied. The court rejected the argument that *Ragan* had been implicitly overruled in *Hanna v. Plumer.*

The United States Court of Appeals for the Tenth Circuit affirmed. That court concluded that Okla. Stat., Tit. 12, § 97 (1971), was in "direct conflict" with Rule 3. However, the Oklahoma statute was "indistinguishable" from the statute involved in *Ragan*, and the court felt itself "constrained" to follow *Ragan.*

We granted certiorari, because of a conflict among the Courts of Appeals. We now affirm.

## II

The question whether state or federal law should apply on various issues arising in an action based on state law which has been brought in federal court under diversity of citizenship jurisdiction has troubled this Court for many years. In the landmark decision of *Erie R. Co. v. Tompkins*, we overturned the rule expressed in *Swift v. Tyson* that federal courts exercising diversity jurisdiction need not, in matters of "general jurisprudence," apply the nonstatutory law of the State. The Court noted that "[diversity] of citizenship jurisdiction was conferred in order to prevent apprehended discrimination in state courts against those not citizens of the State." The doctrine of *Swift v. Tyson* had led to the undesirable results of discrimination in favor of noncitizens, prevention of uniformity in the administration of state law, and forum shopping. In response, we established the rule that "[except] in matters governed by the Federal Constitution or by Acts of Congress, the law to be applied in any [diversity] case is the law of the State."

In *Guaranty Trust Co. v. York*, . . . we concluded that the state statute of limitations should be applied. "Plainly enough, a statute that would completely bar recovery in a suit if brought in a State court bears on a State-created right vitally and not merely formally or negligibly. As to consequences that so intimately affect recovery or non-recovery a federal court in a diversity case should follow State law."

The decision in *York* led logically to our holding in *Ragan v. Merchants Transfer & Warehouse Co., supra.* In *Ragan*, . . . the applicable statute of limitations supplied by Kansas law was two years. Kansas had an additional statute which provided: "An action shall be deemed commenced within the meaning of [the statute of limitations], as to each defendant, at the date of the summons which is served on him. . . . The defendant moved for summary judgment on the ground that the Kansas statute of limitations barred the action since service had not been made within either the 2-year period. . . . It was conceded that had the case been brought in Kansas state court it would have been barred. Nonetheless, the District Court held that the statute had been tolled by the filing of the complaint. The Court of Appeals reversed because "the requirement of service of summons within the statutory period was an integral part of that state's statute of limitations."

We affirmed, relying on *Erie* and *York*. "We cannot give [the cause of action] longer life in the federal court than it would have had in the state court without adding something to the cause of action. We may not do that consistently with *Erie R. Co. v. Tompkins*." We rejected the argument that Rule 3 of the Federal Rules of Civil Procedure governed the manner in which an action was commenced in federal court for purposes of tolling the state statute of limitations. Instead, we held that the service of summons statute controlled because it was an integral part of the state statute of limitations, and under *York* that statute of limitations was part of the state-law cause of action.

*Ragan* was not our last pronouncement in this difficult area, however. In 1965 we decided *Hanna v. Plumer*, holding that in a civil action where federal jurisdiction was based upon diversity of citizenship, Rule 4(d)(1) of the Federal Rules of Civil Procedure, rather than state law, governed the manner in which process was served. Massachusetts law required in-hand service on an executor or administrator of an estate, whereas Rule 4 permits service by leaving copies of the summons and complaint at the defendant's home with some person "of suitable age and discretion." The Court noted that in the absence of a conflicting state procedure, the Federal Rule would plainly control. We stated that the "outcome-determination" test of *Erie* and *York* had to be read with reference to the "twin aims" of *Erie*: "discouragement of forum-shopping and avoidance of inequitable administration of the laws." We determined that the choice between the state in-hand service rule and the Federal Rule "would be of scant, if any, relevance to the choice of a forum," for the plaintiff "was not presented with a situation where application of the state rule would wholly bar recovery; rather, adherence to the state rule would have resulted only in altering the way in which process was served." This factor served to distinguish that case from *York* and *Ragan*.

The Court in *Hanna*, however, pointed out "a more fundamental flaw" in the defendant's argument in that case. The Court concluded that the *Erie* doctrine was simply not the appropriate test of the validity and applicability of one of the Federal Rules of Civil Procedure:

> The *Erie* rule has never been invoked to void a Federal Rule. It is true that there have been cases where this Court had held applicable a state rule in the face of an argument that the situation was governed by one of the Federal Rules. But the holding of each such case was not that *Erie* commanded displacement of a Federal Rule by an inconsistent state rule, but rather that the scope of the Federal Rule was not as broad as the losing party urged, and therefore, there being no Federal Rule which covered the point in dispute, *Erie* commanded the enforcement of state law.

The Court cited *Ragan* as one of the examples of this proposition. The Court explained that where the Federal Rule was clearly applicable, as in *Hanna*, the test was whether the Rule was within the scope of the Rules Enabling Act, 28 U.S.C. § 2072, and if so, within a constitutional grant of power such as the Necessary and Proper Clause of Art. I.

## III

The present case is indistinguishable from *Ragan*. The statutes in both cases require service of process to toll the statute of limitations, and in fact the predecessor to the Oklahoma statute in this case was derived from the predecessor to the Kansas statute in *Ragan*. Here, as in *Ragan*, the complaint was filed in federal court under diversity jurisdiction within the 2-year statute of limitations, but service of process did not occur until after the 2-year period and the 60-day service period had run. In both cases the suit would concededly have been barred in the applicable state court, and in both instances the state service statute was held to be an integral part of the statute of limitations by the lower court more familiar than we with state law. Accordingly, as the Court of Appeals held below, the instant action is barred by the statute of limitations unless *Ragan* is no longer good law.

Petitioner argues that the analysis and holding of *Ragan* did not survive our decision in *Hanna*. Petitioner's position is that Okla. Stat., Tit. 12, § 97 (1971), is in direct conflict with the Federal Rule. Under *Hanna*, petitioner contends, the appropriate question is whether Rule 3 is within the scope of the Rules Enabling Act and, if so, within the constitutional power of Congress. In petitioner's view, the Federal Rule is to be applied unless it violates one of those two restrictions. This argument ignores both the force of *stare decisis* and the specific limitations that we carefully placed on the *Hanna* analysis.

. . . This Court in *Hanna* distinguished *Ragan* rather than overruled it, and for good reason. Application of the *Hanna* analysis is premised on a "direct collision" between the Federal Rule and the state law. In *Hanna* itself the "clash" between Rule 4(d)(1) and the state in-hand service requirement was "unavoidable." The first question must therefore be whether the scope of the Federal Rule in fact is sufficiently broad to control the issue before the Court. It is only if that question is answered affirmatively that the *Hanna* analysis applies.[9]

. . . [T]he present case is an instance where "the scope of the Federal Rule [is] not as broad as the losing party [urges], and therefore, there being no Federal Rule which [covers] the point in dispute, *Erie* [commands] the enforcement of state law." Rule 3 simply states that "[a] civil action is commenced by filing a complaint with the court." There is no indication that the

---

9. This is not to suggest that the Federal Rules of Civil Procedure are to be narrowly construed in order to avoid a "direct collision" with state law. The Federal Rules should be given their plain meaning. If a direct collision with state law arises from that plain meaning, then the analysis developed in *Hanna v. Plumer* applies.

Rule was intended to toll a state statute of limitations, much less that it purported to displace state tolling rules for purposes of state statutes of limitations. In our view, in diversity actions Rule 3 governs the date from which various timing requirements of the Federal Rules begin to run, but does not affect state statutes of limitations.

In contrast to Rule 3, the Oklahoma statute is a statement of a substantive decision by that State that actual service on, and accordingly actual notice by, the defendant is an integral part of the several policies served by the statute of limitations. The statute of limitations establishes a deadline after which the defendant may legitimately have peace of mind; it also recognizes that after a certain period of time it is unfair to require the defendant to attempt to piece together his defense to an old claim. A requirement of actual service promotes both of those functions of the statute. It is these policy aspects which make the service requirement an "integral" part of the statute of limitations both in this case and in *Ragan*. As such, the service rule must be considered part and parcel of the statute of limitations. Rule 3 does not replace such policy determinations found in state law. Rule 3 and Okla. Stat., Tit. 12, § 97 (1971), can exist side by side, therefore, each controlling its own intended sphere of coverage without conflict.

Since there is no direct conflict between the Federal Rule and the state law, the *Hanna* analysis does not apply. Instead, the policies behind *Erie* and *Ragan* control the issue whether, in the absence of a federal rule directly on point, state service requirements which are an integral part of the state statute of limitations should control in an action based on state law which is filed in federal court under diversity jurisdiction. The reasons for the application of such a state service requirement in a diversity action in the absence of a conflicting federal rule are well explained in *Erie* and *Ragan*, and need not be repeated here. It is sufficient to note that although in this case failure to apply the state service law might not create any problem of forum shopping,[15] the result would be an "inequitable administration" of the law. *Hanna v. Plumer*. There is simply no reason why, in the absence of a controlling federal rule, an action based on state law which concededly would be barred in the state courts by the state statute of limitations should proceed through litigation to judgment in federal court solely because of the fortuity that there is diversity of citizenship between the litigants. The policies underlying diversity jurisdiction do not support such a distinction between state and federal plaintiffs, and *Erie* and its progeny do not permit it.

The judgment of the Court of Appeals is Affirmed.

---

15. There is no indication that when petitioner filed his suit in federal court he had any reason to believe that he would be unable to comply with the service requirements of Oklahoma law or that he chose to sue in federal court in an attempt to avoid those service requirements.

## Comments and Questions

1. As in *Hanna*, the Court detected no indication that Walker had shopped for the federal forum in order to avoid the Oklahoma service requirements. *See* footnote 15. Why then the different result in the two cases—the federal rule trumps in *Hanna*, but not in *Walker*? The answer lies in the different tests applied to direct Fed. R. Civ. P. conflicts and "unguided *Erie*" conflicts.

2. *Walker* involves what Professor Burbank refers to as the "twilight zone" between substance and procedure that is not controlled by the Federal Rules. Stephen Burbank, Semtek, *Forum Shopping, and Federal Common Law*, 77 Notre Dame L. Rev. 1027, 1028 (2002). The key to resolving such cases is determining whether the Fed. R. Civ. P. and the state rule that are in *apparent* conflict are truly coextensive (i.e., cover the same ground), and thus in *direct unavoidable collision*.

If they are in direct conflict (as where the Massachusetts rule required in-hand service, but Fed. R. Civ. P. 4(d)(1) did not), *Hanna*'s Rules Enabling Act analysis controls, favoring application of the Fed. R. Civ. P. as long as it is arguably procedural. If there is *no* direct conflict with a Fed. R. Civ. P., and thus the federal practice at stake does not carry the imprimatur of the formal rule-making process (where, for example, it is judge-made), then *Walker* reverts to enforcing *Erie*'s twin aims of discouraging forum shopping and avoiding inconsistent results, achieved through *Guaranty Trust Co. v. York*'s outcome test and usually favoring state practice.

3. *Walker* reflects an inclination to read the Fed. R. Civ. P. narrowly so as to avoid direct conflicts whenever possible, notwithstanding the Court's explicit disavowal in footnote 9. Fed. R. Civ. P. 3's "commenced" language is read to simply refer to the starting point for the time periods set out elsewhere in the Rules, not the tolling of the statute of limitations. This leaves only a conflict between the Okla. Stat. and the federal judicial practice of tolling upon filing of the case.

Critical of this approach, Professor Catherine Struve has argued that "[m]inimizing conflict with the Enabling Act is a worthy goal, but it can invite departure from a Rule's text and Notes." Catherine T. Struve, *The Paradox of Delegation: Interpreting the Federal Rules of Civil Procedure*, 150 U. Pa. L. Rev. 1099, 1150 (2002).

What does *Walker* do to the goal of uniformity of federal procedure articulated by Chief Justice Warren in *Hanna*? What about the Fed. R. Civ. P. rescue operation?

4. In *Harvey's Wagon Wheel, Inc. v. Van Blitter*, 959 F.2d 153 (9th Cir. 1992), a diversity action by a casino to collect on a gambling debt, defendant moved to dismiss because plaintiff failed to bring the case to trial within five years, as required by Nev. R. Civ. P. 41(e). The casino countered that Fed. R. Civ. P. 41(b) should control in the federal action. That rule *permits* dismissal for failure to prosecute but, unlike the Nevada rule, does not set a mandatory time period. Defendant, seeking to come within *Walker* and thus application of the state rule, contended that there was "no direct collision here because

the rules differ somewhat in scope. The federal rule does not require dismissal at any point; the Nevada rule requires dismissal after five years." The Ninth Circuit disagreed:

> While not perfectly coextensive, the federal and Nevada involuntary dismissal rules conflict sufficiently to meet the [*Hanna*] standard. The federal rule is "sufficiently broad to cover the point in dispute" because it permits dismissal at (and before) the time that the Nevada rule requires dismissal. Additionally, both rules aim to promote judicial housekeeping and diligent prosecution. Both rules also incorporate discretion, albeit in different degrees. Accordingly, we hold that the Federal Rule 41(b) and Nevada Rule 41(e) are coextensive.

959 F.2d at 156. Observing that application of the federal rule would not raise forum shopping concerns ("No rational plaintiff would file in federal court based on the expectation that after five years without a trial, dismissal would be discretionary rather than mandatory"), the court applied Fed. R. Civ. P. 41(b) and affirmed the denial of defendant's motion to dismiss. *See also Burlington Northern Railroad v. Woods*, 480 U.S. 1 (1987) (Fed. R. App. P. 38, granting courts of appeals discretion to award costs in the case of frivolous appeals, displaces the Alabama penalty statute mandating damages for an unsuccessful appeal).

6. In *Stewart Organization, Inc. v. Ricoh Corp.*, 487 U.S. 22 (1988), the Court extended *Hanna*'s Fed. R. Civ. P.-friendly approach to federal statutory provisions as well. Defendant filed a motion under 28 U.S.C. § 1404(a) to transfer the diversity action from the Alabama federal district court to the Southern District of New York, invoking a forum selection clause in the dealership contract sued upon which required any litigation to be filed in New York City. The district court denied the motion because Alabama state law refused to enforce forum selection clauses. The Eleventh Circuit Court of Appeals reversed, holding that venue is a procedural matter properly controlled by § 1404(a), under which the forum selection clause was enforceable. (*See* Chapter 7, Part M.)

The Supreme Court agreed, holding that § 1404(a) properly addressed a matter of "practice and procedure," and thus was within the constitutional parameters of Congress to prescribe housekeeping rules for the federal courts. As it directly clashed with state law (by permitting the district court to weigh *all* factors of convenience and fairness, implicitly including the existence of a forum selection clause), § 1404(a) would displace the state rule and control.

Justice Scalia dissented, viewing the conflict as similar to *Walker*, where the federal rule was *not* broad enough to cover the issue in dispute. Absent a direct conflict between federal and state practice, Scalia would apply the *Guaranty Trust Co. v. York* outcome test. He concluded that § 1404 should not displace the Alabama rule against enforcement of forum selection clauses because that would lead to forum shopping to federal court by litigants seeking to enforce such clauses, and inequitable administration of the laws as between the outcome in state and federal court. Scalia's observation that "[t]he decision of an important legal issue should not turn on the accident of diversity of citizenship" brings us back full circle to *Erie v. Tompkins*.

7. Synthesize the line of cases from *Erie* through *Walker*. Articulate the various "tests" for federal/state choice of law where:

1. State practice conflicts *directly and unavoidably* with a Fed. R. Civ. P. or federal statute.
2. State practice conflicts with a judge-made federal practice *not* codified in a Fed. R. Civ. P. or federal statute (the "unguided *Erie* choice").
3. State practice conflicts with a federal practice that, while not found in a Fed. R. Civ. P. or federal statute, nonetheless reflects (as in *Byrd*) an *"essential characteristic"* of federal litigation.

Note again the critical importance of *the source of the federal practice* in resolving federal-state conflicts. You should also be aware that where the U.S. Constitution supplies the federal law, there is no *Erie* choice of law issue because any contrary state practice is displaced by operation of the Supremacy Clause. Thus, for example, if the Seventh Amendment had clearly provided for a jury trial on the issue of whether Byrd was an "employee" (look back again at footnote 10 in *Byrd*), that would have ended the conversation. *See generally* Kevin M. Clermont, *Reverse*-Erie, 82 Notre Dame L. Rev. 1, 9-10 (2006).

---

How does former civil procedure professor Ruth Bader Ginsburg employ all three routes of *Erie* analysis in the following case?

# ■ GASPERINI v. CENTER FOR HUMANITIES, INC.
### *518 U.S. 415 (1996)*

Justice GINSBURG delivered the opinion of the Court:

Under the law of New York, appellate courts are empowered to review the size of jury verdicts and to order new trials when the jury's award "deviates materially from what would be reasonable compensation." N.Y. Civ. Prac. Law and Rules (CPLR) § 5501(c) (McKinney 1995). Under the Seventh Amendment, which governs proceedings in federal court, but not in state court, "the right of trial by jury shall be preserved, and no fact tried by a jury, shall be otherwise reexamined in any Court of the United States, than according to the rules of the common law." U.S. Const., Amdt. 7. The compatibility of these provisions, in an action based on New York law but tried in federal court by reason of the parties' diverse citizenship, is the issue we confront in this case. We hold that New York's law controlling compensation awards for excessiveness or inadequacy can be given effect, without detriment to the Seventh Amendment, if the review standard set out in CPLR § 5501(c) is applied by the federal trial court judge, with appellate control of the trial court's ruling limited to review for "abuse of discretion."

## I

Petitioner William Gasperini, a journalist for CBS News and the Christian Science Monitor, began reporting on events in Central America in 1984. He earned his living primarily in radio and print media and only occasionally sold his photographic work. During the course of his seven-year stint in Central America, Gasperini took over 5,000 slide transparencies, depicting active war zones, political leaders, and scenes from daily life. In 1990, Gasperini agreed to supply his original color transparencies to The Center for Humanities, Inc. (Center) for use in an educational videotape, Conflict in Central America. Gasperini selected 300 of his slides for the Center; its videotape included 110 of them. The Center agreed to return the original transparencies, but upon the completion of the project, it could not find them.

Gasperini commenced suit in the United States District Court for the Southern District of New York, invoking the court's diversity jurisdiction pursuant to 28 U.S.C. § 1332.[1] He alleged several state-law claims for relief, including breach of contract, conversion, and negligence. The Center conceded liability for the lost transparencies and the issue of damages was tried before a jury.

At trial, Gasperini's expert witness testified that the "industry standard" within the photographic publishing community valued a lost transparency at $1,500. This industry standard, the expert explained, represented the average license fee a commercial photograph could earn over the full course of the photographer's copyright, i.e., in Gasperini's case, his lifetime plus 50 years. Gasperini estimated that his earnings from photography totaled just over $10,000 for the period from 1984 through 1993. He also testified that he intended to produce a book containing his best photographs from Central America.

After a three-day trial, the jury awarded Gasperini $450,000 in compensatory damages. This sum, the jury foreperson announced, "is [$]1500 each, for 300 slides." Moving for a new trial under Federal Rule of Civil Procedure 59, the Center attacked the verdict on various grounds, including excessiveness. Without comment, the District Court denied the motion.

The Court of Appeals for the Second Circuit vacated the judgment entered on the jury's verdict. Mindful that New York law governed the controversy, the Court of Appeals endeavored to apply CPLR § 5501(c), which instructs that, when a jury returns an itemized verdict, as the jury did in this case, the New York Appellate Division "shall determine that an award is excessive or

---

1. Plaintiff Gasperini, petitioner here, is a citizen of California; defendant Center, respondent here, is incorporated, and has its principal place of business, in New York.

inadequate if it deviates materially from what would be reasonable compensation." . . . Surveying Appellate Division decisions that reviewed damage awards for lost transparencies, the Second Circuit concluded that testimony on industry standard alone was insufficient to justify a verdict; prime among other factors warranting consideration were the uniqueness of the slides' subject matter and the photographer's earning level.

Guided by Appellate Division rulings, the Second Circuit held that the $450,000 verdict "materially deviates from what is reasonable compensation." Some of Gasperini's transparencies, the Second Circuit recognized, were unique, notably those capturing combat situations in which Gasperini was the only photographer present. But others "depicted either generic scenes or events at which other professional photojournalists were present." No more than 50 slides merited a $1,500 award, the court concluded, after "giving Gasperini every benefit of the doubt." Absent evidence showing significant earnings from photographic endeavors or concrete plans to publish a book, the court further determined, any damage award above $100 each for the remaining slides would be excessive. Remittiturs "present difficult problems for appellate courts," the Second Circuit acknowledged, for court of appeals judges review the evidence from "a cold paper record." Nevertheless, the Second Circuit set aside the $450,000 verdict and ordered a new trial, unless Gasperini agreed to an award of $100,000.

This case presents an important question regarding the standard a federal court uses to measure the alleged excessiveness of a jury's verdict in an action for damages based on state law. We therefore granted certiorari.

## II

Before 1986, state and federal courts in New York generally invoked the same judge-made formulation in responding to excessiveness attacks on jury verdicts: courts would not disturb an award unless the amount was so exorbitant that it "shocked the conscience of the court." . . . In both state and federal courts, trial judges made the excessiveness assessment in the first instance, and appellate judges ordinarily deferred to the trial court's judgment. . . .

In 1986, as part of a series of tort reform measures,[3] New York codified a standard for judicial review of the size of jury awards. Placed in CPLR § 5501(c), the prescription reads:

> In reviewing a money judgment . . . in which it is contended that the award is excessive or inadequate and that a new trial should have been granted unless a stipulation is entered to a different award, the appellate division shall determine that an award is excessive or inadequate if it deviates materially from what would be reasonable compensation.

---

3. The legislature sought, particularly, to curtail medical and dental malpractice, and to contain "already high malpractice premiums." Legislative Findings and Declaration, Ch. 266, 1986 N.Y. Laws 470 (McKinney).

As stated in Legislative Findings and Declarations accompanying New York's adoption of the "deviates materially" formulation, the lawmakers found the "shock the conscience" test an insufficient check on damage awards; the legislature therefore installed a standard "invit[ing] more careful appellate scrutiny." At the same time, the legislature instructed the Appellate Division to state the reasons for the court's rulings on the size of verdicts, and the factors the court considered in complying with § 5501(c). In his signing statement, then-Governor Mario Cuomo emphasized that the CPLR amendments were meant to rachet up the review standard: "This will assure greater scrutiny of the amount of verdicts and promote greater stability in the tort system and greater fairness for similarly situated defendants throughout the State."

. . .

To determine whether an award "deviates materially from what would be reasonable compensation," New York state courts look to awards approved in similar cases. . . .

## III

In cases like Gasperini's, in which New York law governs the claims for relief, does New York law also supply the test for federal-court review of the size of the verdict? The Center answers yes. The "deviates materially" standard, it argues, is a substantive standard that must be applied by federal appellate courts in diversity cases. The Second Circuit agreed. *See* 66 F.3d, at 430. Gasperini, emphasizing that § 5501(c) trains on the New York Appellate Division, characterizes the provision as procedural, an allocation of decision-making authority regarding damages, not a hard cap on the amount recoverable. Correctly comprehended, Gasperini urges, § 5501(c)'s direction to the Appellate Division cannot be given effect by federal appellate courts without violating the Seventh Amendment's Reexamination Clause.

As the parties' arguments suggest, CPLR § 5501(c), appraised under *Erie R. Co. v. Tompkins* and decisions in *Erie*'s path, is both "substantive" and "procedural": "substantive" in that § 5501(c)'s "deviates materially" standard controls how much a plaintiff can be awarded; "procedural" in that § 5501(c) assigns decisionmaking authority to New York's Appellate Division. Parallel application of § 5501(c) at the federal appellate level would be out of sync with the federal system's division of trial and appellate court functions, an allocation weighted by the Seventh Amendment. The dispositive question, therefore, is whether federal courts can give effect to the substantive thrust of § 5501(c) without untoward alteration of the federal scheme for the trial and decision of civil cases.

### A

Federal diversity jurisdiction provides an alternative forum for the adjudication of state-created rights, but it does not carry with it generation of rules of substantive law. As *Erie* read the Rules of Decision Act: "Except in matters governed by the Federal Constitution or by Acts of Congress, the law to be applied in any case is the law of the State." 304 U.S. at 78. Under the *Erie* doctrine, federal courts sitting in diversity apply state substantive law and federal procedural law.

Classification of a law as "substantive" or "procedural" for *Erie* purposes is sometimes a challenging endeavor.[7] *Guaranty Trust Co. v. York*, an early interpretation of *Erie*, propounded an "outcome-determination" test: "Does it significantly affect the result of a litigation for a federal court to disregard a law of a State that would be controlling in an action upon the same claim by the same parties in a State court?" Ordering application of a state statute of limitations to an equity proceeding in federal court, the Court said in *Guaranty Trust*: "Where a federal court is exercising jurisdiction solely because of the diversity of citizenship of the parties, the outcome of the litigation in the federal court should be substantially the same, so far as legal rules determine the outcome of a litigation, as it would be if tried in a State court." *See also Ragan v. Merchants Transfer & Warehouse Co.*, 337 U.S. 530, 533 (1949) (when local law that creates the cause of action qualifies it, "federal court must follow suit," for "a different measure of the cause of action in one court than in the other [would transgress] the principle of *Erie*"). A later pathmarking case, qualifying *Guaranty Trust*, explained that the "outcome-determination" test must not be applied mechanically to sweep in all manner of variations; instead, its application must be guided by "the twin aims of the *Erie* rule: discouragement of forum shopping and avoidance of inequitable administration of the laws." *Hanna v. Plumer*, 380 U.S. 460, 468.

Informed by these decisions, we address the question whether New York's "deviates materially" standard, codified in CPLR § 5501(c), is outcome affective in this sense: Would "application of the [standard] . . . have so important an effect upon the fortunes of one or both of the litigants that failure to [apply] it would [unfairly discriminate against citizens of the forum State, or] be likely to cause a plaintiff to choose the federal court"?

We start from a point the parties do not debate. Gasperini acknowledges that a statutory cap on damages would supply substantive law for *Erie* purposes. *See* Reply Brief for Petitioner 2 ("The state as a matter of its substantive law may, among other things, eliminate the availability of damages for a particular claim entirely, limit the factors a jury may consider in determining damages, or place an absolute cap on the amount of damages available, and

---

7. Concerning matters covered by the Federal Rules of Civil Procedure, the characterization question is usually unproblematic: It is settled that if the Rule in point is consonant with the Rules Enabling Act, 28 U.S.C. § 2072, and the Constitution, the Federal Rule applies regardless of contrary state law. *See Hanna v. Plumer*, 380 U.S. 460 (1965); *Burlington Northern R. Co. v. Woods*, 480 U.S. 1, 4-5 (1987). Federal courts have interpreted the Federal Rules, however, with sensitivity to important state interests and regulatory policies. *See, e.g., Walker v. Armco Steel Corp.*, 446 U.S. 740, 750-752 (1980) (reaffirming decision in *Ragan v. Merchants Transfer & Warehouse Co.*, 337 U.S. 530 (1949), that state law rather than Rule 3 determines when a diversity action commences for the purposes of tolling the state statute of limitations; Rule 3 makes no reference to the tolling of state limitations, the Court observed, and accordingly found no "direct conflict"); *S. A. Healy Co. v. Milwaukee Metropolitan Sewerage Dist.*, 60 F.3d 305, 310-312 (7th Cir. 1995) (state provision for offers of settlement by plaintiffs is compatible with Federal Rule 68, which is limited to offers by defendants).

such substantive law would be applicable in a federal court sitting in diversity."). Although CPLR § 5501(c) is less readily classified, it was designed to provide an analogous control.

New York's Legislature codified in § 5501(c) a new standard, one that requires closer court review than the common law "shock the conscience" test. More rigorous comparative evaluations attend application of § 5501(c)'s "deviates materially" standard. To foster predictability, the legislature required the reviewing court, when overturning a verdict under § 5501(c), to state its reasons, including the factors it considered relevant. *See* CPLR § 5522(b). We think it a fair conclusion that CPLR § 5501(c) differs from a statutory cap principally "in that the maximum amount recoverable is not set forth by statute, but rather is determined by case law." In sum, § 5501(c) contains a procedural instruction, but the State's objective is manifestly substantive.

It thus appears that if federal courts ignore the change in the New York standard and persist in applying the "shock the conscience" test to damage awards on claims governed by New York law, "'substantial' variations between state and federal [money judgments]" may be expected. *See Hanna.* We therefore agree with the Second Circuit that New York's check on excessive damages implicates what we have called *Erie*'s "twin aims." Just as the *Erie* principle precludes a federal court from giving a state-created claim "longer life . . . than [the claim] would have had in the state court," so *Erie* precludes a recovery in federal court significantly larger than the recovery that would have been tolerated in state court.

**B**

CPLR § 5501(c), as earlier noted, is phrased as a direction to the New York Appellate Division. Acting essentially as a surrogate for a New York appellate forum, the Court of Appeals reviewed Gasperini's award to determine if it "deviate[d] materially" from damage awards the Appellate Division permitted in similar circumstances. The Court of Appeals performed this task without benefit of an opinion from the District Court, which had denied "without comment" the Center's Rule 59 motion. Concentrating on the authority § 5501(c) gives to the Appellate Division, Gasperini urges that the provision shifts fact-finding responsibility from the jury and the trial judge to the appellate court. Assigning such responsibility to an appellate court, he maintains, is incompatible with the Seventh Amendment's Reexamination Clause, and therefore, Gasperini concludes, § 5501(c) cannot be given effect in federal court. Although we reach a different conclusion than Gasperini, we agree that the Second Circuit did not attend to "[a]n essential characteristic of [the federal court] system," *Byrd v. Blue Ridge Rural Elec. Cooperative, Inc.*, when it used § 5501(c) as "the standard for [federal] appellate review."

That "essential characteristic" was described in *Byrd*, a diversity suit for negligence in which a pivotal issue of fact would have been tried by a judge were the case in state court. The *Byrd* Court held that, despite the state practice, the plaintiff was entitled to a jury trial in federal court. In so ruling, the Court said that the *Guaranty Trust* "outcome-determination" test was an insufficient guide in cases presenting countervailing federal interests. The Court described the countervailing federal interests present in *Byrd* this way:

> The federal system is an independent system for administering justice to litigants who properly invoke its jurisdiction. An essential characteristic of that system is the manner in which, in civil common-law actions, it distributes trial functions between judge and jury and, under the influence—if not the command—of the Seventh Amendment, assigns the decisions of disputed questions of fact to the jury.

The Seventh Amendment, which governs proceedings in federal court, but not in state court, bears not only on the allocation of trial functions between judge and jury, the issue in *Byrd*; it also controls the allocation of authority to review verdicts, the issue of concern here. The Amendment reads:

> In Suits at common law, where the value in controversy shall exceed twenty dollars, the right of trial by jury shall be preserved, and no fact tried by a jury, shall be otherwise re-examined in any Court of the United States, than according to the rules of the common law.

*Byrd* involved the first Clause of the Amendment, the "trial by jury" Clause. This case involves the second, the "Reexamination" Clause. In keeping with the historic understanding, the Reexamination Clause does not inhibit the authority of trial judges to grant new trials "for any of the reasons for which new trials have heretofore been granted in actions at law in the courts of the United States." Fed. Rule Civ. Proc. 59(a). That authority is large. See 6A Moore's Federal Practice ¶ 59.05[2], pp. 59-44 to 59-46 (2d ed. 1996) ("The power of the English common law trial courts to grant a new trial for a variety of reasons with a view to the attainment of justice was well established prior to the establishment of our Government."). "The trial judge in the federal system," we have reaffirmed, "has . . . discretion to grant a new trial if the verdict appears to [the judge] to be against the weight of the evidence." *Byrd*. This discretion includes overturning verdicts for excessiveness and ordering a new trial without qualification, or conditioned on the verdict winner's refusal to agree to a reduction (remittitur).

In contrast, appellate review of a federal trial court's denial of a motion to set aside a jury's verdict as excessive is a relatively late, and less secure, development. Such review was once deemed inconsonant with the Seventh Amendment's Reexamination Clause. . . . But in successive [cases] we noted, without disapproval, that courts of appeals engage in review of district court excessiveness determinations, "abuse of discretion" as their standard.

[A]ppellate review for abuse of discretion is reconcilable with the Seventh Amendment as a control necessary and proper to the fair administration of justice: . . . "[N]othing in the Seventh Amendment . . . precludes appellate review of the trial judge's denial of a motion to set aside [a jury verdict] as excessive."

### C

In *Byrd*, the Court faced a one-or-the-other choice: trial by judge as in state court, or trial by jury according to the federal practice. In the case before us, a choice of that order is not required, for the principal state and federal interests can be accommodated. The Second Circuit correctly recognized that when New York substantive law governs a claim for relief, New York law and decisions guide the allowable damages. But that court did not take into account the characteristic of the federal-court system that caused us to reaffirm: "The proper role of the trial and appellate courts in the federal system in reviewing the size of jury verdicts is . . . a matter of federal law." "The role of the district court is to determine whether the jury's verdict is within the confines set by state law. . . . The court of appeals should then review the district court's determination under an abuse-of-discretion standard."

New York's dominant interest can be respected, without disrupting the federal system, once it is recognized that the federal district court is capable of performing the checking function, *i.e.*, that court can apply the State's "deviates materially" standard in line with New York case law evolving under CPLR § 5501(c).[22] We recall, in this regard, that the "deviates materially" standard serves as the guide to be applied in trial as well as appellate courts in New York.

Within the federal system, practical reasons combine with Seventh Amendment constraints to lodge in the district court, not the court of appeals, primary responsibility for application of § 5501(c)'s "deviates materially" check. Trial judges have the "unique opportunity to consider the evidence in the living courtroom context," while appellate judges see only the "cold paper record," 66 F.3d at 431.

District court applications of the "deviates materially" standard would be subject to appellate review under the standard the Circuits now employ when inadequacy or excessiveness is asserted on appeal: abuse of discretion. In light of *Erie*'s doctrine, the federal appeals court must be guided by the damage-control standard state law supplies, but as the Second Circuit itself

---

22. Justice Scalia finds in Federal Rule of Civil Procedure 59 a "federal standard" for new trial motions in "'direct collision'" with, and "'leaving no room for the operation of,'" a state law like CPLR § 5501(c). The relevant prescription, Rule 59(a), has remained unchanged since the adoption of the Federal Rules by this Court in 1937. Rule 59(a) is as encompassing as it is uncontroversial. It is indeed "Hornbook" law that a most usual ground for a Rule 59 motion is that "the damages are excessive." Whether damages are excessive for the claim-in-suit must be governed by some law. And there is no candidate for that governance other than the law that gives rise to the claim for relief—here, the law of New York. *See* 28 U.S.C. § 2072(a) and (b) ("Supreme Court shall have the power to prescribe general rules of . . . procedure"; "[s]uch rules shall not abridge, enlarge or modify any substantive right"); *see also* R. Fallon, D. Meltzer, & D. Shapiro, *Hart and Wechsler's The Federal Courts and the Federal System* 729-730 (4th ed. 1996) (observing that Court "has continued since *Hanna v. Plumer*, 380 U.S. 460 (1965) to interpret the federal rules to avoid conflict with important state regulatory policies," *citing Walker v. Armco Steel Corp.*, 446 U.S. 740 (1980)).

has said: "If we reverse, it must be because of an abuse of discretion. . . . The very nature of the problem counsels restraint. . . . We must give the benefit of every doubt to the judgment of the trial judge."

## IV

It does not appear that the District Court checked the jury's verdict against the relevant New York decisions demanding more than "industry standard" testimony to support an award of the size the jury returned in this case. As the Court of Appeals recognized, the uniqueness of the photographs and the plaintiff's earnings as photographer—past and reasonably projected—are factors relevant to appraisal of the award. Accordingly, we vacate the judgment of the Court of Appeals and instruct that court to remand the case to the District Court so that the trial judge, revisiting his ruling on the new trial motion, may test the jury's verdict against CPLR § 5501(c)'s "deviates materially" standard.

[The dissenting opinions of Justices STEVENS and SCALIA (the latter joined by Chief Justice REHNQUIST and Justice THOMAS) are omitted.]

## Comments and Questions

1. Justice Ginsburg pens one of the great understatements in Supreme Court jurisprudence here: "Classification of a law as 'substantive' or 'procedural' for *Erie* purposes is sometimes a challenging endeavor." But *Gasperini* also illustrates another of *Erie*'s illusive distinctions in the post-*Hanna* world—that between direct unavoidable conflicts between a Federal Rule and state practice, and situations where both can coexist.

Ginsburg (as well as Stevens in his dissent, 518 U.S. at 440, n.1)) places *Gasperini* in the latter category, reading Fed. R. Civ. P. 59 as not supplying any substantive content or "federal standard" for the granting of new trials, but merely providing the mechanics of such a motion. Treating this as an unguided *Erie* conflict, she reverts to the outcome test, and concludes that

> if federal courts ignore the change in the New York standard and persist in applying the "shock the conscience" test to damage awards on claims governed by New York law, "'substantial' variations between state and federal [money judgments]" may be expected. We therefore agree with the Second Circuit that New York's check on excessive damages implicates what we have called *Erie*'s "twin aims." Just as the *Erie* principle precludes a federal court from giving a state-created claim "longer life . . . than [the claim] would have had in the state court," so *Erie* precludes a recovery in federal court significantly larger than the recovery that would have been tolerated in state court.

518 U.S. at 429-430.

2. Justice Scalia's dissent flows from his placement of the case in the other category—a direct and unavoidable clash between Fed. R. Civ. P. 59 and New York's "materially deviates" standard:

> [I]n my view, one does not even reach the *Erie* question in this case. The standard to be applied by a district court in ruling on a motion for a new trial is set forth in Rule 59 of the Federal Rules of Civil Procedure, which provides that "[a] new trial may be granted . . . for any of the reasons for which new trials have heretofore been granted in actions at law *in the courts of the United States*." (Emphasis added.) That is undeniably a federal standard. Federal District Courts in the Second Circuit have interpreted that standard to permit the granting of new trials where "it is quite clear that the jury has reached a seriously erroneous result" and letting the verdict stand would result in a "miscarriage of justice." Assuming (as we have no reason to question) that this is a correct interpretation of what Rule 59 requires, it is undeniable that the Federal Rule is "sufficiently broad to cause a direct collision with the state law or, implicitly, to control the issue before the court, thereby leaving no room for the operation of that law." It is simply not possible to give controlling effect both to the federal standard and the state standard in reviewing the jury's award. That being so, the court has no choice but to apply the Federal Rule, which is an exercise of what we have called Congress's "power to regulate matters which, though falling within the uncertain area between substance and procedure, are rationally capable of classification as either." *Hanna.*

518 U.S. at 467-468.

Is Justice Scalia's position here inconsistent with his conclusion in *Stewart Organization, Inc. v. Ricoh* (note 6 following *Walker v. Armco Steel Corp.*, above) that § 1404 was *not* broad enough to displace the state rule against enforcement of forum selection clauses?

3. Can the Supreme Court give meaningful guidance in so complex an area if there is fundamental disagreement even about *which of the competing analyses applies*? Who has the better argument here, Scalia (that Fed. R. Civ. P. 59 is broad enough to displace the state law on the grounds for granting new trials) or Ginsburg (that it is not the Federal Rule, but just judge-made practice, that bumps up against the state standard)?

4. How does Justice Ginsburg invoke *Byrd*'s "essential characteristic" of federal litigation concept to untangle the intricate web of state and federal practice here?

## The Last Words on *Erie*?

*Gasperini v. Center for Humanities, Inc.* seemed an apt end to the *Erie* saga, as Justice Ginsburg was able to neatly divide the law-application authority between the state and federal sovereigns in a manner consistent with the three analyses developed since 1938. But the Supreme Court opted to jump back into the fray six years later, and produced a not-so-neat result.

*Semtek International Inc. v. Lockheed Martin Corp.*, 531 U.S. 497 (2001), involved both vertical and horizontal choice of law issues, and prompted Professor Burbank to observe that it "would be difficult for even the most adept spinner of law school hypotheticals to devise a case more challenging." Stephen B. Burbank, Semtek, *Forum Shopping, and Federal Common Law*, 77 Notre Dame L. Rev. 1027 (2002).

Semtek's breach of contract action was dismissed by the federal district court in California as barred by that state's two-year statute of limitations. It then brought suit in a Maryland state court on the same claims, relying on Maryland's three-year statute. The Maryland court dismissed on grounds of *res judicata*, which (as covered in our next chapter) prevents a plaintiff from relitigating a claim that has already gone to final judgment on the merits. Semtek appealed, arguing that the *res judicata* effect of the federal court's dismissal of the first action should be controlled by California state court doctrine, which would not treat dismissal on statute of limitations grounds as "on the merits."

A unanimous Supreme Court held that federal (not state) law controls the issue, but (with a twist befitting the *Erie* puzzle) concluded that, absent a Fed. R. Civ. P. directly on point, federal law must incorporate state law, so that the same rule would apply whether the dismissal had been ordered by a federal or a state court:

> This is, it seems to us, a classic case for adopting, as the federally prescribed rule of decision, the law that would be applied by state courts in the State in which the federal diversity court sits. [A]ny other rule would produce the sort of "forum-shopping and inequitable administration of the laws" that *Erie* seeks to avoid, since filing in, or removing to, federal court would be encouraged by the divergent effects that the litigants would anticipate from likely grounds of dismissal.

531 U.S. at 508.

We will have more to say about *Semtek* in Chapter 10.

---

What follows is the Supreme Court's *last* last word on *Erie*.

# ■ SHADY GROVE ORTHOPEDIC ASSOC. v. ALLSTATE INS. CO.
### *130 S. Ct. 1431 (2010)*

Justice SCALIA announced the judgment of the Court and delivered the opinion of the Court with respect to Parts I and II-A, an opinion with respect to Parts II-B and II-D, in which The CHIEF JUSTICE, Justice THOMAS, and Justice SOTOMAYOR join, and an opinion with respect to Part II-C, in which The CHIEF JUSTICE and Justice THOMAS join.

New York law prohibits class actions in suits seeking penalties or statutory minimum damages.[1] We consider whether this precludes a federal district court sitting in diversity from entertaining a class action under Federal Rule of Civil Procedure 23.

## I

The petitioner's complaint alleged the following: Shady Grove Orthopedic Associates, P. A., provided medical care to Sonia E. Galvez for injuries she suffered in an automobile accident. As partial payment for that care, Galvez assigned to Shady Grove her rights to insurance benefits under a policy issued in New York by Allstate Insurance Co. Shady Grove tendered a claim for the assigned benefits to Allstate, which under New York law had 30 days to pay the claim or deny it. Allstate apparently paid, but not on time, and it refused to pay the statutory interest that accrued on the overdue benefits (at two percent per month).

Shady Grove filed this diversity suit in the Eastern District of New York to recover the unpaid statutory interest. Alleging that Allstate routinely refuses to pay interest on overdue benefits, Shady Grove sought relief on behalf of itself and a class of all others to whom Allstate owes interest. The District Court dismissed the suit for lack of jurisdiction. It reasoned that N.Y. Civ. Prac. Law Ann. § 901(b), which precludes a suit to recover a "penalty" from proceeding as a class action, applies in diversity suits in federal court, despite Federal Rule of Civil Procedure 23. Concluding that statutory interest is a "penalty" under New York law, it held that § 901(b) prohibited the proposed class action. And, since Shady Grove conceded that its individual claim (worth roughly $500) fell far short of the amount-in-controversy requirement for individual suits under 28 U.S.C. § 1332(a), the suit did not belong in federal court.[3]

The Second Circuit affirmed. The court did not dispute that a federal rule adopted in compliance with the Rules Enabling Act, would control if it conflicted with § 901(b). But there was no conflict because (as we will describe in more detail below) the Second Circuit concluded that Rule 23 and § 901(b)

---

1. N.Y. Civ. Prac. Law Ann. § 901 (West 2006) provides:

(a) One or more members of a class may sue or be sued as representative parties on behalf of all if: 1. the class is so numerous that joinder of all members, whether otherwise required or permitted, is impracticable; 2. there are questions of law or fact common to the class which predominate over any questions affecting only individual members; 3. the claims or defenses of the representative parties are typical of the claims or defenses of the class; 4. the representative parties will fairly and adequately protect the interests of the class; and 5. a class action is superior to other available methods for the fair and efficient adjudication of the controversy.

(b) Unless a statute creating or imposing a penalty, or a minimum measure of recovery specifically authorizes the recovery thereof in a class action, an action to recover a penalty, or minimum measure of recovery created or imposed by statute may not be maintained as a class action.

3. Shady Grove had asserted jurisdiction under 28 U.S.C. § 1332(d)(2), which relaxes, for class actions seeking at least $5 million, the rule against aggregating separate claims for calculation of the amount in controversy. See *Exxon Mobil Corp. v. Allapattah Services, Inc.*, 545 U.S. 546, 571 (2005).

address different issues. Finding no federal rule on point, the Court of Appeals held that § 901(b) is "substantive" within the meaning of *Erie R.R. v. Tomkins*, and thus must be applied by federal courts sitting in diversity.

## II

The framework for our decision is familiar. We must first determine whether Rule 23 answers the question in dispute. If it does, it governs—New York's law notwithstanding—unless it exceeds statutory authorization or Congress's rulemaking power. See *Hanna v. Plumer*, 380 U.S. 460, 463-464 (1965). We do not wade into *Erie*'s murky waters unless the federal rule is inapplicable or invalid.

### A

The question in dispute is whether Shady Grove's suit may proceed as a class action. Rule 23 provides an answer. It states that "[a] class action may be maintained" if two conditions are met: The suit must satisfy the criteria set forth in subdivision (a) (i.e., numerosity, commonality, typicality, and adequacy of representation), and it also must fit into one of the three categories described in subdivision (b). By its terms this creates a categorical rule entitling a plaintiff whose suit meets the specified criteria to pursue his claim as a class action. (The Federal Rules regularly use "may" to confer categorical permission, *see, e.g.*, Fed. Rules Civ. Proc. 8(d)(2)-(3), 14(a)(1), 18(a)-(b), 20(a)(1)-(2), 27(a)(1), 30(a)(1), as do federal statutes that establish procedural entitlements, *see, e.g.*, 29 U.S.C. § 626(c)(1); 42 U.S.C. § 2000e-5(f)(1).) Thus, Rule 23 provides a one-size-fits-all formula for deciding the class-action question. Because § 901(b) attempts to answer the same question—i.e., it states that Shady Grove's suit "may not be maintained as a class action" (emphasis added) because of the relief it seeks—it cannot apply in diversity suits unless Rule 23 is *ultra vires*.

The Second Circuit believed that § 901(b) and Rule 23 do not conflict because they address different issues. Rule 23, it said, concerns only the criteria for determining whether a given class can and should be certified; section 901(b), on the other hand, addresses an antecedent question: whether the particular type of claim is eligible for class treatment in the first place—a question on which Rule 23 is silent. Allstate embraces this analysis.

We disagree. To begin with, the line between eligibility and certifiability is entirely artificial. Both are preconditions for maintaining a class action. Allstate suggests that eligibility must depend on the "particular cause of action" asserted, instead of some other attribute of the suit. But that is not so. Congress could, for example, provide that only claims involving more than a certain number of plaintiffs are "eligible" for class treatment in federal court. In other words, relabeling Rule 23(a)'s prerequisites "eligibility criteria" would obviate Allstate's objection—a sure sign that its eligibility—certifiability distinction is made-to-order.

There is no reason, in any event, to read Rule 23 as addressing only whether claims made eligible for class treatment by some *other* law should be certified as class actions. Allstate asserts that Rule 23 neither explicitly nor implicitly empowers a federal court "to certify a class in each and every case" where the Rule's criteria are met. But that is *exactly* what Rule 23 does: It says that if the prescribed preconditions are satisfied "[a] class action *may be maintained*"—not "*a class action may be permitted*." Courts do not maintain actions; litigants do. The discretion suggested by Rule 23's "may" is discretion residing in the plaintiff: He may bring his claim in a class action if he wishes. And like the rest of the Federal Rules of Civil Procedure, Rule 23 *automatically* applies "in all civil actions and proceedings in the United States district courts," Fed. Rule Civ. Proc. 1.

Allstate points out that Congress has carved out some federal claims from Rule 23's reach, *see, e.g.*, 8 U.S.C. § 1252(e)(1)(B)—which shows, Allstate contends, that Rule 23 does not authorize class actions for all claims, but rather leaves room for laws like § 901(b). But Congress, unlike New York, has ultimate authority over the Federal Rules of Civil Procedure; it can create exceptions to an individual rule as it sees fit—either by directly amending the rule or by enacting a separate statute overriding it in certain instances. The fact that Congress has created specific exceptions to Rule 23 hardly proves that the Rule does not apply generally. In fact, it proves the opposite. If Rule 23 did not authorize class actions across the board, the statutory exceptions would be unnecessary.

Allstate next suggests that the structure of § 901 shows that Rule 23 addresses only certifiability. Section 901(a), it notes, establishes class certification criteria roughly analogous to those in Rule 23 (wherefore it agrees that subsection is pre-empted). But § 901(b)'s rule barring class actions for certain claims is set off as its own subsection, and where it applies § 901(a) does not. . . . Rule 23 permits all class actions that meet its requirements, and a State cannot limit that permission by structuring one part of its statute to track Rule 23 and enacting another part that imposes additional requirements. Both of § 901's subsections undeniably answer the same question as Rule 23: whether a class action may proceed for a given suit.

The dissent argues that § 901(b) has nothing to do with whether Shady Grove may maintain its suit as a class action, but affects only the remedy it may obtain if it wins. Whereas "Rule 23 governs procedural aspects of class litigation" by "prescrib[ing] the considerations relevant to class certification and postcertification proceedings," § 901(b) addresses only "the size of a monetary award a class plaintiff may pursue." Accordingly, the dissent says, Rule 23 and New York's law may coexist in peace.

We need not decide whether a state law that limits the remedies available in an existing class action would conflict with Rule 23; that is not what § 901(b) does. By its terms, the provision precludes a plaintiff from "maintain[ing]" a class action seeking statutory penalties. Unlike a law that sets a ceiling on damages (or puts other remedies out of reach) in properly filed class actions, § 901(b) says nothing about what remedies a court may award; it prevents the class actions it covers from coming into existence at all. Consequently, a court bound by § 901(b) could not certify a class action seeking both statutory penalties and other remedies even if it announces in advance that it will refuse to award the penalties in the event the plaintiffs prevail; to do so would violate the statute's clear prohibition on "maintain[ing]" such suits as class actions.

. . .

The evidence of the New York Legislature's purpose is pretty sparse. But even accepting the dissent's account of the Legislature's objective at face value, it cannot override the statute's clear text. Even if its aim is to restrict the remedy a plaintiff can obtain, § 901(b) achieves that end by limiting a plaintiff's power to maintain a class action. The manner in which the law "could have been written," has no bearing; what matters is the law the Legislature did enact. We cannot rewrite that to reflect our perception of legislative purpose.

. . .

The dissent's approach of determining whether state and federal rules conflict based on the subjective intentions of the state legislature is an enterprise destined to produce "confusion worse confounded." It would mean, to begin with, that one State's statute could survive pre-emption (and accordingly affect the procedures in federal court) while another State's identical law would not, merely because its authors had different aspirations. It would also mean that district courts would have to discern, in every diversity case, the purpose behind any putatively pre-empted state procedural rule, even if its text squarely conflicts with federal law. That task will often prove arduous. Many laws further more than one aim, and the aim of others may be impossible to discern. Moreover, to the extent the dissent's purpose-driven approach depends on its characterization of § 901(b)'s aims as substantive, it would apply to many state rules ostensibly addressed to procedure. Pleading standards, for example, often embody policy preferences about the types of claims that should succeed—as do rules governing summary judgment, pretrial discovery, and the admissibility of certain evidence. Hard cases will abound. . . .

But while the dissent does indeed artificially narrow the scope of § 901(b) by finding that it pursues only substantive policies, that is not the central difficulty of the dissent's position. The central difficulty is that even artificial narrowing cannot render § 901(b) compatible with Rule 23. Whatever the policies they pursue, they flatly contradict each other. Allstate asserts (and the dissent implies) that we can (and must) interpret Rule 23 in a manner that avoids overstepping its authorizing statute. If the Rule were susceptible of two meanings—one that would violate § 2072(b) and another that would not—we would agree. But it is not. Rule 23 unambiguously authorizes any plaintiff, in any federal civil proceeding, to maintain a class action if the Rule's prerequisites are met. We cannot contort its text, even to avert a collision with state law that might render it invalid. See *Walker v. Armco Steel*

*Corp.*, 446 U.S. 740, 750, n. 9 (1980).[8] What the dissent's approach achieves is not the avoiding of a "conflict between Rule 23 and § 901(b)," but rather the invalidation of Rule 23 (pursuant to § 2072(b) of the Rules Enabling Act) to the extent that it conflicts with the substantive policies of § 901. There is no other way to reach the dissent's destination. We must therefore confront head-on whether Rule 23 falls within the statutory authorization.

**B**

*Erie* involved the constitutional power of federal courts to supplant state law with judge-made rules. In that context, it made no difference whether the rule was technically one of substance or procedure; the touchstone was whether it "significantly affect[s] the result of a litigation." *Guaranty Trust Co. v. York.* That is not the test for either the constitutionality or the statutory validity of a Federal Rule of Procedure. Congress has undoubted power to supplant state law, and undoubted power to prescribe rules for the courts it has created, so long as those rules regulate matters "rationally capable of classification" as procedure. *Hanna.* In the Rules Enabling Act, Congress authorized this Court to promulgate rules of procedure subject to its review, 28 U.S.C. § 2072(a), but with the limitation that those rules "shall not abridge, enlarge or modify any substantive right," § 2072(b).

We have long held that this limitation means that the Rule must "really regulat[e] procedure, the judicial process for enforcing rights and duties recognized by substantive law and for justly administering remedy and redress for disregard or infraction of them." The test is not whether the rule affects a litigant's substantive rights; most procedural rules do. What matters is what the rule itself regulates: If it governs only "the manner and the means" by which the litigants' rights are "enforced," it is valid; if it alters "the rules of decision by which [the] court will adjudicate [those] rights," it is not.

Applying that test, we have rejected every statutory challenge to a Federal Rule that has come before us. We have found to be in compliance with § 2072(b) rules prescribing methods for serving process (Fed. Rule Civ. Proc. 4(f)); (Fed. Rule Civ. Proc. 4(d)(1)), and requiring litigants whose mental or physical condition is in dispute to submit to examinations, (Fed. Rule Civ. Proc. 35). Likewise, we have upheld rules authorizing imposition of sanctions upon those who file frivolous appeals, (Fed. Rule App. Proc. 38), or who sign court papers without a reasonable inquiry into the facts asserted, (Fed. Rule Civ. Proc. 11). Each of these rules had some practical effect on the parties' rights, but each undeniably regulated only the process for enforcing those rights; none altered the rights themselves, the available remedies, or the rules of decision by which the court adjudicated either.

Applying that criterion, we think it obvious that rules allowing multiple claims (and claims by or against multiple parties) to be litigated together are also valid. *See, e.g.,* Fed. Rules Civ. Proc. 18 (joinder of claims), 20 (joinder of

---

8. The cases chronicled by the dissent each involved a Federal Rule that we concluded could fairly be read not to "control the issue" addressed by the pertinent state law, thus avoiding a "direct collision" between federal and state law, see *Walker.* But here, as in *Hanna,* a collision is "unavoidable."

parties), 42(a) (consolidation of actions). Such rules neither change plaintiffs' separate entitlements to relief nor abridge defendants' rights; they alter only how the claims are processed. For the same reason, Rule 23—at least insofar as it allows willing plaintiffs to join their separate claims against the same defendants in a class action—falls within § 2072(b)'s authorization. A class action, no less than traditional joinder (of which it is a species), merely enables a federal court to adjudicate claims of multiple parties at once, instead of in separate suits. And like traditional joinder, it leaves the parties' legal rights and duties intact and the rules of decision unchanged.

Allstate contends that the authorization of class actions is not substantively neutral: Allowing Shady Grove to sue on behalf of a class "transform[s] [the] dispute over a five hundred dollar penalty into a dispute over a five million dollar penalty." Allstate's aggregate liability, however, does not depend on whether the suit proceeds as a class action. Each of the 1,000-plus members of the putative class could (as Allstate acknowledges) bring a freestanding suit asserting his individual claim. It is undoubtedly true that some plaintiffs who would not bring individual suits for the relatively small sums involved will choose to join a class action. That has no bearing, however, on Allstate's or the plaintiffs' legal rights. The likelihood that some (even many) plaintiffs will be induced to sue by the availability of a class action is just the sort of "incidental effec[t]" we have long held does not violate § 2072(b).

Allstate argues that Rule 23 violates § 2072(b) because the state law it displaces, § 901(b), creates a right that the Federal Rule abridges—namely, a "substantive right . . . not to be subjected to aggregated class-action liability" in a single suit. To begin with, we doubt that that is so. Nothing in the text of § 901(b) (which is to be found in New York's procedural code) confines it to claims under New York law; and of course New York has no power to alter substantive rights and duties created by other sovereigns. As we have said, the consequence of excluding certain class actions may be to cap the damages a defendant can face in a single suit, but the law itself alters only procedure. In that respect, § 901(b) is no different from a state law forbidding simple joinder. As a fallback argument, Allstate argues that even if § 901(b) is a procedural provision, it was enacted "for *substantive reasons.*" Its end was not to improve "the conduct of the litigation process itself" but to alter "the outcome of that process."

The fundamental difficulty with both these arguments is that the substantive nature of New York's law, or its substantive purpose, makes no difference. A Federal Rule of Procedure is not valid in some jurisdictions and invalid in others—or valid in some cases and invalid in others—depending upon whether its effect is to frustrate a state substantive law (or a state procedural law enacted for substantive purposes). . . .

*Hanna* unmistakably expressed the same understanding that compliance of a Federal Rule with the Enabling Act is to be assessed by consulting the Rule itself, and not its effects in individual applications:

"[T]he court has been instructed to apply the Federal Rule, and can refuse to do so only if the Advisory Committee, this Court, and Congress erred in their prima facie judgment that the Rule in question transgresses neither the terms of the Enabling Act nor constitutional restrictions."

In sum, it is not the substantive or procedural nature or purpose of the affected state law that matters, but the substantive or procedural nature of the Federal Rule. . . . [T]he validity of a Federal Rule depends entirely upon whether it regulates procedure. If it does, it is authorized by § 2072 and is valid in all jurisdictions, with respect to all claims, regardless of its incidental effect upon state-created rights.

. . .

**D**

We must acknowledge the reality that keeping the federal-court door open to class actions that cannot proceed in state court will produce forum shopping. That is unacceptable when it comes as the consequence of judge-made rules created to fill supposed "gaps" in positive federal law. See *Hanna*. For where neither the Constitution, a treaty, nor a statute provides the rule of decision or authorizes a federal court to supply one, "state law must govern because there can be no other law." But divergence from state law, with the attendant consequence of forum shopping, is the inevitable (indeed, one might say the intended) result of a uniform system of federal procedure. Congress itself has created the possibility that the same case may follow a different course if filed in federal instead of state court. Cf. *Hanna*, 380 U.S. at 472-473. The short of the matter is that a Federal Rule governing procedure is valid whether or not it alters the outcome of the case in a way that induces forum shopping. To hold otherwise would be to "disembowel either the Constitution's grant of power over federal procedure" or Congress's exercise of it. Id. at 473-474.

The judgment of the Court of Appeals is reversed, and the case is remanded for further proceedings.

*It is so ordered.*

Justice STEVENS, concurring in part and concurring in the judgment.
The New York law at issue, N.Y. Civ. Prac. Law Ann. (CPLR) § 901(b), is a procedural rule that is not part of New York's substantive law. Accordingly, I agree with Justice Scalia that Federal Rule of Civil Procedure 23 must apply in this case and join Parts I and II-A of the Court's opinion. But I also agree with Justice Ginsburg that there are some state procedural rules that federal courts must apply in diversity cases because they function as a part of the State's definition of substantive rights and remedies.

**I**

. . . Congress has provided for a system of uniform federal rules, under which federal courts sitting in diversity operate as "an independent system for administering justice to litigants who properly invoke its jurisdiction," and not as state-court clones that assume all aspects of state tribunals but are managed by Article III judges. See *Hanna*, 380 U.S. at 473-474. But while Congress may have the constitutional power to prescribe procedural rules that interfere with state substantive law in any number of respects, that is not what Congress has done. Instead, it has provided in the Enabling Act that although "[t]he Supreme Court" may "prescribe general rules of practice and procedure," § 2072(a), those rules "shall not abridge, enlarge or modify any substantive right," § 2072(b). Therefore, "[w]hen a situation is covered by one of the Federal Rules, . . . the court has been instructed to apply the Federal Rule" unless doing so would violate the Act or the Constitution. *Hanna*, 380 U.S. at 471.

. . .

Congress has thus struck a balance: "[H]ousekeeping rules for federal courts" will generally apply in diversity cases, notwithstanding that some federal rules "will inevitably differ" from state rules. *Hanna*, 380 U.S. at 473. But not every federal "rul[e] of practice or procedure," § 2072(a), will displace state law. To the contrary, federal rules must be interpreted with some degree of "sensitivity to important state interests and regulatory policies," *Gasperini v. Center for Humanities, Inc.*, and applied to diversity cases against the background of Congress' command that such rules not alter substantive rights and with consideration of "the degree to which the Rule makes the character and result of the federal litigation stray from the course it would follow in state courts." This can be a tricky balance to implement.

It is important to observe that the balance Congress has struck turns, in part, on the nature of the state law that is being displaced by a federal rule. And in my view, the application of that balance does not necessarily turn on whether the state law at issue takes the *form* of what is traditionally described as substantive or procedural. Rather, it turns on whether the state law actually is part of a State's framework of substantive rights or remedies.

. . .

## II

When both a federal rule and a state law appear to govern a question before a federal court sitting in diversity, our precedents have set out a two-step framework for federal courts to negotiate this thorny area. At both steps of the inquiry, there is a critical question about what the state law and the federal rule mean.

The court must first determine whether the scope of the federal rule is " 'sufficiently broad' " to " 'control the issue' " before the court, "thereby leaving no room for the operation" of seemingly conflicting state law. *Walker v. Armco Steel Corp.*, 446 U.S. 740, 749-750, and n. 9 (1980). If the federal rule does not apply or can operate alongside the state rule, then there is no "Ac[t] of Congress" governing that particular question, 28 U.S.C. § 1652, and the court must engage in the traditional Rules of Decision Act inquiry under *Erie* and its progeny. In some instances, the "plain meaning" of a federal rule will not come into " 'direct collision' " with the state law, and both can operate. *Walker*,

446 U.S. at 750, n. 9, 749. In other instances, the rule "when fairly construed," with "sensitivity to important state interests and regulatory policies," *Gasperini*, 518 U.S. at 427, n. 7, will not collide with the state law.

If, on the other hand, the federal rule is "sufficiently broad to control the issue before the Court," such that there is a "direct collision," *Walker*, 446 U.S. at 749-750, the court must decide whether application of the federal rule "represents a valid exercise" of the "rulemaking authority . . . bestowed on this Court by the Rules Enabling Act." That Act requires, *inter alia*, that federal rules "not abridge, enlarge or modify *any* substantive right." 28 U.S.C. § 2072(b) (emphasis added). Unlike Justice Scalia, I believe that an application of a federal rule that effectively abridges, enlarges, or modifies a state-created right or remedy violates this command. Congress may have the constitutional power "to supplant state law" with rules that are "rationally capable of classification as procedure," but we should generally presume that it has not done so. Indeed, the mandate that federal rules "shall not abridge, enlarge or modify any substantive right" evinces the opposite intent, as does Congress' decision to delegate the creation of rules to this Court rather than to a political branch.

Thus, the second step of the inquiry may well bleed back into the first. When a federal rule appears to abridge, enlarge, or modify a substantive right, federal courts must consider whether the rule can reasonably be interpreted to avoid that impermissible result. See, e.g., *Semtek Int'l Inc. v. Lockheed Martin Corp.*, 531 U.S. 497, 503 (2001) (avoiding an interpretation of Federal Rule of Civil Procedure 41(b) that "would arguably violate the jurisdictional limitation of the Rules Enabling Act" contained in § 2072(b)). And when such a "saving" construction is not possible and the rule would violate the Enabling Act, federal courts cannot apply the rule. See 28 U.S.C. § 2072(b) (mandating that federal rules "shall not" alter "any substantive right" (emphasis added)); *Hanna*, 380 U.S. at 473. A federal rule, therefore, cannot govern a particular case in which the rule would displace a state law that is procedural in the ordinary use of the term but is so intertwined with a state right or remedy that it functions to define the scope of the state-created right. And absent a governing federal rule, a federal court must engage in the traditional Rules of Decision Act inquiry, under the *Erie* line of cases. This application of the Enabling Act shows "sensitivity to important state interests," and "regulatory policies," but it does so as Congress authorized, by ensuring that federal rules that ordinarily "prescribe general rules of practice and procedure," § 2072(a), do "not abridge, enlarge or modify any substantive right," § 2072(b).

Justice Scalia believes that the sole Enabling Act question is whether the federal rule "really regulates procedure," which means, apparently, whether it regulates "the manner and the means by which the litigants' rights are enforced." I respectfully disagree. This interpretation of the Enabling Act is consonant with the Act's first limitation to "general rules of practice and procedure," § 2072(a). But it ignores the second limitation that such rules also "not abridge, enlarge or modify any substantive right," § 2072(b) (emphasis added), and in so doing ignores the balance that Congress struck between uniform rules of federal procedure and respect for a State's construction of its own rights and remedies. It also ignores the separation-of-powers presumption, and federalism presumption, that counsel against judicially created rules displacing state substantive law.[9]

. . .

Although the plurality appears to agree with much of my interpretation of § 2072, it nonetheless rejects that approach for two reasons, both of which are mistaken. First, Justice Scalia worries that if federal courts inquire into the effect of federal rules on state law, it will enmesh federal courts in difficult determinations about whether application of a given rule would displace a state determination about substantive rights. I do not see why an Enabling Act inquiry that looks to state law necessarily is more taxing than Justice Scalia's. But in any event, that inquiry is what the Enabling Act requires: While it may not be easy to decide what is actually a "substantive right," "the designations substantive and procedural become important, for the Enabling Act has made them so." The question, therefore, is not what rule we think would be easiest on federal courts. The question is what rule Congress established. Although, Justice Scalia may generally prefer easily administrable, bright-line rules, his preference does not give us license to adopt a second-best interpretation of the Rules Enabling Act. Courts cannot ignore text and context in the service of simplicity.

. . .

## III

Justice Ginsburg views the basic issue in this case as whether and how to apply a federal rule that dictates an answer to a traditionally procedural question (whether to join plaintiffs together as a class), when a state law that "defines the dimensions" of a state-created claim dictates the opposite answer. As explained above, I readily acknowledge that if a federal rule displaces a state rule that is "'procedural' in the ordinary sense of the term," but sufficiently interwoven with the scope of a substantive right or remedy, there would be an Enabling Act problem, and the federal rule would have to give way. In my view, however, this is not such a case.

. . .

---

9. The plurality's interpretation of the Enabling Act appears to mean that no matter how bound up is a state provision is with the State's own rights or remedies, any contrary federal rule that happens to regulate "the manner and the means by which the litigants' rights are enforced," *ante* at 1442 (internal quotation marks omitted), must govern. There are many ways in which seemingly procedural rules may displace a State's formulation of its substantive law. For example, statutes of limitations, although in some sense procedural rules, can also be understood as a temporal limitation on legally created rights; if this Court were to promulgate a federal limitations period, federal courts would still, in some instances, be required to apply state limitations periods. Similarly, if the federal rules altered the burden of proof in a case, this could eviscerate a critical aspect—albeit one that deals with *how* a right is enforced—of a State's framework of rights and remedies. Or if a federal rule about appellate review displaced a state rule about how damages are reviewed on appeal, the federal rule might be pre-empting a state damages cap. Cf. *Gasperini*, 518 U.S. at 427.

Because Rule 23 governs class certification, the only decision is whether certifying a class in this diversity case would "abridge, enlarge or modify" New York's substantive rights or remedies. § 2072(b). Although one can argue that class certification would enlarge New York's "limited" damages remedy, such arguments rest on extensive speculation about what the New York Legislature had in mind when it created § 901(b). But given that there are two plausible competing narratives, it seems obvious to me that we should respect the plain textual reading of § 901(b), a rule in New York's procedural code about when to certify class actions brought under any source of law, and respect Congress' decision that Rule 23 governs class certification in federal courts. In order to displace a federal rule, there must be more than just a possibility that the state rule is different than it appears.

Accordingly, I concur in part and concur in the judgment.

Justice GINSBURG, with whom Justice KENNEDY, Justice BREYER, and Justice ALITO join, dissenting.

The Court today approves Shady Grove's attempt to transform a $500 case into a $5,000,000 award, although the State creating the right to recover has proscribed this alchemy. If Shady Grove had filed suit in New York state court, the 2% interest payment authorized by New York Ins. Law Ann. § 5106(a), as a penalty for overdue benefits would, by Shady Grove's own measure, amount to no more than $500. By instead filing in federal court based on the parties' diverse citizenship and requesting class certification, Shady Grove hopes to recover, for the class, statutory damages of more than $5,000,000. The New York Legislature has barred this remedy, instructing that, unless specifically permitted, "an action to recover a penalty, or minimum measure of recovery created or imposed by statute may not be maintained as a class action." N.Y. Civ. Prac. Law Ann. § 901(b). The Court nevertheless holds that Federal Rule of Civil Procedure 23, which prescribes procedures for the conduct of class actions in federal courts, preempts the application of § 901(b) in diversity suits.

The Court reads Rule 23 relentlessly to override New York's restriction on the availability of statutory damages. Our decisions, however, caution us to ask, before undermining state legislation: Is this conflict really necessary? Had the Court engaged in that inquiry, it would not have read Rule 23 to collide with New York's legitimate interest in keeping certain monetary awards reasonably bounded. I would continue to interpret Federal Rules with awareness of, and sensitivity to, important state regulatory policies. Because today's judgment radically departs from that course, I dissent.

## I

. . .

### B

In our prior decisions in point, many of them not mentioned in the Court's opinion, we have avoided immoderate interpretations of the Federal Rules that would trench on state prerogatives without serving any countervailing federal interest. "Application of the *Hanna* analysis," we have said, "is premised on a 'direct collision' between the Federal Rule and the state law." *Walker v. Armco Steel Corp.*, 446 U.S. 740, 749-750 (1980) (quoting *Hanna*, 380 U.S. at 472). To displace state law, a Federal Rule, "when fairly construed," must be "'sufficiently broad'" so as "to 'control the issue' before the court, thereby leaving no room for the operation of that law." *Burlington Northern R. Co. v. Woods*, 480 U.S. 1, 4-5 (1987) (quoting *Walker*, 446 U.S. at 749-750, and n. 9); cf. *Stewart Organization, Inc. v. Ricoh Corp.*, 487 U.S. 22, 37-38 (1988) (Scalia, J., dissenting) ("[I]n deciding whether a federal . . . Rule of Procedure encompasses a particular issue, a broad reading that would create significant disuniformity between state and federal courts should be avoided if the text permits.").

In pre-*Hanna* decisions, the Court vigilantly read the Federal Rules to avoid conflict with state laws. . . .

In all of these cases, the Court stated in *Hanna*, "the scope of the Federal Rule was not as broad as the losing party urged, and therefore, there being no Federal Rule which covered the point in dispute, *Erie* commanded the enforcement of state law." 380 U.S. at 470. In *Hanna* itself, the Court found the clash "unavoidable;" the petitioner had effected service of process as prescribed by Federal Rule 4(d)(1), but that "how-to" method did not satisfy the special Massachusetts law applicable to service on an executor or administrator. Even as it rejected the Massachusetts prescription in favor of the federal procedure, however, "[t]he majority in Hanna recognized . . . that federal rules . . . must be interpreted by the courts applying them, and that the process of interpretation can and should reflect an awareness of legitimate state interests."

Following *Hanna*, we continued to "interpre[t] the federal rules to avoid conflict with important state regulatory policies."

. . . The Court veers away from that approach—and conspicuously, its most recent reiteration in *Gasperini*, in favor of a mechanical reading of Federal Rules, insensitive to state interests and productive of discord.

. . .

C

. . .

Section 901(a) allows courts leeway in deciding whether to certify a class, but § 901(b) rejects the use of the class mechanism to pursue the particular remedy of statutory damages. The limitation was not designed with the fair conduct or efficiency of litigation in mind. Indeed, suits seeking statutory damages are arguably best suited to the class device because individual proof of actual damages is unnecessary. New York's decision instead to block class-action proceedings for statutory damages therefore makes scant sense, except as a means to a manifestly substantive end: Limiting a defendant's liability in a single lawsuit in order to prevent the exorbitant inflation of penalties—remedies the New York Legislature created with individual suits in mind.

**D**

. . .

As the Second Circuit well understood, Rule 23 prescribes the considerations relevant to class certification and postcertification proceedings—but it does not command that a particular remedy be available when a party sues in a representative capacity. Section 901(b), in contrast, trains on that latter issue. Sensibly read, Rule 23 governs procedural aspects of class litigation, but allows state law to control the size of a monetary award a class plaintiff may pursue.

In other words, Rule 23 describes a method of enforcing a claim for relief, while § 901(b) defines the dimensions of the claim itself. In this regard, it is immaterial that § 901(b) bars statutory penalties in wholesale, rather than retail, fashion. The New York Legislature could have embedded the limitation in every provision creating a cause of action for which a penalty is authorized; § 901(b) operates as shorthand to the same effect. It is as much a part of the delineation of the claim for relief as it would be were it included claim by claim in the New York Code.

The Court single-mindedly focuses on whether a suit "may" or "may not" be maintained as a class action. Putting the question that way, the Court does not home in on the reason why. Rule 23 authorizes class treatment for suits satisfying its prerequisites because the class mechanism generally affords a fair and efficient way to aggregate claims for adjudication. Section 901(b) responds to an entirely different concern; it does not allow class members to recover statutory damages because the New York Legislature considered the result of adjudicating such claims *en masse* to be exorbitant. The fair and efficient conduct of class litigation is the legitimate concern of Rule 23; the remedy for an infraction of state law, however, is the legitimate concern of the State's lawmakers and not of the federal rulemakers.

. . .

The absence of an inevitable collision between Rule 23 and § 901(b) becomes evident once it is comprehended that a federal court sitting in diversity can accord due respect to both state and federal prescriptions. Plaintiffs seeking to vindicate claims for which the State has provided a statutory penalty may pursue relief through a class action if they forgo statutory damages and instead seek actual damages or injunctive or declaratory relief; any putative class member who objects can opt out and pursue actual damages, if available, and the statutory penalty in an individual action. In this manner, the Second Circuit explained, "Rule 23's procedural requirements for class actions can be applied along with the substantive requirement of CPLR 901(b)." In sum, while phrased as responsive to the question whether certain class actions may begin, § 901(b) is unmistakably aimed at controlling how those actions must end. On that remedial issue, Rule 23 is silent.

Any doubt whether Rule 23 leaves § 901(b) in control of the remedial issue at the core of this case should be dispelled by our *Erie* jurisprudence, including *Hanna*, which counsels us to read Federal Rules moderately and cautions against stretching a rule to cover every situation it could conceivably reach. The Court states that "[t]here is no reason . . . to read Rule 23 as addressing only whether claims made eligible for class treatment by some other law should be certified as class actions." To the contrary, [our precedents] provide good reason to look to the law that creates the right to recover. That is plainly so on a more accurate statement of what is at stake: Is there any reason to read Rule 23 as authorizing a claim for relief when the State that created the remedy disallows its pursuit on behalf of a class? None at all is the answer our federal system should give.

. . .

By finding a conflict without considering whether Rule 23 rationally should be read to avoid any collision, the Court unwisely and unnecessarily retreats from the federalism principles undergirding *Erie*. Had the Court reflected on the respect for state regulatory interests endorsed in our decisions, it would have found no cause to interpret Rule 23 so woodenly—and every reason not to do so.

## II

Because I perceive no unavoidable conflict between Rule 23 and § 901(b), I would decide this case by inquiring "whether application of the [state] rule would have so important an effect upon the fortunes of one or both of the litigants that failure to [apply] it would be likely to cause a plaintiff to choose the federal court." *Hanna*, 380 U.S. at 468, n. 9. See *Gasperini*, 518 U.S. at 428.

. . .

When no federal law or rule is dispositive of an issue, and a state statute is outcome affective in the sense our cases on *Erie* (pre- and post-*Hanna*) develop, the Rules of Decision Act commands application of the State's law in diversity suits. As this case starkly demonstrates, if federal courts exercising diversity jurisdiction are compelled by Rule 23 to award statutory penalties in class actions while New York courts are bound by § 901(b)'s proscription, "substantial variations between state and federal [money judgments] may be expected." The "variation" here is indeed "substantial." Shady Grove seeks class relief that is ten thousand times greater than the individual remedy available to it in state court. As the plurality acknowledges, forum shopping will undoubtedly result if a plaintiff need only file in federal instead of state court to seek a massive monetary award explicitly barred by state law. See *Gasperini*, 518 U.S. at 431 ("*Erie* precludes a recovery in federal court significantly larger than the recovery that would have been tolerated in state court."). The "accident of diversity of citizenship" should not subject a defendant to such augmented liability.

*Gasperini*'s observations apply with full force in this case. By barring the recovery of statutory damages in a class action, § 901(b) controls a defendant's maximum liability in a suit seeking such a remedy. The remedial provision could have been written as an explicit cap: "In any class action seeking statutory damages, relief is limited to the amount the named plaintiff would have recovered in an individual suit." That New York's Legislature used other words to express the very same meaning should be inconsequential.

We have long recognized the impropriety of displacing, in a diversity action, state-law limitations on state-created remedies. . . .

The Court's erosion of *Erie*'s federalism grounding impels me to point out the large irony in today's judgment. Shady Grove is able to pursue its claim in federal court only by virtue of the recent enactment of the Class Action Fairness Act of 2005 (CAFA), 28 U.S.C. § 1332(d). In CAFA, Congress opened federal-court doors to state-law-based class actions so long as there is minimal diversity, at least 100 class members, and at least $5,000,000 in controversy. By providing a federal forum, Congress sought to check what it considered to be the overreadiness of some state courts to certify class actions. In other words, Congress envisioned fewer—not more—class actions overall. Congress surely never anticipated that CAFA would make federal courts a mecca for suits of the kind Shady Grove has launched: class actions seeking state-created penalties for claims arising under state law—claims that would be barred from class treatment in the State's own courts.

. . .

I would continue to approach *Erie* questions in a manner mindful of the purposes underlying the Rules of Decision Act and the Rules Enabling Act, faithful to precedent, and respectful of important state interests. I would therefore hold that the New York Legislature's limitation on the recovery of statutory damages applies in this case, and would affirm the Second Circuit's judgment.

## Comments and Questions

1. Which of the three opinions—the plurality's, Stevens's, or Ginsburg's—best reflects the concerns regarding federalism as originally set forth in *Erie R.R. v. Tomkins*? Or does each simply emphasize certain *Erie* policies over others?

2. Which opinion do you think Chief Justice Earl Warren (author of *Hanna v. Plumer*) would agree with? What about Justice Thurgood Marshall (author of *Walker v. Armco Steel Co.*)? Or Justice Harlan (concurring in *Hanna v. Plumer* with his "primary private activity" test)? Draft the operative two or three short paragraphs of the opinions you think each would have written in *Shady Grove*.

3. *Shady Grove* presents the oddity of one of the Court's most conservative (and often states' rights oriented) members, Antonin Scalia, giving a broad reading to a Federal Rule and thereby displacing the state's judgment that class actions seeking such penalties should not proceed, while the liberal Ruth Bader Ginsburg would deprive plaintiffs of the class action device in deference to New York's statute. Does the *Erie* puzzle now transcend ideology?

Professor Jeffrey W. Stempel writes:

Justice Ruth Bader Ginsburg's more functional approach, arguably too solicitous of state law, prevailed in *Gasperini* only to be relegated to a dissent in *Shady Grove*. By contrast, *Gasperini* dissenter Justice Antonin Scalia emerged victorious in a more formalist, perhaps overly federal court-empowering plurality opinion reminiscent of Chief Justice Earl Warren's *Hanna v. Plumer* majority opinion. Critics might term the Scalia plurality in *Shady Grove* as "*Hanna* on steroids" (or at least a pumped-up *Hanna*) in its aggressive view that federal procedural rules eject contrary state procedural codes, even where they embody substantive state law or policy, so long as the federal rule is actually procedural and on point.

. . .

*Shady Grove* was also a wonderful departure from the Court's seemingly predictable ideological divide that has characterized other close cases in recent years. The majority upholding Federal Rule 23 included conservatives Scalia, Chief Justice John Roberts and Justice Clarence Thomas combined with liberals Sotomayor and Stevens while the dissenters attempting to privilege the state law were liberals Ginsburg and Stephen Breyer joined by conservatives Anthony Kennedy and Samuel Alito. The division of the Court cut against type, which both illustrated the difficulty of *Erie* issues and provided a bit of reassurance that case outcomes are not completely predictable according to the Justices' overall ideology or outcome preferences. The conservative-led majority permitted the plaintiff considerably more leverage over a large commercial defendant than it would have obtained under state law, a result opposed by the liberal-led dissenters.

Shady Grove *and the Potential Democracy-Enhancing Benefits of* Erie *Formalism*, 44 Akron L. Rev. 907, 908-911 (2011).

4. Does the plurality opinion minimize "the threat to the goal of uniformity of federal procedure" that concerned Chief Justice Warren in *Hanna*? If so, at what cost to the principles of federalism?

5. Is the plurality correct when it treats Fed. R. Civ. P. 23 as just another joinder device, like Fed. R. Civ. P. 18 (joinder of claims), 20 (joinder of parties), or 42(a) (consolidation of actions)? Are there substantive implications to allowing small claimants to aggregate their cases in a way that makes them financially feasible to bring?

What about *Erie*'s twin aims of discouraging forum shopping and avoiding inconsistent results between state and federal court on the same matter? Note the apparent success of Shady Grove Orthopedic Associates in shopping for the federal forum, and thereby transforming a $500 individual case into a $5 million class action, as Justice Ginsburg notes in her dissent. Isn't this just what bothered the Court about Harry Tomkins's "gaming" of the system under the *Swift v. Tyson* regime?

6. Professors Stephen Burbank and Tobias Barrington Wolff view *Shady Grove* as a missed opportunity to clarify the murky area of conflicts between the Federal Rules and state law. *See Redeeming the Missed Opportunities of*

Shady Grove, 159 U. Pa. L. Rev. 17 (2010). They complain that the Court's precedents "give some Federal Rules implausibly broad interpretations in order to apply federal law while emptying others of content in order to avoid an Enabling Act challenge." Can you annotate that assertion to the cases we have read?

### Practice Exercise No. 38: Analyzing Vertical Choice of Law Issues in *Carpenter*

Assume there is diversity of citizenship among the parties in *Carpenter v. Dee*, making available either a federal or a state forum for the litigation. In weighing these options, we (as plaintiff's counsel) discover that the Massachusetts legislature has adopted a "tort reform" statute providing that a plaintiff seeking punitive damages in state court must:

1. "plead with particularity the facts and circumstances upon which any claim for punitive damages in based, and may not make any such allegations upon information and belief or on the assertion that there will likely be evidentiary support after reasonable opportunity for discovery."
2. "pay the reasonable attorneys' fees of defendant if the claim for punitive damages is ultimately unsuccessful."
3. "post a security bond in the amount determined by the court to assure that such attorneys' fees will be paid, if so ordered."

The legislative history recites findings that claims for punitive damages are often made without merit, unfairly intimidate defendants into settling, and tend to substantially enlarge the time and expense of litigation.

It's been suggested that if we file in federal district court rather than state court, we would *not* be subject to the tort reform statute. Prepare for a brainstorming session on this forum selection strategy.

### Review Exercise No. 9

You are law clerk to the judge trying a federal diversity action alleging negligence on the part of plaintiff's corporate landlord. The tenant claims he suffered debilitating injuries in a fall down a steep flight of outdoor stairs that had not been cleared of snow and ice.

During voir dire of prospective jurors, the judge asked the group whether they had any experience that would bias them against either party. Venireperson 6 answered that she had recently rented from a landlord who refused to make any necessary repairs. Venireperson 9 is a carpenter who informed the court that landlords have on occasion failed to pay his bills for work he performed at their request.

The judge excused both for cause, over the objection of plaintiff's counsel, who requested permission to ask the venirepersons follow-up questions to ascertain whether their objectivity would actually be compromised. Counsel pointed out that under state practice in that jurisdiction, a litigant has a statutory right to supplement the court's voir dire questions in such a situation to avoid unjustified exclusion of persons from jury service. The state supreme court has ruled that any violation of that statute is presumed to have been prejudicial to the party denied the right to question jurors, and requires reversal.

In effect, plaintiff's counsel argues, defendant has been given two additional peremptory challenges without having to show actual bias, affording the defense a distinct tactical advantage in shaping the jury, and thus both infringing on plaintiff's Seventh Amendment right to a jury trial, and creating the risk of a different outcome than would obtain in state court.

Fed. R. Civ. P. 47 leaves this matter to the judge's discretion ("If the court examines the jurors, it must permit the parties or their attorneys to make any further inquiry *it considers proper*"), and she is inclined not to permit counsel follow-up questions because that would slow down the selection process, especially as it will likely come up again with other members of the panel; it might also give plaintiff's counsel the opportunity to unduly influence the prospective jurors by the nature or manner in which the further questions are posed. But the judge is also concerned about the risk of reversal on this issue if the verdict goes against plaintiff and the issue is pressed on appeal.

The judge has called a recess, and asks for your advice as to whether state or federal practice should control. Be prepared to so advise.

## "Reverse-*Erie*"

The flip side of the vertical choice of law dilemma is the question of when a state court, entertaining a federal claim within its concurrent subject matter jurisdiction, is obligated to apply federal law in place of its own state rule—the so-called reverse-*Erie* scenario.

Assume an arrestee brings a § 1983 action against the police officers in state court, alleging use of excessive force. In such cases, the federal courts apply the usual standard of proof applicable in civil cases, namely preponderance of the evidence. But if the state courts impose on plaintiffs a heightened burden in tort actions against police officers—"clear and convincing" proof—which standard should the state court apply?

The Supreme Court of Wisconsin held that the federal standard must prevail:

> The United States Supreme Court has recognized that just as federal courts are constitutionally obligated to apply state law to state claims, *Erie R.R. Co. v. Tompkins*, 304 U.S. 64, 58 S. Ct. 817, 82 L. Ed. 1188 (1938), so too the Supremacy Clause imposes on state courts a constitutional duty to proceed in such

manner that all the substantial rights of the parties under controlling federal law [are] protected. Inasmuch as the burden of proof is substantive, we hold that under the Supremacy Clause, the lower federal burden of proof applies in § 1983 excessive force cases in state court.

*Shaw v. Leatherberry*, 286 Wis. 2d 380, 395 (2005). Burden of proof was not, the Wisconsin court concluded, "a mere incident" of procedure, but a "substantive aspect" of the cause of action, and the state court could not alter the "substantial rights" which Congress provided in § 1983. *Id.* at 396.

To read more about this topic, see Kevin M. Clermont, *Reverse*-Erie, 82 Notre Dame L. Rev. 1 (2006).

# 10

# *Finality and Preclusion*

## A. INTRODUCTION

Suppose Joe and Sally are involved in an automobile accident. Sally files a lawsuit alleging that Joe's negligence caused the accident and seeking compensation for a broken left headlight. She litigates that case to conclusion, and a final judgment is entered. Sally then files a second negligence lawsuit against Joe arising from the very same accident, but this time seeking recovery for the broken *right* headlight. Could any dispute resolution system tolerate such inefficiency?

The doctrine of *res judicata* (or *claim preclusion*) prevents Sally from litigating successive suits against Joe arising from the same event. Repetition would waste scarce judicial resources, be unfair to the harassed defendant, permit a plaintiff to spin the litigation roulette wheel until she finds a sympathetic jury, and run the risk of inconsistent results.

Claim preclusion thus requires a plaintiff to assert *all* matters arising out ✓ rule of the *same incident or transaction* and against the *same party* in one lawsuit. The doctrine precludes repetitive litigation regardless of whether the plaintiff wins or loses the first case, and even if we now know that the decision was wrong on the law or facts. (The post-verdict or appeals process is the place to remedy such mistakes.) Subsequent litigation is categorically barred in the interest of finality.

But what if Sally also has a gripe against Joe for an unpaid loan that is *unrelated* to the accident? While Sally *could* join the two claims pursuant to Fed. R. Civ. P. 18 (*see* Chapter 3), she is not required to do so because the claims involve different events. Litigating these two cases separately would not require a repetition of the same facts and evidence, nor would it constitute undue harassment of defendant, nor would it risk inconsistent judgments from the very same set of circumstances.

Operation of the doctrine of claim preclusion will obviously depend on the breadth of our definition of "same claim"—the broader the definition, the more joinder we are going to mandate at the time of the litigation, and the more preclusion that will follow later for matters that are left out.

Claim preclusion thus operates in two time frames of critical importance to lawyers and litigants. First, in planning the case, plaintiff's counsel must be careful to include in the complaint *all* matters that might be considered part of the *same claim* against that defendant, or risk preclusion of omitted matters in a future litigation. Second, once final judgment has been entered in a case, subsequent litigation between the same parties may require a determination of whether Case 2 represents impermissible "splitting" of a single claim into two lawsuits; if so, Case 2 will not be permitted to go forward.

Now suppose that Sally and Joe have executed a contract requiring Joe to clear timber from Sally's land every June for ten years. Joe performs on the contract for two years, but then is sued by Sally for failure to clear the land in Year 3. Joe defends by challenging the validity of the contract, asserting he was not of sufficient age and legal capacity to enter into the contract when it was signed. The case is tried and results in a jury verdict and judgment for Sally. Subsequently, Sally sues Joe again, this time for failure to clear the land in Year 7. While this is a *different claim* because it arises out of a different breach (which could not have been anticipated and litigated in Year 3), and thus is not foreclosed by claim preclusion, the doctrine of *collateral estoppel* (or *issue preclusion*) comes into play. If (as is likely) it is determined that the jury in the first case must have resolved the capacity issue against Joe in order to find for Sally, Joe will be foreclosed from asserting that defense again. Once an issue has been adjudicated between adverse parties, that identical issue cannot be relitigated in another lawsuit between the same parties.

While claim preclusion prevents a second litigation from proceeding at all (usually by way of summary judgment), issue preclusion works more narrowly (through, for example, partial summary judgment) to foreclose litigation of an issue that has previously been litigated and resolved between the parties.

The influential American Law Institute (ALI) summarizes the finality doctrines as follows:

## ■ RESTATEMENT (SECOND) OF JUDGMENTS*

### § 17. EFFECTS OF FORMER ADJUDICATION—GENERAL RULES

A valid and final personal judgment is conclusive between the parties, except on appeal or other direct review, to the following extent:

(1) If the judgment is in favor of the plaintiff, the claim is extinguished and merged in the judgment;

(2) If the judgment is in favor of the defendant, the claim is extinguished and the judgment bars a subsequent action on that claim;

[Editors' Note: While the common law assigned different terms to the doctrine of *res judicata* depending on which party prevailed in the suit, i.e., *merger* occurred where plaintiff won and *bar* where defendant won, the very same consequence followed in both scenarios—there could be no subsequent action on that claim.]

(3) A judgment in favor of either the plaintiff or the defendant is conclusive, in a subsequent action between them on the same or a different claim, with respect to any issue actually litigated and determined if its determination was essential to that judgment.

**COMMENT**

d. Erroneous judgment. The general rules stated in this Section are applicable to a valid and final judgment, even if it is erroneous and subject to reversal. If the judgment is erroneous, the unsuccessful party's remedy is to have it set aside or reversed in the original proceedings. Such a remedy may be sought by a motion for a new trial or other relief in the court that rendered the judgment, or by an appeal or other proceedings for review of the judgment in an appellate court.

---

The doctrines of claim and issue preclusion must not be confused with the principle of *stare decisis*, by which courts generally follow past precedent in resolving questions of law. *Stare decisis* "is a basic self-governing principle within the Judicial Branch" designed to ensure that the law will not change erratically; it "permits society to presume that bedrock principles are founded in the law rather than in the proclivities of individuals." *Patterson v. McLean Credit Union*, 491 U.S. 164, 172 (1989). While precedents are not sacrosanct, the burden is on the party seeking reconsideration. In our *Sally v. Joe* automobile collision hypothetical, decisional law holding that contributory negligence is a complete bar to recovery would control unless Sally's lawyers are successful in arguing for departure from precedent. Note that *stare decisis* widely applies to all litigants, whereas claim and issue preclusion constrain only the parties (and those "in privity" with them, as discussed later) from the previous case.

Two other doctrines should be noted: *Law of the case* dictates that once an issue of law has been determined in a case, that issue cannot generally be relitigated in subsequent stages of the same lawsuit. It is premised on obvious concerns of efficiency and consistency. *See* Larry L. Teply and Ralph U. Whitten, *Civil Procedure* 1061-1062 (4th ed. 2009). *Double jeopardy* is a protection applicable in criminal cases against being tried for the same offense twice; unlike preclusion on the civil side, it is derived from the Constitution, specifically the Fifth Amendment.

## B. CLAIM PRECLUSION (*RES JUDICATA*)— "SPEAK NOW OR FOREVER HOLD YOUR PEACE"

To make out the defense of claim preclusion (which you will recall must be pled affirmatively under Fed R. Civ. P. 8(c)), three elements must be shown:

- A prior suit has proceeded to a *final valid judgment on the merits*.
- The present suit arises out of the *same claim* as the prior suit.
- The *parties in both suits are the same, or in privity* (to be discussed).

### 1. What Constitutes the "Same Claim"?

The following excerpt elucidates the prevailing transactional definition of the concept of a "claim":

## ■ RESTATEMENT (SECOND) OF JUDGMENTS

### § 24. DIMENSIONS OF "CLAIM" FOR PURPOSES OF MERGER OR BAR—GENERAL RULE CONCERNING "SPLITTING"

(1) When a valid and final judgment rendered in an action extinguishes the plaintiff's claim pursuant to the rules of merger or bar, the claim extinguished includes all rights of the plaintiff to remedies against the defendant with respect to all or any part of the transaction, or series of connected transactions, out of which the action arose.

(2) What factual grouping constitutes a "transaction," and what groupings constitute a "series," are to be determined pragmatically, giving weight to such considerations as whether the facts are related in time, space, origin, or motivation, whether they form a convenient trial unit, and whether their treatment as a unit conforms to the parties' expectations or business understanding or usage.

#### COMMENT

a. Rationale of a transactional view of claim. In defining claim to embrace all the remedial rights of the plaintiff against the defendant growing out of the relevant transaction (or series of connected transactions), this Section responds to modern procedural ideas which have found expression in the Federal Rules of Civil Procedure and other procedural systems.

"Claim," in the context of *res judicata*, has never been broader than the transaction to which it related. But in the days when civil procedure still bore the imprint of the forms of action and the division between law and equity, the courts were prone to associate claim with a single theory of recovery, so that with respect to one transaction, a plaintiff might have as many claims as there were theories of the substantive law upon which he could seek relief against the defendant. Thus, defeated in an action based on one theory, the plaintiff might be able to maintain another action based on a different theory, even though both actions were grounded upon the defendant's identical act or connected acts forming a single life-situation. In those earlier days there was also some adherence to a view that associated claim with the assertion of a single primary right as accorded by the substantive law, so that, if it appeared that the defendant had invaded a number of primary rights conceived to be held by the plaintiff, the plaintiff had the same number of claims, even though they all sprang from a unitary occurrence. There was difficulty in knowing which rights were primary and what was their extent, but a primary right and the corresponding claim might turn out to be narrow. Thus it was held by some courts that a judgment for or against the plaintiff in an action for personal injuries did not preclude an action by him for property damage occasioned by the same negligent conduct on the part of the defendant—this deriving from the idea that the right to be free of bodily injury was distinct from the property right. Still another view of claim looked to sameness of evidence; a second action was precluded where the evidence to support it was the same as that needed to support the first. Sometimes this was made the sole test of identity of claim; sometimes it figured as a positive but not as a negative test; that is, in certain situations a second action might be precluded although the evidence material to it varied from that in the first action. Even so, claim was not coterminous with the transaction itself.

The present trend is to see claim in factual terms and to make it coterminous with the transaction regardless of the number of substantive theories, or variant forms of relief flowing from those theories, that may be available to the plaintiff; regardless of the number of primary rights that may have been invaded; and regardless of the variations in the evidence needed to support the theories or rights. The transaction is the basis of the litigative unit or entity which may not be split.

. . . A modern procedural system . . . permits the presentation in the action of all material relevant to the transaction without artificial confinement to any single substantive theory or kind of relief and without regard to historical forms of action or distinctions between law and equity. . . . The law of *res judicata* now reflects the expectation that parties who are given the capacity to present their "entire controversies" shall in fact do so.

b. Transaction: application of a pragmatic standard. The expression "transaction, or series of connected transactions," is not capable of a mathematically precise definition; it invokes a pragmatic standard to be applied with attention to the facts of the cases. And underlying the standard is the need to strike a delicate balance between, on the one hand, the interests of the defendant and of the courts in bringing litigation to a close and, on the other, the interest of the plaintiff in the vindication of a just claim.

It should be emphasized that the concept of a transaction is here used in the broad sense. . . . In general, the expression connotes a natural grouping or common nucleus of operative facts. Among the factors relevant to a determination whether the facts are so woven together as to constitute a single claim are their relatedness in time, space, origin, or motivation, and whether, taken together, they form a convenient unit for trial purposes. Though no single factor is determinative, the relevance of trial convenience makes it appropriate to ask how far the witnesses or proofs in the second action would tend to overlap the witnesses or proofs relevant to the first. If there is a substantial overlap, the second action should ordinarily be held precluded. But the opposite does not hold true; even when there is not a substantial overlap, the second action may be precluded if it stems from the same transaction or series.

c. Transaction may be single despite different harms, substantive theories, measures or kinds of relief. A single transaction ordinarily gives rise to but one claim by one person against another. When a person by one act takes a number of chattels belonging to another, the transaction is single, and judgment for the value of some of the goods exhausts the claim and precludes the injured party from maintaining one action for the remainder. In the more complicated case where one act causes a number of harms to, or invades a number of different interests of the same person, there is still but one transaction; a judgment based on the act usually prevents the person from maintaining another action for any of the harms not sued for in the first action. . . .

That a number of different legal theories casting liability on an actor may apply to a given episode does not create multiple transactions and hence multiple claims. This remains true although the several legal theories depend on different shadings of the facts, or would emphasize different elements of the facts, or would call for different measures of liability or different kinds of relief.

---

Consider the application of this transactional definition of "claim" in the next case.

## ■ CAR CARRIERS, INC. v. FORD MOTOR COMPANY
### *789 F.2d 589 (7th Cir. 1989)*

RIPPLE, Circuit Judge:

In this case, we are asked to decide whether the present litigation is barred by an earlier lawsuit under the doctrine of *res judicata*. For the reasons which follow, we hold that the present suit is barred by the earlier judgment and, accordingly, affirm the judgment of the district court.

In 1982, Car Carriers, Inc. (Car Carriers) and six related entities brought an action against Ford Motor Company (Ford) and Nu-Car Carriers, Inc. (Nu-

Car). Count I of the six count complaint (1982 Complaint) accused Ford and Nu-Car of conspiring in violation of the Sherman Act, 15 U.S.C. § 1. The remaining five counts asserted pendent state law claims.

The district court dismissed the entire action. The court found the antitrust claim lacking because the plaintiffs failed "to suffer the type of harm the antitrust laws were designed to recompense." Further, since the court found that this defect was "noncurable," the antitrust claim was dismissed with prejudice. Having dismissed the complaint's only federal claim, the district court declined to exercise pendent jurisdiction over the remaining state law claims and dismissed them without prejudice. On appeal, a panel of this court affirmed the district court's decision in all respects.

Undaunted by their first unfruitful journey through the federal courts, Car Carriers and its related entities filed the present action on October 25, 1983 (1983 Complaint). The 1983 Complaint consisted of twenty-four counts: Counts I-VI alleged violations of the Racketeer Influenced and Corrupt Organizations Act (RICO), 18 U.S.C. § 1961 *et seq.*; Count XXIV alleged a violation of the Interstate Commerce Act, 49 U.S.C. §§ 11902-11904; the remaining seventeen counts alleged violations of Illinois law.

The district court again dismissed the entire action. The court held that the federal claims arose from the same "basic fact situation" as that alleged in support of the 1982 Complaint's antitrust claim and, therefore, were barred by the doctrine of *res judicata*. For reasons which are not relevant here, this dismissal was without prejudice. The state law claims were again dismissed without prejudice as not pendent to any valid federal claim. After unsuccessful attempts to clarify or amend the district court's judgment, this appeal followed.

# I

Before addressing Car Carriers' substantive claims, it will be helpful to set out the occurrences which sparked the 1982 Complaint—the initial litigation in this matter. As set forth in that complaint, from 1968 until 1981, Car Carriers transported new Ford vehicles from Ford's plants and railheads in the Chicago area. As a transport company, Car Carriers was regulated by both the Illinois and Interstate Commerce Commissions; accordingly, Car Carriers' rates were subject to approval by both agencies. The complaint alleged that Ford had the power to control these rates either by formally opposing any rate increase sought before the agencies or by simply terminating the carrier.

According to Car Carriers, as early as 1975, Ford and its alleged coconspirators entered into contracts and continuing combinations which were designed to restrain trade in the business of providing haulaway motor transportation for new Ford automobiles. As explained in this court's earlier opinion, Car Carriers accused Ford of employing the following method to implement its goal:

First, the carrier selected for elimination (the so-called "target carrier") would be required to make substantial investments in new tractor-trailer equipment, real estate, and new terminal facilities. In return, Ford would promise additional transportation traffic and "complete agreement with increased tariff rates necessary to pay for these acquisitions." After the "target" carriers had made these investments, however, Ford would then prevent them from obtaining the rate increases necessary for profitable operations.

Second, Ford, with support of other carriers, "interfered with and prevented [the] target haulaway carriers and their affiliates from selling their businesses and assets as going business concerns or prevented [the] target haulaway carriers from consolidation or merger with other carriers." Finally, Ford would apparently terminate its relationship with the target carrier at this point, thereby allowing the favored carriers to "acquire the businesses and assets of [the target carriers] at distress prices or for less than fair market value as going business concerns."

. . .

In this litigation, the appellants present [two] issues for our review. First, they ask that we reject the district court's fact-oriented test for *res judicata* in favor of an analysis which would differentiate causes of action based on the rights, duties, and injuries allegedly redressed by each claim. Second, assuming we adopt the district court's approach, the appellants ask that we relieve them of their *res judicata* burden because some of their claims were based on facts which—while admittedly in existence prior to the 1982 Complaint—were unknown to them until after judgment on that complaint.

## II

The district court found that the federal claims alleged in the 1983 Complaint arose out of the same factual context as described in the 1982 Complaint. Thus, the court dismissed these claims as barred by the doctrine of *res judicata*. The appellants do not disagree with the district court's finding that both complaints arose out of a common core of operative fact; rather, they attempt to overturn the district court's decision by persuading us to adopt an alternate formulation for determining the application of *res judicata*. Under this alternate test, *res judicata* would not bar a second lawsuit when "an analysis of the rights, duties, and injuries involved in the second lawsuit reveals that they are materially different from those in issue in the first." For the reasons which will be explained in the following section, we decline to adopt the appellants' suggested formulation.

*Res judicata* is designed to ensure the finality of judicial decisions. It is not "a mere matter of practice or procedure inherited from a more technical time than ours. It is a rule of fundamental and substantial justice, of public policy and of private peace, which should be cordially regarded and enforced by the courts." It "encourages reliance on judicial decisions, bars vexatious litigation, and frees the courts to resolve other disputes." "Its enforcement is essential to the maintenance of social order; for, the aid of judicial tribunals would not be invoked for the vindication of rights of person and property, if conclusiveness did not attend the judgments of such tribunals."

**A**

"Under *res judicata*, a final judgment on the merits bars further claims by parties or their privies based on the same cause of action." In determining the scope of a "cause of action," this circuit has utilized the "same transaction" test. Under this test, a "cause of action" consists of "a single core of operative facts which give rise to a remedy." This "same transaction" test is decidedly fact-oriented. Once a transaction has caused injury, all claims arising from that transaction must be brought in one suit or be lost. Thus, "a mere change in the legal theory does not create a new cause of action." Therefore, prior litigation acts as a bar not only to those issues which were raised and decided in the earlier litigation but also to those issues which could have been raised in that litigation. *Federated Department Stores, Inc. v. Moitie*, 452 U.S. 394, 398 (1981).

As the commentators have noted, this approach is consistent with the general litigation scheme established by the Federal Rules of Civil Procedure. Litigants have great latitude in joining claims and amending pleadings. *See* Fed. R. Civ. P. 15, 18. Thus, to further the purpose of the rules, it is appropriate that *res judicata* be defined with sufficient breadth to encourage parties to present all their related claims at one time. Further, we note that the Federal Rules define compulsory counterclaims as those claims which have arisen out of the same transaction or occurrence that prompted the plaintiffs' action. *See* Fed. R. Civ. P. 13(a). By compelling defendants to bring their claims in the same action, the rule encourages the simultaneous and final resolution of all claims which arise from a common factual background. Thus, if the Federal Rules impose this obligation on defendants, we believe that it is appropriate to interpret the doctrine of *res judicata* in such a way as to further that same goal by imposing a similar obligation on plaintiffs.

The appellants argue that, while the "same transaction" test may be the primary test for defining a "cause of action," it is not the universal test. The appellants argue that a more appropriate test in this case would be one which scrutinized the theories of relief (RICO, Interstate Commerce Act, Sherman Act) in search of differences between the rights, duties and injuries addressed by each.

We do not disagree that [the cases relied upon] contain language suggesting that *res judicata* analysis can involve a comparison of the rights, duties and injuries that have been alleged. We believe, however, that this language must be read cautiously lest it undermine the fundamental policies of *res judicata*: "that there be an end of litigation; that those who have contested an issue shall be bound by the result of the contest, and that matters once tried shall be considered forever settled as between the parties." It is no accident that the "same transaction" test has become "the present trend among courts nationwide. It preserves—far more firmly than the alternate formulation—the fundamental policy concerns of the doctrine. In our view, these policy concerns counsel against using in this case the "right-duty" approach which the appellants have suggested. Indeed, . . . an unsuccessful party ought not be able to "frustrate the doctrine of *res judicata* by cloaking the same cause of action in the language of a theory of recovery untried in the previous litigation." Therefore, the "right-duty" approach should not be used as a substitute for the "same transaction" test absent compelling circumstances and a clear showing that such a substitution will not undermine the policies of *res judicata*. Appellants have made absolutely no such showing in this case.

### B

We turn now to an application of the "transactional" test to the facts of this case. We must determine whether Car Carriers' RICO and Interstate Commerce Act claims could have been brought in the earlier litigation; in other words, we must decide whether these claims are part of the same cause of action which spawned the earlier Sherman Act claim. [The three threshold requirements of *res judicata* are (1) an identity of the parties or their privies, (2) an identity of the causes of action, and (3) a final judgment on the merits.]

In this appeal, neither party has contested the "final judgment" element. Further, neither party has questioned the identity of the parties in the two actions. While N & W was a new party defendant in the second action, it did not join in the *res judicata* motion; and even though the named plaintiffs were not identical in both actions, the additional plaintiffs in the second action did "not deny their obvious privity with the plaintiffs in the 1982 Action." Therefore, the only open question concerns the identity of the causes of action involved in both suits.

In concluding that both the 1982 and the 1983 Complaints alleged the same cause of action, the district court first relied on an analysis derived from the doctrine of pendent jurisdiction. As enunciated in *United Mine Workers v. Gibbs*, 383 U.S. 715 (1966), a federal court may exercise pendent jurisdiction over a state law claim if both the state and federal claims derive from a common nucleus of operative fact.

In this case, the alleged pendent claims were virtually identical to the state law claims alleged in the 1982 Complaint. Thus, according to the district court's reasoning, the appellants had admitted that the Sherman Act, RICO, and Interstate Commerce Act claims derived from a common nucleus of operative fact. Therefore, the district court concluded that *res judicata* was appropriate because the 1983 Complaint's RICO and Interstate Commerce Act claims arose out of the same set of facts as did the 1982 Complaint's Sherman Act claim.

There is a good deal of merit to the trial court's position. However, we are reluctant to rely on that ground alone. Mere allegations that state claims are pendent to a federal action do not create pendent jurisdiction. When dismissing both the 1982 Complaint's federal claims and the 1983 Complaint's federal claims, the district court also dismissed the state claims without determining whether they had properly been brought as pendent claims.

Therefore, since the district court's decision did not disclose whether pendent jurisdiction would have been proper had the federal claims survived, we must find a more solid basis for our decision.

As an alternate ground for its decision, the district court also specifically found that the RICO and Sherman Act counts arose out of the same underlying facts. The court stated: "Like the present RICO claims, the earlier antitrust claims alleged Ford induced Car Carriers to make investments it could not recoup. Like the earlier antitrust claims, the current RICO claims allege Car Carriers was terminated due to a sham and predatory bid, and Ford and Nu-Car refused to buy Car Carriers' assets upon its termination." We agree; the RICO and Sherman Act claims arose out of a single core of operative facts and, thus, were parts of the same cause of action.

The district court did not specifically mention the Interstate Commerce Act claim—Count XXIV of the 1983 Complaint. Yet, a brief review of that count makes clear that it too was part of the same cause of action. Paragraph 504, the first paragraph of that count, states in relevant part:

> Count XXIV seeks damages from Ford and Nu-Car as a result of their individual and joint violations of 49 U.S.C. §§ 11902, 11903(a) and (b) and 11904(a)(3) and (b) wherein they both solicited, gave, granted, accepted, received, and offered rebates, concessions and discrimination by various direct and indirect means in a continuing course of conduct from July 1981 until about June 1983, which conduct was designed to replace Car Carriers at Chicago, to install Nu-Car as Ford's driveaway and haulaway carrier, and to secure Nu-Car improvement of Ford owned real estate in Chicago by Nu-Car at no cost to Ford. These Ford/Nu-Car violations grew out of Ford's request for bids to replace CCI in Chicago, Nu-Car's response to that request and Ford's subsequent actions in installing Nu-Car in Chicago and elsewhere with incremental traffic effective October 1981.

This allegation parallels the facts underlying the 1982 Complaint. Accordingly, the district court did not err by dismissing this count.[10]

In sum, we hold that the district court properly applied the "same transaction test" to dismiss all of Car Carriers' federal claims.

## III

As a second ground for appeal, Car Carriers asks that we lift the *res judicata* bar for some of its claims because Car Carriers did not discover the facts supporting those claims until after the 1982 Complaint had been dismissed. In essence, Car Carriers claims that since *res judicata* will not bar

---

10. While we are aware that the actions alleged in Count XXIV extend beyond the time period alleged in the 1982 Complaint, we believe that this discrepancy is unimportant. In this case, it is sufficient that there is some chronological overlap and that the two complaints arise out of the same common nucleus of operative fact. To the extent that Count XXIV addresses events occurring after the first judgment, we note that the 1983 Complaint was dismissed without prejudice specifically to allow such a claim to be brought later.

actions based on facts occurring after the initial judgment,—presumably because those facts were unknown to the plaintiffs when they initiated their first action—*res judicata* should likewise not bar claims based on pre-judgment facts which were unknown to the plaintiffs when they filed. We find this contention to be absolutely without merit.

As we concluded in Part II, *supra*, all of the appellants' claims were part of the same cause of action; they all arose from a single core of operative fact. Since all claims arose from the same factual context and since the appellants had sufficient knowledge to sue on one claim, they also had sufficient knowledge to sue on the rest of their claims. When a litigant files a lawsuit, the courts have a right to presume that he has done his legal and factual homework. It would undermine the basic policies protected by the doctrine of *res judicata* to permit the appellants to once again avail themselves of judicial time and energy while another litigant, who has yet to be heard even once, waits in line behind them. . . .

## IV

In disposing of the 1983 Complaint, the district court properly analyzed the *res judicata* effect of its earlier decision. We note, in addition, that since Counts I and II were properly dismissed as barred by *res judicata*, all actions against the appellee Norfolk & Western Railway Company were properly dismissed inasmuch as they were derivative. Therefore, the decision of the district court is Affirmed.

## Comments and Questions

1. Plaintiff Car Carriers, Inc. argued that *res judicata* should not be controlled by a transactional analysis, but rather by a narrower definition of "same claim" focused on rights, duties, and injuries. As noted previously in the *Restatement* commentary, some jurisdictions following this latter approach concluded that separate claims for property damage and personal injury may arise out of the same accident, since the right to recover for one is distinct from the right to be compensated for the other. Do you see why the modern trend has rejected this view?

2. Car Carriers, Inc. also argued that *res judicata* should not apply because some of the facts supporting the 1983 complaint were not discovered by counsel until after the dismissal of the 1982 complaint. The court rejected this contention as "absolutely without merit." Why? Do you see the difference between *new events* giving rise to a new claim (look back at Sally and Joe's multi-year contract for clearing of timber), and *newly discovered facts* regarding the original claim? Could claim preclusion accommodate an exception of the kind proposed by Car Carriers, Inc. without sacrificing its core purpose? Wouldn't such an exception reward lawyers for failing to do their "legal and factual homework"?

It should be noted that Fed. R. Civ. P. 60(b) allows a district court to set aside a judgment on the basis of "newly discovered evidence that, with reasonable diligence, could not have been discovered in time to move for a new trial under Rule 59(b)." *See* Chapter 5, Part E(7).

3. What is the relationship between Fed. R. Civ. P. 13(a) and claim preclusion? If there were no compulsory counterclaim rule (as in some jurisdictions), would *res judicata* principles achieve the same result—i.e., preclusion of a claim because it was not asserted in a prior case as a counterclaim arising from the same transaction as the plaintiff's claim?

In the absence of a compulsory rule, a defendant in a previous action who now brings a transactionally related claim against the former plaintiff (the parties have, in other words, switched roles) may be foreclosed (1) by operation of issue preclusion from relitigating common issues that were determined in the prior action; or (2) from pursuing his claim at all by operation of claim preclusion if entertaining his claim would undermine the finality of the original judgment. *See* Larry L. Teply and Ralph U. Whitten, *Civil Procedure* 997-999 (4th ed. 2009) (citing *Restatement (Second) of Judgments* § 22). If, for example, A sues B for injuries resulting from a motor vehicle collision, and B defends by denying negligence but omits to assert a counterclaim against A for his own injuries, B may be foreclosed in these ways from asserting that claim in a subsequent action he brings against A.

4. In *Heacock v. Heacock*, 402 Mass. 21 (1988), Carla filed a tort action in Superior Court seeking damages for injuries resulting from an assault allegedly committed by former husband Gregg while they were married. Gregg filed a motion to dismiss, asserting that her claim was precluded by a prior divorce judgment entered in the Probate Court. In the divorce proceeding, Carla had presented evidence of the assault and injuries to support her claim that the marriage should be dissolved because of irretrievable breakdown. The Superior Court judge agreed with Gregg and dismissed Carla's tort action "on the basis of issue preclusion, collateral estoppel, *res judicata*, or any one of those three, whichever happens to be the best one." 402 Mass. at 23. [Warning: Don't try this approach on your Civil Procedure or Bar Examination.]

Can you help the judge determine *which* doctrine would apply? Here's what the Supreme Judicial Court said in reversing the dismissal on Carla's appeal:

> 1. Claim preclusion. The doctrine of claim preclusion makes a valid, final judgment conclusive on the parties and their privies, and bars further litigation of all matters that were or should have been adjudicated in the action. This is so even though the claimant is prepared in a second action to present different evidence or legal theories to support his claim, or seeks different remedies. The doctrine is a ramification of the policy considerations that underlie the rule against splitting a cause of action, and is "based on the idea that the party to be precluded has had the incentive and opportunity to litigate the matter fully in the first lawsuit." As such, it applies only where both actions were based on the same claim.

A tort action is not based on the same underlying claim as an action for divorce. The purpose of a tort action is to redress a legal wrong in damages; that of a divorce action is to sever the marital relationship between the parties, and, where appropriate, to fix the parties' respective rights and obligations with regard to alimony and support, and to divide the marital estate. Although a judge in awarding alimony and dividing marital property must consider, among other things, the conduct of the parties during the marriage, the purposes for which these awards are made do not include compensating a party in damages for injuries suffered. The purpose of an award of alimony is to provide economic support to a dependent spouse; that of the division of marital property is to recognize and equitably recompense the parties' respective contributions to the marital partnership. The plaintiff could not have recovered damages for the tort in the divorce action, as the Probate Court does not have jurisdiction to hear tort actions and award damages.* The policy considerations commonly advanced to justify the doctrine of claim preclusion are not implicated in the circumstances of this case. Maintenance of the tort claim will not subject the defendant and the courts to the type of piecemeal litigation that the doctrine of claim preclusion seeks to prevent. As such, nothing in the doctrine or in the policy considerations underlying it warrants its application in the circumstances of this case.

2. Issue preclusion. To defend successfully on the ground of issue preclusion, the defendant must establish that the issue of fact sought to be foreclosed actually was litigated and determined in a prior action between the parties or their privies, and that the determination was essential to the decision in the prior action. Because a judge in awarding alimony and dividing marital property must consider a number of factors, and the judge who presided over the Heacocks' divorce action did not make any findings of fact to support his judgment, we cannot say that the judge necessarily resolved any issue relating to the defendant's assault of the plaintiff. Accordingly, the doctrine of issue preclusion does not apply.

402 Mass. at 23-25. The Supreme Court of Connecticut reached the same result in *Delahunty v. Massachusetts Mutual Life Ins. Co.,* 236 Conn. 582, 674 A.2d 1290 (1996), where it refused to preclude a wife from bringing a postdivorce tort suit against her former husband for fraudulently converting the proceeds of her life insurance policy.

Had these two decisions gone the other way, a divorce decree would in effect immunize the alleged tortfeasor from any litigation arising from acts committed during the marriage, notwithstanding the inability to seek recovery in the divorce proceeding.

5. **The Single Injury/Single Recovery Rule.** What happens if a plaintiff, who has recovered in a lawsuit from an asbestos manufacturer after proving that his workplace exposure caused his asbestosis, later develops

---

*Eds.' Note:* Claim preclusion does not apply where the "plaintiff was unable to rely on a certain theory of the case or to seek a certain remedy or form of relief in the first action because of the limitations on the subject matter jurisdiction of the courts or restrictions on their authority to entertain multiple theories or demands for multiple remedies or forms of relief in a single action, and the plaintiff desires in the second action to rely on that theory or to seek that remedy or form of relief." *See Restatement (Second) of Judgments* § 26(1)(c).

mesothelioma, a malignant lung cancer also caused by the exposure? Can he file a second suit seeking damages for the far more serious ailment?

Under traditional claim preclusion principles, the answer generally is no. As the Fifth Circuit Court of Appeals explained:

> Once injury results there is but a single tort and not a series of separate torts, one for each resultant harm. The cause of action thus created is for all the damage caused by the single legal wrong, and a plaintiff may not split this cause of action by seeking damages for some of his injuries in one suit and for later-developing injuries in another. The cause of action inheres in the causative aspects of a breach of a legal duty, the wrongful act itself, and not in the various forms of harm which result therefrom. He does not have a discrete cause of action for each harm. . . .
>
> Gideon has but one cause of action for all the damages caused by the defendants' legal wrong; the diseases that have developed *and will in probability develop* are included within this cause of action, for they are but part of the sequence of harms resulting from the alleged breach of legal duty. Gideon could not split his cause of action and recover damages for asbestosis, then later sue for damages caused by such other pulmonary disease as might develop, then still later sue for cancer should cancer appear. His claim includes, without limitation, all damages for future pain and suffering, inability to work in the future, reduced life expectancy, future medical expenses, and future disabilities and diseases that will probably develop from present injuries.

*Gideon v. Johns-Manville Sales Corp.*, 761 F.2d 1129, 1136-1137 (5th Cir. 1985) (emphasis added). As a consequence, a plaintiff in this situation must present expert testimony that there is a reasonable medical probability of his developing and dying from cancer induced by the inhalation of asbestos fibers, and seek appropriate recovery for all present and potential injuries. *Id.*, at 1138. *See also Restatement (Second) of Judgments* § 25 comment c.

Significantly, a few decisions have, however, been willing to construe the "single injury" rule to permit a later suit for a latent disease that had not developed at the time of the first trial. *See, e.g., Hagerty v. L & L Marine Services, Inc.*, 788 F.2d 315, 320-321 (5th Cir. 1986).

## 2. What Constitutes a "Final Valid Judgment on the Merits"?

### ■ RESTATEMENT (SECOND) OF JUDGMENTS

#### § 20. JUDGMENT FOR DEFENDANT—EXCEPTIONS TO THE GENERAL RULE OF BAR

(1) A personal judgment for the defendant, although valid and final, does not bar another action by the plaintiff on the same claim:

(a) When the judgment is one of dismissal for lack of jurisdiction, for improper venue, or for nonjoinder or misjoinder of parties; or

(b) When the plaintiff agrees to or elects a nonsuit (or voluntary dismissal) without prejudice or the court directs that the plaintiff be nonsuited (or that the action be otherwise dismissed) without prejudice; . . .

**ILLUSTRATION**

1. A brings an action against B for personal injuries, and the action is dismissed for improper venue on the ground that the judicial district in which suit was brought was not the district of defendant's residence as required by law. Although A is not barred from maintaining an action on the claim in another district, the rules of issue preclusion are applicable to the determination that venue was improper in the initial action.

2. A brings an action against B for personal injuries in a federal court, basing jurisdiction on diversity of citizenship. The action is dismissed on the ground that the alleged diversity does not in fact exist. A is not barred from bringing another action on the same claim in a court of competent jurisdiction.

---

Note that the *Restatement* does not use the phrase judgment "on the merits," but instead excludes from the operation of claim preclusion dismissals on jurisdictional or misjoinder grounds, in which case it can be refiled in an appropriate court with proper jurisdiction, or with the proper parties. Although the expression connotes a decision on the substantive validity of the plaintiff's claim (such as summary judgment) rather than on a procedural ground (such as improper venue), it has not always been so interpreted. Fed. R. Civ. P. 41(b), for example, presumptively treats dismissals for failure of the plaintiff to prosecute the case or to comply with civil procedure rules as "an adjudication on the merits," even though such dismissals are obviously not directed at the "validity" of the claim. *See* Jack H. Friedenthal, Mary Kay Kane, and Arthur R. Miller, *Civil Procedure* § 14.7 at 689-691 (4th ed. 2005).

*Semtek International, Inc. v. Lockheed Martin Corp.*, 531 U.S. 497 (2001) (discussed in Chapter 9), dealt with the claim-preclusive effect of a dismissal on statute of limitations grounds. The California federal district court characterized its dismissal as "on the merits and with prejudice." Consequently, when Semtek refiled the claim in a state court in Maryland (where the statute had not yet run), that court dismissed on *res judicata* grounds. Reversing, a unanimous Court concluded that even though both Fed. R. Civ. P. 41(b) and the rendering court would treat the prior judgment as "on the merits," that was not conclusive as to whether the second lawsuit was precluded. Rather, California's law of claim preclusion would control the question, and the matter was remanded for that determination.

## 3. *"The Parties Are the Same or Are in Privity"*

Under what circumstances may someone be precluded from litigating on the basis of a prior decision in a case in which they were not a party? When, in other words, may a litigant be deprived of his day in court because *someone else* had it for him?

# ■ BRENT TAYLOR, PETITIONER v. ROBERT A. STURGELL, ACTING ADMINISTRATOR, FEDERAL AVIATION ADMINISTRATION, ET AL.

*553 U.S. 880 (2008)*

Justice GINSBURG delivered the opinion of the Court.

"It is a principle of general application in Anglo-American jurisprudence that one is not bound by a judgment *in personam* in a litigation in which he is not designated as a party or to which he has not been made a party by service of process." *Hansberry v. Lee*, 311 U. S. 32, 40 (1940). Several exceptions, recognized in this Court's decisions, temper this basic rule. In a class action, for example, a person not named as a party may be bound by a judgment on the merits of the action, if she was adequately represented by a party who actively participated in the litigation.. In this case, we consider for the first time whether there is a "virtual representation" exception to the general rule against precluding nonparties. Adopted by a number of courts, including the courts below in the case now before us, the exception so styled is broader than any we have so far approved.

The virtual representation question we examine in this opinion arises in the following context. Petitioner Brent Taylor filed a lawsuit under the Freedom of Information Act seeking certain documents from the Federal Aviation Administration. Greg Herrick, Taylor's friend, had previously brought an unsuccessful suit seeking the same records. The two men have no legal relationship, and there is no evidence that Taylor controlled, financed, participated in, or even had notice of Herrick's earlier suit. Nevertheless, the D. C. Circuit held Taylor's suit precluded by the judgment against Herrick because, in that court's assessment, Herrick qualified as Taylor's "virtual representative."

We disapprove the doctrine of preclusion by "virtual representation," and hold, based on the record as it now stands, that the judgment against Herrick does not bar Taylor from maintaining this suit.

## I

The Freedom of Information Act (FOIA) accords "any person" a right to request any records held by a federal agency. No reason need be given for a FOIA request, and unless the requested materials fall within one of the Act's enumerated exemptions, the agency must "make the records promptly available" to the requester. If an agency refuses to furnish the requested records, the requester may file suit in federal court and obtain an injunction "order[ing] the production of any agency records improperly withheld."

The courts below held the instant FOIA suit barred by the judgment in earlier litigation seeking the same records. Because the lower courts' decisions turned on the connection between the two lawsuits, we begin with a full account of each action.

A

The first suit was filed by Greg Herrick, an antique aircraft enthusiast and the owner of an F-45 airplane, a vintage model manufactured by the Fairchild Engine and Airplane Corporation (FEAC) in the 1930's. In 1997, seeking information that would help him restore his plane to its original condition, Herrick filed a FOIA request asking the Federal Aviation Administration (FAA) for copies of any technical documents about the F-45 contained in the agency's records.

To gain a certificate authorizing the manufacture and sale of the F-45, FEAC had submitted to the FAA's predecessor, the Civil Aeronautics Authority, detailed specifications and other technical data about the plane. Hundreds of pages of documents produced by FEAC in the certification process remain in the FAA's records. The FAA denied Herrick's request, however, upon finding that the documents he sought are subject to FOIA's exemption for "trade secrets and commercial or financial information obtained from a person and privileged or confidential."

In an administrative appeal, Herrick urged that FEAC and its successors had waived any trade-secret protection. The FAA thereupon contacted FEAC's corporate successor, respondent Fairchild Corporation (Fairchild). Because Fairchild objected to release of the documents, the agency adhered to its original decision.

Herrick then filed suit in the U. S. District Court for the District of Wyoming. Challenging the FAA's invocation of the trade-secret exemption, Herrick placed heavy weight on a 1955 letter from FEAC to the Civil Aeronautics Authority. The letter authorized the agency to lend any documents in its files to the public "for use in making repairs or replacement parts for aircraft produced by Fairchild." This broad authorization, Herrick maintained, showed that the F-45 certification records held by the FAA could not be regarded as "secre[t]" or "confidential" within the meaning of [the exemption].

Rejecting Herrick's argument, the District Court granted summary judgment to the FAA. The 1955 letter, the court reasoned, did not deprive the certification documents of trade-secret status, for those documents were never in fact released pursuant to the letter's blanket authorization. The court also stated that even if the 1955 letter had waived trade-secret protection, Fairchild had successfully "reversed" the waiver by objecting to the FAA's release of the records to Herrick.

On appeal, the Tenth Circuit agreed with Herrick that the 1955 letter had stripped the requested documents of trade-secret protection. But the Court of Appeals upheld the District Court's alternative determination—i.e., that Fairchild had restored trade-secret status by objecting to Herrick's FOIA request. On that ground, the appeals court affirmed the entry of summary judgment for the FAA.

In so ruling, the Tenth Circuit noted that Herrick had failed to challenge two suppositions underlying the District Court's decision. First, the District Court assumed trade-secret status could be "restored" to documents that had lost protection. Second, the District Court also assumed that Fairchild had regained trade-secret status for the documents even though the company claimed that status only "after Herrick had initiated his request" for the F-45 records. The Court of Appeals expressed no opinion on the validity of these suppositions.

**B**

The Tenth Circuit's decision issued on July 24, 2002. Less than a month later, on August 22, petitioner Brent Taylor—a friend of Herrick's and an antique aircraft enthusiast in his own right—submitted a FOIA request seeking the same documents Herrick had unsuccessfully sued to obtain. When the FAA failed to respond, Taylor filed a complaint in the U. S. District Court for the District of Columbia. Like Herrick, Taylor argued that FEAC's 1955 letter had stripped the records of their trade-secret status. But Taylor also sought to litigate the two issues concerning recapture of protected status that Herrick had failed to raise in his appeal to the Tenth Circuit.

After Fairchild intervened as a defendant, the District Court in D. C. concluded that Taylor's suit was barred by claim preclusion; accordingly, it granted summary judgment to Fairchild and the FAA. The court acknowledged that Taylor was not a party to Herrick's suit, [yet] held that a nonparty may be bound by a judgment if she was "virtually represented" by a party.

. . .

The record before the District Court in Taylor's suit revealed the following facts about the relationship between Taylor and Herrick: Taylor is the president of the Antique Aircraft Association, an organization to which Herrick belongs; the two men are "close associate[s]"; Herrick asked Taylor to help restore Herrick's F-45, though they had no contract or agreement for Taylor's participation in the restoration; Taylor was represented by the lawyer who represented Herrick in the earlier litigation; and Herrick apparently gave Taylor documents that Herrick had obtained from the FAA during discovery in his suit.

Fairchild and the FAA conceded that Taylor had not participated in Herrick's suit. The D. C. District Court determined, however, that Herrick ranked as Taylor's virtual representative. Accordingly, the District Court held Taylor's suit, seeking the same documents Herrick had requested, barred by the judgment against Herrick.

The D. C. Circuit affirmed. . . .

We granted certiorari to resolve the disagreement among the Circuits over the permissibility and scope of preclusion based on "virtual representation."

**II**

The preclusive effect of a federal-court judgment is determined by federal common law. See *Semtek Int'l Inc. v. Lockheed Martin Corp.*, 531 U. S. 497, 507-508 (2001). For judgments in federal-question cases—for example,

Herrick's FOIA suit—federal courts participate in developing "uniform federal rule[s]" of res judicata, which this Court has ultimate authority to determine and declare. The federal common law of preclusion is, of course, subject to due process limitations.

Taylor's case presents an issue of first impression in this sense: Until now, we have never addressed the doctrine of "virtual representation" adopted (in varying forms) by several Circuits and relied upon by the courts below. Our inquiry, however, is guided by well-established precedent regarding the propriety of nonparty preclusion. We review that precedent before taking up directly the issue of virtual representation.

### A

The preclusive effect of a judgment is defined by claim preclusion and issue preclusion, which are collectively referred to as "res judicata." Under the doctrine of claim preclusion, a final judgment forecloses "successive litigation of the very same claim, whether or not relitigation of the claim raises the same issues as the earlier suit." Issue preclusion, in contrast, bars "successive litigation of an issue of fact or law actually litigated and resolved in a valid court determination essential to the prior judgment," even if the issue recurs in the context of a different claim. By "preclud[ing] parties from contesting matters that they have had a full and fair opportunity to litigate," these two doctrines protect against "the expense and vexation attending multiple lawsuits, conserv[e] judicial resources, and foste[r] reliance on judicial action by minimizing the possibility of inconsistent decisions."

A person who was not a party to a suit generally has not had a "full and fair opportunity to litigate" the claims and issues settled in that suit. The application of claim and issue preclusion to nonparties thus runs up against the "deep-rooted historic tradition that everyone should have his own day in court." Indicating the strength of that tradition, we have often repeated the general rule that "one is not bound by a judgment *in personam* in a litigation in which he is not designated as a party or to which he has not been made a party by service of process." *Hansberry*, 311 U. S., at 40.

### B

Though hardly in doubt, the rule against nonparty preclusion is subject to exceptions. For present purposes, the recognized exceptions can be grouped into six categories.

First, "[a] person who agrees to be bound by the determination of issues in an action between others is bound in accordance with the terms of his agreement." *Restatement (Second) of Judgments* § 40, p. 390 (1980) (hereinafter *Restatement*). For example, "if separate actions involving the same transaction are brought by different plaintiffs against the same defendant, all the parties to all the actions may agree that the question of the defendant's liability will be definitely determined, one way or the other, in a 'test case.'"

Second, nonparty preclusion may be justified based on a variety of preexisting "substantive legal relationship[s]" between the person to be bound and a party to the judgment. Qualifying relationships include, but are not limited to, preceding and succeeding owners of property, bailee and bailor, and assignee and assignor. See 2 Restatement §§ 43-44, 52, 55. These exceptions originated "as much from the needs of property law as from the values of preclusion by judgment."[1]

Third, we have confirmed that, "in certain limited circumstances," a nonparty may be bound by a judgment because she was "adequately represented by someone with the same interests who [wa]s a party" to the suit. Representative suits with preclusive effect on nonparties include properly conducted class actions, see Fed. Rule Civ. Proc. 23, and suits brought by trustees, guardians, and other fiduciaries.

Fourth, a nonparty is bound by a judgment if she "assume[d] control" over the litigation in which that judgment was rendered. Restatement § 39. Because such a person has had "the opportunity to present proofs and argument," he has already "had his day in court" even though he was not a formal party to the litigation. Id., Comment a, p. 382.

Fifth, a party bound by a judgment may not avoid its preclusive force by relitigating through a proxy. Preclusion is thus in order when a person who did not participate in a litigation later brings suit as the designated representative of a person who was a party to the prior adjudication. . . .

Sixth, in certain circumstances a special statutory scheme may "expressly foreclos[e] successive litigation by nonlitigants . . . if the scheme is otherwise consistent with due process." Examples of such schemes include bankruptcy and probate proceedings. . . .

## III

Reaching beyond these six established categories, some lower courts have recognized a "virtual representation" exception to the rule against nonparty preclusion. . . .

The D. C. Circuit purported to ground its virtual representation doctrine in this Court's decisions stating that, in some circumstances, a person may be bound by a judgment if she was adequately represented by a party to the proceeding yielding that judgment. But the D. C. Circuit's definition of "adequate representation" strayed from the meaning our decisions have attributed to that term.

. . .

### B

. . . Fairchild and the FAA argue that preclusion is in order whenever "the relationship between a party and a non-party is 'close enough' to bring the

---

1. The substantive legal relationships justifying preclusion are sometimes collectively referred to as "privity." The term "privity," however, has also come to be used more broadly, as a way to express the conclusion that nonparty preclusion is appropriate on any ground. To ward off confusion, we avoid using the term "privity" in this opinion.

second litigant within the judgment." Courts should make the "close enough" determination, they urge, through a "heavily fact-driven" and "equitable" inquiry . . .

We reject this argument for three reasons. First, our decisions emphasize the fundamental nature of the general rule that a litigant is not bound by a judgment to which she was not a party. Accordingly, we have endeavored to delineate discrete exceptions that apply in "limited circumstances." Respondents' amorphous balancing test is at odds with the constrained approach to nonparty preclusion our decisions advance.

. . .

Our second reason for rejecting a broad doctrine of virtual representation rests on the limitations attending nonparty preclusion based on adequate representation. A party's representation of a nonparty is "adequate" for preclusion purposes only if, at a minimum: (1) the interests of the nonparty and her representative are aligned, see *Hansberry*, 311 U. S., at 43; and (2) either the party understood herself to be acting in a representative capacity or the original court took care to protect the interests of the nonparty. In addition, adequate representation sometimes requires (3) notice of the original suit to the persons alleged to have been represented.

In the class-action context, these limitations are implemented by the procedural safeguards contained in Federal Rule of Civil Procedure 23.

An expansive doctrine of virtual representation, however, would "recogniz[e], in effect, a common-law kind of class action." That is, virtual representation would authorize preclusion based on identity of interests and some kind of relationship between parties and nonparties, shorn of the procedural protections prescribed in *Hansberry* and Rule 23. These protections, grounded in due process, could be circumvented were we to approve a virtual representation doctrine that allowed courts to "create de facto class actions at will."

Third, a diffuse balancing approach to nonparty preclusion would likely create more headaches than it relieves. Most obviously, it could significantly complicate the task of district courts faced in the first instance with preclusion questions. An all-things-considered balancing approach might spark wide-ranging, time-consuming, and expensive discovery tracking factors potentially relevant under seven- or five-prong tests. And after the relevant facts are established, district judges would be called upon to evaluate them under a standard that provides no firm guidance. Preclusion doctrine, it should be recalled, is intended to reduce the burden of litigation on courts and parties. "In this area of the law," we agree, "'crisp rules with sharp corners' are preferable to a round-about doctrine of opaque standards."

**C**

Finally, . . . the FAA maintains that nonparty preclusion should apply more broadly in "public-law" litigation than in "private-law" controversies. To support this position, the FAA offers two arguments. First, the FAA urges, . . . the plaintiff has a reduced interest in controlling the litigation "because of the public nature of the right at issue." The FAA next argues that "the threat of vexatious litigation is heightened" in public-law cases because "the number of plaintiffs with standing is potentially limitless." . . .

But we are not convinced that this risk justifies departure from the usual rules governing nonparty preclusion. First, *stare decisis* will allow courts swiftly to dispose of repetitive suits brought in the same circuit. Second, even when *stare decisis* is not dispositive, "the human tendency not to waste money will deter the bringing of suits based on claims or issues that have already been adversely determined against others." This intuition seems to be borne out by experience: The FAA has not called our attention to any instances of abusive FOIA suits in the Circuits that reject the virtual-representation theory respondents advocate here.

## IV

For the foregoing reasons, we disapprove the theory of virtual representation on which the decision below rested. The preclusive effects of a judgment in a federal-question case decided by a federal court should instead be determined according to the established grounds for nonparty preclusion described in this opinion. See Part II-B, supra.

. . .

### A

It is uncontested that four of the six grounds for non-party preclusion have no application here: There is no indication that Taylor agreed to be bound by Herrick's litigation, that Taylor and Herrick have any legal relationship, that Taylor exercised any control over Herrick's suit, or that this suit implicates any special statutory scheme limiting relitigation. Neither the FAA nor Fairchild contends otherwise.

It is equally clear that preclusion cannot be justified on the theory that Taylor was adequately represented in Herrick's suit. Nothing in the record indicates that Herrick understood himself to be suing on Taylor's behalf, that Taylor even knew of Herrick's suit, or that the Wyoming District Court took special care to protect Taylor's interests. Under our pathmarking precedent, therefore, Herrick's representation was not "adequate."

That leaves only the fifth category: preclusion because a nonparty to an earlier litigation has brought suit as a representative or agent of a party who is bound by the prior adjudication. Taylor is not Herrick's legal representative and he has not purported to sue in a representative capacity. He concedes, however, that preclusion would be appropriate if respondents could demonstrate that he is acting as Herrick's "undisclosed agent."

Respondents argue here, as they did below, that Taylor's suit is a collusive attempt to relitigate Herrick's action. The D. C. Circuit considered a similar question in addressing the "tactical maneuvering" prong of its virtual representation test. The Court of Appeals did not, however, treat the issue as one of agency, and it expressly declined to reach any definitive conclusions due to "the ambiguity of the facts." We therefore remand to give the courts below an opportunity to determine whether Taylor, in pursuing the instant FOIA suit, is acting as Herrick's agent. Taylor concedes that such a remand is appropriate.

We have never defined the showing required to establish that a nonparty to a prior adjudication has become a litigating agent for a party to the earlier case. Because the issue has not been briefed in any detail, we do not discuss the matter elaborately here. We note, however, that courts should be cautious about finding preclusion on this basis. A mere whiff of "tactical maneuvering" will not suffice; instead, principles of agency law are suggestive. They indicate that preclusion is appropriate only if the putative agent's conduct of the suit is subject to the control of the party who is bound by the prior adjudication. See 1 Restatement (Second) of Agency § 14, p. 60 (1957) ("A principal has the right to control the conduct of the agent with respect to matters entrusted to him.").

**B**

On remand, Fairchild suggests, Taylor should bear the burden of proving he is not acting as Herrick's agent. . . . We reject Fairchild's suggestion. Claim preclusion, like issue preclusion, is an affirmative defense. See Fed. Rule Civ. Proc. 8(c). Ordinarily, it is incumbent on the defendant to plead and prove such a defense, and we have never recognized claim preclusion as an exception to that general rule. We acknowledge that direct evidence justifying nonparty preclusion is often in the hands of plaintiffs rather than defendants. But "[v]ery often one must plead and prove matters as to which his adversary has superior access to the proof." In these situations, targeted interrogatories or deposition questions can reduce the information disparity. We see no greater cause here than in other matters of affirmative defense to disturb the traditional allocation of the proof burden.

For the reasons stated, the judgment of the United States Court of Appeals for the District of Columbia Circuit is vacated, and the case is remanded for further proceedings consistent with this opinion.

*It is so ordered.*

## Comments and Questions

1. While *Taylor v. Sturgell* certainly sounds the death knell for the amorphous virtual representation theory of nonparty preclusion, and emphasizes that for due process reasons any such preclusion is clearly the exception and not the rule, it still leaves *some* room for nonparties to be foreclosed in the six situations described in Part IIB.

2. The common law used the term "privity" (a label the *Taylor* Court explicitly eschews, see footnote 1) to describe a relationship between a past litigant and a current litigant such that the latter should be bound by the decision rendered in the former's prior action.

Examples of privity include the following:

- A person acquires an interest in property that has already been the subject of a lawsuit. Thus an heir who inherits land, or a successive buyer, is bound by a prior judgment regarding an easement.
- A party litigates in a representative capacity. A judgment in a suit brought by or against the trustee may, for example, bind the beneficiary in a subsequent action.
- A close familial relationship exists between a party in the prior case and a litigant in the present case *whose claim is derivative of or closely aligned* with the former's. A wife was deemed bound by the outcome of her husband's prior bankruptcy proceeding, even though she was not a party to it, because the claims she asserted in the current action derived exclusively from claims asserted by her husband. *Eubanks v. FDIC*, 977 F.2d 166 (5th Cir. 1992).

In the latter situation it must be emphasized, however, that family relationship and parallel interests are *not* in themselves sufficient to establish privity. Each victim injured in an automobile accident has an independent claim for his or her injuries that is *not* derivative of the others, and thus litigation by one family member will not foreclose such actions by the others. *See, e.g., Freeman v. Lester Coggins Trucking, Inc.*, 771 F.2d 860 (5th Cir. 1985).

For more on privity, *see* Jack H. Friedenthal, Mary Kay Kane, and Arthur R. Miller, *Civil Procedure* § 14.13 (4th ed. 2005), in which the authors suggest that "a more profitable analysis of when nonparties may be bound requires an inquiry into whether the facts and circumstances in the first case raise the presumption that the nonparty's interest was fully and adequately presented."

3. Consider the following excerpts from a pre-*Taylor v. Sturgell* decision taking on what Circuit Judge Bruce Selya describes as the "murky corner of the law" called "privity." A section on virtual representation has been deleted, as *Taylor* takes that concept off the table. Note that as a consequence of this decision, a seven-week jury trial in the district court may in effect be repeated by a new group of plaintiffs asserting parallel claims, underscoring the tension between efficiency and fairness that lurks beneath any question of finality.

## ■ GONZALEZ v. BANCO CENTRAL CORP.
*27 F.3d 751 (1st Cir. 1994)*

Selya, Circuit Judge:

This appeal raises tantalizing questions concerning the application of the doctrine of *res judicata* to nonparties. Because we conclude that appellants cannot lawfully be precluded from bringing their action in the circumstances at bar, we reverse the district court's order of dismissal and remand for further proceedings.

## I. BACKGROUND

In the 1970s, a consortium of real estate developers sold subdivided lots of undeveloped land to approximately 3,000 purchasers, most of whom resided in Puerto Rico. Contrary to the promoters' glowing representations, the real estate proved to be Florida swampland, unsuitable for development.

In 1982, a gaggle of duped purchasers (whom we shall call "the Rodriguez plaintiffs") commenced a civil action in the United States District Court for the District of Puerto Rico. They sued the sellers, the banks that financed the project, and several related individuals. The Rodriguez plaintiffs alleged violations of the Interstate Land Sales Full Disclosure Act ("ILSFDA"), 15 U.S.C. § 1703, the Securities Exchange Act of 1934, 15 U.S.C. § 78j, Rule 10b-5 thereunder, 17 C.F.R. § 240.10b-5, and the Racketeering Influenced and Corrupt Organizations Act ("RICO"), 18 U.S.C. §§ 1961-1964. Some of the plaintiffs then assisted in the formation of the Sunrise Litigation Group. The group's members paid fees that helped defray the costs of the litigation and exchanged information that sometimes proved to be of use in pursuing the litigation.

After several years of discovery and numerous amendments to the pleadings, the Rodriguez plaintiffs, 152 strong, sought to convert their suit to a class action. In April of 1987, the district court refused either to certify a class or to permit additional plaintiffs to intervene. Almost immediately thereafter, several prospective plaintiffs who had tried in vain to join the Rodriguez litigation initiated the instant action. The new coalition of claimants (whom we shall call "the Gonzalez plaintiffs") were represented by the same lawyers who represented the Rodriguez plaintiffs. They sued the same defendants and their complaint mimicked a proposed amended complaint on file (but never allowed) in the Rodriguez litigation. . . .

Despite strong evidence of skullduggery, the Rodriguez plaintiffs frittered away much of their case through a series of pretrial blunders. The Rodriguez plaintiffs ultimately lost what remained of their case after a seven-week jury trial when Judge Fuste directed verdicts for the defendants on the only surviving claims and this court upheld his ruling on appeal, *see Rodriguez v. Banco Central Corp.*, 990 F.2d 7, 14 (1st Cir. 1993).

Following the interment of the Rodriguez litigation, renewed attention focused on the Gonzalez litigation (which was pending before Judge Laffitte). By then, the Gonzalez plaintiffs were pressing certain claims that replicated those pressed and lost by the Rodriguez plaintiffs, e.g., claims under the ILSFDA, Rule 10b-5, and RICO (premised on securities fraud), and certain additional claims that had been neglected or abandoned by the Rodriguez plaintiffs, e.g., RICO claims premised on mail fraud, state-law claims for fraud, and claims for breach of contract.

After silhouetting the Gonzalez plaintiffs' suit against the backdrop of the completed Rodriguez litigation, Judge Laffitte, by way of an unpublished memorandum opinion, dismissed the action in its entirety on grounds of *res judicata*. The Gonzalez plaintiffs appeal.

## II. ANALYSIS

Although appellants were not parties to the earlier litigation, the court below applied *res judicata* in bar of their claims under a theory of privity. The applicability vel non of the doctrine of *res judicata* presents a question of law over which we exercise plenary appellate review. . . .

The accepted formulation of *res judicata* for federal court use teaches that "a final judgment on the merits of an action precludes the parties or their privies from relitigating issues that were or could have been raised in that action." *Allen v. McCurry*, 449 U.S. 90, 94 (1980). Accordingly, the elements of *res judicata* are (1) a final judgment on the merits in an earlier suit, (2) sufficient identicality between the causes of action asserted in the earlier and later suits, and (3) sufficient identicality between the parties in the two suits.

In the present situation, the first element in this tripartite test provokes no controversy; appellants concede that the earlier (Rodriguez) suit resulted in final judgment on the merits. Thus, we concentrate our energies on the remaining two prongs of the test.

### IDENTICALITY OF CAUSES OF ACTION

To determine whether sufficient subject matter identity exists between an earlier and a later suit, federal courts employ a transactional approach. This approach recognizes that a valid and final judgment in an action will extinguish subsequent claims "with respect to all or any part of the transaction, or series of connected transactions, out of which the action arose."

To understand the transactional approach, it is necessary to appreciate that a single transaction or series of transactions can—and often does—give rise to a multiplicity of claims. Phrased another way, "[a] single cause of action can manifest itself in an outpouring of different claims, based variously on federal statutes, state statutes, and the common law." The necessary identity will be found to exist if both sets of claims—those asserted in the earlier action and those asserted in the subsequent action—derive from a common nucleus of operative facts. This principle pertains no matter how diverse or prolific the claims themselves may be. It follows that the omission of a particular statement of claim from the original suit is of no great consequence; if the transaction is the same and the other components of the test are satisfied, principles of *res judicata* will bar all claims that either were or could have been asserted in the initial action. The key is to define the underlying injury.

This definitional process is not a purely mechanical exercise. "What factual grouping constitutes a 'transaction', and what groupings constitute a 'series,' are [matters that should] be determined pragmatically," taking into consideration a wide variety of relevant factors, including but not limited to such things as "whether the facts are related in time, space, origin, or motivation, whether they form a convenient trial unit, and whether their treatment as a unit conforms to the parties' expectations. . . ."

Given these criteria, we believe that there is sufficient identicality here between the earlier and later actions to satisfy the requisite standard.

Without exception, appellants' claims stem from the same series of transactions as the claims asserted in the initial litigation. Although the individual sales contracts are different, all of them arise out of a single course of conduct undertaken by a band of allied defendants. By like token, while each purchaser acquired a different lot at a different price, all the lots are part of the same development and all were sold by means of the same ballyhoo. At the very least, the two sets of claims are closely related in time, origin, and geography.

Moreover, if merged, the two sets of claims would form a well-integrated unit. The same kinds of land sale contracts that the Rodriguez plaintiffs attacked under ILSFDA and sought to characterize as "securities" for purposes of their RICO claim underlie appellants' current claims. To be sure, appellants have negotiated the procedural minefield more nimbly than their predecessors, and have, therefore, assembled a more varied assortment of legal theories; but their claims—including both those that replicate the Rodriguez plaintiffs' claims and those that do not—implicate the same series of interconnected transactions that gave rise to the causes of action litigated in the earlier lawsuit. In short, both sets of claims, though dressed in different legal garb, grow out of a common nucleus of operative facts. No more is exigible.

### IDENTICALITY OF PARTIES

. . .

Under federal law, *res judicata* can sometimes operate to bar the maintenance of an action by persons who, technically, were not parties to the initial action (to which preclusive effect is attributed). Nonetheless, we appreciate that this is a murky corner of the law and caution the district courts to tread gingerly in applying *res judicata* to nonparties.[4]

### PRIVITY

The most familiar mechanism for extending *res judicata* to nonparties without savaging important constitutional rights is the concept of privity— a concept that furnishes a serviceable framework for an exception to the rule that *res judicata* only bars relitigation of claims by persons who were parties to the original litigation. Although privity can be elusive, this case does not require us to build four walls around it. Here, the *res judicata* defense is based not on some exotic doctrinal refinement but on commonly accepted principles of how privity operates to bring about nonparty preclusion. The theory underlying defendants' iteration of the defense is that privity exists (and, therefore, nonparty preclusion potentially obtains) if a nonparty either substantially controlled a party's involvement in the initial litigation or, conversely, permitted a party to the initial litigation to function as his de facto representative. We accept defendants' theoretical

---

4. The perils of nonparty preclusion are real. Prominent among them is the prospect that an overly expansive arrangement of the concept, or too free use of it, may endanger constitutional rights. *See Meza v. General Battery Corp.*, 908 F.2d 1262, 1266 (5th Cir. 1990) (approving concept but noting the due process concerns implicit in the ideal that, in general, every party is entitled to her own "day in court").

premise, but, after close perscrutation of the record as a whole, we conclude that neither stripe of privity exists here.

### SUBSTANTIAL CONTROL

The doctrine of *res judicata* rests upon the bedrock principle that, for claim preclusion to apply, a litigant first must have had a full and fair opportunity to litigate his claim. If a nonparty either participated vicariously in the original litigation by exercising control over a named party or had the opportunity to exert such control, then the nonparty effectively enjoyed his day in court, and it is appropriate to impute to him the legal attributes of party status for purposes of claim preclusion.

Substantial control means what the phrase implies; it connotes the availability of a significant degree of effective control in the prosecution or defense of the case—what one might term, in the vernacular, the power—whether exercised or not—to call the shots. *Restatement (Second) of Judgments* § 39, comment c, at 384 (stating that control, for purposes of issue preclusion, refers to the right to exercise "effective choice as to the legal theories and proofs to be advanced," as well as "control over the opportunity to obtain review").

As the proverb suggests, a picture is sometimes worth a thousand words. Along these lines, we suspect that the concept of substantial control can be illustrated better by examples than by linguistic constructs. For instance, substantial control has been found in the case of a liability insurer that assumes the insured's defense, *see, e.g., Iacaponi v. New Amsterdam Cas. Co.*, 379 F.2d 311, 312 (3d Cir. 1967), *cert. denied*, 389 U.S. 1054 (1968), an indemnitor who participates in defending an action brought against the indemnitee, *see, e.g., Bros., Inc. v. W.E. Grace Mfg. Co.*, 261 F.2d 428, 430-31 (5th Cir. 1958), and the owner of a close corporation who assumes control of litigation brought against the firm, *see, e.g., Kreager v. General Elec. Co.*, 497 F.2d 468, 471-72 (2d Cir.), *cert. denied*, 419 U.S. 1041 (1974). Conversely, courts have refused to find substantial control merely because a nonparty retained the attorney who represented a party to the earlier action, *see Freeman v. Lester Coggins Trucking, Inc.*, 771 F.2d 860, 864 (5th Cir. 1985); *Ramey v. Rockefeller*, 348 F. Supp. 780, 785 (E.D.N.Y. 1972), or because the nonparty assisted in financing the earlier action, *see Rumford Chem.*, 215 U.S. at 159-60; *General Foods Corp. v. Massachusetts Dep't of Pub. Health*, 648 F.2d 784, 787-88 (1st Cir. 1981), or because the nonparty testified as a witness in the earlier action, *see Benson & Ford, Inc. v. Wanda Petroleum Co.*, 833 F.2d 1172, 1174-75 (5th Cir. 1987); *Ponderosa Devel. Corp. v. Bjordahl*, 787 F.2d 533, 536-37 (10th Cir. 1986), or because the nonparty procured witnesses or evidence, *see Carl Zeiss Stiftung v. V.E.B. Carl Zeiss, Jena*, 293 F. Supp. 892, 921 (S.D.N.Y. 1968), *modified*, 433 F.2d 686 (2d Cir. 1970), *cert. denied*, 403 U.S. 905 (1971), or because the nonparty furnished his attorney's assistance, *see Cofax Corp. v. Minn. Mining & Mfg. Co.*, 79 F. Supp. 842, 844 (S.D.N.Y. 1947).

In the last analysis, there is no bright-line test for gauging substantial control. The inquiry must be case-specific, and fact patterns are almost endlessly variable. The critical judgment cannot be based on isolated facts. Consequently, an inquiring court must consider the totality of the circumstances to determine whether they justify a reasonable inference of a nonparty's potential or actual involvement as a decisionmaker in the earlier litigation. The nonparty's participation may be overt or covert, and the evidence of it may be direct or circumstantial—so long as the evidence as a whole shows that the nonparty possessed effective control over a party's conduct of the earlier litigation as measured from a practical, as opposed to a purely theoretical, standpoint. The burden of persuasion ultimately rests with him who asserts that control (or the right to exercise it) existed to such a degree as would warrant invoking nonparty preclusion.

Applying this standard, there is no principled way in which it can be said that the *Gonzalez* plaintiffs substantially controlled the *Rodriguez* plaintiffs in regard to the original litigation. The only facts to which the district court alluded in ruling that nonparty preclusion loomed involve the similarity of the complaints at one point in time, the parties' common legal representation, and the planned use of some discovered materials in both litigations. In our view, these facts do not begin to show that the *Gonzalez* plaintiffs exercised any meaningful degree of control over the course of the *Rodriguez* litigation. Nor did they have either the right or the opportunity to demand such control.

Moreover, the record contains much additional evidence indicating the absence of substantial control. No useful purpose would be served by marshalling this evidence. We do, however, remark the most telling datum: that the *Rodriguez* plaintiffs sought to amend their complaint to add those who later became the *Gonzalez* plaintiffs a full half-decade after the start of the litigation—a datum strongly suggesting that appellants had no involvement in the initial five years of litigation. This lack of participation at the early stages of the *Rodriguez* litigation is particularly probative on the issue of substantial control, for it was during this period that many pivotal strategic decisions were made, resulting in the virtual forfeiture of some especially promising causes of action (including the mail fraud and state-law claims). Obviously, appellant had no chance to share in this decisionmaking.

. . .

### III. Conclusion

We need go no further. Because the appellants were neither parties to the initial action nor in privity with the plaintiffs therein, the district court erred in dismissing their suit under principles of *res judicata*. Reversed and remanded for further proceedings. Costs to appellants.

## Comments and Questions

Given what you now know about the constitutional limitations on preclusion against nonparties, are you surprised by the following excerpt from a recent Supreme Court decision by Anthony Kennedy in which white firefighters in New Haven successfully challenged the City's refusal to promote them from the civil service eligible list because of concerns regarding the discriminatory impact and validity of the tests?

> If, after it certifies the test results, the City faces a disparate-impact suit [from minority firefighters who were not party to the litigation], then in light of our holding today it should be clear that the City would avoid disparate-impact liability based on the strong basis in evidence that, had it not certified the results, it would have been subject to disparate-treatment liability.

*Ricci v. DeStafano*, 129 S. Ct. 2658, 2681 (2009).

An African-American firefighter who was neither a party in *Ricci*, nor represented by either party—the white plaintiffs or the City—filed his own discrimination case against the City, challenging the weighting of the test results which favored the written over the oral component, an issue not litigated in the earlier action. His case was dismissed on the basis of Justice Kennedy's paragraph in the preceding case, even though the district court judge admitted it deprived the plaintiff of his day in court. The Second Circuit reversed. *Briscoe v. City of New Haven*, 654 F.3d 200 (2011).

As Justice Robert Jackson famously said, the Supreme Court is not final because it is infallible, it is infallible because it is final. *See generally* Mark S. Brodin, *Ricci v. DeStefano: The* New Haven Firefighters *Case & the Triumph of White Privilege*, 20 S. Cal. Rev. L. Soc. Just. 161 (2011).

## Practice Exercise No. 39: Applying Claim Preclusion Doctrine in *Carpenter* and *City of Cleveland*

1. Assume that the plaintiffs in *City of Cleveland* lose their case and a final judgment is entered against them. The City subsequently changes the selection procedures for firefighter applicants and develops a new physical agility test, which, like the previous one, results in the exclusion of all female candidates. Can the same plaintiffs sue the City again alleging that the new test unlawfully discriminates against women, or will they be barred by claim preclusion? Can other women who fail the new test bring an action? Might any other finality or related doctrines apply in these litigations?

2. Now suppose instead that the *City of Cleveland* plaintiffs who unsuccessfully sued for gender discrimination are African American. Can these women bring a subsequent suit against the City alleging that the firefighter evaluation procedures that they were subjected to were *racially* discriminatory?

3. Let's turn to *Carpenter v. Dee*. Assume that Twyla Burrell, the owner of the Jeep CJ-7, was in the vehicle with Randall and Charlie at the time of the accident. Shortly afterward, Twyla filed an action against Randall in Small Claims Court for property damage to the jeep, and recovered a judgment of $2,000, the maximum allowed in that court. Three months later, Twyla filed an action against Randall in Superior Court seeking substantial damages for personal injuries she allegedly suffered as a result of the accident. Randall's attorney has moved to dismiss on preclusion grounds. How should the court rule?

The *Restatement* uses a similar scenario to illustrate the operation of claim preclusion:

> In an automobile collision, A is injured and his car damaged as a result of the negligence of B. Instead of suing in a court of general jurisdiction of the state, A brings his action for the damage to his car in a justice's court, which has jurisdiction in actions for damage to property but has no jurisdiction in actions for injury to the person. Judgment is rendered for A for the damage to the car. A cannot thereafter maintain an action against B to recover for the injury to his person arising out of the same collision.

*Restatement (Second) of Judgments* § 24, illustration (14).

From the perspective of efficiency and finality, it certainly seems appropriate to preclude Twyla from relitigating the accident in a court of general jurisdiction after *she chose* to litigate in a court of limited jurisdiction. The Connecticut Supreme Court, however, created an exception in a similar case in the interest of encouraging resort to the prompt and inexpensive process of the Small Claims Court. *See Issac v. Truck Service, Inc.*, 253 Conn. 416 (2000). Should it make a difference if Twyla had not been represented by counsel when she filed in Small Claims Court?

4. Assume that Nancy Carpenter filed an action in Superior Court against the City of Lowell based on the failure of the police officers who had stopped Randall Dee to advise him that the jeep had been illegally and dangerously modified. The action was dismissed on defendant's 12(b)(6) motion, the court relying on precedent holding that municipalities in the Commonwealth are not liable for the negligence of their employees. No appeal was filed, and a final judgment entered for the City.

One month later, the Supreme Judicial Court, in an unrelated case, repudiated the prior precedent and announced a new rule rendering municipalities liable for the negligent acts of their employees. May Nancy Carpenter take advantage of this development and refile her suit against the City? We will revisit this question when we read *Federated Department Stores v. Moitie*, later in this chapter.

## C. ISSUE PRECLUSION (COLLATERAL ESTOPPEL)

### 1. In Operation

### ■ DAVID P. HOULT v. JENNIFER HOULT
*157 F.3d 29 (1st Cir. 1998)*

BOUDIN, Circuit Judge:

In July 1988, when she was 27 years old, Jennifer Hoult brought suit in the district court against her father, David Hoult, alleging assault and battery, intentional infliction of emotional distress, and breach of fiduciary duty. To support these claims, she alleged that her father had sexually abused, raped and threatened her from the time that she was about four years old until she was about sixteen years old.

The statute of limitations presented an obvious obstacle. Jennifer Hoult sought to overcome it by showing that the alleged abuse caused her to repress her memory of the events until she began to recapture those memories during therapy sessions in October 1985. *See* M.G.L. 260 § 4C. The claim of repressed memory was supported at trial by testimony from a psychiatrist, Dr. Renee Brandt, who appeared as an expert witness on repression caused by traumatic abuse.

In June 1993, the district court conducted an eight day jury trial in which Jennifer Hoult testified at length, giving detailed descriptions of extensive alleged abuse by her father; in addition to other forms of abuse, she testified to five specific episodes of rape. Supporting testimony was provided by her former therapist and by Dr. Brandt. In defense, David Hoult testified on his own behalf, flatly denying the allegations, but presented no other witnesses.

On July 1, 1993, the jury returned a verdict in favor of Jennifer Hoult and ordered damages in the amount of $500,000. This verdict was preceded by a separate finding by the jury rejecting the statute of limitations defense; in effect the jury found that Jennifer Hoult had repressed memory of the abuse until it was rediscovered within the limitations period. David Hoult appealed both from the judgment against him and the denial of a motion for a new trial, but both appeals were ultimately dismissed for lack of prosecution.

Later, Jennifer Hoult wrote letters to several professional associations in which she repeated the charge that her father had raped her. David Hoult then brought the present action in the district court against Jennifer Hoult, claiming that her charge of rape against him was defamatory. Jennifer Hoult moved to dismiss on the ground that the jury verdict in her earlier assault action had determined that David Hoult had raped her and that David Hoult was barred by collateral estoppel from relitigating this finding.

Initially, the district court denied the motion to dismiss, saying that the evidence adduced at the trial could have led the jury to impose liability because David Hoult had sexually abused Jennifer Hoult "in ways that did not amount to rape" or could even have done so on the basis of Jennifer Hoult's testimony that David Hoult had "threatened her with murder, chased her around the house with a knife, and fondled her in a sexual manner, among other incidents of violence and assault."

By motion for reconsideration, Jennifer Hoult argued that the jury's finding of repression, in rejecting the statute of limitations defense, was necessarily based on Dr. Brandt's expert opinion that the repression required "repeated acts" of sexual abuse; and the only repeated acts of sexual abuse (Jennifer Hoult argued) were her descriptions of five separate incidents of rape. Accepting this argument, the district court allowed Jennifer Hoult's motion to dismiss the action, and David Hoult now appeals.

The governing legal doctrine of collateral estoppel, which we briefly summarize, is largely undisputed; the problem is one of applying the doctrine to this case. . . . Subject to certain exceptions, the general rule on "issue preclusion" is as follows: When an issue of fact or law is actually litigated and determined by a valid and final judgment, and the determination is essential to the judgment, the determination is conclusive in a subsequent action between the parties, whether on the same or a different claim. *Restatement (Second) of Judgments* § 27 (1982). Neither side disputes that this formulation sets forth the governing law.

David Hoult . . . says—as did the district judge in his original order refusing to dismiss—that there is no proof that the jury ever determined that David Hoult had committed the alleged rapes. The burden is upon Jennifer Hoult, as the party invoking collateral estoppel, to establish that the jury did so determine in the original action.

Admittedly, the jury made no explicit finding that rapes occurred. Nevertheless, "an issue may be 'actually' decided [for collateral estoppel purposes] even if it is not explicitly decided, for it may have constituted, logically or practically, a necessary component of the decision reached." The court in the second case may examine the full record in the earlier one to decide "whether a rational jury could have grounded its verdict upon an issue other than that which the [moving party] seeks to foreclose from consideration." *Ashe v. Swenson*, 397 U.S. 436 (1970).

Whether the jury did find, or must have found, rape in the earlier trial is perhaps a question of fact. But where (as here) the question is answered by looking only at the paper record of the earlier trial, appeals courts tend to review the district court ruling de novo. The more difficult threshold issue is how clear it must be that the jury found the fact in question. The maxim of Lord Coke which is sometimes quoted by courts is that "an estoppel must be certain to every intent."

This is more demanding than the "more likely than not" standard commonly applied in civil matters, but sensibly so. Telling a party that it cannot prove or contest a fact of importance in the case at hand is a severe measure. Courts have been willing to take that step only where it is certain that the issue has already been decided in a prior case (normally one involving the same parties). . . . Confronted with a general verdict in the earlier case, courts commonly ask whether a finding was "necessary" to the judgment, and answer the question by looking primarily to the instructions and the result. But a finding is "necessary" if it was central to the route that led the factfinder to the judgment reached, even if the result "could have been achieved by a different, shorter and more efficient route." And in deciding whether the jury did make and rest centrally upon a finding not expressly made, it is proper to consider not only what was "logically" but also what was "practically" a "necessary component of the decision reached."

Here, the rape charges were the centerpiece of Jennifer Hoult's case. In the opening statement, her counsel said that Jennifer Hoult would have to live with her "memories of the rape, torture, and sexual abuse" by her father and that her father had had "intercourse" with her. Defense counsel answered that Jennifer Hoult could not have been "raped by her father some 3,000 times," as she had once claimed, and he promised evidence to show the unlikelihood that numerous rapes could have occurred without detection by other family members.

Jennifer Hoult then testified specifically to five incidents of rape and said that there were other like rapes whose details she could not recollect. On cross-examination by defense counsel, she said:

> I know based on the specific memories that I have of him attacking me and based on my perceptions, and memories of my life as a whole that he assaulted me regularly, and that rape, even the narrower definition [simple sexual intercourse] was a regular part of the way that he assaulted me.

In closing argument, defense counsel—who argued first—said at the outset:

> Specifically, Jennifer alleges that her father sexually abused her. More specifically, Jennifer claims that her father raped her, and I will call your attention now, as I did in my opening statement, that Jennifer describes rape as forcible vaginal intercourse.

In response, Jennifer Hoult's counsel said: "And this is not about hugging and kissing. She is claiming he assaulted her. He raped her. It's not inappropriate hugging and kissing."

A further consideration, stressed by the district court, is Dr. Brandt's testimony and the jury's finding on the statute of limitations. Dr. Brandt testified that repeated sexual abuse can cause repression of memory of the abuse and that Jennifer Hoult's symptoms "correlated" with such a syndrome. In finding that the statute of limitations had run, the only plausible explanation is that the jury accepted Jennifer Hoult's testimony as to the rapes, which were the salient and specific acts of repeated abuse to which she testified.

Theoretically, the jury could have concluded that Jennifer Hoult had made up or imagined the rapes, and it could then have found repressed memory and awarded the $500,000 judgment because of improper sexual fondlings and threats or acts of violence. But this is a wholly unrealistic assessment of a trial in which the rapes were the central and pivotal issue, the fondlings were the preface to the rapes, and the violence was connected to the rapes (either as part of the rapes or to encourage silence). In our view the jury necessarily decided that rapes had occurred.

The present law suit seeks, in the guise of a defamation action, to retry the central issue in the prior assault case between the same litigants. That issue—ultimately a credibility contest between the two opposing parties—was resolved by the jury at the first trial. Whether the jury was right or wrong, its decision about what happened is not now open to relitigation.

Affirmed.

# Comments and Questions

1. Note that in contrast to claim prelusion, which forecloses further litigation of all matters that *were or should have been adjudicated* in the earlier action, issue preclusion operates more narrowly, to foreclose only those issues that *were actually litigated and resolved* in the prior action.

2. *Hoult* illustrates the difficulty that may arise in applying issue preclusion where the previous judgment is (as it usually is) in the form of a general verdict. How did Judge Boudin reconstruct what the jury had actually decided (in other words, read their collective minds) in reaching the prior verdict? Note that the general verdict in *Hoult* was accompanied by a separate jury finding rejecting David Hoult's statute of limitations defense. What role did this play in Judge Boudin's analysis of the preclusion question?

3. **Alternative defenses.** The difficulty of determining what issues were necessarily resolved by a prior general verdict may be exacerbated where the defendant had raised alternative defenses. Take the earlier example of Sally suing Joe for breach of the multi-year contract to clear her land every June. In her action for breach in Year 3, assume that Joe defended on two grounds: that he was not of sufficient age to enter a valid contract, *and*, in any event, there was no breach. A general verdict for Sally would mean that the jury must have resolved *all* the issues against Joe, and thus his legal capacity defense would be foreclosed if Joe tried to raise it again in the action for breach in Year 7.

But what if the verdict in the first case had been *in favor of Joe*? Since the jury could have reached a defendant's verdict by crediting *either* of his defenses, and thus may have found for Joe solely because there was no breach in Year 3, Joe should not be able to foreclose Sally from relitigating the issue of his legal capacity if he raises it again in the Year 7 case.

4. Fed. R. Civ. P. 49 authorizes the discretionary use of special verdicts, as well as interrogatories accompanying a general verdict (a variation of which was used in *Hoult v. Hoult*). What advantages do these alternatives to the general verdict provide insofar as the operation of issue preclusion is concerned? *See* Mark S. Brodin, *Accuracy, Efficiency, and Accountability in the Litigation Process—The Case for the Fact Verdict*, 59 U. Cin. L. Rev. 15 (1990).

5. Was David Hoult denied due process of law (his "day in court") by operation of issue preclusion?

6. **Epilogue to Hoult litigation**. Winning a verdict of $500,000 and *collecting it* are two very different things. Shortly after the verdict, Jennifer sought and obtained a preliminary injunction to prevent her father, a former researcher at the Massachusetts Institute of Technology, from transferring his assets to protect them from the judgment in violation of the fraudulent conveyance statute. After years of further proceedings in both district court and bankruptcy court, the First Circuit Court of Appeals in 2004 affirmed orders below requiring David to deposit his income and pension benefits into a designated bank account to be used, minus modest living expenses, to pay toward the judgment. 373 F.3d 47 (1st Cir. 2004).

At last report, Jennifer Hoult was working as a Law Guardian in Kings County, NY.

7. *Hoult* lists the requirements for issue preclusion as follows:

- When an *issue of fact or law is actually litigated and determined,*
- by a *valid final judgment,*
- and the determination is *essential to the judgment,*
- then the determination is *conclusive on the identical issue in a subsequent action between the parties.*

Issue preclusion operates only where Case 1 and Case 2 share a common issue—the sexual assault in both *Jennifer v. David Hoult* and *David v. Jennifer Hoult*; the attorney-client relationship in both litigations in *Jarosz v. Palmer*, our next case; the misrepresentations in the proxy statement in the two litigations in *Parklane Hosiery*, the case that follows that. The diagram that follows may help you envision such situations, where Case 2 represents a different claim than Case 1 (and thus is not precluded by *res judicata*), but they share a common Issue D.

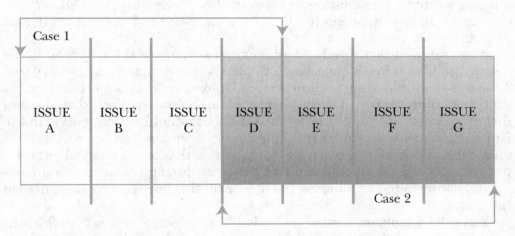

## 2. *"Essential to the Judgment"*

### ■ JAROSZ v. PALMER
*436 Mass. 526 (2002)*

Cowin, J.:

The plaintiff, James Jarosz, appeals from an order of the Superior Court dismissing his claims against the defendants on the basis of issue preclusion. The plaintiff's claims against attorney Stephen L. Palmer and his law firm Warner & Stackpole LLP (Palmer) are premised on the contention that

Palmer represented Jarosz individually in his acquisition of a corporation. A Superior Court judge granted the defendants' motion for judgment on the pleadings after concluding that Jarosz was precluded from arguing that Palmer had represented him individually because, in a separate case brought by Jarosz against his former business partners, another judge of the Superior Court had concluded that Palmer and Jarosz did not have an attorney-client relationship. . . . We reverse the Superior Court's order and remand the case for further proceedings.

1. *Factual background and procedural history.* We summarize the relevant facts from the Superior Court's order on the defendants' motion for judgment on the pleadings. Jarosz and three business partners together agreed to acquire a company known as Union Products. Jarosz hired Palmer, an attorney, to assist in the acquisition and financing of the business. Jarosz and his partners successfully acquired the business and each became twenty-five per cent owners. The relationship between Jarosz and his partners eventually soured, and the partners terminated Jarosz from his position as employee and officer of Union Products. As a result, Jarosz filed suit against both the partners and the Union Products corporation, alleging wrongful termination and breach of fiduciary duty (the *Union Products* case). Palmer represented the three partners and the corporation in this suit.

Jarosz moved to disqualify Palmer from serving as the partners' attorney in the Union Products case on the basis that Palmer had represented Jarosz individually in his acquisition of Union Products, and therefore his continued representation of the partners and the corporation created a conflict of interest. The judge's order on Jarosz's disqualification motion in the Union Products case stated that, for Jarosz to succeed on his motion, "he must meet the threshold burden of establishing that an attorney-client relationship existed between himself and Palmer during the acquisition dealings." Having found that Jarosz failed to meet this burden, the judge denied the motion.

After the commencement of the *Union Products* case, Jarosz filed this suit against Palmer, alleging breach of contract, breach of fiduciary duty, legal malpractice, and violations of G.L. c. 93A. Palmer defended the suit on the ground, inter alia, that he had not represented Jarosz individually. Palmer filed a motion for judgment on the pleadings, claiming that the judge's ruling on Jarosz's motion for disqualification in the Union Products case precluded Jarosz from relitigating the issue whether Palmer had represented Jarosz individually. The judge in the instant case allowed the motion, finding that the three requirements for issue preclusion were met: the issue had been actually litigated, was the subject of a valid and final judgment, and was essential to the judge's decision. Jarosz filed a timely notice of appeal, claiming that the issue had not been actually litigated, was not the subject of a final judgment, and was not essential to the decision. . . .

We conclude that issue preclusion's requirement that the issue decided be "essential to the judgment" requires that the issue be essential to the merits of the underlying case. Because this requirement was not met in this case, we reverse the Superior Court's judgment on this basis. . . .

3. *Issue preclusion.* The doctrine of issue preclusion provides that when an issue has been "actually litigated and determined by a valid and final judgment, and the determination is essential to the judgment, the determination is conclusive in a subsequent action between the parties whether on the same or different claim." Jarosz . . . challenges the . . . conclusion that the issue was both actually litigated and essential to the decision.

a. *Actually litigated.* The Appeals Court concluded correctly that the issue of Jarosz's attorney-client relationship with Palmer was actually litigated in the *Union Products* case. Jarosz claims that the issue was not actually litigated because the judge issued his decision without an evidentiary hearing or full trial, and he did not have the opportunity to conduct discovery or cross-examine witnesses. While it is true that "preclusive effect should not be given to issues or claims that were not actually litigated in [the] prior action," an evidentiary hearing or trial is not required before issue preclusion can apply. The appropriate question is whether the issue was " 'subject to an adversary presentation and consequent judgment' that was not 'a product of the parties' consent. . . .' "

The issue of Jarosz's attorney-client relationship was briefed by the parties and, after a hearing, the judge determined the issue. Jarosz presented an affidavit detailing his contacts with Palmer. The judge considered the facts alleged by Jarosz and determined that, even if taken as true, they did not provide sufficient evidence of an individual attorney-client relationship. During oral argument before this court, Jarosz conceded that he did not request discovery or an evidentiary hearing; he chose to litigate the motion to disqualify on the basis of affidavits. The application of issue preclusion is not conditioned on the opportunity for discovery and an evidentiary hearing. The type of adversary proceeding afforded the parties in this case is sufficient to constitute actual litigation.

The determination of an issue in a prior proceeding has no preclusive effect where "[t]he party against whom preclusion is sought had a significantly heavier burden of persuasion with respect to the issue in the initial action than in the subsequent action; the burden has shifted to his adversary; or the adversary has a significantly heavier burden than he had in the first action." Jarosz argues that because public policy considerations favor the rights of clients to choose their attorneys, the standard for disqualifying an opposing attorney in the initial action was very high, whereas, in the present case, he only needed to prove the attorney-client relationship by a preponderance of the evidence. However, the existence of the attorney-client relationship was the threshold determination in both instances, and the plaintiff's burden of proof was a preponderance of the evidence in both proceedings.

b. *Essential to the judgment.* The issue of Jarosz's attorney-client relationship with Palmer was clearly not essential to a determination of his breach of fiduciary duty and wrongful termination claims against the Union Products defendants; Jarosz could have prevailed on those claims regardless of the outcome of his motion to disqualify. However, the issue was obviously essential to the judge's decision to deny that motion. We therefore must determine whether the requirement that the issue be "essential to the judgment" necessitates that the issue be essential to the underlying case, or whether it is sufficient that the issue is essential to the decision at hand.

We conclude that, in this context, the term "judgment" refers to a final determination on the merits of the proceeding. For a ruling to have preclusive effect, it must have a bearing on the outcome of the case. "If issues are determined but the judgment is not dependent upon the determinations, relitigation of those issues in a subsequent action between the parties is not precluded." . . . The use of the term "case" indicates that the finding must be regarded by the court and the party as essential to a determination on the merits, and not merely essential to a determination of the narrow issue before the court at that time.

The nature of Jarosz's attorney-client relationship with Palmer was clearly not essential to a determination on the merits of his underlying claim. Therefore, the issue was not essential to the judgment, and issue preclusion cannot apply.

## Comments and Questions

1. The requirement that resolution of the issue must have been *essential to the prior judgment* in order to be preclusive in a subsequent litigation is analogous to the rule that *dicta* is not binding precedent. The rationale is that only those matters central to the outcome will likely be given sufficient attention by the litigants and the court to justify according them finality. *See* Fleming James, Jr., Geoffrey C. Hazard, Jr., and John Leubsdorf, *Civil Procedure* § 11.20 (5th ed. 2001).

2. **Burdens of Proof**. Note the significance of the comparative burdens of proof between the prior proceeding and one in which preclusion is sought. The Supreme Judicial Court espouses the general rule (dictated by concerns for fairness) that prior litigation cannot have preclusive effect where the party against whom preclusion is now sought had a significantly heavier burden of persuasion with respect to the particular issue in the prior action, or his adversary has a significantly heavier burden now than in the first action. *See Restatement (Second) of Judgments* § 28(4). Thus a defendant in a criminal prosecution for arson—where proof must be beyond a reasonable doubt—cannot be precluded from litigating his guilt by a prior judgment against him in a civil action—where plaintiff prevailed upon a mere preponderance of the evidence that he was liable for destruction of the building.

What happens in the reverse sequence, where the criminal prosecution precedes the civil trial? Had O.J. Simpson been convicted of murdering Nicole Brown Simpson and Ronald Goldman in the so-called Trial of the Century, instead of being acquitted, as he actually was, that conviction on proof beyond a reasonable doubt would have precluded him from relitigating the issue in the subsequent wrongful death civil action, where the victims' families needed to prove their case by a mere preponderance. *See, e.g., Kowalski v. Gagne*, 914 F.2d 299 (1st Cir. 1990) (defendant's second-degree murder conviction collaterally estopped him from contesting liability under Massachusetts wrongful death statute based on having caused the death of decedent by a willful, wanton, or reckless act; the issue in the murder prosecution as to whether defendant had intentionally inflicted force on decedent in a manner that created strong likelihood of death was identical, for collateral estoppel purposes, with the issue in the wrongful death context).

Note that Simpson could not use his actual acquittal against the civil plaintiffs, because they were neither parties nor in privity with the prosecution in the criminal case, and thus had not had their "day in court."

O.J. Simpson was ultimately found liable in the wrongful death action. *Rufo v. Simpson*, 103 Cal. Rptr. 2d 492 (Ct. App. 2001). But that determination could not be used to preclude him from relitigating the issue of the murders a third time in a subsequent case to determine custody of his children. The standard of proof in the custody proceeding required "clear and convincing" evidence to terminate his parental rights, a higher burden than the mere preponderance of the evidence required in the wrongful death action. *See Guardianship of Simpson*, 79 Cal. Rptr. 2d 389 (1999).

3. Settlement of a lawsuit generally carries no issue preclusive effect because no issue has been actually litigated and determined. *See Arizona v. California*, 530 U.S. 392, 414 (2000).

---

### 3. Nonmutual Issue Preclusion

We know that (with the few narrow exceptions discussed in *Taylor v. Sturgell*) preclusion cannot operate *against* a litigant who was not a party in the prior case, as each party is entitled to his day in court. The next decision deals with the question of whether a nonparty can *invoke* preclusion against a litigant from the earlier case, a matter referred to as nonmutual estoppel.

### ■ PARKLANE HOSIERY CO., INC. v. SHORE
#### *439 U.S. 322 (1979)*

Justice STEWART delivered the opinion of the Court:
This case presents the question whether a party who has had issues of fact adjudicated adversely to it in an equitable action may be collaterally estopped from relitigating the same issues before a jury in a subsequent legal action brought against it by a new party.

The respondent brought this stockholder's class action against the petitioners in a Federal District Court. The complaint alleged that the petitioners, Parklane Hosiery Co., Inc. (Parklane), and 13 of its officers, directors, and stockholders, had issued a materially false and misleading proxy statement in connection with a merger. The proxy statement, according to the complaint, had violated §§ 14(a), 10(b), and 20(a) of the Securities Exchange Act of 1934, as well as various rules and regulations promulgated by the Securities and Exchange Commission (SEC). The complaint sought damages, rescission of the merger, and recovery of costs.

Before this action came to trial, the SEC filed suit against the same defendants in the Federal District Court, alleging that the proxy statement that had been issued by Parklane was materially false and misleading in essentially the same respects as those that had been alleged in the respondent's complaint. Injunctive relief was requested. After a 4-day trial, the District Court found that the proxy statement was materially false and misleading in the respects alleged, and entered a declaratory judgment to that effect. The Court of Appeals for the Second Circuit affirmed this judgment. The respondent in the present case then moved for partial summary judgment against the petitioners, asserting that the petitioners were collaterally estopped from relitigating the issues that had been resolved against them in the action brought by the SEC.[2] The District Court denied the motion on the ground that such an application of collateral estoppel would deny the petitioners their Seventh Amendment right to a jury trial. The Court of Appeals for the Second Circuit reversed, holding that a party who has had issues of fact determined against him after a full and fair opportunity to litigate in a nonjury trial is collaterally estopped from obtaining a subsequent jury trial of these same issues of fact. The appellate court concluded that "the Seventh Amendment preserves the right to jury trial only with respect to issues of fact, [and] once those issues have been fully and fairly adjudicated in a prior proceeding, nothing remains for trial, either with or without a jury." Because of an intercircuit conflict, we granted certiorari.

## I

The threshold question to be considered is whether, quite apart from the right to a jury trial under the Seventh Amendment, the petitioners can be precluded from relitigating facts resolved adversely to them in a prior equitable proceeding with another party under the general law of collateral estoppel. Specifically, we must determine whether a litigant who was not a party to

---

2. A private plaintiff in an action under the proxy rules is not entitled to relief simply by demonstrating that the proxy solicitation was materially false and misleading. The plaintiff must also show that he was injured and prove damages. Since the SEC action was limited to a determination of whether the proxy statement contained materially false and misleading information, the respondent conceded that he would still have to prove these other elements of his prima facie case in the private action. The petitioners' right to a jury trial on those remaining issues is not contested.

a prior judgment may nevertheless use that judgment "offensively" to prevent a defendant from relitigating issues resolved in the earlier proceeding.[4]

## A

Collateral estoppel, like the related doctrine of *res judicata*,[5] has the dual purpose of protecting litigants from the burden of relitigating an identical issue with the same party or his privy and of promoting judicial economy by preventing needless litigation. *Blonder-Tongue Laboratories, Inc. v. University of Illinois Foundation*, 402 U.S. 313, 328-329. Until relatively recently, however, the scope of collateral estoppel was limited by the doctrine of mutuality of parties. Under this mutuality doctrine, neither party could use a prior judgment as an estoppel against the other unless both parties were bound by the judgment. Based on the premise that it is somehow unfair to allow a party to use a prior judgment when he himself would not be so bound,[7] the mutuality requirement provided a party who had litigated and lost in a previous action an opportunity to relitigate identical issues with new parties.

By failing to recognize the obvious difference in position between a party who has never litigated an issue and one who has fully litigated and lost, the mutuality requirement was criticized almost from its inception. Recognizing the validity of this criticism, the Court in *Blonder-Tongue Laboratories, Inc. v. University of Illinois Foundation, supra*, abandoned the mutuality requirement, at least in cases where a patentee seeks to relitigate the validity of a patent after a federal court in a previous lawsuit has already declared it invalid. The "broader question" before the Court, however, was "whether it is any longer tenable to afford a litigant more than one full and fair opportunity for judicial resolution of the same issue." The Court strongly suggested a negative answer to that question:

> In any lawsuit where a defendant, because of the mutuality principle, is forced to present a complete defense on the merits to a claim which the plaintiff has fully litigated and lost in a prior action, there is an arguable misallocation of resources. To the extent the defendant in the second suit may not win by asserting, without contradiction, that the plaintiff had fully and fairly, but unsuccessfully, litigated the same claim in the prior suit, the defendant's time and money are diverted from alternative uses—productive or otherwise—to relitigation of a decided issue. And, still assuming that the issue was resolved correctly in the first suit, there is reason to be concerned about the plaintiff's allocation of resources.

4. In this context, offensive use of collateral estoppel occurs when the plaintiff seeks to foreclose the defendant from litigating an issue the defendant has previously litigated unsuccessfully in an action with another party. Defensive use occurs when a defendant seeks to prevent a plaintiff from asserting a claim the plaintiff has previously litigated and lost against another defendant.

5. Under the doctrine of *res judicata*, a judgment on the merits in a prior suit bars a second suit involving the same parties or their privies based on the same cause of action. Under the doctrine of collateral estoppel, on the other hand, the second action is upon a different cause of action and the judgment in the prior suit precludes relitigation of issues actually litigated and necessary to the outcome of the first action.

7. It is a violation of due process for a judgment to be binding on a litigant who was not a party or a privy and therefore has never had an opportunity to be heard. *Blonder-Tongue Laboratories, Inc. v. University of Illinois Foundation*, 402 U.S. 313, 329; *Hansberry v. Lee*, 311 U.S. 32, 40.

Permitting repeated litigation of the same issue as long as the supply of unrelated defendants holds out reflects either the aura of the gaming table or "a lack of discipline and of disinterestedness on the part of the lower courts, hardly a worthy or wise basis for fashioning rules of procedure." Although neither judges, the parties, nor the adversary system performs perfectly in all cases, the requirement of determining whether the party against whom an estoppel is asserted had a full and fair opportunity to litigate is a most significant safeguard.

*Id.*, at 329 n.10.

**B**

The *Blonder-Tongue* case involved defensive use of collateral estoppel—a plaintiff was estopped from asserting a claim that the plaintiff had previously litigated and lost against another defendant. The present case, by contrast, involves offensive use of collateral estoppel—a plaintiff is seeking to estop a defendant from relitigating the issues which the defendant previously litigated and lost against another plaintiff. In both the offensive and defensive use situations, the party against whom estoppel is asserted has litigated and lost in an earlier action. Nevertheless, several reasons have been advanced why the two situations should be treated differently.

First, offensive use of collateral estoppel does not promote judicial economy in the same manner as defensive use does. Defensive use of collateral estoppel precludes a plaintiff from relitigating identical issues by merely "switching adversaries." Thus defensive collateral estoppel gives a plaintiff a strong incentive to join all potential defendants in the first action if possible. Offensive use of collateral estoppel, on the other hand, creates precisely the opposite incentive. Since a plaintiff will be able to rely on a previous judgment against a defendant but will not be bound by that judgment if the defendant wins, the plaintiff has every incentive to adopt a "wait and see" attitude, in the hope that the first action by another plaintiff will result in a favorable judgment. Thus offensive use of collateral estoppel will likely increase rather than decrease the total amount of litigation, since potential plaintiffs will have everything to gain and nothing to lose by not intervening in the first action.

A second argument against offensive use of collateral estoppel is that it may be unfair to a defendant. If a defendant in the first action is sued for small or nominal damages, he may have little incentive to defend vigorously, particularly if future suits are not foreseeable. Allowing offensive collateral estoppel may also be unfair to a defendant if the judgment relied upon as a basis for the estoppel is itself inconsistent with one or more previous judgments in favor of the defendant.[14] Still another situation where it might be

---

14. In Professor Currie's familiar example, a railroad collision injures 50 passengers all of whom bring separate actions against the railroad. After the railroad wins the first 25 suits, a plaintiff wins in suit 26. Professor Currie argues that offensive use of collateral estoppel should not be applied so as to allow plaintiffs 27 through 50 automatically to recover. Currie, *Mutuality of Estoppel: Limits of the Bernhard Doctrine*, 9 Stan. L. Rev. 281, 304 (1957).

unfair to apply offensive estoppel is where the second action affords the defendant procedural opportunities unavailable in the first action that could readily cause a different result.[15]

### C

We have concluded that the preferable approach for dealing with these problems in the federal courts is not to preclude the use of offensive collateral estoppel, but to grant trial courts broad discretion to determine when it should be applied. The general rule should be that in cases where a plaintiff could easily have joined in the earlier action or where, either for the reasons discussed above or for other reasons, the application of offensive estoppel would be unfair to a defendant, a trial judge should not allow the use of offensive collateral estoppel.

In the present case, however, none of the circumstances that might justify reluctance to allow the offensive use of collateral estoppel is present. The application of offensive collateral estoppel will not here reward a private plaintiff who could have joined in the previous action, since the respondent probably could not have joined in the injunctive action brought by the SEC even had he so desired. Similarly, there is no unfairness to the petitioners in applying offensive collateral estoppel in this case. First, in light of the serious allegations made in the SEC's complaint against the petitioners, as well as the foreseeability of subsequent private suits that typically follow a successful Government judgment, the petitioners had every incentive to litigate the SEC lawsuit fully and vigorously.[18] Second, the judgment in the SEC action was not inconsistent with any previous decision. Finally, there will in the respondent's action be no procedural opportunities available to the petitioners that were unavailable in the first action of a kind that might be likely to cause a different result.[19]

We conclude, therefore, that none of the considerations that would justify a refusal to allow the use of offensive collateral estoppel is present in this case. Since the petitioners received a "full and fair" opportunity to litigate their claims in the SEC action, the contemporary law of collateral estoppel leads inescapably to the conclusion that the petitioners are collaterally estopped

15. If, for example, the defendant in the first action was forced to defend in an inconvenient forum and therefore was unable to engage in full scale discovery or call witnesses, application of offensive collateral estoppel may be unwarranted. Indeed, differences in available procedures may sometimes justify not allowing a prior judgment to have estoppel effect in a subsequent action even between the same parties, or where defensive estoppel is asserted against a plaintiff who has litigated and lost. The problem of unfairness is particularly acute in cases of offensive estoppel, however, because the defendant against whom estoppel is asserted typically will not have chosen the forum in the first action.

18. After a 4-day trial in which the petitioners had every opportunity to present evidence and call witnesses, the District Court held for the SEC. The petitioners then appealed to the Court of Appeals for the Second Circuit, which affirmed the judgment against them. Moreover, the petitioners were already aware of the action brought by the respondent, since it had commenced before the filing of the SEC action.

19. It is true, of course, that the petitioners in the present action would be entitled to a jury trial of the issues bearing on whether the proxy statement was materially false and misleading had the SEC action never been brought—a matter to be discussed in Part II of this opinion. But the presence or absence of a jury as factfinder is basically neutral, quite unlike, for example, the necessity of defending the first lawsuit in an inconvenient forum.

from relitigating the question of whether the proxy statement was materially false and misleading.

## II

The question that remains is whether, notwithstanding the law of collateral estoppel, the use of offensive collateral estoppel in this case would violate the petitioners' Seventh Amendment right to a jury trial.[20]

. . .

The petitioners argue that application of collateral estoppel in this case would violate their Seventh Amendment right to a jury trial. The petitioners contend that since the scope of the Amendment must be determined by reference to the common law as it existed in 1791, and since the common law permitted collateral estoppel only where there was mutuality of parties, collateral estoppel cannot constitutionally be applied when such mutuality is absent.

The petitioners have advanced no persuasive reason, however, why the meaning of the Seventh Amendment should depend on whether or not mutuality of parties is present. . . . The party against whom estoppel is asserted has litigated questions of fact, and has had the facts determined against him in an earlier proceeding. [T]here is no further fact-finding function for the jury to perform, since the common factual issues have been resolved in the previous action.

The Seventh Amendment has never been interpreted in the rigid manner advocated by the petitioners. On the contrary, many procedural devices developed since 1791 that have diminished the civil jury's historic domain have been found not to be inconsistent with the Seventh Amendment. *See Galloway v. United States*, 319 U.S. 372, 388-393 (directed verdict does not violate the Seventh Amendment); *Gasoline Products Co. v. Champlin Refining Co.*, 283 U.S. 494, 497-498 (retrial limited to question of damages does not violate the Seventh Amendment even though there was no practice at common law for setting aside a verdict in part); *Fidelity & Deposit Co. v. United States*, 187 U.S. 315, 319-321 (summary judgment does not violate the Seventh Amendment).

The *Galloway* case is particularly instructive. There the party against whom a directed verdict had been entered argued that the procedure was unconstitutional under the Seventh Amendment. In rejecting this claim, the Court said:

The Amendment did not bind the federal courts to the exact procedural incidents or details of jury trial according to the common law in 1791, any more than it tied them to the common-law system of pleading or the specific rules of evidence then prevailing. Nor were "the rules of the common law" then

---

20. The Seventh Amendment provides: "In Suits at common law, where the value in controversy shall exceed twenty dollars, the right to jury trial shall be preserved. . . ."

prevalent, including those relating to the procedure by which the judge regulated the jury's role on questions of fact, crystallized in a fixed and immutable system. . . .

The more logical conclusion, we think, and the one which both history and the previous decisions here support, is that the Amendment was designed to preserve the basic institution of jury trial in only its most fundamental elements, not the great mass of procedural forms and details, varying even then so widely among common-law jurisdictions.

319 U.S., at 390, 392 (footnote omitted).

The law of collateral estoppel, like the law in other procedural areas defining the scope of the jury's function, has evolved since 1791. Under the rationale of the *Galloway* case, these developments are not repugnant to the Seventh Amendment simply for the reason that they did not exist in 1791. Thus if, as we have held, the law of collateral estoppel forecloses the petitioners from relitigating the factual issues determined against them in the SEC action, nothing in the Seventh Amendment dictates a different result, even though because of lack of mutuality there would have been no collateral estoppel in 1791.

The judgment of the Court of Appeals is Affirmed.

Justice REHNQUIST, dissenting:

It is admittedly difficult to be outraged about the treatment accorded by the federal judiciary to petitioners' demand for a jury trial in this lawsuit. Outrage is an emotion all but impossible to generate with respect to a corporate defendant in a securities fraud action, and this case is no exception. But the nagging sense of unfairness as to the way petitioners have been treated, engendered by the imprimatur placed by the Court of Appeals on respondent's "heads I win, tails you lose" theory of this litigation, is not dispelled by this Court's antiseptic analysis of the issues in the case. It may be that if this Nation were to adopt a new Constitution today, the Seventh Amendment guaranteeing the right of jury trial in civil cases in federal courts would not be included among its provisions. But any present sentiment to that effect cannot obscure or dilute our obligation to enforce the Seventh Amendment, which was included in the Bill of Rights in 1791 and which has not since been repealed in the only manner provided by the Constitution for repeal of its provisions.

The right of trial by jury in civil cases at common law is fundamental to our history and jurisprudence. Today, however, the Court reduces this valued right, which Blackstone praised as "the glory of the English law," to a mere "neutral" factor and in the name of procedural reform denies the right of jury trial to defendants in a vast number of cases in which defendants, heretofore, have enjoyed jury trials. Over 35 years ago, Mr. Justice Black lamented the "gradual process of judicial erosion which in one-hundred-fifty years has slowly worn away a major portion of the essential guarantee of the Seventh Amendment." *Galloway v. United States*, 319 U.S. 372, 397 (1943) (dissenting opinion). Regrettably, the erosive process continues apace with today's decision.[1]

. . .

The founders of our Nation considered the right of trial by jury in civil cases an important bulwark against tyranny and corruption, a safeguard too precious to be left to the whim of the sovereign, or, it might be added, to that of the judiciary. Those who passionately advocated the right to a civil jury trial did not do so because they considered the jury a familiar procedural device that should be continued; the concerns for the institution of jury trial that led to the passages of the Declaration of Independence and to the Seventh Amendment were not animated by a belief that use of juries would lead to more efficient judicial administration. Trial by a jury of laymen rather than by the sovereign's judges was important to the founders because juries represent the layman's common sense, the "passional elements in our nature," and thus keep the administration of law in accord with the wishes and feelings of the community. O. Holmes, *Collected Legal Papers* 237 (1920). Those who favored juries believed that a jury would reach a result that a judge either could not or would not reach. It is with these values that underlie the Seventh Amendment in mind that the Court should, but obviously does not, approach the decision of this case. . . .

Judged by the foregoing principles, I think it is clear that petitioners were denied their Seventh Amendment right to a jury trial in this case. . . .

In my view, it is "unfair" to apply offensive collateral estoppel where the party who is sought to be estopped has not had an opportunity to have the facts of his case determined by a jury. Since in this case petitioners were not entitled to a jury trial in the Securities and Exchange Commission (SEC) lawsuit, I would not estop them from relitigating the issues determined in the SEC suit before a jury in the private action. . . .

The Court accepts the proposition that it is unfair to apply offensive collateral estoppel "where the second action affords the defendant procedural opportunities unavailable in the first action that could readily cause a different result." Differences in discovery opportunities between the two actions are cited as examples of situations where it would be unfair to permit offensive collateral estoppel. But in the Court's view, the fact that petitioners would have been entitled to a jury trial in the present action is not such a "procedural [opportunity]" because "the presence or absence of a jury as factfinder is basically neutral, quite unlike, for example, the necessity of defending the first lawsuit in an inconvenient forum."

. . .

[T]hose who drafted the Declaration of Independence and debated so passionately the proposed Constitution during the ratification period, would indeed be astounded to learn that the presence or absence of a jury is merely

---

1. Because I believe that the use of offensive collateral estoppel in this particular case was improper, it is not necessary for me to decide whether I would approve its use in circumstances where the defendant's right to a jury trial was not impaired.

"neutral," whereas the availability of discovery, a device unmentioned in the Constitution, may be controlling. It is precisely because the Framers believed that they might receive a different result at the hands of a jury of their peers than at the mercy of the sovereign's judges, that the Seventh Amendment was adopted. And I suspect that anyone who litigates cases before juries in the 1970's would be equally amazed to hear of the supposed lack of distinction between trial by court and trial by jury. The Court can cite no authority in support of this curious proposition. The merits of civil juries have been long debated, but I suspect that juries have never been accused of being merely "neutral" factors.

. . .

## Comments and Questions

1. The common law mutuality doctrine, effectively abrogated in federal litigation by *Parklane* (the states are free to continue to insist on mutuality), had limited the parties who could *use* issue preclusion against an adversary to those who were parties in the original case. The idea was that in fairness, only a party who had had "skin in the game" in the prior case should be allowed to benefit from the decision there.

In contrast, the constitutional due process (day-in-court) safeguard prevents estoppel from being *used against* a party who has not had a full and fair opportunity to litigate the matter in the previous case.

2. The demise of the mutuality requirement opened a whole new set of issues that the Court grapples with in *Parklane*, particularly regarding the offensive use of collateral estoppel, which, in contrast to defensive collateral estoppel, may actually encourage multiple litigation.

Take the following scenario. Alan collides with two vehicles on the highway, one driven by Bob and the other by Charlie. Each of the three drivers denies the accident was his fault. When contemplating an action to recover for his damages, Alan must consider that suing Bob or Charlie *separately* would run the risk that if he loses to one at trial, the other could use defensive collateral estoppel against Alan. If, for example, Bob successfully defends *Alan v. Bob* by asserting that Alan was the driver at fault, a jury verdict for Bob could foreclose Alan from relitigating the issue in *Alan v. Charlie*. Note that a verdict *in favor* of Alan could not be used by him in a subsequent suit against Charlie, who has not had his day in court. The incentive for Alan is therefore *to join* Bob and Charlie as co-defendants (Fed. R. Civ. P. 20), and take his best shot at each in a single trial, a result fully consistent with the interest in efficiency and avoiding the multiplicity of suits.

Now consider the very opposite incentive set up by offensive collateral estoppel. Suppose now that Alan was a passenger in Bob's car, which collided with Charlie. Bob sues Charlie for negligence. In contemplating whether to join as a co-plaintiff or intervenor, Alan knows that a decision *against* Bob on the issue of fault could not be used against him by Charlie if

Alan brings his own separate action, as he has not had his day in court. Alan also knows, on the other hand, that he may be able to piggyback on the verdict if it goes *against* Charlie, by using offensive collateral estoppel to prevent Charlie from relitigating the fault issue common to both actions. Alan has, in short, "everything to gain and nothing to lose" by staying out of the first action. Multiple lawsuits from the same incident may thus be encouraged by the unrestricted use of offensive collateral estoppel.

3. The discretionary constraints articulated by *Parklane* are designed to avoid such unfair exploitation of nonmutual offensive collateral estoppel. Thus a court should hesitate to allow its use if:

- the plaintiff could easily have joined in the earlier case, and appears to have played the strategic waiting game; or
- the stakes in the earlier case were considerably smaller, so there was less incentive to litigate the issue then than now; or
- the judgment relied upon is inconsistent with others in which the defendant has prevailed; or
- the second action affords important procedural opportunities that were unavailable to the defendant in the first action.

4. How would Professor Currie's "familiar example" in the Court's footnote 14 be resolved under the *Parklane* analysis?

5. Note that the prior decision which was the source of preclusion in *Parklane* resulted from a bench trial before a judge, and therefore (unlike the jury's general verdict in *Hoult*) conveniently contained specific findings of fact and conclusions of law. *See* Fed. R. Civ. P. 52(a).

6. Issue preclusion may operate when an administrative agency resolves issues in its judicial capacity and the losing party seeks to relitigate those issues in a federal court. *See University of Tennessee v. Elliott*, 478 U.S. 788 (1986) (but unreviewed state administrative proceedings do not have preclusive effect in a Title VII action, because of the structure of that statute requiring resort to the EEOC). It also operates in the reverse, as where an attorney was precluded from relitigating in state disbarment proceedings the issue of whether he had intentionally overbilled a client, which had been resolved against him by summary judgment in the client's federal court action. *See In re Goldstone*, 445 Mass. 551 (2005). The Supreme Judicial Court of Massachusetts observed:

The application of offensive issue preclusion was fair in this case. First, the board was not involved in the initial civil litigation because it had neither a reason, nor an opportunity, to join the proceedings. Second, Goldstone had every incentive to defend the first action vigorously because he was confronting severe financial consequences if [his client's] allegations were found to be true. [His client] had alleged fraud, breach of contract, breach of fiduciary duty, and violation of G.L. c. 93A, seeking not only repayment of all fees that had been paid on the closed cases (more than $833,000), but also multiple damages under G.L. c. 93A. In addition, Goldstone had counterclaimed for the unpaid balance of his bills. As such, the amount in dispute in that action was in excess of $2 million, and Goldstone had an obvious incentive to defend that action vigorously. Third, the judgment relied on by bar counsel is not inconsistent with any previous judgments in favor of Goldstone—the civil case is the only relevant judgment here. Finally, contrary to Goldstone's contention, the bar discipline hearing would not afford him additional procedural opportunities unavailable in the first action that could "readily cause a different result."

445 Mass. at 559-560.

The Court added:

Goldstone argues that, had an affidavit [he unsuccessfully offered into evidence] been admitted in the Federal action, the court could not have [granted summary judgment against him] and offensive issue preclusion would not have been available in the bar discipline hearing. However, issue preclusion is premised on a party's prior opportunity to litigate an issue, not on whether the party made the best use of that opportunity. With hindsight, every litigant who loses a case can point to some additional step that he or she could have taken, and can contend that that step would have made a difference in the outcome. Merely pointing to such steps (here, the step of properly identifying Casson during discovery and submitting his affidavit in opposition to the summary judgment motion) does not operate to avoid issue preclusion. Goldstone had the "opportunity" to submit the Casson affidavit in the prior proceedings, as long as he abided by the procedural requirements for submitting it (i.e., by making proper disclosure in discovery). His own failure to comply with the rules applicable to the Federal proceedings does not mean that he was deprived of a fair opportunity to litigate.

445 Mass. at 560.

7. Given Justice Rehnquist's eloquent invocation of the Seventh Amendment in his *Parklane* dissent, has the Court not elevated the doctrine of finality above the cherished constitutional right to trial by jury? What could possibly justify this result?

8. The tug-of-war between finality and fairness also plays itself out with regard to postconviction relief in criminal cases. Dating back to the Magna Carta, the writ of habeas corpus has permitted collateral review of final convictions. *See generally* Wayne Lafave, Jerold Israel, and Nancy King, *Criminal Procedure* § 28.1 et seq. (5th ed. 2009). Proponents of expansive habeas review have argued that "[c]onventional notions of finality of litigation have no place where life or liberty is at stake and infringement of constitutional rights is alleged." *Sanders v. United States*, 373 U.S. 1, 8 (1963) (Brennan, J.).

But in sharp contrast to his dissent in *Parklane*, Justice Rehnquist came down firmly on the side of finality in habeas matters. *See Herrera v. Collins*, 506 U.S. 390 (1993) (holding that a claim of actual innocence based on newly discovered evidence is not a valid ground for federal habeas relief absent a showing of a constitutional violation during the proceedings).

The tension between finality ("getting it *done*") and fairness ("getting it *right*"), or efficiency vs. equity, is the subject of Part D, The Counterweights to Finality, later in this chapter, and arises perhaps most dramatically in the adjudication of mass torts, as is illustrated by our next case.

### 4. *Issue Preclusion in Mass Tort Litigation*

## ■ C. A. HARDY, et al., Plaintiffs-Appellees, v. JOHNS-MANVILLE SALES CORPORATION, et al., Defendants-Appellants
*681 F.2d 334 (5th Cir. 1982)*

GEE, Circuit Judge:

This appeal arises out of a diversity action brought by various plaintiffs—insulators, pipefitters, carpenters, and other factory workers—against various manufacturers, sellers, and distributors of asbestos-containing products. The plaintiffs, alleging exposure to the products and consequent disease, assert various causes of action, including negligence, breach of implied warranty, and strict liability. The pleadings in each of the cases are substantially the same. No plaintiff names a particular defendant on a case-by-case basis but, instead, includes several—often as many as twenty asbestos manufacturers—in his individual complaint. The rationale offered for this unusual pleading practice is that, given the long latent period of the diseases in question, it is impossible for plaintiffs to isolate the precise exposure period or to identify the particular manufacturer's product responsible. The trial court accepted this rationale and opted for a theory of enterprise- or industry-wide liability (market share apportionment determines a manufacturer's liability unless a given manufacturer exculpates itself by proving that its product could not have caused the injury).

. . .

Defendants' interlocutory appeal is directed at the district court's order which applies collateral estoppel to this mass tort. The order is, in effect, a partial summary judgment for plaintiffs based on nonmutual offensive collateral estoppel derived from this court's opinion in *Borel v. Fibreboard Paper Products Corp.*, 493 F.2d 1076 (5th Cir. 1973) (henceforth *Borel*). *Borel* was a diversity lawsuit in which manufacturers of insulation products containing asbestos were held strictly liable to an insulation worker who developed asbestosis and mesothelioma and ultimately died. The trial court construed *Borel* as establishing as a matter of law and/or of fact that: (1) insulation products containing asbestos as a generic ingredient are "unavoidably unsafe products," (2) asbestos is a competent producing cause of mesothelioma and asbestosis, (3) no warnings were issued by any asbestos insulation manufacturers prior to 1964, and (4) the "warning standard" was not met by the *Borel* defendants in the period from 1964 through 1969. . . . The sole issue on appeal is the validity of the order on grounds of collateral estoppel.

. . .

Under the terms of the order, the plaintiffs need not prove that the defendants either knew or should have known of the dangerous propensities of their products and therefore should have warned consumers of these dangers, defendants being precluded from showing otherwise. On appeal, the defendants contend that the order violates their rights to due process and to trial by jury. Because we conclude that the trial court abused its discretion in applying collateral estoppel, we reverse.

. . .

In *Parklane Hosiery Co. v. Shore*, 439 U.S. 322 (1979), the Supreme Court was asked to determine "whether a party who has had issues of fact adjudicated adversely to it in an equitable action may be collaterally estopped from relitigating the same issues before a jury in a subsequent legal action brought against it by a new party." The Court responded affirmatively, noting offensive collateral estoppel's "dual purpose of protecting litigants from the burden of relitigating an identical issue with the same party or his privy and of promoting judicial economy by preventing needless litigation." The Court reiterated that mutuality is not necessary to proper invocation of collateral estoppel under federal law, and further held that the use of offensive collateral estoppel does not violate a defendant's seventh amendment right to a jury trial. To avoid problems with the use of the doctrine, the Court adopted a general rule of fairness, stating "that in cases where plaintiff could easily have joined in the earlier action or where . . . for other reasons, the application of offensive collateral estoppel would be unfair to a defendant, a trial judge should not allow the use of offensive collateral estoppel."

In the wake of *Parklane*, it is clear that a right, question, or fact distinctly put in issue and directly determined as a ground of recovery by a court of competent jurisdiction collaterally estops a party or his privy from relitigating the issue in a subsequent action. So stated, the doctrine recognizes that a person "cannot be bound by a judgment unless he has had reasonable notice of the claim against him and opportunity to be heard in opposition to that claim. The right to a full and fair opportunity to litigate an issue is, of course, protected by the due process clause of the United States Constitution. While *Parklane* made the doctrine of mutuality effectively a dead letter under federal law, the case left undisturbed the requisite of privity, i.e., that collateral estoppel can only be applied against parties who have had a prior "full and fair opportunity to litigate their claims." The requirement that a person against whom the conclusive effect of a judgment is invoked must be a party or a privy to the prior judgment retains its full vigor after *Parklane*.

## THE NON-*BOREL* DEFENDANTS

This is the first and, in our view, insurmountable problem with the trial court's application of collateral estoppel in the case *sub judice*. The omnibus order under review here does not distinguish between defendants who were parties to *Borel* and those who were not; it purports to estop all defendants because all purportedly share an "identity of interests" sufficient to constitute privity. The trial court's action stretches "privity" beyond meaningful limits. . . .

Federal courts have deemed several types of relationships "sufficiently close" to justify preclusion. First, a nonparty who has succeeded to a party's interest in property is bound by any prior judgments against that party. . . . Second, a nonparty who controlled the original suit will be bound by the resulting judgment. . . . Third, federal courts will bind a nonparty whose interests were represented adequately by a party in the original suit. The rationale for these exceptions is obviously that in these instances the nonparty has in effect had his day in court. In this case, the exceptions are inapplicable. . . .

The fact that all the non-*Borel* defendants, like the *Borel* defendants, are engaged in the manufacture of asbestos-containing products does not evince privity among the parties. The plaintiffs did not demonstrate that any of the non-*Borel* defendants participated in any capacity in the *Borel* litigation—whether directly or even through a trade representative—or were even part of a trustee-beneficiary relationship with any *Borel* defendant. On the contrary, several of the defendants indicate on appeal that they were not even aware of the *Borel* litigation until those proceedings were over and that they were not even members of industry or trade associations composed of asbestos product manufacturers.

. . .

The court's omnibus order here amounts to collateral estoppel based on similar legal positions—a proposition that has been properly rejected by at least one other district court that considered the identical issue. . . . "Privity is not established by the mere fact that persons may happen to be interested in the same question or in proving the same state of facts," and we hold that the trial court's actions here transgress the bounds of due process.

## THE *BOREL* DEFENDANTS

The propriety of estopping the six defendants in this case who were parties to *Borel* poses more difficult questions. In ascertaining the precise preclusive effect of a prior judgment on a particular issue, [t]he party asserting the estoppel must show that: (1) the issue to be concluded is identical to that involved in the prior action; (2) in the prior action the issue was "actually litigated"; and (3) the determination made of the issue in the prior action must have been necessary and essential to the resulting judgment.

If it appears that a judgment may have been based on more than one of several distinctive matters in litigation and there is no indication which issue it was based on or which issue was fully litigated, such judgment will not preclude, under the doctrine of collateral estoppel, relitigation of any of the issues.

Appellants argue that *Borel* did not necessarily decide that asbestos-containing insulation products were unreasonably dangerous because of failure to warn. According to appellants, the general *Borel* verdict, based on general instructions and special interrogatories, permitted the jury to ground strict liability on the bases of failures to test, of unsafeness for intended use, of failures to inspect, or of unsafeness of the product. Strict liability on the basis of failure to warn, although argued to the jury by trial counsel for the plaintiff in *Borel*, was, in the view of the appellants, never formally presented in the jury instructions and therefore was not essential to the *Borel* jury verdict.

Appellants' view has some plausibility. The special interrogatories answered by the *Borel* jury were general and not specifically directed to failure to warn. General instructions to the *Borel* jury on the plaintiff's causes of action did not charge on failure to warn. . . .

The court closely scrutinizes the evidence, theories of the parties, instructions to the jury, and the general verdict and special interrogatory answers. We must ultimately conclude that the judgment in *Borel* cannot estop even the *Borel* defendants in this case for three interrelated reasons.

First, after review of the issues decided in *Borel*, we conclude that *Borel* is ultimately ambiguous as to certain key issues. As the authors of the *Restatement (Second) of Judgments* s.29, comment g (1982), have noted, collateral estoppel is inappropriate where the prior judgment is ambivalent.

. . .

Even if we are wrong as to the ambiguities of the *Borel* judgment, there is a second, equally important, reason to deny collateral estoppel effect to it: the presence of inconsistent verdicts. In *Parklane*, the Court noted that collateral estoppel is improper and "unfair" to a defendant "if the judgment relied upon as a basis for the estoppel is itself inconsistent with one or more previous judgments in favor of the defendant."[2] Not only does issue preclusion in such cases appear arbitrary to a defendant who has had favorable judgments on the same issue, it also undermines the premise that different juries reach equally valid verdicts. One jury's determination should not, merely because it comes later in time, bind another jury's determination of an issue over which there are equally reasonable resolutions of doubt. [The court noted that the asbestos manufacturers had prevailed in 35 of the 70 similar cases litigated.]

Finally, we conclude that even if the *Borel* verdict had been unambiguous and the sole verdict issued on point, application of collateral estoppel would still be unfair with regard to the *Borel* defendants because it is very doubtful that these defendants could have foreseen that their $68,000 liability to plaintiff Borel would foreshadow multimillion dollar asbestos liability. As noted in *Parklane*, it would be unfair to apply collateral estoppel "if a

---

2. The injustice of applying collateral estoppel in cases involving mass torts is especially obvious. Thus, in *Parklane* the Court cited Prof. Currie's "familiar example": "A railroad collision injures 50 passengers all of whom bring separate actions against the railroad. After the railroad wins the first 25 suits, a plaintiff wins in suit 26. Professor Currie argues that offensive use of collateral estoppel should not be applied so as to allow plaintiffs 27 through 50 automatically to recover."

defendant in the first action is sued for small or nominal damages (since) he may have little incentive to defend vigorously, particularly if future lawsuits are not foreseeable." While in absolute terms a judgment for $68,000 hardly appears nominal, the early cases like *Borel* have opened the floodgates to an enormous, unprecedented volume of asbestos litigation. According to a recent estimate, there are over 3,000 asbestos plaintiffs in the Eastern District of Texas alone and between 7,500 and 10,000 asbestos cases pending in United States District Courts around the country. The omnibus order here involves 58 pending cases, and the many plaintiffs involved in this case are each seeking $2.5 million in damages. Such a staggering potential liability could not have been foreseen by the *Borel* defendants.

The trial court's application of issue preclusion to the "fact" that asbestos is in all cases a competent producing cause of mesothelioma and asbestosis involves similar problems. *Borel* dealt with the disease-causing aspects of asbestos dust generated by insulation materials. That case did not determine as a matter of fact that because airborne asbestos dust and fibers from thermal insulation materials are hazardous, all products containing asbestos—in whatever quantity or however encapsulated—are hazardous. The injustice in precluding the "fact" that the generic ingredient asbestos invariably and in every use or mode causes cancer is clearest in the case of appellant Garlock. Garlock points out that its products, unlike the loosely woven thermal insulation materials in *Borel* that, when merely handled, emitted large quantities of airborne asbestos dust and fibers, are linoleum-type products in which the asbestos is encapsulated in a rubber-like coating. According to Garlock, its gasket products do not release significant amounts of dust or fibers into the air and have never been demonstrated to be dangerous in installation, use, or removal. Certainly, defendants ought to be free, even after *Borel*, to present evidence of the scientific knowledge associated with their particular product without being prejudiced by a conclusive presumption that asbestos in all forms causes cancer. The court regarded collateral estoppel in this context as precluding merely the "can it" question rather than the "did it" question. The problem is that the "can it" and "did it" questions cannot in this instance be so easily segregated, and a determination that asbestos generally is hazardous threatens to undermine a defendant's possibly legitimate defense that its product was not scientifically known to be hazardous, now or at relevant times in the past. If the trial court's application of issue preclusion on the generic danger of asbestos is not meant to burden a defendant's ability to present such evidence, then we fail to see the intended usefulness of the court's action.

. . .

We sympathize with the district court's efforts to streamline the enormous asbestos caseload it faces. None of what we say here is meant to cast doubt on any possible alternative ways to avoid reinventing the asbestos liability wheel (joint discovery and consolidation of appropriate groups of cases for trial of particular common issues are some of the possibilities). We hold today only that courts cannot read *Borel* to stand for the proposition that, as matters of fact, asbestos products are unreasonably dangerous or that asbestos as a generic element is in all products a competent producing cause of cancer. To do otherwise would be to elevate judicial expedience over considerations of justice and fair play.

## Comments and Questions

1. Given the press of thousands of nearly identical asbestos cases on the docket, it is not surprising that trial judges would look to issue preclusion (claim preclusion of course being unavailable because each plaintiff is entitled to his own day in court) in an attempt to streamline the process. It is equally unsurprising that expansive privity theories like "identity of interests" would not survive constitutional scrutiny, as in the principal case. *See generally* Michael D. Green, *The Inability of Offensive Collateral Estoppel to Fulfill Its Promise: An Examination of Estoppel in Asbestos Litigation*, 70 Iowa L. Rev. 141 (1984).

2. What if the prior decision was based on expert testimony that is now deemed unreliable, or discredited, or out of date? Should a court for example refuse to foreclose a pharmaceutical manufacturer from relitigating the issue of the hazardous nature of its product where, in the earlier decision against it in a similar case, plaintiffs had presented testimony of a medical researcher whose methods have since been rejected by other courts? Several decisions give an affirmative answer. See *Coburn v. Smithkline Beecham Corp.*, 174 F. Supp. 2d 1235 (D. Utah 2001) (alleging that antidepressant Paxil caused suicide) ("As the scientific landscape changes concerning the evidence for or against the causal connection posited by Plaintiffs, GSK should be free to present—and juries free to evaluate—evidence that makes it more or less likely that Paxil does or does not cause violent reactions in some patients. Simply said, the [prior] verdict should not be—and will not be—the final word on the subject." 174 F. Supp. 2d at 1241); *Rogers v. Ford Motor Co.*, 925 F. Supp. 1413 (N.D. Ind. 1996) (doctrine of offensive collateral estoppel did not bar manufacturer of vehicle's seat belt assembly from relitigating issue of whether assembly was defective, where decision in prior case had been called into doubt by subsequent testing by the National Highway Traffic Safety Administration).

# D. THE COUNTERWEIGHTS TO FINALITY

Are there any circumstances in which countervailing policy concerns outweigh the doctrines of finality? What if the decision in the prior case is based on what is now acknowledged to be an erroneous reading of the law? Does the interest in arriving at the "correct" result trump the interest in putting disputes to rest once and for all? Consider the following case.

# ■ FEDERATED DEPARTMENT STORES, INC. v. MOITIE

*452 U.S. 394 (1981)*

Justice REHNQUIST delivered the opinion of the Court:

The only question presented in this case is whether the Court of Appeals for the Ninth Circuit validly created an exception to the doctrine of *res judicata*. The court held that *res judicata* does not bar relitigation of an unappealed adverse judgment where, as here, other plaintiffs in similar actions against common defendants successfully appeal the judgments against them. We disagree with the view taken by the Court of Appeals for the Ninth Circuit and reverse.

## I

In 1976 the United States brought an antitrust action against petitioners, owners of various department stores, alleging that they had violated § 1 of the Sherman Act, 15 U.S.C. § 1, by agreeing to fix the retail price of women's clothing sold in northern California. Seven parallel civil actions were subsequently filed by private plaintiffs seeking treble damages on behalf of proposed classes of retail purchasers, including that of respondent Moitie in state court (*Moitie I*) and respondent Brown (*Brown I*) in the United States District Court for the Northern District of California. Each of these complaints tracked almost verbatim the allegations of the Government's complaint, though the *Moitie I* complaint referred solely to state law. All of the actions originally filed in the District Court were assigned to a single federal judge, and the *Moitie I* case was removed there on the basis of diversity of citizenship and federal-question jurisdiction. The District Court dismissed all of the actions "in their entirety" on the ground that plaintiffs had not alleged an "injury" to their "business or property" within the meaning of § 4 of the Clayton Act, 15 U.S.C. § 15.

Plaintiffs in five of the suits appealed that judgment to the Court of Appeals for the Ninth Circuit. The single counsel representing Moitie and Brown, however, chose not to appeal and instead refiled the two actions in state court, *Moitie II* and *Brown II*. Although the complaints purported to raise only state-law claims, they made allegations similar to those made in the prior complaints, including that of the Government. Petitioners removed these new actions to the District Court for the Northern District of California and moved to have them dismissed on the ground of *res judicata*. In a decision rendered July 8, 1977, the District Court first denied respondents' motion to remand. It held that the complaints, though artfully couched in terms of state law, were "in many respects identical" with the prior complaints, and were thus properly removed to federal court because they raised "essentially federal law" claims. The court then concluded that because *Moitie II* and *Brown II* involved the "same parties, the same alleged offenses, and the same time periods" as *Moitie I* and *Brown I*, the doctrine of *res judicata* required that they be dismissed. This time, Moitie and Brown appealed.

Pending that appeal, this Court on June 11, 1979, decided *Reiter v. Sonotone Corp.*, 442 U.S. 330, holding that retail purchasers can suffer an "injury" to their "business or property" as those terms are used in § 4 of the Clayton Act. On June 25, 1979, the Court of Appeals for the Ninth Circuit reversed and remanded the five cases which had been decided with *Moitie I* and *Brown I*, the cases that had been appealed, for further proceedings in light of *Reiter*. When *Moitie II* and *Brown II* finally came before the Court of Appeals for the Ninth Circuit, the court reversed the decision of the District Court dismissing the cases.[2] Though the court recognized that a "strict application of the doctrine of *res judicata* would preclude our review of the instant decision," it refused to apply the doctrine to the facts of this case. It observed that the other five litigants . . . had successfully appealed the decision against them. It then asserted that "non-appealing parties may benefit from a reversal when their position is closely interwoven with that of appealing parties," and concluded that "[because] the instant dismissal rested on a case that has been effectively overruled," the doctrine of *res judicata* must give way to "public policy" and "simple justice." We granted certiorari to consider the validity of the Court of Appeals' novel exception to the doctrine of *res judicata*.

## II

There is little to be added to the doctrine of *res judicata* as developed in the case law of this Court. A final judgment on the merits of an action precludes the parties or their privies from relitigating issues that were or could have been raised in that action. Nor are the *res judicata* consequences of a final, unappealed judgment on the merits altered by the fact that the judgment may have been wrong or rested on a legal principle subsequently overruled in another case. As this Court explained in *Baltimore S.S. Co. v. Phillips*, 274 U.S. 316, 325 (1927), an "erroneous conclusion" reached by the court in the first suit does not deprive the defendants in the second action "of their right to rely upon the plea of *res judicata*. A judgment merely voidable because based upon an erroneous view of the law is not open to collateral attack, but can be corrected only by a direct review and not by bringing another action upon the same cause [of action]." We have observed that "[the] indulgence of a contrary

---

2. The Court of Appeals also affirmed the District Court's conclusion that *Brown II* was properly removed to federal court, reasoning that the claims presented were "federal in nature." We agree that at least some of the claims had a sufficient federal character to support removal. As one treatise puts it, courts "will not permit plaintiff to use artful pleading to close off defendant's right to a federal forum . . . [and] occasionally the removal court will seek to determine whether the real nature of the claim is federal, regardless of plaintiff's characterization." 14 C. Wright, A. Miller, & E. Cooper, *Federal Practice and Procedure* § 3722, pp. 564-566 (1976). The District Court applied that settled principle to the facts of this case. After "an extensive review and analysis of the origins and substance of" the two Brown complaints, it found, and the Court of Appeals expressly agreed, that respondents had attempted to avoid removal jurisdiction by "[artfully]" casting their "essentially federal law claims" as state-law claims. We will not question here that factual finding.

view would result in creating elements of uncertainty and confusion and in undermining the conclusive character of judgments, consequences which it was the very purpose of the doctrine of *res judicata* to avert." *Reed v. Allen*, 286 U.S. 191, 201 (1932).

In this case, the Court of Appeals conceded that the "strict application of the doctrine of *res judicata*" required that *Brown II* be dismissed. By that, the court presumably meant that the "technical elements" of *res judicata* had been satisfied, namely, that the decision in *Brown I* was a final judgment on the merits and involved the same claims and the same parties as *Brown II*.[3] The court, however, declined to dismiss *Brown II* because, in its view, it would be unfair to bar respondents from relitigating a claim so "closely interwoven" with that of the successfully appealing parties. We believe that such an unprecedented departure from accepted principles of *res judicata* is unwarranted. Indeed, the decision below is all but foreclosed by our prior case law.

. . . Indeed, this case presents even more compelling reasons to apply the doctrine of *res judicata* than did [prior cases]. Respondents here seek to be the windfall beneficiaries of an appellate reversal procured by other independent parties, who have no interest in respondents' case, not a reversal in interrelated cases procured . . . by the same affected party. Moreover, it is apparent that respondents here made a calculated choice to forgo their appeals.

The Court of Appeals also rested its opinion in part on what it viewed as "simple justice." But we do not see the grave injustice which would be done by the application of accepted principles of *res judicata*. "Simple justice" is achieved when a complex body of law developed over a period of years is evenhandedly applied. The doctrine of *res judicata* serves vital public interests beyond any individual judge's ad hoc determination of the equities in a particular case. There is simply "no principle of law or equity which sanctions the rejection by a federal court of the salutary principle of *res judicata*." The Court of Appeals' reliance on "public policy" is similarly misplaced. This Court has long recognized that "[public] policy dictates that there be an end of litigation; that those who have contested an issue shall be bound by the result of the contest, and that matters once tried shall be considered forever settled as between the parties." We have stressed that "[the] doctrine of *res judicata* is not a mere matter of practice or procedure inherited from a more technical time than ours. It is a rule of fundamental and substantial justice, of public policy and of private peace, which should be cordially regarded and enforced by the courts." The language used by this Court half a century ago is even more compelling in view of today's crowded dockets:

> The predicament in which respondent finds himself is of his own making. . . . [We] cannot be expected, for his sole relief, to upset the general and well-established doctrine of res judicata, conceived in the light of the maxim that the interest of the state requires that there be an end to litigation—a maxim

---

3. The dismissal for failure to state a claim under Federal Rule of Civil Procedure 12(b)(6) is a "judgment on the merits."

which comports with common sense as well as public policy. And the mischief which would follow the establishment of precedent for so disregarding this salutary doctrine against prolonging strife would be greater than the benefit which would result from relieving some case of individual hardship.

*Reed v. Allen*, 286 U.S., at 198-199.

Respondents argue that "the district court's dismissal on grounds of *res judicata* should be reversed, and the district court directed to grant respondent's motion to remand to the California state court." In their view, *Brown I* cannot be considered *res judicata* as to their state-law claims, since *Brown I* raised only federal-law claims and *Brown II* raised additional state-law claims not decided in *Brown I*, such as unfair competition, fraud, and restitution.

It is unnecessary for this Court to reach that issue. It is enough for our decision here that *Brown I* is *res judicata* as to respondents' federal-law claims. Accordingly, the judgment of the Court of Appeals is reversed, and the cause is remanded for proceedings consistent with this opinion. It is so ordered.

Justice BLACKMUN, with whom Justice MARSHALL joins, concurring in the judgment:

While I agree with the result reached in this case, I write separately to state my views on two points.

First, I, for one, would not close the door upon the possibility that there are cases in which the doctrine of *res judicata* must give way to what the Court of Appeals referred to as "overriding concerns of public policy and simple justice." [R]espondents were not "caught in a mesh of procedural complexities." Instead, they made a deliberate tactical decision not to appeal. Nor would public policy be served by making an exception to the doctrine in this case; to the contrary, there is a special need for strict application of *res judicata* in complex multiple party actions of this sort so as to discourage "breakaway" litigation. Finally, this is not a case "where the rights of appealing and non-appealing parties are so interwoven or dependent on each other as to require a reversal of the whole judgment when a part thereof is reversed."

Second, and in contrast, I would flatly hold that *Brown I* is *res judicata* as to respondents' state-law claims. Like the District Court, the Court of Appeals found that those state-law claims were simply disguised federal claims; since respondents have not cross-petitioned from that judgment, their argument that this case should be remanded to state court should be itself barred by *res judicata*. More important, even if the state and federal claims are distinct, respondents' failure to allege the state claims in *Brown I* manifestly bars their allegation in *Brown II*. The dismissal of *Brown I* is *res judicata* not only as to all claims respondents actually raised, but also as to all claims that could have been raised. Since there is no reason to believe that it was clear at the outset of this litigation that the District Court would have declined to exercise pendent jurisdiction over state claims, respondents were obligated to plead those claims if they wished to preserve them. Because they did not do so, I would hold the claims barred.

Justice BRENNAN, dissenting:

In its eagerness to correct the decision of the Court of Appeals for the Ninth Circuit, the Court today disregards statutory restrictions on federal-court jurisdiction, and, in the process, confuses rather than clarifies long-established principles of *res judicata*. I therefore respectfully dissent.

## I

Respondent Floyd R. Brown filed this class action (*Brown II*) against petitioners in California state court. The complaint stated four state-law causes of action: (1) fraud and deceit, (2) unfair business practices, (3) civil conspiracy, and (4) restitution. Plaintiffs' Complaint, paras. 11-14. It alleged "not less than $600" damages per class member, and in addition sought "appropriate multiple damages," exemplary and punitive damages, interest from date of injury, attorney's fees and costs, and other relief. All four of the causes of action rested wholly on California statutory or common law; none rested in any fashion on federal law.

Nonetheless, petitioners removed the suit to the United States District Court for the Northern District of California, where respondent Brown filed a motion to remand on the ground that his action raised no federal question within the meaning of 28 U.S.C. § 1441(b). Respondent's motion was denied by the District Court, which stated that "[from] start to finish, plaintiffs have essentially alleged violations by defendants of federal antitrust laws." The court reasoned that "[artful] pleading" by plaintiffs cannot "convert their essentially federal law claims into state law claims," and held that respondent's complaint was properly removed "because [it] concerned federal questions which could have been originally brought in Federal District Court without satisfying any minimum amount in controversy." The court then dismissed the action, holding that, under the doctrine of *res judicata*, *Brown II* was barred by the adverse decision in an earlier suit in federal court (*Brown I*) involving "the same parties, the same alleged offenses, and the same time periods."

The Court of Appeals affirmed the District Court's decision not to remand, stating that "[the] court below correctly held that the claims presented were federal in nature." However, the Court of Appeals reversed the District Court's order of dismissal, and remanded for trial.

## II

The provision authorizing removal of actions from state to federal courts on the basis of a federal question[2] is found in 28 U.S.C. § 1441(b):

2. As the District Court acknowledged, *Brown II* could not be removed on the basis of diversity of citizenship, because the amount in controversy did not exceed $10,000. The court correctly noted, however, that the action could have been removed without regard to the amount in controversy, if it could have been brought as an original action in federal court without meeting any minimum amount in controversy. Actions under the Clayton Act, 15 U.S.C. § 15, may be brought in federal court without regard to amount in controversy. *See also* 28 U.S.C. § 1331 (1976 ed., Supp. IV), and note following § 1331 (repeal of minimum amount in controversy for federal-question cases pending as of date of enactment).

> Any civil action of which the district courts have original jurisdiction founded on a claim or right arising under the Constitution, treaties or laws of the United States shall be removable without regard to the citizenship or residence of the parties.

Removability depends solely upon the nature of the plaintiff's complaint: an action may be removed to federal court only if a "right or immunity created by the Constitution or laws of the United States [constitutes] an element, and an essential one, of the plaintiff's cause of action." An action arising under state law may not be removed solely because a federal right or immunity is raised as a defense.

An important corollary is that "the party who brings a suit is master to decide what law he will rely upon and therefore does determine whether he will bring a 'suit arising under' the . . . [laws] of the United States" by the allegations in his complaint. Where the plaintiff's claim might be brought under either federal or state law, the plaintiff is normally free to ignore the federal question and rest his claim solely on the state ground. If he does so, the defendant has no general right of removal.

This corollary is well grounded in principles of federalism. So long as States retain authority to legislate in subject areas in which Congress has legislated without pre-empting the field, and so long as state courts remain the preferred forum for interpretation and enforcement of state law, plaintiffs must be permitted to proceed in state court under state law. It would do violence to state autonomy were defendants able to remove state claims to federal court merely because the plaintiff could have asserted a federal claim based on the same set of facts underlying his state claim. . . .

This lawsuit concerns the area of antitrust in which federal laws have not displaced state law. Thus, respondent Brown had the option of proceeding under state or federal law, or both. So far as is apparent from the complaint, which was carefully limited to four California state-law causes of action, this case arises wholly without reference to federal law. Under settled principles of federal jurisdiction, therefore, respondent's lawsuit should not have been removed to federal court.

The Court today nonetheless sustains removal of this action on the ground that "at least some of the claims had a sufficient federal character to support removal." I do not understand what the Court means by this. Which of the claims are federal in character? Why are the claims federal in character? In my view, they are all predicated solely on California law. Certainly, none of them purports to state a claim under the federal antitrust laws, and the mere fact that plaintiffs might have chosen to proceed under the Clayton Act surely does not suffice to transmute their state claims into federal claims.

The Court relies on what it calls a "factual finding" by the District Court, with which the Court of Appeals agreed, that "respondents had attempted to avoid removal jurisdiction by '[artfully]' casting their 'essentially federal law claims' as state-law claims." But this amounts to no more than a pejorative characterization of respondents' decision to proceed under state rather than federal law. "Artful" or not, respondents' complaints were not based on any claim of a federal right or immunity, and were not, therefore, removable. . . .

Even assuming that this Court and the lower federal courts have jurisdiction to decide this case, however, I dissent from the Court's disposition of the *res judicata* issue. Having reached out to assume jurisdiction, the Court inexplicably recoils from deciding the case. The Court finds it "unnecessary" to reach the question of the *res judicata* effect of *Brown I* on respondents' "state-law claims." "It is enough for our decision here," the Court says, "that *Brown I* is *res judicata* as to respondents' federal-law claims." *Ibid*. But respondents raised only state-law claims; respondents did not raise any federal-law claims. Thus, if the Court fails to decide the disposition of respondents' state-law claims, it decides nothing. And in doing so, the Court introduces the possibility—heretofore foreclosed by our decisions—that unarticulated theories of recovery may survive an unconditional dismissal of the lawsuit.

Like Justice Blackmun, I would hold that the dismissal of *Brown I is res judicata* not only as to every matter that was actually litigated, but also as to every ground or theory of recovery that might also have been presented. An unqualified dismissal on the merits of a substantial federal antitrust claim precludes relitigation of the same claim on a state-law theory. The Court's failure to acknowledge this basic principle can only create doubts and confusion where none were before, and may encourage litigants to split their causes of action, state from federal, in the hope that they might win a second day in court.

I therefore respectfully dissent, and would vacate the judgment of the Court of Appeals with instructions to remand to the District Court with instructions to remand to state court.

## Comments and Questions

1. *Moitie* demonstrates the high priority our litigation system places on finality. In reaching the same result in a case invoking Fed. R. Civ. P. 60(b)(5)'s clause permitting a judgment to be reopened when it was "based on an earlier judgment that has been reversed or vacated," the First Circuit Court of Appeals wrote:

> The Federal Rules of Civil Procedure place considerable importance on the finality of judgments, even as legal precedents come and go. Parties who complete litigation must be able to expect that a court's decision will continue to have effect. Accordingly, the Rules preclude reopening cases except in certain narrow circumstances not applicable here.

The plaintiffs had argued unsuccessfully that an intervening Supreme Court decision in effect declaring voluntary public school desegregation plans unconstitutional should change the result of their prior challenge to the plan in Lynn, Massachusetts, which had been dismissed. *See Comfort ex rel. Neumyer v. Lynn School Committee*, 541 F. Supp. 2d 429 (D. Mass. 2008).

2. Do you agree with the Court's explicit equation of finality and "simple justice"? When you read *United States v. Mendoza* in note 7 below and *Martin v. Wilks*, the last case reprinted in this book, consider whether the Court is *always* consistent in treating adjudication as absolutely conclusive.

3. Can you reconcile the Court's suggestion at the end of the *Moitie* opinion that *Brown I* may be *res judicata* only as to the *federal law* claims with the established principle that claim preclusion operates as to *all* transactionally related claims that *could have been raised* in the prior proceeding? Do Justices Blackmun, Marshall, and Brennan stay closer to this principle in their analysis? Note Justice Brennan's concern that the "Court introduces the possibility—heretofore foreclosed by our decisions—that unarticulated theories of recovery may survive an unconditional dismissal of the lawsuit." Why would the majority, which is so enthusiastic about finality, under-enforce *res judicata* in this way?

4. What is the relationship between the preclusion issue and the question of removal in *Moitie*? Is there not a contradiction between the Court's conclusion that *Brown II* was properly removed because of the "federal nature" of its assertedly state-law claims, and its suggestion nonetheless that *Brown II*'s state-law claims may not be precluded by *Brown I* because it set out only federal claims? How could *Brown II* be a "disguised" federal claim for purposes of removal, yet survive preclusion by the prior dismissal of that very federal claim? What does Justice Brennan say about this?

The Court's footnote 2 alludes to the so-called artful pleading doctrine, which prevents a plaintiff from depriving defendant of the right to remove to a federal forum by cleverly pleading the case as a purely state-law claim, when in fact it is "federal in nature." Justice Brennan, harking back to the notion invoked in *Mottley* of the plaintiff as "the master" of his complaint who alone decides what law to rely on, characterizes this artful pleading doctrine as a violation of the "principles of federalism" and an affront to "state autonomy."

Also critical of the doctrine, Professor Arthur Miller concludes that the Supreme Court gave the removal question only "slight attention" in *Moitie*, and that subsequent decisions have raised serious question about the viability of the Court's reasoning in footnote 2. *See* Arthur R. Miller, *Artful Pleading: A Doctrine in Search of Definition*, 76 Tex. L. Rev. 1781 (1998).

5. Four years after *Moitie*, the Supreme Court returned to the claim preclusion question in the context of overlapping state and federal antitrust claims. In *Marrese v. American Academy of Orthopaedic Surgeons*, 470 U.S. 373 (1985), plaintiffs filed a Sherman Act case in federal court (which has exclusive jurisdiction over such claims) following unsuccessful litigation in state court challenging their exclusion from membership in the Academy. The Court held that the federal full faith and credit statute, 28 U.S.C. § 1738 (discussed in our next case), required that the federal court apply the state's law of claim preclusion to determine whether the state court judgment barred

the subsequent federal antitrust claim, even though the latter could not have been raised in the state proceeding.

In so ruling, the Court rejected the position of Judge Cudahy, who, dissenting from the Seventh Circuit's decision below barring the federal antitrust claim, argued in favor of the definition of claim preclusion embodied in the *Restatement (Second) of Judgments*, which requires that the prior court must have been able to exercise jurisdiction over the subsequent claim for preclusion to apply. Given exclusive federal jurisdiction, plaintiffs could not have litigated their Sherman Act claim in state court.

To read more about this topic, *see* Stephen B. Burbank, *Afterwords: A Response to Professor Hazard and a Comment on* Marrese, 70 Cornell L. Rev. 659 (1985); David J. Schulte, *The Claim Preclusive Effect of State Court Judgments on Federal Antitrust Claims:* Marrese v. American Academy of Orthopaedic Surgeons, 71 Iowa L. Rev. 609 (1986).

6. How can plaintiffs avoid risking loss of their federal claim in the *Marrese* situation? What about filing the case in federal court in the first instance and seeking supplemental jurisdiction over the state claims?

7. Writing for the Court in *United States v. Mendoza*, 464 U.S. 154 (1984), Justice Rehnquist (who in *Moitie* insisted there were *no* exceptions to the doctrine of *res judicata*) carved out an exception to the use of issue preclusion against the U.S. government. Like *Moitie* and *Brown*, the government failed to appeal an adverse decision by a U.S. District Court, this one holding that the due process rights of a group of Filipino World War II veterans had been violated when their citizenship naturalization process had been suspended. Mendoza (not a party to the earlier case) later brought a suit raising the same issue, and the Ninth Circuit held the government was estopped from relitigating it. The Supreme Court disagreed:

> A rule allowing nonmutual collateral estoppel against the Government in such cases would substantially thwart the development of important questions of law by freezing the first final decision rendered on a particular legal issue. Allowing only one final adjudication would deprive this Court of the benefit it receives from permitting several courts of appeals to explore a difficult question before this Court grants certiorari.

What happened to strict application of preclusion doctrine?

Should the usual rules of issue preclusion have been suspended as a matter of policy in the next case as well?

## ■ ALLEN v. McCURRY
### *449 U.S. 90 (1980)*

Justice STEWART delivered the opinion of the Court:

At a hearing before his criminal trial in a Missouri court, the respondent, Willie McCurry, invoked the Fourth and Fourteenth Amendments to suppress evidence that had been seized by the police. The trial court denied the suppression motion in part, and McCurry was subsequently convicted after a jury trial. The conviction was later affirmed on appeal. Because he did not assert that the state courts had denied him a "full and fair opportunity" to litigate his search and seizure claim, McCurry was barred by this Court's decision in *Stone v. Powell*, 428 U.S. 465, from seeking a writ of habeas corpus in a federal district court. Nevertheless, he sought federal-court redress for the alleged constitutional violation by bringing a damages suit under 42 U.S.C. § 1983 against the officers who had entered his home and seized the evidence in question. We granted certiorari to consider whether the unavailability of federal habeas corpus prevented the police officers from raising the state courts' partial rejection of McCurry's constitutional claim as a collateral estoppel defense to the § 1983 suit against them for damages.

## I

In April 1977, several undercover police officers, following an informant's tip that McCurry was dealing in heroin, went to his house in St. Louis, Mo., to attempt a purchase. Two officers, petitioners Allen and Jacobsmeyer, knocked on the front door, while the other officers hid nearby. When McCurry opened the door, the two officers asked to buy some heroin "caps." McCurry went back into the house and returned soon thereafter, firing a pistol at and seriously wounding Allen and Jacobsmeyer. After a gun battle with the other officers and their reinforcements, McCurry retreated into the house; he emerged again when the police demanded that he surrender. Several officers then entered the house without a warrant, purportedly to search for other persons inside. One of the officers seized drugs and other contraband that lay in plain view, as well as additional contraband he found in dresser drawers and in auto tires on the porch.

McCurry was charged with possession of heroin and assault with intent to kill. At the pretrial suppression hearing, the trial judge excluded the evidence seized from the dresser drawers and tires, but denied suppression of the evidence found in plain view. McCurry was convicted of both the heroin and assault offenses.

McCurry subsequently filed the present § 1983 action for $1 million in damages against petitioners Allen and Jacobsmeyer, other unnamed individual police officers, and the city of St. Louis and its police department. The complaint alleged a conspiracy to violate McCurry's Fourth Amendment rights, an unconstitutional search and seizure of his house, and an assault on him by unknown police officers after he had been arrested and handcuffed. The petitioners moved for summary judgment. The District Court apparently understood the gist of the complaint to be the allegedly unconstitutional search and seizure and granted summary judgment, holding that collateral estoppel prevented McCurry from relitigating the search-and-seizure question already decided against him in the state courts.

The Court of Appeals reversed the judgment and remanded the case for trial. The appellate court said it was not holding that collateral estoppel was generally inapplicable in a § 1983 suit raising issues determined against the federal plaintiff in a state criminal trial. But noting that *Stone v. Powell* barred McCurry from federal habeas corpus relief, and invoking "the special role of the federal courts in protecting civil rights," the court concluded that the § 1983 suit was McCurry's only route to a federal forum for his constitutional claim and directed the trial court to allow him to proceed to trial unencumbered by collateral estoppel.

## II

The federal courts have traditionally adhered to the related doctrines of *res judicata* and collateral estoppel. Under *res judicata*, a final judgment on the merits of an action precludes the parties or their privies from relitigating issues that were or could have been raised in that action. Under collateral estoppel, once a court has decided an issue of fact or law necessary to its judgment, that decision may preclude relitigation of the issue in a suit on a different cause of action involving a party to the first case. As this Court and other courts have often recognized, *res judicata* and collateral estoppel relieve parties of the cost and vexation of multiple lawsuits, conserve judicial resources, and, by preventing inconsistent decisions, encourage reliance on adjudication.

In recent years, this Court has reaffirmed the benefits of collateral estoppel in particular, finding the policies underlying it to apply in contexts not formerly recognized at common law. Thus, the Court has eliminated the requirement of mutuality in applying collateral estoppel to bar relitigation of issues decided earlier in federal-court suits, and has allowed a litigant who was not a party to a federal case to use collateral estoppel "offensively" in a new federal suit against the party who lost on the decided issue in the first case, *Parklane Hosiery Co. v. Shore*, 439 U.S. 322. But one general limitation the Court has repeatedly recognized is that the concept of collateral estoppel cannot apply when the party against whom the earlier decision is asserted did not have a "full and fair opportunity" to litigate that issue in the earlier case.

The federal courts generally have also consistently accorded preclusive effect to issues decided by state courts. *Res judicata* and collateral estoppel not only reduce unnecessary litigation and foster reliance on adjudication, but also promote the comity between state and federal courts that has been recognized as a bulwark of the federal system. . . .

Indeed, though the federal courts may look to the common law or to the policies supporting *res judicata* and collateral estoppel in assessing the preclusive effect of decisions of other federal courts, Congress has specifically required all federal courts to give preclusive effect to state-court judgments whenever the courts of the State from which the judgments emerged would do so:

> [Judicial] proceedings [of any court of any State] shall have the same full faith and credit in every court within the United States and its Territories and Possessions as they have by law or usage in the courts of such State. . . .

28 U.S.C. § 1738. It is against this background that we examine the relationship of § 1983 and collateral estoppel, and the decision of the Court of Appeals in this case.

## III

This Court has never directly decided whether the rules of *res judicata* and collateral estoppel are generally applicable to § 1983 actions. But the virtually unanimous view of the Courts of Appeals has been that § 1983 presents no categorical bar to the application of *res judicata* and collateral estoppel concepts. These federal appellate court decisions have spoken with little explanation or citation in assuming the compatibility of § 1983 and rules of preclusion, but the statute and its legislative history clearly support the courts' decisions. . . .

[T]he legislative history of § 1983 does not in any clear way suggest that Congress intended to repeal or restrict the traditional doctrines of preclusion. The main goal of the Act was to override the corrupting influence of the Ku Klux Klan and its sympathizers on the governments and law enforcement agencies of the Southern States, and of course the debates show that one strong motive behind its enactment was grave congressional concern that the state courts had been deficient in protecting federal rights. But in the context of the legislative history as a whole, this congressional concern lends only the most equivocal support to any argument that, in cases where the state courts have recognized the constitutional claims asserted and provided fair procedures for determining them, Congress intended to override § 1738 or the common-law rules of collateral estoppel and *res judicata*. Since repeals by implication are disfavored, much clearer support than this would be required to hold that § 1738 and the traditional rules of preclusion are not applicable to § 1983 suits.

As the Court has understood the history of the legislation, Congress realized that in enacting § 1983 it was altering the balance of judicial power between the state and federal courts. But in doing so, Congress was adding to the jurisdiction of the federal courts, not subtracting from that of the state courts. . . . The debates contain several references to the concurrent jurisdiction of the state courts over federal questions, and numerous suggestions that the state courts would retain their established jurisdiction so that they could, when the then current political passions abated, demonstrate a new sensitivity to federal rights.

To the extent that it did intend to change the balance of power over federal questions between the state and federal courts, the 42d Congress was acting in a way thoroughly consistent with the doctrines of preclusion. . . . Congress had intended a federal remedy in three circumstances: where state substantive law was facially unconstitutional, where state procedural law was inadequate to allow full litigation of a constitutional claim, and where state procedural law, though adequate in theory, was inadequate in practice. In short, the federal courts could step in where the state courts were unable or unwilling to protect federal rights. This understanding of § 1983 might well support an exception to *res judicata* and collateral estoppel where state law did not provide fair procedures for the litigation of constitutional claims, or where a state court failed to even acknowledge the existence of the constitutional principle on which a litigant based his claim. Such an exception, however, would be essentially the same as the important general limit on rules of preclusion that already exists: Collateral estoppel does not apply where the party against whom an earlier court decision is asserted did not have a full and fair opportunity to litigate the claim or issue decided by the first court. But [there is] no strength to any argument that Congress intended to allow relitigation of federal issues decided after a full and fair hearing in a state court simply because the state court's decision may have been erroneous. . . .

The only conceivable basis for finding a universal right to litigate a federal claim in a federal district court is hardly a legal basis at all, but rather a general distrust of the capacity of the state courts to render correct decisions on constitutional issues. [This Court has emphatically rejected that position.]

The Court of Appeals erred in holding the doctrine of collateral estoppel inapplicable to his § 1983 suit. Accordingly, the judgment is reversed, and the case is remanded to the Court of Appeals for proceedings consistent with this opinion.

It is so ordered.

Justice BLACKMUN, with whom Justice BRENNAN and Justice MARSHALL join, dissenting:

The legal principles with which the Court is concerned in this civil case obviously far transcend the ugly facts of respondent's criminal convictions in the courts of Missouri for heroin possession and assault.

The Court today holds that notions of collateral estoppel apply with full force to this suit brought under 42 U.S.C. § 1983. In my view, the Court, in so ruling, ignores the clear import of the legislative history of that statute and disregards the important federal policies that underlie its enforcement. It also shows itself insensitive both to the significant differences between the § 1983 remedy and the exclusionary rule, and to the pressures upon a criminal defendant that make a free choice of forum illusory. I do not doubt that principles of preclusion are to be given such effect as is appropriate in a § 1983 action. In many cases, the denial of *res judicata* or collateral estoppel effect would serve no purpose and would harm relations between federal and state tribunals. Nonetheless, the Court's analysis in this particular case is unacceptable to me. It works injustice on this § 1983 plaintiff, and it makes more difficult the consistent protection of constitutional rights, a consideration that was at the core of the enacters' intent. Accordingly, I dissent.

. . .

In this case, the police officers seek to prevent a criminal defendant from relitigating the constitutionality of their conduct in searching his house, after the state trial court had found that conduct in part violative of the defendant's Fourth Amendment rights and in part justified by the circumstances. I doubt that the police officers, now defendants in this § 1983 action, can be considered to have been in privity with the State in its role as prosecutor. Therefore, only "issue preclusion" is at stake.

The following factors persuade me to conclude that this respondent should not be precluded from asserting his claim in federal court. First, at the time § 1983 was passed, a nonparty's ability, as a practical matter, to invoke collateral estoppel was nonexistent. One could not preclude an opponent from relitigating an issue in a new cause of action, though that issue had been determined conclusively in a prior proceeding, unless there was "mutuality." Additionally, the definitions of "cause of action" and "issue" were narrow. As a result, and obviously, no preclusive effect could arise out of a criminal proceeding that would affect subsequent civil litigation. Thus, the 42d Congress could not have anticipated or approved that a criminal defendant, tried and convicted in state court, would be precluded from raising against police officers a constitutional claim arising out of his arrest.

Also, the process of deciding in a state criminal trial whether to exclude or admit evidence is not at all the equivalent of a § 1983 proceeding. The remedy sought in the latter is utterly different. In bringing the civil suit the criminal defendant does not seek to challenge his conviction collaterally. At most, he wins damages. In contrast, the exclusion of evidence may prevent a criminal conviction. A trial court, faced with the decision whether to exclude relevant evidence, confronts institutional pressures that may cause it to give a different shape to the Fourth Amendment right from what would result in civil litigation of a damages claim. Also, the issue whether to exclude evidence is subsidiary to the purpose of a criminal trial, which is to determine the guilt or innocence of the defendant, and a trial court, at least subconsciously, must weigh the potential damage to the truth-seeking process caused by excluding relevant evidence.

A state criminal defendant cannot be held to have chosen "voluntarily" to litigate his Fourth Amendment claim in the state court. The risk of conviction puts pressure upon him to raise all possible defenses. He also faces uncertainty about the wisdom of forgoing litigation on any issue, for there is the possibility that he will be held to have waived his right to appeal on that issue. The "deliberate bypass" of state procedures, which the imposition of collateral estoppel under these circumstances encourages, surely is not a preferred goal. To hold that a criminal defendant who raises a Fourth Amendment claim at his criminal trial "freely and without reservation submits his federal claims for decision by the state courts," is to deny reality. The criminal defendant is an involuntary litigant in the state tribunal, and against him all the forces of the State are arrayed. To force him to a choice between forgoing either a potential defense or a federal forum for hearing his constitutional civil claim is fundamentally unfair.

I would affirm the judgment of the Court of Appeals.

# Comments and Questions

1. What policy concerns are invoked by the dissenters to outweigh strict application of preclusion doctrine in the context of a federal civil rights action following on the heels of a state criminal prosecution? How does the Court answer these concerns?

2. Four years after *Allen v. McCurry*, the Court revisited the question of whether preclusion doctrine should be suspended in order to provide a federal forum for civil rights claims. Dr. Ethel D. Migra brought a state court breach of contract action against the Board of Education when it reneged on its earlier renewal of her contract as supervisor of elementary education. She prevailed, and was awarded reinstatement and compensatory damages. She subsequently filed a § 1983 action in federal court alleging that her nonrenewal was in retaliation for her role as an advocate of desegregation in the school district, thereby depriving her of constitutional rights. The district court granted summary judgment for the defendants on the basis of *res judicata*, and the Supreme Court affirmed. *Migra v. Warren City School District Board of Education*, 465 U.S. 75 (1984):

> The Court in *Allen* left open the possibility . . . that the preclusive effect of a state-court judgment might be different as to a federal issue that a § 1983 litigant could have raised but did not raise in the earlier state-court proceeding. That is the central issue to be resolved in the present case. Petitioner did not litigate her § 1983 claim in state court, and she asserts that the state-court judgment should not preclude her suit in federal court simply because her federal claim could have been litigated in the state-court proceeding. Thus, petitioner urges this Court to interpret the interplay of § 1738 and § 1983 in such a way as to accord state-court judgments preclusive effect in § 1983 suits only as to issues actually litigated in state court.
>
> It is difficult to see how the policy concerns underlying § 1983 would justify a distinction between the issue preclusive and claim preclusive effects of state-court judgments. The argument that state-court judgments should have less preclusive effect in § 1983 suits than in other federal suits is based on Congress' expressed concern over the adequacy of state courts as protectors of federal rights. *Allen* recognized that the enactment of § 1983 was motivated partially out of such concern, but *Allen* nevertheless held that § 1983 did not open the way to relitigation of an issue that had been determined in a state criminal proceeding. Any distrust of state courts that would justify a limitation on the preclusive effect of state judgments in § 1983 suits would presumably apply equally to issues that actually were decided in a state court as well as to those that could have been. If § 1983 created an exception to the general preclusive effect accorded to state-court judgments, such an exception would seem to require similar treatment of both issue preclusion and claim preclusion. Having rejected in *Allen* the view that state-court judgments have no issue preclusive effect in § 1983 suits, we must reject the view that § 1983 prevents the judgment in petitioner's state-court proceeding from creating a claim preclusion bar in this case.

Petitioner suggests that to give state-court judgments full issue preclusive effect but not claim preclusive effect would enable litigants to bring their state claims in state court and their federal claims in federal court, thereby taking advantage of the relative expertise of both forums. Although such a division may seem attractive from a plaintiff's perspective, it is not the system established by § 1738. That statute embodies the view that it is more important to give full faith and credit to state-court judgments than to ensure separate forums for federal and state claims. This reflects a variety of concerns, including notions of comity, the need to prevent vexatious litigation, and a desire to conserve judicial resources. In the present litigation, petitioner does not claim that the state court would not have adjudicated her federal claims had she presented them in her original suit in state court. Alternatively, petitioner could have obtained a federal forum for her federal claim by litigating it first in a federal court. Section 1983, however, does not override state preclusion law and guarantee petitioner a right to proceed to judgment in state court on her state claims and then turn to federal court for adjudication of her federal claims. We hold, therefore, that petitioner's state-court judgment in this litigation has the same claim preclusive effect in federal court that the judgment would have in the Ohio state courts.

465 U.S. at 83-85. *See also Kremer v. Chemical Constr. Corp.*, 456 U.S. 461 (1982) (a state court decision upholding on appeal an administrative agency's rejection of an employment discrimination claim precludes the subsequent filing of a federal Title VII claim in federal court); *University of Tennessee v. Elliott*, 478 U.S. 788 (1986) (where plaintiff has not sought review of the state administrative determinations, they do not have preclusive effect in a Title VII action; preclusive effect is, however, accorded to fact determinations made by a state agency in its judicial capacity when plaintiff seeks to relitigate them in a federal civil rights action under the Reconstruction statutes).

3. What are the lessons of *Allen v. McCurry*, *Migra v. Warren City School District Board of Education*, and *Kremer v. Chemical Constr. Corp.* for lawyers who represent plaintiffs in civil rights cases and seek to do so in federal court? Can supplemental jurisdiction (§ 1367) play a useful role?

## Summary Note on Cross-Jurisdictional Preclusion

As we have seen, the rules of finality operate expansively across many boundary lines—between State *A* and State *B*, between state and federal courts, between civil and criminal cases. A plaintiff cannot generally split her claim into transactionally related federal and state lawsuits. Issues litigated and resolved between litigants in state court are precluded from being relitigated in federal court, and vice versa. Issues resolved against a defendant in a criminal case will usually prelude relitigation by that party in a subsequent civil case. The following list summarizes the line-crossing nature of preclusion doctrine.

**State ⇒ State.** The Full Faith and Credit Clause of the Constitution mandates that a court in State *B* accord a judgment rendered in State *A* the same preclusive effect the judgment would have in State *A*.

**State ⇒ Federal.** 28 U.S.C. § 1738 imposes the same "full faith and credit" obligation on federal courts with regard to judgments of any state court. *See generally San Remo Hotel, L.P. v. City & County of San Francisco*, 545 U.S. 323 (2005).

**Federal ⇒ State.** The preclusive effect in state court of a prior federal court judgment was the subject of *Semtek International, Inc. v. Lockheed Martin Corp.*, 531 U.S. 497 (2001), discussed earlier. Where the judgment was entered in a federal question case (§ 1331), it is accorded the preclusive effect that federal common law provides. For diversity case judgments (§ 1332), *Semtek* mandates that federal common law incorporate the preclusion rules that would be applied by the state courts in the state in which the judgment was rendered. This is in order to avoid the forum shopping and inequitable administration of justice problems underlying the *Erie* doctrine. For a pre-*Semtek* treatment of the topic, *see* Stephen B. Burbank, *Interjurisdictional Preclusion, Full Faith and Credit and Federal Common Law: A General Approach*, 71 Cornell L. Rev. 733 (1986).

## Practice Exercise No. 40: Applying Preclusion Principles

On March 8, 2010, Malcolm-Jinwala Warner (a citizen of Maine) was severely injured in a head-on collision with a Jeep Wrangler driven by Carmen Padros. The accident occurred when Warner was waiting at a stop sign on Main Street in Lowell, MA, and Padros was attempting to make a left turn onto that street; Padros lost control of the jeep and it rolled over on top of Warner's car. Warner's wife, who was following in her own car, saw the entire accident.

Warner's attorney has learned that Padros had been stopped by the Lowell police an hour before the accident and was found to have a blood alcohol level of .11, which is above the legal limit, but was let go when she promised to drive directly home. His attorney also discovered that four months prior to the accident, Padros had modified her jeep with a suspension lift kit and oversized tires purchased from Ultimate Auto. In a criminal prosecution arising out of the accident, Padros was tried for illegally raising the height of her jeep and found guilty. She received a suspended sentence.

Warner has now brought a personal injury action in federal court against Padros, the Lowell police officers who stopped her prior to the accident, the City of Lowell, and Ultimate Auto. Assume that four weeks after Warner filed his complaint, a federal court jury in *Carpenter v. Dee* rendered a general verdict on all counts in favor of Nancy Carpenter and against Dee, the Lowell Police Department, and Ultimate Auto. Judgment entered accordingly and was affirmed on appeal.

Warner's attorney, with whom you are working, believes that the defendants may be collaterally estopped in ways that will significantly help Warner's case. A hearing is scheduled on Warner's motion for partial summary judgment.

1. Identify the issues and defendants that may be estopped.

2. Assume Warner knew about the *Carpenter* case at the time it was filed, and was invited to join as co-plaintiff but refused. Would this in any way change your answer to Question 1?

3. In your research you discover a previous civil case where the Boston Police Department and the City were found grossly negligent after two police officers stopped a driver, measured his blood alcohol level of .10, issued a citation, and then let him continue to drive. The motorist then struck a pedestrian, who brought suit. Would this previous case collaterally estop any of the parties in the *Warner* case? Could you use the case in any other way?

4. Warner alleges that as a result of the accident with Padros his left leg was broken in three places. Padros's attorney learns that a worker's compensation board found that Warner's left leg was broken on March 1, 2010 (seven days before the accident), as result of a work-related incident. Will the board's finding collaterally estop Warner regarding his injuries in the car accident?

5. If Warner prevails against Padros, can Warner's wife successfully sue Padros for negligent infliction of emotional distress, or will *res judicata* bar her claim? If her claim can proceed, can she use collateral estoppel to her advantage against Padros?

## Review Exercise No. 10

To: Law Clerks
From: Trial Judge
Re: *Collector v. Gallery*

In *Charles Collector* (Collector) *v. Cape Gallery, Inc.* (Gallery), commenced June 10, 2010, both sides (subsequent to discovery) have moved for total or partial summary judgment, relying on preclusion law. Our state Supreme Court has, in other cases, affirmed the application of nonmutual collateral estoppel when deemed appropriate. Please tell me how to rule and why.

Collector's complaint alleges in relevant part: (1) On March 4, 2009, he purchased a painting ("Truro Fog") from Gallery for $7,200, which Sally Sales, while working for Gallery, and with authority, guaranteed him in writing was painted by Karl Knaths (Knaths) in 1962; (2) on May 4, 2010, Collector first realized the painting was a forgery; (3) if it were an original Knaths, the painting would be worth $30,000, but instead it is valueless; (4) Gallery owes Collector $30,000 as a result of breach of written guarantee.

Gallery's answer admits all allegations in item 1; states, as to item 2, that it is without sufficient knowledge to answer when Collector realized anything and denies the allegation of forgery; and denies all allegations in items 3 and 4. Gallery asserts the affirmative defense of *res judicata*. Both parties demand a jury trial.

To support its partial summary judgment motion based on issue preclusion, Collector points to the pleadings and has filed three affidavits. One affidavit, signed by Collector, states that each allegation of his complaint is true; he is an experienced appraiser of oil paintings; he has had much experience buying and selling paintings by Knaths; if the Knaths was not a forgery it would be worth $30,000, but if the painting he bought is not a Knaths it is worthless. A second affidavit, signed by Carla Expert, says that she has been a professor of Modern Art at the Museum School for twenty-two years; she has compared "Wellfleet Sunset" and "Provincetown Pier" (both 1962 paintings allegedly by Knaths, which are in the Museum School Collection) with "Truro Fog" and there is no way that the painter of "Truro Fog" was the same painter who painted "Wellfleet Sunset" and "Province-town Pier": the colors, brush strokes, types of paint, and sense of abstraction are too different. The third affidavit is signed by the clerk of the Superior Court and states that the attached docket, pleadings, complete transcript, and opinion are accurate copies. These documents show that in the earlier case of *The Museum School v. Gallery*, commenced January 3, 2007, in the Superior Court (with no jury), an action to rescind (for reason of mutual mistake or fraud) a contract to buy "Wellfleet Sunset" and "Provincetown Pier" on the grounds the paintings were not by Knaths, the judge found in favor of Gallery and wrote in her opinion that "I find in this hotly contested case that was tried for six days in September, 2007, with many witnesses on both sides, that both paintings were painted in 1962 by Karl Knaths. Gallery's experts were persuasive as to the authenticity of the two Knaths." Final judgment was entered for Gallery on October 22, 2007, and no appeal was taken.

Gallery's motion for summary judgment based on claim preclusion is accompanied by an affidavit of the clerk of the Superior Court regarding another case of Collector against Gallery, commenced on August 1, 2010, with copies of the docket, pleadings, defendant's interrogatories, motions, and court order. The complaint stated that from January 1, 2009, through July 31, 2010, Collector had purchased three paintings on three different occasions from Gallery (all modern paintings but only one by Knaths, "Moon over Eastham," allegedly a 1960 painting), each with a separate written guarantee of authenticity, signed by different Gallery employees, and that Collector sought to rescind the purchases for fraud or mutual mistake, on the ground that none of the three were by their purported painters. Gallery admitted the sales and guarantees, denied the fraud and mistake, and alleged that each painting was authentic. The papers showed that, despite a court order, Collector had repeatedly refused to answer interrogatories or show up for depositions, and that the judge ordered the case dismissed with prejudice pursuant to the state counterpart of Fed. R. Civ. P. 37(b)(2)(A).

Gallery also filed an interrogatory answer submitted by Collector in the case presently before me, stating that Collector was paying Carla Expert $100 per hour for all work performed on this case, and an affidavit by Gallery's lawyer that she intended to cross-examine both Collector and Expert at the trial to show their bias, among other things.

# 11

**Class Actions: It All Comes Together**

## A. INTRODUCTION

A class action is a lawsuit brought by a representative plaintiff on behalf of similarly situated people. Individual class members lose control over their lawsuit in exchange for the benefits of collective action. These benefits include the ability to maintain a lawsuit in cases where the remedy is too inconsequential to merit individual litigation or the ability to reform institutions with class-wide injunctive relief. In some ways, the class action is an extension of the doctrine of joinder you learned about in Chapter 3. But unlike joinder, where every plaintiff is present, in the class action context most of the class members are absent from the courtroom. This raises significant questions, such as what justifies one person representing others in a binding litigation? How can the system assure that the representative is reliable? How does the class action mechanism square with the idea expressed in *Taylor v. Sturgell* (discussed in Chapter 10) and other cases that every person is entitled to his or her own day in court? When are class members' claims sufficiently similar to one another that they should all be brought in the same lawsuit?

The class action revisits a good deal of the civil procedure doctrine, concepts, and policies you have already studied in this course. Class actions are also one of the most debated procedural devices and for good reason. All of the anxiety-provoking issues in civil litigation are magnified in the class context, including questions of whether our system enables too much litigation, concerns about the cost of litigation to defendants and the economy, and concerns about trampling plaintiffs' individual rights in the name of efficiency. The doctrine of class actions and the practice of class action litigation also give rise to many questions about attorney incentives, individual rights, and access to justice that can only be understood in the political context of the times.

The evolution of class actions parallels the narrative of much of contemporary civil procedure. Early on, the Federal Rules of Civil Procedure were the embodiment of a philosophy that embraced access to courts through simplified pleading, ease of amendment, liberal discovery, broad joinder of parties, jury trials, and an invitation to lawyer creativity and innovative claims for relief. Over time, as you have seen throughout this book, there has been a retrenchment against the open approach to civil procedure. Courts and legislatures have demanded more particularized pleadings, sanctions have been invigorated, the discovery rules have been narrowed and limited, and jury trials have been replaced with summary judgment, case managers, and forms of alternative dispute resolution (ADR). Similarly, whereas in 1966, when the modern class action rule was ratified by Congress, the rule expressed the more liberal vision of the Federal Rules, it has since come to represent the excesses of our litigation system, and numerous attempts have been made to reform class actions. The length of the current version of Rule 23 and its numerous provisions is a reflection of the rulemakers' concern about the problems created by class action litigation. Courts and legislatures have tightened the requirements for certifying class actions and limited the remedies available in the context of class action litigation. For example, in 1996 Congress limited the ability of legal-services providers that receive federal funds from representing clients in class actions. 42 U.S.C. § 2996(e)(d)(5). The Truth in Lending Act (TILA) limits the available remedies in class actions brought under that law to the lesser of $500,000 or 1 percent of the net worth of the defendant. 15 U.S.C. § 1640(a)(2)(B). The Public Securities Litigation Reform Act (PSLRA) imposed heightened pleading requirements for securities class actions, among other things. Pub. L. No. 104-67, 109 Stat. 737 (1995).

Yet class actions also differ from other areas of procedure you have studied. Many of the assumptions prevalent in the context of binary litigation are turned on their head in the class action context. For example, despite the prevailing view that the federal courts are inundated with cases and that access to the courthouse ought to be limited, Congress actually *expanded* federal subject matter jurisdiction over class actions by passing the Class Action Fairness Act of 2005. *See* 28 U.S.C § 1332(d). This legislation was largely understood to be a defendant-friendly reaction to concerns about state courts being too lenient in certifying national class actions. Similarly, although no defendant wants to be sued, in complex litigation defendants sometimes seek to have class actions certified so that they can preclude future suits, an arrangement that some scholars call "global peace." Finally, while the policy debate about class actions frequently centers on plaintiffs' rights— in other words, are class members getting their due?—defendants are often the ones expressing these concerns.

Because it can bind absent parties, the class action raises substantial due process concerns. The ordinary rule of civil litigation, as you have learned, is that parties cannot be bound by a judgment unless they have actually participated in the suit. Yet in the class action context individuals can be bound even though they have not had their day in court. How can this be? The first case in this chapter, *Hansberry v. Lee*, addresses this fundamental question, returning to the due process concerns addressed in Chapter 1. The plaintiff class may also encompass individual class members from states outside the court's jurisdiction, even those who did not expressly consent to appear. The second case in this chapter, *Phillips Petroleum v. Shutts*, addresses the question of how a court can exercise personal jurisdiction over absent class members, returning to the due process concerns addressed in Chapter 7. Both of these cases were decided during a period when class action litigation was relatively new and rare, but the seeds of the current concerns about class actions had already been planted.

Even if the court's interpretation of due process allows a class action, this does not end the inquiry. In order for a lawsuit to proceed as a class action, it must be certified by a court. To do this, the court must find that the class action meets all the requirements of Rule 23. These requirements will be discussed in detail later in this chapter. As illustrated by the opinion in *Wal-Mart v. Dukes*, class certification is very difficult to achieve, especially in federal court, because the requirements have been tightened over time. Preclusion doctrine plays a critical role in understanding the reasons for the tightening of certification standards. If the class representative succeeds in certifying a class, the results of the class action litigation are binding on all the class members, even those who did not participate in the litigation and even those who did not actually *know* about the litigation.

## B. CLASS ACTION PRACTICE, POLICY, AND CONTEXT

Before delving into the doctrine, it is useful to consider the policy concerns that have driven the evolution of the law in this area. Class actions were a rarely used procedural device until the rule was liberalized in 1966. That year the rules drafters introduced a new structure to the class action rule, one which classified class actions based on remedies. After setting out basic requirements for sustaining a class action (numerosity, commonality, typicality, adequate representation, to be discussed later in this chapter), the class action rule creates three types of class actions: (1) limited fund, (2) injunctive, and (3) money damages class actions. Limited fund class actions are brought, as their name suggests, when there is a limited pot of money to pay a group of individuals with claims against a defendant. Injunctive class actions are often civil rights cases. Money damages class actions can run the gamut from back pay claims in an employment discrimination suit to compensatory damages in a consumer protection suit.

One reason for the liberalization of the class action rule was the desegregation suits of the 1950s and 1960s. The ability to bring such suits was greatly expanded with the passage of the Civil Rights Act of 1964. Injunctive civil rights class actions have until recently been relatively non-controversial. The gender discrimination class action brought by female employees against Wal-Mart, excerpted later in this chapter, signals a change in the more sanguine approach of the courts to civil rights class actions. By contrast, money damages class actions have always been very controversial. If you have ever been a member of a class action, most likely you were a member of a lawsuit brought under a consumer protection law seeking money damages. Concerns about this type of class action include the high attorneys' fees awards relative to the claims of individual class members and concerns that so much is at stake in a class action that it can unduly pressure a defendant to settle even nonmeritorious claims.

Why permit one person to sue on behalf of others? There are three justifications for permitting class actions: efficiency, deterrence, and individual rights. Each of these arguments also raises counterarguments against this procedural device.

*Efficiency.* On the one hand, class actions permit the consolidation of what otherwise would be numerous smaller lawsuits so that courts can adjudicate them more efficiently, clear their dockets, and avoid duplicative motion practice. In doing so, class actions enable litigation, perhaps encouraging cases that would not otherwise be brought. How so? Class actions solve a collective action problem in situations where individuals have legal rights but the recovery is too small to merit a lawsuit. Because class actions aggregate claims and lawyers often receive a percentage of the total recovery, lawyers working on a contingency fee are able to leverage the class action device to garner very substantial fee awards, often in the millions of dollars. Class actions are lucrative for lawyers, and this encourages lawyers to sue. In the scholarly literature, these lawyers are sometimes referred to as "bounty hunters" and other times as "private attorneys general." *See* William B. Rubenstein, *On What a "Private Attorney General" Is—And Why It Matters*, 57 Vand. L. Rev. 2129 (2004). The benefit of this arrangement is that it encourages lawyers to sue (sometimes called "entrepreneurial litigation"). The criticism is similar: it encourages lawyers to bring risky or even meritless lawsuits on the chance that they can obtain a big payoff. For an article analyzing these issues that is as relevant as when it was written, see John C. Coffee, Jr., *The Regulation of Entrepreneurial Litigation: Balancing Fairness and Efficiency in the Large Class Action*, 54 U. Chi. L. Rev. 877 (1987).

*Deterrence.* A closely related argument in favor of class actions is that this procedural device allows plaintiffs to hold defendants responsible for their misconduct. Where individual claims are very small, plaintiffs are unlikely to sue. This means that a large entity would be able to violate the rights of numerous plaintiffs only a little and get away with it. For example, imagine a financial services company overcharges its customers by $1. It would be a rare person who would sue for that dollar. But if the company has overcharged 5 million consumers, there is a potential class action lawsuit worth $5 million, which is a suit worth bringing. Many are concerned that class actions overdeter by encouraging litigation, sometimes without a good basis or on "technical" violations of the law that should not be pursued. Because defendants would rather pay a settlement with large fees to the lawyers than risk litigating a class action and face substantial damages at trial, the concern is that defendants will settle even meritless lawsuits. Although it is widely accepted that most class actions that are certified settle, there are no good empirical studies documenting settlement rates or the quality of settlements. There is some evidence that many of the plaintiffs filing complaints with class allegations never seek certification, and that actual certifications are rare, but the empirical data is limited. The best study is now dated. Deborah Hensler, et al., *Class Action Dilemmas: Pursuing Public Goals for Private Gain* (Rand Institute for Civil Justice, 2000).

*Individual Rights.* You have seen how complicated and expensive pretrial practice, and especially discovery, can be. An ordinary person may not have sufficient funds to pay for such a lawsuit, and it would be unreasonable for that person to bring a lawsuit if the ultimate damages are less than the cost of litigating. Class actions, by aggregating small claims, make it worthwhile for lawyers to represent the class on a contingency basis, enabling individual class members to vindicate rights in a group setting that they could never do alone. At the same time, most commentators agree that class actions are really cases run by lawyers. Class members are largely absent from the litigation. Their rights of participation are limited to the right to opt out or to object at a fairness hearing late in the game. Because participation in them is limited, class actions can also be said to trample on individual rights. Some believe that class actions give lawyers the opportunity to extract rent from the class by settling for high attorneys' fees and lower compensation for class members. To the extent that this happens, as a practical matter it limits litigants' rights. Finally, there is an argument that class actions infringe on defendants' rights by encouraging "blackmail" litigation. This means that the defendant experiences pressure to settle not because the suit has merit, but instead because the defendant calculates that even a very small risk of losing a nonmeritorious suit is too great when the potential loss is very large. For an evaluation of the arguments in favor of and against the idea that class actions force defendants to settle, see Charles M. Silver, *"We're Scared to Death": Class Certification and Blackmail*, 78 N.Y.U. L. Rev. 1357 (2003).

The next section explores the due process foundations of the class action. In addressing the due process issues, courts have largely been concerned with the implications of the class action for plaintiffs' individual rights. As you read the cases presented, consider how the various policy arguments in favor of and against class treatment play out.

## C. DUE PROCESS FOUNDATIONS

In 1938 when the Federal Rules were adopted, the class action was a very seldom used procedural device that originated in English equity practice. *See* Stephen P. Yeazell, *From Medieval Group Litigation to the Modern Class Action* (1987). Today the class action rule is invoked much more often, although class actions still make up a tiny percentage of the federal docket. This change is due to the revision of the class action rule in 1966, which gave us the very useful and often reviled rule that we know today. The first problem posed by class action is the idea of representation—what does it mean for one person to "represent" the interests of another? This is a problem in political life as well as group litigation. The first case you will read, *Hansberry v. Lee*, addresses this question. We begin with some history behind the case.

### 1. Adequacy of Representation

### ■ ALLEN R. KAMP, THE HISTORY BEHIND *HANSBERRY v. LEE*
*20 U.C. Davis L. Rev. 481 (1987)*

#### INTRODUCTION

This Article, investigating *Hansberry v. Lee*'s factual background, grew out of a student's comment after a civil procedure class. In teaching class actions, *Hansberry* is a classic, usually the first case in the class action section of civil procedure textbooks. My class session went according to plan. I initially explained racially restrictive covenants and their validity until *Shelley v. Kraemer* in 1948, and then began a Socratic examination of *Hansberry*. The case sought to enforce a racially restrictive covenant and the covenant's validity turned on the result of a prior case. The question then becomes whether Hansberry is bound by the prior case, *Burke v. Kleiman*, which was a class action. The Court held he was not bound because the class was composed of members with conflicting goals:

> It is quite another to hold that all those who are free alternatively either to assert rights or to challenge them are of a single class, so that any group, merely because it is of the class so constituted, may be deemed adequately to represent any others of the class in litigating their interests in either alternative.

Then the students realized that (a) it is constitutional to have a class action that binds the class members to the class judgment; (b) whether the prior class action binds the class members may be decided collaterally in a subsequent lawsuit; and (c) without "adequate representation" the class members are not bound. I discussed Rule 23's requirements of "adequate representation" and "typicality." Afterward, I upset the students' complacency by asking how much consistency between class members' views is required: what if some members in a prison suit are masochists and like cruel and unusual punishment? What if, in a school desegregation suit, some students do not want to be bussed? I discussed questions of opt-out rights and social policy concerning the advisability of representative lawsuits in general and class actions in particular, and then wrapped up.

This analysis of *Hansberry* was upset by one of my students, Mr. C. O. Travis, who, while working as a garbageman, was attending John Marshall Law School at night. "Professor, did you know that Hansberry in *Hansberry v. Lee* was Lorraine Hansberry's father and that *A Raisin in the Sun* was based on her family's experience?" Lorraine Hansberry had attended Mr. Travis' high school in Chicago. I did not know, and at first did not believe it. Some investigation, however, revealed that Mr. Travis was right. What was the history of the Hansberry family? The answer involves black, Chicago, and legal history, leads to a re-examination of the *Hansberry* case, and provides insights into the judicial process.

## THE BACKGROUND OF THE *HANSBERRY* CASE

The conflict in *Hansberry*, caused by the Hansberrys' move into an all-white neighborhood, derived from Chicago's increasing black population. Between 1900 and 1934, the city's black population grew from 30,000 to 236,000. During this time, however, blacks were continuously more segregated. In 1910, 25% of blacks lived in areas of under 5% black population. None lived in areas of over 90% concentration. By 1934, less than 5% lived in areas of under 5% concentration, while 65% lived in areas that were 90% or more black. Geographically, blacks were concentrated in two narrow corridors stretching westward and southward from downtown Chicago.

This segregation was accomplished in two ways: violence and the racially restrictive covenant. After the violence of the 1910's and 1920's subsided, racially restrictive covenants were developed. "Around these black zones, an organized endeavor was put in place to subject the property to racially restrictive covenants. Although prior to the '20's, several individual owners and developers had placed race restrictions on their deeds, covenants covering entire neighborhoods were uncommon in Chicago." Such covenants were legal—in 1926, the Supreme Court dismissed for want of jurisdiction a case upholding a racially restrictive covenant in *Corrigan v. Buckley*.

After the *Corrigan* decision, the Chicago Real Estate Board started a program to cover neighborhoods with the covenants. They prepared a model covenant. (The *Hansberry* covenant was based on this model.) Then the Board sent out speakers and organizers across the city to get the covenants adopted. Organizing a neighborhood to adopt a covenant was a massive task. Legal descriptions and signatures had to be obtained, and then the covenants had to be filed with the Recorder of Deeds. Notary publics were hired to notarize and then record signatures. Subsequently, if any black persons moved into the area, they were reported, a suit filed against their occupancy, and an injunction obtained. By the late 1920's, black neighborhoods were hemmed in on all sides by the racial covenants. Up to 85 percent of Chicago was covered by such covenants.

The racially restrictive covenants legally prevented occupancy by blacks. They bound the signer and subsequent purchasers, showing up as an "objection" in any title search. Courts would routinely enforce the covenants, ordering vacation of the premises on pain of contempt. . . .

The covenant was useful only if most of the owners had signed it. Thus, a covenant's effectiveness required that a certain percentage of owners participate. Thus, the issue in dispute in *Hansberry*—actual percentage of the signatures in the affected area—was a key requirement:

> This agreement and the restrictions herein contained shall be of no force or effect unless this agreement or a substantially similar agreement, shall be signed by the owners above enumerated of ninety-five per cent of the frontage above described, or their heirs or assigns, and recorded in the office of the Recorder of Deeds of Cook County, Illinois, on or before December 31, 1928.

The covenant challenged by the Hansberrys covered a subdivision known as "South Park" or "Washington Park." This area was a three by four block rectangle bounded on the north by Washington Park, on the east by Cottage Grove, on the south by 63rd Street, and on the west by South Park Avenue. A race track, torn down in 1908, formerly occupied the land. This area was populated by whites, but surrounded on the west and south by black areas.

In 1940, only three black families lived in the area. West of the subdivision, the population went from 10% to 100% nonwhite. To the south, 90 to 100% of the population was nonwhite.

To the east, however, were the white areas of Hyde Park and Woodlawn, where the nonwhite population was only .1 to 9.9%. The South Park subdivision, therefore, was seen as a barrier between the black community and Woodlawn.

In 1928, a group of white businessmen, the Woodlawn Property Owners Association, organized a covenant to cover the South Park neighborhood. The covenant had the support of outside real estate organizations, institutions, banks, and mortgage companies. Contradictory evidence exists about the participation of the University of Chicago, located in Hyde Park. A 1937 article stated that the university was trying to establish a "buffer state," and had contributed funds to the Woodlawn Property Owners Association. The University did not deny this. Robert Hutchins, then president of the university, stated: "However unsatisfactory they [the covenants] may be they are the only means at present available by which the members of the associations [neighborhood associations] can stabilize the conditions under which they desire to live."

The effective system of segregation created by the racially restrictive covenants began to break down in the 1930's. Two phenomena contributed to this breakdown: the growth of Chicago's black population and the

Depression. Together they produced an increased black demand for housing and a depressed market for white housing. Hansberry was able to buy his house because he was the only person who wanted it.

Chicago's black population grew in the first third of the twentieth century. In 1900, it was 30,000; in 1934, 236,000. At the same time, the process of continually increasing segregation restricted blacks to the ghetto. In 1910, 24% of the total black population lived in areas in which 95% of the people were white. In 1934, only 3% of the black population lived in such areas. In 1910, the highest concentration of blacks to the general population was between 60-69%; in 1934, 87% of blacks lived in areas that were over 70% black; 69% lived in areas that were 99% black. In 1937, it was estimated that there were 50,000 more black people than units available. Blacks had to pay 20 to 50% more than whites for comparable housing.

Contemporaneously, the Depression reduced the market for white housing. In the Washington Park subdivision, the population decreased by 13.8 percent between 1930 and 1934. In the 1930's, "there was no market among white people for property in the subdivision." The prior owner of the Hansberry home, Burke, had left the house vacant at the time he moved from the subdivision. Thus, most of those who wanted to rent or buy in white areas were blacks:

> The Supreme Court eventually ruled in favor of the blacks, but even before that ruling [*Hansberry*], other white property owners opened their buildings to blacks and extracted high rentals for accommodations which were unable to attract white tenants. Rather than suffer financial losses, they elected to violate existing covenants and fill their vacant units with blacks.

One of these owners was Burke, who was an officer in the Woodlawn Property Owners Association and whose wife, Olive Ida Burke, had successfully sued, in *Burke v. Kleiman*, to enforce the covenant. Burke afterwards "resigned his position and withdrew from the association with ill feelings, and stated several times that he would put negroes in every block of that property." In order to sell to the Hansberrys, Burke set up a dummy transaction in which Jay D. Crook bought the property to convey to the Hansberrys. In the suit to enforce the covenant against the Hansberrys, it was alleged that

> through fraudulent concealment on the part of the defendants James T. Burke and Harry A. Price, from the Bank [First National Bank of Englewood], of the fact that Hansberry was a negro and that the property was being purchased for him, a deed was produced from the bank to Jay D. Crook who, in fact, purchased for Hansberry.

Thus, Mr. Burke was one of the defendants in *Hansberry*, attacking the decree obtained in a prior suit by his wife, Olive.

The defendant, Carl A. Hansberry, was an active man who had had varied careers, including deputy United States Marshal, businessman, and unsuccessful Republican candidate for Congress. He distributed pamphlets on black civil rights under the name of "The Hansberry Foundation." His daughter Lorraine described him:

> My father was typical of a generation of Negroes who believed that the "American way" could successfully be made to work to democratize the United States. Thus, twenty-five years ago, he spent a small personal fortune, his considerable talents, and many years of his life fighting, in association with NAACP attorneys, Chicago's "restrictive covenants" in one of this nation's ugliest ghettoes.
>
> That fight also required that our family occupy the disputed property in a hellishly hostile "white neighborhood" in which literally howling mobs surrounded our house. . . . One of these missiles almost took the life of the then eight-year old signer of this letter. My memories of this "correct" way of fighting white supremacy in America include being spat at, cursed and pummeled in the daily trek to and from school. And I also remember my desperate and courageous mother, patrolling our household all night with a loaded German luger, doggedly guarding her four children, while my father fought the respectable part of the battle in the Washington court.
>
> The fact that my father and the NAACP "won" a Supreme Court decision, in a now famous case which bears his name in the law books, is—ironically—the sort of "progress" our satisfied friends allude to when they presume to deride the more radical means of struggle. The cost, in emotional turmoil, time and money, which contributed to my father's early death as a permanently embittered exile in a foreign country when he saw that after such sacrificial efforts the Negroes of Chicago were as ghetto-locked as ever, does not seem to figure in their calculations.

The sale generated the lawsuit to enforce the covenant and evict the Hansberrys, *Lee v. Hansberry*. The complaint alleged a conspiracy on the part of the defendants to destroy the agreement by selling or leasing property in the restricted area to Negroes. Plaintiffs were successful below, the court restraining Burke "from leasing or selling any real estate within the restricted area to negroes, or to white persons for the purpose of selling or leasing to negroes, restraining . . . the Supreme Liberty Life Insurance company from making any further loans on real estate in the restricted area to negroes or for occupancy by negroes; declaring the conveyance to Hansberry and wife void and ordering them to remove from the premises, and holding the restrictive agreement valid and in full force and effect."

The main arguments considered by the Illinois Supreme Court concerned the covenant's interpretation and validity under its own terms. No constitutional objection was considered.

The evidentiary basis of the rulings against the defendants below were not challenged except as to one Israel Katz. The court found that his statement that "he would sell his property to anybody, including negroes," was sufficient evidence to enjoin him from doing so.

The appellants argued that enjoining the mortgage company from making loans in the restricted area to Negroes or for Negro occupancy was improper, because mortgages were exempted from the restrictive agreement. The Illinois Supreme Court ruled that the language merely provided that violating the restrictive agreement was an insufficient reason to invalidate a mortgage. "It does not give mortgagees a license to conspire to destroy the agreement, as the evidence shows this insurance company was doing."

The main argument in the case revolved around the question whether the requisite number of owners had signed the agreement. The agreement was to be "of no force or effect" unless signed by owners of 95 percent of the area's frontage. The plaintiffs in *Lee* argued that this question was *res judicata*, determined by the prior case of *Burke*. The trial court in *Hansberry* found that actually only 54 percent had signed the agreement, but that the question was *res judicata*.

The complainant's contention was "that unless an injunction is granted, said neighborhood will become mixed, both white and colored with its attendant evils." In *Burke*, the defense was that conditions had so changed in the area that enforcing the decree would be inequitable. Certain facts were stipulated, including that more than the required 95 percent of frontage owners had signed the covenants. The court in *Burke* found that the neighborhood had not changed materially and affirmed the decree, summarily rejecting the constitutional argument.

The Illinois Supreme Court, in *Lee v. Hansberry*, found that *Burke* "was a class or representative suit." Thus, "other members of the class are bound by the results in the case unless it is reversed or set aside on direct proceedings." That the finding was stipulated did not render the decree any less binding. The court found no evidence of fraud or collusion in procuring the stipulation. Thus the questions of execution and validity were *res judicata*, and *res judicata* extends to all matters that might have been raised. The covenant's validity could not be relitigated and the decree evicting the Hansberrys was affirmed.

Hansberry petitioned for *certiorari* to the Supreme Court. His lawyers hoped to have racially restrictive covenants declared unconstitutional. Their main arguments, however, went to the propriety of the class action—only their last argument went to the purported constitutional violation. . . .

## ■ HANSBERRY v. LEE
### *311 U.S. 32 (1940)*

Justice STONE delivered the opinion of the Court:

The question is whether the Supreme Court of Illinois, by its adjudication that petitioners in this case are bound by a judgment rendered in an earlier litigation to which they were not parties, has deprived them of the due process of law guaranteed by the Fourteenth Amendment.

Respondents brought this suit in the Circuit Court of Cook County, Illinois, to enjoin the breach by petitioners of an agreement restricting the use of land within a described area of the City of Chicago, which was alleged to have been entered into by some five hundred of the land owners. The agreement stipulated that for a specified period no part of the land should be "sold, leased to or permitted to be occupied by any person of the colored race," and provided that it should not be effective unless signed by the "owners of 95 per centum of the frontage" within the described area. The bill of complaint set up that the owners of 95 per cent of the frontage had signed; that respondents are owners of land within the restricted area who have either signed the agreement or acquired their land from others who did sign and that petitioners Hansberry, who are Negroes, have, with the alleged aid of the other petitioners and with knowledge of the agreement, acquired and are occupying land in the restricted area formerly belonging to an owner who had signed the agreement.

To the defense that the agreement had never become effective because owners of 95 per cent of the frontage had not signed it, respondents pleaded that that issue was *res judicata* by the decree in an earlier suit. *Burke v. Kleiman*, 277 Ill. App. 519. To this petitioners pleaded, by way of rejoinder, that they were not parties to that suit or bound by its decree, and that denial of their right to litigate, in the present suit, the issue of performance of the condition precedent to the validity of the agreement would be a denial of due process of law guaranteed by the Fourteenth Amendment. It does not appear, nor is it contended that any of petitioners is the successor in interest to or in privity with any of the parties in the earlier suit.

The circuit court, after a trial on the merits, found that owners of only about 54 per cent of the frontage had signed the agreement, and that the only support of the judgment in the *Burke* case was a false and fraudulent stipulation of the parties that 95 per cent had signed. But it ruled that the issue of performance of the condition precedent to the validity of the agreement was *res judicata* as alleged and entered a decree for respondents. The Supreme Court of Illinois affirmed. We granted certiorari to resolve the constitutional question. . . .

It is a principle of general application in Anglo-American jurisprudence that one is not bound by a judgment in personam in a litigation in which he is not designated as a party or to which he has not been made a party by service of process. *Pennoyer v. Neff*, 95 U.S. 714; 1 *Freeman on Judgments*, 5th Ed., § 407. A judgment rendered in such circumstances is not entitled to the full faith and credit which the Constitution and statute of the United States, R.S. § 905, 28 U.S.C. § 687, 28 U.S.C.A. § 687, prescribe, *Pennoyer v. Neff, supra*; *Lafayette Ins. Co. v. French*, 18 How. 404, 15 L. Ed. 451; *Hall v. Lanning*, 91 U.S. 160; *Baker v. Baker, E. & Co.*, 242 U.S. 394, and judicial action enforcing it against the person or property of the absent party is not that due process which the Fifth and Fourteenth Amendments require. *Postal Telegraph-Cable Co. v. Neport*, 247 U.S. 464; *Old Wayne Mut. L. Ass'n v. McDonough*, 204 U.S. 8.

To these general rules there is a recognized exception that, to an extent not precisely defined by judicial opinion, the judgment in a "class" or "representative" suit, to which some members of the class are parties, may bind members of the class or those represented who were not made parties to it.

The class suit was an invention of equity to enable it to proceed to a decree in suits where the number of those interested in the subject of the litigation is so great that their joinder as parties in conformity to the usual rules of procedure is impracticable. Courts are not infrequently called upon to proceed with causes in which the number of those interested in the litigation is so great as to make difficult or impossible the joinder of all because some are not within the jurisdiction or because their whereabouts is unknown or where if all were made parties to the suit its continued abatement by the death of some would prevent or unduly delay a decree. In such cases where the interests of those not joined are of the same class as the interests of those who are, and where it is considered that the latter fairly represent the former in the prosecution of the litigation of the issues in which all have a common interest, the court will proceed to a decree.

It is evident that the considerations which may induce a court thus to proceed, despite a technical defect of parties, may differ from those which must be taken into account in determining whether the absent parties are bound by the decree or, if it is adjudged that they are, in ascertaining whether such an adjudication satisfies the requirements of due process and of full faith and credit. Nevertheless there is scope within the framework of the Constitution for holding in appropriate cases that a judgment rendered in a class suit is *res judicata* as to members of the class who are not formal parties to the suit. Here, as elsewhere, the Fourteenth Amendment does not compel state courts or legislatures to adopt any particular rule for establishing the conclusiveness of judgments in class suits; nor does it compel the adoption of the particular rules thought by this court to be appropriate for the federal courts. With a proper regard for divergent local institutions and interests, *cf. Jackson County v. United States*, 308 U.S. 343, 351, this Court is justified in saying that there has been a failure of due process only in those cases where it cannot be said that the procedure adopted, fairly insures the protection of the interests of absent parties who are to be bound by it. *Chicago, B. & Q.R. Co. v. Chicago*, 166 U.S. 226, 235.

It is familiar doctrine of the federal courts that members of a class not present as parties to the litigation may be bound by the judgment where they are in fact adequately represented by parties who are present, or where they actually participate in the conduct of the litigation in which members of the class are present as parties, *Plumb v. Goodnow (Plumb v. Crane)*, 123 U.S. 560; *Confectioners' Machinery Co. v. Racine Engine & Mach. Co.*, 7 Cir., 163 F. 914; *Id.*, 7 Cir., 170 F. 1021; *Bryant El. Co. v. Marshall, C.C.*, 169 F. 426, or where the interest of the members of the class, some of whom are present as parties, is joint, or where for any other reason the relationship between the parties present and those who are absent is such as legally to entitle the former to stand in judgment for the latter. *Smith v. Swormstedt, supra*; *cf. Christopher v. Brusselback, supra*, 302 U.S. at pages 503, 504, and cases cited.

In all such cases, so far as it can be said that the members of the class who are present are, by generally recognized rules of law, entitled to stand in judgment for those who are not, we may assume for present purposes that such procedure affords a protection to the parties who are represented though absent, which would satisfy the requirements of due process and full faith and credit. Nor do we find it necessary for the decision of this case to say that, when the only circumstance defining the class is that the determination of the rights of its members turns upon a single issue of fact or law, a state could not constitutionally adopt a procedure whereby some of the members of the class could stand in judgment for all, provided that the procedure were so devised and applied as to insure that those present are of the same class as those absent and that the litigation is so conducted as to insure the full and fair consideration of the common issue. We decide only that the procedure and the course of litigation sustained here by the plea of *res judicata* do not satisfy these requirements.

The restrictive agreement did not purport to create a joint obligation or liability. If valid and effective its promises were the several obligations of the signers and those claiming under them. The promises ran severally to every other signer. It is plain that in such circumstances all those alleged to be bound by the agreement would not constitute a single class in any litigation brought to enforce it. Those who sought to secure its benefits by enforcing it could not be said to be in the same class with or represent those whose interest was in resisting performance, for the agreement by its terms imposes obligations and confers rights on the owner of each plot of land who signs it. If those who thus seek to secure the benefits of the agreement were rightly regarded by the state Supreme Court as constituting a class, it is evident that those signers or their successors who are interested in challenging the validity of the agreement and resisting its performance are not of the same class in the sense that their interests are identical so that any group who had elected to enforce rights conferred by the agreement could be said to be acting in the interest of any others who were free to deny its obligation.

Because of the dual and potentially conflicting interests of those who are putative parties to the agreement in compelling or resisting its performance, it is impossible to say, solely because they are parties to it, that any two of them are of the same class. Nor without more, and with the due regard for the protection of the rights of absent parties which due process exacts, can some be permitted to stand in judgment for all.

It is one thing to say that some members of a class may represent other members in a litigation where the sole and common interest of the class in the litigation is either to assert a common right or to challenge an asserted obligation. *Smith v. Swormstedt, supra; Supreme Tribe of Ben-Hur v. Cauble, supra; Groves v. Farmers State Bank*, 368 Ill. 35, 12 N.E.2d 618. It is quite another to hold that all those who are free alternatively either to assert rights or to challenge them are of a single class, so that any group merely because it is of the class so constituted, may be deemed adequately to represent any others of the class in litigating their interests in either alternative. Such a selection of representatives for purposes of litigation, whose substantial interests are not necessarily or even probably the same as those whom they are deemed to represent, does not afford that protection to absent parties which due process requires. The doctrine of representation of absent parties in a class suit has not hitherto been thought to go so far. Apart from the opportunities it would afford for the fraudulent and collusive sacrifice of the rights of absent parties, we think that the representation in this case no more satisfies the requirements of due process than a trial by a judicial officer who is in such situation that he may have an interest in the outcome of the litigation in conflict with that of the litigants.

The plaintiffs in the *Burke* case sought to compel performance of the agreement in behalf of themselves and all others similarly situated. They did not designate the defendants in the suit as a class or seek any injunction or other relief against others than the named defendants, and the decree which was entered did not purport to bind others. In seeking to enforce the agreement the plaintiffs in that suit were not representing the petitioners here whose substantial interest is in resisting performance. The defendants in the first suit were not treated by the pleadings or decree as representing others or as foreclosing by their defense the rights of others, and even though nominal defendants, it does not appear that their interest in defeating the contract outweighed their interest in establishing its validity. For a court in this situation to ascribe to either the plaintiffs or defendants the performance of such functions on behalf of petitioners here, is to attribute to them a power that it cannot be said that they had assumed to exercise, and a responsibility which, in view of their dual interests it does not appear that they could rightly discharge.

## Comments and Questions

1. Describe the two lawsuits at issue in *Hansberry*. Who sued whom? Who wanted to bind whom and on what theory? What precisely was the constitutional question? How would you describe the holding of *Hansberry*?

2. Hansberry was decided before Rule 23 was promulgated. What procedural rule applied to the *Hansberry* case? Where is it codified?

3. Note that in *Hansberry*, the plaintiffs sought to preclude Mr. Hansberry on the basis of a stipulation from the previous case. Would that stipulation be sufficient to bind parties under modern federal preclusion doctrine? Under *Hansberry*, at what point in a class action lawsuit may the class no longer challenge the adequacy of the named plaintiffs who purported to represent them?

4. Why does it ever make sense for a suit to bind people other than the named parties? How representative must the interests of the class representative be vis-à-vis the rest of the class? The classic suit for which Rule 23 was written in 1966 was the school desegregation action. Yet, as Professor Kamp queried, "What if, in a school desegregation suit, some students do not want to be bussed?" For a discussion of this problem in the integration context, see Derek A. Bell, Jr., *Serving Two Masters: Integration Ideals and Client Interest in School Desegregation Litigation*, 85 Yale L.J. 470 (1976). To consider this same question in the modern era, imagine that one gay couple wishes to file a class action on behalf of all similarly situated

persons arguing that a ban on gay marriage violates the equal protection clause of the state or federal constitutions. What potential conflicts might arise among that class of persons? *See* William B. Rubenstein, *Divided We Litigate: Addressing Disputes Among Group Members and Lawyers in Civil Rights Campaigns*, 106 Yale L.J. 1623 (1997).

## 2. Participation

The biggest change made by the rules drafters in 1966 was to add a new type of class action that had never been available before: the money damages class action. Rule 23(b)(3) permits courts to certify a class action for money damages when the plaintiffs meet the requirements of the class action rule, which are described in more detail later. As you read the next case, *Phillips Petroleum Co. v. Shutts*, consider the different procedural protections available as a matter of due process in the case of money damages class actions as compared with the class action in *Hansberry* (which was decided before the modern class action rule was written). In keeping with the theme of this chapter, this case offers you the opportunity to revisit the doctrine of personal jurisdiction in a new context. As you read, consider the following questions: Why does the Kansas court have personal jurisdiction over absent class members who have no connection with the state? How are plaintiffs and defendants similarly (or differently) situated in class and individual litigation? Do the due process standards articulated in *Hansberry* and *Shutts* differ, and if so, how? Do these cases, read together, indicate that different protections ought to be required to protect absent class members in injunctive as opposed to money damages class actions?

## ■ PHILLIPS PETROLEUM CO. v. SHUTTS
### 472 U.S. 797 (1985)

Justice REHNQUIST delivered the opinion of the Court.

Petitioner is a Delaware corporation which has its principal place of business in Oklahoma. During the 1970's it produced or purchased natural gas from leased land located in 11 different States, and sold most of the gas in interstate commerce. Respondents are some 28,000 of the royalty owners possessing rights to the leases from which petitioner produced the gas; they reside in all 50 States, the District of Columbia, and several foreign countries. Respondents brought a class action against petitioner in the Kansas state court, seeking to recover interest on royalty payments which had been delayed by petitioner. They recovered judgment in the trial court, and the Supreme Court of Kansas affirmed the judgment over petitioner's contentions that the Due Process Clause of the Fourteenth Amendment prevented Kansas from adjudicating the claims of all the respondents, and that the Due Process Clause and the Full Faith and Credit Clause of Article

IV of the Constitution prohibited the application of Kansas law to all of the transactions between petitioner and respondents. We reject petitioner's jurisdictional claim, but sustain its claim regarding the choice of law.

Because petitioner sold the gas to its customers in interstate commerce, it was required to secure approval for price increases from what was then the Federal Power Commission, and is now the Federal Energy Regulatory Commission. Under its regulations the Federal Power Commission permitted petitioner to propose and collect tentative higher gas prices, subject to final approval by the Commission. If the Commission eventually denied petitioner's proposed price increase or reduced the proposed increase, petitioner would have to refund to its customers the difference between the approved price and the higher price charged, plus interest at a rate set by statute. See 18 CFR § 154.102 (1984).

Although petitioner received higher gas prices pending review by the Commission, petitioner suspended any increase in royalties paid to the royalty owners because the higher price could be subject to recoupment by petitioner's customers. Petitioner agreed to pay the higher royalty only if the royalty owners would provide petitioner with a bond or indemnity for the increase, plus interest, in case the price increase was not ultimately approved and a refund was due to the customers. Petitioner set the interest rate on the indemnity agreements at the same interest rate the Commission would have required petitioner to refund to its customers. A small percentage of the royalty owners provided this indemnity and received royalties immediately from the interim price increases; these royalty owners are unimportant to this case.

The remaining royalty owners received no royalty on the unapproved portion of the prices until the Federal Power Commission approval of those prices became final. Royalties on the unapproved portion of the gas price were suspended three times by petitioner, corresponding to its three proposed price increases in the mid-1970's. In three written opinions the Commission approved all of petitioner's tentative price increases, so petitioner paid to its royalty owners the suspended royalties of $3.7 million in 1976, $4.7 million in 1977, and $2.9 million in 1978. Petitioner paid no interest to the royalty owners although it had the use of the suspended royalty money for a number of years.

Respondents Irl Shutts, Robert Anderson, and Betty Anderson filed suit against petitioner in Kansas state court, seeking interest payments on their suspended royalties which petitioner had possessed pending the Commission's approval of the price increases. Shutts is a resident of Kansas, and the Andersons live in Oklahoma. Shutts and the Andersons own gas leases in Oklahoma and Texas. Over petitioner's objection the Kansas trial court granted respondents' motion to certify the suit as a class action under Kansas law. The class as certified was comprised of 33,000 royalty owners who had royalties suspended by petitioner. The average claim of each royalty owner for interest on the suspended royalties was $100.

After the class was certified respondents provided each class member with notice through first-class mail. The notice described the action and informed each class member that he could appear in person or by counsel; otherwise each member would be represented by Shutts and the Andersons, the named plaintiffs. The notices also stated that class members would be included in the class and bound by the judgment unless they "opted out" of the lawsuit by executing and returning a "request for exclusion" that was included with the notice. The final class as certified contained 28,100 members; 3,400 had "opted out" of the class by returning the request for exclusion, and notice could not be delivered to another 1,500 members, who were also excluded. Less than 1,000 of the class members resided in Kansas. Only a minuscule amount, approximately one quarter of one percent, of the gas leases involved in the lawsuit were on Kansas land.

After petitioner's mandamus petition to decertify the class was denied, the case was tried to the court. The court found petitioner liable under Kansas law for interest on the suspended royalties to all class members. . . . The applicable interest rates were: 7% for royalties retained until October 1974; 9% for royalties retained between October 1974 and September 1979; and thereafter at the average prime rate. The trial court did not determine whether any difference existed between the laws of Kansas and other States, or whether another State's laws should be applied to non-Kansas plaintiffs or to royalties from leases in States other than Kansas.

Petitioner raised two principal claims in its appeal to the Supreme Court of Kansas. It first asserted that the Kansas trial court did not possess personal jurisdiction over absent plaintiff class members as required by *International Shoe Co. v. Washington*, 326 U.S. 310 (1945), and similar cases. Related to this first claim was petitioner's contention that the "opt-out" notice to absent class members, which forced them to return the request for exclusion in order to avoid the suit, was insufficient to bind class members who were not residents of Kansas or who did not possess "minimum contacts" with Kansas. Second, petitioner claimed that Kansas courts could not apply Kansas law to every claim in the dispute. The trial court should have looked to the laws of each State where the leases were located to determine, on the basis of conflict of laws principles, whether interest on the suspended royalties was recoverable, and at what rate.

The Supreme Court of Kansas held that the entire cause of action was maintainable under the Kansas class-action statute, and the court rejected both of petitioner's claims. 235 Kan. 195 (1984). . . .

## I

As a threshold matter we must determine whether petitioner has standing to assert the claim that Kansas did not possess proper jurisdiction over the many plaintiffs in the class who were not Kansas residents and had no connection to Kansas. Respondents claim that a party generally may assert only his own rights, and that petitioner has no standing to assert the rights of its adversary, the plaintiff class, in order to defeat the judgment in favor of the class.

Standing to sue in any Article III court is, of course, a federal question which does not depend on the party's prior standing in state court. . . . One of [the] prudential limits on [Article III] standing is that a litigant must normally assert his own legal interests rather than those of third parties.

Respondents claim that petitioner is barred by the rule requiring that a party assert only his own rights; they point out that respondents and petitioner are adversaries and do not have allied interests such that petitioner would be a good proponent of class members' interests. They further urge that petitioner's interference is unneeded because the class members have had opportunity to complain about Kansas' assertion of jurisdiction over their claim, but none have done so.

Respondents may be correct that petitioner does not possess standing jus tertii, but this is not the issue. Petitioner seeks to vindicate its own interests. As a class-action defendant petitioner is in a unique predicament. If Kansas does not possess jurisdiction over this plaintiff class, petitioner will be bound to 28,100 judgment holders scattered across the globe, but none of these will be bound by the Kansas decree. Petitioner could be subject to numerous later individual suits by these class members because a judgment issued without proper personal jurisdiction over an absent party is not entitled to full faith and credit elsewhere and thus has no res judicata effect as to that party. Whether it wins or loses on the merits, petitioner has a distinct and personal interest in seeing the entire plaintiff class bound by res judicata just as petitioner is bound. The only way a class action defendant like petitioner can assure itself of this binding effect of the judgment is to ascertain that the forum court has jurisdiction over every plaintiff whose claim it seeks to adjudicate, sufficient to support a defense of res judicata in a later suit for damages by class members.

While it is true that a court adjudicating a dispute may not be able to predetermine the res judicata effect of its own judgment, petitioner has alleged that it would be obviously and immediately injured if this class-action judgment against it became final without binding the plaintiff class. We think that such an injury is sufficient to give petitioner standing on its own right to raise the jurisdiction claim in this Court. . . .

## II

Reduced to its essentials, petitioner's argument is that unless out-of-state plaintiffs affirmatively consent, the Kansas courts may not exert jurisdiction over their claims. Petitioner claims that failure to execute and return the "request for exclusion" provided with the class notice cannot constitute consent of the out-of-state plaintiffs; thus Kansas courts may exercise jurisdiction over these plaintiffs only if the plaintiffs possess the sufficient "minimum contacts" with Kansas as that term is used in cases involving personal jurisdiction over out-of-state defendants. Since Kansas had no prelitigation contact with many of the plaintiffs and leases involved, petitioner claims that Kansas has exceeded its jurisdictional reach and thereby violated the due process rights of the absent plaintiffs.

In *International Shoe* we were faced with an out-of-state corporation which sought to avoid the exercise of personal jurisdiction over it as a defendant by a Washington state court. We held that the extent of the defendant's due process protection would depend "upon the quality and nature of the activity in relation to the fair and orderly administration of the laws. . . ." 326 U.S., at 319. We noted that the Due Process Clause did not permit a State to make a binding judgment against a person with whom the State had no contacts, ties, or relations. If the defendant possessed certain minimum contacts with the State, so that it was "reasonable and just, according to our traditional conception of fair play and substantial justice" for a State to exercise personal jurisdiction, the State could force the defendant to defend himself in the forum, upon pain of default, and could bind him to a judgment.

The purpose of this test, of course, is to protect a defendant from the travail of defending in a distant forum, unless the defendant's contacts with the forum make it just to force him to defend there. As we explained in [*World Wide Volkswagen v. Woodson*] the defendant's contacts should be such that "he should reasonably anticipate being haled" into the forum. 444 U.S., at 297.

Although the cases like *Shaffer* and *Woodson* which petitioner relies on for a minimum contacts requirement all dealt with out-of-state defendants or parties in the procedural posture of a defendant, petitioner claims that the same analysis must apply to absent class-action plaintiffs. In this regard petitioner correctly points out that a chose in action is a constitutionally recognized property interest possessed by each of the plaintiffs. *Mullane v. Central Hanover Bank & Trust Co.*, 339 U.S. 306 (1950). An adverse judgment by Kansas courts in this case may extinguish the chose in action forever through res judicata. Such an adverse judgment, petitioner claims, would be every bit as onerous to an absent plaintiff as an adverse judgment on the merits would be to a defendant. Thus, the same due process protections should apply to absent plaintiffs: Kansas should not be able to exert jurisdiction over the plaintiff's claims unless the plaintiffs have sufficient minimum contacts with Kansas.

We think petitioner's premise is in error. The burdens placed by a State upon an absent class-action plaintiff are not of the same order or magnitude as those it places upon an absent defendant. An out-of-state defendant summoned by a plaintiff is faced with the full powers of the forum State to render judgment against it. The defendant must generally hire counsel and travel to the forum to defend itself from the plaintiff's claim, or suffer a default judgment. The defendant may be forced to participate in extended and often costly discovery, and will be forced to respond in damages or to comply with some other form of remedy imposed by the court should it lose the suit. The defendant may also face liability for court costs and attorney's fees. These burdens are substantial, and the minimum contacts requirement of the Due Process Clause prevents the forum State from unfairly imposing them upon the defendant.

A class-action plaintiff, however, is in quite a different posture. The Court noted this difference in *Hansberry v. Lee*, 311 U.S. 32, 40-41 (1940), which explained that a "class" or "representative" suit was an exception to the rule that one could not be bound by judgment in personam unless one was made fully a party in the traditional sense. As the Court pointed out in *Hansberry*, the class action was an invention of equity to enable it to proceed to a decree in suits where the number of those interested in the litigation was too great to permit joinder. The absent parties would be bound by the decree so long as the named parties adequately represented the absent class and the prosecution of the litigation was within the common interest.

Modern plaintiff class actions follow the same goals, permitting litigation of a suit involving common questions when there are too many plaintiffs for proper joinder. Class actions also may permit the plaintiffs to pool claims which would be uneconomical to litigate individually. For example, this lawsuit involves claims averaging about $100 per plaintiff; most of the plaintiffs would have no realistic day in court if a class action were not available.

In sharp contrast to the predicament of a defendant haled into an out-of-state forum, the plaintiffs in this suit were not haled anywhere to defend themselves upon pain of a default judgment. As commentators have noted, from the plaintiffs' point of view a class action resembles a "quasi-administrative proceeding, conducted by the judge." 3B J. Moore & J. Kennedy, Moore's Federal Practice ¶ 23.45 (1984); Kaplan, *Continuing Work of the Civil Committee: 1966 Amendments to the Federal Rules of Civil Procedure* (I), 81 Harv. L. Rev. 356, 398 (1967).

A plaintiff class in Kansas and numerous other jurisdictions cannot first be certified unless the judge, with the aid of the named plaintiffs and defendant, conducts an inquiry into the common nature of the named plaintiffs' and the absent plaintiffs' claims, the adequacy of representation, the jurisdiction possessed over the class, and any other matters that will bear upon proper representation of the absent plaintiffs' interest. Unlike a defendant in a civil suit, a class-action plaintiff is not required to fend for himself. The court and named plaintiffs protect his interests. Indeed, the class-action defendant itself has a great interest in ensuring that the absent plaintiff's claims are properly before the forum. In this case, for example, the defendant sought to avoid class certification by alleging that the absent plaintiffs would not be adequately represented and were not amenable to jurisdiction.

The concern of the typical class-action rules for the absent plaintiffs is manifested in other ways. Most jurisdictions, including Kansas, require that a class action, once certified, may not be dismissed or compromised without the approval of the court. In many jurisdictions such as Kansas the court may amend the pleadings to ensure that all sections of the class are represented adequately.

Besides this continuing solicitude for their rights, absent plaintiff class members are not subject to other burdens imposed upon defendants. They need not hire counsel or appear. They are almost never subject to counterclaims or cross-claims, or liability for fees or costs. Absent plaintiff class members are not subject to coercive or punitive remedies. Nor will an adverse judgment typically bind an absent plaintiff for any damages, although a valid adverse judgment may extinguish any of the plaintiff's claims which were litigated.

Unlike a defendant in a normal civil suit, an absent class-action plaintiff is not required to do anything. He may sit back and allow the litigation to run its course, content in knowing that there are safeguards provided for his protection. In most class actions an absent plaintiff is provided at least with an opportunity to "opt out" of the class, and if he takes advantage of that opportunity he is removed from the litigation entirely. This was true of the Kansas proceedings in this case. The Kansas procedure provided for the mailing of a notice to each class member by first-class mail. The notice, as we have previously indicated, described the action and informed the class member that he could appear in person or by counsel, in default of which he would be represented by the named plaintiffs and their attorneys. The notice further stated that class members would be included in the class and bound by the judgment unless they "opted out" by executing and returning a "request for exclusion" that was included in the notice.

Petitioner contends, however, that the "opt out" procedure provided by Kansas is not good enough, and that an "opt in" procedure is required to satisfy the Due Process Clause of the Fourteenth Amendment. Insofar as plaintiffs who have no minimum contacts with the forum State are concerned, an "opt in" provision would require that each class member affirmatively consent to his inclusion within the class.

Because States place fewer burdens upon absent class plaintiffs than they do upon absent defendants in nonclass suits, the Due Process Clause need not and does not afford the former as much protection from state-court jurisdiction as it does the latter. The Fourteenth Amendment does protect "persons," not "defendants," however, so absent plaintiffs as well as absent defendants are entitled to some protection from the jurisdiction of a forum State which seeks to adjudicate their claims. In this case we hold that a forum State may exercise jurisdiction over the claim of an absent class-action plaintiff, even though that plaintiff may not possess the minimum contacts with the forum which would support personal jurisdiction over a defendant. If the forum State wishes to bind an absent plaintiff concerning a claim for money damages or similar relief at law,[3] it must provide minimal procedural due process protection. The plaintiff must receive notice plus an opportunity to be heard and participate in the litigation, whether in person or through counsel. The notice must be the best practicable, "reasonably calculated, under all the circumstances, to apprise interested parties of the pendency of the action and afford them an opportunity to present their objections." *Mullane*, 339 U.S., at 314-315, we hold that due process requires at a minimum that an absent

---

3. Our holding today is limited to those class actions which seek to bind known plaintiffs concerning claims wholly or predominately for money judgments. We intimate no view concerning other types of class actions, such as those seeking equitable relief. Nor, of course, does our discussion of personal jurisdiction address class actions where the jurisdiction is asserted against a defendant class.

plaintiff be provided with an opportunity to remove himself from the class by executing and returning an "opt out" or "request for exclusion" form to the court. Finally, the Due Process Clause of course requires that the named plaintiff at all times adequately represent the interests of the absent class members. *Hansberry*, 311 U.S., at 42-43, 45.

We reject petitioner's contention that the Due Process Clause of the Fourteenth Amendment requires that absent plaintiffs affirmatively "opt in" to the class, rather than be deemed members of the class if they do not "opt out." We think that such a contention is supported by little, if any precedent, and that it ignores the differences between class-action plaintiffs, on the one hand, and defendants in nonclass civil suits on the other. Any plaintiff may consent to jurisdiction. The essential question, then, is how stringent the requirement for a showing of consent will be.

We think that the procedure followed by Kansas, where a fully descriptive notice is sent first-class mail to each class member, with an explanation of the right to "opt out," satisfies due process. Requiring a plaintiff to affirmatively request inclusion would probably impede the prosecution of those class actions involving an aggregation of small individual claims, where a large number of claims are required to make it economical to bring suit. The plaintiff's claim may be so small, or the plaintiff so unfamiliar with the law, that he would not file suit individually, nor would he affirmatively request inclusion in the class if such a request were required by the Constitution. If, on the other hand, the plaintiff's claim is sufficiently large or important that he wishes to litigate it on his own, he will likely have retained an attorney or have thought about filing suit, and should be fully capable of exercising his right to "opt out."

In this case over 3,400 members of the potential class did "opt out," which belies the contention that "opt out" procedures result in guaranteed jurisdiction by inertia. Another 1,500 were excluded because the notice and "opt out" form was undeliverable. We think that such results show that the "opt out" procedure provided by Kansas is by no means pro forma, and that the Constitution does not require more to protect what must be the somewhat rare species of class member who is unwilling to execute an "opt out" form, but whose claim is nonetheless so important that he cannot be presumed to consent to being a member of the class by his failure to do so. . . .

We therefore hold that the protection afforded the plaintiff class members by the Kansas statute satisfies the Due Process Clause. The interests of the absent plaintiffs are sufficiently protected by the forum State when those plaintiffs are provided with a request for exclusion that can be returned within a reasonable time to the court. Both the Kansas trial court and the Supreme Court of Kansas held that the class received adequate representation, and no party disputes that conclusion here. We conclude that the Kansas court properly asserted personal jurisdiction over the absent plaintiffs and their claims against petitioner . . . .

We therefore affirm the judgment of the Supreme Court of Kansas insofar as it upheld the jurisdiction of the Kansas courts over the plaintiff class members in this case, and reverse its judgment insofar as it held that Kansas law was applicable to all of the transactions which it sought to adjudicate. We remand the case to that court for further proceedings not inconsistent with this opinion.

It is so ordered.

## Comments and Questions

1. Why is the *defendant* asserting the plaintiff class members' due process right not to be dragged into Kansas Court? A careful reading of the Court's rationale for permitting defendant to make the personal jurisdiction argument underscores the reasons that class certification is so important. Can you explain why certification is such an important motion for defendants? What are the effects on the defendant if a class is certified?

2. The Court explains in footnote 3 that the holding in *Shutts* that class members must be given the opportunity to opt out is limited to money damages class actions. In injunctive class actions, the court is not required to provide an opportunity for plaintiffs to opt out. Can you think of a policy rationale for the difference? Should plaintiffs be given an opportunity to opt out in injunctive class actions as well? You will want to revisit these questions after reading *Wal-Mart v. Dukes*, reproduced later in this chapter, in which the Court held (unanimously) that plaintiffs bringing injunctive class actions cannot seek back pay (a form of money damages) without certifying a money damages class action, with the greater protections it provides to class members.

3. What type of notice was afforded the class members in *Shutts*? Class action notices are notoriously unfriendly documents and difficult to decipher. You can see models for such notices on the Federal Judicial Center Web site: *www.fjc.gov*. When class notices are difficult to understand and claims forms difficult to fill out, response rates in class actions will predictably be lower than if notices and claims forms were more user friendly. There is little data on claiming rates in class actions because courts rarely require the parties to provide this information. The exception is coupon settlements. A coupon settlement is one in which class members receive the opportunity to purchase a product at a discounted price instead of cash. The Class Action Fairness Act of 2005 (CAFA) requires that in settlements offering coupons to class members, the attorneys' fees are to be calculated based on the coupons actually redeemed. 28 U.S.C. § 1712. This provision, combined with the increased scrutiny of coupon settlements mandated by CAFA, appears to have reduced the number of coupon settlements in the federal courts.

4. The Court in *Shutts* also notes that 1,500 persons were excluded from the class action because their notices and opt-out forms were undeliverable. Does due process require that the notice be actually delivered in order to be adequate under *Mullane*? Today, undelivered notices are usually not considered by courts to require exclusion of those class members. Should they?

5. The second question presented in *Shutts* and not excerpted here concerned what substantive law ought to apply to that class action. In that

case, the majority of the class members were citizens of five states: Texas, Oklahoma, Louisiana, New Mexico, and Wyoming. Which state's law should apply is a horizontal choice of law question. Originally the Kansas courts had applied Kansas law to all the gas leases. The Supreme Court struck down this holding on due process and full faith and credit grounds and explained that "for a State's substantive law to be selected in a constitutionally permissible manner, that State must have a significant contact or significant aggregation of contacts, creating state interests, such that choice of its law is neither arbitrary nor fundamentally unfair." *Shutts*, 472 U.S. at 818 (quoting *Allstate Ins. Co. v. Hague*, 449 U.S. 302 (1981)). The Court remanded to the Kansas Supreme Court. The Kansas Court subsequently analyzed the law of the relevant states and held that it was substantively the same as Kansas law. *Shutts v. Phillips Petroleum Co.*, 240 Kan. 764 (1987).

6. In federal court, one of the biggest impediments to certifying national class actions has been the differing substantive laws of the various states. This problem has become more pronounced since the passage of CAFA, which effectively federalized most class actions and is discussed later in this chapter. *See* Linda Silberman, *The Role of Choice of Law in National Class Actions*, 156 U. Pa. L. Rev. 2001 (2008). Strictly speaking, this is not a choice of law problem, but rather a question of whether, under Rule 23, the class members from different states share enough in common to justify collective treatment. One proposed solution to this problem is to apply the law of the home state of the defendant to all the class members regardless of their home state. *See* Samuel Issacharoff, *Settled Expectations in a World of Unsettled Law: Choice of Law After the Class Action Fairness Act*, 106 Colum. L. Rev. 1839 (2006). How does this proposal square with the rationale of the *Erie* doctrine developed in Chapter 9?

## D. THE CLASS ACTION RULE

In addition to the constitutional requirements imposed by the due process clause, class actions are governed by Federal Rule of Civil Procedure 23. Although the rule has been revised several times since its promulgation, the basic structure of the rule has remained the same. Many state class action rules mirror Rule 23, although judicial interpretations of these rules differ. Other states have more liberal or more restrictive class action rules. New York's rule, addressed in *Shady Grove v. Allstate* (reproduced in Chapter 9), featured the New York state class action rule, which prohibits class actions in particular categories of cases.

### 1. The Contours of the Federal Rule

The first thing a plaintiff who wishes to bring a class action must do is define the class. Who is going to be included and who is not? The class definition will determine who is bound by the adjudication if the class is certified and is antecedent to the application of the remaining requirements of the rule.

The plaintiff must also meet four requirements, set forth in Rule 23(a): (1) numerosity, (2) commonality, (3) typicality, and (4) adequacy of representation. First, he must demonstrate that the class is sufficiently numerous that joinder of all the plaintiffs is impracticable. Second, he must show that there are issues of law and fact in common for all class members. Third, the representative must be typical of the other class members such that he shared interests with them. Fourth and finally, the class representative must show that he can adequately represent the class. These requirements apply regardless of the type of class action plaintiff seeks. Consider how these requirements overlap. For example, can a nontypical plaintiff be an adequate representative? If the class representative is "typical" of the class, does this not imply that the class members have something in common (otherwise, what would his typicality mean)?

The class action rule provides for three different types of class actions, divided by the types of remedies plaintiffs seek. The first type is class actions where the defendant may be subject to incompatible legal standards or there is a limited fund from which plaintiffs seek recovery. Fed. R. Civ. P. 23(b)(1). This is the least common type of class action. The second type of class action is an action where plaintiffs are seeking an injunction. Fed. R. Civ. P. 23(b)(2). This type of class action is often brought in the civil rights context, although not exclusively. The third type is available where plaintiffs are seeking money damages. Fed. R. Civ. P. 23(b)(3). Money damages class actions are the most common type of class action and the most controversial.

Different protections apply to the different types of class actions. Class actions brought under Rule 23(b)(1) and (2)—incompatible standards, limited fund, and injunctive class actions—are *mandatory*. This means that there is no requirement that plaintiffs receive notice or be permitted to opt out of the class action suit. By contrast, when class actions are brought under Rule 23(b)(3) seeking money damages, the class representative must provide notice to the class members of the pending suit and class members must be allowed to opt out. The Supreme Court has held that the plaintiff bears the cost of notice. *Eisen v. Carlisle & Jacquelin*, 417 U.S. 156 (1974). What do you think this means for the financing of class action litigation and the incentives to settle these cases?

Each of these types of class actions is treated differently in terms of due process requirements and the requirements of the rule. For example, (b)(1) and (b)(2) do not permit class members to opt out of the litigation. This limitation appears to have been ratified by the Supreme Court in *Shutts*. Furthermore, in (b)(3) class actions plaintiffs must meet all the requirements of the rule (numerosity, commonality, typicality, and adequacy of representation) plus a number of other requirements. These additional requirements are referred to as "predominance" and "superiority." For example, plaintiffs seeking to certify a money damages class action must show both that the common issues of law and fact *predominate* over any individual issues and that the class action is *superior* to individual litigation. The rule requires courts to consider the following factors when evaluating money damages class actions: (1) the particular interests of the class members to control their own lawsuits; (2) the (prior) commencement of other relevant lawsuits; (3) the desirability of concentrating the litigation into a single forum; and (4) the manageability of the class. In a case such as *Shutts*, where the absent class members are from different states and the claims arise under state law, common issues may not predominate over individual ones if state laws differ from another. Can a class member from California be governed by the same law as a class member from Kansas? The Kansas Supreme Court ruled that they could under Kansas choice of law, but the Supreme Court has not decided this question. Most federal courts refuse to certify class actions when different state laws are implicated because class members are too different from one another. In the same vein, consider whether a court would certify a discrimination class action like that in the *City of Cleveland* case seeking compensatory damages (including emotional distress) which are available under Title VII. What would the defendant in such a case argue to avoid class certification under 23(b)(3)?

As you think about the additional requirements for money damages class actions, consider how they relate to the policy issues described here. What is the impetus for putting additional requirements on money damages class actions? Commentators and the rules drafters have expressed concern that there will be unresolvable conflicts of interest between class members in money damages suits. Should we be worried about the same conflicts of interest in injunctive actions, and if not, why not?

The class action rule also contains a series of provisions that mandate more procedures than those required for ordinary binary litigation to go forward. Consider these differences and what policy considerations justify them:

### 1. *Settlement Approval*

Rule 23(e) requires that before a class action is settled the parties receive court approval. By contrast, the decision to settle is determined by the parties in binary litigation. In a class action, the court must hold a hearing and determine whether the settlement is fair, reasonable, and adequate. If so, the court may approve the settlement.

### 2. *Interlocutory Appeal*

Rule 23(f) permits the losing party to appeal a certification decision prior to a final judgment (called an "interlocutory appeal"). This reflects the rulemakers' understanding of the importance of the certification decision. Interlocutory appeals are very rare in litigation; ordinarily one needs a final judgment in order to appeal. Why are they available in class actions? This is largely because of arguments by defendants that the certification decision *determines* the litigation. If a class action is certified, then the value of the lawsuit, as compared with an individual suit, is very great. This means that the risk of loss for the defendant is also very great.

For example, imagine that there are 1,000 plaintiffs each with a claim worth $500. Compare the effect on a defendant of a series of $500 suits or one class action suit where plaintiffs may recover $500 million if they win. First, not all the eligible plaintiffs are likely to bring their $500 suit, so even if he loses every case the defendant is not likely to be required to pay the full amount of damages that a class action might require. Second, in a series of individual lawsuits, the defendant may win some and lose some. The class action, by contrast, is an all-or-nothing proposition. Either the defendant loses and is liable for the entire amount or the defendant wins and is liable for nothing. Whether the risk of loss should be calculated differently in serial litigation as compared to a one-shot class suit is a question of probability theory that has important real-world implications for defendants. Defendants who are risk averse, risk neutral, or risk seeking will react differently to these probabilities.

### 3. *Appointing the Class Counsel*

Rule 23(g) requires that the *lawyer* demonstrate that he can adequately represent the class. This is largely because the class action is a lawyer-run litigation. Some people even go so far as to call it "entrepreneurial litigation." Lawyers often pick the class representatives, define the parameters of the class, and make all the decisions for the class members. This state of affairs is contrasted with binary litigation, where the lawyer (at least in theory) follows the directions of his client. Who is the client in the class action? Is it the class representative? Or is it the group of disbursed individuals who make up the class?

Plaintiff-side class action lawyers have been the subject of a great deal of criticism and many of the proposals for revising Rule 23 are driven by concerns over their conduct. This is largely because there is a lot of money to be made by lawyers in class suits. The lawyer's entrepreneurial role in class litigation creates an "agent-principal problem." This concept refers to the idea that the lawyer may have interests that are not aligned with those of his client, the class. For example, it may be in the lawyer's interest to obtain a fee by quickly settling a case when a more protracted litigation would provide greater compensation to class members. A lot of scholarship has been devoted to solving the agent-principal problem in class actions. *See, e.g.*, Bruce L. Hay and David Rosenberg, *'Sweetheart' and 'Blackmail' Settlements in Class Actions: Reality and Remedy*, 75 Notre Dame L. Rev. 1377 (2000).

### 4. *Attorneys' Fees*

Rule 23(h) requires the attorneys to make a motion for fees and the court to determine what amount would be fair to award the attorneys for their work on the case. This provision is driven by the concern that class counsel would take advantage of the class if the lawyers were allowed to set their own fees.

There are two methods for calculating attorneys' fees in class actions. First, fees can be calculated on a percentage basis. The court may award a percentage of the fund that is to be awarded to class members rather than the (often much smaller) amount that is actually collected by class members at the end of the day. CAFA also set limits on attorneys' fees in certain situations such as when the class's recovery comes in the form of coupons rather than cash payments. A review of district and appellate opinions reveals that coupon settlements have become rarer in the federal courts since the passage of CAFA.

Second, fees can be calculated on a loadstar basis, that is, based on the number of hours the attorneys worked multiplied by an hourly rate. Courts may also add a "multiplier" when they calculate fees based on a loadstar method; multipliers increase the fees to reflect the risk that the attorneys took in pursuing the litigation. A recent study found that the mean and median fee awards in class actions are around 25 percent of the settlement fund. *See* Brian Fitzpatrick, *An Empirical Study of Class Action Settlements and Their Fee Awards*, 7 J. of Emp. Legal Stud. 811 (2010).

## 2. The Rule in Application

The case brought by Betty Dukes and several other plaintiffs on behalf of all women employed by Wal-Mart garnered an extraordinary amount of publicity, even for a class action. *See* Liza Featherstone, *Selling Women Short: The Landmark Battle for Workers' Rights at Wal-Mart* (2005). This class action, which included from 500,000 to 3 million women (depending on who was doing the counting), projected the concerns about litigation generally and class actions in particular on a very big screen: the nation's largest private employer. The size of the class action, and the plaintiffs' untested theory of liability, made the case extraordinary. Yet the Court's opinion, particularly its interpretation of the commonality requirement of federal rule 23(a), applies to all class actions.

## ■ WAL-MART STORES, INC. v. DUKES
### 131 S. Ct. 2541 (2011)

Justice SCALIA delivered the opinion of the Court.

We are presented with one of the most expansive class actions ever. The District Court and the Court of Appeals approved the certification of a class comprising about one and a half million plaintiffs, current and former female employees of petitioner Wal-Mart who allege that the discretion exercised by their local supervisors over pay and promotion matters violates Title VII by discriminating against women. In addition to injunctive and declaratory relief, the plaintiffs seek an award of backpay. We consider whether the certification of the plaintiff class was consistent with Federal Rules of Civil Procedure 23(a) and (b)(2).

## I

### A

Petitioner Wal-Mart is the Nation's largest private employer. It operates four types of retail stores throughout the country: Discount Stores, Supercenters, Neighborhood Markets, and Sam's Clubs. Those stores are divided into seven nationwide divisions, which in turn comprise 41 regions of 80 to 85 stores apiece. Each store has between 40 and 53 separate departments and 80 to 500 staff positions. In all, Wal-Mart operates approximately 3,400 stores and employs more than one million people.

Pay and promotion decisions at Wal-Mart are generally committed to local managers' broad discretion, which is exercised "in a largely subjective manner." 222 F.R.D. 137, 145 (N.D. Cal.2004). Local store managers may increase the wages of hourly employees (within limits) with only limited corporate oversight. As for salaried employees, such as store managers and their deputies, higher corporate authorities have discretion to set their pay within preestablished ranges.

Promotions work in a similar fashion. Wal-Mart permits store managers to apply their own subjective criteria when selecting candidates as "support managers," which is the first step on the path to management. Admission to Wal-Mart's management training program, however, does require that a candidate meet certain objective criteria, including an above-average performance rating, at least one year's tenure in the applicant's current position, and a willingness to relocate. But except for those requirements, regional and district managers have discretion to use their own judgment when selecting candidates for management training. Promotion to higher office—e.g., assistant manager, co-manager, or store manager—is similarly at the discretion of the employee's superiors after prescribed objective factors are satisfied.

### B

The named plaintiffs in this lawsuit, representing the 1.5 million members of the certified class, are three current or former Wal-Mart employees who allege that the company discriminated against them on the basis of their sex by denying them equal pay or promotions, in violation of Title VII of the Civil Rights Act of 1964, 78 Stat. 253, as amended, 42 U.S.C. § 2000e-1 et seq. . . .

These plaintiffs, respondents here, do not allege that Wal-Mart has any express corporate policy against the advancement of women. Rather, they claim that their local managers' discretion over pay and promotions is exercised disproportionately in favor of men, leading to an unlawful disparate impact on female employees, see 42 U.S.C. § 2000e-2(k). And, respondents say, because Wal-Mart is aware of this effect, its refusal to cabin its managers' authority amounts to disparate treatment, see § 2000e-2(a). Their complaint seeks injunctive and declaratory relief, punitive damages, and backpay. It does not ask for compensatory damages.

Importantly for our purposes, respondents claim that the discrimination to which they have been subjected is common to all Wal-Mart's female employees. The basic theory of their case is that a strong and uniform "corporate culture" permits bias against women to infect, perhaps subconsciously, the discretionary decisionmaking of each one of Wal-Mart's thousands of managers—thereby making every woman at the company the victim of one common discriminatory practice. Respondents therefore wish to litigate the Title VII claims of all female employees at Wal-Mart's stores in a nationwide class action.

### C

Class certification is governed by Federal Rule of Civil Procedure 23. Under Rule 23(a), the party seeking certification must demonstrate, first, that:

"(1) the class is so numerous that joinder of all members is impracticable,

"(2) there are questions of law or fact common to the class,

"(3) the claims or defenses of the representative parties are typical of the claims or defenses of the class, and

"(4) the representative parties will fairly and adequately protect the interests of the class" (paragraph breaks added).

Second, the proposed class must satisfy at least one of the three requirements listed in Rule 23(b). Respondents rely on Rule 23(b)(2), which applies when "the party opposing the class has acted or refused to act on grounds that apply generally to the class, so that final injunctive relief or corresponding declaratory relief is appropriate respecting the class as a whole."

Invoking these provisions, respondents moved the District Court to certify a plaintiff class consisting of "'[a]ll women employed at any Wal-Mart domestic retail store at any time since December 26, 1998, who have been or may be subjected to Wal-Mart's challenged pay and management track promotions policies and practices.'" 222 F.R.D., at 141-142. As evidence that there were indeed "questions of law or fact common to" all the women of Wal-Mart, as Rule 23(a)(2) requires, respondents relied chiefly on three forms of proof: statistical evidence about pay and promotion disparities between men and women at the company, anecdotal reports of discrimination from about 120 of Wal-Mart's female employees, and the testimony of a sociologist, Dr. William Bielby, who conducted a "social framework analysis" of Wal-Mart's "culture" and personnel practices, and concluded that the company was "vulnerable" to gender discrimination. 603 F.3d 571, 601 (9th Cir. 2010) (en banc).

Wal-Mart unsuccessfully moved to strike much of this evidence. It also offered its own countervailing statistical and other proof in an effort to defeat Rule 23(a)'s requirements of commonality, typicality, and adequate representation. Wal-Mart further contended that respondents' monetary claims for backpay could not be certified under Rule 23(b)(2), first because that Rule refers only to injunctive and declaratory relief, and second because the backpay claims could not be manageably tried as a class without depriving Wal-Mart of its right to present certain statutory defenses. With one limitation not relevant here, the District Court granted respondents' motion and certified their proposed class.

### D

A divided en banc Court of Appeals substantially affirmed the District Court's certification order. 603 F.3d 571. The majority concluded that respondents' evidence of commonality was sufficient to "raise the common question whether Wal-Mart's female employees nationwide were subjected to a single set of corporate policies (not merely a number of independent discriminatory acts) that may have worked to unlawfully discriminate against them in violation of Title VII." *Id.*, at 612 (emphasis deleted). It also agreed with the District Court that the named plaintiffs' claims were sufficiently typical of the class as a whole to satisfy Rule 23(a)(3), and that they could serve as adequate class representatives, see Rule 23(a)(4). *Id.*, at 614-615. With respect to the Rule 23(b)(2) question, the Ninth Circuit held that respondents' backpay claims could be certified as part of a (b)(2) class because they did not "predominat[e]" over the requests for declaratory and injunctive relief, meaning they were not "superior in strength, influence, or authority" to the nonmonetary claims. *Id.*, at 616 (internal quotation marks omitted).

Finally, the Court of Appeals determined that the action could be manageably tried as a class action because the District Court could adopt the approach the Ninth Circuit approved in *Hilao v. Estate of Marcos*, 103 F.3d 767, 782-787 (1996). There compensatory damages for some 9,541 class members were calculated by selecting 137 claims at random, referring those claims to a special master for valuation, and then extrapolating the validity and value of the untested claims from the sample set. The Court of Appeals "s[aw] no reason why a similar procedure to that used in *Hilao* could not be employed in this case." *Id.*, at 627. It would allow Wal-Mart "to present individual defenses in the randomly selected 'sample cases,' thus revealing the approximate percentage of class members whose unequal pay or nonpromotion was due to something other than gender discrimination." *Ibid.*, n. 56 (emphasis deleted).

We granted certiorari.

### II

The class action is "an exception to the usual rule that litigation is conducted by and on behalf of the individual named parties only." *Califano v. Yamasaki*, 442 U.S. 682, 700-701 (1979). In order to justify a departure from that rule, "a class representative must be part of the class and 'possess the same interest and suffer the same injury' as the class members." *East Tex.*

*Motor Freight System, Inc. v. Rodriguez*, 431 U.S. 395, 403 (1977). Rule 23(a) ensures that the named plaintiffs are appropriate representatives of the class whose claims they wish to litigate. The Rule's four requirements—numerosity, commonality, typicality, and adequate representation—"effectively 'limit the class claims to those fairly encompassed by the named plaintiff's claims.'" *General Telephone Co. of Southwest v. Falcon*, 457 U.S. 147, 156 (1982).

### A

The crux of this case is commonality—the rule requiring a plaintiff to show that "there are questions of law or fact common to the class." Rule 23(a)(2). That language is easy to misread, since "[a]ny competently crafted class complaint literally raises common 'questions.'" Nagareda, *Class Certification in the Age of Aggregate Proof*, 84 N.Y.U. L. Rev. 97, 131-132 (2009). For example: Do all of us plaintiffs indeed work for Wal-Mart? Do our managers have discretion over pay? Is that an unlawful employment practice? What remedies should we get? Reciting these questions is not sufficient to obtain class certification. Commonality requires the plaintiff to demonstrate that the class members "have suffered the same injury," *Falcon, supra*, at 157. This does not mean merely that they have all suffered a violation of the same provision of law. Title VII, for example, can be violated in many ways—by intentional discrimination, or by hiring and promotion criteria that result in disparate impact, and by the use of these practices on the part of many different superiors in a single company. Quite obviously, the mere claim by employees of the same company that they have suffered a Title VII injury, or even a disparate-impact Title VII injury, gives no cause to believe that all their claims can productively be litigated at once. Their claims must depend upon a common contention—for example, the assertion of discriminatory bias on the part of the same supervisor. That common contention, moreover, must be of such a nature that it is capable of classwide resolution—which means that determination of its truth or falsity will resolve an issue that is central to the validity of each one of the claims in one stroke.

"What matters to class certification . . . is not the raising of common 'questions'—even in droves—but, rather the capacity of a classwide proceeding to generate common answers apt to drive the resolution of the litigation. Dissimilarities within the proposed class are what have the potential to impede the generation of common answers." Nagareda, *supra*, at 132.

Rule 23 does not set forth a mere pleading standard. A party seeking class certification must affirmatively demonstrate his compliance with the Rule—that is, he must be prepared to prove that there are in fact sufficiently numerous parties, common questions of law or fact, etc. We recognized in *Falcon* that "sometimes it may be necessary for the court to probe behind the pleadings before coming to rest on the certification question," 457 U.S., at 160, and that certification is proper only if "the trial court is satisfied, after a rigorous analysis, that the pre-requisites of Rule 23(a) have been satisfied," *id.*, at 161. Frequently that "rigorous analysis" will entail some overlap with the merits of the plaintiff's underlying claim. That cannot be helped. . . . Nor is there anything unusual about that consequence: The necessity of touching aspects of the merits in order to resolve preliminary matters, e.g., jurisdiction and venue, is a familiar feature of litigation.

In this case, proof of commonality necessarily overlaps with respondents' merits contention that Wal-Mart engages in a pattern or practice of discrimination. That is so because, in resolving an individual's Title VII claim, the crux of the inquiry is "the reason for a particular employment decision," *Cooper v. Federal Reserve Bank of Richmond*, 467 U.S. 867, 876 (1984). Here respondents wish to sue about literally millions of employment decisions at once. Without some glue holding the alleged reasons for all those decisions together, it will be impossible to say that examination of all the class members' claims for relief will produce a common answer to the crucial question why was I disfavored.

**B**

[This Court's opinion in] *Falcon* suggested two ways in which [the] conceptual gap [between the individual's claim that she was denied higher pay on discriminatory grounds and the existence of a class of persons who have suffered the same injury] might be bridged. First, if the employer "used a biased testing procedure to evaluate both applicants for employment and incumbent employees, a class action on behalf of every applicant or employee who might have been prejudiced by the test clearly would satisfy the commonality and typicality requirements of Rule 23(a)." *Id.*, at 159, n. 15. Second, "[s]ignificant proof that an employer operated under a general policy of discrimination conceivably could justify a class of both applicants and employees if the discrimination manifested itself in hiring and promotion practices in the same general fashion, such as through entirely subjective decisionmaking processes." *Ibid.* We think that statement precisely describes respondents' burden in this case. The first manner of bridging the gap obviously has no application here; Wal-Mart has no testing procedure or other companywide evaluation method that can be charged with bias. The whole point of permitting discretionary decisionmaking is to avoid evaluating employees under a common standard.

The second manner of bridging the gap requires "significant proof" that Wal-Mart "operated under a general policy of discrimination." That is entirely absent here. Wal-Mart's announced policy forbids sex discrimination and as the District Court recognized the company imposes penalties for denials of equal employment opportunity. The only evidence of a "general policy of discrimination" respondents produced was the testimony of Dr. William Bielby, their sociological expert. Relying on "social framework" analysis, Bielby testified that Wal-Mart has a "strong corporate culture," that makes it "'vulnerable'" to "gender bias." He could not, however, "determine with any specificity how regularly stereotypes play a meaningful role in employment decisions at Wal-Mart. At his deposition . . . Dr. Bielby conceded that he could not calculate whether 0.5 percent or 95 percent of the employment decisions at Wal-Mart might be determined by stereotyped thinking." . . . [E]ven if properly considered, Bielby's testimony does nothing to advance respondents' case. "[W]hether 0.5 percent or 95 percent of the employment decisions at Wal-Mart might be determined by stereotyped thinking" is the essential question on which respondents' theory of commonality depends. If Bielby admittedly has no answer to that question, we can safely disregard what he has to say. It is worlds away from "significant proof" that Wal-Mart "operated under a general policy of discrimination."

C

The only corporate policy that the plaintiffs' evidence convincingly establishes is Wal-Mart's "policy" of allowing discretion by local supervisors over employment matters. On its face, of course, that is just the opposite of a uniform employment practice that would provide the commonality needed for a class action; it is a policy against having uniform employment practices. It is also a very common and presumptively reasonable way of doing business—one that we have said "should itself raise no inference of discriminatory conduct."

To be sure, we have recognized that, "in appropriate cases," giving discretion to lower-level supervisors can be the basis of Title VII liability under a disparate-impact theory—since "an employer's undisciplined system of subjective decisionmaking [can have] precisely the same effects as a system pervaded by impermissible intentional discrimination." But the recognition that this type of Title VII claim "can" exist does not lead to the conclusion that every employee in a company using a system of discretion has such a claim in common. To the contrary, left to their own devices most managers in any corporation—and surely most managers in a corporation that forbids sex discrimination—would select sex-neutral, performance-based criteria for hiring and promotion that produce no actionable disparity at all. Others may choose to reward various attributes that produce disparate impact—such as scores on general aptitude tests or educational achievements. And still other managers may be guilty of intentional discrimination that produces a sex-based disparity. In such a company, demonstrating the invalidity of one manager's use of discretion will do nothing to demonstrate the invalidity of another's. A party seeking to certify a nationwide class will be unable to show that all the employees' Title VII claims will in fact depend on the answers to common questions.

Respondents have not identified a common mode of exercising discretion that pervades the entire company—aside from their reliance on Dr. Bielby's social frameworks analysis that we have rejected. In a company of Wal-Mart's size and geographical scope, it is quite unbelievable that all managers would exercise their discretion in a common way without some common direction. Respondents attempt to make that showing by means of statistical and anecdotal evidence, but their evidence falls well short. . . .

Even if they are taken at face value, these studies are insufficient to establish that respondents' theory can be proved on a classwide basis. . . . A regional pay disparity, for example, may be attributable to only a small set of

Wal-Mart stores, and cannot by itself establish the uniform, store-by-store disparity upon which the plaintiffs' theory of commonality depends.

There is another, more fundamental, respect in which respondents' statistical proof fails. Even if it established (as it does not) a pay or promotion pattern that differs from the nationwide figures or the regional figures in all of Wal-Mart's 3,400 stores, that would still not demonstrate that commonality of issue exists. Some managers will claim that the availability of women, or qualified women, or interested women, in their stores' area does not mirror the national or regional statistics. And almost all of them will claim to have been applying some sex-neutral, performance-based criteria—whose nature and effects will differ from store to store. In the landmark case of ours which held that giving discretion to lower-level supervisors can be the basis of Title VII liability under a disparate-impact theory, the plurality opinion conditioned that holding on the corollary that merely proving that the discretionary system has produced a racial or sexual disparity is not enough. "[T]he plaintiff must begin by identifying the specific employment practice that is challenged." That is all the more necessary when a class of plaintiffs is sought to be certified. Other than the bare existence of delegated discretion, respondents have identified no "specific employment practice"—much less one that ties all their 1.5 million claims together. Merely showing that Wal-Mart's policy of discretion has produced an overall sex-based disparity does not suffice.

Respondents' anecdotal evidence suffers from the same defects, and in addition is too weak to raise any inference that all the individual, discretionary personnel decisions are discriminatory. In *Teamsters v. United States*, 431 U.S. 324 (1977), in addition to substantial statistical evidence of company-wide discrimination, the Government (as plaintiff) produced about 40 specific accounts of racial discrimination from particular individuals . . . [that] represented roughly one account for every eight members of the class. Moreover, the Court of Appeals noted that the anecdotes came from individuals "spread throughout" the company who "for the most part" worked at the company's operational centers that employed the largest numbers of the class members. Here, by contrast, respondents filed some 120 affidavits reporting experiences of discrimination—about 1 for every 12,500 class members—relating to only some 235 out of Wal-Mart's 3,400. . . . Even if every single one of these accounts is true, that would not demonstrate that the entire company "operate[s] under a general policy of discrimination," *Falcon, supra*, at 159, n. 15, which is what respondents must show to certify a companywide class.

The dissent misunderstands the nature of the foregoing analysis. It criticizes our focus on the dissimilarities between the putative class members on the ground that we have "blend[ed]" Rule 23(a)(2)'s commonality requirement with Rule 23(b)(3)'s inquiry into whether common questions "predominate" over individual ones. That is not so. We quite agree that for purposes of Rule 23(a)(2) " '[e]ven a single [common] question' " will do. We consider dissimilarities not in order to determine (as Rule 23(b)(3) requires) whether common questions predominate, but in order to determine (as Rule 23(a)(2) requires) whether there is "[e]ven a single [common] question." And there is not here. Because respondents provide no convincing proof of a companywide discriminatory pay and promotion policy, we have concluded that they have not established the existence of any common question. In sum, we agree with Chief Judge Kozinski that the members of the class:

> held a multitude of different jobs, at different levels of Wal-Mart's hierarchy, for variable lengths of time, in 3,400 stores, sprinkled across 50 states, with a kaleidoscope of supervisors (male and female), subject to a variety of regional policies that all differed. . . . Some thrived while others did poorly. They have little in common but their sex and this lawsuit.

603 F.3d, at 652 (dissenting opinion).

## III

We also conclude that respondents' claims for backpay were improperly certified under Federal Rule of Civil Procedure 23(b)(2). Our opinion in *Ticor Title Ins. Co. v. Brown*, 511 U.S. 117, 121 (1994) (per curiam) expressed serious doubt about whether claims for monetary relief may be certified under that provision. We now hold that they may not, at least where (as here) the monetary relief is not incidental to the injunctive or declaratory relief.

### A

Rule 23(b)(2) allows class treatment when "the party opposing the class has acted or refused to act on grounds that apply generally to the class, so that final injunctive relief or corresponding declaratory relief is appropriate respecting the class as a whole." One possible reading of this provision is that it applies only to requests for such injunctive or declaratory relief and does not authorize the class certification of monetary claims at all. We need not reach that broader question in this case, because we think that, at a minimum, claims for individualized relief (like the backpay at issue here) do not satisfy the Rule. The key to the (b)(2) class is "the indivisible nature of the injunctive or declaratory remedy warranted—the notion that the conduct is such that it can be enjoined or declared unlawful only as to all of the class members or as to none of them." Nagareda, 84 N.Y.U. L. Rev., at 132. In other words, Rule 23(b)(2) applies only when a single injunction or declaratory judgment would provide relief to each member of the class. It does not authorize class certification when each individual class member would be entitled to a different injunction or declaratory judgment against the defendant. Similarly, it does not authorize class certification when each class member would be entitled to an individualized award of monetary damages.

That interpretation accords with the history of the Rule. Because Rule 23 "stems from equity practice" that predated its codification, *Amchem*

*Products, Inc. v. Windsor,* 521 U.S. 591, 613 (1997), in determining its meaning we have previously looked to the historical models on which the Rule was based. As we observed in *Amchem,* "[c]ivil rights cases against parties charged with unlawful, class-based discrimination are prime examples" of what (b)(2) is meant to capture. 521 U.S., at 614. In particular, the Rule reflects a series of decisions involving challenges to racial segregation— conduct that was remedied by a single classwide order. In none of the cases cited by the Advisory Committee as examples of (b)(2)'s antecedents did the plaintiffs combine any claim for individualized relief with their classwide injunction. *See* Advisory Committee's Note, 39 F.R.D. 69, 102 (1966) (citing cases).

Permitting the combination of individualized and classwide relief in a (b)(2) class is also inconsistent with the structure of Rule 23(b). Classes certified under (b)(1) and (b)(2) share the most traditional justifications for class treatment—that individual adjudications would be impossible or unworkable, as in a (b)(1) class, or that the relief sought must perforce affect the entire class at once, as in a (b)(2) class. For that reason these are also mandatory classes: The Rule provides no opportunity for (b)(1) or (b)(2) class members to opt out, and does not even oblige the District Court to afford them notice of the action. Rule 23(b)(3), by contrast, is an "adventuresome innovation" of the 1966 amendments, framed for situations "in which 'classaction treatment is not as clearly called for',". It allows class certification in a much wider set of circumstances but with greater procedural protections. Its only prerequisites are that "the questions of law or fact common to class members predominate over any questions affecting only individual members, and that a class action is superior to other available methods for fairly and efficiently adjudicating the controversy." Rule 23(b)(3). And unlike (b)(1) and (b)(2) classes, the (b)(3) class is not mandatory; class members are entitled to receive "the best notice that is practicable under the circumstances" and to withdraw from the class at their option. *See* Rule 23(c)(2)(B).

Given that structure, we think it clear that individualized monetary claims belong in Rule 23(b)(3). The procedural protections attending the (b)(3) class—predominance, superiority, mandatory notice, and the right to opt out—are missing from (b)(2) not because the Rule considers them unnecessary, but because it considers them unnecessary to a (b)(2) class. When a class seeks an indivisible injunction benefitting all its members at once, there is no reason to undertake a case-specific inquiry into whether class issues predominate or whether class action is a superior method of adjudicating the dispute. Predominance and superiority are self-evident. But with respect to each class member's individualized claim for money, that is not so—which is precisely why (b)(3) requires the judge to make findings about predominance and superiority before allowing the class. Similarly, (b)(2) does not require that class members be given notice and optout rights, presumably because it is thought (rightly or wrongly) that notice has no purpose when the class is mandatory, and that depriving people of their right to sue in this manner complies with the Due Process Clause. In the context of a class action predominantly for money damages we have held that absence of notice and opt-out violates due process. *See Phillips Petroleum Co. v. Shutts,* 472 U.S. 797, 812 (1985). While we have never held that to be so where the monetary claims do not predominate, the serious possibility that it may be so provides an additional reason not to read Rule 23(b)(2) to include the monetary claims here.

**B**

Against that conclusion, respondents argue that their claims for backpay were appropriately certified as part of a class under Rule 23(b)(2) because those claims do not "predominate" over their requests for injunctive and declaratory relief. They rely upon the Advisory Committee's statement that Rule 23(b)(2) "does not extend to cases in which the appropriate final relief relates exclusively or predominantly to money damages." 39 F.R.D., at 102 (emphasis added). The negative implication, they argue, is that it does extend to cases in which the appropriate final relief relates only partially and nonpredominantly to money damages. Of course it is the Rule itself, not the Advisory Committee's description of it, that governs. And a mere negative inference does not in our view suffice to establish a disposition that has no basis in the Rule's text, and that does obvious violence to the Rule's structural features. The mere "predominance" of a proper (b)(2) injunctive claim does nothing to justify elimination of Rule 23(b)(3)'s procedural protections: It neither establishes the superiority of class adjudication over individual adjudication nor cures the notice and opt-out problems. We fail to see why the Rule should be read to nullify these protections whenever a plaintiff class, at its option, combines its monetary claims with a request—even a "predominating request"—for an injunction.

Respondents' predominance test, moreover, creates perverse incentives for class representatives to place at risk potentially valid claims for monetary relief. In this case, for example, the named plaintiffs declined to include employees' claims for compensatory damages in their complaint. That strategy of including only backpay claims made it more likely that monetary relief would not "predominate." But it also created the possibility (if the predominance test were correct) that individual class members' compensatory-damages claims would be precluded by litigation they had no power to hold themselves apart from. If it were determined, for example, that a particular class member is not entitled to backpay because her denial of increased pay or a promotion was not the product of discrimination, that employee might be collaterally estopped from independently seeking compensatory damages based on that same denial. That possibility underscores the need for plaintiffs with individual monetary claims to decide for themselves whether to tie their fates to the class representatives' or go it alone—a choice Rule 23(b)(2) does not ensure that they have.

The predominance test would also require the District Court to reevaluate the roster of class members continually. The Ninth Circuit recognized the necessity for this when it concluded that those plaintiffs no longer employed by Wal-Mart lack standing to seek injunctive or declaratory relief against its employment practices. The Court of Appeals' response to that difficulty, however, was not to eliminate all former employees from the certified class, but to eliminate only those who had left the company's employ by the date the complaint was filed. That solution has no logical connection to the problem, since those who have left their Wal-Mart jobs since the complaint was filed have no more need for prospective relief than those who left beforehand. . . . Of course, the alternative (and logical) solution of excising plaintiffs from the class as they leave their employment may have struck the Court of Appeals as wasteful of the District Court's time. . . . What follows from this, however, is not that some arbitrary limitation on class membership should be imposed but that the backpay claims should not be certified under Rule 23(b)(2) at all.

Finally, respondents argue that their backpay claims are appropriate for a (b)(2) class action because a backpay award is equitable in nature. The latter may be true, but it is irrelevant. The Rule does not speak of "equitable" remedies generally but of injunctions and declaratory judgments. As Title VII itself makes pellucidly clear, backpay is neither.

### C

. . . Contrary to the Ninth Circuit's view, Wal-Mart is entitled to individualized determinations of each employee's eligibility for backpay. . . .

. . . When the plaintiff seeks individual relief such as reinstatement or backpay after establishing a pattern or practice of discrimination, "a district court must usually conduct additional proceedings . . . to determine the scope of individual relief." *Teamsters,* 431 U.S., at 361. At this phase, the burden of proof will shift to the company, but it will have the right to raise any individual affirmative defenses it may have, and to "demonstrate that the individual applicant was denied an employment opportunity for lawful reasons." *Id.,* at 362.

The Court of Appeals believed that it was possible to replace such proceedings with Trial by Formula. A sample set of the class members would be selected, as to whom liability for sex discrimination and the backpay owing as a result would be determined in depositions supervised by a master. The percentage of claims determined to be valid would then be applied to the entire remaining class, and the number of (presumptively) valid claims thus derived would be multiplied by the average backpay award in the sample set to arrive at the entire class recovery—without further individualized proceedings. We disapprove that novel project. Because the Rules Enabling Act forbids interpreting Rule 23 to "abridge, enlarge or modify any substantive right," 28 U.S.C. § 2072(b), a class cannot be certified on the premise that Wal-Mart will not be entitled to litigate its statutory defenses to individual claims. And because the necessity of that litigation will prevent backpay from being "incidental" to the classwide injunction, respondents' class could not be certified even assuming, arguendo, that "incidental" monetary relief can be awarded to a 23(b)(2) class.

* * *

The judgment of the Court of Appeals is Reversed.

Justice GINSBURG, with whom Justice BREYER, Justice SOTOMAYOR, and Justice KAGAN join, concurring in part and dissenting in part.

The class in this case, I agree with the Court, should not have been certified under Federal Rule of Civil Procedure 23(b)(2). The plaintiffs, alleging discrimination in violation of Title VII, 42 U.S.C. § 2000(e) et seq., seek monetary relief that is not merely incidental to any injunctive or declaratory relief that might be available. A putative class of this type may be certifiable under Rule 23(b)(3), if the plaintiffs show that common class questions "predominate" over issues affecting individuals—e.g., qualification for, and the amount of, backpay or compensatory damages—and that a class action is "superior" to other modes of adjudication.

Whether the class the plaintiffs describe meets the specific requirements of Rule 23(b)(3) is not before the Court, and I would reserve that matter for consideration and decision on remand. The Court, however, disqualifies the class at the starting gate, holding that the plaintiffs cannot cross the "commonality" line set by Rule 23(a)(2). In so ruling, the Court imports into the Rule 23(a) determination concerns properly addressed in a Rule 23(b)(3) assessment.

# I

## A

Rule 23(a)(2) establishes a preliminary requirement for maintaining a class action: "[T]here are questions of law or fact common to the class." . . .

A "question" is ordinarily understood to be "[a] subject or point open to controversy." American Heritage Dictionary 1483 (3d ed.1992). *See also* Black's Law Dictionary 1366 (9th ed.2009) (defining "question of fact" as "[a] disputed issue to be resolved . . . [at] trial" and "question of law" as "[a]n issue to be decided by the judge"). Thus, a "question" "common to the class" must be a dispute, either of fact or of law, the resolution of which will advance the determination of the class members' claims.[3]

---

3. The Court suggests Rule 23(a)(2) must mean more than it says. If the word "questions" were taken literally, the majority asserts, plaintiffs could pass the Rule 23(a)(2) bar by "[r]eciting . . . questions" like "Do all of us plaintiffs indeed work for Wal-Mart?" Sensibly read, however, the word "questions" means disputed issues, not any utterance crafted in the grammatical form of a question.

**B**

The District Court, recognizing that "one significant issue common to the class may be sufficient to warrant certification," found that the plaintiffs easily met that test. Absent an error of law or an abuse of discretion, an appellate tribunal has no warrant to upset the District Court's finding of commonality.

The District Court certified a class of "[a]ll women employed at any Wal-Mart domestic retail store at any time since December 26, 1998." The named plaintiffs, led by Betty Dukes, propose to litigate, on behalf of the class, allegations that Wal-Mart discriminates on the basis of gender in pay and promotions. They allege that the company "[r]eli[es] on gender stereotypes in making employment decisions such as . . . promotion[s][and] pay." Wal-Mart permits those prejudices to infect personnel decisions, the plaintiffs contend, by leaving pay and promotions in the hands of "a nearly all male managerial workforce" using "arbitrary and subjective criteria." Further alleged barriers to the advancement of female employees include the company's requirement, "as a condition of promotion to management jobs, that employees be willing to relocate." Absent instruction otherwise, there is a risk that managers will act on the familiar assumption that women, because of their services to husband and children, are less mobile than men. *See* Dept. of Labor, Federal Glass Ceiling Commission, *Good for Business: Making Full Use of the Nation's Human Capital* 151 (1995).

Women fill 70 percent of the hourly jobs in the retailer's stores but make up only "33 percent of management employees." "[T]he higher one looks in the organization the lower the percentage of women." The plaintiffs' "largely uncontested descriptive statistics" also show that women working in the company's stores "are paid less than men in every region" and "that the salary gap widens over time even for men and women hired into the same jobs at the same time."

The District Court identified "systems for . . . promoting in-store employees" that were "sufficiently similar across regions and stores" to conclude that "the manner in which these systems affect the class raises issues that are common to all class members." The selection of employees for promotion to in-store management "is fairly characterized as a 'tap on the shoulder' process," in which managers have discretion about whose shoulders to tap. Vacancies are not regularly posted; from among those employees satisfying minimum qualifications, managers choose whom to promote on the basis of their own subjective impressions.

Wal-Mart's compensation policies also operate uniformly across stores, the District Court found. The retailer leaves open a $2 band for every position's hourly pay rate. Wal-Mart provides no standards or criteria for setting wages within that band, and thus does nothing to counter unconscious bias on the part of supervisors.

Wal-Mart's supervisors do not make their discretionary decisions in a vacuum. The District Court reviewed means Wal-Mart used to maintain a "carefully constructed . . . corporate culture," such as frequent meetings to reinforce the common way of thinking, regular transfers of managers between stores to ensure uniformity throughout the company, monitoring of stores "on a close and constant basis," and "Wal-Mart TV," "broad-cas[t] . . . into all stores."

The plaintiffs' evidence, including class members' tales of their own experiences, suggests that gender bias suffused Wal-Mart's company culture. Among illustrations, senior management often refer to female associates as "little Janie Qs." One manager told an employee that "[m]en are here to make a career and women aren't." A committee of female Wal-Mart executives concluded that "[s]tereotypes limit the opportunities offered to women."

Finally, the plaintiffs presented an expert's appraisal to show that the pay and promotions disparities at Wal-Mart "can be explained only by gender discrimination and not by . . . neutral variables." 222 F.R.D., at 155. Using regression analyses, their expert, Richard Drogin, controlled for factors including, inter alia, job performance, length of time with the company, and the store where an employee worked. The results, the District Court found, were sufficient to raise an "inference of discrimination."

### C

The District Court's identification of a common question, whether Wal-Mart's pay and promotions policies gave rise to unlawful discrimination, was hardly infirm. The practice of delegating to supervisors large discretion to make personnel decisions, uncontrolled by formal standards, has long been known to have the potential to produce disparate effects. Managers, like all humankind, may be prey to biases of which they are unaware.[6] The risk of discrimination is heightened when those managers are predominantly of one sex, and are steeped in a corporate culture that perpetuates gender stereotypes. . . .

We have held that "discretionary employment practices" can give rise to Title VII claims, not only when such practices are motivated by discriminatory intent but also when they produce discriminatory results. . . .

The plaintiffs' allegations state claims of gender discrimination in the form of biased decisionmaking in both pay and promotions. The evidence reviewed by the District Court adequately demonstrated that resolving those claims would necessitate examination of particular policies and practices alleged to affect, adversely and globally, women employed at Wal-Mart's stores. Rule 23(a)(2), setting a necessary but not a sufficient criterion for class-action certification, demands nothing further.

---

6. An example vividly illustrates how subjective decisionmaking can be a vehicle for discrimination. Performing in symphony orchestras was long a male preserve. Goldin and Rouse, *Orchestrating Impartiality: The Impact of "Blind" Auditions on Female Musicians*, 90 Am. Econ. Rev. 715, 715-716 (2000). In the 1970's orchestras began hiring musicians through auditions open to all comers. *Id.*, at 716. Reviewers were to judge applicants solely on their musical abilities, yet subconscious bias led some reviewers to disfavor women. Orchestras that permitted reviewers to see the applicants hired far fewer female musicians than orchestras that conducted blind auditions, in which candidates played behind opaque screens. *Id.*, at 738.

## II

### A

The Court gives no credence to the key dispute common to the class: whether Wal-Mart's discretionary pay and promotion policies are discriminatory. . . . "What matters," the Court asserts, "is not the raising of common 'questions,'" but whether there are "[d]issimilarities within the proposed class" that "have the potential to impede the generation of common answers."

The Court blends Rule 23(a)(2)'s threshold criterion with the more demanding criteria of Rule 23(b)(3), and thereby elevates the (a)(2) inquiry so that it is no longer "easily satisfied," 5 J. Moore et al., Moore's Federal Practice § 23.23[2], p. 23-72 (3d ed.2011). Rule 23(b)(3) certification requires, in addition to the four 23(a) findings, determinations that "questions of law or fact common to class members predominate over any questions affecting only individual members" and that "a class action is superior to other available methods for . . . adjudicating the controversy."

The Court's emphasis on differences between class members mimics the Rule 23(b)(3) inquiry into whether common questions "predominate" over individual issues. And by asking whether the individual differences "impede" common adjudication, the Court duplicates 23(b)(3)'s question whether "a class action is superior" to other modes of adjudication. Indeed, Professor Nagareda, whose "dissimilarities" inquiry the Court endorses, developed his position in the context of Rule 23(b)(3). See 84 N.Y.U.L.Rev., at 131 (Rule 23(b)(3) requires "some decisive degree of similarity across the proposed class" because it "speaks of common 'questions' that 'predominate' over individual ones"). "The Rule 23(b)(3) predominance inquiry" is meant to "tes[t] whether proposed classes are sufficiently cohesive to warrant adjudication by representation." Amchem Products, Inc. v. Windsor, 521 U.S. 591, 623 (1997). If courts must conduct a "dissimilarities" analysis at the Rule 23(a)(2) stage, no mission remains for Rule 23(b)(3).

Because Rule 23(a) is also a prerequisite for Rule 23(b)(1) and Rule 23(b)(2) classes, the Court's "dissimilarities" position is far reaching. Individual differences should not bar a Rule 23(b)(1) or Rule 23(b)(2) class, so long as the Rule 23(a) threshold is met. . . .

### B

The "dissimilarities" approach leads the Court to train its attention on what distinguishes individual class members, rather than on what unites them. Given the lack of standards for pay and promotions, the majority says, "demonstrating the invalidity of one manager's use of discretion will do nothing to demonstrate the invalidity of another's."

Wal-Mart's delegation of discretion over pay and promotions is a policy uniform throughout all stores. The very nature of discretion is that people will exercise it in various ways. A system of delegated discretion, Watson held, is a practice actionable under Title VII when it produces discriminatory outcomes. A finding that Wal-Mart's pay and promotions practices in fact violate the law would be the first step in the usual order of proof for plaintiffs seeking individual remedies for company-wide discrimination. That each individual employee's unique circumstances will ultimately determine whether she is entitled to backpay or damages, § 2000e-5(g)(2)(A) (barring backpay if a plaintiff "was refused . . . advancement . . . for any reason other than discrimination"), should not factor into the Rule 23(a)(2) determination.

\* \* \*

The Court errs in importing a "dissimilarities" notion suited to Rule 23(b)(3) into the Rule 23(a) commonality inquiry. I therefore cannot join Part II of the Court's opinion.

## Comments and Questions

1. As noted earlier, *Wal-Mart v. Dukes* was an extraordinary case, yet the law made here applies to all class actions. Note that the Court unanimously agreed that the plaintiffs' back pay claims could not be certified as part of their injunctive class action. Do you think that class members seeking injunctive relief in an employment discrimination class action should have to meet the more onerous requirements of Rule 23(b)(3) in order to sustain their collective claims for back pay? What effect is this additional burden likely to have on the ability of class members to seek back pay in smaller employment discrimination class actions, if any? What effect will it have on lawyers who bring such class actions? Are plaintiffs like those in *Wal-Mart v. Dukes*, whose back pay claims average around $2,000, likely to bring individual actions? Why or why not? Is fee shifting enough to encourage such lawsuits? Should our society encourage such individual suits?

2. The case presents what appear to be two different interpretations of the "commonality" requirement of Rule 23(a). What are the differences between Justice Scalia's articulation of the "common questions" standard and Justice Ginsburg's? How does the majority's interpretation of the words "common question of law or fact" differ from what you learned about the interpretation of that same language in the context of joinder under Rule 20? How would the standards articulated in these two opinions differ in application in a more routine class action such as the *Shutts* case?

The commonality question is made more complicated by the relationship between the substantive merits and certification. In *Wal-Mart*, the plaintiffs pursued an innovative legal theory: that although Wal-Mart had no policy governing salary and promotions, the company's sexist corporate culture resulted in women receiving lower salaries than similarly situated men. One way to frame the "common question" at issue in the case is to ask whether that theory is viable. Although this was a class certification motion, not a motion to dismiss or a motion for summary judgment, Justice Scalia in effect ruled on the validity of this theory. Because the majority did not accept that the plaintiff's theory was viable, it found no common question. Scholars have debated both whether this theory is consistent with Title VII and whether it ought to be. *Compare* Melissa Hart and Paul M. Secunda, *A Matter of Context: Social Framework Evidence in Employment Discrimination Class Actions*, 78 Fordham L. Rev. 37 (2009), *and* Samuel Bagenstos, *Implicit Bias, "Science" and Antidiscrimination Law*, 1 Harv. L. & Pol'y Rev. 477 (2007), *with* John Monahan, Laurens Walker, and Gregory Mitchell, *Contextual Evidence of Gender Discrimination: The Ascendance of "Social Frameworks,"* 94 Va. L. Rev. 1715 (2008).

3. What are the assumptions of the Justices about how people behave in the workplace? Are they justified? In several other contexts, particularly pleadings, you have seen judicial assumptions driving doctrine. What limits should there be on judges using their common sense and personal observations of the world in framing doctrine? Is it possible to avoid this, even if we wanted to?

4. One question raised by this case is to what extent a court should consider the merits of the litigation on a certification motion. Some scholars have suggested that Rule 23 should be revised to include the litigants' likelihood of success on the merits, an analysis that parallels the test that courts apply in the preliminary injunction context, as part of class certification. Is this a good idea? Why or why not? *See* Robert Bone, *Sorting Through the Certification Muddle*, 63 Vand. L. Rev. En Banc 105 (2010).

5. As mentioned, one of the key questions in class action litigation is what incentives lawyers have to bring such lawsuits. This is because class action lawsuits are generally considered to be driven by lawyers rather than clients. In this case, the plaintiffs were represented both by a prestigious private firm specializing in employment discrimination litigation, Cohen Milstein, and a well-regarded public interest organization, The Impact Fund. Should courts treat cases pursued by public interest organizations differently than those pursued for private gain? Why or why not?

6. In the segment entitled *How to Read a Rule* in Chapter 1, you were introduced to the controversy over interpretation of the Federal Rules and the role of the Advisory Committee Notes. What role do the Advisory Committee Notes play in the analysis in this case? How should the intention of the rule drafters be considered in the proper interpretation of the rule? How does the approach taken by the majority in *Wal-Mart* square with the Court's approach to rule interpretation in *Ashcroft v. Iqbal* (reproduced in Chapter 3)? Is the interpretive mode in the Court's modern jurisprudence consistent?

## Practice Exercise No. 41: Motion for Class Certification in *City of Cleveland*

Prepare for a session before a federal district judge to hear the motion to certify a plaintiff class in the *City of Cleveland*. Students with last names beginning with the letters A-D will be clerks to the judge; E-O should prepare arguments (for the City) in opposition to the motion; and P-Z should prepare arguments (for the class) in support of the motion.

Assume that the class that the plaintiffs seek to certify is as defined in paragraph 5 of the Complaint in the Case Files. Assume for purposes of this exercise that the plaintiffs' firm has the requisite skill, experience, and financial resources to handle this class action.

## Note on Subject Matter Jurisdiction in Class Action and Other Complex Litigation

In the first decade of the twenty-first century, Congress dramatically expanded the federal courts' jurisdiction over class actions and mass tort litigation. The two key statutes were the Class Action Fairness Act ("CAFA"), governing class actions, and the Multiparty, Multiforum Trial Jurisdiction Act, governing tort cases.

### *Subject Matter Jurisdiction over Class Actions*

In 2005, Congress passed CAFA, which among other things amended 28 U.S.C. § 1332 by adding section (d). This section suspends the traditional requirements of complete diversity and the amount in controversy with respect to class actions. Now a class action may be filed in or removed to federal court so long as the total amount in controversy for the entire class is at least $5 million and the case meets a minimal diversity requirement—at least one plaintiff is a citizen of a different state than the defendant. This means that most class actions of any significance can end up in federal court. CAFA contains exceptions for class actions that are entirely or largely local in character. The "local controversy exception" of CAFA limits the district court's removal jurisdiction in cases where more than two-thirds of the class are citizens of the state in which the action was originally filed, and one defendant is a citizen of the state in which the action was originally filed, the principal injuries allegedly caused by all the defendants occurred in the state in which the action was originally filed, and no other action was filed asserting the same or similar factual allegations. § 1332(4)(A). CAFA also includes a "home state exception" providing that the district court "shall decline to exercise jurisdiction" when "two-thirds or more of the members of all proposed plaintiff classes in the aggregate, and the primary defendants, are citizens of the State in which the action was originally filed." § 1332(4)(B). A final provision leaves the exercise of subject matter jurisdiction at the discretion of the district court "in the interests of justice and looking at the totality of the circumstances" where "greater than one-third but less than two-thirds of the members of all proposed plaintiff classes in the aggregate and the primary defendants are citizens of the State in which the action was originally filed." In that case, the district court must consider these factors:

(A)  whether the claims asserted involve matters of national or interstate interest;

(B)  whether the claims asserted will be governed by laws of the State in which the action was originally filed or by the laws of other States;

(C)  whether the class action has been pleaded in a manner that seeks to avoid Federal jurisdiction;

(D)  whether the action was brought in a forum with a distinct nexus with the class members, the alleged harm, or the defendants;

(E)  whether the number of citizens of the State in which the action was originally filed in all proposed plaintiff classes in the aggregate is substantially larger than the number of citizens from any other State, and the citizenship of the other members of the proposed class is dispersed among a substantial number of States; and

(F)  whether, during the 3-year period preceding the filing of that class action, 1 or more other class actions asserting the same or similar claims on behalf of the same or other persons have been filed.

§ 1332(d)(3).

Unlike the Federal Rules of Civil Procedure, the Class Action Fairness Act is a statute passed by Congress. The politics of its enactment are summarized as follows:

Defendants have long complained about the economic pressure that class actions place upon them. Consumer class actions, where individual damages may be minimal, but in the aggregate huge, have been of particular concern. Critics of class actions complained that in such cases consumers received little of value, while class counsel were awarded millions of dollars in fees. Although not specifically responding to these complaints, the federal judiciary, led by the United States Supreme Court in *Amchem Products, Inc. v. Windsor,* tightened up the class certification process, making federal court less attractive to plaintiffs in certain kinds of cases. Additionally, the Court's decisions in the 1986 Trilogy of Summary Judgment cases, together with its decision in *Daubert v. Merrell-Dow Pharmaceuticals* [forbidding the use of "junk science" evidence], have made it tougher for plaintiffs to survive motions for summary judgments in federal courts.

These federal judicial developments led plaintiffs' lawyers to seek out state courts more amenable to class certification and jury trials. In response, defendants increasingly sought to remove cases from state court to federal court, where they hoped to defeat class certification, and more successfully defend their clients' interests. Plaintiffs learned to defeat the right to removal by naming non-diverse parties as defendants to destroy complete diversity, or by alleging an amount in controversy less than the amount required for federal diversity jurisdiction under 28 U.S.C. § 1332.

Neither side could be happy with these developments. While plaintiffs' attorneys complained of being deprived of their chosen state court forums, corporate defendants complained of being sued in "Judicial Hellholes." Although the problem might have been overstated, some state courts, and certain counties within some states, had become magnets for plaintiffs in certain forms of litigation. CAFA is a significant outgrowth of these dynamics. . . .

The purpose of CAFA, as Senator Arlen Specter, Chair of the Senate Judiciary Committee, put it, is

... to prevent judge shopping to States and even counties where courts and judges have a prejudicial predisposition on cases. Regrettably, the history has been that there are some States in the United States and even some counties where there is forum shopping, which means that lawyers will look to that particular State, that particular county to get an advantage.

Georgene M. Vairo, *Developments in the Law: The Class Action Fairness Act of 2005*, 39 Loy. L.A. L. Rev. 979, 980-982 (2006).

## Subject Matter Jurisdiction over Mass Torts

Several years before CAFA, Congress passed the Multiparty, Multiforum Trial Jurisdiction Act of 2002 (MMTJA), 28 U.S.C. § 1369. The MMTJA was designed to redress the perceived inefficiencies and inconsistencies of duplicative litigation arising from a single mass tort. It authorizes federal jurisdiction over mass tort cases deriving from a single accident killing at least seventy-five persons. As one judge described the provisions of this statute:

This new jurisdictional statute, by its terms, expands the original jurisdiction of federal courts to include lawsuits arising from accidents where more than 75 natural persons die at a discrete location, provided that the other requirements of the statute are satisfied. The first part of the statute, § 1369(a), grants the federal district court original jurisdiction over any civil action stemming from such a tragedy with minimal diversity between the parties, provided that one of the following factors is also present: (1) a defendant resides in a different state from where a substantial part of the accident took place, regardless of whether a substantial portion of the accident also took place in his or her own state; (2) any two defendants reside in different states, regardless of whether these defendants happen to reside in the same state as another defendant; or (3) substantial parts of the accident took place in different states. . . .

Section 1369(b), entitled, "Limitation of jurisdiction of district courts," mandates that a district court judge abstain from hearing any civil action meeting the requirements of § 1369(a) where two conditions are both satisfied: abstention is required when (1) "the substantial majority of plaintiffs are citizens of a single State of which the primary defendants are also citizens" and (2) "the claims asserted will be governed primarily by the laws of that State." 28 U.S.C. § 1369(b). . . .

[A]fter reviewing this legislative history, it is clear that in enacting § 1369, Congress intended to create a mechanism whereby litigation stemming from one major disaster could easily be consolidated in one federal court for discovery and trial. It is also clear that Congress' motivation in passing this legislation was to promote judicial efficiency while avoiding multiple lawsuits concerning the same subject matter strewn throughout the country in various state and federal courts. Thus, § 1369 was intended to address these concerns by creating a new statutory grant of original federal jurisdiction aimed exclusively at large accidents resulting in 75 or more deaths. . . .

Subsection (b) of new § 1369 creates an exception to the minimal diversity rule. In brief, a U.S. district court may not hear any case in which a "substantial majority" of the plaintiffs and the "primary" defendants are all citizens of the same state; and in which the claims asserted are governed primarily by the laws of that same state. In other words, only state courts may hear such cases. . . .

[I]t is clear that Congress was concerned about a small subset of disaster cases finding their way into federal court—cases where the substantial majority of the plaintiffs and the "primary" defendants are all from the same state, and where the claims asserted will be governed primarily by the laws of that same state. By creating § 1369(b), Congress attempted to create a statutory exception, or "safeguard" whereby these local disaster cases could continue to be heard in state court, even though more than 75 people died therein and minimal diversity existed between the parties. Thus, in an effort to achieve this balance, the statute directs the federal court to "abstain from accepting jurisdiction in primarily local actions," in favor of state courts. . . .

*Passa v. Derderian*, 308 F. Supp. 2d 43 (D.R.I. 2004) (interpreting the MMTJA in a case arising out of a fire at "The Station" nightclub in Rhode Island in which approximately 100 people died and 200 were injured). In addition to expanding federal subject matter authority by requiring only minimal diversity and no requisite amount-in-controversy, the MMTJA also provides for nationwide service of process and subpoena of witnesses, liberalized venue rules, and open-ended right for claimants to intervene. *See* Peter Adomeit, *The Station Nightclub Fire and Federal Jurisdictional Reach: The Multidistrict, Multiparty, Multiforum Jurisdiction Act of 2002*, 25 W. New Eng. L. Rev. 243 (2003).

The "single accident" at "a discrete location" requirement of the law has prevented application of the MMTJA to the numerous cases arising as a result of the multiple levee breaches caused by Hurricane Katrina. *See, e.g., Case v. ANPAC Louisiana Insurance Co.*, 466 F. Supp. 2d 781 (E.D. La. 2006) (action by homeowners against their insurance companies, removed to federal court by defendants, was remanded to state court). Some of those cases were removed to federal court under CAFA, but the federal courts refused to exercise jurisdiction under the local controversy exception to CAFA. *See Preston v. Tenet Healthsystem Memorial Medical Center*, 485 F.3d 804 (5th Cir. 2007) (stating that "[t]his particular Hurricane Katrina case symbolizes a quintessential example of Congress' intent to carve-out exceptions to CAFA's expansive grant of federal jurisdiction when our courts confront a truly localized controversy").

# E. REVISITING THE JUDICIAL ROLE IN CLASS ACTION SETTLEMENTS

The doctrinal question of when and how to certify large-scale class actions is related to deeper questions about the limits of the judicial role. Limitations on the judicial role may be understood as an imposition of Article III and the idea of "separation of powers" or as a more common law requirement of the role of the judge in the adversarial system. Chapter 6 introduced these ideas in the context of *Brown v. Plata*, two class actions challenging the medical and mental health treatment provided prisoners in California's prison system. That litigation ended with a structural injunction that was affirmed by the Supreme Court. Now that you know a little more about class action doctrine, it is a good time to revisit these theoretical questions about the forms and limits of judging.

## ■ MARTHA MINOW, JUDGE FOR THE SITUATION: JUDGE JACK WEINSTEIN, CREATOR OF TEMPORARY ADMINISTRATIVE AGENCIES
*97 Colum. L. Rev. 2010, 2020-2026 (1997)*

. . . Functionally, court-supervised settlements that establish systems for processing individual claims create temporary administrative agencies without proceeding through the legislative or executive branches. Even without the establishment of such claims facilities, judicial supervision of complex suits resembles administrative agency activity, especially in the use of masters and magistrates authorized to conduct fact-finding hearings, to manage parts of disputes, and to gather expert knowledge. Such solutions provide redress without destroying private defendants and construct flexible procedures and norms intended—by the judge and by the parties' lawyers—to suit particular circumstances. Sometimes, the court-created process is actually integrated into another prepackaged administrative procedure through the bankruptcy framework. At other times, the administrative dimensions of the court-supervised process are illustrated by the reactions of other players; other branches of government, government institutions such as schools, and private actors often send lobbyists to influence the court process, just as administrative agencies have inspired the development of vital advocacy organizations such as the AIDS Action Committee and the Natural Resources Defense Council. Judging for the situation, then, involves contextualized efforts to construct procedures tailored for a particular circumstance; judging for the situation involves generating temporary administrative structures responsive to the claims at hand. . . . Creation of claims processing facilities, use of public hearings, and consultation with community members and experts amount to the establishment of uniquely temporary and contextually specific administrative processes. These devices are framed around the parties to a litigation. The court, and the adjunct actors employed by the court, perform the work of processing claims under simplified procedures and management, seeking to fulfill party expectations swiftly. Exemplifying the range of administrative agencies in this country, some of the court-sponsored processes may be technically competent and efficient while others may be immersed in partisan debates. Typically, the claims-processing activity set up under court approval accomplishes the same shift from fault-based norms to compensation for harms that administrative agencies have adopted in contexts such as black lung disease and workers' compensation for injuries on the job. Yet, while it is fair to point to the similarities between these judicially created claims procedures and legislatively created administrative agencies, the differences between the two are also striking. Two important differences divide court-created administration systems from established administrative agencies: (1) the fact of court creation rather than legislative or executive authorization, and (2) their temporary, collapsible structure as compared to the more enduring, and at times entrenched, bureaucratic nature of traditional administrative agencies. The first invites intense scrutiny and potentially fatal objection on Article III and separation-of-powers grounds; the second may offer an intriguing challenge to other forms of administration. Both are, in my view, valuable contributions to American law and politics.

1. *Separation of Powers.* If a federal court, rather than the legislative or executive branches, creates an administrative agency, it is fair to inquire into the potential breach of separation-of-powers requirements and bounded authority for the judiciary. Has the court strayed into the domain of the executive to enforce the law or taken over the task of the legislature to devise prospective rules and establish government agencies? Have appointed judges stepped into the fray reserved for elected officials? Are the judges making political judgments that require accommodation, bargaining, and the accountability of the electoral sanction for democratic legitimacy and efficacy? Answers to these questions are bound to reflect the political preferences of the observer as much as considered theories of democratic governmental structures. Yet, seeing the inevitable infusion of politics into the question restates the problem. A judge who engages in the process of creating administrative responses to social problems is also inevitably immersed in political views, but lacks the tethering or camouflage of the traditional adjudicatory procedure. Judge Weinstein himself has not been shy in detailing his own support for compensatory, rather than fault-based, approaches to mass torts, and a cost-sharing approach toward defendants' liability. Similarly, Judge Weinstein has tried to reframe debates over the alleged litigation crisis and difficulties of access to the courts by labeling the issues as the challenge of responding to "the mass of cases working their way through the system." This is the language and conception of administration; it also reflects a choice in favor of redistribution and spreading the costs of injuries across broad communities, rather than other potential responses to harms in the world. For those who think these kinds of questions require the tangling and wrangling of legislative debate, such court actions amount to unchecked fiat, beyond the scope of legal authority and in violation of democratic principles. Three modest defenses can be offered on behalf of Judge Weinstein and other judges who use judicial resources to respond to such social problems despite inaction

by the elected branches: the vacuum created by their inaction leaves judges with properly filed, concrete claims, requiring some sort of response. Kenneth R. Feinberg, sometimes a special master in mass tort cases and always an expert in them, has concluded that no sweeping congressional reform is forthcoming on either the procedural or substantive sides of the field, "[s]o in effect the courts must do what they can with the tools at their disposal." These cases warrant utilization of untraditional means, like special masters, community input, and aggressive case management, because they encompass unanticipated problems with wide-ranging social and political ramifications. As Judge Weinstein insightfully notes, "[a] rigid and unresponsive judiciary, blind to the needs of various communities and of society at large, is far more likely to cause an erosion of public confidence in legal institutions than a judiciary perceived as overly interested in resolving the problems before it." Judicial action actually may trigger action by the other branches, and thereby promote the vision of overlapping and checking branches of government that lies behind the separation of powers. Judge Weinstein's *Agent Orange* settlement had this effect; Congress responded with a bill to aid veterans affected by exposure to dioxin, and the Veterans' Administration eventually interpreted its mandate to include responding to the needs of these veterans. Unlocking the logjam in the electoral branches may be a role uniquely assigned to the courts, and thus a basis for justifying judicial action that otherwise seems to interfere with legislative and executive prerogatives. Energetic judging thus may stimulate action by other branches that have been frozen and unresponsive. Second, judicial action may be defended here as continuous, rather than discontinuous, with other forms of adjudication. There is not an obvious or steady line distinguishing the judicial role involved in selecting strict liability as the standard in a particular tort case from the judicial role involved in supervision of a settlement achieving a similar result. Of course, this line of defense may simply expose even more judicial action to critique as invasive of the ambit of legislative or executive authority. Moreover, if the costs of the administrative process include assessments to the government, and not just to private parties, obtaining public revenues and justifying their use calls for resort to the elected branches. Yet, all judicial action requires appropriations and expenditures of public funds, ranging from the salaries of judges and clerks to outlays for paper and computer disks. Enforcement of the simplest damages award requires the use of personnel to process forms and, at times, to execute liens on property. There is no sharp line separating the tasks of adjudication and the tasks of implementing the law. A separation-of-powers objection starts a debate about appropriate judicial behavior; it does not clinch the debate, nor provide an absolute bar to a temporary administrative apparatus. Third, exposure and defense of the boundaries between the branches are necessary for reasoned debate: The initiative of someone like Judge Weinstein can generate public debate and analysis to sharpen understandings of separation of powers, a crucial element of our governmental structure. Jack Weinstein's approach to judging renders immediate what otherwise can remain a remote debate about the proper relationship between law and justice. Weinstein's approach reminds lawyers, judges, and theorists that legal rules—ranging from the most technical procedures to the basic constitutional structure—were devised by human beings as means for governing with justice. In Judge Weinstein's court, it is no defense to argue "that's never been done before"; legitimacy and legality are to be measured as much by results as by concordance with precedent. Accordingly, if governing with justice requires bending the rules and altering precedents, then the rules and the precedents need to be bent and altered. Of course, this is only one of many vigorously competing views about the proper relation between justice and law. As a result, Judge Weinstein's landmark cases afford rich, real examples to test the typically abstract debates over this and other competing views of law. In this way, his decisions benefit even those who find his approach to law to be an appalling disregard of its constraints.

2. *Temporary Administration.* An administrative agency established by the legislature or the executive may have an endpoint or sunset provision terminating its existence, but this is not the common practice. Instead, such administrative agencies, once established, tend to endure and require massive efforts to trim them, much less to close them down. The administrative processes established by courts, in contrast, have very specific time limitations, even if they endure for several years. A claims facility lasts only as long as the fund exists and claims remain to be processed; judicial supervision through masters and magistrates may extend longer than some would like, but it does come to an end when assigned tasks are fulfilled, when the parties complete their assigned duties or successfully move to modify their obligations, or when the judge involved concludes that no more can be done. These are not perfectly calibrated measures for termination, but they do yield endpoints to judicially sponsored administrative action. . . . Inventing flexible, responsive administrative practices may be the only alternative to big, blunt bureaucracies on the one hand, and private market mechanisms on the other.

## Comments and Questions

1. In *Agent Orange*, Judge Weinstein was committed to generating a settlement in the case from the moment it reached his courtroom, even though early settlement discussions had failed. He pressed for settlement by appointing an aggressive special master to push for one, by rejecting requests to bifurcate the trial or to delay it for more time for discovery, by issuing "tentative" rulings on the substantive law that made both sides worried about losing on the merits, and by directing all counsel to appear in chambers on the Saturday morning four days before trial was scheduled to begin for an around-the-clock negotiation session. Ultimately, the amount of settlement ($180 million) came from the judge himself. Does this kind of conduct comport

with desirable court-annexed dispute resolution, or does it demonstrate grave problems with that approach? For a fascinating account of Judge Weinstein's activism and his unconventionally imaginative efforts to force the *Agent Orange* parties to settle, read Peter H. Schuck, *Agent Orange on Trial* (1986).

2. A class action such as the Agent Orange litigation is very unlikely to be certified today. "Class actions seemed to drop out of the available set of tools for attempting to settle most mass torts, absent some extraordinary willingness of a settling defendant to allow some form of future claims to return to the tort system." Samuel Issacharoff, *Private Claims, Aggregate Rights*, 2008 Sup. Ct. Rev. 183, 208. In two cases decided in the late 1990s, the Supreme Court severely limited the ability of the federal courts to certify mass tort class actions like *Agent Orange. See Ortiz v. Fibreboard Corp.*, 527 U.S. 815 (1999); *Amchem Prods. Inc. v. Windsor*, 521 U.S. 591 (1997). Instead, mass tort cases such as the Agent Orange litigation would more likely be brought as individual lawsuits in federal courts all over the country and transferred for purposes of discovery and pre-trial motions to a single court. The Multidistrict Litigation statute provides that a panel of judges (called the Judicial Panel on Multidistrict Litigation) determine whether a given litigation merits consolidation in one courtroom and to which federal court in the country the cases should be sent. *See* 28 U.S.C. § 1407. This means that pre-trial litigation may occur far from the forum that the plaintiff chose.

3. Years after the settlement of the Agent Orange litigation was administered and closed, potential claimants came forward arguing that they had not been adequately represented in the litigation because the settlement did not make adequate provision for people whose injuries had not yet manifested. They succeeded in reopening their case. *See Stephenson v. Dow Chemical Co.*, 273 F.3d 249 (2d Cir. 2001), *affirming judgment in part, vacating in part*, 539 U.S. 111 (2003). The success of the collateral attack on the *Agent Orange* settlement is one reason that class actions are no longer considered good vehicles for achieving "global peace" in mass torts. Ultimately these plaintiffs' suits failed. Once they were back in Judge Weinstein's courtroom, the plaintiffs lost on summary judgment. *See In re Agent Orange Product Liability Litigation*, 517 F.3d 76 (2008) (holding that government contractor defense barred plaintiffs' claims).

# F. PRECLUSION IN CLASS ACTIONS

You have now reached the point where you should be able to grapple with a case that integrates almost all of the rules introduced in this chapter. Moreover, the case will force you to reconsider many of the underlying purposes of a procedural system, due process, and discrimination law. After you read *Martin v. Wilks*, study the applicable section of the Civil Rights Act of 1991 (which is printed after the case) and prepare for the final practice exercise.

## ■ MARTIN v. WILKS
### 490 U.S. 755 (1989)

Chief Justice REHNQUIST delivered the opinion of the Court:

A group of white firefighters sued the city of Birmingham, Alabama (City), and the Jefferson County Personnel Board (Board) alleging that they were being denied promotions in favor of less qualified black firefighters.* They claimed that the City and the Board were making promotion decisions on the basis of race in reliance on certain consent decrees, and that these decisions constituted impermissible racial discrimination in violation of the Constitution and federal statute. The District Court held that the white firefighters were precluded from challenging employment decisions taken pursuant to the decrees, even though these firefighters had not been parties to the proceedings in which the decrees were entered. We think this holding contravenes the general rule that a person cannot be deprived of his legal rights in a proceeding to which he is not a party.

The litigation in which the consent decrees were entered began in 1974, when the Ensley Branch of the National Association for the Advancement of Colored People and seven black individuals filed separate class-action complaints against the City and the Board. They alleged that both had engaged in racially discriminatory hiring and promotion practices in various public service jobs in violation of Title VII of the Civil Rights Act of 1964, 42 U.S.C. § 2000e *et seq.*, and other federal law. After a bench trial on some issues, but before judgment, the parties entered into two consent decrees, one between the black individuals and the City and the other between them and the Board. These proposed decrees set forth an extensive remedial scheme, including long-term and interim annual goals for the hiring of blacks as firefighters. The decrees also provided for goals for promotion of blacks within the fire department.

The District Court entered an order provisionally approving the decrees and directing publication of notice of the upcoming fairness hearings. Notice of the hearings, with a reference to the general nature of the decrees, was published in two local newspapers. At that hearing, the Birmingham Firefighters Association (BFA) appeared and filed objections as *amicus curiae*. After the hearing, but before final approval of the decrees, the BFA and two of its members also moved to intervene on the ground that the decrees would adversely affect their rights. The District Court denied the motions as untimely and approved the decrees. *United States v. Jefferson County*, 28 F.E.P. Cases 1834 (N.D. Ala. 1981). Seven white firefighters, all members of the BFA, then filed a complaint against the City and the Board seeking injunctive relief against enforcement of the decrees. The seven argued that the decrees would operate to illegally discriminate against them; the District Court denied relief.

---

*Eds.' Note:* For more information about the history of race relations in Birmingham, *see* Chapter 2.

Both the denial of intervention and the denial of injunctive relief were affirmed on appeal. *United States v. Jefferson County*, 720 F.2d 1511 (11th Cir. 1983). The District Court had not abused its discretion in refusing to let the BFA intervene, thought the Eleventh Circuit, in part because the firefighters could "institut[e] an independent Title VII suit, asserting specific violations of their rights." *Id.*, at 1518. And, for the same reason, petitioners had not adequately shown the potential for irreparable harm from the operation of the decrees necessary to obtain injunctive relief. *Id.*, at 1520.

A new group of white firefighters, the Wilks respondents, then brought suit against the City and the Board in District Court. They too alleged that, because of their race, they were being denied promotions in favor of less qualified blacks in violation of federal law. The Board and the City admitted to making race conscious employment decisions, but argued that the decisions were unassailable because they were made pursuant to the consent decrees. A group of black individuals, the Martin petitioners, were allowed to intervene in their individual capacities to defend the decrees.

The defendants moved to dismiss the reverse discrimination cases as impermissible collateral attacks on the consent decrees. The District Court denied the motions, ruling that the decrees would provide a defense to claims of discrimination for employment decisions "mandated" by the decrees, leaving the principal issue for trial whether the challenged promotions were indeed required by the decrees. After trial the District Court granted the motion to dismiss. The court concluded that "if in fact the City was required to [make promotions of blacks] by the consent decree, then they would not be guilty of [illegal] racial discrimination" and that the defendants had "establish[ed] that the promotions of the black individuals . . . were in fact required by the terms of the consent decree."

On appeal, the Eleventh Circuit reversed. It held that, "[b]ecause . . . [the Wilks respondents] were neither parties nor privies to the consent decrees, . . . their independent claims of unlawful discrimination are not precluded." . . .

We granted certiorari, and now affirm the Eleventh Circuit's judgment. All agree that "[i]t is a principle of general application in Anglo-American jurisprudence that one is not bound by a judgment in personam in a litigation in which he is not designated as a party or to which he has not been made a party by service of process." *Hansberry v. Lee*, 311 U.S. 32, 40 (1940). *See, e.g., Parklane Hosiery Co. v. Shore*, 439 U.S. 322, 327, n.7. This rule is part of our "deep-rooted historic tradition that everyone should have his own day in court." 18 C. Wright, A. Miller, & E. Cooper, *Federal Practice and Procedure* § 4449, p. 417 (1981) (18 Wright). A judgment or decree among parties to a lawsuit resolves issues as among them, but it does not conclude the rights of strangers to those proceedings.[2]

---

2. We have recognized an exception to the general rule when, in certain limited circumstances, a person, although not a party, has his interests adequately represented by someone with the same interests who is a party. Additionally, where a special remedial scheme exists expressly foreclosing successive litigation by nonlitigants, as for example in bankruptcy or probate, legal proceedings may terminate

Petitioners argue that, because respondents failed to timely intervene in the initial proceedings, their current challenge to actions taken under the consent decree constitutes an impermissible "collateral attack." They argue that respondents were aware that the underlying suit might affect them, and if they chose to pass up an opportunity to intervene, they should not be permitted to later litigate the issues in a new action. The position has sufficient appeal to have commanded the approval of the great majority of the Federal Courts of Appeals, but we agree with the contrary view expressed by the Court of Appeals for the Eleventh Circuit in this case.

We begin with the words of Justice Brandeis in *Chase National Bank v. Norwalk*, 291 U.S. 431 (1934): "The law does not impose upon any person absolutely entitled to a hearing the burden of voluntary intervention in a suit to which he is a stranger. . . . Unless duly summoned to appear in a legal proceeding, a person not a privy may rest assured that a judgment recovered therein will not affect his legal rights." *Id.*, at 441. While these words were written before the adoption of the Federal Rules of Civil Procedure, we think the Rules incorporate the same principle; a party seeking a judgment binding on another cannot obligate that person to intervene; he must be joined. Against the background of permissive intervention set forth in *Chase Nat'l Bank*, the drafters cast Rule 24, governing intervention, in permissive terms. *See* Fed. R. Civ. P. 24(a) (intervention as of right) ("Upon timely application anyone shall be permitted to intervene"); Fed. R. Civ. P. 24(b) (permissive intervention) ("Upon timely application anyone may be permitted to intervene"). They determined that the concern for finality and completeness of judgments would be "better [served] by mandatory joinder procedures." 18 Wright § 4452, p. 453. Accordingly, Rule 19(a) provides for mandatory joinder in circumstances where a judgment rendered in the absence of a person may "leave . . . persons already parties subject to a substantial risk of incurring . . . inconsistent obligations . . ." Rule 19(b) sets forth the factors to be considered by a court in deciding whether to allow an action to proceed in the absence of an interested party.

Joinder as a party, rather than knowledge of a lawsuit and an opportunity to intervene, is the method by which potential parties are subjected to the jurisdiction of the court and bound by a judgment or decree. The parties to a lawsuit presumably know better than anyone else the nature and scope of relief sought in the action, and at whose expense such relief might be granted. It makes sense, therefore, to place on them a burden of bringing in additional parties where such a step is indicated, rather than placing on potential additional parties a duty to intervene when they acquire knowledge of the lawsuit. The linchpin of the "impermissible collateral attack" doctrine—the attribution of preclusive effect to a failure to intervene—is therefore quite inconsistent with Rule 19 and Rule 24 . . . preclusive effect might be attributed to a failure to intervene. 390 U.S., at 114-15.

---

preexisting rights if the scheme is otherwise consistent with due process. Neither of these exceptions, however, applies in this case.

Petitioners contend that a different result should be reached because the need to join affected parties will be burdensome and ultimately discouraging to civil rights litigation. Potential adverse claimants may be numerous and difficult to identify; if they are not joined, the possibility for inconsistent judgments exists. Judicial resources will be needlessly consumed in relitigation of the same question.

Even if we were wholly persuaded by these arguments as a matter of policy, acceptance of them would require a rewriting rather than an interpretation of the relevant Rules. But we are not persuaded that their acceptance would lead to a more satisfactory method of handling cases like this one. It must be remembered that the alternatives are a duty to intervene based on knowledge, on the one hand, and some form of joinder, as the Rules presently provide, on the other. No one can seriously contend that an employer might successfully defend against a Title VII claim by one group of employees on the ground that its actions were required by an earlier decree entered in a suit brought against it by another, if the later group did not have adequate notice or knowledge of the earlier suit.

The difficulties petitioners foresee in identifying those who could be adversely affected by a decree granting broad remedial relief are undoubtedly present, but they arise from the nature of the relief sought and not because of any choice between mandatory intervention and joinder. Rule 19's provisions for joining interested parties are designed to accommodate the sort of complexities that may arise from a decree affecting numerous people in various ways. We doubt that a mandatory intervention rule would be any less awkward. As mentioned, plaintiffs who seek the aid of the courts to alter existing employment policies, or the employer who might be subject to conflicting decrees, are best able to bear the burden of designating those who would be adversely affected if plaintiffs prevail; these parties will generally have a better understanding of the scope of likely relief than employees who are not named but might be affected. Petitioners' alternative does not eliminate the need for, or difficulty of, identifying persons who, because of their interests, should be included in a lawsuit. It merely shifts that responsibility to less able shoulders.

Nor do we think that the system of joinder called for by the Rules is likely to produce more relitigation of issues than the converse rule. The breadth of a lawsuit and concomitant relief may be at least partially shaped in advance through Rule 19 to avoid needless clashes with future litigation. And even under a regime of mandatory intervention, parties who did not have adequate knowledge of the suit would relitigate issues. Additional questions about the adequacy and timeliness of knowledge would inevitably crop up. We think that the system of joinder presently contemplated by the rules best serves the many interests involved in the run of litigated cases, including cases like the present one.

Petitioners also urge that the congressional policy favoring voluntary settlement of employment discrimination claims, referred to in cases such as *Carson v. American Brands, Inc.*, 450 U.S. 79 (1981), also supports the "impermissible collateral attack" doctrine. But once again it is essential to note just what is meant by "voluntary settlement." A voluntary settlement in the form of a consent decree between one group of employees and their employer cannot possibly "settle," voluntarily or otherwise, the conflicting claims of another group of employees who do not join in the agreement. This is true even if the second group of employees is a party to the litigation: "[P]arties who choose to resolve litigation through settlement may not dispose of the claims of a third party . . . without that party's agreement. A court's approval of a consent decree between some of the parties therefore cannot dispose of the valid claims of nonconsenting intervenors." *Firefighters v. Cleveland*, 478 U.S. 501, 529 (1986).

Insofar as the argument is bottomed on the idea that it may be easier to settle claims among a disparate group of affected persons if they are all before the court, joinder bids fair to accomplish that result as well as a regime of mandatory intervention.

For the foregoing reasons we affirm the decision of the Court of Appeals for the Eleventh Circuit. That court remanded the case for trial of the reverse discrimination claims. *In re Birmingham Reverse Discrimination*, 833 F.2d, at 1500-02. Petitioners point to language in the District Court's findings of fact and conclusions of law which suggests that respondents will not prevail on the merits. We agree with the view of the Court of Appeals, however, that the proceedings in the District Court may have been affected by the mistaken view that respondents' claims on the merits were barred to the extent they were inconsistent with the consent decree.

Affirmed.

Justice STEVENS with whom Justice BRENNAN, Justice MARSHALL, and Justice BLACKMUN join, dissenting:

As a matter of law there is a vast difference between persons who are actual parties to litigation and persons who merely have the kind of interest that may as a practical matter be impaired by the outcome of a case. Persons in the first category have a right to participate in a trial and to appeal from an adverse judgment; depending on whether they win or lose, their legal rights may be enhanced or impaired. Persons in the latter category have a right to intervene in the action in a timely fashion, or they may be joined as parties against their will. But if they remain on the sidelines, they may be harmed as a practical matter even though their legal rights are unaffected. One of the disadvantages of sideline-sitting is that the bystander has no right to appeal from a judgment no matter how harmful it may be.

In these cases the Court quite rightly concludes that the white firefighters who brought the second series of Title VII cases could not be deprived of their legal rights in the first series of cases because they had neither intervened nor been joined as parties. *See Firefighters v. Cleveland*, 478 U.S. 501, 529-530 (1986); *Parklane Hosiery Co. v. Shore*, 439 U.S. 322, 327, n.7 (1979). The consent decrees obviously could not deprive them of any contractual rights, such as seniority, *cf. W. R. Grace & Co. v. Rubber Workers*, 461 U.S. 757 (1983), or accrued vacation pay, *cf. Massachusetts v. Morash*, 490 U.S. 107 (1989), or of any other legal rights, such as the right to have their employer comply with federal statutes like Title VII, *cf. Firefighters v. Cleveland, supra*, 478 U.S., at 529. There is no reason, however, why the consent decrees might not produce changes in conditions at the white firefighters' place of employment that, as a practical matter, may have a serious effect on their opportunities for employment or promotion even though they are not bound by the decrees in any legal sense. The fact that one of the effects of a decree is to curtail the job opportunities of nonparties does not mean that the nonparties have been deprived of legal rights or that they have standing to appeal from that decree without becoming parties.

Persons who have no right to appeal from a final judgment—either because the time to appeal has elapsed or because they never became parties to the case—may nevertheless collaterally attack a judgment on certain narrow grounds. If the court had no jurisdiction over the subject matter, or if the judgment is the product of corruption, duress, fraud, collusion, or mistake, under limited circumstances it may be set aside in an appropriate collateral proceeding. *See Restatement (Second) of Judgments* §§ 69-72 (1982). This rule not only applies to parties to the original action, but also allows interested third parties collaterally to attack judgments. In both civil and criminal cases, however, the grounds that may be invoked to support a collateral attack are much more limited than those that may be asserted as error on direct appeal. Thus, a person who can foresee that a lawsuit is likely to have a practical impact on his interests may pay a heavy price if he elects to sit on the sidelines instead of intervening and taking the risk that his legal rights will be impaired.

In these cases there is no dispute about the fact that respondents are not parties to the consent decrees. It follows as a matter of course that they are not bound by those decrees. Those judgments could not, and did not, deprive them of any legal rights. The judgments did, however, have a practical impact on respondents' opportunities for advancement in their profession. For that reason, respondents had standing to challenge the validity of the decrees, but the grounds that they may advance in support of a collateral challenge are much more limited than would be allowed if they were parties prosecuting a direct appeal.

The District Court's rulings in this case have been described incorrectly by both the Court of Appeals and this Court. The Court of Appeals repeatedly stated that the District Court had "in effect" held that the white firefighters were "bound" by a decree to which they were not parties. And this Court's opinion seems to assume that the District Court had interpreted its consent decrees in the earlier litigation as holding "that the white firefighters were precluded from challenging employment decisions taken pursuant to the decrees." It is important, therefore, to make clear exactly what the District Court did hold and why its judgment should be affirmed.

# I

The litigation in which the consent decrees were entered was a genuine adversary proceeding. In 1974 and 1975, two groups of private parties and the United States brought three separate Title VII actions against the city of Birmingham (City), the Personnel Board of Jefferson County (Board), and various officials, alleging discrimination in hiring and promotion in several areas of employment, including the fire department. After a full trial in 1976, the District Court found that the defendants had violated Title VII and that a test used to screen job applicants was biased. After a second trial in 1979 that focused on promotion practices—but before the District Court had rendered a decision—the parties negotiated two consent decrees, one with the City defendants and the other with the Board. The United States is a party to both decrees. The District Court provisionally approved the proposed decrees and directed that the parties provide notice "to all interested persons informing them of the general provisions of the Consent Decrees . . . and of their right to file objections." App. 695. Approximately two months later, the District Court conducted a fairness hearing, at which a group of black employees objected to the decrees as inadequate and a group of white firefighters—represented in part by the Birmingham Firefighters Association (BFA)—opposed any race-conscious relief. *Id.*, at 727. The District Court overruled both sets of objections and entered the decrees in August 1981.

In its decision approving the consent decrees, the District Court first noted "that there is no contention or suggestion that the settlements are fraudulent or collusive." *Id.*, at 238a. The court then explained why it was satisfied that the affirmative-action goals and quotas set forth in the decrees were "well within the limits upheld as permissible" in *Steelworkers v. Weber*, 443 U.S. 193 (1979), and other cases. It pointed out that the decrees "do not preclude the hiring or promotion of whites and males even for a temporary period of time," and that the City's commitment to promote blacks and whites to the position of fire lieutenant at the same rate was temporary and was subject both to the availability of qualified candidates and "to the caveat that the decree is not to be interpreted as requiring the hiring or promotion of a person who is not qualified or of a person who is demonstrably less qualified according to a job-related selection procedure." It further found that the record provided "more than ample reason" to conclude that the City would eventually be held liable for discrimination against blacks at high-level positions in the fire and police departments. Based on its understanding of the wrong committed, the court concluded that the remedy embodied in the consent decrees was "reasonably commensurate with the nature and extent of the indicated discrimination." The District Court then rejected other specific objections, pointing out that the decrees would not impinge on any contractual rights of the unions or their members. Finally, after noting that it had fully considered the white firefighters' objections to the settlement, it denied their motion to intervene as untimely.

Several months after the entry of the consent decrees, the Board certified to the City that five black firefighters, as well as eight whites, were qualified to full six vacancies in the position of lieutenant. A group of white firefighters then filed suit against the City and Board challenging their policy of "certifying candidates and making promotions on the basis of race under the assumed protection of consent settlements." The complaint alleged, in the alternative, that the consent decrees were illegal and void, or that the defendants were not properly implementing them. The plaintiffs filed motions for a temporary restraining order and a preliminary injunction. After an evidentiary hearing, the District Court found that the plaintiffs' collateral attack on the consent decrees was "without merit" and that four of the black officers were qualified for promotion in accordance with the terms of the decrees. Accordingly, it denied the motions, and, for the first time in its history, the City had a black lieutenant in its fire department.

The plaintiffs' appeal from that order was consolidated with the appeal that had been previously taken from the order denying the motion to intervene filed in the earlier litigation. The Court of Appeals affirmed both orders. *See United States v. Jefferson C.*, 720 F.2d 1511 (11th Cir. 1983). While that appeal was pending, in September 1983, the Wilks respondents filed a separate action against petitioners. The Wilks complaint alleged that petitioners were violating Title VII, but it did not contain any challenge to the validity of the consent decrees. After various preliminary proceedings, the District Court consolidated these cases, along with four other reverse discrimination actions brought against petitioners, under the caption *In re: Birmingham Reverse Discrimination Litigation*. In addition, over the course of the litigation, the court allowed further parties to intervene.

On February 18, 1985, the District Court ruled on the City's motion for partial summary judgment and issued an opinion that, among other things, explained its understanding of the relevance of the consent decrees to the issues raised in the reverse discrimination litigation. After summarizing the proceedings that led up to the entry of the consent decrees, the District Court expressly "recognized that the consent decrees might not bar all claims of 'reverse discrimination' since [the plaintiffs] had not been parties to the prior suits." The court then took a position with respect to the relevance of the consent decrees that differed from that advocated by any of the parties. The plaintiffs contended that the consent decrees, even if valid, did not constitute a defense to their action, and, in the alternative, that the decrees did not authorize the promotion of black applicants ahead of higher scoring white applicants and thus did not justify race-conscious promotions. The City, on the other hand, contended that the promotions were immunized from challenge if they were either required or permitted by the terms of the decrees. The District Court took the intermediate position that promotions required by—and made because of—the decrees were justified. However, it denied the City's summary judgment motion because it raised factual issues requiring a trial.

In December 1985, the court conducted a 5-day trial limited to issues concerning promotions in the City's fire and engineering departments. At that trial, respondents challenged the validity of the consent decrees; to meet that challenge, petitioners introduced the records of the 1976 trial, the 1979 trial, and the fairness hearing conducted in 1981. Respondents also tried to prove that they were demonstrably better qualified than the black fire-fighters who had been promoted ahead of them. At the conclusion of the trial, the District Court entered a partial final judgment dismissing portions of the plaintiffs' complaints. The judge explained his ruling in an oral opinion dictated from the bench, supplemented by the adoption, with some changes, of detailed findings and conclusions drafted by the prevailing parties.

In his oral statement, the judge adhered to the legal position he had expressed in his February ruling. He stated: "The conclusions there expressed either explicitly or implicitly were that under appropriate circumstances, a valid consent decree appropriately limited can be the basis for a defense against a charge of discrimination, even in the situation in which it is clear that the defendant to the litigation did act in a racially conscious manner. In that February order, it was my view as expressed then, that if the City of Birmingham made promotions of blacks to positions as fire lieutenant, fire captain and civil engineer, because the City believed it was required to do so by the consent decree, and if in fact the City was required to do so by the Consent Decree, then they would not be guilty of racial discrimination, either under Title 7, Section 1981, 1983 or the 14th Amendment. That remains my conclusion given the state of the law as I understand it." He then found as a matter of fact that petitioners had not promoted any black officers who were not qualified or who were demonstrably less qualified than the whites who were not promoted. He thus rejected respondents' contention that the City could not claim that it simply acted as required by terms of the consent decree.

> In this case, under the evidence as presented here, I find that even if the burden of proof be placed on the defendants, they have carried that proof and that burden of establishing that the promotions of the black individuals in this case were in fact required by the terms of the consent decree.

The written conclusions of law that he adopted are less clear than his oral opinion. He began by unequivocally stating: "The City Decree is lawful." He explained that "under all the relevant case law of the Eleventh Circuit and the Supreme Court, it is a proper remedial device, designed to overcome the effects of prior, illegal discrimination by the City of Birmingham." In that same conclusion, however, he did state that "plaintiffs cannot collaterally attack the Decree's validity." Yet, when read in context—and particularly in light of the court's finding that the decree was lawful under Eleventh Circuit and Supreme Court precedent—it is readily apparent that, at the extreme, this was intended as an alternative holding. More likely, it was an overstatement of the rule that collateral review is narrower in scope than appellate review. In any event, and regardless of one's reading of this lone sentence, it is absolutely clear that the court did not hold that respondents were bound by the decree. Nowhere in the District Court's lengthy findings of fact and conclusions of law is there a single word suggesting that respondents were bound by the consent decree or that the court intended to treat them as though they had been actual parties to that litigation and not merely as persons whose interests, as a practical matter, had been affected. Indeed, respondents, the Court of Appeals, and the majority opinion all fail to draw attention to any point in this case's long history at which the judge may have given the impression that any nonparty was legally bound by the consent decree.

## II

Regardless of whether the white firefighters were parties to the decrees granting relief to their black co-workers, it would be quite wrong to assume that they could never collaterally attack such a decree. If a litigant has standing, he or she can always collaterally attack a judgment for certain narrowly defined defects. On the other hand, a district court is not required to retry a case—or to sit in review of another court's judgment—every time an interested nonparty asserts that some error that might have been raised on direct appeal was committed. Such a broad allowance of collateral review would destroy the integrity of litigated judgments, would lead to an abundance of vexatious litigation, and would subvert the interest in comity between courts. Here, respondents have offered no circumstance that might justify reopening the District Court's settled judgment.

The implementation of a consent decree affecting the interests of a multitude of nonparties, and the reliance on that decree as a defense to a charge of discrimination in hiring and promotion decisions, raise a legitimate concern of collusion. No such allegation, however, has been raised. Moreover, there is compelling evidence that the decrees were not collusive. In its decision approving the consent decrees over the objection of the BFA and individual white firefighters, the District Court observed that there had been "no contention or suggestion" that the decrees were fraudulent or collusive. The record of the fairness hearing was made part of the record of this litigation, and this finding was not contradicted. More significantly, the consent decrees were not negotiated until after the 1976 trial and the court's finding that the City had discriminated against black candidates for jobs as police officers and firefighters, and until after the 1979 trial, at which substantial evidence was presented suggesting that the City also discriminated against black candidates for promotion in the fire department. Like the record of the 1981 fairness hearing, the records of both of these prior proceedings were made part of the record in this case. Given this history, the lack of any indication of collusion, and the District Court's finding that "there is more than ample reason for . . . the City of Birmingham to be concerned that [it] would be in time held liable for discrimination against blacks at higher level positions in the police and fire departments," it is evident that the decree was a product of genuine arm's-length negotiations.

Nor can it be maintained that the consent judgment is subject to reopening and further litigation because the relief it afforded was so out of line with settled legal doctrine that it "was transparently invalid or had only a frivolous pretense to validity." *Walker v. Birmingham*, 388 U.S. 307, 315 (1967) (suggesting that a contemner might be allowed to challenge contempt citation on ground that underlying court order was "transparently invalid"). To the contrary, the type of race-conscious relief ordered in the consent decrees is entirely consistent with this Court's approach to affirmative action. Given a sufficient predicate of racial discrimination, neither the Equal Protection Clause of the Fourteenth Amendment nor Title VII of the Civil Rights Act of 1964 erects a bar to affirmative action plans that benefit non-victims and have some adverse effect on nonwrongdoers. As Justice O'Connor observed in *Wygant v. Jackson Bd. of Educ.*, 476 U.S. 267 (1986): "This remedial purpose need not be accompanied by contemporaneous findings of actual discrimination to be accepted as legitimate as long as the public actor has a firm basis for believing that remedial action is required." *Id.*, at 286 (opinion concurring in part and concurring in judgment). Such a belief was clearly justified in these cases. After conducting the 1976 trial and finding against the City and after listening to the five days of testimony in the 1979 trial, the judge was well qualified to conclude that there was a sound basis for believing that the City would likely have been found to have violated Title VII if the action had proceeded to a litigated judgment.

Hence, there is no basis for collaterally attacking the judgment as collusive, fraudulent, or transparently invalid. Moreover, respondents do not claim—nor has there been any showing of—mistake, duress, or lack of jurisdiction. Instead, respondents are left to argue that somewhat different relief would have been more appropriate than the relief that was actually granted. Although this sort of issue may provide the basis for a direct appeal, it cannot, and should not, serve to open the door to relitigation of a settled judgment.

## III

The facts that respondents are not bound by the decree and that they have no basis for a collateral attack, moreover, do not compel the conclusion that the District Court should have treated the decree as nonexistent for purposes of respondents' discrimination suit. That the decree may not directly interfere with any of respondents' legal rights does not mean that it may not affect the factual setting in a way that negates respondents' claim. The fact that a criminal suspect is not a party to the issuance of a search warrant does not imply that the presence of a facially valid warrant may not be taken as evidence that the police acted in good faith. Similarly, the fact that an employer is acting under court compulsion may be evidence that the employer is acting in good faith and without discriminatory intent. Indeed, the threat of a contempt citation provides as good a reason to act as most, if not all, other business justifications.

After reviewing the evidence, the District Court found that the City had in fact acted under compulsion of the consent decree. Based on this finding, the court concluded that the City carried its burden of coming forward with a legitimate business reason for its promotion policy, and, accordingly, held that the promotion decisions were "not taken with the requisite discriminatory intent" necessary to make out a claim of disparate treatment under Title VII or the Equal Protection Clause. For this reason, and not because it thought that respondents were legally bound by the consent decree, the court entered an order in favor of the City and defendant-intervenors.

Of course, in some contexts a plaintiff might be able to demonstrate that reference to a consent decree is pretextual. For example, a plaintiff might be able to show that the consent decree was collusive and that the defendants simply obtained the court's rubber stamp on a private agreement that was in no way related to the eradication of pervasive racial discrimination. The plaintiff, alternatively, might be able to show that the defendants were not bound to obey the consent decree because the court that entered it was without jurisdiction. Similarly, although more tenuous, a plaintiff might argue that the parties to the consent judgment were not bound because the order was "transparently invalid" and thus unenforceable. If the defendants were as a result not bound to implement the affirmative-action program, then the plaintiff might be able to show that the racial preference was not a product of the court order.

In a case such as this, however, in which there has been no showing that the decree was collusive, fraudulent, transparently invalid, or entered without jurisdiction, it would be "unconscionable" to conclude that obedience to an order remedying a Title VII violation could subject a defendant to additional liability. Rather, all of the reasons that support the Court's view that a police officer should not generally be held liable when he carries out the commands in a facially valid warrant apply with added force to city officials, or indeed to private employers, who obey the commands contained in a decree entered by a federal court. In fact, Equal Employment Opportunity Commission regulations concur in this assessment. They assert: "The Commission interprets Title VII to mean that actions taken pursuant to the direction of a Court Order cannot give rise to liability under Title VII." 29 C.F.R. § 1608.8 (1989). Assuming that the District Court's findings of fact were not clearly erroneous—which of course is a matter that is not before us—it seems perfectly clear that its judgment should have been affirmed. Any other conclusion would subject large employers who seek to comply with the law by remedying past discrimination to a never-ending stream of litigation and potential liability. It is unfathomable that either Title VII or the Equal Protection Clause demands such a counter-productive result.

## IV

The predecessor to this litigation was brought to change a pattern of hiring and promotion practices that had discriminated against black citizens in Birmingham for decades. The white respondents in this case are not responsible for that history of discrimination, but they are nevertheless beneficiaries of the discriminatory practices that the litigation was designed to correct. Any remedy that seeks to create employment conditions that would have obtained if there had been no violations of law will necessarily have an adverse impact on whites, who must now share their job and promotion opportunities with blacks. Just as white employees in the past were innocent beneficiaries of illegal discriminatory practices, so is it inevitable that some of the same white employees will be innocent victims who must share some of the burdens resulting from the redress of the past wrongs.

There is nothing unusual about the fact that litigation between adverse parties may, as a practical matter, seriously impair the interests of third persons who elect to sit on the sidelines. Indeed, in complex litigation this Court has squarely held that a sideline-sitter may be bound as firmly as an actual party if he had adequate notice and a fair opportunity to intervene and if the judicial interest in finality is sufficiently strong.

There is no need, however, to go that far in order to agree with the District Court's eminently sensible view that compliance with the terms of a valid decree remedying violations of Title VII cannot itself violate that statute or the Equal Protection Clause. The city of Birmingham, in entering into and complying with this decree, has made a substantial step toward the eradication of the long history of pervasive racial discrimination that has plagued its fire department. The District Court, after conducting a trial and carefully considering respondents' arguments, concluded that this effort is lawful and should go forward. Because respondents have thus already had their day in court and have failed to carry their burden, I would vacate the judgment of the Court of Appeals and remand for further proceedings consistent with this opinion.

## ■ CIVIL RIGHTS ACT OF 1991
*Pub. L. No. 102-166, § 402(a), 105 Stat. 1071, 1099, reprinted at 42 U.S.C. § 2000e-2(n)(1) (Supp. V, 1993)*

§ 108. [A]n employment practice that implements and is within the scope of a litigated or consent judgment or order that resolves a claim of employment discrimination under the Constitution or Federal civil rights laws may not be challenged . . . in a claim under the Constitution or Federal civil rights laws:

(i) by a person who, prior to the entry of the judgment or order . . . had—

(1) actual notice of the proposed judgment or order sufficient to apprise such person that such judgment or order might adversely affect the interests and legal rights of such person and that an opportunity was available to present objections to such judgment or order by a future date certain; and

(2) a reasonable opportunity to present objections to such judgment or order;
  or
  (ii) by a person whose interests were adequately represented by another person who had previously challenged the judgment or order on the same legal grounds and with a similar factual situation, unless there has been an intervening change in law or fact.

## Comments and Questions

1. It is noteworthy that *Martin v. Wilks* arose out of a dispute in Birmingham, Alabama. You will recall from Chapter 2 that Birmingham is the location from which Rev. Martin Luther King, Jr., penned his famous *Letter from Birmingham City Jail*. Reverend King referred to Birmingham as America's most segregated city, and it was among the cities that witnessed some of the most violent struggles of the civil rights movement.

2. As you reach the end of this course, revisit the question that we first addressed in Chapter 1: Is giving individuals their "day in court" an important procedural value? Does requiring parties who are aware of litigation that could potentially affect their interests to intervene adequately respect, protect, or advance that value? What other, competing values ought courts to consider?

### Practice Exercise No. 42: The Supreme Court Addresses the Constitutionality of Preclusion Under the Civil Rights Act

Assume that the year is 2016 and that there are a number of new Justices on the Supreme Court of the United States. Moreover, the provisions of the Civil Rights Act of 1991 dealing with *Martin v. Wilks*, which are printed immediately after that case, are still in effect. Assume further that the *City of Cleveland* case, with essentially the same facts and same parties that you have studied throughout this course, was commenced in January 2012 in federal court and resulted, after a full trial before a judge without a jury, in a verdict and judgment for the plaintiffs under Title VII and an injunction ordering the City of Cleveland to use a non-gender-biased written and physical examination in the future, which results in qualified women being hired for the Cleveland fire department, and granting them as of the hiring date (if they have previously taken the discriminatory tests, and now passed the new tests) seniority, pay, and the positions that they would have had if they had previously passed the test and been hired at that time. The judgment entered and decree ordered as a result of that suit were appealed to the Court of Appeals and affirmed. This decree has adversely affected some current male members of the fire department, who have, in effect, placed lower on the seniority scale and who have been prejudiced already, they argue, by a reduced opportunity to become officers in the department. Fifteen women have already been hired since the new nondiscriminatory tests have been administered, and three of these are already captains. Moreover, the women who were now hired at larger salaries left a diminished salary pool from which current male members could receive raises.

The current male members of the Cleveland Fire Department, claiming that they were prejudiced by the initial suit, brought a class action against the women on the Department and the City of Cleveland to void the judgment and the injunction on the grounds that they were indispensable parties to the initial suit brought in behalf of the women. The named white male class representatives admitted in depositions that within six months of the commencement of the 2012 suit they had read about it in the newspapers, but they also said that they did not realize the impact that "victory for the women" would have on them. They allege that the district court in the 2012 class action knew about them and their concerns at least by January 2014, three months before the trial commenced in that case, which is when they moved to intervene for the first time; their motion to intervene was denied, and that decision was affirmed by the appeals court, after hearing their argument. They further argued that they cannot be bound and harmed by a suit to which they were not a party. The district court granted summary judgment to the women on the force and to the City of Cleveland, on the grounds that the initial verdict and judgment were valid, the male fire-fighters were not necessary and indispensable parties, the *Martin v. Wilks* amendment found in the Civil Rights Act is dispositive, and that the trial judge in the initial suit acted within his appropriate discretion in denying the late attempt to intervene. The court of appeals affirmed on all points. The Supreme Court has granted certiorari.

The plaintiffs in the current class action suit, the male firefighters, argue that *Martin v. Wilks* governs, that the initial decree is invalid on Rule 19 and due process grounds, that they had a right to intervene and the denial to grant their motion was improper, and that the *Martin v. Wilks* amendment found in the Civil Rights Act of 1991 is unconstitutional on due process grounds for it purports to bind them without formal notice, service, and the right to be heard. The women firefighters and the City of Cleveland argue that this suit is in a procedurally incorrect posture, that *Martin v. Wilks* doesn't apply to their initial case or to this one because it is distinguishable, that the current court should decide the *Martin v. Wilks* issue differently for it was wrongly decided in 1989 (regardless of the Civil Rights Act of 1991), that the Civil Rights Act of 1991 does apply and is constitutional, and that the plaintiffs in the current suit lost any rights they might otherwise have had because of their tardy attempt to intervene in the first suit (the district court judge did not abuse her discretion in denying the motion to intervene and that preclusion law prevents their now appealing a motion denied in the prior lawsuit).

The women firefighters and the City of Cleveland have hired the same lawyer. Students with last names beginning with the letters A-M will argue for the appellees; all others will argue for the male appellants. Each student should be prepared to give a complete oral argument before the Supreme Court, unless you chose the option that follows. You will be picked at random. Appellants' counsel will be called upon first.

**Option:** You may wish to prepare your arguments as a team (of three or fewer). Make sure you team with students representing the same party (or parties). If any member of your team is selected, all should come forward to argue; divide the allotted time as you see fit.

# Case Files

# Case Files
## *Carpenter v. Dee*
## Contents

*Initial Memorandum*

To:      Associates

From:   Carol Coblentz (senior partner)

Re:      Nancy Carpenter—potential client of Needham, Shaker & Coblentz

At 7:00 P.M. on August 31, 2011, 25-year-old Charlie Carpenter was riding as a passenger with his friend Randall Dee in Dee's Jeep CJ-7. They were on their way to pick up their swimming trunks so they could return to a friend's barbecue and pool party. On the corner of Palmer and Franklin Streets in Lowell, MA, Dee lost control of the jeep and it rolled over. Dee suffered only minor injuries, but Charlie Carpenter was pinned under the vehicle and killed.

Charlie Carpenter was survived by his wife Nancy who was pregnant and later delivered a premature but healthy son on January 10, 2012. She named the boy Charlie Jr. At the time of the accident Mr. Carpenter was employed as a custodian at Forsythe University, where he received benefits, which applied to his wife and would have covered his child as well. Charlie Sr. was killed just prior to qualifying for University-funded life insurance benefits. Prior to his custodian job, Charlie worked as an auto mechanic for a variety of local auto body shops.

Months prior to the incident Randall Dee had modified the jeep with a suspension lift kit and oversize tires. These modifications affected the jeep's handling characteristics and were a significant factor in the rollover of the jeep. Dee had been stopped by Lowell police on several occasions prior to the accident for various suspected motor vehicle offenses. However, we believe that the police never advised him that the jeep was illegally modified and that the authorities took no other action to prevent the jeep from being driven in its dangerously modified condition.

On July 28, 2012, Randall Dee was convicted in criminal court on four counts in relation to the incident on August 31, 2011: (1) negligent homicide; (2) failing to slow at an intersection; (3) speeding; and (4) altering the height of a motor vehicle. He received a one-year suspended sentence for the homicide count and was required to serve two years' probation and 200 hours of community service. Fines for the other charges amounted to $100.

The jeep that Dee was driving was owned by his ex-girlfriend, Twyla Burrell. Ms. Burrell maintained a minimum liability insurance policy on the jeep in the amount of $10,000. Ms. Burrell had lived with Dee for more than a year, and when she moved out, she left the jeep with Dee, ostensibly because he had done so much work on it.

We'll need to investigate further to discover the extent of the modifications made to the jeep, but Ms. Carpenter knows that they included a suspension lift and hugely oversized tires. I'm not entirely clear about the next bit, but Ms. Carpenter insists that the body of the jeep was lifted even further off the frame by using hockey pucks that were bolted to the frame at various points around the vehicle. A Massachusetts statute prohibits raising the height of a vehicle more than two inches off of the frame, and Ms. Carpenter says she's certain that the jeep was lifted at least a foot. Although she believes that the rollover was caused by the modifications— and from what I hear in the news about hiked-up vehicles, this sounds plausible—none of these modifications broke or were damaged as a part of the accident.

We know that Dee had been stopped by uniformed Lowell police officers previously and that on one prior occasion he was found guilty of the offense of driving while intoxicated (for which his license was suspended for thirty days). Further, we know that at some time prior to that conviction (but still subsequent to the modifications of the jeep) Dee was stopped by a uniformed Lowell police officer for driving without a side view mirror and instructed not to drive the jeep until he got a mirror. Dee was stopped on at least one other occasion by Lowell police for driving an unregistered, uninsured vehicle—at which time it was taken from him and towed away; Dee later proved that there was insurance on the jeep and was fined only for driving it unregistered.

From what we can tell, Randall Dee is not a wealthy man. He is unmarried and lives in his family home with his brother, Peter. Ms. Carpenter believes they bought the house from the estate of their deceased father. Ms. Carpenter says that she thought the brothers both owned the house, but a mutual friend told her recently that Peter says he owns the house alone. To date, we don't know where Randall Dee bought the parts he used to modify the jeep, nor do we know if he received any warnings from anyone about creating a dangerous propensity to tip over by raising the jeep off the frame. We also don't know if he knew the jeep was too high under the Mass. Code, nor do we know yet where he had his car inspected for its annual inspection sticker required under Massachusetts law.

Please be prepared to discuss with me who the parties might be in a lawsuit, and what the causes of action might be. Should we take the case?

Note—I advised Ms. Carpenter that if we take the case we would pursue it on a contingent fee basis.

[*Eds.' Note:* The names of the parties have been changed to protect their privacy. The dates of certain events (including the enactment and effective dates of certain Massachusetts regulations) have been modified for pedagogical reasons. With other minor exceptions, the pleadings, motions, and discovery in the Case Files are identical to those filed in the actual case.]

## ■ MASS. GEN. LAWS CH. 229 § 2
## (WRONGFUL DEATH)*

A person who

(1) by his negligence causes the death of a person, or

(2) by willful, wanton or reckless act causes the death of a person under such circumstances that the deceased could have recovered damages for personal injuries if his death had not resulted, or

(3) operates a common carrier of passengers and by his negligence causes the death of a passenger, or

(4) operates a common carrier of passengers and by his willful, wanton or reckless act causes the death of a passenger under such circumstances that the deceased could have recovered damages for personal injuries if his death had not resulted, or

(5) is responsible for a breach of warranty arising under Article 2 of chapter one hundred and six which results in injury to a person that causes death, shall be liable in damages in the amount of:

(1) the fair monetary value of the decedent to the persons entitled to receive the damages recovered, as provided in section one, including but not limited to compensation for the loss of the reasonably expected net income, services, protection, care, assistance, society, companionship, comfort, guidance, counsel, and advice of the decedent to the persons entitled to the damages recovered;

(2) the reasonable funeral and burial expenses of the decedent;

(3) punitive damages in an amount of not less than five thousand dollars in such case as the decedent's death was caused by the malicious, willful, wanton or reckless conduct of the defendant or by the gross negligence of the defendant;

except that:

(1) the liability of an employer to a person in his employment shall not be governed by this section,

(2) a person operating a railroad shall not be liable for negligence in causing the death of a person while walking or being upon such railroad contrary to law or to the reasonable rules and regulations of the carrier and

(3) a person operating a street railway or electric railroad shall not be liable for negligence for causing the death of a person while walking or being upon that part of the street railway or electric railroad not within the limits of a highway.

A person shall be liable for the negligence or the willful, wanton or reckless act of his agents or servants while engaged in his business to the same extent and subject to the same limits as he would be liable under this section for his own act. Damages under this section shall be recovered in an action of tort by the executor or administrator of the deceased. An action to recover

---

*Eds.' Note: At common law, the death of the victim abated the victim's claim for the personal injuries. Beginning in the mid-1800s, "wrongful death statutes" were enacted by states to prevent tortfeasors from escaping liability in circumstances where the victim happened to die.

damages under this section shall be commenced within three years from the date of death or within such time thereafter as is provided by section four, four B, nine or ten or chapter two hundred and sixty.

[The survivorship provisions of Mass. Gen. Laws ch. 229 § 1 are as follows:

(1) If the deceased shall have been survived by a wife or husband and no children or issue surviving, then to the use of such surviving spouse.

(2) If the deceased shall have been survived by a wife or husband and by one child or by the issue of one deceased child, then one half to the use of such surviving spouse and one half to the use of such child or his issue by right of representation.

(3) If the deceased shall have been survived by a wife or husband and by more than one child surviving either in person or by issue, then one third to the use of such surviving spouse and two thirds to the use of such surviving children or their issue by right of representation.

(4) If there is no surviving wife or husband, then to the use of the next of kin.]

# ■ MASS. GEN. LAWS CH. 229 § 6 (CONSCIOUS SUFFERING)

In any civil action brought under [the Wrongful Death section reprinted above], damages may be recovered for conscious suffering resulting from the same injury, but any sum so recovered shall be held and disposed of by the executors or administrators as assets of the estate of the deceased.

# ■ MASS. GEN. LAWS CH. 109A §§ 1-10 (FRAUDULENT CONVEYANCE)*

§ 1 Definitions. In this chapter "Assets" of a debtor means property not exempt from liability for his debts. To the extent that any property is liable for any debts of the debtor, such property shall be included in his assets.

"Conveyance" includes every payment of money, assignment, release, transfer, lease, mortgage or pledge of tangible or intangible property, and also the creation of any lien or encumbrance.

"Creditor" is a person having any claim, whether matured or unmatured, liquidated or unliquidated, absolute, fixed or contingent.

"Debt" includes any legal liability, whether matured or unmatured, liquidated or unliquidated, absolute, fixed or contingent.

§ 2 Insolvency of persons. A person is insolvent within the meaning of this chapter when the present fair salable value of his assets is less than the

---

*Eds.' Note:* This was the law at the time the actual lawsuit was brought. Massachusetts has since adopted the Uniform Fraudulent Transfer Act, which has similar provisions. *See* Mass. Gen. Laws ch. 109A.

amount that will be required to pay his probable liability on his existing debts as they become absolute and matured. . . .

§ 3 Fair consideration. Fair consideration is given for property or obligation—

(a) When in exchange for such property or obligation, as a fair equivalent therefor, and in good faith, property is conveyed or an antecedent debt is satisfied, or

(b) When such property or obligation is received in good faith to secure a present advance or antecedent debt in amount not disproportionately small as compared with the value of the property or obligation obtained. . . .

§ 4 Conveyances by insolvent. Every conveyance made and every obligation incurred by a person who is or will be thereby rendered insolvent is fraudulent as to creditors without regard to his actual intent if the conveyance is made or the obligation is incurred without a fair consideration. . . .

§ 6 Conveyances by person about to incur debts beyond ability to pay. Every conveyance made and every obligation incurred without fair consideration when the person making the conveyance or entering into the obligation intends or believes that he will incur debts beyond his ability to pay as they mature is fraudulent as to both present and future creditors.

§ 7 Conveyances made with intent to defraud. Every conveyance made and every obligation incurred with actual intent, as distinguished from intent presumed in law, to hinder, delay or defraud either present or future creditors, is fraudulent as to both present and future creditors . . .

§ 9 Rights of creditors; matured claims.

(1) Where a conveyance or obligation is fraudulent as to a creditor, such creditor, when his claim has matured, may, as against any person except a purchaser for fair consideration without knowledge of the fraud at the time of the purchase, or one who has derived title immediately or immediately from such a purchaser—

(a) Have the conveyance set aside or obligation annulled to the extent necessary to satisfy his claim, or

(b) Disregard the conveyance and attach or levy execution upon the property conveyed.

(2) A purchaser who without actual fraudulent intent has given less than a fair consideration for the conveyance or obligation may retain the property or obligation as security for repayment.

§ 10 Rights of creditors; immature claims. Where a conveyance made or obligation incurred is fraudulent as to a creditor whose claim has not matured, he may proceed in the supreme judicial or superior court against any person against whom he could have proceeded had his claim matured, and the court may—

(a) Restrain the defendant from disposing of his property,

(b) Appoint a receiver to take charge of the property,

(c) Set aside the conveyance or annul the obligation, or

(d) Make any order which the circumstances of the case may require.

## COMMONWEALTH OF MASSACHUSETTS

MIDDLESEX, SS

NANCY CARPENTER, As
Administratrix of the Estate
of Charles Carpenter,
  Plaintiff

    vs.

RANDALL DEE and
PETER DEE,
  Defendants.

SUPERIOR COURT DEPARTMENT
OF THE TRIAL COURT CIVIL
ACTION NO. 12-6144

COMPLAINT

PLAINTIFF CLAIMS
TRIAL BY JURY

**PARTIES**

1. The plaintiff Nancy Carpenter is a resident of Lowell, Middlesex County, Massachusetts. She brings this action in her capacity as the administratrix of the estate of Charles Carpenter, her late husband, of Lowell, Middlesex County, Massachusetts. She was duly appointed as administratrix by the Middlesex Probate Court, docket number 11P3875A.

2. The defendant Randall Dee is a resident of Lowell, Middlesex County, Massachusetts.

3. The defendant Peter Dee is a resident of Lowell, Middlesex County, Massachusetts.

**FACTS**

4. On or about August 31, 2011, the plaintiff's intestate, Charles Carpenter, was riding as a passenger in a 1986 Jeep CJ-7 (hereinafter "the jeep").

5. The jeep was owned by one Twyla Burrell, and operated by the defendant Randall Dee.

6. At or near the intersection of Palmer and Franklin Streets in Lowell, the operator lost control of the jeep, and it rolled over, pinning Charles Carpenter beneath it.

7. The loss of control and resulting accident was caused by the negligent and/or grossly negligent and/or wanton and willful, and reckless conduct of

the defendant Randall Dee as operator of the jeep including, but not limited to, the following acts and omissions:

a. excessive speed;
b. failing to stop at an intersection; and
c. illegal and dangerous alteration of the chassis, causing unsafe handling characteristics.

## COUNT I—WRONGFUL DEATH

8. The plaintiff repeats and incorporates herein the allegations of paragraphs 1 through 7.

9. As a result of the negligent and/or grossly negligent and/or wanton, willful, and reckless conduct of the defendant Randall Dee, the plaintiff's intestate was killed on August 31, 2011.

## COUNT II—CONSCIOUS SUFFERING

10. The plaintiff repeats and incorporates herein the allegations of paragraphs 1 through 7.

11. As a result of the conduct of the defendant Randall Dee, as described above, the plaintiff's intestate sustained serious personal injuries, from which he suffered consciously, prior to his death on August 31, 2011.

## COUNT III—FRAUDULENT CONVEYANCE

12. The plaintiff repeats and incorporates herein the allegations of paragraphs 1 through 7.

13. At the time of the accident on August 31, 2011, the defendant Randall Dee and the defendant Peter Dee owned as joint tenants a certain parcel of land at 91 Birch Hill Road, Lowell, Massachusetts, containing approximately 11,604 square feet.

14. The defendants Randall Dee and Peter Dee had purchased said property from the estate of their deceased father Rick Dee, for the amount of $80,000 on or about February 13, 2011.

15. On or about October 8, 2011, the defendant Randall Dee conveyed all his right, title and interest in the above property to Peter Dee for "nominal consideration."

16. On information and belief, the transfer of such interest was fraudulent as to creditors, including, but not limited to, the plaintiff, within the meaning of Mass. Gen. Laws ch. 109A, in that:

(a) The conveyance was made without fair consideration, and Randall Dee was thereby rendered insolvent, within the meaning of Mass. Gen. Laws ch. 109A, § 4; and/or

(b) The conveyance was made without fair consideration at a time when the defendant Randall Dee believed that he would incur debts beyond his ability to pay, within the meaning of Mass. Gen. Laws ch. 109A, § 6; and/or

(c) The transfer was made with an actual intent to hinder, delay, or defraud creditors, including but not limited to the plaintiff, within the meaning of Mass. Gen. Laws ch. 109A, § 7.

**WHEREFORE, the plaintiff prays for the following relief:**

1. Judgment on Count I against the defendant Randall Dee

(a) To compensate the survivors of the plaintiff's intestate for the fair monetary value of the deceased for reasonably expected net income lost, services, protection, care, assistance, society, companionship, comfort, guidance, counsel, and advice of the deceased;

(b) Reasonable funeral and burial expenses;

(c) Punitive damages in an amount of at least $5,000.00, pursuant to Mass. Gen. Laws ch. 229, § 2.

2. Judgment on Count II against the defendant Randall Dee to compensate the estate of Charles Carpenter for his pain and conscious suffering.

3. That the Court issue a temporary restraining order enjoining the defendant, Randall Dee, until further order of this court, from conveying, encumbering, or in any other manner transferring any interest, legal or equitable, in any of his assets, including but not limited to real estate, bank accounts, certificates of deposit, securities, valuables, and any other asset not immune from execution, except in the ordinary course of business.

4. That the Court issue a preliminary injunction enjoining the defendant Randall Dee, until the disposition of this action on the merits, from conveying, encumbering, or in any other manner transferring any interest, legal or equitable, in any of his assets, including but not limited to real estate, bank accounts, certificates of deposit, securities, valuables, and any other asset not immune from execution, except in the ordinary course of business.

5. That the Court issue a temporary restraining order enjoining the defendant Peter Dee, until further order of this court, from conveying,

encumbering, or in any other manner transferring any interest, legal or equitable, in the real estate at 91 Birch Hill Road, Lowell, MA.

6. That the Court issue a preliminary injunction, enjoining the defendant Peter Dee, until the disposition of this action on the merits, from conveying, encumbering, or in any other manner transferring any interest, legal or equitable, in the real estate at 91 Birch Hill Road, Lowell, MA.

7. That the Court, under Count III, declare null and void the conveyance of the interest of Randall Dee in the property at 91 Birch Hill Road, Lowell, and/or allow satisfaction of any judgment in this action against Randall Dee to be satisfied against the interest he held in said property prior to the fraudulent conveyance.

8. That the Court issue a temporary restraining order enjoining the defendants, until further order of the Court, from selling, or transferring in any way the jeep vehicle involved or in any way modifying it, or changing its present condition.

9. That the Court issue a preliminary injunction enjoining the defendants, until the disposition of this action on the merits, from selling, or transferring in any way the jeep vehicle involved or in any way modifying it, or changing its present condition.

By her attorneys,

By: /s/ Carol Coblentz
Carol Coblentz (BBO#304321)
Needham, Shaker and Coblentz
44 Park Place
Boston, MA 02100
(617) 555-5555

Dated: /d/

[*Eds.' Note:* Notice that at the beginning of this complaint, there is a civil action number, No. 12-6144. Practices vary among jurisdictions, but here the "12" represents the year this case filed, 2012. The remainder of the number is a unique identification number issued by the clerk of the court upon filing of the complaint. This "docket number" will then appear on all subsequent court filings. Docket numbers may also include a letter or a set of initials that indicate to what judge or court session the case is assigned.

You will also notice another number in the signature block of the filing attorney. Upon admission to the bar in Massachusetts, new lawyers are issued a unique identification number by the Board of Bar Overseers (BBO). Here, attorney Carol Coblentz has a "BBO Number" of 304321. Various state (federal) rules may require lawyers to identify themselves with an identification number on documents filed with that court.]

# COMMONWEALTH OF MASSACHUSETTS

MIDDLESEX, SS

SUPERIOR COURT DEPARTMENT
OF THE TRIAL COURT CIVIL
ACTION NO. 12-6144

NANCY CARPENTER, As
Administratrix of the Estate
of Charles Carpenter,
  Plaintiff

    vs.

MOTION TO DISMISS

RANDALL DEE and
PETER DEE,
  Defendants.

The defendant Randall Dee moves to dismiss Counts I, II, and III (Wrongful Death, Conscious Suffering, and Fraudulent Conveyance) of the Complaint against said defendant pursuant to Mass. R. Civ. P. 12(b)(6) for failure to state claims upon which relief can be granted.

In support thereof Randall Dee says that the Complaint alleges three causes of action against said defendant. It is further alleged that on August 31, 2011, the Plaintiff's intestate was injured and killed while a passenger in a Jeep CJ-7 that rolled over because said jeep was being driven at an excessive speed while failing to stop at an intersection and with illegal and dangerous alteration of the chassis. The specific allegations against the defendants include the following:

(a) On Count I, the defendant's conduct was negligent and/or grossly negligent and/or wanton, willful, and reckless;

(b) On Count II, the defendant's conduct resulted in serious personal injuries to the plaintiff's intestate which resulted in conscious suffering; and

(c) On Count III, the defendant fraudulently conveyed a certain parcel of land that was purchased for the amount of $80,000; and that defendant Randall Dee conveyed all his right, title, and interest in said property to Peter Dee for nominal consideration and that transfer of such interest was fraudulent.

All three counts should be dismissed for the two reasons hereunder set forth:

(1) Randall Dee was not the owner of said Jeep CJ-7.

(2) The complaint does not allege that Randall Dee owed a duty to Charles Carpenter.

Count III should also be dismissed for failure to plead the circumstances with particularity.

RANDALL DEE, by his attorney,

By: _____ /s/ Robert Orthwein _____
Robert Orthwein (BBO#627841)
Chaudhuri, Brown, Orthwein & Guinto
11 Boardwalk
Boston, MA 02100
(617) 555-1111

Dated: /d/

## COMMONWEALTH OF MASSACHUSETTS

MIDDLESEX, SS

NANCY CARPENTER, As
Administratrix of the Estate
of Charles Carpenter,
  Plaintiff

    vs.

RANDALL DEE and
PETER DEE,
  Defendants.

SUPERIOR COURT DEPARTMENT
OF THE TRIAL COURT CIVIL
ACTION NO. 12-6144

MOTION FOR MORE DEFINITE
STATEMENT

The defendant Randall Dee moves the Court to issue an order for a more definite statement pursuant to Mass. R. Civ. P. 12(e).

The complaint is so vague and ambiguous that defendant should not reasonably be required to prepare a responsive pleading. Plaintiff should be ordered to furnish a more definite statement of the nature of her claim as set forth in her complaint in the following respects:

1. With respect to the allegations contained in Paragraph 7, page 1 of the complaint, plaintiff should be required to state the facts supporting her conclusion that on August 31, 2011, Randall Dee lost control of the 1986 Jeep CJ-7 because of his negligent and/or grossly negligent and/or wanton and willful, conduct by stating the circumstances surrounding the accident: weather conditions, speed of vehicle, proximity to other vehicles, condition and experience of defendant-driver.

2. With respect to the prayer for relief, plaintiff has failed to provide the amount which she is claiming for loss of the value of the decedent's net income, services, protection, care, assistance, society, companionship, comfort, guidance, counsel, and advice of the deceased.

RANDALL DEE, by his attorney,

By: _____ /s/ Robert Orthwein _____
Robert Orthwein (BBO#627841)
Chaudhuri, Brown, Orthwein & Guinto
11 Boardwalk
Boston, MA 02100
(617) 555-1111

Dated: /d/

COMMONWEALTH OF MASSACHUSETTS

MIDDLESEX, SS                           SUPERIOR COURT DEPARTMENT
OF THE TRIAL COURT CIVIL
ACTION NO. 12-6144

NANCY CARPENTER, As
Administratrix of the Estate
of Charles Carpenter,
   Plaintiff                              ANSWER OF RANDALL DEE
(AS TO COUNTS I AND II ONLY)

     vs.

                                     DEFENDANT RANDALL DEE
RANDALL DEE and                      CLAIMS JURY TRIAL
PETER DEE,
   Defendants.

**PARTIES**

1. The Defendant, Randall Dee, admits the allegations contained in Paragraph One of Plaintiff's Complaint.

2. The Defendant, Randall Dee, admits the allegations contained in Paragraph Two of Plaintiff's Complaint.

3. The Defendant, Randall Dee, admits the allegations contained in Paragraph Three of Plaintiff's Complaint.

**FACTS**

4. The Defendant, Randall Dee, admits the allegations contained in Paragraph Four of Plaintiff's Complaint.

5. The Defendant, Randall Dee, admits the allegations contained in Paragraph Five of Plaintiff's Complaint.

6. The Defendant, Randall Dee, denies each and every allegation contained in Paragraph Six of Plaintiff's Complaint.

7. The Defendant, Randall Dee, denies each and every allegation contained in Paragraph Seven of Plaintiff's Complaint.

**COUNT I—WRONGFUL DEATH**

8. The Defendant, Randall Dee, repeats and realleges his answers contained in Paragraphs One through Seven, as if fully stated herein.

9. The Defendant, Randall Dee, denies each and every allegation contained in Paragraph Nine of Plaintiff's Complaint.

## COUNT II—CONSCIOUS SUFFERING

10. The Defendant, Randall Dee, repeats and realleges his answers contained in Paragraphs One through Seven, as if fully stated herein.

11. The Defendant, Randall Dee, denies each and every allegation contained in Paragraph Eleven of Plaintiff's Complaint.

### FIRST DEFENSE

And further answering, the Defendant says that the Plaintiff's intestate's own negligence caused or contributed to the accident and damages alleged, and therefore the Plaintiff cannot recover.

### SECOND DEFENSE

And further answering, the Defendant says that the Plaintiff's intestate was more than 50 percent negligent in causing or contributing to the accident and damages alleged, and therefore the Plaintiff either cannot recover or any verdict or finding in his favor must be reduced by the percentage of negligence attributed to the said Plaintiff's intestate.

### THIRD DEFENSE

And further answering, the Defendant says that the Plaintiff's intestate assumed the risk of the accident and damages alleged, and therefore the Plaintiff cannot recover.

### FOURTH DEFENSE

And further answering, the Defendant says that the Plaintiff's intestate was in violation of the law at the time and place of the alleged accident, which violation of the law caused or contributed to the happening of said accident, and therefore the Plaintiff cannot recover.

### FIFTH DEFENSE

And further answering, the Defendant says that the Plaintiff's intestate's alleged injuries and subsequent death were caused by persons other than the

Defendant, his agents, servants, or employees, and plaintiff's intestate's alleged injuries, if any, were caused by persons for whose conduct the defendant is not responsible, and therefore, the Plaintiff cannot recover.

## SIXTH DEFENSE

And further answering, the Defendant says that the Plaintiff's intestate's alleged injuries, and subsequent death, do not come within one of the exceptions to the Massachusetts No-Fault Insurance Law, being Massachusetts General Laws, Chapter 231, Section 6D, and therefore the Plaintiff is barred from bringing this action and cannot recover.

## SEVENTH DEFENSE

And further answering, the Defendant says that the alleged cause of action referred to in the Plaintiff's complaint falls within the purview of Massachusetts General Laws, Chapter 90, Section 34(m), and therefore this action is brought in violation of the law and the Plaintiff cannot recover.

WHEREFORE, the Defendant, Randall Dee, demands judgment against the Plaintiff and further demands that said action be dismissed.

AND FURTHER, the Defendant, Randall Dee, claims a trial by jury on all the issues.

RANDALL DEE, by his attorney,

By: _____ /s/ Robert Orthwein _____
Robert Orthwein (BBO#627841)
Chaudhuri, Brown, Orthwein & Guinto
11 Boardwalk
Boston, MA 02100
(617) 555-1111

Dated: /d/

[*Eds.' Note:* Randall Dee did not answer the allegations in Count III of the complaint. One possible explanation for this is that the parties may have reached an agreement on what to do about the alleged fraudulent conveyance pending a trial on the merits. It also is conceivable that Randall Dee intended later to answer Count III, but the parties then simply forgot. To be sure, unusual things happen during litigation.

We also wish to emphasize that Randall Dee's third defense, assumption of the risk, is not a defense under Massachusetts comparative negligence law.

The sixth and seventh affirmative defenses are completely baseless. The statutory provisions cited relate to Massachusetts no-fault insurance, and the defenses do not apply in this case. We reprint the Answer in full, however, because we want you to see what was filed. It also is instructive to learn what happens when one blindly follows forms.]

## COMMONWEALTH OF MASSACHUSETTS

MIDDLESEX, SS

NANCY CARPENTER, As
Administratrix of the Estate
of Charles Carpenter,
  Plaintiff

    vs.

RANDALL DEE and
PETER DEE,
  Defendants.

SUPERIOR COURT DEPARTMENT
OF THE TRIAL COURT CIVIL
ACTION NO. 12-6144

MOTION TO AMEND

    Now comes the plaintiff and moves for leave to file an Amended Complaint, a copy of which is attached hereto.

By her attorneys,

By: _____ /s/ Carol Coblentz _____
Carol Coblentz (BBO#304321)
Needham, Shaker and Coblentz
44 Park Place
Boston, MA 02100
(617) 555-5555

Dated: /d/

## COMMONWEALTH OF MASSACHUSETTS

MIDDLESEX, SS

NANCY CARPENTER, As
Administratrix of the Estate
of Charles Carpenter,
    Plaintiff

    vs.

RANDALL DEE, PETER DEE;
ULTIMATE AUTO, INC;
and CITY OF LOWELL,
    Defendants.

SUPERIOR COURT DEPARTMENT
OF THE TRIAL COURT CIVIL
ACTION NO. 12-6144

AMENDED COMPLAINT

PLAINTIFF CLAIMS
TRIAL BY JURY

## PARTIES

1. The plaintiff Nancy Carpenter is a resident of Lowell, Middlesex County, Massachusetts. She brings this action in her capacity as the administratrix of the estate of Charles Carpenter, her late husband, of Lowell, Middlesex County, Massachusetts. She was duly appointed as administratrix by the Middlesex Probate Court, docket number 11P3875A.

2. The defendant Randall Dee is a resident of Lowell, Middlesex County, Massachusetts.

3. The defendant Peter Dee is a resident of Lowell, Middlesex County, Massachusetts.

4. Ultimate Auto, Inc. is a Massachusetts corporation, with a usual place of business in Lowell, Middlesex County, Massachusetts.

5. The City of Lowell ("the City"), is a body politic and corporate, with executive offices at 100 Main Street, Lowell, Middlesex County, Massachusetts.

## FACTS

6. On or about August 31, 2011, the plaintiff's intestate, Charles Carpenter, was riding as a passenger in a 1986 Jeep CJ-7 (hereinafter "the jeep").

7. The jeep was owned by one Twyla Burrell, and operated by the defendant Randall Dee.

8. At or near the intersection of Palmer and Franklin Streets in Lowell, the operator lost control of the jeep, and it rolled over, pinning Charles Carpenter beneath it.

9. The loss of control and resulting accident was caused by the negligent and/or grossly negligent and/or wanton, willful, and reckless conduct of the defendant Randall Dee as operator of the jeep including, but not limited to; the following acts and omissions:

(a) Excessive speed;
(b) Failing to stop at an intersection; and
(c) Illegal and dangerous alteration of the chassis, causing unsafe handling characteristics.

10. The defendant Randall Dee modified the jeep, by means of a suspension lift kit and oversize tires. He purchased both items at a retail store owned and operated by the defendant Ultimate Auto.

11. The raised suspension and oversized tires markedly affected the handling characteristics (including, but not limited to, propensity to roll over) of the jeep, and such modifications were a substantial contributing cause to the accident on August 31, 2011.

12. On several occasions prior to August 31, 2011, police officers of the City of Lowell, acting within the scope of their employment, stopped the defendant Randall Dee while operating the jeep, in connection with suspected motor vehicle offenses. On no occasion, did any of the officers advise the defendant Dee that the vehicle was illegally modified, or take any other action to prevent the vehicle from being operated in its dangerous condition. The failure of the police to act was a substantial contributing cause to the accident on August 31, 2011.

## COUNT I (Wrongful Death, Randall Dee)

13. The plaintiff repeats and incorporates herein the allegations of paragraphs 1-9.

14. As a result of the negligent and/or grossly negligent and/or wanton, willful, and reckless conduct of the defendant Randall Dee, the plaintiff's intestate was killed on August 31, 2011.

## COUNT II (Conscious Suffering, Randall Dee)

15. The plaintiff repeats and incorporates herein the allegations of paragraphs 1-9.

16. As a result of the conduct of the defendant Randall Dee, as described above, the plaintiff's intestate sustained serious personal injuries, from which he suffered consciously, prior to his death on August 31, 2011.

### COUNT III (Fraudulent Conveyance)

17. The plaintiff repeats and incorporates herein the allegations of paragraphs 1-9.

18. At the time of the accident on August 31, 2011, the defendant Randall Dee and the defendant Peter Dee owned as joint tenants a certain parcel of land at 91 Birch Hill Road, Lowell, Massachusetts, containing approximately 11,604 square feet.

19. The defendants Randall Dee and Peter Dee had purchased said property from the estate of their deceased father Richard Dee, for the amount of $80,000.00 on or about February 13, 2011.

20. On or about October 8, 2011, the defendant Randall Dee conveyed all his right, title, and interest in the above property to Peter Dee for "nominal consideration."

21. On information and belief, the transfer of such interest was fraudulent as to the creditors, including, but not limited to, the plaintiff, within the meaning of Mass. Gen. Laws ch. 109A, in that:

(a) The conveyance was made without fair consideration and Randall Dee was thereby rendered insolvent, within the meaning of Mass. Gen. Laws ch. 109A, § 4; and/or

(b) The conveyance was made without fair consideration at a time when the defendant Randall Dee believed that he would incur debts beyond his ability to pay, within the meaning of Mass. Gen. Laws ch. 109A, § 6; and/or

(c) The transfer was made with an actual intent to hinder, delay or defraud creditors, including but not limited to the plaintiff, within the meaning of Mass. Gen. Laws ch. 109A, § 7.

### COUNT IV (Wrongful Death, Ultimate Auto)

22. The plaintiff repeats and incorporates herein the allegations of paragraphs 1-11.

23. The defendant Ultimate Auto as a retailer of automotive parts, owed a duty to Randall Dee (and to the public generally) to provide appropriate

technical advice with regard to the sale of products that could be used to modify vehicles.

24. In breach of that duty, the defendant Ultimate Auto was guilty of negligent and/or grossly negligent and/or wanton, willful, and reckless conduct, including, but not limited to, the following acts and omissions:

(a) Selling a suspension lift kit and oversized tires which, individually and in combination, altered the height of the jeep, affecting its handling characteristics (including, but not limited to, its propensity to roll over) and rendered it unsafe;

(b) Failing to give any kind of warning or instruction to Randall Dee, with respect to the effect of such parts on the handling characteristics of the jeep;

(c) Selling automotive parts which constituted per se a violation of Mass. Gen. Laws ch. 90, § 7P, with regard to modification of vehicle height;

(d) Failing to advise Randall Dee that the installation of the parts constituted a violation of Mass. Gen. Laws ch. 90, § 7P.

25. As a result of the above acts and omissions, the defendant Randall Dee installed the suspension lift kit and oversized tires, and the acts and omissions of Ultimate Auto were a substantial contributing cause to the loss of control and resulting accident on August 31, 2011.

26. As a result of the negligent and/or grossly negligent and/or wanton, willful, and reckless conduct of the defendant, Ultimate Auto, the plaintiff's intestate was killed on August 31, 2011.

## COUNT V (Conscious Suffering, Ultimate Auto)

27. The plaintiff repeats and incorporates herein the allegations of paragraphs 1-11 and 23-26.

28. As a result of the conduct of the defendant Ultimate Auto, as described above, the plaintiff's intestate sustained serious personal injuries, from which he suffered consciously, prior to his death on August 31, 2011.

## COUNT VI (Wrongful Death, Warranties, Ultimate Auto)

29. The plaintiff repeats and incorporates herein the allegations of paragraphs 1-11 and 23-26.

30. The defendant Ultimate Auto was a merchant with respect to sale of the suspension lift kit and oversized tires. The defendant Ultimate Auto

breached implied warranties of merchantability and fitness for a particular purpose, by selling to the defendant Randall Dee, a suspension lift kit and oversized tires which, individually and in combination, rendered the jeep unreasonably dangerous and/or by selling the suspension lift kit and oversized tires, without adequate warning or instruction with regard to their dangerous propensity.

31. As a result of the said breaches of warranty, the defendant Randall Dee installed the suspension lift kit and oversized tires. The breaches of the defendant Ultimate Auto were a substantial contributing cause to the loss of control and resulting accident on August 31, 2011. As a result of the defendant's breaches of warranty, the plaintiff's intestate was killed on August 31, 2011.

## COUNT VII (Conscious Suffering, Warranties, Ultimate Auto)

32. Plaintiff repeats and incorporates herein the allegations of paragraphs 1-11, 23-26, and 29-31.

33. As a result of the breaches of warranty of the defendant Ultimate Auto, as described above, the plaintiff's intestate sustained serious personal injuries, from which he suffered consciously, prior to his death on August 31, 2011.

## COUNT VIII (Wrongful Death, City of Lowell)

34. Plaintiff repeats and incorporates herein the allegations of paragraphs 1-12.

35. On or about February 19, 2012, the year after the accident, the plaintiff, through her attorney and pursuant to Mass. Gen. Laws ch. 258, § 4, gave written notice of its claim to the City. No substantive response to that notice has been forthcoming.

36. The modification of the jeep represented an imminent danger to all persons who might be affected by it, in particular, its occupants, and a clear violation of Mass. Gen. Laws ch. 90, § 7P. As such, it created a special duty of care to those who might be affected by it, including the plaintiff's intestate.

37. Despite the obvious danger of immediate and foreseeable injury presented by the jeep, police officers of the City of Lowell failed to take any effective action to reduce or eliminate the danger.

38. As a result, the jeep was being operated in a condition of imminent danger on August 31, 2011, and the negligence of the City, through its police

officers, was a substantial contributing cause to the loss of control and resulting accident on that date.

39. As a result of the negligence of the City, its agents and employees, the plaintiff's intestate was killed on August 31, 2011.

### COUNT IX (City of Lowell, Conscious Suffering)

40. The plaintiff repeats and incorporates herein the allegations of paragraphs 1-12 and 34-39.

41. As a result of the conduct of the defendant City as described above, the plaintiff's intestate sustained serious personal injuries, from which he suffered consciously, prior to his death on August 31, 2011.

**WHEREFORE** the plaintiff prays for the following relief:

1. Judgment on Counts I, IV, VI, and VIII against the defendants Randall Dee, Ultimate Auto, and City of Lowell.

(a) To compensate the survivors of the plaintiff's intestate for the fair monetary value of the deceased for reasonably expected net income lost, services, protection, care, assistance, society, companionship, comfort, guidance, counsel, and advice of the deceased.
(b) Reasonable funeral and burial expenses.
(c) Punitive damages in an amount of at least $5,000.00, pursuant to Mass. Gen. Laws ch. 229, § 2.

2. Judgment on Counts II, V, VII, and IX against the defendants Randall Dee, Ultimate Auto, and City of Lowell to compensate the estate of Charles Carpenter for his pain and conscious suffering.

3. That the Court issue a temporary restraining order enjoining the defendant, Randall Dee, until further order of this court, from conveying, encumbering, or in any other manner transferring any interest, legal or equitable, in any of his assets, including but not limited to real estate, bank accounts, certificates of deposit, securities, valuables, and any other asset not immune from execution, except in the ordinary course of business.

4. That the Court issue a preliminary injunction enjoining the defendant Randall Dee, until the disposition of this action on the merits, from conveying, encumbering, or in any other manner transferring any interest, legal or equitable, in any of his assets, including but not limited to real estate, bank accounts, certificates of deposit, securities, valuables, and any other asset not immune from execution, except in the ordinary course of business.

5. That the Court issue a Temporary Restraining Order enjoining the defendant Peter Dee, until further order of this court, from conveying, encumbering, or in any other manner transferring any interest, legal or equitable, in the real estate at 91 Birch Hill Road, Lowell, Massachusetts.

6. That the Court issue a preliminary injunction enjoining the defendant, Peter Dee, until the disposition of this action on the merits, from conveying, encumbering, or in any other manner transferring any interest, legal or equitable, in the real estate at 91 Birch Hill Road, Lowell, Massachusetts.

7. That the Court, under Count III, declare null and void the conveyance of the interest of Randall Dee in the property at 91 Birch Hill Road, Lowell and/or allow satisfaction of any judgment in this action against Randall Dee to be satisfied against the interest he held in said property prior to the fraudulent conveyance.

8. That the Court issue a temporary restraining order enjoining the defendants, until further Order of the Court, from selling or transferring in any way the jeep vehicle involved or in any way modifying it or changing its present condition.

9. That the Court issue a preliminary injunction enjoining the defendants, until the disposition of this action on the merits, from selling or transferring in any way the jeep vehicle involved or in any way modifying it or changing its present condition.

10. PLAINTIFF CLAIMS TRIAL BY JURY.

By her attorneys,

By: _____ /s/ Carol Coblentz _____
Carol Coblentz (BBO#304321)
Needham, Shaker and Coblentz
44 Park Place
Boston, MA 02100
(617) 555-5555

Dated: /d/

# ■ UNIFORM COMMERCIAL CODE § 2-314. IMPLIED WARRANTY: MERCHANTABILITY; USAGE OF TRADE

(1) Unless excluded or modified . . . , a warranty that the goods shall be merchantable is implied in a contract for their sale if the seller is a merchant with respect to goods of that kind. . . .

(2) Goods to be merchantable must be at least such as

(a) pass without objection in the trade under the contract description; and

(b) in the case of fungible goods, are of fair average quality within the description; and

(c) are fit for the ordinary purposes for which such goods are used; and

(d) run, within the variations permitted by the agreement, of even kind, quality and quantity within each unit and among all units involved; and

(e) are adequately contained, packaged, and labeled as the agreement may require; and

(f) conform to the promises or affirmations of fact made on the container or label if any.

(3) Unless excluded or modified . . . other implied warranties may arise from course of dealing or usage of trade.

## COMMENT

1. The seller's obligation applies to present sales as well as to contracts. . . .

2. The question when the warranty is imposed turns basically on the meaning of the terms of the agreement as recognized in the trade. . . .

3. In an action based on breach of warranty, it is of course necessary to show not only the existence of the warranty but the fact that the warranty was broken and that the breach of the warranty was the proximate cause of the loss sustained. In such an action an affirmative showing by the seller that the loss resulted from some action or event following his own delivery of the goods can operate as a defense. Equally, evidence indicating that the seller exercised care in the manufacture, processing or selection of the goods is relevant to the issue of whether the warranty was in fact broken. Action by the buyer following an examination of the goods which ought to have indicated the defect complained of can be shown as matter bearing on whether the breach itself was the cause of the injury.

# ■ UNIFORM COMMERCIAL CODE § 2-315. IMPLIED WARRANTY: FITNESS FOR PARTICULAR PURPOSE

Where the seller at the time of contracting has reason to know any particular purpose for which the goods are required and that the buyer is relying on the seller's skill or judgment to select or furnish suitable goods, there is unless excluded or modified under the next section an implied warranty that the goods shall be fit for such purpose.

COMMENT

1. Whether or not this warranty arises in any individual case is basically a question of fact to be determined by the circumstances of the contracting. Under this section the buyer need not bring home to the seller actual knowledge of the particular purpose for which the goods are intended or of his reliance on the seller's skill and judgment, if the circumstances are such that the seller has reason to realize the purpose intended or that the reliance exists. . . .

2. A "particular purpose" differs from the ordinary purpose for which the goods are used in that it envisages a specific use by the buyer which is peculiar to the nature of his business whereas the ordinary purposes for which goods are used are those envisaged in the concept of merchantability and go to uses which are customarily made of the goods in question. For example, shoes are generally used for the purpose of walking upon ordinary ground, but a seller may know that a particular pair was selected to be used for climbing mountains.

A contract may of course include both a warranty of merchantability and one of fitness for a particular purpose. . . .

# ■ MASS. GEN. LAWS CH. 90 § 7P. HEIGHT OF MOTOR VEHICLES; ALTERATION RESTRICTED

No person shall alter, modify or change the height of a motor vehicle with an original manufacturer's gross vehicle weight rating of up to and including ten thousand pounds, by elevating or lowering the chassis or body by more than two inches above or below the original manufacturer's specified height by use of so-called "shackle lift kits" for leaf springs or by use of lift kits for coil springs, tires, or any other means or device.

The registrar shall establish such rules and regulations for such changes in the height of motor vehicles beyond said two inches. No motor vehicle that has been so altered, modified or changed beyond the provisions of this section or the rules and regulations established by the registrar shall be operated on any way.

# ■ MASS. GEN. LAWS CH. 231B § 85. COMPARATIVE NEGLIGENCE; LIMITED EFFECT OF CONTRIBUTORY NEGLIGENCE AS DEFENSE

Contributory negligence shall not bar recovery in any action by any person or legal representative to recover damages for negligence resulting in death or in injury to person or property, if such negligence was not greater than the total amount of negligence attributable to the person or persons against whom recovery is sought, but any damages allowed shall be diminished in proportion to the amount of negligence attributable to the person for whose injury, damage or death recovery is made. In determining by what amount the plaintiff's damages shall be diminished in such a case, the negligence of each plaintiff shall be compared to the total negligence of all persons against whom recovery is sought. The combined total of the plaintiff's negligence taken together with all of the negligence of all defendants shall equal one hundred per cent.

The violation of a criminal statute, ordinance or regulation by a plaintiff which contributed to said injury, death or damage, shall be considered as evidence of negligence of that plaintiff, but the violation of said statute, ordinance or regulation shall not as a matter of law and for that reason alone, serve to bar a plaintiff from recovery.

The defense of assumption of risk is hereby abolished in all actions hereunder.

The burden of alleging and proving negligence which serves to diminish a plaintiff's damages or bar recovery under this section shall be upon the person who seeks to establish such negligence, and the plaintiff shall be presumed to have been in the exercise of due care.

# ■ MASS. GEN. LAWS CH. 231B §§ 1-4. CONTRIBUTION AMONG JOINT TORTFEASORS

§ 1. (a) Except as otherwise provided in this chapter, where two or more persons become jointly liable in tort for the same injury to person or property, there shall be a right of contribution among them even though judgment has not been recovered against all or any of them.

(b) The right of contribution shall exist only in favor of a joint tortfeasor, hereinafter called tortfeasor, who has paid more than his pro rata share of the common liability, and his total recovery shall be limited to the amount paid by him in excess of his pro rata share. No tortfeasor shall be compelled to make contribution beyond his own pro rata share of the entire liability.

(c) A tortfeasor who enters into a settlement with a claimant shall not be entitled to recover contribution from another tortfeasor in respect to any amount paid in a settlement which is in excess of what was reasonable.

(d) A liability insurer, who by payment has discharged in full or in part the liability of a tortfeasor and has thereby discharged in full its obligation as insurer, shall be subrogated to the tortfeasor's right of contribution to the extent of the amount it has paid in excess of the tortfeasor's pro rata share of the common liability. This provision shall not limit or impair any right of subrogation arising from any other relationship.

(e) This chapter shall not impair any right of indemnity under existing law. Where one tortfeasor is entitled to indemnity from another, the right of the indemnity obligee shall be for indemnity and not contribution, and the indemnity obligor shall not be entitled to contribution from the obligee for any portion of his indemnity obligation.

§ 2. In determining the pro rata shares of tortfeasors in the entire liability (a) their relative degrees of fault shall not be considered; (b) if equity requires, the collective liability of some as a group shall constitute a single share; and (c) principles of equity applicable to contribution generally shall apply.

§ 3. (a) Whether or not judgment has been entered in an action against two or more tortfeasors for the same injury, contribution may be enforced by separate action.

(b) Where a judgment has been entered in an action against two or more tortfeasors for the same injury, contribution may be enforced in that action by judgment in favor of one against other judgment defendants by motion upon notice to all parties to the action.

(c) If there is a judgment for the injury against the tortfeasor seeking contribution, any separate action by him to enforce contribution must be commenced within one year after the judgment has become final by lapse of time for appeal or after appellate review.

(d) If there is no judgment for the injury against the tortfeasor seeking contribution, his right of contribution shall be barred unless he has either (1) discharged by payment, the common liability within the statute of limitations period applicable to claimant's right of action against him and has commenced his action for contribution within one year after payment, or (2) agreed, while action is pending against him, to discharge the common liability and has, within one year after the agreement, paid the liability and commenced his action for contribution.

(e) The recovery of a judgment for an injury against one tortfeasor shall not, of itself, discharge the other tortfeasors from liability for the injury unless the judgment is satisfied. The satisfaction of the judgment shall not impair any right of contribution.

(f) The judgment of the court in determining the liability of the several defendants to the claimant for an injury shall be binding as among such defendants in determining their right to contribution.

§ 4. When a release or covenant not to sue or not to enforce judgment is given in good faith to one or two or more persons liable in tort for the same injury:

(a) It shall not discharge any of the other tortfeasors from liability for the injury unless its terms so provide; but it shall reduce the claim against the others to the extent of any amount stipulated by the release or the covenant, or in the amount of the consideration paid for it, whichever is the greater; and

(b) It shall discharge the tortfeasor to whom it is given from all liability for contribution to any other tortfeasor.

# ■ WALTER VANBUSKIRK,* "LIFTING" A TRUCK

Driving around on the streets, it is not uncommon to see trucks that are higher off the ground and have larger tires than normal trucks. The process truck owners go through to achieve this effect is called "lifting" the truck. There are three basic ways to life a truck: body lifts, suspension lifts, and larger tires. Each of these types of lifts have different uses and have different effects on the center of gravity of the truck.

## BODY LIFTS

All trucks and some cars have frames as the main structural member. The frame is the base which most everything else bolts onto. The body of the truck bolts onto the frame at numerous locations (apparently twelve locations on Randall Dee's jeep). Normally, there is a small rubber spacer approximately 1 inch in thickness, called a body mount, between the frame and the body at each of these locations. A body lift uses larger spacers between the body and the frame to raise the body up off the frame. This has the effect of raising the fenders up higher which allows the use of larger tires.

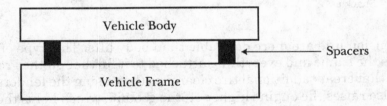

In the case, Randall Dee used hockey pucks as the spacers between the body and the frame. Although this may sound absurd, it is actually very common. However, most people will use spacers made of steel or some specially designed composite material when putting in more than 2 inches of lift. This approach is preferred, because the rubber hockey pucks are too compressible. Dee used four hockey pucks at each body mount location to achieve approximately 4 inches of lift.

## SUSPENSION LIFTS

Between the truck's axle and frame is the suspension. The suspension is made up of four main components: the shackle, the leaf spring, the shock absorber, and the U-bolt. (Note that the following graphic does not have

---

* Walter VanBuskirk, a 1999 graduate of Boston College Law School, is now a partner at the law firm of Sullivan & Worcester in Boston, Massachusetts.

shock absorbers or U-Bolts.) The shackle attaches the leaf spring to the frame. The leaf spring is a series of "arched" strips of metal welded together, which flex to allow the vehicle to move somewhat independently of the tires. If left alone, after a vehicle hits a bump the leaf spring would continue to bounce. The shock absorber stops the leaf spring from bouncing. Finally, the U-bolt attaches the leaf spring to the axle.

To raise the suspension in a truck there are numerous options: longer shackles, larger leaf springs, or a spacer between the axle and the leaf spring (you would never use hockey pucks here). Randall Dee used larger leaf springs.

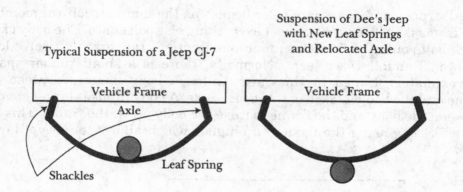

Typical Suspension of a Jeep CJ-7

Suspension of Dee's Jeep with New Leaf Springs and Relocated Axle

Suspension lifts are more desirable than body lifts. This type of lift actually raises the frame and everything attached to it further off the ground. Not only does that create additional tire clearance (by raising the fenders over the axle), it also raises the engine higher off the ground, which helps the truck in off-road situations. Dee used a 2½-inch larger spring. This does not always give exactly a 2½-inch lift; the spring is flexible, and the weight of the vehicle has a large effect on the actual lift. In this case Dee actually achieved a 3-inch lift. It should also be noted that jeeps are strange in that they are one of the only trucks that have the axle mounted on top of the leaf spring. Most other trucks mount the axle under the leaf spring, which allows the use of a spacer between the axle and leaf spring to lift the truck. Randall Dee remounted the axle under the leaf springs. This is a common step performed when lifting a jeep.

### LARGER TIRES

Basically the major use of body lifts and suspension lifts is to allow the use of bigger tires. Bigger tires give the truck more total clearance (they can drive through deeper mud and over bigger rocks). Average tires are around 28 inches in diameter. The tires Randall Dee put on his jeep were 40 inches in diameter. This is a 12-inch increase in diameter, which leads to 6 inches of additional height over his previous tires.

## DEE'S JEEP

In the case of Dee's jeep, he put in 4 inches of body lift, a 3-inch suspension lift replacing the leaf springs, 3 inches of additional suspension lift by remounting the axle, and larger tires adding 6 inches. In total, Dee's jeep is at least 16 inches higher than a regular jeep.

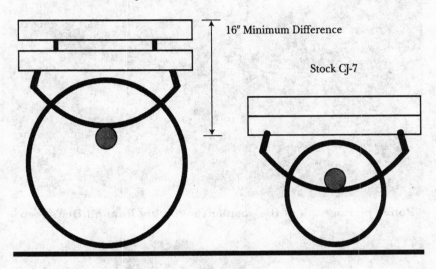

Randall Dee's CJ-7

16″ Minimum Difference

Stock CJ-7

## ■ PHOTOGRAPHS

Police photograph of the accident involving Randall Dee's jeep

Police photograph of the accident involving Randall Dee's jeep

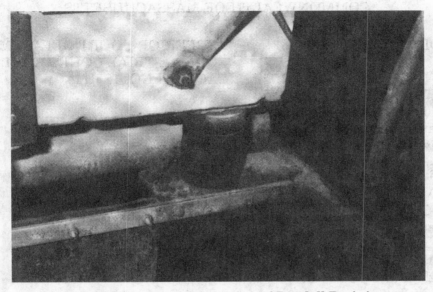

**Close up of the raised suspension of Randall Dee's jeep**

## COMMONWEALTH OF MASSACHUSETTS

MIDDLESEX, SS

NANCY CARPENTER, As
Administratrix of the Estate
of Charles Carpenter,
  Plaintiff

    vs.

RANDALL DEE; PETER DEE;
CITY OF LOWELL,
  Defendants.

---

ULTIMATE AUTO, INC.,
Defendant and Third-Party
  Plaintiff

    vs.

DALE MCGILL and
MCGILL'S GARAGE, INC.,
  Third-Party Defendants.

SUPERIOR COURT DEPARTMENT
OF THE TRIAL COURT CIVIL
ACTION NO. 12-6144

MOTION OF DEFENDANT
ULTIMATE AUTO, INC.
TO FILE A THIRD-PARTY
COMPLAINT

The defendant, Ultimate Auto, Inc., moves that the Court allow it to file the attached third-party complaint for contribution against Dale McGill and McGill's Garage, Inc.

In support thereof, the defendant Ultimate Auto, Inc. states that discovery has shown that the vehicle, which was allegedly in a defective condition at the time of the accident, had been issued an inspection sticker by the third-party defendants and that the issuance of said inspection sticker was in violation of applicable Massachusetts regulations. Accordingly, the third-party defendants would be liable as joint tortfeasors for the claims made by the plaintiff.

By its Attorneys,

_____ /s/ Bertram Cohen _____
Bertram Cohen (BBO#641311)
Roth, McKnight & Zimmerman
111 Milk Street
Boston, MA 02100
(617) 555-0000

Dated: /d/

## COMMONWEALTH OF MASSACHUSETTS

| | |
|---|---|
| MIDDLESEX, SS | SUPERIOR COURT DEPARTMENT OF THE TRIAL COURT CIVIL ACTION NO. 12-6144 |
| NANCY CARPENTER, As Administratrix of the Estate of Charles Carpenter,   Plaintiff | |
|    vs. | |
| RANDALL DEE; PETER DEE; CITY OF LOWELL,   Defendants. | THIRD-PARTY COMPLAINT OF ULTIMATE AUTO, INC. |
| ULTIMATE AUTO, INC.,   Defendant and Third-Party   Plaintiff | |
| vs. | |
| DALE MCGILL and MCGILL'S GARAGE, INC.,   Third-Party Defendants. | |

### COUNT I

1. The third-party defendant, Dale McGill, is an individual residing station doing business as McGill's Garage, Inc., in Watertown, Massachusetts.

2. The defendant/third-party plaintiff, Ultimate Auto, Inc., has been named as a party defendant in an action sounding in tort against it and in which it is alleged that the negligence of the defendant/third-party plaintiff entitled the plaintiff to recover for damages allegedly sustained as a result of a motor vehicle accident on August 31, 2011.

3. If the plaintiff did sustain injuries and damages as alleged, such injuries and damages occurred as a direct and proximate result of the negligence and carelessness of the third-party defendant, Dale McGill in approving an inspection sticker on the vehicle involved in the accident alleged in the plaintiff's complaint.

4. The third-party defendant is jointly liable for the injuries and damages allegedly sustained by the plaintiff pursuant to Mass. Gen. Laws ch. 231B, §§ 1-3.

WHEREFORE, the defendant/third-party plaintiff, Ultimate Auto, Inc., says that if it is found liable to the plaintiff, the third-party defendant, Dale McGill, is liable to the defendant/third-party plaintiff as a joint tortfeasor.

## COUNT II

5. The third-party defendant, McGill's Garage, Inc., is a Massachusetts corporation with a usual place of business in Watertown, Massachusetts, and at all time material was in the business of conducting motor vehicle inspections.

6. The defendant/third-party plaintiff, Ultimate Auto, Inc., has been named as a party defendant in an action sounding in tort against it and in which it is alleged that the negligence of the defendant/third-party plaintiff entitled the plaintiff to recover for damages allegedly sustained as a result of a motor vehicle accident on August 31, 2011.

7. If the plaintiff did sustain injuries and damages as alleged, such injuries and damages occurred as a direct and proximate result of the negligence and carelessness of employees or agents of the third-party defendant, McGill's Garage, Inc., in approving or issuing an inspection sticker on the vehicle involved in the accident alleged in the plaintiff's complaint.

8. The third-party defendant is jointly liable for the injuries and damages allegedly sustained by the plaintiff pursuant to Mass. Gen. Laws ch. 231B, §§ 1-3.

WHEREFORE, the defendant/third-party plaintiff, says that if it is found liable to the plaintiff, the third-party defendant, McGill's Garage, Inc., is liable to the defendant/third-party plaintiff as a joint tortfeasor.

By its Attorneys,

_____ /s/ Bertram Cohen _____
Bertram Cohen (BBO 641311)
Roth, McKnight & Zimmerman
111 Milk Street
Boston, MA 02100
(617) 555-0000

Dated: /d/

## COMMONWEALTH OF MASSACHUSETTS

MIDDLESEX, SS

SUPERIOR COURT DEPARTMENT
OF THE TRIAL COURT CIVIL
ACTION NO. 12-6144

NANCY CARPENTER, As
Administratrix of the Estate
of Charles Carpenter,
  Plaintiff

    vs.

RANDALL DEE; PETER DEE;
CITY OF LOWELL,
  Defendants.

ANSWER AND CROSS-CLAIMS
OF ULTIMATE AUTO, INC.

TRIAL BY JURY

ULTIMATE AUTO, INC.,
Defendant and Third-Party
  Plaintiff

    vs.

DALE MCGILL and
MCGILL'S GARAGE, INC.,
  Third-Party Defendants.

## FIRST DEFENSE

The Defendant, Ultimate Auto, Inc. ("Ultimate Auto") addresses the separately numbered paragraphs of the Complaint as follows:

1. The Defendant is without knowledge or information sufficient to form a belief as to the truth of the allegations contained in Paragraph 1.

2. The Defendant is without knowledge or information sufficient to form a belief as to the truth of the allegations contained in Paragraph 2.

3. The Defendant is without knowledge or information sufficient to form a belief as to the truth of the allegations contained in Paragraph 3.

4. The Defendant admits the allegations contained in Paragraph 4.

5. The Defendant admits the allegations contained in Paragraph 5.

6. The Defendant is without knowledge or information sufficient to form a belief as to the truth of the allegations contained in Paragraph 6.

7. The Defendant is without knowledge or information sufficient to form a belief as to the truth of the allegations contained in Paragraph 7.

8. The Defendant is without knowledge or information sufficient to form a belief as to the truth of the allegations contained in Paragraph 8.

9. The Defendant denies the allegations contained in Paragraph 9.

10. The Defendant denies the allegations contained in Paragraph 10.

11. The Defendant denies the allegations contained in Paragraph 11.

12. The Defendant is without knowledge or information sufficient to form a belief as to the truth of the allegations contained in Paragraph 12.

13-21. The Defendant makes no answer to the allegations of these Paragraphs because they do not purport to make a claim against it.

22. The Defendant repeats and realleges its answers to Paragraphs 1-11.

23. The Defendant denies the allegations contained in Paragraph 23.

24. The Defendant denies the allegations contained in Paragraph 24.

25. The Defendant denies the allegations contained in Paragraph 25.

26. The Defendant denies the allegations contained in Paragraph 26.

27. The Defendant repeats and realleges its answers to Paragraphs 1-11 and 23-26.

28. The Defendant denies the allegations contained in Paragraph 28.

29. The Defendant repeats and realleges its answers to Paragraphs 1-11 and 23-26.

30. The Defendant denies the allegations contained in Paragraph 30.

31. The Defendant denies the allegations contained in Paragraph 31.

32. The Defendant repeats and realleges its answers to Paragraphs 1-11, 23-26, and 29-31.

33. The Defendant denies the allegations contained in Paragraph 33.

34-41. The Defendant makes no answer to the allegations of these Paragraphs because they do not purport to make a claim against it.

## SECOND DEFENSE

This action is barred by operation of the applicable statute of limitations.

## THIRD DEFENSE

If the Plaintiff is entitled to recover against the Defendant, any such recovery must be reduced in accordance with the comparative negligence statute as enacted in the Commonwealth, since the Plaintiff's own negligence was the proximate cause of the injury sustained.

## FOURTH DEFENSE

Any loss sustained by the Plaintiff resulted from his own negligence, which was greater in degree than any negligence of the Defendant and therefore the Plaintiff is barred from recovery in this action.

## FIFTH DEFENSE

The Defendant is exempt from liability to the extent provided by the Massachusetts "no fault" statutes, Mass. Gen. Laws ch. 90, § 34m, and Mass. Gen. Laws ch. 231 § 6d.

## SIXTH DEFENSE

The Plaintiff has failed to give notice of breach of warranty, and the Defendant has thereby been prejudiced.

## CROSS-CLAIM AGAINST RANDALL DEE, PETER DEE AND THE CITY OF LOWELL

1. If the Plaintiff's decedent was injured as alleged by the Plaintiff, he was injured as a result of the negligence of the Defendants, Randall Dee, Peter Dee, and/or the City of Lowell.

2. The Defendants, Randall Dee, Peter Dee, and the City of Lowell, are liable to the Defendant, Ultimate Auto, Inc. for contribution pursuant to Mass. Gen. Laws ch. 231B.

WHEREFORE, the Defendant Ultimate Auto, Inc., demands judgment for contribution against the Defendants, Randall Dee and Peter Dee.

THE DEFENDANT, ULTIMATE AUTO, INC., DEMANDS TRIAL BY JURY ON ALL CLAIMS.

By its Attorneys,

_____ /s/ Bertram Cohen _____
Bertram Cohen (BBO#641311)
Roth, McKnight & Zimmerman
111 Milk Street
Boston, MA 02100
(617) 555-0000

Dated: /d/

## COMMONWEALTH OF MASSACHUSETTS

MIDDLESEX, SS

SUPERIOR COURT DEPARTMENT
OF THE TRIAL COURT CIVIL
ACTION NO. 12-6144

NANCY CARPENTER, As
Administratrix of the Estate
of Charles Carpenter,
  Plaintiff

PLAINTIFF'S REQUEST FOR
PRODUCTION OF DOCUMENTS
BY ULTIMATE AUTO, INC.

    vs.

RANDALL DEE; PETER DEE;
ULTIMATE AUTO, INC.;
and CITY OF LOWELL,
  Defendants.

The plaintiff, Nancy Carpenter, hereby requests of defendant, Ultimate Auto, Inc., that the plaintiff be permitted to inspect and copy the originals and copies of the following designated documents, writings, photographs, or tangible things. Production, inspection and copying shall take place at the office of defendant's counsel, within thirty days of the receipt of this notice or at such other place and time as may be agreed upon by counsel for the parties.

If, in response to any of the following requests, production of a document is denied on the basis of attorney-client privilege or trial-preparation/work-product materials, kindly indicate sufficient information concerning said document and the claimed privilege to enable the court to assess the applicability of said privilege, including the nature of the document withheld, the identity of its author, the current custodian of the document, the date the document was prepared, and the exact privilege being asserted.

### DEFINITIONS

A. "The accident" refers to the alleged accident described in plaintiff's complaint as occurring on or about August 31, 2011.

B. "The motor vehicle" means the jeep alleged to have caused the plaintiff's injuries and described in the plaintiff's complaint.

C. "Ultimate Auto, Inc." means the defendant Ultimate Auto, Inc., its officers, agents, and employees.

D. The term "documents" as used herein includes writings of any sort, drawings, graphs, charts, photographs, and other data compilations.

## REQUESTS

1. All promotional and descriptive material in your possession relating in any way to oversize tires.

2. All promotional and descriptive material in your possession relating in any way to suspension lift kits.

3. All documents in your possession which comment upon, or relate in any way to, Mass. Gen. Laws ch. 90, § 7P.

4. A copy of all warnings and instructions which accompany suspension lift kits and/or oversize tires.

5. All warranties pertaining to the above products.

6. All complaints, letters, notices, claims or suit papers which constitute, reflect or relate to any claims as described in plaintiff's Interrogatory No. 11.*

7. All studies, reports, literature, research, or documents of any other kind and description, relating in any way to the alteration in vehicle handling or driving characteristics (including, but not limited to change in its propensity to roll over) as result of alteration of vehicle height.

8. Copies of all industry and trade standards which reflect, or relate in any way to, the design, construction, or configuration of automobile parts which have the purpose or effect of altering vehicle height.

9. Copies of all insurance policies (primary or excess) affording coverage to the defendant for this loss.

10. Copies of all statements secured at any time from plaintiff, or from any member of the plaintiff's family, and whether such statements be recorded or written, signed or unsigned.

11. All written warnings or instructions, which you have ever furnished to any customer, relating in any way to alteration of the handling or driving

---

*Eds.' Note: Plaintiff's Interrogatory No. 11 can be found reprinted in Ultimate Auto's Answers to Interrogatories in these case files.

characteristics of the vehicle (including, but not limited to, its propensity to roll over) as a result of modification of vehicle height.


By her Attorneys,


By: _____ /s/ Carol Coblentz _____
Carol Coblentz (BBO#304321)
Needham, Shaker and Coblentz
44 Park Place
Boston, MA 02100
(617) 555-5555

Dated: /d/

## COMMONWEALTH OF MASSACHUSETTS

MIDDLESEX, SS

SUPERIOR COURT DEPARTMENT
OF THE TRIAL COURT CIVIL
ACTION NO. 12-6144

NANCY CARPENTER, As
Administratrix of the Estate
of Charles Carpenter,

  Plaintiff

  vs.

RANDALL DEE; PETER DEE;
ULTIMATE AUTO, INC.;
and CITY OF LOWELL,
  Defendants.

RESPONSE OF DEFENDANT
ULTIMATE AUTO, INC. TO PLAIN-
TIFF'S REQUEST FOR PRODUC-
TION OF DOCUMENTS

1. Catalogue and specification sheet to be produced.

2. Manufacturer's brochure to be produced.

3. Registry of Motor Vehicle regulation to be produced.

4. The defendant has no such documents in his possession, custody, or control other than the documents produced in response to requests no. 1 and 2.

5. The defendant has no such documents in his possession, custody, or control.

6. The defendant has no such documents in his possession, custody, or control.

7. The defendant has no such documents in his possession, custody, or control.

8. The defendant, by its attorney, objects to this request on the grounds that it is vague and does not specify with particularity the documents sought.

9. Insurance policy to be produced.

10. The defendant has no such documents in his possession, custody, or control.

11. The defendant has no such documents in his possession, custody, or control.

By its Attorneys,

_____ /s/ Bertram Cohen _____
Bertram Cohen (BBO#641311)
Roth, McKnight & Zimmerman
111 Milk Street
Boston, MA 02100
(617) 555-0000

Dated: /d/

# COMMONWEALTH OF MASSACHUSETTS

MIDDLESEX, SS

SUPERIOR COURT DEPARTMENT
OF THE TRIAL COURT CIVIL
ACTION NO. 12-6144

NANCY CARPENTER, As
Administratrix of the Estate
of Charles Carpenter,
 Plaintiff

ANSWERS OF DEFENDANT
ULTIMATE AUTO, INC. TO
PLAINTIFF'S INTERROGATORIES

vs.

RANDALL DEE; PETER DEE;
ULTIMATE AUTO, INC.;
and CITY OF LOWELL,
 Defendants.

1. Please identify yourself by stating your full name, residential address, business address, employer, occupation and job title.*

Adam Jenkins, 11 Weeping Willow Road, Lexington, MA, President of Ultimate Auto, Inc.

2. Before proceeding further, please consult with all necessary persons, and review all necessary documents, to answer the remaining interrogatories. Have you done so?

Yes.

3. If you are a member of any trade associations, related in any way in whole or in part to the design, manufacture, sale, or use of automotive parts, which have the purpose or effect of modifying the height of vehicles, please identify all such organizations including: (a) name; (b) address; (c) inclusive dates of your membership; and (d) the name of any publications which you regularly receive from such organizations.

Specialty Equipment Manufacturers Associations.

4. Were you, or anyone employed by your company, aware of the existence of Massachusetts General Laws ch. 90 section 7P. Unless the answer is in the unqualified negative, kindly state the name, residential address and position with your company of all persons who were so aware.

Yes. Cecil Sylvester.

---

*Eds.' Note:* The local rules of many courts require that answers to interrogatories also contain the questions being answered. This makes it easier for judges and lawyers to comprehend and use the answers.

5. If you expect to call any person as an expert witness at the trial of this case, kindly state (a) the name and address of each person whom you expect to call as an expert witness at trial; (b) the subject matter on which each person whom you expect to call as an expert witness at trial is expected to testify, and his qualifications as an expert in that area; (c) the substance of the facts and opinions to which each expert is expected to testify and a summary of the grounds for each such opinion; and (d) the formal education (including the college and postgraduate education) of each such expert, each job or position such person has held in his area of expertise and the dates of such employment, membership in professional societies of each such expert, and identify all publications of each such subject in his field of expertise.

Unknown at the present time.

6. With respect to any primary or excess liability insurance applicable to the plaintiff's claim, please state the insurer, effective dates of the policy, and applicable coverage limits.

$500,000/$500,000 single limit bodily injury coverage, The Travelers Insurance Company, effective on the date of the loss alleged in the plaintiff's complaint.

7. Please identify all automotive parts ever purchased by the defendant, Randall Dee, at your company, including the exact description of such parts, date of purchase, and purchase price.

It is unknown what, if any, automotive parts were ever purchased by Randall Dee from Ultimate Auto. This question is presently being investigated by my attorney in connection with discovery in this action.

8. If you provided Randall Dee with any oral or written warning or instruction, relating in any way to change in the driving characteristics of modified vehicles (including, but not limited to, an increased propensity to roll over) please state (a) the exact content of such warning; (b) the date; and (c) the person or persons who gave such warning or instruction.

It is unknown what, if any, instructions were ever provided to Randall Dee by Ultimate Auto. This question is presently being investigated by my attorney in this action.

9. Are you, or is anyone in your company, aware that Monster Tire's 38 inch "Monster Mudder" tires (hereinafter "the Monster Tires") if mounted on a 1986 Jeep CJ7 (with necessary modifications to allow the mounting of such tires) could alter the driving and handling characteristics of the vehicle? Unless the answer is in the unqualified negative, kindly state (a) when you first became aware of this; (b) the name, address, and company position of all persons with such awareness; and (c) in as much detail as possible, please describe what characteristics you were aware could be affected.

The defendant, by his attorney, objects to this interrogatory on the grounds that it is not clear what modifications are included in the term "necessary." Without waiving this objection the defendant states that both at, and after, the date of the accident, alleged in the plaintiff's complaint Adam Jenkins was aware that any modification to the center of gravity of a vehicle by the addition of tires could, depending on the vehicle, and other variables, affect the handling of the vehicle.

10. Are you, or is anyone in your company, aware that Rodeo Suspension lift kits, if mounted on a 1986 Jeep CJ7 could alter the driving and handling characteristics of the vehicle. Unless the answer is in the unqualified negative, kindly state (a) when you first became aware of this; (b) the name, address, and company position of all persons with such awareness; and (c) in as much detail as possible, please describe what characteristics you were aware could be affected.

No.

11. If you have ever received any claim or lawsuit, relating in any way to a vehicle rolling over, after the installation of any parts (including, but not limited to suspension lift kits and tires) purchased at your company, please state as to each such claim or lawsuit (a) the name of the person or persons involved in such claim or lawsuit; (b) name of plaintiff's attorney, if any; (c) date of receipt of the claim or lawsuit; (d) date of the incident; (e) the current status of such claim or lawsuit; and (f) the court, caption, and docket number of each such claim which resulted in litigation.

Not applicable.

12. Please identify the officers, directors, agent, servant, or employee of the defendant with the most knowledge as to each of the following topics, including such individuals' full name, residential address, business address and position; (a) training of your company's sales personnel; (b) warnings or instructions issued to customers with regard to changes in handling or driving characteristics as a result of altering the height of a vehicle; and (c) the status of any claims or lawsuits described in Interrogatory No. 11 above.

Cecil Sylvester.

Signed under the pains and penalties of perjury
ULTIMATE AUTO, INC.

By: _____ /s/ Adam Jenkins _____
Adam Jenkins

# COMMONWEALTH OF MASSACHUSETTS

MIDDLESEX, SS

SUPERIOR COURT DEPARTMENT
OF THE TRIAL COURT CIVIL
ACTION NO. 12-6144

NANCY CARPENTER, As
Administratrix of the Estate
of Charles Carpenter,
   Plaintiff

      vs.

RANDALL DEE; PETER DEE;
ULTIMATE AUTO, INC.;
and CITY OF LOWELL,
   Defendants.

TRANSCRIPT OF DEPOSITION
OF DEFENDANT RANDALL DEE

Deposition of Randall Dee, taken on behalf of the Plaintiff, pursuant to Notice
under the applicable Rules of the Massachusetts Rules of Civil Procedure,
before Rochelle D. Baron, a Shorthand Reporter and Notary Public in and for
the Commonwealth of Massachusetts, at the Offices of Needham, Shaker &
Coblentz on Thursday, xxxxx, xx,* commencing at 10:30 A.M.

APPEARANCES
   ROSEMARY NEEDHAM, ESQ. and CAROL COBLENTZ, ESQ., For
     Plaintiff.
   GWENDOLYN FRANCIS, ESQ., For Defendant Randall Dee.
   BERTRAM COHEN, ESQ., For Defendant Ultimate Auto, Inc.
   CAITLIN TALBOT, ESQ., For Defendant City of Lowell.

. . .

---

*Eds.' Note:* In the actual case, this deposition was taken six months after the complaint was filed and
prior to the addition of Ultimate Auto, Inc. and the City of Lowell as defendants.

MS. COBLENTZ: Let me propose the following stipulations. The witness will read and sign the deposition. We will waive the notarization, sealing and filing; reserve all objections, except as to form, and reserve all motions to strike, except as to form.

RANDALL DEE, a witness called by the plaintiff, having been first duly sworn, was examined and testified as follows:

DIRECT EXAMINATION BY MS. COBLENTZ: Mr. Dee, my name is Carol Coblentz. I represent the plaintiff in this action. I'm going to be asking you a series of questions. It is not my intent to trick you in any way. If you, therefore, don't understand a question or it's unclear to you, please let me know, and I'll rephrase it or repeat it. And if you don't ask me to do that, I will assume you understand it.

If you hear an objection from your attorney, you go ahead and answer unless I instruct you not to answer. And if you want a break at any time, just let me know about that as well. Would you state your name, please?

A: Randall Dee
Q: Where do you live, sir?
A: 91 Birch Hill Road, Lowell.
Q: And how long have you lived at that house?
A: Twenty-five years.
Q: And that's the house that you grew up in that your parents owned?
A: Yes.
Q: What's your Social Security number?
A: I'm not—I don't know it by heart.
Q: Do you have a driver's license with you today?

A: Yes.
Q: Is this your driver's license?
A: Yes.
Q: And is your Social Security number on your driver's license as well?
A: Yes.
Q: Mr. Dee, are your parents both deceased?
A: Yes.
Q: And what were their names?
A: Dorothy Dee and Richard Dee.
Q: And do you know approximately when they purchased the house that you live in now, approximately?
A: Twenty-five years ago—about twenty-five years ago.

[We have omitted three pages of deposition regarding the transfer of the Dee house to Randall and his three siblings.]

Q: Mr. Dee, tell me when you first got your driver's license, approximately.
A: Five years ago.
Q: And what's your current age?
A: Twenty-five.
Q: So it was several years after you were first entitled to apply that you got it.
A: Yes. I think it was about—it might have been two years after or—I'm not sure. I forget. I think I might have been nineteen.
Q: Did you take driver's education in school?
A: No.
Q: Did you graduate from high school?
A: Yes.
Q: Lowell?
A: Lowell Vocational High School.
Q: And what course did you take there?

*A:* Auto body.

*Q:* And you are presently employed?

*A:* Yes.

*Q:* By whom?

*A:* Raytheon of Waltham.

*Q:* And what do you do, sir?

*A:* I am a plater, metal finisher.

*Q:* And how long have you been at Raytheon?

*A:* Four years.

*Q:* And your present rate of pay is what?

*A:* What do you mean?

*Q:* Are you paid on an hourly basis?

*A:* Yes.

*Q:* What do you make an hour?

*A:* I think it's around $12 or something.

*Q:* And you work a forty-hour week?

*A:* Yes.

*Q:* Do you get overtime as well?

*A:* Very little but I do.

*Q:* And that's time and a half?

*A:* Yes.

*Q:* Did you take driving instruction from anyone?

*A:* No.

*Q:* Just kind of learned O.J.T., as they say?

*A:* Yes.

*Q:* Have you ever held a job in which driving was a part of your duties?

*A:* No.

*Q:* What was the first car that you owned?

*A:* I never owned a car. I had never actually owned a car.

*Q:* The jeep that you were driving at the time of this accident was registered to whom?

*A:* Twyla Burrell.

*Q:* And Burrell was an old girlfriend of yours?

*A:* Yes.

*Q:* And did you, in fact, live with her at some time?

*A:* Yes.

*Q:* Was her legal address 91 Birch Hill Road?

*A:* For a while before the accident.

*Q:* Now, when did you and she stop living together, approximately?

*A:* I'm not—

*Q:* It was before the accident?

*A:* Yes.

*Q:* A year or so before, something like that?

*A:* Yes.

*Q:* When was that vehicle purchased by Twyla Burrell?

*A:* Would have to be around 2009 or 2010, I'd say.

*Q:* And it was a 1986 Jeep CJ-7?

*A:* Yes.

*Q:* Where was it purchased from?

*A:* Some car auction, I think, in Concord maybe.

[We have omitted the portion of the deposition regarding Randall's acquisition of the jeep from Twyla Burrell.]

*Q:* Can you help me at all in terms of the specific date when the jeep was purchased?

*A:* I'm not too sure. It had to be late 2009 maybe. I could find out, but I'm not too sure.

*Q:* Now, were any modifications made to the jeep?

*A:* Yes.

*Q:* I want to talk about those in as much detail as we can and to talk about each of them separately. First of all, let me start with tires. When the jeep was purchased, what kind of tires did it have, if you know?

*A:* It had stock tires.

*Q:* And do you know the size of those tires?

*A:* Fifteen inch.

*Q:* Would that be stock for a Jeep CJ-7?

*A:* Yes.

*Q:* At some point, much larger tires were put on, is that right?

*A:* Yes.

*Q:* Were the stock tires that were on it in good condition?

*A:* No. They were worn out.

*Q:* So they needed to be replaced anyway.

*A:* Yes.

*Q:* Did you immediately replace them with larger tires?

*A:* I had to lift the jeep before I could put the bigger tires on.

*Q:* And when you say "lift the jeep," you mean raise the suspension?

*A:* Yes.

*Q:* And we'll get to that. When and where did you purchase the larger tires?

*A:* I purchased them at Ultimate Auto, Inc.

*Q:* And these tires are called Monster Tires, is that right?

*A:* Yes.

*Q:* Is that a brand name, or do you know what the brand was?

*A:* That may be the brand. Though it might be technically something else.

*Q:* And what size tires were these?

*A:* They were 40 inch, 15's but 40 inch.

*Q:* In other words, the inner radius—

*A:* The rim was 15-inch rim.

*Q:* Fifteen-inch rim which is the same as the stock rim?

*A:* Yes.

*Q:* But the diameter of the tire is much larger.

*A:* Yes.

*Q:* And is 40 inch the diameter of the tire?

*A:* Yes.

*Q:* So it's over three feet. And the suspension needs to be raised to accommodate that.

*A:* Yes.

*Q:* Had you previously raised the suspension before you purchased the tires?

*A:* Yes.

*Q:* And tell me what you did to do that.

*A:* Well, I bought a lift kit, a suspension—a suspension lift kit from the same place, Ultimate Auto and then I—and that raised it, I think, 3 inches—

*Q:* The lift kit alone raised it 3 inches.

*A:* —and stiffened up the suspension. And then I raised the body from the frame 4 inches with spaces underneath the body of the jeep to the frame and that gave—

*Q:* So that was a total of 7 inches—

*A:* Yes.

*Q:* —which gave you enough clearance to fit the tires.

*A:* Fit the tires.

*Q:* And now, having raised it 7 inches, could the car then work? I mean I understand it would have looked silly. Would it have worked on stock tires?

*A:* Yes.

*Q:* And if it had stock tires, say, at the roof line, it still would have been 7 inches higher.

*A:* Yes.

*Q:* And with the Monster Tires, how much additional height was added?

*A:* It probably raised a foot?

*Q:* So that overall, it had been lifted as much as 1 foot 7 inches, am I right?

*A:* Approximately.

*Q:* What I want to do, Mr. Dee, is go into this in detail, and you have to bear with me because I'm not an auto mechanic. And I want to understand it as much as I can.

*MS. FRANCIS:* Can I just interject. I don't think there's anything to show that there's actual figures or that this is on his own estimate. I understand you've given us your best judgment about the height, and I understand you haven't measured them to the fraction of an inch.

*A:* Yes.

*Q:* Did you purchase the lift kit at the same time as you purchased tires to raise the body? Was that all done at the same time?

*A:* What do you mean?

*Q:* Okay. The lift kit contained some specific materials that are used to raise the suspension.

*A:* Are we talking about now the suspension or the body?

*Q:* The suspension.

*A:* They're just springs that are arced greater than a stock spring, and that's what gives you the lift.

*Q:* And you also purchased a kind of rubber disc as a spacer.

*A:* Not for the suspension; that's for the body.

*Q:* Did you do the work yourself?

*A:* Yes.

*Q:* Did anyone help you?

*A:* Charlie did a little bit, but it was mostly me.

*Q:* Charlie Carpenter?

*A:* Yes.

*Q:* Where did you do the work?

*A:* I did it in my backyard, my driveway.

*Q:* Did you need a lift to do any of this work?

*A:* Just a floor jack.

*Q:* And how long did it take you to do that work?

*A:* A couple of months, two months.

*Q:* Let's start by having you describe for me what parts you purchased from Ultimate Auto.

*A:* Okay. I purchased the Monster Tires, right—

*Q:* Four of them?

*A:* Four of them, yes—and—

*Q:* What was the cost of those? [Discussion off the record.]

*Q:* Is it your best memory that the tires were $300 each?

*A:* No. The tires were $200 each and the rims were $50 each for a rim. So four—four rims was $200 and the tires were $200 each.

*Q:* So that's a thousand.

*A:* Yes, plus the tax or whatever. It came to roughly—I guess I got the receipt—$1200. Gee, and if I had gone to New Hampshire, I would have saved the tax.

*Q:* So it was about $1200 just for the tires and rims?

*A:* Yes.

*Q:* And with tax, excise tax and so forth.

*A:* Yes.

*Q:* Am I correct that you purchased those after you had already done the work to lift the car?

*A:* Yes.

*Q:* So the first thing you purchased was what?

*A:* The leaf spring, the suspension lift at Ultimate Auto.

*MS. COBLENTZ:* I have a pretty good idea what a leaf spring looks like but let's go off the record a minute. [Discussion off the record.]

*Q:* We're to do this by drawing of words as opposed to pictures.

*A:* Yes.

*Q:* The first thing that you did was you replaced the stock leaf spring with a more arced spring.

*A:* Yes.

*Q:* And the upper part of the spring connects to the frame of the jeep and the lower part connects to the axle.

*A:* Right.

*Q:* So that by increasing the arc, it has the effect of raising the frame relative to the axle, is that correct?

*A:* Yes.

*Q:* And the stiffer and more arced spring raises the frame relative to the axle by how much, approximately?

*A:* I think it was a 3-inch, 2½ inch it says on the—2½-inch suspension lift they call it.

*Q:* So there is a box that calls it a 2½-inch lift.

*A:* Yes, Rodeo is the name.

*Q:* Rodeo?

*A:* Yes.

*Q:* Do you, by any chance, have any of the boxes or any of the instructions for that equipment?

*A:* Probably not.

*Q:* But it was called Rodeo?

*A:* Yes.

*Q:* And this was purchased at Ultimate Auto?

*A:* Yes.

*Q:* Now, did you purchase the body lift materials at the same time?

*A:* No.

*Q:* Did you buy four springs?

*A:* Yes.

*Q:* And what was the cost, approximately?

*A:* I think it cost $350 or $300 and change.

*Q:* So about $80 or $85 per spring, correct?

*A:* About that.

*Q:* Was that the first thing you purchased to do the modification?

*A:* Yes.

*Q:* And then at a subsequent time, you purchased the kit to lift the body relative to the frame.

*A:* Yes.

*Q:* And what is that called?

*A:* It's called a body lift.

*Q:* And is the term "hockey puck" sometimes used to describe that?

*A:* Well, what happened is I called Crazy Larry's, a place where they sell body lifts. I called the place to purchase it, and they— I don't know who the guy was, but he said, "Everybody's using hockey pucks. It's the hardest rubber in the world." He was buying hockey pucks and using them as body lifts so that's what I did. I went out and I bought a bunch of hockey pucks.

*Q:* An actual hockey puck in a sporting goods store?

*A:* Yes.

*Q:* Do you know where you bought them?

*A:* City Sports in Waltham.

*Q:* So you literally used hockey pucks.

*A:* Yes.

*Q:* Did you get this advice over the phone?

*A:* Yes.

*Q:* From Crazy Larry's?

*A:* Yes.

*Q:* Who gave you the advice about the body lifts?

*A:* I don't remember who it was because I was calling around a bunch of places looking for a body lift.

*Q:* Did Ultimate Auto sell body lifts?

*A:* Yes everybody did.

*Q:* Do you have any way of remembering who you talked to there?

*A:* No, no. I called so many locations. I forget who told me. I'm not too sure who said, but he said everybody's using hockey pucks so—

*Q:* Do you know what that body lift kit looks like?

*A:* Yes.

*Q:* Does it, in fact, consist of a rubber—

*A:* They are spacers; they're round; some are made out of aluminum; some are made out of steel. And they're just round pieces of metal with a hole through the middle. You just put—you just lift the body a little from the frame and fill it in and put body bolts back in.

*Q:* So it's just a cylinder really.

*A:* That's all.

*Q:* Okay. And does Ultimate Auto specialize in conversion of vehicles?

*A:* I don't know if—they don't do it themselves. They sell the parts, but they don't actually do any of the work.

*Q:* And they sell racing tires and so forth.

*A:* They sell everything.

*Q:* So it's a specialty store—

*A:* Yes.

*Q:* —for people who want to modify cars either in terms of racing them or speeding them up or things of that sort.

*A:* Or four-wheeling.

*Q:* Or four-wheeling. Now, when you bought the hockey pucks, what did you do, did you drill out a hole in them?

*A:* Yes.

*Q:* And you pile—

*A:* Four on—

*Q:* —four on top of each other.

*A:* Yes.

*Q:* So let's say a hockey puck's about an inch and a half thick.

*A:* No, an inch thick.

*Q:* So that raised it 4 inches.

*A:* Yes.

*Q:* When you purchased the hockey pucks, did you, by any chance, tell City Sports what you were going to use them for?

*A:* No. I told them I owned a hockey team.

*Q:* So you bought sixteen pucks.

*A:* I bought about fifty of them.

*Q:* Fifty of them?

*A:* Sure.

*Q:* Because they wear out?

*A:* No. You got—

*Q:* I thought you said four on each wheel.

*A:* No. We're talking about the body now. From the frame, you got—you got about twelve mount—twelve spots where the body bolts to the frame so you got to put four, four, four, and four.

*Q:* So at every point where the body bolts to the frame you put four hockey pucks as a spacer.

A:  Yes.

Q:  Is that something you had heard about before, the use—

A:  Everybody was doing it.

Q:  —the use of hockey pucks?

A:  Everybody was doing it. They were cheaper, for one thing. And you are better off having rubber in between to absorb the shock rather than metal, metal to metal.
Everybody was using the hockey pucks.

MS. COBLENTZ:  Off the record.
[Discussion off the record.]

Q:  And then after you did that, you then went back and purchased the Monster Tires.

A:  Yes.

Q:  Do you remember the names of the persons you dealt with at Ultimate Auto?

A:  No. They changed. He never gets the same salesmen. They come and go at that place. I wouldn't remember.

Q:  Is the place still in existence?

A:  Yes.

Q:  Are Monster Tire tires designed specifically for jeeps?

A:  No.

MS. FRANCIS:  I don't know if he'd know that information anyway.

Q:  If you know. Are they made for four-wheel-drive vehicles?

A:  They're made for anything, any type of vehicle.

Q:  Are they designed for off-road use?

A:  Yes.

Q:  They're pretty knobby?

A:  Yes.

Q:  But they will also operate on the road?

A:  Yes.

Q:  And I am correct that with a tire of that size that you would be unable to accommodate it without doing both the suspension lift and the body lift?

A:  Yes.

Q:  Had you ever had prior experience modifying vehicles?

A:  No.

Q:  Did you teach yourself to do this?

A:  Yes.

Q:  Did you use any printed materials to learn how to do it?

A:  No. I looked in books, but like Off Road magazine or something. It was a fad. Everybody was lifting.

Q:  Did you subscribe to any of those magazines?

A:  No.

Q:  You just purchased them someplace?

A:  Yes.

Q:  Do you know the name of any specific ones that you used?

A:  Magazine?

Q:  Yes.

A:  Off Road, I think it's called.

Q:  Did you use an article in Off Road as a kind of "how to" or a manual to help you do this?

A:  No.

Q:  Had you gotten any instruction in this during your high school vocational training?

A:  No.

Q:  I take it that from a mechanical point of view it wasn't terribly complicated.

A:  No.

Q:  Now, did you ever learn in high school or from any source that jeeps were known to have a rollover problem?

A:  Yes.

*Q:* And where did you first learn that?

*A:* I think I seen it on the TV, 20/20.

*Q:* On 20/20 or Sixty Minutes?

*A:* Something like that there was an article.

*Q:* Was that before this accident, if you know?

*A:* I think it was after. I'm not sure.

*Q:* Did you know at the time when you made the modifications that raising the height of a vehicle can affect its handling characteristics?

*A:* Yes.

*Q:* And did you know that raising the height of a vehicle can, among other things, affect its propensity to roll over?

*A:* I didn't know. I figured it would make it better because the tires were heavier. You got heavy tires at the bottom. Now you got more weight at the bottom of the vehicle now than the top so I figured it would roll less.

*Q:* You actually thought it would roll less because of the weight of the tires—

*A:* Yes.

*Q:* —even though the overall height was raised as much as it was?

*A:* Yes.

*Q:* When you purchased the Monster Tires at Ultimate Auto did the salesman give you any instructions concerning their use?

*A:* No.

*Q:* Did he tell you about anything to watch out for?

*A:* No.

*Q:* Did he ask you what vehicle you were putting them on?

*A:* No.

*Q:* Just sold them to you?

*A:* That's all.

*Q:* You paid the money and they went out.

*A:* You got it, right, yes.

*Q:* Same question with respect to the suspension raiser, suspension lift kit, did you get any warnings or instructions when you purchased that?

*A:* No, no.

*Q:* And were there any questions about what use you were going to put these parts to?

*A:* What do you mean, any questions?

*Q:* Did he give you any instructions?

*A:* Oh, the same man?

*Q:* Yes, the same man.

*A:* No, they just hand them to you and you give them the money.

*Q:* Were there any warnings or instructions in the suspension lift kits concerning their use?

*A:* Not that I know of. I didn't see any.

*Q:* I may have asked you and I forgot the answer, the manufacturer of the Monster Tires?

*A:* I think that's their name.

*Q:* Do they make other kinds of tires? It's not a name that's familiar to me.

*A:* I'm not too sure. It's not a familiar name. I'm not sure if that's all they make.

*Q:* Are these tires still on the car?

*A:* Yes.

*Q:* And the car is where?

*A:* It's in my driveway.

*Q:* And you know that you're not allowed to modify it.

*A:* I don't even think—it's rotting there.

*Q:* Did you do maintenance work on the jeep yourself?

*A:* Yes.

*Q:* Did you ever have maintenance work on it performed anywhere else?

*A:* No.

*Q:* Did you do all the work on it yourself?

*A:* Yes.

*Q:* Do you remember any of the maintenance you did on it?

*A:* Changed the oil, spark plugs.

*Q:* Did you do any engine work on it at all?

*A:* No. It's basically stock. I put a header on it, but other than that, it was all stock.

*Q:* So, to the best of your judgment, that car never saw the inside of an auto mechanic's door after you got it.

*A:* No.

*Q:* Do you remember where the vehicle was inspected?

*A:* Yes.

*Q:* Where was that?

*A:* McGill's.

*Q:* If I suggest to you December of 2010, does that sound about right as the last inspection?

*A:* I can't recall.

*Q:* But you know that it was inspected prior to the accident.

*A:* Yes.

*Q:* Now, by December 2010, had the modifications all been done?

*A:* That means before it's been inspected, you mean?

*Q:* Yes.

*A:* Oh, yes.

*Q:* So if, in fact, it was inspected in December of 2010, the inspector was looking at a very modified vehicle, correct—

*A:* Yes.

*Q:* —and with all of the modifications we've talked about.

*A:* Yes.

*Q:* I'd just like to talk about your driving history. You indicated that you started driving, you thought, about age nineteen, approximately.

*A:* I think it was nineteen.

*Q:* Prior to this accident, were you charged with any motor vehicle violations, excluding parking.

*A:* Yes.

*Q:* And I'd like to talk about them in order, starting with the earliest that you can recall.

*A:* Let me think. I think the only one was drunk driving.

*Q:* And do you recall when that was?

*MS. FRANCIS:* Approximate time.

*A:* I forget.

*MS. FRANCIS:* Do you want to go off the record to refresh your recollection?

[Discussion off the record.]

*Q:* I have some information suggesting that in April of 2011 you were charged with driving under the influence. Does that sound correct?

*A:* Yes.

*Q:* Do you know any of the officers involved?

*A:* Yes.

*Q:* And who were they? I'm talking about that stop now.

*A:* With the drunk driving?

*Q:* Drunk driving, right.

*MS. FRANCIS:* Do you want to go off the record to refresh your recollection?

*A:* Ricky Murdoch, the officer was Ricky Murdoch.

*Q:* M-U-R-D-O-C-H?

*A:* That's close enough.

*Q:* Do you know any other of the officers involved with that?

*A:* No.

*Q:* Were you driving the jeep at that time?

*A:* Yes.

*Q:* And it had, of course, been modified?

*A:* Yes.

*Q:* Did the officers at that time make any comments to you about the jeep?

*A:* No.

*Q:* What was the outcome of that charge?

*A:* What did they do to me?

*Q:* Yes.

*A:* I was found guilty of DWI and I lost my license—loss of license for thirty days, and I had to go to school, drunk driving school, for so many hours. I'm not sure how many hours.

*Q:* Now, when your license is pulled, do you physically give up your license?

*A:* Yes.

*Q:* You hand it, what, to the clerk or something in court?

*A:* Yes.

*Q:* And then you get it back later?

*A:* In thirty days from the date you give it to them, they'll give it back to you providing you go to that—

*Q:* Now, as I understand it, at the time of this accident, you didn't have your license in your possession, is that correct?

*A:* Yes.

*Q:* Am I correct?

*A:* Yes.

*Q:* But you did, in fact, have a license at that time.

*A:* Yes.

*Q:* It had been returned?

*A:* Oh, are we talking about—

*Q:* At the time of this accident that we're here for.

*A:* I didn't have it on me, but I did have a license.

*Q:* You mentioned another incident. There was something about there not being a side mirror.

*A:* Well, I was never cited for that.

*Q:* But were you pulled over for it?

*A:* Yes.

*Q:* Do you know the name of the officer who did that?

*A:* No.

*Q:* But it was a uniformed Lowell police officer?

*A:* Yes.

*Q:* And when was that, first of all?

*A:* It was prior to the accident. I'm not too sure.

*Q:* Was it prior to the drunk driving charge?

*A:* Yes.

*Q:* Was it in 2010?

*A:* Yes.

*Q:* So it was—and so at that time, the vehicle had been modified again.

*A:* Yes.

*Q:* And could you tell me what the officer said?

*A:* He told me to—he told me—he said, "Take the vehicle home and don't take it back out on the road till you get a mirror on it, a rear view mirror." So I took it home and I put a mirror on it.

*Q:* You're talking about a side mirror—

*A:* Yes.

*Q:* —not the inner rear view mirror.

*A:* No.

*Q:* The driver's side mirror.

*A:* Yes.

*Q:* And you did that?

*A:* Yes.

*Q:* And did that officer make any comment on the height of the vehicle or anything related to its height?

*A:* No.

*Q:* And again, that was in 2010?

*A:* Yes.

*Q:* Now, were there any other motor vehicle violations; that you have had up to this accident?

*A:* Yes.

*Q:* And what was that?

*A:* I was pulled over for being unregistered, uninsured in that jeep. What happened is it was insured, but the little sticker that goes on your plate there— you know how they send you a card, renewal-registration renewal, well, either I never got the card or something so I didn't notice that little sticker had expired. So I was pulled over in that jeep. They towed the vehicle, and they cited me for unregistered, uninsured.

*Q:* And when was that?

*A:* That was prior to the accident. It could have been in 2000 or 2001.

*Q:* You mean 2010.

*A:* I'm sorry, 2010.

*Q:* But it was after the vehicle had been modified.

*A:* Yes.

*Q:* Am I correct that you did the modification fairly shortly after you got the jeep?

*A:* Yes.

*Q:* So let me recap. On at least three occasions prior to the accident this vehicle, in its modified form, came under the scrutiny of the Lowell Police Department.

*A:* Yes.

*Q:* And on none of those occasions did the police officers comment to you at all about its height, am I correct?

*A:* Yes.

*Q:* Was there any court appearance involved with that unregistered, uninsured charge?

*A:* Yes.

*Q:* What was the outcome of that?

*A:* I proved that it was insured. I brought in proof that it was insured so he dismissed that charge, but he did fine me for being unregistered, and that's it.

*Q:* So, in fact, for whatever reason, you couldn't show that the car was registered.

*A:* It had expired.

*Q:* It had expired.

*A:* But it was insured.

*Q:* Okay. Were you fined?

*A:* Yes.

*Q:* So presumably there are court records relating to that.

*A:* Yes.

*Q:* Who was your insurance agent?

*A:* I don't remember.

*Q:* Is the jeep insured now?

*A:* No.

*Q:* Is it in a driveable condition?

*A:* No.

*Q:* Because?

*A:* The windshield broke, it's missing the hood and fender.

*Q:* So it hasn't been driven since the day of the accident.

*A:* No.

*Q:* How did it get from the accident site back to you house?

*A:* Towed.

*Q:* Do you know who towed it?

*A:* McGill's.

*Q:* Do you know how it was towed?

*A:* Just a normal—

Q: Was it dollied?

A: No. It was just towed, lift the front end.

Q: Towed on the rear wheels?

A: Yes.

Q: I'd like to turn to the happening of the accident itself. The date of the accident, sir, was what, do you recall?

A: August, 2011.

MS. COBLENTZ: Off the record a second.

[Discussion off the record.]

Q: What day of the week was that, do you know?

A: Saturday.

Q: And what did you do that morning?

A: What did I do?

Q: Yes.

A: I got up—

Q: Do you remember anything special about the day?

A: No, just regular day.

Q: Did you have plans for the day?

A: Well, it was my brother's birthday.

Q: Peter's?

A: Yes. They invited a few friends over to his girlfriend's house. It was a hot day. She has a pool in the backyard, which is about a hundred—a hundred feet away from the accident where she lives.

Q: And her name is what?

A: Keisha Ramsay.

Q: How do you spell that?

A: K-E-I-S-H-A, R-A-M-S-A-Y.

MS. COBLENTZ: Off the record.
[Discussion off the record.]

Q: Does she still live there?

A: Yes.

Q: Do you know the address?

A: No.

Q: Does your brother still go out with her?

A: Yes.

Q: Who was present at the party?

A: There was myself, my wife, my brother, his girlfriend Keisha, her mother—was that—her brother-in-law with his two children.

Q: What's his name?

A: Stony; that's his last name, Stony. I'm not sure of his first name.

Q: And she has been here with us today.

A: Yes.

Q: When were you married?

A: [No response.]

Q: Nobody ever remembers that. Don't feel bad.

A: That's a toughie.

Q: Were you married at the time of this accident?

A: No.

Q: I should never have asked.

A: I'm in trouble now.

Q: It's just the pressure of the occasion. When did you arrive at the party?

A: I'd say around 4:30 or 5.

Q: And was Charlie invited to the party?

A: Yes.

Q: Did you invite him?

A: No, my brother did.

Q: Was Charlie more your friend or your brother's friend?

A: He was both.

Q: And you had known him for a long time?

A: Oh, yes. We were like brothers.

Q: Did Charlie arrive separately from you?

A: Yes.

Q: How did he get to the party?

*A:* His car.

*Q:* And what kind of car did he have?

*A:* I think he had a green Mustang.

*Q:* How long were you at the party?

*A:* About an hour before he came.

*Q:* You were there an hour before Charlie came?

*A:* About that.

*Q:* So Charlie would have come around 5:30 or so.

*A:* Yes.

*Q:* Was this party for a dinner?

*A:* It was a cookout, barbecue, whatever.

*Q:* And did you, in fact, have dinner?

*A:* Yes.

*Q:* Was there any alcohol served at this party?

*A:* There was beer.

*Q:* Did you have beer?

*A:* No.

*Q:* You had none?

*A:* No.

*Q:* How do you remember that?

*A:* I just was—just didn't drink. I wasn't drinking that day, I remember.

*Q:* How much did you drink then? Did you have an occasional beer?

*A:* That's all; on the weekends, maybe a Saturday.

*Q:* Have you ever had any kind of drinking problem?

*A:* No.

*Q:* Did Charlie have anything to drink?

*A:* I don't know.

*Q:* What time did you leave the party?

*A:* Let's see. I'd say around 6:30-7 or—we were just leaving to get our bathing suits to go swimming, me and Charlie.

*Q:* Were you going to go back to each of your houses to get suits?

*A:* Yes.

*Q:* And where were you on your way first, to your house or his?

*A:* Probably his; his was—let me think—yes, his house would be closer.

[Discussion off the record.]

*Q:* And the accident happened at the corner of Palmer and Franklin, is that right?

*A:* Yes.

*Q:* I'd like you to draw, just if you could, a little map showing the path from the party to where the accident happened.

*A:* Okay.

[Witness drawing.]

*MS. FRANCIS:* May I just inquire, are you intending to use this for future reference, this sketch, or is it just for questions?

*MS. COBLENTZ:* Well, I'll mark it.

*MS. FRANCIS:* Of course, it's completely out of scale.

*MS. COBLENTZ:* I want to get the relationship of one street to the other.

*THE WITNESS:* I'm not too sure of the spelling or whatever, but I think that's how it was, basically.

*MS. COBLENTZ:* Let me mark this sketch as the next exhibit.

[A sketch drawn by the witness was marked as Exhibit No. 4 for identification.]

*Q:* Exhibit 4 is your sketch indicating the house where—

*A:* Yes.

*Q:* And the accident happened in the course of the left turn onto Franklin Street; is that correct?

*A:* Yes.

*Q:* Now, before we get into that, in previous occasions when you had driven the vehicle, had there been any time when you felt it leaning or starting to roll over?

*A:* No.

*Q:* Had you driven it off the road at all?

*A:* Very little, a few times.

*Q:* Where did you drive it off road?

*A:* Prospect Hill.

*Q:* Prospect Hill in Waltham?

*A:* Yes.

*Q:* Did you drive up the hill there or just kind of around those grounds there?

*A:* Around the grounds.

*Q:* Had you ever driven it off road under conditions where you had any real need for the extra clearance that all the modifications had given you?

*A:* Yes.

*Q:* And are there, for example, rocks and boulders there that you need to clear?

*A:* There's rocks and boulders and muddy, and I took it up there in the snow. And you need the clearance or you'd get hung up in the snow. You know what I mean, you'd actually be stuck in the snow if you weren't that high.

*Q:* But the primary use that you made of the vehicle was on the road?

*A:* Yes.

*Q:* Now, is Palmer and Franklin a regulated intersection? Is there a stop sign or traffic light there?

*A:* No traffic light; I think there's a stop sign. I'm not sure, but not—I didn't have a stop sign. I think there is the stop sign.

*Q:* On Franklin?

*A:* On Franklin.

*Q:* Can you give me your best estimate of your speed as you were going down Palmer Street before you got to the corner?

*A:* I'd say it couldn't be no more than 20 because that jeep with the big tire, I didn't change the gear ratio so it didn't have no power. It took a long time to pick up speed so I say—the distance from about a hundred yards—

*Q:* Do you remember what gear you were in?

*A:* First gear, because it was a slight climb, like I said. When I put on the big tires, it took all the power away from it.

*Q:* You were in first gear all that time?

*A:* Yes, because it's real short. I don't think I got out of first gear.

*Q:* Were you in first gear as you made the corner?

*A:* Yes.

*Q:* When the jeep rolled, you were in first gear?

*A:* I'm pretty sure.

*Q:* Do you remember turning the corner excessively sharply?

*MS. FRANCIS:* I object.

*Q:* Let me rephrase it. Did you turn the corner more sharply than you usually turn a corner?

*A:* No.

*Q:* Tell me exactly what happened, as you remember it.

*A:* I was going down Palmer Street and then that intersection or that turn, it's real sharp—no. I wouldn't say sharp. It's a real dangerous turn or something.

It dips and then—it dips toward—it's—I don't know. It's a bad—everybody cuts it. No one ever takes the turn. Everybody crosses the yellow line.

Q: In other words, you cut the corner a little bit onto Franklin.

A: You have to. That's the land of—

Q: Is it, for instance, a 90-degree turn?

MS. FRANCIS: I don't think he'd have any knowledge of that.

Q: If you know.

A: I don't know.

Q: You know what I mean when I say that? Is it more than like a square corner? Are you land of doubling back when you—

A: I don't think so.

Q: Is there something about the pitch on Franklin Road *that* creates any difficulty?

A: I would say there is, but—

Q: Have you ever heard about any other accidents at that corner?

A: I seen—the bushes that I hit, a couple of—maybe a month ago, the same bushes, the exact same spot, the bushes were dug up again.

Q: Okay. I'd like you to draw another diagram for me showing the same intersection in larger scale, and I'll draw the streets.

[Ms. Coblentz draws a diagram.]

Q: This is Palmer and this is Franklin. The jeep is coming from here and making this turn [indicating], correct?

A: Okay.

Q: Right?

A: Yes.

Q: First of all, describe it in words and then we'll figure out what we want on the sketch. You indicated that you had to cut the corner crossing the yellow line as you did so.

A: Yes, very—yes.

Q: And what was the first sensation you had of any problem?

A: I didn't. It just—I don't remember.

Q: Do you remember applying the brakes?

A: Yes, I think so. It happened— you know, I'd say so fast but just—I don't remember. I tried to, you know, block it out. I just can't recall.

Q: As you think back on it, do you have a memory of the vehicle rolling?

A: Barely.

Q: And I take it rolled—if you were looking at the vehicle from behind, it rolled clockwise? In other words, it rolled toward the right?

A: It rolled toward the passenger side.

Q: Right. And do you have any sense about when it started to roll in relation to where you were, on Palmer or Franklin?

A: No.

Q: It was shortly after you had started the turn though, is that right?

A: Oh, yes.

Q: Were you pretty much onto Franklin when it began to roll?

A: I was probably right in the middle of the turn maybe.

Q: What I'd like you to draw for me, as best you can, and try to get the jeep somewhat in scale, at least relative to the intersection itself, the position of the jeep at the moment when it first seemed to begin to turn. And the way we draw cars in the law business is like this with a "V" on the front end like that.

*A:* And what do you want me to do?

*Q:* I want you to draw the position of the jeep when it first started to roll.

*MS. FRANCIS:* Is that what he felt?

*Q:* When you felt that it first started to roll, as best you can. But I just want to get some sense of where it was in relation to the intersection.

*A:* I'm coming down here [indicating].

*Q:* Down here turning onto Franklin like that?

*A:* And there was a house here. There was bushes here, shrubs.

*Q:* Why don't you draw the shrubs.

*A:* How do you—

*Q:* Just kind of a wavy line to indicate the shrubs.
[Witness complies.]

*Q:* Those are the shrubs on that corner?

*A:* I'd say right about—maybe right there.

*Q:* And can you draw for me the final position that the jeep was in when it came to rest?

*MS. FRANCIS:* Can we mark that position with some kind of letter or something?

*MS. COBLENTZ:* Yes.

*Q:* Why don't you put "1" inside that. And then draw the position of the jeep when it came to rest.

*MS. FRANCIS:* The location, you mean?

*MS. COBLENTZ:* Yes, the position.

*MS. FRANCIS:* Because position means situation.
[Witness complies.]

*A:* Something like that.

*Q:* So it came to rest partly on the road in these bushes.

*A:* Yes.

*MS. FRANCIS:* Can we mark that position with a "2"?

*MS. COBLENTZ:* Yes.

*Q:* Can you put a "2" on there?
[Witness complies.]

*Q:* And at that point, the vehicle was completely flipped over.

*A:* Yes.

*Q:* And Charlie was pinned under the roll bar?

*A:* Yes.

*Q:* Did it have the roll bar when you got it?

*A:* Yes.

*Q:* Were you thrown out of the vehicle?

*A:* No.

*Q:* Were you belted in?

*A:* No.

*Q:* You were inside the vehicle?

*A:* Yes. I had the steering wheel, you know, to hold me in. So when it rolled, I slid out of it, like fell out toward the passenger side.

*Q:* And what did you do when you got out? First of all, you were conscious.

*A:* Yes.

*Q:* Were you hurt at all?

*A:* Yes.

*Q:* How had you gotten hurt?

*A:* I think I banged up my knee.

*Q:* But you weren't seriously hurt at all?

*A:* No.

*Q:* Were there people around?

*A:* Yes.

*Q:* What's the first thing you did?

*A:* I checked—I looked to see where Charlie was.

*Q:* And you saw him pinned under the roll bar.

*A:* Yes.

*Q:* What did you do next?

*A:* I flipped out. I tried to push the jeep. I just didn't know what to do.

*Q:* Did you get some people to help you?

*A:* Some—somebody came over. I just—I don't remember. I know—

*Q:* Do you remember at some point the vehicle being pushed onto its side?

*A:* I don't—I'm not sure. It must have been.

*Q:* Do you remember it being on its side when the police arrived?

*A:* Yes, I think so.

*Q:* Do you remember having any conversation with the police that night?

*A:* No.

*Q:* What do you mean, after the accident?

*A:* Yes. They put me in the traffic safety van and—

*MS. FRANCIS:* Do you remember talking to the police was the question.

*A:* Yes.

*MS. FRANCIS:* Was that the question, just talking to the police?

*MS. COBLENTZ:* Yes.

*Q:* Well, let me ask this. At some point, you knew you were being charged with some crime.

*A:* Correct, yes.

*Q:* Were you informed of it that night?

*A:* No.

*Q:* Were you taken to the hospital?

*A:* Yes.

*Q:* Was that Lowell's Community Hospital?

*A:* Yes.

*Q:* Were you treated and released?

*A:* What happened is I was waiting—I was waiting to be treated and then I heard that Charlie died. I just flipped out. I refused treatment, and I just walked out of the hospital and went home.

*Q:* You walked home?

*A:* Yes.

*Q:* How far is that?

*A:* About a mile.

*Q:* Was the car in the two-wheel drive or four-wheel drive position?

*A:* Two.

*Q:* Did you ever use four-wheel drive on the road?

*A:* Only in the winter in the snow.

*Q:* Did you tell the police that you had some steering difficulty?

*A:* I thought there was, but—I'm not sure. I said something about that.

*Q:* Is it your belief today that there was any steering difficulty?

*A:* I'm still not sure. I haven't touched the jeep. I don't know.

*Q:* Am I correct that at the moment when the vehicle began to roll over, up to that time, you had not been aware of any steering problem?

*A:* No.

*Q:* It began to negotiate the curve and accepted steering input as you made it, right?

*A:* Repeat that.

*Q:* Yes. You turned the wheel and the vehicle responded to your turning the wheel.

*A:* Yes, as far as I—yes.

*Q:* And you're not aware of any braking problem, is that right?

*A:* No.

*Q:* Do you remember the names of the officers you spoke to that night?

*A:* [No response.]

*A:* The officers?

*Q:* Yes.

*A:* No. I have it at home.

*Q:* Had you ever seen either of them before?

*A:* No.

*Q:* Were you or Charlie yelling anything just prior to the accident?

*A:* No.

*Q:* Did you ever hear any information of a witness that said you were?

*A:* Yes.

*Q:* How did you hear that?

*A:* He said it at the probable cause hearing.

*Q:* And your testimony is that you were not yelling?

*A:* No.

*Q:* Were there any repairs made to the jeep after the accident?

*A:* No.

*Q:* At what time was it towed back to your house, do you know?

*A:* I think it was two days after. It was towed to McGill's Garage, and it was stored back there, I think, for a couple of days, And then it was towed to my house.

*Q:* I just want to go through the charges and what happened. You were charged with a number of different offenses as a result of this, weren't you—

*A:* Right.

*Q:* —of which the most serious, of course, was motor vehicle homicide. You were found guilty of that.

*A:* I think so, yes.

*MS. FRANCIS:* Do you recall?

*Q:* And do you remember what your penalty was for that?

*A:* Two years suspended sentence.

*Q:* So that the two years has now elapsed.

*A:* No. I think it's—I got until May, I think.

*Q:* And the driving to endanger was dismissed and merged into the count for motor vehicle homicide.

*A:* Yes.

*Q:* And you were found not guilty of operating after license had been revoked.

*A:* Yes.

*Q:* And you were found guilty for failing to slow at the intersection.

*A:* Yes.

*Q:* And you were found guilty of speeding, right?

*A:* Yes.

*Q:* And you were found guilty of altering the height of a motor vehicle.

*A:* Yes.

*Q:* At the time, sir, when you deeded your interest in your house to your brother, did you have any other substantial property?

*A:* No.

*Q:* So it's fair to say that the house was really your sole significant asset.

*A:* That's it.

*Q:* And what was your motor vehicle liability insurance at the time of this accident?

*A:* What option, you mean?

*Q:* Yes.

*A:* I think it was option 3.

*Q:* Do you remember how much liability coverage you had?

*A:* I think it was 10/20, something like that.

*MS. COBLENTZ:* Off the record. [Discussion off the record.]

*Q:* So you knew that you had the minimum amount of liability insurance, correct?

*A:* Yes.

*Q:* And you knew at the time, did you not, that one who negligently causes the death of another can be responsible civilly as well as criminally for that?

*MS. FRANCIS:* I object to that. I don't think he even has the answer to that.

*MS. COBLENTZ:* I think it relates.

*MS. FRANCIS:* He knew at which time?

*MS. COBLENTZ:* At the time he conveyed the house. That's what this goes to.

*MS. FRANCIS:* That he knew— what was the question again?

*Q:* At the time when you conveyed the house, you knew that someone who is negligent and causes the death of another person can be responsible to the estate of that person civilly or criminally.

*A:* I didn't know that.

*Q:* You didn't know that?

*A:* No.

*Q:* You had no concerns whatever about possibly losing an asset?

*A:* No. I just needed money. I didn't have nowhere to turn. I don't have any credit at all. I needed money before he'd represent me.

*Q:* Does Raytheon have a credit union?

*A:* Yes.

*Q:* Had you gone to the credit union?

*A:* No.

*Q:* Did you ever ask?

*A:* No. I didn't think they'd lend you that much money.

*Q:* But you didn't inquire.

*A:* No.

*MS. COBLENTZ:* I'm done.

*MS. FRANCIS:* I have a couple of questions.

CROSS EXAMINATION BY
MS. FRANCIS

*Q:* Was there any damage to the jeep that you described to us?

*A:* Right now? From the accident, you mean?

*Q:* From the accident.

*A:* The windshield broke and the nose—the nose is crushed, like the hood and the two fenders and that's—

*Q:* Was it driveable after the accident?

*A:* I don't think so.

*Q:* Was there any damage to this new suspension that you installed?

*A:* No, not that I know of.

*Q:* In other words, those hockey pucks were still in place?

*A:* Yes.

*Q:* Did you have to put separate bolts that you purchased to go through the center of those hockey pucks?

*A:* Did I, yes.

*Q:* Longer ones—

*A:* Yes.

*Q:* —than were there? Were they still intact after the accident?

*A:* Yes, yes.

*Q:* And the springs that you installed, were they still intact?

*A:* Yes. The whole undercarriage is intact?

*Q:* Was there any damage to any of the parts that you installed?

*A:* No, nothing; It didn't roll that hard.

*MS. FRANCIS:* I have no further questions.

REDIRECT EXAMINATION BY MS. COBLENTZ

*Q:* Where did you purchase the bolts?

*A:* A hardware store.

*Q:* But you didn't get them at a specialty auto store.

*A:* No.

*MS. COBLENTZ:* That's all I have.

*MS. FRANCIS:* We're all set. [Whereupon, the deposition was concluded at 12:08 P.M.]

## COMMONWEALTH OF MASSACHUSETTS

MIDDLESEX, SS

SUPERIOR COURT DEPARTMENT
OF THE TRIAL COURT CIVIL
ACTION NO. 12-6144

NANCY CARPENTER, As
Administratrix of the Estate
of Charles Carpenter,
   Plaintiff

    vs.

THIRD-PARTY DEFENDANT DALE
MCGILL'S AND MCGILL'S GAR-
AGE, INC.'S MOTION FOR SUM-
MARY JUDGMENT

RANDALL DEE; PETER DEE;
CITY OF LOWELL,
   Defendants.
ULTIMATE AUTO, INC.,
Defendant and Third-Party
   Plaintiff

vs.

DALE MCGILL and MCGILL'S
GARAGE, INC.,
   Third-Party Defendants.

Now come the third-party defendants, Dale McGill and McGill's Garage, Inc., by and through counsel and move this court pursuant to Rule 56 for Summary Judgment in their behalf on the basis that there is no genuine issue of material fact as to whether the third-party defendants owed a duty to Plaintiff's decedent, rather, this is a question of law to be decided by this court, as more fully set forth in the third-party defendants' memorandum filed in support of this motion.

Third-party defendants request oral argument of this motion.

Attorney for third-party defendants,

_____ /s/ Lisa Scottoline _____
Lisa Scottoline (BBO#393689)
Scottoline & Turow
One Federal Street
Boston, MA 02100
617/555-7777

Dated: /d/

## COMMONWEALTH OF MASSACHUSETTS

MIDDLESEX, SS

SUPERIOR COURT DEPARTMENT
OF THE TRIAL COURT CIVIL
ACTION NO. 12-6144

NANCY CARPENTER, As
Administratrix of the Estate
of Charles Carpenter,
  Plaintiff

  vs.

RANDALL DEE; PETER DEE;
CITY OF LOWELL,
  Defendants.
ULTIMATE AUTO, INC.,
  Defendant and Third-Party
  Plaintiff

  vs.

DALE MCGILL and MCGILL'S
GARAGE, INC.,
  Third-Party Defendants.

MEMORANDUM IN SUPPORT OF
THIRD-PARTY DEFENDANT
DALE MCGILL'S AND MCGILL'S
GARAGE, INC.'S MOTION FOR
SUMMARY JUDGMENT

Now come the third-party defendants, Dale McGill and McGill's Garage, Inc., and in support of their Motion for Summary Judgment, pursuant to Rule 56 state as follows:

## I. INTRODUCTION

This instant action arises out of a one-vehicle auto incident where a 1986 Jeep CJ-7 (hereinafter referred to as "the jeep"), operated by defendant, Randall Dee, "rolled-over," allegedly causing the death of plaintiff's decedent, Charles Carpenter, on August 31, 2011. Some time prior to August 31, 2011, Randall Dee allegedly modified the suspension on the jeep by installing oversize tires and a suspension kit manufactured and sold by the defendant, Ultimate Auto, Inc. It is alleged by the plaintiff that Ultimate Auto was negligent when it sold the tires and suspension kit which allegedly altered the height of the jeep and affected its handling characteristics rendering it unsafe. The plaintiff sets forth various specific allegations of negligence in support of its alleged cause of action. (Plaintiff's Complaint Count IV, ¶¶ 22-25.)

Ultimate Auto later added McGill's Garage, Inc., and Dale McGill as third-party defendants demanding contribution and alleging that Dale McGill, as agent or employee, of McGill's Garage, Inc. was negligent in approving an inspection sticker on said vehicle prior to the date of the accident. At the time alleged McGill's Garage, Inc., was a duly licensed inspection station for the Commonwealth of Massachusetts and engaged, among other things, in inspecting vehicles and either passing or rejecting said vehicles in accordance with the Code of Massachusetts Regulations, 540 Mass. Regs. Code, §§ 4.00 through 4.08 then in effect.

It is alleged that a safety inspection sticker was issued by McGill's Garage, Inc., to the Dee vehicle in December 2010, several months prior to the incident in question and after Dee had altered due jeep with the tires and suspension kit purchased from Ultimate Auto.

## II. ARGUMENTS AND POINTS OF LAW

Neither Dale McGill (hereinafter called "McGill") nor McGill's Garage, Inc., (hereinafter called "McGill's Garage") are liable to Ultimate Auto as joint tortfeasor for contributions to any loss proved by the plaintiff against Ultimate Auto for the reason that at the time of the alleged incident no duty was owing by either Dale McGill or McGill's Garage to the plaintiff, plaintiff's decedent, or anyone else.

Without a duty owing by McGill and/or McGill's Garage to plaintiff or plaintiff's decedent, neither McGill or McGill's Garage are liable to plaintiff or plaintiff's decedent in tort. Because neither McGill nor McGill's Garage are liable in tort to plaintiff or plaintiff's decedent, neither is a joint tortfeasor against whom contribution can be had by Ultimate Auto.

Massachusetts General Laws, Chapter 231B, Section 1(a), inserted by Stat. 1962, Chapter 730, Section 1, provides in pertinent parts: "[W]here two or more persons become jointly liable in tort for the same injury to person or property, there shall be a right of contribution among them." The language of this statute requires that the potential contributor be directly liable to the plaintiff. Without liability in tort, there is no right to contribution.

It therefore follows that only if McGill's Garage and Dale McGill are directly liable to the plaintiff's decedent can the defendant/third-party plaintiff state a claim for contribution from McGill's Garage and Dale McGill.

At the time of the alleged issuance of the inspection sticker, December 2010, McGill's Garage, and its employee McGill were required to inspect vehicles in accordance with 540 Mass. Regs. Code, §§ 4.00 through 4.08 effective March 31, 2004.*

Said regulations did not require McGill's Garage, nor McGill, as employee acting within the scope of his employment when issuing the inspection sticker, to inspect and/or reject any vehicle for alleged violations of any height or suspension alteration requirement.

Although Mass. Gen. Laws, ch. 90, § 7P may have prohibited any person from modifying or changing the height of a motor vehicle, with some exceptions, as alleged by the plaintiff, neither McGill nor McGill's Garage altered the jeep and, therefore, they were not governed by that statute in the issuance of the December 2006 inspection sticker.

As 540 Mass. Regs. Code, §§ 4.00 through 4.08 effective March 31, 2008, did not require inspection for altered height, neither McGill nor McGill's Garage had a duty to do so. In fact, pursuant to 540 Mass. Regs. Code §§ 4.00 through 4.08, neither McGill nor McGill's Garage had any right to inspect and/or reject the subject jeep as the regulations set forth those specific areas only which were governed by the inspection procedure and did not authorize any inspection station to act beyond the specific directions of the regulations.

540 Mass. Regs. Code § 4.00 effective March 31, 2008, was not amended until May 27, 2012 [the year after the accident], after the death of Charlie Carpenter and after the issuance of the sticker in question. At that time the inspection guidelines were changed to include inspection and/or rejection of certain altered height vehicles. 540 Mass. Regs. Code § 4.04(13)(a).

## III. CONCLUSION

There is only a question of law before this Court; that is, whether an inspection station, in December 2010 had a duty to, through its agents and/or employees, reject a 1986 Jeep CJ-7 vehicle which had been modified with a suspension kit and tires to alter the height of the vehicle. Dispositive questions of law are properly heard on Motion for Summary Judgment. Clearly, the answer is no. 540 Mass. Regs. Code § 4.00 effective March 31, 2008, through May 27, 2012, set forth the standards for vehicle inspection and was silent as to altered height vehicles. Therefore, neither Dale McGill nor McGill's Garage through any other agent and/or employee had a duty owing to plaintiff or plaintiff's decedent relative to Dee vehicle.

---

*Eds.' Note:* For this exercise we have changed the effective dates of these regulations in order to make this simulation conform with the sequence of events as they occurred in the actual case.

Having no duty owing to the plaintiff or plaintiff's decedent, neither McGill nor McGill's Garage can be held as a joint tortfeasor with Ultimate Auto and others regarding the loss claimed by plaintiff in this action. As neither McGill nor McGill's Garage can be held as joint tortfeasor, neither can be liable to Ultimate Auto for contribution as alleged in the Third-Party Complaint.

WHEREFORE, Dale McGill and McGill's Garage, Inc., move this Court for entry of summary judgment in their respective favors and against the third-party plaintiff, Ultimate Auto, Inc.

Attorney for third-party defendants,

_____ /s/ Lisa Scottoline _____
Lisa Scottoline (BBO#393689)
Scottoline & Turow
One Federal Street
Boston, MA 02100
617/555-7777

Dated: /d/

# COMMONWEALTH OF MASSACHUSETTS

MIDDLESEX, SS

SUPERIOR COURT DEPARTMENT
OF THE TRIAL COURT CIVIL
ACTION NO. 12-6144

NANCY CARPENTER, As
Administratrix of the Estate
of Charles Carpenter,
  Plaintiff

vs.

RANDALL DEE; PETER DEE;
CITY OF LOWELL,
  Defendants.

ULTIMATE AUTO, INC.,
  Defendant and Third-Party
  Plaintiff

vs.

DALE MCGILL and MCGILL'S
GARAGE, INC.,
  Third-Party Defendants.

STIPULATION OF THIRD-PARTY
PLAINTIFF, ULTIMATE AUTO,
INC., AND THIRD-PARTY
DEFENDANTS, DALE MCGILL
AND MCGILL'S GARAGE, INC.

Defendant and Third-Party Plaintiff, Ultimate Auto, Inc., and Third-Party Defendants, Dale McGill and McGill's Garage, Inc., hereby stipulate as follows:

1. At all relevant times. McGill's Garage, Inc., was a duly licensed inspection station for the Commonwealth of Massachusetts, which was engaged in, among other things, passing or rejecting vehicles; and Dale McGill was a certified inspector.

2. A safety inspection sticker was issued by McGill's Garage, Inc., to the Dee vehicle in question in December 2010, several months prior to the incident in question and after Dee had altered the jeep with the tires and suspension kit purchased from Ultimate Auto. Randall Dee paid $15.00 for the inspection and sticker.

3. Dale McGill was at all relevant times the President of, and Chief Mechanic and Inspector at, McGill's Garage, Inc. As of December 2010, he

had been a gas station owner for fifteen years; he worked in other gas stations as a mechanic and helper for eight years prior to that.

4. The Commonwealth of Massachusetts Periodic Annual Inspection of All Motor Vehicles regulations [reprinted in the Case Files] were in effect at the time of the December 2010 inspection. Mass. Gen. Laws ch. 90 § 7P [also in the Case Files] also was in effect at all relevant times, including at the time of the inspection.

5. At all relevant times, McGill's Garage had large external signs that said: "Full Service Center," "Gas Station," and "Massachusetts Inspection Station."

6. At several times during 2010 Randall Dee bought gas at McGill's Garage, and Dale McGill was often the individual who pumped the gas into the jeep. On at least one occasion prior to December 2010, Randall Dee got a change of oil and lubrication for the jeep at McGill's Garage.

7. The following discovery [not reprinted in the Case Files] has occurred:

(a) In a deposition, Randall Dee said that when he went to McGill's Garage for the December 2010 inspection, he said to Dale McGill words to the effect that "I want my jeep inspected for a safety sticker." He further states in that deposition that "I thought a safety sticker meant my jeep was safe."

(b) Randall Dee and Dale McGill both say in depositions that Dale McGill inspected the jeep in question in December 2010 and put the sticker showing that the vehicle had passed inspection on the front windshield of the jeep; both further say that neither Randall Dee nor Dale McGill mentioned the modifications to the jeep to each other in December 2010 or at any other time.

(c) Plaintiff's lawyers have provided an affidavit during the discovery process in this case from an engineer who states that she has had extensive education and experience in vehicle design and safety. The affidavit further says that in the expert's opinion, based on what she has learned through extensive discovery in the case, inspection of the jeep in question, and a visit to the relevant site, "a substantial cause of the accident in question was the elevated height of the modified jeep which made the jeep a good deal less stable than it would be without the modifications."

Executed by the parties as of this ____/d/____ day of ____/m/____, ____/y/____.

ULTIMATE AUTO, INC.,
Third-Party Plaintiff

DALE MCGILL and
MCGILL'S GARAGE, INC.,
Third-Party Defendant

By its Attorney,
_____ /s/ Bertram Cohen _____
Bertram Cohen (BBO#641311)
Roth, McKnight & Zimmerman
111 Milk Street
Boston, MA 02100
(617) 555-0000

By its Attorney,
_____ /s/ Lisa Scottoline _____
Lisa Scottoline (BBO#393689)
Scottoline & Turow
One Federal Street
Boston, MA 02100
617/555-7777

# ■ THE COMMONWEALTH OF MASSACHUSETTS, SECRETARY OF STATE, REGULATION FILING AND PUBLICATION*

1. **REGULATION CHAPTER NUMBER AND HEADING:** 540 Mass. Regs. Code § 4.00 Periodic Annual Staggered Safety and Combined Safety and Emissions Inspection of All Motor Vehicles.

2. **NAME OF AGENCY: Registry of Motor Vehicles**

3. **READABLE LANGUAGE SUMMARY:** States the general purposes and requirements of this regulation as well as the persons, organizations and businesses affected.

The purpose of 540 Mass. Regs. Code § 4.00 is to provide for a periodic staggered safety and combined safety and emissions inspection of all motor vehicles registered in the Commonwealth of Massachusetts and to establish licensing procedures for inspection stations, fleet inspection stations and safety inspection stations only authorized to participate in the inspection program. 540 Mass. Regs. Code § 4.00 establishes regulations and procedures for the issuance of various certificates to owner/operators in accordance with inspection procedures. 540 Mass. Regs. Code § 4.00 shall affect all persons owning, operating, purchasing and selling automobiles in the Commonwealth and shall affect many businesses relating to motor vehicle industry.

### CODE OF MASSACHUSETTS REGULATIONS: REGISTRY OF MOTOR VEHICLES

#### 4.00 PERIODIC ANNUAL STAGGERED SAFETY AND COMBINED SAFETY AND EMISSION INSPECTION OF ALL MOTOR VEHICLES

. . . The purpose of 540 Mass. Regs. Code § 4.00 is to provide rules and regulations and to establish inspection procedures for a periodic annual staggered safety and combined safety and emissions inspection of all motor vehicles in accordance with the General Laws of the Commonwealth of Massachusetts.

#### 4.01 SCOPE AND APPLICABILITY

540 Mass. Regs. Code § 4.00 is adopted by the Registrar of Motor Vehicles in accordance with the authority of Mass. Gen. Laws ch. 90 § 31 to establish rules and regulations governing the use and operation of motor vehicles and trailers. 540 Mass. Regs. Code § 4.00 establishes rules and regulations which provide for a periodic staggered safety and combined safety and emission inspection of all motor vehicles registered in the Commonwealth of Massachusetts under the authority of Mass. Gen. Laws ch. 90 § 7A establishing

---

*Eds.' Note:* These were the applicable regulations at the time of the inspection.

regulations for issuance of various certificates in accordance with proper inspection of a motor vehicle pursuant to Mass. Gen. Laws ch. 90 § 7V(a)(b)(c) and establishes rules and regulations for licensing stations which are approved to perform safety or combined safety and emissions inspections on motor vehicles pursuant to Mass. Gen. Laws ch. 90 § 7W.

### 4.02 SPECIAL DEFINITIONS

In addition to the definitions set forth in Mass. Gen. Laws ch. 90 § 1, the following special definitions shall also apply. . . .

**Certificate of Inspection** shall mean a serially numbered, adhesive sticker, device or symbol, as may be prescribed by the registrar indicating a motor vehicle has met the inspection requirements established by the registrar for issuance of a certificate. The registrar may prescribe the use of one or more categories of certificate of inspection in accordance with Mass. Gen. Laws ch. 90 § 1.

**Certified Inspector** shall mean an individual certified by the commissioner as properly trained to perform an emissions inspection as delineated by the manufacturer of the emissions analyzer in accordance with Mass. Gen. Laws ch. 90 § 1. . . .

**Exempt Vehicles** shall mean motor vehicles whose curb weight exceeds eight thousand pounds, motorcycles, diesel powered vehicles, motor vehicles more than twenty-five model years old before the date of inspection, motor vehicles not capable of a speed greater than twenty-five miles per hour under any condition of operation or loading on a level surface and any class of vehicles exempted by the commissioner of Department of Environmental Quality Engineering which present prohibitive inspection problems. . . .

**Inspection Station** shall mean a proprietorship, partnership, or corporation licensed by the registrar to perform safety or combined safety and emissions inspections on motor vehicles. . . .

**Safety Inspection Station Only** shall mean a proprietorship, partnership or corporation whose principal business is unique to a particular exempt vehicle.

### 4.03 REQUIREMENTS FOR INITIAL AND SUBSEQUENT STAGGERED ANNUAL INSPECTION

(1) **General Provisions.** Every owner or person in control of a Massachusetts registered motor vehicle shall submit the vehicle for inspection under the following rules: . . .

(c) **Inspection upon Registration.** Every owner or person in control of a motor vehicle which is newly registered in the Commonwealth shall submit such motor vehicle for certificate of inspection within seven days of the date on which the motor vehicle is first registered to said owner in the Commonwealth. . . .

(2) **Subsequent Inspection.** Subsequent to initial inspection, every owner or person in control of a Massachusetts registered motor vehicle shall submit the vehicle for inspection annually during the monthly expiration of the previously issued Certificate of Inspection.

(3) **Validity of Certificates of Inspection.** Certificates of Inspection are valid until such time as they expire or ownership of the vehicle transferred.

**4.04** PROCEDURES FOR INSPECTION OF ALL MOTOR VEHICLES

(1) **Prior to beginning inspection,** a visual check of the vehicle should be made to determine that ice and snow accumulation, condition of the suspension, etc., will not impede or interfere with the proper aiming of headlamps. Inspectors shall collect the established inspection fee and remove any inspection sticker from the wind-shield of the motor vehicle.

(2) **Check registration certificate** for date of expiration. . . .

(3) **Inspect number plate(s)** to see that they are undamaged, securely mounted, clean and clearly visible. No bumper, trailer hitch or other accessory may interfere with a clear view of them. The number plate must be mounted in the proper location on the rear of the vehicle if the vehicle has been issued one plate. Both number plates must be mounted in the proper location on the rear and front of the vehicle, if the vehicle has been issued two plates.

Any decorative number plate or number plate replica not issued by the Registry of Motor Vehicles on which the word Massachusetts appears must be removed from the vehicle.

(4) **Perform Emission Testing Requirements and Procedures.** . . .

(5) **Test Brakes.**

(a) The adjuster may operate the vehicle in the inspection bay and test the parking and service brake. The parking brake on all vehicles will be tested by accelerating the motor to approximately 1200 to 1300 RPMs with the vehicle in gear in both forward and reverse positions against the brake in the applied position. . . .

(b) Brakes shall be adequate to stop the vehicle from a speed of 20 MPH in not more than the following distances:

| | | |
|---|---|---|
| Service (foot) Brake | Pleasure Vehicles | 25 feet |
| | Trucks and Buses | 35 feet |
| Parking (hand) Brake | All Vehicles | 75 feet |

(6) **Examine Muffler and Exhaust System.** Accelerate motor to test for prevention of unnecessary noise and emission of any unreasonable amount of smoke. The exhaust system, exhaust manifold(s), exhaust pipe(s), muffler(s) and tailpipe(s), if designed to be so equipped, shall be tight and free of leaks.

(7) **Check Steering and Suspension**

(a) Check for free steering by turning the steering wheel through a full right and left turn. Reject a vehicle if binding or interference occurs during the procedure. With the front wheels in the straight ahead position (and the engine running on vehicle equipped with power steering) measure lash or lost movement at the steering wheel rim.

(b) Lash or lost movement on passenger cars and station wagons, as measured at the steering wheel rim, should not exceed 2 inches if the vehicle is equipped with manual steering. Lash or lost movement on antique motor vehicles, trucks, vans and buses will be measured in the same manner with the allowable tolerance on trucks, vans and buses to be determined by steering wheel diameter in accordance with the following schedule:

| Steering Wheel Diameter | Lash (shall not exceed) |
|---|---|
| 16″ | 2″ |
| 18″ | 2¼″ |
| 20″ | 2½″ |
| 22″ | 2¾″ |

(c) The front end of all vehicles will be raised by jacking or hoisting and visually examined. Vehicles equipped with ball joints will be raised and checked in accordance with the instructions and recommendations of the Automobile Manufacturers Association. Ball joint tolerance shall not exceed those established by the vehicle manufacturer.

(d) Reject a vehicle with excessive wear or play in any part of the steering mechanism or of the vehicle that would affect proper steering. . . .

(8) **Sound Horn.** Sound horn to test for adequate signal. The horn must be securely fastened to the vehicle.

(9) **Examine Windshield and Rear Windows**

(a) **Clear Windshield. . . .**

(b) **Ornaments.** Ornaments forward of the operator's line of vision through the windshield must be removed. No poster or sticker shall be attached to the windshield in such a manner so as to obstruct the vision of the operator.

(c) **Rear Windows.** Rear windows must allow an unobstructed view to the rear. On convertible type vehicles, the rear window must be inspected and if clouded, the vehicle must be rejected.

(d) **Windshield Cleaner(s).** Test for proper operation. . . .

(10) **Examine Lighting Devices.**

(a) **Tail Lights.** Every motor vehicle, except a two wheeled motorcycle, an antique motor car and a farm tractor, shall be equipped with two red lights (tail lamps) mounted one at each side of the rear of the vehicle so as to show two red lights from behind and equipped with two stop lights (stop lamps) mounted and displayed in a like manner. A single lamp may combine both the above functions. Every motor vehicle shall be equipped with a white light so arranged as to illuminate the rear number plate so that it is plainly visible at sixty feet.

(b) **Directionals.** Front and rear directional signals will be operable on every vehicle originally equipped with such signals. Every motor vehicle registered in the Commonwealth which was manufactured for the model year 1967 and for subsequent model years, shall be equipped with a device to permit the front and rear directional signals to flash simultaneously.

(c) **Headlamps.** Headlamps shall be aimed in accordance with the Registrar's specifications. Said specifications shall be forwarded to licensees by the Registry of Motor Vehicles.

(11) **Examine Tires.**

(a) No tire mounted on a motor vehicle or trailer shall be deemed to be in safe operating condition unless it meets the visual and tread depth requirements set forth in these regulations.

1. **Tread Depth.** The amount of tread design on the tire. Tread depth includes both the original, retread and recap tread design; and, in respect to special mileage commercial tires, recut and regrooved tread design. Truck and bus tires having a wheel diameter over 16 inches, having sufficient original tread rubber above the breaker strip may be siped and classed as a siped tread design 2/32 of an inch siped depth shall be considered equal to 2/32 of an inch original tread depth, provided that the cords of the tire are not damaged by the process.

2. **Special Mileage Commercial Tire.** A tire manufactured with an extra layer of rubber between the cord body and original tread design, which extra layer is designed for the purpose of recutting or regrooving, and which tire is specifically labeled as a special mileage commercial tire.

3. **Visual Requirements.** No tire shall be deemed to be in safe operating condition if such tire has:

a. **Fabric Break.** A fabric break, or a cut in excess of one inch in any direction as measured on the outside of the tire and deep enough to reach the body cords, or has been repaired temporarily by the use of blowout patches or boots; or

b. **Bulges.** Any bump, bulge or knot related to separation or partial failure of the tire, structure; or

c. **Exposed Cord.** Any portion of the ply or cord structure exposed; or

d. **Worn Tread.** A portion of the tread design completely worn, provided such worn portion is of sufficient size to affect substantially the traction and stopping ability of the tire.

4. **Method of Measuring Tread Depth.** Tire tread depth shall be measured by a tread depth gauge which shall be of a type calibrated in thirty-seconds of an inch. Readings shall be taken in a major tread groove of the tire nearest the center at two points of the circumference at least fifteen inches apart. Readings for a tire which has the tread design running across the tire or for a siped tire, where such tread design is permitted, shall be taken at or near the center of the tire at two points of the circumference of at least fifteen inches apart.

5. **Tread Depth Requirements.** No tire shall be deemed to be in safe operating condition if such tire is worn to the point where less than two-thirty-seconds (2/32) of an inch of tread design remains at both points at which gauge readings are obtained.

6. **Tire Intermix.** The vehicle will be rejected if a radial ply tire is used on the same axle with a conventional non-radial tire. The vehicle will be rejected if bias or bias belted ply tires are used on the rear axle when non-radial tires are used on the front axle. . . .

(12) **Examine Bumpers, Fenders, External Sheet Metal and Fuel Tank.** Any motor vehicle will be rejected if any of the following conditions are evident:

(a) **Bumpers.** Broken or bent bumpers, fenders, exterior sheet metal or mouldings having sharp edges or abnormal protrusions extending beyond normal vehicle extremities so as to constitute a danger to pedestrians and other motor vehicle traffic. If bumper face plates are removed, bumper brackets must also be removed. The vehicle hood, door and luggage compartment lid and battery or engine compartment doors or lids, if so equipped, must fully and properly close and be capable of being firmly latched.

(b) **Fenders.** Front and rear fenders must be in place. . . .

(c) **Floor Pans.** Floor pans which are rusted through or otherwise would permit passage of exhaust gases into the passenger or trunk area.

(d) **Fuel Tanks.** Fuel tanks which are not securely attached to the vehicle's body or chassis. . . .

#### 4.07 ISSUANCE OF CERTIFICATES OF INSPECTION, REJECTION, AND WAIVER PROCEDURE

(1) **General Provisions.**

(a) A separate and distinct charge, as established by the Registrar and Commissioner, shall be made for each inspection.

(b) All required entries on certificates and periodic inspection reports must be legibly completed in ink, ball point pen or indelible pencil by the inspection station owner/operator or employee performing the inspection.

(2) **Certificate of Inspection.**

(a) Any motor vehicle subject to Safety Inspection Only or Combined Safety and Emissions Inspection, which, after inspection, is found to be in compliance with all safety or safety and emissions inspection requirements will be issued a Certificate of Inspection. . . .

(3) **Certificate of Rejection.**

(a) Any motor vehicle subject to the Combined Safety and Emissions Inspection which is not in compliance with all safety and emissions inspection requirements and any motor vehicle subject to Safety Inspection Only which is not in compliance with all safety inspection requirements, will be issued a Certificate of Rejection.

(b) **Requirements.** When a Certificate of Rejection is issued on a motor vehicle, entries pertaining to the date of inspection and vehicle registration number of the motor vehicle will be completed by the inspection station owner/operator or employee performing the inspection on the Certificate of Inspection, that would normally have been issued to the motor vehicle, and on the periodic inspection report. The certificate will be retained at the inspection station for a period of twenty days for potential issuance to the affected motor vehicle. If issued to the affected motor vehicle, all required entries on said certificate and on the periodic inspection report will be completed. At the expiration of the twenty day period, unissued certificates with partial entries will be held in an open file for return to the Registry of Motor Vehicles.

**4.08** LICENSURE OF INSPECTION STATION

(1) **General Provisions: Licensing Requirements.** Effective April 1, 1983, all inspection stations, which shall include Inspection Stations for Combined Safety and Emissions Testing, Fleet Inspection Stations and Safety Inspection Stations Only shall be licensed by the Registry of Motor Vehicles to carry out the annual staggered Safety or Safety and Emissions Inspection Program. . . .

(g) **Requirements for Personnel Who Administer Inspections.** Inspections must be performed by the licensee or permanent employees of the licensee who are in possession of a Massachusetts Motor Vehicle Operators License. Persons performing inspections must be able to demonstrate their proficiency in inspecting motor vehicles and in operating, calibrating and maintaining items or equipment required for the inspection of motor vehicles, to personnel of the Registry of Motor Vehicles and the Massachusetts Department of Environmental Quality Engineering assigned to program administration and enforcement. Persons performing Emissions inspections must be certified by the Commissioner. A permanent employee is herein defined as a person carried on the payroll records of the applicant, regularly employed on the premises for a minimum of twenty hours a week. . . .

# ■ RESTATEMENT (SECOND) OF CONTRACTS

### § 201. WHOSE MEANING PREVAILS.

(1) Where the parties have attached the same meaning to a promise or agreement or a term thereof, it is interpreted in accordance with that meaning.

(2) Where the parties have attached different meanings to a promise or agreement or a term thereof, it is interpreted in accordance with the meaning attached by one of them if at the time the agreement was made

(a) that party did not know of any different meaning attached by the other, and the other knew the meaning attached by the first party; or

(b) that party had no reason to know of any different meaning attached by the other, and the other had reason to know the meaning attached by the first party. . . .

## § 202. Rules in Aid of Interpretation.

(1) Words and other conduct are interpreted in the light of all the circumstances, and if the principal purpose of the parties is ascertainable it is given great weight.

(2) A writing is interpreted as a whole, and all writings that are part of the same transaction are interpreted together.

(3) Unless a different intention is manifested,

(a) where language has a generally prevailing meaning, it is interpreted in accordance with that meaning;

(b) technical terms and words of art are given their technical meaning when used in a transaction within their technical field.

. . . (5) Wherever reasonable, the manifestations of intention of the parties to a promise or agreement are interpreted as consistent with each other and with any relevant course of performance, course of dealing, or usage of trade.

## . . . § 207. Interpretation Favoring the Public.

In choosing among the reasonable meanings of a promise or agreement or a term thereof, a meaning that serves the public interest is generally preferred.

# ■ RESTATEMENT (SECOND) OF TORTS

## § 299A. Undertaking in Profession or Trade.

Unless he represents that he has greater or less skill or knowledge, one who undertakes to render services in the practice of a profession or trade is required to exercise the skill and knowledge normally possessed by members of that profession or trade in good standing in similar communities.

### OFFICIAL COMMENTS

a. Skill, as the word is used in this Section, is something more than the mere minimum competence required of any person who does an act, under the rule stated in § 299. It is that special form of competence which is not part of the ordinary equipment of the reasonable man, but which is the result of acquired learning, and aptitude developed by special training and experience. All professions, and most trades, are necessarily skilled, and the word is used to refer to the special competence which they require.

b. *Profession or trade.* This Section is thus a special application of the rule stated in § 299. It applies to any person who undertakes to render services to another in the practice of a profession, such as that of physician or surgeon, dentist, pharmacist, oculist, attorney, accountant, or engineer. It applies also to any person who undertakes to render services to others in the practice of a skilled trade, such as that of airplane pilot, precision machinist, electrician, carpenter, blacksmith, or plumber. This Section states the minimum skill and knowledge which the actor undertakes to exercise, and therefore to have. If he has in fact greater skill than that common to the profession or trade, he is required to exercise that skill, as stated in § 299, Comment e.

c. *Undertaking.* In the ordinary case, the undertaking of one who renders services in the practice of a profession or trade is a matter of contract between the parties, and the terms of the undertaking are either stated expressly, or implied as a matter of understanding. The rule here stated does not, however, depend upon the existence of an enforceable contract between the parties. It applies equally where professional services are rendered gratuitously, as in the case of a physician treating a charity patient, or without any definite understanding, as in the case of one who renders services to a patient who is unconscious, in an emergency. The basis of the rule is the undertaking of the defendant, which may arise apart from contract.

This undertaking is not necessarily a matter of the requirements of the particular task undertaken, although that task will of course have its bearing upon what is understood. A highly skilled individual, as for example, a certified public accountant, may undertake to perform services which normally require little skill, as for example to do ordinary bookkeeping, and in performing those services he may, or may not, undertake to exercise his unusually high skill. On the other hand a bookkeeper with little or no accounting skill may undertake to do work which would normally call for a certified public accountant, and he may, or may not, undertake in doing it to exercise the skill of such an accountant. It is a matter of the skill which he represents himself to have, or is understood to undertake to have, rather than of the skill which he actually possesses, or which the task requires.

d. *Special representation.* An actor undertaking to render services may represent that he has superior skill or knowledge, beyond that common to his profession or trade. In that event he incurs an obligation to the person to whom he makes such a representation, to have, and to exercise, the skill and knowledge which he represents himself to have. Thus a physician who holds himself out as a specialist in certain types of practice is required to have the skill and knowledge common to other specialists. On the other hand the actor may make it clear that he has less than the minimum of skill common to the profession or trade; and in that case he is required to exercise only the skill which he represents that he has. Thus a layman who attempts to perform a surgical operation in an emergency, in the absence of any surgeon, and who makes it clear that he does not have the skill or knowledge of a surgeon, is not required to exercise such skill or knowledge. The rule stated in this Section applies only where there is no such special representation.

e. *Standard normally required.* In the absence of any such special representation, the standard of skill and knowledge required of the actor who practices a profession or trade is that which is commonly possessed by members of that profession or trade in good standing. It is not that of the most highly skilled, nor is it that of the average member of the profession or trade, since those who have less than median or average skill may still be competent and qualified. Half of the physicians of America do not automatically become negligent in practicing medicine at all, merely because their skill is less than the professional average. On the other hand, the standard is not that of the charlatan, the quack, the unqualified or incompetent individual who has succeeded in entering the profession or trade. It is that common to those who are recognized in the profession or trade itself as qualified, and competent to engage in it.

f. *Schools of thought.* Where there are different schools of thought in a profession, or different methods are followed by different groups engaged in a trade, the actor is to be judged by the professional standards of the group to which he belongs. The law cannot undertake to decide technical questions of proper practice over which experts reasonably disagree, or to declare that those who do not accept particular controversial doctrines are necessarily negligent in failing to do so. There may be, however, minimum requirements of skill applicable to all persons, of whatever school of thought, who engage in any profession or trade. Thus any person who holds himself out as competent to treat human ailments must have a minimum skill in diagnosis, and a minimum knowledge of possible methods of treatment. Licensing statutes, or those requiring a basic knowledge of science for the practice of a profession, may provide such a minimum standard.

g. *Type of community.* Allowance must be made also for the type of community in which the actor carries on his practice. A country doctor cannot be expected to have the equipment, facilities, experience, knowledge or opportunity to obtain it, afforded him by a large city. The standard is not, however, that of the particular locality. If there are only three physicians in a small town, and all three are highly incompetent, they cannot be permitted to set a standard of utter inferiority for a fourth who comes to town. The standard is rather that of persons engaged in similar practice in similar localities, considering geographical location, size, and the character of the community in general.

Such allowance for the type of community is most frequently made in professions or trades where there is a considerable degree of variation in the skill and knowledge possessed by those practicing it in different localities. It has commonly been made in the cases of physicians or surgeons, because of the difference in the medical skill commonly found in different parts of the United States, or in different types of communities. In other professions, such as that of the attorney, such variations either do not exist or are not as significant, and allowance for them has seldom been made. A particular profession may be so uniform, in different localities, as to the skill and knowledge of its members, that the court will not feel required to instruct the jury that it must make such allowance.

## ■ ECONOMICS SPECIALISTS OF BOSTON, INC.*

**282 Huntington Ave., Boston, MA 02115, (617) 555-0505**

/d/

Carol Coblentz, Esq.
Needham, Shaker and Coblentz      **CONFIDENTIAL**
44 Park Place
Boston, MA 02100

Re: Damages in Nancy Carpenter Case

Dear Carol,

Before we meet with you to discuss our final report in this case, I wanted to provide you with my current thinking about the damages resulting from the tragic death of Charles Carpenter. First, I should report that I have had no success in finding jury verdicts in Middlesex County, or even in Massachusetts, for similar cases during the past five years. No reported case has involved the tipping of a jeep or other car that had been raised. The tipped vehicle cases we have found in which there have been jury verdicts involved products liability with respect to an unaltered vehicle or alleged negligent work done by repair shops and plaintiffs who survived with severe injuries. There were four such cases in Middlesex County in the past five years: two resulted in defendants' verdicts, and the other two had plaintiffs' verdicts for $1,800,000 and $2,150,000, respectively; but again, these were plaintiffs who were still alive. Both of those cases, I am told, settled while still on appeal. The two plaintiffs' victories were plaintiffs with horrendous injuries, and each had a fairly large earning history and earning potential (one engineer and one accountant). On the other hand, those plaintiffs were older than Charles Carpenter at the time of his death, and none involved a retailer who sold parts or tires. There are wrongful death verdicts for plaintiffs in a number of cases in Middlesex during the past five years, but the circumstances of each case are so unique with respect to the deceased, surviving heirs, and the circumstances of death that we do not think they provide any real guidance. Those verdicts range from $180,000 to $7,125,000. You know better than we, but we do not think previous jury verdicts are very helpful in assessing the value of this case.

As you and I have discussed, the Massachusetts Wrongful Death Statute permits damages for categories of harm that are beyond the realm of our

---

*Eds.' Note:* This document has been invented for this case in order to help students think about damages for various practice exercises. It does draw, in part, from economist reports, discovery, and other information in the actual case.

expertise as economists. We can give you estimates for net lost earnings (after subtracting for direct personal consumption of the deceased, Charles Carpenter (hereafter "Charles")), as well as lost household services that would have been provided by Carpenter to his family. The statute also covers compensation for the loss of the "reasonably expected . . . protection, care, assistance, society, companionship, comfort, guidance, counsel and advice of the decedent to the persons entitled to the damages recovered. . . ." You (and a jury) will have to consider the value of those intangibles without the guidance of an economist.

Additional losses that we will not consider for purposes of our economic opinion (but you will undoubtedly wish to include) are the money paid to the hospital to which Carpenter was taken after the accident ($1,682.35); the ambulance charge ($363.00); funeral home expense ($1,950.00); monument company expense ($1,442.50); law firm charge for appointment of administratrix ($320.00); and uncertain additional expenses for the filling out and filing of the Massachusetts Department of Revenue estate tax return (this should probably run no more than $1,000.00 and perhaps as low as $500.00).

After interviewing the plaintiff widow and her sister, we ascertained that Charles was a very good high school student, involved in a number of extracurricular activities. He received training as an auto mechanic in high school, and after high school and before his job as a custodian at Forsythe University, he had two jobs as a mechanic: one at an auto dealer and one for a bus company. He took the job at Forsythe in order to be closer to home, and to work an evening shift so that when the baby arrived, his wife could work during the day, while he cared for the baby. He loved children, and was very close to his nieces and nephews; he worked with an autistic child while in high school. He adored his wife. So far as we can tell, the marriage was solid and they were very much in love and reliant on each other. He hoped eventually to have more schooling, and to get into the computer field.

His work as a custodian was covered by a union contract. His salary at Forsythe during the year he died would have been $22,298; in the following year, it would have been $23,587. We are assuming a forty-hour week, fifty-two weeks a year. We will assume that his benefits for retirement and insurance equal the average percent of wages for unionized employees in service industries nationally—16 percent.

His wages would have grown throughout his work life. We have made two alternative assumptions concerning the rate of growth of his wages: 1.5 percent in real, inflation-adjusted terms for the remainder of his life (based on raises in this type of work during the past twenty years) and 2.5 percent based on his above-average motivation and his future plan to move into the higher-paying computer field.

We have back-up for the following assumptions. He would work 33.2 more years, and live an additional 46.4 years. His effective average tax rate (state and federal combined) would be 15 percent over the course of his expected life. His personal consumption of his after-tax income would be 35.5 percent. Based on conversations with his wife, we assume he worked approximately twenty hours a week around the house, and would continue to do so. We use a conservative $5.00 per hour for that work, or an annual total of $5,200. We assume that the value of these services would remain constant in real terms over the remainder of his life.

Assuming the net lost earnings will be paid in a lump sum, which will be able to earn interest, future losses must be discounted to present value using a real discount rate. The real discount rate is estimated by subtracting the average historical inflation rate from the average historical long-term interest rate. A real discount rate of 2.5 percent is used.

We'll give you a year by year chart, but here are the bottom lines. We estimate that the discounted net after-tax economic loss to Carpenter's wife and son resulting from his death would lie between $589,069 and $634,176, depending upon the assumptions concerning his future growth in wages. These figures are composed first of the total lost earnings calculated as I have described (having subtracted his anticipated personal consumption) of $428,139 (1.5 percent growth) or $473,246 (2.5 percent growth). To each of these one should add $160,931 for household services. The two figures added together are how we arrived at our total estimates.

Please give me a call if you want us to consider other variables or other figures before we meet.

                                        Very truly yours,

                                        /s/
                                        Jocelyn Q. Russo

## Case Files
### *City of Cleveland Firefighters*
## Contents

## Initial Memorandum*

To: Firm Associates

From: Elisabeth Julia Jennifer, Senior Partner of Jennifer, Berton & Abrahams

Re: Strategy Session Preparing to Draft a Complaint in the Cleveland Fire-fighters Case

Date: September 8, 2012

Several women who recently took the City of Cleveland Entry Level Fire-fighters Exam have asked our office to represent them in a civil action against the City of Cleveland, et al. With the assistance of the Cleveland Coalition for Job Equity ("the Coalition") they previously filed a charge with the Equal Employment Opportunity Commission and have recently received a "Notice of Right to Sue" from the U.S. Department of Justice.

The women believe that the City of Cleveland has engaged in discrimi-nation against females regarding recruiting, training, testing, hiring, and employment of firefighters. If true, such discrimination is in violation of rights guaranteed by the Constitution of the United States and applicable civil rights statutes. In addition, there is possibly an additional claim for violation of state laws regarding civil service rules and regulations.

The suit we are contemplating will allege violations of: Civil Rights Act of 1877, 42 U.S.C. §§ 1983 and 1985(3) and Title VII of the Civil Rights Act of 1964, 42 U.S.C. § 2000e. Subject matter jurisdiction in federal court is found under 28 U.S.C. § 1343(a), as well as under the general federal question subject matter jurisdiction provision of 28 U.S.C. § 1331. The supplemental claim under state law involves a violation of Ohio Revised Code § 124.58 and presents a more complicated subject matter jurisdiction problem (28 U.S.C. § 1367), but don't worry about subject matter jurisdiction issues at this time, nor about the class action aspects of the case.

### FACTS

I do pro bono work for the Coalition. The information in paragraphs A, B, C, and D below has been derived from various news sources, reports, and

---

*Eds.' Note: This memorandum, and the following documents in these Case Files are based on an actual case brought many years earlier. We invented the initial memorandum in order to introduce you to the case. The names, dates, and a few of the facts have been changed, and the law, when it has changed in the interim, has been brought up to date. At the time the actual case was commenced, there were no women firefighters in the Cleveland Fire Department. Today there are several women firefighters in the depart-ment. For purposes of this course, use the facts that are in these Case Files.

signed statements in the Coalition files, and I believe that we have evidentiary support for those facts.

A. There are presently no women employed by the city as firefighters, although several cities (such as New York, Columbus, and Seattle) do have female firefighters. The city of Cleveland uses a rank-order written and physical abilities test ostensibly to select candidates who possess the highest skills required to perform the job. Candidates are graded on their test performance, and an eligibility list is compiled in which scores are ranked from high to low. Although the test used by the city is supposed to be designed to eliminate discriminatory hiring, such rank-order tests (as opposed to tests resulting in a non-ranked list of those who are qualified to serve) have been shown to have a disparate impact on women. The test used by the city can perhaps be challenged on the grounds that the test measures attributes in which men traditionally excel, such as speed and strength, while it ignored those in which women excel, such as stamina and endurance. This exam also tested for attributes not necessarily related to the skills that the job of firefighting requires.

B. The city hired a consultant to design, administer, and score the entry-level firefighter examination in question. No women were hired after those exams were scored and ranked. Several years ago, the same consultant was hired to design an exam for entry-level firefighters and to administer it. Cognizant of the fact that no women had yet scored high enough to be ranked at a level that even remotely provided an opportunity to be selected a firefighter, the consultant prepared a new job analysis and designed his test based on the new job analysis.

C. After the test was developed, but prior to the exam, the city embarked on a program to recruit and train female firefighters. As part of its recruitment program, the city provided potential female recruits with a free twelve-week training course. According to the initial interviews held with the women, this course did not include all components of what eventually would be on the exam.

D. On April 30, 2011, the city administered the written portion of the test, and on May 7 through 13, the physical portion of the test. Although there were originally 3,612 applicants, only 2,212 took the written part of the exam (285 of whom were females) and of those only 1,233 were allowed to take the physical part of the exam. Out of that group 29 females scored high enough to be placed on an eligibility list with 1,069 males. The highest ranking woman was 334 on the list, thus precluding any possibility that a female would be selected for one of the 35 available openings.

I have affidavits from three potential plaintiffs. Here are summaries, although Pat Moss has not yet consented to be a named plaintiff.

Barbara Zoll is a 24-year-old white female and a resident of the City of Cleveland. She is a graduate of Kent State University with a Bachelor's Degree in aerospace technology. She took the written exam, and received a score high enough to be permitted to take the physical agility test.

In January 2011, while watching a local television news show she became aware of the recruitment program. After calling the Fire Department and asking for additional information she was referred to another program targeted toward minorities. She attended classes as part of the minority program for three weeks until discovering, on her own, the program directed to women recruits. She then began attending the women's recruitment classes four nights a week for four hours each. The classes included physical conditioning as well as academic aspects of the exam.

On the day of the civil service exam she arrived at 9:00 A.M. as instructed, with her yellow admission card indicating name, address, and seat number. There was no additional identification required or requested. On the answer sheet handed her at that time the pertinent information (name, address, and other information) was already filled out. Although it was announced that once testing began no one would be allowed to leave the test area, Zoll witnessed other candidates coming and going from the exam area with no apparent control. During the exam, an exam monitor personally told her of several typographical errors, however no general announcements were made to this effect. The plaintiff found the exam tested for areas of knowledge not previously announced in the civil service posting, or covered by the recruitment program classes. Despite two attempts to receive a copy of her graded exam she has not been allowed to do so.

Although Barbara Zoll was an exceptionally good athlete, the special class for women did not prepare her for the physical portion of the test. The barbell exercise caught her off guard, and the men had a distinct advantage in the dummy-pull. Despite the fact that she was in great shape, Barbara Zoll did much worse on the physical portion than she did on the written portion.

Pat Moss is a 33-year-old, white female, who has a Bachelor of Arts in Social Studies and a teaching certificate. She has taken three other civil service exams within the last six months in other smaller communities and has placed eighth (8th), seventh (7th), and fifteenth (15th), respectively. She originally heard about the special women's training program over the local television news. She received additional information from a friend who is a current Cleveland firefighter. On average she attended the classes two (2) days a week, beginning about three (3) weeks after they started. Ten days prior to the exam she saw the consultant and the Civil Service Personnel Administrator attend and observe a class. At the next class she attended, certain aspects of the physical conditioning program were made more rigorous, however it was not until the week before the actual physical exam that she and the other program participants were notified that weight training would be part of the exam.

In addition to the official women's training program, Moss also attended a special private training program. This course was run by a former police chief and cost $500.00. Included in that course of study were a number of general areas not covered in the official training program, but which were eventually on the exam. It was intimated by the facilitator of the private classes that he was in contact with the consultant.

Moss also notes that there were no security measures followed during the administering of the exam. She also had a test monitor point out a typographical error regarding the mislabeling of answers. After the exam, she spoke with a male applicant who informed her that he had been notified about three (3) typographical errors. Her test answer sheet had been filled out in advance with her name, address, and other pertinent personal information.

Because Moss scored a 45 she was allowed to take the physical agility test, scheduled for a Sunday, May 11, at 4:00 P.M. Upon arriving on the day the exam was scheduled she was notified by a note posted on the door that the exam was postponed until May 13 due to rain and cold. On the rescheduled test date the identification system was limited to signing an entry log and receiving a card with her name on it. At the conclusion of each event the monitors wrote down her times and would then initial them. After completing all of the test events the cards were returned by placing them on a pile at a desk. Nobody was able to explain to her how the raw scores would be converted into a final rating for the agility test.

A number of the back tanks (I think this refers to self-contained breathing apparatus or air tanks), required to be worn while dragging a hose to the opposite end from where one starts, were inoperative. This resulted in a line-up at that particular event and a resting period for only some of the test participants. On the day she took the agility test the weather was sunny, dry, and cool.

Moss ranked 587 on the eligibility list. After learning her score she wrote letters to the Mayor and the Director of Public Safety questioning a rumor she heard that minority candidates would be scored differently. The Director of Public Safety responded that the procedure for choosing firefighters is designated by the Charter of the City; however, selection of minority candidates has been modified by court order. White female candidates are not considered as minorities under the court order.

Jennifer Grimes is 24 years old, white, married, and at the time the exam was given, a resident of Parma, Ohio. She attended the official training program for women firefighters about two nights a week, and she also attended the private class for six weeks prior to the written test being administered. She learned of the private classes through a firefighter neighbor. The private classes are distinguishable from the official classes because they covered specific technical instruction concerning fire fighting techniques and other material taught at the Fire Academy. Two weeks prior to the exam the instructor notified the class that he had received certain information about the exam's content and then proceeded to instruct the class on tips to answer certain types of comprehension questions.

The official training sessions she attended did not cover this material, indeed, she recalls the classes as being focused on basic English, basic math, and story problems. These classes appeared to come directly from a generic commercial outline.

The private classes did not focus as heavily on physical conditioning as the official class. However, they were scheduled to practice a simulated physical exam for six Saturdays prior to the exam. One week before the actual physical component of the examination she, along with all the other qualifying applicants, received a copy of the physical test program. The events listed included a barbell event, requiring that a 33-pound barbell be pressed 35 times without bending knees.

While attending the official women's training sessions she overheard an instructor inform several women that they could not get into the private class because it was full. Furthermore, she heard this same instructor characterize the women's training sessions as equal to the other classes. The son of this instructor was enrolled in the private classes to prepare for the firefighters exam.

Upon arriving at the written exam the yellow entry card was being made available to those individuals who had arrived without one. Her test answer sheet had been filled out in advance with her name, address, etc. She had been informed that the applicants would be filling out this information themselves.

During the exam she observed people changing seats from their assigned seats, smoking, and talking. Errors on the exam were corrected by individual monitors assigned to areas of the Convention Center where the exam was held.

Grimes scored high enough to be eligible for the physical agility test. At the physical exam on May 9, 2011, she was informed that she was to proceed directly from one event to another without stopping in between; if she was found to be out of sequence with other candidates she would be disqualified. However, she observed other persons stopping to rest or being permitted to complete events even though they were out of sequence. Additionally, she observed lines forming at certain events, thus allowing some people the opportunity to rest.

## Legal Analysis

Here is a summary of the legal research I have done so far in this case. I see four potential claims:

### 1. Section 1983

One potential remedy for a deprivation of civil rights is 42 U.S.C. § 1983, which provides:

> Every person who, under color of any statute, ordinance, regulation, custom or usage, of any State or Territory or the District of Columbia, subjects, or causes to be subjected, any citizen of the United States or other person within the jurisdiction thereof to the deprivation of any rights, privileges, or immunities secured by the Constitution and laws, shall be liable to the party injured in an action at law, suit in equity, or other proper proceeding for redress. . . .

The plain language of 42 U.S.C. § 1983 mandates that a plaintiff must satisfy two essential requisites to state an actionable claim. First, there must be an alleged violation of a right secured by federal constitutional or statutory laws, such as the Fourth Amendment right to be free from unreasonable searches or the Fourteenth Amendment right to the equal protection of the laws. Second, a § 1983 plaintiff must show that the alleged deprivation was caused by a person acting under color (or pretense) of state law. (Most rights secured by the Constitution are protected only against infringement by public entities or their officials, not private parties.)

There is case law holding that a municipality (like the City of Cleveland) is "a person" (and thus an appropriate defendant) for purposes of § 1983. In order to make out a claim against a local governmental body, it must be shown that the deprivation of rights complained of grows out of either the official policy or the custom and practice of the municipality. Actions by subordinate city officials acting on their own are not covered, unless they are acting in an official policy-making role.

The federal right that we will claim implicates § 1983 is the right to equal protection for women under the Fourteenth Amendment. The Supreme Court has held that a plaintiff claiming a violation of the Fourteenth Amendment Equal Protection Clause must prove *discriminatory intent* (i.e., that the challenged action was *deliberately* designed to disadvantage a protected group). *Discriminatory effect* alone is not sufficient to make out an Equal Protection violation. *See Washington v. Davis*, 426 U.S. 229 (1976); *Village of Arlington Heights v. Metropolitan Housing Development Corp.*, 429 U.S. 252 (1977). A plaintiff asserting an equal rights violation in a Section 1983 claim must be prepared to meet both production and persuasion burdens as to discriminatory intent. In *Black v. City of Akron, Ohio*, 831 F.2d 131 (6th Cir. 1987), however, the court held that "statistical proof may be used in actions under 42 U.S.C. § 1983" and that "allegations of statistical evidence of an adverse impact might be sufficient to survive summary judgment." *Id.* at 133.

Unless the only relief sought is equitable, the parties have the right to claim a jury in § 1983 cases. Section 1983 plaintiffs are entitled to compensatory damages, and also to punitive damages where "evil motive or intent" or "reckless or callous indifference to federally protected rights" is proven. *Smith v. Wade*, 461 U.S. 30 (1983). The court has discretion to allow a prevailing plaintiff (but not the United States) to recover "a reasonable attorney's fee as part of costs" in § 1983 cases. (42 U.S.C. § 1988).

### 2. Section 1985

Another potential remedy is found in 42 U.S.C. § 1985(3):

If two or more persons in any State or Territory conspire or go in disguise on the highway or on the premises of another, for the purpose of depriving, either directly or indirectly, any person or class of persons of the equal protection of the laws, or of equal privileges and immunities under the laws; or for the purpose of preventing or hindering the constituted authorities of any State or Territory from giving or securing to all persons within such State or Territory the equal protection of the laws; or if two or more persons conspire to prevent by force, intimidation, or threat, any citizen who is lawfully entitled to vote, from giving his support or advocacy in a legal manner, toward or in favor of the election of any lawfully qualified person as an elector for President or Vice President, or as a Member of Congress of the United States; or to injure any citizen in person or property on account of such support or advocacy; in any case of conspiracy set forth in this section, if one or more persons engaged therein do, or cause to be done, any act in furtherance of the object of such conspiracy, whereby another is injured in his person or property, or deprived of having and exercising any right or privilege of a citizen of the United States, the party so injured or deprived may have an action for the recovery of damages occasioned by such injury or deprivation, against any one or more of the conspirators.

A claim asserted under § 1985(3) may be based on a purely private conspiracy (with no government involvement) if it was motivated by "some racial, or perhaps otherwise class-based, invidiously discriminatory animus." *Griffin v. Breckenridge*, 403 U.S. 88, 102 (1971). The conspiracy must be aimed at interfering with rights that are protected in 42 U.S.C. § 1985 against encroachment, such as "equal protection of the laws, or of equal privileges and immunities under the laws," so this probably will get us back into having to prove discriminatory animus even when the conspiracy involves state actors. "It remains uncertain whether gender-based motivation qualifies as an actionable animus. . . ." under § 1985(3). 1 Harold S. Lewis, Jr., *Litigating Civil Rights and Employment Discrimination Cases* § 1.5 (1996). "The Court [in *Great American Fed. S. & L Assn. v. Novotny*, 442 U.S. 366 (1979)] held that § 1985(3) is unavailable to enforce rights created by Title VII, 'expressing the fear that it might be used to bypass the detailed state and local administrative procedures, conciliation mechanisms and judicial remedies that Congress specified in the modern statute.'" Lewis, Jr., *id.* But, as I read *Novotny*, we can use § 1985(3) to recover for a conspiracy to violate the equal protection clause; unlike *Novotny*, we have state action in our case.

Section 1985(3) provides a civil remedy, and consequently the elements of what constitute a civil conspiracy are probably relevant to defining "conspiracy" for § 1985(3) purposes. These elements are: "(1) two or more persons; (2) an object to be accomplished; (3) a meeting of the minds on the object or course of action; (4) one or more unlawful, overt acts; and (5) damages as the proximate result." *Nelson v. Fontenot*, 784 F. Supp. 1528 (E.D. Tex. 1992) (action brought by deputy sheriffs against county officials alleging conspiracy to prohibit deputies from organizing a union).

### 3. Ohio Civil Service Statute

The Ohio statutory provisions relating to "frauds in examination prohibited" (Title I, Ch. 124, § 124.58) are as follows:

No person or officer shall willfully or corruptly, by himself or in cooperation with one or more persons, defeat, deceive, or obstruct any person in respect of his right of examination, appointment, or employment according to sections

124.01 to 124.64 of the Revised Code, or to any rules or regulations prescribed pursuant to such sections; or willfully or corruptly, falsely mark, grade, estimate, or report upon the examination or proper standing of any person examined, registered, or certified pursuant to such sections, or aid in so doing; or willfully or corruptly make any false representations concerning the same, or concerning the person examined; or willfully or corruptly furnish to any person any special or secret information for the purpose of either improving or injuring the prospects or chances of any person so examined, registered, or certified, or personate any other person, or permit or aid in any manner any person to personate him, in connection with any examination, registration, appointment, application, or request to be examined, registered, or appointed; or shall furnish any false information about himself, or any other person, in connection with any examination, registration, appointment, application, or request to be examined, registered, or appointed.

There is very little case law interpreting this portion of the Ohio civil service statutory provisions or the predecessor Ohio statute. The word "fraud" in its title, and the repetition of words such as "willfully or corrupt," "defeat, deceive, or obstruct," "falsely mark," "personate," and "willfully or corruptly furnish to any person any special or secret information" with respect to civil service examinations suggest to me that the purpose of these provisions is to protect the integrity of the civil service examination system by prohibiting cheating of any kind or the intentional distortion of results by dishonest behavior, such as providing people with the exam in advance, or taking the exam in someone else's name, or altering the true results. In *Resek v. Seven Hills*, 9 Ohio App. 3d 224, 227 (1963), the statutory provisions are cited in a case in which the Chief of Police was removed from his office for, among other things, illegally trying to help a friend who had failed the civil service exam for lieutenant. The Chief of Police had tried to influence a member of the Civil Service Commission (whom he had helped get appointed) to award the person who had failed undeserved credits for efficiency and seniority in service. The Chief of Police also tried to stop other people from getting the promotion to lieutenant, thus making room for his friend. Such behavior, in violation of the civil service provisions, was part of the justification for his removal. Under the predecessor statute to Title I, Ch. 124, § 124.58, a civil service commissioner who made a false certificate that an applicant had satisfactorily passed an examination, which was untrue, was found guilty of corrupt use of his office. *Kerr v. Hinkle*, 12 OD (NP) 365 (1902).

### 4. Title VII

Title VII is, of course, another possibility. 42 U.S.C. §§ 2000e et seq. The statute prohibits discrimination in both private and public employment, and provides in pertinent part:

(a) It shall be an unlawful employment practice for an employer—
(1) to fail or refuse to hire or to discharge any individual or otherwise to discriminate against any individual with respect to his compensations,

terms, conditions, or privileges of employment, because of such individual's race, color, religion, sex, or national origin; or

(2) to limit, segregate, or classify his employees or applicants for employment in any way which would deprive or tend to deprive any individual of employment opportunities or otherwise adversely affect his status as an employee, because of such individual's race, color, religion, sex, or national origin. . . .

(h) Notwithstanding any other provision of this subchapter, it shall not be an unlawful employment practice for an employer . . . to give and to act upon the results of any professionally developed ability test provided that such test, its administration or action upon the results is not designed, intended or used to discriminate because of race, color, religion, sex or national origin. . . .

Generally speaking, a violation of Title VII may be established by showing that (1) a covered employer (fifteen or more employees), (2) discriminated, (3) on one of the prohibited bases of discrimination, (4) with respect to an employment practice covered by the Act. Title VII prohibits two forms of discrimination: (I) disparate treatment, the familiar form of intentional conduct motivated by race, color, religion, sex, or national origin; and (II) disparate impact, the use of ostensibly neutral selection practices which have an adverse effect on a protected group and are not justified by a showing that the device predicts successful job performance. An example of the latter is a written examination that excludes disproportionate numbers of minorities and has no substantial relation to the skills and attributes necessary to perform the job in question.

In a *disparate treatment* case the plaintiff may prove discriminatory intent through circumstantial evidence. To do so, she first must establish a prima facie case of discrimination; the elements of which are:

(1) membership in a protected group;
(2) application and qualification for a job for which the employer was seeking applicants;
(3) rejection, despite the applicant's qualifications; and
(4) the employer's continued solicitation of applicants with qualifications equal to the plaintiff's.

Such a showing raises a rebuttable inference that the rejection was discriminatorily motivated. *See McDonnell Douglas Corp. v. Green*, 411 U.S. 792 (1973); *Texas Dept. of Community Affairs v. Burdine*, 450 U.S. 248 (1981). The defendant must then articulate (merely a burden of production) a nondiscriminatory explanation for the rejection. Employers might introduce evidence of the plaintiff's inferior qualifications, insubordination, or inability to get along with others. After the employer meets its production burden on nondiscriminatory purpose, the plaintiff has the opportunity to demonstrate that the articulated reason is merely a pretext to cover the discriminatory motivation. The plaintiff ordinarily attempts to accomplish this by comparing his/her record and qualifications with that of individuals of the opposite race or gender who were favorably treated by the employer. The ultimate burden of proof remains with the plaintiff to prove (both in the production and persuasion senses) discriminatory intent on the part of the defendant. In *St. Mary's Honor Center v. Hicks*, 509 U.S. 502 (1993), the Supreme Court held that even if the plaintiff meets its burden in proving pretext (i.e., the factfinder is persuaded that the reason or reasons given by the employer are not the real reasons why the defendant-employer rejected the plaintiff), the plaintiff may still lose unless the factfinder is persuaded that it was pretext for discrimination, as opposed to some other reason the employer is trying to hide. This holding in a 5-4 decision has been highly controversial, and courts disagree as to when the plaintiff's initial prima facie case, accompanied by the factfinder's disbelief of the employer's stated reason (i.e., a finding of pretext) is sufficient to permit an inference of discriminatory intent. Mark S. Brodin, *The Demise of Circumstantial Proof in Employment Discrimination Litigation:* St. Mary's Honor Center v. Hicks, *Pretext, and the "Personality Excuse,"* 18 Berkeley J. Employment & Lab. L. 183 (1997). *See also Reeves v. Sanderson Plumbing Prods., Inc.*, 530 U.S. 133 (2000).

The theory of *disparate impact* was adopted by the Supreme Court in *Griggs v. Duke Power Co.*, 401 U.S. 424, 432 (1971), in which the plaintiffs challenged the employer's requirement of a high school diploma and a passing grade on a standardized general intelligence test in order to be employed at the North Carolina power plant. Evidence presented indicated that because of the inferior educational opportunities afforded to black citizens of the state, these selection requirements disproportionately excluded black applicants. Moreover, the requirements were not shown to have any relation to the performance of jobs at the plant. The Supreme Court held that in order to establish a disparate impact violation of Title VII, "a plaintiff need only show that the facially neutral standards in question select applicants for hire in a significantly discriminatory pattern." The burden of proof then shifts to the employer to prove (with both production and persuasion burdens) that the challenged requirement had "a manifest relationship to the employment in question." If the employer is successful in proving that the requirement was job-related, the plaintiff may still prevail by proving that alternative selection devices would serve the employer's legitimate interests without a similar discriminatory effect.

Physical qualifications for employment which are ostensibly gender-neutral may nonetheless have a discriminatory impact on one sex. In *Dothard v. Rawlinson*, 433 U.S. 321 (1977), for example, the Court struck down height/weight minimums for the position of prison guard because they excluded disproportionate numbers of female applicants, and were not shown to be job-related.

Disparate impact cases involve some tricky burden of proof problems, which were addressed by the Civil Rights Act of 1991 and now are part of Title VII:

> (k)(1)(A)(i) An unlawful employment practice based on disparate impact is established under this title only if—a complaining party demonstrates that a

respondent uses a particular employment practice that causes a disparate impact on the basis of race, color, religion, sex, or national origin and the respondent fails to demonstrate that the challenged practice is job related for the position in question and consistent with business necessity . . . .

(B)(i) With respect to demonstrating that a particular employment practice causes a disparate impact as described in subparagraph (A)(i), the complaining party shall demonstrate that each particular challenged employment practice causes a disparate impact, except that if the complaining party can demonstrate to the court that the elements of a respondent's decisionmaking process are not capable of separation for analysis, the decisionmaking process may be analyzed as one employment practice.

(B)(ii) If the respondent demonstrates that a specific employment practice does not cause the disparate impact, the respondent shall not be required to demonstrate that such practice is required by business necessity. . . .

42 U.S.C. § 2000e-2.

The Civil Rights Act of 1991 reaffirms the prior case law that even if the factfinder is persuaded that the defendant's stated "job related" employment practice is "consistent with business necessity," the plaintiff can win if it proves (production and persuasion burdens) that there is an alternative employment practice that the defendant refuses to adopt that would meet the employer's business needs without having a similar discriminatory impact. (Sec. 105(a)(ii) and (C).)

The Civil Rights Act of 1991 also clarified the burden of proof in so-called mixed-motive disparate treatment cases:

> Sec. 107. Clarifying Prohibition Against Impermissible Consideration of Race, Color, Religion, Sex, or National Origin in Employment Practices.
>
> Except as otherwise provided in this title, an unlawful employment practice is established when the complaining party demonstrates that race, color, religion, sex, or national origin was a motivating factor for any employment practice, even though other factors also motivated the practice.
>
> On a claim in which an individual proves a violation under section 703 (m) and a respondent demonstrates that the respondent would have taken the same action in the absence of the impermissible motivating factor, the court—
>
> (i) may grant declaratory relief, injunctive relief (except as provided in clause (ii)), and attorney's fees and costs demonstrated to be directly attributable only to the pursuit of a claim under section 703 (m); and
>
> (ii) shall not award damages or issue an order requiring any admission, reinstatement, hiring, promotion, or payment, described in subparagraph (A). . . .

One other provision of the Civil Rights Act of 1991 may be of interest:

> Sec. 106. Prohibition Against Discriminatory Use of Test Scores.
>
> (1) It shall be an unlawful employment practice for a respondent, in connection with the selection or referral of applicants or candidates for employment or promotion, to adjust the scores of, use different cutoff scores for, or

otherwise alter the results of, employment related tests on the basis of race, color, religion, sex, or national origin. . . .

Under Title VII, a plaintiff can recover compensatory and punitive damages by proving intentional discrimination, but cannot do so in a disparate impact case. Reinstatement and back pay are considered equitable remedies that are available in both disparate impact and disparate treatment cases. In a disparate treatment case, compensatory damages (including damages for future pecuniary losses, emotional pain, suffering, inconvenience, mental anguish, loss of enjoyment of life, and other nonpecuniary losses) and punitive damages are limited for each complaining party to $300,000 against employers with more than 500 employees; but, in addition, the complaining party can be awarded equitable relief. In a case in which the plaintiff seeks compensatory damages (which will be a disparate treatment case requiring the plaintiff to prove intentional discrimination), any party may claim a jury. Parties do not have the right to demand a jury in disparate impact cases. Under Title VII, prevailing plaintiffs can be awarded attorney fees. Civil Rights Act of 1991, §§ 102-103.

# IN THE UNITED STATES DISTRICT COURT
## FOR THE NORTHERN DISTRICT OF OHIO
### EASTERN DIVISION

BARBARA ZOLL
902 East 61st Street, Apt. #5
Cleveland, Ohio 44103

JENNIFER GRIMES
1992 Brookdale Road
Parma, Ohio 44134

On behalf of themselves and
all others similarly situated

   Plaintiffs

   vs.

CITY OF CLEVELAND
City Hall
601 Lakeside Avenue
Cleveland, Ohio 44114

JAMES KOSOLSKY, MAYOR
City of Cleveland
City Hall
601 Lakeside Avenue
Cleveland, Ohio 44114
   Individually and in his official capacity as Mayor

HARRY N. TARPLEY, DIRECTOR
Department of Public Safety
City of Cleveland
City Hall
601 Lakeside Avenue
Cleveland, Ohio 44114
   Individually and in his official capacity as Director
   of the Department of Public Safety

STEVEN SAPERS, PRESIDENT
Civil Service Commission
4210 Cable Avenue
Cleveland, Ohio 44127
   Individually and in his official capacity as a Civil
   Service Commission member and officer

C.A. No. 12-2371

**COMPLAINT**
**CLASS ACTION**

EVAN W. SPANIOG, VICE PRESIDENT
Civil Service Commission
15089 Harland Avenue
Cleveland, Ohio 44119
   Individually and in his official capacity as a Civil
   Service Commission member and officer

ALICE Q. SIMMONS, SECRETARY
Civil Service Commission
Room 119, City Hall, 601 Lakeside Avenue
Cleveland, Ohio 44114
   Individually and in her official capacity as a Civil
   Service Commission member and officer

BETTY SMITH
1400 Henley Avenue
Cleveland, Ohio 44109
   Individually and in her official capacity as a Civil
   Service Commission member

SAMUEL HAWKINS
4823 East 74th Street
Cleveland, Ohio 44104
   Individually and in his official capacity as a Civil
   Service Commission member

KAREN SHELTON
PERSONNEL ADMINISTRATOR
Civil Service Commission
City of Cleveland
Room 119, City Hall
601 Lakeside Avenue
Cleveland, Ohio 44114
   Individually and in her official capacity as Personnel
   Administrator of the Civil Service Commission

THOMAS McGINNIS, FIRE CHIEF
City of Cleveland
1535 Superior Avenue
Cleveland, Ohio 44114
   Individually and in his official capacity as Fire Chief

SHELDON O. MARSHALL
Personnel Testing and Statistical Analysis
1701 Erie Ave.
Cleveland, Ohio 44114
   Acting as an agent and/or representative of the City of
   Cleveland in devising and administering its Civil
   Service Commission test, and for the Fire Department
   of the City of Cleveland, Defendants.

# PRELIMINARY STATEMENT

1. This is a class action for declaratory and equitable relief and damages brought by the Plaintiffs against the City of Cleveland, Ohio, and several municipal officials and an agent and/or representative of the City of Cleveland on the grounds that the Defendants have engaged in unlawful discrimination against females with respect to the Defendants' policies and practices concerning the recruiting, training, testing, hiring, and employment of firefighters.

The Plaintiffs seek a judgment and decree that the practices complained of are in violation of rights guaranteed by the Constitution of the United States and applicable civil rights statutes.

Plaintiffs also seek to invoke the Court's supplemental jurisdiction with respect to common law claims arising out of the same common nucleus of facts as her federal claims. In connection with this claim, the Plaintiffs seek a judgment or decree that the practices complained of herein are in violation of the laws of the State of Ohio, ordinances, rules and regulations of the City of Cleveland and its Civil Service Commission.

# PARTIES

## A. Plaintiffs

2. (a) Plaintiff, Barbara Zoll, is a citizen of the United States residing at 902 East 61st Street, Apt. #5, Cleveland, Ohio 44103.

(b) Barbara Zoll is a white female.

(c) On April 30, 2011, Plaintiff took the City of Cleveland Civil Service Commission written test for eligibility for appointment as a Cleveland firefighter.

(d) Barbara Zoll received a score of 48.50 on the written test and took the physical agility test administered from May 7 through May 13, 2011.

(e) Plaintiff is No. 642 on the current eligibility list for appointment as a Cleveland firefighter.

(f) Barbara Zoll attended classes in a specially funded training program for female applicants for the April 30, 2011, firefighters' Civil Service Commission Test.

3. (a) Plaintiff, Jennifer Grimes, is a citizen of the United States residing at 1992 Brookdale Road, Parma, Ohio 44134. In late January or early February

2011, when she applied to take the City of Cleveland Civil Service Commission test for eligibility for appointment as a Cleveland firefighter, Plaintiff was a bona fide resident of 3448 West 94th Street, Cleveland, Ohio 44102.

(b) Jennifer Grimes is a white female.

(c) On April 30, 2011, Plaintiff took the City of Cleveland Civil Service Commission written test for eligibility for appointment as a Cleveland firefighter.

(d) Jennifer Grimes received a score of 39.50 on the written test, plus an additional 5 points because she is a veteran, and was permitted to take the physical agility test administered on May 9, 2011.

(e) Jennifer Grimes received a score of 28.24 on the physical agility test, and was given an additional 10 points because she was a resident of the City of Cleveland.

(f) Jennifer Grimes is No. 952 on the current eligibility list for appointment as a Cleveland firefighter.

(g) Because of her ranking as No. 952 on the current eligibility list, it is unlikely that Plaintiff will be appointed as a Cleveland firefighter.

(h) Jennifer Grimes attended classes in a specially funded training program for female applicants for the firefighters Civil Service Commission Test.

## B. Class Action

4. Plaintiffs bring this action on their own behalf and pursuant to Rules 23(a) and (b)(2), Fed. R. Civ. P. on behalf of all others similarly situated.

5. The class which Plaintiffs represent includes all females who at any time applied to take the Civil Service Commission Examination for eligibility for appointment as a Cleveland firefighter offered on April 30, 2011, and also all females who attended the special training class offered by the City of Cleveland from approximately mid-January 2011 to late-April, 2011, for the purpose of training actual and potential female applicants for the April 30, 2011, Civil Service Examination. The class also includes all females who have been or will be deterred from applying for employment, and also all females who will be employed, or who will apply for employment as firefighters with the City of Cleveland at any time in the future.

6. (a) The Defendants have restricted eligibility of applicants for the position of firefighter to persons eighteen years of age or more, who are citizens of the United States and who possess a high school diploma, or the equivalent.

(b) The population of the Standard Metropolitan Statistical Area (SMSA) of Cleveland includes 1,384,025 persons eighteen years of age or more.

(c) Of these 1,384,025 persons, approximately 53% are female.

(d) Two hundred eighty-five (285) women took the Civil Service Commission written test for eligibility for appointment as a Cleveland firefighter on April 30, 2011. The number of women who will apply for employment in the future, or who have been or will be deterred from applying is unknown.

(e) The class is so numerous that joinder of all members is impracticable.

7. (a) Defendants issue notices of all Civil Service examinations for the position of firefighter.

(b) Defendants require written tests of all firefighter applicants and agility tests of those who pass the written test.

(c) No (0) female has ever been employed by the City of Cleveland as a firefighter in its history; the woman scoring highest on the examination that began April 30, 2011, is No. 334 on the eligibility list.

(d) A special training program for female applicants or potential applicants was held by the Defendant City of Cleveland for the April 30, 2011, Civil Service Commission examination for the position of Cleveland firefighter. While this program was open to anyone who wished to attend, free of charge, it was referred to as being especially for women.

(e) The above facts are common to the class.

8. Questions of law common to the members of the class concern whether the acts herein alleged to have been committed by the Defendants constitute violations of the United States Constitution and the Civil Rights Acts of 1871, and 1964, as amended.

9. (a) Plaintiff Barbara Zoll applied to take, participated in, and passed the Civil Service Commission written test for eligibility for appointment as a Cleveland firefighter offered on April 30, 2011, and scored a 33.2 on the physical portion.

(b) Plaintiff Jennifer Grimes applied to take, and passed the Civil Service Commission written tests for eligibility for appointment as a Cleveland firefighter offered on April 30, 2011. She attained a score of less than 35 (the requisite passing score) on the physical agility test offered from May 7, 2011, through May 13, 2011, although her name is, nevertheless, listed on the eligibility list for appointment as a Cleveland firefighter.

(c) The City of Cleveland plans to appoint approximately thirty-five (35) firefighters immediately from the current firefighter eligibility list.

(d) The highest-ranking woman who passed both the written test and the physical agility test is ranked Number 334 on the eligibility list.

(e) The City of Cleveland will not reach any woman on the current eligibility list for appointment as a Cleveland firefighter unless it takes women from the eligibility list out of their rank order.

(f) All the named Plaintiffs attended some classes of a specially-funded training program for the April 30, 2011, Cleveland Firefighters Civil Service Commission Examination.

(g) Plaintiffs' claims are typical of the class.

10. (a) Plaintiffs have pursued available administrative remedies by filing charges of employment discrimination based on their sex with the Cleveland Regional Office of the Equal Employment Opportunity Commission.

(b) Plaintiffs have retained counsel and are able fairly and adequately to represent and protect the interests of the class.

11. The Defendants' policies regarding hiring and employment have been and will continue to be generally applicable to the class thereby making appropriate final injunctive and declaratory relief with respect to the class as a whole. A common relief is sought. A class action is the only practical method of fair and efficient adjudication of this controversy.

## C. Defendants

12. (a) Defendant City of Cleveland is a municipal corporation organized and established pursuant to laws of the State of Ohio.

(b) Defendant City of Cleveland, through its mayor and council, formulates, adopts, and implements policies, practices, and procedures with regard to hiring and employment by the municipality.

(c) Defendant City of Cleveland is an employer within the meaning of Title 42 U.S.C. § 2000e(a) and (b), as amended.

13. Defendant James Kosolsky is Mayor of the City of Cleveland and, as such, is vested with the authority to enforce the City's ordinances, regulations, and policies. He is sued in his official capacity and individually.

14. Defendant Harry N. Tarpley is the Director of the Department of Public Safety of the City of Cleveland. As an appointee of the mayor, he is

vested with authority to oversee and direct the operations and policies of the various safety divisions of the City of Cleveland, including the Fire Department. He is sued in his official capacity and individually.

15. Steven Sapers is President of the Civil Service Commission of the City of Cleveland. He is vested with the authority to carry out the ordinances, rules, regulations, and policies of the Civil Service Commission. He is sued in his official capacity and individually.

16. Evan W. Spaniog is Vice President of the Civil Service Commission of the City of Cleveland. He is vested with the authority to carry out the ordinances, rules, regulations, and policies of the Civil Service Commission. He is sued in his official capacity and individually.

17. Alice Q. Simmons is the Secretary of the Civil Service Commission of the City of Cleveland. She is vested with the authority to carry out the ordinances, rules, regulations, and policies of the Civil Service Commission. She is being sued in her official capacity and individually.

18. Betty Smith is a member of the Civil Service Commission of the City of Cleveland. She is vested with the authority to carry out the ordinances, rules, regulations, and policies of the Civil Service Commission. She is being sued in her official capacity and individually.

19. Samuel Hawkins is a member of the Civil Service Commission of the City of Cleveland. He is vested with the authority to carry out the ordinances, rules, regulations, and policies of the Civil Service Commission. He is being sued in his official capacity and individually.

20. Karen Shelton is Personnel Administrator of the Civil Service Commission of the City of Cleveland. She is vested with the authority to carry out the ordinances, rules, regulations, and policies of the Civil Service Commission. She is being sued in her official capacity and individually.

21. (a) Defendant Fire Chief Thomas McGinnis is a sworn officer of the Fire Department of the City of Cleveland.

(b) The Fire Chief supervises approximately 1,000 persons who serve as firefighters for the City.

(c) Defendant Fire Chief McGinnis is an agent of an employer within the meaning of. Title 42 U.S.C. § 2000e(a) and (b), as amended.

22. (a) Defendant Sheldon O. Marshall is a professor of psychology at Case-Western Reserve University, Cleveland, Ohio, who offers consulting

services in the area of devising, administering, evaluating, and scoring civil service examinations on behalf of local, state, and federal governments.

(b) Pursuant to an agreement with the Defendant City of Cleveland, Defendant Marshall prepared, administered, scored, and evaluated the Civil Service Commission written test for eligibility for appointment as a Cleveland firefighter offered on April 30, 2011, and also the physical agility test of the same examination, offered from May 7 through 13, 2011.

(c) Defendant Marshall is an agent and/or representative of an employer within the meaning of Title 42 U.S.C. § 2000e(a) and (b) as amended.

## STATEMENT OF THE CLAIM

### A. Count One: Title VII

23. On or about October 6, 2007, Sheldon O. Marshall submitted a Proposal to provide a job-related entry-level examination for the position of firefighter—City of Cleveland.

24. Pursuant to Ordinance No. 2618-94 enacted December 6, 2007, the Council of the City of Cleveland selected Defendant Marshall to provide his professional services in preparing, administering, and defending a job-related, entry-level examination for the position of firefighter.

25. (a) On or about March 15, 2008, pursuant to Ordinance No. 2618-94 enacted by the Council of the City of Cleveland on December 6, 2007, the City of Cleveland entered into a formal agreement with Defendant Marshall that he provide the professional services necessary to prepare, administer, and defend a job-related, entry-level examination for the position of firefighter.

(b) In return, the City of Cleveland has paid or will pay Defendant Marshall an amount equal to or in excess of Thirty-Seven Thousand Five Hundred Fifty Dollars ($37,550.00).

26. On or about January 1, 2011, the Civil Service Commission of the City of Cleveland issued an announcement of an open competitive examination for the position of firefighter, the written portion of which would be administered on April 30, 2011. Said announcement stated:

The written test is designed to measure basic reading and math skills, the ability to follow directions, the ability to recall basic factual materials, and a variety of judgment and skills related to firefighter performance. Knowledge of firefighting procedures is not required on the test.

27. (a) During January 2011, or February 2011, the exact date unknown, the City of Cleveland commenced a program allegedly intended to prepare women successfully to pass all phases of the 2011 firefighter entry-level tests.

(b) Classes in this program were free of charge and described as a women's training course.

(c) Classes in the women's training program were supervised by Lt. Kevin Kelly, an agent of the Defendant City of Cleveland.

(d) The content of the classes in this program did not provide adequate preparation for the content of the written test administered on April 30, 2011.

(e) The content of the classes in the women's training program did not include all aspects of the physical agility test administered May 7 through 12, 2011.

28. (a) For several months prior to April 30, 2011, the exact dates being unknown, Buddy Casey offered a program of classes to prepare candidates for the firefighter tests.

(b) Enrollees in Buddy Casey's classes were charged a fee of Five Hundred Dollars ($500.00).

(c) Only eight (8) women attended Casey's classes.

(d) The content of Casey's classes closely paralleled the content of the written test offered on April 30, 2011.

29. On or about April 30, 2011, at the Cleveland Convention Center commencing at 9:30 A.M., the Civil Service Commission administered the written portion of the entry-level firefighters test to all candidates.

30. Those persons determined by the City of Cleveland to have passed the written test successfully were notified to take the physical agility test.

31. Physical agility tests were administered to groups of twenty-five (25) candidates at scheduled half hour intervals commencing May 7, 2011 through May 13, 2011.

32. (a) Sometime during the second half of May, 2011, the Civil Service Commission issued an eligibility list of one thousand ninety-eight (1,098) names of persons who had taken both written and physical portions of the City of Cleveland's entry-level firefighter examination during April-May, 2011.

(b) Of the one thousand ninety-eight (1,098) names appearing on the eligibility list, the names of only twenty-nine (29) women appear.

(c) The highest ranking woman on the May, 2011 eligibility list is F. Huilbert, who is ranked No. 334.

(d) Women have been informed by agents, officers, and representatives of the City of Cleveland that no women will be hired as Cleveland firefighters.

33. (a) The Cleveland firefighter entry-level examination has a disparate adverse impact upon female applicants with respect to both the written and the physical agility portions of the examination.

34. (a) The content of the written portion of the entry-level firefighter test administered April 30, 2011, is not job-related and/or performance predictive.

(b) The content of the written test does not accord with the content of the Civil Service announcement of January 3, 2011.

(c) Nor was the written test administered April 30, 2011, related to the content of the special women's firefighter training program offered by the City of Cleveland in early 2011.

(d) The firefighter written test discriminates against female applicants on the basis of their sex.

(e) Alternative job-related methods of testing were available, which would not have had as adverse a disparate effect upon females and which would not have discriminated against females on the basis of their sex.

35. (a) The administration of the written test was not in accordance with laws, ordinances, regulations, and policies applicable to the Defendants in this action.

(b) Security for the administration of the test was not uniformly applied to all candidates.

36. (a) The method of grading and evaluating the written test scores discriminated against females upon the basis of their sex.

(b) The method of grading, evaluation, and weighting questions within the written test was not selected until after the candidates had completed and turned in their completed tests.

(c) Five (5) extra points for eligible veterans were added immediately to veterans' written scores thereby enabling many men who otherwise would not have passed the written test to attain a passing grade of thirty-five (35).

(d) Methods of correcting errors in the written test were not uniformly applied to all candidates.

(e) Although various female candidates requested the right to review their graded written tests, their requests were denied.

37. (a) The content of the physical agility test administered from May 7 through May 13, 2011, was not job-related and/or performance predictive of the skills required of an entry-level Cleveland firefighter.

(b) The physical agility test was not related to the content of the special women's firefighter training program offered by the City of Cleveland in early 2011.

(c) The physical agility test was of such difficulty that it was predictable that women would be more likely than men to be eliminated by it.

(d) The physical agility test included items with respect to which women are known to be disadvantaged while excluding those with respect to which females generally are advantaged.

38. The administration of the physical agility test from May 7 through May 13, 2011, was neither consistent, uniform, nor fair.

39. (a) The grading of the physical agility test has had a disparate adverse impact upon women and a discriminatory effect upon women based upon their sex.

(b) Times for each physical agility event were evaluated against the times of other participants, rather than for minimum competency.

(c) The methods of evaluating candidates' time scores varied significantly and without adequate reason, on the different days the physical test was administered.

(d) The method of weighting, evaluating, and scoring the physical agility test was not determined until after the candidates had completed their tests.

(e) The method of determining the physical agility test score sufficient for placement on the eligibility list was not in accordance with the stated requirement set forth in the instruction sheet issued to candidates taking the agility test (see Exhibit A *attached*).

40. The City of Cleveland, through its officers, agents, and representatives has made statements intended to discourage females from seeking employment with the City of Cleveland's Fire Department.

41. The City of Cleveland and the other named Defendants knew, or should have known, that the written and physical agility firefighters' tests would have a disparate adverse impact and discriminatory effect upon females because of their sex.

42. The procedures described above for the selection of entry-level firefighters were intended by the Defendants to eliminate female candidates from consideration for firefighter positions.

43. By all the acts set forth in paragraphs 23 through 42 above, the Defendants have violated Title VII of the Civil Rights Act of 1964, 42 U.S.C. §§ 2000e, et seq.

44. Plaintiffs have fulfilled the conditions precedent to filing a civil action pursuant to Title VII of the Civil Rights Act of 1964. Both Named Plaintiffs have filed timely charges of discrimination with the Equal Employment Opportunity Commission and requested their Notices of Right to Sue.

## RELIEF PRAYED

45. WHEREFORE, Plaintiffs respectfully pray that this Honorable Court:

(a) Declare unlawful the policies and practices of the Defendants set forth in paragraphs 23 through 42 above, as depriving Plaintiffs and the members of the class they represent, employment opportunities protected by Title VII of the Civil Rights Act of 1964, 42 U.S.C. §§ 2000e, et seq.;

(b) Enjoin the Defendants, both preliminarily and permanently, from declaring the Plaintiffs and others of their class to be either ineligible or too low ranking on the eligibility list for appointment to entry-level firefighter positions on the basis of unvalidated tests which have a disparate effect upon females solely because of their sex;

(c) Direct that the Defendant City of Cleveland, its Mayor, department directors, civil service commission, and others undertake a program to formulate, promulgate, and implement a uniform and nondiscriminatory procedure and policy with respect to the recruiting, hiring, and training of female firefighters;

(d) Make Plaintiffs and the members of their class whole by appropriate back pay, including pre-judgment and post-judgment interest at prevailing rates on the amount awarded, and front pay;

(e) Grant Plaintiffs and the members of their class the costs of this action and reasonable attorneys' fees pursuant to 42 U.S.C. § 1988, including interest at prevailing rates on all sums awarded;

(f) After a prompt hearing of this action according to law, issue an order retaining jurisdiction of this claim until such time as the Court is assured from the activity of the Defendants and their agents that the violations of rights complained of herein have ceased and are no longer threatened and that the effect of past violations has been remedied; and

(g) Grant such other affirmative relief as the Court deems just and appropriate.

## B. Count Two: § 1983

46-65. As paragraphs 46 through 65, Plaintiffs restate, as if fully stated herein, paragraphs 23 through 42 of this complaint.

66. By all the acts set forth in paragraphs 46 through 65 above, the Defendants have violated the Civil Rights Act of 1871, 42 U.S.C. § 1983, and the Due Process and Equal Protection Clause of the Fourteenth Amendment of the United States Constitution.

## RELIEF PRAYED

67. WHEREFORE, Plaintiffs respectfully pray that this Honorable Court:

(a) Pursuant to Title 28 U.S.C. §§ 2201 and 2202, declare unlawful the actions, policies, practices, customs, and usages herein challenged, as being violative of the Civil Rights Act of 1871, 42 U.S.C. § 1983, and the Fourteenth Amendment to the United States Constitution;

(b) Enjoin, both preliminarily and permanently, all use of veterans' preference points for male firefighters with respect to the scoring of the City of Cleveland's entry-level firefighter test;

(c) Enjoin the Defendants, both preliminarily and permanently, from declaring the Plaintiffs and others of their class to be either ineligible or too low ranking on the eligibility list for appointment to entry-level firefighter positions on the basis of unvalidated tests which have a disparate effect upon females solely because of their sex;

(d) Direct that the Defendant City of Cleveland, its Mayor, department directors, civil service commission, and others undertake a program to formulate, promulgate, and implement a uniform and nondiscriminatory procedure and policy with respect to the recruiting, hiring, and training of female firefighters;

(e) Make Plaintiffs and the members of their class whole by appropriate back pay, including pre-judgment and post-judgment interest at prevailing rates on the amount awarded, and front pay;

(f) Grant Plaintiffs and the members of their class the costs of this action and reasonable attorneys' fees pursuant to 42 U.S.C. § 1988, including interest at prevailing rates on all sums awarded;

(g) Award Plaintiffs and the members of the class they represent compensatory and punitive damages;

(h) After a prompt hearing of this action according to law, issue an order retaining jurisdiction of this claim until such time as the Court is assured from the activity of the Defendants and their agents that the violations of rights complained of herein have ceased and are no longer threatened and that the effect of past violations has been remedied; and

(i) Grant such other affirmative relief as the Court deems just and appropriate.

## C. Count Three: Conspiracy Under § 1985(3)

68-87. As paragraphs 68 through 87, Plaintiffs restate, as if fully stated herein, paragraphs 23 through 42 of this complaint.

88. (a) Defendants the City of Cleveland, the officers and members of the Civil Service Commission and Fire Chief McGinnis and other unnamed co-conspirators each and with the others determine the employment needs of the City.

(b) Similarly, the Defendants determine the methods used to publicize the fact that hiring of firefighters for the City will take place.

(c) Further, the above-named Defendants, together with Defendant Sheldon Marshall, select the testing procedures, administer the examination, and evaluate the results.

(d) Finally, the above-named Defendants, together with Defendant Sheldon Marshall, are responsible for deciding which applicants will be hired for available entry-level firefighter position.

89. Defendants employed by the City of Cleveland have conspired with Defendant Marshall and with each other to deprive directly or indirectly,

candidates for firefighter positions for the City of Cleveland of their rights to equal employment opportunity guaranteed by the Fourteenth Amendment to the United States Constitution and 42 U.S.C. §§ 1983 and 2000e, et seq.

90. Defendants employed by the City of Cleveland, Defendant Marshall, and any unnamed co-conspirators have met and acted in concert to deprive the Plaintiffs and members of their class equal opportunities for employment with the City of Cleveland, thereby causing irreparable injury to them in violation of rights guaranteed by the Due Process and Equal Protection Clauses of the Fourteenth Amendment to the United States Constitution and 42 U.S.C. §§ 1983 and 2000e, et seq.

91. By these multiple acts, some of which were taken outside the scope of authority and the official capacities of the Defendants, as set forth in paragraphs 75 through 95 above, the Defendants have violated the Civil Rights Act of 1871, 42 U.S.C. § 1985(3).

## RELIEF PRAYED

92. WHEREFORE, Plaintiffs respectfully pray that this Honorable Court:

(a) Pursuant to Title 28 U.S.C. §§ 2201 and 2202 declare unlawful the actions taken in concert by the Defendants conspiring to deprive the Plaintiffs and the members of the class they represent of nondiscriminatory training programs, preparation, development, administration, grading, evaluation, and purported validation of both the written firefighters' test offered on April 30, 2011, and the physical agility firefighters' test offered May 7 through May 13, 2011, and declare unlawful, null and void these same actions and the eligibility list(s) resulting from said tests as being violative of 42 U.S.C. § 1985(3);

(b) Enjoin, both preliminarily and permanently, all use of veterans' preference points for male firefighters with the scoring of the City of Cleveland's entry-level firefighter test;

(c) Enjoin the Defendants, both preliminarily and permanently, from declaring the Plaintiffs and others of their class to be either ineligible or too low ranking on the eligibility list for appointment to entry-level firefighter positions on the basis of unvalidated tests which have a disparate effect upon females solely because of their sex;

(d) Direct that the Defendant City of Cleveland, its Mayor, department directors, civil service commission, and others undertake a program to formulate, promulgate, and implement a uniform and nondiscriminatory procedure and policy with respect to the recruiting, hiring, and training of female firefighters;

(e) Make Plaintiffs and the members of their class whole by appropriate back pay, including pre-judgment and post-judgment interest at prevailing rates on the amount awarded, and front pay;

(f) Grant Plaintiffs and the members of their class the costs of this action and reasonable attorneys' fees pursuant to 42 U.S.C. § 1988, including interest at prevailing rates on all sums awarded;

(g) Award Plaintiffs and the members of the class they represent compensatory and punitive damages;

(h) After a prompt hearing of this action according to law, issue an order retaining jurisdiction of this claim until such time as the Court is assured from the activity of the Defendants and their agents that the violations of rights complained of herein have ceased and are no longer threatened and that the effect of past violations has been remedied; and

(i) Grant such other affirmative relief as the Court deems just and appropriate.

## D. Count Four: Ohio Civil Service Fraud Statute

93-112. As paragraphs 93 through 112, Plaintiffs restate, as if fully stated herein, paragraphs 23 through 42 of this complaint.

113. Rule 4.00 of the Civil Service Rules of the City of Cleveland provide procedures for the conduct of civil service competitive examinations.

114. The importance of proper administrative procedures with respect to the conduct of civil service examinations is underscored by Ohio Rev. Code § 124.58, which prohibits fraud with respect to defeating, deceiving, or obstructing any person in respect of his right of examination, appointment, or employment. This statute also prohibits willful, corrupt, or false grading of examinations and other matters.

115. Defendants made material representations to the Plaintiffs, falsely and fraudulently, that the City of Cleveland was seeking to appoint women firefighters, thereby inducing Plaintiff to apply to take the firefighter examination.

116. These representations, whether oral or in writing, by the Defendants were known to be false by some or all of the Defendants at the time these

representations were made and were made willfully and maliciously with intent to induce Plaintiffs to take the firefighter examination and to deceive and deny Plaintiffs their civil rights.

117. Plaintiffs, relying upon the false representations and the representation of the Defendants that the women's training program would adequately prepare them for the firefighter examination, enrolled in the women's training program, spent substantial time preparing for the Civil Service Commission firefighting examination, and completed those tests which they were permitted to take in their attempt to qualify for firefighter positions.

118. The Defendants, having induced the Plaintiffs to take tests which discriminated against women based upon their sex, then also administered and evaluated these tests in a discriminatory, willful, and malicious fashion.

119. As a result of these false and fraudulent representations of the Defendants, Plaintiffs were proximately injured and suffered economic loss, loss of career opportunity, humiliation, and emotional distress.

## RELIEF PRAYED

120. WHEREFORE, Plaintiffs respectfully pray that this Honorable Court:

(a) Declare unlawful the policies and practices of the Defendants set forth in paragraphs 23 through 42 above;

(b) Enjoin the Defendants, both preliminarily and permanently, from declaring the Plaintiffs and others of their class to be either ineligible or too low ranking on the eligibility list for appointment to entry-level firefighter positions on the basis of unvalidated tests which have a disparate effect upon females solely because of their sex;

(c) Direct that the Defendant City of Cleveland, its Mayor, department directors, civil service commission, and others undertake a program to formulate, promulgate, and implement a uniform and nondiscriminatory procedure and policy with respect to the recruiting, hiring, and training of female firefighters;

(d) Enjoin, both preliminarily and permanently, all additions of veterans' preference points to written test scores;

(e) Award Plaintiffs and the members of the class they represent compensatory damages, also including back pay;

(f) Award Plaintiffs and the members of the class they represent punitive damages, also including costs and attorneys' fees; and

(g) Grant such other affirmative relief as the Court deems just and appropriate.

Respectfully Submitted
By Their Attorney


_____ /s/ E. Julia Jennifer _____
Elisabeth Julia Jennifer
Jennifer, Berton & Abrahams
56 Joan Street
Cleveland, Ohio 44114

Dated: /d/

## EXHIBIT A

## CLEVELAND ENTRY LEVEL EXAM FOR FIREFIGHTERS
## PART II—PHYSICAL STRENGTH, ENDURANCE,
## AND ABILITY TEST

Place: Cleveland Fire Academy, 3250 Lakeside Avenue
Date: May 7—May 13, 2011

Your scheduled date and time are marked on your $3 \times 5$ ticket. . . .

(1) If it is impossible for you to appear at the date and time scheduled on your white ticket, stop at the re-scheduling desk as you leave.

(2) Parking near the Academy is limited, allow time to park and reach the Academy by your scheduled time.

(3) Bring your ticket; it is your ticket of admission to the Academy testing area. You will get no other notice concerning the physical test unless you fail to qualify on the written exam. Persons not scheduled for testing during that specific half-hour session will not be admitted to the Academy testing area.

(4) Wear comfortable clothing and sneakers or rubber-soled shoes similar to those you would wear when participating in a demanding athletic event.

(5) Check with your doctor before participating in the physical ability test if you have circulatory, respiratory, or other problems that have required medical attention, if you have a blood pressure of 150/100 or higher, or if you are taking medication.

(6) Avoid eating, drinking coffee, or smoking for at least two hours before your scheduled testing session. It is also advisable to allow yourself ten minutes of warm-up and stretching exercises before signing in to begin the test.

The physical abilities exam is designed to measure aerobic fitness, muscular strength and endurance, balance, and speed as these factors relate to frequently encountered tasks involved in firefighting and rescue. Where possible we have tried to simulate firefighter activities which do not require special prior training. Where special training, safety concerns, or physical constraints exist, test elements have been modified to measure the same skills and abilities in a more practical and standardized manner.

In all cases it is the responsibility of the candidate to complete the exercises as rapidly as possible without risking personal injury through carelessness or reckless actions. Falls and/or minor injuries incurred during an event can cost you far more than one or two extra seconds spent exercising caution.

There are three events as described below. In each case you will earn from 0 to the maximum points listed (in fractional steps), based on your performance. There is no absolute pass/fail cut-off on each individual event, but you must score a total of 35 out of 50 points (70 percent) to pass the agility test.

Event 1—Upper arm and shoulder muscular endurance—(10 pts.) Raise bar bell (approx. 33 lb.) to chin level. On signal raise barbell overhead to full arm extension and then lower to chin level. Repeat rapidly for 60 seconds or until a maximum of 35 lifts are completed. Score will be based on total successful lifts in one minute up to the maximum of 35. Lifts involving the bending of knees and/or use of legs will be discounted. You must proceed immediately to Event 2. If you delay being tested so that you drop out of the testing sequence, you will be disqualified.

Events 2 and 3 will be run with the applicant carrying a standard self-contained breathing apparatus on his/her back (excluding mask and regulator), weighing approximately 40 lb.

Event 2—Fire scene set-up and building entry—(25 pts.) Grab one end and drag 100 ft. of 4.5 in. hose 90 ft.; drop and run to other end of hose; pick up and drag 90 ft. back to start area; run to fire apparatus (70 ft.); remove 12 ft. extension ladder (35 lb.); enter fire tower (45 ft. away), place ladder against wall of first landing; continue up the inside stairwell to the fourth story above ground level; return to first landing; remove ladder and replace on fire apparatus. Approximately 340 ft. total run plus 40 ft. vertical ascent and descent. Score based on total time required from beginning of hose drag to return of ladder to side of fire apparatus.

Event 3—Simulated interior fire rescue—(15 pts.) Grasp handle of dead weight (100 lb); pull 20 ft to low headroom drag area (30 in. high, 40 in. wide); crawl and drag weight through low headroom area (36 ft.); drag weight 16 ft. past marker; return to start area through low headroom drag area. Distance approx. 144 ft. Score based on total time.

All distances, weights, and other measures are approximate. Minor procedural, equipment, and/or measurement changes may be invoked at the time of the exam.

## Memorandum Re Directed Verdict*

To:        Judicial Clerks

From:   Judge Paz, United States District Court for the Northern District of
            Ohio

Re:        Defendant City of Cleveland's Directed Verdict (Judgement as a
            Matter of Law) Motion in Barbara Zoll, et al. v. City of Cleveland.

As you know, I have been hearing plaintiff's evidence in this case for the
past week. I am sure that the city will move for a directed verdict (now a Fed.
R. Civ. P. 50 motion for judgment as a matter of law) as soon as the plaintiffs
rest, which should be any hour now. I want to decide the motion fairly quickly,
once plaintiffs rest, so that counsel, witnesses, and the jury know what to do.
So please be prepared to advise me on a moment's notice.

What I will do now is bring you up to date on the case, and at the end of
this memo I will give you a photostat of the relevant portions of my trial
notebook summarizing the evidence. If more evidence comes in the next
few hours that I think is at all relevant to the motion I will tell you later.

You've seen the complaint previously, and you have told me that during
your civil procedure course you were exposed to civil rights actions under
Sections 1983 and 1985, and Title VII cases. This is a class action brought
on behalf of entry-level female firefighters in the City of Cleveland, challenging the rank-order written and physical capabilities selection examination
established by the city as perpetuating the exclusion of women from firefighting positions.

The plaintiffs have proceeded under four causes of action. Count One is
for alleged violations of Title VII of the Civil Rights Act of 1964, as amended.
Count Two alleges a violation of 42 U.S.C. § 1983, based upon violations of the
Due Process and Equal Protection Clauses of the Fourteenth Amendment of
the United States Constitution. Count Three alleges a conspiracy under 42
U.S.C. § 1985(3) to deprive the plaintiffs of their rights under the Due Process
and Equal Protection Clauses of the Fourteen Amendment of the U.S. Constitution. Count Four alleges violations of the Ohio Revised Code § 124.58
("Frauds in examinations prohibited").

The only defendant remaining in the case is the City of Cleveland. The
plaintiffs have settled with Sheldon Marshall, the expert who devised the

*Eds.' Note: This memorandum and the following trial notebook are based on the actual trial, but
have been drafted solely for the purposes of this book. Some testimony has been modified, added, and
eliminated for pedagogical purposes.

tests in question, and have now dismissed against all other defendants except the city. Nonetheless, to the extent that a city official's or agent's activity is relevant to making the city liable, such activity can be considered. I assume that the city will move for directed verdict on all four counts. Ignore that this is a class action, and treat the named plaintiffs as individuals for purposes of this motion. Also ignore any issues relating to the type or amount of damages, for I have bifurcated liability from questions of damages or types of injunctive relief.

I have already decided that I will deny any motion for directed verdict against the Title VII count, because I am sure that the plaintiffs' statistics with respect to virtually no hiring of females ("disparate impact") shifts the burdens of production and persuasion to the defendants to prove the "business necessity defense." In the words of the Cook and Sobieski treatise, "Under the 1991 Act, an employer may successfully defend a disparate impact resulting from an employment practice by demonstrating 'that the challenged practice is job related for the position in question and consistent with business necessity.'" I am confident that the plaintiffs' statistical evidence has placed that burden on defendants.

I have asked counsel to consider (i) whether they are entitled to a trial by jury on only the Title VII count; and (ii) whether they would be willing to have me decide the Title VII count alone, without a jury, since it involves so much detailed information about testing. I think the lawyers are leaning in that direction—proceeding without a jury—if only Title VII remains.

I suspect that the defendant's motion for directed verdict on the other three counts will rely on the following potential weaknesses in plaintiffs' case, which I will explain.* As to the Ohio statute (Ohio Rev. Code, Sec. 124.58), take a look at the exact wording of the statute. The term "frauds" in the title, and the repeated use of such words as "willfully or corruptly" and "deceive," "falsely," and "false" suggest to me that defendants will say there is no evidence of misstatements of existing facts with intent to deceive. My clerks with last names beginning with the letters A-G should particularly be prepared to advise me on the directed verdict motion relating to that count. It is critical that you read each clause of the statute and analyze the evidence as to each clause. Do the plaintiffs have a stronger shot at surviving the directed verdict motion as to any particularly clause? What evidence makes you think so?

It seems to me that the plaintiffs may have trouble with "conspiracy" aspects of the 42 U.S.C. § 1985(3) count, but I want you to also consider what else they have to prove substantively in this count. My clerks with

---

*Eds.' Note:* Students may also find it useful to reread the legal analysis portions of the Initial Memorandum in these *City of Cleveland* Case Files.

last names beginning with the letters H-P should particularly analyze plaintiffs' production burden with respect to that count. The law is clear that all conspirators do not have to be named as co-defendants, nor do they have to remain in the case for the jury to consider whether there was a conspiracy within the meaning of § 1985(3). In other words, you will have to analyze the activity of the Mayor, Dr. Marshall, fire department officials, etc., to the extent there is evidence about them, even though the only defendant is now the City. A conspiracy is often defined as follows: "a combination, or an agreement between two or more persons, for accomplishing an unlawful end or a lawful end by unlawful means."

I suspect that 42 U.S.C. § 1983 may present the closest case with respect to whether or not the plaintiffs can survive a directed verdict motion. My clerks with last names beginning with the letters Q-Z should concentrate on any directed verdict motion directed to that count. On this cause of action, I suspect the plaintiffs may have problems with both intent and causation. In other words, the prima facie case under § 1983 requires that the plaintiffs produce evidence that directly and/or circumstantially (through the use of inferences) would permit a reasonable jury to find that a defendant "purposefully and intentionally" discriminated against women and that the defendant's activity caused the harm claimed, which I take it is the failure of women to secure positions as firefighters. With respect to the city, it is not enough that some official unilaterally had an animus against women, or did not like the idea of women becoming firefighters. The city or the fire department must have had a policy to discriminate, which is different from a series of isolated events. The question is whether a reasonable jury on the evidence could find such a policy, bearing in mind that such a policy need not be articulated in writing or orally; it could be inferred, if such an inference is a reasonable one.

## Portions of Judge Paz's Trial Notebook

Evidence Admitted in *Barbara Zoll, Jennifer Grimes, et al. v. City of Cleveland* which might be relevant to directed verdict motion.

Plaintiffs' first witness, Mayor James Kosolsky: testifies that he has been mayor of the City of Cleveland for about eight years. Doesn't know exactly when he found out, but "I certainly knew that the fire department was absent of any women firefighters." (Pl. Ex. 1: "Mayor Policy Statement of Affirmative Action and Equal Employment Opportunity.") He made "a commitment to the city to develop and implement result-oriented goals, procedures and programs to reduce the underutilization of minorities and women and to achieve equity throughout the city's workforce." Wanted testing procedures that "would not preclude women from being members of the Cleveland Fire Department, but at the same time would guarantee that the dept. would have qualified individuals." Knows there are now women firefighters in other fire departments in the U.S. "Hammered away at his people that I want this to be the best doggone test there can be. I don't want anybody charging that we are trying to discriminate or preclude anybody from being a member of any of our departments or the city service." Reads from document that says "Fire Division has set a goal to hire seven blacks and two Hispanics as firefighters." Admits that no number of women specifically listed as a goal. Two years later, a document says: goal to hire one woman as typist in fire department. Testifies that reason number set for black and Hispanic firefighters was result of consent decree in another case. Fire department had 1,010 paid members. Three were women, none as uniformed firefighters.

Cross-examination by city attorney (as on direct): Firefighters job is "to protect the health, safety and welfare of the citizens of Cleveland. That's the overriding thing that we are trying to get done. We are in the service business, and want to get the best service that we can possibly provide and have the best people we can to provide the service."

*Q:* "Mayor, did you ever intentionally discriminate with respect to the female applicants who sought employment in the Division of Fire?"
*A:* "Absolutely not."

Re-direct of mayor (as on cross): He's not suggesting in any way that the objective of bringing women into the firefighters' workforce is in conflict with the goal of bringing in firefighters for protection of the health and safety and welfare of the citizens of Cleveland.

Plaintiffs read to the jury certain requests for admission that have been admitted by all defendants, as well as certain stipulations agreed to by all parties. My summary of data on the written and physical examinations to become a uniform firefighter in Cleveland, Ohio (these are the examinations being challenged in this lawsuit): There were initially 3,612 applicants. 2,212 took the written part of the test. 1,233 took the physical part. Each portion of the examination was worth a raw score of 50 points, with a maximum achievable score (with the two tests combined) of 100. The raw scores on the written portion were adjusted by capping the scores from the different sections, by awarding 5 extra points to qualifying veterans, by awarding 10 extra points to city residents, and by adding 6 points to the scores of minority candidates. The veteran and resident point adjustments were made pursuant to provisions in the city charter. The minority adjustment was undertaken as a means of complying with a consent decree entered against the city in a suit by minority candidates alleging bias in hiring. Only those applicants with adjusted-score of at least 35 were eligible to take the physical portion of the exam. 285 females took the written portion; 122 passed. 1,927 males took the written portion; 1,206 passed. The maximum attainable score for candidates on the physical portion of the exam was 50. 35 was considered a passing score. Of the 1,125 men taking the physical test, 1,002 passed. Of the 101 women taking the physical test, 15 passed. After taking the physical portion of the examination, 29 females and 1,069 males scored high enough on both portions of the exam to be placed on the eligibility list. The woman with the highest score ranked 334 on the eligibility list, which was too low to be hired. The class of 35 firefighters hired in the two year period as a result of the exam in question contained no women.

Percentage of males passing the written examination was 62.5%. Percentage of females was 42.8%. 89.3% of males received a score of 35 or higher on the physical portion of the exam in question; 14.0% of the females who took it had 35 or higher on this portion.

The eligibility list is compiled of those whose combined scores on both tests (including the adjustments on the written portion) was 69.5 or higher. The general practice, based on the city's charter, is for the director of public safety to hire in strict top/down rank numerical order from the eligibility list, the only exception being for the hiring of a black/Hispanic quota pursuant to a court decree, designed to remedy intentional and egregious racial discrimination. After establishment of the eligibility list, further selection components include a medical test, a psychological test, and a background check. These three procedures are conducted only upon the highest ranking candidates who have any realistic chance of being hired.

The rate at which women received a combined written and physical score high enough to be placed upon the eligibility list was dramatically less than the rate at which men received a combined written and physical score high enough to be placed on the eligibility list.

According to the most relevant United States Census, the workforce in the Cleveland Standard Metropolitan Statistical Area is 46% female.

Plaintiffs' next witness was Janet Quigley. Worked for the Employment Litigation Section, Civil Rights Division, U.S. Department of Justice, Washington, D.C. A mathematical statistician. Based on education and experience, I qualified her as an expert in statistical analysis. She is trained to compute standard deviation numbers—"a measure of fluctuation from what actually occurred in an event from what is expected to occur under normal circumstances or due to chance." She computed standard deviations for the physical performance examination in question. 1,233 applicants took it; of those, 108 or 8.3% were female. On the final eligibility list, 29 or 2.6% were female. In normal circumstances or due to chance, we'd expect to have 91 of those females scoring high enough on the examination. The difference is 62, and the number of standard deviations acquired is 6.76. "The probability of this event is 1 in 10 billion, approximately zero." Used the same method to calculate standard deviation for those applicants (1017) who scored 35 or higher on physical examination. 1,002 or 98.5% were male and 15 or 1.5% were female. Using the same methodology as before, we would have expected 84 females to have scored 35 or higher. The probability of what in fact happened was 1 in 10,000 billion, approximately zero (other similar statistics).

Cross-examination by counsel for the city. Witness admits she just looked at numbers. Didn't know the physical or the mental ability of anyone who took the examinations. Admits that five times as many women took the physical exam in the year in question than when the exam was previously given two years before.

Summary of testimony about the test itself, compiled from testimony of several witnesses, including Dr. Marshall: Test was prepared by Dr. Marshall, who has extensive experience in the area of job analysis and examination development for safety forces, including the position of entry-level firefighter. Interviewed hundreds of firefighters and high ranking officers, read firefighting manuals and books, made and analyzed questionnaires to ascertain the frequency and importance of firefighting tasks. Based on women failing to rank high on previous eligibility lists, he was concerned about gender differences, and wanted to minimize adverse impact tests had on females. At same time, wants test to show best people for job.

Based upon extensive research, and comparison of his findings with manuals and lists of tasks used in other cities, Dr. Marshall developed final written and physical components of the examination. The written component was designed to test reading comprehension, the ability to follow directions, mathematical skills, and other forms of cognitive reasoning. Much of the information tested came from the Ohio Fire Service Training Manual. The physical component consisted of three events:

Event 1: **Overhead Lift**—using a 33 lb. barbell, candidates must lift the barbell overhead repeatedly for one minute or up to a maximum of 35 lifts. Cannot bend knees; must be locked.

Event: 2: **Fire Scene Set Up and Tower Climb**—while wearing a custom-tailored self-contained breathing apparatus, candidates must drag two lengths of standard 2 1/2 inch hose 180 feet (90 feet one way, drop coupling, run to the other end of the hose, pick up and return 90 feet, drop coupling in designated area), run 75 feet to pumper, remove a one-person ladder (approximately 35 lb.) from the side of the pumper, carry the ladder into the fire tower, place it against the back rail of the first landing and continue up the inside stairwell to the fifth floor where a monitor observes the candidates' arrival. Then, candidates return to the first landing, retrieve the ladder and place it on the pumper.

Event 3: **Dummy Drag**—still wearing their self-contained breathing apparatus, candidates must drag a 100 lb. bag 70 feet (40 of which includes low headroom), turn and, still dragging the bag, return to the starting point.

Dr. Marshall was paid by the city, and worked closely with fire department officers from the city. Worked most with Assistant Chief Adams on this test, and on previous ones. Marshall had worked for the city many times previously. He knew that the barbell event was "something most women wouldn't be familiar with at all." When he saw how badly women did on the event, he decided on his own late one evening after the event to add one and three-quarter points for each women on this event. Many firemen told him and he believes that strength and speed are critical to firefighters, particularly in the first few minutes after the uniform firefighters arrive at a fire. His test concentrated on anaerobic abilities, and he knows women do better on aerobic exercises. But aerobic capacity is tested in the physical given to those whose names have been taken from the eligibility list. The sequencing of the three events is not related to how it is done in actually fighting fires. Marshall knew before he created the barbell test that introducing above-your-head lifting had eliminated women from the Cleveland Emergency Medical Technician testing. For the barbell test, applicants were not permitted to bend their knees. Firefighters bend their knees ordinarily when carrying ladders and other heavy objects.

Testimony of Alice Simons, Secretary of the Civil Service Division, Cleveland. She gave out applications and advice re: tests and openings in question. May have said under her breath to a woman applicant: "Why don't you stay home and have babies." (Other witness testifies she said this.) Yes, she did ask one female applicant why she wanted to be a firefighter. Did allow two men to apply late, but they were already in the building when it closed at the end of the last permitted day. Told them to come back first thing the next day the building was open, even though it was beyond the date. "After all, they were already in the building." Late-filing woman was different; she hadn't been in building.

Testimony of William M. Adams. Direct: Employed by Division of Fire for twenty-seven years. Now assistant-chief. In charge of fire suppression forces on one shift for the entire City of Cleveland. Cleveland is one of few cities in state with their own fire training academy. Cleveland part of nationwide program to rate all firefighters into groups, according to proficiency. Group One less proficiency than Two, Two less than Three and Four, etc. The National Fire Protection Association (NFPA) sets standards for fire instruction, equipment, and other matters. NFPA and our department agree you can train firefighters to be better throughout their careers. Cleveland has a firefighters' training manual. Worked extensively with Dr. Marshall in months just before the test in question. He suggested to Dr. Marshall that barbell lifts might be one way to test for important physical skills for firefighters. Doesn't remember if talked about locking the knees. May have suggested the running and dragging event. Can't recall. He had taken prior exams where they had to pick up 120 to 150 pound dummies. Often have to carry heavy things in hurry. Sometimes have to do it crawling. "Hand straps" can be used to carry people out. They weren't used in the physical exam.

Witness had talked to Dr. Marshall before Marshall prepared the tests in question, and they had discussed matters taken directly from the Ohio Fire Service Training Manual. He identifies differences between the ARCO training book and the Fire Service Training Manual. Question: "Now, if someone knew that Dr. Marshall was going to use the Fire Service Training Manual, he or she could do a better job in taking the written test, isn't that true?" Answer: "I don't know if that would be a true statement or not." He did tell the women at the Fire Service Training Academy that "if they study hard the Arco book, they would do well on the exam." He knew that in the Buddy Casey course, which applicants paid to take, they were told to study from the Fire Service Training Manual.

Jury is read answers to interrogatories showing that women who took the Casey course did significantly better on both portions of the exam than women who only took the free course that was designed specifically to help women prepare for the exams. The free course specifically designed for women was given by Kevin Kelly.

Yes, he did think that women would be chosen from a different list. This was the "scuttlebutt." Question: "But you communicated to the women that they were going to be hired off the list. Women will testify that they heard you say that. Do you recall making those statements?" Answer: "Yes. Again I wasn't speaking as a Cleveland Fire Department official. I was telling them this is my belief." Yes, he has observed women actually performing, fighting live fires. Maybe 15 to 20 times. Probably all types. Probably saw them using pipe poles and saw them dragging hoses. Probably saw them in two story fires and probably saw them take ladders off the hook and ladder. Probably some of them had higher and some lower scores than men. Question: "And would you rate some of the woman firefighters better than other male cadets?" Answer: "Well they are probably better than some and worse than others, yes." Some of the women observed were lower on eligibility lists then men. Admits in former deposition saying: "Some of these women who were firefighters ranked lower than male cadets, but performed better than those male cadets." Now adds: "On certain tasks they did."

Jury shown the announcement given to all applicants about the tests in question. It did not mention barbells. It said: "The physical agility portion will measure endurance, upper and lower body strength, and hand/eye coordination. Candidates will be required to perform a series of events using actual firefighting equipment and such equipment may have to be carried up and down stairs. You will have to perform a simulated rescue with a dummy of adult body weight. You are recommended to increase your physical endurance in order to maximize your performance on the examination." Previous announcements, also shown to the jury, had been more specific about each aspect of the physical test.

Testimony of Kevin Kelly. Direct. In the department for 22 years. Now a Lieutenant. Has heard firefighters, assistant chiefs, and other officers say many times that women don't belong in fire department, that they aren't strong and fast enough; that they "can't come through in a pinch." Heard such stuff from Assistant Chief Adams as recently as one year before the test in question. Can't recall exact words. He knows women firefighters are presently in the cities of Columbus, Ohio; New York, New York; Seattle, Washington; and other major cities. Some fire departments don't choose by rank order on exams. Instead, they put everyone together who has passed the exams, basically a pass/fail test. Some attempt to achieve diversity from that larger pool. Some have random selection from all those who have passed, pure chance.

Was at meeting when Safety Director Harry Tarpley expressed his view that objections to women as firefighters because of their physical capacity "were invalid." Kelly testifies that Tarpley "expressed his belief that it is an operational need for the City's Fire Department to have a personnel force reflective of Cleveland's population, male and female, because the community expects this kind of reflection—it provides awareness, a sensitivity to community problems and enhances the division's ability to function within the community." Safety Director Tarpley did not recommend any new criteria for the employment of firefighters from those applied in prior years except for an effort to recruit minorities and women. Tarpley had said he was satisfied with the qualifications of applicants on the eligibility list prepared three years before the one in question. He didn't suggest that either the written or physical components of the exam be made more difficult.

Kelly, continuing: Sometime after Marshall's tests had been developed, but before they were administered, the city started a program to recruit and train female firefighters. As part of the recruitment program, the city advertised and gave a free twelve-week training program. There was also a minority pre-test training program conducted by the city which was attended by both males and females. Also there was the $500 course given by Buddy Casey, a retired lieutenant from the department. He had been doing this for years. Because of his interest, and previous experience teaching firefighters, Kelly was chosen to design and implement a pre-examination recruitment and training program for women interested in becoming firefighters. "I undertook this program under the direction of Chief McGinnis, Assistant Chief Gainsley and Safety Director Tarpley." I sought and received funding from the Comprehensive Employment and Training Act (CETA) program for the women's training program to pay for textbooks, equipment, and instructors. I was assigned this project as part of my regular duties, and relieved from doing some other things. But I spent hundreds more hours on this than what I got paid for; "I wanted to do it. It made sense to me."

My course met twelve times, four hours each. Two and a half hours were on physical activities, and the rest on cognitive. Written portion was based primarily on the then current edition of the ARCO Civil Service Test training manual. I thought this would work best and didn't know of Dr. Marshall's reliance on the Ohio Fire Service Training Manual. Physical portion of my course based primarily on the content of previous examinations, including training in such activities as dummy lift and carry, dummy drag, hose drag, tower run, fence climb, ladder lift, balance beam walk, and hose coupling. The program didn't include training in the use of barbells, and I didn't recommend to any of the women that she work with barbells prior to the examination. One week before the actual physical examination, the city notified all applicants of the content of the examination, including the barbell event. I obtained a set of barbells and made them available to my students. "In my opinion, with additional training, the women could have become more proficient with barbells." Chief McGinnis—Chief of the Cleveland Fire Department—never came to any of the classes, and "pretty much left me to design my own course."

Testimony of Buddy Casey: Former lieutenant, Cleveland Fire Department. Father was a policeman. Been giving my course for over ten years. In year in question, 485 persons enrolled in my Police and Fire School. My curriculum based on prior examinations and from study guide previously prepared by Dr. Marshall. These materials indicated to me that mechanical reasoning and technical subjects would be covered on the written component of the exam, including material from the Ohio Fire Training Manual. Based on Marshall's earlier tests, my training included a dummy drag, a hose drag (2 1/2 inch hose), and a stair climb carrying a donut roll of hose. I recommended weight lifting to develop biceps and forearms to enable candidates to carry the donut roll up 5 to 6 flights of stairs. Of the top 100 persons on the eligibility list in question, 48 were my students. Of the top 200, 92 or 93 were mine. Of the top 300, 134 took my class. Six of the nine women who took my course were on the eligibility list. "I am charging them a lot of money. I have a real incentive to give the best course possible."

Testimony of Barbara Zoll: Lives in Cleveland. Applied for and took entry level firefighter examination for year in question. Saw announcement by mayor that city looking for more minorities and women in fire department. Reads from announcement: "Contact our minority and women special recruitment office at 10539 St. Clair, weekdays 9:00 to 8:00 and Saturdays 9:00 to 1:00. You must be 18 or older with a high school diploma or GED. For more information call 555-2000." I thought I'd be good at firefighting. I'm pretty athletic, and run 40 to 60 miles a week. Have been doing it for several years. Had run and finished in D.C. marathon, 26.2 miles. Three years before test, I had finished a marathon in four hours. Had run Honolulu, Revco, Montreal (in 323), and Boston marathons. Friend told me of pretest training program for women—free, I liked that. Went to some of them. I also took the Casey paid course. ARCO manual given me at women's class. Casey went over tests he had prepared, concentrated on tools, electricity, currents, math, physics, fulcrums, pulleys, stuff that appeared on the actual exam. Casey took us at the end of each class to lift weights at Cleveland State. Had us put weights in backpack and run up stairs. Moved to Cleveland proper so I'd get ten more points. I was crazy to pass. I thought they'd for sure hire women, from what I heard. First given details about physical portion right after the written exam. Surprised that barbells now appeared. My physical was eleven days later. Afraid to go work on barbells now, because "if you pull something, you're going to be out of the competition." Got 48.5 out of 50 on the written portion. I felt adequately prepared on that part, had even taken books out of library. Barbell was first part of physical. I did about 22 in allotted time. "When I didn't make the required 35 lifts, I just felt like I had blown all my chances. Really depressed about it." But still did other events. Women's training program didn't teach the sequencing of events—the second test— like it was given. Then had to pull a hundred pound dummy under tables. The training programs did not have this particular dummy event. In the test, every time you got too high the tank caught, and you got stuck. Cost time. I watched others do it. Many of the later people took off their shoes, and went under first (ducking). It was definitely something you easily could have been taught to do better, faster. With shoes off, some people's feet slipped. "So the guys took their shoes off and their socks and were doing it in their bare feet. Your feet are moist, you are not going to slip and they go right through there right underneath." No monitors told them not to do this. These techniques were not taught at the women's training program. Some candidates had more time between three physical tests than others.

I took other city and towns' tests, too, and passed. But not hired. Not large enough departments to have openings. I was ecstatic when I found out I passed the Cleveland exam. Later a neighbor told me I got something from Civil Service. I ran home; was number 642 on list. Overwhelmed, started crying.

Cross-examination. Got 33.32 on physical portion. Not get veteran points. Women's times on marathons not as good as men. Flier she read didn't talk of preferential treatment for women. Thought might get hired because they gave special course for women, and she did well compared to other women in the course. Admits she "washed out" when took Parma, Ohio physical test. Slipped on the water. Disqualified on very first test in Parma. And slipped and lost momentum in Cleveland dummy drag too. Shown exhibit of announcement of test. Admits that it lists she should be prepared to carry equipment up and down stairs. And should be prepared to rescue dummies of adult body weight. Did all or part of the preparatory courses. Ran marathons. Worked a little on Nautilus machines. Worked on upper body strength. Two out of three tests concentrate on leg muscles. Was told could rip dummy so could have handle. Those who had more time between tests was random, luck of the draw. No sign said men could take off shoes, and women couldn't on the dummy-drag. No problem on application process itself.

Re-direct. Announcement said to wear sneakers or rubber-sole shoes "similar to those you would wear when participating in a demanding athletic event." Would have removed shoes if knew it was allowed for the dummy drag event.

Testimony of Jennifer Grimes: Read article in Plain Dealer saying fire department wanted women to apply. Attracted to fact that there would be special training program for women. Was member of Scandinavia Club, and already working on nautilus. Worked on arms and legs. Went to special Kelly free course for women once or twice every week given. ARCO book used exclusively in that class, "I studied it." Went to Community College and took some math. Eager to prepare for exam in question. "My understanding was that the city intended to hire women and that I believed that they had a certain number that they wanted to hire." I got this understanding at the special women's course. First learned of actual physical events after we finished the written portion. Surprised that barbells listed. Not worked on any types of weights in the special program. Had from April 30 (written) to May 9th to prepare for actual events. Physical given me on May 9. (period was May 7 through May 13; I was given 9th) Didn't start barbell training then; not want to strain self.

Never told to study from Fire Training Manual. ARCO book never mentioned classifications and uses of fire extinguishers. When I took exam, I could see I wasn't adequately trained. I did 33 of 35 barbells, and felt very shaky afterwards. I was surprised how my body acted. Nothing in training prepared me for this. On hose and ladder run, we had trained separately in the class, but never in that type of sequence. If it would have been pass/fail and I could have paced myself, I could have passed that portion. The required speed made it difficult. Dummy had a ring at the end of it. It was different than the one we had in training. One in training the weight was distributed in a way it was easier to pull. Never told I could take off shoes to do the dummy drag.

Took exams in four other towns. Brook Park written exam was more just reading comprehension. Was 13 out of 400 in Brook Park, including both physical and written. More balance and agility tests. Also mile or mile and a half run. Many were pass/fail events.

Not aware that one could apply for Cleveland exam after the date given. Got veteran points in Cleveland. Was 952 on eligibility list. Surprised they didn't hire women after the training programs they put us through.

Cross-examination: No trouble getting or completing application. Never discouraged by any Cleveland official. Was given sample questions by the city. City sent her notice of special training program. Nothing in newspaper article said they would hire women regardless of performance on exams. Would have still taken exam even if hadn't got impression women would be on a separate list. Didn't have to pay for women's course. Knew about $500 course by Buddy Casey. Even though women's course met four times a week for twelve weeks, only went once or twice a week. Sometimes left classes early. Had opportunity in class to do dummy drag. Given practice lifting ladders, and running up tower. Maybe missed some things when not there. And had opportunity to drag a hose at the women's class. And it was timed, like in the exam. And given practice carrying objects, like in the exam. Maybe missed other materials besides the ARCO book when she was absent. Instructors encouraged her to believe in self at the women's course. No males in course when she practiced running the tower and doing the dummy drag and dummy carry.

N.B. There was other evidence from other members of the plaintiff class, but it was cumulative, and didn't add anything for directed verdict purposes.

I asked plaintiffs' counsel whether they were going to put in their expert evidence on alleged deficiencies in the tests during their case in chief. They said that as a matter of strategy, and because the United States Government controlled the expert witnesses, their basic attacks on the content, criterion-related, and construct validity of the tests would await the defendants' defending the tests in the second tier of the Title VII case. In other words, the plaintiffs would use their statistics to shift the burden of going forward to the city on the business necessity defense, and the plaintiffs would then attack the business necessity and try to show "pretext" in the third tier. I suggested that the evidence on pretext might be relevant to "intent" and "purpose" in the Section 1983 case, and that such evidence might be critical to meet their production burden as to the non-Title VII counts. They said they thought the statistics and their other evidence would be sufficient at this stage of the case. I assume they didn't want to tip their hand to the city on test-validity evidence, before the city had to defend their tests at the second tier of the Title VII case.

IN THE UNITED STATES DISTRICT COURT*
FOR THE NORTHERN DISTRICT OF OHIO
EASTERN DIVISION

| | |
|---|---|
| UNITED STATES OF AMERICA,<br>Plaintiff, | C.A. No. 12-4773<br>Judge Arthur L. Paz |
| vs. | MOTION OF THE PLAINTIFF<br>UNITED STATES TO BIFURCATE |
| CITY OF CLEVELAND, et al.,<br>Defendants. | FOR TRIAL THE ISSUES OF<br>LIABILITY AND INDIVIDUAL<br>RELIEF |

Plaintiff United States hereby moves this Court under Rule 42(b) of the Federal Rules of Civil Procedure to bifurcate the trial of this case into two stages: liability stage (Stage I) and an individual relief stage (Stage II).

The Supreme Court in *International Brotherhood of Teamsters v. United States*, 431 U.S. 324 (1977) has specifically approved such a bifurcated trial of cases of this nature. Moreover, division of the trial into a liability stage and an individual relief stage will serve the interests of judicial economy and accelerate the disposition of this case.

The attached memorandum provides points and authorities in support of this motion. Also attached is a proposed order providing for the bifurcation.

Respectfully submitted,

_____ /s/ Ruggero Calipari _____
Ruggero Calipari
Attorney, U.S. Dept. of Justice
Civil Rights Division
Employment Litigation Section
Washington, D.C. 20530
(202) 555-4171

Dated: /d/

*Eds.' Note:* This was the case brought by the United States government on the same facts as the Zoll and Grimes case, but the government sued only under Title VII. The cases were consolidated for trial.

IN THE UNITED STATES DISTRICT COURT*
FOR THE NORTHERN DISTRICT OF OHIO
EASTERN DIVISION

| | |
|---|---|
| UNITED STATES OF AMERICA,<br>  Plaintiff, | C.A. No. 12-4773<br>Judge Arthur L. Paz |
| vs. | MEMORANDUM IN SUPPORT<br>OF MOTION OF THE PLAINTIFF |
| CITY OF CLEVELAND, et al.,<br>  Defendants. | UNITED STATES TO BIFURCATE<br>FOR TRIAL THE ISSUES OF<br>LIABILITY AND INDIVIDUAL<br>RELIEF |

## BACKGROUND

The United States filed this action against the City of Cleveland, the Cleveland Civil Service Commission, the Cleveland Fire Department, and in their official capacities, the Director of the Department of Public Safety, the Fire Chief of the Cleveland Fire Department and the members of the Cleveland Civil Service Commission (hereinafter collectively referred to as "City," "Cleveland" or "City of Cleveland"), alleging, inter alia, that the City of Cleveland was engaged in a pattern or practice of employment discrimination in violation of Title VII of the Civil Rights Act of 1964, as amended, 42 U.S.C. § 2000e et seq. against women with respect to entry level employment opportunities as sworn firefighters in the Cleveland Fire Department.

The complaint alleges that the City of Cleveland's employment practices violate Title VII by the use of selection devices that unlawfully discriminate against female applicants for the fire department because they have an adverse impact based upon sex and are not predictors of successful job performance.

## ARGUMENT

Plaintiff United States has moved this Court for an order bifurcating the trial with regard to the issues concerning Defendants' liability and general injunctive relief (Stage I) and the issues concerning the entitlement of individuals to monetary and other individual make-whole relief (Stage II). Rule

---

*Eds.' Note:* This was the case brought by the United States government on the same facts as the Zoll and Grimes case, but the government sued only under Title VII. The cases were consolidated for trial.

42(b) of the Federal Rules of Civil Procedure provides for such a bifurcated procedure. Rule 42(b) states in relevant part:

> (b) **Separate Trials**. The court, in furtherance of convenience or to avoid prejudice, or when separate trials will be conducive to expedition and economy, may order a separate trial of any . . . issues. . . .

In *International Brotherhood of Teamsters v. United States*, 431 U.S. 324 (1977), the Supreme Court recognized the appropriateness of a bifurcated procedure in pattern or practice suits. The Court explained the first stage of a pattern or practice suit as follows:

> The plaintiff in a pattern-or-practice action is the government, and its initial burden is to demonstrate that unlawful discrimination has been a regular procedure or policy followed by an employer or group of employers. . . . At the initial, "liability" stage of a pattern-or-practice suit the Government is not required to offer evidence that each person for whom it will ultimately seek relief was a victim of the employer's discriminatory policy. Its burden is to establish a prima facie case that such a policy existed. The burden then shifts to the employer to defeat the prima facie showing of a pattern-or-practice by demonstrating that the Government's proof is either inaccurate or insignificant. 431 U.S. 360.

> When the Government seeks individual relief for the victims of the discriminatory practice, a district court must usually conduct additional proceedings after the liability phase of the trial to determine the scope of individual relief. *Id*. at 361. *See also Equal Employment Opportunity Commission v. Monarch Pattern Tool Co.*, 737 F.2d 1444 (6th Cir. 1984).

The United States submits that the two-stage trial procedure recognized in *Teamsters* should be used in this pattern or practice litigation as well. In so doing, the interests of judicial economy would be served. By reserving the determination of the scope and extent of individual relief for Stage II proceedings, the court will expedite the disposition of this case. Part of the relief sought is make-whole relief for potentially numerous individual women who have been harmed by the discriminatory employment practices alleged in the complaint. *See* Section 706(g), 42 U.S.C. § 2000e(g); *Albemarle Paper Go. v. Moody*, 422 U.S. 405 (1975).

It is common practice in employment discrimination cases, where, as here, there are a large number of potential individual claimants, for courts to try liability issues separately from those issues involving individual relief. *See, e.g., United States v. Lee Way Motor Freight, Inc.*, 7 FEP Cases 710, 750 (W.D. Okla. 1973), *aff'd in relevant part*, 625 F.2d 918 (10th Cir. 1979); *United States v. U.S. Steel Corp.*, 520 F.2d 1043, 1052-1056 (5th Cir. 1975); *Love v. Pullman Co.*, 12 FEP Cases 331 (D. Colo. 1975), *aff'd*, 569 F.2d 1074 (10th Cir.

1976); *Ellison v. Rock Hill Printing & Finishing Co.*, 64 F.R.D. 415 (D.S.C. 1974). The rationale for bifurcation was explained by the district court in *Love v. Pullman Co., supra*, this way:

If we order bifurcation and if plaintiffs fail to establish liability, then lengthy discovery and complex evidentiary problems concerning individual membership in the class and individual damages will be unnecessary. Of course, should liability be proved, then a subsequent proceeding will, absent a settlement, be required to determine the validity and amount of individual claims. But we are not persuaded by defendant's contention that bifurcation will somehow delay final disposition of the case, assuming liability is established. By limiting discovery to issues of liability, the trial of those issues may be accelerated in time. Then if liability is found, the parties may resume discovery on damages. We do not believe that evidence relating to the fact of damage, as an element of liability for class-wide discrimination, and proof of individual claims overlaps to any significant extent.

From the foregoing, we conclude that separation for trial of the liability issues from the damages issues in the instant case would be "conducive to expedition and economy" and that defendant will suffer no prejudice thereby. *Love v. Pullman Co.*, 12 FEP Cases at 332.

The United States is aware that a private class action, the Barbara Zoll action, has been consolidated with the United States's action for trial. It should be pointed out, however, that courts typically bifurcate the proceedings in private class actions into a liability stage and an individual relief stage, just as is done in government pattern or practice actions.

As in other cases of this type, the United States anticipates that the City of Cleveland's discrimination may entitle a substantial number of persons to individual relief. Little or no discovery has been taken by any of the parties concerning individual make-whole relief. Naturally, we recognize our threshold burden to establish defendants' liability. To avoid the possibility of expending unnecessary efforts by the Court and the parties concerning matters of discovery and evidence related to individual damages, the Court should reserve issues on individual relief for a Stage II proceeding.

Respectfully submitted,

_____ /s/ Ruggero Calipari _____
Ruggero Calipari
Attorney, U.S. Dept. of Justice
Civil Rights Division
Employment Litigation Section
Washington, D.C. 20530
(202) 555-4171

Dated: /d/

## Transcript of Jury Instructions (on § 1983 Action)

*THE COURT:* Ladies and gentlemen of the jury, we now come to the part of the trial where I will tell you the law.

My charge has been broken down into three laws.

First, the law that applies in just about every civil case, and then I will tell you the law in this case, and then I will tell you about your deliberations.

Now, as I said many times to you, you are the triers of the facts, and I tell you what the law is.

And these instructions are for your guidance in arriving at a verdict in this case. They don't intend to reflect any opinion on the part of the Court, and don't single out any one instruction alone but consider them in their entirety.

You are not concerned with the wisdom of any rule of law, and you are not permitted any personal interpretation. It is your duty to take the law that I give you, and you recall when I picked the jury I said that you must follow the jury instructions regardless of what it was.

Now, in this case it is to be considered as between equal parties. Under our system of law the law is no respector of titles or situations like that, so we have a class of women who are applicants for firefighter against the City of Cleveland.

You are supposed to consider them equal in their standing before the Court.

During the course of the trial the lawyers may have made objections to questions. If I have sustained an objection, you never heard the answer, and don't speculate on what the answer was.

If I overruled the objection, you heard the answer. The lawyers have an obligation to object when they believe an improper question has been asked, so don't hold that against the lawyers because they may have objected.

You are the determiners of the credibility of the witnesses and that really means believability. You can believe all, some of the witnesses' testimony or none of the witnesses' testimony.

Now, witnesses may be discredited or impeached by contradictory evidence, and you heard during the course of the trial that sometimes a witness who had previously been deposed was examined about apparently inconsistent statements between the deposition and now, and you consider all of that in determining the credibility of the witness.

Now, evidence is all of the testimony from the witnesses in the case and usually including exhibits.

In this case it is your combined recollection of all the testimony that will be with you in the jury room, and for simplicity you will rely on your collective recollection of what the evidence is, which is the live testimony of witnesses, and that is how we decide this case.

If a lawyer happens to ask a question in an assertive voice, that is not evidence. The evidence is not what the lawyer says. The lawyer may ask the question, and it may appear to be in the form of testimony, but don't consider the lawyer's statements. It is not evidence, and that includes both opening and closing statements. I told you those were only the lawyer's views of the evidence in the case, and I also permitted the lawyers to tell you before each witness testified, to tell you the purpose of the witness being sworn and testifying, and that you should not consider that as evidence, only the lawyer's view to give you a brief summary of what is to come and give you a better understanding of the witness's testimony.

It is the witness's testimony that is evidence and not the lawyer's preliminary statement.

Now, generally speaking, we have two types of evidence called direct and circumstantial. Now, direct evidence is the testimony or recital of facts by witnesses who have actual knowledge of the incident.

The other is circumstantial or indirect evidence. Circumstantial evidence is evidence of facts or circumstances from which the jury may infer other connected facts which immediately and reasonably follow according to common experience.

There is no distinction between the two. All the law requires is that you find the facts in accordance with a preponderance of all the evidence in the case, both direct and circumstantial.

Now, you heard me mention the word "inference," and while you are to consider only the evidence in the case, you are not limited to the mere bald statements of the witnesses. In other words, you are not limited solely to what you see and hear as the witnesses testify.

In other words, you are permitted to draw from the facts which you find have been proved such reasonable inferences as seem justified in the light of your experiences.

In other words, an inference is a reasonable deduction of fact which logically follows from other facts established by the evidence. In other words, inferences are deductions or conclusions which reason and common sense lead the jury to draw from facts which have been established by the evidence in the case.

The existence of an inference does not change or shift the burden of proof from one party to another. The inference must be weighed along with all the evidence to determine if the issue to which it applies has been established by a preponderance of the evidence.

You are permitted to make any logical and immediate inference from the facts which you find have been established, but you can't make an inference on an inference. You can make an inference or inferences only from the facts.

I already told you about credibility.

Now, burden of proof. That means as follows:

In our system of society when people can't resolve their difference, they resort to litigation, and a person who feels aggrieved will file a lawsuit. That person is the plaintiff.

The other person responds. That's the defendant or defendants.

Now, the plaintiff usually files a complaint in making certain allegations. The allegations of the complaint are not evidence. It only puts the other side on notice what the charges are against them. The other side responds in the form of an answer.

Now, the person who asserts a claim in a complaint has what we call the burden of proof and then must prove the facts that they allege by a preponderance of the evidence, and that's known as burden of proof.

While the burden rests upon the party who asserts an affirmative action to claim by a preponderance of the evidence, they have to prove that claim by the preponderance. It doesn't require absolute certainty, only a preponderance of the evidence.

Simply stated, it is evidence that is more probable, more persuasive and of great probative value. It is the quality of the evidence that must be weighed, and quality may or may not be identical with the quantity, that is, with the greater number of witnesses.

In determining whether or not an issue has been proved by a preponderance of the evidence, you should consider all of the evidence bearing upon that issue regardless of who produced it.

If the evidence is equally balanced or if you are unable to determine which side of an issue has the preponderance, then the party who has the burden of proof has not established such issue by a preponderance of the evidence. That's the simple facts of it.

So that is the general law that is applicable in just about every case, and I am now going to tell you a little bit about the particular law in this case.

This case started with a complaint filed by the plaintiffs. The only defendant now is the City of Cleveland for you to consider, and that would be the only person liable, although we still have some individual—what we call state actors, and I will tell you about that shortly.

Your main concern is whether the City of Cleveland intentionally discriminated against these women firefighters, applicants.

Now, the plaintiffs filed a complaint in which they made the allegations, and I told you about the complaint earlier and you heard the lawyers make reference to the complaint. The allegations in the complaint are not evidence as I told you before.

The City has filed an answer in the form of a general denial which places the simple issues before you as to whether or not the City of Cleveland purposely or purposefully and intentionally discriminated against these women applicants for firefighters in the 2011 examination in the design, preparation and the administration of the test and in making the eligibility list

Now, in this case, we are dealing with Title 42, Section 1983. That's what we call a civil rights action, and it provides, in substance, that no person shall be denied his or her constitutional rights under color of law, and if somebody violates their constitutional rights under color of law, they are liable.

Now, the constitutional right alleged to have been violated in this case is under the Fourteenth Amendment, the due process clause—I mean, equal protection clause that says that no state shall make or enforce any law which shall abridge the privileges or immunities of citizens in the United States, nor shall any state deprive any person of life, liberty or property without due process of law nor deny any person within its jurisdiction the equal protection of laws, and I will explain that to you very, very shortly.

Now, this amendment provides in substance, that there shall be no infringement of a person of his constitutional right of equal protection. Now, this applies to classes of people, and all members of a particular class are entitled to equal protection and they should be treated equally.

I already defined this class to you, and it is simply the applicants for firefighters who were women in the City of Cleveland in 2011, and that's basically what you will consider. And the principal allegation is that they were discriminated against by the defendants, the City of Cleveland, in this examination.

Obviously, as I told you about the purpose, the plaintiff has the burden of proving each and every element of the case by a preponderance of the evidence, and I will define various terms for you and other words that have common meaning so I won't necessarily go over them with you.

The three elements that must be proven in this type of case is whether the defendant purposely or intentionally committed the acts which were charged against him and whether they were under color of law and whether they were the proximate cause of the plaintiffs not being placed higher on the examination and so forth.

Now, under color of law, I am telling you is a matter of law that all the action here was under color of law, so you don't have to concern yourself with that, but our main concern is whether we have a constitutional violation which was under the equal protection clause.

I reviewed with you the statute and the constitutional violation.

Now, an employment practice is not unconstitutional as a violation of equal protection simply because it has a disproportionately adverse impact upon one group or another. In this case, the mere fact that the firefighter entry level examination resulted in males scoring higher than females does not make that examination unconstitutional.

The plaintiffs must prove purposeful discrimination. That is, the plaintiffs must prove by a preponderance of the evidence there was purposeful discrimination and this examination was designed, prepared and administered and so forth to discriminate against females.

Now, what do we mean by purposeful, knowingly, intentional?

An act is done knowingly if it is done voluntarily and intentionally and not because of mistake, accident, negligence or other innocent reason.

Now, an act is intentional if it is done knowingly and done voluntarily and done deliberately and not because of mistake, accident, negligence or other innocent reason.

In determining whether the defendant acted intentionally, we can't get in the mind of people, and you will have to take a look at that and make that determination from all of the facts and circumstances. The City of Cleveland can only be liable if the city policy was one of discrimination against women firefighters, and that's the only way the City can be liable.

We have some municipal actors here. They are not parties in the case, so we are only talking about the City of Cleveland and liability can only come from a policy of the City that would make the City liable.

Now, a policy in simple terms is the general principles or rules by which a government is guided in its management of public affairs. We can have statutes, ordinances, rules, regulations or just operative practices and procedures.

All of these can be considered policies, and it is different than just isolated events. It must be a policy.

Now, you could have one series of events. It could be a policy, but the City can only be liable if its policy was to discriminate against women intentionally or purposefully.

Now, I want to tell you about some things that you heard about in the case, but before I do that, you have heard the word "discrimination" referred to over and over again.

Now, it means the effect of an established practice which confers particular privileges on a class arbitrarily selected from a large number of persons. It is unfair treatment or denial of normal privileges to persons because of their sex and applies in this case, a failure to treat all persons equally where no reasonable distinction can be found between those favored and those not favored.

All of you are familiar with the word "discrimination," so it doesn't need any expert advice to tell you what the word "discrimination" means.

Now, equal protection simply means that all persons shall be treated equally under our laws and under our government procedures.

Now, in order to avoid some confusion, there was a lot of testimony and disputed evidence here and terms and words were used and I better tell you about the legal significance of any of them. The fact that I discuss this with you doesn't mean I have an opinion on them, just what the law is.

Reference was made in the testimony here about other cases and about blacks and Hispanics. Now, this is a case of sex discrimination against women applicant firefighters. Now, I let that testimony in because it may or may not have had an impact on the women applicant firefighters. If you find that it had some relevance and effect on the women firefighters in this case under the charge in this case, then you can consider that along with all the other evidence.

If you find it is totally irrelevant and has no relationship to the issues in this case, you will totally disregard it. The fact that the court of law in another court put an order on the City of Cleveland to give some preferences to black or Hispanic firefighters has no effect on this case unless that policy by that court decree was wrongfully administered to such an extent that it discriminated against women, but to that extent, the City complied, they had to. But don't decide this case based on the facts in that case. You are only dealing with the sex discrimination charge.

Now, you heard some questions about quotas. I am telling you as a matter of law a governmental agency is not required to have a numbered quota, so the fact there was no quota for women has no legal significance.

You heard testimony about affirmative action plan. The City isn't even required to have an affirmative action plan, but once they have such a plan, they are required to implement the plan and comply with the stated policies of the plan.

The City of Cleveland, like all governmental agencies and all private agencies, they are required—prohibited from discriminating against women because of discrimination, because this is a marketplace and a job place and that's the job of the City.

So in regard to the test, you heard a lot of testimony about the test and how it was designed and how it was prepared, how it was administered, how it was graded and how the list was made.

Now, it is for you to decide from all the evidence whether, based on everything you heard, the City policy purposefully and intentionally discriminated against women in regard to the test, and that's what the allegation is.

Once again, I want to remind you we have a thing in law called the totality of the circumstances. You are to decide this based on all of the evidence in the case and all of the direct evidence, all of the circumstantial evidence and all of the inferences that come from the facts that you find have been proven.

Now, the purpose of these tests are they are designed, prepared and administered to select from an adult application pool those candidates most likely to be successful in training and to be successful firefighters, and that's what we call job-related. You heard testimony about job-related in regard to these tests.

Now, you also heard a lot of testimony about the City hiring an expert to prepare the tests. Now, the municipal government has the obligation like the defendant here, to get a qualified testmaker and give him instructions in regard to his guidelines as to the qualifications for the job and the duties to be performed on both the mental and physical aspect of the test, and he should understand what he is doing.

And it is his obligation to develop a test or tests for mental and physical skills that will be job-related and be a fair and reasonable test for skills and abilities and a predictor of successful performance in training as well as a firefighter.

Now, you heard testimony about events and sequence of events, and it is for you to determine from all of the evidence whether there was something in the events that were chosen and the selection of the sequence of whether it resulted in a discriminatory—intentionally discriminatory impact or effect on the women.

If the sequence of the physical test events was not reasonably or rationally related to job announcement or the training program or the training materials or manuals and that the sequence was not designed and/or administered in such a manner as would objectively illustrate that the applicant would be a successful trainee and/or a successful firefighter and that such sequence of events, in addition to being non-job-related, was more difficult for women than for men, all of this can be considered in determining whether there was intentional discrimination. Obviously, you will consider the corollary of that, and as to numerical ranking, you heard some evidence about numerical ranking.

I am telling you as a matter of law the City of Cleveland charter and the Civil Service Commission requires there be a numerical ranking. There must be a numerical ranking, and it is required that the Civil Service Commission, after they do the written test scoring and the physical test scoring and the other components of the test and the other procedures they then prepare a numerical listing. And then for the number of applicants or for the number of jobs to be filled, they give three names to the appointing authority for each one job.

If there were 35 jobs, they would give them 105 names, and the appointing authority then has to appoint from that list. It is a 1-2-3 rule.

Now, you heard testimony about study materials, study manuals, training material. The City was not obligated to give any training manuals or study materials. They could have just had the announcement for the test. The announcement must be related to the testing.

You can't have an announcement for one purpose to give a test for another. The announcement was to give people general notice of what the test would be and must be reasonably or rationally related to the test, and it is for you to determine whether that was done.

The City was not required to give training material, but once they did, there must be a direct relationship between the training material and what's on the test.

Now, they are not required to give copies of the test or give precisely the exact questions for the written, and they are not required to give precisely or tell the sequence of events. They do it in a very general way.

Obviously, the type of thing on the written and the type of thing on the physical must be reasonably or rationally related to the duties of firefighter and give reasonable notice to the applicants of the general areas to be covered, not the precise areas but the general areas.

They must be done in such a way that the average person would understand them. So while the City is not required to give training material, once they give it, certainly it should be reasonably and rationally related to the test and not be designed in such a way as to be misleading or result in discrimination purposefully and intentionally against women.

The written and physical material for the test should have been designed, prepared and administered in a manner that both men and women should have been treated equally. The test should not have been designed, prepared and/or administered in such a manner that favors one group of applicants over another group of applicants.

In other words, the test should not be designed, prepared or administered in such a fashion or manner that it discriminates against one group of applicants. It must be consistent, as I just said, with the general terms of the announcement by the Civil Service Commission, and the test must be consistent with the job announcement.

All of this, and I am not trying to emphasize any one point, all of this may be or must be considered by you in determining whether the City actually intentionally discriminated.

Now, job related, you have heard that term, and the tests or test must relate or bear a relationship to the work or duties normally performed by the average firefighter in daily firefighting activities. It relates to actual job tasks.

In other words, it relates to actual job tasks, and you heard a lot of testimony about barbells. Now, the fact that the applicants in training classes did not work with barbells and did not practice the physical exercise in the same sequence as they did on the test in and of itself does not mean that the City discriminated against the plaintiffs.

However, this evidence can be considered together with all of the other evidence in determining whether any defendant intentionally discriminated against women firefighter applicants in the design, preparation and administration of the firefighting test in 2011.

So if you, the jury, find by a preponderance of the evidence that the 2011 test was designed, prepared or administered in such a manner or in such a way that it discriminated against women applicants, then you find that the women applicants' constitutional rights to equal protection was denied by the defendant.

On the other hand, if you find by a preponderance of the evidence that the plaintiffs proved that any one of the defendants* violated their constitutional right to equal protection under color of law, you

---

*Eds.' Note:* We do not know why the judge talked about "defendants" here, since only the City of Cleveland remained in this case as a defendant.

shall find for that plaintiff and against that defendant.

On the other hand, if you find that the plaintiffs failed to prove by a preponderance of the evidence any one of the elements discussed above, you shall return a verdict for that defendant and against the plaintiffs.

One other thing, each applicant for the firefighters examination has the obligation and is required to prepare himself or herself for the written and physical agility tests. The City has no obligation to train the applicants, and the City is not the guarantor of the success of any applicant for the firefighters examination.

However, if the City does give its notice, which it did about the test as I told you before and they do undertake training, then the training should relate to the subject matter generally that will be on the test, and I told you that before.

The City's obligation is to give a fair and reasonable and physical agility test that tests skills and abilities of the applicants and predicts the probability of a successful training followed by the probability that the applicant will be a successful firefighter and it must be job-related.

Now, that generally is the law on the 1983 equal protection case.

Now, in order for the plaintiffs to prevail, he must have another element, and that is there must be a proximate cause. If you find there was a constitutional violation, you must then find there was a proximate cause by a preponderance of the evidence.

In other words, the action of the City was a proximate cause of the firefighters' applicants who were women for not being placed higher on the list or being hired as fire-fighters, so if you find all three elements, in other words, that the City violated their constitutional rights and its violation was a proximate cause of them not being—women not being hired on the list, then you will render a verdict for the plaintiff against the defendant.

On the other hand, if the plaintiff failed to prove any one of these elements, you will end up returning a verdict for the defendant.

Now, you will retire very shortly to the jury room and begin your deliberations and elect one of your members as a foreperson to speak for you.

You heard all of the evidence, and you may not remember all of it individually but you will find collectively you will remember all of it.

The admonition I give you not to form or express an opinion about the case is no longer with you. Otherwise you couldn't deliberate.

You can also talk to each other about the case. You will do all your deliberations in the jury room and only with all of you present.

If any of you has to leave to go to the bathroom, you will stop your deliberations.

Now, I have here—I am going to give you one interrogatory, and the question is, "Did you find that the City of Cleveland intentionally or purposely discriminated against women applicants for the position of firefighters in the design, preparation, administration, scoring and the construction of the eligibility list of the 2011 City of Cleveland fire-fighters examination?"

And it will be yes or no and it must be signed by all nine of you. You will do your deliberations, and when all nine of you have reached a verdict, it must be unanimous, I have two verdict forms.

One is in favor of the plaintiff and one is in favor of the City. It only has to be signed by the foreperson, and the first one—there is no significance by the order which I read them—"We, the jury in the above-captioned case, unanimously find by a preponderance of the evidence for the plaintiffs Barbara Zoll et al. and against the defendant City of Cleveland in the 42 U.S.C. § 1983 case."

The other one is, "We, the jury in the above-captioned case, unanimously find for the defendant City of Cleveland and against the plaintiffs Barbara Zoll et al. in the 42 U.S.C. § 1983 case."

We have concluded that we are going to decide this case. You have heard the evidence, and you heard some discussion about the exhibits as we went along, but for expediting the proceeding, we are not going to give you any exhibits, just the interrogatory and the verdict form. . . .

Remember, you will elect one of your members as foreperson, and your principal charge is based on these instructions to decide if the City of Cleveland by its policies purposely and intentionally discriminated against women firefighters in this whole procedure, the 2011 firefighters examination.

## Excerpts from Transcript of Closing Arguments Made to the Judge in the Title VII Case

*MR. CALIPARI:* First of all, the only issue in this case of litigation is whether the [test in question] was job-related ... Another point I want to make briefly, your Honor, is under *Connecticut versus Teal*, where any aspect of a selection procedure has an adverse impact, the employer must relate [it to the] job.

[This] Court has also asked a question about whether under Title VII [the] United States was required to show intent. We state that the Supreme Court has expressly ruled showing of discriminatory purpose for intent is not required under Section 7 of Title VII.

However, in this case I think it's pretty clear that even though the burden is not there to show intent, there certainly was intent on the part of the City to exclude women from being part of the fire department. First of all, 2011 was the first time the City set out to recruit women for the job of firefighting. 2011 was also the first year the items on the test were not identified prior to the examination or prior to examination ... with sufficient time so women could train and all the expert physiologists, experts in exercise physiology agreed that there's a vast improvement with training for women.

In fact, as you recall, the testimony of Dr. Marshall and [the] Chief, the City took steps, intentionally took steps to mislead individuals as to exactly what was going to be on that examination. The City also went and hired somebody who was not an expert in exercise physiology, or an expert in gender differences. In fact as you recall, the job analysis conducted by Dr. Marshall showed the hand/eye coordination, balance and aerobic capacity were critical and important elements of the job of firefighter. To test for these items would have reduced the gender differences between males and females. They were in fact not tested for, although Dr. Marshall does in his linkage of the abilities to the individual items, his table indicates that those abilities, hand/eye coordination, balance and aerobic capacity, were in fact tested for. But in fact, [our experts] disagreed as did the expert exercise physiologist for the City. ...

Job analysis conducted by Dr. Marshall concluded in part that firefighters must possess a high level of aerobic capacity and aerobic fitness, muscular strength, muscular endurance, flexibility, coordination, muscular balance and speed. In fact, Dr. Marshall indicated that he intended to have the firefighters exams test for muscular endurance and aerobic capacity because those traits become particularly important in life-threatening situations.

No one's contraindicated that aerobic capacity and aerobic fitness are critical to the job of firefighting. However, all the experts in exercise physiology do agree these tests were primarily anaerobic in nature and did not test and measure the aerobic energy system. The 2011 examination of three events, barbell event, the fire scene setup, tire climb and the dummy drag, there's no evidence that this test is validated on the basis of content validity.

Event number one, barbell event, first of all, there's no evidence that the barbell or overhead lift is an activity performed by firefighters in performance of their duty. Dr. Marshall testified he included the barbell lift to measure absolute muscular endurance of shoulder and upper limbs, not specifically to replicate tasks performed by firefighters. This event had the most adverse impact upon women when you consider its use in a rank order selection procedure. . . .

Event two involved sprinting up and down stairs, performing other tasks in a fashion that is not only dangerous but does not replicate the manner in which firefighters perform their duties. As the Chief indicated, firefighting lasts many hours. It's a coordinated and choreographed activity, and if a firefighter is exhausted, he's unable to perform further firefighting duties.

You recall . . . the City's expert [testified] that these types of events in the way they are run results in a build-up of lactic acid and a build-up of lactic acid results in a person becoming exhausted and, as the Chief testified, once a person is exhausted, he's of no use to save lives or put out fires.

We heard testimony that event number three was designed to replicate rescues in smoke-filled rooms. While even Dr. Marshall testified, firefighters do not and are not trained to run in smoke-filled rooms to perform rescues. The doctor testified that event number three, the dummy drag, measures a nonspecific item or activity. He says it's a

measurement of strength and ability to drag or pull. And he's in direct contradiction to what Dr. Marshall testifies to with that event. You recall Dr. Marshall testified a good time for that event would be dragging a dummy 2 feet per second. One must point out to him in trial that the actual time required in order to pass the test was 4 feet per second, then he changed his opinion.

The event was administered in a nonstandard fashion and you recall Dr. Barrett testifying that a test should be standardized. It was nonstandard because individuals in event number three were able to wrap the rope and the ring around the wrists, his or her wrists, to aid in the dragging. Others were not instructed to do so. Similarly, individuals were allowed to remove shoes to gain better traction. Others were not instructed to do so.

The Court heard testimony that the dummy they used, the fact it was nonarticulated, disadvantages persons with other strengths. You recall a doctor testified although someone may not have the grip strength necessary to pull it, he or she could compensate by using the arms or dragging the dummy in a different manner. If it was an articulated dummy, you'd be able to take advantage of that. The manner in which these three test items are designed to perform does not replicate or approximate the critical and coordinant tasks necessary to perform the job of firefighting.

Your Honor, the United States is seeking three things with respect to these proceedings. First, that the Court find these tests and City selection procedures are unlawful under Title VII. Second, that the Court order the City not to discriminate against women in the future. And third, that the Court order the City to develop a valid, fair and job-related examination for the position of eventual firefighter in the future. As a result of this test, zero women were hired in a position of firefighter . . . there would be no women on the fire department today.

Dr. Marshall, the developer of the examination, developed both written and physical portions of the examination. He has absolutely no expertise in the area of exercise physiology. Dr. Marshall developed the examination and his testimony and that evidence which he sets forth in his report is contradicted by the city's own experts in exercise physiology. The examination was a test for aerobic capacity, aerobic fitness, muscular strength, and so on. No one's been at disagreement with that, but those are the critical and important elements of firefighting. The City, in fact, did not test for those elements. . . .

Finally, your Honor, the United States asks that the Court strike down these examinations as being not job related or valid under Title VII and find the City has not carried its burden to show that these examinations are job related. Thank you.

*MS. JENNIFER:* Your Honor, I'll try not to be repetitive of arguments that have been made by Mr. Calipari. . . .

The City has cited to [the] sixth circuit case . . . [of] *Grano Department of Development versus City of Columbus.* . . . Reading through this is an exercise in credulity in that the statements that are made presumably are in there in an attempt to make it appear they apply to our case. Grano is a disparate treatment case, not a disparate impact case, and the language of the opinion specifically points out the difference of standard between the disparate treatment and the disparate impact case. Why it's in here, I don't know. There is a paucity of sixth circuit authority in the conclusions of law that the City has submitted.

One of the other cases . . . is *Louisville Black Police Officers Organization versus the City of Louisville.* There's a citation to the Western District of Kentucky for the proposition that the content validity of employment selection device can be demonstrated, even though all the uniform guidelines are not satisfied. And it indicates that it was affirmed by the sixth circuit.

If one checks the sixth circuit opinion involved, all but [*sic*] the sixth circuit opinion is the award of attorney's fees to plaintiff's counsel in that case. We, of course, concur in the importance of that particular sixth circuit opinion, but not for the proposition for which it appears to be cited here in the City's conclusions of law.

With respect to the omissions from the conclusions of law, we don't see any references to *Williams v. Vukavich.* We don't see references to any of the cases that—

*MR. SOLMINE:* Objection, your Honor. I thought this was closing.

*THE COURT:* Go ahead.

*MS. JENNIFER:* That in fact are at issue in this case, *Columbus v.*

*Vukavich*, and I think that in looking at the law that we have here, it's very important to point out that *Williams versus Vukavich* particularly cites with approval the second circuit's decision, in *Guardians*, which is, of course, the Seminole [*sic*] case, dealing with a need to validate. If you have a case that you're using—test that you're using in rank order, that you must validate for the use with respect to rank order.

Now, in looking at the standards for determining liability in this case, we of course are looking primarily at a disparate impact case. We put forward evidence with respect to some instances of disparate treatment as well, but they are simply illustrative to show examples of the kind of treatment that was going on during the period of time that the issues concerning this test were before us.

In looking at the disparate impact of the exam, I noticed with interest for the first time in the City's conclusions of law number four, the City now admits that the differential selection rate of males versus females in fact does constitute adverse impact, [a] conclusion they weren't willing to stipulate to at any time. Now, given the fact they've omitted that disparate impact, it appears to be an omission with respect to tests as a whole, or I should say the selection process as a whole, not with respect to the individual components of the test. . . .

Now, in looking at the standards that we have of disparate impact case [*sic*] with respect to our burden of proof, once the disparate impact is established, then it's up to the defendants to in fact carry a burden

of proof, not production, as is set forth in the disparate treatment case, but the burden of proof to be able to show the job necessity for using the procedure that they have used.

Now, that's normally shown through use of validation to show the job-relatedness of the test. But one of the things that's been brought up and that I want to reiterate is that in this case they have used a rank order score which includes components in addition to the written and the physical, and it includes veterans points and includes residents points. If we look at the Court's opinion, *Connecticut versus Teal*, not only is it clear that the individual components must be validated under the circumstances, but it is the entire selection process, the entire selection procedure. And I might add that this is a situation, of course, where the bottom line did not show adverse impact in the *Teal* case. But if we look at even the dissenting opinion in this case, it's clear that it is the total selection procedure that must be validated, and here we have basically an admission from the City that they haven't attempted to do so.

But in any event, we have a system here in which the use of the capping system and the use of a variable number of minority points led to an adverse impact on the rank order of the women on the list, particularly adversely affecting women at the top of the list, the only women who stood a chance of being hired. And that particular problem, the differential effect upon the people at the top of the list, is not unique in this case if we look at *Thomas versus City of Evanston.* We see that the Court there is very attentive to the fact that the importance is the ranking. It's not the average scores. That's a meaningless indication in a case of this kind. It's the position on the list that's all important. Now, in addition to using veteran points, capping and racial points that created a disparate impact, we also had the irregularities in the administration development of the written test. . . .

Finally, in the last section of the test, the judgment section, we had only 14 questions, and three of them Dr. Marshall reluctantly admitted that, perhaps because he developed this himself, he reluctantly admitted that there were alternate answers that were equally logical to the ones he selected and gave people credit for.

And then there was one question in this section in which Dr. Marshall simply said the answer was wrong. . . . Four of the 14 items of this last section, which supposedly tested judgment, was the only section that did test judgment. We assume judgment is very important in the job of firefighter, but close to 30 percent of these items were deficient.

Now, in looking at the physical, . . . there was no measure established, no specific measure established for the amount of physical strength that the job of firefighter required.

If we look at Supreme Court authority on this point, the height and weight requirement that was at issue in *Dothard versus Rawlinson* felt and the Supreme Court there point out, I'm quoting, that

the defendants had produced no evidence correlating the height and weight requirement with the requisite amount of strength thought essential to firefighters and some men at the fire academy that you had to make the written more difficult. So instead, what he does is he sets up a system that weights the physical twice as much as the written.

Now, with respect to pretext, I think it's important to point out that what we've got here is an enormous amount of evidence that deals with intentional discrimination. . . .

When we look at all these things, the effect is foreseeable. That's evidence and intent. The fact that *Penick* was a 1983 case isn't relevant. The fact that evidence comes in here at the last stage as the plaintiff's rebuttal of defendant's case is sufficient for our purposes in making our Title VII case. Thank you, your Honor.

*MR. SOLIMINE:* Good afternoon, your Honor. I want to begin, your Honor, by thanking the Court, first of all, for giving us so much latitude in trying this case and also for the Court's attentiveness to the issues and testimony herein. Given that I only have about 20 minutes, there are a couple of issues that I do want to address that Ms. Jennifer raised. I want to do that very briefly.

First of all, she indicated that there was [*sic*] some problems with the written part of the examination, that, for example, she noted there were people who during the administration of the written examination, about 300 people have both parts of the—that the first part of the test, they had both the exam answer sheet and the booklet. Again, there's been no evidence that this particular occurrence in any way benefited males or females. . . .

I need not remind this Court we spent nearly four weeks listening to various witnesses testify in this case. We had nearly 30 witnesses, over 2,500 pages of transcript in this case. That's quite a bit, your Honor. But it was essential that we get what the true issues were that were involved. This Court made clear early on there is a very narrow issue involved here and that issue is whether or not the examination in 2011, the entire examination in 2011 and the hiring processes for firefighters discriminated against women. That's the issue that's presented here, your Honor. This is not a case about whether women can do the job of firefighting, this is not a case of race discrimination. We are not called here to address, your Honor, whether or not the inherent order is improper. The controlling issue is whether or not the City's testing and hiring procedures were discriminatory against women.

Now, your Honor, in my summation, I'm going to talk of principally two points: The first one being adverse impact and the second one being the job-relatedness and validity of the 2011 examination. . . .

Your Honor, I'd be hard pressed to stand here now and argue that the selection rate for females as a result of the 2011 examination did not have an adverse impact or did not reflect adverse impact. In fact, your Honor, any City which gave a valid test for firefighting would be faced with the same dilemma. That's been evidenced in Columbus,

Buffalo, New York, New York City, and other cities. That's the reality that we have to live with. When the City hired firefighters . . . , all those hired were males, all those hired were talked down, no females were hired. What we have is the inexorable zero the Courts talk about. We'll have to live with that.

Your Honor, that's the only point we're going to concede and that's the only point that the evidence mandates that we concede. The bottom line, your Honor, is that in this particular case, we have submitted nearly four weeks—strike that. We have spent nearly four years before this Court on this case, four weeks actually in the courtroom, trying this case. There have been numerous depositions. In fact, Dr. Marshall himself has been deposed over eight times. There's countless exhibits, reams and reams of paper, trial transcripts, deposition transcripts, and the bottom line, your Honor, in spite of all of that is that the test is valid.

Your Honor, we could have learned this three years ago, four years ago. We didn't have to wait four years to arrive at that. And another reality, your Honor, that it seems to have taken the plaintiffs four years to get to, is the reality that females didn't score high enough to be selected, that is because like anybody else who didn't score high enough to be selected that they lack the abilities required of the job, principally the physical abilities involved in the job of firefighting. Those are tough realities, your Honor, but that's the way it is.

Now, we accept it as our burden to show that the 2011 examination was job related. . . . We've been at this for four years, [and] might as well go ahead and remind the Court what the evidence shows.

During the trial your Honor, we had one witness that this Court remarked had broken the record for testifying. That witness was Dr. Marshall. We saw him again today. He was on the stand for I believe what amounted to about five days' testifying because he was the one who developed the 2011 examination. . . . [H]e developed the examination[] not because we couldn't find anyone better, but because he was the best person for the job. And other court's [sic] in this district had knowledge of that skill and experience and competency in test developing. . . .

[Dr. Marshall testified that his] first objective was to make sure that the abilities that were measured were those abilities that were required for the job of firefighter. . . . He also testified that the second objective . . . was to make sure that the tests actually used the kinds of tasks that firefighters performed. . . . Dr. Marshall then identified a third objective . . . and that was to make sure that the test picked those people who do well on the job. . . . By the testimony we know of now, your Honor, all three of these forms of validity are interrelated and Dr. Marshall's goal at that point was to as best as possible be [sic] all three of these objectives.

. . .

Now, there has been some talk, I guess I have to say more than talk, real serious efforts to turn the 2011 examination into two examinations. Your Honor, there was only one

examination. And that is what the candidates had to score high enough on in order to make it on the eligibility list, the entire examination, the cognitive and intellectual part and as well the physical part of the examination.

What's principally at issue here, your Honor, is the physical part of that test, the physical events. We've had some testimony about problems with the written, but no evidence to show that there is even a need to focus soley [sic] on the written or soley [sic] on the physical. But given the fact, your Honor, that that is what the plaintiffs have sought to do, we certainly have to address the challenge to the physical events. . . .

[E]vent number one was [the] overhead lift or barbell lift. Plaintiffs didn't like event number [one]. And they gave a number of reasons why they didn't like event number one and viewed it as being detrimental to women. Well, there are principally three reasons why they don't like event number one. First of all, they say firefighters don't lift barbells in conduct to perform firefighting task[s]. Your Honor, no one ever said they did.

Number two, they complain about the fact candidates were prohibited [sic] bending knees while doing this event.

Third, they claim women are not very familiar with barbells, and therefore, Dr. Marshall specifically put in this event to weed out women. Your Honor, the evidence in this case screens [sic] to the contrary.

First of all, the evidence is clear and unequivocal there are tasks firefighters have to perform wherein they use their upper body muscles exclusively, and that's what event number one was capping the candidates upper body strength. . . . They do have to lift fire-fighting equipment overhead, and we had quite a bit of testimony with respect to what it is that firefighters have to do.

We had testimony to the effect that there are times when they use those upper body muscles and cannot use their legs in order to get the job done. We heard testimony from the Chief in terms of the critical and important tasks that firefighters have to perform in the first few minutes of arriving. He talked about having to perform ventilation. That was something that had to be done quickly. And that the objective is [to] get that done in five minutes.

We heard testimony also from the Chief that when firefighters arrive at the scene, they have to get a ladder off the truck. They have to use those upper body muscles to get that ladder off. They have to go up and straddle a roof and begin to chop a hole in order to ventilate, because as I said before, the straddle method, they're using their upper body muscles exclusively.

We had another firefighter testify here, that was Ken Naig. Ken Naig talked about pulling ceilings, using a pipe pole, and he testified the objective was to get plaster and wood and everything removed so you could check to see where the fires is spreading. If that isn't done as quickly as possible, you're going to be in trouble.

Ken Naig testified that in a minute he's been able to do 50 movements up and down on his ceiling using a pipe pole. We had Ken Naig in court and used with his pipe pole, he was able to do 80 pushes up and down in a minute using the pipe pole.

There was another thing upon mentioning Ken Naig at this point, your Honor, is Dave Hall by his testimony made it clear that firefighters do their job as quickly as possible, be it ventilating, be it performing a rescue, be it getting the supply— they work very hard to get the job done as quickly as possible. That fact, your Honor, the sincerity and dedication of Ken Naig as a firefighter was reflected in a newspaper article that was in today's paper regarding a rescue, and although the article didn't mention it, the firefighter attempted to rescue that six year old, who in fact did get her out. It was Ken Naig, your Honor.

Now, we also heard, as I said before, about a lot of equipment the firefighters have to carry. We heard testimony from Scott Keefe about the fact that since he's only 5 feet 4 inches tall that he has to compensate for his height because he knows the job of firefighter requires him to be strong in his upper body. So he lifts weights to keep himself in shape.

Now, we've had women come in who testified and complained about the bar lift, but most of the women who testified were able to do 35 lifts. Your Honor, I'm not sure what the beef is there.

They have complaints about event number three as well and—but before I go to that it was their expert's view that what you really should do if you want to see whether someone can chop or lift or carry a ladder is you ought to have them do that.

Your Honor, common sense tells us that is ridiculous. Can you imagine the carnage at the exam site when you have novices swinging axes and carrying ladders and trying to raise 60-pound fans overhead? It's ridiculous. . . .

Now, event number [two, the] hose drag. Now, they had several complaints, a couple principal complaints about event two. They were timing and intention. They didn't like the fact that the events measured there were timed. Well, your Honor, the reality is that that event needs to be timed. . . . [A] pump in Cleveland has only about two minutes of water, so it's important the fire department get that line laid out and connected to the hydrant as soon as possible. Hook and ladder people engage in rescue, ventilation work, and it's important that ventilation be done simultaneously with efforts to hook up that line so by the time the line is hooked up, the water is ready to go, the building is ventilated, the heat and smoke is coming out. You can't waste your time doing those activities, your honor. . . .

Now, on to event number three. They have principally three complaints about that. First, they don't like the fact this event was timed. Second, they don't like the weight of the dummy. Again, event number three was timed for the same reason event number two was timed. It demonstrates tasks, it has to be done as quickly as possible. We're talking, event number two, about being able to measure, the candidate's ability to drive themselves by pulling their weight a certain required distance. It's a simulated rescue. It's something that has to be done as quickly as possible. . . .

They didn't like the weight of the dummy. . . . They offered in lieu of the dummy use of an articulated dummy, something with arms and legs your Honor.

We saw the description of how the event number three was set up. There was an overhead barrier they had to crawl up. You can have the legs and arms and everything flailing all over the place. What's the sense of having an articulated dummy. The plaintiff's own witness, Buddy Casey, said he tried using an articulated dummy for his course, five or six people go through with that thing, arms are torn off, legs are torn off. Imagine the complaints we'd have from the plaintiffs had we used an articulated dummy and that dummy was not the exact weight and specification for each candidate that went through. Clearly, their complaints about the weight are ridiculous.

Third is the grip. This is a real surprise. They didn't like the handle. They wanted to be able to have a dummy or weight designed so each candidate could grab it however they please. What they're ignoring here, your Honor, is they're introducing differentiation, they're eliminating the standardization of this event. If you leave it up to a candidate to figure out how they're going to grab the dummy, imagine the variance you're going to get in your examination. . . .

Again, back to time. I forgot to mention we talked about the time issue. We have firefighters [who talked] about the criticality of rescues. Talked about how when a structure is burning and he goes in to perform a rescue, there are two people's lives at steak [*sic*], his and the life of the victim. He's going to do everything to make sure he gets the victim out and himself out and alive as soon as possible. . . .

The City of Cleveland is not a laboratory, your Honor, they are real people in this town, real people who when their homes are on fire or the lives of their children—maybe that's funny to some people, but the reality is it's a serious situation when someone's home is on fire and the City cannot afford to experiment with a job that involves such serious dangers to the public. The City certainly deserves to have the best qualified for the job and their very lives depend on that. Thank you.

# Table of Cases

# *Table of Statutes and Rules*

# Index